American Stories

A History of the United States

Combined Volume

Second Edition

H. W. Brands
University of Texas

T. H. Breen
Northwestern University

R. Hal Williams
Southern Methodist University

Ariela J. Gross
University of Southern California

Boston Columbus Indianapolis New York San Francisco Upper Saddle River
Amsterdam Cape Town Dubai London Madrid Milan Munich Paris Montréal Toronto
Delhi Mexico City São Paulo Sydney Hong Kong Seoul Singapore Taipei Tokyo

Editorial Director: Craig Campanella
Editor-in-Chief: Dickson Musslewhite
Executive Editor: Ed Parsons
Assistant Editor: Alex Rabinowitz
Editorial Assistant: Emily Tamburri
Senior Manufacturing and Operations
  Manager for Arts & Sciences: Mary Fischer
Operations Specialist: Christina Amato
Director of Marketing: Brandy Dawson
Senior Marketing Manager: Maureen E. Prado Roberts
Marketing Assistant: Samantha Bennett
Senior Managing Editor: Ann Marie McCarthy
Senior Project Manager: Denise Forlow

Director of Media and Assessment: Brian Hyland
Media Project Manager: Nikhil Bramhavar
Digital Media Editor: Andrea Messineo
Senior Art Director: Maria Lange
Cover and Interior Design: T-9 Design
Cover Image: Bottom, ArtPix/Alamy; top, ClassicStock/Alamy
Cartographer: Maps.com
AV Project Manager: Mirella Signoretto
Full-Service Production, Interior Design,
  and Composition: PreMediaGlobal
Printer/Binder: R.R.D./Crawfordsville
Cover Printer: Lehigh-Phoenix Color/Hagerstown
Text Font: 10/12.5 Minion Pro

Credits and acknowledgments borrowed from other sources and reproduced, with permission, in this textbook appear on appropriate page within text (or on pages C-1–C-2).

Many of the designations by manufacturers and seller to distinguish their products are claimed as trademarks. Where those designations appear in this book, and the publisher was aware of a trademark claim, the designations have been printed in initial caps or all caps.

Library of Congress Cataloging-in-Publication Data
  American stories : a history of the United States / H.W. Brands . . . [et al.].—2nd ed.
    p. cm.
  Includes index.
  ISBN 978-0-205-24361-7 (combined)
  978-0-205-03656-1 (vol. 1)
  978-0-205-03655-4 (vol. 2)
  1. United States—History. I. Brands, H. W.
  E178.A5544 2011
  973—dc23

2011023657

10 9 8 7 6 5 4

Combined Volume
ISBN 10: 0-205-24361-4
ISBN 13: 978-0-205-24361-7

Examination Copy
ISBN 10: 0: 0-205-06483-3
ISBN 13: 978-0-205-06483-0

Volume 1
ISBN 10: 0-205-03656-2
ISBN 13: 978-0-205-03656-1

Books a la carte Volume 1
ISBN 10: 0-205-20642-5
ISBN 13: 978-0-205-20642-1

Volume 2
ISBN 10: 0-205-03655-4
ISBN 13: 978-0-205-03655-4

Books a la carte Volume 2
ISBN 10: 0-205-20645-X
ISBN 13: 978-0-205-20645-2

PEARSON

Brief **Contents**

Contents

Maps, Figures, and Tables

FIGURES

TABLES

New to the Second Edition

Teachers familiar with the first edition of *American Stories* will find that this second edition is different in many important ways. The major changes are:

- **Better Integration with MyHistoryLab** This edition is tied more closely to *MyHistoryLab* than ever before. *MyHistoryLab* icons appear throughout the text, connecting the main narrative to a strong array of *MyHistoryLab* resources, including primary source documents, analytical video segments, interactive maps, and more. A new *MyHistoryLab Connections* feature at the end of each chapter prompts students to follow the Study Plan for the chapter. Central to the new release of *MyHistoryLab*, the Study Plan guides students through activities that develop higher-order thinking.

- **New Format** The second edition appears in a new compact format that is more affordable and easier for students to carry and handle.

- **New Map Program** Every one of the more than 80 maps in the second edition has been redrawn for greater clarity and visual impact.

- **New Key Term Questions** Building on the innovative instructional design of its predecessor, the second edition now treats the key terms for each chapter in a unique way. A list of *Key Term Questions* appears at the end of each chapter, placing each key term in the context of a probing question. These encourage students to think critically about the term, rather than simply memorize it. Page references connect each term to where it is first discussed in the text.

- **Improved Narrative** The narrative has been extensively edited and rewritten to bring the story of American history into sharper focus. For example, all maps, figures, and tables are now numbered for easier reference and to integrate them more closely to the text. Content has been added and improved in every chapter. For instance, Chapter 2 discusses the founding of the colonies of New Jersey, Delaware, New Hampshire, and North Carolina; Chapter 1 now includes a discussion and table about the Columbian Exchange; and Chapters 21 and 24 have more detail on empire and American foreign policy before World War I. Other substantive changes are described below.

- **Greater Emphasis on Native Americans** The coverage of Native Americans has been increased throughout the text. New sections discuss the diverse life-ways of native peoples in North America before the arrival of the Europeans (Chapter 1); the role of Native Americans in the American Revolution (Chapter 5); the infamous Trail of Tears in the 1830s (Chapter 10); reservation life and the efforts at forced assimilation in the late nineteenth and early twentieth centuries (Chapter 17); and the role of Native American troops in World War II (Chapter 27).

- **Greater Emphasis on the Spanish** The discussion of the Spanish role in the American story has been enhanced with new coverage of Spanish colonization and Spanish interaction with the Native Americans (Chapters 1 and 4); Spain's role in the American Revolution (Chapter 5); and life in the Spanish-speaking borderlands of the Southwest (Chapter 17).

- **Greater Emphasis on African Americans** The history of African Americans has been expanded with new graphics in Chapter 11 and a major new section in Chapter 19 on the spread of Jim Crow in both the South and North after Reconstruction.

- **Thoroughly Updated** Chapters 31 and 32 have been rewritten to bring the American story up to 2011, with new sections on the elections of 2008 and 2010, health care reform, the Great Recession, gay marriage and gays in the military, and the changes revealed in the 2010 census.

A Note to my Fellow Teachers

From H. W. Brands

I've been teaching American history for thirty years now (I started young—really), and in that time I've noticed something that almost certainly has occurred to many of you: that our students come to our classrooms with increasingly varied backgrounds. Some students are better prepared than ever, having taken advanced placement courses and acquired a solid grounding in historical facts, interpretations, and methods. Other students arrive less well prepared. Many of these are international students; some are students for whom English is a second or third language. Some of these, and some others, simply never took American history in high school. Some, finally, just didn't do well in the history courses they did take.

Different students require different methods of teaching, including different textbooks. Students well versed in American history do best with a book that presupposes their preparation and takes them beyond it. Students for whom the subject is new or otherwise challenging are more likely to succeed with a book that is more selective in its coverage, that focuses on essential themes, and that offers features designed to facilitate the learning process. Any textbook can be intimidating, as even my best students have reminded me over the years. The hundreds of pages and thousands of facts can put anyone off. For that reason, whatever reduces the intimidation factor can help students succeed.

This is the philosophy behind *American Stories: A History of the United States*. A single purpose has motivated the creation of this book: to enhance the accessibility of American history and thereby increase students' chances of success. This goal is what brought me to the classroom, it's what keeps me there, and it's one I think I share with you. If *American Stories: A History of the United States* contributes to achieving this goal, we all—teachers and students—will be the winners.

APPROACH AND THEMES

The most frequent complaint I get from students regarding history textbooks is that the mass of information is overwhelming. There are too many facts and ideas, and it is difficult to determine what to focus on. Many students need help pulling the key concepts from the narrative. This complaint provided the starting point for *American Stories*, which differs from standard textbooks in two fundamental respects.

First, we reduced the number of topics covered, retaining the essential elements of the American story while eliminating others. We surveyed over five hundred instructors from across the country to find out what topics were most commonly covered in a typical survey classroom. Every subject in the U.S. history course was rated according to what respondents thought must be covered. Once we received the results, we culled the most commonly taught topics and selected them for inclusion in *American Stories*. Making choices wasn't easy; at times it was painful. But we considered it necessary. Some topics are simply not taught as often as others, and our job as historians is to let students know what they need to know.

Second, we integrated a variety of study aids into the text. These were originally developed with the assistance of Dr. Kathleen T. McWhorter and Debby Kalk. Kathleen is a professor and author with more than 40 years of experience at both two- and four-year colleges, including Niagara Community College, and specializes in developmental reading, writing, composition, and study skills. Debby is an instructional designer and author with more than 20 years of experience producing materials for educational publishers, corporate training, and public education and who speaks frequently on instructional design at workshops and conferences. With the help of both Kathleen and Debby, *American Stories* is the first college-level U.S. history survey completely designed to meet the needs of the instructor and the student.

Beyond this, *American Stories* places great emphasis on a compelling narrative. We—I and my fellow authors—have used significant incidents and episodes to reflect the dilemmas, the choices, and the decisions made by the American people as well as by their leaders. Our story of the American past includes the major events that have shaped the nation—the wars fought, the presidents elected, the legislation enacted, the treaties signed—but it doesn't stop there. We examine the ways in which the big events influenced the lives of ordinary people. How did the American Revolution alter the fortunes and prospects of men, women, and children around the country? What was it like for blacks and whites to live in a plantation society? How did the shift from an agrarian to an industrial economy transform daily life? What impact did technology, in such forms as the automobile and computer, have on patterns of living in the twentieth century?

Each chapter begins with a vignette that launches the narrative of that chapter and identifies its themes. Some of the vignettes have special meaning for the authors. The account in Chapter 18 of the 1876 Centennial Exposition in Philadelphia, for example, recalls to my mind the 1962 World's Fair in Seattle. I and my brother and sisters traveled by train with my grandfather from our home in Portland to Seattle to see the fair. I remember riding the Monorail and ascending the Space Needle; these two icons of the fair were supposed to point the way to the future of urban life. Things didn't work out quite that way, just as the forecasts from the 1876 exposition missed the mark in some respects. But the excitement the world's fair brought to my eight-year-old life was similar to that experienced by the children who attended the exposition.

The vignette that opens Chapter 26, on the Great Depression of the 1930s, reminds me of the stories my father used to tell about his experiences during that trying decade. His family wasn't nearly as hard hit as many in the 1930s; like Pauline Kael, he was a college student. And like her, he saw how hard it was for many of his classmates to stay in school. He himself was always working at odd jobs, trying to make ends meet. Times were hard, yet he learned the value of a dollar—something he impressed on me as I was growing up.

By these means and others, I and my fellow authors have attempted to bring history to life for students. We believe that while history rarely repeats itself, the story of the American past is profoundly relevant to the problems and challenges facing the nation today.

PEDAGOGICAL FEATURES

The pedagogical elements in *American Stories* have been carefully constructed to be accessible to students and to support a better, deeper understanding of U.S. history. These elements fall into two categories, Textual Pedagogy that appears throughout the main body of each chapter, and Study Resources collected at the ends of chapters.

■ **Textual Pedagogy** Each chapter follows a consistent pedagogy that maximizes student learning. *Spotlight Questions* in the chapter openers preview the main idea for each major section and provide a framework for the entire chapter. As a reminder to students, these questions are repeated in the margins after each major section. *Quick Check Questions* follow each subsection for immediate reinforcement of key ideas presented in each section. If students are unable to answer these questions, they know to go back and reread the subsection for the main idea. *Key Terms* are highlighted throughout each chapter and are defined in the text's glossary. *MyHistoryLab Icons* appear in the margins, identifying additional resources that students may find in the program. (See below for more on *MyHistoryLab*.)

■ **Study Resources** Each chapter concludes with a series of study resources. A chapter *Timeline* surveys the chronology of key events, with page references for easy look-up of information. The *Chapter Review* connects back to the Spotlight Questions, providing brief answers that summarize the main points of each section. *Key Term Questions* place each key term in the context of a probing question, encouraging students to think critically about the term, rather than simply memorizing it. Here too, page references support easy look-up of information. A *MyHistoryLab Connections* feature caps off the study resources for each chapter. These provide questions for analysis drawn from the chapter Study Plan in *MyHistoryLab*.

A FINAL WORD

My fellow authors and I, with the assistance of the professionals at Pearson, have devoted a great deal of effort to making a textbook of which we are all very proud. Our goal with *American Stories* is to convey our excitement for history to our students in the most accessible manner possible. We've done what we can toward this goal, but we realize that our success depends on you, the classroom instructors. Our job is to make your job easier. All of us—authors and instructors—are in this together. So keep up the good work, and thanks!

A Note to Students: Tips for Studying History

Every autumn for many years I have taught an introductory course in American history. Over that time I've come to appreciate the value of devoting the first class session to the fundamentals of studying and learning history. Every subject—mathematics, chemistry, psychology, English, art—has its peculiarities; each reveals itself to students in particular ways. And different students have different learning styles. But the experiences of the many students I've taught have convinced me that certain general techniques produce good results.

I always tell students that these techniques aren't the only way to study; they may have their own methods. But I also tell them that these techniques have worked for a lot of students in the past, and might work for them. Here they are:

1. **History is a *story*,** not just an assortment of facts. The connections are critical. How do the events and people you are reading or hearing about relate to one another? This is what historians want to know, and what distinguishes them from chroniclers, who simply list events and leave it at that. Therefore:

   Find the story line, the plot. Identify the main characters, the turning points. How did the story—or the part of the story you are studying in a given chapter or lecture—turn out? Why did it turn out that way and not some other?

2. **Dates matter, but order matters more.** Students often get the idea that history is all about dates. It's not. It's about what caused what (as in a story: see Rule 1 above). Dates are useful only in that they help you remember what happened before what else. This is crucial, because the thing that came first might have caused, or at least influenced, the thing that came later. Therefore:

   Concentrate on the order of events. If you do, the dates will fall into place by themselves.

3. **History takes time**—to happen, and to learn. History is nothing more or less than how people deal with each other (again, it's a story). But like any richly detailed story, it can take time to absorb.
   Therefore:

   Spread out your studying. If you have three hours of reading to do, do it over three days for an hour a day. If you have a test coming up, give yourself two weeks to study, allocating a half hour each day. You'll learn more easily; you'll retain more. And you'll have a better chance to enjoy the story.

4. **History's stories are both spoken and written.** That's why most classes involve both lectures and readings. In the typical syllabus, readings—chapters of the text, supplementary documents and articles—are keyed to the lectures, with the readings chosen to complement the lectures, and vice versa.
   Therefore:

   Read the assigned materials before the corresponding lectures. It's tempting not to—to let the reading slide. But resist the temptation. Advance reading makes the lectures far more understandable—and far more enjoyable.

5. **Less is more,** at least in note-taking. Not every word in the text or other reading is equally important; not every word uttered by your instructor in a lecture has equal value. The point of notes is to distill a chapter or a lecture into a smaller, more manageable size.
   Therefore:

   Hit the high points. Focus on where the text and lecture overlap. Write down key phrases and words; don't write complete sentences. And if you are using a highlighter on a book, be sparing. If yellow (or pink or whatever color you prefer) starts to become the prevailing motif of your pages, you've gone too far.

6. **History is a twice-told tale.** History is both what happened and how we've remembered what happened. Think of your first exposure to a particular historical topic as history *happening*, and your second exposure as history *being remembered*. An awareness of both is necessary to making the history stick in your head.
   Therefore:

   Take a rest after reading a chapter or attending a lecture. **Then go back and review**. Your class notes should not be comprehensive (see Rule 5), but as you go back over them, you will remember details that will help you fill out your notes. While you are reviewing a chapter, ask yourself what your notes on the chapter mean, and why you highlighted this particular phrase or that.

   To summarize, when approaching a history course:

- **Find the story line.**
- **Concentrate on the order of events.**
- **Spread out your studying.**
- **Read the assignments before the lectures.**
- **Hit the high points in taking notes.**
- **Take a rest, then review.**

A final suggestion: Allow enough time for this course so you aren't rushed. If you give yourself time to get into the story, you'll come to enjoy it. And what you enjoy, you'll remember.

Best wishes,

H. W. Brands

Supplements for Qualified College Adopters

MyHistoryLab

MyHistoryLab (www.myhistorylab.com) The moment you know Educators know it. Students know it. It's that inspired moment when something that was difficult to understand suddenly makes perfect sense. Our MyLab products have been designed and refined with a single purpose in mind: to help educators create that moment of understanding with their students.

Instructor's Resource Manual with Test Bank Available at the Instructor's Resource Center, at **www.pearsonhighered.com/irc**, the Instructor's Resource Manual with Test Bank contains chapter outlines, summaries, key points and vital concepts, and information on audio-visual resources that can be used in developing and preparing lecture presentations. The Test Bank includes multiple choice questions and essay questions and is text specific.

PowerPoint Presentation Available at the Instructor's Resource Center, at **www.pearsonhighered.com/irc**, the PowerPoints contain chapter outlines and full-color images of maps and arts. They are text specific and available for download.

MyTest Available at **www.pearsonmytest.com**, MyTest is a powerful assessment generation program that helps instructors easily create and print quizzes and exams. Questions and tests can be authored online, allowing instructors ultimate flexibility and the ability to efficiently manage assessments anytime, anywhere! Instructors can easily access existing questions and edit, create, and store using simple drag-and-drop and Word-like controls.

Supplements for Students

MyHistoryLab

MyHistoryLab (www.myhistorylab.com) The moment you know Educators know it. Students know it. It's that inspired moment when something that was difficult to understand suddenly makes perfect sense. Our MyLab products have been designed and refined with a single purpose in mind: to help educators create that moment of understanding with their students.

CourseSmart www.coursemart.com CourseSmart eTextbooks offer the same content as the printed text in a convenient online format—with highlighting, online search, and printing capabilities. You **save 60% over the list price** of the traditional book.

Books à la Carte Books à la Carte editions feature the exact same content as the traditional printed text in a convenient, three-hole-punched, loose-leaf version at a discounted price—allowing you to take only what you need to class. You'll **save 35% over the net price of the traditional book. V1 - ISBN: 0205206425; ISBN-13: 9780205206421; V2 - ISBN: 020520645X; ISBN-13: 9780205206452**

Library of American Biography Series **www.pearsonhighered.com/educator/series/Library-of-American-Biography/10493.page** Pearson's renowned series of biographies spotlighting figures who had a significant impact on American history. Included in the series are Edmund Morgan's *The Puritan Dilemma: The Story of John Winthrop*, B. Davis Edmund's *Tecumseh and the Quest for Indian Leadership*, J. William T. Youngs, *Eleanor Roosevelt: A Personal and Public Life*, John R. M. Wilson's *Jackie Robinson and the American Dilemma* and Sandra Opdycke's *Jane Addams and her Vision for America*.

Supplements for Qualified College Adopters	Supplements for Students
Retreiving the American Past Available through the Pearson Custom Library (**www.pearsoncustom.com**, keyword search | rtap), the *Retrieving the American Past* (RTAP) program lets you create a textbook or reader that meets your needs and the needs of your course. RTAP gives you the freedom and flexibility to add chapters from several best-selling Pearson textbooks, in addition to *The American Nation, 14/e,* and/or 100 topical reading units written by the History Department of Ohio State University, all under one cover. Choose the content you want to teach in depth, in the sequence you want, at the price you want your students to pay.	**Penguin Valuepacks www.pearsonhighered.com/penguin** A variety of Penguin-Putnam texts is available at discounted prices when bundled with *American Stories, 2/e.* Texts include Benjamin Franklin's *Autobiography and Other Writings*, Nathaniel Hawthorne's *The Scarlet Letter*, Thomas Jefferson's *Notes on the State of Virginia*, and George Orwell's *1984*.
	A Short Guide to Writing About History, 7/e Written by Richard Marius, late of Harvard University, and Melvin E. Page, Eastern Tennessee State University, this engaging and practical text helps students get beyond merely compiling dates and facts. Covering both brief essays and the documented resource paper, the text explores the writing and researching processes, identifies different modes of historical writing, including argument, and concludes with guidelines for improving style. **ISBN-10: 0205118607; ISBN-13: 9780205118601**
	Longman American History Atlas This full-color historical atlas designed especially for college students is a valuable reference tool and visual guide to American history. This atlas includes maps covering the scope of American history from the lives of the Native Americans to the 1990s. Produced by a renowned cartographic firm and a team of respected historians, the Longman American History Atlas will enhance any American history survey course. **ISBN: 0321004868; ISBN-13: 9780321004864**

MyHistoryLab (www.myhistorylab.com)

The Moment You Know

Educators know it. Students know it. It's that inspired moment when something that was difficult to understand suddenly makes perfect sense. MyHistoryLab has been designed and refined with a single purpose in mind: to help history teachers create that moment of understanding with their students.

Features of MyHistoryLab

MyHistoryLab provides **engaging experiences** that personalize, stimulate, and measure learning for each student.

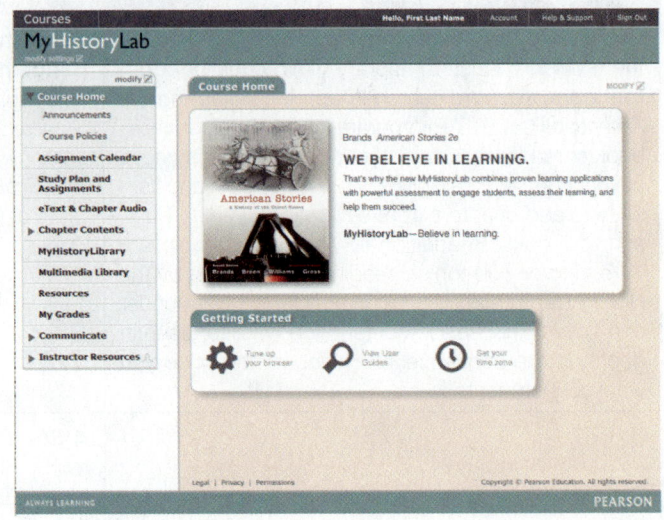

- *Closer Look tours*—walk students through a variety of images, maps, and primary sources in detail, helping them to uncover their meaning and understand their context.
- **A History Bookshelf**—enables students to read, download, or print up to 100 of the most commonly assigned history works, like Thomas Paine's, *Common Sense*, Booker T. Washington's, *Up From Slavery*, and Andrew Carnegie's, *Autobiography*.
- **The Pearson eText**— lets students access their textbook anytime, anywhere, and any way they want—including listening online or downloading to their iPad.
- **A personalized study plan** for each student, based on a chapter Pre-Test, arranges content from less complex thinking—like remembering basic facts—to more complex critical thinking—like understanding connections and analyzing the past. This layered approach promotes better critical-thinking skills, and helps students succeed in the course and beyond.
- **Assessment** tied to every chapter enables both instructors and students to track progress and get immediate feedback. With results flowing into a powerful gradebook, the assessment program helps instructors identify student challenges early—and find the best resources with which to help students.
- **An assignment calendar** allows instructors to assign graded activities, with specific deadlines, and measure student progress.
- *ClassPrep* collects the very best class presentation resources in one convenient online destination, so instructors can keep students engaged throughout every class.
- **Audio Files**—Full audio of the entire text is included to suit the varied learning styles of today's students. In addition there are audio clips of speeches, readings, and music that provide another engaging way to experience history.
- **Text and Visual Documents**—Over 1,500 primary source documents, images, and maps are available organized by chapter in the text. Primary source documents are also available in

the MyHistoryLibrary and can be searched by author, title, theme, and topic. Many of these documents include critical thinking questions.

- **Lecture and Archival Videos**—Lectures by leading scholars on provocative topics give students a critical look at key points in history. Videos of speeches, news footage, key historical events, and other archival video take students back to the moment in history.
- **MySearchLab**—This website provides students access to a number of reliable sources for online research, as well as clear guidance on the research and writing process.
- **Gradebook**—Students can follow their own progress and instructors can monitor the work of the entire class. Automated grading of quizzes and assignments helps both instructors and students save time and monitor their results throughout the course.

NEW In-text References to MyHistoryLab Resources

Read, View, See, Watch, Hear, Study, and Review Icons integrated in the text connect resources on MyHistoryLab to specific topics within the chapters. The icons are not exhaustive; many more resources are available than those highlighted in the book, but the icons draw attention to some of the most high-interest resources available on MyHistoryLab.

Read the **Document** on **myhistorylab.com** Points students to primary and secondary source documents related to the chapter.

View the **Image** on **myhistorylab.com** Identifies primary and secondary source images, including photographs, fine art, and artifacts to provide students with a visual perspective on history.

View the **Map** on **myhistorylab.com** Directs students to atlas and interactive maps; these present both broad overviews and detailed examinations of historical developments.

Watch the **Video** on **myhistorylab.com** Notes pertinent archival videos and videos of Pearson History authors that probe various topics.

Listen to the **Audio File** on **myhistorylab.com** Marks audio clips from historically significant songs and speeches that enrich students' engagement with history.

View the **Closer Look** on **myhistorylab.com** Alerts students to study resources for each chapter of the textbook available online through www.myhistorylab.com. These resources include practice tests and flashcards.

NEW MyHistoryLab Connections

At the end of each chapter a new feature called *MyHistoryLab Connections* prompts students to follow the Study Plan for the chapter, and provides a list of the resources that are marked with icons in the text.

Acknowledgments

The authors acknowledge with special gratitude the contribution of Kathleen T. McWhorter and Debby Kalk for their work in developing a sound pedagogical plan. We are also most grateful to our consultants and reviewers whose thoughtful and constructive work contributed greatly to this edition. Their many helpful suggestions led to significant improvements in the final product.

Jeffrey Adler, *University of Florida*; Edward Andrews, *University of New Hampshire*; Guy Aronoff, *California State University–Channel Islands*; Andrew Bacha, *Harrisburg Area Community College*; Frank M. Baglione, *Tallahassee Community College*; John Baick, *Western New England College*; Brett Barker, *University of Wisconsin–Marathon County*; Jonathan Beagle, *Western New England College*; Marjorie Berman, *Red Rocks Community College*; David Darryl Bibb, *University of Great Falls*; Brian Black, *Penn State Altoona*; Deborah Blackwell, *Texas A&M International University*; Marcia Schmidt Blaine, *Plymouth State University*; Chuck Boening, *Shelton State Community College*; Edward Bond, *Alabama A&M University*; Barbara Booth, *Santa Ana College*; Wesley Borucki, *Palm Beach Atlantic University*; Jeff Bremer, *Stephen F. Austin State University*; Jeff Broadwater, *Barton College*; Robert E. Brown, *Tunxis Community College*; John Burch, *Campbellsville University*; J. Michael Butler, *South Georgia College*; Don Butts, *Gordon College*; Shvonnie R. Caffey, *Bishop State Community College*; Jeff Carlisle, *Oklahoma City Community College*; Roger Carpenter, *University of Louisiana, Monroe*; Charles L. Cohen, *University of Wisconsin–Madison*; John Condon, *Merrimack College*; P. Scott Corbett, *Ventura College*; Robert Cray, *Montclair State University*; Andria Crosson, *University of Texas at San Antonio*; Thomas A. DeBlack, *Arkansas Tech University*; Andrea DeKoter, *State University of New York at Cortland*; Terrence Delaney, *Three Rivers Community College*; Rick Dodgson, *Lakeland College*; Dean Dohrman, *University of Central Missouri*; Gary Donato, *Massachusetts Bay Community College*; Lisa Linquist Dorr, *University of Alabama*; Shawn Dry, *Oakland Community College*; David Dzurec, *University of Scranton*; Scotty Edler, *North Central Texas College*; Damon Eubank, *Campbellsville University*; Gabrielle Everett, *Jefferson College*; Richard M. Filipink, *Western Illinois University*; Daniel Finn, *Seminole State College*; Michael Fitzgerald, *Franciscan University*; Amy Forss, *Metropolitan Community College*; Arthur Friedman, *Montclair State University*; Hal M. Friedman, *Henry Ford Community College*; Michael Gabriel, *Kutztown University*; Jeff Gall, *Truman State University;* George Gerdow, *Northeastern Illinois University*; Michael Gherke, *Glenville State College*; John Glen, *St. Louis Community College, Wildwood Campus*; Janet Golden, *Rutgers University*; Susan Gonda, *Grossmont College*; Larry Goodrich, *Northwest Vista College*; Kathleen Gorman, *Minnesota State University, Mankato*; Matthew Greider, *Lake Land College*; Aldo Garcia Guevara, *Worcester State College*; Edward Gutierrez, *University of Hartford*; Karen Hagan, *The Victoria College*; Dixie Ray Haggard, *Valdosta State University*; Charlotte Haller, *Worcester State College*; Gregory M. Havrilcsak, *The University of Michigan–Flint*; David M. Head, *John Tyler Community College*; Matthew Hiner, *Lakeland Community College*; Andrew G. Hollinger, *Tarrant County College*; Charles W. Hope, *Tarrant County College–Southeast Campus*; Wallace H. Hutcheon, *Northern Virginia Community College*; Ross Huxoll, *University of Nebraska–Kearney*; Diane B. Jackson, *Los Angeles Trade Technical College*; Thomas Jodziewicz, *University of Dallas*; Andrew Johns, *Brigham Young University*; Juli A. Jones, *San Diego Mesa College*; Russell Jones, *Eastern Michigan University*; Sandra Jowers-Barber, *University of the District of Columbia*; Mark S. Joy, *Jamestown College*; Jennifer Fish Kashay, *Colorado State University*; John S. Kemp, *Truckee Meadows Community College*; Don Knox, *Wayland Baptist University*; Raymond Krohn, *University of Northern Colorado*; Melissa LaPrelle, *Collin County Community College*; William P. Leeman, *Providence College*; Daniel Lewis, *California State Polytechnic University, Pomona*; Stephen Lowe, *Olivet*

Nazarene University; John Maddox, *Los Angeles Valley Community College;* Robert W. Malick, *Harrisburg Area Community College;* Evelyn DeLong Mangie, *University of South Florida;* Edwin Martini, *Western Michigan University;* Louis McDermott, *Solano Community College;* Brian McKnight, *Angelo State University;* Peter C. Messer, *Mississippi State University;* Michael Messner, *Skyline College;* Mary M. McClendon, *Chipola College;* Greg Miller, *Hillsborough Community College;* Sarah E. Miller, *University of South Carolina–Salkehatchie;* Russell Mitchell, *Tarrant County College Southeast;* Caryn Neumann, *Miami University of Ohio;* Dave O'Grady, *University of Southern Indiana;* Gary B. Ostrower, *Alfred University;* Edgar Pacas, *Pasadena City College;* Chris Padgett, *American River College;* David Parker, *Kennesaw State University;* Donald Parkerson, *East Carolina University;* Elaine Pascale, *Suffolk University;* Ronnie Peacock, *Metropolitan State College of Denver;* Katherine Pierce, *Sam Houston State University;* Jeffrey J. Pilz, *North Iowa Area Community College;* Ann Marie Plane, *University of California at Santa Barbara;* Brian K. Plummer, *Azusa Pacific University;* Charlotte Power, *Black River Technical College;* William Price, *North Country Community College*; Daniel Prosterman, *Salem College;* Steven Rauch, *Augusta State University;* David B. Raymond, *Northern Maine Community College;* Jonathan Rees, *Colorado State University, Pueblo;* Miriam Reumann, *The University of Rhode Island;* Paul Rorvig, *University of Central Missouri;* Rodney Ross, *Harrisburg Area Community College;* Tara Ross, *Onondaga Community College;* Mary Ellen Rowe, *University of Central Missouri;* Wendy Maier Sarti, *Oakton Community College;* John C. Savagian, *Alverno College;* Sandra Schackel, *Boise State University;* James Schick, *Pittsburg State University;* Don Schwegler, *SUNY New Paltz;* Earl A. Shoemaker, *University of Wisconsin–Eau Claire;* Terry L. Shoptaugh, *Minnesota State University Moorhead;* James Showalter, *Langston University;* Jeffrey Smith, *Lindenwood University;* Kris Smith, *Lindenwood University;* David L. Snead, *Liberty University;* Jean A. Stuntz, *West Texas A&M University;* James Taw, *Valdosta State University;* Jon Taylor, *University of Central Missouri;* Brad Tennant, *Presentation College;* James Treu, *North Central Missouri College;* John Turner, *University of Southern Alabama;* Marcus S. Turner, *San Jacinto College Central;* Jennifer Wallach, *University of North Texas;* Kenneth A. Watras, *Park University's College of Distance Learning;* Paul Weinstein, *The University of Akron Wayne College;* Pam West, *Jefferson State Community College;* Cheryl White, *Louisiana State University Shreveport;* Scott M. Williams, *Weatherford College;* David Williams, *Valdosta State University;* Larry C. Wilson, *San Jacinto College;* Julie Winch, *University of Massachusetts–Boston;* Deborah Wood, *SUNY Brockport;* Chad Wooley, *Tarrant County College;* Cristina Zaccarini, *Adelphi University;* Colleen Shaughnessy Zeena, *Endicott College;* and Patricia Zelman, *Tarleton State University.*

The staff at Pearson continued its generous support and assistance for our efforts. We thank our Executive Editor Ed Parsons for his attention, support, and thoughtful guidance throughout this revision; Development Editor Gerald Lombardi, who helped us augment and enhance the appeal of the text; and Executive Marketing Manager Maureen Prado Roberts, who worked zealously to convey the message and vision of the authors to the Pearson sales force and to the marketplace. Production Manager Denise Forlow, Cover Design Manager/Cover Designer Maria Lange, and Lindsay Bethoney and the staff at PreMediaGlobal put the finishing touches on this new edition and deftly guided it through the many phases of production.

Finally, each author received aid and encouragement from many colleagues, friends, and family members. T. H. Breen thanks Strother Roberts for his splendid help with this edition. Hal Williams extends thanks to Carole S. Cohen, Jacqueline Bradley, and Susan Harper-Bisso for their help with revisions for this edition. Ariela Gross extends thanks to Riaz Tejani for invaluable help with this edition.

H. W. Brands

T. H. Breen

R. Hal Williams

Ariela J. Gross

About the **Authors**

H. W. Brands

H. W. Brands is the Dickson Allen Anderson Centennial Professor of History at the University of Texas at Austin. He is the author of numerous works of history and international affairs, including *The Devil We Knew: Americans and the Cold War* (1993), *Into the Labyrinth: The United States and the Middle East* (1994), *The Reckless Decade: America in the 1890s* (1995), *TR: The Last Romantic* (a biography of Theodore Roosevelt) (1997), *What America Owes the World: The Struggle for the Soul of Foreign Policy* (1998), *The First American: The Life and Times of Benjamin Franklin* (2000), *The Strange Death of American Liberalism* (2001), *The Age of Gold: The California Gold Rush and the New American Dream* (2002), *Woodrow Wilson* (2003), *Andrew Jackson* (2005), *Traitor to His Class: The Privileged Life and Radical Presidency of Franklin Delano Roosevelt* (2008), and *American Colossus: The Triumph of Capitalism, 1865–1900* (2010). His writing has received popular and critical acclaim; several of his books have been bestsellers, and *The First American* and *Traitor to His Class* were finalists for the Pulitzer Prize. He lectures frequently across North America and in Europe. His essays and reviews have appeared in the *New York Times*, the *Wall Street Journal*, the *Washington Post*, the *Los Angeles Times*, *Atlantic Monthly*, and elsewhere. He is a regular guest on radio and television, and has participated in several historical documentary films.

T. H. Breen

T. H. Breen is the Director of the Nicholas D. Chabraja Center for Historical Studies and William Smith Mason Professor of American History at Northwestern University. He received his Ph.D. from Yale University in 1968. He has taught at Northwestern since 1970. Breen's major books include *The Character of the Good Ruler: A Study of Puritan Political Ideas in New England* (1974); *Puritans and Adventurers: Change and Persistence in Early America* (1980); *Tobacco Culture: The Mentality of the Great Tidewater Planters on the Eve of Revolution* (1985); *Marketplace of Revolution: How Consumer Politics Shaped American Independence* (2004); and, with Stephen Innes of the University of Virginia, *"Myne Owne Ground": Race and Freedom on Virginia's Eastern Shore* (1980). His *Imagining the Past* (1989) won the 1990 Historic Preservation Book Award. In addition to receiving several awards for outstanding teaching at Northwestern, Breen has been the recipient of research grants from the American Council of Learned Societies, the Guggenheim Foundation, the Institute for Advanced Study (Princeton), the National Humanities Center, and the Huntington Library. He has served as the Fowler Hamilton Fellow at Christ Church, Oxford University (1987–1988), the Pitt Professor of American History and Institutions, Cambridge University (1990–1991), the Harmsworth Professor of American History at Oxford University (2000–2001), and was a recipient of the Humboldt Prize (Germany). He has recently published *American Insurgents, American Patriots: The Revolution of the People* (2010). He is now working on a book to be entitled *Journey to a Nation: George Washington's Campaign to Bring the New Federal Government to the People, 1789–1791.*

R. Hal Williams

R. Hal Williams is professor of history at Southern Methodist University. He received his A.B. from Princeton University in 1963 and his Ph.D. from Yale University in 1968. His books include *The Democratic Party and California Politics, 1880–1896* (1973); *Years of Decision: American Politics in the 1890s* (1978); *The Manhattan Project: A Documentary Introduction to the Atomic Age* (1990); and *Realigning America: McKinley, Bryan, and the Remarkable Election of 1896* (2010). A specialist in American political history, he taught at Yale University from 1968 to 1975 and came to SMU in 1975 as chair of the Department of History. From 1980 to 1988, he served as dean of Dedman College, the school of humanities and sciences, at SMU, and from 2002 to 2006 as dean of Research and Graduate Studies. In 1980, he was a visiting professor at University College, Oxford University. Williams has received grants from the American Philosophical Society and the National Endowment for the Humanities, and he has served on the Texas Committee for the Humanities. He is currently working on a biography of James G. Blaine, the late-nineteenth-century speaker of the House, secretary of state, and Republican presidential candidate.

Ariela J. Gross

Ariela Gross is John B. and Alice R. Sharp Professor of Law and History, and Co-Director of the Center for Law, History and Culture, at the University of Southern California. She has been a visiting Professor at Tel Aviv University, the École des Hautes Études en Sciences Sociales, and Kyoto University. She is the author of *Double Character: Slavery and Mastery in the Antebellum Southern Courtroom* (2000) and *What Blood Won't Tell: A History of Race on Trial in America* (2008), winner of the Willard Hurst Prize from the Law and Society Association; the Lillian Smith Award for the best book on the South, and the American Political Science Association Best Book on Race, Ethnicity, and Politics. Gross has received fellowships from the American Council of Learned Societies, the Guggenheim Foundation, and the National Endowment for the Humanities, and is now working on several comparative projects about law, race, and slavery in the Americas, and law, contemporary politics, and the memory of slavery in the U.S. and Europe.

1 NEW WORLD ENCOUNTERS

Preconquest–1608

Contents and Spotlight Questions

((•─ **Listen** to the **Chapter Audio** for Chapter 1 on **myhistorylab.com**

DIVERSE CULTURES: DE VACA'S JOURNEY THROUGH NATIVE AMERICA

The diversity of Native American peoples astonished the Europeans who first voyaged to the New World. Early sixteenth-century Spanish adventurer Álvar Núñez Cabeza de Vaca offered a sample of this

De Vaca and His Fellow Shipwreck Survivors In 1528, a hurricane destroyed a fleet transporting over 300 Spanish soldiers from Florida to Cuba. Shipwrecked on the Florida coast, the survivors set out over land for Spain's holdings in Mexico. Eight years later only De Vaca and three companions survived to stumble into the Spanish outpost at Culiacán.

striking diversity in his La *Relacion (The Account)*. Shipwrecked in Florida in 1528, De Vaca had made his way overland to Texas. During his eight year trek, De Vaca met and lived among Indians belonging to over twenty unique cultures.

The Apalachees of Florida cultivated "great fields of maize" as well as beans and squash. "The Indians of southeastern Texas, whom De Vaca called "the People of the Figs," did not cultivate the soil." Instead, they relied upon fishing and gathering the fruit of the prickly pear cactus, which De Vaca called "figs." To harvest this fruit, the "fig" people traveled great distances, trading with other Indians along their journey. On the plains of northern Mexico, De Vaca encountered the "People of the Cows," who hunted bison for food and clothing.

Other Europeans echoed De Vaca's observations. Throughout the Americas they encountered rich cultural diversity. Language, physical attributes, social organization, and local foodways separated the Indians of North America into unique nations. Each of these nations, in its own way, would have to come to terms with the arrival of Europeans.

Europeans sailing in the wake of Admiral Christopher Columbus—explorers and conquerors like De Vaca—constructed a narrative of superiority that survived long after they themselves passed from the scene. The standard narrative recounted first in Europe and then in the United States depicted heroic adventurers, missionaries, and soldiers sharing Western civilization with the peoples of the New World and opening a vast virgin land to economic development. This familiar tale celebrated material progress, the inevitable spread of European values, and the taming of frontiers. It was a history crafted by the victors and their descendants to explain how they had come to inherit the land.

This narrative of events no longer provides an adequate explanation for European conquest and settlement. It is not so much wrong as partisan, incomplete, even offensive. History recounted from the perspective of the victors inevitably silences the voices of the victims, the peoples who, in the victors' view, foolishly resisted economic and technological progress. Heroic tales of the advance of Western values only deflect modern attention away from the rich cultural and racial diversity that characterized North American societies for a very long time. More disturbing, traditional tales of European conquest also obscure the sufferings of the millions of Native Americans who perished and the millions of Africans sold in the New World as slaves.

By placing these complex, often unsettling, experiences within an interpretive framework of *creative adaptations*—rather than of *exploration* or *settlement*—we go a long way toward recapturing the full human dimensions of conquest and resistance. While the New World often witnessed tragic violence and systematic betrayal, it allowed ordinary people of three different races and many different ethnic identities opportunities to shape their own lives as best they could within diverse, often hostile environments.

Neither the Native Americans nor the Africans were passive victims of European exploitation. Within their own families and communities, they made choices, sometimes rebelling, sometimes accommodating, but always trying to make sense in terms of their own cultures of what was happening to them.

NATIVE AMERICANS BEFORE THE CONQUEST

As almost any Native American could have informed the first European adventurers, the peopling of America did not begin in 1492. In fact, although the Spanish invaders who followed Columbus proclaimed the discovery of a "New World," they really brought into contact three worlds—Europe, Africa, and the Americas—that had existed for thousands years. Indeed, the first migrants reached the North American continent some 15,000–20,000 years ago.

Environmental conditions played a major part in this great human trek. Twenty thousand years ago, during the last Ice Age, the earth's climate was colder than it is today. Huge glaciers, often more than a mile thick, extended as far south as the present states of Illinois and Ohio and covered much of western Canada. Much of the world's moisture was transformed into ice, and the oceans dropped hundreds of feet below their current levels. The receding waters created a land bridge connecting Asia and North America, a region now submerged beneath the Bering Sea that archaeologists named Beringia.

Even at the height of the last Ice Age, much of the far north remained free of glaciers. Small bands of spear-throwing Paleo-Indians pursued giant mammals (megafauna)—woolly mammoths and mastodons, for example—across the vast tundra of Beringia. These hunters were the first human beings to set foot on a vast, uninhabited continent. Because these migrations took place over a long time and involved small, independent bands of highly nomadic people, the Paleo-Indians never developed a sense of common identity. Each group focused on its own immediate survival, adjusting to the opportunities presented by various microenvironments.

The tools and weapons of the Paleo-Indians differed little from those of other Stone Age peoples found in Asia, Africa, and Europe. In terms of human health, however, something occurred on the Beringian tundra that forever altered the history of Native Americans. The members of these small migrating groups stopped hosting a number of communicable diseases—smallpox and measles being the deadliest. Although Native Americans experienced illnesses such as tuberculosis, they no longer suffered the major epidemics that under normal conditions would have killed much of their population every year. The physical isolation of these bands may have protected them from the spread of contagious disease. Another theory notes that epidemics have frequently been associated with prolonged contact with domestic animals such as cattle and pigs. Since the Paleo-Indians did not domesticate animals, not even horses, they may have avoided the microbes that caused virulent European and African diseases.

Whatever the explanation for this curious epidemiological record, Native American populations lost immunities that later might have protected them from many contagious germs. Thus, when they first came into contact with Europeans and Africans, Native Americans had no defense against the great killers of the Early Modern World. And, as medical researchers have discovered, dislocations resulting from war and famine made the Indians even more vulnerable to infectious disease.

What explains cultural differences among Native American groups before European conquest?

View the **Image**
Clovis Points on
myhistorylab.com

The Environmental Challenge: Food, Climate, and Culture

Some 12,000 years ago, global warming reduced the glaciers, allowing nomadic hunters to pour into the heart of the North America (see Map 1.1). Within just a few thousand years, Native Americans had journeyed from Colorado to the southern tip of South America.

Blessed with a seemingly inexhaustible supply of meat, the early migrants experienced rapid population growth. As archaeologists have discovered, however, the sudden expansion of human population coincided with the loss of scores of large mammal species, many of them the spear-throwers' favorite sources of food: mammoths and mastodons, camels, and, amazingly, horses were eradicated from the land. The peoples of the Great Plains did not obtain horses until the Spanish reintroduced them in the New World in 1547. Some archaeologists have suggested that the early Paleo-Indian hunters were responsible for the mass extinction of so many animals. However, climatic warming, which transformed well-watered regions into arid territories, probably put the large mammals under severe stress. Early humans simply contributed to an ecological process over which they ultimately had little control.

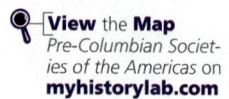

View the **Map**
Pre-Columbian Societies of the Americas on
myhistorylab.com

The Indian peoples adjusted to the changing environment. As they dispersed across North America, they developed new food sources, at first smaller mammals and fish, nuts and berries, and then about 5,000 years ago, they discovered how to cultivate certain plants. Knowledge of maize (corn), squash, and beans spread north from central Mexico. The peoples living in the Southwest acquired cultivation skills long before the bands living along the Atlantic Coast. The shift to basic crops—a transformation that is sometimes termed the Agricultural Revolution—profoundly altered Native American societies.

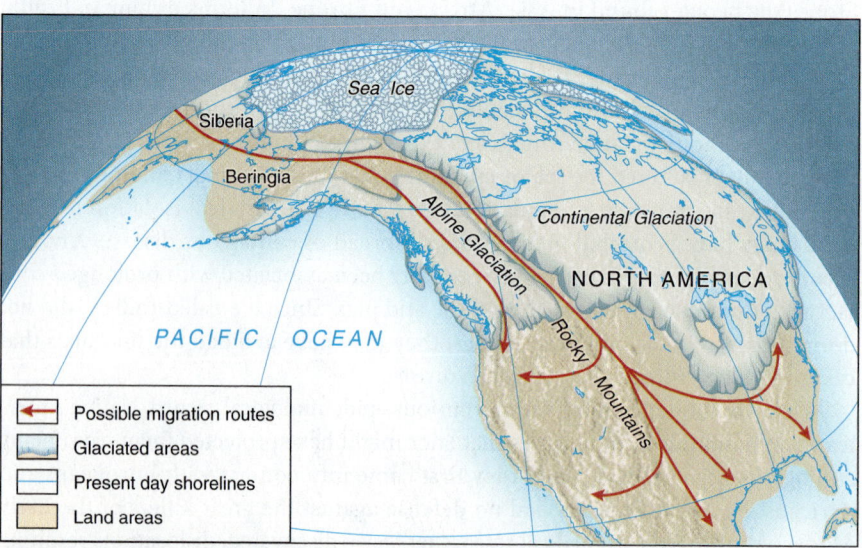

Map 1.1 *Routes of the First Americans*   The peopling of North America began about 20,000 years ago, during the last Ice Age, and continued for millennia.

The availability of a more reliable store of food helped liberate nomadic groups from the insecurities of hunting and gathering. During this period, Native Americans began to produce ceramics, a valuable technology for storing grain. The harvest made permanent villages possible, which often were governed by clearly defined hierarchies of elders and kings, and as the food supply increased, the population greatly expanded, especially around urban centers in the Southwest and the Mississippi Valley. Although the evidence is patchy, scholars currently estimate that approximately 4 million Native Americans lived north of Mexico when the Europeans arrived.

The vast distances and varied climates of North America gave rise to a great diversity of human cultures employing a wide variety of ingenuous strategies for dealing with their unique regional environments. (See Map 1.2.) Some native peoples were unable to take advantage of the Agricultural Revolution. In the harsh climate of the far north, Inuit living in small autonomous kin-based bands developed watertight vessels called kayaks that allowed them to travel and hunt seals in frigid Arctic waters. Many Indian peoples, like those of the Great Plains, combined agriculture with hunting, living most of the year in permanent villages built along river valleys with the men dispersing to seasonal hunting camps at certain times. To attract game animals, especially the buffalo, Plains Indian communities burned the grasslands annually to promote the growth of fresh, green vegetation. Some Native American groups were even more dramatic in their efforts to reshape their natural environment. In the southwest, in what would become New Mexico, the Anasazi culture built massive pueblo villages and overcame the aridity of their desert home by developing a complex society that could sustain a huge, technologically sophisticated network of irrigation canals.

Quick Check

✓ What was life like for the first humans living in North America and what role did the Earth's climate play in shaping their experiences?

Aztec Dominance

As with the Anasazi, the stability the Agricultural Revolution brought allowed the Indians of Mexico and Central America to structure more complex societies. Like the Inca, who lived in what is now Ecuador, Peru, and northern Chile, the Mayan and Toltec peoples of Central Mexico built vast cities, formed government bureaucracies that dominated large tributary populations, and developed hieroglyphic writing and an accurate solar calendar. Their cities, which housed several hundred thousand people, impressed the Spanish conquerors. Bernal Díaz del Castillo reported, "When we saw all those [Aztec] towns and villages built in the water, and other great towns on dry land, and that

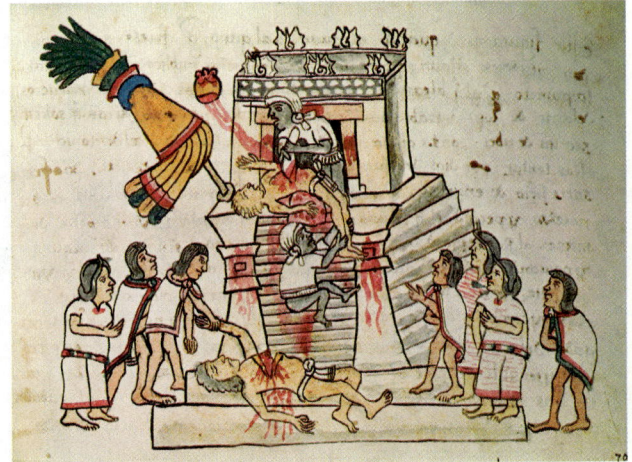

The Aztecs This image from the *Codex Magliabechiano* depicts Aztec priests engaged in human sacrifice.

Map 1.2 *The First Americans: Locations of Major Indian Groups and Culture Areas in the 1600s* The Native American groups scattered across North America into the 1600s had strikingly diverse cultures.

straight and level causeway leading to Mexico, we were astounded…. Indeed, some of our soldiers asked whether it was not all a dream."

Not long before Columbus's first voyage across the Atlantic, the Aztec, an aggressive, warlike people, swept through the Valley of Mexico, conquering the great cities that their enemies had constructed. Aztec warriors ruled by force, reducing defeated rivals to tributary status. In 1519, the Aztecs' main ceremonial center, Tenochtitlán (on the site of modern Mexico City), contained as many as 250,000 people, compared with only 50,000 in Seville, the port from which the early Spanish explorers of the Americas had sailed. Elaborate human sacrifice associated with Huitzilopochtli, the Aztec sun god, horrified Europeans, who apparently did not find the savagery of their own civilization so objectionable. The Aztec ritual killings were connected to the agricultural cycle, and the Indians believed the blood of their victims possessed extraordinary fertility powers. A fragment of an Aztec song-poem captures the indomitable spirit that once pervaded this militant culture:

> Proud of itself
>
> is the city of Mexico—Tenochtitlán.
>
> Here no one fears to die in war.
>
> This is our glory. . . .
>
> Who could conquer Tenochtitlán?
>
> Who could shake the foundation of heaven?

Quick Check

✓ What most impressed Spanish explorers about Aztec culture?

Eastern Woodland Cultures

In northeastern North America along the Atlantic coast, the Indians did not practice intensive agriculture. These peoples, numbering less than a million at the time of conquest, generally supplemented farming with seasonal hunting and gathering. Most belonged to what ethnographers term the Eastern Woodland Cultures. Small bands formed villages during the summer. The women cultivated maize and other crops while the men hunted and fished. During the winter, difficulties associated with feeding so many people forced the communities to disperse. Each family lived off the land as best it could.

Seventeenth-century English settlers were most likely to have encountered the Algonquian-speaking peoples who occupied much of the Atlantic coast from North Carolina to Maine. Included in this large linguistic family were the Powhatan of Tidewater, Virginia, the Narragansett of Rhode Island, and the Abenaki of northern New England.

Algonquian groups exploited different resources in different regions and spoke different dialects. They did not develop strong ties of mutual identity. When their own interests were involved, they were more than willing to ally themselves with Europeans or "foreign" Indians against other Algonquian speakers. Divisions among Indian groups would facilitate European conquest. Native American peoples greatly outnumbered the first settlers, and had the Europeans not forged alliances with the Indians, they could not so easily have gained a foothold on the continent.

However divided the Indians of eastern North America may have been, they shared many cultural values and assumptions. Most Native Americans, for example, defined their place in society through kinship. Such personal bonds determined the character of economic and political relations. The farming bands living in areas eventually claimed by England were often matrilineal, which meant in effect that the women owned the fields and houses, maintained tribal customs, and had a role in tribal government. Among the native communities of Canada and the northern Great Lakes, patrilineal forms were more common. In these groups, the men owned the hunting grounds that the family needed to survive.

Eastern Woodland communities organized diplomacy, trade, and war around reciprocal relationships that impressed Europeans as being extraordinarily egalitarian, even democratic. Chains of native authority were loosely structured. Native leaders were such renowned public speakers because persuasive rhetoric was often their only effective source of power. It required considerable oratorical skills for an Indian leader to persuade independent-minded warriors to support a proposed policy.

Before the arrival of the white settlers, Indian wars were seldom very lethal. Young warriors attacked neighboring bands largely to exact revenge for an insult or the death of a relative, or to secure captives. Fatalities, when they did occur, sparked cycles of revenge. Some captives were tortured to death; others were adopted into the community to replace fallen relatives.

Quick Check

✓ How was society structured among the Eastern Woodland Indians before the arrival of Europeans?

CONDITIONS OF CONQUEST

How did Europeans and Native Americans interact during the period of first contact?

The arrival of large numbers of white men and women on the North American continent profoundly altered Native American cultures. Change did not occur at the same rates in all places. Indian villages on the Atlantic coast came under severe pressure almost immediately; inland groups had more time to adjust. Wherever Indians lived, however, conquest strained traditional ways of life, and as daily patterns of experience changed almost beyond recognition, native peoples had to devise new answers, responses, and ways to survive in physical and social environments that eroded tradition.

Cultural Negotiations

Native Americans were not passive victims of geopolitical forces beyond their control. So long as they remained healthy, they held their own in the early exchanges, and although they eagerly accepted certain trade goods, they generally resisted other aspects of European cultures. The earliest recorded contacts between Indians and explorers suggest curiosity and surprise rather than hostility.

What Indians desired most was peaceful trade. The earliest French explorers reported that natives waved from shore, urging the Europeans to exchange metal items for beaver skins. In fact, the Indians did not perceive themselves at a disadvantage in these dealings. They could readily see the technological advantage of guns over bows and arrows. Metal knives made daily tasks much easier. And to acquire such goods they gave up pelts, which to them seemed in abundant supply. "The English have no sense," one Indian informed a French priest. "They give us twenty knives like this for one Beaver skin." Another native announced that "the Beaver does everything perfectly well: it makes kettles, hatchets, swords, knives, bread … in short, it makes everything." The man who recorded these observations reminded French readers—in case they had missed the point—that the Indian was "making sport of us Europeans."

Trading sessions along the eastern frontier were really cultural seminars. The Europeans tried to make sense out of Indian customs, and although they may have called the natives "savages," they quickly discovered that the Indians drove hard bargains. They demanded gifts; they set the time and place of trade.

Communicating with the Indians was always difficult for the Europeans, who did not understand the alien sounds and gestures of the Native American cultures. In the absence of meaningful conversation, Europeans often concluded that the Indians held them in high regard, perhaps seeing the newcomers as gods. Such one-sided encounters involved a lot of projection, a mental process of translating alien sounds and gestures into what Europeans wanted to hear. Sometimes the adventurers did not even try to communicate with the Indians, assuming from superficial observation—as did the sixteenth-century explorer Giovanni da Verrazzano—"that they have no religion, and that they live in absolute freedom, and that everything they do proceeds from Ignorance."

Ethnocentric Europeans tried repeatedly to "civilize" the Indians. In practice that meant persuading natives to dress like the colonists, attend white schools, live in permanent structures, and, most important, accept Christianity. The Indians listened more or less patiently, but in the end, they usually rejected European values. One South Carolina trader explained that when Indians were asked to become more English, they said no, "for they thought it hard, that we should desire them to change their manners and customs, since they did not desire us to turn Indians."

Some Indians were attracted to Christianity, but most paid it lip service or found it irrelevant to their needs. As one Huron told a French priest, "It would be useless for me to repent having sinned, seeing that I never have sinned." Another Huron announced that he did not fear punishment after death since "we cannot tell whether everything that appears faulty to Men, is so in the Eyes of God."

Among some Indian groups, gender figured significantly in a person's willingness to convert to Christianity. Native men who traded animal skins for European goods had more frequent contact with the whites and proved more receptive to the missionaries' arguments. But native women jealously guarded traditional culture, a system that often sanctioned polygamy—a husband having several wives—and gave women substantial authority over the distribution of food within the village.

The white settlers' educational system proved no more successful than their religion in winning cultural converts. Young Indians deserted stuffy classrooms at the first opportunity. In 1744, Virginia offered several Iroquois boys a free education at the College of William and Mary. The Iroquois leaders rejected the invitation because they found that boys who had gone to college "were absolutely good for nothing being neither acquainted with the true methods of killing deer, catching Beaver, or surprising an enemy."

Even matrimony seldom eroded the Indians' attachment to their own customs. When Native Americans and whites married—unions the English found less desirable

Read the **Document**
Thomas Hariot, The Algonquian Peoples on **myhistorylab.com**

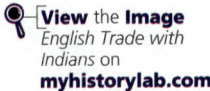
View the **Image**
English Trade with Indians on **myhistorylab.com**

Quick Check

✓ Why did Europeans insist on trying to "civilize" the Indians?

than did the French or Spanish—the European partner usually elected to live among the Indians. Impatient settlers who regarded the Indians simply as an obstruction to progress sometimes developed more coercive methods, such as enslavement, to achieve cultural conversion. Again, from the white perspective, the results were disappointing. Indian slaves ran away or died. In either case, they did not become Europeans.

Threats to Survival: Columbian Exchange

Over time, cooperative encounters between the Native Americans and Europeans became less frequent. The Europeans found it almost impossible to understand the Indians' relation to the land and other natural resources. English planters cleared the forests and fenced the fields and, in the process, radically altered the ecological systems on which the Indians depended. The European system of land use inevitably reduced the supply of deer and other animals essential to traditional native cultures.

Dependency also came in more subtle forms. The Indians welcomed European commerce, but like so many consumers throughout history, they discovered that the objects they most coveted inevitably brought them into debt. To pay for the trade goods, the Indians hunted more aggressively and even further reduced the population of fur-bearing mammals.

Commerce eroded Indian independence in other ways. After several disastrous wars—the Yamasee War in South Carolina (1715), for example—the natives learned that demonstrations of force usually resulted in the suspension of normal trade, on which the Indians had grown dependent for guns and ammunition, among other things. A hardened English businessman made the point bluntly. When asked if the Catawba Indians would harm his traders, he responded that "the danger would be … little from them, because they are too fond of our trade to lose it for the pleasure of shedding a little English blood."

It was disease, however, that ultimately destroyed the cultural integrity of many North American tribes. European adventurers exposed the Indians to bacteria and viruses against which they possessed no natural immunity. Smallpox, measles, and influenza decimated the Native American population. Other diseases such as alcoholism took a terrible toll.

The decimation of Native American peoples was an aspect of ecological transformation known as the Columbian Exchange. European conquerors exposed the Indians to new fatal diseases; the Indians adopted European plants and domestic animals and introduced the invaders to marvelous plants such as corn and potatoes that changed European history. (See Table 1.1.)

The Algonquian communities of New England experienced appalling death rates. One Massachusetts colonist reported in 1630 that the Indian peoples of his region "above twelve years since were swept away by a great & grievous Plague … so that there are verie few left to inhabite the Country." Settlers possessed no knowledge of germ theory—it was not formulated until the mid-nineteenth century—and speculated that the Christian God had providentially cleared the wilderness of heathens.

TABLE 1.1 New Opportunities, New Threats: The Columbian Exchange

From the Americas to Eurasia and Africa

Maize, Potatoes, Sweet Potatoes, Tomatoes, Beans, Cinchona Tree (the source of quinine), Many Types of Beans, Pineapples, Blueberries, Papaya, Pecans, Tobacco, Cacao, Vanilla, Peanuts, Peppers, Cassava, Squash, Avocadoes, Sunflowers, Turkeys, and (maybe) Syphilis

From Eurasia and Africa to the Americas

Cereals (wheat, rice, barley, etc.), Sugar, Bananas, Coconuts, Orchard Trees (apples, oranges, lemons, etc.), Olives, Wine Grapes, Coffee, Lettuces, Black Pepper, Livestock (horses, sheep, swine, cattle, goats, chickens, etc.), Honey Bees, Many Epidemic Diseases (smallpox, influenza, chicken pox, etc.)

Historical demographers now estimate that some tribes suffered a 90 to 95 percent population loss within the first century of European contact. The population of the Arawak Indians of the island of Hispaniola (modern Haiti and the Dominican Republic), for example, dropped from about 3,770,000 in 1496 to only 125 in 1570. The death of so many Indians decreased the supply of indigenous laborers, whom the Europeans needed to work the mines and grow staple crops such as sugar and tobacco. The decimation of native populations may have persuaded colonists throughout the New World to seek a substitute labor force in Africa. Indeed, the enslavement of blacks has been described as an effort by Europeans to "repopulate" the New World.

Indians who survived the epidemics often found that the fabric of traditional culture had come unraveled. The enormity of the death toll and the agony that accompanied it called traditional religious beliefs and practices into question. The survivors lost not only members of their families, but also elders who might have told them how to bury the dead properly and give spiritual comfort to the living.

Some native peoples, such as the Iroquois, who lived a long way from the coast and thus had more time to adjust to the challenge, withstood the crisis better than did those who immediately confronted the Europeans and Africans. Refugee Indians from the hardest-hit eastern communities were absorbed into healthier western groups. However horrific the crisis may have been, it demonstrated just how much the environment—a source of opportunity as well as devastation—shaped human encounters throughout the New World.

View the **Map**
Native American Population Loss, 1500–1700 on **myhistorylab.com**

Quick Check
✓ What effect did the introduction of Old World diseases such as smallpox have on Native American societies and cultures?

WEST AFRICA: ANCIENT AND COMPLEX SOCIETIES

The first Portuguese who explored the African coast during the fifteenth century encountered many different political and religious cultures. Centuries earlier, Africans in this region had come into contact with Islam, the religion the Prophet Muhammad founded in the seventh century. Islam spread slowly from Arabia into West Africa. Not until A.D. 1030 did a kingdom in the Senegal Valley accept Islam. Many other West Africans, such as those in ancient Ghana, continued to observe traditional religions.

What was the character of the West African societies that European traders first encountered?

As Muslim traders from North Africa and the Middle East brought a new religion to West Africa, they expanded sophisticated trade networks that linked the villagers of Senegambia with urban centers in northwest Africa, Morocco, Tunisia, and Libya. Camel caravans regularly crossed the Sahara carrying goods that were exchanged for gold and slaves. Sub-Saharan Africa's well-developed links with Islam surprised a French priest who in 1686 observed African pilgrims going "to visit Mecca to visit Mahomet's tomb, although they are eleven or twelve hundred leagues distance from it."

West Africans spoke many languages and organized themselves into diverse political systems. Several populous states, sometimes termed "empires," exercised loose control over large areas. Ancient African empires such as Ghana were vulnerable to external attack and internal rebellion, and the oral and written histories of this region record the rise and fall of several large kingdoms. When European traders first arrived, the major states would have included Mali, Benin, and Kongo. Many other Africans lived in what are known as stateless societies, largely autonomous communities organized around lineage structures. In these respects, African and Native American cultures had much in common.

The Portuguese journeyed to Africa in search of gold and slaves. Mali and Joloff officials (see Map 1.3) were willing partners in this commerce but insisted that Europeans respect African trade regulations. They required the Europeans to pay tolls and other fees and restricted the conduct of their business to small forts or castles on the coast. Local merchants acquired slaves and gold in the interior and transported them to the coast, where they exchanged them for European manufactures. Transactions were calculated in local African currencies: A slave would be offered to a European trader for so many bars of iron or ounces of gold.

European slave traders accepted these terms, largely because they had no other choice. The African states fielded formidable armies, and outsiders soon discovered they could not impose their will on the region simply through force. Moreover, local diseases such as malaria and yellow fever proved so lethal for Europeans—six out of ten of whom would die within a single year's stay in Africa—that they were

happy to avoid dangerous trips to the interior. Most slaves were men and women taken captive during wars; others were victims of judicial practices designed specifically to supply the growing American market. By 1650, most West African slaves were destined for the New World rather than the Middle East.

Even before Europeans colonized the New World, the Portuguese were purchasing almost 1,000 slaves a year on the West African coast. The slaves were frequently forced to work on the sugar plantations of Madeira (Portuguese) and the Canaries (Spanish), Atlantic islands on which Europeans experimented with forms of unfree labor

Read the **Document** *Ghana and its People in the Eleventh Century* on **myhistorylab.com**

Slave Factories Cape Coast Castle was one of many so-called slave factories European traders built on the West African coast.

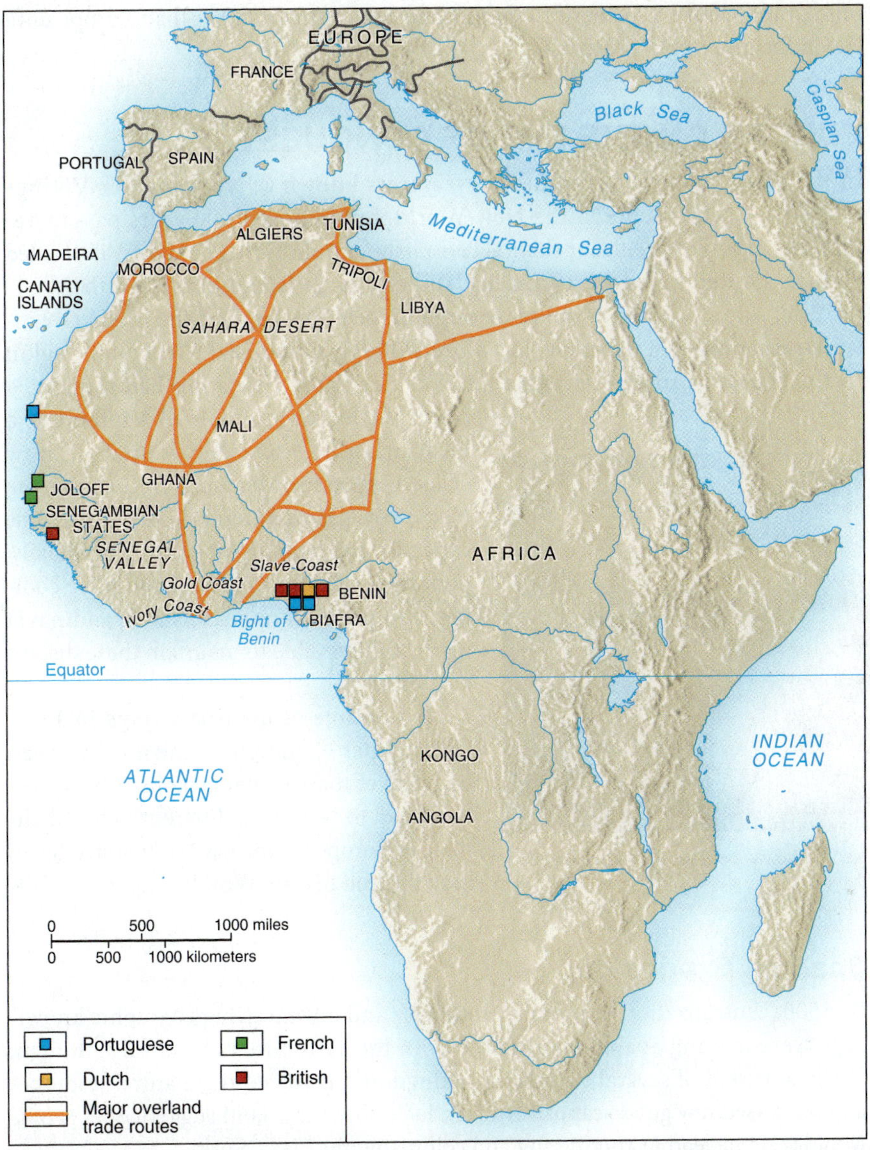

Map 1.3 *Trade Routes in Africa* This map of African trade routes in the 1600s illustrates the existence of a complex economic system.

that would later be more fully and ruthlessly established in the American colonies. Approximately 10.7 million Africans were taken to the New World as slaves. The figure for the eighteenth century alone is about 5.5 million, of which more than one-third came from West Central Africa. The Bight of Benin, the Bight of Biafra, and the Gold Coast supplied most of the others.

The peopling of the New World is usually seen as a story of European migrations. But in fact, during every year between 1650 and 1831, more Africans than Europeans came to the Americas. As historian Davis Eltis wrote, "In terms of

View the **Image**
Purchasing Slaves on the African Shore on
myhistorylab.com

immigration alone … America was an extension of Africa rather than Europe until late in the nineteenth century."

EUROPE ON THE EVE OF CONQUEST

What factors explain Spain's central role in New World exploration and colonization?

In the tenth century, Scandinavian seafarers known as Norsemen or Vikings established settlements in the New World, but almost 1,000 years passed before they received credit for their accomplishment. In 984, a band of Vikings led by Eric the Red sailed west from Iceland to a large island in the North Atlantic. Eric, who possessed a fine sense of public relations, named the island Greenland, reasoning that others would more willingly colonize the icebound region "if the country had a good name." A few years later, Eric's son Leif founded a small settlement he named Vinland at a location in northern Newfoundland now called L'Anse aux Meadows. At the time, the Norse voyages went unnoticed by other Europeans. The hostility of Native Americans, poor lines of communication, climatic cooling, and political upheavals in Scandinavia made it impossible to maintain these distant outposts.

At the time of his first voyage in 1492, Christopher Columbus seems to have been unaware of these earlier exploits. His expeditions had to wait for a different political climate in Europe in which a newly united Spain took the lead in New World conquest.

L'Anse aux Meadows Located on Newfoundland, L'Anse aux Meadows was the site of a Norse settlement.

Spanish Expansion

By 1500, centralization of political authority and advances in geographic knowledge were making Spain a world power. In the early fifteenth century, though, Spain consisted of several autonomous kingdoms. It lacked rich natural resources and possessed few good seaports. In fact, little about this land suggested its people would take the lead in conquering and colonizing the New World.

By the end of the 1400s, however, Spain suddenly came alive with creative energy. The marriage of Spain's two principal Christian rulers, King Ferdinand of Aragon and Queen Isabella of Castile, sparked a drive for political consolidation that, because of the monarchs' fervid Catholicism, took on the characteristics of a religious crusade. Spurred by the militant faith of their monarchs, the armies of Castile and Aragon waged holy war—known as the *Reconquista*—against the kingdom of Granada, the last independent Muslim state in Spain. In 1492, Granada fell, and, for the first time in seven centuries, the entire Iberian Peninsula was under Christian rulers. Spanish authorities showed no tolerance for people who rejected the Catholic faith.

During the *Reconquista*, thousands of Jews and Moors (Spanish Muslims) were driven from the country. Indeed, Columbus undoubtedly encountered such refugees as he was preparing for his famous voyage. From this volatile social and political environment came the **conquistadores**, men eager for personal glory and material gain, uncompromising in religion, and loyal to the crown. They were prepared to employ fire and sword in any cause sanctioned by God and king, and these adventurers carried European culture to the most populous regions of the New World.

Long before Spaniards ever reached the West Indies, they conquered the indigenous peoples of the Canary Islands, a strategically located archipelago in the eastern Atlantic. The harsh labor systems the Spanish developed in the Canaries served as models of subjugation in America. An early fifteenth-century Spanish chronicle described the Canary natives as "miscreants … [who] do not acknowledge their creator and live in part like beasts." Many islanders died of disease; others were killed in battle or enslaved. The new Spanish landholders introduced sugar, a labor-intensive plantation crop. They forced slaves captured in Africa to provide the labor. Dreams of wealth drove this oppressive process. Through the centuries, European colonists would repeat it many times.

Quick Check

✓ Who were the *conquistadores*, and what were their motivations in the New World?

The Strange Career of Christopher Columbus

If it had not been for Christopher Columbus (Cristoforo Colombo), Spain might never have gained an American empire. Little is known about his early life. Born in the Italian city of Genoa in 1451 of humble parentage, Columbus soon devoured the classical learning that had so recently been rediscovered and made available in print. He mastered geography, and—perhaps while sailing the coast of West Africa—he became obsessed with the idea of voyaging west across the Atlantic Ocean to reach Cathay, as China was then known to Europeans.

In 1484, Columbus presented his plan to the king of Portugal. However, while the Portuguese were just as interested as Columbus in reaching Cathay, they elected to voyage around the continent of Africa instead of following the route Columbus suggested. They suspected that Columbus had underestimated the circumference of the earth and that he would starve before reaching Asia. The Portuguese decision eventually paid off handsomely. In 1498, one of their captains, Vasco da Gama, returned from India with a fortune in spices and other luxury goods.

Undaunted by rejection, Columbus petitioned Isabella and Ferdinand for financial backing. They were initially no more interested in his grand design than the Portuguese had been. But time was on Columbus's side. Spain's aggressive new monarchs envied the success of their neighbor, Portugal. Columbus played on the rivalry between the countries, talking of wealth and empire. Indeed, for a person with little success or apparent support, he was supremely confident. One contemporary reported that when Columbus "made up his mind, he was as sure he would discover what he did discover, and find what he did find, as if he held it in a chamber under lock and key."

Columbus's stubborn lobbying for the "Enterprise of the Indies" wore down opposition in the Spanish court, and the two sovereigns provided him with a small

Watch the **Video**
How Should We Think of Columbus? on
myhistorylab.com

fleet of three ships: the *Niña*, the *Pinta*, and the *Santa Maria*. The indomitable admiral set sail for Cathay in August 1492, the same year that Grenada fell.

Educated Europeans of the fifteenth century knew the world was round. No one seriously believed that Columbus and his crew would tumble off the edge of the earth. The concern was with size, not shape. Columbus estimated the distance to the mainland of Asia to be about 3,000 nautical miles, a voyage his small ships would have no difficulty completing. The actual distance is 10,600 nautical miles, however, and had the New World not been in his way, he and his crew would have run out of food and water long before they reached China, as the Portuguese had predicted.

After stopping in the Canary Islands to refit the ships, Columbus continued westward in early September. When the tiny Spanish fleet sighted an island in the Bahamas after only 33 days at sea, the admiral concluded he had reached Asia. Since his mathematical calculations had obviously been correct, he assumed he would soon encounter the Chinese. It never occurred to Columbus that he had stumbled upon a New World. He assured his men, his patrons, and perhaps himself that the islands were indeed part of the fabled "Indies." Or, if not the Indies themselves, then they were surely an extension of the great Asian landmass. He searched for the splendid cities Marco Polo had described in his accounts of China in the thirteenth century, but instead of wealthy Chinese, Columbus encountered Native Americans, whom he appropriately, if mistakenly, called "Indians."

After his first voyage of discovery, Columbus returned to the New World three more times. But despite his courage and ingenuity, he could never find the treasure his financial supporters in Spain demanded. Columbus died in 1506 a frustrated but wealthy entrepreneur, unaware that he had reached a previously unknown continent separating Asia from Europe. The final disgrace came in December 1500 when an ambitious falsifier, Amerigo Vespucci, published a sensational account of his travels across the Atlantic that convinced German mapmakers he had proved America was distinct from Asia. Before the misconception could be corrected, the name *America* gained general acceptance throughout Europe.

Watch the **Video**
What is Columbus's Legacy? on
myhistorylab.com

Quick Check

✔ What did educated Europeans believe about the shape and size of the Earth prior to 1492?

SPAIN IN THE AMERICAS

How did Spanish conquest of Central and South America transform Native American cultures?

Only two years after Columbus's first voyage, Spain and Portugal almost went tlo war over the anticipated treasure of Asia. Pope Alexander VI negotiated a settlement that pleased both kingdoms. Portugal wanted to exclude the Spanish from the west coast of Africa and, what was more important, from Columbus's new route to "India." Spain insisted on maintaining complete control over lands discovered by Columbus, which were still regarded as extensions of China. The **Treaty of Tordesillas** (1494) divided the entire world along a line located 270 leagues west of the Azores. Any lands discovered west of the line belonged to Spain. At the time, no European had ever seen Brazil, which turned out to be on Portugal's side of the line. (Brazilians speak Portuguese.) The treaty failed to discourage future English, Dutch, and French adventurers from trying their luck in the New World.

The *Conquistadores*: Faith and Greed

Spain's new discoveries unleashed a horde of *conquistadores* on the Caribbean. These independent adventurers carved out small settlements on Cuba, Hispaniola, Jamaica, and Puerto Rico in the 1490s and early 1500s. They were not interested in creating a permanent society in the New World. Rather, they came for instant wealth, preferably in gold, and were not squeamish about the means they used to get it. Bernal Díaz, one of the first Spaniards to migrate to the region, explained he had traveled to America "to serve God and His Majesty, to give light to those who were in darkness, and to grow rich, as all men desire to do." In less than two decades, the Indians who had inhabited the Caribbean islands had been exterminated, victims of exploitation and disease.

For a quarter century, the *conquistadores* concentrated their energies on the major islands that Columbus had discovered. Rumors of fabulous wealth in Mexico, however, aroused the interest of many Spaniards, including Hernán Cortés, a minor government functionary in Cuba. Like so many members of his class, he dreamed of glory, military adventure, and riches that would transform him from an ambitious court clerk into an honored nobleman or *hidalgo*. On November 18, 1518, Cortés and a small army left Cuba to verify the stories of Mexico's treasure. Events soon demonstrated that Cortés was a leader of extraordinary ability.

His adversary was the legendary Aztec emperor Montezuma. The confrontation between the two powerful personalities is one of the more dramatic stories of early American history. A fear of competition from rival *conquistadores* coupled with a burning desire to conquer a new empire drove Cortés forward. Determined to push his men through any obstacle, he burned the ships that had carried them to Mexico to prevent them from retreating. Cortés led his 600 followers across rugged mountains and gathered allies from among the Tlaxcalans, a tributary people eager to free themselves from Aztec domination.

In war, Cortés possessed obvious technological superiority over the Aztec. The sound of gunfire initially frightened the Indians. Moreover, Aztec troops had never seen horses, much less armored horses carrying sword-wielding Spaniards. But these elements would have counted for little had Cortés not also gained a psychological advantage over his opponents. At first, Montezuma thought that the Spaniards were gods, representatives of the fearful plumed serpent, Quetzalcoatl. Instead of resisting, the emperor hesitated. When Montezuma's resolve hardened, it was too late. Cortés's victory in Mexico, coupled with other conquests in South America, transformed Spain, at least temporarily, into the wealthiest state in Europe (see Map 1.4).

View the **Closer Look**
An Early European Image of Native Americans on **myhistorylab.com**

Quick Check
✓ How did Cortés and his small band of Spanish soldiers manage to conquer the Aztec empire?

From Plunder to Settlement

With the conquest of Mexico, renamed New Spain, the Spanish crown confronted a difficult problem. Ambitious *conquistadores*, interested chiefly in their own wealth and glory, had to be brought under royal authority. Adventurers like Cortés were

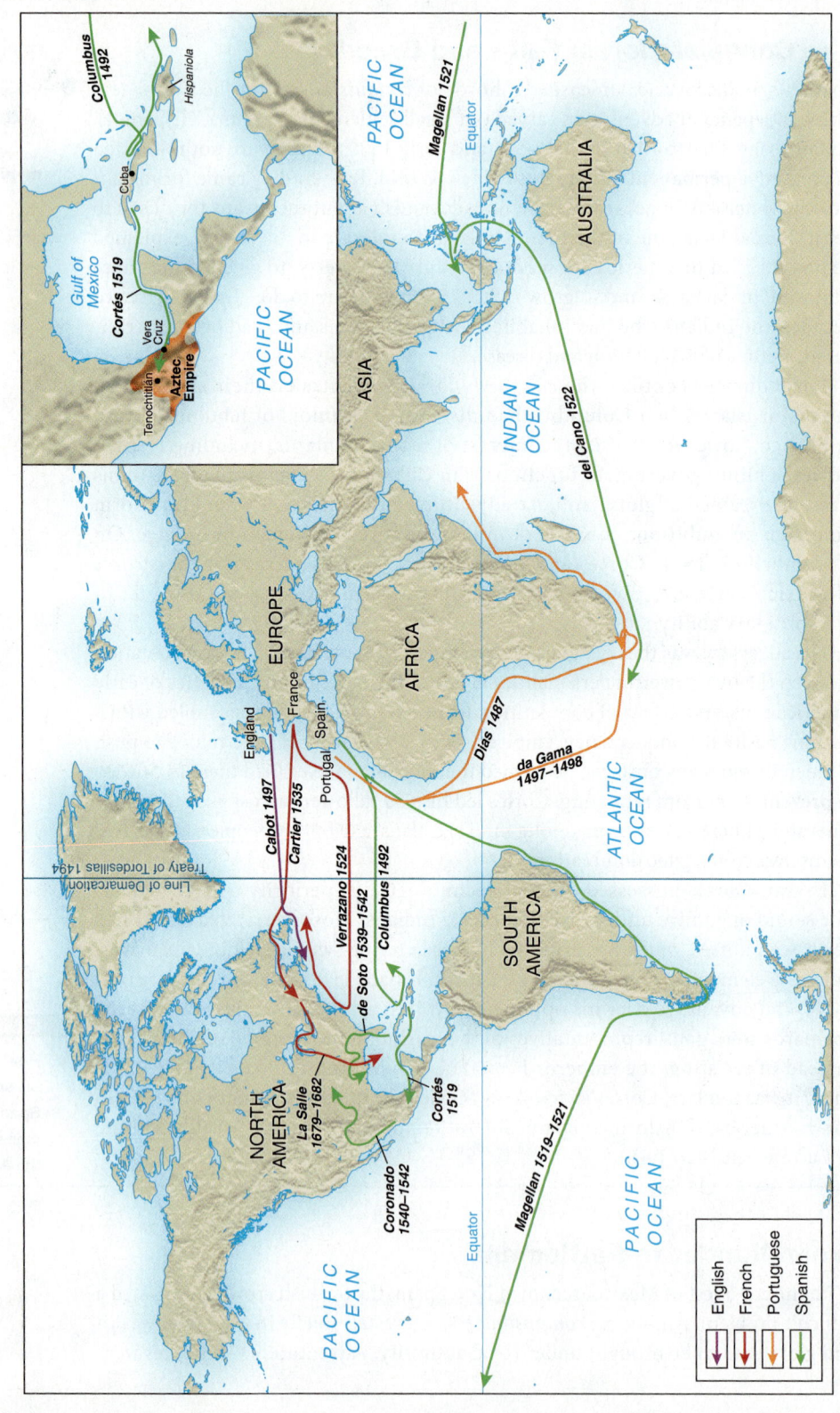

Map 1.4 Voyages of European Exploration New World discovery sparked intense competition among the major European states.

PACIFIC OCEAN

Columbus 1492

Hispaniola

Cuba

Gulf of Mexico

Cortés 1519

Vera Cruz

Tenochtitlán

Aztec Empire

PACIFIC OCEAN

PACIFIC OCEAN

Magellan 1521

Equator

AUSTRALIA

INDIAN OCEAN

del Cano 1522

ASIA

AFRICA

Dias 1487

da Gama 1497–1498

ATLANTIC OCEAN

EUROPE

England

France

Spain

Portugal

Line of Demarcation

Treaty of Tordesillas 1494

Cabot 1497

Cartier 1535

Verrazano 1524

Columbus 1492

de Soto 1539–1542

Cortés 1519

La Salle 1679–1682

Coronado 1540–1542

NORTH AMERICA

SOUTH AMERICA

Magellan 1519–1521

Equator

PACIFIC OCEAN

PACIFIC OCEAN

English

French

Portuguese

Spanish

20

stubbornly independent, quick to take offense, and thousands of miles away from the seat of imperial government.

The crown found a partial solution in the *encomienda* system. The monarch rewarded the leaders of the conquest with Indian villages. The people who lived in the settlements provided the *encomenderos* with labor tribute in exchange for legal protection and religious guidance. The system, of course, cruelly exploited Indian laborers. One historian concluded, "The first encomenderos, without known exception, understood Spanish authority as provision for unlimited personal opportunism." Cortés alone was granted the services of more than 23,000 Indian workers. The *encomienda* system made the colonizers more dependent on the king, for it was he who legitimized their title. The new economic structure helped to transform "a frontier of plunder into a frontier of settlement."

Indian Slaves In 1595, Theodore de Bry depicted the harsh Spanish labor discipline on a sugar plantation on the Island of Hispaniola.

Spain's rulers attempted to maintain tight control over their American possessions. The volume of correspondence between the two continents, much of it concerning mundane matters, was staggering. All documents were duplicated several times by hand. Because the trip to Madrid took months, a year often passed before a simple request was answered. But somehow the cumbersome system worked. In Mexico, officials appointed in Spain established a rigid hierarchical order, directing the affairs of the countryside from urban centers.

The Spanish also brought Catholicism to the New World. The Dominicans and Franciscans, the two largest religious orders, established Indian missions throughout New Spain. Some friars tried to protect the Native Americans from the worst exploitation. One courageous Dominican, Fra Bartolomé de las Casas, published an eloquent defense of Indian rights, *Historia de las Indias*, that questioned the legitimacy of European conquest of the New World. Las Casas's work provoked heated debate in Spain and initiated reforms designed to bring greater "love and moderation" to Spanish–Indian relations. It is impossible to ascertain how many converts the friars made. In 1531, however, a newly converted Christian Indian reported a vision of the Virgin Mary, a dark-skinned woman of obvious Indian ancestry, who became known throughout the region as the Virgin of Guadalupe. This figure—the result of a creative blending of Indian and European cultures—became a powerful symbol of Mexican nationalism in the wars for independence fought against Spain almost three centuries later.

Read the **Document**
Bartolome de las Casas, "Of the Islands of Hispaniola" on **myhistorylab.com**

View the **Image**
Cruel Conquistadors Torturing Native Americans on **myhistorylab.com**

The Virgin of Guadalupe The Virgin of Guadalupe, depicted here in a 1531 representation, is a popular religious symbol of Mexico. Like the Indian Juan Diego, to whom she is said to have appeared and offered comfort, the Virgin is dark-skinned.

Quick Check

✓ Describe the character of Spanish-Indian relations following the conquest of Mexico.

About 250,000 Spaniards migrated to the New World during the sixteenth century. Another 200,000 made the journey between 1600 and 1650. Most colonists were single males in their late twenties seeking economic opportunities. They generally came from the poorest agricultural regions of southern Spain—almost 40 percent migrating from Andalusia. Since so few Spanish women migrated, especially in the sixteenth century, the men often married Indians and blacks, unions that produced mixed-race descendents known as *mestizos* and *mulattos*. The frequency of interracial marriage indicated that the people of New Spain were more tolerant of racial differences than were the English who settled in North America. For the people of New Spain, economic worth affected social standing as much if not more than skin color did. Persons born in the New World, even those of Spanish parentage (*criollos*), were regarded as socially inferior to natives of the mother country (*peninsulares*).

Spain claimed far more of the New World than it could manage. Spain's rulers regarded the American colonies primarily as a source of precious metals, and between 1500 and 1650, an estimated 200 tons of gold and 16,000 tons of silver were shipped back to the Spanish treasury in Madrid. This great wealth, however, proved a mixed blessing. The sudden acquisition of so much money stimulated a horrendous inflation that hurt ordinary Spaniards. They were hurt further by long, debilitating European wars funded by American gold and silver. Moreover, instead of developing its own industry, Spain became dependent on the annual shipment of bullion from America. In 1603, one insightful Spaniard declared, "The New World conquered by you, has conquered you in its turn." This weakened, although still formidable, empire would eventually extend its territorial claims north to California and the Southwest (see Chapter 4).

THE FRENCH CLAIM CANADA

What was the character of the French empire in Canada?

French interest in the New World developed slowly. More than three decades after Columbus's discovery, King Francis I sponsored the unsuccessful efforts of Giovanni da Verrazzano to find a short water route to China via a northwest passage around or through North America. In 1534, the king sent Jacques Cartier on a similar quest. The rocky, barren coast of Labrador depressed the explorer. He grumbled, "I am rather inclined to believe that this is the land God gave to Cain."

Discovery of a large, promising waterway the following year raised Cartier's spirits. He reconnoitered the Gulf of Saint Lawrence, traveling up the magnificent river as far as modern Montreal. But Cartier got no closer to China, and, discouraged by the harsh winters, he headed home in 1542. Not until 65 years later did Samuel de Champlain resettle this region for France. He founded Quebec in 1608.

As with other colonial powers, the French declared they had migrated to the New World in search of wealth and to convert the Indians to Christianity. As it turned out, these economic and spiritual goals required full cooperation between the French and the Native Americans. In contrast to the English settlers, who established independent farms and regarded the Indians at best as obstacles to civilization, the French viewed the natives as necessary economic partners. Furs were Canada's most valuable export, and to obtain the pelts of beaver and other animals, the French were absolutely dependent on Indian hunters and trappers. French traders lived among the Indians, often taking native wives and studying local cultures.

Frenchmen known as *coureurs de bois*, following Canada's great river networks, paddled deep into the heart of the continent for fresh sources of furs. Some intrepid traders penetrated beyond the Great Lakes into the Mississippi Valley. In 1673, Père Jacques Marquette journeyed down the Mississippi River, and nine years later, Sieur Robert de La Salle reached the Gulf of Mexico. In the early eighteenth century, the French established small settlements in Louisiana, the most important being New Orleans. The spreading French influence worried English colonists living along the Atlantic coast, for the French seemed to be cutting them off from the trans-Appalachian west.

Catholic missionaries also depended on Indian cooperation. Canadian priests were drawn from two orders, the Jesuits and the Recollects, and although measuring their success in the New World is difficult, it seems they converted more Indians than did their English Protestant counterparts to the south. Like the fur traders, the missionaries lived among the Indians and learned their languages.

The French dream of a vast American empire suffered from serious flaws. The crown remained largely indifferent to Canadian affairs. Royal officials in New France received limited and sporadic support from Paris. An even greater problem was the decision to settle what many peasants and artisans considered a cold, inhospitable land. Throughout the colonial period, Canada's European population remained small. A census of 1663 recorded only 3,035 French residents. By 1700, there were only 15,000. Men far outnumbered women, thus making it hard for settlers to form new families. Moreover, because of the colony's geography, all exports and imports had to go through Quebec. It was relatively easy, therefore, for crown officials to control that traffic, usually by awarding fur-trading monopolies to court favorites. Such practices created political tensions and hindered economic growth.

THE ENGLISH TAKE UP THE CHALLENGE

The first English visit to North America remains shrouded in mystery. Fishermen working out of Bristol and other western English ports may have landed in Nova Scotia and Newfoundland as early as the 1480s. The huge stock of codfish of the Grand Banks undoubtedly drew vessels of all nations, and during summers sailors probably

Read the **Document** *Jacques Cartier, First Contact with the Indians (1534)* on **myhistorylab.com**

Why did England not participate in the early competition for New World colonies?

dried and salted their catches on Canada's convenient shores. John Cabot (Giovanni Caboto), a Venetian sea captain, completed the first recorded transatlantic voyage by an English vessel in 1497, while attempting to find a northwest passage to Asia.

Cabot died during a second voyage in 1498. Although Sebastian Cabot continued his father's explorations in the Hudson Bay region in 1508–1509, England's interest in the New World waned. For the next three-quarters of a century, the English people were preoccupied with more pressing domestic and religious concerns. When curiosity about the New World revived, however, Cabot's voyages established England's belated claim to American territory.

Birth of English Protestantism

Read the **Document**
Henry VII, Letters of Patent Granted to John Cabot on **myhistorylab.com**

At the time of Cabot's death, England was not prepared to compete with Spain and Portugal for the riches of the Orient. Although Henry VII, the first Tudor monarch, brought peace to England in 1485 after a bitter civil war, the country still contained too many "over-mighty subjects," powerful local magnates who maintained armed retainers and often paid little attention to royal authority. Henry possessed no standing army; his small navy intimidated no one. The Tudors gave nominal allegiance to the pope in Rome, but unlike the rulers of Spain, they were not crusaders for Catholicism.

International diplomacy also worked against England's early entry into New World colonization. In 1509, to cement an alliance between Spain and England, the future Henry VIII married Catherine of Aragon, daughter of Ferdinand and Isabella. As a result of this marital arrangement, English merchants enjoyed limited rights to trade in Spain's American colonies, but any attempt by England at independent colonization would have threatened those rights and jeopardized the alliance.

By the end of the sixteenth century, however, conditions within England had changed dramatically, in part because of the Protestant Reformation. The English began to consider their former ally, Spain, to be the greatest threat to English aspirations. Tudor monarchs, especially Henry VIII (r. 1509–1547) and his daughter Elizabeth I (r. 1558–1603), developed a strong central administration, while England became increasingly Protestant. The merger of English Protestantism and English nationalism helped propel England into a central role in European affairs and was crucial in creating a powerful sense of an English identity among all classes of people.

Popular anticlericalism helped spark religious reformation in England. Although they observed traditional Catholic ritual, the English people had long resented paying monies to a pope who lived in far-off Rome. Early in the sixteenth century, criticism of the clergy grew increasingly vocal. Cardinal Thomas Wolsey, the most powerful prelate in England, flaunted his immense wealth and unwittingly became a symbol of spiritual corruption. Parish priests were objects of ridicule; they seemed theologically ignorant and eager to line their own pockets. Anticlericalism did not run as deep in England as it had in Martin Luther's Germany, but by the late 1520s, the Catholic Church could no longer take for granted the allegiance of the great mass of the population. The people's growing anger is central to understanding the English Reformation. Put simply, if ordinary English men and women had not accepted separation from Rome, then Henry VIII could not have forced them to leave the church.

The catalyst for Protestant Reformation in England was the king's desire to rid himself of his wife, Catherine of Aragon. Their marriage had produced a daughter,

Mary, but no son. The need for a male heir obsessed Henry. He and his counselors assumed a female ruler could not maintain domestic peace, and England would fall again into civil war. The answer seemed to be remarriage. Henry petitioned Pope Clement VII for a divorce (technically, an annulment), but the Spanish were unwilling to tolerate the public humiliation of Catherine. They forced the pope to procrastinate. In 1527, time ran out. The king fell in love with Anne Boleyn and moved to divorce Catherine with or without papal consent. Anne would become his second wife in 1533 and would later deliver a daughter, Elizabeth.

The final break with Rome came swiftly. Between 1529 and 1536, the king, acting through Parliament, severed all ties with the pope, seized church lands, and dissolved many of the monasteries. In March 1534, the Act of Supremacy announced, "The King's Majesty justly and rightfully is supreme head of the Church of England." The entire process, which one historian termed a "state reformation," was conducted with impressive efficiency. Land formerly owned by the Catholic Church passed quickly into private hands, and within a short period, property holders throughout England had acquired a vested interest in Protestantism. Beyond breaking with the papacy, Henry showed little enthusiasm for theological change. Many Catholic ceremonies survived.

The split with Rome, however, opened the door to increasingly radical religious ideas. In 1539, an English translation of the Bible first appeared in print. Before then, Scripture had been widely available only in Latin, the language of an educated elite. For the first time in English history, ordinary people could read the word of God in the vernacular. It was a liberating experience that persuaded some men and women that Henry had not sufficiently reformed the English church.

With Henry's death in 1547, England entered a period of political and religious instability. Edward VI, Henry's young son by his third wife, Jane Seymour, came to the throne, but he was a sickly child. Militant Protestants took control, insisting the Church of England remove every trace of its Catholic origins. When young Edward died in 1553, these ambitious efforts came to a sudden halt. Henry's eldest daughter, Mary I, ascended the throne. Fiercely loyal to the Catholic faith of her mother, Catherine of Aragon, Mary vowed to return England to the pope.

Hundreds of Protestants were executed; others scurried off to the safety of Geneva and Frankfurt, where they absorbed the most radical Calvinist doctrines of the day. When Mary died in 1558 and was succeeded by Elizabeth I, the "Marian exiles" flocked back to England, more eager than ever to rid the Tudor church of Catholicism. Queen Elizabeth governed the English people from 1558 to 1603, an intellectually exciting period during which some of her subjects took the first halting steps toward colonizing the New World. Elizabeth recognized that her most urgent duty as queen was to end the religious turmoil that had divided the country for a generation. She established a unique church, Catholic in much of its ceremony and government but clearly Protestant in doctrine. Under her so-called Elizabethan settlement, the queen assumed the title "Supreme Governor of the Church in England." Some churchmen urged her to abolish all Catholic rituals, but she ignored these strident reformers. The young queen understood that she could not rule effectively without the full support of her people, and that neither radical change nor widespread persecution would gain a monarch lasting popularity.

Quick Check
✓ What was the impact of the Protestant Reformation on English politics?

Religion, War, and Nationalism

Slowly, but steadily, English Protestantism and English national identity merged. A loyal English subject in the late sixteenth century loved the queen, supported the Church of England, and hated Catholics, especially those who lived in Spain. Elizabeth herself came to symbolize this militant new chauvinism. Her subjects adored the Virgin Queen and applauded when her famed "Sea Dogs"—dashing figures such as Sir Francis Drake and Sir John Hawkins—seized Spanish treasure ships in American waters. These raids were little more than piracy, but in this undeclared state of war, such harassment passed for national victories. There seemed to be no reason patriotic Elizabethans should not share in the wealth of the New World. With each engagement, each threat, each plot, English nationalism took deeper root. By the 1570s, it had become obvious that powerful ideological forces similar to those that had moved the Spanish subjects of Isabella and Ferdinand almost a century earlier were driving the English people.

In the mid-1580s, Philip II, who had united the empires of Spain and Portugal in 1580, decided that England's arrogantly Protestant queen could be tolerated no longer. He ordered the construction of a mighty fleet, hundreds of transport vessels designed to carry Spain's finest infantry across the English Channel. When one of Philip's lieutenants viewed the Armada at Lisbon in May 1588, he described it as la *felicissima armada*, the invincible fleet. The king believed that with the support of England's oppressed Catholics, Spanish troops would sweep Elizabeth from power.

The Spanish Armada was a grand scheme; it was an even grander failure. In 1588, a smaller, more maneuverable English navy dispersed Philip's Armada, and severe storms finished it off. Spanish hopes for Catholic England lay wrecked along the rocky coasts of Scotland and Ireland. English Protestants interpreted victory in providential terms: "God breathed and they were scattered."

Even as the Spanish military threat grew, Sir Walter Ralegh, one of the Queen's favorite courtiers, launched a settlement in North America. He diplomatically named his enterprise Virginia, in honor of his patron Elizabeth, the Virgin Queen. In 1587 Ralegh dispatched colonists under the command of John White to Roanoke, a site on the coast of present-day North Carolina, but poor planning, preparation for war with Spain, and hostilities with Native Americans doomed the experiment. When English vessels finally returned to Roanoke, the settlers had disappeared. No one has ever explained what happened to the "lost" colonists.

Read the
Document
John White, Letter to Richard Hakluyt (1590) on
myhistorylab.com

Quick Check

✓ How did Protestantism and English national identity become merged under Queen Elizabeth I?

CONCLUSION: CAMPAIGN TO SELL AMERICA

Had it not been for Richard Hakluyt the Younger, who publicized explorers' accounts of the New World, the dream of American colonization might have died in England. Hakluyt never saw America. Nevertheless, his vision of the New World powerfully shaped English public opinion. He interviewed captains and sailors and collected their stories in a massive book titled *The Principall Navigations, Voyages, and Discoveries of the English Nation* (1589).

The work appeared to be a straightforward description of what these sailors had seen across the sea. That was its strength. In reality, Hakluyt edited each piece so it would drive home the book's central point: England needed American colonies. Indeed, they were essential to the nation's prosperity and independence. In Hakluyt's America, there were no losers. "The earth bringeth fourth all things in aboundance, as in the first creations without toil or labour," he wrote of Virginia. His blend of piety, patriotism, and self-interest proved popular, and his *Voyages* went through many editions.

Hakluyt's enthusiasm for the spread of English trade throughout the world may have blinded him to the aspirations of other peoples who actually inhabited those distant lands. He continued to collect testimony from adventurers and sailors who claimed to have visited Asia and America. In a popular new edition of his work published between 1598 and 1600 and entitled the *Voyages*, he catalogued in extraordinary detail the commercial opportunities awaiting courageous and ambitious English colonizers. Hakluyt's entrepreneurial perspective obscured other aspects of the European Conquest, which would soon transform the face of the New World. He paid little attention, for example, to the rich cultural diversity of the Native Americans; he said not a word about the pain of the Africans who traveled to North and South America as slaves. Instead, he and many other polemicists for English colonization led the ordinary men and women who crossed the Atlantic to expect a paradise on earth. By fanning such unrealistic expectations, Hakluyt persuaded European settlers that the New World was theirs for the taking, a self-serving view that invited ecological disaster and human suffering.

Indian Fishing Techniques John White depicted fishing techniques practiced by the Indians of the present-day Carolinas. In the canoe, Indians use dip nets and multipronged spears. In the background, they stab at fish with long spears. At left, a weir traps fish by taking advantage of the river current's natural force.

1 STUDY RESOURCES

((•—|**Listen** to the **Chapter Audio** for Chapter 1 on **myhistorylab.com**

TIMELINE

CHAPTER REVIEW

NATIVE AMERICANS BEFORE THE CONQUEST

What explains cultural differences among Native American groups before European conquest?

Paleo-Indians crossed into North America from Asia 20,000 years ago. During the migrations, they divided into distinct groups, often speaking different languages. The Agricultural Revolution sparked population growth, allowing some groups, such as the Aztecs, to establish complex societies. The Eastern Woodland Indians, who lived along the Atlantic coast, had just begun to practice agriculture when the Europeans arrived. (*p. 5*)

CONDITIONS OF CONQUEST

How did Europeans and Native Americans interact during the period of first contact?

Native Americans initially welcomed the opportunity to trade with the Europeans. The newcomers insisted on "civilizing" the Indians. Neither Christianity nor European-style education held much appeal for Native Americans, and they resisted efforts to transform their cultures. Contagious Old World diseases, such as smallpox, decimated the Indians, leaving them vulnerable to cultural imperialism. (*p. 10*)

WEST AFRICA: ANCIENT AND COMPLEX SOCIETIES

What was the character of the West African societies European traders first encountered?

West Africans had learned of Islam long before European traders arrived looking for slaves. The earliest Europeans found powerful local rulers who knew how to profit from commercial exchange. Slaves who had been captured in distant wars were taken to so-called slave factories where they were sold to Europeans and then shipped to the New World. (*p. 13*)

EUROPE ON THE EVE OF CONQUEST

What factors explain Spain's central role in New World exploration and colonization?

The unification of Spain under Ferdinand and Isabella, and the experience of the *Reconquista*, provided Spain with advantages in its later conquest of the New World. The Spanish crown supported the explorations of Christopher Columbus, who thought he had discovered a new route to Asia. His voyages gave the Spanish a head start in claiming American lands. (*p. 16*)

SPAIN IN THE AMERICAS

How did Spanish conquest of Central and South America transform Native American cultures?

Spanish *conquistadores* conquered vast territories in the Caribbean, Mexico, and Central and South America during the sixteenth century. Catholic missionaries followed the *conquistadores* to convert the Indians to Christianity. Although the Spanish conquerors cruelly exploited the Indians as laborers, intermarriage between the groups created a new culture blending Spanish and Indian elements. (*p. 18*)

THE FRENCH CLAIM CANADA

What was the character of the French empire in Canada?

The French in Canada focused on building a trading empire rather than on settlement. The *coureurs de bois* and Catholic missionaries lived among the Indians, learning their languages and customs. French explorers followed the extensive river networks of North America and claimed vast stretches of land along the St. Lawrence and Mississippi Rivers. (*p. 22*)

THE ENGLISH TAKE UP THE CHALLENGE

Why did England not participate in the early competition for New World colonies?

During the early 1500s, religious turmoil preoccupied England's monarchs. After ascending the throne in 1558, Queen Elizabeth I ended internal religious struggle by establishing an English Church that was Protestant in doctrine but Catholic in ceremony. Under Elizabeth, English nationalism merged with anti-Catholicism to challenge Spanish control of the Americas. (*p. 23*)

KEY TERM QUESTIONS

1. How did environmental conditions lead to the formation of Beringia? (p. 5)

2. How did the Agricultural Revolution change Native American societies? (p. 6)

3. How did the Indians of the Eastern Woodland Cultures differ from Indians living in other regions? (p. 9)

4. How did the Columbian Exchange threaten the existence of Native Americans? (p. 12)

5. Who were the *conquistadores*, and what where their motivations in the New World? (p. 17)

6. What were the successes and failures of the Treaty of Tordesillas? (p. 18)

7. How did the *encomienda* system exploit Indian laborers? (p. 21)

8. Why was the Virgin of Guadalupe a significant symbol for Mexicans? (p. 21)

9. What were the *coureurs de bois* looking for while following Canada's river networks? (p. 23)

10. How did the Protestant Reformation change the relationship between England and Spain? (p. 24)

11. What was the significance of the failure of The Spanish Armada's invasion of England? (p. 26)

MyHistoryLab CONNECTIONS

Visit **www.myhistorylab.com** for a customized Study Plan to build your knowledge of *New World Encounters*.

Question for Analysis

1. What were the challenges facing Pre-Columbian societies in the New World?

   View the **Map** *Pre-Columbian Societies of the Americas* p. 6

2. How does this image represent a European stereotype of Native Americans?

   View the **Closer Look** *An Early European Image of Native Americans* p. 19

3. How much of a factor did new technology play in Columbus's 1492 voyage?

   Watch the **Video** *How Should We Think of Columbus?* p. 17

4. How does Las Casas characterize the native peoples?

   Read the **Document** *Bartolome de las Casas, "Of the Island of Hispaniola"* p. 21

5. What motivated King Henry VII to grant the patent to John Cabot?

   Read the **Document** *Henry VII, Letters of Patent Granted to John Cabot* p. 24

Other Resources from this Chapter

View the **Image** *Clovis Points*

Read the **Document** *Thomas Hariot, The Algonquian Peoples*

View the **Image** *English Trade with Indians*

View the **Map** *Native American Population Loss, 1500–1700*

Read the **Document** *Ghana and its people in the Eleventh Century*

View the **Image** *Purchasing Slaves on the African Shore*

View the **Image** *Cruel Conquistadors Torturing Native Americans*

Read the **Document** *Jacques Cartier, First Contact with the Indians*

Read the **Document** *John White Letter to Richard Hakuyt*

Watch the **Video** *What is Columbus's Legacy?*

Contents and Spotlight Questions

((●─ **Listen** to the **Chapter Audio** for Chapter 2 on **myhistorylab.com**

PROFIT AND PIETY: COMPETING VISIONS FOR ENGLISH SETTLEMENT

In spring 1644, John Winthrop, governor of Massachusetts Bay, learned that Native Americans had overrun the scattered tobacco plantations of Virginia, killing some 500 colonists. Winthrop never thought much of the Chesapeake settlements. He regarded the people who had migrated to that part of America as grossly materialistic, and because Virginia had recently expelled several Puritan ministers, Winthrop decided the hostilities were God's way of punishing the tobacco planters for their worldliness: "It was observable that this massacre came upon them soon after they had driven out the godly ministers we had sent to them." When Virginians appealed to Massachusetts for military supplies, they received a cool reception. "We were weakly provided ourselves," Winthrop explained, "and so could not afford them any help of that kind."

Captain John Smith and Powhatan The story of Pocahontas rescuing Capt. John smith just as he was about to be executed by her father Powhatan is well-known. In all likelihood the ceremony, pictured here, was never intended to end in Smith's death. Instead, Powhatan symbolically spared Smith's life in order to emphasize the werowance's authority over Smith and the Jamestown settlers who had come to live in his lands.

In 1675, the tables turned. Native Americans declared all-out war against the New Englanders, and soon reports of the destruction of Puritan communities reached Virginia. "The Indians in New England have burned Considerable Villages," wrote one leading tobacco planter, "and have made them [the New Englanders] desert more than one hundred and fifty miles of those places they had formerly seated."

News of New England's adversity did not displease Sir William Berkeley, Virginia's royal governor. He and his friends held the Puritans in contempt. Indeed, the New Englanders reminded them of the religious fanatics who had provoked civil war in England and who in 1649 had executed King Charles I. Berkeley noted that he might have shown more pity for the New Englanders "had they deserved it of the King." The governor, sounding like a Puritan himself, described the Indians as the "Instruments" with which God intended "to destroy the King's Enemies." For good measure, Virginia outlawed the export of foodstuffs to its embattled northern neighbors.

Such extraordinary disunity in the colonies—not to mention lack of compassion— may surprise anyone searching for the roots of modern nationalism in this early period. English colonization in the seventeenth century did not spring from a desire to build a centralized empire in the New World similar to that of Spain or France. Instead, the English crown awarded colonial charters to a wide variety of entrepreneurs, religious idealists, and aristocratic adventurers who established separate and profoundly different colonies. Not only did New Englanders have little in common with the earliest Virginians and Carolinians, but they were often divided among themselves.

Migration itself helps to explain this striking competition and diversity. At different times, different colonies appealed to different sorts of people. Men and women moved to the New World for various reasons, and as economic, political, and religious conditions changed on both sides of the Atlantic during the seventeenth century, so too did patterns of English migration.

BREAKING AWAY: DECISIONS TO MOVE TO AMERICA

Why did the Chesapeake colonies not prosper during the earliest years of their settlement?

English colonists crossed the Atlantic for many reasons. Some wanted to institute a purer form of worship, more closely based on their interpretation of Scripture. Others dreamed of owning land and improving their social position. A few came to the New World to escape bad marriages, jail terms, or the dreary prospect of lifelong poverty. Since most seventeenth-century migrants, especially those who transferred to the Chesapeake colonies, left almost no records of their lives in England, it is futile to try to isolate a single cause or explanation for their decision to leave home.

In the absence of detailed personal information, historians usually have assumed that poverty, or the fear of soon falling into poverty, drove people across the Atlantic. No doubt economic considerations figured heavily in the final decision to leave England. But so did religion, and the poor of early modern England were often among those demanding the most radical ecclesiastical reform. As a recent historian of seventeenth-century migration concluded, "Individuals left for a variety of motives, some idealistic, others practical, some simple, others complex, many perhaps contradictory and imperfectly understood by the migrants themselves."

Whatever their reasons for crossing the ocean, English migrants to America in this period left a nation wracked by recurrent, often violent political and religious controversy. During the 1620s, autocratic Stuart monarchs—James I (r. 1603–1625) and his son Charles I (r. 1625–1649)—who succeeded Queen Elizabeth I on the English throne fought constantly with the members of Parliament over rival notions of constitutional and representative government.

Regardless of the exact timing of departure, English settlers brought with them ideas and assumptions that helped them make sense of their everyday experiences in an unfamiliar environment. Their values were tested and sometimes transformed in the New World, but they were seldom destroyed. Settlement involved a complex process of adjustment. The colonists developed different subcultures in America, and in each it is possible to trace the interaction between the settlers' values and the physical elements, such as the climate, crops, and soil, of their new surroundings. The Chesapeake, the New England colonies, the Middle Colonies, and the Southern Colonies formed distinct regional identities that have survived to the present day.

The Chesapeake: Dreams of Wealth

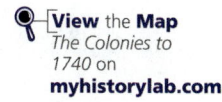

View the **Map**
The Colonies to 1740 on
myhistorylab.com

After the Roanoke debacle in 1590, English interest in American settlement declined, and only a few aging visionaries such as Richard Hakluyt kept alive the dream of colonies in the New World. These advocates argued that the North American mainland contained resources of incalculable value. An innovative group, they insisted, might reap great profits and supply England with raw materials that it would otherwise be forced to purchase from European rivals: Holland, France, and Spain.

Moreover, any enterprise that annoyed Catholic Spain or revealed its weakness in America seemed a desirable end in itself to patriotic English Protestants. Anti-Catholicism and hatred of Spain became an integral part of English national identity during this period, and unless one appreciates just how deeply those sentiments ran in the popular mind, one cannot fully understand why ordinary people who had no direct financial stake in the New World so generously supported English efforts to colonize America. Soon after James I ascended to the throne (1603), adventurers were given an opportunity to put their theories into practice in the colonies of Virginia and Maryland, an area known as the Chesapeake, or later, as the Tobacco Coast.

Quick Check

✓ Why did some people continue to advocate colonies in the New World?

Entrepreneurs in Virginia

During Elizabeth I's reign, the major obstacle to successful colonization of the New World had been raising money. No single person, no matter how rich or well connected, could underwrite the vast expenses a New World settlement required. The solution to this financial problem was the joint-stock company, a business organization in which many people could invest without fear of bankruptcy. A merchant or landowner could purchase a share of stock at a stated price, and at the end of several years, the investor could anticipate recovering the initial amount plus a portion of whatever profits the company had made. Joint-stock ventures sprang up like mushrooms. Affluent English citizens, and even some of more modest fortunes, rushed to invest in the companies, and, as a result, some projects amassed large amounts of capital, enough certainly to launch a new colony in Virginia.

On April 10, 1606, King James issued the first Virginia charter, which authorized the London Company to establish plantations in Virginia. The London Company was an ambitious business venture. Its leader, Sir Thomas Smith, was reputedly London's wealthiest merchant. Smith and his partners gained possession of the territory lying between present-day North Carolina and the Hudson River. These were generous but vague boundaries, to be sure, but the Virginia Company—as the London Company soon called itself—set out immediately to find the treasures Hakluyt had promised.

In December 1606, the *Susan Constant*, the *Godspeed*, and the *Discovery* sailed for America. The ships carried 104 men and boys who had been instructed to establish a fortified outpost some hundred miles up a large navigable river. The natural beauty and economic potential of the region were apparent to everyone. A voyager on the expedition reported seeing "faire meaddowes and goodly tall trees, with such fresh waters running through the woods, as almost ravished [us] at first sight."

The leaders of the colony selected—without consulting resident Native Americans—what the Europeans considered a promising location more than 30 miles from the mouth of the James River. A marshy peninsula jutting out into the river became the site for one of America's most unsuccessful villages, Jamestown. Modern historians have criticized the choice, for the low-lying ground proved to be a disease-ridden death trap; even the drinking water was contaminated with salt. But Jamestown seemed the ideal place to build a fort, since surprise attack by Spaniards or Native Americans rather than sickness appeared the more serious threat in the early months of settlement.

However, avarice soon became an issue. Virginia's adventurers had traveled to the New World in search of the sort of instant wealth they imagined the Spaniards had found in Mexico and Peru. Tales of rubies and diamonds lying on the beach probably inflamed their expectations. Even when it must have been apparent that such expectations were unfounded, the first settlers often behaved in Virginia as if they expected to become rich. Instead of cooperating for the common good—guarding or farming, for example—individuals pursued personal interests. They searched for gold when they might have helped plant corn. No one would take orders, and those who were supposed to govern the colony looked after their private welfare while disease, war, and starvation ravaged the settlement.

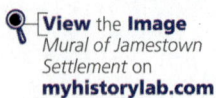

View the **Image**
Mural of Jamestown Settlement on
myhistorylab.com

Quick Check
✓ Why did Jamestown come so close to failing in its early years?

Threat of Anarchy

Virginia might have failed had it not been for Captain John Smith. Before coming to Jamestown, he had traveled throughout Europe and fought with the Hungarian army against the Turks—and, if Smith is to be believed, he was saved from certain death by various beautiful women. Because of his reputation for boasting, historians have discounted Smith's account of life in early Virginia. Recent scholarship, however, has affirmed the truthfulness of his curious story.

In Virginia, Smith brought order out of anarchy. While members of the council in Jamestown debated petty politics, he traded with the local Indians for food, mapped the Chesapeake Bay, and may even have been rescued from execution by a young Indian girl, Pocahontas. In the fall of 1608, he seized control of the ruling council and instituted tough military discipline. Under Smith, no one enjoyed special privilege. Those whom he forced to work came to hate him. But he managed to keep them alive, no small achievement in such a deadly environment.

Leaders of the Virginia Company in London recognized the need to reform the entire enterprise. After all, they had spent considerable sums and had received nothing in return. In 1609, the company directors obtained a new charter from the king, which completely reorganized the Virginia government. Henceforth all commercial and political decisions affecting the colonists rested with the company, a fact that had not been made sufficiently clear in the 1606 charter. Moreover, in an effort to raise scarce capital,

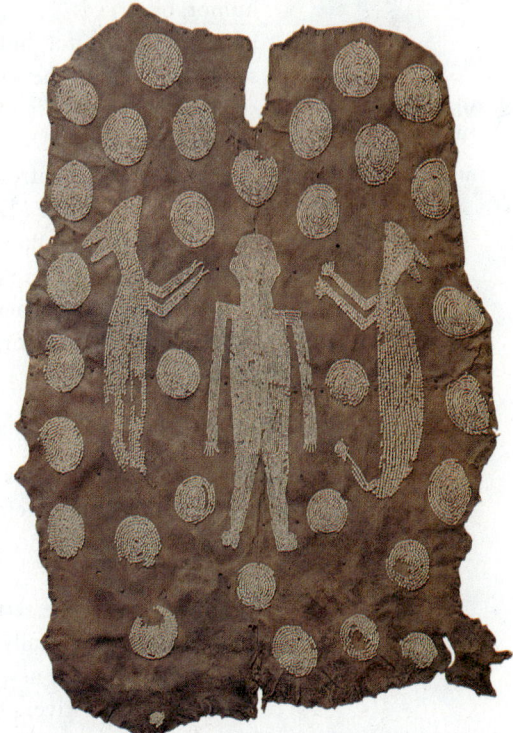

Powhatan Ceremonial Cloak In 1608, Powhatan, the father of Pocahontas, gave this shell-decorated ceremonial cloak to Captain Christopher Newport, commander of the fleet that brought the first English settlers to Jamestown. (*Source: Ashmolean Museum, Oxford, England, U.K.*)

the original partners opened the joint-stock company to the general public. For a little more than £12—approximately one year's wages for an unskilled English laborer—a person or group of persons could purchase a stake in Virginia. It was anticipated that in 1616 the profits from the colony would be distributed among the shareholders. The company sponsored a publicity campaign; pamphlets and sermons extolled the colony's potential and exhorted patriotic English citizens to invest in the enterprise.

The burst of energy came to nothing. Bad luck and poor planning plagued the Virginia Company. A vessel carrying additional settlers and supplies went aground in Bermuda, and while this misadventure did little to help the people at Jamestown, it provided Shakespeare with the idea for his play *The Tempest*.

Between 1609 and 1611, the remaining Virginia settlers lacked capable leadership, and, perhaps as a result, they lacked food. The terrible winter of 1609–1610 was termed the "starving time." A few desperate colonists were driven to cannibalism, an ironic situation since early explorers had assumed that only Native Americans would eat human flesh. In England, Smith heard that one colonist had killed his wife, powdered (salted) her, and "had eaten part of her before it was known; for which he was executed." The captain, who possessed a droll sense of

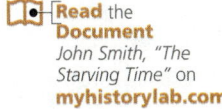

Read the **Document**
John Smith, "The Starving Time" on **myhistorylab.com**

humor, observed, "Now, whether she was better roasted, broiled, or carbonadoed [sliced], I know not, but such a dish as powdered wife I never heard of." Other settlers simply lost the will to live.

The presence of so many Native Americans was an additional threat to Virginia's survival. The first colonists found themselves living—or attempting to live—in territory controlled by what was probably the most powerful Indian confederation east of the Mississippi River. Under the leadership of their paramount chief or *werowance*, Powhatan, these Indians had by 1608 created a loose association of some 30 tribes. When Captain John Smith arrived to lead several hundred adventurers, the Powhatans (named for their king) numbered some 14,000 people, including 3,200 warriors. These people hoped to enlist the Europeans as allies against native enemies.

When it became clear that the two groups, holding such different notions about labor and property and about exploiting the natural environment, could not coexist in peace, the Powhatans tried to drive the invaders out of Virginia, once in 1622 and again in 1644. Their numbers sapped by losses from European diseases, the Powhatan failed both times. The failure of the second campaign destroyed the Powhatan empire.

In June 1610, the settlers who had survived despite starvation and conflicts with the Indians actually abandoned Virginia. Through a stroke of luck, however, a new governor and new colonists arrived from England just as they were sailing down the James River. The governor and the deputy governors who succeeded him, Sir Thomas Gates and Sir Thomas Dale, ruled by martial law. The new colonists, many of them male and female servants employed by the company, were marched to work by the beat of the drum. Such methods saved the colony but could not make it flourish. In 1616, company shareholders received no profits. Their only reward was the right to a piece of unsurveyed land located 3,000 miles from London.

View the Image
Powhatan in Longhouse on
myhistorylab.com

Quick Check

✔ Why did the first Virginia settlers not cooperate for the common good?

Tobacco Saves Virginia

The economic solution to Virginia's problems grew in the vacant lots of Jamestown. Only Indians bothered to cultivate tobacco until John Rolfe, a settler who achieved notoriety by marrying Pocahontas, realized this local weed might be a valuable export. Rolfe experimented with the crop, eventually growing in Virginia a milder variety that had been developed in the West Indies that was more appealing to European smokers.

Virginians suddenly possessed a means to make money. Tobacco proved relatively easy to grow, and settlers who had avoided work now threw themselves into its production with single-minded diligence. In 1617, one observer found that Jamestown's "streets and all other spare places [are] planted with tobacco … the Colony dispersed all about planting tobacco." Although King James I originally considered smoking immoral and unhealthy, he changed his mind when the duties he collected on tobacco imports began to mount.

The Virginia Company sponsored another ambitious effort to transform the colony into a profitable enterprise. In 1618, Sir Edwin Sandys (pronounced Sands) led a faction of stockholders that began to pump life into the dying organization by instituting sweeping reforms and eventually ousting Sir Thomas Smith and his friends. Sandys wanted private investors to develop their own estates in Virginia. Before 1618, there had been little incentive to do so, but by relaxing Dale's martial law and promising an elective representative assembly called the **House of Burgesses**, Sandys thought he could make the colony more attractive to wealthy speculators.

Even more important was Sandys's method for distributing land. Colonists who covered their own transportation cost to America were guaranteed a **headright**, a 50-acre lot for which they paid only a small annual rent. Adventurers were granted additional headrights for each servant they brought to the colony. This allowed prosperous planters to build up huge estates while they also acquired dependent laborers. This land system persisted long after the ompany's collapse. So too did the notion that the wealth of a few justified the exploitation of many others.

Sandys also urged the settlers to diversify their economy. Tobacco alone, he argued, was not a sufficient base. He envisioned colonists busily producing iron and tar, silk and glass, sugar and cotton. There was no end to his suggestions. He scoured Europe for skilled artisans and exotic plants. To finance such a huge project, Sandys relied on a lottery, a game of chance that promised a continuous flow of capital into the company's treasury. The final element in the grand scheme was people. Sandys sent English settlers by the thousand to Jamestown, ordinary men and women swept up by the same hopes that had carried the colonists of 1607 to the New World.

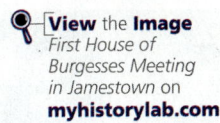
View the **Image**
First House of Burgesses Meeting in Jamestown on **myhistorylab.com**

Quick Check
✓ In what sense did tobacco save the Chesapeake colonies?

Time of Reckoning

Company records reveal that between 1619 and 1622, 3,570 individuals were sent to the colony. People seldom moved to Virginia as families. Although the first women arrived in Jamestown in 1608, most emigrants were single males in their teens or early twenties who came to the New World as **indentured servants**. In exchange for transportation across the Atlantic, they agreed to serve a master for a stated number of years. The length of service depended in part on the age of the servant. The younger the servant, the longer he or she served. In return, the master promised to give the laborers proper care and, at the conclusion of their contracts, provide them with tools and clothes according to "the custom of the country."

Powerful Virginians corrupted the system. Poor servants wanted to establish independent tobacco farms. As they discovered, however, headrights were awarded not to the newly freed servant, but to the great planter who had paid for the servant's transportation to the New World and for his or her food and clothing during the indenture. And even though indentured servants were promised land when they were freed, they were most often cheated, becoming members of a growing, disaffected landless class in seventeenth-century Virginia.

Life in the Chesapeake Shown here is a reconstruction of a free white planter's house from the late seventeenth-century Chesapeake.

Whenever possible, planters in Virginia purchased able-bodied workers, in other words, persons (preferably male) capable of hard agricultural labor. This preference skewed the colony's sex ratio. In the early decades, men outnumbered women by as much as six to one. Such gender imbalance meant that even if a male servant lived to the end of his indenture—an unlikely prospect—he could not realistically expect to start his own family. Moreover, despite apparent legal safeguards, masters could treat dependent workers as they pleased; after all, these people were legally considered property. Servants were sold, traded, even gambled away. It does not require much imagination to see that a society that tolerated such an exploitative labor system might later embrace slavery.

Most Virginians did not live long enough to worry about marriage. Death was omnipresent. Indeed, extraordinarily high mortality was a major reason the Chesapeake colonies developed so differently from those of New England. On the eve of the 1618 reforms, Virginia's population stood at approximately 700. The Virginia Company sent at least 3,500 more people, but by 1622 only 1,240 were still alive. "It Consequentilie followes," declared one angry shareholder, "that we had then lost 3000 persons within those 3 yeares." The major killers were contagious diseases. Salt in the water supply also took a toll. And on Good Friday, March 22, 1622, the Powhatan Indians slew 347 Europeans in a well-coordinated surprise attack.

No one knows for certain how such a horrendous mortality rate affected the survivors. At the least, it must have created a sense of impermanence, a desire to escape Virginia with a little money before sickness or violence ended the adventure. The settlers who drank to excess aboard the tavern ships anchored in the James River described the colony "not as a place of Habitacion but only of a short sojourninge."

On both sides of the Atlantic people wondered whom to blame. The burden of responsibility lay largely with the Virginia Company. In fact, its scandalous mismanagement embarrassed James I, and in 1624 he dissolved the bankrupt enterprise and transformed Virginia into a royal colony. The crown appointed a governor and a council. No provision was made, however, for continuing the House of Burgesses. While elections to the Burgesses were hardly democratic, it did provide wealthy planters a voice in government. Even without the king's authorization, the representatives gathered annually after 1629, and in 1639, King Charles I recognized the body's existence.

Read the **Document**
Wessell Webling, His Indenture (1622) on **myhistorylab.com**

Quick Check

✓ What explains the extraordinary death rate in early Virginia?

Maryland: A Catholic Refuge

By the end of the seventeenth century, Maryland society looked remarkably like that of its Chesapeake neighbor, Virginia. At the time of its first settlement in

1634, however, no one would have predicted that Maryland, a colony wholly owned by a Catholic nobleman, would have survived, much less become a flourishing tobacco colony (see Map 2.1).

The driving force behind the founding of Maryland was Sir George Calvert, later Lord Baltimore. Calvert, a talented and well-educated man, enjoyed the patronage of James I. He was awarded lucrative positions in the government, the most important being the king's secretary of state. In 1625, however, Calvert shocked almost everyone by publicly declaring his Catholicism; in this fiercely anti-Catholic society, persons who openly supported the Church of Rome were immediately stripped of civil office. Although forced to resign as secretary of state, Calvert retained the crown's favor.

Before resigning, Calvert sponsored a settlement on the coast of Newfoundland, but after visiting it, he concluded that no English person, whatever his or her religion, would transfer to a place where the "ayre [is] so intolerably cold." He turned his attention to the Chesapeake, and on June 30, 1632, Charles I granted George Calvert's son, Cecilius, a charter for a colony to be located north of Virginia. The boundaries of the settlement, named Maryland in honor of Charles's queen, were so vaguely defined that they generated legal controversies not fully resolved until the 1760s when Charles Mason and Jeremiah Dixon surveyed their famous boundary line between Pennsylvania and Maryland.

Map 2.1 *Chesapeake Colonies, 1640* The many deep rivers flowing into the Chesapeake Bay provided English planters with a convenient transportation system, linking them directly by sea to European markets.

Cecilius, the second Lord Baltimore, wanted to create a sanctuary for England's persecuted Catholics. He also intended to make money. Without Protestant settlers, it seemed unlikely Maryland would prosper, and Cecilius instructed his brother Leonard, the colony's governor, to do nothing that might frighten off hypersensitive Protestants. The governor was ordered to "cause all Acts of the Roman Catholic Religion to be done as privately as may be and ... [to] instruct all Roman Catholics to be silent upon all occasions of discourse concerning matters of Religion." On March 25, 1634, the *Ark* and *Dove*, carrying about 150 settlers, landed safely, and within days, the governor purchased from the Yaocomico Indians a village that became St. Mary's City, the first capital of Maryland.

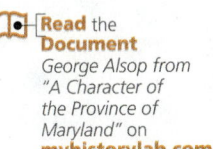

Read the Document
George Alsop from "A Character of the Province of Maryland" on **myhistorylab.com**

The colony's charter was a throwback to an earlier feudal age. It transformed Lord Baltimore into a "palatine lord," a proprietor with almost royal powers. Settlers swore an oath of allegiance not to the king of England but to Lord Baltimore. In England, such practices had long ago been abandoned. As the proprietor, Lord Baltimore owned outright almost six million acres and had absolute authority over anyone living in his domain.

On paper, at least, everyone in Maryland was assigned a place in an elaborate social hierarchy. Members of a colonial ruling class, persons who purchased 6,000 acres from Baltimore, were called lords of the manor. These landed aristocrats were permitted to establish local courts of law. People holding less acreage enjoyed fewer privileges, particularly in government. Baltimore figured that land sales and rents would finance the entire venture.

Baltimore's feudal system never took root in Chesapeake soil. People refused to play the social roles the lord proprietor had assigned them. These tensions affected Maryland's government. Baltimore assumed that his brother, acting as his deputy in America, and a small appointed council of local aristocrats would pass laws and carry out routine administration. When an elected assembly first convened in 1635, Baltimore allowed the delegates to discuss only those acts he had prepared. The members of the assembly bridled at such restrictions, insisting on exercising traditional parliamentary privileges. Neither side gained a clear victory in the assembly, and for almost 25 years, legislative squabbling contributed to the political instability that almost destroyed Maryland.

The colony drew both Protestants and Catholics, and the two groups might have lived in harmony had civil war not broken out in England in the 1640s. When Oliver Cromwell and the Puritan faction executed King Charles I in 1649, transforming England briefly into a republic, it seemed Baltimore might lose his colony. To head this off and placate Maryland's restless Protestants, the proprietor drafted the famous "Act concerning Religion" in 1649, which extended toleration to everyone who accepted the divinity of Christ. At a time when European rulers regularly persecuted people for their religious beliefs, Baltimore championed liberty of conscience.

However laudable the act may have been, it did not heal religious divisions in Maryland, and when local Puritans seized the colony's government in 1650, they repealed the act. For almost two decades, vigilantes roamed the countryside, and one armed group temporarily drove Leonard Calvert out of Maryland. In 1655, civil war flared again, and the Calvert family did not regain control until 1658.

In this troubled sanctuary, ordinary planters and their workers cultivated tobacco on plantations dispersed along riverfronts. In 1678, Baltimore complained that he could not find 50 houses in a space of 30 miles. Tobacco affected almost every aspect of local culture. "In Virginia and Maryland," one member of the Calvert family explained, "Tobacco, as our Staple, is our all, and indeed leaves no room for anything Else." A steady stream of indentured servants supplied the plantations with dependent laborers—until African slaves replaced them at the end of the seventeenth century.

Europeans sacrificed much by coming to the Chesapeake. For most of the seventeenth century, their standard of living there was primitive compared with that of people of the same social class who had remained in England. Two-thirds of the planters, for example, lived in houses of only two rooms and of a type associated with the poorest classes in contemporary English society.

Quick Check

✓ What motives led Lord Baltimore to establish the colony of Maryland?

A "NEW" ENGLAND IN AMERICA

The Pilgrims enjoy almost mythic status in American history. These brave refugees crossed the cold Atlantic in search of religious liberty, signed a democratic compact aboard the *Mayflower*, landed at Plymouth Rock, and gave us our Thanksgiving Day. As with most legends, this one contains only a core of truth.

The Pilgrims were not crusaders out to change the world. Rather, they were humble English farmers. Their story began in the early 1600s in Scrooby Manor, a small community located approximately 150 miles north of London. Many people in this area believed the Church of England, or Anglican Church, retained too many traces of its Catholic origin. Its very rituals compromised God's true believers. So, early in the reign of James I, the Scrooby congregation formally left the established state church. Like others who followed this logic, they were called Separatists. Since English law required citizens to attend Anglican services, the Scrooby Separatists moved to Holland in 1608–1609 rather than compromise their beliefs.

The Netherlands provided the Separatists with a good home—too good. The members of the little church feared they were losing their identity; their children were becoming Dutch. In 1617, therefore, some of the original Scrooby congregation vowed to sail to America. Included in this group was William Bradford, a wonderfully literate man who later wrote *Of Plymouth Plantation*, one of the first and certainly most poignant accounts of an early American settlement.

Poverty presented the major obstacle to the Pilgrims' plans. They petitioned for a land patent from the Virginia Company of London. They also looked for someone willing to underwrite the staggering costs of colonization. The negotiations went well, or so it seemed. After stopping in England to take on supplies and laborers, the Pilgrims set off for America in 1620 aboard the *Mayflower*, armed with a patent to settle in Virginia and indebted to English investors who were only marginally interested in religious reform.

Because of an error in navigation, the Pilgrims landed not in Virginia but in what is today Massachusetts in New England. The patent for which they had worked so diligently had no validity there. In fact, the crown had granted New England to another company. Without a patent, the colonists possessed no authorization to form a civil government, a serious matter since some sailors who were not Pilgrims threatened mutiny. To preserve the struggling community from anarchy, 41 men signed an agreement known as the **Mayflower Compact** to "covenant and combine our selves together into a civil body politick."

How did differences in religion affect the founding of the New England colonies?

Read the **Document** *Mayflower Replica Plymouth, Massachusetts* on **myhistorylab.com**

Although later praised for its democratic character, the Mayflower Compact could not ward off disease and hunger. During the first months in Plymouth, death claimed approximately half of the 102 people who had initially set out from England. Moreover, debts contracted in England severely burdened the new colony. To their credit, the Pilgrims honored their financial obligations, but it took almost 20 years to satisfy the English investors. Without Bradford, whom they elected as governor, the settlers might have been overwhelmed. Through strength of will and self-sacrifice, however, Bradford persuaded frightened men and women that they could survive in America.

Bradford had help. Almost anyone who has heard of the Plymouth Colony knows of Squanto, a Patuxet Indian who welcomed the first Pilgrims in excellent English. In 1614 unscrupulous adventurers had kidnapped Squanto and sold him in Spain as a slave. Somehow he escaped bondage, making his way to London, where merchants who owned land in Newfoundland taught him to speak English. They apparently hoped that he would deliver moving public testimonials about immigrating to the New World. In any case, Squanto returned to the Plymouth area just before the Pilgrims arrived. Squanto joined Massasoit, a Native American leader, in teaching the Pilgrims much about hunting and agriculture, a debt that Bradford acknowledged. Although evidence for the so-called First Thanksgiving is sketchy, it is certain that without Native American support the Europeans would have starved.

European diseases had destroyed many of the Indian villages near Plymouth before the Pilgrims arrived. Now the Pilgrims were able to move onto cleared land left empty by the disappearance of the Indians. In time, the Pilgrims replicated the humble little farm communities they had known in England. They formed Separatist congregations to their liking, and the population slowly increased. But because Plymouth offered only limited economic prospects, it attracted few new settlers. In 1691, the colony was absorbed into its larger and more prosperous neighbor, Massachusetts Bay.

The Puritan Migration to Massachusetts

Read the **Document** *Reasons for the Plantation in New England* on **myhistorylab.com**

In the early seventeenth century, an extraordinary spirit of religious reform burst forth in England, and before it burned itself out, Puritanism had transformed the face of England and America. Modern historians have difficulty comprehending this powerful spiritual movement. Some consider the Puritans neurotic individuals who condemned liquor and sex, dressed in drab clothes, and minded their neighbors' business.

This crude caricature is based on a profound misunderstanding of the actual nature of this broad popular movement. The seventeenth-century Puritans were more like today's radical political reformers, men and women committed to far-reaching institutional change, than like naive do-gooders or narrow fundamentalists. To their enemies, of course, the Puritans were irritants, always pointing out civil and ecclesiastical imperfections and urging everyone to try to fulfill the commands of Scripture. Many people, however, shared their vision, and their values remained a dominant element in American culture at least until the Civil War.

The Puritans were products of the Protestant Reformation. They accepted a notion advanced by the sixteenth-century French-Swiss theologian John Calvin that an omnipotent God predestined some people to salvation and condemned others to eternal damnation no matter how good or sinful their lives were. But instead of waiting passively for Judgment Day, the Puritans examined themselves for signs of grace, for hints that God had placed them among his "elect." A member of the elect, they argued, would try to live according to Scripture, to battle sin and eradicate corruption.

For the Puritans, the logic of everyday life was clear. If the Church of England contained unscriptural elements—clerical vestments associated with Catholic ritual, for example—then they must be eliminated. If the pope in Rome was in league with the Antichrist foretold in the Bible, then Protestant kings should not ally with Catholic states. If God condemned licentiousness and intoxication, then local officials should punish whores, adulterers, and drunks. There was nothing improper about an occasional beer or passionate physical love within marriage, but when sex and drink became ends in themselves, the Puritans thought England's ministers and magistrates should speak out. Persons of this temperament were more combative than the Pilgrims had been. They wanted to purify the Church of England from within, and before the 1630s at least, separatism held little appeal for them.

From the Puritan perspective, James I and Charles I seemed unconcerned about the spiritual state of the nation. James tolerated corruption within his court and condoned gross public extravagance. Charles I persecuted Puritan ministers, forcing them either to conform to his theology or lose their licenses to preach. As long as Parliament met, Puritan voters in the various boroughs and counties of England elected men sympathetic to their point of view. These outspoken representatives criticized royal policies. Because of their defiance, Charles decided in 1629 to rule England without Parliament and four years later named William Laud, who represented everything the Puritans detested, archbishop of Canterbury, the leading position within the Church of England. The doors of reform slammed shut. The corruption remained.

John Winthrop, the future governor of Massachusetts Bay, was caught up in these events. Little about his background suggested such an auspicious future. He owned a small manor in Suffolk, one that never produced sufficient income to support his growing family. He dabbled in law. But the core of Winthrop's life was a faith in God so intense that his contemporaries immediately identified him as a Puritan. The Lord, he concluded, was displeased with England. Time for reform was running out. In May 1629, he wrote to his wife, "I am verily perswaded God will bring some heavye Affliction upon this lande, and that speedylye." He was, however, confident that the Lord would "provide a shelter and a hidinge place for us."

Read the **Document**
John Winthrop, "A Model of Christian Charity" (1630) on **myhistorylab.com**

Quick Check

✓ Why did the Puritans choose to leave England?

"A City on a Hill"

A fleet bearing Puritan settlers, John Winthrop among them, departed England in March 1630. By the end of the Puritan colony's first year, almost 2,000 people had arrived in Massachusetts Bay, and before the "Great Migration" concluded in the early 1640s, more than 16,000 men and women had arrived there.

Historians know a lot about the background of these settlers. Many of them originated in an area northeast of London called East Anglia, where Puritan ideas had taken deep root. London, Kent, and the West Country also contributed to the stream of emigrants. In some instances, entire villages were reestablished across the Atlantic. Many Bay Colonists had been farmers in England, but a surprisingly large number came from industrial centers, such as Norwich, where cloth was manufactured for the export trade.

Whatever their backgrounds, they moved to Massachusetts as nuclear families—fathers, mothers, and their dependent children—a form of migration strikingly different from the one that peopled Virginia and Maryland. Moreover, because the settlers had already formed families in England, the colony's sex ratio was more balanced than that found in the Chesapeake colonies. Finally, and perhaps more significantly, once they had arrived in Massachusetts, these men and women survived. Indeed, their life expectancy compares favorably to that of modern Americans. Many factors help explain this phenomenon—clean drinking water and a healthy climate, for example. While the Puritans could not have planned to live longer than did colonists in other parts of the New World, this remarkable accident reduced the emotional shock of long-distance migration.

The first settlers possessed another source of strength and stability. They were bound together by a common sense of purpose. God, they insisted, had formed a special covenant with the people of Massachusetts Bay. The Lord expected them to live according to Scripture and reform the church—in other words, to create an Old Testament "City on a Hill" that would stand as a beacon of righteousness for the rest of the Christian world. If they fulfilled their side of the bargain, the settlers could anticipate peace and prosperity.

The Bay Colonists developed an innovative form of church government known as Congregationalism. Under this system, each village church was independent of outside

Old Ship Meetinghouse This early Puritan meetinghouse in Hingham, Massachusetts, was called the Old Ship Meetinghouse because its interior design resembled the hull of a ship. The oldest surviving wooden church in the United States, it could accommodate about 700 people.

interference. The American Puritans, of course, wanted nothing of bishops. The people were the church, and as a body, they pledged to uphold God's law. In the Salem Church, for example, the members covenanted "with the Lord and with one another and do bind ourselves in the presence of God to walk together in all his ways."

Simply because a person happened to live in a certain community did not mean he or she automatically belonged to church. The churches of Massachusetts were voluntary institutions. To join one a man or woman had to provide testimony—a confession of faith—before neighbors who had already been admitted as full members. It was a demanding process. But most men and women in early Massachusetts aspired to full membership, which entitled them to receive the sacraments and gave some of them responsibility for choosing ministers, disciplining sinners, and settling difficult questions of theology. Although women and blacks could not vote for ministers, they did become members of the Congregational churches.

The government of Massachusetts was neither a democracy nor a theocracy. The magistrates elected in Massachusetts did not believe they represented the voters, much less the whole populace. They ruled in the name of the electorate, but their responsibility was to God. In 1638, Winthrop warned against overly democratic forms, since "the best part [of the people] is always the least, and of that best part the wiser is always the lesser." The Congregational ministers possessed no formal political authority in Massachusetts Bay and could not even hold civil office. Voters often ignored the recommendations of their ministers.

In New England, the town became the center of public life. In other regions of British America, where the county was the focus of local government, people did not experience the same density of social and institutional interaction. In Massachusetts, groups of men and women voluntarily covenanted together to observe common goals. The community constructed a meetinghouse where religious services and town meetings were held. This powerful sense of shared purpose—something that later Americans have greatly admired—should not obscure the fact that the founders of New England towns also had a keen eye for personal profit. Seventeenth-century records reveal that speculators often made a good deal of money from selling "shares" in village lands. But acquisitiveness never got out of control, and recent studies have shown that entrepreneurial practices rarely disturbed the peace of the Puritan communities. Inhabitants generally received land sufficient to build a house and support a family. Although villagers escaped the kind of feudal dues collected in other parts of America, they were expected to contribute to the minister's salary, pay local and colony taxes, and serve in the militia.

Quick Check

✓ What did the founders of Massachusetts mean when they referred to their colony as a "City on a Hill"?

Competing Truths in New England

The European settlers of Massachusetts Bay managed to live in peace—at least with each other. This was a remarkable achievement considering the chronic instability that plagued other colonies. The Bay Colonists disagreed over many issues, sometimes vociferously; towns disputed with neighboring villages over boundaries. But the people inevitably relied on the civil courts to mediate differences. They believed in a rule of law, and in 1648 the colonial legislature, called the General Court, drew up the *Lawes and Liberties*, the first alphabetized code of law printed in English. In clear prose, it explained to ordinary colonists their rights and responsibilities as citizens of the commonwealth. The code engendered public trust in government and discouraged magistrates from the arbitrary exercise of authority.

The Puritans never supported religious toleration. They transferred to the New World to preserve *their own* freedom of worship. They expressed little concern for the religious freedom of those they deemed heretics. The most serious challenges to Puritan orthodoxy in Massachusetts Bay came from two charismatic people. The first, Roger Williams, arrived in 1631 and immediately attracted loyal followers. Indeed, everyone seemed to have liked him as a person.

Williams's *religious ideas*, however, created controversy. He preached extreme separatism. The Bay Colonists, he exclaimed, were impure in the sight of the Lord so long as they remained even nominal members of the Church of England. More-over, he questioned the validity of the colony's charter, since the king had not first purchased the land from the Indians, a view that threatened the integrity of the entire colonial experiment. Williams also insisted that the civil rulers of Massa-chusetts had no business punishing settlers for their religious beliefs. Monitoring people's consciences was God's responsibility, not men's. The Bay magistrates were prepared neither to tolerate heresy nor to accede to Williams's other demands, and in 1636, after failing to reach a compromise with him, they banished him from the colony. Williams then worked out the logic of his ideas in Providence, a village he founded in what would become Rhode Island.

The Bay magistrates rightly concluded that Anne Hutchinson, posed an even graver threat to the peace of the commonwealth than Williams had. This intelli-gent woman, her husband William, and her children arrived in the New World in 1634. Even contemporaries found her religious ideas, which consisted of a highly personal form of spirituality, usually termed antinomianism, confusing.

Hutchinson shared her thoughts with other Bostonians, many of them women. Her outspoken views scandalized orthodox leaders of church and state. She suggested that all but two ministers in the colony had lost touch with the "Holy Spirit" and were preaching a doctrine in the Congregational churches that was little better than that of Archbishop Laud. When authorities demanded she explain her unusual opinions, she suggested that she experienced divine inspira-tion independently of either the Bible or the clergy. In other words, Hutchinson's teachings could not be tested by Scripture, a position that seemed dangerously subjective. Indeed, her theology threatened the very foundation of Massachusetts Bay. Without clear, external standards, one person's truth was as valid as anyone else's, and from Winthrop's perspective, Hutchinson's teachings invited civil and religious anarchy. But her challenge to authority was not simply theological. As a woman, her aggressive speech sparked a deeply misogynist response from the colony's male leaders.

When this woman described Congregational ministers—some of them the lead-ing divines of Boston—as unconverted men, the General Court intervened. For two days in 1637, the ministers and magistrates of Massachusetts Bay cross-examined

Hutchinson. In this intense theological debate, she more than held her own. She knew as much about the Bible as did her inquisitors.

Hutchinson defied the ministers and magistrates to demonstrate exactly where she had gone wrong. Just when it appeared Hutchinson had outmaneuvered—indeed, embarrassed—her opponents, she let down her guard, declaring that what she knew of God came "by an immediate revelation.... By the voice of his own spirit to my soul." Here was what her accusers had suspected but could not prove. She had confessed in open court that the Spirit can live without the Moral Law. This antinomian statement fulfilled the worst fears of the Bay rulers, and they were relieved to exile Hutchinson and her followers to Rhode Island.

Quick Check

✓ In what ways did Roger Williams and Anne Hutchinson pose a threat to the Massachusetts Bay Colony?

Mobility and Division

Massachusetts Bay spawned four new colonies, three of which survived to the American Revolution (see Map 2.2). New Hampshire became a separate colony in 1677. Its population grew slowly, and for much of the colonial period, New Hampshire remained economically dependent on Massachusetts, its commercial neighbor to the south.

Far more people were drawn to the fertile lands of the Connecticut River Valley. In 1636, settlers founded the villages of Hartford, Windsor, and Wethersfield. No one forced these men and women to leave Massachusetts, and in their new surroundings, they recreated a society that looked much like the one they had known in the Bay Colony. Through his writings, Thomas Hooker, Connecticut's most prominent minister, helped all New Englanders define Congregational church policy. Puritans on both sides of the Atlantic read Hooker's beautifully crafted works. In 1639, representatives from the Connecticut towns passed the Fundamental Orders, a blueprint for civil government, and in 1662, King Charles II awarded the colony its own charter.

In 1638, another group, led by Theophilus Eaton and the Reverend John Davenport, settled New Haven and several adjoining towns along Long Island Sound. These emigrants, many of whom had come from London, lived briefly in Massachusetts Bay but then insisted on forming a Puritan commonwealth of their own, one that established a closer relationship between church and state than the Bay

Map 2.2 New England Colonies, 1650 The early settlers quickly carved up New England. New Haven briefly flourished as a separate colony before being taken over by Connecticut in 1662. Long Island later became part of New York; Massachusetts absorbed Plymouth; and in 1677, New Hampshire became a separate colony.

Colonists had allowed. The New Haven colony never prospered, and in 1662, it was absorbed into Connecticut.

Rhode Island experienced a different history. From the beginning, it drew people of an independent mind, and according to one Dutch visitor, Rhode Island was "the receptacle of all sorts of riff-raff people…. All the cranks of New-England retire thither." This, of course, was an exaggeration. Roger Williams founded Providence in 1636; two years later, Anne Hutchinson took her followers to Portsmouth. Other groups settled around Narragansett Bay. Not surprisingly, these men and women appreciated the need for toleration. No one was persecuted in Rhode Island for his or her religious beliefs.

One might have thought the separate Rhode Island communities would cooperate for the common good. They did not. Villagers fought over land and schemed with outside speculators to divide the tiny colony into even smaller pieces. In 1644, Parliament issued a patent for the "Providence Plantations," and in 1663, the Rhode Islanders obtained a royal charter. But for most of the seventeenth century, colony-wide government existed in name only. Despite their constant bickering, however, the settlers of Rhode Island built up a profitable commerce in agricultural goods.

Quick Check

✓ What religious and economic factors led to the settlement of other New England colonies beyond Masschusetts Bay?

DIVERSITY IN THE MIDDLE COLONIES

How did ethnic diversity shape the development of the Middle Colonies?

New York, New Jersey, Pennsylvania, and Delaware were settled for different reasons (see Map 2.3). William Penn, for example, envisioned a Quaker sanctuary; the Duke of York worried chiefly about his own income. Despite the founders' intentions, however, some common characteristics emerged. Both colonies developed a strikingly heterogeneous population, men and women of different ethnic and religious backgrounds. This cultural diversity influenced the economic, political, and ecclesiastical institutions of the Middle Colonies. The raucous, partisan public life of the Middle Colonies foreshadowed later American society.

Anglo-Dutch Rivalry on the Hudson

Read the **Document**
Father Isaac Jogues' Description of New York, 1640 on **myhistorylab.com**

By the early seventeenth century, the Dutch were Europe's most aggressive traders. The Netherlands—a small, loosely federated nation—possessed the world's largest merchant fleet. Its ships vied for the commerce of Asia, Africa, and the Americas. Dutch rivalry with Spain, a fading though still formidable power, was largely responsible for the settlement of New Netherland. While searching for the elusive Northwest Passage in 1609, Henry Hudson, an English explorer employed by a Dutch company, sailed up the river that now bears his name. Further voyages led to the establishment of trading posts in what became the colony of New Netherland, although permanent settlement did not occur until 1624. The area also seemed an excellent base from which to attack Spain's colonies in the New World.

The directors of the Dutch West India Company sponsored two small outposts, Fort Orange (Albany), located well up the Hudson River, and New Amsterdam (New York City) on Manhattan Island. The first Dutch settlers were salaried employees, not colonists, and their superiors in Europe expected them to spend most of their time gathering furs. They did not receive land for their troubles. Needless to say, this arrangement attracted few Dutch immigrants.

The colony's European population may have been small—only 270 in 1628—but its ethnic mix was extraordinary. One visitor to New Amsterdam in 1644 maintained he had heard "eighteen different languages" spoken there. Even if this report was exaggerated, there is no doubt the Dutch colony drew English, Finns, Germans, and Swedes. By the 1640s, a sizable community of free blacks (probably former slaves who had gained their freedom through self-purchase) had developed in New Amsterdam, adding African tongues to the cacophony of languages. New England Puritans who left Massachusetts and Connecticut to stake out farms on eastern Long Island further fragmented the colony's culture.

New Netherland lacked capable leadership. The company sent a number of director-generals to oversee judicial and political affairs. Without exception, these men were temperamentally unsuited to govern an American colony. They adopted autocratic procedures, lined their own pockets, and, in one case, blundered into a war that killed scores of Indians and settlers. The company made no provision for an elected assembly. As much as they could, the scattered inhabitants living along the Hudson River ignored company directives. They felt no loyalty to the trading company that had treated them so shabbily. Long Island Puritans complained bitterly about the absence of representative institutions. The Dutch system has been described as "unstable pluralism."

In August 1664, the Dutch lost their tenuous hold on New Netherland. The English crown, eager to score an easy victory over a commercial rival, dispatched a fleet of warships to New Amsterdam. The commander of this force, Colonel Richard Nicolls, ordered the colonists to surrender. The last director-general, a colorful character named Peter Stuyvesant, rushed wildly about the city urging the settlers to resist the English. But no one obeyed. Even the Dutch remained deaf to his appeals. Instead, they accepted the Articles of Capitulation, a generous agreement that allowed Dutch nationals to remain in the province and retain their property under English rule.

Charles II had already granted his brother James, the Duke of York, a charter for the newly captured territory and much else besides. The duke became absolute proprietor over Maine, Martha's Vineyard, Nantucket, Long Island, and the rest of New York all the way south to Delaware Bay. The king perhaps wanted to encircle New England's potentially disloyal Puritan population, but he also created a bureaucratic nightmare.

Map 2.3 *Middle Colonies, 1685* New York and Philadelphia became colonial America's most important commercial ports.

t' Fort nieuw Amsterdam op de Manhatans

New Amsterdam Dutch colonization in the first half of the seventeenth century extended from New Amsterdam (New York City) up the Hudson River to Fort Orange (Albany).

Quick Check

✓ Why were the Dutch unable to establish a permanent colony in what became New York?

The Duke of York had acquired a thorough aversion to representative government. He had no intention of letting such a participatory system take root in New York. "I cannot *but* suspect," he announced, that an assembly "would be of dangerous consequence." The Long Islanders felt betrayed. In part to appease these outspoken critics, Governor Nicolls—one of the few competent administrators to serve in the Middle Colonies—drew up in March 1665 a legal code known as the Duke's Laws. It guaranteed religious toleration and created local governments.

There was no provision, however, for an elected assembly or for democratic town meetings. The legal code disappointed the Puritan migrants on Long Island, and when the duke's officers attempted to collect taxes, these people protested that they were "inslav'd under an Arbitrary Power."

The Dutch kept silent. For decades they remained a large unassimilated ethnic group. They continued to speak their own language, worship in their own churches (Dutch Reformed Calvinist), and eye their English neighbors with suspicion. In fact, the colony seemed little different from what it had been under the Dutch West India Company: a loose collection of independent communities ruled by an ineffectual central government.

Confusion in New Jersey

Only three months after receiving a charter for New York, the Duke of York gifted its southernmost lands to two courtiers who had served Charles II during the English Civil War. The land between the Hudson and Delaware Rivers went to John, Lord Berkeley and Sir George Carteret to form a colony named New Jersey (in honor of Carteret's birthplace, the Isle of Jersey in the English Channel). But before learning of James's decision, the governor of the colony had allowed migrants from New England to take up farms west of the Hudson River. In exchange for small annual rents to the duke, these settlers were granted the rights to establish an elected assembly, a headright system, and liberty of conscience. Berkeley and Carteret recruited colonists on similar terms, assuming that that they would receive the rent money. Soon it was not clear who owned what in New Jersey.

The result was chaos. Some colonists insisted that the governor had authorized their assembly. Others, equally insistent, claimed that Berkeley and Carteret had done so. Both sides were wrong. Neither the proprietors nor the governor possessed any legal right to set up a colonial government. James could transfer land to favorite courtiers, but no matter how many times the land changed hands, the government remained his personal responsibility. Knowledge of the law failed to quiet the controversy. Through it all, the duke showed not the slightest interest in the peace and welfare of the people of New Jersey.

Berkeley grew tired of the venture. It generated headaches rather than income. In 1674, he sold his proprietary rights to a group of surprisingly quarrelsome Quakers. The sale necessitated the division of the colony into two separate governments known as East and West Jersey. Neither half prospered. Carteret and his heirs tried unsuccessfully to turn a profit in East Jersey. The Quaker proprietors fought among themselves with such intensity that not even William Penn could bring tranquility to their affairs. Penn wisely turned his attention to the unclaimed territory across the Delaware River. The West Jersey proprietors went bankrupt, and in 1702 the Crown reunited the two Jerseys into a single royal colony.

Quick Check
✓ What caused chaos during the settlement of New Jersey?

Quakers in America

The founding of Pennsylvania cannot be separated from the history of the Quaker movement. Believers in an extreme form of antinomianism, the **Quakers** saw no need for a learned ministry, since one person's interpretation of Scripture was as valid as anyone else's. This radical religious sect gained its name from the derogatory term that English authorities sometimes used to describe those who quake or "tremble at the word of the Lord." The name persisted even though the Quakers preferred being called Professors of the Light or, more commonly, Friends.

Quakers practiced humility in their daily lives. They wore simple clothes and employed old-fashioned forms of address that set them apart from their neighbors. Friends refused to honor worldly position and accomplishment or to swear oaths in courts of law. They were also pacifists. Quakers considered all persons equal in the sight of the Lord, a belief that generally annoyed people of rank and achievement.

Moreover, the Quakers never kept their thoughts to themselves. They preached conversion constantly, spreading the "Truth" throughout England, Ireland, and America. The Friends played important roles in the early history of New Jersey, Rhode Island, and North Carolina, as well as Pennsylvania. In some places, the "publishers of Truth" wore out their welcome. English authorities harassed the Quakers. Thousands were jailed, and in Massachusetts Bay between 1659 and 1661, Puritan magistrates ordered several Friends put to death. But persecution only inspired the persecuted Quakers to redouble their efforts.

Quick Check
✓ What explains Puritan hostility toward the Quakers?

Penn's "Holy Experiment"

William Penn, the founder of Pennsylvania, dedicated his life to the Quaker faith, a commitment that led to the founding of Pennsylvania. His personality was complex. He was an athletic person who threw himself into intellectual pursuits. He was a bold visionary capable of making pragmatic decisions. He came from an aristocratic family and yet spent his adult life involved with a religious movement associated with the lower class.

In 1688, Penn negotiated one of the more impressive land deals in the history of American real estate. Charles II awarded Penn a charter making him the sole proprietor of a vast area called Pennsylvania (literally, "Penn's woods"). The name embarrassed the modest Penn, but he knew better than to look the royal gift horse in the mouth. In 1682, the new proprietor purchased from the Duke of York the so-called Three Lower Counties that eventually became Delaware. Traders in Swedish employ had begun establishing trading posts along the river in the 1630s. In 1655, the Dutch took over full control of these New Sweden territories, but the Duke of York pushed them out in 1664. Penn's astute purchase of these Lower Counties guaranteed that Pennsylvania would have access to the Atlantic and determined even before Philadelphia had been established that it would become a commercial center.

Read the Document
William Penn, "Model for Government" (1681) on myhistorylab.com

Penn lost no time in launching his "Holy Experiment." In 1682, he set forth his ideas in an unusual document known as the Frame of Government. The royal charter gave Penn the right to create any form of government he desired, and his imagination ran wild. His plan blended traditional notions about the privileges of a landed aristocracy with daring concepts of personal liberty. Penn guaranteed that settlers would enjoy, among other things, liberty of conscience, freedom from persecution, no taxation without representation, and due process of law.

Penn promoted his colony aggressively throughout England, Ireland, and Germany. He had no choice. His only source of revenue was the sale of land and the collection of quitrents. Penn commissioned pamphlets in several languages extolling the quality of Pennsylvania's rich farmland. The response was overwhelming. People poured into Philadelphia, the new city Penn had laid out, and the surrounding area. In 1685 alone, 8,000 immigrants arrived. Most of the settlers were Irish, Welsh, and English Quakers, and they generally moved to America as families. But Penn opened the door to men and women of all nations. He asserted that the people of Pennsylvania "are a collection of divers nations in Europe, as French, Dutch, Germans, Swedes, Danes, Finns, Scotch, Irish, and English."

The settlers were by no means all Quakers. The founder of Germantown, Francis Daniel Pastorius, called the ship that brought him to the New World a "Noah's Ark" of religions, and within his own household, there were servants who subscribed "to the Roman [Catholic], to the Lutheran, to the Calvinistic, to the Anabaptist, and to the Anglican church, and only one Quaker." Ethnic and religious diversity was crucial in the development of Pennsylvania's public institutions, and its politics were more quarrelsome than those in more homogeneous colonies such as Virginia and Massachusetts.

In 1701, legal challenges in England forced Penn to depart for the mother country. Just before he sailed, Penn signed the Charter of Liberties, a new frame of government that established a unicameral or one-house legislature (the only one in colonial America) and gave the representatives the right to initiate bills. Penn also allowed the assembly to conduct its business without proprietary interference. The charter provided for the political separation of the Three Lower Counties (Delaware), whose settlers had never shown any enthusiasm for Penn's "Holy Experiment" and who had been demanding autonomy. This hastily drafted document served as Pennsylvania's constitution until the American Revolution.

Quick Check

✓ How did the Quaker religion influence the development of Pennsylvania?

PLANTING THE SOUTHERN COLONIES

In some ways, Carolina society looked much like the one that had developed in Virginia and Maryland. In both areas, white planters forced African slaves to produce staple crops for a world market. But such superficial similarities masked substantial regional differences. In fact, "the South"—certainly the fabled solid South of the early nineteenth century—did not exist during the colonial period. The Carolinas, joined much later by Georgia, stood apart from their northern neighbors (see Map 2.4). As a historian of colonial Carolina explained, "the southern colonies were never a cohesive section in the same way that New England was. The great diversity of population groups … discouraged southern sectionalism."

How was the founding of the Carolinas different from the founding of Georgia?

Founding the Carolinas

On March 24, 1663, Charles II granted a group of eight courtiers, styled the Proprietors of Carolina, a charter to the vast territory between Virginia and Spanish-ruled Florida running west as far as the "South Seas," even though no one knew where that was. After initial setbacks, the most energetic proprietor, Anthony Ashley Cooper, later Earl of Shaftesbury, realized that without an infusion of new money Carolina would fail. In 1669, he persuaded other Carolinian proprietors to invest their own capital in the colony. Once he received sufficient funds, he dispatched 300 English colonists to Port Royal under the command of Joseph West. The fleet put in briefly at the Caribbean island of Barbados to pick up additional recruits, and in March 1670, after being punished by Atlantic gales that destroyed one ship, the expedition arrived at its destination. Only 100 people were still alive. The unhappy settlers did not remain long at Port Royal, an unappealing, low-lying place badly exposed to Spanish attack. They moved northward, locating eventually along the more secure Ashley River. Later the colony's administrative center, Charles Town (it did not become Charleston until 1783) was established at the junction of the Ashley and Cooper rivers.

Before 1680, almost half the men and women who settled in the Port Royal area came from Barbados. This small Caribbean island, which produced an annual fortune in

Charles Town This engraving from 1671 of the fortified settlement at Charleston, South Carolina, shows the junction of the Ashley and Cooper rivers. Many of Charleston's settlers came from the sugar plantations of Barbados.

Map 2.4 *The Carolinas and Georgia* Caribbean sugar planters migrated to the Goose Creek area, where they eventually mastered rice cultivation. Poor harbors in North Carolina retarded the spread of European settlement there.

sugar, depended on slave labor. By the third quarter of the seventeenth century, Barbados had become overpopulated. Wealthy families could not provide their sons and daughters with sufficient land to maintain social status, and as the crisis intensified, Barbadians looked to Carolina for relief.

These migrants, many of whom were rich, traveled to Carolina both as individuals and as family groups. Some even brought gangs of slaves with them to the American mainland. The Barbadians carved out plantations on the tributaries of the Cooper River and established themselves immediately as the colony's most powerful political faction. "So it was," wrote historian Richard Dunn, "that these Caribbean pioneers helped to create on the North American coast a slave-based plantation society closer in temper to the islands they fled from than to any other mainland English settlement."

Much of the planters' time was taken up with the search for a profitable crop. The early settlers experimented with several plants: tobacco, cotton, mulberry trees for silk, and grapes. The most successful items turned out to be beef, animal skins, and naval stores (especially tar used to maintain ocean vessels). By the 1680s, some Carolinians had built up great herds of cattle—700 or 800 head in some cases. Traders who dealt with Indians brought back thousands of deerskins from the interior. They also often returned with Indian slaves. These commercial resources, together with tar and turpentine, enjoyed a good market. The planters did not fully appreciate the value of rice until the 1690s, but once they did, it quickly became the colony's main staple.

Proprietary Carolina was in a constant political uproar. Factions vied for special privilege. The Barbadian settlers, known locally as the Goose Creek Men, resisted the proprietors' policies at every turn. A large community of French Protestant Huguenots located in Craven County distrusted the Barbadians. The proprietors—an ineffectual group after Cooper died in 1683—appointed incompetent governors who only made things worse. One visitor observed that "the Inhabitants of Carolina should be as free from Oppression as any [people] in the Universe … if their own Differences amongst themselves do not occasion the contrary." By the end of the seventeenth century, the Commons House of Assembly had assumed the right to initiate legislation. In 1719, the colonists overthrew the last proprietary governor. In 1729, the king created separate royal governments for North and South Carolina, hoping that splitting the colonies would help lead to more effective (and more peaceable) governance.

Quick Check

✓ How did the Barbadian background of the early settlers shape the economic development of the Carolinas?

Founding of Georgia

The early history of Georgia was strikingly different from that of Britain's other mainland colonies. Its settlement was really an act of aggression against Spain, which had as good a claim to this area as did the English. During the eighteenth century, the two nations were often at war (see Chapter 4), and South Carolinians worried that the Spaniards moving up from bases in Florida would occupy the disputed territory between Florida and the Carolina grant.

The colony owed its existence primarily to James Oglethorpe, a British general and member of Parliament who believed that he could thwart Spanish designs on the area south of Charles Town while providing a fresh start for London's worthy poor, saving them from debtors' prison. (Until the nineteenth century, debtors could be imprisoned if they could not repay what they owed.) Although Oglethorpe envisioned Georgia as an asylum as well as a garrison, the military aspects of his proposal appealed to the British government. In 1732, King George II granted Oglethorpe and a board of trustees a charter for a new colony named after him to be located between the Savannah and Altamaha rivers and from "sea to sea." The trustees living in the mother country were given complete control over Georgia politics, a condition the settlers soon found intolerable.

During the first years of colonization, Georgia fared no better than had earlier utopian experiments. The English poor showed little desire to move to an inclement frontier, and the trustees, in their turn, provided little incentive for emigration. Each colonist received only 50 acres. Another 50 acres could be added for each servant transported to Georgia, but no settler could amass more than 500 acres. Moreover, land could be passed only to an eldest son, and if a planter had no sons when he died, the holding reverted to the trustees. Slavery was prohibited. So was rum.

Almost as soon as they arrived in Georgia, the settlers complained. The colonists demanded slaves, pointing out to the trustees that without an unfree labor force they could not compete economically with their South Carolina neighbors. The settlers also wanted a voice in local government. In 1738, 121 people living in the new colony's capital, Savannah, petitioned for fundamental reforms in the colony's constitution. Oglethorpe responded angrily, "The idle ones are indeed for Negroes. If the petition is countenanced, the province is ruined." In 1741, the settlers again petitioned Oglethorpe, addressing him as "our Perpetual Dictator."

While the colonists grumbled about restrictions, Oglethorpe tried and failed to capture the Spanish fortress at St. Augustine in Florida (1740). This disappointment coupled with the growing popular unrest destroyed his interest in Georgia. The trustees were forced to compromise their principles. In 1738, they eliminated restrictions on the amount of land a man could own and allowed women to inherit land. In 1750, they permitted the settlers to import slaves. Soon Georgians could drink rum. In 1751, the trustees returned Georgia to the king, undoubtedly relieved to be free of what had become a hard-drinking, slave-owning plantation society much like that in South Carolina. The king authorized an assembly in 1751, but Georgia still attracted few new settlers.

Quick Check
✓ Why did Georgia settlers object to the government imposed upon them by James Oglethorpe?

TABLE 2.1   England's Principal Mainland Colonies

Name	Original Purpose	Date of Founding	Principal Founder	Major Export	Estimated Population ca. 1700
Virginia	Commercial venture	1607	Captain John Smith	Tobacco	64,560
New Amsterdam (New York)	Commercial venture	1613 (made English colony, 1664)	Peter Stuyvesant, Duke of York	Furs, grain	19,107
Plymouth	Refuge for English Separatists	1620 (absorbed by Massachusetts, 1691)	William Bradford	Grain	Included with Massachusetts
New Hampshire	Commercial venture	1623	John Mason	Wood, naval stores	4,958
Massachusetts	Refuge for English Puritans	1628	John Winthrop	Grain, wood	55,941
Maryland	Refuge for English Catholics	1634	Lord Baltimore (George Calvert)	Tobacco	34,100
Connecticut	Expansion of Massachusetts	1635	Thomas Hooker	Grain	25,970
Rhode Island	Refuge for dissenters from Massachusetts	1636	Roger Williams	Grain	5,894
Delaware	Commercial venture	1638 (included in Penn grant, 1681; given separate assembly, 1703)	William Penn	Grain	2,470
North Carolina	Commercial venture	1663	Anthony Ashley Cooper	Wood, naval stores, tobacco	10,720
South Carolina	Commercial venture	1663	Anthony Ashley Cooper	Naval stores, rice, indigo	5,720
New Jersey	Consolidation of new English territory, Quaker settlement	1664	Sir George Carteret	Grain	14,010
Pennsylvania	Refuge for English Quakers	1681	William Penn	Grain	18,950
Georgia	Discourage Spanish expansion; charity	1733	James Oglethorpe	Rice, wood, naval stores	5,200 (in 1750)

Sources: U.S. Bureau of the Census, *Historical Statistics of the United States: Colonial Times to 1970,* Washington, D.C., 1975; John J. McCusker and Russell R. Menard, *The Economy of British America, 1607–1789,* Chapel Hill, 1985.

CONCLUSION: LIVING WITH DIVERSITY

Long after he had returned from his adventures in Virginia, Captain John Smith reflected on the difficulty of establishing colonies in the New World. It was a task for which most people were not suited. "It requires," Smith counseled, "all the best parts of art, judgment, courage, honesty, constancy, diligence, and industry, [even] to do neere well." On another occasion, Charles I warned Lord Baltimore that new settlements "commonly have rugged and laborious beginnings."

In the seventeenth century, women and men had followed leaders such as Baltimore, Smith, Winthrop, Bradford, Penn, and Berkeley to the New World in anticipation of creating a successful new society. Some migrants were religious visionaries; others were hardheaded businessmen. The results of their efforts, their struggles to survive in an often hostile environment, and their interactions with various Native American groups yielded a spectrum of settlements along the Atlantic coast, from the quasi-feudalism of South Carolina to the Puritan commonwealth of Massachusetts Bay.

The diversity of early English colonization must be emphasized precisely because it is so easy to overlook (see Table 2.1). Even though the colonists eventually banded together and fought for independence, persistent differences separated New Englanders from Virginians, Pennsylvanians from Carolinians. The interpretive challenge, of course, is to comprehend how European colonists managed during the eighteenth century to overcome fragmentation and develop the capacity to imagine themselves a nation.

2 STUDY RESOURCES

((•—Listen to the **Chapter Audio** for Chapter 2 on **myhistorylab.com**

TIMELINE

1607 First English settlers arrive at Jamestown, p. 37

1608–1609 Scrooby congregation (Pilgrims) leaves England for Holland, p. 41

1609–1611 "Starving time" in Virginia threatens survival of the colonists, p. 35

1619 Virginia assembly, called House of Burgesses, meets for the first time, p. 37

1620 Pilgrims sign the Mayflower Compact, p. 41

1622 Indian attack devastates Virginia, p. 38

1624 Dutch investors create permanent settlements along Hudson River, p. 48
• James I, king of England, dissolves Virginia Company, p. 38

1625 Charles I ascends English throne, p. 33

1634 Colony of Maryland is founded, p. 39

1636 Puritan settlers found Hartford and other Connecticut Valley towns, p. 47

1638 Anne Hutchinson exiled to Rhode Island, p. 47
• Theophilus Eaton and John Davenport lead settlers to New Haven Colony, p. 47

1639 Connecticut towns accept Fundamental Orders, p. 47

1644 Second major Indian attack in Virginia, p. 36

1649 Charles I executed during English Civil War, p. 40

1663 Rhode Island obtains royal charter, p. 48
  • Proprietors receive charter for Carolina, p. 53

1664 English conquer New Netherland, p. 49

1677 New Hampshire becomes a royal colony, p. 47

1681 William Penn granted patent for his "Holy Experiment," p. 52

1732 James Oglethorpe receives charter for Georgia, p. 55

CHAPTER REVIEW

BREAKING AWAY: DECISIONS TO MOVE TO AMERICA

Why did the Chesapeake colonies not prosper during the earliest years of settlement?

Poor governance in early Virginia, founded in 1607, led to starvation and hostilities with the Powhatan Indians. Founded in 1634 as a refuge for Catholics, Maryland's early politics were plagued by religious tensions that sometimes led to large-scale violence. Both colonies imported predominately young, male indentured servants as laborers and suffered high mortality rates from disease. This resulted in transient and unruly societies with few stable families. *(p. 32)*

A "NEW" ENGLAND IN AMERICA

What role did differences in religion play in the founding of the New England colonies?

Religious persecution drove thousands of Puritans to New England. John Winthrop hoped the settlers would reform English Protestantism and create a "City on a Hill." The Puritans did not welcome dissent. They exiled Roger Williams and Anne Hutchinson to Rhode Island for their religious beliefs. Stable nuclear families and good health helped Puritans avoid the social turmoil that plagued the Chesapeake colonies. *(p. 41)*

DIVERSITY IN THE MIDDLE COLONIES

How did ethnic diversity shape the development of the Middle Colonies?

After conquering the Dutch colony of New Netherland in 1664, the English renamed it New York. Despite the conquest, the Dutch remained an influential minority in the colony, and ethnic rivalries shaped the politics of New York for decades. In 1681, Charles II granted William Penn, a Quaker, a charter to establish Pennsylvania. Penn's guarantee to respect all Christian settlers' liberty of conscience drew immigrants from across Northern Europe. *(p. 48)*

PLANTING THE SOUTHERN COLONIES

How was the founding of the Carolinas different from that of Georgia?

Immigrants from Barbados began settling in the Carolinas in the 1670s. Barbadian immigrants to the Carolinas, many of whom were wealthy planters seeking new lands for plantations, brought slavery with them when they moved. Georgia was founded in 1732 as an alternative to debtors' prison for impoverished Englishmen and as a military outpost to guard against the Spanish in Florida. *(p. 53)*

KEY TERM QUESTIONS

1. How did the joint-stock company make possible the launching of a new colony in Virginia? (p. 33)

2. What was the purpose of creating the House of Burgesses in Virginia? (p. 37)

3. How did the headright system help to establish the colony in Virginia? (p. 37)

4. Why were most indentured servants unable to reap the benefits of coming to the New World? (p. 37)

5. What purpose did the Mayflower Compact serve when it was signed in 1620? (p. 41)

6. How did the Protestant Reformation influence the Puritans? (p. 42)

7. What were the backgrounds of the Puritans participating in the "Great Migration"? (p. 44)

8. Why did antinomianism threaten many in the Massachusetts Bay Colony? (p. 46)

9. How did the Quakers' religious beliefs differ from that of the Puritans? (p. 51)

MyHistoryLab Connections

Visit **www.myhistorylab.com** for a customized Study Plan to build your knowledge of *New World Experiments*.

Question for Analysis

1. How similar were the settlers that founded the first colonies in the New World?

   View the **Map** *The Colonies to 1740* p. 33

2. What stereotypes of Native Americans does John Smith evoke in *The Starving Time*?

   Read the **Document** *John Smith, The Starving Time* p. 35

3. How important was tobacco to the economy of Maryland?

   Read the **Document** *George Alsop, From a Character of the Province of Maryland* p. 39

4. How does Winthrop portray the Puritan purpose in America as a divine mandate?

   Read the **Document** *John Winthrop, A Model of Christian Charity* p. 43

Other Resources from this Chapter

View the **Image** *Mural of Jamestown Settlement*

View the **Image** *Powhattan in Longhouse*

View the **Image** *First House of Burgessess Meeting in Jamestown*

Read the **Document** *Wessell Webling, His Indenture*

View the **Image** *Mayflower Replica Plymouth, Massachusetts*

Read the **Document** *Reasons for the Plantation in New England*

Read the **Document** *Father Isaac Jogues Description of New York, 1640*

Read the **Document** *William Penn "Model for Government"*

Read the **Document** *James Oglethorpe to the Trustees*

3 Putting Down Roots

Opportunity and Oppression in Colonial Society, 1619–1692

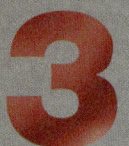

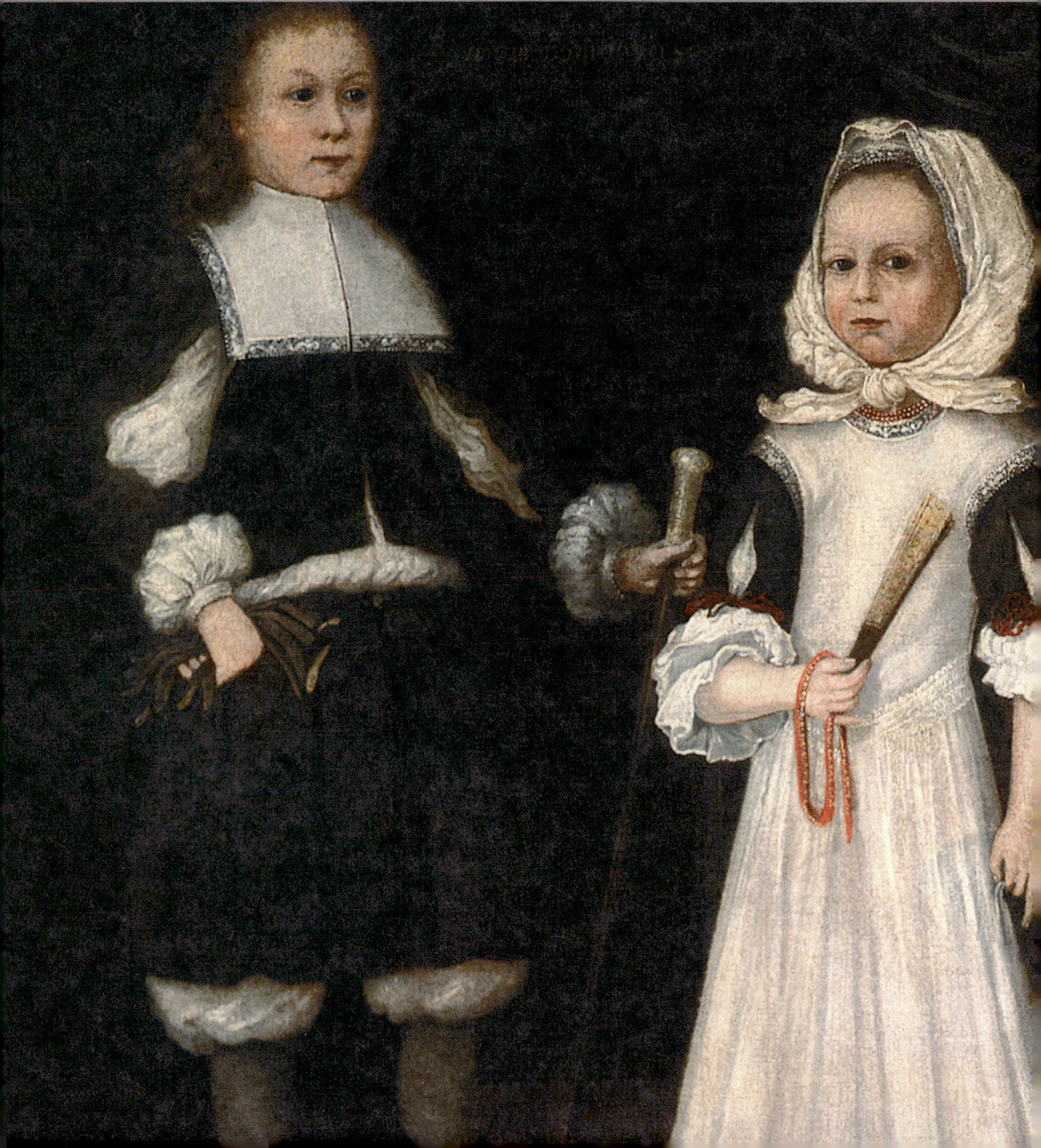

Contents and Spotlight Questions

((•─ Listen to the **Chapter Audio** for Chapter 3 on **myhistorylab.com**

FAMILIES IN AN ATLANTIC EMPIRE

The Witherspoon family moved from Great Britain to the South Carolina backcountry early in the eighteenth century. Although otherwise indistinguishable from the thousands of other ordinary families that put down roots in English America, the Witherspoons were made historical figures by the candid account of pioneer life produced by their son, Robert, who was only a small child at the time of their arrival.

The Mason Children David, Joanna, and Abigail, c. 1670. An early portrait of three children from a wealthy Massachusetts Bay Colony family.
(*Source: The Freake-Gibbs Painter, American. "The Mason Children: Davis, Joanna and Abigail," 1670. Oil on canvas, 39-1/2" 42-11/16". The Fine Arts Museum of San Francisco, San Francisco, CA. Gift of Mr. and Mrs. John D. Rockefeller, III.*)

The Witherspoons' initial reaction to the New World—at least, that of the mother and children—was utter despondence. "My mother and us children were still in expectation that we were coming to an agreeable place," Robert confessed, "but when we arrived and saw nothing but a wilderness and instead of a fine timbered house, nothing but a very mean dirt house, our spirits quite sunk." For many years, the Witherspoons feared they would be killed by Indians, become lost in the woods, or be bitten by snakes.

Yet the Witherspoons managed to survive the early difficult years on the Black River. To be sure, the Carolina backcountry did not look much like the world they had left behind, but the difference apparently did not discourage Robert's father. He had a vision of what the Black River settlement might become. "My father," Robert recounted, "gave us all the comfort he [could] by telling us we would get all these trees cut down and in a short time [there] would be plenty of inhabitants, [and] that we could see from house to house."

Robert Witherspoon's account reminds us how the early history of colonial America was an intimate story of families, and not, as some commentators would have us believe, just of individuals. The peopling of the Atlantic frontier—the cutting down of the forests and the creation of new communities where one could see from "house to house"—was not a process that involved what we would today recognize as state policy. Family considerations influenced men and women as they made the important decisions that would shape their new lives in the colonies. It was within this primary social unit that most colonists earned their livelihoods, educated their children, defined gender, sustained religious tradition, and nursed each other in sickness. In short, the family was the source of their societal and cultural identities.

Early colonial families did not exist in isolation. They were part of larger societies. As we have already seen, the character of the first English settlements in the New World varied substantially (see Chapter 2). During much of the seventeenth century, these initial differences grew stronger as each region responded to different environmental conditions and developed its own traditions. The various local societies in which families like the Witherspoons put down roots reflected several critical elements: supply of labor, abundance of land, unusual demographic patterns, and commercial ties with European markets. In the Chesapeake, for example, an economy based almost entirely on a single staple—tobacco—created an insatiable demand for indentured servants and black slaves. In Massachusetts Bay, the extraordinary longevity of the founders generated a social and political stability that Virginians and Marylanders did not attain until the very end of the seventeenth century.

By 1660, it seemed regional differences had undermined the idea of a unified English empire in America. During the reign of Charles II (r. 1660–1685), however, a trend toward cultural convergence began. Although subcultures had evolved in strikingly different directions, countervailing forces such as common language and religion gradually pulled English American settlers together. Parliament took advantage of this trend and began to establish uniform rules for the expanding American empire. The process was slow and uneven, often sparking violent colonial resistance. By the end of the seventeenth century, however, England had made significant progress toward transforming the New World provinces into an empire that produced needed raw materials and purchased manufactured goods. If a person was black and enslaved, however, he or she was likely to experience oppression rather than opportunity in British America.

SOCIAL STABILITY: NEW ENGLAND COLONIES OF THE SEVENTEENTH CENTURY

Seventeenth-century New Englanders replicated a traditional social order they had known in England. The transfer of a familiar way of life to the New World seemed less difficult for these Puritan migrants than it did for the many English men and women who settled in the Chesapeake colonies. Their contrasting experiences, fundamental to understanding the development of both cultures, can be explained, at least in part, by the extraordinary strength and resilience of New England families.

What factors explain the remarkable social stability achieved in early New England?

Immigrant Families and New Social Order

Early New Englanders believed God ordained the family for human benefit. It was essential to the maintenance of social order, since outside the family, men and women succumbed to carnal temptation. Such people had no one to sustain them or remind them of Scripture. "Without Family care," declared the Reverend Benjamin Wadsworth, "the labour of Magistrates and Ministers for Reformation and Propagating Religion, is likely to be in great measure unsuccessful."

The godly family, at least in theory, was ruled by a patriarch, father to his children, husband to his wife, the source of authority and object of unquestioned obedience. The wife shared responsibility for raising children, but in important decisions, especially those about property, she was expected to defer to her spouse.

The New Englanders' concern about the character of the godly family is not surprising. This institution was central in shaping their society. In contrast to those who migrated to Virginia and Maryland, New Englanders crossed the Atlantic within nuclear families. That is, they moved within established units consisting of a father, mother, and their dependent children. People who migrated to America within families preserved local English customs more fully than did the youths who traveled to other parts of the continent as single men and women. The comforting presence of immediate family members reduced the shock of adjusting to a strange environment 3,000 miles from home. Even in the 1630s, the ratio of men to women in New England was fairly well balanced, about three males for every two females. Persons who had not already married in England before coming to the New World could expect to form nuclear families of their own.

Early New England marriage patterns did not differ substantially from those in seventeenth-century England. The average age for men at first marriage was the mid-twenties. Wives were slightly younger than their husbands, the average age being about 22. There is no evidence that New Englanders favored child brides. Nor, for that matter, were Puritan families unusually large by European standards of the period.

The explanation for the region's impressive growth turned out to be survival rather than fertility. Put simply, people who, under normal conditions, would have died in contemporary Europe lived in New England. Indeed, the life expectancy of seventeenth-century settlers was not much less than our own. Males who survived infancy might expect to see their seventieth birthday. Twenty percent of the men of the first generation reached age 80. The figures for women were only slightly lower. Why the early settlers lived so long is not entirely clear. No doubt, pure drinking water, a cool climate that retarded the spread of fatal contagious disease, and a dispersed population promoted good health.

Longer life altered family relations. New England males lived to see not only their own children reach adulthood but the birth of grandchildren. This may have been one of the first societies in recorded history in which a person could reasonably anticipate knowing his or her grandchildren, a demographic surprise that contributed to social stability. The traditions of particular families and communities literally remained alive in the memories of the colony's oldest citizens.

Quick Check

✓ How did families contribute to social order in seventeenth-century New England?

Puritan Women in New England

New England relied heavily on the work of women. They did not, however, necessarily do the same jobs that men performed. Women usually handled separate tasks, including cooking, washing, clothes making, dairying, and gardening. Their production of food was essential to the survival of most households. Sometimes wives—and the overwhelming majority of adult seventeenth-century women were married—raised poultry, and by selling surplus birds, they achieved some economic independence. When people in one New England community chided a man for allowing his wife to peddle her fowl, he responded, "I meddle not with the geese nor turkeys for they are hers." In fact, during this period women were often described as "deputy husbands," a label that drew attention both to their dependence on family patriarchs and to their roles as decision makers.

More women than men also joined churches. Within a few years of founding, many New England congregations contained two female members for every male, a process historians describe as the "feminization of colonial religion." Contemporaries offered different explanations for the gender shift. Cotton Mather, the leading Congregational minister of Massachusetts Bay, argued that God had created "far more *godly Women*" than men. Others thought that the life-threatening experience of childbirth gave women a deeper appreciation of religion.

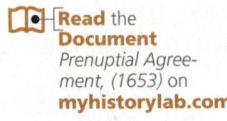 **Read** the **Document** *Prenuptial Agreement, (1653)* on **myhistorylab.com**

In political and legal matters, society sharply curtailed the rights of colonial women. According to English common law, a wife exercised no control over property. She could not, for example, sell land, although her husband could dispose of their holdings without her permission. Divorce was extremely difficult to obtain in any colony before the American Revolution. Indeed, a person married to a cruel or irresponsible spouse had little recourse but to run away or accept the unhappy situation.

Yet most women were neither prosperous entrepreneurs nor abject slaves. Letters indicate that men and women generally accommodated themselves to the gender roles they thought God had ordained. One of early America's most creative poets, Anne Bradstreet, wrote movingly of the fulfillment she had found with her husband. In "To my Dear and loving Husband," Bradstreet declared:

> If ever two were one, then surely we.
> If ever man were lovíd by wife, then thee;
> If ever wife was happy in a man,
> Compare with me ye woman if you can.

Although Puritan couples worried that the affection they felt for a spouse might turn their thoughts away from God's perfect love, this was a danger they were willing to risk.

Read the **Document**
"Anne Bradstreet, "Before the Birth of One of Her Children" on **myhistorylab.com**

Quick Check
✓ What was life like for women in seventeenth-century New England?

Establishing a New Social Order

During the seventeenth century, New England colonists gradually sorted themselves out into distinct social groupings. Persons who would never have been "natural rulers" in England became provincial gentry in the northern colonies. It helped, of course, to be wealthy and educated, but these attributes alone could not guarantee a newcomer's acceptance into the local ruling elite, at least not during the early decades of settlement. In Massachusetts and Connecticut, Puritan voters expected their leaders to join Congregational churches and defend orthodox religion.

While most New Englanders accepted a hierarchical view of society, they disagreed over their assigned places. Both Massachusetts Bay and Connecticut passed sumptuary laws—statutes that limited wearing fine apparel to the wealthy and prominent—to curb the pretensions of those of lower status. Yet such restraints could not prevent some people from rising and others from falling within the social order.

Most northern colonists were yeomen (independent farmers) who worked their own land. While few became rich, even fewer fell hopelessly into debt. Their daily lives, especially for those who settled New England, centered on scattered little communities where they participated in village meetings, church affairs, and militia training. Owning land gave agrarian families a sense of independence from external authority. As one man bragged to those who had stayed behind in England, "Here are no hard landlords to rack us with high rents or extorting fines. . . . Here every man may be master of his own labour and land . . . and if he have nothing but his hands he may set up his trade, and by industry grow rich."

Many northern colonists worked as servants at some point in their lives. This system of labor differed greatly from the pattern of servitude that developed in seventeenth-century Virginia and Maryland. New Englanders seldom recruited servants from the Old World. The forms of agriculture practiced in this region, mixed cereal and dairy farming, made employing large gangs of dependent workers uneconomic. Rather, New England families placed their adolescent children in nearby homes. These young persons contracted for four or five years and seemed more like apprentices than servants. Servitude was not simply a means by which one group exploited another. It was a form of vocational training in which the children of both the rich and the poor participated.

By the end of the seventeenth century, the New England Puritans had developed a compelling story about their own history in the New World. The founders had been extraordinarily godly men and women, and in a heroic effort to establish a purer form of religion, pious families had passed "over the vast ocean into this vast and howling wilderness." Although the children and grandchildren of the first generation sometimes questioned their own ability to please the Lord, they recognized the mission to the New World had been a success: They were "as Prosperous as ever, there is Peace & Plenty, & the Country flourisheth."

Quick Check

✔ What counted more in determining social status in early New England—piety or wealth?

THE CHALLENGE OF THE CHESAPEAKE ENVIRONMENT

What factors contributed to political unrest in the Chesapeake region during this period?

A different regional society developed in England's Chesapeake colonies, Virginia and Maryland. This contrast with New England seems puzzling. After all, the two areas were founded at roughly the same time by men and women from the same mother country. In both regions, settlers spoke English, accepted Protestantism, and gave allegiance to one crown. And yet, seventeenth-century Virginia looked nothing like Massachusetts Bay. To explain the difference, colonial historians have studied environmental conditions, labor systems, and agrarian economies. The most important reason for the distinctiveness of these early southern plantation societies, however, turned out to be the Chesapeake's death rate, a frighteningly high mortality that tore at the very fabric of traditional family life.

Families at Risk

Unlike New England's settlers, the men and women who emigrated to the Chesapeake region did not move in family units. They traveled to the New World as young unmarried servants, youths cut off from the security of traditional kin relations. Although these immigrants came from a cross section of English society, most had been poor to middling farmers. It is now estimated that 70 to 85 percent of the white colonists who went to Virginia and Maryland during the seventeenth century were not free; that is, they owed four or five years' labor in exchange for the cost of passage to America. If the servant was under age 15, he or she had to serve seven years. Most of these laborers were males between the ages of 18 and 22. In fact, before 1640, the ratio of males to females was 6 to 1. This figure dropped to about 2.5 to 1 by the end of the century, but the sex ratio in the Chesapeake was never as favorable as it had been in early Massachusetts.

Most immigrants to the Chesapeake region died soon after arriving. It is difficult to ascertain the exact cause of death in most cases, but malaria and other diseases took a frightful toll. Life expectancy for Chesapeake males was about 43, some ten to 20 years less than for men born in New England! For women, life was even shorter. Twenty-five percent of all children died in infancy; another 25 percent did not see their twentieth birthdays. The survivors were often weak or ill, unable to perform hard physical labor.

Because of the unbalanced sex ratio, many adult males could not find wives. Migration not only cut them off from their English families but also deprived them of an opportunity to form new ones. Without a constant flow of immigrants, the population of Virginia and Maryland would have actually declined.

High mortality compressed the family life cycle into a few years. One partner in a marriage usually died within seven years. Only one in three Chesapeake marriages survived for as long as a decade. Not only did children not meet grandparents—they often did not even know their own parents. Widows and widowers quickly remarried, bringing children by former unions into their new homes, and a child often grew up with persons to whom he or she bore no blood relation.

Women were in great demand in the early southern colonies. Some historians have argued that scarcity heightened the woman's bargaining power in the marriage market. An immigrant did not have to obtain parental consent to marry. She was on her own in the New World and could select whomever she pleased. If a woman lacked beauty or strength, or if she were of low moral standards, she could still be confident of finding an American husband. Such negotiations may have provided Chesapeake women with a means of improving their social status.

Nevertheless, liberation from traditional restraints on seventeenth-century women must not be exaggerated. Women servants were vulnerable to sexual exploitation by their masters. Moreover, in this unhealthy environment, childbearing was extremely dangerous, and women in the Chesapeake usually died 20 years earlier than their New England counterparts.

Quick Check

✓ How did the high mortality rates in the early Chesapeake colonies affect economic and family life?

The Structure of Planter Society

Colonists who managed to survive grew tobacco—as much tobacco as they could. This crop became the Chesapeake staple, and since it was relatively easy to cultivate, anyone with a few acres of cleared land could harvest leaves for export. Cultivation of tobacco did not, however, produce a society roughly equal in wealth and status. To the contrary, tobacco generated inequality. Some planters amassed fortunes; others barely subsisted. Labor made the difference, for to succeed in this staple economy, one had to control the labor of other men and women. More workers in the fields meant larger harvests and, of course, larger profits. Since free persons showed no interest in growing another man's tobacco, not even for wages, wealthy planters relied on white laborers who were not free and on slaves. The social structure that developed in the seventeenth-century Chesapeake reflected a wild, often unscrupulous scramble to bring men and women of three races—black, white, and Indian—into various degrees of dependence.

Great planters dominated Chesapeake society. The group was small, only a trifling portion of the population of Virginia and Maryland. During the early seventeenth century, the composition of Chesapeake gentry was continually in flux. Some gentlemen died before they could establish a secure claim to high social status; others returned to England, thankful to have survived. Not until the 1650s did the family names of those who would become famous eighteenth-century gentry appear in the records. The first gentlemen were not—as genealogists sometimes discover to their dismay—dashing cavaliers who had fought in the English Civil War for King Charles I. Rather, such Chesapeake gentry as the Burwells, Byrds, Carters, and Masons consisted originally of the younger sons of English merchants and artisans.

Freemen formed the largest class in Chesapeake society. Their origins were strikingly different from those of the gentry, or from those of New England's yeomen farmers. Chesapeake freemen traveled to the New World as indentured servants, signing contracts in which they sold their labor for a set number of years in exchange for passage from Europe. If they had dreamed of becoming great planters, they were disappointed. Most seventeenth-century freemen lived on the edge of poverty. Some freemen, of course, did better in America than they would have in England, but in both Virginia and Maryland, historians have found a sharp economic division separating the gentry from the rest of white society.

Read the
Document
*Virginia Law on
Indentured Servitude*
on
myhistorylab.com

Below the freemen came indentured servants. Membership in this group was not demeaning; after all, servitude was a temporary status. But servitude in the Chesapeake colonies was not the benign institution it was in New England. Great planters purchased servants to grow tobacco. No one seemed overly concerned whether these laborers received decent food and clothes, much less whether they acquired trade skills. Young people, thousands of them, cut off from family ties, sick often to the point of death, unable to obtain normal sexual release, regarded their servitude as a form of slavery. Not surprisingly, the gentry worried that unhappy servants and impoverished freemen, what the planters called the "giddy multitude," would rebel at the slightest provocation, a fear that turned out to be justified.

The character of social mobility—and this observation applies only to whites—changed during the seventeenth century. Until the 1680s, it was relatively easy for a newcomer who possessed capital to join the planter elite. No one paid much attention to the reputation or social standing of one's English family.

After the 1680s, however, a demographic shift occurred. Although infant mortality remained high, life expectancy for those who survived childhood in the Chesapeake improved significantly, and for the first time in the history of Virginia and Maryland, important leadership positions went to men who had been born in America. A political historian described this transition as the "emergence of a creole majority," in other words, as the rise of an indigenous ruling elite. Before this time, immigrant leaders had died without heirs or had returned as quickly as possible to England. The members of the new creole class took a greater interest in local government. Their activities helped give the tobacco colonies the political and cultural stability that had eluded earlier generations of planter adventurers.

The key to success in this creole society was ownership of slaves. Those planters who held more blacks could grow more tobacco and thus could acquire fresh capital to purchase even more laborers. Over time, the rich not only became richer; they formed a distinct ruling elite that newcomers found increasingly difficult to enter.

Opportunities for advancement also decreased for freemen in the region. Studies of mid-seventeenth-century Maryland reveal that some servants managed to become moderately prosperous farmers and small officeholders. But as the gentry consolidated its hold on political and economic institutions, ordinary people discovered it was much harder to rise in Chesapeake society. Those men and women with more ambitious dreams headed for Pennsylvania, North Carolina, or western Virginia.

Social institutions that figured importantly in the daily experience of New Englanders were either weak or nonexistent in the Chesapeake colonies. In part, the sluggish development resulted from the continuation of high infant mortality rates. There was little incentive to build elementary schools, for example, if half the children would die before reaching adulthood. The great planters sent their sons to England or Scotland for their education, and even after the founding of the College of William and Mary in Virginia in 1693, the gentry continued to patronize English schools. As a result, higher education in the South languished for much of the colonial period.

Tobacco influenced the spread of other institutions in the region. Planters were scattered along the rivers, often separated from their nearest neighbors by miles of poor roads. Since the major tobacco growers traded directly with English merchants, they had no need for towns.

Quick Check

✓ Why did the great planters purchase so many indentured servants during this period?

RACE AND FREEDOM IN BRITISH AMERICA

Many people who landed in the colonies had no desire to come to the New World. They were Africans taken as slaves to cultivate rice, sugar, and tobacco. As the Native Americans were exterminated and the supply of white indentured servants dried up, European planters demanded ever more African laborers.

How did African American slaves preserve an independent cultural identity in the New World?

Roots of Slavery

Much is known about the transfer of African peoples across the Atlantic. During the entire history of this human commerce, between the sixteenth and nineteenth centuries, slave traders carried almost 11 million blacks to the Americas. Most of these men and women were sold in Brazil or the Caribbean. A relatively small number of Africans reached British North America, and of this group, most arrived after 1700. Because slaves performed hard physical labor, planters preferred purchasing young males. In many early slave communities, men outnumbered women by a ratio of two to one.

English colonists did not hesitate to enslave black people or, for that matter, Native Americans. While the institution of slavery had long died out in England itself, New World settlers quickly discovered how well slave labor operated in the Spanish and Portuguese colonies. The decision to bring African slaves to the colonies, therefore, was primarily economic.

English masters, however, seldom justified the practice purely in terms of planter profits. Indeed, they adopted a different pattern of rhetoric. English writers associated blacks in Africa with heathen religion, barbarous behavior, sexual promiscuity—with evil itself. From such a racist perspective, the enslavement of Africans seemed unobjectionable. The planters argued that the Bible

Virginian Luxuries   Undated, unsigned, and hidden on the back of another painting, the two-part painting *Virginian Luxuries* depicts a white man kissing a black woman and whipping a black man.

condoned slavery and maintained that if black slaves converted to Christianity, shedding their supposedly savage ways, they would actually benefit from their loss of freedom.

Africans first landed in Virginia in 1619 as a cargo of slaves a Dutch trader stole from a Spanish ship in the Caribbean. For the next 50 years, the status of the colony's black people remained unclear. English settlers classified some black laborers as slaves for life, as chattel to be bought and sold at the master's will. But other Africans became servants, presumably for stated periods of time, and a few blacks even purchased their freedom. Several seventeenth-century Africans became successful Virginia planters.

One reason Virginia lawmakers tolerated such confusion was that the black population remained small. By 1660, fewer than 1,500 people of African origin lived in the entire colony (compared to 26,000 whites), and it hardly seemed necessary for the legislature to draw up an elaborate slave code to control so few men and women. If the planters could have obtained more black laborers, they certainly would have. There is no evidence that the great planters preferred white indentured servants to black slaves. The problem was supply. During this period, slave traders sold their cargoes on Barbados or the other sugar islands of the West Indies, where they fetched higher prices than Virginians could afford to pay. In fact, before 1680, most blacks who reached England's colonies on the North American mainland came from Barbados or through New Netherland rather than directly from Africa. (See Map 3.1.)

By the end of the seventeenth century, the legal status of Virginia's black people was no longer in doubt. They were slaves for life, and so were their children after them. This transformation reflected changes in the supply of Africans to British North America. After 1672, the Royal African Company was chartered to meet the colonial planters' demands for black laborers. Historian K. G. Davies terms this organization "the strongest and most effective of all European companies formed exclusively for the African trade." Between 1695 and 1709, more than 11,000 Africans were sold in Virginia alone; many others went to Maryland and the Carolinas. Although American merchants—most of them based in Rhode Island—entered the trade during the eighteenth century, the British supplied the bulk of the slaves to the mainland market for the entire colonial period.

The expanding black population apparently frightened white colonists, for as the number of Africans increased, lawmakers drew up ever stricter slave codes. During

View the **Closer Look**
Plan and Sections of a Slave Ship and Illustration of a Slave Camp on
myhistorylab.com

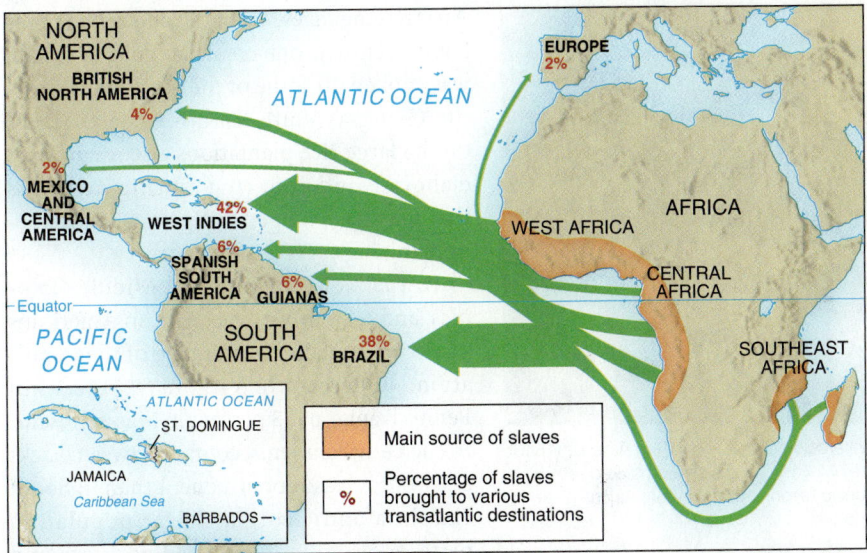

Map 3.1 *Origins and Destinations of African Slaves, 1619–1760* Although many African slaves were carried to Britain's North American colonies, far more slaves were sold in the Caribbean sugar colonies and Brazil, where, because of horrific health conditions, the death rate far exceeded that of the British mainland colonies.

this period, racism, always latent in New World societies, was fully revealed. By 1700, slavery was unequivocally based on the color of a person's skin. Blacks fell into this status simply because they were black. A vicious pattern of discrimination had been set in motion. Even conversion to Christianity did not free the African from bondage. The white planter could deal with his black property as he alone saw fit, and one revolting Virginia statute excused masters who killed slaves, on the grounds that no rational person would purposely "destroy his own estate." Black women constantly had to fear sexual violation by a master or his sons. Children born to a slave woman became slaves regardless of the father's race. Unlike the Spanish and French colonies, where persons of lighter color enjoyed greater privileges in society, the English colonies tolerated no mixing of the races. Mulattoes and pure Africans received the same treatment.

Quick Check

✓ Why did the slave population in British North America remain relatively small for most of the seventeenth century?

Constructing African American Identities

The slave experience varied from colony to colony. The daily life of a black person in South Carolina, for example, was different from that of an African American who lived in Pennsylvania or Massachusetts Bay. The size and density of the slave population largely determined how successfully blacks could maintain a separate cultural identity. In the lowlands of South Carolina during the eighteenth century, 60 percent of the population was black. The men and women were placed on large, isolated rice plantations and had limited contact with whites. In these areas blacks developed creole languages that mixed basic English vocabulary with words from

Aboard a Slave Ship This watercolor, *Slave Deck of the Albanoz* (1846), by naval officer Lieutenant Godfrey Meynell, shows slaves packed with cargo in the hold of a ship after being taken captive in West Africa.

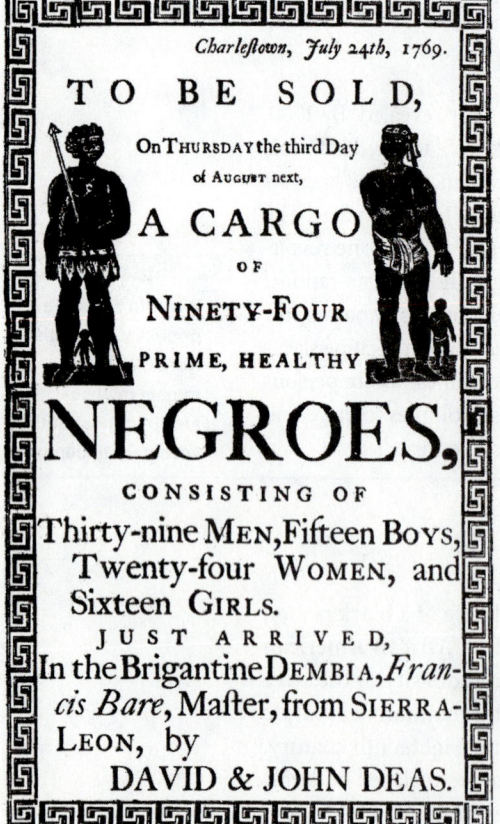

Charlestown, July 24th, 1769.

TO BE SOLD,

On THURSDAY the third Day
of AUGUST next,

A CARGO

OF

NINETY-FOUR

PRIME, HEALTHY

NEGROES,

CONSISTING OF

Thirty-nine MEN, Fifteen BOYS,
Twenty-four WOMEN, and
Sixteen GIRLS.

JUST ARRIVED,

In the Brigantine DEMBIA, *Francis Bare*, Master, from SIERRA-
LEON, by

DAVID & JOHN DEAS.

Slave Auctions This public notice announces a slave auction to be held at the Charles Town wharf (1769).

African languages. Until the end of the nineteenth century, one creole language, Gullah, was spoken on some of the Sea Islands along the Georgia–South Carolina coast. Slaves on the large rice plantations also established elaborate and enduring kinship networks that may have helped mitigate the more dehumanizing aspects of bondage.

In the New England and Middle Colonies, and even in Virginia, African Americans made up a smaller percentage of the population: 40 percent in Virginia, 8 percent in Pennsylvania, and 3 percent in Massachusetts. In such environments, contact between blacks and whites was more frequent than in South Carolina and Georgia. These population patterns profoundly affected northern and Chesapeake blacks, for while they escaped the physical drudgery of rice cultivation, they found it more difficult to preserve an independent African identity. In northern cities, slaves working as domestics and living in their masters' houses saw other blacks but had little opportunity to develop creole languages or reaffirm a common African past.

The process of establishing African American traditions involved reshaping African and European customs into something that was neither African nor European. It was African American. The slaves accepted Christianity but did so on their own terms— terms their masters seldom fully understood. Blacks transformed Christianity into an expression of religious feeling in which an African element remained vibrant. In music and folk art, they gave voice to a cultural identity that even the most degrading conditions could not eradicate.

A major turning point in the history of African Americans occurred during the early eighteenth century. The number of live births exceeded deaths, and from this time on, the expansion of the African American population owed more to natural increase than to the importation of new slaves. Thousands of new Africans arrived each year, but the creole population was always much larger than that of the immigrant blacks. This demographic shift did not occur in the Caribbean or South American colonies until much later. Historians believe that North American blacks enjoyed a healthier climate and better diet than did other New World slaves.

Although mainland blacks lived longer than those of Jamaica or Barbados, they were still slaves. They protested their debasement in many ways, some in individual acts of violence, others in organized revolt. The most serious slave rebellion of the colonial period was the Stono Uprising, when 150 South Carolina blacks seized guns and ammunition and murdered white planters in September 1739. "With Colours displayed, and two Drums beating," they marched toward Spanish Florida, where they had been promised freedom. The militia overtook the rebellious slaves and killed most of them. Although the uprising was short-lived, such incidents helped persuade whites everywhere that their own blacks might secretly be planning bloody revolt.

Read the
Document
James Oglethorpe,
The Stono Rebellion
(1739) on
myhistorylab.com

Quick Check

✓ How did African American slaves preserve cultural practices associated with West African societies?

BLUEPRINT FOR EMPIRE

Until the mid-seventeenth century, English political leaders largely ignored the American colonists. Private companies and aristocratic proprietors had created these societies, some for profit, others for religious sanctuary, but in no case did the crown provide financial or military assistance. After the Restoration of Charles II in 1660, Englishmen of various sorts—courtiers, merchants, parliamentarians—concluded that the colonists should be brought more tightly under the control of the mother country. The regulatory policies that evolved during this period formed a framework for an empire that survived with only minor adjustment until 1765.

Why did England discourage free and open trade in colonial America?

Response to Economic Competition

By the 1660s the dominant commercial powers of Europe adopted economic principles that later critics would term mercantilism. Mercantilists argued that since trading nations were competing for the world's resources—mostly for raw materials from dependent colonies—one nation's commercial success translated directly into a loss for its rivals. It seemed logical, therefore, that England would want to protect its own markets from France or Holland by passing mercantilist trade policies discouraging its colonies from trading with other European powers. For seventeenth-century planners, free markets made no sense. They argued that trade tightly regulated by the central government represented the only way to increase the nation's wealth at the expense of competitors.

National interest alone, however, did not shape public policy. Instead, the needs of powerful interest groups led to the rise of English commercial regulation. Each group looked to colonial commerce to solve a different problem. The king wanted money. English merchants were eager to exclude Dutch rivals from lucrative American

Wedding in the Slave Quarters *Old Plantation*, a watercolor by an unknown artist (about 1800), shows that African wedding customs survived plantation slavery.

Quick Check

✓ Why did seventeenth-century English rulers support mercantilism?

markets and needed government assistance to compete with the Dutch, even in Virginia or Massachusetts Bay. For the landed gentry who sat in Parliament, England needed a stronger navy, and that in turn meant expanding the domestic shipbuilding industry. And almost everyone agreed England should establish a more favorable balance of trade, that is, increase exports, decrease imports, and grow richer at the expense of other European states. None of these ideas was particularly innovative, but taken together they provided a blueprint for England's first empire.

Regulating Colonial Trade

Parliament passed a Navigation Act in 1660. The statute was the most important piece of imperial legislation drafted before the American Revolution. Colonists from New Hampshire to South Carolina and the Caribbean islands paid close attention to this statute, which stated (1) that no ship could trade in the colonies unless it had been constructed in either England or America and carried a crew that was at least 75 percent English (for these purposes, colonists counted as Englishmen), and (2) that certain **enumerated goods** of great value that were not produced in England—tobacco, sugar, cotton, indigo, etc.—could be transported from the colonies only to an English or another colonial port. In 1704, Parliament added rice and molasses to the enumerated list; in 1705, rosins, tars, and turpentine for shipbuilding were included.

The 1660 act was masterfully conceived. It encouraged the development of domestic shipbuilding and prohibited European rivals from obtaining enumerated goods anywhere except in England. Since the Americans had to pay import duties in England (for this purpose colonists did not count as Englishmen) on such items as sugar and tobacco, the legislation also gave the crown another source of income.

In 1663, Parliament passed a second Navigation Act known as the Staple Act, which stated that, with a few exceptions, nothing could be imported into the colonies unless it had first been transshipped through England, a process that greatly increased the price colonial consumers ultimately paid.

The **Navigation Acts** attempted to eliminate the Dutch, against whom the English fought three wars in this period (1652–1654, 1664–1667, and 1672–1674), as the intermediaries of American commerce. Just as English merchants were celebrating their victory, however, an unanticipated rival appeared: New England merchant ships sailed out of Boston, Salem, and Newport to become formidable competitors in maritime commerce.

During the 1660s, the colonists showed little enthusiasm for the new imperial regulations. Reaction to the Navigation Acts varied from region to region. Virginians bitterly protested them. The collection of English customs on tobacco reduced the planters' profits. Moreover, excluding the Dutch from the trade reduced competition and meant that growers often had to sell their crops at artificially low prices. The Navigation Acts hit the small planters especially hard, for they were least able to absorb increased production costs. Even though the governor of Virginia lobbied on the planters' behalf, the crown turned a deaf ear.

At first, New Englanders simply ignored the commercial regulations. Indeed, one Massachusetts merchant reported in 1664 that Boston entertained "near one hundred sail of ships, this year, of ours and strangers." The strangers, of course, were the Dutch, who had no intention of obeying the Navigation Acts so long as they could reach colonial ports. Some New England merchants found clever ways to circumvent the Navigation Acts. These crafty traders picked up cargoes of enumerated goods such as sugar or tobacco, sailed to another colonial port (thereby fulfilling the letter of the law), and then made directly for Holland or France. Along the way they paid no customs.

To plug the loophole, Parliament passed the Navigation Act of 1673. This statute established a plantation duty, a sum of money equal to normal English customs duties to be collected on enumerated products at the various colonial ports. New Englanders could now sail wherever they pleased within the empire, but they could not escape paying customs.

Parliament passed the last major piece of imperial legislation in 1696. It tightened enforcement procedures, putting pressure on the colonial governors to exclude England's competitors from American ports. It also expanded the American customs service and set up vice-admiralty courts in the colonies. Established to settle disputes that occurred at sea, vice-admiralty courts required neither juries nor oral cross-examination, both traditional elements of the common law. But they were effective and even popular for resolving maritime questions quickly enough to send ships to sea again with little delay. One other significant change in the imperial system occurred in 1696. King William III replaced the ineffective Lords of Trade with a body of advisers that came to be known as the Board of Trade. This group was expected to monitor colonial affairs closely and give government officials the best advice on commercial and other problems. For decades, it energetically carried out its responsibilities.

The members of Parliament believed these reforms would compel the colonists to accept the Navigation Acts, and they were largely correct. By 1700, American goods transshipped through the mother country accounted for a quarter of all English exports, an indication that the colonists found it profitable to obey the commercial regulations. In fact, during the eighteenth century, smuggling from Europe to America dried up almost completely.

> **Quick Check**
> ✓ How did the Navigation Acts establish the foundation for a commercial empire?

COLONIAL POLITICAL REVOLTS

The Navigation Acts created an illusion of unity. English administrators superimposed a system of commercial regulation on different, often unstable American colonies and called it an empire. But these statutes did not remove long-standing differences. Within each colony's society, men and women struggled to bring order out of disorder, establish stable ruling elites, defuse ethnic and racial tensions, and cope with population pressures that imperial planners only dimly understood. During the late seventeenth century, these efforts sometimes sparked revolt.

> **How** did colonial revolts affect the political culture of Virginia and New England?

First, the Virginians rebelled, and then a few years later, political violence swept through Maryland, New York, and Massachusetts Bay, England's most populous mainland colonies. Historians once interpreted these events as rehearsals for the American Revolution, or even for Jacksonian democracy in the 1830s. They perceived the rebels as frontier democrats, rising against an entrenched aristocracy.

Research suggests, however, that this view misconstrued these late-seventeenth-century rebellions. The uprisings were not confrontations between ordinary people and their rulers. Indeed, the events were not in any modern sense of the word ideological. In each colony, the local gentry split into factions, usually the "outs" versus the "ins," and each side proclaimed its political legitimacy.

Civil War in Virginia: Bacon's Rebellion

After 1660, the Virginia economy suffered a prolonged depression. Returns from tobacco had not been good for some time, and the Navigation Acts reduced profits even further. Indentured servants complained about lack of food and clothing. No wonder that Virginia's governor, Sir William Berkeley, despaired of ever ruling "a People where six parts of seven at least are Poor, Endebted, Discontented and Armed." In 1670, he and the House of Burgesses disfranchised all landless freemen, persons they regarded as troublemakers, but the threat of social violence remained.

Things changed when Nathaniel Bacon arrived in Virginia in 1674. This ambitious young man came from a respectable English family and set himself up immediately as a substantial planter. But he wanted more. Bacon envied the government patronage monopolized by Berkeley's cronies, a group known locally as the Green Spring faction. When Bacon attempted to obtain a license to engage in the fur trade, he was rebuffed. This lucrative commerce was reserved for the governor's friends. If Bacon had been willing to wait, he probably would have been accepted into the ruling clique, but as events would demonstrate, he was not a patient man.

Read the
Document
Nathaniel Bacon's Declaration (July 30, 1676) on
myhistorylab.com

Events beyond Bacon's control thrust him suddenly into the center of Virginia politics. In 1675, Indians reacting to white encroachment attacked outlying plantations, killing colonists, and Virginians expected the governor to send an army to retaliate. Instead, early in 1676, Berkeley called for constructing a line of defensive forts, a plan that the settlers considered both expensive and ineffective. Indeed, the strategy raised embarrassing questions. Was Berkeley protecting his own fur monopoly? Was he planning to reward his friends with contracts to build useless forts?

While people speculated, Bacon offered to lead a volunteer army against the Indians at no cost to the hard-pressed Virginia taxpayers. All he demanded was an official commission from Berkeley giving him military command and the right to attack other Indians, not just the hostile Susquehannocks. The governor refused. With some justification, Berkeley regarded his upstart rival as a fanatic on the subject of Indians. The governor saw no reason to exterminate peaceful tribes simply to avenge the death of a few white settlers.

What followed would have been comic had not so many people died. Bacon thundered against the governor's treachery; Berkeley labeled Bacon a traitor. Both men appealed to the populace for support. On several occasions, Bacon marched his followers to the frontier, but they either failed to find the enemy or, worse, massacred friendly Indians. At one point, Bacon burned Jamestown to the ground, forcing the governor to flee to the colony's Eastern Shore. Bacon's bumbling lieutenants chased Berkeley across Chesapeake Bay only to be captured themselves. Thereupon, the governor mounted a new campaign.

Read the
Document
Declaration Against Nathaniel Bacon (1676) on
myhistorylab.com

As Bacon's Rebellion dragged on, it became apparent that Bacon and his gentry supporters had only the vaguest notion of what they were trying to achieve. The members of the planter elite never seemed to appreciate that the rank-and-file soldiers, often black slaves and poor white servants, had legitimate grievances against Berkeley's corrupt government and were demanding reforms, not just a share in the governor's fur monopoly.

When Charles II learned of the fighting in Virginia, he dispatched 1,000 regular soldiers to Jamestown. By the time they arrived, Berkeley had regained control over the colony's government. In October 1676, Bacon died after a brief illness, and his followers soon dispersed.

Berkeley, now old and embittered, was recalled to England in 1677. His successors, especially Lord Culpeper (1680–1683) and Lord Howard of Effingham (1683–1689), seemed interested primarily in enriching themselves at the expense of the Virginia planters. Their self-serving policies, coupled with the memory of near anarchy, helped heal divisions within Virginia's ruling class. For almost a century, in fact, the local gentry formed a united front against greedy royal appointees.

Quick Check

✓ What were the underlying causes of Bacon's Rebellion?

The Glorious Revolution in the Bay Colony

During John Winthrop's lifetime (1588–1649), Massachusetts settlers developed an inflated sense of their independence from the mother country. After 1660, however, it became difficult even to pretend that the Puritan colony was a separate state. Royal officials demanded full compliance with the Navigation Acts. Moreover, the growth of commerce attracted new merchants to the Bay Colony, men who were Anglicans rather than Congregationalists and who maintained close business contacts in London. These persons complained loudly of Puritan intolerance. The Anglican faction was never large, but its presence divided Bay leaders. A few Puritan ministers and magistrates regarded compromise with England as treason, a breaking of the Lord's covenant. Other spokesmen, recognizing the changing political realities within the empire, urged a more moderate course.

In 1675, amid this ongoing political crisis, the Indians dealt the New Englanders a terrible setback. Metacomet, a Wampanoag chief the whites called King Philip, declared war against the colonists. The powerful Narragansett Indians, whose lands the settlers had long coveted, joined Metacomet, and in little more than a year of fighting the Indians destroyed scores of frontier villages, killed hundreds of colonists, and disrupted the entire regional economy. More than 1,000 Indians and New Englanders died in the conflict. The war left the people of Massachusetts deeply in debt and more than ever uncertain of their future. As in other parts of colonial America, the defeated Indians were forced off their lands, compelled by events to become either refugees or economically marginal figures in white society.

In 1684, the debate over the Bay Colony's relation to the mother country ended abruptly. The Court of Chancery, sitting in London and acting on a petition from the king, annulled the charter of the Massachusetts Bay Company. In one stroke of a pen, the patent that Winthrop had so lovingly carried to America in 1630, the foundation for a "City on a Hill," was gone. The decision forced the most stubborn Puritans to recognize they were part of an empire run by people who did not share their religious vision.

James II, who succeeded Charles II in 1685, disliked representative institutions. He decided to restructure the government of the entire region in the Dominion of New England. Between 1686 and 1689, the Dominion incorporated Massachusetts, Connecticut, Rhode Island, Plymouth, New York, New Jersey, and New Hampshire under a single appointed royal governor. For this demanding position, James selected Sir Edmund Andros (pronounced Andrews), a military veteran of tyrannical temperament. Andros arrived in Boston in 1686, and within months he had alienated everyone: Puritans, moderates, even Anglican merchants. Not only did Andros abolish elective assemblies, he also enforced the Navigation Acts with such rigor that he brought about a commercial depression. Andros declared normal town meetings illegal, collected taxes the people never approved, and packed the courts with supporters who detested the local population. Eighteenth-century historian and royal governor Thomas Hutchinson compared Andros unfavorably with the Roman tyrant Nero.

In late 1688, the ruling class of England deposed James II, an admitted Catholic, and placed his Protestant daughter, Mary, and her husband, William of Orange, on the throne as joint monarchs, who reigned as William III and Mary II. As part of the settlement, William and Mary accepted a Bill of Rights, stipulating the constitutional rights of all Englishmen. When news of this Glorious Revolution reached Boston, the Bay colonists overthrew the hated Andros regime. The New England version of the Glorious Revolution (April 18, 1689) was so popular that no one came to the governor's defense. Andros was jailed without a shot having been fired.

Thanks largely to the lobbying of Increase Mather, who pleaded the colonists' case in London, William III abandoned the Dominion of New England, and in 1691 granted Massachusetts a new royal charter. This document differed substantially from the company patent of 1629. The freemen no longer selected their governor. The choice now belonged to the king. Membership in the General Court was determined by annual election, and these representatives in turn chose the men who sat in the governor's council or upper house, subject always to the governor's veto. Moreover, the franchise, restricted here as in other colonies to adult males, was determined on the basis of personal property rather than church membership, a change that brought Massachusetts into conformity with general English practice. Town government remained much as it had been in Winthrop's time.

Quick Check

✓ Why did colonists overthrow the Dominion of New England in 1689?

Contagion of Witchcraft

The instability of the Massachusetts government following Andros's arrest—what Reverend Samuel Willard described as "the short Anarchy accompanying our late Revolution"—allowed what under normal political conditions would have been an isolated, though ugly, local incident to become a major crisis. Fearful men and women living in Salem Village, a small, unprosperous farming community, nearly overwhelmed the new rulers of Massachusetts Bay.

Accusations of witchcraft were not uncommon in seventeenth-century New England. Puritans believed that an individual might make a compact with the devil, but during the first decades of settlement, authorities had executed only about 15 alleged witches. Sometimes villagers simply ignored suspected witches. Never before had fears of witchcraft plunged an entire community into panic.

The terror in Salem Village began in late 1691, when several adolescent girls started to behave strangely. They cried out for no apparent reason; they twitched on the ground. When neighbors asked what caused their suffering, the girls said they were victims of witches, seemingly innocent persons who lived in the community. The arrest of several alleged witches did not relieve the girls' "fits," nor did prayer solve the problem. More accusations were made, and at least one person confessed, providing a frightening description of the devil as "a thing all over hairy, all the face hairy, and a long nose." In June 1692, a special court began to send men and women to the gallows. By the end of

Read the **Document**
Cotton Mather, Memorable Providences Relating to Witchcraft on **myhistorylab.com**

the summer, the court had hanged 19 people; another person was pressed to death with heavy rocks. Other suspects died in jail.

Then suddenly, the storm was over. Led by Increase Mather, prominent Congregational ministers belatedly urged leniency and restraint. Especially troubling to the clergymen was the court's decision to accept spectral evidence, that is, reports of dreams and visions in which the accused appeared as the devil's agent. Worried about convicting people on such dubious testimony, Mather declared, "It were better that ten suspected witches should escape, than that one innocent person should be condemned." The colonial government accepted the ministers' advice and convened a new court that acquitted, pardoned, or released the remaining suspects. After the Salem nightmare, witchcraft ceased to be a capital offense.

No one knows exactly what sparked the terror in Salem Village. The community had a history of religious discord, and during the 1680s the people split into angry factions over the choice of a minister. Economic tensions also played a part. Poorer, more traditional farmers accused members of prosperous, commercially oriented families of being witches. The underlying misogyny of the entire culture meant that more victims were women than men. Terror of attack by Native Americans may also have influenced this ugly affair. Indians in league with the French in Canada had recently raided nearby communities, killing people related to the bewitched Salem girls and, significantly, during the trials some victims described the Devil as a "tawny man."

Cotton Mather The publication of Cotton Mather's *Memorable Providences, Relating to Witchcrafts and Possessions* (1689) contributed to the hysteria that resulted in the Salem witchcraft trials. Mather is shown here surrounded by some of the forms a demon assumed in the "documented" case of an English family besieged by witches.

Quick Check

✓ Why were so many apparently innocent people convicted of witchcraft in Salem from 1691 to 1692?

CONCLUSION: FOUNDATIONS OF AN ATLANTIC EMPIRE

"It is no little Blessing of God," Cotton Mather announced proudly in 1700, "that we are part of the *English* nation." A half century earlier, John Winthrop would not have spoken these words, at least not with such enthusiasm. The two men were, of course, products of different political cultures. It was not so much that the character of Massachusetts society had changed. In fact, the Puritan families of 1700 were much like those of the founding generation. Rather, the difference was in England's attitude toward the colonies. Rulers living more than 3,000 miles away now made political and economic demands that Mather's contemporaries could not ignore.

The creation of a new imperial system did not, however, erase sectional differences. By 1700, for example, the Chesapeake colonies were more, not less, committed to cultivating tobacco and to slave labor. Although the separate regions were being pulled slowly into England's commercial orbit, they had little to do with each other. The elements that sparked a powerful sense of nationalism among colonists dispersed over a huge territory would not be evident for a long time. It would be a mistake, therefore, to anticipate the coming of the American Revolution.

3 STUDY RESOURCES

((•─**Listen** to the **Chapter Audio** for Chapter 3 on **myhistorylab.com**

TIMELINE

1619 First blacks arrive in Virginia, p. 70

1660 Charles II is restored to the English throne, p. 73
• Parliament passes the First Navigation Act, p. 75

1663 Second Navigation (Staple) Act passed, p. 74

1673 Plantation duty imposed to close loopholes in commercial regulations, p. 75

1675 King Philip's (Metacomet's) War devastates New England, p. 77

1676 Bacon's Rebellion threatens Governor Berkeley's government in Virginia, p. 77

1684 Charter of the Massachusetts Bay Company revoked, p. 77

1686 Dominion of New England established, p. 78

1688 James II driven into exile during Glorious Revolution, p. 78

1689 Rebellion in Massachusetts, p. 78

1692 Witch trials wrack Salem Village, p. 79

1696 Parliament establishes Board of Trade, p. 75

1739 Stono Uprising of South Carolina slaves terrifies white planters, p. 73

CHAPTER REVIEW

SOCIAL STABILITY: NEW ENGLAND COLONIES OF THE SEVENTEENTH CENTURY

What factors explain the remarkable social stability achieved in early New England?

Seventeenth-century New Englanders migrated to America in family groups, ensuring that the ratio of men to women remained roughly even, making it easier for young people to marry and start families. Stable marriage, together with New England's healthy climate, led to rapid population growth. While many young New Englanders served as servants, most seventeenth-century colonists eventually acquired property. (p. 63)

THE CHALLENGE OF THE CHESAPEAKE ENVIRONMENT

What factors contributed to political unrest in the Chesapeake region during this period?

Most immigrants to the early Chesapeake colonies were single young male indentured servants. Disease killed many of them shortly after arriving. Men outnumbered women, making it difficult for freemen to marry. Because of the short life expectancy, marriages did not last long. Economic inequality and family instability contributed to political unrest. (p. 66)

RACE AND FREEDOM IN BRITISH AMERICA

How did African American slaves preserve an independent cultural identity in the New World?

Slaves, especially those in the South, developed new creole languages that blended English with African languages. They established enduring kinship networks that helped mitigate the hardships of slavery. Enslaved Africans also developed new forms of music and folk art that drew upon African roots and adapted the Christianity taught them by their masters to include African religious elements. (p. 69)

BLUEPRINT FOR EMPIRE

Why did England discourage free and open trade in colonial America?

During the seventeenth century, Parliament passed mercantilist laws declaring that colonial raw materials and commerce would benefit only the mother country and not a European rival. These commercial regulations represented England's new blueprint for the empire. (p. 73)

COLONIAL POLITICAL REVOLTS

How did colonial revolts affect the political culture of Virginia and New England?

During Bacon's Rebellion, landless freemen rose up against the governor and demanded Indian lands.

Although the rebellion failed, it unified Virginia's ruling elite. In 1684, James II restructured the northern colonies to increase crown authority. New Englanders threw off the Dominion of New England in 1689 and negotiated for government charters that allowed significant local autonomy. (*p. 75*)

KEY TERM QUESTIONS

1. What was life like for a yeoman farmer in the northern colonies? (p. 65)

2. How did the life of an indentured servant differ from that of a member of the gentry? (p. 68)

3. How did the chartering of the Royal African Company solidify slavery in Virginia? (p. 70)

4. What argument did proponents of mercantilism employ? (p. 73)

5. Why did England seek to control the distribution of enumerated goods from the colonies? (p. 74)

6. Why did Parliament pass the Navigation Acts? (p. 74)

7. What were the underlying causes of Bacon's Rebellion? (p. 76)

8. Why did colonists overthrow the Dominion of New England in 1689? (p. 77)

9. How did the colonists respond to the Glorious Revolution? (p. 78)

10. Why would clergymen find the court's acceptance of spectral evidence troubling? (p. 79)

MYHISTORYLAB CONNECTIONS

Visit **www.myhistorylab.com** for a customized Study Plan to build your knowledge of *Putting Down Roots*.

Question for Analysis

1. Why was cruelty such an important element of the slave capturing process?

   View the **Closer Look** *Plan and Sections of a Slave Ship and an Illustration of a Slave Camp* p. 70

2. What happened to the Slaves who participated in the Stono Rebellion?

   Read the **Document** *James Oglethorpe, The Stono Rebellion* p. 73

3. What was the purpose of issuing a declaration against Nathaniel Bacon?

   Read the **Document** *Declaration Against Nathaniel Bacon (1676)* p. 76

4. Why would Mather include a description of the signs of witchcraft in his account?

   Read the **Document** *Cotton Mather, Memorable Providences Relating to Witchcraft* p. 78

Other Resources from This Chapter

Read the **Document** *Prenuptial Agreement, 1653*

Read the **Document** *Anne Bradstreet Before the Birth of One of Her Children*

Read the **Document** *Nathaniel Bacon's Declaration*

Read the **Document** *Virginia Law on Indentured Servitude*

4 Experience of Empire

Eighteenth-Century America, 1680–1763

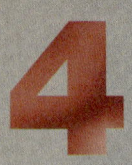

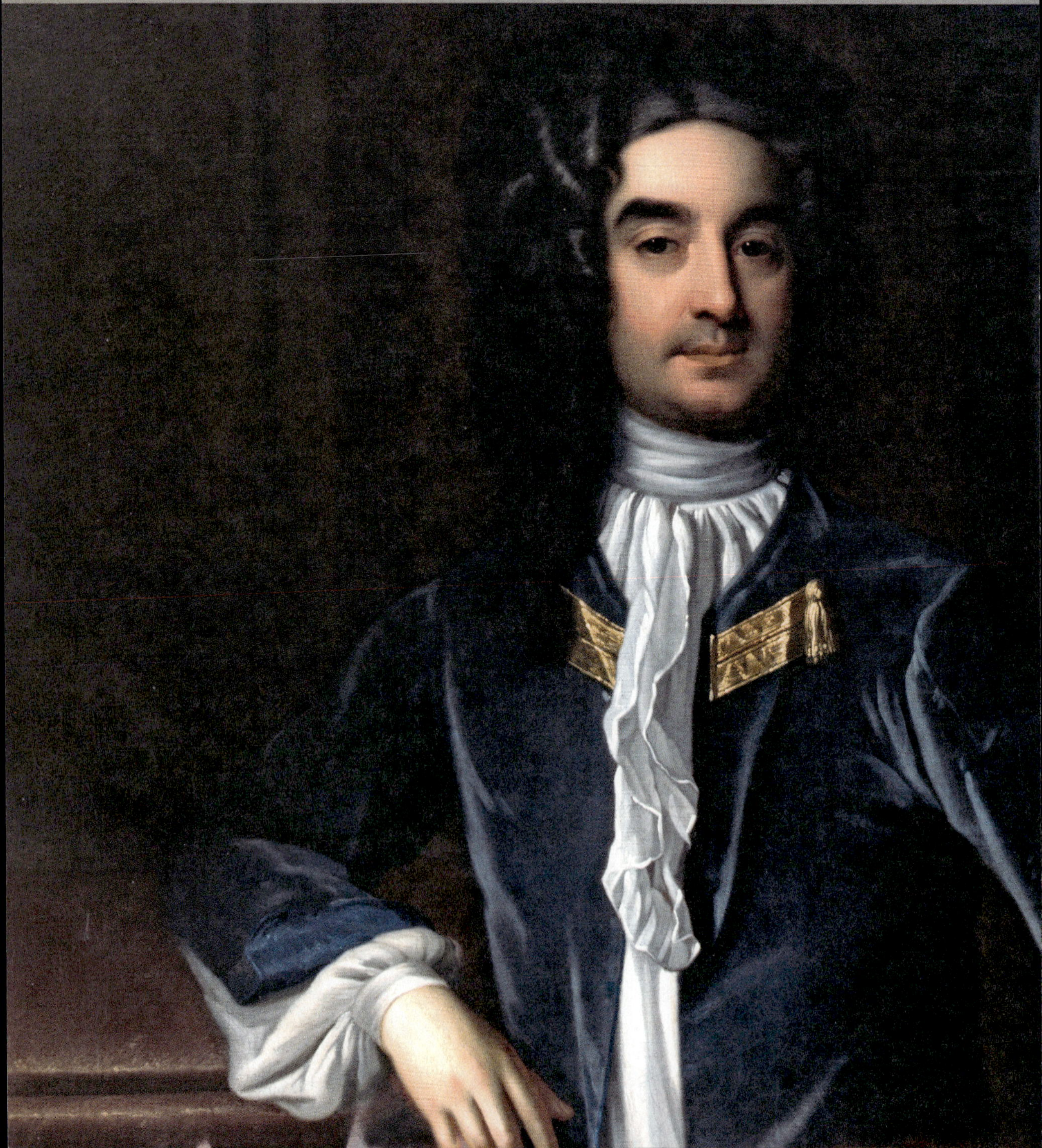

Contents and Spotlight Questions

((•—[Listen to the **Chapter Audio** for Chapter 4 on **myhistorylab.com**

William Byrd III Byrd's *History of the Dividing Line Run in the Year 1728* contains a marvelously satirical account of the culture of poor country farmers in eighteenth-century North Carolina.

CONSTRUCTING AN ANGLO-AMERICAN IDENTITY: THE JOURNAL OF WILLIAM BYRD

William Byrd II (1674–1744) was a type of British American one would not have encountered during the earliest years of settlement. This successful Tidewater planter was a product of a new, more cosmopolitan environment, and as an adult, Byrd seemed as much at home in London as in his native Virginia. In 1728, at the height of his political influence in Williamsburg, the capital of colonial Virginia, Byrd accepted a commission to help survey a disputed boundary with North Carolina. During his long journey into the backcountry, Byrd kept a journal, a satiric, often bawdy chronicle of daily events that is now regarded as a classic of early American literature.

On his trip into the wilderness, Byrd met many different people. No sooner had he left the familiar world of tobacco plantations than he came across a self-styled "Hermit," an Englishman who apparently preferred the freedom of the woods to the constraints of society. "He has no other Habitation but a green Bower or Harbour," Byrd reported, "with a Female Domestick as wild & as dirty as himself."

As the boundary commissioners pushed farther into the backcountry, they encountered highly independent men and women of European descent, small frontier families that Byrd regarded as living no better than savages. He attributed their uncivilized behavior to a diet of too much pork. "The Truth of it is, these People live so much upon Swine's flesh ... [that it] makes them ... extremely hoggish in their Temper, & many of them seem to Grunt rather than Speak in their ordinary conversation." The wilderness journey also brought Byrd's party into contact with Native Americans, whom he properly distinguished as Catawba, Tuscarora, Usheree, and Sapponi Indians.

Byrd's journal invites us to view the rapidly developing eighteenth-century backcountry from a fresh perspective. It was not a vast empty territory awaiting the arrival of European settlers. Maps often sustain this false impression. Depicting cities and towns, farms and plantations clustered along the Atlantic coast, they suggest a "line of settlement" pushing outward into a huge blank area with no mark of civilization. The people Byrd met on his journey into the backcountry would not have understood such maps. The empty space on the maps was their home. They experienced the frontier as populous zones of many cultures stretching from the English and French settlements in the north all the way to the Spanish borderlands in the far southwest.

The point is not to discount the significance of the older Atlantic settlements. During the eighteenth century, Britain's 13 mainland colonies were transformed. Their population grew at unprecedented rates. German and Scots-Irish immigrants arrived in huge numbers. So, too, did African slaves.

Wherever they lived, colonial Americans of this period were less isolated from one another than colonists had been during the seventeenth century. Indeed, after 1690, men and women expanded their cultural horizons, becoming part of a larger Anglo-American empire. The change was striking. Colonists whose parents or grandparents had come to the New World to confront a "howling wilderness" now purchased European manufactures, read English journals, participated in imperial wars, and sought favors from a growing number of resident royal officials. No one—not even the inhabitants of the distant frontiers—could escape Britain's influence. The cultural, economic, and political links connecting the colonists to the imperial center in London grew stronger with time.

This surprising development raises a difficult question. If the eighteenth-century colonists were so powerfully attracted to Great Britain, why did they ever declare independence? The answer may be that as the colonists became more British, they also inevitably became more American. This helps explain the appearance after midcentury of genuine nationalist sentiment. Political, commercial, and military links that brought the colonists into more frequent contact with Britain also made them more aware of other colonists. It was within an expanding, prosperous empire that they first began seriously to consider what it meant to be American.

TENSIONS IN THE BACKCOUNTRY

Accurate population data from the colonial period are difficult to find. The first national census did not occur until 1790. Still, pre-Revolutionary sources indicate that the total white population of Britain's 13 mainland colonies rose from about 250,000 in 1700 to 2,150,000 in 1770, an annual growth rate of 3 percent.

Few societies in recorded history have expanded so rapidly. If the growth rate had not dropped during the nineteenth and twentieth centuries, the United States today would have more than one billion people. Natural reproduction was responsible for most of the growth. More families bore children who in turn lived long enough to have children of their own. Because of this sudden expansion, the colonial population was strikingly young; approximately one-half of the populace at any given time was under age 16.

Not only was the total population increasing rapidly; it also was becoming more dispersed and heterogeneous. Each year thousands of non-English Europeans arrived. Unlike those seventeenth-century English settlers in search of religious sanctuary or instant wealth (see Chapter 2), the newcomers generally hoped to obtain their own land and become independent farmers. These people often traveled to the backcountry, a region stretching approximately 800 miles from western Pennsylvania to Georgia. Although they planned to follow the customs they had known in Europe, they found it far more demanding than they had anticipated to survive on the British frontier. They plunged into a complex, fluid, often violent society that included Native Americans, African Americans, as well as other Europeans. (See Map 4.1.)

Read the **Document**
William Byrd—An American Gentleman on **myhistorylab.com**

What difficulties did Native Americans face in maintaining their cultural independence on the frontier?

Map 4.1 *Distribution of European and African Immigrants in the Thirteen Colonies* A flood of non-English immigrants swept the British colonies between 1700 and 1775.

Scots-Irish Flee English Oppression

During the seventeenth century, English rulers thought they could dominate Catholic Ireland by transporting thousands of lowland Scottish Presbyterians to northern Ireland. These settlers became known as the Scots-Irish. The plan failed. Anglican English officials discriminated against the Presbyterians. They passed laws that placed the Scots-Irish at a disadvantage when they traded in England; they taxed them exorbitantly.

After several poor harvests in the 1720s, many Scots-Irish began to emigrate to America, where they hoped to find the freedom and prosperity that had been denied them in Ireland. Often entire Presbyterian congregations followed charismatic ministers to the New World, intent on replicating a distinctive, fiercely independent culture on the frontier. An estimated 150,000 Scots-Irish migrated to the colonies before the Revolution.

Most Scots-Irish immigrants landed in Philadelphia, but instead of remaining there, they carved out farms on Pennsylvania's western frontier. The colony's proprietors welcomed the new settlers, for it seemed they would form an ideal barrier between the Indians and the older, coastal communities. The Penn family soon had second thoughts, however. The Scots-Irish squatted on whatever land looked best. When colony officials pointed out that large tracts had already been reserved, the immigrants retorted that "it was against the laws of God and nature that so much land should be idle when so many Christians wanted it to labour on and to raise their bread." Wherever they located, the Scots-Irish challenged established authority.

Quick Check

✓ Why did so many Scots-Irish migrate to America during the eighteenth century?

Germans Search for a Better Life

A second large body of non-English settlers, more than 100,000 people, came from the upper Rhine Valley, the German Palatinate. Some of the migrants, especially those who relocated to America around 1700, belonged to small pietistic Protestant sects whose religious views were similar to those of the Quakers. These Germans moved to the New World primarily to find religious toleration. Under the guidance of Francis Daniel Pastorius (1651–1720), Mennonites established a prosperous community in Pennsylvania known as Germantown.

By midcentury, however, the characteristics of the German migration had begun to change. Many Lutherans transferred to the Middle Colonies. Unlike members of the pietistic sects, these men and women were not in search of religious freedom. Rather, they traveled to the New World to improve their material lives. The Lutheran Church in Germany initially tried to control the distant congregations, but although the migrants fiercely preserved much of traditional German culture, they were eventually forced to accommodate to new social conditions. Henry Melchior Mühlenberg (1711–1787), a tireless leader, helped German Lutherans through a difficult cultural adjustment. In 1748, Mühlenberg organized a meeting of local pastors and lay delegates that ordained ministers of their own choosing, an act of spiritual independence that has been called "the most important single event in American Lutheran history."

The German migrants—mistakenly called Pennsylvania Dutch because the English confused *deutsch* (meaning "German") with *Dutch* ("a person from Holland")—began reaching Philadelphia in large numbers after 1717. By 1766, persons of German stock accounted for more than one-third of Pennsylvania's population. Even their most vocal detractors admitted the Germans were the best farmers in the colony.

After 1730, Germans and Scots-Irish pushed south from western Pennsylvania into the Shenandoah Valley, thousands of them settling in the backcountry of Virginia and the Carolinas. The Germans usually remained wherever they found unclaimed fertile land. By contrast, the Scots-Irish often moved two or three times, acquiring a reputation as a rootless people.

Wherever the newcomers settled, they often found themselves living beyond the effective authority of colonial governments. To be sure, backcountry residents petitioned for assistance during wars against the Indians, but they preferred to be left alone. These conditions heightened the importance of religious institutions within the small ethnic communities. Although the stimulus for coming to America may have been a desire for economic independence and prosperity, backcountry families—especially the Scots-Irish—flocked to evangelical Protestant preachers, to Presbyterian and later Baptist and Methodist ministers, who not only fulfilled the settlers' spiritual needs but also gave these scattered communities a moral character that survived long after the colonial period.

Read the Document
Peter Kalm, a Swedish Visitor to Philadelphia 1748 on **myhistorylab.com**

Quick Check

✓ Why did the new German and Scots-Irish immigrants to America move west after they arrived in the colonies?

Native Americans Stake Out a Middle Ground

During much of the seventeenth century, various Indian groups who contested the English settlers for control of coastal lands suffered terribly, sometimes from war, but more often from contagious diseases such as smallpox. The two races found it difficult to live in close proximity. As one Indian informed the Maryland assembly in 1666, "Your hogs & Cattle injure Us, You come too near Us to live & drive Us from place to place. We can fly no farther; let us know where to live & how to be secured for the future from the Hogs & Cattle."

Against such odds the Indians managed to survive. By the eighteenth century, the site of the most intense and creative contact between the races had shifted to the huge territory between the Appalachian Mountains and the Mississippi River, where several hundred thousand Native Americans made their homes.

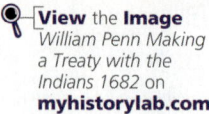

View the **Image**
*William Penn Making
a Treaty with the
Indians 1682* on
myhistorylab.com

Many Indians had only recently migrated to the area. The Delaware, for example, retreated to far western Pennsylvania and the Ohio Valley to escape almost continuous confrontation with advancing European invaders. Other Indians drifted west in less happy circumstances. They were refugees, the remnants of Native American groups who had lost so many people that they could no longer sustain an independent cultural identity. These survivors joined with other Indians to establish new multiethnic communities. Stronger groups of Indians, such as the Creek, Choctaw, Chickasaw, Cherokee, and Shawnee, generally welcomed the refugees. Strangers were formally adopted to replace relatives killed in battle or overcome by sickness.

The concept of a middle ground—a geographical area where two district cultures interacted with neither holding a clear upper hand—helps us understand how eighteenth-century Indians held their own in the backcountry beyond the Appalachian Mountains. The Native Americans never intended to isolate themselves completely from European contact. They relied on white traders, French and English, to provide essential metal goods and weapons. The goal of the Indian confederacies was rather to maintain a strong independent voice in these commercial exchanges, whenever possible playing the French against the British. So long as they had sufficient military strength they compelled everyone who came to negotiate in the "middle ground" to give them proper respect. Native Americans took advantage of rivals when possible; they compromised when necessary. It is best to imagine the Indians' middle ground as an open, dynamic process of creative interaction.

However desirable they may have appeared, European goods subtly eroded traditional Native American authority structures. During the period of earliest encounter with white men, Indian leaders reinforced their own power by controlling the character and flow of commercial exchange. If a trader wanted a rich supply of animal skins, for example, he soon learned that he had better negotiate directly with a chief or tribal elder. But as more European traders operated within the "middle ground," ordinary Indians began to bargain for themselves, obtaining colorful and durable manufactured items without first consulting a Native American leader. Independent commercial dealings of this sort weakened the Indians' ability to resist organized white aggression. As John Stuart, a superintendent of Indian affairs, explained in 1761, "A modern Indian cannot subsist without Europeans; And would handle a Flint Ax or any other rude utensil used by his ancestors very awkwardly; So that what was only convenience at first is now become Necessity."

The survival of the middle ground depended ultimately on factors over which the Native Americans had little control. Imperial competition between France and Great Britain enhanced the Indians' bargaining position. But after the British defeated the French in 1763, the Indians no longer received the same solicitous attention. Keeping old allies happy seemed to the British a needless expense. Moreover, contagious disease continued to take a fearful toll. In the southern backcountry between 1685 and 1790, the Indian population dropped an astounding 72 percent. In the Ohio Valley, the numbers suggest similar rates of decline.

Quick Check

✓ How did Native Americans manipulate the "middle ground" to their advantage?

SPANISH BORDERLANDS OF THE EIGHTEENTH CENTURY

The Spanish empire continued to shape borderlands societies into the eighteenth century. As anyone who visits the modern American Southwest discovers, Spanish administrators and priests—not to mention ordinary settlers—left a lasting imprint on its cultural landscape.

Until 1821, when Mexico declared independence from Madrid, Spanish authorities struggled to control a vast northern frontier. During the eighteenth century, the Spanish empire in North America included widely dispersed settlements such as San Francisco and San Diego in California; Santa Fe, New Mexico; San Antonio, Texas; and St. Augustine, Florida (see Map 4.2). In these borderland communities, European colonists mixed with peoples of other races and backgrounds, forming multicultural societies.

Why was the Spanish empire unable to control its northern frontier?

Conquering the Northern Frontier

In the late sixteenth century, Spanish settlers, led by Juan de Oñate, established European communities north of the Rio Grande. The Pueblo Indians resisted the invasion of colonists, soldiers, and missionaries, and in a major rebellion in 1680 led by El Popé, the native peoples drove the whites out of New Mexico. The Spanish did not reconquer this fiercely contested area until 1692. By then, Native American

Read the **Document** *Testimony of Pedro Naranjo to Spanish Authorities* on **myhistorylab.com**

Map 4.2 *The Spanish Borderlands, ca. 1770* In the eighteenth century, Spain's North American empire extended across what is now the southern United States from Florida through Texas and New Mexico to California.

hostility coupled with the failure to find precious metal had cooled Spain's enthusiasm for the northern frontier.

Concern over French encroachment in the Southeast led Spain to colonize St. Augustine (Florida) in 1565. This was the first permanent European settlement in what would become the United States, predating the founding of Jamestown and Plymouth by decades. Pedro Menéndez de Avilés brought some 1,500 soldiers and settlers to St. Augustine, where they constructed an impressive fort, but the colony failed to attract additional Spanish migrants.

California also never figured prominently in Spain's plans for the New World. Early explorers reported finding only impoverished Indians along the Pacific coast. Adventurers saw no natural resources worth mentioning, and since the area was difficult to reach from Mexico City—the overland trip could take months—California received little attention. Fear that the Russians might seize the entire region belatedly sparked Spanish activity, however, and after 1769, two indomitable servants of empire, Fra Junípero Serra and Don Gaspar de Portolá, organized permanent missions and *presidios* (forts) at San Diego, Monterey, San Francisco, and Santa Barbara.

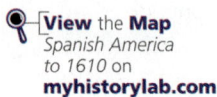

View the **Map**
*Spanish America
to 1610 on*
myhistorylab.com

Quick Check

✓ Why did the Spanish not more aggressively develop California and the Southwest?

Spanish Mission Baroque-style eighteenth-century Spanish mission at San Xavier del Bac outside present-day Tucson, Arizona. Spanish missions dotted the frontier of northern New Spain from Florida to California.

Peoples of the Spanish Borderlands

In contrast to the English frontier settlements of the eighteenth century, the Spanish outposts in North America grew slowly. A few Catholic priests and imperial administrators traveled to the northern provinces, but the danger of Indian attack and a harsh physical environment discouraged ordinary colonists. Most European migrants were soldiers in the pay of the empire. Although some colonists came directly from Spain, most had been born in other Spanish colonies such as the Canaries or New Spain, and because European women rarely appeared on the frontier, Spanish males formed relationships with Indian women, fathering mestizos, children of mixed race.

As in other eighteenth-century frontiers, encounters with Spanish soldiers, priests, and traders altered Native American cultures. The experience here was quite different from that of the whites and Indians in the British backcountry. The Spanish exploited Native American labor, reducing entire Indian villages to servitude. Many Indians moved to the Spanish towns, and although they lived alongside the Europeans—something rare in British America—they were consigned to the lowest social class, objects of European contempt. However much their material conditions changed, the southwestern Indians resisted efforts to convert them to Catholicism. The Pueblo maintained their own religious forms—often at great personal risk—and they sometimes murdered priests who became too intrusive. Angry Pueblo Indians at Taos reportedly fed the hated Spanish friars corn tortillas containing urine and mouse meat.

The Spanish empire never had the resources necessary to secure the northern frontier. The small military posts were intended primarily to discourage other European powers such as France, Britain, and Russia from taking territory claimed by Spain. It would be misleading, however, to stress the fragility of Spanish colonization. The urban design and public architecture of many southwestern cities still reflect the vision of the early Spanish settlers, and the old borderlands largely remain Spanish speaking to this day.

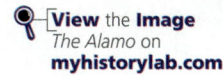

View the Image
The Alamo on
myhistorylab.com

Quick Check

✓ How successful were the Spanish in assimilating the Pueblos to imperial rule?

THE IMPACT OF EUROPEAN IDEAS ON AMERICAN CULTURE

The character of the older, more established British colonies changed almost as rapidly as that of the backcountry. The rapid growth of an urban cosmopolitan culture impressed eighteenth-century commentators, and although most Americans still lived on scattered farms, they had begun to participate aggressively in an exciting consumer marketplace that expanded their imaginative horizons.

How did European ideas affect eighteenth-century American life?

American Enlightenment

European historians often refer to the eighteenth century as an Age of Reason. During this period, a body of new, often radical, ideas swept through the salons and universities, altering how educated Europeans thought about God, nature, and society. This intellectual revolution, called the **Enlightenment**, involved the work of Europe's greatest minds, men such as Newton and Locke, Voltaire and Hume. Their writings received a mixed reception in the colonies. On the whole, the American Enlightenment was tamer than its European counterpart, for while the colonists welcomed experimental science, they defended traditional Christianity.

Enlightenment thinkers shared basic assumptions. Philosophers of the Enlightenment replaced the concept of original sin with a much more optimistic view of human nature. A benevolent God, having set the universe in motion, gave human beings the power of reason to enable them to comprehend the orderly workings of His creation. Everything, even human society, operated according to these mechanical rules. The responsibility of right-thinking men and women, therefore, was to make certain that institutions such as church and state conformed to self-evident natural laws. It was possible to achieve perfection in this world. In fact, human suffering was the result of people's losing touch with the fundamental insights of reason.

For many Americans, the appeal of the Enlightenment was its focus on a search for useful knowledge, ideas, and inventions to improve the quality of human life. What mattered was practical experimentation. A speech delivered in 1767 before the members of the American Society in Philadelphia reflected the new utilitarian spirit: "Knowledge is of little Use when confined to mere Speculation, But when speculative Truths are reduced to Practice, when Theories grounded upon Experiments ... and the Arts of Living made more easy and comfortable ... Knowledge then becomes really useful."

The Enlightenment spawned scores of earnest scientific tinkerers, people who dutifully recorded changes in temperature, strange plants and animals, and astronomic phenomena. While these eighteenth-century Americans made few earth-shattering discoveries, they did encourage their countrymen, especially those who attended college, to apply reason to the solution of social and political problems.

Quick Check

✓ What were the basic intellectual assumptions of the American Enlightenment?

Benjamin Franklin

Benjamin Franklin (1706–1790) absorbed the new cosmopolitan culture. European thinkers regarded him as a fellow *philosophe*, a person of reason and science, a role that he self-consciously cultivated when he visited England and France in later life. Franklin had little formal education, but as a young man working in his brother's print shop, he kept up with the latest intellectual currents. In his *Autobiography*, Franklin described the excitement of discovering a new British journal. It was like a breath of fresh air to a boy growing up in Puritan New England: "I met with an odd volume of *The Spectator* ... I had never before seen any of them. I bought it, read it over and over, and was much delighted with it. I thought the writing excellent, and wished if possible to imitate it."

After he moved to Philadelphia in 1723, Franklin devoted himself to the pursuit of useful knowledge, ideas that would increase the happiness of his fellow Americans. Franklin never denied the existence of God. Rather, he pushed the Lord aside, making room for the free exercise of human reason. Franklin tinkered, experimented, and reformed. Almost everything aroused his curiosity. His investigation of electricity brought him world fame, but Franklin was never satisfied with his work in this field until it yielded practical application. In 1756, he invented the lightning rod. He also designed an efficient stove that is still used today. In modern America, Franklin has become exactly what he would have wanted to be, a symbol of material progress through human ingenuity.

Benjamin Franklin Franklin exemplified the scientific curiosity and search for practical knowledge characteristic of Enlightenment thinkers of the eighteenth century. His experiments on electricity became world famous and inspired others to study the effects of the strange force.

Franklin promoted the spread of reason. In Philadelphia, he organized groups that discussed the latest European literature, philosophy, and science. In 1727, for example, he "form'd most of my ingenious Acquaintances into a Club for mutual Improvement, which we call'd the Junto." Four years later Franklin helped found the Library Company, a voluntary association that for the first time allowed people like him to pursue "useful knowledge." The members of these societies communicated with Americans in other colonies, providing them not only with new information but also with models for their own clubs and associations. Such efforts broadened the intellectual horizons of many colonists, especially those who lived in cities.

Read the **Document**
Franklin, Observations Concerning the Increase of Mankind on **myhistorylab.com**

Quick Check

✓ What characteristics did Benjamin Franklin possess that made him an Enlightenment figure?

Economic Transformation

The colonial economy kept pace with the stunning growth in population. During the first three-quarters of the eighteenth century, the population increased at least eightfold. Yet even with so many additional people to feed and clothe, the per

![Boston Harbor engraving]

Boston Harbor This engraving of a work by William Burgis depicts the port of Boston at mid-century.

capita income did not decline. Indeed, except for poor urban dwellers, such as sailors whose employment varied with the season, white Americans did well. Abundant land and the growth of agriculture accounted for their economic success. New farmers could not only provide for their families' well-being but could also sell their crops in European and West Indian markets. Each year, more Americans produced more tobacco, wheat, or rice—to cite just the major export crops—and thus maintained a high level of individual prosperity without developing an industrial base.

At midcentury, colonial exports flowed along well-established routes. More than half of American goods produced for export went to Britain. The Navigation Acts (see Chapter 3) were still in effect, and "enumerated" items such as tobacco had to be landed first at a British port. Furs were added to the restricted list in 1722. The White Pines Acts passed in 1711, 1722, and 1729 forbade Americans from cutting white pine trees without a license. The purpose of this legislation was to reserve the best trees for the Royal Navy. The Molasses Act of 1733—also called the Sugar Act—placed a heavy duty on molasses imported from foreign ports; the Hat and Felt Act of 1732 and the Iron Act of 1750 attempted to limit the production of colonial goods that competed with British exports.

((•—Listen to the
Audio File
*The Connecti-
cut Peddler* on
myhistorylab.com

These statutes might have created tensions between the colonists and the mother country had they been rigorously enforced. Crown officials, however, generally ignored the new laws. New England merchants imported molasses from French Caribbean islands without paying the full customs; iron masters in the Middle Colonies continued to produce iron. Even without the Navigation Acts, however, most colonial exports would have been sold on the English market. The emerging consumer society in Britain was creating a new generation of buyers who possessed enough income to purchase American goods, especially sugar and tobacco. This rising demand was the major market force shaping the colonial economy.

Quick Check

✓ Why did Americans in the first half of the eighteenth century not complain about the Navigation Acts?

Birth of a Consumer Society

After midcentury, Americans began buying more English goods than their parents or grandparents had done, giving birth to a consumer revolution. Between 1740 and 1770, English exports to the American colonies increased by an astounding 360 percent.

In part, this new American market shift reflected a transformation in the British economy. The pace of the British economy picked up dramatically after 1690. Small factories produced certain goods more efficiently and more cheaply than the colonists could. The availability of these products altered the lives of most Americans, even those with modest incomes. Staffordshire china replaced crude earthenware; imported cloth replaced homespun. Franklin noted in his *Autobiography* how changing consumer habits affected his life. For years, he had eaten his breakfast in an earthenware bowl with a pewter spoon, but one morning it was served "in a china bowl, with a spoon of silver." Franklin observed that "this was the first appearance of plate and china in our house which afterwards in the course of years, as our wealth increased, augmented gradually to several hundred pounds in value." In this manner, British industrialization undercut American handicraft and folk art.

To help Americans purchase manufactured goods, British merchants offered generous credit. Colonists deferred final payment by paying interest on their debts. The temptation to acquire English finery blinded many people to hard economic realities. They gambled on the future, hoping bumper crops would reduce their dependence on the large merchant houses of London and Glasgow. Some persons lived within their means, but the aggregate American debt continued to grow. Colonial leaders tried various expedients to remain solvent—issuing paper money, for example—and while these efforts delayed a crisis, the balance-of-payments problem was clearly very serious.

Intercoastal trade also increased in the eighteenth century. Southern planters sent tobacco and rice to New England and the Middle Colonies, where these staples were exchanged for meat, wheat, and goods imported from Britain. By 1760, approximately 30 percent of the colonists' total tonnage capacity was involved in this "coastwise" commerce. Backcountry farmers in western Pennsylvania and the Shenandoah Valley also carried their grain to market along an old Iroquois trail that became known as the Great Wagon Road, a rough, hilly highway that by the time of the Revolution stretched 735 miles along the Blue Ridge Mountains to Camden, South Carolina (see Map 4.3). Long, graceful Conestoga wagons carried most of their produce. German immigrants in the Conestoga River Valley in Lancaster County, Pennsylvania, had invented these "wagons of empire."

Map 4.3   *The Great Wagon Road* By the mid-eighteenth century, the Great Wagon Road had become a major highway for the settlers in Virginia and the Carolina backcountry.

The shifting patterns of trade had immense effects on the development of an American culture. First, the flood of British imports eroded local and regional identities. Commerce helped to "Anglicize" American culture by exposing colonial consumers to a common range of British manufactured goods. Deep sectional differences remained, but Americans from New Hampshire to Georgia were increasingly drawn into a sophisticated economic network centered in London. Second, the expanding coastal and overland trade brought colonists of different backgrounds into more frequent contact. Ships that sailed between New England and South Carolina, and between Virginia and Pennsylvania, provided dispersed Americans with a means to exchange ideas and experiences on a more regular basis. Mid-eighteenth-century printers, for example, established dozens of new journals. These weekly newspapers carried information not only about the mother country and world commerce but also about the colonies.

Quick Check

✓ How did Americans manage to pay for so many new consumer goods?

RELIGIOUS REVIVALS IN PROVINCIAL SOCIETIES

How did the Great Awakening transform the religious culture of colonial America?

A sudden, spontaneous series of Protestant revivals in the mid-eighteenth century, known as the Great Awakening, profoundly affected the lives of ordinary people. This new, highly personal appeal to a "new birth" in Christ caused men and women of all backgrounds to rethink basic assumptions about church and state, institutions and society.

George Whitefield The fervor of the Great Awakening was intensified by the eloquence of itinerant preachers such as George Whitefield, the most popular evangelical of the mid-eighteenth century. (*Source*: John Wollaston, "George Whitefield," ca. 1770. National Portrait Gallery, London.)

Read the **Document** *Jonathan Edwards, "Sinners in the Hands of an Angry God" on* **myhistorylab.com**

The Great Awakening

Whatever their origins, the seeds of the Great Awakening were generally sown on fertile ground. In the early eighteenth century, many Americans—especially New Englanders—complained that organized religion had lost vitality. They looked back at Winthrop's generation with nostalgia, assuming that common people at that time must have possessed greater piety than did later, more worldly colonists. Congregational ministers seemed obsessed with dull, scholastic matters; they no longer touched the heart. And in the Southern Colonies, there were simply not enough ordained ministers to tend to the religious needs of the population.

The Great Awakening arrived unexpectedly in Northampton, a small farm community in western Massachusetts. It was sparked by Jonathan Edwards, the local Congregational minister. Edwards accepted the traditional teachings of Calvinism, reminding his parishioners that an omnipotent God had determined their eternal fate. There was nothing they could do to save themselves. They were totally dependent on the Lord's will. He thought his fellow ministers had grown soft. They left men and women with the mistaken impression that sinners might somehow avoid damnation by performing good works.

Although Edwards was an outstanding theologian, he did not possess the dynamic personality to sustain the revival. That role fell to George Whitefield, a young, inspiring preacher from England who toured the colonies from New Hampshire to Georgia. While Whitefield was not an original thinker, he was an extraordinarily effective public speaker. And like his friend Benjamin Franklin, he symbolized the cultural forces that were transforming the Atlantic world.

Whitefield's audiences came from all groups of American society: rich and poor, young and old, rural and urban. While he described himself as a Calvinist, Whitefield welcomed all Protestants. He spoke from any available pulpit: "Don't tell me you are a Baptist, an Independent, a Presbyterian, a dissenter, tell me you are a Christian, that is all I want."

Whitefield was a brilliant entrepreneur. Like Franklin, with whom he published many popular volumes, the itinerant minister possessed an almost intuitive sense of how to turn this burgeoning consumer society to his own advantage, and he embraced the latest merchandising techniques. He appreciated, for example, the power of the press in selling the revival, and he regularly advertised his own work in British and American newspapers. The crowds flocked to hear Whitefield, while his critics grumbled about the commercialization of religion. One anonymous writer in Massachusetts noted that there was "a very wholesome law of the province to discourage Pedlars in Trade," and it seemed high time "to enact something for the discouragement of Pedlars in Divinity also."

Read the **Document**
Benjamin Franklin on George Whitefield (1771) on **myhistorylab.com**

Quick Check

✓ What explains the Reverend George Whitefield's extraordinary popularity among colonial Americans?

Evangelical Religion

Other American-born itinerant preachers, who traveled from settlement to settlement throughout the colonies to spread their message, followed Whitefield's example. The most famous was Gilbert Tennent, a Scots-Irish Presbyterian who had been educated in the Middle Colonies. His sermon "On the Danger of an Unconverted Ministry," printed in 1741, set off a storm of protest from established ministers who were insulted by assertions that they did not understand true religion. Lesser-known revivalists traveled from town to town, colony to colony, challenging local clergymen who seemed hostile to evangelical religion. Men and women who thronged to hear the itinerants were called "New Lights." During the 1740s and 1750s, many congregations split between defenders of the new emotional preaching and those who regarded the movement as dangerous nonsense.

Despite Whitefield's successes, many ministers remained suspicious of the itinerants and their methods. Some complaints may have just been sour grapes. One "Old Light" spokesman labeled Tennent "a monster! impudent and noisy." He claimed Tennent told anxious Christians that "they were damned! damned! damned! This charmed them; and, in the most dreadful winter I ever saw, people wallowed in snow, night and day, for the benefit of his beastly brayings; and many ended their days under these fatigues." Charles Chauncy, minister of the prestigious First Church of Boston, raised more troubling issues. How could the revivalists be certain God had sparked the Great Awakening? Perhaps the itinerants had relied too much on emotion? "Let us esteem those as friends of religion," Chauncy advised, "… who warn us of the danger of enthusiasm, and would put us on our guard, that we may not be led aside by it."

Despite occasional anti-intellectual outbursts, the New Lights founded several important centers of higher learning. They wanted to train young men to carry on the good works of Edwards, Whitefield, and Tennent. In 1746, New Light Presbyterians established the College of New Jersey, which later became Princeton University. Just before his death, Edwards was appointed its president. The evangelical minister Eleazar Wheelock launched Dartmouth (1769); other revivalists founded Brown (1764) and Rutgers (1766).

The Great Awakening also encouraged men and women who had been taught to remain silent before traditional authority figures to speak up, to take an active role in their salvation. They could no longer rely on ministers or institutions. The individual alone stood before God. Knowing this, New Lights shattered the old harmony among Protestant sects. In its place, they introduced a noisy, often bitter competition. As one New Jersey Presbyterian complained, "There are so many particular *sects* and *Parties* among professed Christians … that we know not … in which of these different *paths*, to steer our course for *Heaven*."

View the **Image**
*Richard Allen
Portrait* on
myhistorylab.com

Expressive evangelicalism struck a particularly responsive chord among African Americans. Itinerant ministers frequently preached to large, sympathetic audiences of slaves. Richard Allen (1760–1831), founder of the African Methodist Episcopal Church (AME), reported he owed his freedom in part to a traveling Methodist minister who persuaded Allen's master that slavery was sinful. Allen himself was converted, as were thousands of other black colonists. According to one historian, evangelical preaching "shared enough with traditional African styles and beliefs such as spirit possession and ecstatic expression … to allow for an interpenetration of African and Christian religious beliefs."

With religious contention came an awareness of a larger community, a union of fellow believers that extended beyond the boundaries of town and colony. In fact, evangelical religion was one of several forces at work during the mid-eighteenth century that brought scattered colonists into contact with one another for the first time. In this sense, the Great Awakening was a "national" event long before a nation actually existed.

People who had been touched by the Great Awakening shared an optimism about the future of America. With God's help, social and political progress was possible, and from this perspective, the New Lights did not sound much different than the mildly rationalist American spokesmen of the Enlightenment. Both groups prepared the way for the development of a revolutionary mentality in colonial America.

Quick Check

✓ What message did evangelical ministers bring to ordinary Americans?

CLASH OF POLITICAL CULTURES

Why were the eighteenth-century colonial assemblies not fully democratic?

The political history of the eighteenth century illuminates a growing tension within the empire. Americans of all regions repeatedly stated their desire to replicate British political institutions. Parliament, they claimed, provided a model for the American assemblies. Although England has never had a formal written constitution, it did develop over the centuries a system of legal checks and balances that, in theory at least, kept the monarch from becoming a tyrant. The colonists claimed that this unwritten constitution preserved their rights and liberties. However, the more the colonists studied British political theory and practice—in other words, the more they attempted to become British—the more aware they became of major differences.

Governing the Colonies: The American Experience

The colonists assumed—perhaps naively—that their own governments were modeled on Britain's balanced constitution. They argued that within their political systems, the governor corresponded to the king and the governor's council to the House of Lords. They saw colonial assemblies as American reproductions of the House of Commons and expected them to preserve the people's interests against those of the monarch and aristocracy. As the colonists discovered, however, general theories about a mixed constitution were even less relevant in America than they were in Britain.

By midcentury, most of the mainland colonies had royal governors appointed by the crown. Many of these governors were career army officers who through luck, charm, or family connection had gained the ear of someone close to the king. These patronage posts did not generate enough income to interest the most powerful or talented personalities of the period, but they did draw mid-level bureaucrats who were ambitious, desperate, or both. It is perhaps not surprising that most governors decided simply not to "consider any Thing further than how to sit easy."

Whatever their demerits, royal governors possessed enormous powers. In fact, they could do things in America that a king could not do in eighteenth-century Britain, such as veto legislation and dismiss judges. The governors also served as military commanders in each province.

Political practice in America differed from the British model in another crucial respect. Royal governors were advised by a council, usually a body of about 12 wealthy colonists selected by the Board of Trade in London on the recommendation of the governor. During the seventeenth century, the council had played an important role in colonial government, but its ability to exercise independent authority declined during the eighteenth century. Its members did not represent a distinct aristocracy within American society the way the House of Lords did in Britain.

If royal governors did not look like kings, nor American councils look like the House of Lords, colonial assemblies bore little resemblance to the eighteenth-century House of Commons. The major difference was the size of the American franchise. In most colonies, adult white males who owned a little land could vote in colonywide elections. One historian estimates that 95 percent of this group in Massachusetts were eligible to vote. In Virginia it was about 85 percent. These figures—much higher than those in contemporary England—have led scholars to view the colonies as "middle-class democracies," societies run by moderately prosperous yeomen farmers who—in politics at least—exercised independent judgment. There were too many of them to bribe, no "rotten" boroughs with few or no voters as there were in Britain, and when these people moved west, colonial assemblies usually created new electoral districts to represent them.

Colonial governments were not democracies in the modern sense. Possessing the right to vote was one thing, exercising it another. Americans participated in elections when major issues were at stake—the formation of banks in mid-eighteenth-century Massachusetts, for example—but usually they were content to let members of the rural and urban gentry represent them in the assemblies. To be sure, unlike modern democracies, colonial politics excluded women and nonwhites from voting. The point to remember, however, is that American voters always had the power to expel legislative rascals. This political reality kept autocratic gentlemen from straying too far from the will of the people.

Quick Check

✓ What was the structure of royal government in eighteenth-century America?

Colonial Assemblies

Elected members of the colonial assemblies believed that they had an obligation to preserve colonial liberties. They perceived any attack on the legislature as an assault on the rights of Americans. The representatives brooked no criticism, and several colonial printers were jailed because they criticized actions taken by a lower house.

So aggressive were these bodies in seizing privileges, determining procedures, and controlling money bills that historians have described the political development of eighteenth-century America as "the rise of the assemblies." No doubt this is exaggerated, but the long series of imperial wars against the French, demanding large public expenditures, transformed the small, amateurish assemblies of the seventeenth century into the more professional, vigilant legislatures of the eighteenth.

This political system seemed designed to generate hostility. Colonial legislators had no reason to cooperate with appointed royal governors. Alexander Spotswood, Virginia's governor from 1710 to 1722, for example, attempted to institute a new land program backed by the crown. When persuasion and gifts failed, he tried chicanery. But the members of the House of Burgesses refused to support a plan that did not suit their own interests. Before leaving office, Spotswood gave up trying to carry out royal policy. Instead, he allied himself with the gentry who controlled the House and the Council and became a wealthy man because they rewarded their new friend with large tracts of land.

A few governors managed briefly to recreate in America the political culture of patronage, a system that eighteenth-century Englishmen took for granted. Most successful in this endeavor was William Shirley, who held office in Massachusetts from 1741 to 1757. The secret to his political successes in America was connection to people who held high office in Britain. But Shirley's practices—and those of men like him—clashed with the colonists' perception of politics. They really believed in the purity of the balanced constitution. They insisted on complete separation of executive and legislative authority.

A major source of shared political information was the weekly journal, a new and vigorous institution in American life. In New York and Massachusetts especially, weekly journals urged readers to preserve civic virtue and be vigilant against the spread of privileged power.

The rise of the assemblies also shaped American culture in subtler ways. During the century, the law became increasingly English in character. The Board of Trade, the Privy Council that advised the king in London and acted as a court of appeals for the colonies, and Parliament scrutinized court decisions and legislative actions from all 13 mainland colonies. As a result, local legal practices that had been widespread during the seventeenth century became standardized. Indeed, according to one historian, the colonial legal system by 1750 "was substantially that of the mother country." Not surprisingly, many men who served in colonial assemblies were either lawyers or had received legal training. When Americans from different regions met—as they frequently did before the Revolution— they discovered that they shared a commitment to preserving the English common law.

As political developments drew the colonists closer to the mother country, they also made Americans more aware of each other. As their horizons widened, they learned they operated within the same general imperial system. Like the revivalists and merchants—people who crossed old boundaries—colonial legislators laid the foundation for a larger cultural identity.

Quick Check

✓ Why were the plans of royal governors so often defeated by colonial assemblies?

CENTURY OF IMPERIAL WAR

Warfare in the colonies changed radically during the eighteenth century. The founders of England's mainland colonies had engaged in intense local conflicts with the Indians, such as King Philip's War (1675–1676) in New England. But after 1690, the colonists were increasingly involved in hostilities that originated on the other side of the Atlantic, in political and commercial rivalries between Britain and France. The external threat to security forced people in different colonies to devise unprecedented measures of military and political cooperation. (See Table 4.1.)

Why did colonial Americans support Great Britain's wars against France?

View the **Map**
European Claims in America, C. 1750 on
myhistorylab.com

The French Threat

On paper, at least, the British colonies enjoyed military superiority over the settlements of New France. King Louis XIV of France (r. 1643–1715) had an army

TABLE 4.1   A Century of Conflict: Major Wars, 1689–1763

Dates	European Name	American Name	Major Allies	Issues	Major American Battle	Treaty
1689–1697	War of the League of Augsburg	King William's War	Britain, Holland, Spain, their colonies, and Native American allies against France, its colonies, and Native American allies	Opposition to French bid for control of Europe	New England troops assault Quebec under Sir William Phips (1690)	Treaty of Ryswick (1697)
1702–1713	War of the Spanish Succession	Queen Anne's War	Britain, Holland, their colonies, and Native American allies against France, Spain, their colonies, and Native American allies	Austria and France hold rival claims to Spanish throne	Attack on Deerfield (1704)	Treaty of Utrecht (1713)
1743–1748	War of the Austrian Succession (War of Jenkins' Ear)	King George's War	Britain, its colonies, and Native American allies, and Austria against France, Spain, their Native American allies, and Prussia	Struggle among Britain, Spain, and France for control of New World territory; among France, Prussia, and Austria for control of central Europe	New England forces capture Louisbourg under William Pepperell (1745)	Treaty of Aix-la-Chapelle (1748)
1756–1763	Seven Years' War	French and Indian War	Britain, its colonies, and Native American allies against France, its colonies, and Native American allies	Struggle among Britain, Spain, and France for worldwide control of colonial markets and raw materials	British and Continental forces capture Quebec under Major General James Wolfe (1759)	Peace of Paris (1763)

Theyanoguin Native Americans often depended on British trade goods and sometimes adopted British dress. Here the Mohawk chief Theyanoguin, called King Hendrick by the British, wears a cloak he received from Queen Anne of England during a visit to London in 1710. During the Seven Years' War, Theyanoguin mobilized Mohawk support for the British.

Quick Check

✓ Why during the eighteenth century did Britain's American colonists come to view the French as a serious threat?

of 100,000 well-armed troops, but he dispatched few of them to the New World. He left the defense of Canada and the Mississippi Valley to the companies engaged in the fur trade. Although France sent more troops to Canada in the mid-eighteenth century, meeting this defensive challenge seemed almost impossible for the French outposts strung out along the St. Lawrence River and the Great Lakes. In 1754, New France contained only 75,000 inhabitants compared to 1.2 million people in Britain's mainland colonies.

For most of the eighteenth century, the theoretical advantages the English colonists enjoyed did them little good. While the British settlements possessed a larger and more prosperous population, they were divided into separate governments that sometimes seemed more suspicious of each other than of the French. When war came, French officers and Indian allies skillfully exploited these jealousies. Moreover, although the population of New France was comparatively small, it was concentrated along the St. Lawrence, so that while the French found it difficult to mount effective offensives against the English, they could easily mass the forces to defend Montreal and Quebec.

During the early eighteenth century, English colonists came to believe that the French planned to "encircle" them, to confine the English to a narrow strip of land along the Atlantic coast. The English noted as early as 1682 that La Salle had claimed for the king of France a territory—Louisiana—that included all the people and resources located on "streams and Rivers" flowing into the Mississippi River. To make good on their claim, the French constructed forts on the Chicago and Illinois rivers. In 1717, they established a military post 200 miles up the Alabama River, within striking distance of the Carolina frontier. In 1718, they settled New Orleans. One New Yorker declared in 1715 that "it is impossible that we and the French can both inhabit this Continent in peace but that one nation must at last give way to the other."

On their part, the French suspected their rivals intended to seize all of North America. Land speculators and frontier traders pushed into territory claimed by the French and owned by the Native Americans. In 1716, one Frenchman urged his government to hasten the development of Louisiana, since "it is not difficult to guess that their [the British] purpose is to drive us entirely out … of North America."

King George's War and Its Aftermath

In 1743, after many small frontier engagements, the Americans were dragged into King George's War (1743–1748), known in Europe as the War of the Austrian Succession, in which the colonists scored a magnificent victory over the French. Louisbourg, a gigantic fortress on Cape Breton Island, the easternmost promontory of Canada, guarded the approaches to the Gulf of St. Lawrence and Quebec. It was described as the Gibraltar of the New World. New England troops under William

Pepperell captured Louisbourg in June 1745, a feat that demonstrated the British colonists could fight and mount effective joint operations.

The French were not prepared to surrender an inch. But the English colonies were growing more populous, and the English possessed a seemingly inexhaustible supply of manufactured goods to trade with the Indians. The French decided in the early 1750s, therefore, to seize the Ohio Valley before the Virginians could do so. They established forts throughout the region, the most formidable being Fort Duquesne, located at a strategic fork in the Ohio River and later renamed Pittsburgh. (See Map 4.4.)

Although France and Britain had not officially declared war, British officials advised the governor of Virginia to "repell force by force." The Virginians needed little encouragement. They were eager to make good their claim to the Ohio Valley. In 1754, militia companies under a promising young officer, George Washington, constructed Fort Necessity not far from Fort Duquesne. The plan failed. The French and their Indian allies overran the exposed outpost (July 3, 1754). The humiliating setback revealed that a single colony could not defeat the French.

Benjamin Franklin, for one, appreciated the need for intercolonial cooperation. When British officials invited representatives from Virginia, Maryland, and the northern colonies to Albany (June 1754) to discuss relations with the Iroquois, Franklin used the occasion to present a blueprint for colonial union. His Albany Plan envisioned the formation of a Grand Council, made up of elected delegates from the colonies, to oversee matters of common defense, western expansion, and Indian affairs. A President General appointed by the king would preside.

First reaction to the Albany Plan was enthusiastic. To take effect, however, it required the support of the separate colonial assemblies and Parliament. It received

Map 4.4 *North America, 1750* By 1750, the French had established a chain of settlements southward through the heart of the continent from Quebec to New Orleans. The British saw this as a threat to their own seaboard colonies, which were expanding westward.

The Albany Plan The first political cartoon to appear in an American newspaper was created by Benjamin Franklin in 1754 to emphasize the importance of the Albany Plan.

neither. The assemblies were jealous of their fiscal authority, and the British thought the scheme undermined the crown's power over American affairs.

In 1755, the Ohio Valley again became the scene of fierce fighting. Even though there was still no formal declaration of war, the British resolved to destroy Fort Duquesne, and to that end, they dispatched units of the regular army to America. In command was Major General Edward Braddock, an obese, humorless veteran who inspired neither fear nor respect. One colonist described Braddock as "very indolent, Slave to his passions, women & wine, as great an Epicure as could be in his eating, tho a brave man."

On July 9, Braddock led 2,500 British redcoats and colonists to humiliating defeat. The French and Indians opened fire as Braddock's army waded across the Monongahela River, about eight miles from Fort Duquesne. Along a narrow road congested with wagons and confused men, Braddock ordered a counterattack, described by one of his officers as "without any form or order but that of a parcell of school boys coming out of s[c]hool." Nearly 70 percent of Braddock's troops were killed or wounded. The general himself died in battle. The French, who suffered only light casualties, remained in firm control of the Ohio Valley.

Quick Check

✓ Why did Benjamin Franklin's Albany Plan receive so little support?

Seven Years' War

Britain's imperial war effort had hit bottom. No one in England or America seemed to possess the leadership necessary to drive the French from the Mississippi Valley. The cabinet of George II (r. 1727–1760) lacked the will to organize and finance a sustained military campaign in the New World, and colonial assemblies balked every time Britain asked them to raise men and money. On May 18, 1756, the British officially declared war on the French, a conflict called the French and Indian War in America and the Seven Years' War in Europe.

Had it not been for William Pitt, the most powerful minister in King George's cabinet, the military stalemate might have continued. This self-confident Englishman believed he alone could save the British empire, an opinion he publicly expressed. When he became effective head of the ministry in December 1756, Pitt could demonstrate his talents.

In the past, warfare on the European continent had worked mainly to France's advantage. Pitt saw no point in concentrating on Europe, and in 1757 he advanced a new imperial policy based on commercial assumptions. In Pitt's judgment, the critical confrontation would take place in North America, where Britain and France were struggling to control colonial markets and raw materials. Indeed, according to Pitt, America was "where England and Europe are to be fought for." He was determined to expel the French from the continent, however great the cost.

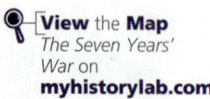 **View** the **Map**
The Seven Years' War on
myhistorylab.com

To direct the grand campaign, Pitt selected two relatively obscure officers, Jeffrey Amherst and James Wolfe. It was a masterful choice, one that a less self-assured man would never have risked. Both officers were young, talented, and ambitious. On July 26, 1758, forces under their direction recaptured Louisbourg, the same fortress the colonists had taken a decade earlier!

This victory cut the Canadians' main supply line with France. The small population of New France could no longer meet the military demands placed on it. As the situation became increasingly desperate, the French forts in the Ohio Valley and the Great Lakes began to fall. Duquesne was abandoned late in 1758 as French and Indian troops under the Marquis de Montcalm retreated toward Quebec and Montreal. During the summer of 1759, the French surrendered key forts at Ticonderoga, Crown Point, and Niagara. Quebec itself fell in September 1759. (See Map 4.5.)

The **Peace of Paris of 1763**, signed on February 10, almost fulfilled Pitt's grandiose dreams. Britain took possession of an empire that stretched around the globe. Only Guadeloupe and Martinique, the Caribbean sugar islands, were given back to the French. After a century-long struggle, the French had been driven from the mainland of North America. Even Louisiana passed out of France's control into Spanish hands. The treaty gave Britain title to Canada, Spanish Florida, and all the land east of the Mississippi River. Moreover, with the stroke of a diplomat's pen, 80,000 French-speaking Canadians, most of them Catholics, became the subjects of George III. (See Map 4.6.)

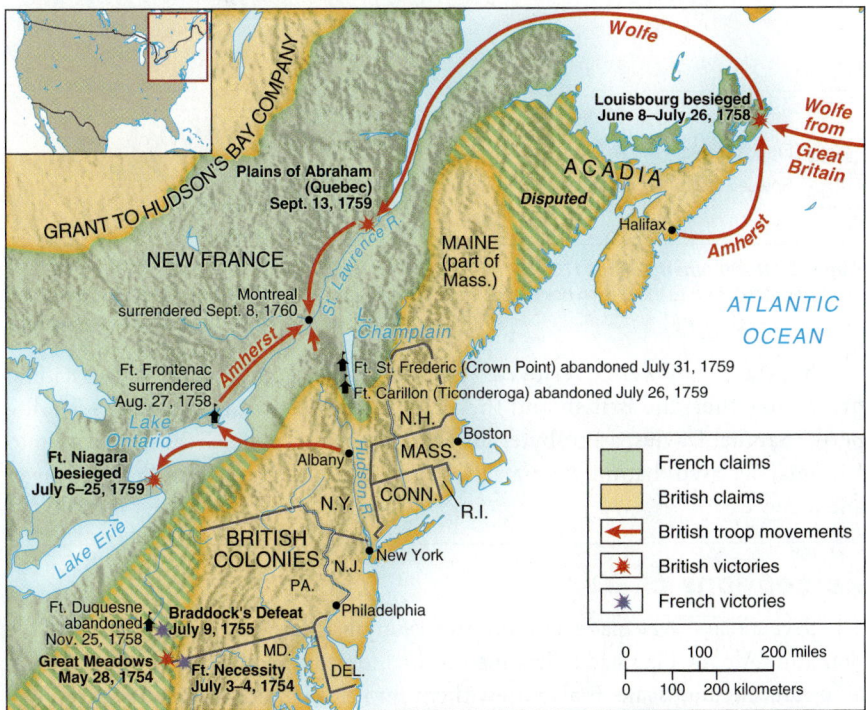

Map 4.5 *The Seven Years' War, 1756–1763 Major Battle Sites* The conflict ended with Britain driving France from mainland North America.

Map 4.6   *North America After 1763*   The Peace of Paris of 1763 redrew the map of North America. Great Britain received all the French holdings except for a few islands in the Atlantic and some sugar-producing islands in the Caribbean.

Quick Check

✓ How did the Peace of Paris of 1763 transform North American politics?

The Americans were overjoyed. It was a time of good feelings and national pride. Together, the British and their colonial allies had thwarted the "Gallic peril." Samuel Davies, a Presbyterian who had brought the Great Awakening to Virginia, declared that the long-awaited victory would inaugurate "a new heaven and a new earth."

Perceptions of War

The Seven Years' War made a deep impression on American society. Even though Franklin's Albany Plan had failed, the war had forced the colonists to cooperate on an unprecedented scale. It also drew them into closer contact with Britain. They became aware of being part of a great empire, military and commercial, but in the process of waging war, they acquired a more intimate sense of an America that lay beyond the plantation and the village. Conflict had carried thousands of young men across colonial boundaries, exposing them to a vast territory full of opportunities for a booming population. Moreover, the war trained a corps of American officers, people like George Washington, who learned that the British were not invincible.

British officials later accused the Americans of ingratitude. Britain, they claimed, had sent troops and provided funds to liberate the colonists from the threat of French attack. The Americans cheered on the British but dragged their feet at every stage, refusing to pay the bills. These charges were later incorporated into a general argument justifying parliamentary taxation in America.

The British had a point. The colonists were, in fact, slow to provide the men and materials to fight the French. Nevertheless, they did contribute to the war effort, and it was reasonable for Americans to regard themselves as at least junior partners in the empire.

Quick Check

✓ Why did victory over France not generate greater mutual respect between American colonists and the British?

CONCLUSION: RULE BRITANNIA?

James Thomson, an Englishman, understood the hold of empire on the popular imagination of the eighteenth century. In 1740, he composed words that British patriots have proudly sung for more than two centuries:

> Rule Britannia, Britannia rule the waves,
> Britons never will be slaves.

Colonial Americans—at least, those of British background—joined this chorus. By midcentury they took their political and cultural cues from Great Britain. They fought in its wars, purchased its consumer goods, flocked to hear its evangelical preachers, and read its publications. The empire gave the colonists a compelling source of identity.

An editor justified the establishment of New Hampshire's first newspaper in precisely these terms: "By this Means, the spirited *Englishman*, the mountainous *Welshman*, the brave *Scotchman*, and *Irishman*, and the loyal *American*, may be firmly united and mutually RESOLVED to guard the glorious Throne of BRITANNIA … as *British Brothers*, in defending the Common Cause." Even new immigrants, the Germans, Scots-Irish, and Africans, who felt no political loyalty to Britain and no affinity for its culture, had to assimilate to some degree to the dominant English culture of the colonies.

Americans hailed Britannia. In 1763, they were the victors, the conquerors of the backcountry. In their moment of glory, the colonists assumed that Britain's rulers saw the Americans as "Brothers," equal partners in the business of empire. Only slowly would they learn the British had a different perception. For them, "American" was a way of saying "not quite English."

4 STUDY RESOURCES

((•—[Listen to the **Chapter Audio** for Chapter 4 on **myhistorylab.com**

TIMELINE

1680 El Popé leads Pueblo Revolt against the Spanish in New Mexico, p. 89

1706 Birth of Benjamin Franklin, p. 92

1734–1736 First expression of the Great Awakening at Northampton, Massachusetts, p. 96

1740 George Whitefield electrifies listeners at Boston, p. 96

CHAPTER REVIEW

TENSIONS IN THE BACKCOUNTRY

What difficulties did Native Americans face in maintaining their cultural independence on the frontier?

Britain's American colonies experienced extraordinary growth during the eighteenth century. German and Scots-Irish migrants poured into the backcountry, where they clashed with Native Americans. The Indians played off French and British imperial ambitions in the "middle ground," but disease and encroachment by European settlers undermined the Indians' ability to resist. *(p. 85)*

SPANISH BORDERLANDS OF THE EIGHTEENTH CENTURY

Why was the Spanish empire unable to control its northern frontier?

During the late 1600s and early 1700s, the Spanish empire expanded its authority north of Mexico. New settlements were established in the Southwest and California. Although the Spanish constructed missions and forts, a lack of settlers and troops made it impossible for them to impose effective imperial authority. Much of the territory they claimed remained under the control of Indian peoples. *(p. 89)*

THE IMPACT OF EUROPEAN IDEAS ON AMERICAN CULTURE

How did European ideas affect eighteenth-century American life?

During the Enlightenment, educated Europeans and American colonists, like Benjamin Franklin, brought scientific reason to the study of religion, nature, and society. By midcentury, economic growth sparked a consumer revolution that introduced colonists to an unprecedented array of imported manufactured items. New ideas and goods helped integrate the American colonies into mainstream British culture. *(p. 91)*

RELIGIOUS REVIVALS IN PROVINCIAL SOCIETIES

How did the Great Awakening transform the religious culture of colonial America?

The Great Awakening brought a new form of evangelical religion to ordinary Americans. It emphasized personal salvation through a "New Birth" and membership in a large community of believers. Itinerant preachers such as George Whitefield drew huge crowds throughout the colonies. Other ministers followed Whitefield, inviting ordinary Americans to question traditional religious authorities. *(p. 96)*

CLASH OF POLITICAL CULTURES

Why were the eighteenth-century colonial assemblies not fully democratic?

Most eighteenth-century colonial governments were comprised of a royal governor, an appointed governor's council, and an elected assembly. Although these representative assemblies did not allow women, blacks, or the poor to vote, they did enfranchise most of the white adult male population. Assemblies guarded their privileges and powers, often conflicting with royal governors who tried to expand their authority. *(p. 98)*

CENTURY OF IMPERIAL WAR

Why did colonial Americans support Britain's wars against France?

France and Britain waged almost constant war in North America. By 1750, Britain's American colonists believed the French in Canada planned to encircle their settlements, cutting them off from the rich lands of the Ohio Valley. The Seven Years' War drove the French from Canada, a victory that generated unprecedented enthusiasm for the British Empire in the colonies. *(p. 101)*

KEY TERM QUESTIONS

1. Why did tensions arise in the backcountry? (p. 85)

2. How did the formation of a "middle ground" help Native Americans survive in the backcountry? (p. 88)

3. What were the basic beliefs of Enlightenment thinkers? (p. 91)

4. How did the consumer revolution affect the British economy? (p. 94)

5. How did the Great Awakening transform the religious culture of colonial America? (p. 96)

6. Why were many ministers suspicious of itinerant preachers? (p. 97)

7. Why did Benjamin Franklin's Albany Plan fail? (p. 103)

8. Why did it take so long for Britain to defeat the French in the Seven Years' War? (p. 104)

9. How did the Peace of Paris of 1763 transform North American politics? (p. 105)

MyHistoryLab Connections

Visit **www.myhistorylab.com** for a customized Study Plan to build your knowledge of *Experience of Empire.*

Question for Analysis

1. How does Peter Kalm's description of Philadelphia give us a feel for what life was like in the 18th Century?

   Read the **Document** Peter Kalm, A Swedish Visitor to Philadelphia, 1748 p. 87

2. According to Naranjo, what transpired on the first day of the uprising?

   Read the **Document** Testimony of Pedro Naranjo to Spanish Authorities p. 89

3. What was Franklin's assessment of the contributions the colonies made to the British Empire?

   Read the **Document** Franklin, Observations Concerning the Increase of mankind p. 93

4. Why did audiences respond so favorably to Jonathan Edwards' preaching?

   Read the **Document** Jonathan Edwards, Sinners in the Hands of an Angry God p. 96

5. What were the effects of The Seven Years War?

   View the **Map** The Seven Years War p. 104

Other Resources from this Chapter

Read the **Document** William Byrd, Diary— An American Gentlemen

View the **Image** William Penn Making a Treaty with the Indians, 1682

View the **Map** Spanish America to 1610

View the **Image** The Alamo

Listen to the **Audio File** The Connecticut Peddler

View the **Image** Richard Allen Portrait

View the **Image** European Claims in America, c. 1750

Read the **Document** Benjamin Franklin on George Whitefield (1771)

5 THE AMERICAN REVOLUTION

From Elite Protest to Popular Revolt, 1763–1783

Contents and Spotlight Questions

((•─┤**Listen** to the **Chapter Audio** for Chapter 5 on **myhistorylab.com**

MOMENT OF DECISION: COMMITMENT AND SACRIFICE

Even as the British army poured into Boston in 1774, demanding obedience to king and Parliament, few Americans welcomed the possibility of revolutionary violence. For many colonial families, it would have been easier, certainly safer, to accede to imperial demands for taxes enacted without their representation. But they did not do so.

For the Patten family, the time of reckoning arrived in spring 1775. Matthew Patten had been born in Ulster, a Protestant Irishman, and with Scots-Irish friends and relatives, he migrated to New Hampshire, where they founded a settlement of 56 families known as Bedford. Matthew farmed the unpromising, rocky soil that he, his wife Elizabeth, and their children called home. In time, distant decisions about taxes and representation shattered the peace of Bedford. The Pattens found themselves drawn into a war not

The Patten family farmstead in Bedford, New Hampshire The Patten Family Farmstead in Bedford, New Hampshire. Scots-Irish immigrants and others on the colonial frontier in the 1770s, worked to keep their farms running and struggled to live normal lives even as Revolution engulfed the country.

of their own making but which, nevertheless, compelled them to sacrifice the security of everyday life for liberty.

On April 20, 1775, accounts of Lexington and Concord reached Bedford. Matthew noted in his diary, "I Received the Melancholy news in the morning that General Gage's troops had fired on our Countrymen at Concord yesterday." His son John marched with neighbors to support the Massachusetts soldiers. The departure was tense. "Our Girls sit up all night baking bread and fitting things for him," Matthew wrote.

The demands of war had only just begun. In late 1775 John volunteered for an American march on British Canada. On the long trek over impossible terrain, the boy died. The father recorded his emotions in the diary. John "was shot through his left arm at Bunker Hill fight and now was lead after suffering much fategue to the place where he now lyes in defending the just Rights of America to whose end he came in the prime of life by means of that wicked Tyrannical Brute (nea worse than Brute) of Great Britain [George III]. He was Twenty four years and 31 days old."

The initial stimulus for rebellion came from the gentry, from the rich and well-born, who resented Parliament's efforts to curtail their rights within the British empire. But as these influential planters, wealthy merchants, and prominent clergymen discovered, the revolutionary movement generated a momentum that they could not control. As relations with Britain deteriorated, particularly after 1765, the traditional leaders of colonial society encouraged ordinary folk to join the protest—as rioters, petitioners, and, finally, soldiers. Newspapers, sermons, and pamphlets helped transform what had begun as a squabble among the gentry into a mass movement. Once the people became involved in shaping the nation's destiny, they could never again be excluded.

Had it not been for ordinary militiamen like John Patten, the British would have easily crushed American resistance. Although some accounts of the Revolution downplay the military side of the story, leaving the impression that a few famous "Founding Fathers" effortlessly carried the nation to independence, a more persuasive explanation must recognize the centrality of armed violence in achieving nationhood.

The American Revolution involved a massive military commitment. If common American soldiers had not been willing to stand up to seasoned British troops, to face the terror of the bayonet charge, independence would have remained a dream of intellectuals. Proportionate to the population, a greater percentage of Americans died in military service during the Revolution than in any war in American history, except the Civil War.

The concept of liberty so magnificently expressed in revolutionary pamphlets was not, therefore, simply an abstraction, an exclusive concern of political theorists such as Thomas Jefferson and John Adams. It also motivated ordinary folk—the Patten family, for example—to fight and risk death. Those who survived the ordeal were never the same, for the experience of fighting, of assuming responsibility in battle and perhaps even of killing British officers, gave new meaning to the idea of social equality.

STRUCTURE OF COLONIAL SOCIETY

Colonists who were alive during the 1760s did not anticipate national independence. For many Americans, it was an era of optimism. The population grew. In 1776, approximately 2.5 million people, black and white, were living in Britain's 13 mainland colonies. The ethnic and racial diversity of these men and women amazed European visitors.

The American population on the eve of independence was also extraordinarily young, an important fact in understanding the development of political resistance. Nearly 60 percent of the American people were under age 21. At any given time, most people in this society were small children. Many of the young men who fought the British during the Revolution either had not been born or had been infants during the Stamp Act crisis. Any explanation for the coming of independence, therefore, must include the political mobilization of so many young people.

Americans also experienced prosperity after the Seven Years' War ended in 1763. To be sure, some ports went through a difficult period as colonists who had been employed during the war were thrown out of work. Sailors and ship workers were especially vulnerable to layoffs of this sort. In general, however, white Americans did very well. Their standard of living was not substantially lower than that of the English. A typical white family of five—a father, mother, and three dependent children—not only could have afforded decent food, clothing, and housing but would have had money left over with which to buy consumer goods. Even the poorest colonists seem to have benefited from a rising standard of living. Although they may not have done as well as their wealthier neighbors, they too wanted to preserve gains they had made.

Why did Americans resist parliamentary taxation?

Breakdown of Political Trust

Ultimate responsibility for preserving the empire fell to King George III (r. 1760–1820). When he became king, he was only age 22 but was determined to play an aggressive role in government. This dismayed England's political leaders. For decades, a powerful though loosely associated group of aristocrats who called themselves Whigs had set policy and controlled patronage. King George II (r. 1727–1760) had accepted their dominance. So long as the Whigs in Parliament did not meddle with his beloved army, he had let them run the nation.

George III destroyed this time-tested arrangement. He selected as his chief minister the Earl of Bute, a Scot whose chief qualification for office was his friendship with the young king. The Whigs who dominated Parliament were outraged. Bute had no ties with the members of the House of Commons; he owed them no favors.

By 1763 Bute, despairing of public life, left office. His departure, however, neither restored the Whigs to preeminence nor dampened the king's enthusiasm for domestic politics. Everyone agreed George could select whomever he desired for cabinet posts, but until 1770, no one seemed able to please him for long. Ministers came and went, often for no other reason than George's personal distaste. Because of this chronic instability, bureaucrats who directed routine colonial affairs did not know what was expected of them. In the absence of clear long-range policy, ministers made narrow decisions or did nothing. With such turbulence around him, the king showed little interest in the American colonies.

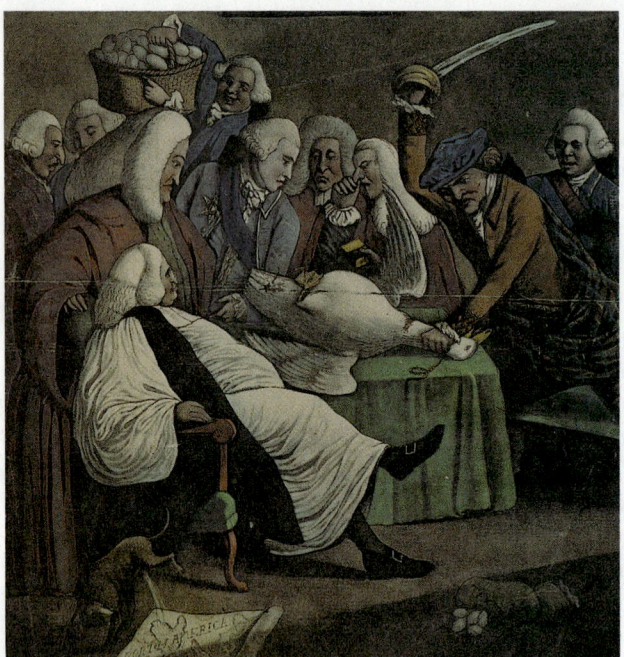

Political Cartoons Cartoons became a popular way of criticizing government during this period. Here, King George III watches as the kilted Lord Bute slaughters the goose America. A cabinet member holds a basket of golden eggs at rear. At front left, a dog urinates on a map of British America.

The king, however, does not bear the sole responsibility for Britain's loss of empire. The members of Parliament who actually drafted the statutes that gradually drove a wedge between the colonies and Britain must share the blame. They failed to resolve the explosive constitutional issues of the day.

The central element in the Anglo-American debate was a concept known as parliamentary sovereignty, the doctrine that Parliament enjoyed absolute legislative authority throughout Britain and its colonies. According to this theory, parliamentary decisions superceded any legislation passed by colonial assemblies. The British ruling classes had an historic view of the role of Parliament that most colonists never shared. They insisted that Parliament was the dominant element within the constitution. It protected rights and property from an arbitrary monarch. Under the Stuart monarchs, especially Charles I (r. 1625–1649), the authority of Parliament had been challenged. But the crown did not formally recognize Parliament's supreme authority in matters such as taxation until the Glorious Revolution of 1688. Almost no one, including George III, would have dissented from a speech made in 1766 before the House of Commons, in which a representative declared, "The parliament hath, and must have, from the nature and essence of the constitution, has had, and ever will have a sovereign supreme power and jurisdiction over every part of the dominions of the state, *to make laws in all cases whatsoever.*"

Such a constitutional position did not leave much room for compromise. Most members of Parliament took a hard line on this issue. The notion of dividing or sharing sovereignty made no sense to the British ruling class. As Thomas Hutchinson, royal governor of Massachusetts, explained, no middle ground existed "between the supreme authority of Parliament and the total dependence of the colonies: it is impossible there should be two independent legislatures in one and the same state."

Quick Check

✔ Why were members of the British government adamant in their defense of parliamentary sovereignty?

No Taxation Without Representation: The American Perspective

Americans did not see it in their "interest" to maintain the "supremacy of Parliament." The crisis in imperial relations forced the colonists first to define and then defend principles rooted in their own political culture. For more than a century, their ideas about the colonies' role within the British empire had remained a vague, untested bundle of assumptions about personal liberties, property rights, and representative institutions.

By 1763, however, certain fundamental American beliefs had become clear. From Massachusetts to Georgia, colonists defended the powers of the provincial assemblies. They drew on a rich legislative history of their own. In the eighteenth century, the American assemblies had expanded their authority over taxation and expenditure. Since no one in Britain bothered to clip their legislative wings, these provincial bodies assumed a major role in policymaking and routine administration. In other words, by midcentury the assemblies looked like American copies of Parliament. It seemed unreasonable, therefore, for the British suddenly to insist on the supremacy of Parliament. As the legislators of Massachusetts observed in 1770, "This house has the same inherent rights in this province as the house of commons in Great Britain."

The constitutional debate turned ultimately on the meaning of representation itself. In 1764, a British official informed the colonists that even though they had not elected members to Parliament—indeed, even though they had had no direct contact with the current members—they were nevertheless "virtually" represented by that august body. The members of Parliament, he declared, represented the political interests of everyone who lived in the British empire. It did not really matter whether everyone had cast a vote.

The colonists ridiculed this notion of virtual representation. The only representatives the Americans recognized as legitimate were those actually chosen by the people for whom they spoke. On this crucial point they would not compromise. As John Adams insisted, a representative assembly should mirror its constituents: "It should think, feel, reason, and act like them." Since the members of Parliament could not possibly "think" like Americans, it followed logically they could not represent them. And if they were not genuine representatives, the members of Parliament—pretensions to sovereignty notwithstanding—had no business taxing the American people. Thus, in 1764 the Connecticut Assembly declared in bold letters, "NO LAW CAN BE MADE OR ABROGATED WITHOUT THE CONSENT OF THE PEOPLE BY THEIR REPRESENTATIVES."

Quick Check

✓ How did Parliament and the American colonists differ in their ideas about representative government?

Justifying Resistance

The political ideology that had the greatest popular appeal among the colonists contained a strong moral component, one that British rulers and American **Loyalists** (people who sided with the king and Parliament during the Revolution) never fully understood. The precise origins of this highly religious perspective on civil government are difficult to locate, but the Great Awakening created a general awareness of an obligation to conduct public and private affairs according to Scripture (see Chapter 4).

Americans expressed their political beliefs in language borrowed from English writers. The person most frequently cited was John Locke, the influential seventeenth-century philosopher. His *Two Treatises of Government* (1690) seemed, to colonial readers at least, a brilliant description of what was in fact American political practice. Locke claimed that all people possessed natural and inalienable rights. To preserve these God-given rights—life, liberty, and property, for example—free men (the status of women in Locke's work was less clear) formed contracts. These agreements were the foundation of human society and civil government. They required the consent of the people who were actually governed. There could be no coercion. Locke justified rebellion against arbitrary government that was by its very nature unreasonable. Americans delighted in Locke's

Read the **Document**
James Otis, An American Colonist Opposes New Taxes on **myhistorylab.com**

ability to unite traditional Protestant religious values with a spirited defense of popular government. They seldom missed a chance to quote "the Great Mr. Locke."

Revolutionary Americans also endorsed ideas associated with the so-called Commonwealthmen. These radical eighteenth-century English writers helped persuade the colonists that *power* was dangerous, a force that would destroy liberty unless it was countered by *virtue*. Persons who shared this charged moral outlook regarded bad policy as not simply the result of human error. Rather, it indicated sin and corruption.

Insistence on public virtue—sacrifice of self-interest to the public good—became the dominant theme of revolutionary political writing. American pamphleteers seldom took a dispassionate, legalistic approach to their analysis of power and liberty. Instead, they exposed plots hatched by corrupt courtiers, such as the Earl of Bute. None of them—or their readers—doubted that Americans were more virtuous than the British.

During the 1760s, however, popular writers were not certain how long the colonists could hold out against arbitrary taxation, standing armies, and Anglican bishops—in other words, against a host of external threats designed to crush American liberty. In 1774, for example, the people of Farmington, Connecticut, declared that "the present ministry, being instigated by the devil and led by their wicked and corrupt hearts, have a design to take away our liberties and properties, and to enslave us forever." These Connecticut farmers described Britain's leaders as "pimps and parasites." This highly emotional, conspiratorial rhetoric sometimes shocks modern readers who assume that America's revolutionary leaders were products of the Enlightenment, persons who relied solely on reason to solve social and political problems. Whatever the origins of their ideas may have been, the colonial pamphleteers successfully roused ordinary men and women to resist Britain with force of arms.

Colonial newspapers spread these ideas through a large dispersed population. Most adult white males—especially those in the northern colonies—were literate, and the number of journals published in this country increased dramatically during the revolutionary period. For the first time in American history, persons throughout the colonies could follow events in distant American cities. The availability of newspapers meant that the details of Bostonians' confrontations with British authorities were known throughout the colonies. These shared political experiences drew Americans together, allowing—in the words of John Adams—"Thirteen clocks … to strike together—a perfection of mechanism which no artist had ever before effected."

Quick Check

✓ How did American colonists justify their resistance to parliamentary sovereignty?

ERODING THE BONDS OF EMPIRE

What events eroded the bonds of empire during the 1760s?

The Seven Years' War saddled Britain with a national debt so huge that more than half the annual budget went to pay the interest on it. Almost everyone in government assumed that with the cessation of hostilities, most of the troops in America would be disbanded, thus saving money. George III, however, insisted on keeping the largest peacetime army in British history on active duty, supposedly to protect Indians from predatory American frontiersmen.

Colonists doubted the value of this expensive army. Britain did not leave enough troops in America to ensure peace on the frontier. The army's weakness was dramatically demonstrated in spring 1763.

The native peoples of the backcountry—the Seneca, Ottawa, Miami, Creek, and Cherokee—had begun discussing how to turn back the tide of white settlement. The powerful spiritual leader Neolin, known as the Delaware Prophet and claiming visions from the "Master of Life," urged the Indians to restore their cultures to the "original state that they were in before the white people found out their country." If moral regeneration required violence, so be it. Neolin converted Pontiac, an Ottawa warrior, to the cause. Pontiac, in turn, coordinated an uprising among the western Indians who had been French allies and hated the British—even those sent to protect them from land-grabbing colonists. This formidable Native American resistance was known as Pontiac's Rebellion. In May, Pontiac attacked Detroit; other Indians harassed the Pennsylvania and Virginia frontiers. In 1764, after his followers began deserting, Pontiac sued for peace. During even this brief outbreak, the British army could not defend exposed colonial settlements, and thousands were killed.

For the Native Americans who inhabited the Ohio Valley, this was a period of almost unmitigated disaster. In fact, more than any other group, the Indians suffered from imperial reorganization. The French defeat made it impossible for native peoples to play off one imperial power against European rivals in the middle ground (see Chapter 4). The British now regarded their former Indian allies as little more than a nuisance. Diplomatic gifts stopped; humiliating restrictions were placed on trade.

Even worse, Pontiac's rising unloosed vicious racism along the colonial frontier. American colonists often used any excuse to attack local Indians, peaceful or not. Late in 1763, vigilantes known as the Paxton Boys murdered Christian Indians, women and children, near Lancaster, Pennsylvania. White neighbors treated the killers as heroes, and the atrocity ended only after the Paxton Boys threatened to march on Philadelphia in search of administrators who dared to criticize such cold-blooded crimes. One of the administrators, Benjamin Franklin, observed sadly, "It grieves me to hear that our Frontier People are yet greater Barbarians than the Indians, and continue to murder them in time of Peace."

Whatever happened to the Indians, the colonists intended to settle the fertile region west of the Appalachian Mountains. After the British government issued the Proclamation of 1763, which prohibited governors from granting land beyond the headwaters of rivers flowing into the Atlantic, disappointed Americans viewed the army as an obstruction to legitimate economic development, an expensive domestic police force.

Paying Off the National Debt

The task of reducing England's debt fell to George Grenville, the rigid, unimaginative chancellor of the exchequer (finance minister) who replaced Bute in 1763 as the king's first minister. After reviewing Britain's finances, Grenville concluded that the colonists would have to contribute to the maintenance of the army. The first bill he steered through Parliament was the Revenue Act of 1764, known as the Sugar Act.

This legislation placed a new burden on the Navigation Acts that had governed the flow of colonial commerce for almost a century (see Chapter 3). Those acts had forced Americans to trade almost exclusively with Britain. They were not, however, primarily intended to raise money for the British government. The Sugar Act—and the acts that followed—redefined the relationship between America and Britain. Parliament now expected the colonies to generate revenue. The preamble of the Sugar Act proclaimed explicitly: "It is just and necessary that a revenue be raised … in America for defraying the expenses of defending, protecting, and securing the same."

The Americans immediately protested Grenville's scheme as unconstitutional. The Rhode Island Assembly said that the Sugar Act taxed the colonists in a manner "inconsistent with their rights and privileges as British subjects." James Otis, a fiery orator from Massachusetts, exclaimed the legislation deprived Americans of "the right of assessing their own taxes."

The act generated no violence, however. Ordinary men and women were only marginally involved in drafting formal petitions. The protest was still confined to the colonial assemblies, merchants, and the well-to-do who had personal interests in commerce.

Quick Check

✓ Why did Parliament think that the colonies should contribute to paying off Britain's national debt?

The Protest Spreads

The **Stamp Act of 1765**, which placed a tax on newspapers and printed matter produced in the colonies, transformed a debate among gentlemen into a mass political movement. Colonial agents had presented Grenville with alternative schemes for raising money in America, but he rejected them. The majority of the House of Commons assumed that Parliament possessed the right to tax the colonists. They responded with enthusiasm when the chancellor announced a plan to squeeze £60,000 annually out of the Americans by requiring them to purchase special seals or stamps to validate legal documents. The Stamp Act was scheduled to go into effect on November 1, 1765, and in anticipation of brisk sales, Grenville appointed stamp distributors for every colony.

Some members of Parliament warned that the act would raise a storm of protest in the colonies. Colonel Isaac Barré, a veteran of the Seven Years' War, warned his colleagues that the Americans would not surrender their rights without a fight. But Barré's appeal fell on deaf ears. Throughout the colonies, extra-legal, semi-secret groups known as the "Sons of Liberty" put political and economic pressure on neighbors who wanted to remain neutral in the contest with Britain.

Word of the Stamp Act reached America in May. It was soon clear that Barré had gauged the colonists' response correctly. The most dramatic reaction occurred in Virginia's House of Burgesses. Patrick Henry, young and eloquent, whose fervor contemporaries compared to evangelical preachers, introduced five resolutions protesting the Stamp Act on the floor of the assembly. He timed his move carefully. It was late in the session; many of the more conservative burgesses had departed for their plantations. Even then, Henry's resolves declaring that Virginians had the right to tax themselves as they alone saw fit passed by narrow margins. The fifth resolution, stricken almost immediately from the legislative records, announced that any attempt to collect stamp revenues in America was "illegal, unconstitutional, and unjust, and has a manifest tendency to destroy British as well as American liberty."

Henry's five resolutions, known popularly as the Virginia Resolves, might have remained a local matter had if not for the colonial press. Newspapers throughout America printed Henry's resolutions, but, perhaps because editors did not really know what had happened in Williamsburg, they reported that all five resolutions had received the burgesses' full support. Several journals even carried two resolves that Henry had not dared to introduce. A result of this misunderstanding was that the Virginians appeared to have taken a radical position on the supremacy of Parliament, one that other Americans now trumpeted before their own assemblies. No wonder Francis Bernard, royal governor of Massachusetts, called the Virginia Resolves an "alarm bell."

Not to be outdone, Massachusetts called a general meeting to protest Grenville's policy. Nine colonies sent representatives to the **Stamp Act Congress** in New York City in October 1765. It was the first intercolonial gathering since the abortive Albany Congress of 1754. The delegates drafted petitions to the king and Parliament that restated the colonists' belief "that no taxes should be imposed on them, but with their own consent, given personally, or by their representatives." The tone of the meeting was restrained, even conciliatory. The congress studiously avoided any mention of independence or disloyalty to the crown.

Resistance to the Stamp Act soon spread to the streets. By taxing deeds, marriage licenses, and playing cards, the act touched the lives of ordinary women and men. Anonymous artisans and seamen, angered by Parliament's insensitivity and fearful that the statute would increase unemployment and poverty, organized mass protests in the major ports.

By November 1, 1765, stamp distributors in almost every American port had publicly resigned. Without distributors, the hated revenue stamps could not be sold. The courts soon reopened; most newspapers were published. Daily life in the colonies was undisturbed, with one exception: The Sons of Liberty persuaded—some said coerced—colonial merchants to boycott British goods until Parliament repealed the Stamp Act. The merchants showed little enthusiasm for such tactics, but the threat of tar and feathers stimulated cooperation.

The boycott was a masterful political innovation. Never before had a resistance movement organized itself so centrally around ordinary consumers' market decisions. The colonists depended on British imports—cloth, metal goods, and ceramics. Each year they imported more consumer goods than they could afford. In this charged atmosphere, one in which ordinary people talked constantly of conspiracy and corruption, it is not surprising that Americans of different classes and backgrounds advocated a radical change in buying habits. Private acts suddenly became part of the public sphere. Personal excess threatened to contaminate the political community. This logic explains the power of an appeal made in a Boston newspaper: "Save your money and you can save your country." In 1765 the boycott had little effect on the sale of British goods in America. By 1773, however, it had seriously reduced the flow of British commerce, especially the trade for tea. (See Map 5.1.)

The boycotts mobilized colonial women. They could not vote or hold civil office, but such legal discrimination did not mean that women were not part of the broader political culture. Since wives and mothers spent their days involved with household chores, they assumed special responsibility to reform consumption, root out luxury, and promote frugality. Indeed, in this realm they possessed real power; they monitored the ideological commitment of the entire family. Throughout the colonies, women altered styles of dress, made homespun cloth, and shunned imported items on which Parliament had placed a tax.

Read the **Document**
Benjamin Franklin, Testimony Against the Stamp Act (1766) on **myhistorylab.com**

View the **Image**
1765 Stamp Act Protest on **myhistorylab.com**

View the **Image**
Women Signing an Anti-tea Agreement on **myhistorylab.com**

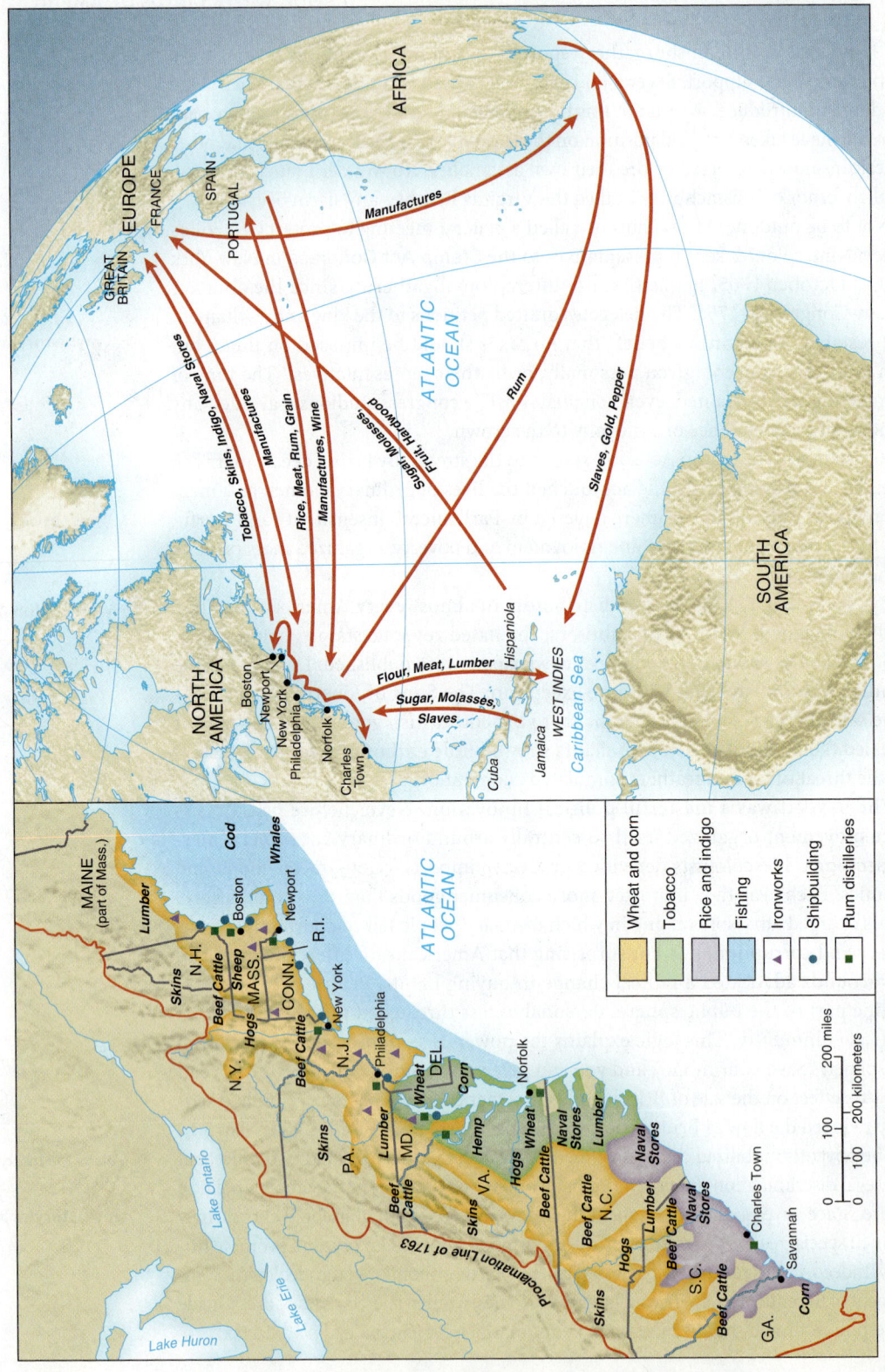

Map 5.1 Colonial Products and Trade Although the American colonists produced many agricultural staples that were valuable to Britain, they were dependent on British manufactures such as cloth, metal goods, and ceramics.

Labels on map (upper globe):

AFRICA
EUROPE
SPAIN
PORTUGAL
FRANCE
GREAT BRITAIN
NORTH AMERICA
SOUTH AMERICA
ATLANTIC OCEAN
Caribbean Sea
WEST INDIES
Hispaniola
Cuba
Jamaica

Boston
Newport
New York
Philadelphia
Norfolk
Charles Town

Manufactures
Tobacco, Skins, Indigo, Naval Stores
Manufactures
Rice, Meat, Rum, Grain
Manufactures, Wine
Fruit, Hardwood
Sugar, Molasses,
Rum
Slaves, Gold, Pepper
Flour, Meat, Lumber
Sugar, Molasses, Slaves

Labels on map (lower regional):

Lake Huron
Lake Erie
Lake Ontario
MAINE (part of Mass.)
N.H.
MASS.
CONN.
R.I.
Newport
Boston
New York
N.Y.
N.J.
PA.
Philadelphia
MD.
DEL.
VA.
Norfolk
N.C.
S.C.
GA.
Charles Town
Savannah
ATLANTIC OCEAN
Proclamation Line of 1763

Cod
Whales
Lumber
Skins
Beef Cattle
Sheep
Hogs
Beef Cattle
Skins
Lumber
Beef Cattle
Wheat
Corn
Hemp
Hogs
Wheat
Beef Cattle
Naval Stores
Lumber
Skins
Hogs
Beef Cattle
Lumber
Naval Stores
Beef Cattle
Naval Stores
Corn
Beef Cattle

Legend:
Wheat and corn
Tobacco
Rice and indigo
Fishing
Ironworks
Shipbuilding
Rum distilleries

0   100   200 miles
0   100   200 kilometers

120

On March 18, 1766, the House of Commons voted 275 to 167 to rescind the Stamp Act. Lest this retreat be interpreted as weakness, Parliament simultaneously passed the Declaratory Act, a shrill defense of its supremacy over the Americans "in all cases whatsoever." The colonists' insistence on no taxation without representation failed to impress British rulers. British merchants, supposedly America's allies, claimed sole responsibility for the Stamp Act repeal. The colonists' behavior had only complicated the task, the merchants lectured. If the Americans knew what was good for them, they would keep quiet.

The Stamp Act crisis eroded the colonists' respect for imperial officeholders in America. Suddenly, these men—royal governors, customs collectors, soldiers—appeared alien, as if their interests were not those of the people over whom they exercised authority. One person who had been forced to resign as stamp distributor for South Carolina noted: "The Stamp Act had introduc'd so much Party Rage, Faction, and Debate that the ancient Harmony, Generosity, and Urbanity for which these People were celebrated is destroyed, and at an End."

Quick Check

✓ Was the repeal of the Stamp Act a victory for the American cause?

Fueling the Crisis

Charles Townshend, the new chancellor of the exchequer, claimed he could solve the American controversy. In January 1767, he surprised everyone by blithely announcing that he knew a way to obtain revenue from the Americans. The members of the House of Commons were so pleased with the news that they voted to lower taxes in Britain, an action that threatened fiscal chaos.

A budgetary crisis forced Townshend to make good on his boast. His scheme was a grab bag of duties on American imports of paper, glass, paint, lead, and tea, collectively known as the Townshend Revenue Acts (June–July 1767). He hoped to generate sufficient funds to pay the salaries of royal governors and other imperial officers, freeing them from dependence on the colonial assemblies.

The chancellor recognized that without tough enforcement his duties would not produce the promised revenues. Therefore, he created an American Board of Customs Commissioners, a body based in Boston, supported by reorganized vice-admiralty courts in Boston, Philadelphia, and Charles Town. For good measure, Townshend persuaded Parliament to order the governor of New York to veto all bills that colony's assembly passed until it supplied resident British troops in

Daughters of Liberty   The boycott movement drew many colonial women into popular politics. In this 1774 woodcut, a Daughter of Liberty stands ready to resist British oppression.

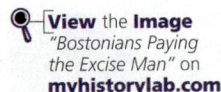
Listen to the
Audio File
*The Liberty
Song* on
myhistorylab.com

Quick Check

✓ Why did Charles
Townshend so
badly misread the
American situation?

accordance with the Quartering Act (May 1765). This law required the colonies to house soldiers in barracks, taverns, and vacant buildings and provide the army with firewood, candles, and beer, among other items. Many Americans regarded this as more taxation without representation, and in New York, at least, colonists refused to pay.

Americans showed no more willingness to pay Townshend's duties than they had to buy Grenville's stamps. The Sons of Liberty organized boycotts of British goods. Men and women took oaths before neighbors promising not to purchase certain goods until Parliament repealed their unconstitutional taxation.

Surge of Force

In October 1768, British rulers made another mistake, one that raised tensions almost to the pitch they had reached during the Stamp Act riots. The issue at the heart of the trouble was the army. To save money and intimidate troublemakers, the ministry transferred 4,000 regular troops (redcoats) from Nova Scotia and Ireland to Boston. To make relations with the Bostonians worse, redcoats—men who were ill treated and underpaid—competed in their spare time for jobs with dockworkers and artisans. Work was already in short supply in Boston, and the streets crackled with tension.

View the **Image**
*"Bostonians Paying
the Excise Man"* on
myhistorylab.com

When colonists questioned why the army had been sent to a peaceful city, pamphleteers responded that it was there to further a conspiracy originally conceived by Bute to oppress Americans, take away their liberties, and collect illegal revenues. Such rhetoric may sound excessive, but to Americans who had absorbed the political theories of the Commonwealthmen, a pattern of tyranny seemed obvious.

Colonists had no difficulty interpreting the violence that erupted in Boston on March 5, 1770. In the gathering dusk of that afternoon, young boys and street toughs threw rocks and snowballs at a small, isolated patrol of soldiers outside the offices of the hated customs commissioners in King Street. The details are obscure, but it appears that as the mob became more threatening, the soldiers panicked and fired, killing five Americans.

Pamphleteers promptly labeled the incident the Boston Massacre. The victims were seen as martyrs and were memorialized in extravagant terms. In one eulogy, Joseph Warren addressed the dead men's widows and children, dramatically re-creating the gruesome scene in King Street: "Behold thy murdered husband gasping on the ground … take heed, ye orphan babes, lest, whilst your streaming eyes are fixed upon the ghastly corpse, your feet slide on the stones bespattered with your father's brains." To

The Boston Massacre This etching by Paul Revere shows British redcoats firing on ordinary citizens, an event know as the Boston Massacre. In subsequent editions, the blood spurting from the dying Americans became more conspicuous.

propagandists like Warren, it mattered little that the five civilians had been bachelors! Paul Revere's blood-splattered engraving of the massacre became an instant best-seller. Confronted with such intense reactions and the possibility of massive armed resistance, crown officials removed the army to an island in Boston Harbor.

At this critical moment, the king's new first minister restored a measure of tranquility. Lord North, congenial, well-meaning, but not very talented, became chancellor of the exchequer after Townshend's death in 1767. North was appointed the first minister in 1770, and for the next 12 years—indeed, throughout most of the American crisis—he retained his office. The secret to his success seems to have been an ability to get along with George III and build a majority in Parliament.

One of North's first recommendations to Parliament was to repeal the Townshend duties. These ill-conceived duties had unnecessarily angered the colonists and hurt English manufacturers. By taxing British exports such as glass and paint, Parliament had only encouraged the Americans to develop their own industries. Without much prodding, Parliament dropped all the Townshend duties—except for tea. The tax on tea was retained, not for revenue purposes, North insisted, but as a reminder that Britain's rulers still subscribed to the principles of the Declaratory Act. They would not compromise the supremacy of Parliament.

Samuel Adams (1722–1803) refused to accept the notion that the repeal of the Townshend duties had secured American liberty. During the early 1770s, while colonial leaders turned to other matters, Adams kept the cause alive with a drum-fire of publicity. He reminded Bostonians that the tax on tea remained in force. He organized public anniversaries commemorating the repeal of the Stamp Act and the Boston Massacre. Adams was a revolutionary, an ideologue burning with indignation at the real and alleged wrongs his countrymen suffered.

With each new attempt by Parliament to assert its supremacy over the colonists, more Bostonians listened to Adams. He observed ominously that the British intended to use the tea revenue to pay judicial salaries, thus freeing colonial judges from dependence on the assemblies. When in November 1772 Adams suggested forming a committee of correspondence to communicate grievances to villagers throughout Massachusetts, he received broad support. Americans in other colonies copied his idea. It was a brilliant stroke. Adams developed a structure of political cooperation independent of royal government.

Read the
Document
Boston Gazette
*Description of the
Boston Massacre* on
myhistorylab.com

Quick Check
✓ Why was it a mistake for the British to station regular troops in Boston?

The Final Provocation: The Boston Tea Party

In May 1773, Parliament passed the Tea Act, legislation the Americans might have welcomed. After all, it lowered the price for their favorite beverage. Parliament wanted to save one of Britain's largest businesses, the East India Company, from bankruptcy. This commercial giant imported Asian tea into Britain, where it was resold to wholesalers. The tea was also subject to heavy duties. The company tried to pass these charges on to consumers, but American tea drinkers preferred cheaper leaves smuggled in from Holland.

The Tea Act changed the rules. Parliament not only allowed the company to sell directly to American retailers, thus cutting out intermediaries, but also eliminated the duties paid in Britain. If all had gone according to plan, the agents of the East India Company in America would have undersold their competitors, including the Dutch smugglers, and the new profits would have saved the company.

But Parliament's logic was flawed. First, since the tax on tea, collected in American ports, remained in effect, this new act seemed a devious scheme to win popular support for Parliament's right to tax the colonists without representation. Second, the act threatened to undercut powerful colonial merchants who sold smuggled Dutch tea. The British government might have been well advised to devise another plan to rescue the ailing company. In Philadelphia and New York City, colonists turned back the tea ships before they could unload.

Read the
Document
*Hewes, "A Retrospect
on the Boston Tea
Party"* on
myhistorylab.com

In Boston, however, the issue was less easily resolved. Governor Hutchinson, a strong-willed man, would not let the vessels return to England. Patriots would not let them unload. So, crammed with tea, the ships sat in Boston Harbor waiting for the colonists to make up their minds. On the night of December 16, 1773, they did so. Men disguised as Mohawk Indians boarded the ships and pitched 340 chests of tea worth £10,000 over the side. John Adams sensed the event would have far-reaching significance. "This Destruction of the Tea," he scribbled in his diary, "is so bold, so daring, so firm, intrepid, and inflexible, and it must have so important consequences, and so lasting, that I can't but consider it as an epocha in history."

News of the **Boston Tea Party** stunned the North ministry. The Bostonians had treated parliamentary supremacy with contempt. British rulers saw no humor whatsoever in the destruction of private property by subjects of the crown dressed in costume. To quell such rebelliousness, Parliament passed the **Coercive Acts**. (In America, they were called the Intolerable Acts.) The legislation (1) closed the port of Boston until the city compensated the East India Company for the lost tea; (2) restructured the Massachusetts government by transforming the upper house of the legislature from an elective to an appointed body and restricting the number of town meetings to one a year; (3) allowed the royal governor to transfer British officials arrested for offenses committed in the line of duty to England, where there was little likelihood they would be convicted; and (4) authorized the army to quarter troops wherever they were needed, even if this required the compulsory requisition of uninhabited private buildings. George III enthusiastically supported this tough policy; he appointed General Thomas Gage as the colony's new royal governor. Gage apparently won the king's favor by announcing that in America, "Nothing can be done but by forcible means."

The sweeping denial of constitutional liberties confirmed the colonists' worst fears. To men like Samuel Adams, it seemed as if Britain intended to enslave the American people. Colonial moderates found their position shaken by the Coercive Acts' vindictiveness. Edmund Burke, one of America's last friends in Parliament, noted sadly in the Commons, that "this is the day, then, that you wish to go to war with all America, in order to conciliate that country to this."

If in 1774 Parliament thought it could isolate Boston from the rest of America, it was in for a rude surprise. Colonists in other parts of the continent recognized immediately that the principles at stake in Boston affected all Americans. Charity suddenly became a political act. People from Georgia to New Hampshire sent livestock, grain, and money to Boston. Ordinary colonists showed they were prepared to make a personal sacrifice for the cause of America.

The sticking point remained—as it had been in 1765—the sovereignty of Parliament. No one in Britain could think of a way around this constitutional impasse. In 1773, Benjamin Franklin had offered a suggestion: "The Parliament has no right to make any law whatever, binding on the colonies … the king, and not the king, lords, and commons collectively, is their sovereign." But so long as it seemed possible to coerce the Americans into obedience, Britain's rulers had little incentive to accept such a humiliating compromise.

Quick Check

✓ Did the coercive acts represent an overreaction by Parliament to the Boston Tea Party?

STEPS TOWARD INDEPENDENCE

During the summer of 1774, committees of correspondence analyzed the perilous situation in which the colonists found themselves. The committees endorsed a call for a Continental Congress, a gathering of 55 elected delegates from 12 colonies (Georgia sent none but agreed to support the action taken). This First Continental Congress convened in Philadelphia on September 5. It included some of America's most articulate, respected leaders; John Adams, Samuel Adams, Patrick Henry, Richard Henry Lee, Christopher Gadsden, and George Washington.

Differences of opinion soon surfaced. Delegates from the Middle Colonies—Joseph Galloway of Pennsylvania, for example—wanted to proceed with caution, but Samuel Adams and other more radical members pushed the moderates toward confrontation. Boston's master politician engineered congressional acceptance of the Suffolk Resolves, a statement drawn up in Suffolk County, Massachusetts, that encouraged forcible resistance to the Coercive Acts.

This decision established the tone of the meeting. Moderates introduced conciliatory measures, which received polite discussion but failed to win a majority vote. Just before returning to their homes (September 1774), the delegates created the "Association," an inter-colonial agreement to halt commerce with Britain until Parliament repealed the Intolerable Acts. This was a brilliant revolutionary decision. The Association authorized a vast network of local committees to enforce nonimportation, a policy by which colonial consumers and shopkeepers promised not to buy British goods. Violators were denounced, shamed, forced either to apologize publicly or to be shunned by their patriot neighbors. In many of the communities, the committees were the government, distinguishing, in the words of James Madison, "Friends from Foes." George III sneered at these activities: "I am not sorry that the line of conduct seems now chalked out … the New England Governments are in a state of Rebellion, blows must decide whether they are to be subject to this country or independent."

What events in 1775 and 1776 led to the colonists' decision to declare independence?

Shots Heard Around the World

The king was correct. Before Congress reconvened, "blows" fell at Lexington and Concord, two small villages in eastern Massachusetts. On the evening of April 18, 1775, General Gage dispatched troops from Boston to seize rebel supplies.

📖 **Read** the
Document
*Joseph Warren,
'Account of the Battle
of Lexington' on*
myhistorylab.com

Paul Revere, a renowned silversmith and patriot, warned the colonists that the redcoats were coming. The Lexington militia, a collection of ill-trained farmers, boys, and old men, decided to stand on the village green on the following morning, April 19, as the British soldiers passed on the road to Concord. No one planned to fight, but in a moment of confusion, someone fired; the redcoats discharged a volley, and eight Americans lay dead.

Word of the incident spread rapidly. By the time the British force reached its destination, the countryside swarmed with "minutemen," special companies of Massachusetts militia prepared to respond instantly to military emergencies. The redcoats found nothing significant in Concord and left. Their long march back to Boston became a rout. Lord Percy, a British officer who brought up reinforcements, remarked more in surprise than bitterness that "whoever looks upon them [the American soldiers] as an irregular mob, will find himself much mistaken." On June 17, colonial militiamen again held their own against seasoned troops at the Battle of Bunker Hill near Boston. The British finally took the hill, but after this costly "victory" in which he suffered 40 percent casualties, Gage complained that the Americans had displayed "a conduct and spirit against us, they never showed against the French."

Quick Check

✓ Why did the British general Thomas Gage underestimate the Americans' military resolve?

BEGINNING "THE WORLD OVER AGAIN"

Members of the Second Continental Congress gathered in Philadelphia in May 1775. They faced an awesome responsibility. British government in the mainland colonies had almost ceased to function, and with Americans fighting redcoats, the country desperately needed strong central leadership. Slowly, often reluctantly, Congress took control of the war. The delegates formed a Continental Army and appointed George Washington its commander, in part because he seemed to have military experience than anyone else available and in part because he looked like he should be commander in chief. The delegates were also eager to select someone who was not from Massachusetts, a colony that seemed already to possess too much power in national councils. Congress purchased military supplies and, to pay for them, issued paper money. But while Congress was assuming the powers of a sovereign government, the congressmen refused to declare independence. They debated and fretted, listened to the moderates who played on the colonists' loyalty to Britain, and then did nothing.

Convinced that force could make up for earlier failures of policy, the British government found a way to transform colonial moderates into angry rebels. In December 1775, Parliament passed the Prohibitory Act, declaring war on American commerce. Until the colonists begged for pardon, they could not trade with the rest of the world. The British navy blockaded their ports and seized American ships on the high seas. (See Table 5.1.) Lord North also hired German mercenaries to help put down the rebellion. And in America, Virginia's royal governor Lord Dunmore further undermined the possibility of reconciliation by urging the colony's slaves to take up arms against their masters. Few did so, but the effort to stir up black rebellion infuriated the Virginia gentry.

Thomas Paine (1737–1809) pushed the colonists closer to forming an independent republic. In England, Paine had failed at various jobs, but while still in

TABLE 5.1   Chronicle of Colonial-British Tension

Legislation	Date	Provisions	Colonial Reaction
Sugar Act	April 5, 1764	Revised duties on sugar, coffee, tea, wine, other imports; expanded jurisdiction of vice-admiralty courts	Several assemblies protest taxation for revenue
Stamp Act	March 22, 1765; repealed March 18, 1766	Printed documents (deeds, newspapers, marriage licenses, etc.) issued only on special stamped paper purchased from stamp distributors	Riots in cities; collectors forced to resign; Stamp Act Congress (October 1765)
Quartering Act	May 1765	Colonists must supply British troops with housing, other items (candles, firewood, etc.)	Assemblies protest; New York Assembly punished for failure to comply, 1767
Declaratory Act	March 18, 1766	Parliament declares its sovereignty over the colonies "in all cases whatsoever"	Ignored in celebration over repeal of the Stamp Act
Townshend Revenue Acts	June 26, 29, July 2, 1767; all repealed—except duty on tea, March 1770	New duties on glass, lead, paper, paints, tea; customs collections tightened in America	Nonimportation of British goods; assemblies protest; newspapers attack British policy
Tea Act	May 10, 1773	Parliament gives East India Company right to sell tea directly to Americans; some duties on tea reduced	Protests against favoritism shown to monopolistic company; tea destroyed in Boston (December 16, 1773)
Coercive Acts (Intolerable Acts)	March–June 1774	Closes port of Boston; restructures Massachusetts government; restricts town meetings; troops quartered in Boston; British officials accused of crimes sent to England or Canada for trial	Boycott of British goods; First Continental Congress (September 1774)
Prohibitory Act	December 22, 1775	Declares British intention to coerce Americans into submission; embargo on American goods; American ships seized	Drives Continental Congress closer to decision for independence

England, Paine had the good fortune to meet Benjamin Franklin, who presented him with letters of introduction to the leading patriots of Pennsylvania. At the urging of his new American friends, Paine produced *Common Sense* in 1776, an essay that became an instant best-seller. In only three months, it sold more than 120,000 copies. Paine confirmed in forceful prose what the colonists had not yet been able to state coherently.

Common Sense stripped kingship of historical and theological justification. For centuries, the English had maintained the legal fiction that the monarch could do no wrong. When the government oppressed the people, the royal counselors were blamed. The crown was above suspicion. To this, Paine cried nonsense. Monarchs

Read the **Document**
Thomas Paine, A Freelance Writer Urges his Readers to use Common Sense on **myhistorylab.com**

Congress Voting Independence Oil painting by Robert Edge Pine and Edward Savage, 1785. The committee Congress appointed to draft a declaration on independence included (center, standing) John Adams, Roger Sherman, Robert Livingston, Thomas Jefferson, and (center foreground, seated) Benjamin Franklin. The committee members are shown submitting Jefferson's draft to the speaker.

ruled by force. George III was a "royal brute," who by his arbitrary behavior had surrendered his claim to the colonists' obedience. All power came from the people. *Common Sense* was a powerful democratic manifesto.

Paine's greatest contribution to the revolutionary cause was persuading ordinary folk to sever their ties with Britain. It was not reasonable, he argued, to regard England as the mother country: "Europe, and not England, is the parent country of America. This new world hath been the asylum for the persecuted lovers of civil and religious liberty from *every part* of Europe." No doubt that message impressed Pennsylvania's German population. The time had come for the colonists to form an independent republic: "We have it in our power to begin the world over again … the birthday of a new world is at hand."

On July 2, 1776, after a long and tedious debate, Congress finally voted for independence: 12 states for, none against (New York abstained). Thomas Jefferson, a young Virginia planter who enjoyed a reputation as a graceful writer, drafted a formal declaration that was accepted with alterations two days later. Much of the Declaration of Independence consisted of a list of specific grievances against George III and his government. Like a skilled lawyer, Jefferson presented the evidence for independence. But the document did not become famous for those passages. Long after the establishment of the new republic, the Declaration challenged Americans to make good on the principle that "all men are created equal." John Adams expressed the patriots' fervor when he wrote on July 3, "Yesterday the greatest question was decided, which ever was debated in America, and a greater perhaps, never was or will be decided among men."

Quick Check

✓ Why do you think Thomas Paine's *Common Sense* became an instant bestseller?

FIGHTING FOR INDEPENDENCE

Why did it take eight years of warfare for the Americans to gain independence?

Only fools and visionaries expressed optimism about America's prospects of winning independence in 1776. The Americans had taken on a formidable military power. Britain's population was perhaps four times that of its former colonies. Britain also possessed a strong manufacturing base, a well-trained regular army supplemented by thousands of German mercenaries (Hessians), and a navy that dominated the seas. Many British officers were battlefield veterans. They already knew what the Americans would slowly learn: Waging war requires discipline, money, and sacrifice.

The British government was confident that it could beat the Americans. In 1776, Lord North and his colleagues regarded the war as a police action. A mere show of force would intimidate the upstart colonists. As soon as the rebels in Boston had been humbled, the British argued, other colonies would desert the cause for independence. General Gage, for example, told the king that the colonists "will be Lions, whilst we are Lambs ... if we take a resolute part they will undoubtedly prove very weak." Since this advice confirmed George's views, he called Gage "an honest determined man."

As later events demonstrated, of course, Britain had become involved in an impossible military situation. Three separate elements neutralized the larger power's advantages over its adversary. First, the British had to transport men and supplies across the Atlantic, a logistic challenge of unprecedented complexity. Unreliable lines of communication broke down under the strain of war.

Second, America was too vast to be conquered by conventional military methods. Redcoats might gain control over the major ports, but as long as the Continental Army remained intact, the rebellion continued. As Washington explained, "the possession of our Towns, while we have an Army in the field, will avail them little.... It is our Arms, not defenceless Towns, they have to subdue." Even if Britain had recruited enough soldiers to occupy the entire country, it would still have lost the war. As one Loyalist instructed the king, "if all America becomes a garrison, she is not worth your attention." Britain could only win by crushing the American will to resist.

And third, British strategists never appreciated the depth of the Americans' commitment to a political ideology. In the wars of eighteenth-century Europe, such beliefs had seldom mattered. European troops before the French Revolution broke out in 1789 served because they were paid or because the military was a vocation, not because they hoped to advance a set of constitutional principles. Americans were different. To be sure, some young men were drawn to the military by bounty money or the desire to escape unhappy families. A few were drafted. But the American troops still had a remarkable commitment to republican ideals. One French officer reported from the United States, "It is incredible that soldiers composed of men of every age, even of children of fifteen, of whites and blacks, almost naked, unpaid, and rather poorly fed, can march so well and withstand fire so steadfastly."

Building a Professional Army

Washington insisted on organizing a regular well-trained field army. Some advisers urged the commander in chief to wage a guerrilla war in which small partisan bands would sap Britain's will to fight. But Washington recognized that the Continental Army was not just a fighting force but a symbol of the republican cause. Its very existence would sustain American hopes, and so long as the army survived, American agents could plausibly solicit foreign aid. This thinking shaped Washington's wartime strategy; he studiously avoided "general actions" in which the Continental Army might be destroyed. Critics complained about Washington's caution, but as they soon discovered, he understood better than they what independence required.

If the commander in chief was correct about the army, however, he failed to comprehend the political importance of the militia. These scattered, almost amateur, military units seldom altered the outcome of battle, but they did maintain control over large areas not directly occupied by the British army. Throughout the war, they compelled men and women who would rather have remained neutral to support the American effort.

For the half million African American colonists, most of them slaves, the fight for independence was poignant. After all, they wanted to achieve personal and political freedom. Many African Americans supported whichever side seemed most likely to deliver them from bondage. An estimated 5,000 African Americans took up arms to fight the British. The Continental Army included two all-black units, one from Massachusetts, the other from Rhode Island. In 1778, the Rhode Island legislature voted to free any slave who volunteered to serve. According to the lawmakers, history taught that "the wisest, the freest, and bravest nations … liberated their slaves, and enlisted them as soldiers to fight in defence of their country." In the South, especially in Georgia and South Carolina, more than 10,000 African Americans supported the British. After the patriots won the war, these men and women relocated to Nova Scotia, Florida, and Jamaica. Some eventually resettled in West Africa.

Quick Check

✓ Why did George Washington insist on organizing a regular field army?

"Times That Try Men's Souls"

🔍 **View** the **Map**
The American Revolution on
myhistorylab.com

After the embarrassing defeats in Massachusetts, Sir William Howe replaced the ill-fated Gage. British rulers now understood that a simple police action would not crush the American rebellion. Parliament authorized sending more than 50,000 troops to the mainland colonies. After evacuating Boston—an untenable position—British forces stormed ashore at Staten Island in New York Harbor on July 3, 1776. From this more central location, Howe believed he could cut the New Englanders off from the rest of America. (See Map 5.2.)

When Washington learned the British were planning to occupy New York City, he transferred many of his inexperienced soldiers to Long Island, where they suffered a major defeat (August 27, 1776). Howe then drove the Continental Army across the Hudson River into New Jersey.

These swift victories persuaded Howe that few Americans enthusiastically supported independence. He issued a general pardon to anyone who would swear allegiance to George III. More than 3,000 men and women who lived in areas occupied by the British took the oath. This group included one frightened signer of the Declaration of Independence. Howe perceived that a lasting peace in America would require his troops to treat "our enemies as if they might one day become our friends." A member of Lord North's cabinet grumbled that this was "a sentimental manner of making war." The pardon plan failed not because Howe lacked toughness, but because his soldiers and officers treated loyal Americans as inferior, an attitude that did little to promote good relations. In any case, as soon as the redcoats left a pardoned region, the rebel militia retaliated against those who had deserted the patriot cause.

In December 1776, Washington's bedraggled army retreated across the Delaware River into Pennsylvania. American prospects appeared bleaker than at any other time during the war. The Continental Army lacked basic supplies, and many men who had signed up for short-term enlistments prepared to go home. "These are the times that try men's souls," Paine wrote in a pamphlet titled *American Crisis*. "The summer soldier and the sunshine patriot will, in this crisis, shrink from the service of their country, but he that stands it *now* deserves … love and thanks… ." Washington determined to attempt a desperate stroke.

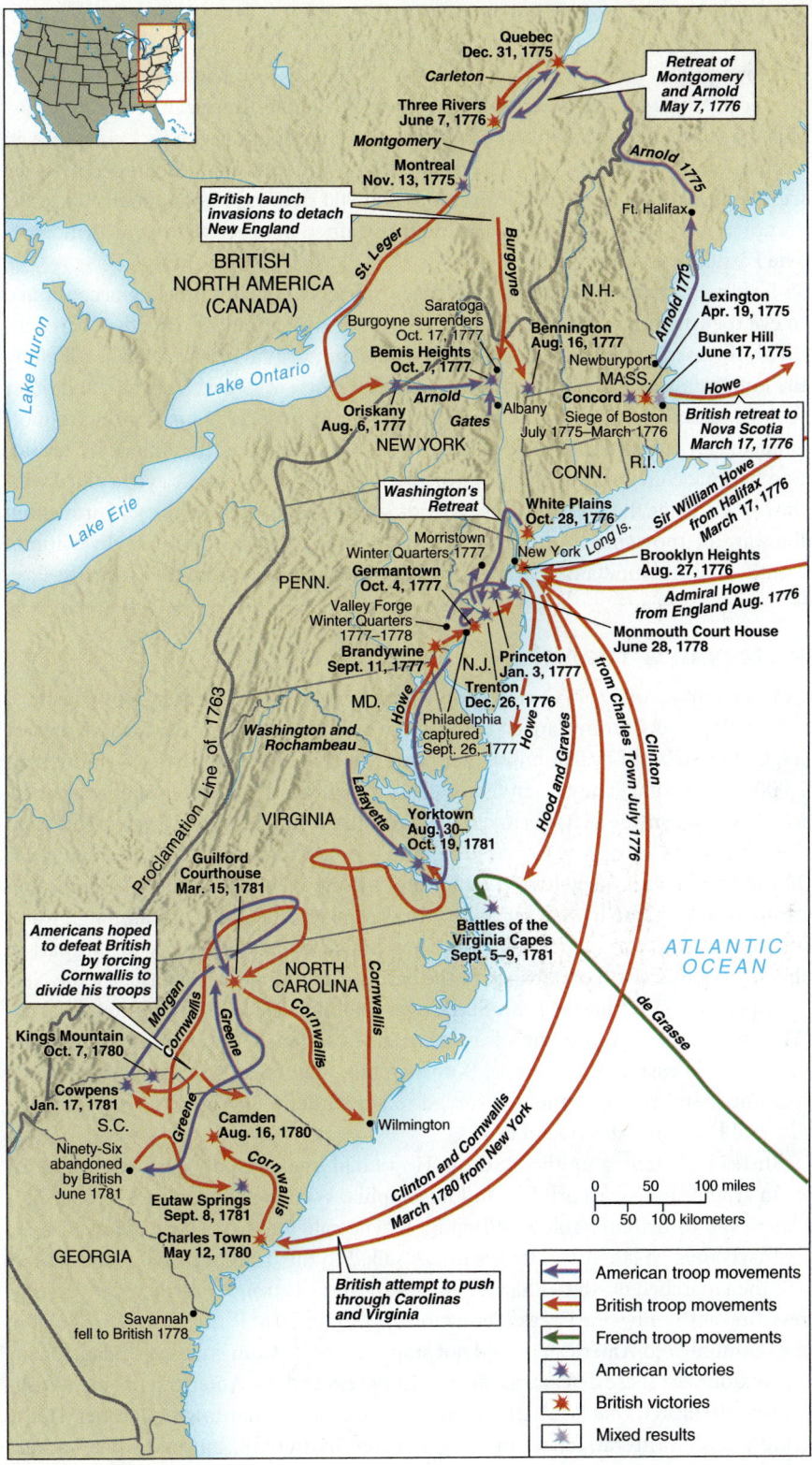

Map 5.2 *The American Revolution, 1775–1781* Battles were fought in the colonies, on the western frontier, and along the Gulf of Mexico. The major engagements of the first years of the war, from the spontaneous rising at Concord in 1775 to Washington's well-coordinated attack on Trenton in December 1776, were fought in the northern colonies. In the middle theater of war, Burgoyne's attempt in 1777 to cut New England off from the rest of the colonies failed when his army was defeated at Saratoga. Action in the final years of the war, from the battles at Camden, Kings Mountain, Cowpens, and Guilford Courthouse to the final victory at Yorktown, occurred in the South.

Howe played into Washington's hands. The British forces were dispersed for the winter in small garrisons across New Jersey. While the Americans could not possibly have defeated the combined British army, they could—with luck—capture an exposed post. On the night of December 25, Continental soldiers slipped over the ice-filled Delaware River and at Trenton took 900 sleeping Hessian mercenaries by complete surprise. In January, Washington gained another victory, at Princeton. The Patriot cause revived.

If this victory in the east served to cheer Patriots on, many Americans continued to eye their frontiers with trepidation. Many Indian nations, fearing the encroachment of American settlers, had cast their lots militarily with the British. All along the long frontier, warriors from the Cherokee, Choctaw, Creek, Shawnee, and other nations raided American settlements and garrisons from 1776 on. For the Iroquois Confederacy, a two-century-old alliance of six related nations, the American Revolution became a civil war as the Mohawk, Seneca, Onondaga, and Cayuga allied with the British, while the Tuscarora and Oneida supported to the rebel cause. Throughout the war, the movements of Native American forces would require the diversion of Continental and militia troops toward the frontier and away from the war in the East.

Quick Check

✓ Why did the first year of war go so badly for the Americans?

Victory in a Year of Defeat

In the summer of 1777, General John Burgoyne, a dashing though overbearing officer, descended from Canada with a force of British regulars, German mercenaries, Canadian and Loyalist militiamen, and Native American warriors—more than 7,000 troops total. They intended to clear the Hudson Valley of rebel resistance; join Howe's army, which was to come up to Albany; and cut New England off from the other states. Burgoyne fought in a grand style. Accompanied by a German band, 30 carts filled with the general's liquor and belongings, and 2,000 dependents and camp followers, the British set out to thrash the Americans. The campaign was a disaster. Military units, mostly from New England, cut the enemy force apart in the deep woods north of Albany. At the battle of Bennington (August 16), the New Hampshire militia under John Stark overwhelmed 1,000 German mercenaries. After this setback, Burgoyne's forces struggled forward, desperately hoping that Howe would rush to their rescue. But when his situation at Saratoga became hopeless, the haughty Burgoyne was forced to surrender 5,800 men to the American General Horatio Gates (October 17).

Instead of moving up the Hudson, Howe had unexpectedly decided to take his main army from New York City to Philadelphia. What he hoped to achieve was not clear, even to Britain's rulers. When Burgoyne called for assistance, Howe was in Pennsylvania. In late July, Howe's forces sailed to the head of the Chesapeake Bay and then marched north to Philadelphia. Washington's troops obstructed their progress, first at Brandywine Creek (September 11) and then at Paoli (September 20), but the outnumbered Americans could not stop the British from entering Philadelphia.

Anxious lest these defeats discourage Congress and the American people, Washington attempted one last battle before winter. At Germantown (October 4), the Americans counterattacked on a fog-covered battlefield, but just when success seemed assured, they broke off the fight. "When every thing gave the most flattering hopes of victory," Washington complained, "the troops began suddenly to retreat." Bad luck, confusion, and incompetence contributed to the failure. A discouraged Continental Army dug in at Valley Forge, 20 miles outside of Philadelphia, where diseases killed 2,500 Americans. Few of the soldiers realized their situation was not nearly as desperate as it had been in 1776.

Quick Check

✓ What role did poor British planning play in the American victory at Saratoga?

The French Alliance

Even before the Americans declared their independence, French agents began to explore ways to aid the colonists, not because the French monarchy favored the republican cause but because it hoped to embarrass the British. The French deeply resented their defeat during the Seven Years' War. During the early months of the Revolution, the French covertly sent tons of military supplies to the Americans. The negotiations for these arms involved secret agents and fictitious trading companies, a type of clandestine operation more typical of modern times than of the eighteenth century. But when American representatives, Benjamin Franklin for one, pleaded for official recognition of American independence or for outright military alliance, the French advised patience. The international stakes were too great for King Louis XVI openly to back a cause that had little chance of success.

Some adventurous French military men embraced the American cause despite their nation's official neutrality. The most famous of these men, the Marquis de Lafayette, set sail in spring 1777, despite being expressly forbidden to do so by King Louis XVI. Once in the United States, Lafayette became an aide-de-camp to George Washington, serving as a trusted advisor, able administrator, and effective diplomat.

It was the victory at Saratoga in 1778 that finally earned the Americans official support from France. It convinced the French that the rebels had formidable forces and were serious in their resolve. Franklin hinted to French officials in Paris that the Americans might accept a British peace initiative. If the French wanted the war to continue, if they really wanted to embarrass their old rival, then they had to do what the British refused to do: formally recognize the independence of the United States.

Map 5.3   Spain entered the Revolutionary War as an ally of France in 1779. By 1781, Spanish forces operating out of New Orleans and St. Louis had captured British forts in the Mississippi Valley and the Midwest from Baton Rouge and Natchez to as far north as the modern state of Michigan. On the Gulf Coast, Spanish amphibious forces led by Count Bernardo de Galvez had also overran British posts from what is now Mobile, Alabama to Pensacola in what was then the British colony of West Florida. Spain retained these Gulf Coast ports and regained all of Florida in the Treaty of Paris in 1783.

The stratagem paid off. On February 6, 1778, the French presented American representatives with two separate treaties. The Treaty of Amity and Commerce established commercial relations with the United States. It tacitly accepted the existence of a new, independent republic. The Treaty of Alliance was even more generous, considering America's obvious military and economic weaknesses. If France and Britain went to war (they did so on June 14, as everyone expected), the French agreed to reject "either Truce or Peace with Great Britain ... until the independence of the United States shall have been formally or tacitly assured by the Treaty or Treaties that shall terminate the War." Even more amazing, France surrendered its claim to all British territories east of the Mississippi. The Americans pledged not to sign a separate peace with Britain without first informing their new ally. France also made no claim to recover Canada, asking only for British islands in the Caribbean. Never had Franklin worked his magic to greater effect.

French intervention instantly transformed British strategy. A colonial rebellion became a world conflict. British and French forces clashed in the Mediterranean, in India and the Indian Ocean, in the Caribbean, and on the coast of West Africa. To counter the French, Britain had to divert scarce military resources, especially newer warships, from the American theater to the English Channel. In fact, there was talk in London of a French invasion. French diplomacy also convinced the Spanish, eager to benefit from Britain's seeming weakness, to enter the world conflict in 1779. More British ships and troops had to be diverted to the West Indies and Florida to counter Spanish threats. The navies of its imperial rivals threatened the overextended British fleet. By concentrating their warships in a specific area, the French or Spanish could hold off or even defeat British squadrons, an advantage that figured significantly in the war's final victory at Yorktown.

Quick Check

✓ What role did French support play in the winning of the Revolutionary War?

The Final Campaign

Strategists calculated that Britain's last chance of winning the war lay in the southern colonies, a region largely untouched in the early fighting. Intelligence reports indicated that Georgia and South Carolina contained many Loyalists who would take up arms for the crown if only they received support from the regular army. The southern strategy British leaders devised in 1779 turned the war into a bitter guerrilla conflict. During the last months of battle, British officers worried that their search for an easy victory had inadvertently opened a Pandora's box of uncontrollable partisan furies.

The southern campaign opened in spring 1780. Savannah, Georgia had already fallen in 1779. General Sir Henry Clinton, who had replaced Howe after Saratoga, now reckoned that if the British could take Charles Town, they could control the entire South. A fleet carrying nearly 8,000 redcoats reached South Carolina in February. Complacent Americans had allowed the city's fortifications to decay. In a desperate effort to save the city, General Benjamin Lincoln's forces dug trenches and reinforced walls, but to no avail. Clinton and his second in command, Lord Cornwallis, encircled the city, and on May 12, Lincoln surrendered an American army of almost 6,000 men.

Despite this victory, partisan warfare weakened the British army. Tory raiders showed little interest in serving as regular soldiers. They preferred night riding, indiscriminate plundering, or murdering neighbors against whom they harbored ancient grudges. The British had unleashed a horde of bandits across South Carolina. Men who supported independence or who had fallen victim to Loyalist guerrillas bided their time. Their chance came on October 7 near Kings Mountain, North Carolina. In the most vicious fighting of the Revolution, the backwoodsmen annihilated a force of British regulars and Tory raiders that had strayed too far from base. One witness reported that when a British officer tried to surrender, at least seven Americans shot him down.

Battle of Yorktown French assistance on land and sea helped the Americans to defeat the British in the American Revolution. In this French print of the battle at Yorktown, French ships block the entrance of Chesapeake Bay, preventing British vessels from resupplying their troops on land. Yorktown, which was unknown to the French artist who made this print, is depicted as a European walled city.

Cornwallis, confused by the enemy's guerilla tactics and poorly supplied, squandered his strength chasing American forces across the Carolinas. He abandoned whatever military strategy had compelled him to leave Charles Town. In early 1781, Cornwallis informed Clinton, "Events alone can decide the future Steps." Events, however, did not run in the British favor. Congress sent General Nathanael Greene to the South with a new army. This young Rhode Islander was the most capable general on Washington's staff. Greene joined Daniel Morgan, leader of the famed Virginia Riflemen. In tactically brilliant engagements, they sapped the strength of Cornwallis's army, at Cowpens, South Carolina (January 17, 1781), and Guilford Courthouse, North Carolina (March 15). Clinton fumed that the inept Cornwallis had left "two valuable colonies behind him to be overrun and conquered by the very army which he boasts to have completely routed but a week or two before."

Cornwallis pushed north into Virginia, shadowed by about 4,500 American troops under the command of the Marquis de Lafayette. Planning, apparently, to establish a base on the coast, Cornwallis began to fortify Yorktown, a sleepy tobacco market on a peninsula bounded by the York and James rivers. Washington watched these maneuvers closely. The canny Virginia planter knew this territory intimately. He sensed that Cornwallis had made a blunder. When Washington learned the French fleet could gain temporary dominance in the Chesapeake Bay, he rushed south from New Jersey to join Lafayette, who was now maneuvering to contain the British forces. With Washington went thousands of well-trained French troops under the Comte de Rochambeau. All the pieces fell into place. The French admiral, the Comte de Grasse, cut Cornwallis off from the sea, while Washington and his lieutenants encircled the British on land. On October 19, 1781, Cornwallis surrendered his entire army of 6,000 men. When Lord North heard of the defeat at Yorktown, he moaned, "Oh God! It is all over." The British still controlled New York City, Charles Town, and Savannah but except for a few skirmishes,

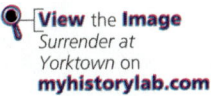 View the Image
Surrender at Yorktown on
myhistorylab.com

Quick Check

✓ Why did the "South-
ern Campaign" not
work out as British
strategists had
anticipated?

the fighting ended. The task of securing the independence of the United States was now in the hands of the diplomats. The preliminary agreement signed in Paris on September 3, 1783, not only guaranteed the independence of the United States; it also transferred all the territory east of the Mississippi River, except Florida, which Britain surrendered to Spain, to the new republic. The Treaty of Paris of 1783 established generous boundaries on the north and south (effectively ceding away the land of their erstwhile Indian allies) and gave the Americans important fishing rights in the North Atlantic.

The Loyalist Dilemma

No one knows how many Americans supported the crown during the Revolution. Some Loyalists undoubtedly avoided making a public commitment that might have led to banishment or loss of property. But for many, neutrality proved impossible. Almost 100,000 men and women permanently left America. While some of these exiles had been imperial officeholders—Thomas Hutchinson, for example— they came from all ranks and backgrounds. More than 30,000 farmers resettled in Canada. Others relocated to England, the West Indies, or Africa.

The political ideology of the Loyalists was not substantially different from that of their opponents. Like other Americans, they believed that men and women were entitled to life, liberty, and the pursuit of happiness. But the Loyalists were convinced that independence would destroy those values by promoting disorder. By turning their backs on Britain, a source of tradition and stability, the rebels seemed to have encouraged licentiousness, even anarchy in the streets. The Loyalists suspected that Patriot demands for freedom were self-serving, even hypocritical, for as Perserved Smith, a Loyalist from Ashfield, Massachusetts, observed, "Sons of liberty … did not deserve the name, for it was evident all they wanted was liberty from oppression that they might have liberty to oppress!"

The Loyalists were caught in a bind. The British never trusted them. After all, they were Americans. During the early stages of the war, Loyalists organized militia companies and hoped to pacify large areas of the countryside with the support of the regular army. The British generals were unreliable partners, however, for no sooner had they called on loyal Americans to come forward than the redcoats marched away, exposing the Tories to rebel retaliation. And in Britain, they were treated as second-class citizens. While many received monetary compensation for their sacrifice, they were never regarded as the equals of native-born British citizens. The Loyalist community in London was gradually transformed into a collection of bitter men and women who felt unwelcome on both sides of the Atlantic.

Although many Loyalists eventually returned to their homes, a sizable number could not do so. For them, the sense of loss was a heavy emotional burden. Perhaps the most poignant testimony came from a young mother living in exile in Nova Scotia: "I climbed to the top of Chipman's Hill and watched the sails disappear in the distance, and such a feeling of loneliness came over me that though I had not shed a tear through all the war I sat down on the damp moss with my baby on my lap and cried bitterly."

Quick Check

✓ Why did so many
loyalists decide to
leave the United
States during the
Revolution?

CONCLUSION: PRESERVING INDEPENDENCE

Watch the **Video**
*The American Revo-
lution as Different
Americans Saw It* on
myhistorylab.com

The American people had waged war against the most powerful nation in Europe and emerged victorious. The Treaty of Paris marked the conclusion of a colonial rebellion, but it remained for the men and women who had resisted taxation without representation to work out the full implications of republicanism. What would be the new government look like? What powers would be delegated to the people, the states, the federal authorities? How far would the wealthy, well-born leaders of the rebellion be willing to extend political, social, and economic rights?

For many Americans the challenge of nation building appeared more formidable than waging war against Britain. As Philadelphia physician Dr. Benjamin Rush explained, "There is nothing more common than to confound the terms of American Revolution with those of the late American war. The American war is over, but this is far from being the case with the American Revolution. On the contrary, nothing but the first act of the great drama is closed."

5 STUDY RESOURCES

Listen to the **Chapter Audio** for Chapter 5 on **myhistorylab.com**

TIMELINE

1764 Parliament passes Sugar Act to collect American revenue, p. 118

1765 Stamp Act receives support of House of Commons (March), p. 118
- Stamp Act Congress meets in New York City (October), p. 119

1766 Stamp Act repealed; Declaratory Act becomes law (March 18), p. 121

1767 Townshend Revenue Acts anger Americans (June–July), p. 121

1770 Parliament repeals Townshend duties except one on tea (March), p. 122
- British troops fire on civilians during "Boston Massacre" (March), p. 122

1772 Samuel Adams forms committee of correspondence, p. 123

1773 Lord North's government passes Tea Act (May), p. 123
- Bostonians hold Tea Party (December), p. 124

1774 Parliament punishes Boston with Coercive Acts (March–June), p. 124
- First Continental Congress convenes (September), p. 125

1775 Patriots take stand at Lexington and Concord (April), p. 125
- Second Continental Congress gathers (May), p. 126
- Americans hold their own at Bunker Hill (June), p. 126

1776 Declaration of Independence signed, p. 128
- British defeat Washington at Long Island (August), p. 130
- American victory at Trenton (December), p. 130

1777 Burgoyne surrenders at Saratoga (October), p. 132

1778 French treaties recognize independence of the United States (February), p. 133

1780 British take Charles Town (May), p. 134

1781 Cornwallis surrenders at Yorktown (October), p. 135

1783 Peace treaty signed (September), p. 136

CHAPTER REVIEW

STRUCTURE OF COLONIAL SOCIETY

Why did Americans resist parliamentary taxation?

During the 1760s British rulers claimed that Parliament could make laws for the colonists "in all cases whatsoever." Americans challenged this "parliamentary sovereignty." Drawing on the work of John Locke, the English philosopher, they insisted that God had given them certain natural and inalienable rights. By attempting to tax them without representation, Parliament threatened those rights. *(p. 113)*

ERODING THE BONDS OF EMPIRE

What events eroded the bonds of empire during the 1760s?

Wars in America were expensive. Parliament established the Proclamation Line of 1763 to reduce the costs of protecting the frontier, but this angered colonists seeking new lands in the west. Parliament also concluded that the colonists should help reduce the national debt, but when it passed the Stamp Act (1765), Americans protested. Colonists boycotted British manufactured goods. Taken aback, Parliament repealed the hated statute, while maintaining in the Declaratory Act (1766) its complete legislative authority over the Americans. *(p. 116)*

STEPS TOWARD INDEPENDENCE

What events in 1775 and 1776 led to the colonists' decision to declare independence?

In 1775, following battles at Lexington and Concord, militiamen from throughout New England descended upon Boston, besieging the British troops encamped there. In response, the Continental Congress formed the Continental Army and appointed George Washington commander. In 1776, Thomas Paine's *Common Sense* convinced colonists that a republic was a better form of government than monarchy, and Congress declared independence. *(p. 125)*

FIGHTING FOR INDEPENDENCE

Why did it take eight years of warfare for the Americans to gain independence?

To win their independence, the colonies first had to overcome the formidable military power of Great Britain. Britain had four times the population of the colonies, was the world's leading manufacturer, had a well-trained and experienced army and the world's best navy. The outgunned colonists had to rely on a war of attrition. It was only after the victory at Saratoga in 1777 convinced the French to enter into an alliance that the colonists were able to win conclusive battles and successfully end the war. *(p. 128)*

KEY TERM QUESTIONS

1. How did the confrontation between King George III and the Whigs lead to political turmoil (p. 113)

2. Why was the British government adamant in its defense of parliamentary sovereignty? (p. 114)

3. How would Loyalists have disputed the reasons Americans offered for resisting British authority? (p. 115)

4. Was the repeal of the Stamp Act of 1765 a victory for the American cause? (p. 118)

5. How did delegates to the Stamp Act Congress present their views to the King and Parliament? (p. 119)

6. How did the Boston Massacre affect colonial loyalty to Britain? (p. 122)

7. How did the committees of correspondence influence colonial resistance to Britain? (p. 123)

8. How did Parliament respond to the Boston Tea Party? (p. 124)

9. Were the Coercive Acts an overreaction by Parliament to the Boston Tea Party? (p. 124)

10. What differences of opinion arose during the First Continental Congress? (p. 125)

11. What did the Second Continental Congress accomplish? (p. 126)

12. Why was Thomas Paine's Common Sense so important? (p. 127)

13. Why was the French role at Yorktown so significant? (p. 135)

14. What was the significance of the Treaty of Paris of 1783? (p. 136)

MyHistoryLab Connections

Visit **www.myhistorylab.com** for a customized Study Plan to build your knowledge of *The American Revolution.*

Question for Analysis

1. What important details concerning the Boston Tea Party are mentioned in Hewes, "A Retrospect on the Boston Tea Party"?

   Read the **Document** *Hewes, A Retrospect on the Boston Tea Party* p. 124

2. According to Joseph Warren, who was the aggressor in the Battle of Lexington?

   Read the **Document** *Joseph Warren, Account of the Battle of Lexington* p. 126

3. Why did the British have such a difficult time fighting against the colonists?

   View the **Map** *The American Revolution* p. 130

4. Did the colonists fight the British as an entirely unified people?

   Watch the **Video** *The American Revolution as Different Americans Saw It* p. 137

Other Resources from this Chapter

Read the **Document** *James Otis, An American Colonist Opposes New Taxes*

Read the **Document** *Benjamin Franklin, Testimony Against the Stamp Act*

View the **Image** *1765 Stamp Act Protest*

View the **Image** *Women Signing Anti-Tea Agreement*

Listen to the **Audio File** *The Liberty Song*

Read the **Document** *Boston Gazette Description of the Boston Massacre*

View the **Image** *Bostonians Paying the Excise Man*

Read the **Document** *Thomas Paine, A Freelance Writer Urges His Readers*

View the **Image** *Surrender at Yorktown*

6 THE REPUBLICAN EXPERIMENT
1783–1788

Contents and Spotlight Questions

((●—[**Listen** to the **Chapter Audio** for Chapter 6 on **myhistorylab.com**

A NEW POLITICAL MORALITY

In 1788, Lewis Hallam and John Henry petitioned the General Assembly of Pennsylvania to open a theater in Philadelphia. Although a 1786 state law banned the performance of stage plays and "disorderly sports," many Philadelphia leaders favored the request to hold "dramatic representations" in their city. A committee appointed to study the issue concluded that a theater would contribute to "the general refinement of manners and the polish of society." Some supporters even argued that the sooner the United States had a professional theater the sooner it would escape the "foreign yoke" of British culture.

Quakers dismissed these claims: Such "seminaries of lewdness and irreligion" would quickly undermine "the virtue of the people.... [N]o sooner is a playhouse opened than it becomes surrounded with ... brothels." Since

Liberty Displaying the Arts and Sciences The Library Company of Philadelphia commissioned this painting by Samuel Jennings in 1792. The broken chain at the feet of the goddess Liberty is meant to demonstrate her opposition to slavery. (*Source: The Library Company of Philadelphia.*)

Pennsylvania was already suffering from a "stagnation of commerce [and] a scarcity of money"—unmistakable signs of God's displeasure—it seemed unwise to risk further divine punishment by encouraging new "hot-beds of vice."

Other citizens interpreted the revolutionary experience from an entirely different perspective. At issue, they insisted, was not popular morality, but state censorship. If the government silenced the stage, then "the same authority... may, with equal justice, dictate the shape and texture of our dress, or the modes and ceremonies of our worship." Depriving those who wanted to see plays of an opportunity to do so, they argued, "will abridge the natural right of every freeman, to dispose of his time and money, according to his own tastes and dispositions." The General Assembly apparently agreed. By 1789, Philadelphians were once again enjoying the liberty of attending the theater.

Throughout post-Revolutionary America everyday matters such as opening a new playhouse provoked passionate debate. The divisions were symptomatic of a new, uncertain political culture struggling to find the proper balance between public morality and private freedom. During the long fight against Britain, Americans had defended individual rights. But they also believed that a republic that compromised its virtue could not preserve liberty and independence.

In 1776, Thomas Paine had reminded ordinary men and women that "the sun never shined on a cause of greater worth.....'Tis not the concern of a day, a year, or an age; posterity are virtually involved in the contest, and will be more or less affected, even to the end of time, by the proceedings now." During the 1780s Americans understood their responsibility not only to each other, but also to history. They worried, however, that they might not meet the challenge. Individual states seemed intent on looking out for local interests rather than the national welfare. Revolutionary leaders such as George Washington and James Madison concluded that the United States needed a strong central government to protect rights and property. Their quest for solutions brought forth a new and enduring constitution.

DEFINING REPUBLICAN CULTURE

What were the limits of equality in the "republican" society of the new United States?

Today, the term *republican* no longer possesses the evocative power it did for most eighteenth-century Americans. For them, it defined not a political party, but a political culture. Those Americans who read deeply in ancient and renaissance history knew that most republics had failed, often within a few years, replaced by tyrants who cared not at all what ordinary people thought about the public good. To preserve their republic from such a fate, victorious revolutionaries such as Samuel Adams recast fundamental political values. For them, republicanism represented more than a form of government. It was a way of life, a core ideology, an uncompromising commitment to maintain liberty and equality, while guarding against the corruptions of power and self-interest.

White Americans emerged from the Revolution with an almost euphoric sense of the nation's destiny. This expansive outlook, encountered among so many ordinary men and women, owed much to the spread of Protestant evangelicalism. However skeptical Jefferson, Franklin, and other leaders may have been about revealed religion, most Americans subscribed to an almost utopian vision of the country's future. To this new republic, God had promised progress and prosperity.

However, the celebration of liberty met with a mixed response. Some Americans—often the very men who had resisted British tyranny—worried that the citizens of the new nation were caught up in a wild, destructive scramble for material wealth. Democratic excesses seemed to threaten order and endanger property rights. Surely a republic could not survive unless its citizens showed greater self-control. For these people, the state assemblies appeared to be the greatest source of instability. Popularly elected representatives lacked what men of property defined as civic virtue, an ability to work for the common good rather than their private interests.

Working out the tensions between order and liberty, between property and equality, generated an outpouring of political genius. At other times in American history, persons of extraordinary talent have been drawn to theology, commerce, or science, but during the 1780s, the country's intellectual leaders—Thomas Jefferson, James Madison, Alexander Hamilton, and John Adams, among others—focused on the problem of how republicans ought to govern themselves.

Read the **Document**
George Washington, Manners and Etiquette on **myhistorylab.com**

Social and Political Reform

Following the war, Americans aggressively ferreted out and, with republican fervor, denounced any traces of aristocratic pretense. As colonists, they had resented the claim that English aristocrats were privileged simply because of noble birth. Even so committed a republican as George Washington had to be reminded that artificial status was contrary to republican principles. In 1783, he and the officers who had served during the Revolution formed the Society of the Cincinnati, a hereditary organization in which membership passed from father to eldest son. The soldiers wanted to maintain old friendships, but anxious republicans throughout America let out a howl of protest. One South Carolina legislator, Aedanus Burke, warned that the Society intended to create "an hereditary peerage … [which would] undermine the Constitution and destroy civil liberty." After an embarrassed Washington called for reforming the Society's bylaws, the Cincinnati

Questions of Equality in the New Republic In this illustration, which appeared as the frontispiece in the 1792 issue of *The Lady's Magazine and Repository of Entertaining Knowledge*, the "Genius of the Ladies Magazine" and the "Genius of Emulation" (holding in her hand a laurel crown) present to Liberty a petition for the rights of women. (*Source: The Library Company of Philadelphia.*)

crisis receded. The fear of privilege remained, however. Wealthy Americans dropped honorific titles such as "esquire." Lawyers of republican persuasion chided judges who had adopted the English custom of wearing great flowing wigs to court.

The appearance of equality was as important as its achievement. In fact, the distribution of wealth in postwar America was more uneven than it had been in the mid-eighteenth century. The sudden accumulation of large fortunes by new families made other Americans particularly sensitive to aristocratic display. It seemed intolerable that a revolution waged against a monarchy should produce a class of persons legally, or even visibly, distinguished from their fellow citizens.

To root out the notion of a privileged class, states abolished laws of primogeniture and entail. In colonial times, these laws allowed a landholder either to pass his entire estate to his eldest son or to declare that his property could never be divided, sold, or given away. Jefferson claimed that the repeal of these practices would eradicate "antient [sic] and future aristocracy; a foundation [has been] laid for a government truly republican." He may have exaggerated the social impact of this reform, but its symbolism counted as much as real social practice. Republican legislators wanted to cleanse traces of the former feudal order from the statute books.

Republican ferment also encouraged states to lower property requirements for voting. After the break with Britain, this seemed logical. As one group of farmers declared, no man can be "free & independent" unless he possesses "a voice … in the choice of the most important Officers in the Legislature." Pennsylvania and Georgia allowed all white male taxpayers to vote. Other states were less democratic, but except for Massachusetts, they reduced property qualifications.

The most important changes in voting patterns were the result of western migration. As Americans moved to the frontier, they received full political representation in their state legislatures. Because new districts tended to be poorer than established coastal settlements, their representatives seemed less cultured, less well trained than those eastern voters elected. Moreover, western delegates resented traveling so far to attend legislative meetings. They lobbied to transfer state capitals to more convenient locations. During this period, Georgia moved the seat of its government from Savannah to Augusta, South Carolina from Charles Town to Columbia, North Carolina from New Bern to Raleigh, Virginia from Williamsburg to Richmond, New York from New York City to Albany, and New Hampshire from Portsmouth to Concord.

After gaining independence, Americans also reexamined the relation between church and state. Republican spokesmen such as Thomas Jefferson insisted that rulers had no right to interfere with the free expression of religious beliefs. As governor of Virginia, he advocated disestablishing the Anglican Church, which had received tax monies and other benefits during the colonial period. Jefferson and his allies regarded such privilege not only as a denial of religious freedom—rival denominations did not receive tax money—but also as a vestige of aristocratic society.

In 1786, Virginia cut the last ties between church and state. Other southern states also disestablished the Anglican Church, but in Massachusetts, Connecticut, and New Hampshire, Congregational churches continued to enjoy special status. Moreover, while Americans championed toleration, they seldom favored philosophies that radically challenged Christian values.

Quick Check

✓ During the 1780s, why were Americans so sensitive to the dangers of "aristocratic display"?

African Americans in the New Republic

Revolutionary fervor forced Americans to confront the most appalling contradiction to republican principles—slavery. The Quaker John Woolman (1720–1772) probably did more than any other white person of the era to remind people of the evils of this institution. A trip he took through the southern colonies as a young man impressed upon Woolman "the dark gloominess" of slavery. In a sermon, the outspoken humanitarian declared "that Men having Power too often misapplied it; that though we made Slaves of the Negroes, and the Turks made Slaves of the Christians, I believed that Liberty was the natural Right of all Men equally."

During the revolutionary period, abolitionist sentiment spread. Both in private and public, people began to criticize slavery in other than religious language. No doubt, the double standard of their own political rhetoric embarrassed many white Americans. They demanded liberation from parliamentary enslavement but held hundreds of thousands of blacks in bondage.

By keeping the issue of slavery before the public through writing and petitioning, African Americans undermined arguments in favor of human bondage. They demanded freedom, reminding white lawmakers that African American men and women had the same natural right to liberty as did other Americans. In 1779, for example, African Americans in Connecticut asked the state assembly "whether it is consistent with the present Claims, of the United States, to hold so many Thousands, of the Race of Adam, our Common Father, in perpetual Slavery." In New Hampshire, 19 persons who called themselves "natives of Africa" reminded legislators that "private or public tyranny and slavery are alike detestable to minds conscious of the equal dignity of human nature."

The scientific accomplishments of Benjamin Banneker (1731–1806), Maryland's African American astronomer and mathematician, and the international fame of Phillis Wheatley (1753–1784), Boston's celebrated "African muse," made it difficult for white Americans to maintain that African Americans could not hold their own in a free society. Wheatley's poems went through many editions. After reading her work, the great French philosopher Voltaire rebuked a friend who had claimed "there never would be Negro poets." As Voltaire discovered, Wheatley wrote "excellent verse in English." Banneker enjoyed a well-deserved reputation as a scientist. After receiving a copy of an almanac that Banneker had published in Philadelphia, Jefferson concluded "that nature has given to our black brethren, talents equal to those of the other colors of men."

In the northern states, there was no real economic justification for slavery. White laborers, often recent European immigrants, resented having to compete against slaves. This economic situation, combined with the acknowledgment of the double standard slavery represented, contributed to the establishment of antislavery societies. In 1775, Franklin helped organize in Philadelphia the Society for the Relief of Free Negroes, Unlawfully Held. John Jay, Alexander Hamilton, and other prominent New Yorkers founded a Manumission Society in 1785. By 1792, antislavery societies were meeting from Virginia to Massachusetts. In the northern states at least, these groups, working for the same ends as Christian evangelicals, put slaveholders on the intellectual defensive for the first time in American history.

Read the **Document**
Slave Petition to the General Assembly in Connecticut (1779) on **myhistorylab.com**

Phillis Wheatley This engraving of Wheatley appeared in her volume of verse, *Poems on Various Subjects, Religious and Moral* (1773), the first book published by an African American.

📖 **Read** the **Document**
Phillis Wheatley, Religious and Moral Poems on **myhistorylab.com**

📖 **Read** the **Document**
Richard Allen, "Address to the Free People of Colour" on **myhistorylab.com**

In states north of Virginia, the abolition of slavery took different forms. Even before achieving statehood in 1791, Vermont drafted a constitution (1777) that prohibited slavery. In 1780, the Pennsylvania legislature passed a law for gradual emancipation. Although the Massachusetts assembly refused to address the issue directly, the state courts liberated its African Americans. A judge ruled slavery unconstitutional in Massachusetts because it conflicted with a clause in the state bill of rights declaring "all men ... free and equal." According to one enthusiast, this decision freed "a Grate number of Blacks ... who ... are held in a state of slavery within the bowels of a free and christian Country." By 1800, slavery was on the road to extinction in the northern states.

These positive developments did not mean that white people accepted blacks as equals. In the very states that outlawed slavery, African Americans faced systematic discrimination. Free blacks were generally excluded from voting, juries, and militia duty—they were denied rights and responsibilities associated with full citizenship. They rarely enjoyed access to education. In cities such as Philadelphia and New York, where African Americans went to look for work, they ended up living in segregated wards or neighborhoods. Even in the churches—institutions that had often attacked slavery—free African Americans were denied equal standing with white worshippers. Humiliations of this sort persuaded African Americans to form their own churches. In Philadelphia, Richard Allen, a former slave, founded the Bethel Church for Negro Methodists (1793) and later organized the African Methodist Episcopal Church (1814), an institution of cultural and religious significance for nineteenth-century American blacks.

Even in the South, where African Americans made up much of the population, slavery disturbed thoughtful white republicans. Some planters simply freed their slaves. By 1790, 12,766 free blacks lived in Virginia. By 1800, there were 30,750. This trend reflected uneasiness among white masters. Richard Randolph, one of Virginia's wealthier planters, explained that he freed his slaves "to make restitution, as far as I am able, to an unfortunate race of bond-men, over whom my ancestors have usurped and exercised the most lawless and monstrous tyranny." George Washington also freed his slaves in his will after his death. But most southern slaveholders, especially in South Carolina and Georgia, rejected manumission. Their well-being depended on slave labor. Perhaps more significant, however, is that no southern leader during the era of republican experimentation defended slavery as a positive good. Such racist rhetoric did not become part of the public discourse until the nineteenth century.

Despite promising starts, the southern states did not abolish slavery. The economic incentives to maintain a servile labor force, especially after the invention of the cotton gin in 1793 and the opening up of the Alabama and Mississippi frontier, overwhelmed the initial abolitionist impulse. An opportunity to translate the principles of the American Revolution into social practice had been lost, at least temporarily. Jefferson reported in 1805, "I have long since given up the expectation of any early provision for the extinction of slavery among us." Unlike some contemporary Virginians, the man who wrote the Declaration of Independence condoned slavery on his own plantation, even fathering children by a woman who, since she was his slave, had little choice in her pregnancies.

Quick Check

✓ Why did the new republican governments not bring liberty and equality to African Americans living in the United States?

The Challenge of Women's Rights

The revolutionary experience accelerated changes in how ordinary people viewed the family. At the beginning of the eighteenth century, fathers claimed authority over their families simply because they were fathers. As patriarchs, they demanded obedience. Fathers could treat wives and children however they pleased. John Locke had powerfully undermined arguments of this sort. In *Some Thoughts Concerning Education* (1693), Locke insisted that the mind was not formed at birth. Children learned from experience. If the infant witnessed violent, arbitrary behavior, then the baby would become an abusive adult. As Locke warned parents, "If you punish him [the child] for what he sees you practice yourself, he will not think that Severity to proceed from Kindness in you careful to amend a Fault in him; but will be apt to interpret it, as Peevishness and Arbitrary Imperiousness of a Father." Enlightened eighteenth-century parents—especially fathers—condemned tyranny in the home.

In this changing intellectual environment, American women began making new demands not only on their husbands but on republican institutions. Abigail Adams, wife of future President John Adams and one of the era's most articulate women, instructed her husband, as he set off for the Second Continental Congress: "I desire you would Remember the Ladies, and be more generous and favourable to them than your ancestors. Do not put such unlimited power into the hands of the Husbands." John responded condescendingly. The "Ladies" would have to wait until the country achieved independence. In 1777, Lucy Knox took an even stronger line with her husband, General Henry Knox. When he was about to return home from the army, she warned him, "I hope you will not consider yourself as commander in chief in your own house—but be convinced … that there is such a thing as equal command."

📖 **Read** the **Document**
John Adams to Abigail Adams, July 3, 1776 on **myhistorylab.com**

If Knox accepted Lucy's argument, he did so because she was a good republican wife and mother. In fact, women justified their assertiveness largely on the basis of political ideology. If survival of republics really depended on the virtue of their citizens, they argued, then it was the special responsibility of women as mothers to nurture the right values in their children and as wives to instruct their husbands in proper behavior. Contemporaries claimed that the woman who possessed "virtue and prudence" could easily "mold the taste, the manners, and the conduct of her admirers, according to her pleasure." In fact, "nothing short of a general reformation of manners would take place, were the ladies to use their power in discouraging our licentious manners."

Ill-educated women could not fulfill these expectations. Women required education that was at least comparable to what men received. Many female academies were established during this period to meet what many Americans, men as well as women, now regarded as a pressing social need. The schools may have received widespread encouragement precisely because they did not radically challenge traditional gender roles. The educated republican woman of the late eighteenth century did not pursue a career; she followed a familiar routine as wife and mother. The frustration of not being allowed to develop her talents may explain the bitterness of a graduation oration an otherwise obscure woman delivered in 1793: "Our high and mighty Lords … have denied us the means of knowledge, and then reproached us for want of it.… They doom'd the sex to servile or frivolous employments, on purpose to degrade their minds, that they themselves might hold unrivall'd, the power and pre-eminence they had usurped."

During this period, women began to petition for divorce on new grounds. One case reveals changing attitudes toward women and the family. In 1784, John Backus, an undistinguished Massachusetts silversmith, was hauled before a court and asked why he beat his wife. He responded that "it was Partly owing to his Education for his father treated his mother in the same manner." The difference between Backus's case and his father's was that Backus's wife refused to tolerate such abuse, and she sued successfully for divorce. Divorce patterns in Connecticut and Pennsylvania show that after 1773, women divorced on about the same terms as men.

The war itself presented some women with fresh opportunities. In 1780, Ester DeBerdt Reed founded a large volunteer women's organization in Philadelphia—the first of its kind in the United States—that raised more than $300,000 for Washington's army. Other women ran farms and businesses while their husbands fought the British. And in 1790, the New Jersey legislature allowed women who owned property to vote.

Despite these scattered gains, republican society still defined women's roles exclusively in terms of mother, wife, and homemaker. Other pursuits seemed unnatural, even threatening. It is perhaps not surprising, therefore, that in 1807, New Jersey lawmakers—angry that

▶◀ **Read** the **Document**
Molly Wallace, Valedictory Address (1792) on
myhistorylab.com

Abigail Adams Benjamin Blyth painted this portrait of Abigail Adams, wife of the future President John Adams, c. 1766.

women voters had apparently determined the result of a close election—repealed female suffrage in the interests of "safety, quiet, and good order and dignity of the state." Even such an allegedly progressive thinker as Jefferson could not imagine allowing women to participate in serious politics. When in 1807 his secretary of the treasury, Albert Gallatin, called attention to the shortage of educated people to serve in government jobs and suggested recruiting women, Jefferson responded sharply: "The appointment of a woman to office is an innovation for which the public is not prepared, nor am I."

Quick Check

✓ What evidence argues that this was a period of significant progress for women in the United States?

The States: Experiments in Republicanism

In May 1776, the Second Continental Congress invited the states to adopt constitutions. The old colonial charters filled with references to king and Parliament were no longer adequate, and within a few years, most states had acted. Rhode Island and Connecticut already enjoyed republican government through their unique seventeenth-century charters that allowed the voters to select both governors and legislators. Eleven other states plus Vermont created new political structures. Their deliberations reveal how Americans in different regions and reacting to different social pressures defined fundamental republican principles.

Several constitutions were experimental, and states rewrote documents that had been drafted in the first flush of independence. These early constitutions nevertheless provided the framers of the federal Constitution of 1787 with insights into the strengths and weaknesses of government based on the will of the people.

Despite disagreements over details, Americans who wrote the various state constitutions shared two political assumptions. First, they insisted on *written* documents. This represented a major break with English practice. Political philosophers in the mother country had long boasted of Britain's unwritten constitution, a collection of judicial decisions and parliamentary statutes. But this vaunted system had not protected the colonists from oppression; hence, after declaring independence, Americans demanded that their state constitutions explicitly define the rights of the people and the power of their rulers.

Second, the authors of the state constitutions believed men and women possessed certain natural rights over which government exercised no control whatsoever. So that future rulers—potential tyrants—would know the exact limits of authority, these fundamental rights were carefully spelled out. Indeed, the people of Massachusetts rejected the proposed state constitution of 1778 largely because it lacked a full statement of their basic rights. They demanded a guarantee of "rights of conscience, and … security of persons and property, which every member in the State hath a right to expect from the supreme power."

Eight state constitutions contained specific declarations of rights. The length and character of these lists varied, but, in general, they affirmed three fundamental freedoms: religion, speech, and press. They protected citizens from unlawful searches and seizures and upheld trial by jury.

Quick Check

✓ Following independence, why did the states insist on drafting *written* constitutions?

STUMBLING TOWARD A NEW NATIONAL GOVERNMENT

Why did many Americans regard the Articles of Confederation as inadequate?

When the Second Continental Congress convened in 1775, the delegates found themselves waging war in the name of a country that did not yet exist. As the military crisis deepened, Congress gradually—often reluctantly—assumed greater authority over national affairs. But everyone agreed such narrow measures were a poor substitute for a legally constituted government. The separate states could not deal with the range of issues that the American people now confronted. Indeed, if independence meant anything in a world of sovereign nations, it implied the creation of a central authority able to conduct war, borrow money, regulate trade, and negotiate treaties.

Articles of Confederation

Creating a viable central government proved more difficult than anyone anticipated. Congress appointed a committee to draw up a plan for confederation. John Dickinson, the lawyer who had written an important revolutionary pamphlet titled *Letters from a Farmer in Pennsylvania*, headed the committee. Dickinson envisioned a strong central government. The report his committee presented on July 12, 1776, shocked delegates who assumed that the constitution would authorize a loose confederation of states. Dickinson's plan placed the western territories, land the separate states claimed for themselves, under congressional control. His committee also called for equal state representation in Congress.

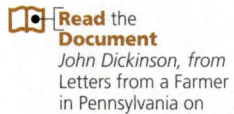
Read the **Document** *John Dickinson, from* Letters from a Farmer in Pennsylvania on **myhistorylab.com**

Since some states, such as Virginia and Massachusetts, were more populous than others, this fueled tensions between large and small states. Also unsettling was Dickinson's recommendation that taxes be paid to Congress on the basis of a state's total population, black as well as white, a formula that angered southerners who did not think slaves should be counted for purposes of taxation.

The Articles of Confederation that Congress finally approved in November 1777 bore little resemblance to Dickinson's original plan. The Articles jealously guarded the sovereignty of the states. The delegates who drafted the framework shared a republican conviction that power—especially power so far removed from the people—was dangerous. The only way to preserve liberty was to place as many constraints as possible on federal authority.

The result was a government that many people regarded as powerless. The Articles provided for a single legislative body consisting of representatives selected annually by the state legislatures. Each state had one vote in Congress. It could send as many as seven delegates, or as few as two, but if they divided evenly on an issue, the state lost its vote. There was no independent executive and no veto over legislative decisions. The Articles also denied Congress the power of taxation, a serious oversight in time of war. To obtain funds, the national government had to ask the states for contributions, called requisitions. If a state failed to cooperate—and many did—Congress limped along without financial support. All 13 states had to assent to amendments to this constitution. The authors expected the weak national government to handle foreign relations, military and Indian affairs, and interstate disputes. They did not award Congress ownership of the lands west of the Appalachians.

The new constitution sent to the states for ratification met apathy and hostility. Most Americans were far more interested in local affairs than in the acts of Congress. When a British army marched through a state, creating a need for immediate military aid, people spoke positively about central government, but as soon as the threat passed, they sang a different tune. During this period, even the slightest encroachment on state sovereignty rankled republicans who feared centralization would promote corruption.

Quick Check

✓ During the Revolution, why did Congress not create a stronger federal government?

Western Land: Key to the First Constitution

The major bone of contention with the Articles, however, was the disposition of the vast, unsurveyed territory west of the Appalachians. Although various states claimed the region, most of it actually belonged to Native Americans. In land grabs that federal negotiators called treaties, the United States government took much of modern Ohio, Indiana, Illinois, and Kentucky. Since the Indians had put their faith in the British during the war, they could do little to resist these humiliating agreements. As John Dickinson, then serving as the president of the Supreme Executive Council of Pennsylvania, told the Indians, since Britain has surrendered "the back country with all the forts … that they [the Indians] must now depend upon us for the preservation." If they dared to resist, "we will instantly turn upon them our armies … and extirpate them from the land where they were born and now live."

Some states, such as Virginia and Georgia, claimed land from the Atlantic Ocean to the elusive "South Seas," in effect extending their boundaries to the Pacific coast by virtue of royal charters. State legislators—their appetites whetted by aggressive land speculators—anticipated large revenues through land sales. Connecticut, New York, Pennsylvania, and North Carolina also announced intentions to seize western land.

Other states were not blessed with vague or ambiguous royal charters. The boundaries of Maryland, Delaware, and New Jersey had been established years earlier. It seemed as if people in these states would be cut off from the anticipated bounty. In protest, these "landless" states refused to ratify the Articles of Confederation. Marylanders were particularly vociferous. All the states had sacrificed for the common good during the Revolution, they complained. It appeared only fair that all states should profit from the fruits of victory, in this case, from the sale of western lands. Maryland's spokesmen feared that if Congress did not void Virginia's excessive claims to all of the Northwest Territory (the land west of Pennsylvania and north of the Ohio River) and to a large area south of the Ohio, beyond the Cumberland Gap, known as Kentucky, then Marylanders would desert their home state in search of cheap Virginia farms, leaving Maryland an underpopulated wasteland.

View the **Map**
Western Land Claims Ceded by the States on **myhistorylab.com**

The states resolved the controversy in 1781 as much by accident as by design. Virginia agreed to cede its holdings north of the Ohio River to the Confederation if Congress nullified land companies' purchases from the Indians. A practical consideration had softened Virginia's resolve. Republicans such as Jefferson worried about expanding their state beyond the mountains; with poor transportation links, it seemed impossible to govern such a large territory from Richmond.

Quick Check

✓ Why did the question of the western lands cause such conflict between the states under the Articles of Confederation?

The western settlers might even come to regard Virginia as a colonial power insensitive to their needs. Marylanders who dreamed of making fortunes on the land market grumbled, but when a British army appeared on their border, they accepted the Articles (March 1, 1781). Congress required another three years to work out the details of the Virginia cession. Other landed states followed Virginia's example. These transfers established an important principle. After 1781, it was agreed that the West belonged not to the separate states but to the United States. (See Map 6.1.)

Northwest Ordinance: The Confederation's Major Achievement

However weak Congress may have been, it did score one impressive triumph. Congressional action brought order to western settlement, especially in the Northwest Territory, and incorporated frontier Americans into an expanding federal system. In 1781, the prospects for success did not seem promising. For years, colonial authorities had ignored people who migrated far inland, sending neither money nor soldiers to protect them from Indian attack. Tensions between the seaboard colonies and the frontier regions sometimes flared into violence. Disorders occurred in South Carolina in 1767, in North Carolina in 1769, and in Vermont in 1777. With thousands of men and women, most of them squatters, pouring across the Appalachians, Congress had to act quickly to avoid the errors of royal and colonial authorities.

The initial attempt to deal with this explosive problem came in 1784. Jefferson, then serving as a member of Congress, drafted an ordinance that became the basis for more enduring legislation. He recommended carving ten new states out of the western lands north of the Ohio River that Virginia had recently ceded to the United States. He specified that each new state establish a republican form of government. When the population of a territory equaled that of the smallest state already in the Confederation, the region could apply for full statehood. In the meantime, free white males could participate in local government, a democratic guarantee that frightened some of Jefferson's more conservative colleagues.

The impoverished Congress was eager to sell off the western territory as quickly as possible. The frontier represented income that did not depend on the unreliable generosity of the states. In 1785, the Land Ordinance established an orderly process for laying out new townships and marketing public lands. Public response

Map 6.1 *Northwest Territory*   The U.S. government auctioned off the land in the Northwest Territory, the region defined by the Ohio River, the Great Lakes, and the Mississippi River. Proceeds from the sale of one section in each township were set aside for the construction of public schools.

disappointed Congress. Surveying the lands took longer than anticipated, and few persons possessed enough hard currency to make even the minimum purchase. Nevertheless, small homesteaders settled wherever they pleased, refusing to pay either government or speculators for the land.

Congress worried about the excess liberty on the frontier. In the 1780s, the West seemed to be filling up with people who by eastern standards were uncultured. Timothy Pickering, a New Englander, declared that "the emigrants to the frontier lands are the least worthy subjects in the United States. They are little less savage than the Indians; and when possessed of the most fertile spots, for want of industry, live miserably." The charge was as old as the frontier itself. Seventeenth-century Englishmen had said the same things of the earliest Virginians. The lawless image stuck, however. Even a sober observer such as Washington insisted that the West crawled with "banditti." The Ordinance of 1784 placed the government of the territories in the hands of people about whom congressmen and speculators had second thoughts.

These various currents shaped the Ordinance of 1787, one of the final acts passed under the Confederation. The bill, also called the Northwest Ordinance, provided a new structure for government of the Northwest Territory. It authorized creating between three and five territories, each to be ruled by a governor, a secretary, and three judges appointed by Congress. When the population of a territory reached 5,000, voters who owned property could elect an assembly, but its decisions were subject to the governor's absolute veto. Once 60,000 persons resided in a territory, they could write a constitution and petition for full statehood. While these procedures represented a retreat from Jefferson's original proposal, the Ordinance of 1787 contained several significant features. A bill of rights guaranteed the settlers the right to trial by jury, freedom of religion, and due process of law. The act also outlawed slavery, which freed the future states of Ohio, Indiana, Illinois, Michigan, and Wisconsin from the curse of human bondage. (See Map 6.2.)

By contrast, Congress paid less attention to settlement south of the Ohio River. Thousands of Americans had already streamed into a part of Virginia known as Kentucky. The most famous of these settlers was Daniel Boone. In 1775, the population of Kentucky was approximately 100; by 1784, it had jumped to 30,000.

Quick Check
How did the Northwest Ordinance resolve the problem of the western lands?

"HAVE WE FOUGHT FOR THIS?"

By 1785, the country seemed to have lost direction. The optimism that sustained revolutionary patriots had dissolved into pessimism and doubt. Many Americans, especially those who had provided leadership during the Revolution, agreed something had to be done. In 1786, Washington observed, "What astonishing changes a few years are capable of producing. Have we fought for this? Was it with these expectations that we launched into a sea of trouble, and have bravely struggled through the most threatening dangers?"

Why did Constitutional delegates compromise on representation and slavery?

Map 6.2 *Western Land* Claims ceded by the states after winning the war, the major issue facing the Continental Congress under the Articles of Confederation was mediating conflicting states' claims to rich western land. By 1802, the states had ceded all rights to the federal government.

The Genius of James Madison

The conviction of people such as Washington that the nation was in crisis reflected tensions within republican thought. They supported open elections and the right of individuals to advance their own economic well-being. But when these elements seemed to undermine social and political order, they feared that liberty had been carried too far. The situation had changed rapidly. As recently as the 1770s, republicans had insisted that the greatest threat to the American people was concentration of power in the hands of unscrupulous rulers. They therefore transformed state governors into figureheads and weakened the Confederation.

By the mid-1780s, persons of property and standing saw the problem in a different light. Recent experience suggested that ordinary citizens did not possess sufficient virtue to sustain a republic. The states had been plagued not by executive tyranny but by an excess of democracy, by a failure of the majority to preserve the property rights of the minority, by an unrestrained individualism that promoted anarchy rather than order.

Many state leaders did not seem concerned about the fiscal health of the national government. Presses churned out worthless paper currency, and in some state assemblies impeded the collection of debt. In Rhode Island, legislators made it illegal for merchants to reject Rhode Island money even though everyone knew it had no value. No wonder Governor William Livingston of New Jersey declared in 1787, "We do not exhibit the virtue that is necessary to support a republican government."

As Americans tried to interpret these experiences within a republican framework, they were checked by the most accepted political wisdom of the age. Baron de Montesquieu (1689–1755), a French political philosopher of immense reputation and author of *The Spirit of the Laws* (1748), declared flatly that a republican government could not flourish in a large territory. The reasons were clear. If the people lost direct control over their representatives, they would fall prey to tyrants. Large distances allowed rulers to hide their corruption; physical separation presented aristocrats with opportunities to seize power.

In the United States, most learned men treated Montesquieu's theories as self-evident truths. His writings seemed to demonstrate the importance of preserving the sovereignty of the states. However much these small republics abused the rights of property and ignored minority interests, it was plainly unscientific to maintain that a republic of 13 states, millions of people, and vast territory could survive.

James Madison rejected Montesquieu's argument and helped Americans think of republican government in radical new ways. This soft-spoken, unprepossessing Virginian was the most brilliant American political thinker of his generation. One French official described Madison as "a man one must study a long time in order to make a fair appraisal." Those who listened carefully to what Madison said, however, soon recognized his genius for translating theory into practice.

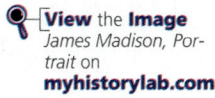

View the **Image**
James Madison, Portrait on
myhistorylab.com

Madison delved into the writings of a group of Scottish philosophers, the most prominent being David Hume (1711–1776). From their works he concluded that Americans need not fear an expanded republic. Madison perceived that "inconveniences of popular States contrary to prevailing Theory, are in proportion not to the extent, but to the narrowness of their limits." Indeed, it was in small states such as Rhode Island that legislative majorities tyrannized the propertied minority. In a large territory, Madison explained, "the Society becomes broken into a greater variety of interest, of pursuits, of passions, which check each other, whilst those who may feel a common sentiment have less opportunity of communication and contact."

Quick Check
✓ How did James Madison respond to republican fears that a nation as large as the United States could never be successfully governed as a republic?

Constitutional Reform

A movement to overhaul the Articles of Confederation began in 1786, when Madison and his friends persuaded the Virginia assembly to recommend a convention to explore creating a unified system of "commercial regulations." Congress supported the idea. In September, delegates from five states arrived in Annapolis, Maryland, to discuss issues that extended far beyond commerce. The small turnout was disappointing, but nationalists hatched an even bolder plan. The delegates advised Congress to hold a second meeting in Philadelphia "to take into consideration the situation of the United States, to devise such further provisions as shall appear to them necessary to render the constitution of the Federal Government adequate to the exigencies of the Union." Staunch states' rights advocates in Congress may not have known what was afoot, but Congress authorized a grand convention to gather in May 1787.

Events played into Madison's hands. Soon after the Annapolis meeting, an uprising known as Shays's Rebellion, involving thousands of impoverished farmers, erupted in western Massachusetts. No matter how hard these men worked, they found themselves in debt to eastern creditors. They complained of high taxes and interest rates and, most of all, of a state government insensitive to their problems. In 1786, Daniel Shays, a veteran of the battle of Bunker Hill, and his armed neighbors closed a county courthouse where creditors were suing to foreclose farm mortgages. The insurgents threatened to seize the federal arsenal in Springfield. Congress did not have funds sufficient to support an army, and the arsenal might have fallen. But wealthy Bostonians raised 4,000 troops to suppress the insurrection. The victors were in for a surprise. At the next general election, Massachusetts voters selected representatives sympathetic to Shays's demands, and a new liberal assembly reformed debtor law.

Nationalists throughout the United States were less forgiving. Shays's Rebellion symbolized the breakdown of law and order that they had predicted. "Great commotions are prevailing in Massachusetts," Madison wrote. "An appeal to the

Read the
Document
*Military Reports of
Shays's Rebellion* on
myhistorylab.com

Shays's Rebellion This 1787 woodcut portrays Daniel Shays with one of his chief officers, Jacob Shattucks. Shays led farmers in western Massachusetts in revolt against a state government that seemed insensitive to the needs of poor debtors. Their rebellion frightened conservative leaders, who demanded a strong new federal government.

sword is exceedingly dreaded." The time had come for sensible people to speak up for a strong national government. The unrest in Massachusetts persuaded persons who might have ignored the Philadelphia meeting to participate in drafting a new constitution.

Quick Check

✓ What role did Shays's Rebellion play in bringing about consitutional reform?

The Philadelphia Convention

In the spring of 1787, 55 men representing 12 states traveled to Philadelphia. Rhode Island refused to take part, which Madison attributed to its "wickedness and folly." Jefferson described the convention as an "assembly of demi-Gods," but this flattering depiction is misleading. However much modern Americans revere the Constitution, they should remember that its authors did not possess divine insight into the nature of government. They were practical people—lawyers, merchants, and planters—many of whom had fought in the Revolution and served in the Congress of the Confederation. Most were in their thirties or forties. The gathering included George Washington, James Madison, George Mason, Robert Morris, James Wilson, John Dickinson, Benjamin Franklin, and Alexander Hamilton, to name some of the more prominent participants. Absent were John Adams and Thomas Jefferson, who were conducting diplomacy in Europe; Patrick Henry, a localist suspicious of strong central government, "smelled a rat" and remained in Virginia.

As soon as the Constitutional Convention opened on May 25, the delegates made two important procedural decisions. First, they voted "that nothing spoken in the House be printed, or communicated without leave." The rule was stringently enforced. Sentries kept out uninvited visitors, windows stayed shut in the sweltering heat to prevent sound from either entering or leaving the chamber, and members were forbidden to copy the daily journal without official permission. As Madison explained, the secrecy rule saved "both the convention and the community from a thousand erroneous and perhaps mischievous reports." It also has made it difficult for modern lawyers and judges to determine what the delegates had in mind when they wrote the Constitution.

Second, the delegates decided to vote by state. But to avoid the problems that had plagued the Confederation, key proposals needed the support of only a majority of the states instead of the nine states the Articles required.

Quick Check

✓ Why were the men who drafted the consitution so concerned with secrecy?

Inventing a Federal Republic

Even before all the delegates had arrived, Madison drew up a framework for a new federal system known as the Virginia Plan. It envisioned a national legislature of two houses, one elected *directly* by the people, the other chosen by the first house from nominations made by the state assemblies. Representation in both houses was proportional to the state's population. The Virginia Plan also provided for an executive elected by Congress. Madison persuaded Edmund Randolph, Virginia's popular governor, to present this scheme to the convention on May 29. Randolph claimed that the Virginia Plan merely revised sections of the Articles, but everyone, including Madison, knew better. "My ideas," Madison confessed, "strike … deeply at the old Confederation." He was determined to restrain the state assemblies, and in the original Virginia Plan, Madison gave the federal government power to veto state laws. Since most delegates at the Philadelphia convention sympathized with the nationalist position, Madison's blueprint for a strong federal government was referred for further study and debate. Men who allegedly had come together to reform the Confederation found themselves discussing the details of "a *national* Government … consisting of a *supreme* Legislature, Executive, and Judiciary."

The Virginia Plan had been pushed through the convention so fast that opponents hardly had an opportunity to object. On June 15, they spoke up. William Paterson, a New Jersey lawyer, advanced the so-called New Jersey Plan, which retained the unicameral legislature in which each state possessed one vote but gave Congress new powers to tax and regulate trade. Paterson argued that these revisions, while more modest than Madison's plan, would have greater appeal for the American people: "I believe that a little practical virtue is to be preferred to the finest theoretical principles, which cannot be carried into effect." The delegates listened politely but only New Jersey, New York, and Delaware voted in favor of it.

Rejecting this framework did not resolve the most controversial issue before the convention. Paterson and others feared that under the Virginia Plan, small states would lose their separate identities. They maintained that unless each state possessed an equal vote in Congress, the small states would find themselves at the mercy of their larger neighbors.

This argument outraged delegates who favored a strong federal government. It awarded too much power to the states. "For whom [are we] forming a Government?" James Wilson of Pennsylvania cried. "Is it for men, or for the imaginary beings called States?" It seemed absurd that 68,000 Rhode Islanders should have the same voice in Congress as 747,000 Virginians.

Quick Check

✓ Did the New Jersey plan represent a significant retreat from the main points of the Virginia plan?

Compromise Saves the Convention

Mediation was the only way to overcome what Roger Sherman of Connecticut called "a full stop in proceedings." On July 2, the convention elected a "grand committee" of one person from each state to resolve differences between the large and small states. Franklin, at age 81 the oldest delegate, served as chair. The two fiercest supporters of proportional representation, Madison and Wilson, were left off the committee, a sign that the small states would salvage something from the compromise.

The committee recommended equal representation for the states in the upper house of Congress and proportionate representation in the lower house. Only the lower house could initiate money bills. One member of the lower house should be selected for every 30,000 inhabitants of a state. Southern delegates insisted that this number include slaves. In the so-called three-fifths rule, the committee agreed that to determine representation in the lower house, every five slaves in a congressional district would count as three free voters, This gave the South much greater power in the new government than it would have otherwise received. As with most compromises, the

👁 **Watch** the **Video**
Slavery and the Constitution on
myhistorylab.com

one Franklin's committee negotiated fully satisfied no one. It did, however, overcome a major impasse. After the small states gained an assured voice in the upper house, the Senate, they cooperated enthusiastically in creating a strong central government.

Despite these advances, in late August, a disturbing issue came before the convention. It was a harbinger of the great sectional crisis of the nineteenth century. Many northern representatives wanted to end the slave trade immediately. They despised the three-fifths rule that seemed to award slaveholders extra power simply because they owned slaves. "It seemed now to be pretty well understood," Madison jotted in his private notes, "that the real difference of interest lay, not between the large and small but between the N. and Southn. States. The institution of slavery and its consequences formed a line of discrimination."

Whenever northern delegates—and on this point they were not united—pushed too aggressively, southerners threatened to bolt the convention, thereby destroying any hope of establishing a strong national government. Curiously, even recalcitrant southerners avoided using the word *slavery*. They seemed embarrassed to call the institution by its true name. In the Constitution itself, slaves were described as "other persons," "such persons," "persons held to Service or Labour," as everything but slaves.

A few northern delegates such as Roger Sherman sought to mollify the southerners, especially the South Carolinians, who spoke passionately about preserving slavery. Gouverneur Morris, a Pennsylvania representative, would have none of it. He reminded the convention that "the inhabitant of Georgia and S.C. who goes to the Coast of Africa, and in defiance of the most sacred laws of humanity tears away his fellow creatures from their dearest connections and damns them to the most cruel bondage, shall have more votes in a Government instituted for the protection of the rights of mankind, than the Citizen of Pa. or N. Jersey."

Ignoring Morris's attacks, the delegates reached an uneasy compromise on the slave trade. Southerners feared that the new Congress would pass commercial regulations that hurt the planters—export taxes on rice and tobacco, for example. They demanded a two-thirds majority of the federal legislature be required to pass trade laws. They backed down on this point, however, in exchange for guarantees that Congress would not interfere with the slave trade until 1808 (see Chapter 8). The South even won a clause assuring the return of fugitive slaves. "We have obtained," Charles Cotesworth Pinckney told the planters of South Carolina, "a right to recover our slaves in whatever part of America they may take refuge, which is a right we had not before."

Although these deals disappointed many northerners, they conceded that establishing a strong national government was of greater immediate importance than ending the slave trade. "Great as the evil is," Madison wrote, "a dismemberment of the union would be worse."

Read the **Document**
The Debates in the Federal Convention of 1787 on **myhistorylab.com**

Quick Check
✓ Why did the delegates think a compromise on slavery and states' rights was necessary to achieve the ratification of a new constituion?

The Last Details

On July 26, the convention formed a Committee of Detail, a group that prepared a rough draft of the Constitution. After the committee completed its work—writing a document that still, after so much debate, preserved the fundamental points of the Virginia Plan— the delegates reconsidered each article. The task required the better part of a month.

During these sessions, the convention concluded that the president, as they now called the chief executive, should be selected by an electoral college, a body of prominent men in each state chosen by local voters. The number of "electoral" votes each state held equaled its number of representatives and senators. This awkward device guaranteed that the president would not be indebted to the Congress for his office. Whoever received the second most votes in the electoral college automatically became vice president. If no person received a majority of the votes, the lower house—the House of Representatives—would decide the election, with each state casting a single vote. Delegates also gave the president veto power over legislation and the right to nominate judges. Both privileges would have been unthinkable a decade earlier, but the state experiments revealed the importance of having an independent executive to maintain a balanced system of republican government.

As the meeting was concluding, delegates expressed concern about the absence of a bill of rights. Most state constitutions included such declarations. Virginians such as George Mason insisted that the states and their citizens needed explicit protection from excesses by the federal government. While many delegates sympathized with Mason's appeal, they noted that the hour was late and, in any case, that the proposed Constitution provided security for individual rights. During the hard battles over ratification, the delegates may have regretted passing over the issue so lightly.

Quick Check

✔ Why did the delegates to the Constitutional Convention fail to Include a formal Bill of Rights?

We the People

Now that many issues were settled, the delegates had to overcome the hurdle of ratifying the Constitution. They adopted an ingenious procedure. Instead of submitting the Constitution to the state legislatures, all of which had a vested interest in the status quo and most of which had two houses, either of which could block approval, they called for electing 13 state conventions to review the new federal government. Moreover, the Constitution would take effect after the assent of only nine states. There was no danger that the proposed system would fail simply because a single state like Rhode Island withheld approval.

The convention asked the urbane Gouverneur Morris to make final stylistic changes in the wording of the Constitution. When Morris examined the working draft, he discovered that it spoke of the collection of states forming a new government. This wording presented problems. Ratification required only nine states. No one knew whether all the states would accept the Constitution and, if not, which nine would. New England states, for example, might reject the document. Morris's brilliant phrase "We the People of the United States" eliminated this difficulty. The new nation was a republic of the people, not of the states.

On September 17, 39 men signed the Constitution. A few delegates, like Mason, could not support it. Others had gone home. For more than three months, Madison had been the convention's driving intellectual force. He now generously summarized the experience: "There never was an assembly of men, charged with a great and arduous trust, who were more pure in their motives, or more exclusively or anxiously devoted to the object committed to them."

Quick Check

✔ What was the "ingenious procedure for ratification" adopted by the Constitutional Convention delegates?

WHOSE CONSTITUTION? STRUGGLE FOR RATIFICATION   161

WHOSE CONSTITUTION? STRUGGLE FOR RATIFICATION

Supporters of the Constitution recognized that ratification would not be easy. After all, the convention had been authorized only to revise the Articles. Instead it produced a new plan that fundamentally altered relations between the states and the central government. (See Table 6.1.) The delegates dutifully dispatched copies of the Constitution to the Congress of Confederation, then meeting in New York City. That powerless body referred the document to the separate states without any recommendation. The fight for ratification had begun.

Federalists and Antifederalists

Proponents of the Constitution enjoyed great advantages over the unorganized opposition. In the contest for ratification, they took no chances. Their most astute move was to adopt the label Federalist. The term cleverly suggested that they stood for a confederation of states rather than for a supreme national authority. In fact, they envisioned a strong centralized national government able to field a formidable army. Critics of the Constitution, who tended to be poorer, less urban, and less well educated than their opponents, cried foul, but they were stuck with the name Antifederalist, a misleading term that made their cause seem a rejection of the very notion of a federation of the states.

The Federalists recruited the most prominent public figures of the day. In every state convention, speakers favoring the Constitution were more polished and fully prepared than their opponents. In New York, the campaign to win ratification sparked publication of *The Federalist*, a brilliant series of essays written by Madison, Hamilton, and John Jay in 1787 and 1788. The nation's newspapers overwhelmingly supported the new government. Few journals even carried Antifederalist writings. In some states, the Federalists adopted questionable tactics to gain ratification. In Pennsylvania, for example, they achieved a quorum for a crucial vote by dragging opposition delegates into the meeting from the streets. In New York, Hamilton threatened upstate Antifederalists that New York City would secede from the state unless the state ratified the Constitution.

In these battles, the Antifederalists articulated a political philosophy that had popular appeal. Like the extreme republicans who drafted the first state constitutions, the Antifederalists were suspicious of political power. They warned that public officials, however selected, would scheme to expand their authority.

Preserving individual liberty required constant vigilance. The larger the republic, the greater the opportunity for political corruption. Local voters could not know what their representatives in a distant national capital were doing. The government the Constitution outlined invited precisely the kinds of problems that Montesquieu had described in *The Spirit of the Laws*: "In so extensive a republic," one Antifederalist declared, "the great officers of government would soon become above the control of the people, and abuse their power."

Antifederalists demanded direct, personal contact with their representatives. Elected officials should reflect the character of their constituents as closely as possible. It seemed unlikely that in large congressional districts, the people could preserve such close ties with their representatives. According to the Antifederalists, the Constitution favored persons wealthy enough to have forged a reputation that extended

What issues separated Federalists from Antifederalists during debates over ratification?

Read the **Document** *Publius James Madison Federalist Paper Number 10* on **myhistorylab.com**

TABLE 6.1   Revolution or Reform? The Articles of Confederation and the Constitution Compared

Political Challenge	Articles of Confederation	Constitution
Mode of ratification or amendment	Require confirmation by every state legislature	Requires confirmation by three-fourths of state conventions or legislatures
Number of houses in legislature	One	Two
Mode of representation	Two to seven delegates represent each state; each state holds only one vote in Congress	Two senators represent each state in upper house; each senator holds one vote. One representative to lower house represents every 30,000 people (in 1788) in a state; each representative holds one vote
Mode of election and term of office	Delegates appointed annually by state legislatures	Senators chosen by state legislatures for six-year term (direct election after 1913); representatives chosen by vote of citizens for two-year term
Executive	No separate executive: Delegates annually elect one of their number as president, who possesses no veto, no power to appoint officers or conduct policy. Administrative functions of government theoretically carried out by Committee of States, practically by various single-headed departments	Separate executive branch: President elected by electoral college to four-year term; granted veto, power to conduct policy and appoint ambassadors, judges, and officers of executive departments established by legislation
Judiciary	Most adjudication left to state and local courts; Congress is final court of appeal in disputes between states	Separate branch consisting of Supreme Court and inferior courts established by Congress to enforce federal law
Taxation	States alone can levy taxes; Congress funds the Common Treasury by making requisitions for state contributions	Federal government granted powers of taxation
Regulation of commerce	Congress regulates foreign commerce by treaty but holds no check on conflicting state regulations	Congress regulates foreign commerce by treaty; all state regulations must obtain congressional consent

beyond a single community. Samuel Chase told the members of the Maryland ratifying convention that under the new system, "the distance between the people and their representatives will be so great that there is no probability of a farmer or planter being chosen … only the *gentry*, the *rich*, and the well-born will be elected."

Federalist speakers mocked their opponents' localist perspective. The Constitution deserved general support precisely because it ensured that future Americans would be represented by "natural aristocrats," individuals possessing greater insights, skills, and training than did the ordinary citizen. These talented leaders could discern the entire population's interests. They were not tied to the selfish needs of local communities. "The little demagogue of a petty parish or county will find his importance annihilated [under the Constitution] and his intrigues useless," predicted Charles Cotesworth Pinckney, a South Carolina Federalist.

Historians have generally accepted the Federalist critique. It would be a mistake, however, to see the Antifederalists as "losers" or as persons who could not comprehend social and economic change. Although their rhetoric echoed an older moral view of political culture, they accepted more easily than did many Federalists a liberal marketplace in which ordinary citizens competed as equals with the rich and well-born. They believed the public good was best served by allowing individuals like themselves to pursue their own private interests. They had been doing that on the local level during the 1780s and resented the imposition of elite controls over their affairs. Although the Antifederalists lost the battle over ratification, their ideas about political economy found many champions in the age of Andrew Jackson.

Many different types of people supported the Constitution. Historians have been unable to discover sharp correlations between wealth and occupation on the one hand and attitudes toward the proposed system of central government on the other. In general, Federalists lived in more commercialized areas than did their opponents. In the cities, artisans as well as merchants called for ratification. Farmers who were only marginally involved in commercial agriculture frequently voted Antifederalist.

Despite passionate pleas from Patrick Henry and other Antifederalists, most state conventions quickly adopted the Constitution. Delaware acted first (December 7, 1787). Within eight months of the Philadelphia meeting, eight of the nine states required to launch the government had ratified the document. The contests in Virginia (June 1788) and New York (July 1788) generated bitter debate, but they too joined the Union, leaving only North Carolina and Rhode Island outside the United States. Eventually (November 21, 1789, and May 29, 1790), even these states ratified the Constitution. Still, the vote had been close. The Constitution was ratified in New York by a tally of 30 to 27, in Massachusetts by 187 to 168, and in Virginia by 89 to 79. A few votes in key states could have defeated the new government. (See Map 6.3.)

While the state conventions sparked angry rhetoric, Americans soon closed ranks behind the Constitution. An Antifederalist who represented one Massachusetts village explained that "he had opposed the adoption of this Constitution; but that he had been overruled … by a majority of wise and understanding men [and that now] he should endeavor to sow the seeds of union and peace among the people he represented."

Read the **Document** *Patrick Henry, Against Ratification of the Constitution (1788)* on **myhistorylab.com**

Quick Check

✓ What were the major political issues separating Federalists from Antifederalists?

Adding the Bill of Rights

The first ten amendments to the Constitution are the major legacy of the Antifederalist argument. In almost every state convention, opponents of the Constitution pointed to the need for greater protection of individual liberties, rights that people presumably had possessed in a state of nature. "It is necessary," wrote one Antifederalist, "that the sober and industrious part of the community should be defended from the rapacity and violence of the vicious and idle. A bill of rights, therefore, ought to set forth the purposes for which the compact is made, and serves to secure the minority against the usurpation and tyranny of the majority." The list of fundamental rights varied from state to state, but most Antifederalists demanded guarantees for jury trial and freedom of religion. They wanted prohibitions against cruel and unusual punishments. There was also considerable support for freedom of speech and of the press.

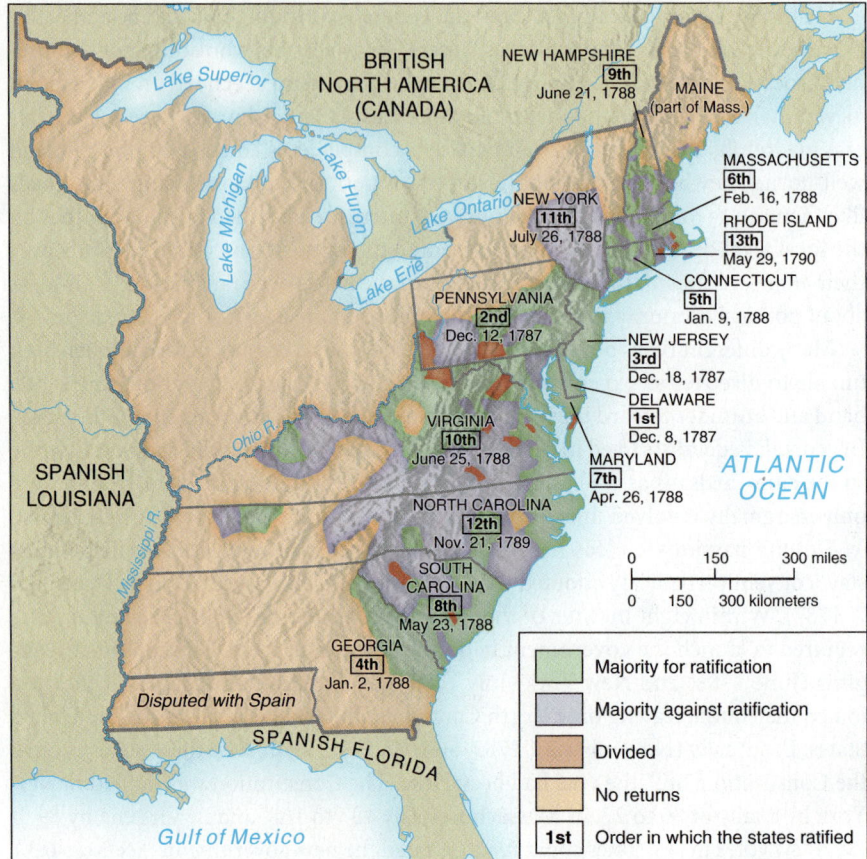

Map 6.3 *Ratification of the Constitution* Advocates of the new Constitution called themselves Federalists, and those who opposed its ratification were known as Antifederalists.

Madison and others regarded the proposals with little enthusiasm. In *The Federalist* No. 84, Hamilton reminded the American people that "the constitution is itself … a BILL OF RIGHTS." But after the adoption of the Constitution had been assured, Madison moderated his stand. A bill of rights would appease able men such as George Mason and Edmund Randolph, who might otherwise remain alienated from the new federal system. "We have in this way something to gain," Madison concluded, "and if we proceed with caution, nothing to lose."

The crucial consideration was caution. People throughout the nation advocated a second constitutional convention to take Antifederalist criticism into account. Madison wanted to avoid such a meeting. He feared that members of the first Congress might use a bill of rights as an excuse to revise the entire Constitution.

Madison carefully reviewed these recommendations and the declarations of rights that had appeared in the early state constitutions. On June 8, 1789, he placed before the House of Representatives a set of amendments to protect individual rights from government interference. Madison told Congress that the greatest dangers to popular liberties came from "the majority [operating] against the minority."

A committee compressed his original ideas into ten amendments that were ratified and became known collectively as the Bill of Rights. For many modern Americans these amendments are the most important section of the Constitution. Madison had hoped that additions would be inserted into the text of the Constitution at the appropriate places, not tacked onto the end, but he was overruled.

The Bill of Rights protected the freedoms of assembly, speech, religion, and the press; guaranteed speedy trial by an impartial jury; preserved the people's right to bear arms; and prohibited unreasonable searches. Other amendments dealt with legal procedure. Some opponents of the Constitution urged Congress to provide greater safeguards for states' rights, but Madison had no intention of backing away from a strong central government. Only the Tenth Amendment addressed the states' relation to the federal system. To calm Antifederalist fears, this crucial article specified that those "powers not delegated to the United States by the Constitution, nor prohibited by it to the States, are reserved to the States respectively, or to the people."

On September 25, 1789, both houses of Congress passed the Bill of Rights. By December 15, 1791, three-fourths of the states had ratified the amendments. Madison was proud of his achievement. He had secured individual rights without undermining the Constitution. When he asked his friend Jefferson for his opinion of the Bill of Rights, Jefferson responded with typical republican candor: "I like [it] … as far as it goes; but I should have been for going further."

Read the **Document**
The Bill of Rights (1789) on **myhistorylab.com**

Quick Check

✓ Why did the men who originally drafted the Constitution not include a Bill of Rights?

CONCLUSION: SUCCESS DEPENDS ON THE PEOPLE

By 1789, one phase of American political experimentation had ended. The people gradually, often haltingly, had learned that in a republican society, they themselves were sovereign. They could no longer blame government failures on inept monarchs or greedy aristocrats. They bore a great responsibility. Americans had demanded a government of the people only to discover during the 1780s that in some situations, the people could not always be trusted with power, majorities could tyrannize minorities, and the best government could abuse individual rights.

Contemporaries had difficulty deciding just what had been accomplished. A writer in the *Pennsylvania Packet* thought the American people had preserved order: "The year 1776 is celebrated for a revolution in favor of liberty. The year 1787 … will be celebrated with equal joy, for a revolution in favor of Government." But aging Patriots grumbled that perhaps order had been achieved at too high a price. In 1788, Richard Henry Lee remarked, "'Tis really astonishing that the same people, who have just emerged from a long and cruel war in defense of liberty, should now agree to fix an elective despotism upon themselves and their posterity."

But most Americans probably would have accepted the optimistic assessment of Benjamin Franklin. As he watched the delegates to the Philadelphia convention sign the Constitution, he noted a sun carved on the back of George Washington's chair. "I have," the aged philosopher noted, "… often in the course of the session … looked at [the sun] behind the President without being able to tell whether it was rising or setting; but now at length I have the happiness to know that it is a rising and not a setting sun."

6 STUDY RESOURCES

((•—Listen to the **Chapter Audio** for Chapter 6 on **myhistorylab.com**

TIMELINE

1776 Second Continental Congress authorizes colonies to create republican government (May), p. 149
- Eight states draft new constitutions; two others already enjoy republican government by virtue of former colonial charters, p. 149

1777 Congress accepts Articles of Confederation (November), p. 150

1781 States ratify Articles of Confederation following settlement of Virginia's western land claims, p. 151

1783 Society of the Cincinnati raises a storm of criticism, p. 143

1785 Congress passes Land Ordinance for Northwest Territory, p. 152

1786 Annapolis Convention suggests revising the Articles of Confederation (September), p. 155
- Shays's Rebellion frightens American leaders, p. 156

1787–1788 All states except North Carolina and Rhode Island ratify Constitution, p. 163

1791 Bill of Rights (first ten amendments to the Constitution) ratified, p. 165

CHAPTER REVIEW

DEFINING REPUBLICAN CULTURE

What were the limits of equality in the "republican" society of the new United States?

Some Americans worried that the scramble for material wealth would undermine republican values in the new nation. Disparities in wealth made some worry that a hereditary aristocracy might grow up to dominate government. Elites worried that democratic excesses would lead to men without property, and the personal independence and stability that came with it, rising to power. Enslaved African Americans and most women were denied the rights to property and the independence required to become full citizens of a republican society. *(p. 142)*

STUMBLING TOWARD A NEW NATIONAL GOVERNMENT

Why did many Americans regard the Articles of Confederation as inadequate?

During the Revolution, Americans showed little interest in establishing a strong national government. Under the Articles of Confederation (1777), an underfunded Congress limped along without direction, while the states competed over western lands. Only after Virginia ceded its claims could Congress draft the Northwest Ordinance, which provided an orderly plan for settling the Ohio Valley. The weak Congress was not even able to force the British to live up to their obligations under the Treaty of Paris of 1783. *(p. 150)*

"HAVE WE FOUGHT FOR THIS?"

Why did Constitutional delegates compromise on representation and slavery?

James Madison's Virginia Plan for the Constitution called for representation in both houses of Congress to be proportional to a state's population. Small states objected that this would put them at the mercy of larger states. Southern states feared that more populous northern states might vote to outlaw slavery. To prevent a breakdown, the delegates compromised. Each state would have an equal number of representatives in the Senate and slaves would be counted as three-fifths of a person when determining representation for the federal government. *(p. 153)*

WHOSE CONSTITUTION? STRUGGLE FOR RATIFICATION

What issues separated Federalists from Antifederalists during debates over ratification?

During the debates of 1787–88, Federalists, who favored stronger national government, defended the Constitution against Antifederalists, who opposed centralized authority. By the end of 1791, enough state conventions had endorsed the Constitution for ratification. To appease the Antifederalists, Congress in 1789 added a Bill of Rights to protect the freedoms of citizens against the power of the national government. *(p. 161)*

KEY TERM QUESTIONS

1. What did republicanism represent for most eighteenth-century Americans? (p. 142)

2. Why did African Americans form the African Methodist Episcopal Church? (p. 146)

3. Why were the authors of the state constitutions so concerned with natural rights? (p. 149)

4. Why did the Articles of Confederation favor the sovereignty of the states rather than that of the federal government? (p. 150)

5. How did the Northwest Ordinance resolve the problem of the western lands? (p. 153)

6. Did Shays's Rebellion betray or uphold the spirit of the American Revolution? (p. 156)

7. How did the New Jersey Plan differ from the Virginia Plan? (p. 157)

8. Why was the three-fifths rule necessary to achieve ratification of a new constitution? (p. 158)

9. What issues separated Federalists from Antifederalists during debates over ratification? (p. 161)

10. Why did Antifederalists oppose the Constitution? (p. 161)

11. Why did the men who originally drafted the Constitution not include a Bill of Rights? (p. 165)

MyHistoryLab CONNECTIONS

Visit www.myhistorylab.com for a customized Study Plan to build your knowledge of *The Republican Experiment*.

Question for Analysis

1. What drove Phillis Wheatley to write on the subjects discussed in her poetry?

   Read the Document *Phill is Wheatley, Religious and Moral Poems* p. 146

2. Why did the disposition of western lands cause an impasse in the ratification of the Articles of Confederation?

   View the Map *Western Land Claims Ceded by the States* p. 151

3. What motivated Daniel Shays to lead a rebellion?

   Read the Document *Military Reports of Shays's Rebellion* p. 156

4. Was slavery protected by the Constitution?

   Watch the Video *Slavery and the Constitution* p. 158

5. Why was Patrick Henry against ratification of the Constitution?

   Read the Document *Patrick Henry, Against Ratification of the Constitution?* p. 163

Other Resources from this Chapter

Read the Document *George Washington, Manners and Etiquette*

Read the Document *Slave Petition to the General Assembly in Connecticut*

Read the Document *Richard Allen, "Address to the Free People of Colour"*

Read the Document *John Adams to Abigail Adams, July 3, 1776*

Read the Document *Molly Wallace Valedictory Address, 1792*

Read the Document *John Dickinson, Letters from a Farmer in Pennsylvania*

View the Image *James Madison, Portrait*

Read the Document *The Debates in the Federal Convention of 1787*

Read the Document *Publius James Madison Federalist Paper Number 10*

Read the Document *The Bill of Rights*

7 DEMOCRACY AND DISSENT

The Violence of Party Politics, 1788–1800

Contents and Spotlight Questions

((•— **Listen** to the **Chapter Audio** for Chapter 7 on **myhistorylab.com**

FORCE OF PUBLIC OPINION

While presiding over the first meeting of the U.S. Senate in 1789, Vice President John Adams called the senators' attention to a pressing procedural question: How would they address George Washington, the newly elected president? Adams insisted that Washington deserved an impressive title to lend dignity and weight to his office. The vice president warned the senators that if they called Washington simply "president of the United States," the "common people of foreign countries [as well

The Hero of Trenton Well-wishers spread flowers in front of George Washington as he rides through Trenton, New Jersey, on his way from Virginia to New York for his inauguration as the first president of the United States in 1789.

as] the sailors and soldiers [would] despise him to all eternity." Adams recommended "His Highness, the President of the United States, and Protector of their Liberties." Some senators favored "His Elective Majesty" or "His Excellency."

Adams's initiative caught many persons, including Washington, by surprise. They regarded the debate as ridiculous. James Madison, a member of the House of Representatives, announced that pretentious European titles were ill-suited to the "genius of the people" and "the nature of our Government." Thomas Jefferson, who was then working as a diplomat in Paris, could not comprehend what motivated the vice president. In private correspondence, he repeated Benjamin Franklin's judgment that Adams "means well for his Country, is always an honest Man, often a wise one, but sometimes, and in some things, absolutely out of his senses." When the senators learned that their efforts embarrassed Washington, they dropped the topic. The leader of the new republic would be called president of the United States. One wag, however, dubbed the portly Adams "His Rotundity."

The comic-opera quality of the debate about how to address Washington should not obscure the participants' concern about setting government policy. The members of the first Congress could not take the survival of republican government for granted. All of them, of course, wanted to secure the Revolution. The recently ratified Constitution transferred sovereignty from the states to the people, a bold and unprecedented decision that many Americans feared would generate chronic instability. Translating constitutional abstractions into practical legislation would have been difficult, even under the most favorable conditions. But these were trying times. Britain and France, rivals again in a century of war, put nearly unbearable pressures on the leaders of the new republic and, in the process, made foreign policy a bitterly divisive issue.

Although no one welcomed them, political parties gradually took shape. Neither the Jeffersonians (also called the Republicans) nor the Federalists—as the two major groups were called—doubted that the United States would one day become a great commercial power. They differed, however, on how best to manage the transition from an agrarian household economy to an international system of trade and industry. The Federalists encouraged rapid integration of the United States into a world economy, but however enthusiastic they were about capitalism, they did not trust the people or local government to do the job effectively. A modern economy, they insisted, required strong national institutions that would be directed by a social elite who understood the financial challenge and would work in the best interests of the people.

Such claims frightened persons who came to identify themselves as Jeffersonians. Strong financial institutions, they thought, had corrupted the government of Britain from which they had just separated themselves. They searched for alternative ways to accommodate the needs of commerce and industry. Unlike the Federalists, the Jeffersonians put their faith in the people, defined for the most part politically as white yeoman farmers. The Jeffersonians insisted that ordinary entrepreneurs, if they could be freed from intrusive government regulations, could be trusted to resist greed and crass materialism and to sustain the virtue of the republic.

During the 1790s, former allies were surprised to discover themselves at odds over such basic issues. One person—Hamilton, for example—would stake out a position. Another, such as Jefferson or Madison, would respond, perhaps speaking a little more extravagantly than a specific issue demanded, goaded by the rhetorical nature of public debate. The first would then rebut the new position passionately. By the mid-1790s, this dialectic had almost spun out of control, taking the young republic to the brink of political violence.

Leaders of every persuasion had to learn to live with "public opinion." The revolutionary elite had invited the people to participate in government, but the gentlemen assumed that ordinary voters would automatically defer to their social betters. Instead, the Founders discovered they had created a rough-and-tumble political culture, a robust public sphere of cheap newspapers and street demonstrations. The newly empowered "public" followed the great debates of the period through articles they read in hundreds of highly partisan journals and magazines.

PRINCIPLE AND PRAGMATISM: ESTABLISHING A NEW GOVERNMENT

In 1788, George Washington enjoyed great popularity. The people remembered him as the selfless leader of the Continental Army. Even before the states had ratified the Constitution, everyone assumed he would be chosen president of the United States. He received the unanimous support of the electoral college, an achievement that no subsequent president has duplicated. John Adams, a respected Massachusetts lawyer who had championed independence in 1776, was elected vice president.

Why was George Washington unable to overcome division within the new government?

Getting Started

Washington owed much of his success as the nation's first president to an instinctive feeling for the symbolic possibilities of political power. Although he possessed only modest speaking abilities and never matched the intellectual brilliance of some contemporaries, Washington sensed that he had come to embody the hopes and fears of the new republic. Without ever displaying the attributes necessary to achieve charisma—an instinctive ability that some leaders have to merge their own personality with the abstract goals of the government—he carefully monitored his official behavior. Washington knew that if he did not demonstrate the existence of a strong republic, people who championed the sovereignty of the individual states would attempt to weaken federal authority before it was ever established.

View the **Image**
Washington Taking the Oath of Office on
myhistorylab.com

The first Congress quickly established executive departments. Some congressmen wanted to prohibit presidents from dismissing cabinet-level appointees without Senate approval, but James Madison—still a voice for a strong, independent executive—successfully resisted this restriction on presidential authority. The chief executive could not function unless he had confidence in the people with whom he worked. In 1789, Congress created the Departments of War, State, and the Treasury, and as secretaries, Washington nominated Henry Knox, Thomas Jefferson,

View the **Image**
*Washington's First
Cabinet* on
myhistorylab.com

and Alexander Hamilton, respectively. Edmund Randolph served as part-time attorney general, a position that ranked slightly lower than the head of a department.

To modern Americans accustomed to a huge federal bureaucracy, Washington's government seems amazingly small. When Jefferson arrived in New York, the first national capital, to take over the State Department, for example, he found two chief clerks, two assistants, and a part-time translator. With this tiny staff, he not only maintained contacts with the representatives of foreign governments, collected information about world affairs, and communicated with U.S. officials overseas, but also organized the first federal census in 1790.

Congress also provided for a federal court system. The Judiciary Act of 1789 created a Supreme Court staffed by a chief justice and five associate justices. It also set up 13 district courts authorized to review the decisions of the state courts. John Jay, a leading figure in New York politics, became chief justice. But since federal judges in the 1790s were expected to travel hundreds of miles over terrible roads to attend sessions of the inferior courts, few persons of outstanding talent and training joined Jay on the federal bench.

Remembering the financial insecurity of the old Confederation government, the new Congress passed the tariff of 1789, a tax of approximately 5 percent on imports. The new levy generated considerable revenue for the young republic. Even before it went into effect, however, the act sparked controversy. Southern planters, who relied heavily on European imports and the northern shippers who could control the flow of imports into the South, claimed that the tariff discriminated against southern interests in favor of those of northern merchants.

Quick Check

✓ What was the
structure of the
federal government
under President
Washington?

Conflicting Visions: Jefferson and Hamilton

Washington's first cabinet included two extraordinary personalities, Alexander Hamilton and Thomas Jefferson. Both had served with distinction during the Revolution, were recognized by contemporaries as men of genius and ambition, and brought to public office a vision of how the American people could achieve greatness.

However much these two men had in common, serious differences emerged. Washington's secretaries disagreed on how the United States should fulfill its destiny. As head of the Treasury Department, Hamilton urged his fellow citizens to think in terms of bold commercial development, of farms and factories embedded within a complex financial network that would reduce the nation's reliance on foreign trade. Because Britain already had an elaborate banking and credit system, Hamilton looked to that country for economic models that might be reproduced on this side of the Atlantic.

Hamilton was also concerned about the people's role in public policy. His view of human nature caused him to fear democratic excess. He assumed that in a republican society, the gravest threat to political stability was anarchy rather than monarchy. The best hope for the survival of the republic, Hamilton believed, lay with the country's moneyed classes. If the wealthiest people could be persuaded that their economic self-interest could be advanced—or at least made less insecure—by the central government, then they would work to strengthen it, and thus bring more prosperity to the common people. Hamilton saw no conflict between private greed and public good; one was the source of the other.

On almost every detail, Jefferson challenged Hamilton's analysis. The secretary of state assumed that the strength of the American economy lay not in its industrial potential but in its agricultural productivity. The "immensity of land" represented the country's major economic resource. Contrary to the claims of some critics, Jefferson did not advocate agrarian self-sufficiency or look back nostalgically to a golden age dominated by simple yeomen. He recognized the necessity of change. While he thought that those who worked the soil were more responsible citizens than those who labored in factories for wages, he encouraged the nation's farmers to participate in an expanding international market. Americans could exchange raw materials "for finer manufactures than they are able to execute themselves."

Unlike Hamilton, Jefferson had faith in the American people's ability to shape policy. He instinctively trusted the people, feared that uncontrolled government power might destroy their liberties, and insisted that public officials follow the letter of the Constitution, a frame of government he described as "the wisest ever presented to men." The greatest threat to the young republic, he argued, came from the corrupt activities of pseudo-aristocrats, persons who placed the protection of "property" and "civil order" above the preservation of "liberty." To tie the nation's future to the selfish interests of a privileged class—bankers, manufacturers, and speculators—seemed cynical and dangerous. He despised speculators who encouraged "the rage of getting rich in a day." Such "gaming" promoted the kinds of vice that threatened republican government. To mortgage the future of the common people by creating a large national debt struck Jefferson as insane. But the responsibility for shaping the economy of the new nation fell mainly to Alexander Hamilton as the first secretary of the treasury.

> **Quick Check**
> ✓ Why did Alexander Hamilton and Thomas Jefferson find it so difficult to cooperate as members of Washington's cabinet?

HAMILTON'S PLAN FOR PROSPERITY AND SECURITY

The unsettled state of the nation's finances was a staggering challenge for the new government. Hamilton threw himself into the task. He read deeply in economic literature. He developed a questionnaire to find out how the U.S. economy worked and sent it to commercial and political leaders throughout the country. But when Hamilton's three major reports—on public credit, banking, and manufacturers—were complete, they bore the stamp of his own creative genius. The secretary synthesized a vast amount of information into an economic blueprint so complex, so innovative that even his allies were baffled.

Hamilton presented his *Report on the Public Credit* to Congress on January 14, 1790. His research revealed that the nation's outstanding debt was approximately $54 million. This sum represented obligations that the U.S. government had incurred during the Revolutionary War. It included foreign loans and loan certificates the government had issued to its own citizens and soldiers. But that was not all.

> **Why** did many Americans oppose Alexander Hamilton's blueprint for national prosperity?

The states owed creditors approximately $25 million. During the 1780s, Americans desperate for cash had sold government certificates to speculators at greatly discounted prices. Approximately $40 million of the nation's debt was owed to 20,000 people, only 20 percent of whom were the original creditors.

Debt as a Source of National Strength

Hamilton's *Report on the Public Credit* contained two major recommendations covering funding and assumption. First, under his plan, the United States promised to fund its foreign and domestic obligations at full face value. Current holders of loan certificates, whoever they were and no matter how they had obtained them, could exchange the old certificates for new government bonds bearing a moderate rate of interest. Second, the secretary urged the federal government to assume responsibility for paying the remaining state debts.

Hamilton reasoned that his credit system would accomplish several goals. It would reduce the power of the individual states in shaping national economic policy, something Hamilton regarded as essential in maintaining a strong federal government. Moreover, the creation of a fully funded national debt would signal to foreign and domestic investors that the United States was now solvent, that its bonds represented a good risk. Hamilton argued that investment capital, which might otherwise flow to Europe, would remain in this country, providing money for commercial and industrial investment. In short, he invited the country's wealthiest citizens to invest in the future of the United States. Critics claimed that the only people who stood to profit from the scheme were Hamilton's friends—some of whom sat in Congress and who had purchased many public securities at very low prices.

To Hamilton's surprise, Madison—his friend and collaborator in writing *The Federalist*—attacked the funding scheme in the House of Representatives. The Virginia congressman agreed that the United States should honor its debts. He worried, however, about the citizens and soldiers who, because of financial hardship, had been compelled to sell their certificates at prices far below face value. If the government treated the current holders of certificates less generously, Madison declared, then there might be sufficient funds to provide equitable treatment for the distressed Patriots. Whatever its moral justification, Madison's plan proved unworkable. Too many records had been lost since the Revolution for the Treasury Department to identify all the original holders. In February 1790, Congress defeated Madison's proposal.

The assumption portion of Hamilton's plan unleashed even greater criticism. Some states had already paid their revolutionary debts. Hamilton's program seemed designed to reward certain states—Massachusetts and South Carolina, for example—simply because they had failed to put their finances in order. The secretary's congressional opponents also became suspicious that assumption was merely a ploy to increase the power and wealth of Hamilton's friends.

On April 12, a rebellious House led by Madison defeated assumption. The victory was short-lived. Hamilton and his supporters resorted to legislative horse trading to pass his program. In exchange for locating the new federal capital on the Potomac River, a move that would stimulate the depressed economy of northern Virginia, key congressmen who shared Madison's political philosophy changed their votes on assumption. Hamilton may also have offered Virginia more federal money than it deserved. In August, Washington signed assumption and funding into law. The first element of Hamilton's design was now in place.

Quick Check

✓ What did Alexander Hamilton hope his new credit system would accomplish?

Interpreting the Constitution: The Bank Controversy

Hamilton submitted his second report to Congress in January 1791. He proposed that the government charter a national bank. This private institution would be funded in part by the federal government. Indeed, since the Bank of the United States would own millions of dollars of new U.S. bonds, its financial stability would be tied directly to the strength of the federal government and, of course, to the success of Hamilton's program. The secretary of the treasury argued that a growing financial community required a central bank to facilitate complex commercial transactions. The bank not only would serve as the main depository of the U.S. government but also would issue currency acceptable to pay federal taxes. Because of that guarantee, the money would maintain its value while in circulation.

Madison and others in Congress raised a howl of protest. While they were not oblivious to the services a national bank might provide for a growing country, they suspected that banks—especially those modeled on British institutions—might "perpetuate a large monied interest" in the United States. The Constitution said nothing about chartering financial corporations. Critics warned that if Hamilton and his supporters were allowed to stretch fundamental law on this occasion, they could not be held back in the future. Popular liberties would be at the mercy of whoever held office. "To take a single step," Jefferson warned, "beyond the boundaries thus specifically drawn around the powers of Congress is to take possession of a boundless field of power, no longer susceptible to definition." On this issue, Hamilton refused to compromise: "This is the first symptom of a spirit which must either be killed or will kill the constitution of the United States."

Even though the bank bill passed Congress (February 8), Washington considered vetoing it on constitutional grounds. Before doing so, however, he requested written opinions from his cabinet. Jefferson's rambling, wholly predictable attack on the bank was not one of his more persuasive performances. By contrast, Hamilton wrote a masterful essay. He assured the president that Article I, Section 8 of the Constitution— "The Congress shall have Power … To make all Laws which shall be necessary and proper for carrying into Execution the foregoing Powers"—justified issuing charters to national banks. The "foregoing Powers" on which Hamilton placed so much weight were taxation, regulation of commerce, and making war. He articulated a doctrine of implied powers that the Constitution did not explicitly grant to the federal government, but which it could be interpreted to grant. His interpretation of the Constitution was something that neither Madison nor Jefferson had anticipated. Hamilton's "loose construction" carried the day. Washington signed the bank act into law.

Hamilton triumphed in Congress, but the general public reacted with fear and hostility. When news of his proposal to fund the national debt at full face value

Quick Check

✓ How did Hamilton justify the creation of the Bank of the United States?

leaked out, for example, speculators rushed to rural areas to buy loan certificates from unsuspecting citizens at bargain prices. To backcountry farmers, making money without physical labor appeared immoral, unrepublican, and un-American. When the greed of a former Treasury official led to several serious bankruptcies in 1792, ordinary citizens began to listen more closely to what Madison, Jefferson, and their associates were saying about corruption in high places.

Setback for Hamilton

In his third major report, *Report on Manufactures*, submitted to Congress in December 1791, Hamilton revealed the final details of his grand design for the economic future of the United States. This lengthy document suggested ways the federal government might stimulate manufacturing. To free itself from dependence on European imports, Hamilton observed, the country had to develop its own industry—textile mills, for example. Without government intervention, however, the process would take decades. Americans would continue to invest in agriculture. But protective tariffs and industrial bounties would accelerate the growth of a balanced economy. With proper planning, the United States would soon hold its own with Britain and France.

📖 **Read** the **Document**
Alexander Hamilton, Opposing Visions for the New Nation on **myhistorylab.com**

In Congress, the battle lines were drawn. Hamilton's opponents—not yet a disciplined party but a loose coalition of men who shared Madison's and Jefferson's misgivings about the secretary's program—ignored his economic arguments. Instead, they engaged him on moral and political grounds. Madison railed against the dangers of "consolidation," which threatened to concentrate power in the federal government, leaving the states defenseless.

Jefferson attacked the *Report on Manufactures* from a different angle. He assumed—largely because Europe's urban poverty had horrified him—that cities breed vice. The government, Jefferson argued, should not promote their development. He believed that Hamilton's proposal guaranteed that American workers would leave the countryside and crowd into urban centers: "I think our government will remain virtuous for many centuries as long as they [the people] are chiefly agricultural … When they get piled upon one another in large cities, as in Europe, they will become corrupt as in Europe." Southern congressmen also saw tariffs and bounties as vehicles for enriching Hamilton's northern friends at the planters' expense. The recommendations in the *Report on Manufactures* were soundly defeated in the House of Representatives.

Quick Check

✓ Why did Congress reject Hamilton's *Report on Manufactures*?

CHARGES OF TREASON: THE BATTLE OVER FOREIGN AFFAIRS

How did foreign affairs affect domestic politics during the 1790s?

During Washington's second term (1793–1797), war in Europe thrust foreign affairs into the forefront of American life. The impact of this development on domestic politics was devastating. Officials who had disagreed on economic policy now began to identify their interests with either Britain or France, Europe's most powerful nations. Political differences, however trivial, were suddenly cited as evidence that one group or the other had entered into treasonous correspondence with external enemies eager to compromise the independence and prosperity of the United States.

Formal political organizations—the Federalists and Republicans—were born in this poisonous atmosphere. The clash between the groups developed over how best to preserve the new republic. The Republicans (Jeffersonians) advocated states' rights, strict interpretation of the Constitution, friendship with France, and vigilance against "the avaricious, monopolizing Spirit of Commerce and Commercial Men." The Federalists urged a strong national government, central economic planning, closer ties with Britain, and maintenance of public order, even if that meant calling out federal troops.

The Peril of Neutrality

Britain treated the United States arrogantly. The young republic could not even compel its old adversary to comply with the Treaty of 1783, in which the British had agreed to vacate military posts in the Northwest Territory. In 1794, approximately 1,000 British soldiers still occupied American land, an obstruction that Governor George Clinton of New York claimed had excluded U.S. citizens "from a very valuable trade to which their situation would naturally have invited them." Moreover, even though 75 percent of American imports came from Britain, that country refused to grant the United States full commercial reciprocity. Among other provocations, it barred American shipping from the lucrative West Indian trade.

France presented a different challenge. In May 1789, Louis XVI, desperate for revenue, authorized a meeting of a representative assembly known as the

Execution of Louis XVI The execution of the king by French revolutionaries deepened the growing political division in America. Although they deplored the excesses of the Reign of Terror, Jeffersonian Republicans continued to support the French people. Federalists feared that the violence and lawlessness would spread to the United States.

Estates General. By so doing, the king unleashed revolutionary forces that eventually toppled the monarchy and cost him his life (January 1793). The men who seized power—and they came and went rapidly—were militant republicans, ideologues eager to liberate all Europe from feudal institutions. In the early years of the French Revolution, France drew on the American experience. Thomas Paine and the Marquis de Lafayette enjoyed great popularity. But the French could not stop the revolutionary violence. Constitutional reform turned into bloody purges. One radical group, the Jacobins, guillotined thousands of its opponents and suspected monarchists during the so-called Reign of Terror (October 1793–July 1794). These horrific events left Americans confused. While those who shared Jefferson's views cheered the spread of republicanism, others who sided with Hamilton condemned French expansionism and political excess.

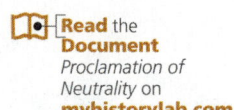

Read the **Document**
Proclamation of Neutrality on **myhistorylab.com**

In the face of growing international tension, neutrality seemed the most prudent course for the United States. But that policy was easier for a weak country to proclaim than defend. In February 1793, France declared war on Britain—what the leaders of revolutionary France called the "war of all peoples against all kings." These powerful European rivals immediately challenged the official American position on shipping: "free ships make free goods," meaning that belligerents should not interfere with the shipping of neutral carriers. To make matters worse, no one was certain whether the Franco-American treaties of 1778 (see Chapter 5) legally bound the United States to support its old ally against Britain.

Both Hamilton and Jefferson wanted to avoid war. The secretary of state, however, believed that nations desiring American goods should be forced to honor American neutrality. If Britain treated the United States as a colonial possession, if the Royal Navy stopped American ships on the high seas and forced seamen to serve the king—in other words, if it impressed American sailors—then the United States should award France special commercial advantages. Hamilton thought Jefferson's scheme insane. He pointed out that Britain had the largest navy in the world and was not likely to be coerced by American threats. The United States, he counseled, should appease the former mother country even if that meant swallowing national pride.

Quick Check

✓ Why could America's political leaders not ignore the French Revolution?

Jay's Treaty Sparks Domestic Unrest

Britain's refusal to abandon its forts in the Northwest Territory remained a source of tension. In June 1793, a new element was added. The London government blockaded French ports to neutral shipping. In November, the Royal Navy captured hundreds of American vessels trading in the French West Indies. The British had not even given the United States advance warning of a change in policy. Outraged members of Congress, especially those who identified with Jefferson and Madison, demanded retaliation: an embargo, stopping debt payment, even war.

Before this rhetoric produced armed struggle, Washington made an effort to preserve peace. In May 1794, he sent Chief Justice John Jay to London to negotiate a formidable list of grievances. Jay's main objectives were removal of the British forts on U.S. territory, payment for ships taken in the West Indies, improved commercial relations, and acceptance of the American definition of neutral rights.

Jefferson's supporters—by now called the Republican interest—anticipated a treaty favorable to the United States. After all, they explained, the war with France had not gone well for Britain, and the British people were surely desperate for American foodstuffs. Even before Jay departed, however, his mission stood little chance of success. Hamilton, anxious as ever to placate the British, had secretly informed British officials that the United States would compromise on most issues.

When Jay reached London, he encountered polite but firm resistance. His efforts resulted in a political humiliation known as **Jay's Treaty**. The chief justice did persuade the British to abandon their frontier posts and allow small American ships to trade in the British West Indies, but the British rejected outright the U.S. position on neutral rights. The Royal Navy would continue to search American vessels for contraband and impress sailors suspected of being British citizens. There would be no compensation for the ships seized in 1793 until the Americans paid British merchants for debts contracted before the Revolution. And to the annoyance of southerners, not a word was said about the slaves the British had carried off at the conclusion of the war. While Jay salvaged peace, he appeared to have betrayed the national interest.

News of Jay's Treaty produced an outcry. Even Washington was apprehensive. He submitted the document to the Senate without recommending ratification, a sign that the president was not happy with the results of Jay's mission. After a bitter debate, the Senate, controlled by Federalists, accepted a revised version of the treaty. The vote was 20 to 10, the bare two-thirds majority the Constitution required.

The details of the Jay agreement soon leaked to the press. The popular journals sparked a firestorm of objection. Throughout the country, people who had formerly been apathetic about national politics were swept up in a wave of protest. Urban mobs condemned Jay's alleged sellout; rural settlers burned him in effigy. Jay jokingly told friends he could find his way across the country simply by following the light of those fires. Southerners announced they would not pay prerevolutionary debts to British merchants. The Virginia legislature proposed a constitutional amendment reducing the Senate's role in treaty-making.

In the House, Republican congressmen, led by Madison, thought they could stop Jay's Treaty by refusing to appropriate funds to implement it. They demanded that Washington show the House state papers relating to Jay's mission. The challenge raised complex constitutional issues. The House was claiming a voice in treaty ratification, a power explicitly reserved to the Senate. There was also the question of executive secrecy in the interest of national security. Washington told the rebellious representatives that "the nature of foreign negotiations requires caution; and their success must often depend on secrecy."

The president played a trump card. He raised the possibility that the House was contemplating his impeachment. This, of course, was unthinkable. Even criticizing Washington in public was politically dangerous. As soon as he redefined the issue before Congress, petitions supporting the president flooded into the nation's

Read the Document
The Jay Treaty on
myhistorylab.com

capital. The Maryland legislature, for example, declared its "unabated reliance on the integrity, judgment, and patriotism of the President of the United States," a statement that called into question the patriotism of certain Republican congressmen. The Federalists won a stunning tactical victory over the opposition. Had a less popular man than Washington occupied the presidency, however, they would not have fared so well. The division between the two parties was now beyond repair. The Republicans labeled the Federalists "the British party"; Federalists believed that the Republicans were in league with the French.

By the time Jay's Treaty became law (June 14, 1795), the two giants of Washington's first cabinet had retired. Late in 1793, Jefferson returned to his Virginia plantation, Monticello. Despite his separation from day-to-day political affairs, he remained the chief spokesman for the Republican party. His rival, Hamilton, left the Treasury in January 1795 to practice law in New York City. He maintained close ties with important Federalists. Even more than Jefferson, Hamilton concerned himself with the details of party organization.

Quick Check

✓ Why did Jay's Treaty spark such hostility throughout the nation?

Pushing the Native Americans Aside

Before Britain finally withdrew its troops from the Great Lakes and Northwest Territory, British officers encouraged local Indian groups—the Shawnee, Chippewa, and Miami—to attack American settlers and traders. The Indians, who even without British encouragement knew that the newcomers intended to seize their land, won several impressive victories over federal troops in the area that would become western Ohio and Indiana. In 1790, General Josiah Harmar led his soldiers into an ambush. The following year, an army under General Arthur St. Clair suffered more than 900 casualties near the Wabash River. But the Indians were militarily more vulnerable than they realized. When confronted with a U.S. army under General Anthony Wayne, they received no support from the British. At the Battle of Fallen Timbers (August 20, 1794), Wayne's forces crushed Indian resistance in the Northwest Territory. The native peoples were compelled to sign the Treaty of Greenville, formally ceding to the U.S. government the land that became Ohio. In 1796, the last British soldiers departed for Canada.

Shrewd negotiations mixed with pure luck helped secure the nation's southwestern frontier with Spain. For complex reasons involving European diplomacy, Spanish officials in 1795 encouraged the U.S. representative in Madrid, Thomas Pinckney, to discuss the navigation of the Mississippi River. Before this initiative, the Spanish government not only had closed the river to American commerce but had incited the Indians to harass American settlers. Relations between the two countries probably would have deteriorated further had the United States not signed Jay's Treaty. The Spanish assumed—erroneously—that Britain and the United States had formed an alliance to strip Spain of its North American possessions.

To avoid this imagined disaster, officials in Madrid offered Pinckney extraordinary concessions: the opening of the Mississippi, the right to deposit goods in New Orleans without paying duties, a secure southern boundary on the 31st parallel (a line roughly parallel to the northern boundary of Florida and running west to the Mississippi), and a promise to stay out of Indian affairs. An amazed Pinckney signed the Treaty of San Lorenzo (Pinckney's Treaty) on October 27, 1795. In March 1796, the Senate ratified it without a single dissenting vote. Pinckney, who came from a prominent South Carolina family, became the hero of the Federalist party. (See Map 7.1.)

Quick Check

✓ Why did "The opening of the Mississippi" figure so prominently in American Politics during the 1790s?

POPULAR POLITICAL CULTURE

More than any other event during Washington's administration, ratification of Jay's Treaty generated intense political strife. Even as members of Congress voted as Republicans or Federalists, they condemned the rising partisan spirit as a threat to the stability of the United States. Popular writers equated "party" with "faction" and "faction" with "conspiracy to overthrow legitimate authority." Party conflict

Why was it hard for Americans to accept political dissent as a part of political activity?

Map 7.1 *Conquest of the West* Withdrawal of the British, defeat of Native Americans, and negotiations with Spain secured the nation's frontiers.

also suggested that Americans had lost the common purpose that had united them during the Revolution. Contemporaries did not appreciate the beneficial role that parties could play in presenting alternative solutions to foreign and domestic problems. Organized opposition smacked of disloyalty and therefore had to be eliminated by any means—fair or foul.

Whiskey Rebellion: Charges of Republican Conspiracy

Political tensions became explosive in 1794. The Federalists convinced themselves that the Republicans were actually prepared to employ violence against the U.S. government. Although the charge was baseless, it took on plausibility in the context of growing party strife.

Read the
Document
*George Washington,
Whiskey Rebellion
Address to the Congress (1794)* on
myhistorylab.com

The crisis developed when farmers in western Pennsylvania protested a federal excise tax on distilled whiskey that Congress had passed in 1791. They did not relish paying any taxes, but this tax struck them as particularly unfair. They made a good deal of money distilling their grain into whiskey, and the excise threatened to put them out of business.

Largely because the Republican governor of Pennsylvania refused to suppress the angry farmers, Washington and other leading Federalists assumed that the insurrection represented a direct political challenge. The president called out 15,000 militiamen and, accompanied by Hamilton, he marched against the rebels. The expedition was a fiasco. The distillers disappeared. Predictably, no one in the Pittsburgh region seemed to know where the troublemakers had gone. Two supposed rebels were convicted of high crimes against the United States; one was reportedly a "simpleton" and the other insane. Washington pardoned both men. As peace returned to the frontier, Republicans gained electoral support from voters the Federalists had alienated.

In the national political forum, however, the Whiskey Rebellion had just begun. Spokesmen for both parties offered sinister explanations for the seemingly innocuous affair. Washington blamed the Republican clubs for promoting civil unrest. He apparently believed that the opposition party had dispatched French agents to western Pennsylvania to undermine the federal government. In November 1794, Washington informed Congress that these "self-created societies"—the Republican political clubs—had inspired "a spirit inimical to all order." Indeed, the Whiskey Rebellion had been "fomented by combinations of men who … have disseminated, from an ignorance or perversion of facts, suspicions, jealousies, and accusations of the whole Government."

Quick Check

✓ Why did Washington and his supporters see the Whiskey Rebellion as something more sinister than just an "embarassing fiasco"?

The president's interpretation of this rural tax revolt was no more charitable than the conspiratorial explanation the Republicans offered. Jefferson labeled the entire episode a Hamiltonian device to create an army to intimidate Republicans.

Washington's Farewell

In September 1796, Washington published his Farewell Address, formally declaring his intention to retire from the presidency. In the address, printed in newspapers throughout the country, Washington warned against political factions. Written largely by Hamilton, who drew on a draft Madison had prepared years earlier, the

The Whiskey Rebellion Tarring and feathering federal officials was one way western Pennsylvanians protested the tax on whiskey in 1794. Washington's call for troops to put down the insurrection drew more volunteers than he had been able to raise during most of the Revolution. (*Source: Whiskey Rebellion, c. 1790s, hand-colored woodcut/North Wind Picture Archives.*)

address served narrowly partisan ends. The product of growing political strife, it sought to advance the Federalist cause in the forthcoming election. By waiting until September to announce his retirement, Washington denied the Republicans time to organize an effective campaign. There was an element of irony in this initiative. Washington had always maintained he stood above party. While he may have done so early in his presidency, events such as Jay's Treaty and the suppression of the Whiskey Rebellion transformed him in the eyes of many Americans into a spokesman solely for Hamilton's Federalist party.

Washington also spoke about foreign policy in the address. He counseled the United States to avoid permanent alliances with distant nations that had no real interest in American security. This statement guided foreign relations for years and became the credo of American isolationists, who argued that the United States should steer clear of foreign entanglements.

Quick Check

✓ In what ways was Washington's Farewell Address in 1796 a piece of party propaganda?

THE ADAMS PRESIDENCY: POLITICS OF MISTRUST

The election of 1796 took place in an atmosphere of mutual distrust. Jefferson, soon to be the vice president, informed a friend that "an Anglican and aristocratic party has sprung up, whose avowed object is to draw over us the substance, as they have already done the forms, of British government." The Federalists were convinced their Republican opponents wanted to hand the government over to French radicals.

During the campaign, the Federalists sowed the seeds of their eventual destruction. Party stalwarts agreed that John Adams should stand against the Republican candidate, Thomas Jefferson. Hamilton, however, schemed to deprive Adams of the

Why were some Federalists willing to sacrifice political freedoms for party advantage?

presidency. He apparently feared that an independent-minded Adams would be difficult to manipulate. He was correct.

Hamilton exploited an awkward feature of the electoral college. In accord with the Constitution, each elector cast two ballots. The person who gained the most votes became president. The runner-up, regardless of party affiliation, became vice president. Ordinarily the Federalist electors would have cast one vote for Adams and one for Thomas Pinckney, the hero of the negotiations with Spain and the party's choice for vice president. Everyone hoped, of course, there would be no tie. Hamilton secretly urged southern Federalists to support only Pinckney, even if that meant throwing away an elector's second vote. If everything had gone according to plan, Pinckney would have received more votes than Adams. But when New Englanders loyal to Adams heard of Hamilton's maneuvering, they dropped Pinckney. When the votes were counted, Adams had 71, Jefferson 68, and Pinckney 59. (See Table 7.1.) Hamilton's treachery angered the new president and heightened tensions within the Federalist party.

The XYZ Affair and Domestic Politics

Foreign affairs immediately occupied Adams's attention. The French regarded Jay's Treaty as an affront. By allowing Britain to define the conditions for neutrality, the United States had in effect sided with that nation against France.

Relations between France and the United States had deteriorated. The French refused to receive Charles Cotesworth Pinckney, the U.S. representative in Paris. Pierre Adet, the French minister in Philadelphia, openly tried to influence the 1796 election in favor of the Republicans. His meddling not only embarrassed Jefferson, it offended the American people. The situation then took a violent turn. In 1797, French privateers began seizing American ships. Since neither the United States nor France declared war, the hostilities came to be known as the Quasi-War.

Hamilton and his friends welcomed an outpouring of anti-French sentiment. The High Federalists—Hamilton's wing of the party—counseled the president to prepare for all-out war, hoping that war would purge the United States of French influence. Adams would not escalate the conflict. He dispatched a special

TABLE 7.1	The Election of 1796	
Candidate	**Electoral Vote**	**Party**
J. Adams	Federalist	71
Jefferson	Republican	68
T. Pinckney	Federalist	59
Burr	Republican	30

commission to Paris in an attempt to remove the sources of antagonism. This famous negotiating team consisted of Charles Pinckney, John Marshall, and Elbridge Gerry. They were instructed to obtain compensation for the ships French privateers had seized and release from the treaties of 1778. Federalists still worried that this old agreement might oblige the United States to defend French colonies in the Caribbean against British attack, which they were reluctant to do. In exchange, the commission offered France the same commercial privileges Jay's Treaty granted to Britain. While the diplomats negotiated, Adams talked of strengthening American defenses, rhetoric that pleased militant Federalists.

The outrageous treatment it received in France shocked the commission. Instead of dealing directly with Talleyrand, the French foreign minister, they met with obscure intermediaries who demanded a huge bribe. The commission reported that Talleyrand would not open negotiations unless he was given $250,000. The French government also expected a "loan" of millions of dollars. The Americans refused to play this insulting game. Pinckney replied, "No, no, not a sixpence," and with Marshall he returned to the United States. When they arrived home, Marshall offered his much-quoted toast: "Millions for defense, but not one cent for tribute."

President Adams John Adams in the suit and sword he wore for his 1797 inauguration. The portrait is by English artist William Winstanley, 1798.

Diplomatic humiliation set off a political explosion. When Adams presented the commission's official correspondence to Congress—the names of Talleyrand's lackeys were labeled X, Y, and Z—the Federalists burst out with a war cry. At last, they would be able to even old scores with the Republicans. In April 1798, a Federalist newspaper in New York City announced that any American who refused to censure France "must have a soul black enough to be *fit for treasons, strategems, and spoils.*" Rumors of conspiracy, referring to the incident as the XYZ Affair, spread through the country. Friendships between Republicans and Federalists were shattered. Jefferson described the tense political atmosphere in a letter to an old colleague: "You and I have formerly seen warm debates and high political passions. But gentlemen of different politics would then speak to each other, and separate the business of the Senate from that of society. It is not so now. Men who have been intimate all their lives, cross the streets to avoid meeting, and turn their heads another way, lest they should be obliged to touch their hats."

Quick Check

✓ During the XYZ affair, why did representatives of the French Government treat American diplomats with such disrespect?

Crushing Political Dissent

In spring 1798, High Federalists assumed that Adams would ask Congress for a declaration of war. In the meantime, they pushed for rearmament, new warships, harbor fortifications, and, most important, an expanded U.S. Army. About the need for land forces, Adams remained skeptical. He saw no likelihood of French invasion.

The president missed the political point. The Federalists wanted the army not to thwart French aggression but to stifle internal opposition. Indeed, militant Federalists used the XYZ Affair to institute what Jefferson termed the "reign of witches." The threat to the Republicans was not simply a figment of the vice president's overwrought imagination. When Theodore Sedgwick, a Federalist senator from Massachusetts, learned of the commission's failure, he observed in words that capture the High Federalists' vindictiveness, "It will afford a glorious opportunity to destroy faction. Improve it."

During summer 1798, a provisional army gradually came into existence. Washington agreed to lead the troops, but only if Adams appointed Hamilton second in command. This demand placed the president in a dilemma. Several revolutionary veterans—Henry Knox, for example—outranked Hamilton. Moreover, the former secretary of the treasury had consistently undermined Adams's authority. To give Hamilton a powerful position seemed awkward at best. When Washington insisted, however, Adams was forced to appoint Hamilton.

The chief of the High Federalists threw himself into recruiting and supplying the troops. No detail escaped his attention. He and Secretary of War James McHenry made certain that in this political army, only loyal Federalists received commissions. They even denied Adams's son-in-law a post. The entire enterprise took on an air of unreality. Hamilton longed for military glory. He may have contemplated attacking Spain's Latin American colonies. His obsession, however, was to restore political order. No doubt he agreed with a Federalist senator from Connecticut who predicted that the Republicans "never will yield till violence is introduced; we must have a partial civil war … and the bayonet must convince some, who are beyond the reach of other arguments."

Hamilton should not have treated Adams with such open contempt. Adams was still the president. Without presidential cooperation, Hamilton could not fulfill his grand military ambitions. Yet whenever pressing questions concerning the army arose, Adams was nowhere to be found. He let commissions lie on his desk unsigned; he took overlong vacations to New England. He made it clear his first love was the navy. In May 1798, the president persuaded Congress to establish the Navy Department. For this new cabinet position, he selected Benjamin Stoddert, who did not take orders from Hamilton. Moreover, Adams further infuriated the High Federalists by refusing to ask Congress for a declaration of war. When they pressed him, Adams threatened to resign, making Jefferson president. As the weeks passed, the American people increasingly regarded the idle army as an expensive extravagance.

Quick Check

✓ Why were the high Federalists willing to place party advantage over the welfare of the entire nation?

Silencing Political Opposition: The Alien and Sedition Acts

The Federalists did not rely solely on the army to crush dissent. During the summer of 1798, Congress passed four bills known collectively as the **Alien and Sedition Acts**. This legislation authorized using federal courts and the powers of the presidency to silence the Republicans. The acts were born of fear and vindictiveness. To punish Jefferson's followers, the Federalists created the nation's first major crisis over civil liberties.

Congress drew up three Alien Acts. The first, the Alien Enemies Law, vested the president with extraordinary wartime powers. On his own authority, he could detain or deport citizens of nations with which the United States was at war and who behaved in a manner he thought suspicious. Since Adams refused to ask for a declaration of war, this legislation never went into effect. A second act, the Alien Law, empowered the president to expel any foreigner from the United States by executive decree. Congress limited the acts to two years. While Adams did not attempt to enforce them, the mere threat of arrest caused Frenchmen to flee the country. The third act, the Naturalization Law, was the most flagrantly political. It established a 14-year probationary period before foreigners could apply for U.S. citizenship. Recent immigrants, especially the Irish, tended to vote Republican. The Naturalization Law, therefore, was designed to keep "hordes of wild Irishmen" away from the polls for as long as possible.

The Sedition Law struck at the heart of free political exchange. It defined criticism of the U.S. government as criminal libel; citizens found guilty by a jury were

Party Conflict In the early years of the republic, political dissent sometimes escalated to physical violence. This fistfight took place on the floor of Congress, February 15, 1798. The combatants are Republican Matthew Lyon and Federalist Roger Griswold.

Read the
Document
*The Alien and Sedi-
tion Acts (1798)* on
myhistorylab.com

subject to fines and imprisonment. Congress entrusted enforcement of the act to the federal courts. Republicans justly worried that the Sedition Law undermined rights guaranteed by the First Amendment. The High Federalists dismissed their complaints: The Constitution, they declared, did not condone "the most ground-less and malignant lies, striking at the safety and existence of the nation." They were determined to shut down the opposition press and were willing to give the govern-ment almost dictatorial powers to do so. The Jeffersonians also expressed concern over the federal judiciary's expanded role in punishing sedition. They believed such matters were best left to state officials.

Quick Check

✓ Why did leaders of
the Federalist party
not appreciate that
the Alien and Sedi-
tion Acts undermined
the Constitution of
the United States?

The Federalists' enforcement of the Sedition Law did not silence opposition—indeed, it sparked even greater criticism and created martyrs. The administration's actions persuaded Republicans that the survival of free government was at stake. Time was running out. "There is no event," Jefferson warned, "... however atro-cious, which may not be expected."

Kentucky and Virginia Resolutions

By the fall of 1798, Jefferson and Madison were convinced that the Federalists envisioned the creation of a police state. According to Madison, the Sedition Law "ought to produce universal alarm." It threatened the free communication of ideas that he "deemed the only effectual guardian of every other right." Extreme Repub-licans such as John Taylor of Virginia recommended secession from the Union; others advocated armed resistance. But Jefferson counseled against such strategies. "This is not the kind of opposition the American people will permit," he reminded his desperate supporters. The last best hope for American freedom lay in the state legislatures.

Read the
Document
*The Kentucky and
Virginia Resolutions
(1798, 1799)* on
myhistorylab.com

As the crisis deepened, Jefferson and Madison drafted separate protests known as the **Kentucky and Virginia Resolutions**. Both statements defended the right of individual state assemblies to interpret the constitutionality of federal law. Jeffer-son wrote the Kentucky Resolutions in November 1798. In an outburst of partisan anger, he flirted with a doctrine of nullification that was as dangerous to the survival of the United States as anything Hamilton and his High Federalist friends advanced.

In the Kentucky Resolutions, Jefferson described the federal union as a compact. The states transferred certain explicit powers to the national government, but they retained full authority over all matters the Constitution did not specifically men-tion. Jefferson rejected Hamilton's broad interpretation of the "general welfare" clause.

When Madison drafted the Virginia Resolutions in December, he took a more temperate stand. Madison urged the states to defend the rights of the American people, but he resisted the notion that a single state legislature could or should overthrow federal law.

The Virginia and Kentucky Resolutions were not intended as statements of abstract principles and most certainly not as a justification for southern seces-sion. They were pure political party propaganda. Jefferson and Madison reminded

American voters during a period of severe domestic tension that the Republicans offered an alternative to Federalist rule. No other state legislatures passed the Resolutions. Even in Virginia, where the Republicans enjoyed broad support, important figures such as John Marshall and George Washington criticized the states' rights argument.

Quick Check

✓ How did the Kentucky and Virginia Resolutions propose to protect American freedoms?

Adams's Finest Hour

In February 1799, President Adams belatedly declared his independence from the Hamiltonian wing of the Federalist party. Throughout the confrontation with France, Adams had shown little enthusiasm for war. Following the XYZ debacle, he began to receive reports that Talleyrand had changed his tune. The French foreign minister told Elbridge Gerry and other Americans that the bribery episode had been an unfortunate misunderstanding. If the United States sent new representatives, he would negotiate in good faith. The High Federalists ridiculed this report. But Adams threw his waning prestige behind peace. In February, he asked the Senate to confirm William Vans Murray as U.S. representative to France.

When the new negotiators—Oliver Ellsworth and William Davie joined Murray—arrived in France in November 1799, they discovered that yet another group had come to power there. This government, headed by Napoleon Bonaparte, cooperated in drawing up an agreement known as the Convention of Mortefontaine. The French refused to compensate the Americans for vessels taken during the Quasi-War, but they declared the treaties of 1778 null and void. Moreover, the convention removed annoying French restrictions on U.S. commerce. Not only had Adams avoided war, he had created an atmosphere of mutual trust that paved the way for the purchase of the Louisiana Territory.

Quick Check

✓ Was the Convention of Mortefontaine a victory for American diplomacy?

The Peaceful Revolution: The Election of 1800

On the eve of the election of 1800, the Federalists were fatally divided. Adams enjoyed wide popularity among the rank and file, especially in New England, but articulate party leaders such as Hamilton vowed to punish the president for betraying their militant policies. The former secretary of the treasury attempted to rig the voting in the electoral college, so that the party's vice presidential candidate, Charles Cotesworth Pinckney, would receive more ballots than Adams and America would be saved from "the fangs of Jefferson." As in 1796, the conspiracy backfired. The Republicans gained 73 votes while the Federalists trailed with 65.

However, the election was not resolved in the electoral college. When the ballots were counted, Jefferson and his running mate, Aaron Burr, had tied. This accident—a Republican elector should have thrown away his second vote—sent the selection of the next president to the House of Representatives, a lame-duck body that the Federalist party still controlled. (See Table 7.2.)

As the House began its work on February 27, 1801, excitement ran high. Each state delegation cast a single vote, with nine votes needed for election. On the first

((•─ **Listen** to the **Audio File** *Jefferson and Liberty* on **myhistorylab.com**

TABLE 7.2   The Election of 1800

Candidate	Electoral Vote	Party
Jefferson	Republican	73
Burr	Republican	73
J. Adams	Federalist	65
C. Pinckney	Federalist	64

ballot, Jefferson received the support of eight states, Burr six, and two states divided evenly. People predicted a quick victory for Jefferson, but after dozens of ballots, the House had still not selected a president. The drama dragged on for six days. To add to the confusion, Burr refused to withdraw. Contemporaries thought his ambition had overcome his good sense.

The logjam finally broke when leading Federalists decided that Jefferson, whatever his faults, would make a more responsible president than would the shifty Burr. Even Hamilton labeled Burr "the most dangerous man of the community." On the thirty-sixth ballot, Representative James A. Bayard of Delaware announced he no longer supported Burr. This decision, coupled with Burr's inaction, gave Jefferson the presidency, ten states to four.

The Twelfth Amendment, ratified in 1804, saved the American people from repeating this potentially dangerous turn of events. Henceforth, the electoral college cast separate ballots for president and vice president.

During the final days of his presidency, Adams appointed as many Federalists as possible to the federal bench. Jefferson protested the hasty manner in which these "midnight judges" were selected. One of them, John Marshall, became chief justice of the United States, a post he held with distinction for 34 years. But behind the last-minute flurry of activity lay bitterness and disappointment. Adams never forgave Hamilton. The Federalist party was left splintered and dispirited. On the morning of Jefferson's inauguration, Adams slipped away from the capital—now located in Washington, D.C.—unnoticed and unappreciated.

In the address that Adams missed, Jefferson attempted to quiet partisan fears. "We are all republicans; we are all federalists," the new president declared. By this statement, he did not mean to suggest that party differences were no longer important. Jefferson reminded his audience that whatever the politicians might say, the people shared a deep commitment to a federal union based on republican ideals set forth during the American Revolution. Indeed, the president interpreted the election of 1800 as revolutionary, the fulfillment of the principles of 1776.

Recent battles, of course, colored Jefferson's judgment. The contests of the 1790s had been hard fought, the outcome often in doubt. Jefferson looked back at this period as a confrontation between the "advocates of republican and those of kingly government." He believed that only his own party's vigilance had saved the country from Federalist "liberticide."

Read the **Document**
Jefferson's First Inaugural Address (1801) on
myhistorylab.com

Quick Check

✓ What did Jefferson mean when he claimed in his first inaugural address that "We are all Republicans; we are all Federalists"?

CONCLUSION: DANGER OF POLITICAL EXTREMISM

From a broader historical perspective, the election of 1800 seems noteworthy for what did not occur. There were no riots, no attempted coup, no secession from the Union, only the peaceful transfer of government from the leaders of one political party to those of the opposition.

Americans had weathered the Alien and Sedition Acts, the meddling by predatory foreign powers in domestic affairs, the shrill partisan rhetoric of hack journalists, and now, at the start of a new century, they were impressed with their own achievement. As one woman who attended Jefferson's inauguration noted, "The changes of administration which in every government and in every age have most generally been epochs of confusion, villainy and bloodshed, in this our happy country take place without any species of distraction, or disorder." But as she understood—indeed, as modern Americans must constantly relearn—extremism in the name of partisan political truth can easily unravel the delicate fabric of representative democracy and leave the republic at the mercy of those who would manipulate the public for private benefit.

7 STUDY RESOURCES

((•—Listen to the **Chapter Audio** for Chapter 7 on **myhistorylab.com**

TIMELINE

Chapter Review

PRINCIPLE AND PRAGMATISM: ESTABLISHING A NEW GOVERNMENT

Why was George Washington unable to overcome division within the new government?

Despite his huge popularity among all segments of the American population, President Washington was unable to bridge the differences between the two most brilliant and strong-willed members of his cabinet: Thomas Jefferson and Alexander Hamilton. These two men fought throughout Washington's presidency over their different visions for the future of the republic. Hamilton imagined an urban commercial nation with a strong central government; Jefferson championed a simple agrarian republic. *(p. 171)*

HAMILTON'S PLAN FOR PROSPERITY AND SECURITY

Why did many Americans oppose Alexander Hamilton's blueprint for national prosperity?

Many citizens – especially farmers and former soldiers felt resented that Hamilton's plan to fund state loan certificates at full value would reward the immoral, unrepublican and un-American actions of speculators by allowing them to make money without physical labor. Many also complained that this plan rewarded the financial irresponsibility of states like Massachusetts and South Carolina. Supporters of Jefferson rejected Hamilton's vision of the United States as a commercial and manufacturing nation, feared that his plan for a Bank of the United States would "perpetuate a large monied interest," and protested that his doctrine of implied powers would lead to the steady growth of governmental power. *(p. 173)*

CHARGES OF TREASON: THE BATTLE OVER FOREIGN AFFAIRS

How did foreign affairs affect domestic politics during the 1790s?

The French Revolution split American opinion. Republicans cheered it; Federalists condemned it. When France declared war on Britain (1793), The French Revolution split American opinion. Republicans cheered it; Federalists condemned it. The extremely unpopular Jay's Treaty (1794) with Britain provoked heated political debate between its Federalist supporters and Republican opponents. Disagreements over how to deal with French aggression and insults during the Quasi-War and the XYZ Affair drove a wedge between the peace-seeking President John Adams and the High Federalists who called for war and military expansion. This divide helped Jefferson win the election of 1800. *(p. 176)*

POPULAR POLITICAL CULTURE

Why was it hard for Americans to accept political dissent as a part of political activity?

In the 1790s, many Americans equated political dissent with disloyalty. During the Whiskey Rebellion (1794), both Federalists and Republicans feared the other party planned to use violence to crush political opposition. In the 1790s, many Americans lamented the loss of unity that had tied them together during the struggle for independence. Moreover, because equated political dissent with disloyalty, they feared that partisan politics might lead to a conspiracy to overthrow the legitimately elected government. During the Whiskey Rebellion (1794), both Federalists and Republicans feared the other party planned to use violence to crush political opposition. *(p. 181)*

THE ADAMS PRESIDENCY: POLITICS OF MISTRUST

Why were some Federalists willing to sacrifice political freedoms for party advantage?

Many Republicans believed that the support of Jeffersonian Republicans for France had compromised American sovereignty. Hamilton and the High Federalists believed that a standing army was necessary to defend against invasion and to silence domestic dissent so that it could not split the republic apart. They rationalized that the sacrifice of political liberties entailed in the Alien and Sedition Acts were necessary to protect the Republic from corrupting foreign (particularly French influences). This was especially important since they anticipated the onset of a war with France. They used the rationale of national security to justify their pursuit of party power. *(p. 183)*

KEY TERM QUESTIONS

1. How did Hamilton justify the creation of the Bank of the United States? (p. 175)

2. Why did Hamilton articulate a doctrine of implied powers? (p. 175)

3. Why could America's leaders not ignore the French Revolution? (p. 178)

4. Why did Jay's Treaty spark such hostility? (p. 179)

5. Why did Washington and his supporters see the Whiskey Rebellion as more sinister than just an "embarrassing fiasco"? (p. 182)

6. Why was Washington's Farewell Address in 1796 a piece of party propaganda? (p. 182)

7. Why did the United States and France fight a Quasi-War rather than a declared war in 1797? (p. 184)

8. During the XYZ Affair, why did representatives of the French government treat American diplomats with such disrespect? (p. 185)

9. Why did Federalist leaders not understand that the Alien and Sedition Acts undermined the Constitution? (p. 187)

10. How did the Kentucky and Virginia Resolutions propose to protect American freedoms? (p. 188)

MyHISTORYLAB CONNECTIONS

Visit **www.myhistorylab.com** for a customized Study Plan to build your knowledge of *Democracy and Dissent*.

Question for Analysis

1. How did Hamilton's vision for the nation differ from Jefferson?

   Read the **Document** *Alexander Hamilton, Opposing Visions for the New Nation* p. 176

2. What was the significance of the Jay Treaty?

   Read the **Document** *The Jay Treaty* p. 179

3. What did Washington seek to accomplish with address to Congress regarding the Whiskey Rebellion?

   Read the **Document** *George Washington, Whiskey Rebellion Address to Congress (1794)* p. 181

4. What were the Alien and Sedition Acts designed to do?

   Read the **Document** *The Alien and Sedition Acts (1798)* p. 188

5. How did the Kentucky and Virginia Resolutions propose to protect American freedoms?

   Read the **Document** *The Kentucky and Virginia Resolutions (1798, 1799)* p. 188

Other Resources from this Chapter

View the **Image** *Washington Taking the Oath of Office*

View the **Image** *Washington's First Cabinet*

Read the **Document** *Proclamation of Neutrality*

Listen to the **Audio File** *Jefferson and Liberty*

Read the **Document** *Jefferson's First Inaugural Address*

Contents and Spotlight Questions

((•─ **Listen** to the **Chapter Audio** for Chapter 8 on **myhistorylab.com**

LIMITS OF EQUALITY

British visitors often expressed contempt for Jeffersonian society. Wherever they traveled in the young republic, they met ill-mannered people inspired with a passion for liberty and equality. Charles William Janson, an Englishman who lived in the United States for 13 years, recounted an exchange he found particularly unsettling that had occurred at the home of an American acquaintance: "On knocking at the door, it was opened by a servant maid, whom I had never before seen." The woman's behavior astonished Janson: "The following is the dialogue, word for word, which took place on this occasion:— 'Is your master at home?'— 'I have no

President Jefferson In 1800, Thomas Jefferson and Aaron Burr each received 73 electoral votes. The election was finally decided in February 1801 when the House of Representatives, on the thirty-sixth ballot, chose Jefferson by a vote of 10 to 4. This flag commemorates Jefferson's victory in the election.

master.'—'Don't you live here?'—'I stay here.'—'And who are you then?'—'Why, I am Mr.—'s *help*. I'd have you know, *man*, that I am no *sarvant* [sic]; none but *negers* [sic] are *sarvants*.'"

In this exchange, Janson encountered the authentic voice of Jeffersonian republicanism—self-confident, assertive, racist, and status conscious. The maid believed she was her employer's equal, perhaps not in wealth but surely in character. She may have even dreamed of owning a house staffed with "*help*." American society fostered such ambition. In the early nineteenth century, thousands of settlers poured across the Appalachians or moved to cities in search of opportunity. Thomas Jefferson and men who stood for public office under the banner of the Republican party claimed to speak for these people.

The limits of the Jeffersonian vision were obvious even to contemporaries. The people who spoke most eloquently about equal opportunity often owned slaves. As early as the 1770s, the famed English essayist Samuel Johnson had chided Americans for their hypocrisy: "How is it that we hear the loudest yelps for liberty from the drivers of Negroes?" Little had changed since the Revolution. African Americans, who represented one-fifth of the population of the United States, were excluded from the new opportunities opening up in the cities and the West. Indeed, the maid Janson encountered insisted—with no apparent sense of inconsistency—that her position was superior to that of blacks, who were brought involuntarily to lifelong servitude.

It is not surprising that in this highly charged racial climate Federalists accused the Republicans, especially those who lived in the South, of hypocrisy. In 1804, a Massachusetts Federalist sarcastically defined "Jeffersonian" as "an Indian word, signifying '*a great tobacco planter, who had herds of black slaves.*'" Race was always just beneath the surface of political maneuvering. Indeed, the acquisition of the Louisiana Territory and the War of 1812 fanned fundamental disagreement about the spread of slavery to the western territories.

In other areas, the Jeffersonians did not fulfill even their own high expectations. As members of an opposition party during the presidency of John Adams, they insisted on a strict interpretation of the Constitution, peaceful foreign relations, and reducing the federal government's role in the lives of average citizens. But once in power after the election of 1800, Jefferson and his supporters discovered that unanticipated pressures, foreign and domestic, forced them to moderate these goals. Before he retired from office in 1809, Jefferson interpreted the Constitution in a way that permitted the government to purchase the Louisiana Territory when the opportunity arose; he regulated the national economy with a rigor that would have surprised Alexander Hamilton; and he led the country to the brink of war.

How did the Republic's growth shape the market economy and relations with Native Americans?

THE REPUBLIC EXPANDS

During the early nineteenth century, the population of the United States grew substantially. The 1810 census counted 7,240,000 Americans, a jump of almost 2 million in ten years. Of this total, approximately 20 percent were black slaves, most of whom lived in the South. The large population increase was the result primarily of natural reproduction. During Jefferson's presidency few immigrants moved to the New World. The largest single group in this society was children under the age of 16, boys and girls who were born after Washington's election and who defined their own futures at a time when the nation's boundaries were rapidly expanding. For white Americans, it was a time of optimism. Many people with entrepreneurial skills or engineering capabilities aggressively advanced in a society that seemed to rate personal merit higher than family background.

Even as Americans defended the rights of individual states, they were forming strong regional identifications. In commerce and politics, they perceived themselves as representatives of distinct subcultures—southerners, New Englanders, or westerners. These broadening geographic horizons reflected improved transportation links that enabled people to travel more easily. But the growing regional mentality was also the product of defensiveness. While local writers celebrated New England's cultural distinctiveness, for example, they were uneasy about the region's rejection of the democratic values that were sweeping the rest of the nation. Moreover, people living south of the Potomac River began describing themselves as southerners, not as citizens of the Chesapeake or the Carolinas as they had done in colonial times.

This shifting focus of attention resulted not only from an awareness of shared economic interests but also from a sensitivity to outside attacks on slavery. Several times during the first 15 years of the nineteenth century, conspirators advocated secession. Though the schemes failed, they revealed powerful sectional loyalties that threatened national unity.

Westward the Course of Empire

The most striking changes occurred in the West. Before the end of the American Revolution, only Indian traders and a few hardy settlers had ventured across the Appalachians. After 1790, however, a flood of people rushed west to stake out farms on the rich soil. Many settlers followed the so-called northern route across Pennsylvania or New York into the old Northwest Territory. Pittsburgh and Cincinnati, both strategically located on the Ohio River, became important commercial ports. In 1803, Ohio joined the Union. Territorial governments were formed in Indiana (1800), Louisiana (1805), Michigan (1805), Illinois (1809), and Missouri (1812).

Pittsburgh *View of the City of Pittsburgh in 1817,* painted by a Mrs. Gibson while on her honeymoon. As the frontier moved west, Pittsburgh became an important commercial center.

Southerners poured into the new states of Kentucky (1792) and Tennessee (1796). Wherever they located, Westerners depended on water transportation. Because of the extraordinarily high cost of hauling goods overland, riverboats represented the only economical means of carrying agricultural products to distant markets. The Mississippi River was the crucial commercial link for the entire region. Westerners did not feel secure so long as Spain controlled New Orleans, the southern gate of the Mississippi.

Families that moved west attempted to transplant familiar eastern customs to the frontier. In areas such as the Western Reserve, a narrow strip of land along Lake Erie in northern Ohio, the influence of New England remained strong. In general, however, a creative mixing of peoples of different backgrounds in a strange environment generated distinctive folkways. Westerners developed their own heroes, such as Mike Fink, the legendary keelboatman of the Mississippi River; Daniel Boone, the famed trapper and Indian fighter; and the eye-gouging "alligatormen" of Kentucky and Tennessee. Americans who crossed the mountains were ambitious and self-confident, excited by the challenge of almost unlimited geographic mobility.

Quick Check

✓ What was the appeal of the West for so many Americans after 1790?

Tenskwatawa Tenskwatawa, known as the Prophet, provided spiritual leadership for the union of the native peoples he and his brother Tecumseh organized to resist white encroachment on Native American lands.

Native American Resistance

At the beginning of the nineteenth century, a substantial number of Native Americans lived in the greater Ohio Valley; the land belonged to them. The tragedy was that the Indians, many dependent on trade with the white people and ravaged by disease, lacked unity. Small groups of Native Americans, allegedly representing the interests of an entire tribe, sold off huge pieces of land, often for whiskey and trinkets.

Such fraudulent transactions disgusted the Shawnee leaders Tenskwatawa (known as the Prophet) and his brother Tecumseh. Tecumseh rejected classification as a Shawnee and may have been the first native leader to identify himself self-consciously as "Indian." These men attempted to revitalize native cultures. Against overwhelming odds, they briefly persuaded Native Americans living in the Indiana Territory to avoid contact with whites, resist alcohol, and, most important, hold on to their land. White intruders saw Tecumseh as a threat to progress. During the War of 1812, they shattered the Indians' dream of cultural renaissance. The populous Creek nation, located in the modern states of Alabama and Mississippi, also resisted the settlers' advance, but its warriors were crushed by Andrew Jackson's Tennessee militia at the Battle of Horseshoe Bend (March 1814).

Well-meaning Jeffersonians disclaimed any intention to destroy the Indians. The president talked of creating a vast reservation beyond the Mississippi River, just as the British had talked before the Revolution of a sanctuary beyond the Appalachians. He sent federal agents to "civilize" the Indians, to transform them into yeoman farmers. But even the most enlightened white thinkers did not believe Indians cultures were worth preserving. In fact, in 1835, the Democratic national convention selected a vice presidential candidate, Richard Johnson of Kentucky, whose major qualification for high office seemed to be that he had killed Tecumseh. And as early as 1780, Jefferson himself—then serving as the governor of Virginia—instructed a military leader on the frontier, "If we are to wage a campaign against these Indians the end proposed should be their extermination, or their removal beyond the lakes of the Illinois river. The same world will scarcely do for them and us."

Read the **Document**
Pennsylvania Gazette Indian Hostilities on **myhistorylab.com**

Quick Check

✓ What would Tecumseh have thought of Federal attempts to "civilize" the Indians?

Commercial Life in the Cities

Before 1820, the prosperity of the United States depended primarily on agriculture and trade. Jeffersonian America was by no stretch of the imagination an industrial economy. Most of the population—84 percent in 1810—was directly involved in agriculture. Southerners concentrated on the staple crops of tobacco, rice, and cotton, which they sold on the European market. In the North, people generally produced livestock and grain.

The cities of Jeffersonian America functioned chiefly as depots for international trade. Only about 7 percent of the nation's population lived in urban centers. Most of these people owed their livelihoods either directly or indirectly to the carrying trade. Major port cities of the early republic—New York, Philadelphia, and Baltimore, for example—had some of the highest population densities ever recorded in this country's history. In 1800, more than 40,000 New Yorkers crowded into only 1.5 square miles; in Philadelphia, some 46,000 people were packed into less than one square mile. As is common today, many city dwellers rented living space. Since the demand for housing exceeded the supply, the rents were high.

American cities exercised only a marginal influence on the nation's vast hinterland. Because of the high cost of land

Spinning Mill Although cotton was an important trade in the early nineteenth century, technological advances in textile production were slow to take hold. Some spinning mills, such as the one pictured here, were built in New England, but what historians call the "Industrial Revolution" did not begin for several more decades.

transportation, urban merchants seldom purchased goods for export—flour, for example—from a distance of more than 150 miles. The separation between rural and urban Americans was far more pronounced during Jefferson's presidency than it was after the development of canals and railroads a few decades later (see Chapter 9).

There was some technological advancement. Samuel Slater, an English-born designer of textile machinery, established cotton-spinning mills in New England, but until the 1820s, these plants employed few workers. In fact, during this period households produced far more cloth than factories did. Another far-sighted inventor, Robert Fulton, sailed the first American steamship up the Hudson River in 1807. In time, this marvelous innovation opened new markets for domestic manufacturers, especially in the West. At the end of the War of 1812, however, few people anticipated how power generated by fossil fuel would transform the American economy.

Ordinary workers often felt threatened by the new machines. Skilled artisans who had spent years mastering a trade and took pride in producing an object that expressed their own personalities found the industrial workplace alienating. Moreover, they rightly feared that innovative technology designed to improve efficiency might throw traditional craftspeople out of work or transform independent entrepreneurs into dependent wage laborers.

Quick Check

✓ What was the character of cities in an expanding Republican economy?

JEFFERSON AS PRESIDENT

How did practical politics challenge Jefferson's political principles?

The District of Columbia seemed an appropriate capital for a Republican president. At the time of Jefferson's first inauguration in 1801, Washington was still an isolated rural village, a far cry from crowded Philadelphia and New York. Jefferson fit comfortably into Washington society. He despised ceremony and shocked foreign dignitaries by meeting them in his slippers or a threadbare jacket. He spent as much time as his duties allowed in reading and reflection.

But Jefferson was also a politician to the core. He ran for the presidency to achieve specific goals: reduce the size and cost of federal government, repeal obnoxious Federalist legislation such as the Alien Acts, and maintain international peace. To accomplish his program, Jefferson needed the full cooperation of congressional Republicans, some of whom were fiercely independent. Over such figures Jefferson exercised political mastery. He established close ties with the leaders of Congress. While he seldom announced his plans in public, his legislative lieutenants knew exactly what he desired. Contemporaries who described Jefferson as a weak president—and some Federalists did just that—did not read the scores of memoranda he sent to political friends or witness the meetings he held with important Republicans. In two terms as president, Jefferson never had to veto an act of Congress.

Jefferson carefully selected the members of his cabinet. During Washington's administration, he had witnessed—even provoked—severe infighting; as president, he nominated only those who enthusiastically supported his programs. James Madison, the leading figure at the Constitutional Convention, became secretary of state. For the Treasury, Jefferson chose Albert Gallatin, a Swiss-born financier who understood the complexities of the federal budget. "If I had the universe to choose from," the president announced, "I could not change one of my associates to my better satisfaction."

Political Reforms

A top priority of the new government was cutting the national debt. Throughout American history, presidents have advocated such reductions, but their rhetoric has seldom yielded tangible results. Jefferson succeeded. He and Gallatin regarded a large federal deficit as dangerous. Both men associated debt with Alexander Hamilton's Federalist financial programs, measures they considered harmful to republicanism. Jefferson claimed that legislators elected by the current generation did not have the right to mortgage the future of unborn Americans.

Jefferson also wanted to diminish the activities of the federal government. He urged Congress to repeal all direct taxes, including the tax that had sparked the Whiskey Rebellion in 1794. Secretary Gallatin calculated that customs receipts could fund the entire cost of national government. As long as commerce flourished, revenues were sufficient. When war closed foreign markets, however, the funds dried up.

To help pay the debt inherited from the Adams administration, Jefferson cut the national budget. He closed several American diplomatic missions in Europe and slashed military spending. In his first term, Jefferson reduced the size of the U.S. Army by 50 percent. Only 3,000 soldiers were left to guard the entire frontier. He also retired most of the navy's warships. When New Englanders claimed these cuts left the country defenseless, Jefferson countered with a glib argument. As ships of the U.S. Navy sailed the oceans, he claimed, they were liable to provoke hostilities, even war; by reducing the size of the fleet, he promoted peace.

More than budgetary considerations prompted Jefferson's military reductions. He was suspicious of standing armies. The militia could defend the republic if it were attacked. No doubt, his experiences during the Revolution influenced his thinking on military affairs, for in 1776, an aroused populace had taken up arms against the British. To ensure that the citizen soldiers would receive professional leadership, Jefferson created the Army Corps of Engineers and the military academy at West Point in 1802.

Political patronage was a burden for the new president. Republicans had worked hard for Jefferson's victory. As soon as he took office, they stormed the executive mansion seeking federal jobs. While the president controlled several hundred jobs, he refused to dismiss all the Federalists. To be sure, he acted quickly to remove the so-called midnight appointees, partisan selections that Adams had made after Jefferson's election. But to transform federal hiring into an undisciplined spoils system, especially at the highest levels of the federal bureaucracy, seemed to Jefferson to be shortsighted. Moderate Federalists might be converted to the Republican party. In any case, the government needed their expertise. At the end of his first term, half of the people holding federal office were appointees of Washington and Adams.

Jefferson's political moderation hastened the demise of the Federalist party. This loose organization had nearly destroyed itself during the election of 1800. After Adams's defeat, prominent Federalists such as Fisher Ames and John Jay withdrew from national affairs. They refused to adopt the popular forms of campaigning that the Republicans had developed so successfully during the late 1790s. The mere prospect of flattering the common people was odious enough to drive Federalists into political retirement.

Many of them also sensed that national expansion worked against their interests. The creation of new states and congressional reapportionment increased

Republican representatives in Washington. By 1805, the Federalists retained only a few seats in New England and Delaware. "The power of the [Jefferson] Administration," confessed John Quincy Adams in 1802, "rests upon the support of a much stronger majority of the people throughout the Union than the former administrations ever possessed since the first establishment of the Constitution."

After 1804, younger Federalists attempted to pump life into the dying party. They experimented with popular election techniques. In some states, they tightened party organization, held nominating conventions, and campaigned energetically for office. These were essential reforms, but except for a brief Federalist revival in the Northeast between 1807 and 1814, the results were disappointing. Even the younger Federalists thought it demeaning to appeal for votes. Diehards such as Timothy Pickering promoted wild secessionist schemes in New England. The most promising moderates—John Quincy Adams, for example—joined the Republicans.

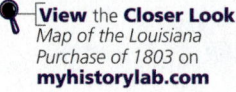

Quick Check

✓ Why did Jefferson find it so difficult to reduce the size of the federal government?

The Louisiana Purchase

When Jefferson took office, he was confident that Louisiana and Florida would eventually become part of the United States. Spain owned these territories, and Jefferson assumed he could persuade the rulers of that notoriously weak nation to sell their colonies. If that peaceful strategy failed, the president was prepared to threaten forcible occupation.

View the **Closer Look** Map of the Louisiana Purchase of 1803 on **myhistorylab.com**

In May 1801, however, prospects for the easy or inevitable acquisition of Louisiana darkened. Jefferson learned that Spain had transferred title to the entire region to France, its powerful northern neighbor. To make matters worse, the French leader Napoleon seemed intent on reestablishing an empire in North America. Even as Jefferson sought more information about the transfer, Napoleon was dispatching an army to suppress a rebellion in France's sugar-rich Caribbean colony, Haiti. From that island stronghold, French troops could occupy New Orleans and close the Mississippi River to American trade.

Watch the **Video** Lewis and Clark: What Were They Trying to Accomplish? on **myhistorylab.com**

A sense of crisis enveloped Washington. Congressmen urged Jefferson to prepare for war against France. Tensions increased when the Spanish officials who still governed New Orleans announced the closing of that port to American commerce (October 1802). Jefferson assumed that the Spanish had acted on orders from France. Despite this provocation, the president preferred negotiations to war. In January 1803, he asked James Monroe, a loyal Republican from Virginia, to join the American minister, Robert Livingston, in Paris and explore the possibility of purchasing New Orleans.

By the time Monroe joined Livingston in France, Napoleon had lost interest in an American empire. The army he sent to Haiti succumbed to tropical diseases. By the end of 1802, more than 30,000 veteran troops had died there. The diplomats from the United States knew nothing of these developments. They were surprised, therefore, in April 1803 when Talleyrand, the French foreign minister, offered to sell the entire Louisiana Territory for only $15 million. The Louisiana Purchase doubled the size of the United States.

Read the **Document** Constitutionality of the Louisiana Purchase (1803) on **myhistorylab.com**

The American people responded enthusiastically to the news. Only a few disgruntled New England Federalists thought the United States was already too large. Jefferson was relieved. The nation had avoided war with France. Nevertheless, he worried that the purchase might be unconstitutional. The president pointed out that the Constitution did not specifically authorize acquiring vast new territories and thousands of foreign citizens. To escape this apparent legal dilemma, Jefferson proposed amending the Constitution. Few persons, even his closest advisers, shared the president's scruples. Events in France soon forced Jefferson to adopt a more pragmatic course. When he heard that Napoleon had become impatient for his money, Jefferson rushed the treaty to a Senate eager to ratify it. Nothing more was said about amending the Constitution.

Quick Check

✓ Did the Louisiana Purchase represent a compromise by Jefferson in his interpretation of the constitution? Why or why not?

The Lewis and Clark Expedition

In the midst of the Louisiana controversy, Jefferson dispatched a secret message to Congress requesting $2,500 to explore the Far West (January 1803). How closely this decision was connected to the Paris negotiations is not clear. Whatever the case, the president asked his private secretary, Meriwether Lewis, to discover whether the Missouri River "may offer the most direct & practicable water communication across this continent for the purposes of commerce." The president also regarded the expedition as an opportunity to collect data about plants and animals. He personally instructed Lewis in the latest techniques of scientific observation. While preparing for this adventure, Lewis's second in command, William Clark, assumed such a prominent role that it became known as the Lewis and Clark Expedition. The effort owed much of its success to a young Shoshoni woman known as Sacagawea. She served as a translator and helped persuade suspicious Native Americans that the explorers meant no harm. As Clark explained, "A woman with a party of men is a token of peace."

The expedition set out from St. Louis up the Missouri River in May 1804. They barely survived crossing the snow-covered Rocky Mountains and then proceeded down the Columbia River. With their food supply running low, the Americans reached the Pacific Ocean in November 1805. The group returned safely the following September. The expedition fulfilled Jefferson's scientific expectations and reaffirmed his faith in the future prosperity of the United States. (See Map 8.1.)

Read the **Document**
Sacagawea Interprets for Lewis and Clark on **myhistorylab.com**

Quick Check

✓ How did the Lewis and Clark expedition reinforce Jefferson's faith in the future of the New Republic?

RACE AND DISSENT UNDER JEFFERSON

Jefferson concluded his first term on a wave of popularity. He had maintained the peace, reduced taxes, and expanded the United States. He overwhelmed his Federalist opponent Charles Cotesworth Pinckney in the presidential election of 1804 (see Table 8.1). Republicans also controlled Congress. John Randolph, the most articulate member of the House of Representatives, exclaimed, "Never was there an administration more brilliant than that of Mr. Jefferson up to this period. We were indeed in the full tide of successful experiment!"

But a perceptive observer might have seen signs of serious division within the Republican party and the country. The president's heavy-handed attempts to reform the federal courts stirred deep animosities. Republicans had begun sniping at other Republicans. Congressional debates over the slave trade revealed powerful sectional loyalties and profound disagreement.

How did Jeffersonians deal with the difficult problems of party politics and slavery?

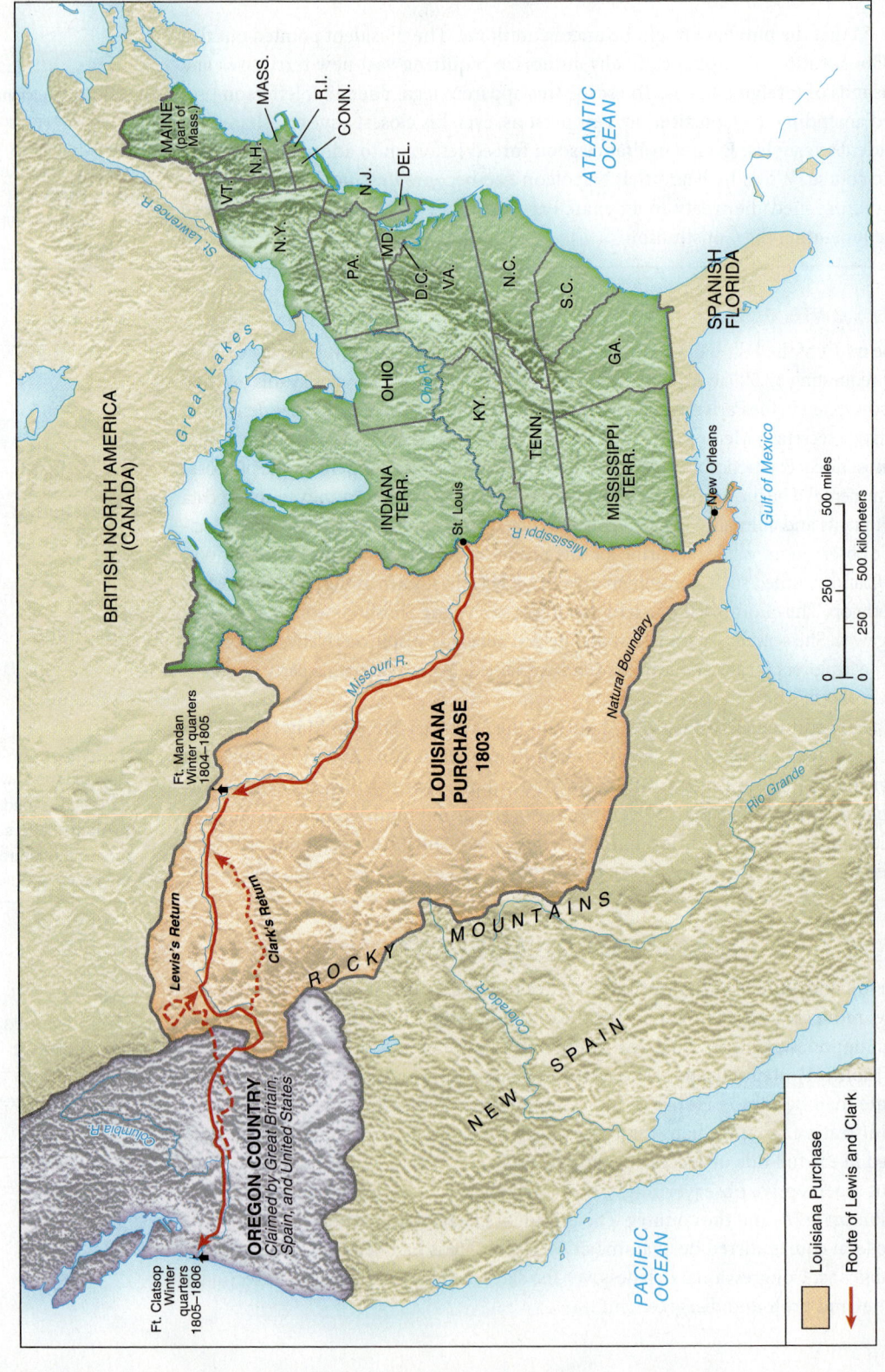

Map 8.1 The Louisiana Purchase and the Route of Lewis and Clark Not until Lewis and Clark had explored the Far West did citizens of the United States realize just how much territory Jefferson had acquired through the Louisiana Purchase.

TABLE 8.1 The Election of 1804		
Candidate	**Party**	**Electoral Vote**
Jefferson	Republican	162
C. Pinckney	Federalist	14

Attack on the Judges

Jefferson's controversy with the federal bench commenced the moment he became president. The Federalists, realizing they would soon lose control over the executive branch, had passed the Judiciary Act of 1801. This law created circuit courts and 16 new judgeships. Through his "midnight" appointments, Adams had filled these positions with Federalist stalwarts. Such blatant partisan behavior angered Jefferson. In the courts, he explained, the Federalists hoped to preserve their political influence, and "from that battery all the works of Republicanism are to be beaten down and erased." Even more infuriating was Adams's appointment of John Marshall as the new chief justice. This shrewd, largely self-educated Virginian of Federalist background could hold his own against the new president.

In January 1802, Jefferson's congressional allies called for repeal of the Judiciary Act. In public debate, they studiously avoided the obvious political issue. The new circuit courts should be closed not only because they were staffed by Federalists but also because they were needlessly expensive. The judges did not hear enough cases to warrant continuance. The Federalists mounted an able defense. The Constitution provided for removing federal judges only when they were found guilty of high crimes and misdemeanors. By repealing the Judiciary Act, the legislative branch would in effect be dismissing judges without a trial, a violation of their constitutional rights. This argument made little impression on the Republicans. In March, the House, following the Senate, voted for repeal.

While Congress debated the Judiciary Act, another battle erupted. One of Adams's "midnight" appointees, William Marbury, complained that the new administration would not give him his commission for the office of justice of the peace for the District of Columbia. He sought redress before the Supreme Court, demanding that the justices compel James Madison, the secretary of state, to deliver the necessary papers. The Republicans were furious when Marshall agreed to hear the case. Apparently the chief justice wanted to provoke a confrontation with the executive branch.

Marshall was too clever to jeopardize the independence of the Supreme Court over such a relatively minor issue. In his celebrated *Marbury v. Madison* decision (February 1803), Marshall berated the secretary of state for withholding Marbury's commission. Nevertheless, he concluded that the Supreme Court did not possess jurisdiction over such matters. Marbury was out of luck. The Republicans were so pleased with the outcome that they failed to examine the logic of Marshall's decision. He had ruled that part of the earlier act of Congress, the one on which Marbury based his appeal, was unconstitutional. This was the first time the Supreme Court asserted its right to judge the constitutionality of congressional acts. While contemporaries did not fully appreciate the significance of Marshall's doctrine, *Marbury v. Madison* later served as an important precedent for judicial review, the Supreme Court's authority to determine the constitutionality of federal statutes.

Neither Marbury's defeat nor repeal of the Judiciary Act placated extreme Republicans. They insisted that federal judges be made more responsive to the will of the people. One solution, short of electing federal judges, was impeachment. This clumsy device enabled the legislature to remove particularly offensive officeholders. In 1803, John Pickering, an incompetent judge from New Hampshire, presented the Republicans with a curious test case. This Federalist appointee was an insane alcoholic. While his outrageous behavior on the bench embarrassed everyone, Pickering had not committed any high crimes against the U.S. government. Ignoring such legal niceties, Jefferson's congressional allies pushed for impeachment. Although the Senate convicted Pickering (March 1804), many senators refused to compromise the letter of the Constitution and were conspicuously absent for the final vote.

Jefferson was apparently so eager to purge the courts of Federalists that he failed to heed these warnings. By the spring of 1803, he had set his sights on a target far more important than John Pickering. In a Baltimore newspaper, the president stumbled on the transcript of a speech allegedly delivered before a federal grand jury. The words seemed almost treasonous. The speaker was Samuel Chase, a justice of the Supreme Court, who had frequently attacked Republican policies. Jefferson leapt at the chance to remove Chase from office. The moment he learned of Chase's actions, the president asked a leading Republican congressman, "Ought the seditious and official attack on the principles of our Constitution … go unpunished?" The congressman took the hint. Within weeks, the Republican-controlled House of Representatives indicted Chase.

Even at this early stage of the impeachment, members of Congress expressed uneasiness. The charges against Chase were purely political. There was no doubt that his speech had been indiscreet. He had told the Baltimore jurors that "our late reformers"—in other words, the Republicans—threatened "peace and order, freedom and property." But while Chase lacked judgment, his attack on the administration hardly seemed criminal. If the Senate convicted Chase, every member of the Supreme Court, including Marshall, might also be dismissed.

Chase's trial before the Senate was one of the most dramatic events in American legal history. Chase and his lawyers conducted a masterful defense. By contrast, John Randolph, the congressman who served as chief prosecutor, behaved erratically, betraying repeatedly his ignorance of the law. While most Republican senators disliked the arrogant Chase, they refused to expand the constitutional definition of impeachable offenses to suit Randolph's argument. On March 1, 1805, the Senate acquitted the justice of all charges. The experience apparently convinced Chase of the need for greater moderation. After returning to the Court, he refrained from attacking Republican policies. His Jeffersonian opponents also learned something important. American politicians did not like tampering with the Constitution to get rid of judges, even an imprudent one like Chase.

Read the **Document**
Opinion for the Supreme Court for Marbury v. Madison on **myhistorylab.com**

Quick Check

✓ Why did the federal courts become the focus of party controversy under Jefferson?

The Slave Trade

Slavery sparked angry debate at the Constitutional Convention of 1787 (see Chapter 6). If delegates from the northern states had refused to compromise on this issue, southerners would not have supported the new government. The slave states demanded much in return for cooperation. According to an agreement that determined the size of a state's congressional delegation, a slave counted as three-fifths of a free white male. This formula meant that while blacks did not vote, they increased the number of southern representatives. The South in turn agreed only that after 1808 Congress *might consider* banning the importation of slaves into the United States. Slaves even influenced the outcome of national elections. Without the three-fifths rule, for example, Adams would have had the electoral votes to defeat Jefferson in 1800.

In December 1806, Jefferson urged Congress to prepare legislation outlawing the slave trade. In early 1807, legislators debated how to end the embarrassing commerce. The issue cut across party lines. Northern representatives generally favored a strong bill; some even wanted to make smuggling slaves into the country a capital offense. But the northerners could not figure out what to do with black people captured by the customs agents who would enforce the legislation. To sell these Africans would involve the federal government in slavery, which many northerners found morally repugnant. Nor was there much sympathy for freeing them. Ignorant of the English language and lacking personal possessions, these blacks seemed unlikely to long survive free in the South.

The Internal Slave Trade Although the external slave trade was officially outlawed in 1808, the commerce in humans persisted. An estimated 250,000 African slaves were brought illicitly to the United States between 1808 and 1860. The internal slave trade also continued. Folk artist Lewis Miller sketched this slave coffle marching from Virginia to new owners in Tennessee under the watchful eyes of mounted white overseers.

Read the
Document
*Congress Prohibits
Importation of
Slaves* on
myhistorylab.com

Quick Check

✓ Why did the United
States government
not outlaw slavery
altogether in 1807?

Southern congressmen responded with threats and ridicule. They told their northern colleagues that no one in the South regarded slavery as evil. It was naive, therefore, to expect planters to enforce a ban on the slave trade or inform federal agents when they spotted a smuggler. The notion that these culprits deserved capital punishment seemed viciously inappropriate.

The bill that Jefferson finally signed in March 1807 probably pleased no one. The law prohibited importing slaves into the United States after January 1, 1808. When customs officials captured a smuggler, the slaves were to be turned over to state authorities and disposed of according to local custom. Southerners did not cooperate. African slaves continued to pour into southern ports. Even more blacks would have been imported had Britain not also outlawed the slave trade in 1807. The Royal Navy then captured American slave smugglers off the coast of Africa. When anyone complained, the British explained that they were merely enforcing the laws of the United States.

EMBARRASSMENTS OVERSEAS

Why did the
United States find
it difficult to avoid
military conflict
during this period?

During Jefferson's second term (1805–1809), the United States found itself in the midst of a world at war. A brief peace in Europe ended abruptly in 1803. The two military giants of the age, France and Great Britain, then fought for supremacy on land and sea. This was a kind of total war unknown in the eighteenth century. Napoleon's armies carried the ideology of the French Revolution across the Continent. The emperor—as Napoleon Bonaparte called himself after December 1804—transformed conquered nations into French satellites. Only Britain offered effective resistance.

At first, the United States profited from European adversity. As "neutral carriers," American ships transported goods to any port in the world where they could find a buyer. American merchants grew wealthy serving Britain and France. Since the Royal Navy did not allow direct trade between France and its colonies, American captains conducted "broken voyages," during which American vessels sailing out of French ports in the Caribbean would put in briefly to an American port, pay nominal customs, and then sail to France. For years, the British did little to halt this obvious subterfuge.

Napoleon's success on the battlefield, however, strained Britain's resources. In July 1805, a British admiralty court announced in the *Essex* decision that "broken voyages" were illegal. The Royal Navy began seizing American ships in record number. Moreover, as the war continued, the British stepped up the impressment of sailors on ships flying the U.S. flag. Estimates of the number of men impressed ranged as high as 9,000.

Beginning in 1806, the British government issued trade regulations known as the Orders in Council. These forbade neutral commerce with the Continent and threatened seizure of any ship that violated the orders. The declarations created what were in effect "paper blockades"; on paper commerce was prohibited. In reality the rival powers lacked the resources to enforce those blockades. Even the powerful British navy could not monitor every Continental port.

Napoleon responded with his own paper blockade called the Continental System. In the Berlin Decree of November 1806 and the Milan Decree of December 1807, he closed all Continental ports to British trade. Neutral vessels carrying British goods were liable to seizure. The Americans were caught between two conflicting systems.

This unhappy turn of international events baffled Jefferson. He had assumed that justice obliged civilized countries to respect neutral rights. Appeals to reason, however, made little impression on states at war. "As for France and England," the president growled, "... the one is a den of robbers, the other of pirates." In a desperate attempt to avoid hostilities for which the United States was ill prepared, Jefferson ordered James Monroe and William Pinckney to negotiate a commercial treaty with Britain. But the document they signed on December 31, 1806, said nothing about impressment. An angry president refused to submit the treaty to the Senate for ratification.

The United States soon suffered an even greater humiliation. A ship of the Royal Navy, the *Leopard*, sailing off the coast of Virginia, commanded an American warship to submit to a search for deserters (June 22, 1807). When the captain of the *Chesapeake* refused to cooperate, the *Leopard* opened fire, killing three men and wounding 18. The attack violated American sovereignty. Official protests received only a perfunctory apology from the British government, and the American people demanded revenge.

Embargo Divides the Nation

Jefferson found what he regarded as a satisfactory way to deal with European predators with a policy he called "peaceable coercion." If Britain and France refused to respect the rights of neutral carriers, then the United States would keep its ships at home. This protected them from seizure and deprived the European powers of needed American goods, especially food. The president predicted that a total embargo of American commerce would soon force Britain and France to negotiate with the United States in good faith: "Our commerce is so valuable to them that they will be glad to purchase it when the only price we ask is to do us justice." The Embargo Act became law on December 22, 1807.

But "peaceable coercion" became a Jeffersonian nightmare. The president naively believed the American people would enthusiastically support the embargo. Instead, compliance required enforcement acts that became increasingly harsh.

By mid-1808, Jefferson and Gallatin were regulating the smallest details of American economic life. The federal government supervised the coastal trade, lest a ship sailing between two states slip away to Europe or the West Indies. Overland trade with Canada was proscribed. When violations still occurred, Congress gave customs collectors the right to seize a vessel merely on suspicion of wrongdoing. A final desperate act in January 1809 prohibited the loading of any U.S. vessel,

The Embargo Act The Ograbme (embargo spelled backward) snapping turtle, created by cartoonist Alexander Anderson, is shown here biting an American tobacco smuggler who is breaking the embargo.

regardless of size, without authorization from a customs officer who was supported by the army, navy, and local militia.

Northerners hated the embargo. Persons near Lake Champlain in upper New York State simply ignored the regulations and roughed up customs officers who interfered with the Canadian trade. The administration was determined to stop the smugglers. Jefferson urged the governor of New York to call out the militia and sent federal troops to overawe the citizens of New York.

New Englanders considered the embargo lunacy. New England merchants were willing to take their chances on the high seas, but for reasons that few people understood, the president insisted that it was better to preserve ships from possible seizure than to make profits. Sailors and artisans were thrown out of work. The popular press maintained a constant howl of protest. Not surprisingly, the Federalist party revived in New England. Extremists suggested that state assemblies nullify federal law.

By 1809, Jefferson's foreign policy was bankrupt. The embargo never seriously damaged the British economy. In fact, British merchants took over lucrative markets that the Americans had been forced to abandon. Napoleon liked the embargo, since it seemed to harm Britain more than France. Faced with growing opposition, the Republicans in Congress panicked. One representative declared that "peaceful coercion" was a "miserable and mischievous failure" and joined his colleagues in repealing the embargo a few days before James Madison's inauguration. Relations between the United States and the great European powers were worse in 1809 than they had been in 1805. During his second term, the pressures of office weighed heavily on Jefferson. After so many years of public service, he welcomed retirement to Monticello.

Quick Check

✓ Why was Jefferson's embargo policy such a failure?

A New Administration Goes to War

In the election of 1808, the former secretary of state, James Madison, defeated the Federalist Charles Cotesworth Pinckney. The margin of victory was substantially lower than Jefferson's had been in 1804, a warning of political troubles ahead. (See Table 8.2.) The Federalists also doubled their seats in the House, from 24 to 48.

The new president confronted the same foreign policy problems that Jefferson had. Neither Britain nor France showed the slightest interest in respecting American neutral rights. Threats against either nation rang hollow so long as

TABLE 8.2   The Election of 1808

Candidate	Party	Electoral Vote
Madison	Republican	122
C. Pinckney	Federalist	47

the United States failed to develop its military strength. In May 1810, Congress passed Macon's Bill Number Two, sponsored by Nathaniel Macon of North Carolina. In a complete reversal of strategy, this poorly drafted legislation reestablished trade with *both* Britain and France. It also contained a curious carrot-and-stick provision. As soon as either of these states repealed restrictions on neutral shipping, the U.S. government promised to halt all commerce with the other.

Napoleon spotted a rare opportunity. He informed the U.S. minister in Paris that France would no longer enforce the hated Berlin and Milan Decrees. Madison reacted impulsively. Without waiting for further information from Paris, he announced that unless Britain repealed the Orders in Council by November, the United States would cut off commercial relations. Only later did the president learn that Napoleon had no intention of living up to his side of the bargain; his agents continued to seize American ships. Madison decided to ignore the French provocations, to pretend the emperor was behaving honestly. The British could not understand why the United States tolerated such obvious deception. No one in London would have suspected that the president really had no other options left.

Events unrelated to international commerce fueled anti-British sentiment in the western United States. Westerners believed—incorrectly—that British agents from Canada had persuaded Tecumseh's warriors to resist American settlement. According to rumors that ran through the region, the British dreamed of monopolizing the fur trade. In any case, General William Henry Harrison, governor of the Indiana Territory, marched an army to the edge of a large Shawnee village at the mouth of Tippecanoe Creek near the banks of the Wabash River. On November 7, 1811, the American troops routed the Indians at the Battle of Tippecanoe. Harrison became a national hero. In 1840 the American people would elect "Tippecanoe" president. This incident forced Tecumseh to seek British military assistance against the Americans, something he probably would not have done had Harrison left him alone.

Quick Check

Why did the American government find it so hard to avoid entanglements in European affairs?

Fumbling Toward Conflict

In 1811, the anti-British mood of Congress intensified. Militant representatives, some elected to Congress for the first time in 1810, announced they would no longer tolerate national humiliation. They called for action, for resistance to Britain, for any course that promised to achieve respect for the United States and security

TABLE 8.3	The Election of 1812	
Candidate	**Party**	**Electoral Vote**
Madison	Republican	128
Clinton	Republican* (antiwar faction)	89

*Clinton was nominated by a convention of antiwar Republicans and endorsed by the Federalists.

for its republican institutions. These aggressive nationalists, many of them from the South and West, have sometimes been labeled the War Hawks. They included Henry Clay, an earthy Kentucky congressman who served as speaker of the House, and John C. Calhoun, a brilliant South Carolinian. These fiery orators spoke of honor and pride, as if foreign relations were a sort of duel between gentlemen. While the War Hawks were Republicans, they repudiated Jefferson's policy of peaceful coercion.

Madison surrendered to the War Hawks. On June 1, 1812, he sent Congress a declaration of war against Britain. The timing was peculiar. Over the preceding months, tensions between the two nations had relaxed. No new attacks had occurred. Indeed, at the very moment Madison called for war, the British government was suspending the Orders in Council, a conciliatory gesture that probably would have preserved the peace.

However inadequately Madison communicated his goals, he does seem to have had a plan. His major aim was to force the British to respect American maritime rights, especially in Caribbean waters. The president's problem was to figure out how a small, militarily weak nation like the United States could bring effective pressure on Britain. Madison's answer seemed to be Canada. This colony supplied Britain's Caribbean possessions with foodstuffs. The president reasoned, therefore, that by threatening to seize Canada, the Americans might compel the British to make concessions on maritime issues.

View the **Image**
British Impressment, 1812 on
myhistorylab.com

Congressional War Hawks may have had other goals. Some expansionists were probably more concerned about conquering Canada than they were about the impressment of American seamen. For others, the whole affair may have truly been about national pride. Andrew Jackson wrote, "For what are we going to fight? … [W]e are going to fight for the reestablishment of our national character, misunderstood and vilified at home and abroad." New Englanders in whose commercial interests the war would supposedly be waged ridiculed such chauvinism. The vote for war in Congress was close, 79 to 49 in the House, 19 to 13 in the Senate. With this doubtful mandate, the country marched to war against the most powerful maritime nation in Europe. The election of 1812 reflected division over the war. Antiwar Republicans nominated De Witt Clinton of New York, who was endorsed by the Federalists. Nevertheless, Madison won narrowly (see Table 8.3).

Quick Check

✔ Why were the War Hawks so intent on pushing the New Republic into a war with Great Britain?

THE STRANGE WAR OF 1812

Optimism for the War of 1812 ran high. The War Hawks apparently believed that even though the United States possessed only a small army and navy, it could sweep the British out of Canada. Such predictions flew in the face of reality. Not only did the Republicans fail to appreciate how unprepared the country was for war, but they also refused to mobilize needed resources. The House rejected direct taxes and authorized naval appropriations only with reluctance. Indeed, even as they planned for battle, the consequences of their political and economic convictions haunted the Republicans in Congress. They did not seem to understand that a weak, decentralized government—the one that Jeffersonians championed—was incapable of waging an expensive war against the world's greatest sea power. (See Map 8.2.)

Why is the War of 1812 sometimes thought of as a "second war of independence"?

View the **Map**
The War of 1812 on
myhistorylab.com

Fighting the British

American military operations focused initially on the western forts. The results were discouraging. On August 16, 1812, General William Hull surrendered an army to a smaller British force at Detroit. Michilimackinac was also lost. Marches against Niagara and Montreal achieved nothing. The militia, led by aging officers with little military aptitude, no matter how enthusiastic, was no match for well-trained European veterans. On the sea, the United States did better. In August, Captain Isaac Hull's *Constitution* defeated the *Guerrière* in a fierce battle, and American privateers destroyed or captured British merchant ships. These successes were deceptive, however. So long as Napoleon threatened the Continent, Britain could spare few warships for service in America. But when peace returned to Europe in 1814, Britain redeployed its fleet and easily blockaded the tiny U.S. Navy.

The campaigns of 1813 revealed that conquering Canada would be more difficult than the War Hawks ever imagined. Both sides recognized that whoever controlled the Great Lakes controlled the West. On Lake Erie, the Americans won the race for naval superiority. On September 10, 1813, Oliver Hazard Perry destroyed a British fleet at

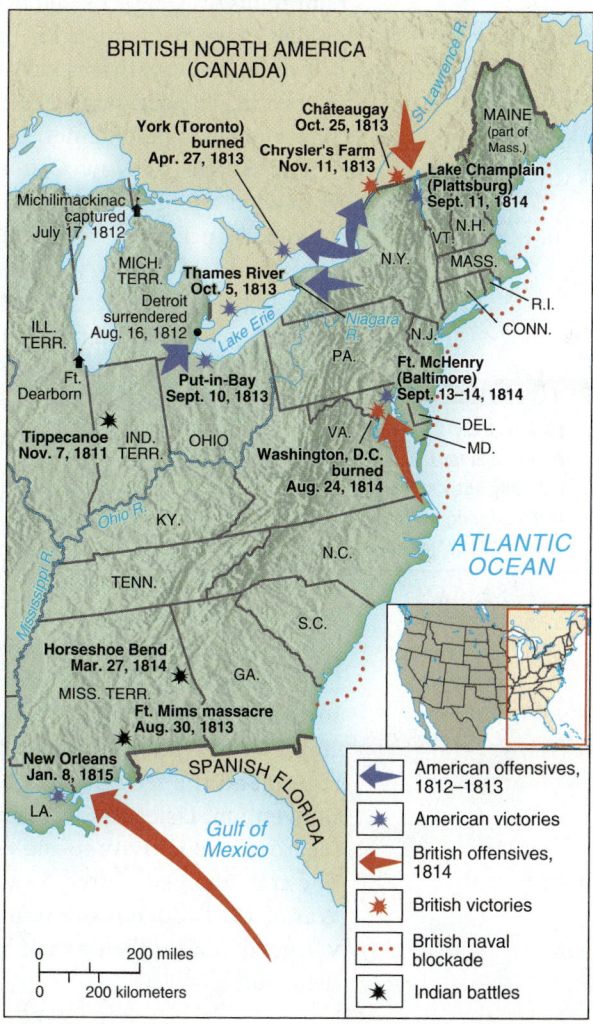

Map 8.2 *The War of 1812* The major battles of the War of 1812 brought few lasting gains to either the British or the Americans.

Put-in-Bay. In a much-quoted letter written after the battle, Perry exclaimed, "We have met the enemy; and they are ours." On October 5, General Harrison overran British troops and Indian warriors at the Battle of Thames River. During this engagement, Tecumseh was killed. On the other fronts, however, the war went badly for the Americans. General Wilkinson suffered an embarrassing defeat near Montreal (Battle of Chrysler's Farm, November 11), and the British navy held its own on Lake Ontario.

((•—| **Listen** to the
Audio File
*Star Spangled
Banner* on
myhistorylab.com

Throughout 1814, British warships harassed the Chesapeake coast. To their surprise, the British found the region almost totally undefended. On August 24, 1814, in retaliation for the Americans' destruction of the capital of Upper Canada (York, Ontario), a small British force burned the American capital, a victory more symbolic than strategic. Encouraged by their easy success and contemptuous of America's ragtag soldiers, the British launched a full-scale attack on Baltimore (September 13–14). To everyone's surprise, the fort guarding the harbor held out against a heavy naval bombardment, and the British gave up the operation. The survival of Fort McHenry inspired Francis Scott Key to write "The Star-Spangled Banner."

View the **Image**
*Burning of the White
House, 1814* on
myhistorylab.com

The **Battle of New Orleans** should never have occurred. The British landed a large assault force under General Edward Pakenham just when diplomats in Europe were preparing the final drafts of a peace treaty. The combatants, of course, knew nothing of these distant developments. On January 8, 1815, Pakenham ordered a frontal attack against General Andrew Jackson's well-defended positions. Pakenham was killed, and the British lost over 2,000 killed and wounded. The Americans suffered only light casualties. The victory not only made Jackson a national folk hero, but it also gave the people of the United States a much needed source of pride. Even in military terms, the battle was significant. If the British had managed to occupy New Orleans, the key to the trade of the Mississippi River Valley, they would have been difficult to dislodge regardless of the peace treaty.

Quick Check

✓ How well did the
Americans fare
militarily against the
British during the
War of 1812?

Hartford Convention: The Demise of the Federalists

In late 1814, leading New England politicians, most of them moderate Federalists, gathered in Hartford, Connecticut, to discuss relations between their region and the federal government in what became known as the **Hartford Convention**. Delegates were angry and hurt by the Madison administration's seeming insensitivity to the economic interests of the New England states. The embargo had soured New Englanders on Republican foreign policy. The War of 1812 added insult to injury. When British troops occupied the coastal villages of Maine, then part of Massachusetts, the president did nothing to drive them out.

The men who met at Hartford on December 15 did not advocate secession. Although people in other sections of the country cried treason, the delegates only recommended changing the Constitution. They drafted amendments that reflected the New Englanders' growing frustration. One proposal suggested that congressional representation be calculated on the basis of the number of white males living in a state. New England congressmen were tired of the three-fifths rule that gave southern slaveholders a disproportionately large voice in the House. The convention also wanted to limit each president to a single term, which New Englanders hoped might end Virginia's monopoly of the presidency. And finally, the delegates insisted that a two-thirds majority be necessary before Congress could declare war, pass commercial regulations, or admit new states to the Union. The moderate Federalists of New England were confident these changes would protect their region from the tyranny of southern Republicans.

The Battle of New Orleans This engraving by Joseph Yeager (c. 1815) depicts the Battle of New Orleans and the death of British Major General Edward Pakenham. The death of the British commander was a turning point in the battle, in which more than 2,000 British soldiers were killed or wounded at the hands of General Andrew Jackson and the American army.

Quick Check

✓ What factors led to the calling of the Hartford Convention and the drafting of the Hartford resolutions?

The convention dispatched its resolutions to Washington, but soon after an official delegation reached the federal capital, the situation became awkward. Everyone was celebrating the victory of New Orleans and the announcement of peace. Republicans in Congress accused the hapless New Englanders of disloyalty. People throughout the country were persuaded that wild secessionists had attempted to destroy the Union. The Hartford Convention accelerated the demise of the Federalist party.

CONCLUSION: THE "SECOND WAR OF INDEPENDENCE"

In August 1814, the United States dispatched a distinguished negotiating team to Ghent, a Belgian city, to open peace talks. At first, the British made impossible demands. They insisted on territorial concessions from the United States, the right to navigate the Mississippi River, and the creation of an Indian buffer state in the Northwest Territory. The Americans rejected the entire package. In turn, they lectured the British about maritime rights and impressment. Fatigue finally broke the deadlock. The British government realized that military force could not significantly alter the outcome of the war. Weary negotiators signed the Treaty of Ghent on Christmas Eve 1814. The document dealt with virtually none of the topics in Madison's war message to Congress. Neither side surrendered territory; Britain refused even to discuss impressment. The adversaries merely agreed to stop fighting, postponing the vexing issues of neutral rights until a later date. The Senate apparently concluded that stalemate was preferable to continued conflict and ratified the treaty 35 to 0.

Still, most Americans viewed the War of 1812 as a success. The country's military accomplishments had been unimpressive, but the people of the United States had been swept up in a contagion of nationalism. "The war," reflected Gallatin, had made Americans "feel and act more as a nation; and I hope that the permanency of the Union is thereby better secured."

8 STUDY RESOURCES

((•─[Listen to the **Chapter Audio** for Chapter 8 on **myhistorylab.com**

TIMELINE

CHAPTER REVIEW

THE REPUBLIC EXPANDS

How did the Republic's growth shape the market economy and relations with Native Americans?

During Jefferson's administration, a rapidly growing population flooded into the Ohio and Mississippi valleys. Family farms produced crops for a robust international market. Cities served as centers, not of industry, but of commerce. When Native Americans such as Tecumseh resisted expansion, the United States government and ordinary white settlers pushed them aside. *(p. 196)*

JEFFERSON AS PRESIDENT

How did practical politics challenge Jefferson's political principles?

Jefferson brought to the presidency a commitment to a small, less expensive federal government. In office, however, he discovered that practical politics demanded compromises with Republican principles. He needed a government capable of responding to unexpected challenges and opportunities throughout the world. Although he worried that the Louisiana Purchase (1803) might exceed his authority under the Constitution, Jefferson accepted the French offer and sent Lewis and Clark to explore this vast territory. *(p. 200)*

RACE AND DISSENT UNDER JEFFERSON

How did Jeffersonians deal with the difficult problems of party politics and slavery?

To end Federalist control of the judiciary, Jefferson denied commissions to judges appointed at the end of the Adams administration and attempted to remove others from office. That failed, and the impeachment of Supreme Court Justice Samuel Chase embarrassed the administration. In 1807, after considerable debate and compromise, Jefferson signed into law a bill outlawing the international slave trade. *(p. 203)*

EMBARRASSMENTS OVERSEAS

Why did the United States find it difficult to avoid military conflict during this period?

During Jefferson's second term, Britain and France waged a world war. Both nations tried to manipulate the United States into taking sides. Recognizing that his country possessed only a weak navy and small army, Jefferson supported the Embargo Act (1807), which closed American ports to foreign commerce. This angered New Englanders who regarded open trade as the key to their region's prosperity. *(p. 208)*

THE STRANGE WAR OF 1812

Why is the War of 1812 sometimes thought of as a "second war of independence"?

Prior to the war, Britain treated the United States as though it were still a colonial possession and regularly seized sailors on American ships. In 1813, American troops failed to conquer Canada. In 1814, British troops burned Washington, D.C., in retaliation. In 1815, General Andrew Jackson won a stunning victory in the Battle of New Orleans. The resolutions of the Hartford Convention, criticizing the war and the Constitution, proved an embarrassment for the Federalists and accelerated their demise as a political party. *(p. 213)*

KEY TERM QUESTIONS

1. What would Tecumseh have thought of federal attempts to "civilize" the Indians? (p. 198)

2. Did the Louisiana Purchase represent a compromise by Jefferson in his interpretation of the Constitution? (p. 202)

3. How did the Lewis and Clark Expedition reinforce Jefferson's faith in the future of the new Republic? (p. 203)

4. What role did the Supreme Court's *Marbury v. Madison* decision play in the party controversy under Jefferson? (p. 205)

5. How did the *Marbury v. Madison* decision establish the principle of judicial review? (p. 206)

6. Why was the Embargo Act such a failure? (p. 209)

7. Why were the War Hawks so intent on pushing the new Republic into a war with Great Britain? (p. 212)

8. How well did the Americans fare militarily against the British during the War of 1812? (p. 213)

9. Why was the Battle of New Orleans fought after the War of 1812 had officially ended? (p. 214)

10. What factors led to the calling of the Hartford Convention and the drafting of the Hartford resolutions? (p. 214)

MYHISTORYLAB CONNECTIONS

Visit **www.myhistorylab.com** for a customized Study Plan to build your knowledge of *Republican Ascendancy*.

Question for Analysis

1. Why was the Louisiana Purchase so crucial for the United States?

   View the **Closer Look** *Map of the Louisiana Purchase of 1803* p. 202

2. How did the Lewis and Clark expedition fit into the idea that expansion was essential to liberty?

   Watch the **Video** *Lewis and Clark: What Were They Trying to Accomplish?* p. 202

Other Resources from this Chapter

Read the **Document** *Pennsylvania Gazette Indian Hostilities*

Read the **Document** *Constitutionality of the Louisiana Purchase*

Read the **Document** *Sacagawea Interprets for Lewis and Clark*

View the **Image** *British Impressment*

3. Why was the Supreme Court's ruling for Marbury v. Madison so significant?

   📖 **Read** the **Document** *Opinion of the Supreme Court for* Marbury v. Madison p. 205

4. Why did the United States government not outlaw slavery altogether in 1807?

   📖 **Read** the **Document** *Congress Prohibits the Importation of Slaves* p. 208

5. Why did the battles of the War of 1812 bring little lasting gain to either the British or the Americans?

   🔍 **View** the **Map** *The War of 1812* p. 212

🔍 **View** the **Image** *Burning of the White House, 1814*

((•— **Listen** to the **Audio File** *Star Spangled Banner*

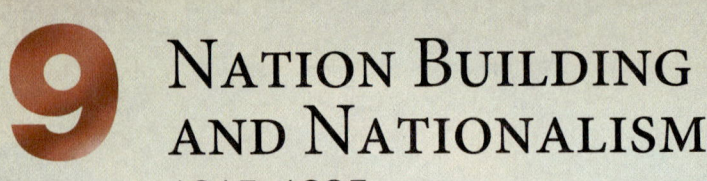

9 NATION BUILDING AND NATIONALISM

1815–1825

Contents and Spotlight Questions

((•─ **Listen** to the **Chapter Audio** for Chapter 9 on **myhistorylab.com**

A REVOLUTIONARY WAR HERO REVISITS AMERICA IN 1824

When the Marquis de Lafayette returned to the United States in 1824 he found a peaceful and prosperous nation. For more than a year, the great French hero of the American Revolution toured the country that he had helped to create and marveled at how much had changed since he had fought beside George Washington more than 40 years before. Lafayette hailed "the immense improvements" and "admirable communications" and was moved by "all the grandeur and prosperity of these happy United States, which ... reflect on every part of the world the light of a far superior political civilization."

Americans had good reasons to make Lafayette's return the occasion for patriotic celebration and reaffirmation. Since the War of 1812, the nation had been free from serious foreign threats to its independence and way of life. Its population, size, and wealth were growing rapidly. Its republican

Election Day in Philadelphia (1815) An exuberant crowd celebrates in the square outside Independence Hall in this painting by German American artist John Lewis Krimmel.

form of government, which many had considered a risky experiment, was apparently working well. James Monroe, the current president, had proclaimed in his first inaugural address that "the United States have flourished beyond example. Their citizens individually have been happy and the nation prosperous." Expansion "to the Great Lakes and beyond the sources of the great rivers which communicate through our whole interior" meant that "no country was ever happier with respect to its domain." As for the government, it was so near to perfection that "in respect to it we have no essential improvement to make."

Beneath the optimism and self-confidence, however, lay undercurrents of doubt and anxiety. The visit of the aged Lafayette signified the passing of the Founders. Less than a year after his departure, Thomas Jefferson and John Adams—who along with James Madison were the last of the great Founders still living—died within hours of each other on the fiftieth anniversary of the Declaration of Independence. Most Americans saw the coincidence as a good omen for the nation. But some asked if their republican virtue and self-sacrifice could be maintained in an increasingly prosperous and materialistic society. And what about the place of black slavery in a "perfect" democratic republic? Lafayette himself was disappointed that the United States had not freed the southern slaves.

But the peace following the War of 1812 did open the way for a surge of nation building. As new lands were acquired or opened up for settlement, hordes of pioneers often rushed in. Improved transportation soon gave many of them access to distant markets, and advances in processing raw materials led to the first stirrings of industrialization. Politicians looked for ways to encourage growth and expansion, and an active judiciary promoted economic development and asserted the priority of national over state and local interests. To guarantee the peace and security essential for internal progress, statesmen proclaimed a foreign policy designed to insulate America from external involvements. A new nation of great potential wealth and power was emerging.

EXPANSION AND MIGRATION

What key forces drove American expansion westward during this period?

Peace with Great Britain in 1815 allowed Americans to shift their attention from Europe and the Atlantic to the vast interior of North America.

Between the Appalachians and the Mississippi, settlement had already begun, especially in the new states of Ohio, Kentucky, and Tennessee. In the lower Mississippi Valley, the former French colony of Louisiana had been admitted as a state in 1812, and a thriving settlement existed around Natchez in the Mississippi Territory. Elsewhere in the trans-Appalachian west, white settlement was sparse, and much land remained in Indian hands. U.S. citizens, eager to expand into lands held by Indian nations and Spain, used diplomacy, military action, force, and fraud to "open" lands for settlement and westward migration.

Extending the Boundaries

Postwar expansionists turned their attention first to Spanish holdings, which included Florida and much of the present-day American West. The Spanish claimed possession of land extending along the Gulf Coast from Florida to the Mississippi. Between 1810 and 1812, however, the United States had annexed the area between the Mississippi and the Perdido River in what became Alabama, claiming that it was part of the Louisiana Purchase. The remainder, known as East Florida, became a prime object of territorial ambition for President James Monroe and his energetic secretary of state, John Quincy Adams. Adams had a grand design for continental expansion that required nullifying or reducing Spanish claims west and east of the Mississippi; he eagerly awaited an opportunity to apply pressure for that purpose.

General Andrew Jackson provided that opportunity. In 1816, U.S. troops crossed into East Florida in pursuit of hostile Seminole Indians. This raid touched off a wider conflict, and after taking command in late 1817, Jackson went beyond his official orders and occupied East Florida in April and May 1818. This operation became known as the First Seminole War.

In November 1818, Secretary Adams informed Spain that the United States had acted in self-defense and that further conflict would be avoided only if it ceded East Florida to the United States. The Madrid government, weakened by Latin American revolutions and the breaking up of its empire, was in no position to resist American bullying. As part of the **Adams–Onís Treaty**, signed on February 22, 1819, Spain relinquished Florida. In return, the United States assumed $5 million of the financial claims of American citizens against Spain.

A strong believer that the United States had a continental destiny, Adams also made Spain give up its claim to the Pacific coast north of California, thus opening a path for future American expansion. Taking advantage of Spain's desire to keep its title to Texas—part of which the United States had claimed as part of the Louisiana Purchase—Adams induced the Spanish minister Luis de Onís to agree to a new boundary between American and Spanish territory that ran north of Texas but extended to the Pacific. Great Britain and Russia still had competing claims to the Pacific Northwest, but the United States was now in a better position to acquire a Pacific coastline.

Interest in exploiting the Far West grew during the second and third decades of the nineteenth century. In 1811, a New York merchant, John Jacob Astor, founded the fur-trading post of Astoria at the mouth of the Columbia River in the Oregon Country. Astor's American Fur Company operated out of St. Louis in the 1820s and 1830s, with fur traders working their way up the Missouri River to the northern Rockies and beyond. First they limited themselves to trading for furs with the Indians, but later, businesses such as the Rocky Mountain Fur Company, founded in 1822, relied on trappers or "mountain men" who went after game on their own and sold the furs to company agents at an annual meeting or "rendezvous."

However, the area beyond the Mississippi did not draw substantial immigration during this period. The focus of attention between 1815 and the 1840s was the nearer west, the rich agricultural lands between the Appalachians and the

North America, 1819 Treaties with Britain following the War of 1812 setting the border between the United States and Canada (British North America) made this border the longest unfortified boundary line in the world.

Mississippi that were inhabited by numerous Indian tribes. Settlers poured across the Appalachians and filled the agricultural heartland of the United States. In 1810, only about one-seventh of the American population lived beyond the Appalachians; by 1840, more than one-third did. During that period, Illinois grew from a territory with 12,282 inhabitants to a state with 476,183; Mississippi's population of about 40,000 increased tenfold; and Michigan grew from a remote frontier area with fewer than 5,000 people into a state with more than 200,000. Eight new western states joined the Union during this period.

While some of the original buyers were land speculators, most of the new land did find its way into the hands of actual cultivators. In some areas, squatters arrived before the official survey and formed claims associations that policed land auctions to prevent "outsiders" from bidding up the price and buying their farms out from under them. Squatters also agitated for formal right of first purchase or preemption from the government. Between 1799 and 1830, Congress granted squatters in specific areas the right to purchase at the minimum price the land that they had already improved. In 1841, Congress formally acknowledged the right to farm on public lands with the assurance of a *future* preemption right.

Quick Check

✓ What territories did the United States acquire under secretary Adams, and how did it obtain them?

Native American Societies Under Pressure

Five Indian nations, with a combined population of nearly 60,000, occupied much of what later became Mississippi, Alabama, Georgia, and Florida. These nations—the Cherokee, Chickasaw, Choctaw, Creek, and Seminole—became known as the "Five Civilized Tribes" because by 1815 they had adopted many of the features of the surrounding white southern society: an agricultural economy, a republican government, and slavery. Indeed, the cultural transformation of the southeastern Indians was part of a conscious strategy to respond to Jeffersonian exhortations toward "civilization" and the promise of citizenship that came with it. But between 1815 and 1833, it became increasingly clear that however "civilized" Indians had become, most white Americans were not interested in incorporating them into U.S. society, whether as nations or as individuals.

The five nations varied in their responses to white encroachment on their lands. So-called mixed-blood leaders such as John Ross convinced the Cherokee to adopt a strategy of accommodation to increase their chances of survival; the Creek and Seminole, by contrast, forcibly resisted.

The Cherokee were the largest of the five nations. Traditional Cherokee society had combined hunting by men and subsistence farming by women. In the early nineteenth century, the shift to a more agrarian, market-based economy eroded the traditional matrilineal kinship system, in which a person belonged to his or her mother's clan. The new order replaced matrilineal inheritance with the U.S. system of patriarchy in which fathers headed the household and property passed from father to son. Emphasis on the nuclear family with the husband as producer and the wife as domestic caretaker diminished the clan's role.

The shift toward agriculture also helped introduce American-style slavery to Cherokee society. As the Cherokee adopted plantation-style agriculture, they also began to adopt white attitudes toward blacks. By the time of Indian Removal in the 1830s and 1840s, a few Cherokee owned plantations with hundreds of slaves, and there were more than 1,500 slaves in the Cherokee Nation. Discrimination against Africans in all five nations grew under pressure of contact with whites. Beginning in the 1820s, the Cherokee Council adopted rules regulating slaves. Whereas a few Africans in the eighteenth century had been adopted into the tribe and become citizens, under the new laws, slaves could not intermarry with Cherokee citizens, engage in trade or barter, or hold property.

To head off encroachments by southern states, the Cherokee also attempted to centralize power in a republican government. As Cherokee historian William McLoughlin has described, "A series of eleven laws passed between 1820

📖 **Read** the **Document**
The Cherokee Treaty of 1817 on **myhistorylab.com**

Cherokee Literacy Sequoyah's invention of the Cherokee alphabet enabled thousands of Cherokees to read and write primers and newspapers in their own language.

and 1823 ... constituted a political revolution in the structure of Cherokee government. Under these laws the National Council created a bicameral legislature, a district and superior court system, an elective system of representation by geographical district rather than by town, and a salaried government bureaucracy." This process culminated in the 1827 adoption of a formal written constitution modeled on the U.S. Constitution.

Sequoyah's invention of a written Cherokee language in 1821–1822 spurred a renaissance of Cherokee culture. He used a phonetic system, representing each syllable in the Cherokee language with symbols, eventually comprising 86 letters. While this alphabet was complicated and lacked punctuation marks, "Sequoyan" gave the Cherokee a new means of self-expression and a reinvigorated sense of their identity. The first American Indian newspaper, the *Cherokee Phoenix*, was published in Sequoyan in 1828. By the time of Indian Removal, Cherokee leaders like John Ross and Elias Boudinot could point with pride to high levels of Cherokee acculturation, education, and economic success at American-style "civilization."

The Seminole, the smallest of the five nations, present perhaps the starkest cultural contrast to the Cherokee, both because the Seminole reacted to pressure from white settlers with armed resistance rather than accommodation, and because their multicultural history gave them a different relationship to slavery.

The Seminole Nation in Florida, which formed after the European conquest of America, was an amalgam of many different peoples with roots in Africa and the New World. Disparate groups of Creek Indians migrating from Georgia and Alabama in the wake of war and disease mingled with the remnants of native Floridians to form the new tribe known as the Seminole. Spain had also granted asylum to runaway African American slaves from the Carolinas, who created autonomous "maroon communities" in Florida, allying with the Seminole to ward off slave-catchers. African Americans and Native Americans intermingled, and by the late eighteenth century, some African Americans were already known as "Seminole Negroes" or *estelusti*. The word *Seminole* itself meant "wild" or "runaway" in the Creek language.

Although the Seminoles adopted African slavery in the early nineteenth century, it was different from slavery as it existed among whites, or even among the Cherokee and Creek. Seminole "slaves" lived in separate towns, planted and cultivated fields in common, owned large herds of livestock, and paid their "owners" only an annual tribute, similar to what Seminole towns paid to the *micco*, or chief.

During the 1820s and 1830s, the es-telusti and the Seminoles were allies in wars against the Americans; however, their alliance came under increasing strain. In 1823, six Seminole leaders, including one of some African ancestry known as "Mulatto King," signed the Treaty of Moultrie Creek, removing the tribe from their fertile lands in northern Florida to swampland south of Tampa. The signers took bribes and believed unfulfilled promises that they would be allowed to stay on their lands. The treaty also required the Seminoles to return runaway slaves and turn away future runaways. During the 1830s, black Seminoles were some of the staunchest opponents of Indian Re-

Competing Land Claims *View of the Great Treaty Held at Prairie du Chien (1825).* Representatives of eight Native American tribes met with government agents at Prairie du Chien, Wisconsin, in 1825 to define the boundaries of their respective land claims. The United States claimed the right to make "an amicable and final adjustment" of the claims. Within 25 years, most of the tribes present at Prairie du Chien had ceded their land to the government.

moval, and they played a major role in the Second Seminole War, which was fought to resist removal from 1835 to 1842. General Thomas W. Jesup, the leader of the U.S. Army, claimed, "This, you may be assured is a negro and not an Indian war."

Treaties like the one signed at Moultrie Creek in 1823 reduced tribal holdings; the federal government used deception, bribery, and threats to induce land cessions. When this did not yield results fast enough to suit southern whites who coveted Indian land for mining, speculation, and cotton production, state governments began to act on their own, proclaiming state jurisdiction over lands federal treaties still allotted to Indians within the state's borders. The stage was thus set for the forced removal of the Five Civilized Tribes to the trans-Mississippi West during the administration of President Andrew Jackson in the 1830s (see Chapter 10).

Farther north, in the Ohio Valley and the Northwest Territory, Native Americans had already suffered military defeat in the conflict between Britain and the United States, leaving them only a minor obstacle to white settlers and land speculators. When the British withdrew from the Old Northwest in 1815, they left their former Indian allies virtually defenseless before the tide of whites who rushed into the region. Consigned by treaty to reservations outside the main lines of white advance, most of the tribes were eventually forced west of the Mississippi.

The last stand of the Indians in this region occurred in 1831–1832, when a faction of the confederated Sac and Fox under Chief Black Hawk refused to abandon their lands east of the Mississippi. Federal troops and Illinois militia drove the Indians back to the river, where they were almost exterminated while attempting to cross to the western bank.

Uprooting Indian communities of the Old Northwest was part of a national program for removing Indians of the eastern part of the country to an area beyond the Mississippi. Many whites viewed Indian society and culture as radically inferior to their own and doomed by "progress." Furthermore, Indians based

Read the **Document**
Black Hawk, from "The Life of Black Hawk" (1833) on
myhistorylab.com

property rights to land on use rather than absolute ownership. Whites saw this as an insuperable obstacle to economic development. Moving Indians west helped many Americans reap fortunes through land speculation. Andrew Jackson got rich speculating on lands he bought from the Chickasaws after negotiating a treaty with them and opening an area along the Mississippi to white settlement in 1814. Land he bought for $100, he later sold for $5,000. Jackson made his name fighting the Creeks in the 1810s. After victory in that conflict, he wrote to General Thomas Pinckney, "I must destroy these deluded victims doomed to distruction by their own restless and savage conduct," and added that he had "on all occasions preserved the scalps of my killed."

As originally conceived by Thomas Jefferson, removal would have allowed those Indians who became "civilized" to remain behind on individually owned farms and qualify for American citizenship. This policy would reduce Indian holdings without appearing to violate American standards of justice. Not everyone agreed with Jefferson's belief that Indians, unlike blacks, had the natural ability to adopt white ways and become useful citizens. People living on the frontier who coveted Indian land and risked violent retaliation for trying to take it were more likely to think of Native Americans as irredeemable savages or vermin to be exterminated if necessary. During the Monroe era (1817–1825), it became clear that white settlers wanted to remove all Indians, "civilized" or not. As president, Andrew Jackson presided over a far more aggressive Indian removal policy.

Quick Check

✓ In what ways did the Cherokee attempt to Increase their chances of survival in the face of American settlement, and how did they differ from the Seminoles?

TRANSPORTATION AND THE MARKET ECONOMY

How did developments in transportation support the growth of agriculture and manufacturing?

It took more than the spread of settlements to bring prosperity to new areas and ensure that the inhabitants would identify with older regions or with the country as a whole. Land transportation was so primitive that in 1813 it took 75 days for one wagon of goods drawn by four horses to travel about 1,000 miles from Worcester, Massachusetts, to Charleston, South Carolina. Coastal shipping eased the problem to some extent in the East and stimulated the growth of port cities. Traveling west over the mountains, however, meant months on the trail.

After the War of 1812, political leaders realized that national security, economic progress, and political unity more or less depended on an improved transportation network. Accordingly, President Madison called for a federally supported program of "internal improvements" in 1815. In the ensuing decades, the nationalists realized their vision of a transportation revolution to a considerable extent, although the direct role of the federal government proved to be less important than anticipated.

Roads and Steamboats

The first great federal transportation project was building the National Road between Cumberland, Maryland, on the Potomac and Wheeling, Virginia, on the Ohio (1811–1818). This impressive gravel-surfaced toll road was extended to Vandalia, Illinois, in 1838. By about 1825, thousands of miles of turnpikes—privately owned toll roads chartered by the states—crisscrossed southern New England, upstate New York, Pennsylvania, and northern New Jersey.

View the Map
Expanding America and Internal Improvements on
myhistorylab.com

The toll roads, however, failed to meet the demand for low-cost transportation over long distances. Travelers benefited more than transporters of bulky freight, for whom the turnpikes proved expensive.

Even the National Road could not offer the low freight costs required for the long-distance hauling of wheat, flour, and the other bulky agricultural products of the Ohio Valley. These commodities needed water transportation.

The United States' natural system of river transportation was one of the most significant reasons for its rapid economic development. The Ohio–Mississippi system in particular provided ready access to the rich agricultural interior and a natural outlet for its products. By 1815, flatboats loaded with wheat, flour, and salt pork were making part of the 2,000-mile trip from Pittsburgh to New Orleans. Even after the coming of the steamboat, flatboats still carried much of the downriver trade.

The flatboat trade, however, was necessarily one-way. A farmer from Ohio or Illinois, or someone hired to do the job, could float down to New Orleans easily enough, but to get back, he usually had to walk overland through rough country. Until the problem of upriver navigation was solved, the Ohio–Mississippi could not carry the manufactured goods that farmers desired in exchange for their crops.

Fortunately, a solution was readily at hand: steam power. Late in the eighteenth century, American inventors had experimented with steam-driven riverboats. John Fitch even exhibited an early model to delegates at the Constitutional Convention in 1788. But making a commercially successful craft required further refinement. In 1807, Robert Fulton, backed by Robert R. Livingston—a prominent wealthy New Yorker—demonstrated the potential of the steamboat by propelling the *Clermont* 150 miles from New York City up the Hudson River. The first steamboat launched in the West was the *New Orleans*, which made the long trip from Pittsburgh to New Orleans in 1811–1812. Besides becoming a principal means of passenger travel on the inland waterways of the East, the river steamboat revolutionized western commerce. In 1815, the *Enterprise* made the first return trip from New Orleans to Pittsburgh. By 1820, 69 steamboats with a total capacity of 13,890 tons were plying western waters.

Steam transport reduced costs, moved goods and people faster, and allowed a two-way commerce on the Mississippi and Ohio rivers. The steamboat captured the American imagination. Great paddle wheelers became luxurious floating hotels, the natural habitats of gamblers, confidence men, and mysterious women. For the pleasure of passengers and

River Transport *The Clermont on the Hudson (1830–1835)* by Charles Pensee. Although some called his *Clermont* "Fulton's Folly," Robert Fulton reduced the cost and increased the speed of river transport.

onlookers, steamboats sometimes raced against each other, and their more skillful pilots became folk heroes. But the boats also had a lamentable safety record, frequently running aground, colliding, or blowing up. The most publicized disasters of antebellum America were spectacular boiler explosions that killed hundreds of passengers. As a result, the federal government began in 1838 to attempt to regulate steamboats and monitor their construction and operation. The legislation, which failed to create an agency capable of enforcing minimum safety standards, was virtually the only federal effort before the Civil War to regulate domestic transportation.

A transportation system based solely on rivers and roads had one enormous gap—it did not provide an economical way to ship western farm produce directly east to ports engaged in transatlantic trade or to the growing urban market of the seaboard states. The solution the politicians and merchants of the Middle Atlantic and midwestern states offered was to build a system of canals that linked seaboard cities directly to the Great Lakes, the Ohio, and ultimately the Mississippi.

At 364 miles long, 40 feet wide, and 4 feet deep, and containing 84 locks, the Erie Canal, which opened in 1825 and linked Lake Erie to Buffalo, New York, was the most spectacular engineering achievement of the young republic. Furthermore, it was a great economic success and inspired numerous other canal projects in other states.

The canal boom ended when it became apparent that most of the waterways were unprofitable. State credit had been overextended, and the panic and depression of the late 1830s and early 1840s forced retrenchment. Moreover, railroads were competing for the same traffic, and a new phase in the transportation revolution was beginning. However, canals, while they failed to turn a profit for most investors, provided a vital service to those who used them and contributed to the new nation's economic development.

((•—[Listen to the
Audio File
The Erie Canal on
myhistorylab.com

Quick Check
✓ How did water transportation affect economic development, and how did this influence expansion westward?

The Canal Boom Illustration of a lock on the Erie Canal at Lockport, New York, 1838. The canal facilitated trade by linking the Great Lakes regions to the eastern seaports.

Emergence of a Market Economy

The desire to reduce the cost and increase the speed of shipping heavy freight over great distances laid the groundwork for a new economic system. Canals made it less expensive and more profitable for western farmers to ship wheat and flour to New York and Philadelphia and also gave manufacturers in the East ready access to an interior market. Steamboats reduced shipping costs on the Ohio and Mississippi and put farmers in the enviable position of receiving more for their crops and paying less for the goods they needed to import. Hence improved transport increased farm income and stimulated commercial agriculture.

At the beginning of the nineteenth century, the typical farming household consumed most of what it produced and sold only a small surplus in nearby markets. Most manufactured articles were produced at home. Easier and cheaper access to distant markets decisively changed this pattern. Between 1800 and 1840, agricultural output increased at an annual rate of approximately 3 percent, and a rapidly growing portion of this production consisted of commodities grown for sale rather than for home consumption. The rise in productivity was partly due to technological advances. Iron or steel plows proved better than wooden ones; the grain cradle displaced the scythe for harvesting; and better varieties or strains of crops, grasses, and livestock were introduced. But the availability of good land and the revolution in marketing were the most important spurs to profitable commercial farming. Good land made for high yields, at least for a time, and when excessive planting wore out the soil, a farmer could migrate to more fertile lands farther west. Transportation facilities made distant markets available and plugged farmers into a commercial network that provided credit and relieved them of the need to do their own selling.

The emerging exchange network encouraged movement away from diversified farming and toward regional concentration on staple crops. Wheat was the main cash crop of the North, and the center of its cultivation moved westward as soil depletion, pests, and plant diseases lowered yields in older regions. In 1815, the heart of the wheat belt was New York and Pennsylvania. By 1839, Ohio was the leading producer, and Indiana and Illinois were beginning to come into their own. On the rocky hillsides of New England, sheep raising was displacing mixed farming. But the prime examples of successful staple production in this era were in the South. Tobacco remained a major cash crop of the upper South (despite declining fertility and a shift to wheat in some areas); rice was important in coastal South Carolina; and sugar was a staple of southern Louisiana. Cotton, however, was the "king" crop in the lower South. It became the nation's principal export commodity and brought wealth and prosperity from South Carolina to Louisiana.

Five factors made the Deep South the world's greatest producer of cotton. First was the great demand generated by the rise of textile manufacturing in England and, to a lesser extent, in New England. Second was the cotton gin. Invented by Eli Whitney in 1793, this simple device cut the labor costs involved in cleaning the seeds from short-staple cotton, thus making it an easily marketable commodity.

A third reason for the rise of cotton was the availability of good land in the Southeast. As yields fell in the original areas of cultivation—mainly South Carolina and Georgia—the opening of the rich and fertile plantation areas or "black belts" of Alabama, Mississippi, and Louisiana shifted the Cotton Kingdom westward and vastly increased total production. In 1816, New Orleans, the great marketing center for western crops, received 37,000 bales of cotton (a bale of cotton weighs 480 pounds); in 1830, 428,000 arrived; in 1840, the annual number had reached 923,000. Between 1817 and 1840, the amount of cotton the South produced tripled from 461,000 to 1,350,000 bales.

View the **Image**
A Patent Drawing of Eli Whitney's Cotton Gin on **myhistorylab.com**

A fourth factor—slavery, which provided a flexible system of forced labor—permitted operations on a scale impossible for the family labor system of the agricultural North. Finally, the cotton economy benefited from the South's splendid natural transportation system—its great network of navigable rivers extending deep into the interior from the cotton ports of Charleston, Savannah, Mobile, and, of course, New Orleans. The South had less need than other agricultural regions for artificial internal improvements such as canals and good roads. Planters could simply establish themselves on or near a river and ship their crops to market via natural waterways.

Quick Check

✓ What was the main agricultural crop of the South, and what factors made it so successful?

Early Industrialism

The growth of a market economy also created new opportunities for industrialists. In 1815, most manufacturing in the United States was carried on in households, in the workshops of skilled artisans, or in small mills that used waterpower to turn wheat into flour or timber into boards. The factory form of production, in which supervised workers tended or operated machines under one roof, was rare. It was found mainly in southern New England, where small spinning mills, relying heavily on the labor of women and children, accomplished one step in the manufacture of cotton textiles. But women working at home still spun most thread and wove, cut, and sewed most cloth.

As late as 1820, about two-thirds of the clothing Americans wore was made entirely in households by female family members—wives and daughters. However, they were producing a growing proportion of it for market rather than direct home consumption. Under the "putting-out" system of manufacturing, merchant capitalists provided raw material to people in their own homes, picked up finished or semifinished products, paid the workers, and took charge of distribution. Items such as simple shoes and hats were also made under the putting-out system. Home manufacturing of this type was centered in the Northeast, often done by farm families making profitable use of their slack seasons. It did not usually challenge the economic preeminence of agriculture or seriously disrupt rural life.

Artisans in small shops in towns made most articles that required greater skill—such as high-quality shoes and boots, carriages or wagons, mill wheels, and barrels or kegs. But after 1815, shops grew bigger; masters tended to become entrepreneurs rather than working artisans; and journeymen often became wage earners rather than aspiring masters. The growing market for low-priced goods also emphasized speed, quantity, and standardization in production. Even where no substantial mechanization was involved, shops dealing in handmade goods for a local clientele tended to become small factories turning out cheaper items for a wider public.

A fully developed factory system emerged first in textile manufacturing. The first cotton mills utilizing the power loom and spinning machinery—thus making it possible to turn fiber into cloth in a single factory—resulted from the efforts of three Boston merchants: Francis Cabot Lowell, Nathan Appleton, and Patrick Tracy Jackson. On a visit to England in 1810–1811, Lowell memorized the closely guarded industrial secret of how to construct a power loom. In Boston, he joined with Appleton and Jackson to acquire a site with water power at nearby Waltham and obtain a corporate charter for textile manufacturing on a new and expanded scale.

Under the name of the Boston Manufacturing Company, the associates began their Waltham operation in 1813. Its phenomenal success led to the erection of a larger and even more profitable mill at Lowell, Massachusetts, in 1822 and another at Chicopee in 1823. Lowell became the great showplace for early American industrialization. Its large and seemingly contented workforce of unmarried young women residing in supervised dormitories, its unprecedented scale of operation, its successful mechanization of almost every stage of the production process—all captured the American middle-class imagination in the 1820s and 1830s. But in the

Read the **Document** *The Harbinger, "Female Workers at Lowell" (1836)* on **myhistorylab.com**

late 1830s and 1840s, conditions in the mills changed for the worse as the owners began to require more work for lower pay, and some of the mill women became militant labor activists. One of them, Sarah Bagley, helped found the Lowell Female Labor Reform Association in 1844. She led protests against long hours and changes that required more work from each operative. Other mills using similar labor systems sprang up throughout New England, which became the first important manufacturing area in the United States.

The shift in textile manufacture from domestic to factory production also shifted the locus of women's economic activity. As the New England textile industry grew, the putting-out system declined. Between 1824 and 1832, household production of textiles dropped from 90 to 50 percent in most parts of New England. The shift to factory production changed capitalist activity in the region. Before the 1820s, New England merchants concentrated mainly on international trade, and Boston mercantile houses made great profits. A major source of capital was the lucrative China trade carried on by fast, well-built New England vessels. When the success of Waltham and Lowell became clear, many merchants shifted their capital from oceanic trade to manufacturing. This had important political consequences, as leading politicians such as Daniel Webster no longer advocated a low tariff that favored importers over exporters. Many politicians now supported a high duty to protect manufacturers from foreign competition.

Early Industrialism Lowell, Massachusetts, became America's model industrial town in the first half of the nineteenth century. In this painting of the town in 1814 (when it was still called East Chelmsford), a multistory brick mill is prominent on the river. Textile mills sprang up throughout Lowell in the 1820s and 1830s, employing thousands of workers, mostly women. Below, a photograph from c. 1848 shows a Lowell mill worker operating a loom.

The development of other "infant industries" after the War of 1812 was less dramatic and would not come to fruition until the 1840s and 1850s. Technology to improve rolling and refining iron was imported from England; it gradually encouraged a domestic iron industry centered in Pennsylvania. The use of interchangeable parts in manufacturing small arms, pioneered by Eli Whitney and Simeon North, helped modernize the weapons industry and contribute to the growth of new forms of mass production.

One should not assume, however, that America had already experienced an industrial revolution by 1840. In that year, 63.4 percent of the nation's labor force was still employed in agriculture. Only 8.8 percent of workers were directly involved in factory production (others worked in trade, transportation, and the professions). Although this represented a significant shift since 1810, when the figures were 83.7 and 3.2 percent, the numbers would have to change much more before it could be said that industrialization had really arrived. The revolution that did occur during these years was essentially one of distribution rather than production. The growth of a market economy of national scope—still based mainly on agriculture but involving a rapid flow of capital, commodities, and services from region to region— was the major economic development of this period. And it had vast repercussions for American life.

For those who benefited from it most directly, the market economy provided firm evidence of progress and improvement. But many of those who suffered from its periodic panics and depressions regretted the loss of the individual independence and security that a localized economy of small producers had provided. These victims of boom and bust were receptive to politicians and reformers who attacked corporations and "the money power."

Quick Check

✓ Which manufacturing sector first fully adopted industrial production, and where was it centered?

THE POLITICS OF NATION BUILDING AFTER THE WAR OF 1812

What decisions did the federal government face as the country expanded?

Geographic expansion, economic growth, and the changes in American life that accompanied them were bound to generate political controversy. Farmers, merchants, manufacturers, and laborers were affected by the changes in different ways. So were northerners, southerners, and westerners. Federal and state policies that were meant to encourage or control growth and expansion did not benefit all these groups or sections equally, and unavoidable conflicts of interest and ideology occurred.

But, for a time, the national political arena did not prominently reflect these conflicts. A myth of national harmony prevailed, culminating in the Era of Good Feeling during James Monroe's two terms as president. Behind this facade, individuals and groups fought for advantage, as always, but without the public accountability and need for broad popular approval that a party system would have required. As a result, popular interest in national politics fell.

The absence of party discipline and programs did not immobilize the federal government. The president took important initiatives in foreign policy; Congress legislated on matters of national concern; and the Supreme Court made far-reaching decisions. The common theme of the public policies that emerged between the War of 1812 and the age of Andrew Jackson, which began in 1829, was an awakening nationalism—a sense of American pride and purpose that reflected the expansionism and material progress of the period.

The Missouri Compromise

In 1817, the Missouri territorial assembly applied for statehood. Since there were 2,000–3,000 slaves in the territory and the petition made no provision for emancipating them or for curbing slave imports, Missouri would enter the Union as a slave state unless Congress blocked it. Missouri was the first state, other than Louisiana, to be carved out of the Louisiana Purchase, and resolving the status of slavery there would have implications for the rest of the trans-Mississippi West.

When the question came before Congress in early 1819, sectional fears and anxieties bubbled to the surface. Many northerners resented southern control of the presidency and the fact that the three-fifths clause of the Constitution, by which every five slaves were counted as three persons in figuring the state's population, gave the South's free population added weight in the House of Representatives and the electoral college. The South, on the other hand, feared for the future of what it regarded as a necessary balance of power between the sections. Until 1819, a strict equality had been maintained by alternately admitting slave and free states; in that year, there were eleven of each. But the northern population was growing more rapidly than the southern, and the North had a decisive majority in the House. Hence the South saw its equal vote in the Senate as essential for preserving the balance.

In February 1819, Congressman James Tallmadge of New York introduced an amendment to the statehood bill, banning further introduction of slaves into Missouri and requiring the gradual elimination of slavery within the state. The House approved his amendment by a narrow margin. The Senate, however, voted it down. The issue remained unresolved until a new Congress convened in December. In the great debate that ensued in the Senate, Federalist leader Rufus King of New York argued that Congress was within its rights to require restricting slavery before Missouri could become a state. Southern senators protested that denying Missouri's freedom in this matter attacked the principle of equality among the states and showed that northerners were conspiring to upset the balance of power between the sections. They were also concerned about the future of African American slavery and the white racial privilege that went with it.

View the Map
The Missouri
Compromise on
myhistorylab.com

A statehood petition from the people of Maine, who were seeking to separate from Massachusetts, suggested a way out of the impasse. In February 1820, the Senate passed the Missouri Compromise, voting to couple the admission of Missouri as a slave state with the admission of Maine as a free state. An amendment

Map 9.1 *The Missouri Compromise, 1820–1821*   The Missouri Compromise kept the balance of power in the Senate by admitting Missouri as a slave state and Maine as a free state. The agreement temporarily settled the argument over slavery in the territories.

prohibited slavery in the rest of the Louisiana Purchase north of the southern border of Missouri, or above the latitude of 36°30', but allowed it below that line. The Senate's compromise then went to the House, where it was initially rejected. Through the adroit maneuvering of Henry Clay—who broke the proposal into three separate bills—it won House approval. The measure authorizing Missouri to frame a constitution and apply for admission as a slave state passed by the razor-thin margin of 90 to 87, with most northern representatives opposed (see Map 9.1).

A major sectional crisis had been resolved. But the Missouri affair was ominous for the future of North–South relations. Jefferson described the controversy as "a fire bell in the night," threatening the Union. In 1821, he wrote prophetically: "All, I fear, do not see the speck on our horizon which is to burst on us as a tornado, sooner or later. The line of division lately marked out between the different portions of our confederacy is such as will never, I fear, be obliterated." The congressional furor had shown that when slavery or its extension came directly before the people's representatives, regional loyalties took precedence over party or other considerations. Both sides used an emotional rhetoric of morality and fundamental rights, and votes followed sectional lines much more closely than on any other issue. If the United States were to acquire any new territories in which Congress had to determine the status of slavery, renewed sectional strife would be unavoidable.

Read the **Document**
Thomas Jefferson Reacts to The Missouri Compromise on **myhistorylab.com**

Quick Check

✓ What was the Missouri Compromise, and what problems did it resolve?

Postwar Nationalism and the Supreme Court

While the Monroe administration was proclaiming national harmony and congressional leaders were struggling to reconcile sectional differences, the third branch of government—the Supreme Court—was making a more substantial and enduring contribution to the growth of nationalism and a strong federal government. Much of this achievement was due to the firm leadership and fine legal mind of the chief justice of the United States, John Marshall.

A Virginian, a Federalist, and the devoted disciple and biographer of George Washington, Marshall served as chief justice from 1801 to 1835, and during that entire period, he dominated the Court as no other chief justice has ever done. Discouraging dissent and seeking to hammer out a single opinion on almost every case that came before the Court, he has been compared to a symphony conductor who was also composer of the music and principal soloist.

As the author of most of the major opinions the Court issued during its formative period, Marshall gave shape to the Constitution and clarified the crucial role of the Court in the American system of government. He placed the protection of individual liberty, especially the right to acquire property, above the attainment of political, social, or economic equality. Ultimately he was a nationalist, believing that the strength, security, and happiness of the American people depended mainly on economic growth and the creation of new wealth.

The role of the Supreme Court, in Marshall's view, was to interpret and enforce the Constitution in a way that encouraged economic development, especially against state legislatures' efforts to interfere with the constitutionally protected rights of individuals or combinations of individuals to acquire property through productive activity. To limit state action, he cited the contract clause of the Constitution, which prohibited a state from passing a law "impairing the obligation of contracts." As the legal watchdog of an enterprising, capitalist society, the Court could also approve a liberal grant of power for the federal government, so that the latter could fulfill its constitutional responsibility to promote the general welfare by encouraging economic growth and prosperity.

In major decisions between 1819 and 1824, the Marshall Court enhanced judicial power and used the contract clause of the Constitution to limit the power of state legislatures. It also strengthened the federal government by sanctioning a broad or loose construction of its constitutional powers and by affirming its supremacy over the states.

In Dartmouth College v. Woodward (1819), the Court was asked to rule whether the New Hampshire legislature could meddle in the governance of Dartmouth College, a private institution. Daniel Webster, arguing for the college and against the state, contended that Dartmouth's original charter of 1769 was a valid and irrevocable contract between the state and the trustees of the college. The Court accepted his argument. Speaking for all the justices, Marshall made the far-reaching

Read the **Document**
Dartmouth College V. Woodward on **myhistorylab.com**

determination that the Constitution's contracts clause fully protected any charter a state granted to a private corporation.

In practical terms, the Court's ruling in the Dartmouth case meant that the kinds of business enterprises state governments were incorporating—such as turnpike or canal companies and textile manufacturers—could hold on indefinitely to any privileges or favors that their original charters had granted. The decision therefore increased the power and independence of business corporations by weakening states' ability to regulate them or withdraw their privileges. The ruling fostered the growth of the modern corporation as a profit-making enterprise with only limited public responsibilities.

About a month after the Dartmouth ruling, in March 1819, the Marshall Court handed down its most important decision. The case of McCulloch v. Maryland arose because the state of Maryland had levied a tax on the Baltimore branch of the Bank of the United States, which had been rechartered for 25 years in 1816. The unanimous opinion of the Court, delivered by Marshall, was that the Maryland tax was unconstitutional. The two main issues were whether Congress had the right to establish a national bank and whether a state had the power to tax or regulate an agency or institution Congress created.

In response to the first question, Marshall set forth his doctrine of "implied powers." Conceding that the Constitution contained no specific authorization to charter a bank, the chief justice argued that such a right could be deduced from more general powers and from an understanding of the "great objects" for which the federal government had been founded. Marshall thus struck a blow for a loose construction of the Constitution and a broad grant of power to the federal government to encourage economic growth and stability.

In answer to the second question—the right of a state to tax or regulate a federal agency—Marshall held that the bank was indeed such an agency and that giving a state the power to tax it would also give the state the power to destroy it. In an important assertion of the supremacy of the national government, Marshall argued that the American people "did not design to make their government dependent on the states." This opinion ran counter to the view of many Americans, particularly in the South, that the Constitution did not take away sovereignty from the states. The debate over federal–state relations was not resolved until the northern victory in the Civil War decisively affirmed the dominance of federal authority. But Marshall's decision gave great new weight to a nationalist constitutional philosophy.

The *Gibbons v. Ogden* decision of 1824 bolstered Congress's power to regulate interstate commerce. A competing ferry service operating between New York and New Jersey challenged a steamboat monopoly granted by the state of New York. The Court declared the New York grant unconstitutional because it amounted to state interference with Congress's exclusive right to regulate interstate commerce. The Court's ruling went a long way toward freeing private interests engaged in furthering the transportation revolution from state interference.

This case showed the dual effect of Marshall's decision making. It broadened the power of the federal government at the expense of the states and encouraged the growth of a national market economy. The Court's actions provide the clearest and most consistent example of the main nationalistic trends of the period—the acknowledgment of the federal government's role in promoting a powerful and prosperous America and the rise of a nationwide capitalist economy.

Quick Check

✓ What did John Marshall believe the Supreme Court's role should be, and how did he help to create It?

Nationalism in Foreign Policy: The Monroe Doctrine

Foreign affairs also reflected the new spirit of nationalism. The main diplomatic challenge facing Monroe after his reelection in 1820 was how to respond to the successful revolt of most of Spain's and Portugal's Latin American colonies after the Napoleonic wars. In Congress, Henry Clay called for immediate recognition of the new states. In doing so, he expressed the belief of many Americans that their neighbors to the south were simply following the example of the United States in its own struggle for independence.

Before 1822, the administration stuck to a policy of neutrality. Monroe and Secretary of State Adams feared that recognizing the revolutionary governments would antagonize Spain and impede negotiations to acquire Florida. But pressure for recognition grew in Congress; in 1821, the House of Representatives, responding to Clay's impassioned oratory, passed a resolution of sympathy for Latin American revolutionaries and made it clear that the president would have the support of Congress if and when he decided to accord recognition. After the Adams–Onís Treaty ceding Florida to the United States had been formally ratified in 1821, Monroe agreed to recognition and diplomatic ties with the Latin American states. The U.S. recognized Mexico and Colombia in 1822, Chile and Argentina in 1823, Brazil (which had separated from Portugal) and the Federation of Central American States in 1824, and Peru in 1826.

Recognizing the Latin American states put the United States on a possible collision course with the major European powers. Austria, Russia, and Prussia were committed to rolling back the tides of liberalism, self-government, and national self-determination that had arisen during the French Revolution and its Napoleonic aftermath. After Napoleon's first defeat in 1814, the monarchs of Europe had joined in a "Grand Alliance" to protect "legitimate" authoritarian governments from democratic challenges. Great Britain was originally a member of this concert of nations but withdrew when its own interests conflicted with those of the other members. In 1822, the remaining alliance members, joined now by the restored French monarchy, authorized France to invade Spain and restore a Bourbon regime that might be disposed to reconquer the empire. This prospect alarmed both Great Britain and the United States.

Particularly troubling to American policymakers was the role of Czar Alexander I of Russia. Not only was the czar an outspoken and active opponent of Latin

American independence, but he was attempting to extend Russian claims on the Pacific coast of North America south to the 51st parallel—into the Oregon Country, which the United States wanted for itself.

The threat from the Grand Alliance pointed to a need for American cooperation with Great Britain, which had its own reasons for wanting to prevent a restoration of Spanish, Portuguese, or French power in the New World. Independent nations offered better and more open markets for British manufactured goods than the colonies of other nations, and the spokesmen for burgeoning British industrial capitalism anticipated a profitable economic dominance over Latin America. In early 1823, the British foreign secretary, George Canning, tried to exact from the French a pledge that they would not try to acquire territories in Spanish America. When that venture failed, he sought to involve the United States in a policy to prevent the Grand Alliance from intervening in Latin America.

In August 1823, Canning broached the possibility of joint Anglo-American action against the Alliance to Richard Rush, U.S. minister to Great Britain. Rush referred the suggestion to the president. Monroe welcomed the British initiative because he believed the United States should take an active role in transatlantic affairs by playing one European power against another. However, Secretary of State Adams favored a different approach. Adams distrusted the British and believed that avoiding entanglements in European politics while also discouraging European intervention in the Americas would best serve the national interest.

⬛ Read the
Document
*The Monroe Doctrine
(1823)* on
myhistorylab.com

Political ambition also predisposed Adams against joint action with Great Britain; he hoped to be the next president and did not want to give his rivals the chance to label him as pro-British. He therefore advocated unilateral action by the United States rather than a joint declaration with the British. As he told the cabinet in November, "It would be more candid, as well as more dignified, to avow our principles explicitly to Russia and France, than to come in as a cock-boat of the British man-of-war."

Adams managed to swing Monroe and the cabinet around to his viewpoint. In his annual message to Congress on December 2, 1823, Monroe included a far-reaching statement on foreign policy that was actually written mainly by Adams, who did become president in 1824. What came to be known as the **Monroe Doctrine** solemnly declared that the United States opposed further colonization in the Americas or any effort by European nations to extend their political systems outside their own hemisphere.

In return, the United States pledged not to involve itself in the internal affairs of Europe or to take part in European wars. The statement envisioned a North and South America composed entirely of independent states—with the United States preeminent among them.

Quick Check

✓ How and why did America's recognition of the Latin American republics change its relationship with the European Powers?

Although the Monroe Doctrine made little impression on the great powers of Europe when it was proclaimed, it signified the rise of a new sense of independence and self-confidence in American attitudes toward the Old World. The United States would now go its own way free of involvement in European conflicts and would protect its own sphere of influence from European interference.

CONCLUSION: THE END OF THE ERA OF GOOD FEELING

The consensus on national goals and leadership that Monroe had represented could not sustain itself. The Era of Good Feeling turned out to be a passing phase and something of an illusion. Although the pursuit of national greatness would continue, there would be sharp divisions over how to achieve it. A general commitment to the settlement of the West and the development of agriculture, commerce, and industry would endure despite differences over what role government should play in the process; but the idea that an elite of nonpartisan statesmen could define common purposes and harmonize competing elements—the concept of leadership that Monroe and Adams had advanced—would no longer be viable in the more contentious and democratic America of the Jacksonian era.

9 STUDY RESOURCES

((•—[Listen to the **Chapter Audio** for Chapter 9 on **myhistorylab.com**

TIMELINE

1813 Boston Manufacturing Company founds cotton mill at Waltham, Massachusetts, p. 223

1815 War of 1812 ends, p. 222

1818 Andrew Jackson invades Spanish Florida, p. 223

1819 Supreme Court hands down far-reaching decisions in Dartmouth College case and in *McCulloch v. Maryland,* p. 238
- Adams–Onís Treaty cedes Spanish territory to the United States, p. 238

1820 Missouri Compromise resolves nation's first sectional crisis, p. 235
- Monroe reelected president almost unanimously, p. 239

1823 Monroe Doctrine proclaimed, p. 240

1824 Lafayette revisits the United States, p. 221
- Supreme Court decides *Gibbons v. Ogden,* p. 238
- John Quincy Adams elected president, p. 240

1825 Erie Canal completed; canal era begins, p. 230

CHAPTER REVIEW

EXPANSION AND MIGRATION

What key forces drove American expansion westward during this period?

Westward expansion was fueled by the ambition to expand American territory and to economically exploit and develop the Far West. The First Seminole War gave Monroe and Adams a chance to push Spain from the southeast under the Adams–Onís Treaty, while entrepreneurs established a fur trade in the North and an aggressive "removal" policy forced Indian tribes from the South. *(p. 222)*

TRANSPORTATION AND THE MARKET ECONOMY

How did developments in transportation support the growth of agriculture and manufacturing?

New turnpikes, canals, steamboats, and eventually railroads expanded the access of farmers and small manufacturers to a regional and even national market. Farmers began to produce staple crops to sell rather than subsistence crops for their own families. Textile factories developed to turn southern cotton into clothing. In the North, industrialization increased efficiency but crowded workers into factories for long hours. *(p. 222)*

THE POLITICS OF NATION BUILDING AFTER THE WAR OF 1812

What decisions did the federal government face as the country expanded?

The government decided whether new states would allow slavery, how the Supreme Court would function, and how the United States would deal with the European powers. The Missouri Compromise established the 36°30' line dividing slave from free states, while the Court became the supreme constitutional interpreter. The Monroe Doctrine held that the United States and European powers should each control their respective hemispheres. *(p. 228)*

KEY TERM QUESTIONS

1. Why did Spain agree to the Adams–Onís Treaty in 1819? (p. 223)

2. Why did squatters push for formal preemption rights from the government? (p. 225)

3. Is the Era of Good Feeling an appropriate name for James Monroe's years as President of the United States? (p. 234)

4. What issues did the Missouri Compromise resolve? (p. 235)

5. What principle did Chief Justice John Marshall establish in his ruling in *Dartmouth College v. Woodward*? (p. 237)

6. What principle did Chief Justice John Marshall establish in his ruling in *McCulloch v. Maryland*? (p. 238)

7. What principle did Chief Justice John Marshall establish in his ruling in *Gibbons v. Ogden*? (p. 238)

8. What were the short- and long-term effects of the Monroe Doctrine? (p. 240)

MYHISTORYLAB CONNECTIONS

Visit **www.myhistorylab.com** for a customized Study Plan to build your knowledge of *Nation Building and Nationalism*.

Question for Analysis

1. What were some of the disadvantages of using rivers to transport products?

   View the **Map** *Expanding America and Internal Improvements* p. 229

2. What was a typical day like for female factory workers?

   Read the **Document** *The Harbinger, Female Workers at Lowell (1836)* p. 233

Other Resources from this Chapter

Read the **Document** *The Cherokee Treaty of 1817*

Read the **Document** *Black Hawk, from "The Life of Black Hawk"*

Listen to the **Audio File** *The Erie Canal*

View the **Image** *A Patent Drawing of Eli Whitney's Cotton Gin*

3. What was the most significant outcome of the Missouri Compromise?

🔍 **View** the **Map** *The Missouri Compromise* p. 235

4. What influence did the Monroe Doctrine have on the great powers of Europe?

📖 **Read** the **Document** *The Monroe Doctrine* p. 240

📖 **Read** the **Document** *Thomas Jefferson Reacts to Missouri*

📖 **Read** the **Document** *Dartmouth College v. Woodward*

10 THE TRIUMPH OF WHITE MEN'S DEMOCRACY

1824–1840

Contents and Spotlight Questions

((•─┤**Listen** to the **Chapter Audio** for Chapter 10 on **myhistorylab.com**

DEMOCRATIC SPACE: THE NEW HOTELS

During the 1820s and 1830s, the United States became a more democratic country for at least some of its population. The emerging spirit of popular democracy found expression in a new institution—the large hotel with several stories and hundreds of rooms. President-elect Andrew Jackson, the political figure who best represented the spirit of the age, stayed in the new National Hotel when he arrived in Washington in 1829 to prepare for his administration. After a horde of well-wishers made a shambles of the White House during his inaugural reception in March 1829, Jackson retreated to the hotel again for a little peace and a chance to consult with his advisers. The National was only one of several large "first-class"

Fine Accommodations New York's Astor House, completed in 1836, was one of the grandest of the new American hotels, offering fine accommodations to travelers who could afford to pay for them.

hotels that opened immediately before or during Jackson's presidency. Among the others were the Tremont House in Boston, the Baltimore City Hotel, and New York's Astor House.

The hotel boom responded to Americans' increasing tendency to move about the country. Entrepreneurs built these large places of accommodation to service the rising tide of travelers, transients, and new arrivals. The hotels provided lodging, food, and drink on an unprecedented scale and were as different from the inns of the eighteenth century as the steamboat was from the flatboat.

According to historian Doris Elizabeth King, "the new hotels were so obviously 'public' and 'democratic' in their character that foreigners were often to describe them as a true reflection of American society." Their very existence showed that many people, white males in particular, were on the move geographically and socially. Among the hotels' patrons were traveling salesmen, ambitious young men seeking to establish themselves in a new city, and restless pursuers of "the main chance" (unexpected economic opportunities) who were not ready to put down roots. Hotel managers shocked European visitors by failing to enforce traditional social distinctions among their clientele. Under the "American plan," guests were required to pay for their meals and eat at a common "table d'hôte" with anyone who happened to be there, including servants traveling with their employers. Ability to pay was the only requirement for admission (unless one was an unescorted woman or dark-skinned). Every white male patron, regardless of social background and occupation, enjoyed the personal service previously available only to a privileged class.

The hotel culture also revealed the limitations of the new democratic era. African Americans, Native Americans, and women were excluded or discriminated against, just as they were denied suffrage. The poor—of whom there were more than most European visitors recognized—could not afford the hotels and were consigned to squalid rooming houses. If the social equality *within* the hotel reflected a decline in traditional status distinctions, the broad gulf between potential patrons and those who could not pay what the hotels charged signaled growing inequality based on wealth rather than inherited status.

Hotel life also reflected the emergence of democratic politics. A new breed of professional politicians spent much of their time in hotels as they traveled about. Congressmen or state legislators often stayed in hotels during sessions, making deals and bargains. The hotel was thus a symbol for the democratic spirit of the age, one that shows its shortcomings and its strengths. The new democracy was first of all political. Amost all white males now had the right to vote, and modern political parties arose appealing to a mass electorate. It was also social. Democracy undermined the habit of deferring to people because of their birth or ancestry. People born in relatively humble circumstances increasingly hoped to climb the ladder of success. But the ideals of equal citizenship and opportunity did not extend across the lines of race and gender, which actually hardened during this period.

DEMOCRACY IN THEORY AND PRACTICE

During the 1820s and 1830s, *democracy* first became a generally accepted term to describe how American institutions were supposed to work. Although the Founders had defined democracy as direct rule by the people, most of them rejected this approach to government because it conflicted with their concept of a well-balanced republic led by a "natural aristocracy." For champions of popular government in the Jacksonian period, however, the people were sovereign and could do no wrong: "The voice of the people is the voice of God." Conservatives were less certain of the wisdom of the common folk. But even they were recognizing that they had to win over public opinion before making major decisions.

Besides evoking "popular sovereignty," the democratic impulse seemed to stimulate social leveling. Earlier Americans had usually assumed that the rich and wellborn were the natural leaders of the community and guardians of its culture and values. But by the 1830s, the disappearance of inherited social ranks and clearly defined aristocracies or privileged groups struck European visitors such as Alexis de Tocqueville as the most radical feature of democracy in America. Historians have described this development as a decline of the spirit of "deference."

The decline of deference meant that "self-made men" of lowly origins could more readily acquire power and influence and that exclusiveness and aristocratic pretensions were likely to provoke hostility or scorn. But economic equality—an equitable sharing of wealth—was not part of the mainstream agenda of the Jacksonian period. This was a competitive capitalist society. The watchword was equality of *opportunity*, not equality of *reward*. Life was a race. So long as all white males appeared to have an equal start, there could be no reason for complaint if some were winners and others losers. Historians now generally agree that economic inequality—the gap between rich and poor—actually increased during this period.

> **How** did the relationship between the government and the people change during this time?

Democratic Culture

Although some types of inequality persisted or even grew during the age of democracy, they did so despite a growing belief that equality was the governing principle of American society.

One example of this was the decline of distinctive modes of dress for upper and lower classes. The elaborate periwigs and knee breeches of eighteenth-century gentlemen gave way to short hair and pantaloons for men of all classes. Fashionable dress among women also ceased to be a sure index of gentility; serving girls on their day off wore the same kind of finery as the wives and daughters of the wealthy—or at least reasonable imitations.

Yet in the cities, the rise of industrialization was also creating a permanent class of low-paid, unorganized wage earners. In rural areas, there was a significant division between successful commercial farmers and small holders, or tenants who subsisted on marginal land, as well as enormous inequality of status between southern planters and their black slaves.

Changes in the organization and status of the learned professions also showed that traditional forms of privilege and elitism were under attack. Under Jacksonian pressure, state legislatures abolished the licensing requirements for physicians that local medical societies had administered. As a result, quacks and folk healers could compete freely with established medical doctors.

The democratic tide also struck the legal profession. Local bar associations continued to set the qualifications for practicing attorneys, but in many places, they admitted persons with little or no formal training and the most rudimentary knowledge of the law. The clergy responded to the new democratic spirit by developing a more popular and emotional style of preaching to please their public.

In this atmosphere of democratic leveling, the popular press was increasingly important as a source of information and opinion. Written and read by common folk, hundreds of newspapers and magazines ushered the mass of white Americans into the political arena. New political views—which those in power might once have silenced—could now find an audience. Reformers of all kinds could easily publicize their causes, and the press became the venue for the great national debates on issues such as the government's role in banking and the status of slavery in new states and territories. As a profession, journalism was open to those who were literate and thought they had something to say. The editors of newspapers with a large circulation were the most influential opinion makers of the age.

The democratic spirit also found expression in new forms of literature and art for a mass audience. The intentions of individual artists and writers varied considerably. Some pandered to popular taste in defiance of traditional standards of high culture. Others tried to capture the spirit of the age by portraying the everyday life of ordinary Americans rather than the traditional subjects of "aristocratic" art. A few hoped to use literature and art to improve popular taste and instill deeper moral and spiritual values. But all of them were aware that their audience was the broad citizenry of a democratic nation rather than a refined elite.

A rise in literacy and a revolution in printing technology made a mass market for popular literature possible. More potential readers and lower publishing costs led to a flood of lurid and sentimental novels, some of which became the first American best-sellers. By the 1840s and 1850s, writers such as George Lippard, Mrs. E. D. E. N. Southworth, and Augusta Jane Evans had perfected the formulas that led to commercial success. Gothic horror and the perils of virtuous heroines threatened by dastardly villains were among the ingredients that readers came to expect from popular fiction.

Many of the new sentimental novels were written by and for women. Some women writers implicitly protested their situation by portraying men as tyrannical, unreliable, or vicious and the women they abandoned or failed to support as resourceful individualists able to make their own way in a man's world. But the standard happy endings sustained the convention that a woman's place was in the home: A virtuous and protective man usually turned up and saved the heroine from independence.

In the theater, melodrama became the dominant genre. Despite religious objections, theater-going was popular in the cities during the Jacksonian era. The standard fare involved the inevitable trio of beleaguered heroine, mustachioed villain, and a hero who asserted himself in the nick of time. Patriotic comedies extolling the common sense of the rustic Yankee who foiled the foppish European aristocrat were also popular and aroused the audience's democratic sympathies. Men and women of all classes went to the theater, and those in the cheap seats often became raucous and even violent when they did not like what they saw. Unpopular actors or plays could provoke riots. In 1849, in New York, 23 people were killed in disorders over an English actor who was the rival of Edwin Forrest, the era's most popular American thespian.

"Popular sovereignty" expressed itself less dramatically in the visual arts, but its influence was still felt. Beginning in the 1830s, painters turned from portraying great events and famous people to depicting everyday life. Democratic genre painters such as William Sidney Mount and George Caleb Bingham captured the lives of plain folk with skill and understanding. Mount, who painted lively rural scenes, expressed the credo of the democratic artist: "Paint pictures that will take with the public—never paint for the few but the many." Bingham was noted for his graphic images of Americans voting, carrying goods on riverboats, and engaging in other everyday activities.

Exponents of a higher culture and a more refined sensibility sought to enlighten or uplift the new public. The "Brahmin poets" of New England—Henry Wadsworth Longfellow, James Russell Lowell, and Oliver Wendell Holmes—offered lofty sentiments and moral messages to a receptive middle class. Ralph Waldo Emerson carried his philosophy of spiritual self-reliance to lyceums and lecture halls across the country. Great novelists such as Nathaniel Hawthorne and Herman Melville experimented with popular romantic genres. But Hawthorne and Melville failed to gain a large readership. Their ironic and pessimistic view of life clashed with the optimism of the age. For later generations of American critics, however, the works of Melville and Hawthorne became centerpieces of the American literary "renaissance" of the mid-nineteenth century. Hawthorne's *The Scarlet Letter* (1850) and Melville's *Moby-Dick* (1851) are now regarded as masterworks of fiction.

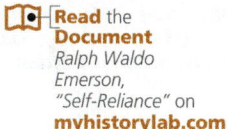

Read the **Document**
Ralph Waldo Emerson, "Self-Reliance" on **myhistorylab.com**

Quick Check

✓ How did American culture reflect a growing spirit of "popular sovereignty"?

Democratic Political Institutions

The supremacy of democracy was most obvious in the new politics of universal white manhood suffrage and mass political parties. By the 1820s, most states had removed the last barriers to voting for all white males. This change was not as radical or controversial as it would be later in nineteenth-century Europe; so many Americans owned land that most voters were still men of property.

The proportion of public officials who were elected rather than appointed also increased. "The people" increasingly chose judges, as well as legislators and executive officers. A new style of politicking developed. Politicians had to get out and campaign, demonstrating in their speeches on the stump that they could mirror voters' fears and concerns. Electoral politics became more festive and dramatic.

Skillful and farsighted politicians—such as Martin Van Buren in New York—began in the 1820s to build stable statewide political organizations out of what had been loosely organized factions. Before the rise of effective national parties,

Stump Speeches Political candidates of the Jacksonian era traveled from town to town giving stump speeches. The political gatherings at which they spoke provided entertainment and were an excellent source of political news. This painting, *Stump Speaking* (1853/1854), is by George Caleb Bingham, one of the most prolific democratic genre painters.

politicians created true party organizations on the state level by dispensing government jobs to friends and supporters and attacking rivals as enemies of popular aspirations. Earlier politicians had regarded parties as a threat to republican virtue and had embraced them only as a temporary expedient, but Van Buren regarded a permanent two-party system as essential to democratic government. In his opinion, parties restricted the temptation to abuse power, a tendency deeply planted in the human heart. The major breakthrough in American political thought during the 1820s and 1830s was the idea of a "loyal opposition," ready to capitalize politically on the mistakes or excesses of the "ins" without denying the ins' right to act the same way when they became the "outs."

Changes in the method of nominating and electing a president fostered the growth of a national two-party system. By 1828, voters rather than state legislatures were choosing presidential electors in all but two of the 24 states. The new need to mobilize grassroots voters behind particular candidates required national organization. Coalitions of state parties that could agree on a single standard-bearer evolved into the great national parties of the Jacksonian era—the Democrats and the Whigs. When national nominating conventions appeared in 1831, representative party assemblies, not congressional caucuses or ad hoc political alliances, selected presidential candidates.

New political institutions and practices encouraged popular interest and participation. In the presidential election of 1824, less than 27 percent of adult white males voted. From 1828 to 1836, 55 percent did. Then it shot up to 78 percent in 1840—the first election in which two fully organized national parties each nominated a single candidate and campaigned in every state in the Union.

Quick Check

✓ What changed during the 1820s and 1830s in the way politicians were elected to public office?

Economic Issues

Economic questions dominated politics in the 1820s and 1830s. The Panic of 1819 and the subsequent depression heightened popular interest in government economic policy. No one really knew how to solve the problems of a market economy that went through cycles of boom and bust, but many still thought they had the answer. Some, especially small farmers, favored a return to a simpler and more "honest" economy without banks, paper money, and the easy credit that encouraged speculation. Others, particularly emerging entrepreneurs, saw salvation in government aid and protection for venture capital. Entrepreneurs appealed to state governments for charters that granted special privileges to banks, transportation enterprises, and manufacturing corporations. The economic distress of the early 1820s fostered the rapid growth of state-level political activity and organizations that foreshadowed the rise of national parties organized around economic programs.

Party disputes involved more than the direct economic concerns of particular interest groups. They also reflected the republican ideology that feared conspiracy against American liberty and equality. Whenever any group appeared to be exerting decisive influence over public policy, its opponents were quick to charge its members with corruption and the unscrupulous pursuit of power.

The notion that the American experiment was fragile, constantly threatened by power-hungry conspirators, took two principal forms. Jacksonians believed that "the money power" endangered the survival of republicanism; their opponents feared that populist politicians like Jackson himself—"rabble-rousers"—would gull the electorate into ratifying high-handed and tyrannical actions contrary to the nation's true interests.

The role of the federal government concerned both sides. Should it foster economic growth, as the National Republicans and later the Whigs contended, or should it simply attempt to destroy what Jacksonians decried as "special privilege" or "corporate monopoly"? Almost everyone favored equality of opportunity. The question was whether the government should actively support commerce and industry or stay out of the economy in the name of laissez-faire (the idea that the government should keep its hands off the economy) and free competition.

> **Quick Check**
>
> ✓ How did the Jacksonians differ from their opponents in their opinions about the New American Experiment?

JACKSON AND THE POLITICS OF DEMOCRACY

The public figure who symbolized the triumph of democracy was Andrew Jackson of Tennessee. Jackson lost the presidential election of 1824, but his victory four years later, his actions as president, and the great political party that formed around him refashioned national politics in a more democratic mold.

> **What** political conflicts did President Andrew Jackson face and how did he resolve them?

Jackson Comes to Power

In the election of 1824, Jackson won a plurality of the electoral votes, but not a majority. (See Table 10.1) The contest was thrown into the House of Representatives, where the legislators were to choose from among the three top candidates: John Quincy Adams of Massachusetts, Jackson, and William Crawford, a Georgian who favored limited government. Adams won when Henry Clay of Kentucky, who had come in fourth, threw his support behind Adams. When Adams appointed Clay secretary of state, Jacksonians charged that a "corrupt bargain" had cost their favorite the presidency. Although there was no evidence that Clay had bartered votes for the promise of a high office, many believed the charge. Adams assumed office under a cloud of suspicion.

TABLE 10.1   The Election of 1824

Candidate	Party	Popular Vote	Electoral Vote*
J. Q. Adams	No party designations	108,740	84
Jackson		153,544	99
Clay		47,136	37
Crawford		46,618	41

*No candidate received a majority of the electoral votes. The House of Representatives elected Adams.

Adams had a frustrating presidency. The political winds were blowing against nationalistic programs, partly because the country was just recovering from a depression that many thought federal banking and tariff policies had caused or made worse. But Adams refused to bow to public opinion and called for expanding federal activity. He had a special interest in government support for science and wanted a national university in Washington. Advocates of states' rights and a strict construction of the Constitution were aghast, and congressional opponents turned the administration's domestic program into a pipe dream.

Men hostile to the administration and favorable to Jackson controlled the Congress elected in 1826. The tariff issue was the main business on their agenda. Pressure for greater protection from foreign imports came not only from manufacturers but also from farmers, especially wool and hemp growers, who would supply critical votes in the presidential election of 1828. The cotton-growing South—the only section where tariffs of all kinds were unpopular—was assumed to be safely in Jackson's camp regardless of his stand on the tariff. Therefore, his supporters felt safe in promoting a high tariff to swing critical votes his way. Jackson himself had never categorically opposed protective tariffs so long as they were "judicious."

As it turned out, the resulting tariff law was anything but judicious. Congress tried to provide something for everybody. Those favoring protection for farmers agreed to protect manufacturers and vice versa. This across-the-board increase in duties, however, angered southern free traders and became known as the tariff of abominations.

The campaign of 1828 actually began with Adams's election in 1824. Rallying around the charge of a corrupt bargain between Adams and Clay, Jackson's supporters began to organize on the state and local level with an eye to reversing the outcome of the election. By late 1827, virtually every county and important town or city in the nation had a Jackson committee. Influential state or regional leaders who had supported other candidates in 1824 now created a formidable coalition behind the Tennessean.

The most significant of these were Vice President John Calhoun of South Carolina, who spoke for the militant states' rights sentiment of the South;

Senator Martin Van Buren, who dominated New York politics through the political machine known as the Albany Regency; and two Kentucky editors, Francis P. Blair and Amos Kendall, who mobilized opposition in the West to Henry Clay and his "American System," which advocated government encouragement of economic development through protective tariffs and federally funded internal improvements. As they prepared for 1828, these leaders and their local followers laid the foundations for the first modern American political party—the Democrats. That the Democratic party was founded to promote the cause of a particular presidential candidate revealed a central characteristic of the emerging two-party system. From this time on, according to historian Richard P. McCormick, national parties existed primarily "to engage in a contest for the presidency." Without this great prize, there would have been less incentive to create national organizations out of the parties and factions developing in the several states.

The election of 1828 saw the birth of a new era of mass democracy. The mighty effort for Jackson featured such electioneering techniques as huge public rallies, torchlight parades, and lavish barbecues or picnics that the candidate's supporters paid for. Many historians believe that the massive turnout at such events during much of the rest of the nineteenth century revealed a deeper popular engagement with politics than at other times in American history. But others have argued that it may merely have showed that politicians had learned that entertainment and treats could lure people to the polls.

Personalities and mudslinging dominated the campaign. The Democratic press and a legion of pamphleteers viciously attacked Adams and praised "Old Hickory," as Jackson was called. Adams' supporters responded in kind; they even accused Jackson's wife, Rachel, of bigamy and adultery because she had unwittingly married Jackson before being officially divorced from her first husband. The Democrats then came up with the utterly false charge that Adams's wife was born out of wedlock.

What gave Jacksonians the edge was their portrayal of Jackson as an authentic man of the people, despite his wealth in land and slaves. His backwoods upbringing, record as a military hero and Indian fighter, and even lack of education were touted as evidence that he was a true representative of the common people, especially the plain folk of the South and the West. Adams, according to Democrats, was the exact opposite—an overeducated aristocrat, more at home in the salon and the study than among plain people. Nature's nobleman was pitted against the aloof New England intellectual. Adams never had a chance.

Jackson won by a popular vote margin of 150,000 and by more than 2 to 1 in the electoral college. But outside the Deep South, voters divided fairly evenly. Adams, in fact, won a majority of the electoral vote in the North. (See Map 10.1) Furthermore, Jackson's mandate was unclear. Most of the politicians in his camp favored states' rights and limited government against the nationalism of Adams and Clay, but Jackson himself had never taken a clear public stand on such issues as banks, tariffs, and internal improvements. He did, however, support removing Indians from the Gulf states, a key to his immense popularity in that region.

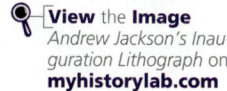

View the **Image**
Andrew Jackson's Inauguration Lithograph on **myhistorylab.com**

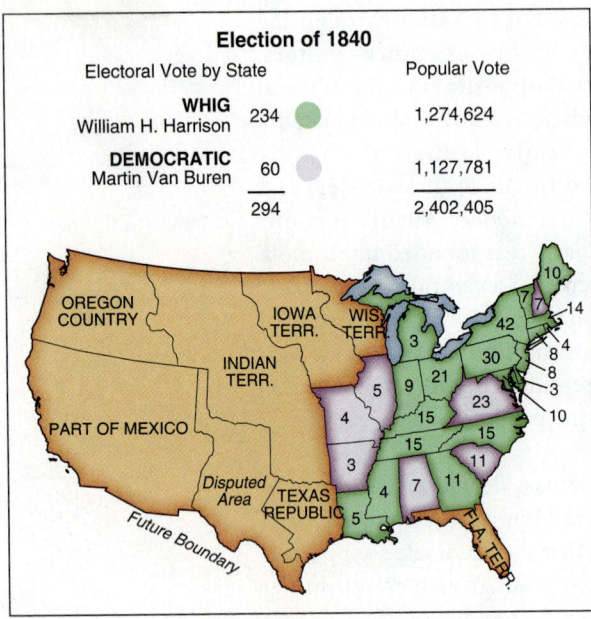

Election of 1840

Electoral Vote by State		Popular Vote
WHIG William H. Harrison	234 🟢	1,274,624
DEMOCRATIC Martin Van Buren	60 ⚪	1,127,781
	294	2,402,405

Map 10.1

Jackson was one of the most forceful and domineering American presidents. His most striking traits were an indomitable will, an intolerance of opposition, and a prickly pride that would not permit him to forgive or forget an insult or supposed act of betrayal. It is sometimes hard to determine whether principle or personal spite motivated his political actions. As a young man on the frontier, he had learned to fight his own battles. Violent in temper and action, he fought duels and battled the British, Spanish, and Indians with a zeal his critics found excessive. He was tough and resourceful, but he lacked the flexibility successful politicians usually show. Yet he generally got what he wanted.

Jackson's presidency commenced with his open endorsement of the rotation of officeholders, or what critics called "the spoils system." Although he did not actually replace many more federal officeholders with his supporters than his predecessors had, he was the first president to defend this practice openly as a legitimate democratic doctrine.

Midway through his first administration, however, Jackson did replace almost all of his original cabinet appointees. At the root of this upheaval was a feud between Jackson and Vice President Calhoun, but the Peggy Eaton affair in 1831 brought it to a head. Peggy O'Neale Eaton, the daughter of a Washington tavern owner, married Secretary of War John Eaton in 1829. Because of gossip about her moral character, other cabinet wives, led by Mrs. Calhoun, refused to receive her socially. Jackson became her fervent champion, partly because he found the charges against her reminiscent of the slanders against his late wife, who had died in 1828. When he raised the issue of Mrs. Eaton's social status at a cabinet meeting, only Secretary of State Van Buren, a widower, supported his stand. This seemingly trivial incident led to the resignation of all but one of the cabinet members (including Eaton), so the president could begin again with a fresh slate. Although Van Buren resigned with the rest to allow a thorough reorganization, Jackson rewarded his loyalty by appointing him minister to Britain and then choosing him as his vice president in 1832.

Quick Check

✓ What lessons do his sweeping electoral victory and his handling of The Peggy Eaton affair teach us about Andrew Jackson? What other political developments of the era helped him win election?

Indian Removal

View the **Closer Look** *Indian Removals* on **myhistorylab.com**

The first major policy question facing the Jackson administration concerned the fate of Native Americans. Jackson had long favored removing eastern Indians to lands beyond the Mississippi. In his military service on the southern frontier, he had already persuaded and coerced tribal groups to emigrate. Jackson's support of removal was no different from the policy of previous administrations. The only real issues were how rapidly and thoroughly it should be carried out and by what means. Georgia, Alabama, and Mississippi were clamoring for action.

Immediately after Jackson's election, Georgia extended its state laws over the Cherokee within its borders. Georgia declared that all Cherokee laws and customs were null and void, made all white people living in the Cherokee Nation subject to Georgia's laws, declared the Cherokee mere tenants at will on their land, and made it a crime for any Cherokee to try to influence another Cherokee to stay in Georgia. State officials also authorized the Georgia militia to use violence against the Cherokee to pressure them to give up their land and move west. Before Jackson's inauguration, Alabama and Mississippi also abolished the sovereignty of the Creeks and Choctaw, and declared state control of the tribes.

This legislation defied both the constitutional provisions giving the federal government exclusive jurisdiction over Indian affairs and specific treaties. But Jackson endorsed the state actions. He regarded Indians as children when they did the white man's bidding and savage beasts when they resisted. He was also aware of his political debt to the land-hungry states of the South. Consequently, in December 1829, he advocated a new and more coercive removal policy. Denying Cherokee autonomy, he asserted the

A Falling House? Jackson's resigning cabinet members were, according to this cartoon, rats deserting a falling house. Jackson is seated on a collapsing chair, while the "altar of reform" and "public confidence in the stability of this administration" pillars topple to his left, and "resignations" flutter behind him. The president's foot is on the tail of the Secretary of State Martin Van Buren rat.

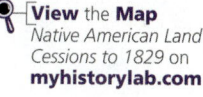
View the **Map**
Native American Land Cessions to 1829 on
myhistorylab.com

primacy of states' rights over Indian rights and called for the speedy and thorough removal of all eastern Indians to designated areas beyond the Mississippi. Chief John Ross warned his people that "the object of the President is … to create divisions among ourselves." President Jackson rejected Ross's appeal against Georgia's violation of federal treaty, and in 1830, the president's congressional supporters introduced a bill to implement the removal policy. Despite heated debate, the Indian Removal Act passed with strong support from the South and western border states.

Jackson then concluded the necessary treaties, using the threat of unilateral state action to bludgeon the tribes into submission. The treaty for Cherokee removal

Trail of Tears Robert Lindneux, *The Trail of Tears* (1942). Cherokee Indians, carrying their few possessions, are prodded along by U.S. soldiers on the Trail of Tears. Thousands of Native Americans died on the ruthless forced march from their homelands in the East to the new Indian Territory in Oklahoma. (*Source: Robert Lindneux, American. "Trail of Tears." Courtesy of the Newberry Library, Chicago/Woolaroc Museum, Bartlesville, Oklahoma.*)

was negotiated with 75 out of 17,000 Cherokees, and none of the tribal officers was present. By 1833, all the southeastern tribes except the Cherokee had agreed to evacuate their ancestral homelands. Choctaw Chief David Folsom wrote, "We are exceedingly tired. We have just heard of the ratification of the Choctaw Treaty. Our doom is sealed. There is no course for us but to turn our faces to our new homes in the setting sun." Alexis de Tocqueville, the French author of *Democracy in America*, watched the troops driving the Choctaws across the Mississippi River in the winter of 1831. He wrote that Americans had deprived Indians of their rights "with singular felicity, tranquilly, legally, philanthropically.... It is impossible to destroy men with more respect for the laws of humanity."

Yet President Jackson was not always concerned with respect for the law. In 1832, he condoned Georgia's defiance of a Supreme Court decision (*Worcester v. Georgia*) that denied a state's right to jurisdiction over tribal lands. Georgia had arrested and sentenced to four years' hard labor a missionary who violated state law by going on tribal land without Georgia's permission. The Supreme Court declared the law unconstitutional. Jackson's legendary declaration that Chief Justice Marshall had "made his decision, now let him enforce it" is almost certainly apocryphal, as there was nothing for either Jackson or Marshall to "enforce"; the decision only required Georgia to release Worcester from custody, which it eventually did. But the story reflects Jackson's general attitude toward the Court's decisions on federal jurisdiction. He would not protect Indians from state action, no matter how violent or coercive, and he put the weight of the federal government behind removal policy.

The Cherokee held out until 1838, when military pressure forced them to march to the territory that is now Oklahoma. This trek—known as the Trail of Tears— was made under such harsh conditions that almost 4,000 of approximately 16,000 marchers died on the way. (See Map 10.2) The final chapter of Indian Removal was the Second Seminole War, which lasted from 1834 to 1841. Although the government had convinced a few Seminoles to sign a treaty in 1834 agreeing to removal, most Seminoles renounced it and resisted for years, making the bloody conflict the most expensive Indian war in U.S. history. The removal of the southeastern Indians exposed the prejudiced and greedy side of Jacksonian democracy.

View the **Map**
Native American Land Cessions, 1840 on
myhistorylab.com

Quick Check

✓ What did the Indian Removal policy demonstrate about Jacksonian democracy?

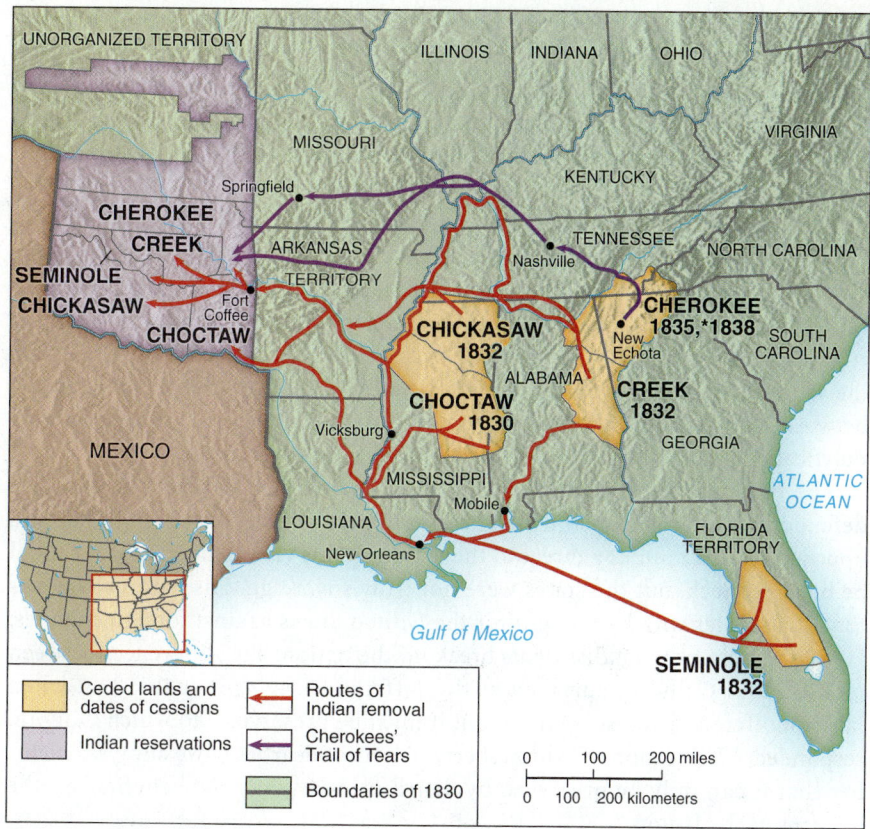

Map 10.2 *Indian Removal*   Because so many Native Americans, uprooted from their lands in the East, died on the forced march to Oklahoma, the route they followed became known as the Trail of Tears.

The Nullification Crisis

During the 1820s, southerners became increasingly fearful of federal encroachment on states' rights. Behind this concern, in South Carolina at least, was a strengthened commitment to slavery and anxiety about the use of federal power to strike at the "peculiar institution." Hoping to keep slavery itself out of the political limelight, South Carolinians seized on another grievance—the protective tariff—as the issue on which to take their stand in favor of a state veto power over federal actions they viewed as contrary to their interests. Tariffs that increased the prices that southern agriculturists paid for manufactured goods and that threatened to undermine their foreign markets by inciting other countries to erect their own protective tariffs hurt the staple-producing and exporting South.

Vice President Calhoun emerged as the leader of the states' rights insurgency in South Carolina, abandoning his earlier support of nationalism and the American System. After the tariff of abominations passed in 1828, the South

Carolina legislature declared the new duties unconstitutional and endorsed a lengthy affirmation—written anonymously by Calhoun—of nullification, or an individual state's right to set aside federal laws. Calhoun supported Jackson in 1828 and planned to serve amicably as his vice president, expecting Jackson to support his native region on the tariff and states' rights. He also hoped to succeed Jackson as president.

In the meantime, however, a bitter personal feud developed between Jackson and Calhoun. The vice president and his wife were prime movers in ostracizing Peggy Eaton. Evidence also came to light that Calhoun, as secretary of war in Monroe's cabinet in 1818, had advocated punishing Jackson for his incursion into Spanish-ruled Florida. As Calhoun lost favor, it became clear that Van Buren rather than the vice president would be Jackson's designated successor. The personal breach between Jackson and Calhoun colored and intensified their confrontation over nullification and the tariff.

The two men also differed on matters of principle. Although generally a defender of states' rights and strict construction of the Constitution, Jackson opposed nullification as a threat to the Union. In his view, federal power should be held in check, but the states were not truly sovereign. His nationalism was that of a soldier who had fought for the United States against foreign enemies. He was not about to let dissidents break up the nation. The differences between Jackson and Calhoun surfaced at the Jefferson Day dinner in 1830, when Jackson offered the toast "Our Union: It must be preserved," to which Calhoun responded, "The Union. Next to Liberty, the most dear. May we always remember that it can only be preserved by distributing equally the benefits and the burdens of the Union."

In 1830 and 1831, the movement against the tariff grew in South Carolina. Calhoun openly took the lead, arguing that states could set aside federal laws. In 1832, a new tariff lowered the rates slightly but retained the principle of protection. Supporters of nullification argued that the new law simply demonstrated that they could expect no relief from Washington. The South Carolina legislature then called a special convention. In November 1832, its members voted to nullify the tariffs of 1828 and 1832 and forbid the collection of customs duties within the state.

Jackson reacted with characteristic decisiveness. He alerted the secretary of war to prepare for military action, denounced nullification as treasonous, and asked Congress for authority to use the army to enforce the tariff. He also sought to pacify the nullifiers by recommending a lower tariff. Congress responded by enacting the Force Bill—which gave the president the military powers he sought—and the compromise tariff of 1833. The latter was primarily the work of Jackson's enemy Henry Clay, but the president signed it anyway. Faced with Jackson's intention to use force and appeased by the lower tariff, South Carolina suspended the nullification ordinance in January 1833 and rescinded it in March, after the new tariff had been enacted. To demonstrate that they had not conceded their constitutional position, however, the convention delegates also nullified the Force Bill.

Read the
Document
*South Carolina
Refuses the Tariff* on
myhistorylab.com

The nullification crisis revealed that South Carolinians would not tolerate federal acts that seemed contrary to their interests or interfered with slavery. The nullifiers' philosophy implied the right of secession and the right to declare laws of Congress null and void. As events would show, a fear of northern meddling with slavery was the main spur to the growth of a militant doctrine of state sovereignty in the South. At the time of the nullification crisis, the other slave states were less anxious about the future of the "peculiar institution" and did not embrace South Carolina's radical conception of state sovereignty. Jackson was himself a southerner, a slaveholder, and in general, a proslavery president.

But the Unionist doctrines that Jackson propounded in his proclamation against nullification alarmed farsighted southern loyalists. More strongly than any previous president, Jackson had asserted that the federal government was supreme over the states and that the Union was indivisible. He had also justified using force against states that denied federal authority.

Quick Check

✓ What was nullification, and why did it emerge in the south? How did Jackson respond to that crisis?

THE BANK WAR AND THE SECOND-PARTY SYSTEM

Jackson's most controversial use of executive power was his successful attack on the Bank of the United States. After it failed to recharter the original Bank of the United States in 1811, Congress chartered a second Bank of the United States in 1816, which became the object of Jackson's antagonism. The Bank War revealed some of the deepest concerns of Jackson and his supporters and expressed their concept of democracy. It also aroused intense opposition, which crystallized in a new national party—the Whigs. The destruction of the Bank and the ensuing economic disruption highlighted the issue of the government's relationship to the nation's financial system. Differences on this question strengthened the new two-party system.

What were the arguments for and against the Bank of the United States?

The Bank Veto and the Election of 1832

Jackson had strong reservations about banking and paper money in general—in part because of his own brushes with bankruptcy after accepting promissory notes

TABLE 10.2 The Election of 1832

Candidate	Party	Popular Vote	Electoral Vote
Jackson	Democratic	688,242	219
Clay	National Republican	473,462	49
Wirt	Anti-Masonic	101,051	7
Floyd	Independent Democratic	*	11

*Electors chosen by South Carolina legislature.

that depreciated in value. He also harbored suspicions that branches of the Bank of the United States had illicitly supported Adams in 1828. In 1829 and 1830, Jackson called on Congress to curb the Bank's power.

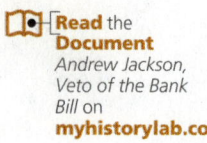

Read the
Document
*Andrew Jackson,
Veto of the Bank
Bill* on
myhistorylab.com

Nicholas Biddle, the president of the Bank, began to worry about its charter, which was to come for up for renewal in 1836. Jackson was also listening to his "Kitchen Cabinet," especially Amos Kendall and Francis P. Blair, who thought an attack on the Bank would be a good party issue for the election of 1832. Biddle then made a fateful blunder. He sought recharter by Congress in 1832, four years ahead of schedule. Senator Henry Clay, leader of the anti-administration forces on Capitol Hill, encouraged this move because he was convinced that Jackson had chosen the unpopular side of the issue and that a congressional endorsement of the Bank would embarrass or even discredit the president. The bill to recharter was introduced in early 1832. Despite Jackson's opposition, it easily passed.

Bur Jackson vetoed the bill with ringing statements of principle. After repeating his opinion that the Bank was unconstitutional, notwithstanding a ruling by the Supreme Court, he argued that it violated the fundamental rights of the people in a democratic society.

Jackson thus called on the common people to fight the "monster" corporation. His veto message was the first to use more than strictly constitutional arguments and deal directly with social and economic issues. Attempts to override the veto failed, and Jackson resolved to take the issue to the people in the upcoming presidential election.

The 1832 election, the first in which national nominating conventions chose the candidates, pitted Jackson against Henry Clay, standard-bearer of the National Republicans. Although the Democrats did not adopt a formal platform, the party firmly opposed rechartering the Bank. Clay and the National Republicans attempted to marshal the pro-Bank sentiment that was strong in many parts of the country. But Jackson won a personal triumph over Clay (see Table 10.2). His share of the popular vote was not as high as in 1828, but he still interpreted it as a mandate for continuing the war against the Bank.

Quick Check

✓ What were Jackson's reasons for opposing the bank, and to whom did he turn for support in that effort?

Killing the Bank

Jackson now resolved to attack the Bank directly by removing federal deposits from Biddle's vaults. The Bank had used all the political influence it could muster to prevent Jackson's reelection, and Old Hickory regarded Biddle as a personal enemy.

To remove the deposits from the Bank, Jackson had to overcome resistance in his own cabinet. When one secretary of the treasury refused to support the policy, he was shifted to another cabinet post. When a second also balked, Roger B. Taney, a Jackson loyalist and opponent of the Bank, replaced him. In September 1833, Taney, as acting secretary of the treasury, ceased depositing government money in the Bank and began to withdraw the funds already there. Although Jackson had suggested that the government keep its money in some kind of public bank, he had never worked out the details or made a specific proposal to Congress. Instead, the funds were placed in 23 state banks. Opponents charged that these banks had been selected for political rather than fiscal reasons and dubbed them Jackson's "pet banks." Since Congress refused to regulate the credit policies of these banks, the way the state banks used the new deposits nullified Jackson's efforts to shift to a hard-money economy. They extended credit recklessly and increased the paper money in circulation.

The Bank of the United States counterattacked by calling in outstanding loans and instituting a policy of credit contraction that helped bring on a recession. Biddle hoped to show that weakening the Bank would hurt the economy. With justification, Jacksonians accused Biddle of deliberately and unnecessarily causing distress out of personal resentment and a desire to maintain his unchecked powers and privileges. The Bank never regained its charter.

A Hydra-Headed Bank Aided by Van Buren (center), Jackson wields his veto rod against the Bank of the United States, whose heads represent the directors of the state branches. Bank president Nicholas Biddle is wearing the top hat. In ancient mythology the Hydra was a snake with many heads; each time one was cut another would sprout up and it would not die.
(Source: Collection of The New-York Historical Society. Negative number 42459.)

View the **Image**
Jackson's Bank Crisis on
myhistorylab.com

Opposition to Jackson's fiscal policies grew in Congress. Clay and his supporters contended that the president had violated the Bank's charter and exceeded his constitutional authority when he removed the deposits. The Senate approved a motion of censure. Jacksonians in the House blocked similar action, but the president was further humiliated when the Senate refused to confirm Taney as secretary of the treasury. (Jackson later named him chief justice of the Supreme Court.) Congressmen who had defended Jackson's veto now thought he had abused the powers of his office.

Quick Check
✓ What did Jackson do to "kill the bank"?

The Emergence of the Whigs

The coalition that passed the censure resolution in the Senate provided the nucleus for a new national party—the Whigs. Its leadership and most of its support came from National Republicans associated with Clay and New England ex-Federalists led by Senator Daniel Webster of Massachusetts. Southern proponents of states' rights who had been upset by Jackson's stand on nullification and saw his withdrawal of federal deposits from the Bank as an unconstitutional abuse of power also supported the Whigs. Even Calhoun and his nullifiers occasionally cooperated with the Whig camp. The rallying cry for this diverse anti-Jackson coalition was "executive usurpation." The Whig label was chosen because of its associations with British and American revolutionary opposition to royal power and prerogatives. In their propaganda, the Whigs attacked the tyrannical designs of "King Andrew" and his court.

The Whigs also gradually absorbed the Anti-Masonic party, a surprisingly strong political movement that had arisen in the Northeast in the late 1820s and early 1830s. Capitalizing on the hysteria aroused by the 1826 disappearance and apparent murder of a New Yorker who had threatened to reveal the secrets of the Masonic order, the Anti-Masons exploited traditional American fears of secret societies and conspiracies. They also appealed to the moral concerns of the northern middle class under the sway of an emerging evangelical Protestantism. Anti-Masons detested Jacksonianism mainly because it tolerated diverse lifestyles. They believed that the government should restrict such "sinful" behavior as drinking, gambling, and breaking the Sabbath. But this diverse Whig coalition could not agree on a single candidate and lost the 1836 presidential election to Jackson's designated successor, Martin Van Buren. Nevertheless, the Whigs ran even with the Democrats in the South. (See Table 10.3)

President Van Buren immediately faced a catastrophic depression, known as the Panic of 1837. This was not exclusively, or even primarily, the result of government policies. It was international and reflected complex changes in the world economy that American policymakers could not control. But the Whigs blamed the state of the economy on Jacksonian finance, and the administration had to respond. Since Van Buren and his party were committed to a policy of laissez-faire on the federal level, they could do little or nothing to relieve economic distress through subsidies or relief measures. But Van Buren could try to salvage the federal funds deposited in shaky state banks and devise a new system of public finance that would not contribute to future panics by fueling speculation and credit expansion.

The economy doomed Van Buren's chances for reelection in 1840. The Whigs had the chance to offer alternative policies that promised to restore prosperity.

((•—Listen to the
Audio File
Van Buren on
myhistorylab.com

View the **Image**
1840 Campaign Ad on
myhistorylab.com

TABLE 10.3   The Election of 1836

Candidate	Party	Popular Vote	Electoral Vote
Van Buren	Democratic	764,198	170
Harrison	Whig	549,508	73
White	Whig	145,342	26
Webster	Whig	41,287	14
Mangum	Independent Democratic	*	11

*Electors chosen by South Carolina legislature.

They passed over the true leader of their party, Henry Clay, and nominated William Henry Harrison, an old military hero who was associated in the public mind with the Battle of Tippecanoe and the winning of the West. To increase the ticket's appeal in the South, they chose John Tyler of Virginia, a states' rights Democrat, as Harrison's running mate.

Using the slogan "Tippecanoe and Tyler, too," the Whigs pulled out all the stops. They organized rallies and parades, complete with posters, placards, campaign hats and emblems, special songs, and even log cabins filled with coonskin caps and barrels of cider for the faithful. Imitating the Jacksonian propaganda against Adams in 1828, they portrayed Van Buren as a luxury-loving aristocrat and compared him with their own homespun candidate. There was an enormous turnout on election day—78 percent of those eligible to vote. When it was over, Harrison had parlayed a narrow edge in the popular vote into a landslide in the electoral college. (See Map 10.3) The Whigs also won control of both houses of Congress.

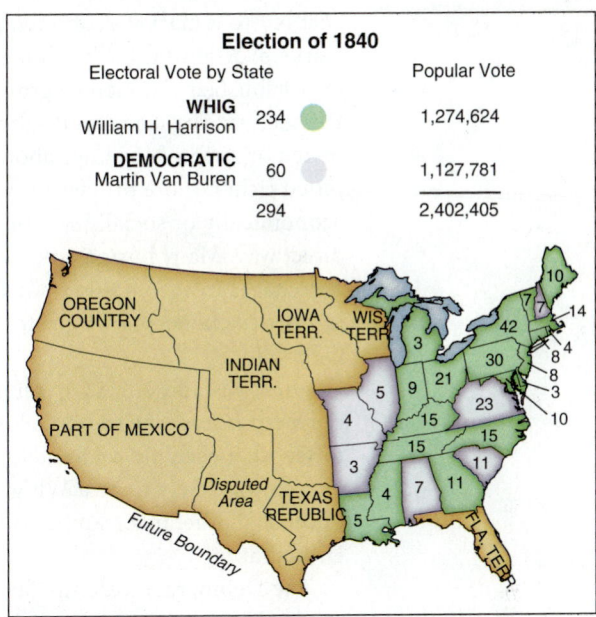

Map 10.3

Quick Check

✓ Who came together to form the Whig Party, and how did they gain power in 1840?

HEYDAY OF THE SECOND-PARTY SYSTEM

America's second-party system came of age in the election of 1840. Unlike the earlier competition between Federalists and Jeffersonian Republicans, the rivalry between Democrats and Whigs made the two-party pattern a normal feature of electoral politics. During the 1840s, the two national parties competed on fairly equal terms for the support of the electorate. Allegiance to one party or the other became a source of personal identity for many Americans and increased their interest and participation in politics.

The parties offered voters a real choice of programs and ideologies. Whigs stood for a "positive liberal state"—which meant government had the right and duty to subsidize or protect enterprises that could contribute to general prosperity and economic growth. Democrats normally advocated a "negative liberal state" in which government kept its hands off the economy.

Economic issues helped determine each party's base of support. In the Whig camp were industrialists who wanted tariff protection, merchants who favored internal improvements to stimulate commerce, and farmers and planters who had

What was the two-party system, and how were the parties different?

adapted to a market economy. Democrats appealed mainly to smaller farmers, workers, declining gentry, and emerging entrepreneurs who were excluded from the established commercial groups that would benefit most from Whig programs. Democratic rhetoric about monopoly and privilege appealed to those who had mixed or negative feelings about a national market economy. This division also pitted richer, more privileged Americans against those who were poorer and less economically or socially secure. But it did not follow class lines in any simple or direct way. Many businessmen were Democrats; many wage earners voted Whig. Merchants in the import trade hated Whiggish high tariffs, whereas workers in industries clamoring for protection often concluded that such duties protected their jobs.

Lifestyles and ethnic or religious identity influenced party loyalties. In the northern states, one way to tell the typical Whig from the typical Democrat was to see what each did on Sunday. A person who went to an evangelical Protestant church was likely to be a Whig. The person who attended a ritualized service—Catholic, Lutheran, or Episcopalian—or did not go to church at all was probably a Democrat.

The Democrats were the favored party of immigrants, Catholics, freethinkers, backwoods farmers, and all those who enjoyed traditional amusements that the new breed of moral reformers condemned. One thing all these groups had in common was a desire to be left alone, free to think and behave as they liked. The Whigs enjoyed strong support among old-stock Protestants in smaller cities, towns, and prosperous rural areas devoted to market farming. In general, the Whigs welcomed a market economy but wanted to restrain the individualism and disorder it created by enforcing cultural and moral values derived from the Puritan tradition.

Nevertheless, party conflict in Congress centered on national economic policy. Whigs stood for a loose construction of the Constitution and federal support for business and economic development. Democrats defended strict construction, states' rights, and laissez-faire. Debates over tariffs, banking, and internal improvements remained vital during the 1840s.

True believers in both parties saw deep ideological or moral meaning in the clash over economic issues. Whigs and Democrats had conflicting views of the good society, and their policies reflected these differences. The Democrats were the party of white male equality and personal liberty. They perceived the American people as a collection of independent and self-sufficient white men. Government's job was to ensure that the individual was not interfered with—in his economic activity, his personal habits, or his religion (or lack of it). Democrats were ambivalent about the market economy because it threatened individual independence. The Whigs, on the other hand, were the party of orderly progress under the guidance of an enlightened elite. They believed that the propertied, the well-educated, and the pious should guide the masses toward the common good. Believing that a market economy would benefit everyone in the long run, they had no qualms about the rise of a commercial and industrial capitalism.

CONCLUSION: TOCQUEVILLE'S WISDOM

The French traveler Alexis de Tocqueville, author of the most influential account ever written of the emergence of American democracy, visited the United States in 1831 and 1832. He left before the presidential election and had little to say about national politics and political parties. For him, the essence of American democracy was local self-government, such as he observed in New England town meetings. The participation of ordinary citizens in the affairs of their communities impressed him. He praised Americans for not conceding their liberties to a centralized state, as he believed the French had done.

Yet Tocqueville was acutely aware of the limitations of American democracy. He knew that the kind of democracy men were practicing was not meant for women. Observing how women were strictly assigned to a separate domestic sphere, he concluded that Americans had never supposed "that democratic principles should undermine the husband's authority and make it doubtful who is in charge of the family." He also believed the nullification crisis foreshadowed destruction of the Union and predicted that slavery would lead to civil war and racial conflict. He noted the power of white supremacy, providing an unforgettable firsthand description of the sufferings of an Indian community during forced migration to the West, and a graphic account of how free blacks were segregated and driven from the polls in northern cities such as Philadelphia. White Americans, he believed, were deeply prejudiced against people of color, and he doubted it was possible "for a whole people to rise … above itself." A despot might force the equality and mingling of the races, but "while American democracy remains at the head of affairs, no one would dare attempt any such thing, and it is possible to foresee that the freer the whites in America are, the more they will seek to isolate themselves." Tocqueville clearly saw that Jacksonian democracy and equality were meant for only some of the people. His belief that slavery would endanger the union was prophetic.

10 STUDY RESOURCES

((•—Listen to the **Chapter Audio** for Chapter 10 on **myhistorylab.com**

TIMELINE

1824 House of Representatives elects John Quincy Adams president, p. 251

1828 Congress passes "tariff of abominations," p. 252
• Andrew Jackson elected president, p. 254

1830 Congress passes Indian Removal Act, p. 255

1831 Jackson reorganizes his cabinet, p. 254
• First national nominating conventions meet, p. 250

1832 Jackson vetoes the bill rechartering the Bank of the United States, p. 260
• Jackson reelected, p. 259

1832–1833 Nullification crisis, p. 259

1833 Jackson removes federal deposits from the Bank of the United States, p. 260

1834 Whig party formed, p. 261

1836 Martin Van Buren elected president, p. 262

1837 Financial panic triggers depression, p. 262

1840 William Henry Harrison elected president, p. 263

CHAPTER REVIEW

DEMOCRACY IN THEORY AND PRACTICE

How did the relationship between the government and the people change during this time?

The federal government grew more accountable to the people it represented. "Popular sovereignty" meant that men of modest backgrounds could attain new social status, while cultural expression reflected this "decline in deference." More public officials now had to seek popular election, but public opinion divided over the role of government in the economy. *(p. 247)*

JACKSON AND THE POLITICS OF DEMOCRACY

What political conflicts did Jackson face and how did he resolve them?

Jackson resolved political conflicts with iron-fisted authority. During the Peggy Eaton affair, he sacked his entire cabinet, and he handled the Indian dilemma by evicting Native Americans from their homeland. During the nullification crisis, he threatened South Carolina with military force. *(p. 251)*

THE BANK WAR AND THE SECOND-PARTY SYSTEM

What were the arguments for and against the Bank of the United States?

Nicholas Biddle believed that the Bank of the United States was essential to American economic stability. Jackson believed the federal bank to be unconstitutional and saw it as a personal enemy and "monster corporation." Bank proponents believed that Jackson's "Bank War" exceeded his constitutional authority, and the Whig party emerged in opposition to his policies. *(p. 259)*

HEYDAY OF THE SECOND-PARTY SYSTEM

What was the two-party system, and how were the parties different?

The "second-party system" was the rivalry between Whigs and Democrats. The Whigs included industrialists, merchants, and farmers who favored stimulus to commerce. Democrats included smaller farmers, wage workers, and declining gentry—individuals the new market economy had left behind. The division also marked cultural differences in religion, ethnicity, and lifestyle. *(p. 263)*

KEY TERM QUESTIONS

1. Why did Congress pass the tariff of abominations in 1828? (p. 252)

2. What does the Trail of Tears and Indian Removal policy in general tell us about Jacksonian democracy? (p. 256)

3. Why did nullification emerge in the South and how did Jackson respond to it? (p. 258)

4. Why was Jackson so intent on waging a Bank War? (p. 259)

5. What were the causes of the Panic of 1837? (p. 262)

6. How did America's second-party system arise? (p. 263)

MYHISTORYLAB CONNECTIONS

Visit **www.myhistorylab.com** for a customized Study Plan to build your knowledge of *The Triumph of White Men's Democracy*.

Question for Analysis

1. What political, economic, and cultural forces contributed to the forced migration of Indians in the 1830s?

   View the **Closer Look** *Indian Removals* p. 254

2. In what areas of the country were Native Americans forced to give up their land?

   View the **Map** *Native American Land Cessions, 1840* p. 255

3. What was the central reason for which South Carolina rejected the tariff?

   Read the **Document** *South Carolina Refuses the Tariff* p. 258

4. What were Jackson's major objections to the national bank?

   Read the **Document** *Andrew Jackson, Veto of the Bank Bill* p. 260

Other Resources from this Chapter

Read the **Document** *Ralph Waldo Emerson, Self-Reliance*

View the **Image** *Andrew Jackson's Inauguration Lithograph*

View the **Map** *Native American Land Cessions to 1829*

View the **Image** *Jackson's Bank Crisis*

Listen to the **Audio File** *Van Buren*

View the **Image** *1840 Campaign Ad*

Contents and Spotlight Questions

((•—Listen to the **Chapter Audio** for Chapter 11 on **myhistorylab.com**

NAT TURNER'S REBELLION: A TURNING POINT IN THE SLAVE SOUTH

On August 22, 1831, the worst nightmare of southern slaveholders became reality. Slaves in Southampton County, Virginia, rose in bloody rebellion. Their leader was Nat Turner, a preacher and prophet who believed God had given him a sign that the time was ripe to strike for freedom; a vision of black and white angels wrestling in the sky had convinced him that divine wrath was about to be visited upon the white oppressor.

Rallying followers as he went along, Turner led his band from plantation to plantation, killing of nearly 60 whites. The rebellion was short-lived; after only 48 hours, white forces dispersed the rampaging slaves. The rebels were then rounded up and executed, along with dozens of other slaves who were suspected of complicity. Turner was the last to be captured. He went to the gallows unrepentant, convinced he had acted in accordance with God's will.

Horrid Massacre in Virginia (1831) A composite of scenes of Nat Turner's Rebellion, an illustration from a book entitled "Authentic and impartial narrative of the tragical scene which was witnessed in Southampton County [New York, 1831].

After the initial panic and rumors of a wider insurrection had passed, white southerners went about the grim business of ensuring such an incident would never happen again. The emergence of a more militant northern abolitionism strengthened their anxiety and determination. Just two years after African American abolitionist David Walker published his *Appeal to the Colored Citizens of the World* in 1829, calling for blacks to take up arms against slavery, William Lloyd Garrison put out the first issue of his newspaper, *The Liberator*, the first publication by a white author to demand immediate abolition of slavery rather than gradual emancipation. Southerners saw Turner and Garrison as two prongs of a revolutionary attack on the southern way of life. Although no evidence came to light that abolitionist propaganda had directly influenced Turner, many whites believed that it must have or that future rebels might be. Consequently, they launched a massive campaign to quarantine the slaves from exposure to antislavery ideas and attitudes.

⊡▢▸ **Read** the **Document**
The Confessions of Nat Turner (1831) on **myhistorylab.com**

New laws restricted the ability of slaves to move about, assemble without white supervision, or learn to read and write. The repression did not stop at the color line; laws and the threat of mob action prevented white dissenters from publicly criticizing or even questioning slavery. The South became a closed society with a closed mind. Loyalty to the region was identified with defense of it, and proslavery agitators sought to create a mood of crisis and danger requiring absolute unity and single-mindedness among the white population. This embattled attitude fostered a more militant sectionalism and inspired threats to secede from the Union unless the South's peculiar institution could be made safe from northern or abolitionist attack.

The repression after the Nat Turner rebellion succeeded. Between 1831 and the Civil War, no further uprisings resulted in the mass killing of whites. This once led some historians to conclude that African American slaves were brainwashed into docility. But resistance to slavery simply took less dangerous forms than open revolt. The brute force employed to suppress the Turner rebellion and the elaborate precautions taken against its recurrence showed slaves that it was futile to confront white power directly. Instead, they asserted their humanity and maintained their self-esteem in other ways. The heroic effort to endure slavery without surrendering to it gave rise to an African American culture of lasting value.

THE WORLD OF SOUTHERN BLACKS

What factors made living conditions for southern blacks more or less difficult?

Most African Americans of the early to mid-nineteenth century experienced slavery on plantations, estates owned by planters who had 20 or more slaves. To ensure their personal safety and the profitability of their enterprises, the masters of these agrarian communities used all the means—physical and psychological—at their command to make slaves docile and obedient. Despite these pressures, most African Americans managed to retain an inner sense of their own worth and dignity. When conditions were right, they asserted their desire for freedom and equality and showed their disdain for white claims that slavery was a positive good. Although slave culture did not normally provoke violent resistance to the slaveholders' regime, the inner world that slaves made for themselves gave them the spiritual strength to thwart the masters' efforts to dominate their hearts and minds. Much of what we know about the world of Southern slaves comes from interviews ex-slaves gave in the 1930s, decades after slavery ended. While the transcriptions of these interviews often reflect the prejudices of the white interviewers, and are colored by the circumstances in which they were given, they remain an invaluable window into the lives of slaves.

View the **Map**
Slavery in the South on
myhistorylab.com

Slaves' Daily Life and Labor

Slaves' daily life varied with the region in which they lived and the type of plantation or farm on which they worked. On large plantations in the Cotton Belt, most slaves worked in "gangs" under an overseer. White overseers, sometimes helped by black "drivers," enforced a workday from sunup to sundown, six days a week. There was never a slack season under "King Cotton." Cultivation required year-round labor. Enslaved women and children also worked in the fields. Parents often brought babies and young children to the fields, where older children could care for them and mothers could nurse them during brief breaks. Older children worked in "trash gangs," weeding and yard cleaning. Life on the sugar plantations of Louisiana was much harsher: Slaves had to work into the night during harvest season, and mortality rates were high.

View the **Image**
Slave Quarters, Hermitage Plantation on
myhistorylab.com

Not all slaves in agriculture worked in gangs. In the low country of South Carolina and Georgia, slaves who cultivated rice worked under a "task system" that gave them more control over the pace of labor. With less supervision, they could complete their tasks within an eight-hour day. Slaves on small farms often worked side by side with their masters rather than in slave gangs, although such intimacy did not necessarily affect power relationships. While about three-quarters of slaves were field workers, slaves performed many other kinds of labor. They dug ditches, built houses, worked on boats and in mills (often hired out by their masters for a year), and were house servants, cooking, cleaning, and gardening. Some slaves, especially women, also worked within the slave community as preachers, caretakers of children, and healers. A few slaves, about 5 percent, worked in industry in the South, including mills, iron works, and railroad building. Slaves in cities did a wider range of jobs than plantation slaves, and in general enjoyed more autonomy. They worked in restaurants and saloons, in hotels, and as skilled tradesmen. Some urban slaves even lived apart from their masters and hired out their own time, returning part of their wages to their owners.

Picking Cotton Although cotton cultivation required constant attention, many of the tasks involved were relatively simple. On a cotton plantation most slaves, including women and children, were field hands who performed the same tasks. Here a slave family stands behind baskets of picked cotton in a Georgia cotton field.

Quick Check

✓ What were the differences between "gang" and "task" labor?

Most slaves also kept gardens or small farm plots for themselves to supplement their diets. They fished, hunted, and trapped animals. Many slaves also worked "overtime" for their own masters on Sundays or holidays in exchange for money or goods, or hired out their overtime hours to others. This "underground economy" suggests slaves' overpowering desire to provide for their families, sometimes even earning enough to purchase their freedom.

Slave Families, Kinship, and Community

More than any other institution, the African American family prevented slavery from becoming utterly demoralizing. Slaves had a strong and abiding sense of family and kinship. But the nature of the families or households that predominated on plantations or farms varied with circumstances. On large plantations with relatively stable slave populations, most slave children lived in two-parent households, and many marriages lasted for 20 to 30 years. The death or sale of one of the partners broke up more marriages than voluntary dissolutions did. Here mothers, fathers, and children were bonded closely, and parents shared child-rearing responsibilities (within the limits masters allowed). Masters and churches encouraged marital fidelity: Stable unions produced more offspring, and adultery and divorce were sinful.

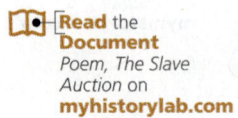

Read the **Document**
Poem, The Slave Auction on
myhistorylab.com

But in areas where most slaves lived on farms or small plantations, and especially in the upper South where slaves were often sold or hired out, a different pattern seems to have prevailed. Under these circumstances, slaves' spouses frequently resided on other plantations or farms, often some distance away, and ties between husbands and wives were looser and more fragile. Female-headed families were the norm, and mothers, assisted in most cases by female relatives and friends, took responsibility for child rearing. Mother-centered families with weak conjugal ties were a natural response to the absence of fathers and the prospect of their being moved or sold beyond visiting distance. Where sale or relocation could break up unions at any time, it did not pay to invest all of one's emotions in a conjugal relationship. But whether the basic family form was nuclear or matrifocal (female-headed), it created infinitely precious ties for its members. The threat of breaking up a family through sale was a disciplinary tool that gave masters great power over their slaves.

View the **Image**
Slave Dealers on
myhistorylab.com

The anguish that accompanied the breakup of families through sale showed the depth of kinship feelings. The first place that masters looked for a fugitive was near a family member who had been sold away. Indeed, many slaves tried to be sold with family members or to the same neighborhood. After emancipation, thousands of freed slaves wandered about looking for spouses, children, or parents from whom they had been forcibly separated years before. The famous spiritual "Sometimes I Feel Like a Motherless Child" expressed far more than religious need; it reflected slaves' family anxieties and personal tragedies.

Kinship and mutual obligation extended beyond the primary family. Slaves often knew their grandparents, uncles, aunts, and even cousins through direct contact or family lore. The names that slaves gave to their children or took for themselves revealed a sense of family continuity over three or four generations. Infants were frequently named after grandparents, and those slaves who took surnames often chose that of an ancestor's owner rather than the family name of a current master.

Kinship ties were not limited to blood relations. When sales broke up families, individuals who found themselves on plantations far from home were likely to be "adopted" into new kinship networks. New families quickly absorbed orphans or children without responsible parents. Soon after the Civil War, one Reconstruction official faced an elderly ex-slave named Roger, who demanded land "to raise crop on" for his "family of sixty 'parents,' that is, relations, children included." A family with 60 parents made no sense to this official, but it did in a community in which ties of affection and cooperation rather than "blood" relation often defined families.

Kinship provided a model for personal relationships and the basis for a sense of community. Everyone addressed elderly slaves as "uncle" and "aunty," and younger unrelated slaves commonly called each other "brother" or "sister." Slave culture was a family culture, which was one of its greatest sources of strength and cohesion. Strong kinship ties, whether real or fictive, meant slaves could depend on one another in times of trouble. The kinship network also helped transmit African American folk traditions from one generation to the next. Together with slave religion, kinship gave African Americans a sense that they were members of a community, not just a collection of oppressed individuals.

A Slave Family Though death or sale broke up many slave families, some families, especially those on large, stable plantations, managed to stay together. This 1862 photograph by Timothy H. O'Sullivan shows five generations of a slave family, all born on the plantation of J. J. Smith in Beaufort, South Carolina.

Quick Check
✓ How did slave communities maintain kinship ties?

Resistance and Rebellion

Open rebellion, bearing arms against the oppressors by organized groups of slaves, was the most dramatic and clear-cut form of slave resistance. Between 1800 and 1831, slaves participated in revolts that showed their willingness to risk their lives in a desperate bid for liberation. In 1800, a Virginia slave named Gabriel Prosser mobilized a large band to march on Richmond. But a violent storm dispersed "Gabriel's army," and the uprising was suppressed without any loss of white life.

In 1811, hundreds of Louisiana slaves marched on New Orleans brandishing guns, waving flags, and beating drums. It took 300 soldiers of the U.S. Army, aided by armed planters and militiamen, to stop the advance and end the rebellion. In 1822, whites in Charleston, South Carolina, uncovered an extensive and well-planned conspiracy that a free black man named Denmark Vesey had organized to seize armories, arm the slaves, and burn the city. Although the **Vesey conspiracy** was nipped in the bud, it convinced South Carolinians that blacks were "the Jacobins of the country [a reference to the militants of the French Revolution] against whom we should always be on guard."

As we have already seen, the most bloody and terrifying slave revolt was the Nat Turner insurrection of 1831. Although it was the last slave rebellion of this kind before the Civil War, armed resistance had not ended. Indeed, the most sustained and successful effort of slaves to win their freedom by force took place in Florida between 1835 and 1842, when hundreds of black fugitives fought the U.S. Army in the Second Seminole War alongside the Indians who had given them a haven. The Seminoles were resisting removal to Oklahoma, but for the blacks who took part in it, the war was a struggle for their own freedom. When it ended, most of them were allowed to accompany their Indian allies to the trans-Mississippi West.

Few slaves ever took part in organized acts of violent resistance against white power. Most realized that the odds against a successful revolt were high. Bitter experience had shown them that the usual outcome was death to the rebels. As a consequence, they resisted white dominance in safer, more ingenious ways.

Watch the **Video**
Underground Railroad
on
myhistorylab.com

One way was to run away, and thousands of slaves did so. Most fugitives never got beyond the neighborhood of the plantation; after "lying out" for a time, they would return, often after negotiating immunity from punishment. But many escapees remained free for years, hiding in swamps or other remote areas. Others escaped to freedom in the North or Mexico. Fugitives stowed away aboard ships heading to northern ports or traveled over land for hundreds of miles, avoiding patrols and inquisitive whites by staying off the roads and moving only at night. Light-skinned blacks sometimes made it to freedom by passing for white. Some escaped with the help of the **Underground Railroad**, an informal network of sympathetic free blacks (and a few whites) who helped fugitives make their way North. The Underground Railroad had an estimated 3,200 active workers. It is estimated that 130,000 refugees (out of 4 million slaves) escaped the slave South between 1815 and 1860. By the 1850s, substantial numbers of Northerners had been in open violation of federal law by hiding runaways for a night. One resourceful slave even had himself packed in a box and shipped to the North. Henry "Box" Brown, like other successful fugitives, published an account of his life in slavery and his daring escape, and fashioned his story as a plea to support the antislavery cause. Such narratives by fugitive slaves are an important source of information about life under slavery.

The typical fugitive was a young, unmarried male from the upper South. For most slaves, however, flight was not an option. Either they lived too deep in the South to reach free soil, or they were reluctant to leave family and friends behind. Slaves who did not or could not leave the plantation had to oppose the masters' regime while remaining under the yoke of bondage.

The normal way of expressing discontent was through indirect or passive resistance. Many slaves worked slowly and inefficiently, not because they were naturally lazy (as whites supposed) but as a gesture of protest or alienation. As the words of a popular slave song said, "You may think I'm working/But I ain't." Others feigned illness or injury. Stealing provisions—a common activity—was another way to flout authority. According to the code of ethics prevailing in the slave quarters, theft from the master simply enabled slaves to get a larger share of the fruits of their own labors.

Many slaves committed acts of sabotage. Tools and agricultural implements were deliberately broken, animals were willfully neglected or mistreated, and barns or other outbuildings were set afire. Often masters could not identify the culprits because slaves did not readily inform on one another. The ultimate act of clandestine resistance was poisoning the master's food. Some slaves, especially the "conjure" men and women who practiced a combination of folk medicine and witchcraft, knew how to mix rare, virtually untraceable poisons, and many plantation whites became suddenly and mysteriously ill. Whole families died from obscure "diseases" that did not infect the slave quarters.

The folktales that slaves passed from generation to generation revealed the attitude behind such actions. The famous Br'er Rabbit stories showed how a small, apparently defenseless animal could outwit a bigger and stronger one through cunning and deceit. Although these tales often had an African origin, they also served as an allegory for the black view of the master–slave relationship. Other stories— which were not told in front of whites—openly portrayed the slave as a clever trickster outwitting the master.

Finally, slave religion, often practiced secretly at night and led by black preachers, gave African Americans a chance to create their own world. Religion seldom inspired slaves to open rebellion, but it encouraged community, solidarity, and self-esteem by giving them something infinitely precious of their own. Many religious songs referred to the promise of freedom, or demanded that an oppressor "let my people go." Nat Turner was a free black preacher.

Quick Check

✓ How successful were the Vesey Conspiracy and Nat Turner Insurrection?

Free Blacks in the Old South

Free blacks occupied an increasingly precarious position in the antebellum South. White southerners' fears of free blacks (like Turner) inciting slave revolts, and their reaction to abolitionists' attacks, led slaveholders after 1830 to defend slavery as a positive good rather than a necessary evil. This defense was racist, emphasizing a dual image of the black person: Under the "domesticating" influence of a white master, the slave was a happy child; outside of this influence, he was a savage beast. As whites strove to convince themselves and northerners that blacks were happy in slavery, they more frequently portrayed free blacks as savages who needed to be reined in.

Beginning in the 1830s, all the southern states cracked down on free blacks. Laws forced free people of color to register or have white guardians who were responsible for their behavior. Free blacks had to carry papers proving their status. In some states, they needed permission to move from one county to another. Licensing laws excluded blacks from several occupations, and the authorities often prevented blacks from holding meetings or forming organizations. Vagrancy and apprenticeship laws forced free blacks into economic dependency barely distinguishable from outright slavery.

Read the
Document
*Runaway Slave
Advertisements* on
myhistorylab.com

Although beset by special problems of their own, most free blacks identified with the suffering of the slaves; when they could, they protested against the peculiar institution and worked for its abolition. Many of them had once been slaves themselves or were the children of slaves; often their relatives were still in bondage. They knew that the discrimination from which they suffered was rooted in slavery and the racial attitudes that accompanied it. So long as slavery existed, their own rights were likely to be denied. Even their freedom was at risk; former slaves who could not prove they had been legally freed could be reenslaved. This threat existed even in the North: Under federal fugitive slave laws, escaped slaves had to be returned to bondage. Even blacks who were born free were not safe. Kidnapping or fraudulent seizure by slave-catchers was always a risk.

Because of the elaborate system of control and surveillance, free blacks in the South could do little to work against slavery. Most found that survival depended on creating the impression of loyalty to the planter regime. In the Deep South, relatively privileged free people of color, mostly of racially mixed origin, were sometimes persuaded that it was to their advantage to preserve the status quo. As skilled artisans and small-business owners dependent on white favors and patronage, they had little incentive to risk everything by taking the side of the slaves. In southern Louisiana, a few mulatto planters even lived in luxury, supported by the labor of other African Americans.

However, although some free blacks created niches of relative freedom, their position in southern society became increasingly precarious. Beginning in the 1830s, southern whites sought to make the line between free and unfree a line between black and white. Free blacks were an anomaly in this system; increasingly, the southern answer was to exclude, degrade, and even enslave those free people of color who remained within their borders. Just before the Civil War, a campaign developed to carry the repression and discrimination to its logical conclusion: State legislatures proposed forcing free people of color to choose between leaving the state or being enslaved.

Quick Check

✓ What was life like for freed slaves in the South?

WHITE SOCIETY IN THE ANTEBELLUM SOUTH

What divided and united white southern society?

Those who know the Old South only from novels, films, and television are likely to imagine a land filled with majestic plantations. Pillared mansions behind oak-lined carriageways are portrayed as scenes of aristocratic splendor, where courtly gentlemen and elegant ladies, attended by hordes of uniformed black servants, lived in refined luxury. Such images suggest that the typical white southerner was an aristocrat whose family owned many slaves.

The great houses existed—many of them can still be seen in Virginia, the low country of South Carolina, and the lower Mississippi Valley—and some wealthy slaveholders' lifestyle was as aristocratic as any ever seen in the United States. But census returns indicate that this was the world of only a tiny percentage of slaveowners and of the total white population. In 1860, only one-quarter of all white southerners belonged to slave-owning families. Even in the Cotton Belt, only about

40 percent of whites were slaveholders on the eve of the Civil War. Planters were the minority of a minority, just 4 percent of the total white population of the South in 1860. Large planters who could build great houses and entertain lavishly, those who owned at least 50 slaves, comprised less than 1 percent of all whites.

Most southern whites, three-fourths of the white population, were non-slaveholding yeoman farmers or artisans. Yet even those who owned no slaves depended on slavery, whether economically, because they hired slaves, or psychologically, because having a degraded class of blacks below them made them feel better about their own place in society. However, the class divisions between slaveholders and non-slaveholders did contribute to the political rifts that became increasingly apparent on the eve of the Civil War.

The Planters' World

The great planters, although few in number, had a disproportionate influence on southern life. They set the tone and values for much of the rest of society, especially for the less wealthy slaveowners who sought to imitate the planters' style of living to the extent their resources allowed. Although many wealthy planters were too busy tending to their plantations to become openly involved in politics, they held more than their share of high offices and often exerted a decisive influence on public policy. In regions where plantation agriculture predominated, they were a ruling class in every sense of the term. Contrary to legend, most of the great planters of the pre–Civil War period were self-made rather than descendants of the old colonial gentry. Some were ambitious young men who married planters' daughters. Others started as lawyers and used their fees and connections to acquire plantations.

As the Cotton Kingdom spread west from South Carolina and Georgia to Alabama, Mississippi, Louisiana, and Texas, the men who became the largest slaveholders were less and less likely to have come from old, well-established planter families. Many of them began as hard-driving businessmen who built up capital from commerce, land speculation, banking, and even slave trading. They then used their profits to buy plantations. Sharp dealing and business skills were more important than genealogy in the competitive, boom-or-bust economy of the western Gulf states.

To succeed, a planter had to be a shrewd entrepreneur who kept a careful eye on the market, the prices of slaves and land, and his debts. Few planters could be men of leisure.

Likewise, the responsibility of running an extended household that produced much of its own food and clothing kept plantation

Plantation Mansion Painting by Adrien Persac depicting the back of a plantation house in Louisiana as seen from the bayou. Persac was commissioned to paint some of the great houses in the region, and in 1858 he published a map showing the plantations along the Mississippi River from Natchez to New Orleans.

mistresses from being the idle ladies of legend. Not only were plantation mistresses a tiny minority of the women who lived and worked in the slave states before the Civil War, but even women from the planter elite rarely lived lives of leisure.

A few of the richest and most secure plantation families did aspire to live like a traditional landed aristocracy, and visiting English nobility accepted them as equals. Big houses, elegant carriages, fancy-dress balls, and multitudes of house servants all reflected aristocratic aspirations. Dueling, despite efforts to repress it, remained the standard way to settle "affairs of honor" among gentlemen. Another sign of gentility was the tendency of planters' sons to avoid "trade" as a primary or secondary career in favor of law or the military. Planters' daughters were trained from girlhood to play the piano, speak French, dress in the latest fashions, and sparkle in the drawing room or on the dance floor. The aristocratic style originated among the older gentry of the seaboard slave states, but by the 1840s and 1850s, it had spread southwest as a second generation of wealthy planters began to displace the rough-hewn pioneers of the Cotton Kingdom.

Quick Check

✔ In what ways did members of the planter society shape themselves as an aristocracy?

Planters, Racism, and Paternalism

No assessment of the planters' outlook or "worldview" can be made without considering their relations with their slaves. Planters owned more than half of all the slaves in the South and set standards for treatment and management. Most planters liked to think of themselves as benevolent masters and often referred to their slaves as if they were members of an extended patriarchal family—a favorite phrase was "our people." According to this paternalistic ideology, blacks were a race of perpetual children requiring constant care and supervision by superior whites. Paternalistic rhetoric increased after abolitionists began to charge that slaveholders were sadistic monsters.

Paternalism went hand in hand with racism. In a typical proslavery apology, Georgia lawyer Thomas Reade Cobb wrote that "a state of bondage, so far from doing violence to the law of [the African's] nature, develops and perfects it; and that, in that state, he enjoys the greatest amount of happiness, and arrives at the greatest degree of perfection of which his nature is capable." The supposed mental and moral inferiority of Africans justified slavery. While some Europeans had drawn negative associations with blackness for centuries, a full-blown modern racism only developed on both sides of the Atlantic in the 1830s and 1840s. Racial "scientists" related skull size to mental ability, and some proslavery apologists even developed religious theories of "polygenesis," arguing that blacks were not descended from Adam and Eve. This racial ideology helped slaveholders believe that a benevolent Christian could justly enslave another human being.

While some historians have argued that paternalism was part of a social system that was organized like a family hierarchy rather than a brutal, profit-making arrangement, there was no inconsistency between planters' paternalism and capitalism. Slaves were a form of capital; that is, they were both the main tools of production for a booming economy and an asset in themselves, valuable for their rising prices, like shares in the stock market today. The ban on the transatlantic slave trade in 1808 was effective enough to make it economically necessary for the slave population to reproduce itself if slavery were to continue. Rising slave prices also inhibited extreme physical abuse and deprivation. It was in masters' self-interest to see that their slave property remained in good enough condition to work hard and produce children. Furthermore, a good return on their investment enabled southern planters to spend more on slave maintenance than masters in less prosperous plantation economies like the Caribbean or Brazil could.

Much of the slaveholders' "paternalist" writing discussed "the coincidence of humanity and interest," by which they meant that treating slaves well (including firm discipline) was in their best economic interest. There was a grain of truth in the planters' claim that their slaves were relatively well provided for. Comparative studies have suggested that pre–Civil War North American slaves enjoyed a higher standard of living than those in other New World slave societies, such as Brazil and Cuba. Their food, clothing, and shelter were normally sufficient to sustain life and labor at slightly above a bare subsistence level, and the rapid increase of the slave population in the Old South stands in sharp contrast to the usual failure of slave populations to reproduce themselves.

Watch the **Video**
Moonlight and Magnolias: Creating the Old South on
myhistorylab.com

But some planters did not behave rationally. They lost their temper or tried to work more slaves than they could afford to maintain. Consequently, there were more cases of physical abuse and undernourishment than a purely economic calculation would lead us to expect.

The testimony of slaves themselves and of independent white observers suggests that masters of large plantations generally did not have close and intimate relationships with the mass of field slaves. The affection and concern associated with a father figure appears to have been limited mainly to relationships with a few favored house servants or other elite slaves, such as coachmen and skilled artisans. The field hands on large estates dealt mostly with overseers who were hired or fired because of their ability to meet production quotas.

The slave market revealed the limits of paternalism. Planters who looked down on slave traders as less than respectable gentlemen nevertheless broke apart families by selling slaves "down river" when they needed money. Even slaveholders who claimed not to participate in the slave market themselves often mortgaged slaves to secure debts; one-third of all slave sales in the South were court-ordered sheriff's auctions when masters defaulted on their debts.

While paternalism may have moderated planters' behavior, especially when economic self-interest reinforced "humanity," most departures from unremitting labor and harsh conditions were concessions that slaves' defiance and resistance wrested from owners at great personal risk.

Furthermore, when they were being realistic, planters conceded that the ultimate basis of their authority was fear, rather than the natural obedience of a loving parent–child relationship. Scattered among their statements are admissions that they relied on the "principle of fear," "more and more on the power of fear," or—most graphically—that it was necessary "to make them stand in fear." Devices for inspiring fear included whipping—a common practice on most plantations—and the threat of sale away from family and friends. Planters' manuals and instructions to overseers reveal that certain and swift punishment for any infraction of the rules or even for a surly attitude was the preferred method for maintaining order and productivity.

Slaves had little recourse against masters' abuse. They lacked legal protection because courts would not accept their testimony. Abolitionists were correct in condemning slavery on principle because it gave one human being nearly absolute power over another. This system was bound to result in atrocities and violence. Even Harriet Beecher Stowe acknowledged in *Uncle Tom's Cabin*, her celebrated antislavery novel of 1852, that most slaveholders were not as sadistic and brutish as Simon Legree. But—and this was her real point—an institution that made a Simon Legree possible was wrong in and of itself.

Quick Check

✓ How did whites see themselves in relation to their slaves?

Small Slaveholders

In 1860, 88 percent of all slaveholders owned fewer than 20 slaves and thus were not truly planters. Of these, most had fewer than ten. Some small slaveholders were urban merchants or professional men whose slaves were domestic servants, but more typical were farmers who used one or two slave families to ease the burden of their own labor. We know relatively little about life on these small slaveholding farms; unlike the planters, the owners left few records. But we do know that life was Spartan. Masters lived in log cabins or small frame cottages. Slaves lived in lofts or sheds that were not usually up to plantation housing standards.

For better or worse, relations between such owners and their slaves were more intimate than on larger estates. Unlike planters, these farmers often worked in the fields alongside their slaves and sometimes ate at the same table or slept under the same roof. But such closeness did not necessarily result in better treatment. Slave testimony reveals that both the best and the worst of slavery could be found on these farms, depending on the character and disposition of the master. Given a choice, most slaves preferred to live on plantations because they offered the sociability, culture, and kinship of the slave quarters and better food, clothing, and shelter.

Quick Check

✓ Why would most slaves prefer plantation life to small farms given the choice?

Yeoman Farmers

Just below the small slaveholders on the social scale was a substantial class of yeoman farmers who owned land they worked themselves. Contrary to another myth about the Old South, most of these people were not degraded, shiftless poor whites. Poor whites did exist, mainly as squatters on barren or sandy soil that no one else wanted. In parts of the South, many of those working the land were tenants; some of these were "shiftless poor whites," but others were ambitious young men seeking to accumulate the capital to become landowners. Most of the nonslaveholding rural population were proud, self-reliant farmers whose way of life did not differ markedly from that of family farmers in the Midwest during the early stages of settlement. If they were disadvantaged compared with farmers elsewhere in the United States, it was because the lack of economic development and urban growth perpetuated frontier conditions and prevented them from producing a substantial surplus for market.

The yeomen were mostly concentrated in the backcountry, where slaves and plantations were rare. Every southern state had hilly sections unsuitable for plantation agriculture. The foothills or interior valleys of the Appalachians and Ozarks offered reasonably good soils for mixed farming, and long stretches of piney barrens along the Gulf Coast were suitable for raising livestock. In such regions slaveless farmers concentrated, giving rise to the "white counties" that complicated southern politics. A distinct group was the genuine mountaineers, who lived too high up for farming and relied on hunting, lumbering, and distilling whiskey.

Read the
Document
Hinton Helper, A
White Southerner
Speaks on
myhistorylab.com

Yeoman women, much more than their wealthy counterparts, participated in every dimension of household labor. They grew vegetables and chickens, made handicrafts and clothing, and even labored in the fields. The poorest women even worked for wages in small businesses or on nearby farms. They also raised much larger families than their wealthier neighbors because children were a valuable labor pool for the family farm.

More lower-class women also lived outside of male-headed households. Despite the pressures of respectability, there was more acceptance and sympathy in less affluent communities for women who bore illegitimate children or were abandoned by their husbands. Working women created a broader definition of "proper households" and held families together in precarious conditions. The lack of transportation, more than a failure of energy or character, limited the prosperity of the yeomen. They mostly grew subsistence crops, mainly corn. They did raise some of the South's cotton and tobacco, but the difficulty of marketing severely limited their production. Their main source of cash was livestock, especially hogs. Hogs could be walked to market over long distances, and massive droves from the backcountry to urban markets were commonplace. But southern livestock was of poor quality and did not bring high prices or big profits.

Although they did not benefit directly from the peculiar institution, most yeomen and other non-slaveholders fiercely opposed abolitionism. A few antislavery southerners, most notably Hinton R. Helper of North Carolina, tried to convince the yeomen that they were victimized by planter dominance and should work for its overthrow. These dissenters pointed out that slavery and the plantation system created a privileged class and limited the economic opportunities of the non-slaveholding white majority.

Most yeomen were staunch Jacksonians who resented aristocratic pretensions and feared concentrations of power and wealth in the hands of the few. They disdained "cotton snobs" and rich planters. In state and local politics, they sometimes voted against planter interests on issues involving representation, banking, and internal improvements. Why, then, did they fail to respond to antislavery appeals that called on them to strike at the real source of planter power and privilege?

One reason was that some non-slaveholders hoped to get ahead, and in the South this meant acquiring slaves. Just enough more prosperous yeomen broke into the slaveholding classes to make this dream seem believable. Planters, anxious to

Yeoman Household Carl G. Von Iwonski, *Block House, New Braunfels*. Most slaveholders in the South were not large plantation owners but small farmers of modest means who lived not in pillared mansions but in small, rough log cabins. Many others were yeoman farmers who owned no slaves.

Quick Check

✓ What was the yeoman's attitude toward slavery?

ensure the loyalty of non-slaveholders, encouraged the notion that every white man was a potential master.

Even if they did not aspire to own slaves, white farmers often viewed black servitude as providing a guarantee of their own liberty and independence. A society that gave them the right to vote and the chance to be self-sufficient on their own land encouraged the feeling that they were fundamentally equal to the largest slaveholders. Although they had no natural love of planters and slavery, they believed—or could be induced to believe—that abolition would threaten their liberty and independence. In part, their anxieties were economic; freed slaves would compete with them for land or jobs. But racism deepened their fears and made their opposition to black freedom implacable. Emancipation was unthinkable because it would remove the pride and status that automatically went with a white skin in this acutely race-conscious society. Slavery, despite its drawbacks, kept blacks "in their place" and made all whites, however poor and uneducated they might be, feel they were free and equal members of a master race.

A Closed Mind and a Closed Society

Despite the tacit assent of most non-slaveholders, the dominant planters never lost their fear that lower-class whites would turn against slavery. They felt threatened from two sides: from the slave quarters where a new Nat Turner might arise, and from the backcountry where yeomen and poor whites might heed the abolitionists' call and overthrow planter domination. Beginning in the 1830s, the ruling element tightened the screws of slavery and used their control of government and communications to create a mood of impending catastrophe to ensure that all southern whites were of one mind on the slavery issue.

Before the 1830s, the rights or wrongs of slavery had been openly discussed in much of the South. Apologists commonly described the institution as "a necessary evil." In the upper South, as late as the 1820s, there had been significant support for the American Colonization Society, with its program of gradual voluntary emancipation accompanied by deportation of the freedmen. In 1831 and 1832—in the wake of the Nat Turner uprising—the Virginia legislature debated gradual emancipation. Representatives of the yeoman farmers living west of the Blue Ridge Mountains supported getting rid of both slavery and blacks to ensure white safety. But the argument that slavery was "a positive good"—rather than an evil slated for gradual elimination—won the day, and emancipation was defeated.

The "positive good" defense of slavery was an answer to the abolitionist charge that the institution was inherently sinful. A host of books, pamphlets, and newspaper editorials published between the 1830s and the Civil War carried the message. Who was it meant to persuade? Partly, the argument was aimed at the North, to bolster anti-abolitionist sentiment. But the message was also clearly calculated to resolve the doubts and misgivings that southerners themselves had freely expressed before the 1830s. Much of the message may have been over the heads of non-slaveholders, many of whom were semiliterate, but some of the arguments, in popularized form, were used to arouse racial anxieties that tended to neutralize antislavery sentiment among the lower classes.

The proslavery argument had three main propositions. The first and foremost was that enslavement was the natural and proper status for people of African descent. Blacks were innately inferior to whites and suited only for slavery. Biased scientific and historical evidence supported this claim. Second, the Bible and Christianity were said to sanction slavery—a position made necessary by the abolitionist appeal to Christian ethics. Ancient Hebrew slavery was held up as a divinely sanctioned model. Saint Paul was quoted endlessly on the duty of servants to obey their masters. Third, efforts were made to show that slavery was consistent with the humanitarian spirit of the nineteenth century. The premise that blacks were naturally dependent led to the notion that they needed "family government" or a special regime equivalent to the asylums for the few whites who were also incapable of caring for themselves. The plantation allegedly provided such an environment, as benevolent masters guided and ruled this race of "perpetual children."

Read the Document George Fitzhugh, "The Blessings of Slavery" (1857) on myhistorylab.com

By the 1850s, the proslavery argument had gone beyond mere apology for the South and its peculiar institution to attack the free-labor system of the North. According to Virginian George Fitzhugh, the master–slave relationship was more humane than the one between northern employers and wage laborers. Slaves had security against unemployment and a guarantee of care in old age, whereas free workers might face destitution and even starvation at any time. Worker insecurity in free societies led inevitably to strikes, class conflicts, and socialism; slave societies, on the other hand, could better protect property rights and maintain other traditional values because their laboring class was better treated and more firmly controlled.

Proslavery southerners also attempted to seal off their region from antislavery ideas and influences. Whites who criticized slavery publicly were mobbed or persecuted. One of the last and bravest of the southern abolitionists, Cassius M. Clay of Kentucky, armed himself with a brace of pistols when he gave speeches, until the threat of mob violence finally forced him across the Ohio River. In 1856, a University of North Carolina professor was fired because he admitted he would vote for the moderately antislavery Republican party if he had a chance. Clergymen who questioned the morality of slavery were driven from their pulpits. Northern travelers suspected of being abolitionist agents were tarred and feathered. When abolitionists tried to send their literature through the mails during the 1830s, it was seized in southern post offices and publicly burned.

Fears that non-slaveholding whites and slaves would get subversive ideas about slavery partly explain such flagrant denials of free speech and civil liberties. Hinton R. Helper's book *The Impending Crisis of the South*, an 1857 appeal to non-slaveholders to resist the planter regime, was suppressed with particular vigor; those found with copies were beaten up or even lynched. But the deepest fear was that abolitionist talk or antislavery literature would incite slaves to rebel. The Nat Turner rebellion raised such anxieties to panic pitch. Laws made it a crime to teach slaves to read and write. Other repressive legislation banned meetings unless a white man was present, restricted the activities of black preachers, and suppressed independent black churches. Free blacks thought to be potential instigators of slave revolt were watched and harassed.

Quick Check

✓ What were some of the strategies used by southern whites to fight antislavery efforts?

But repression did not allay planters' fears of abolitionist subversion, lower-class white dissent, and, above all, slave revolt. Proslavery propaganda and national events in the 1850s created panic and desperation. More southerners became convinced that safety from abolitionism and its terrors required a formal withdrawal from the Union—secession.

SLAVERY AND THE SOUTHERN ECONOMY

How was slavery related to economic success in the South?

Despite their internal divisions, white southerners from all regions and classes came to perceive that their interests were tied up with slavery, whether because they owned slaves themselves or because they believed slavery was essential to the "southern way of life" or "white men's democracy." The expansion of slavery can largely be attributed to the rise of "King Cotton"—the number of slaves in the South more than tripled between 1810 and 1860 to nearly 4 million. The cotton-growing areas of the South were becoming more dependent on slavery, while agriculture in the upper South was moving away from the institution. Yet slavery remained important to the economy of the upper South through the slave trade. To understand southern thought and behavior, it is necessary to bear in mind this major regional difference between a slave plantation society and a farming and slave-trading region.

Sales Lewis Miller, *Slave Sale, Virginia*, probably 1853. Slave auctions, such as the one depicted in Lewis Miller's sketchbook, were an abomination and embarrassment to many Americans.

The Internal Slave Trade

Tobacco, the original plantation crop of the colonial period, remained the principal slave-cultivated commodity of the upper tier of southern states. But markets were often depressed, and profitable tobacco cultivation was hard to sustain for long in one place because the crop depleted the soil. As slave prices rose (because of high demand in the lower South) and demand for slaves in the upper South fell, the "internal" slave trade took off. Economic historians have concluded that the most important crop the tobacco kingdom produced was not the "stinking weed" but human beings cultivated for the auction block. The most profitable business for slaveholders in Virginia, Kentucky, Maryland, and the Carolinas was selling "surplus" slaves from the upper South to the Deep South, where staple crop production was more profitable. This interstate slave trade sent 600,000–700,000 slaves in a southwesterly direction between 1815 and 1860. (See Table 11.1.) A slave child born in the upper South in the 1820s had a 30 percent chance of being "sold downriver" by 1860. Such sales not only split families, but made it unlikely that the slaves sold would ever see friends or family again.

The slave trade provided crucial capital in a period of transition and innovation in the upper South. Nevertheless, the declining importance of slave labor in that region meant the peculiar institution had a weaker hold on public loyalty there than in the cotton states. More rapid urban and industrial development than elsewhere in the South accompanied this diversification of agriculture. As a result, Virginians, Marylanders, and Kentuckians were divided on whether their future lay with the Deep South's plantation economy or with the industrializing free-labor system that was flourishing north of their borders.

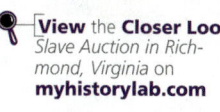

View the **Closer Look**
Slave Auction in Richmond, Virginia on
myhistorylab.com

Quick Check

✓ In what region did "internal" slave trading become the most profitable industry? why?

The Rise of the Cotton Kingdom

The warmer climate and good soils of the lower tier of southern states made it possible to raise crops more suited than tobacco or cereals to plantation agriculture and slave labor. Since the colonial or revolutionary periods, rice and long-staple fine cotton had been grown profitably on vast estates along the coast of South Carolina and Georgia. In Louisiana, between New Orleans and Baton Rouge, sugar was the cash crop. As in the West Indies, sugar production required heavy investment and backbreaking labor—in other words, large, well-financed plantations and small armies of slaves. But cultivation of rice, long-staple cotton, and sugar was limited to peripheral, semitropical areas. It was the rise of short-staple cotton as the South's major crop that strengthened the hold of slavery and the plantation on the southern economy.

Short-staple cotton differed from the long-staple variety in two important ways: Its bolls contained seeds that were much more difficult to extract by hand, and it could be grown almost anywhere south of Virginia and Kentucky—the main requirement was a guarantee of 200 frost-free days. Before the 1790s, the seed extraction problem had prevented short-staple cotton from becoming a major market crop. Eli Whitney's invention of the cotton gin, a machine that separates the seeds from raw cotton fibers, in 1793 resolved that difficulty, however, and the subsequent westward expansion opened vast areas for cotton cultivation. Unlike rice and sugar, cotton could be grown on small farms and plantations. But large planters enjoyed advantages that made them the main producers. Only relatively large operators could afford their own gins or possessed the capital to acquire the fertile bottomlands that brought the highest cotton yields. They also had lower transportation costs because they could monopolize land along rivers and streams that were the South's natural transportation arteries.

The first major cotton-producing regions were inland areas of Georgia and South Carolina, but the center of production shifted rapidly west. By the 1830s,

View the **Image**
Cotton Gin on a Plantation in Louisiana on
myhistorylab.com

TABLE 11.1   U.S. Slave Population, 1820 and 1860

	1820	1860
United States	1,538,125	3,953,760
North	19,108	64
South	1,519,017	3,953,696
Upper South	965,514	1,530,229
Delaware	4,509	1,798
Kentucky	127,732	225,483
Maryland	107,397	87,189
Missouri	10,222	114,931
North Carolina	205,017	331,059
Tennessee	80,107	275,719
Virginia	425,153	490,865
Washington, D.C.	6,377	3,185
Lower South	553,503	2,423,467
Alabama	41,879	435,080
Arkansas	1,617	111,115
Florida	*	61,745
Georgia	149,654	462,198
Louisiana	69,064	331,726
Mississippi	32,814	436,631
South Carolina	258,475	402,406
Texas	*	182,566

*Florida and Texas were not states in 1820.
Figure originally appeared in SLAVES WITHOUT MASTERS: THE FREE NEGRO IN THE ANTEBELLUM SOUTH
Copyright (c) 1974, 2007 by Ira Berlin. Reprinted by permission of The New Press. www.thenewpress.com.

Alabama and Mississippi had surpassed Georgia and South Carolina as cotton-growing states. By the 1850s, Arkansas, northwest Louisiana, and east Texas were the most prosperous and growing plantation regions. The rise in production that accompanied this expansion was phenomenal. Between 1792 and 1817, the South's output of cotton rose from about 13,000 bales to 461,000; by 1840, it was 1.35

million. In 1860, it peaked at a colossal 4.8 million bales. (Each bale weighed 480 pounds.) Most of the cotton was exported to the booming British textile industry. (See Figure 11.1.)

But the rise of the Cotton Kingdom did not bring uniform or steady prosperity to the lower South. Many planters worked the land until it was exhausted and then took their slaves west to richer soils, leaving depressed and ravaged areas behind them. Fluctuations in markets and prices also ruined planters. Depressions, including a wave of bankruptcies, followed boom periods. But during the rising output and high prices of the 1850s, the planters began to imagine they were immune to economic disasters.

Despite the insecurities, cotton production represented the Old South's best chance for profitable investment. Hence planters had little incentive to seek alternatives to slavery, the plantation, and dependence on a single cash crop. Slavery was an

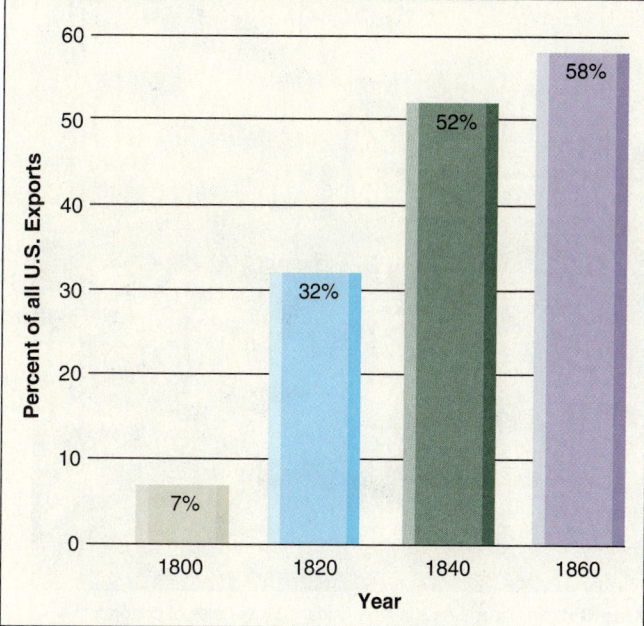

Cotton as a Percentage of All U.S. Exports, 1800–1860
Hine, Darlene, Clark, Hine, William, C., Harrold, Stanley, C. AFRICAN-AMERICAN ODYSSEY: THE COMBINED VOLUME, 4/E (c) 2008 Printed and Electronically reproduced by permission of Pearson Education, Inc., Upper Saddle River, New Jersey.

economically sound institution in 1860 and showed no signs of imminent decline. In the 1850s, planters could normally expect an annual return of 8 to 10 percent on capital invested. This was roughly equivalent to what could be obtained from the most lucrative sectors of northern industry and commerce.

Yet just because the system made slaveholders wealthy does not mean that the benefits trickled down to the rest of the population—to the majority of whites who owned no slaves and to the slaves themselves—nor that it promoted efficiency and progressive change. Large plantation owners were the only segment of the population to enjoy the full benefits of the slave economy. Small slaveholders and non-slaveholders shared only to a limited extent in the bonanza profits of the cotton economy. The South's economic development was skewed in favor of a single route to wealth, open only to the minority with white skin and access to capital. Concentrating capital and business energies on cotton production foreclosed the diversified industrial and commercial growth that would have provided wider opportunities. Thus, compared to the industrializing North, the South was an underdeveloped region in which much of the population had little incentive to work hard.

Quick Check

✓ Why was the cotton gin so useful, and what effect did it have on southern agriculture?

CONCLUSION: WORLDS IN CONFLICT

If slaves lived in a distinct world of their own, so did planters, less affluent whites, and free blacks. The Old South was a divided society. The observations of northern traveler Frederick Law Olmsted in the 1850s bear this out. On a great plantation, he watched the

King Cotton Steamboats in New Orleans await bales of cotton for shipment. By 1860 production of "King Cotton" in the South peaked at 4.8 million bales.

slaves stop working when the overseer turned away; on a small farm, he saw a slave and his owner working in the fields together. Olmsted heard non-slaveholding whites damn the planters as "cotton snobs" but also call blacks "niggars" and express fear of interracial marriages if slaves were freed. He received hospitality from poor whites living in crowded one-room cabins and from wealthy planters in pillared mansions; life in the backcountry was radically different from that in the plantation belts.

The South was a kaleidoscope of groups divided by class, race, culture, and geography. What held it together and provided some unity were a booming plantation economy and a web of customary relationships and loyalties that could obscure the underlying cleavages and antagonisms. The fractured and fragile nature of this society would soon become apparent under the pressures of civil war.

11 STUDY RESOURCES

((•— **Listen** to the **Chapter Audio** for Chapter 11 on **myhistorylab.com**

TIMELINE

CHAPTER REVIEW

THE WORLD OF SOUTHERN BLACKS

What factors made living conditions for southern blacks more or less difficult?

Living conditions were difficult because slaves performed many types of labor. Some worked from sunup to sundown in gangs; others maintained more work control through the "task system"; urban slaves and free blacks had more autonomy. Family and community helped ease slave life, while some slaves resisted oppression by running away, sabotage, and even armed rebellion. *(p. 270)*

WHITE SOCIETY IN THE ANTEBELLUM SOUTH

What were the divisions and unities in white southern society?

While great planters were a tiny minority of the population, they set the tone for white southern society, propagating the ideology of "paternalism," that slaves were children who required a stern but loving parent. Most whites owned few or no slaves, but a political system of "white man's democracy" and the ideology of white supremacy united them with large slaveholders. *(p. 276)*

SLAVERY AND THE SOUTHERN ECONOMY

How was slavery related to economic success in the South?

Slavery dominated the economy of the South: Tobacco gave way to the internal slave trade as the biggest business in the upper South, while the cotton gin made large-scale staple agriculture a booming economic machine in the Deep South, fueling the growth of a world textile industry and enriching the planter class. *(p. 284)*

KEY TERM QUESTIONS

1. Why did the Vesey conspiracy fail? (p. 274)

2. Who operated the Underground Railroad? (p. 274)

3. What was the yeoman's attitude toward slavery? (p. 280)

4. Why did the American Colonization Society transport so few slaves to Africa? (p. 282)

5. Why did the cotton gin transform southern agriculture? (p. 285)

MyHistoryLab Connections

Visit **www.myhistorylab.com** for a customized Study Plan to build your knowledge of *Slaves and Masters.*

Question for Analysis

1. What caused Nat Turner to lead the slave revolt?

   Read the **Document** *Confessions of Nat Turner* p. 270

2. What impact did large concentrations of slaves have on white Southerners?

   View the **Map** *Slavery in the South* p. 271

3. What was the Underground Railroad?

   Watch the **Video** *Underground Railroad* p. 274

4. What factors might have influenced George Fitzhugh's position on slavery?

   Read the **Document** *George Fitzhugh, The Blessings of Slavery* p. 283

5. How did the economy of the internal slave trade contribute to the Civil War?

   View the **Closer Look** *Slave Auction in Richmond, Virginia* p. 285

Other Resources from this Chapter

View the **Image** *Slave Quarters, Hermitage Plantation*

Read the **Document** *Poem, The Slave Auction*

View the **Image** *Slave Dealers*

Read the **Document** *Runaway Slave Advertisements*

Watch the **Video** *Moonlight and Magnolias*

Read the **Document** *Hinton Helper, A White Southerner Speaks*

View the **Image** *Cotton Gin on a Plantation in Louisiana*

12

The Pursuit of Perfection

1800–1861

Contents and Spotlight Questions

((•—[**Listen** to the **Chapter Audio** for Chapter 12 on **myhistorylab.com**

REDEEMING THE MIDDLE CLASS

In the winter of 1830–1831, a wave of religious revivals swept the northern states. The most dramatic and successful took place in Rochester, New York. For six months, Presbyterian evangelist Charles G. Finney preached almost daily, emphasizing that every man and woman had the power to choose Christ and a godly life.

Finney broke with his church's traditional belief that God's inscrutable will decided who would be saved when he preached that "sinners ought to be made to feel that they have something to do, and that something is to repent. That is something that no other being can do for them, neither God nor man, and something they can do and do now." Finney converted hundreds, and church membership doubled during his stay. The awakened Christians of Rochester were urged to convert relatives, neighbors, and employees. If enough people enlisted in the evangelical crusade, Finney proclaimed, the millennium would be achieved within months.

Finney's call for religious and moral renewal fell on fertile ground in Rochester. The bustling boomtown on the Erie Canal was suffering from

Revival Meeting, **1850** Christians respond emotionally at an open-air revival meeting. Oil on panel by Jeremiah Paul, c1850. The Granger Collection, NYC.

growing pains and tensions arising from rapid economic development. Leading families were divided into quarreling factions. Workers were threatening to break free from the control their employers had exerted over their lives. Most of the early converts were from the middle class. Businessmen who had been heavy drinkers and irregular churchgoers now abstained from alcohol and went to church at least twice a week. They pressured the employees in their workshops, mills, and stores to do likewise. More rigorous standards of proper behavior and religious conformity unified Rochester's elite and increased its ability to control the rest of the community. As in other cities the revival swept, evangelical Protestantism gave the middle class a stronger sense of identity and purpose.

But the war on sin was not always so unifying. Among those converted in Rochester and elsewhere were some who could not rest easy until the whole nation conformed to the pure Christianity of Christ's Sermon on the Mount. Finney expressed such a hope himself, but he concentrated on individual religious conversion and moral uplift, trusting that the purification of American society and politics would automatically follow. Other religious and moral reformers, however, were inspired to crusade against those social and political institutions that failed to achieve Christian perfection. These reformers attacked such collective "sins" as whiskey, war, slavery, and even government.

Religiously inspired reformism cut two ways. On the one hand, it imposed a new order and cultural unity on divided and troubled communities like Rochester. But it also inspired more radical movements or experiments that threatened to undermine established institutions that failed to live up to the more idealistic reformers' principles. One of these movements—abolitionism—challenged the central social and economic institution of the southern states and helped trigger political upheaval and civil war.

THE RISE OF EVANGELICALISM

How did the evangelical revivalism of the early nineteenth century spur reform movements?

American Protestantism was in ferment during the early nineteenth century. Denominations turned to revivalism to strengthen religious values and increase church membership. Mobilization of the faithful into associations to spread the gospel and reform American morals often followed spiritual renewals.

The Second Great Awakening

The Second Great Awakening, a wave of religious revivals, began in earnest on the southern frontier around 1800. In 1801, nearly 50,000 people gathered at Cane Ridge, Kentucky. According to a contemporary observer:

The noise was like the roar of Niagara. The vast sea of human beings seemed to be agitated as if by a storm. I counted seven ministers all preaching at once… . Some of the people were singing, others praying, some crying for mercy … while others were shouting most vociferously…. At one time I saw at least five hundred swept down in a moment, as if a battery of a thousand guns had been opened upon them, and then followed immediately shrieks and shouts that rent the heavens.

Emotional camp meetings, spontaneous religious gatherings organized usually by Methodists or Baptists but sometimes by Presbyterians, became a regular feature of religious life in the South and lower Midwest. On the frontier, the camp meeting met social and religious needs. In the sparsely settled southern backcountry, it was difficult to sustain local churches with regular ministers. Methodists sent out circuit riders. Baptists licensed uneducated farmers to preach to their neighbors. But for many people, the only way to get baptized or married or to have a communal religious experience was to attend a camp meeting.

Read the
Document
Reverand Peter Cartwright, Cane Ridge on
myhistorylab.com

In the South, Baptists and Presbyterians eventually deemphasized camp meetings in favor of "protracted meetings" in local churches that featured guest preachers holding forth day after day for up to two weeks. Southern evangelical churches, especially Baptist and Methodist, grew rapidly in membership and influence during the first half of the nineteenth century and became the focus of rural life. Although they fostered societies to improve morals—to encourage temperance and discourage dueling, for example—they generally shied away from social reform. The conservatism of a slaveholding society discouraged radical efforts to change the world.

Reformist tendencies were more evident in the distinctive revivalism that originated in New England and western New York. Northern evangelists were mostly Congregationalists and Presbyterians, influenced by New England Puritan traditions. Their greatest successes were not in rural or frontier areas but in small- to medium-sized towns and cities. Their revivals could be stirring affairs but were less extravagantly emotional than the camp meetings of the South. The northern brand of evangelism led to the formation of societies devoted to redeeming the human race in general and American society in particular.

The reform movement in New England began as an effort to defend Calvinism against the liberal views of religion fostered by the Enlightenment. The younger generation's growing acceptance of the belief that the Deity was the benevolent master architect of a rational universe, rather than an all-powerful, mysterious God, alarmed the Reverend Timothy Dwight, who became president of Yale College in 1795. Those religious liberals whose rationalism reached the point of denying the divinity of Jesus and the doctrine of the Trinity, and who therefore proclaimed themselves to be "Unitarians," particularly disturbed him.

To Dwight's horror, Unitarians captured fashionable and sophisticated New England congregations and even won control of the Harvard Divinity School. He fought back by preaching to Yale undergraduates that they were "dead in sin" and provoked campus revivals. But the harsh pessimism of orthodox Calvinist doctrine, with its stress on original sin and predestination, had limited appeal in a republic committed to freedom and progress.

Younger Congregational ministers reshaped New England Puritanism to increase its appeal to people who shared the prevailing optimism about human capabilities. The first great practitioner of the new evangelical Calvinism was Lyman Beecher, one of Dwight's pupils. Just before and after the War of 1812, Beecher promoted revivals in the Congregational churches of New England. He induced thousands—in his home church in Litchfield, Connecticut, and in other churches that offered him their pulpits—to acknowledge their sinfulness and surrender to God.

During the late 1820s, Beecher was forced to confront the new and more radical form of revivalism Charles G. Finney was practicing in western New York. Upstate New York was a hotbed of religious enthusiasms. Most its population consisted of transplanted New Englanders who had left behind their close-knit villages and ancestral churches but not their Puritan consciences. Troubled by rapid economic changes and the social dislocations that went with them, they were ripe for a new faith and fresh moral direction.

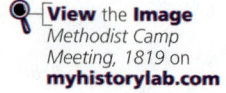
View the **Image**
*Methodist Camp
Meeting, 1819* on
myhistorylab.com

Although he worked within Congregational and Presbyterian churches (which were cooperating under a plan of union established in 1804), Finney was relatively indifferent to theological issues. His appeal was to emotion or the heart rather than to doctrine or reason. He wanted converts to feel the power of Christ and become new men and women. He eventually adopted the extreme view that redeemed Christians could be free of sin—as perfect as their Father in Heaven. This **perfectionism** led many evangelicals into moral reform movements.

Beginning in 1823, Finney conducted successful revivals in towns and cities of western New York, culminating in his triumph in Rochester in 1830–1831. Even more controversial than his freewheeling approach to theology was how he won converts. Finney sought instantaneous conversions. He held meetings that lasted all night or for days in a row, placing an "anxious bench" in front of the congregation where those who were repenting could receive special attention, and encouraged women to pray publicly for male relatives.

Finney's new methods and the emotionalism that accompanied them disturbed Beecher and eastern evangelicals. Finney also violated Christian tradition by allowing women to pray aloud in church. An evangelical summit meeting between Beecher and Finney, in New Lebanon, New York, in 1827, failed to resolve these and other issues. Beecher threatened to stand on the state line if Finney tried to bring his crusade to Connecticut. But it soon became clear that Finney was not merely stirring people up; he was leaving strong, active churches behind him. Opposition weakened. Finney eventually founded a tabernacle in New York City that became a rallying point for evangelical efforts to reach the urban masses.

Quick Check

✓ What made Revivalism such an effective means to win converts to religion?

From Revivalism to Reform

The northern wing of the Second Great Awakening, unlike the southern, inspired a great movement for social reform. Converts were organized into voluntary associations that sought to stamp out sin and social evil and win the world for Christ. Most of the converts of northern revivalism were middle-class citizens already active in their communities. They were seeking to adjust to the bustling world of the market revolution in ways that would not violate their traditional moral and social values. Their generally optimistic and forward-looking attitudes led to hopes that a wave of conversions would save the nation and the world.

In New England, Beecher and his evangelical associates established a network of missionary and benevolent societies. In 1810, Presbyterians and Congregationalists founded a Board of Commissioners for Foreign Missions and soon sent two missionaries to India. In 1816, the Reverend Samuel John Mills organized the American Bible Society. By 1821, it had distributed 140,000 Bibles, mostly in the West where churches and clergymen were scarce.

Another major effort went into publishing and distributing religious tracts, mainly by the American Tract Society, founded in 1825. Special societies targeted groups beyond the reach of regular churches, such as seamen, Native Americans, and the urban poor. In 1816–1817, middle-class women in New York, Philadelphia, Charleston, and Boston formed societies to spread the gospel in lower-class wards—where, as one of their missionaries put it, there was "a great mass of people beyond the restraints of religion."

Evangelicals also founded moral reform societies. Some of these aimed at curbing irreligious activity on the Sabbath; others sought to stamp out dueling, gambling, and prostitution. In New York in 1831, a zealous young clergyman claimed there were 10,000 prostitutes in the city laying their snares for innocent young men. As a result of this expose, an asylum was established to redeem "abandoned women." Middle-class women shifted the focus of this crusade to the men who patronized prostitutes and proposed that observers record and publish the names of men seen entering brothels. The plan was abandoned because it offended those who thought that suppressing public discussion and investigation of sexual vices would better serve the cause of virtue.

Beecher was especially influential in the **temperance movement**, the most successful reform crusade; his sermons against drink were the most important and widely distributed of the early tracts calling for total abstinence from "demon rum." The temperance movement was directed at a real social evil. Since the Revolution, whiskey had become the most popular American beverage. Made from corn by farmers or, by the 1820s, in commercial distilleries, it was cheaper than milk or beer and safer than water (which was often contaminated). In some areas, rum and brandy were also popular. Hard liquor was frequently consumed with food as a table beverage, even at breakfast, and children sometimes imbibed along with adults. Per capita annual consumption of distilled beverages in the 1820s was almost triple what it is today, and alcoholism had reached epidemic proportions.

The temperance reformers viewed drinking as a threat to public morality. Drunkenness was seen as a loss of self-control and moral responsibility that spawned crime, vice, and disorder. Above all, it threatened the family. Drinking was mainly a male vice, and the main target of temperance propaganda was the husband and father who abused, neglected, or abandoned his wife and children because he

THE DRUNKARD'S PROGRESS.

Temperance Propaganda warned that the drinker who began with "a glass with a friend" would inevitably follow the direct path to poverty, despair, and death. (*Source: "The Drunkard's Progress," Fruitlands Museum, Harvard, Massachusetts.*)

Read the **Document**
Lyman Beecher, "Six Sermons on Intemperance" (1828) on **myhistorylab.com**

View the **Image**
Temperance Pledge on **myhistorylab.com**

Quick Check

✓ What was the temperance movement, and why did it attract so many followers in this period?

was a slave to the bottle. Women played a vital role in the movement and in making it a crusade for protecting the home. The drinking habits of the poor or laboring classes also aroused concern. Particularly in urban areas, "respectable" and propertied people lived in fear that drunken mobs would attack private property and create chaos.

Many evangelical reformers regarded intemperance as the greatest obstacle to a republic of God-fearing, self-disciplined citizens. In 1826, clergymen active in mission work organized the American Temperance Society to coordinate and extend the work local churches and moral reform societies had begun. The original aim was to encourage abstinence from "ardent spirits" or hard liquor; there was no agreement on the evils of beer and wine. The society sent out lecturers, issued a flood of literature, and sponsored essay contests. Its agents organized revival meetings and called on attendees to pledge to abstain from spirits. The campaign was effective. By 1834, its 5,000 local branches had more than a million members, many of them women.

Some workingmen defiantly insisted on their right to drink, and built their own autonomous social life in grog halls and taverns, with heavy drinking an important part of it. But others joined temperance societies of their own. The Washingtonian Society, born in 1840, sought out the confirmed drunkard and offered him salvation. The Washingtonians held weekly experience meetings to testify to their own struggles with "Demon Drink" and tried to recreate the enjoyable community aspects of tavern life with temperance songs, poems, and theatre. Washingtonian Societies spread like wildfire among young men, women, and children, including African Americans.

Although it may be doubted whether many confirmed drunkards were cured, the movement did alter the drinking habits of middle-class American males by making temperance a mark of respectability. Per capita consumption of hard liquor declined more than 50 percent during the 1830s, and by 1850 it was down to one-third of what it had been in 1830.

Cooperating missionary and reform societies—collectively known as the "benevolent empire"—were a major force in American culture by the early 1830s. Efforts to modify American attitudes and institutions seemed to be bearing fruit. The middle class was embracing self-control and self-discipline, equipping individuals to confront a new world of economic growth and social mobility without losing their cultural and moral bearings.

DOMESTICITY AND CHANGES IN THE AMERICAN FAMILY

The evangelical culture of the 1820s and 1830s influenced the family as an institution and inspired new conceptions of its role in American society. Women—regarded as particularly susceptible to religious and moral influences—were increasingly confined to the domestic circle, but they became more important within it. Many parents viewed rearing children as essential preparation for a self-disciplined Christian life, and they did it with serious self-consciousness.

What was the doctrine of "separate spheres," and how did it change family life?

The Cult of Domesticity

The notion that women belonged in the home while the public sphere belonged to men has been called the ideology of "separate spheres." In particular, the view that women had a special role to play in the domestic sphere as guardians of virtue and spiritual heads of the home has been described as the **Cult of Domesticity**, or the "Cult of True Womanhood." For most men, a woman's place was in the home and on a pedestal. The ideal wife and mother was "an angel in the house," a model of piety and virtue who exerted a wholesome moral and religious influence over men and children. An 1846 poem expressed a masculine view of the true woman:

View the **Image**
Marriage Certificate, 1848 on
myhistorylab.com

Read the **Document**
Matthew Carey, Rules for Husbands and Wives on
myhistorylab.com

> I would have her as pure as the snow on the mount—
>
> As true as the smile that to infancy's given—
>
> As pure as the wave of the crystalline fount,
>
> Yet as warm in the heart as the sunlight of heaven.

The sociological reality behind the Cult of True Womanhood was a growing division between the working lives of middle-class men and women. In the eighteenth century and earlier, most economic activity had been centered in and near the home, and husbands and wives often worked together in a common enterprise. By the mid-nineteenth century, however, this way of life was declining, especially in the Northeast. In towns and cities, factories and counting-houses severed the home from the workplace. Men went forth every morning to their places of labor, leaving their wives at home to tend the house and the children. Married women were increasingly deprived of a productive economic role. The cult of domesticity made a virtue of the fact that men were solely responsible for running the world and building the economy.

A new conception of gender roles justified and glorified this pattern. The doctrine of "separate spheres"—set forth in novels, advice literature, and the new women's magazines—sentimentalized the woman who kept a spotless house, nurtured her children, and offered her husband a refuge from the heartless world of commerce and industry. From a modern point of view, it is easy to condemn the Cult of Domesticity as a rationalization for male dominance, and it largely was. Yet confinement to the home did not necessarily imply that women were inferior. By the standards of evangelical culture, women in the domestic sphere could be viewed as superior to men, since women could cultivate the "feminine" virtues of love and self-sacrifice and thus act as official guardians of religious and moral values.

Furthermore, many women used domestic ideology to fashion a role for themselves in the public sphere. The evangelical movement encouraged women's roles as the keepers of moral virtue. The revivals not only gave women a role in converting men but endowed Christ with stereotypical feminine characteristics. A nurturing, loving, merciful savior, mediating between a stern father and his erring children, provided the model for woman's new role as spiritual head of the home. Membership in evangelical church associations prepared women for new roles as civilizers of men and guardians of domestic culture and morality. Female reform societies taught women the strict ethical code they were to instill in other family members; mothers' groups showed them how to build character and encourage piety in children.

View the **Image**
Woman's Sphere on
myhistorylab.com

While many working-class women aspired to the ideal of True Womanhood, domestic ideology only affected the daily lives of relatively affluent women. Working-class wives were not usually employed outside the home during this period, but they labored long and hard within it. Besides cleaning, cooking, and taking care of many children, they often took in washing or piecework to supplement a meager family income. Their endless domestic drudgery made a sham of the notion that women had the time and energy for the "higher things of life." Life was especially hard for African American women. Most of those who were "free Negroes" rather than slaves did not have husbands who made enough to support them. They had to serve in white households or work at home doing other people's washing and sewing.

In urban areas, unmarried working-class women often lived on their own and toiled as household servants, in the sweatshops of the garment industry, and in factories. Barely able to support themselves and at the mercy of male sexual predators, they were in no position to identify with the middle-class ideal of elevated, protected womanhood. For some, the relatively well-paid and gregarious life of the successful prostitute seemed an attractive alternative to loneliness and privation.

For middle-class women whose husbands or fathers earned a good income, freedom from industrial or farm labor offered tangible benefits. They had the leisure to read the new literature directed primarily at housewives, participate in female-dominated charities, and cultivate deep friendships with other women. The result was a feminine subculture emphasizing "sisterhood" or "sorority." This growing sense of solidarity with other women and of the importance of sexual identity could transcend the private home and even the barriers of social class. Beginning in the 1820s, urban middle- and upper-class women organized societies for the relief and rehabilitation of poor or "fallen" women. Their aim was not economic and political equality with men but the elevation of all women to true womanhood.

For some women, the domestic ideal even sanctioned efforts to extend their sphere until it conquered the masculine world outside the home. This domestic feminism was reflected in crusades to stamp out such masculine sins as intemperance, gambling, and sexual vice.

In the benevolent societies and reform movements of the Jacksonian era, especially those designated as women's organizations, women handled money, organized meetings and public appeals, made contracts, and even gave orders to male subordinates. The desire to extend the feminine sphere motivated Catharine Beecher's campaign to make school teaching a woman's occupation. A prolific and influential writer on the theory and practice of domesticity, this unmarried daughter of Lyman Beecher saw the spinster-teacher as equivalent to a mother. By instilling in young males the virtues that only women could teach, the schoolmarm could help liberate America from corruption and materialism.

But the main focus of Beecher and other domestic feminists remained the role of married women who stayed home and did their part simply by being wives and mothers. Reforming husbands was difficult: They were away much of the time and tended to be preoccupied with business. But this very fact gave women primary responsibility for rearing children—to which nineteenth-century Americans attached almost cosmic significance. Since women were considered particularly well qualified to transmit piety and morality to future citizens of the republic, the Cult of Domesticity exalted motherhood and encouraged a new concern with childhood as the time when "character" was formed.

Quick Check

✓ What was the doctrine of "separate spheres," and How did women extend the reach of the domestic sphere to encompass activities of public concern?

The Discovery of Childhood

The nineteenth century has been called "the century of the child." More than ever, childhood was seen as a distinct stage of life requiring the special and sustained attention of adults at least until the age of 13 or 14. The middle-class family now became "child-centered": The care, nurture, and rearing of children was viewed as the family's main function. Earlier, adults had treated children more casually, often sending them away from home for education or for apprenticeship at a young age. Among the well-to-do, children spent more time with servants or tutors than with their parents.

By the early nineteenth century, however, children were staying at home longer and receiving more attention from parents, especially mothers. The colonial custom of naming a child after a sibling who had died in infancy became much less common. Each child was now seen as a unique, irreplaceable individual.

New customs and fashions heralded the "discovery" of childhood. Books were published specifically for juveniles. Parents became more self-conscious about their responsibilities and sought help from experts on child rearing.

The new concern for children resulted in more intimate relations between parents and children. In advice manuals and sentimental literature, affection, not authority, bound the ideal family together. Discipline remained at the core of "family government," but the preferred method of enforcing good behavior changed. Shaming or withholding affection partially displaced corporal punishment. Disobedient middle-class children were now more likely to be confined to their rooms to reflect on their sins than to receive a thrashing. Discipline could no longer be justified as the constant application of physical force over naturally wayward beings. In an age of moral perfectionism, the role of discipline was to induce repentance and change basic attitudes. The goal was often described as "self-government"; to achieve it, parents used guilt, rather than fear, as their main source of leverage. A mother's sorrow or a father's stern silence was deemed more effective in forming character than blows or angry words.

Shared realities of childhood cut across class and ethnic lines. For example, mortality for infants and young children was high throughout the nineteenth century. Even wealthy families could expect to lose one child out of five or six before age five. But class and region made a big difference in children's lives. Farm children tended livestock, milked cows, churned butter, scrubbed laundry, harvested crops, and hauled water; working-class urban children did "outwork" in textiles, worked in street markets, and scavenged.

One important explanation for the growing focus on childhood is the smaller size of families. If nineteenth-century families had remained as large as those of earlier times, parents could not have lavished so much care and attention on individual offspring. For reasons not completely understood, the average number of children born to each woman during her fertile years dropped from 7.04 in 1800 to 5.42 in 1850. As a result, the average number of children per family declined about 25 percent, beginning a trend lasting to the present day.

Birth control contributed to this demographic revolution. Ancestors of the modern condom and diaphragm were openly advertised and sold during the pre–Civil War period, but most couples probably controlled family size by practicing the withdrawal method or having intercourse less often. Abortion was also common and on the rise. By 1850, there may have been one abortion for every five or six live births.

Parents seemed to understand that having fewer children meant they could provide their offspring with a better start in life. This was appropriate in a society that was shifting from agriculture to commerce and industry. For rural households short of labor, large families were an economic asset. For urban couples who hoped to send their children into a competitive world that demanded special talents and training, large families were a financial liability.

Quick Check

✓ How did notions of childhood change during the nineteenth century, and what difference did that make for family life?

The Extension of Education

Another change affecting children was the growing belief that the family could not carry the whole burden of socializing and reforming individuals, *and* that children needed schooling as well as parental nurturing. To extend the advantages of "family government" beyond the domestic circle, reformers established or improved public institutions that were designed to shape character and instill self-discipline. Between 1820 and 1850, the number of free public schools grew enormously. The new resolve to put more children in school for longer periods reflected many of the same values that exalted the child-centered family. Up to a certain age, children could be effectively nurtured and educated in the home. But after that they needed formal training at a character-molding institution that would prepare them to make a living and bear the burdens of republican citizenship. Intellectual training at school was regarded as less important than moral indoctrination.

Sometimes the school was a substitute for the family, since many children were thought to lack a proper home environment. The masses of poor and immigrant children who allegedly failed to get proper nurturing at home alarmed educational reformers. Schools had to make up for this disadvantage. Otherwise, people "incapable of self-government" would endanger the republic.

Before the 1820s, schooling in the United States was a haphazard affair. The wealthy sent their children to private schools, while some of the poor sent their children to charity or "pauper" schools that local governments financed. Public education was most highly developed in New England, where towns were required by law to support elementary schools. It was weakest in the South, where almost all education was private.

Demand for more public education began in the 1820s and early 1830s as a central focus of the workingmen's movements in eastern cities. These hard-pressed artisans viewed free schools open to all as a way to counter the growing gap between rich and poor. Affluent taxpayers, who did not see why they should pay to educate other people's children, opposed the demands. But middle-class reformers seized the initiative, shaped educational reform to fit their own end of social discipline, and provided the momentum for legislative success.

The most influential supporter of the common school movement was Horace Mann of Massachusetts. As a lawyer and state legislator, Mann worked tirelessly to establish a state board of education and tax support for local schools. In 1837, he persuaded the legislature to enact his proposals and subsequently became the first secretary of the new board, an office he held with distinction until 1848. He believed teachers and school officials could mold children like clay to a state of perfection. Like advocates of child rearing through moral influence rather than physical force, he discouraged corporal punishment except as a last resort. His position on this issue led to a bitter controversy with Boston schoolmasters who retained a Calvinist sense of original sin and favored a freer use of the rod.

Against those who argued that school taxes violated property rights, Mann contended that private property was actually held in trust for the good of the community: "The property of this commonwealth is pledged for the education of all its youth up to such a point as will save them from poverty and vice, and prepare them for the adequate performance of their social and civil duties." Mann's conception of public education as a means of social discipline converted the middle and upper classes to the cause. By teaching middle-class morality and respect for order, the schools could turn potential rowdies and

Watch the **Video**
Who was Horace Mann and Why are so many schools Named after him? on
myhistorylab.com

Read the **Document**
Horace Mann, Report of the Massachusetts Board of Education on
myhistorylab.com

revolutionaries into law-abiding citizens. Schools could also encourage social mobility by opening doors for lower-class children who were determined to do better than their parents.

In practice, new or improved public schools often alienated working-class pupils and their families rather than reforming them. Compulsory attendance laws deprived poor families of needed wage earners without guaranteeing jobs for those with an elementary education. As the laboring class became increasingly immigrant and Catholic in the 1840s and 1850s, dissatisfaction arose over the evangelical Protestant tone of "moral instruction" in the schools. Mann and his disciples were deliberately trying to impose a uniform culture on people who valued differing traditions.

In addition to the "three Rs" ("reading, 'riting, and 'rithmetic"), mid-nineteenth-century public schools taught the "Protestant ethic"—industry, punctuality, sobriety, and frugality. These were the virtues the famous *McGuffey's Eclectic Readers*, which first appeared in 1836, stressed. Millions of children learned to read by digesting McGuffey's parables about the terrible fate of those who gave in to sloth, drunkenness, or wastefulness. Such moral indoctrination helped produce generations of Americans with personalities and beliefs adapted to the needs of an industrializing society—people who could be depended on to adjust to the precise and regular routines of the factory or the office. But as an education for self-government—in the sense of learning to think for oneself—it left much to be desired.

Fortunately, however, education was neither limited to the schools nor devoted solely to children. Every city and almost every town or village had a lyceum, a debating society, or a mechanics' institute where adults of all social classes could broaden their intellectual horizons. Lyceums featured lectures on such subjects as "self-reliance" and "the conduct of life" by creative thinkers such as Ralph Waldo Emerson; explanations and demonstrations of the latest scientific discoveries; and debates on controversial issues.

Young Abraham Lincoln, who had received less than two years of formal schooling as a child in backwoods Indiana, sharpened his intellect in the early 1830s as a member of the New Salem, Illinois, debating society. In 1838, after moving to Springfield, he set forth his political principles when he spoke at the local lyceum on "The Perpetuation of Our Political Institutions." More than the public schools, the lyceums and debating societies fostered independent thought and encouraged new ideas.

Quick Check

✓ How did Horace Mann change ideas about public schooling in America?

REFORM TURNS RADICAL

What were some of the major antebellum reform movements?

During the 1830s, dissension split the great reform movement spawned by the Second Great Awakening. Efforts to promote evangelical piety, improve personal and public morality, and shape character through familial or institutional discipline continued and even flourished. But bolder spirits set their sights on the total liberation and perfection of the individual.

The Rise of Radical Abolitionism

The new perfectionism had its most important success within the antislavery movement. Before the 1830s, most people who expressed religious and moral concern over slavery were affiliated with the American Colonization Society. Most colonizationists admitted that slavery was an evil, but they also viewed it as a deeply rooted social and economic institution that could be eliminated only gradually and with the cooperation of slaveholders. Reflecting racial prejudice, they proposed to provide transportation to Africa for free blacks who chose to go, or were emancipated for that purpose, to relieve southern fears that a race war would erupt if freed slaves remained in America. In 1821, the society established the colony of Liberia in West Africa, and in the 1830s, a few thousand African Americans were settled there.

Colonization proved to be grossly inadequate as a step toward eliminating slavery. Many of the blacks transported to Africa were already free, and those liberated by masters whom the colonization movement influenced represented only a tiny percentage of the natural increase of the southern slave population. Northern blacks denounced the enterprise because it denied the prospect of racial equality in America. Black opposition to colonizationism helped persuade William Lloyd Garrison and other white abolitionists to repudiate the Colonization Society and support immediate emancipation without emigration. Garrison launched a more radical antislavery movement in 1831 in Boston, when he began to publish a journal called *The Liberator*. Besides calling for immediate and unconditional emancipation, Garrison denounced colonization as a slaveholder's plot to remove troublesome free blacks and an ignoble surrender to un-Christian prejudices. His rhetoric was as severe as his proposals were radical. As he wrote in the first issue of *The Liberator*, "I will be as harsh as truth and as uncompromising as justice…. I am in earnest—I will not equivocate—I will not excuse—I will not retreat a single inch—And I WILL BE HEARD!" Heard he was. In 1833, Garrison and other abolitionists founded the American Anti-Slavery Society. "We shall send forth agents to lift up the voice of remonstrance, of warning, of entreaty, and of rebuke," its Declaration of Sentiments proclaimed. The colonization movement was placed on the defensive, and many of its most active northern supporters became abolitionists.

The abolitionist movement, like the temperance crusade, was a direct outgrowth of the Second Great Awakening. Leading abolitionists had undergone conversion experiences in the 1820s and were already committed to Christian activism before they dedicated themselves to freeing the slaves. Several were ministers or divinity students seeking a mission that would fulfill spiritual and professional ambitions.

Theodore Dwight Weld personified the connection between revivalism and abolitionism. Weld came from a long line of New England ministers. After dropping out of divinity school because of physical and spiritual ailments, he migrated to western New York. There he fell under the influence of Charles G. Finney and, after a long struggle, underwent a conversion experience in 1826. He then became an itinerant lecturer for reform causes. By the early 1830s, he

Read the **Document**
Abolitionist Demands Immediate End on **myhistorylab.com**

focused his attention on the moral issues raised by the institution of slavery. After a flirtation with colonization, Weld was converted to abolitionism in 1832, recognizing that colonizationists did not accept blacks as equals or "brothers-in-Christ." In 1834, he instigated what amounted to abolitionist revivals at Lane Theological Seminary in Cincinnati. When the seminary's trustees attempted to suppress discussion of immediate emancipation, Weld led most students in a walkout. The "Lane rebels" subsequently founded Oberlin College as a center for abolitionist activity.

In 1835 and 1836, Weld toured Ohio and western New York preaching abolitionism. He also supervised and trained other agents and orators to convert the region to immediate emancipation. The tried-and-true methods of the revival—fervent preaching, protracted meetings, and the call for individuals to come forth and announce their redemption—were put at the service of the antislavery movement. Weld and his associates often had to face angry mobs, but they left behind them tens of thousands of new abolitionists and hundreds of antislavery societies. Northern Ohio and western New York became hotbeds of abolitionist sentiment.

Antislavery orators and organizers tended to have their greatest successes in the small- to medium-sized towns of the upper North. The typical convert came from an upwardly mobile family engaged in small business, the skilled trades, or market farming. In larger towns and cities, or when they ventured close to the Mason–Dixon Line, abolitionists were more likely to encounter fierce and effective opposition. In 1835, Garrison was almost lynched in Boston. In New York City, the Tappan brothers—Lewis and Arthur—were frequently threatened and attacked. These two successful merchants used their wealth to finance antislavery activities. In 1835–1836, they supported a massive effort to distribute antislavery pamphlets through the U.S. mails. But most New Yorkers regarded them as dangerous radicals.

Abolitionists who thought of taking their message to the fringes of the South had reason to pause, given the fate of the antislavery editor Elijah Lovejoy. In 1837, while defending himself and his printing press from a mob in Alton, Illinois, just across the Mississippi River from slaveholding Missouri, Lovejoy was shot and killed.

Racism was a major cause of anti-abolitionist violence in the North. Rumors that abolitionists advocated or practiced interracial marriage could easily incite an urban crowd. If it could not find white abolitionists, the mob was likely to turn on local blacks. Working-class whites tended to fear that economic and social competition with blacks would increase if abolitionists freed the slaves and made them citizens. But "gentlemen of property and standing" dominated many of the mobs. Solid citizens resorted to violence, it would appear, because abolitionism threatened their conservative notions of social order and hierarchy.

By the end of the 1830s, the abolitionist movement was under stress. Besides the burden of external repression, there was internal dissension. Becoming an abolitionist required an exacting conscience and an unwillingness to compromise. These traits also made it difficult for abolitionists to work together and maintain a united front. During the late 1830s, Garrison, the most visible abolitionist, began to adopt positions that other abolitionists found extreme and divisive. He embraced the nonresistant or "no-government" philosophy of Henry C. Wright and urged abolitionists to abstain from voting or participating in a corrupt political system. He attacked the clergy and the churches for refusing to take an antislavery stand and encouraged his followers to "come out" of the established denominations rather than work within them.

These positions alienated members of the Anti-Slavery Society who hoped that abolitionists could influence or take over organized religion and the political system. But Garrison's stand on women's rights led to an open break at the national convention of the American Anti-Slavery Society in 1840. Following their leader's principle that women should be equal partners in the crusade, a Garrison-led majority elected a woman to the society's executive committee. A minority, led by Lewis Tappan, then formed a competing organization—the American and Foreign Anti-Slavery Society.

The new organization never amounted to much, but the schism weakened Garrison's influence. When he repudiated the Constitution as a proslavery document and called for northern secession from the Union, few antislavery people in the Middle Atlantic or Midwestern states went along. Outside New England, most abolitionists worked within the churches and avoided controversial side issues such as women's rights and nonresistant pacifism. Some antislavery advocates became political activists. The Liberty party, organized in 1840, was their first attempt to enter the electoral arena under their own banner; it signaled a new effort to turn antislavery sentiment into political power.

Quick Check

✓ Who were the leading opponents of slavery, and What different approaches did they take to politics as they put forward demands for slavery's immediate abolition?

Black Abolitionists

From the beginning the abolitionist movement depended on the northern free black community. Most of the early subscribers to Garrison's *Liberator* were African Americans. Black orators, especially escaped slaves such as Frederick Douglass, brought home the realities of bondage to northern audiences. But relations between white and black abolitionists were often tense. Blacks protested that they did not have their fair share of leadership positions or influence over policy. Eventually a black antislavery movement emerged that was largely independent of the white-led crusade. In addition to Douglass, prominent black male abolitionists were Charles Remond, William Wells Brown, Robert Purvis, and Henry Highland Garnet. Outspoken women such as Sojourner Truth, Maria Stewart, and Frances Harper also played a significant role in black antislavery activity. The Negro Convention movement, which sponsored national meetings of black leaders beginning in 1830, provided an important forum for independent black expression. Their most eloquent statement came in 1854, when black leaders met in Cleveland to declare their faith in a separate identity, proclaiming, "We pledge our integrity to use all honorable means, to unite us, as one people, on this continent."

Read the **Document**
Maria Stewart, "The Miseries We Tasted" on **myhistorylab.com**

Read the **Document**
David Walker, A Black Abolitionist Speaks Out (1829) on **myhistorylab.com**

Black newspapers, such as *Freedom's Journal*, first published in 1827, and the *North Star*, founded by Douglass in 1847, enabled black writers to preach liberation to black readers. African American authors also wrote books and pamphlets attacking slavery, refuting racism, and advocating resistance. One of the most influential publications was David Walker's *Appeal … to the Colored Citizens of the World*, which appeared in 1829. Walker denounced slavery in the most vigorous language and called for a black revolt against white tyranny.

Free blacks in the North were also the main conductors on the fabled Underground Railroad, which opened a path for fugitives from slavery. Ex-slaves such as Harriet Tubman and Josiah Henson made regular forays into the slave states to lead other blacks to freedom, and free blacks ran many of the "stations" along the way. In northern towns and cities, free blacks organized "vigilance committees" to protect fugitives and thwart the slave-catchers. Blacks even used force to rescue recaptured fugitives from the authorities. In Boston in 1851, one such group seized a slave named Shadrack from a U.S. marshal who was returning him to bondage. In deeds and words, free blacks showed unyielding hostility to slavery and racism.

Historians have debated whether the abolitionist movement of the 1830s and early 1840s was a failure. It failed to convince most Americans that slavery was a sinful institution that should be abolished immediately. This position, which implied that blacks should be granted equality as American citizens, ran up against a commitment to white supremacy in all parts of the country. In the South, abolitionism helped inspire a more militant defense of slavery. The belief that peaceful agitation, or what abolitionists called "moral suasion," would convert slaveholders and their northern sympathizers to abolition was unrealistic.

But in another sense the crusade was successful. It made the public conscious of the slavery issue and convinced many northerners that the South's peculiar institution was morally wrong and dangerous to the American way of life. The South helped the antislavery cause in the North by responding hysterically and repressively to abolitionist agitation. In 1836, southern congressmen forced adoption of a "gag rule" requiring that abolitionist petitions be tabled without being read; the post office

Abolitionist Frederick Douglass, who escaped from slavery in 1838, became one of the most effective voices in the crusade against slavery.

Freedom Calling Harriet Tubman, far left, is shown here with some of the slaves she helped escape on the Underground Railroad. Born a slave in Maryland, she escaped to Philadelphia in 1849. She is said to have helped 300 African Americans flee slavery. She led many of them all the way to Canada, where they would be beyond the reach of the Fugitive Slave Law. (*Source: Smith College, Sophia Smith Collection, Northampton, Massachusetts.*)

refused to deliver antislavery literature in the slave states. Prominent northerners who had been unmoved by abolitionist depictions of slave suffering became more responsive when their own civil liberties were threatened. The politicians who later mobilized the North against the expansion of slavery into the territories drew strength from the antislavery and anti-southern sentiments that abolitionists had already called forth.

Quick Check

✓ What was the Underground Railroad, and who were its main operators?

From Abolitionism to Women's Rights

Abolitionism also was a catalyst for the women's rights movement. From the beginning, women participated actively in the abolitionist crusade. Between 1835 and 1838, the American Anti-Slavery Society bombarded Congress with petitions, mostly calling for abolition of slavery in the District of Columbia. More than half of the thousands of these petitions included women's signatures.

Some antislavery women defied conventional ideas of their proper sphere by becoming public speakers and demanding an equal role in the leadership of antislavery societies. The most famous of these were the Grimké sisters, Sarah and Angelina, who attracted enormous attention as the rebellious daughters of a South Carolina slaveholder. When male abolitionists objected to their speaking in public to mixed audiences of men and women, Garrison defended them and helped forge a link between blacks' and women's struggles for equality.

A Mother's Movement Elizabeth Cady Stanton, a leader of the women's rights movement, reared seven children. In addition to her pioneering work, especially for woman suffrage, she also lectured on family life and child care.

⊙ **Watch** the **Video**
The Women's Rights Movement in the nineteenth Century on
myhistorylab.com

Quick Check

✓ What goals did The Seneca Falls Convention seek to accomplish?

The battle to participate equally in the antislavery crusade made women abolitionists acutely aware of male dominance and oppression. For them, the same principles that justified the liberation of the slaves also applied to emancipating women from restrictions on their rights as citizens. In 1840, Garrison's American followers withdrew from the first World's Anti-Slavery Convention in London because the sponsors refused to seat the women in their delegation. Among the women excluded were Lucretia Mott and Elizabeth Cady Stanton.

Wounded by men's reluctance to extend the cause of emancipation to include women, Stanton and Mott began discussing plans for a women's rights convention. They returned to New York, where a campaign was already under way to reform the state's laws limiting the rights of married women. Ernestine Rose, a young Jewish activist, and Judge Thomas Herttell, a political radical and freethinker who had introduced the first bill to reform the state's marriage laws to the New York legislature, spearheaded this campaign. It came to a head at the famous Seneca Falls Convention, which Stanton and Mott organized in upstate New York in 1848. These early feminists, in their first national gathering, issued a Declaration of Sentiments, modeled on the Declaration of Independence, charging that "the history of mankind is a history of repeated injuries and usurpations on the part of man toward woman, having in direct object the establishment of an absolute tyranny over her." They demanded that all women be given the right to vote and that married women be freed from unjust laws giving husbands control of their property, persons, and children. Rejecting the Cult of Domesticity with its doctrine of separate spheres, these women and their male supporters launched the modern movement for gender equality.

CONCLUSION: COUNTERPOINT ON REFORM

Nathaniel Hawthorne was a great American writer who observed the perfectionist ferment of the age but suggested in his novels and tales that pursuit of the ideal led to a distorted view of human nature and possibilities.

He illustrated the dangers of pursuing perfection too avidly in his tale of a father who kills his beautiful daughter by trying to remove her one blemish, a birthmark. His greatest novels, *The Scarlet Letter* (1850) and *The House of the Seven Gables* (1851), probed New England's Puritan past and the shadows it cast on Hawthorne's own age. By dwelling on original sin as a psychological reality, Hawthorne told his contemporaries that they could never escape from guilt and evil. One had to accept the world as an imperfect place. Although he did not openly attack humanitarian reformers and cosmic optimists, Hawthorne's parables and allegories implicitly questioned the assumptions of pre–Civil War reform.

One does not have to agree with Hawthorne's pessimistic view of the human condition to acknowledge that perfectionist reformers promised more than they could deliver. Revivals could not make all men like Christ; temperance could not solve all social problems; and abolitionist agitation could not end slavery peacefully. The consequences of perfectionist efforts were often far different from what their proponents expected. In defense of the reformers, however, one could argue that Hawthorne's skepticism and fatalism were a prescription for doing nothing about intolerable evils. If the reform impulse was long on inspirational rhetoric but short on durable, practical achievements, it did at least disturb the complacent and opportunistic surface of American life and open the way to necessary changes. Nothing would improve unless people were willing to dream of improvements.

12 STUDY RESOURCES

((•—Listen to the **Chapter Audio** for Chapter 12 on **myhistorylab.com**

TIMELINE

1801 Massive revival held at Cane Ridge, Kentucky, p. 292

1826 American Temperance Society organized, p. 296

1830–1831 Charles G. Finney evangelizes Rochester, New York, p. 294

1831 William Lloyd Garrison publishes first issue of *The Liberator*, p. 303

1833 Abolitionists found American Anti-Slavery Society, p. 303

1835–1836 Theodore Weld advocates abolition in Ohio and upstate New York, p. 304

1837 Massachusetts establishes a state board of education, p. 301

1840 American Anti-Slavery Society splits over women's rights and other issues, p. 305

1848 Feminists found the women's rights movement at Seneca Falls, New York, p. 308

CHAPTER REVIEW

THE RISE OF EVANGELICALISM

How did the evangelical revivalism of the early nineteenth century spur reform movements?

Evangelical revivalists preached the perfectibility of individual moral agents, encouraging each person to choose his or her own moral and political destiny. This perfectionism led evangelical Christians to organize voluntary associations and benevolent societies that would teach people moral and social values. The most important of these reform efforts was the temperance movement. *(p. 292)*

DOMESTICITY AND CHANGES IN THE AMERICAN FAMILY

What was the doctrine of "separate spheres," and how did it change family life?

The doctrine of "separate spheres" glorified women's role in caring for the home and family, guarding religious and moral values while men went into the public sphere to earn money and participate in politics. Smaller families and more leisure time for middle-class families also emphasized children's development, including new public schools open to all. *(p. 297)*

REFORM TURNS RADICAL

What were the major antebellum reform movements?

Religious revivalism inspired movements for temperance, abolition of slavery, and women's rights. These movements grew more radical over time, turning to the political sphere in the 1840s as they lost confidence that changing men's hearts could transform society. The abolitionists organized the Liberty party in 1840, and feminists held their first convention at Seneca Falls in 1848. *(p. 302)*

KEY TERM QUESTIONS

1. What was the Second Great Awakening? (p. 292)

2. Why did the temperance movement attract so many followers in the early nineteenth century? (p. 295)

3. What was the Cult of Domesticity? (p. 297)

4. How did Charles G. Finney's belief in perfectionism influence American Protestantism? (p. 294)

5. How did the "benevolent empire" affect American society? (p. 296)

6. What took place at the Seneca Falls Convention and why was it significant? (p. 308)

7. How did the Second Great Awakening help to bring about the abolitionist movement? (p. 303)

MYHISTORYLAB CONNECTIONS

Visit **www.myhistorylab.com** for a customized Study Plan to build your knowledge of *The Pursuit of Perfection*

Question for Analysis

1. Why did Beecher view alcohol consumption as such a threat to the nation?

   Read the **Document** *Lyman Beecher, Six Sermons on Intemperance* p. 296

Other Resources from this Chapter

Read the **Document** *Reverend Peter Cartwright, Cane Ridge*

View the **Image** *Methodist Camp Meeting, 1819*

2. Why was Horace Mann so important?

   👁—Watch the **Video** *Who Was Horace Mann and Why are So Many Schools Named After Him?* p. 301

3. How does Simon Legree treat Uncle Tom during the trip to the plantation?

   📖—Read the **Document** *New England Writer Portrays Slavery, 1852* p. 304

4. What is the tone of David Walker's Appeal?

   📖—Read the **Document** *David Walker, A Black Abolitionist Speaks Out (1829)* p. 306

5. How was the Women's Rights Movement of the Nineteenth Century connected to the abolitionist movement of the same period?

   👁—Watch the **Video** *The Women's Rights Movement in Nineteenth Century America* p. 308

🔍—View the **Image** *Marriage Certificate, 1848*

📖—Read the **Document** *Matthew Carey, Rules for Husbands and Wives* p. 297

🔍—View the **Image** *Woman's Sphere*

📖—Read the **Document** *Horace Mann Report on the Massachusetts Board of Education*

📖—Read the **Document** *Abolitionist Demands Immediate End to Slavery*

📖—Read the **Document** *Maria Stewart, The Miseries We Tasted*

Contents and Spotlight Questions

((•─┤**Listen** to the **Chapter Audio** for Chapter 13 on **myhistorylab.com**

THE SPIRIT OF YOUNG AMERICA

In the 1840s and early 1850s, politicians, writers, and entrepreneurs frequently proclaimed themselves champions of Young America. One of the first to use the phrase was the famous author and lecturer Ralph Waldo Emerson, who told an audience in 1844 that the nation was entering a new era of commercial development, technological progress, and territorial expansion. Emerson suggested that a progressive new generation—the Young Americans—would lead this surge of physical development. More than a slogan but less than an organized movement, Young America favored the market economy and industrial growth, a more aggressive foreign policy, and a celebration of America's unique strengths and virtues.

Young Americans favored enlarging the national market by acquiring new territory. They called for the annexation of Texas, claimed all of Oregon, and urged the seizure of vast territories from Mexico. They also celebrated the technological advances that would knit this new empire together, especially the telegraph and the railroad.

Young America was both a cultural and intellectual movement and an economic and political one. In 1845, a Washington journal hailed the

Ambition and Ambivalence Herman Melville, shown here in an 1870 portrait by Joseph Oriel Eaton, shaped the knowledge he gained as a merchant sailor into *Moby-Dick*, a cautionary saga about the dark side of human ambition.

313

49-year-old James K. Polk, the youngest man to have been elected president, as a sign that youth will "dare to take antiquity by the beard, and tear the cloak from hoary-headed hypocrisy. Too young to be corrupt … it is Young America, awakened to a sense of her own intellectual greatness by her soaring spirit. It stands in strength, the voice of the majority." During the Polk administration, Young American writers and critics—mostly based in New York City—called for a distinctive national literature, free of subservience to European themes or models and expressive of the democratic spirit. Their organ was the *Literary World*, a magazine founded in 1847. Its ideals influenced two of the greatest writers America has produced: Walt Whitman and Herman Melville.

Whitman captured the exuberance and expansionism of Young America in his "Song of the Open Road":

From this hour I ordain myself loos'd of limits and imaginary lines,
Going where I list, my own master total and absolute,
…………………………
I inhale great draughts of space,
The east and the west are mine, and the north and the south are mine.
I am larger, better than I thought.

Songs of Ourselves Walt Whitman in the "carpenter portrait" that appeared in the first edition of his great work, *Leaves of Grass*, in 1855. The poet's rough clothes and slouch hat signify his identification with the common people.

In *Moby-Dick*, Herman Melville produced a novel original enough in form and concept to more than fulfill the demand of Young Americans for "a New Literature to fit the New Man in the New Age." But Melville was too deep a thinker not to see the perils behind the soaring ambition and aggressiveness of the new age. The whaling captain Ahab, whose relentless pursuit of the white whale destroys himself and his ship, symbolized—among other things—the dangers facing a nation that was overreaching itself by indulging its pride and exalted sense of destiny with too little concern for the moral and practical consequences.

The Young American ideal—the idea of a young country led by young men into new paths of prosperity and greatness—appealed to many people and found support across party lines. But it came to be identified primarily with young Democrats who wanted to move their party away from its traditional fear of commerce and industry. Unlike old-line Jeffersonians and Jacksonians, Young Americans had no qualms about the market economy and the speculative, materialistic spirit it called forth.

Before 1848, the Young American impulse focused mainly on the great expanse of western lands that lay just beyond the nation's borders. After the Mexican-American War, when territorial gains extended the nation's boundaries from the Atlantic to the Pacific, attention shifted to internal development. Discoveries of gold in the nation's western territories fostered economic growth, technological advances spurred industrialization, and increased immigration brought more people to populate the lands newly acquired—by agreement or by force.

TEXAS, MANIFEST DESTINY, AND THE MEXICAN-AMERICAN WAR

The rush of settlers beyond the nation's borders in the 1830s and 1840s inspired politicians and propagandists to call for annexing those areas. Some proclaimed it was the Manifest Destiny of the United States to absorb all of North America, including Canada and Mexico. Such ambitions—and the policies they inspired—led to a diplomatic confrontation with Britain over claims to Oregon and a war with Mexico. (See Map 13.1)

Why did the U.S. annex Texas and the Southwest?

The Texas Revolution

While U.S. expansionists also clashed with Britain over territory in the Pacific Northwest, the major terrain of conflict was between the United States and Mexico in the Southwest. In 1821, Mexico, which then included areas that currently make up the states of Texas, New Mexico, Arizona, California, Nevada, Utah, and much of Colorado, declared its independence from Spain.

View the **Map**
Texas Revolution, 1836 on
myhistorylab.com

Map 13.1 *Territorial Expansion by the Mid-Nineteenth Century* Fervent nationalists promoted the growth of America through territorial expansion as the divinely ordained "Manifest Destiny" of a chosen people.

Newly independent Mexico encouraged trade with the United States and wooed American settlers to Texas, which was sparsely populated. It granted Stephen F. Austin, son of a one-time Spanish citizen, a huge piece of land there in hopes he would help attract and settle new colonists from the United States. Some 15 other Anglo-American *empresarios* received similar land grants in the 1820s. In 1823, 300 families from the United States were settled on the Austin grant. Within a year, the colony's population was 2,021. The offer of fertile and inexpensive land attracted many American immigrants.

But friction soon developed between the Mexican government and the Anglo-American colonists over slavery and the authority of the Catholic Church. Anglo-American settlers were not willing to become Mexicans. Yet under the terms of settlement, all people living in Texas had to become Mexican citizens and Roman Catholics. Slavery presented another problem. In 1829, Mexico freed all slaves under its jurisdiction. The Mexican government gave slaveholders in Texas an exemption that allowed them to emancipate their slaves and then force them to sign lifelong contracts as indentured servants, but many Texans refused to limit their ownership rights in any way. Settlers either converted to Catholicism in name only or ignored the requirement.

A Mexican commission reported in 1829 that Americans in Texas were flagrantly violating Mexican law—refusing to emancipate their slaves, evading import duties on goods from the United States, and not converting to Catholicism. In 1830, the Mexican Congress prohibited further American immigration and importation of slaves to Texas.

But the new law was feebly enforced, and the flow of settlers, slaves, and smuggled goods continued. Texans complained about the lack of local self-government. Under the Mexican federal constitution, Texas was part of the state of Coahuila, and Texan representatives were outnumbered three to one in the state legislature. In 1832, the colonists showed their displeasure by rioting in protest against the arrest of Anglo-Americans by a Mexican commander.

The Texans' status as "tolerated guests" was threatened in 1834 when General Antonio López de Santa Anna made himself dictator of Mexico and abolished its federal system. News of these developments reached Texas late in the year, along with rumors that the American immigrants were going to be disenfranchised or even expelled. The Texans, already aroused by earlier restrictive policies, prepared to resist Santa Anna's effort to enforce tariff regulations.

Santa Anna sent reinforcements. On June 30, 1835, before they arrived, settlers led by William B. Travis captured the Mexican garrison at Anahuac without firing a shot. The Texans first fought Mexican troops at Gonzales in October and forced a cavalry detachment to retreat. Shortly thereafter, Austin captured San Antonio along with most of the Mexican troops then in Texas.

Quick Check

✓ Why were Austin and the settlers so dissatisfied with Mexican rule over Texas?

The Republic of Texas

While this early fighting was going on, delegates from the American communities in Texas declared their independence on March 2, 1836. A constitution, based on that of the United States, was adopted for the new Republic of Texas, and a temporary government was installed to carry on the struggle. Although the ensuing conflict largely pitted Americans against Mexicans, some Texas Mexicans, or *Tejanos*, sided with the Anglo rebels. They too wanted to be free of Santa Anna's heavy-handed rule.

Within days after Texas declared itself a republic, rebels and Mexican troops in San Antonio fought the famous battle of the Alamo. Myths about this battle have magnified the Anglo rebels' valor at the Mexicans' expense. The folklore is based on fact—only 187 rebels fought off a far larger number of Mexican soldiers for more than a week before capitulating—but not all rebels fought to the death. The folk hero Davy Crockett and seven other survivors were captured and executed. Nevertheless, a tale that combined actual and mythical bravery inside the Alamo gave the insurrection inspiration, moral sanction, outside support, and the rallying cry "Remember the Alamo."

The revolt ended with an exchange of slaughters. A few days after the Alamo battle, another Texas detachment was captured near the San Antonio River and marched to the town of Goliad, where most of its 350 members were executed. The next month, on April 21, 1836, the main Texas army, under Sam Houston, assaulted Santa Anna's troops at an encampment near the San Jacinto River during the siesta hour. The final count showed that 630 Mexicans and only a handful of Texans had been killed. Santa Anna was captured and forced to sign treaties recognizing the independence of Texas and its claim to territory all the way to the Rio Grande. (See Map 13.2)

Houston became the first president of Texas. He immediately sent an emissary to Washington to test the waters for annexation. Houston's agent found sympathy for Texas's independence, but Andrew Jackson and others told him that domestic politics and fear of a war with Mexico made immediate annexation impossible. The most that he could win from Congress and the Jackson administration was formal recognition of Texas sovereignty.

In its ten-year existence as the Lone Star Republic, Texas drew settlers from the United States. The Panic of 1837 impelled many debt-ridden and land-hungry farmers to take advantage of the free grants of 1,280 acres that Texas offered immigrating heads of white families. By 1844, Texas's population had soared from 30,000 to 142,000. Both newcomers and old settlers assumed that they would soon be annexed and restored to American citizenship.

Map 13.2 *Major Battles of the Texas Revolution* The Texans suffered severe losses at the Alamo and Goliad, but they scored a stunning victory at San Jacinto.

View the Image
The Alamo on
myhistorylab.com

Quick Check

✓ What aspects of the Alamo folklore are true, and which are fictionalized?

Battle of San Jacinto In this panorama of the Texas Revolution's decisive battle at San Jacinto by H. A. McArdle, Sam Houston leads the charge against Santa Anna's forces.

The Annexation of Texas

◉ ⌐**Watch** the **Video**
The Annexation of
Texas on
myhistorylab.com

President John Tyler initiated the politics of Manifest Destiny by making Texas annexation a major issue. As an "accidental president," a vice president who became president in 1841 when William Henry Harrison died after scarcely a month in office, Tyler needed an issue people could rally around. In 1843, he put the full weight of his administration behind the annexation of Texas, which he thought would solidify his support in the South. Secretary of State John C. Calhoun negotiated an annexation treaty that was brought before the Senate in 1844.

The strategy of linking annexation explicitly to the interests of the South and slavery led northern antislavery Whigs to charge that the whole scheme was a pro-slavery plot to advance the interests of one section of the nation against the other. The Senate rejected the annexation treaty by a decisive vote of 35 to 16 in June 1844. Tyler then attempted to admit Texas as a state through a joint resolution of both houses of Congress, but Congress adjourned before the issue came to a vote. The whole question was deferred in anticipation of the election of 1844.

Texas became the central issue in the 1844 campaign. But party lines held firm, and Tyler himself could not capitalize on the issue because neither party supported his stand. He tried to run as an independent but could not gain significant support and withdrew.

If the Democratic convention had been held in 1843—as originally scheduled—ex-President Martin Van Buren would have won the nomination. But postponing the conclave until May 1844 weakened his chances. The annexation question came to the fore, and Van Buren had to take a stand. He persisted in the view he had held as president—incorporating Texas would risk war with Mexico, arouse sectional strife, and destroy the unity of the Democratic party. These fears seemed

TABLE 13.1 The Liberty Party Swings an Election

Candidate	Party	Actual Vote in New York	National Electoral Vote	If Liberty Voters Had Voted Whig	Projected Electoral Vote
Polk	Democratic	237,588	170	237,588	134
Clay	Whig	232,482	105	248,294	141
Birney	Liberty	15,812	0	—	—

confirmed in 1844 when the dominant party faction in Van Buren's home state of New York opposed Tyler's Texas policy. To keep the issue out of the campaign, Van Buren struck a gentleman's agreement with Henry Clay, the overwhelming favorite for the Whig nomination, that both of them would publicly oppose immediate annexation.

Van Buren's opposition to annexation cost him the nomination. Southern delegates, who secured a rule requiring approval by a two-thirds vote, blocked Van Buren's nomination. After eight ballots, a dark horse candidate—James K. Polk of Tennessee—emerged triumphant. Polk, a protégé of Andrew Jackson, had been speaker of the House and governor of Tennessee.

An expansionist, Polk ran on a platform calling for the simultaneous annexation of Texas and assertion of American claims to all of Oregon. He identified himself and his party with the popular cause of turning the United States into a continental nation, an aspiration that attracted support from all parts of the country.

Polk won the election by a relatively narrow popular margin. He secured his triumph in the electoral college by winning New York and Michigan, where the Liberty party candidate, James G. Birney, took enough Whig antislavery votes away from Clay to affect the outcome. (See Tables 13.1 and 13.2) The close election did not prevent the Democrats from claiming that the people had backed an aggressive campaign to extend the borders of the United States.

After Polk's victory, Congress reconsidered the annexation of Texas. The mood had changed, and leading senators from both parties who had opposed Tyler's scheme for annexation by joint resolution changed their position. Congress approved annexation a few days before Polk took office. By contrast, the expansionist claim to all of the Oregon Country, jointly occupied by the U.S. and Britain, was

Read the **Document**
James K. Polk, First Inaugural Address on **myhistorylab.com**

TABLE 13.2 The Election of 1844

Candidate	Party	Popular Vote	Electoral Vote
Polk	Democratic	1,338,464	170
Clay	Whig	1,300,097	105
Birney	Liberty	62,300	—

Quick Check

✔ Why and how did
Texas cost Van
Buren his party's
nomination?

abandoned. Polk settled the Oregon question in 1846 with a treaty that garnered the U.S. its first deepwater port on the Pacific in Puget Sound, but ceded to Britain all of the Oregon territory above the 49th parallel. To northerners, who had hoped for more free states to balance the admission of Texas as a slave state, this concession demonstrated that Polk would be a southern president.

The Doctrine of Manifest Destiny

The expansionist mood that accompanied Polk's election and the annexation of Texas was given a name and a rationale in 1845. John L. O'Sullivan, a proponent of the Young America movement and editor of the influential *United States Magazine and Democratic Review*, charged that foreign governments were conspiring to block the annexation of Texas to thwart "the fulfillment of our manifest destiny to overspread the continent allotted by providence for the free development of our yearly multiplying millions."

Besides coining the phrase *Manifest Destiny*, O'Sullivan pointed to the three main ideas that lay behind it. One was that God favored American expansionism. This notion came naturally out of the long tradition, going back to the New England Puritans, that identified the growth of America with the divinely ordained success of a chosen people. Second, the phrase "free development" implied that the spread of American rule meant "extending the area of freedom." Democratic institutions and local self-government would follow the flag if the United States annexed areas claimed by autocratic foreign governments. O'Sullivan's third premise was that population growth required territorial acquisitions.

In its most extreme form, Manifest Destiny meant that the United States would occupy the entire North American continent. Nothing less would appease its land-hungry population.

Quick Check

✔ What was America's
"Manifest Destiny,"
and what were the
origins of this
concept?

War with Mexico

Although Mexico had offered to recognize Texas independence in 1845 to forestall annexation to the United States, it rejected the Lone Star Republic's dubious claim to the unsettled territory between the Nueces River and the Rio Grande. When the United States annexed Texas and assumed its claim to the disputed area, Mexico broke off diplomatic relations and prepared for war.

Polk responded by placing troops in Louisiana on alert and dispatching John Slidell to Mexico City to resolve the boundary dispute and persuade the Mexicans to sell New Mexico and California to the United States. The Mexican government refused to receive Slidell because his appointment ignored the break in regular diplomatic relations. While Slidell was cooling his heels in Mexico City, in January 1846, Polk ordered General Zachary Taylor to advance beyond the Nueces and proceed toward the Rio Grande, thus encroaching on territory both sides claimed.

By April, Taylor was near Matamoros on the Rio Grande. On the opposite bank of the river, Mexican forces had erected a fort. On April 24, 1,600 Mexican soldiers crossed the river and the following day attacked a small American detachment,

View the **Map**
*Mexican-American
War, 1846–1848* on
myhistorylab.com

killing 16 and capturing the rest. Taylor told the president: "Hostilities may now be considered as commenced."

The news was neither unexpected nor unwelcome. Polk was already preparing his war message to Congress when he learned of the fighting on the Rio Grande. A short and decisive war would force the cession of California and New Mexico.

The Mexican-American War lasted much longer than expected because the Mexicans refused to make peace despite military defeats. In the first major campaign of the conflict, Taylor took Matamoros and overcame fierce resistance to capture the city of Monterrey.

Taylor's decision to allow the Mexican garrison there to go free and his unwillingness or inability to advance farther into Mexico angered Polk and led him to adopt a new strategy to win the war and a new commander to implement it. He ordered General Winfield Scott to attack Veracruz and place an American army within striking distance of Mexico City. With half his forces detached for this invasion, Taylor was left in northern Mexico. But this did not deprive him of a final moment of glory. At Buena Vista, in February 1847, he claimed victory over a sizable Mexican army sent to dislodge him. Despite his unpopularity with the administration, Taylor became a national hero and the Whig candidate for president in 1848.

Meanwhile, an expedition led by Stephen Kearny captured Santa Fe, proclaimed the annexation of New Mexico, and set off for California. There they found that American settlers, in cooperation with an exploring expedition under John C. Frémont, had declared independence as the Bear Flag Republic. The U.S. Navy had also captured Monterey on the California coast. With the addition of Kearny's troops, a relatively few Americans took possession of California by 1847 against weak Mexican opposition.

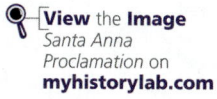

View the Image
*Santa Anna
Proclamation* on
myhistorylab.com

The decisive Veracruz campaign required massive and careful preparations. But in March 1847, the city fell after a 20-day siege. Then Scott began his advance on Mexico City. In the most important battle of the war, he defeated Santa Anna at Cerro Gordo on April 17 and 18. The Mexicans occupied an apparently impregnable position on high ground blocking the way to Mexico City. A daring flank attack that required soldiers to scramble up mountainsides enabled Scott to win a decisive victory. By August, American troops were in front of Mexico City. After a temporary armistice, which the Mexicans used to improve their defenses, Scott captured the city on September 14.

Quick Check
✓ How did the United
States obtain New
Mexico and
California?

Settlement of the Mexican-American War

Accompanying Scott's army was a diplomat, Nicholas P. Trist, who was authorized to negotiate a peace treaty whenever the Mexicans decided they had had enough. But despite the unbroken American victories, no Mexican leader was willing to invite the wrath of a proud and patriotic citizenry by agreeing to the terms that Polk wanted to impose. Even after the capture of Mexico City, Trist found it difficult to exact an acceptable treaty from the Mexican government. In November, Polk ordered Trist to return to Washington.

Trist ignored Polk's instructions and lingered in Mexico City. On February 2, 1848, he finally signed a treaty that gained all the territory he had been commissioned to obtain. The **Treaty of Guadalupe Hidalgo** ceded New Mexico and California to the United States for $15 million, established the Rio Grande as the border between Texas and Mexico, and promised that the U.S. government would assume the financial claims of American citizens against Mexico. The 80,000 Mexican residents of the new territories would become U.S. citizens. When the agreement reached Washington, Polk censured Trist for disobeying orders but still sent the treaty to the Senate, which ratified it by a vote of 38 to 14 on March 10.

The United States gained 500,000 square miles of territory from the Mexican-American War. The size of the nation expanded by about 20 percent, adding the present states of California, Utah, New Mexico, Nevada, Arizona, and parts of Colorado and Wyoming. Those interested in a southern route for a transcontinental railroad pressed for even more territory. That pressure led in 1853 to the Gadsden Purchase, through which the United States acquired the southernmost parts of present-day Arizona and New Mexico. (See Map 13.3)

But why, given the expansionist spirit of the age, did the U.S. not just annex *all* of Mexico? According to historian Frederick Merk, a peculiar combination of racism and anti-colonialism dominated American opinion. It was one thing to acquire thinly populated areas where "Anglo-Saxon" pioneers could settle. It was something else to incorporate millions of mixed Spanish and Indian people. These "mongrels," charged racist opponents of the "All Mexico" movement, could never be fit citizens of a self-governing republic. They would have to be ruled the way the British governed India, and the possession of colonial dependencies was contrary to American ideals and traditions.

Merk's thesis sheds light on why the general public had little appetite for swallowing all of Mexico, but those actually making policy had more mundane and practical reasons for being satisfied with what Guadalupe Hidalgo obtained. What they had really wanted all along, historian Norman Graebner contends, were the great California harbors of San Francisco and San Diego. From these ports, Americans could trade directly with Asia and dominate the commerce of the Pacific. Once California had been acquired, policymakers had little incentive to press for more Mexican territory.

The war with Mexico provoked political dissension. Most of the Whig party opposed the war in principle, arguing that the United States had no valid claims to the area south of the Nueces. Whig congressmen voted for military appropriations while the conflict was going on, but they criticized the president for starting it. More ominous, northerners from both parties charged that the real purpose of the war was to spread slavery and increase the power of the southern states. While battles were being fought in Mexico, Congress was debating the Wilmot Proviso, a proposal to prohibit slavery in any territories acquired from Mexico. A bitter sectional quarrel over slavery was a legacy of the Mexican-American War (see Chapter 14).

Map 13.3 *The Mexican-American War* The Mexican-American War added 500,000 square miles of territory to the United States, but the cost was high: $100 million and 13,000 lives.

The domestic controversies the war aroused and the propaganda of Manifest Destiny revealed the limits of mid-nineteenth-century American expansionism and put a damper on efforts to extend the nation's boundaries further. Concerns about slavery and race impeded acquisition of new territory in Latin America and the Caribbean. Resolution of the Oregon dispute clearly indicated that the United States was not willing to fight a powerful adversary to obtain large chunks of British North America, and the old ambition of incorporating Canada faded. From 1848 until expansionism revived in the late nineteenth century, American growth usually took the form of populating and developing the vast territory already acquired. Although the treaty guaranteed the rights of the former inhabitants of Mexico, they in effect became second-class citizens of the United States.

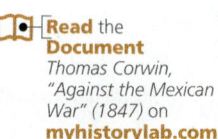

Read the Document
Thomas Corwin, "Against the Mexican War" (1847) on **myhistorylab.com**

Quick Check

✓ Why, given the expansionist spirit, did the United States not annex Mexico in its entirety?

INTERNAL EXPANSIONISM AND THE INDUSTRIAL REVOLUTION

How did developments in transportation foster industrialization and encourage immigration?

Young America expansionists saw a clear link between new territory and other forms of material growth and development. In 1844, Samuel F. B. Morse perfected and demonstrated his electric telegraph, a device that would make it possible to communicate rapidly over the continent. Simultaneously, the railroad was becoming a more important means of moving people and goods over the same great distances. Improvements in manufacturing and agriculture increased the volume and range of internal trade. The beginnings of mass immigration were providing human resources for exploiting new areas and economic opportunities.

The discovery of gold in newly acquired California in 1848 attracted a flood of emigrants from the East and foreign nations. The gold they unearthed spurred the national economy, and the rapid growth of population on the Pacific Coast inspired projects for transcontinental telegraph lines and railroad tracks.

Manifest Destiny and the thirst for new territory waned after the Mexican-American War. The expansionist impulse was channeled instead into internal development. Although the boundaries of the nation ceased to expand, the technological advances and population increase of the 1840s continued during the 1850s. The result was faster economic growth, more industrialization and urbanization, and a new American working class.

The Triumph of the Railroad

The railroad transformed the American economy during the 1840s and 1850s. The technology came from England, where steam locomotives were first used to haul cars along tracks in 1804. In 1830 and 1831, two American railroads began commercial operation—the Charleston and Hamburg in South Carolina and the Baltimore and Ohio in Maryland. After these pioneer lines had shown that steam locomotion was practical and profitable, other railroads were built and began to carry passengers and freight during the 1830s. But this early success was limited, because canals were strong competitors, especially for the freight business. Passengers might prefer the speed of trains, but the lower unit cost of transporting freight on the canal boats prevented most shippers from changing their habits. Furthermore, states such as New York and Pennsylvania had invested heavily in canals and resisted chartering a competitive form of transportation.

During the 1840s, rails extended beyond the northeastern and Middle Atlantic states, and mileage increased more than threefold, totaling more than 9,000 miles by 1850. By 1860, all the states east of the Mississippi had rail service. (See Map 13.4) In the 1840s and 1850s, railroads drove many of the canals out of business. Better tracks and more powerful locomotives that could haul more cars decreased the cost of hauling goods. Railroads had an enormous effect on the economy. Although English imports originally met the demand for iron rails, it eventually spurred development of the domestic iron industry. Since railroads required an enormous capital outlay, their promoters pioneered new methods for financing business enterprise. At a time when families or partnerships still owned most manufacturing and mercantile concerns, the railroad companies sold stock to the public and helped set the pattern for separating ownership from control that characterizes the modern corporation. They also developed new types of securities, such as "preferred stock" (with no voting rights but the assurance of a fixed rate of return) and long-term bonds at a set rate of interest.

Private capital did not fully meet the needs of the early railroad barons. State and local governments, convinced that railroads were the key to their prosperity, loaned them money, bought their stock, and guaranteed their bonds. Despite the dominant philosophy of laissez-faire, the federal government surveyed the routes of projected lines and provided land grants. In 1850, for example, the Illinois Central was granted millions of acres of public land. Forty companies received such aid before 1860, setting a precedent for the massive post–Civil War land grants to the railroads.

Read the **Document**
Senate Report on the Railroads (1852) on **myhistorylab.com**

Quick Check

✓ What new political and financial arrangements emerged to encourage the growth of the railroads?

The Industrial Revolution Takes Off

While railroads were revolutionizing transportation, American industry was growing rapidly. The factory mode of production, which had originated before 1840 in the cotton mills of New England, was extended to other products (see Chapter 9). Instead of being done in different locations, wool was woven and processed in single production units beginning in the 1830s. By 1860, some of the largest textile mills in the country were producing wool cloth. In eastern Pennsylvania, iron was being forged and rolled in factories by 1850. The industries producing firearms, clocks, and sewing machines also adopted the factory system during this period.

The essential features of the emerging mode of production were gathering a supervised workforce in a single place, paying cash wages to workers, using interchangeable parts, and manufacturing by "continuous process." Within a factory setting, a sequence of continuous operations could rapidly and efficiently assemble standardized parts, manufactured separately and in bulk, into a final product. Mass production, which involved the division of labor into a series of relatively simple and repetitive tasks, contrasted sharply with the traditional craft mode of production, in which a single worker produced the entire product out of raw materials.

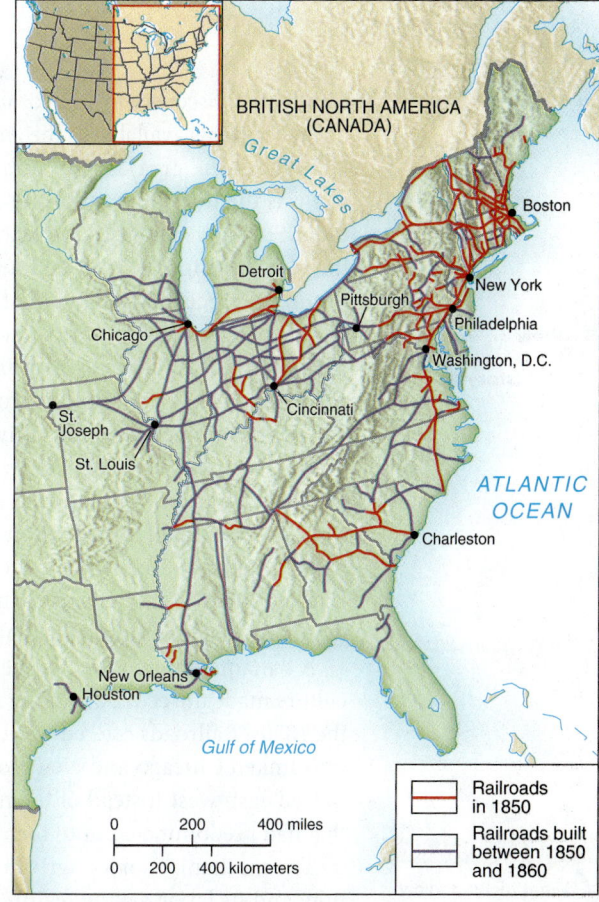

Map 13.4 *Railroads, 1850 and 1860* During the 1840s and 1850s, railroad lines moved rapidly westward. By 1860, more than 30,000 miles of track had been laid.

Labor Advancements A revolution in farming followed the introduction of new farm implements such as Cyrus McCormick's reaper, which could do ten times the work of a single person. The lithograph, by an anonymous artist, is titled *The Testing of the First Reaping Machine near Steele's Tavern, Virginia, 1831.*

The transition to mass production often depended on new technology. Just as power looms and spinning machinery had made textile mills possible, new and more reliable machines or industrial techniques revolutionized other industries. Elias Howe's invention of the sewing machine in 1846 laid the basis for the ready-to-wear clothing industry and contributed to the mechanization of shoemaking. During the 1840s, iron manufacturers adopted the British practice of using coal rather than charcoal for smelting and thus produced a metal better suited to industrial needs. Charles Goodyear's discovery in 1839 of the process for vulcanizing rubber made new manufactured items available to the American consumer, most notably the overshoe.

Perhaps the greatest triumph of mid-nineteenth-century American technology was the development of the world's most sophisticated and reliable machine tools. Such inventions as the extraordinarily accurate measuring device known as the vernier caliper in 1851 and turret lathes in 1854 were signs of an American aptitude for precision toolmaking that was essential for efficient industrialization.

But progress in industrial technology and organization did not mean the United States had become an industrial society by 1860. Factory workers remained a small fraction of the workforce, and agriculture retained first place both as a source of livelihood for individuals and as a contributor to the gross national product. But farming itself, at least in the North, was undergoing its own technological revolution. John Deere's steel plow, invented in 1837 and mass produced by the 1850s, enabled midwestern farmers to cultivate the tough prairie soils that had resisted cast-iron implements. The mechanical reaper, patented by Cyrus McCormick in 1834, made harvesting grain much easier. Seed drills, cultivators, and threshing machines also came into widespread use before 1860. (See Table 13.3)

A dynamic interaction between advances in transportation, industry, and agriculture made the economy of the northern states stronger and more resilient during the 1850s. Railroads offered western farmers better access to eastern markets. After rails linked Chicago and New York in 1853, most midwestern farm commodities flowed east–west instead of the north–south direction based on riverborne traffic that had predominated until then.

The mechanization of agriculture also gave additional impetus to industrialization, and its labor-saving features released workers for other economic activities. The growth of industry and the modernization of agriculture were thus mutually reinforcing aspects of a single process of economic growth.

View the **Image**
Calico Factory, 1854 on
myhistorylab.com

Quick Check

✓ What technological developments contributed to the new "mass production"?

TABLE 13.3 The Age of Practical Invention

Year*	Inventor	Contribution	Importance/Description
1787	John Fitch	Steamboat	First successful American steamboat
1793	Eli Whitney	Cotton gin	Simplified process of separating fiber from seeds; helped make cotton a profitable staple of southern agriculture
1798	Eli Whitney	Jig for guiding tools	Facilitated manufacture of interchangeable parts
1802	Oliver Evans	Steam engine	First American steam engine; led to manufacture of high-pressure engines used throughout eastern United States
1813	Richard B. Chenaworth	Cast-iron plow	First iron plow to be made in three separate pieces, thus making possible replacement of parts
1830	Peter Cooper	Railroad locomotive	First steam locomotive built in America
1831	Cyrus McCormick	Reaper	Mechanized harvesting; early model could cut six acres of grain a day
1836	Samuel Colt	Revolver	First successful repeating pistol
1837	John Deere	Steel plow	Steel surface kept soil from sticking; farming thus made easier on rich prairies of Midwest
1839	Charles Goodyear	Vulcanization of rubber	Made rubber much more useful by preventing it from sticking and melting in hot weather
1842	Crawford W. Long	First administered ether	Reduced pain and risk of shock during operations in surgery
1844	Samuel F. B. Morse	Telegraph	Made long-distance communication almost instantaneous
1846	Elias Howe	Sewing machine	First practical machine for automatic sewing
1846	Norbert Rillieux	Vacuum evaporator	Improved method of removing water from sugar cane; revolutionized sugar industry and was later applied to many other products
1847	Richard M. Hoe	Rotary printing press	Printed an entire sheet in one motion; vastly speeded up printing process
1851	William Kelly	"Air-boiling process"	Improved method of converting iron into steel (usually known as Bessemer process because English inventor Bessemer had more advantageous patent and financial arrangements)
1853	Elisha G. Otis	Passenger elevator	Improved movement in buildings; when later electrified, stimulated development of skyscrapers
1859	Edwin L. Drake	First American oil well	Initiated oil industry in the United States
1859	George M. Pullman	Pullman passenger car	First railroad sleeping car suitable for long-distance travel

*Dates refer to patent or first successful use.

Source: Allan Weinstein and Frank Gatell, one table, "The Age of Practical Invention" in FREEDOM AND CRISIS, 3/E Copyright (c) 1983. Reprinted with permission of The McGrawHill Companies, Inc.

Mass Immigration Begins

The incentive to mechanize northern industry and agriculture came in part from a shortage of cheap labor. Compared to the industrializing nations of Europe, the economy of the United States in the early nineteenth century was labor-scarce. Since it was difficult to attract able-bodied men to work for low wages in factories or on farms, women and children were used extensively in the early textile mills, and commercial farmers had to rely on the labor of their family members. Labor-saving machinery eased but did not solve the labor shortage. Factories required more operatives. Railroad builders needed construction gangs. The growth of industrial work attracted many European immigrants during the two decades before the Civil War.

Between 1820 and 1840, an estimated 700,000 immigrants arrived in the United States, mainly from the British Isles and German-speaking areas of continental Europe. During the 1840s, this substantial flow became a flood. No fewer than 4.2 million people crossed the Atlantic between 1840 and 1860, and about 3 million of these arrived between 1845 and 1855. This was the greatest influx in proportion to total population—about 20 million—that the nation has ever experienced. (See Figure 13.1) The largest single source of the new mass immigration was Ireland, but Germany was not far behind. Smaller contingents came from Switzerland, Norway, Sweden, and the Netherlands.

The massive transatlantic movement had many causes; some people were "pushed" out of their homes; others were "pulled" toward America. The push factor that caused 1.5 million Irish to forsake the Emerald Isle between 1845 and 1854 was the great potato blight, which brought famine to a population that subsisted on this single crop. The low fares then prevailing on sailing ships bound from England to North America made escape to America possible. Ships involved in the timber trade carried their bulky cargoes from Boston or Halifax to Liverpool; as an alternative to returning to America partly in ballast, they packed Irish immigrants into their holds. The squalor and misery in these steerage accommodations were almost beyond belief.

Because of the ports involved in the lumber trade—Boston, Halifax, Saint John's, and Saint Andrews—the Irish usually arrived in Canada or the Northeast. Immobilized by poverty and a lack of the skills required for pioneering in the West, most of them remained in the Northeast. By the 1850s, they constituted much of the total population of Boston, New York, Philadelphia, and many smaller New England and

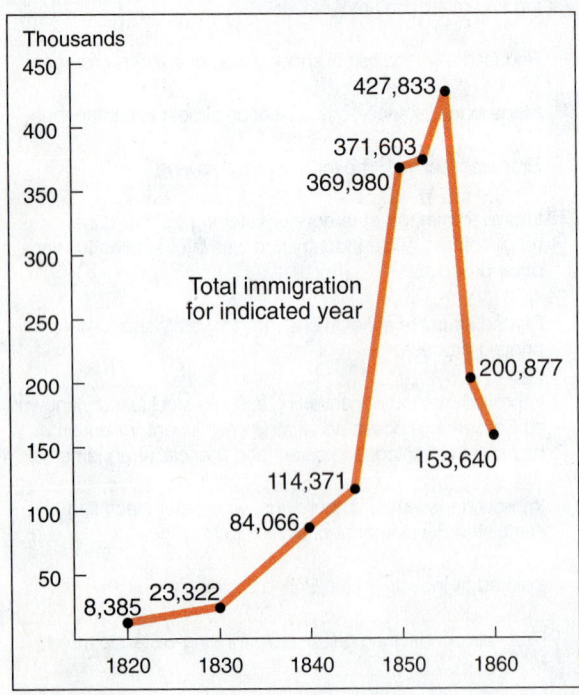

Figure 13.1 Immigration to the United States, 1820–1860

Middle Atlantic cities. Forced into low-paid menial labor and crowded into festering urban slums, they were looked down on by most native-born Americans. Their devotion to Catholicism aroused Protestant resentment and mob violence. Racists even doubted that the Irish were "white" like other northern Europeans. (See Chapter 14 for a discussion of nativism and anti-Catholicism.)

The million or so Germans who also came in the late 1840s and early 1850s were more fortunate. Most of them were also peasants, but unlike the Irish, they had fled hard times rather than outright catastrophe. Changes in German landholding patterns and a fluctuating market for grain squeezed small farmers. Those whose mortgages were foreclosed—or who could no longer make the regular payments to landlords that were the price of emancipation from feudal obligations—frequently immigrated to America. Again unlike the Irish, they often escaped with a little capital to make a fresh start in the New World.

Many German immigrants were artisans and sought to ply their trades in cities such as New York, St. Louis, Cincinnati, and Milwaukee—all of which became German American centers. But many peasants went back to the land. Their diversified agricultural skills and small amounts of capital enabled them to become successful midwestern farmers. In general, Germans encountered less prejudice and discrimination than the Irish. For Germans who were Protestant, religious affinity with their American neighbors made for relative tolerance. But even Catholic Germans normally escaped the scorn heaped on the Irish, perhaps because they were less poverty-stricken and were not members of an ethnic group Anglo-Americans had learned to despise from their English ancestors and cousins.

Economic opportunity attracted most of the Irish, German, and other European immigrants to America. A minority, like some German revolutionaries of 1848, chose the United States because they admired its democratic political system. But most immigrants were more interested in making a decent living than in voting or running for office. Peak periods of immigration—1845 to 1854 is a prime example—coincided closely with times of domestic prosperity and high demand for labor. During depressed periods, immigration dropped off.

The immigrants exacerbated the problems of America's rapidly growing cities. The old "walking city" in which rich and poor lived in close proximity near the center of town was giving way to a more segregated environment. Railroads and horse-drawn streetcars enabled the affluent to move to the first American suburbs, while areas nearer commercial and industrial centers became the congested abode of newcomers from Europe. Slums such as the notorious Five Points district in New York City were characterized by overcrowding, poverty, disease, and crime. Recognizing that these conditions created potential dangers for the entire urban population, middle-class reformers worked to professionalize police forces, introduce sanitary water and sewage disposal systems, and upgrade housing. They made some progress before the Civil War, but the lot of the urban poor, mainly immigrants, was not dramatically improved. Most urban immigrants' lives remained unsafe, unhealthy, and unpleasant.

Read the **Document**
Samuel Morse, Foreign Immigration (1835) on **myhistorylab.com**

Quick Check
✓ What were the new immigrants' reasons for migrating, and what conditions did they face on arrival?

The New Working Class

Most immigrants ended up as wage workers in factories, mines, and construction camps or as casual day laborers doing the many unskilled tasks urban and commercial growth required. By providing a vast pool of cheap labor, they fueled and accelerated the Industrial Revolution. During the 1850s, factory production in Boston and other port cities previously devoted to commerce grew—partly because thousands of recent Irish immigrants worked for the kind of low wages that almost guaranteed large profits for entrepreneurs.

In established industries and older mill towns of the Northeast, immigrants added to, or displaced, the native-born workers who had predominated in the 1830s and 1840s. The changing workforce of the textile mills in Lowell, Massachusetts, provided a striking example of this process. In 1836, only 3.7 percent of the workers in one Lowell mill were foreign born; most were young unmarried women from New England farms. By 1860, immigrants constituted 61.7 percent of the workforce. This trend reveals much about the changing character of the American working class. In the 1830s, most male workers were artisans. Factory work was still largely the province of women and children. Both groups were predominantly of American stock. In the 1840s, more men worked in factories, although women predominated in the textile industry. During that decade, conditions in many mills deteriorated. Relations between management and labor became more impersonal, and workers were pushed to increase their output. Workdays of 12–14 hours were common.

The result was an upsurge of labor militancy involving female and male factory workers. Mill girls in Lowell, for example, formed a union—the Female Labor Reform Association—and agitated for shorter working hours. On a broader front, workers' organizations petitioned state legislatures for laws limiting the workday to ten hours. Some such laws were actually passed, but they were ineffective because employers could still require a prospective worker to sign a contract agreeing to longer hours.

The increasing employment of immigrants between the mid-1840s and the late 1850s made it more difficult to organize industrial workers. Impoverished fugitives from the Irish potato famine tended to have lower economic expectations and more conservative social attitudes than did native-born workers. Consequently, the Irish

Greater Fortunes This 1854 cartoon, titled "The Old World and the New," shows a shabbily dressed man in Ireland examining posters for trips to New York (left). At right, he is shown later, in America, wearing finer clothes and looking at posters advertising trips for emigrants returning to Dublin. As was the case for many immigrants seeking economic opportunities in the "New World," his situation has apparently changed for the better.

immigrants were initially willing to work for less and were less prone to protest working conditions.

However, the new working class of former rural folk did not make the transition to industrial wage labor easily or without subtle and indirect protests. Tardiness, absenteeism, drunkenness, loafing, and other resistance to factory discipline reflected hostility to the unaccustomed and seemingly unnatural routines of industrial production. The adjustment to new styles and rhythms of work was painful and slow.

> **Quick Check**
> ✓ How did the constitution and behavior of the working class change in this period?

CONCLUSION: THE COSTS OF EXPANSION

By 1860, industrial expansion and immigration had created a working class of men and women who seemed destined for a life of low-paid wage labor. This reality stood in contrast to America's self-image as a land of opportunity and upward mobility. This ideal still had some validity in rapidly developing regions of the western states, but it was mostly myth for the increasingly foreign-born industrial workers of the Northeast.

Internal and external expansion had come at a heavy cost. Tensions associated with class and ethnic rivalries were only part of the price of rapid economic development. The acquisition of new territories was politically divisive and soon led to a catastrophic sectional controversy. In the late 1840s and early 1850s, Democratic Senator Stephen A. Douglas of Illinois (called the Little Giant because of his small stature and large presence) sought political power for himself and his party by combining an expansionist foreign policy with the economic development of the territories already acquired. Recognizing that the slavery question was the main obstacle to his program, he sought to neutralize it through compromise and evasion (see Chapter 14). His failure to win the presidency or even the Democratic nomination before 1860 showed that Young America's dream of a patriotic consensus for headlong expansion and economic development could not withstand the tensions and divisions that expansionist policies created and brought to light.

13 STUDY RESOURCES

((•—[Listen to the **Chapter Audio** for Chapter 13 on **myhistorylab.com**

TIMELINE

1823 American settlers arrive in Texas, p. 316

1830 Mexico attempts to halt American migration to Texas, p. 316

1831 American railroads begin commercial operation, p. 324

1834 Cyrus McCormick patents mechanical reaper, p. 326

1835 Revolution in Texas, p. 316

1836 Texas becomes independent republic, p. 316

1837 John Deere invents steel plow, p. 326

CHAPTER REVIEW

TEXAS, MANIFEST DESTINY, AND THE MEXICAN-AMERICAN WAR

Why did the U.S. annex Texas and the Southwest?

The annexation of Texas and the Southwest had several causes. Early settlers of Texas grew dissatisfied with the Catholic, antislavery Mexican administration. Many Americans believed that it was America's "Manifest Destiny" to expand across the continent. This ideology was a useful rallying cry for politicians willing to go to war with Mexico to gain new territory. (*p. 315*)

INTERNAL EXPANSIONISM AND THE INDUSTRIAL REVOLUTION

How did developments in transportation foster industrialization and encourage immigration?

Rail transportation allowed the swift movement of people and goods. Other advances in technology permitted the new "mass production." The new industries drew many immigrants from Ireland and Germany, who were fleeing famine and persecution. Immigration made labor more plentiful and thus cheaper, so working conditions declined. (*p. 324*)

KEY TERM QUESTIONS

1. Why were politicians, writers, and entrepreneurs so interested in championing Young America? (p. 313)

2. What was Manifest Destiny? (p. 315)

3. What elements of the Alamo folklore are true, and which are fictionalized? (p. 317)

4. What were the causes of the Mexican-American War? (p. 321)

5. What were the results of the Treaty of Guadalupe Hidalgo? (p. 322)

MyHistoryLab Connections

Visit **www.myhistorylab.com** for a customized Study Plan to build your knowledge of *An Age of Expansionism*

Question for Analysis

1. How did Texas join the Union?

   👁 **Watch** the **Video** *The Annexation of Texas* p. 318

2. Where did the U.S. win battles in the Mexican-American War?

   🔍 **View** the **Map** *Mexican-American War, 1846-1848* p. 320

3. What were the main reasons for increasing railroad construction?

   📖 **Read** the **Document** *Senate Report on Railroads, 1852* p. 325

4. Why was Samuel Morse so fervently against immigration?

   📖 **Read** the **Document** *Samuel Morse, Foreign Immigration* p. 329

Other Resources from this Chapter

🔍 **View** the **Map** *Texas Revolution, 1836*

🔍 **View** the **Image** *The Alamo*

📖 **Read** the **Document** *James K. Polk, First Inaugural Address*

🔍 **View** the **Image** *Santa Anna Proclamation*

📖 **Read** the **Document** *Thomas Corwin, Against the Mexican War*

🔍 **View** the **Image** *Calico Factory, 1854*

14 THE SECTIONAL CRISIS

1846–1861

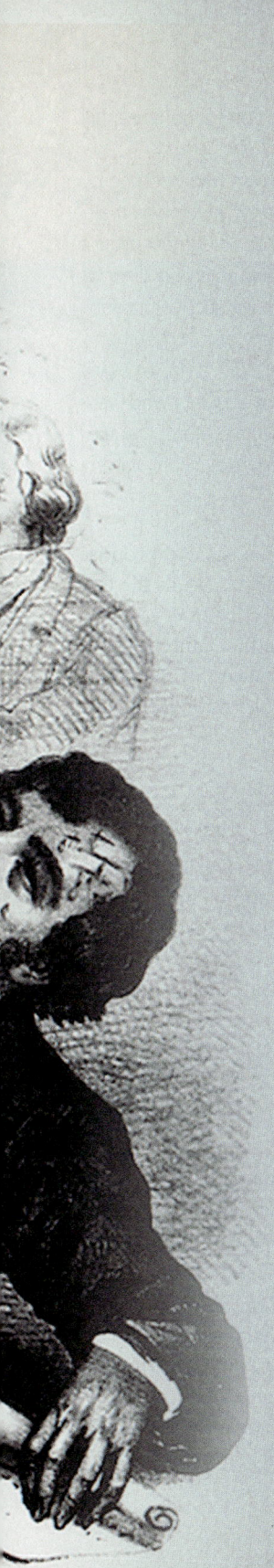

Contents and Spotlight Questions

((•—[**Listen** to the **Chapter Audio** for Chapter 14 on **myhistorylab.com**

BROOKS ASSAULTS SUMNER IN CONGRESS

On May 22, 1856, Representative Preston Brooks of South Carolina walked onto the floor of the Senate with a rattan cane in his hand. Charles Sumner, the antislavery senator from Massachusetts who had recently given a fiery oration condemning the South for plotting to extend slavery to the Kansas Territory, was seated at his desk. What was worse, the speech had insulted Senator Andrew Butler of South Carolina, Brooks' kinsman. When he reached Sumner, Brooks beat him over the head with the cane. Stunned, Sumner made a desperate effort to rise and ripped his bolted desk from the floor. He then collapsed under a torrent of blows as the cane shattered in Brooks' hand.

Sumner was so badly injured that he did not return to the Senate for three years. But Massachusetts reelected him in 1857 and kept his seat vacant as a reproach to southern brutality and "barbarism." In parts of the North, Sumner was hailed as a martyr to the cause of "free soil," and Brooks was denounced as a bully. But his fellow southerners lionized Brooks. When he

Dubious Support After his constituents learned of Preston Brooks's caning of Senator Sumner, they sent Brooks a gold-handled cowhide whip to use on other antislavery advocates.

resigned from the House after southern congressmen blocked a vote of censure, his constituents reelected him unanimously.

These contrasting reactions show how bitter sectional antagonism had become by 1856. Sumner spoke for the radical wing of the new Republican party, which was making a bid for national power by mobilizing the North against the alleged aggressions of "the slave power." Southerners viewed the very existence of this party as an insult to the South and a threat to its interests. Sumner came closer to being an abolitionist than any other member of Congress. Nothing created greater fear and anxiety among southerners than their belief that antislavery forces were plotting against their way of life. To many northerners, "bully Brooks" stood for all the arrogant and violent slaveholders who were allegedly conspiring to extend their barbaric labor system. By 1856, therefore, the sectional cleavage that would lead to the Civil War had already undermined national unity.

The crisis of the mid-1850s came only a few years after the elaborate compromise of 1850 had seemingly resolved the dispute over the future of slavery in the territories acquired in the Mexican War. The Kansas-Nebraska Act of 1854 renewed the agitation over the extension of slavery, revived sectional conflict, and led to the emergence of the Republican Party. From that point on, sectional confrontation increased and destroyed the prospects for a new compromise. Violence on the Senate floor foreshadowed violence on the battlefield.

THE COMPROMISE OF 1850

How did territorial expansion intensify the conflict over slavery

The conflict over slavery in the territories began in the late 1840s. During the early phase of the sectional controversy, the leaders of two strong national parties, each with substantial followings in both the North and the South, had a vested interest in resolving the crisis. Furthermore, the less tangible features of sectionalism—emotion and ideology—were less divisive than they later became. Hence, in 1850, a kind of give-and-take achieved a fragile compromise that would not be possible in the changed environment of the mid-1850s.

The Problem of Slavery in the Mexican Cession

As the price of union between states committed to slavery and those in the process of abolishing it, the Founders had attempted to limit the role of the slavery issue in national politics. The Constitution gave the federal government the right to abolish the international slave trade but no authority to regulate or destroy the institution where it existed under state law. It was easy to condemn slavery in principle but difficult to develop a practical program to eliminate it without defying the Constitution.

Radical abolitionists acknowledged this problem and resolved it by rejecting the law of the land in favor of a "higher law" prohibiting human bondage. In 1844, William Lloyd Garrison publicly burned the Constitution, condemning it as "a Covenant with Death, an Agreement with Hell." But Garrison spoke for a small minority dedicated to freeing the North, at whatever cost, from the sin of condoning slavery.

During the 1840s, most northerners showed that while they disliked slavery, they also detested abolitionism. They were inclined to view slavery as a backward and unwholesome institution, much inferior to their own free-labor system, and could be persuaded that slaveholders were power-hungry aristocrats seeking more than their share of national political influence. But they regarded the Constitution as a binding contract between slave and free states and were likely to be prejudiced against blacks and reluctant to accept them as free citizens. They saw no legal or desirable way to bring about emancipation within the southern states.

But the Constitution had not predetermined the status of slavery in *future* states. Since Congress could admit new states to the Union under any conditions it wished to impose, the price of admission could include the abolition of slavery. This had led to the Missouri crisis of 1819–1820 (see Chapter 9). The resulting compromise was designed to decide whether new states would be admitted as slave states or free by drawing a line between slave and free states and extending it westward through the unsettled portions of what was then American soil. When specific territories were settled, organized, and prepared for statehood, slavery would be permitted south of the line of 36°30' and prohibited north of it.

The tradition of providing both the free North and the slave South with opportunities to expand and create new states broke down when new territories were wrested from Mexico in the 1840s. The acquisition of Texas, California, and New Mexico—all south of the Missouri Compromise line—threatened to upset the parity between slave and free states. Since it was generally assumed in the North that Congress could prohibit slavery in new territories, a movement developed in Congress to do just that.

Quick Check

✓ What role did the Constitution play in the debates over slavery in existing states as well as in newly acquired territories?

The Wilmot Proviso Launches the Free-Soil Movement

The Free-Soil crusade began in August 1846, only three months after the start of the Mexican-American War, when Representative David Wilmot, a Pennsylvania Democrat, proposed an amendment to the military appropriations bill that would ban slavery in any territory acquired from Mexico. Wilmot spoke for the many northern Democrats who felt neglected and betrayed by the party's choice of Polk over Van Buren in 1844 and by Polk's "prosouthern" policies. Wilmot also proposed prohibiting free African Americans from settling in the new territories. This would enhance the economic opportunities of the North's common folk by preventing competition from slaves and free blacks. By thus linking racism with resistance to the spread of slavery, Wilmot appealed to a broad spectrum of northern opinion.

Northern Whigs shared Wilmot's concern about unregulated competition between slave and free labor in the territories. Voting for the measure also provided an outlet for their frustration at being unable to halt the annexation of Texas and the Mexican-American War. Whig leaders preferred that there be no expansion at all, but when expansion could not be avoided, northern Whigs endorsed the view that territory acquired from Mexico should not be used to increase the power of the slave states.

In the first House vote on the Wilmot Proviso, a sectional cleavage replaced party lines. Every northern congressman except for two Democrats voted for the

Read the **Document**
John C. Calhoun's Proposal to Preserve the Union on
myhistorylab.com

Quick Check

✓ What was the Wilmot Proviso, and what effect did it have on existing party lines?

amendment, and every southerner except two Whigs voted against it. After passing the House, the Proviso was blocked in the Senate by a combination of southern influence and Democratic loyalty to the administration. When the appropriations bill went back to the House without the Proviso, the administration's arm-twisting changed enough northern Democratic votes to pass the bill and thus defeat the Proviso.

Forging a Compromise

One early compromise reached on the Mexican cession was a formula known as "squatter sovereignty" that would enable the actual settlers to determine the status of slavery in a territory. The North and the South interpreted this proposal differently. For northern Democrats, squatter sovereignty—or popular sovereignty, as it was later called—meant the settlers could vote slavery up or down at the first meeting of a territorial legislature. For the southern wing of the party, it meant a decision would be made only when a convention drew up a constitution and applied for statehood. The chief proponent of squatter sovereignty was Senator Lewis Cass of Michigan, the Democratic nominee for president in 1848. Cass lost to General Zachary Taylor, who ran as a Whig war hero without a platform. (See Table 14.1) Taylor refused to commit himself on the status of slavery in the territories, although he promised not to veto any congressional legislation on the subject. Northern supporters of the Wilmot Proviso backed former President Van Buren, who ran under the new Free-Soil Party, the first broad, sectional, antislavery party. After Taylor won, he sought to bypass congressional debate by admitting California and New Mexico immediately as states, skipping the territorial stage; this triggered such strong southern opposition that others stepped in to seek a compromise.

Hoping again to play the role of "great pacificator" as he had in the Missouri Compromise of 1820, Senator Henry Clay of Kentucky tried to reduce sectional tension by providing mutual concessions on a range of divisive issues. On the critical territorial question, his solution was to admit California as a free state and organize the rest of the Mexican cession with no explicit prohibition of slavery—in other words, without the Wilmot Proviso. Noting that Mexican law had already abolished slavery in New Mexico, he also pointed out that its arid climate made it unsuitable for cotton culture and slavery. He also sought to resolve a boundary dispute between New Mexico and Texas by granting the disputed region to New Mexico while compensating Texas by having the federal government take over its state debt. As another concession to the North, he recommended prohibiting slave sales at auction in the District of Columbia and permitting the District's white inhabitants to abolish slavery if they saw fit. To appease the South, he called for a more effective Fugitive Slave Law.

TABLE 14.1   The Election of 1848

Candidate	Party	Popular Vote	Electoral Vote
Taylor	Whig	1,360,967	163
Cass	Democratic	1,222,342	127
Van Buren	Free-Soil	291,263	—

A Fragile Compromise Henry Clay, shown here addressing the Senate, helped negotiate the Compromise of 1850 to settle the dispute over the extension of slavery in territories
acquired in the Mexican-American War. Daniel Webster, seated at left resting his head on
his hand, supported Clay's proposed compromise. Ardent states' rightist John C. Calhoun,
standing third from right, led the opposition.

These proposals provided the basis for the **Compromise of 1850**. Proposed in
February 1850, it took months to get through Congress. One obstacle was President
Taylor's resistance; although a southerner slaveholder, Taylor opposed extending
slavery into the new western territories. Another obstacle was getting congressmen
to vote for the compromise as a single package or "omnibus bill." Few politicians
from either section were willing to go on record as supporting the key concessions
to the *other* section. In July, two developments broke the logjam: President Taylor
died and was succeeded by Millard Fillmore, who favored the compromise; and the
omnibus strategy was abandoned in favor of a series of measures that could be voted
on separately. After the breakup of the omnibus bill, some of Clay's proposals were
modified to make them more acceptable to the South and the Democrats. Senator
Stephen A. Douglas maneuvered the separate provisions through Congress.

As the price of Democratic support, the bills organizing New Mexico and Utah as
territories included the popular sovereignty principle. Territorial legislatures in the
Mexican cession were explicitly granted power over "all rightful subjects of legislation,"
which might include slavery. Half of the compensation to Texas for giving up its claims
to New Mexico was paid directly to holders of Texas bonds. (See Map 14.1)

Read the
Document
*The Fugitive Slave Act
(1850)* on
myhistorylab.com

Abolition of the slave trade—but not slavery itself—in the District of Columbia and a new Fugitive Slave Law were also enacted. The latter was an outrageous piece of legislation. As the result of southern pressures and amendments, suspected fugitives were now denied a jury trial, the right to testify in their own behalf, and other basic constitutional protections. This removed any effective safeguards against accusers making false claims that a black person was an escaped slave—or even kidnapping free blacks.

The compromise passed because northern Democrats, southern Whigs, and representatives of both parties from the border states supported its key measures. A majority of congressmen from both sections did not support any single bill, and few senators or representatives actually voted for the entire package. Many northern Whigs and southern Democrats thought the end result conceded too much to the other section. Doubts lingered over the value or workability of a "compromise" that was more like an armistice or a cease-fire.

Yet the Compromise of 1850 did temporarily restore sectional peace. In southern state elections during 1850–1851, moderate coalitions defeated the radicals who viewed the compromise as a sellout to the North. But this emerging "unionism" was conditional. Southerners demanded strict northern adherence to the compromise, especially to the Fugitive Slave Law, as the price for suppressing threats of secession. In the North, the compromise received greater support. The Fugitive Slave Law was unpopular in areas where abolitionism was strong because it required northerners to enforce slavery, and there were sensational rescues or attempted rescues of

Map 14.1 *The Compromise of 1850* The "compromise" was actually a series of resolutions granting some concessions to the North—especially admission of California as a free state—and some to the South, such as a stricter Fugitive Slave Law.

escaped slaves. But the northern states largely adhered to the law during the next few years. When the Democrats and Whigs approved or condoned the compromise in their 1852 platforms, it seemed that sharp differences on the slavery issue had been banished from national politics again.

Quick Check

✓ What were the key provisions of the Compromise of 1850?

POLITICAL UPHEAVAL, 1852–1856

The second-party system—Democrats versus Whigs—survived the crisis over slavery in the Mexican cession, but the Compromise of 1850 may have fatally weakened it. Although both national parties had been careful during the 1840s not to alienate

How did the two-party system change during this period?

CAUTION!!

COLORED PEOPLE OF BOSTON, ONE & ALL,

You are hereby respectfully CAUTIONED and advised, to avoid conversing with the **Watchmen and Police Officers of Boston,**

For since the recent ORDER OF THE MAYOR & ALDERMEN, they are empowered to act as

KIDNAPPERS

AND

Slave Catchers,

And they have already been actually employed in KIDNAPPING, CATCHING, AND KEEPING SLAVES. Therefore, if you value your LIBERTY, and the *Welfare of the Fugitives* among you, *Shun* them in every possible manner, as so many *HOUNDS* on the track of the most unfortunate of your race.

Keep a Sharp Look Out for KIDNAPPERS, and have TOP EYE open.

APRIL 24, 1851.

THEODORE PARKER'S PLACARD

Placard written by Theodore Parker and printed and posted by the Vigilance Committee of Boston after the rendition of Thomas Sims to slavery in April, 1851.

Caution! This abolitionist broadside was printed in response to a ruling that fugitive slave Thomas Sims must be returned to his master in Georgia.

their supporters in either section of the country, they had in fact offered voters alternative ways of dealing with slavery. Democrats had endorsed headlong territorial expansion with the promise of a fair division of the spoils between slave and free states. Whigs had generally opposed annexations or acquisitions, because they were likely to raise the slavery question and threaten sectional harmony. Each strategy could be presented to southern voters as a good way to protect slavery and to northerners as a good way to contain it.

The consensus meant the two major parties had to find other issues on which to base their distinctive appeals. Their failure to do so encouraged voter apathy and disenchantment with them. When the Democrats sought to revive the Manifest Destiny issue in 1854, they reopened the explosive issue of slavery in the territories. By this time, the Whigs were too weak and divided to respond with a policy of their own, and a purely sectional Free-Soil party—the Republicans—gained prominence. The collapse of the second-party system released sectional agitation from the constraints the competition of strong national parties had imposed.

The Party System in Crisis

The presidential campaign of 1852 was devoid of major issues. Whigs tried to revive interest in nationalistic economic policies, but with business thriving under the Democratic program of limited government involvement, a protective tariff, a national bank, and internal improvements got little support.

Another tempting issue was immigration. The massive influx from Europe upset many Whigs, partly because most of the new arrivals were Catholics, and the Whig following was largely evangelical Protestant. The immigrants also voted overwhelmingly Democratic. The Whig leadership was divided on whether to compete with the Democrats for the immigrant vote or restrict immigrant voting rights.

The Whigs nominated General Winfield Scott of Mexican-American War fame, who supported the faction that resisted nativism and sought to broaden the party's appeal. But Scott and his supporters could not sway Catholic immigrants from their Democratic allegiance, and nativist Whigs sat out the election to protest their party's disregard of their cultural prejudices.

But the main cause for Scott's crushing defeat was the support he lost in the South when he allied himself with the dominant northern antislavery wing of the party, led by Senator William Seward of New York. Democrat Franklin Pierce of New Hampshire, a colorless nonentity compared to his rival, swept the Deep South and edged out Scott in most of the free states. (See Table 14.2) The outcome revealed that the Whig party lacked a program that would distinguish it from the Democrats and appeal to voters in both sections of the country. The Whigs had declined to such an extent that even a war hero like General Scott could not give the party a victory the way Taylor had four years earlier.

TABLE 14.2   The Election of 1852

Candidate	Party	Popular Vote	Electoral Vote
Pierce	Democratic	1,601,117	254
Scott	Whig	1,385,453	42
Hale	Free-Soil	155,825	—

Despite their overwhelming victory in 1852, the Democrats had reasons for anxiety about their supporters' loyalty. Because the major parties had ceased to offer clear-cut alternatives to the electorate, voter apathy or alienation was growing. The Democrats won majorities in both North and South in 1852 primarily because the public viewed them as the most reliable supporters of the Compromise of 1850, not because of firm party allegiance.

Quick Check

✓ Why did the democrats win the election of 1852, and why were they uneasy despite this victory?

The Kansas-Nebraska Act Raises a Storm

In January 1854, Senator Stephen A. Douglas of Illinois proposed a bill to organize the territory west of Missouri and Iowa. Since this region fell within the area where the Missouri Compromise had banned slavery, Douglas hoped to head off southern opposition and keep the Democratic party united by disregarding the compromise line and setting up the territorial government in Kansas and Nebraska on the basis of popular sovereignty.

Douglas wanted to organize the Kansas-Nebraska area quickly because he supported the expansion of settlement and commerce. He hoped a railroad would soon be built to the Pacific with Chicago (or another midwestern city) as its eastern terminus. A controversy over slavery in the new territory would slow down the process of organization and settlement and hinder building the railroad. As a leader of the Democrats, Douglas also hoped his Kansas-Nebraska bill would revive the spirit of Manifest Destiny that had given the party cohesion and electoral success in the mid-1840s (see Chapter 13). As the main advocate for a new expansionism, he expected to win the Democratic nomination and the presidency in 1856.

The price of southern support, Douglas soon discovered, was an amendment explicitly repealing the Missouri Compromise. Although he realized this would "raise a hell of a storm," he agreed. In this more provocative form, the bill passed the Senate by a large margin and the House by a narrow one. Douglas had split his party: Half of the northern Democrats in the House voted against the legislation. (See Map 14.2)

The Democrats who broke ranks created the storm that Douglas had predicted but underestimated. "Independent Democrats" denounced the bill as "a gross violation of a sacred pledge." A memorial from 3,000 New England ministers described it as a craven and sinful surrender to the slave power. For many northerners, probably most, the Kansas-Nebraska Act was an abomination because it permitted the possibility of slavery in an area where it had been prohibited. Except for an aggressive minority, southerners had not pushed for such legislation or even shown much interest in it, but now they felt obliged to support it. Their support provided

View the **Image**
Stephen Douglas on **myhistorylab.com**

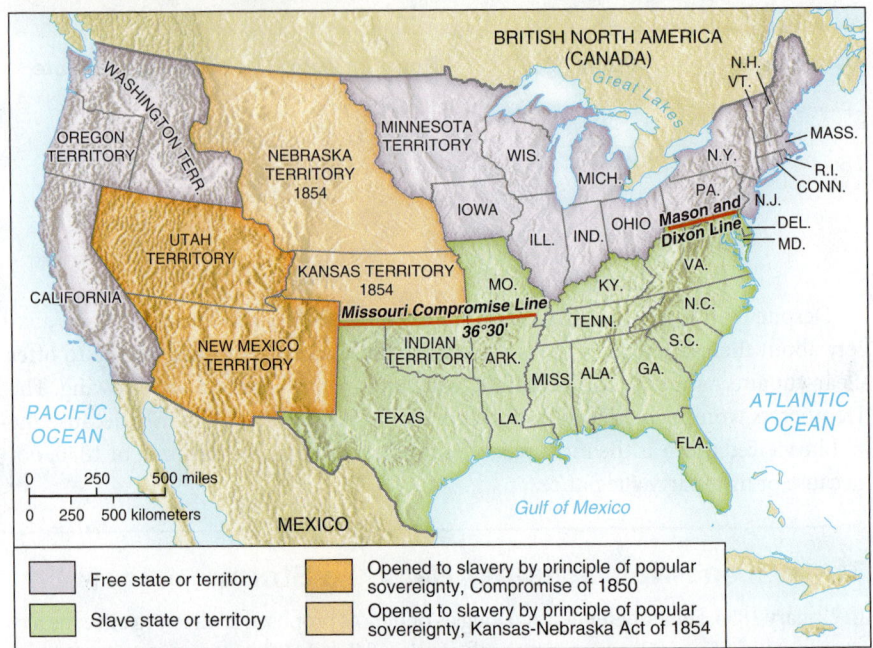

Map 14.2 *The Kansas-Nebraska Act of 1854*   The Kansas-Nebraska Act applied the principle of popular sovereignty to voters in the Kansas and Nebraska territories, allowing them to decide for themselves whether to permit slavery in their territories. The act repudiated the Missouri Compromise of 1820, which had prohibited slavery in the territory of the Louisiana Purchase north of 36°30' latitude.

ammunition to those who were seeking to convince the northern public of a conspiracy to extend slavery.

Douglas's bill was a catastrophe for sectional harmony. It repudiated a compromise that many in the North regarded as a binding sectional compact, almost as sacred and necessary to the survival of the Union as the Constitution itself. In defiance of the whole compromise tradition, it made a concession to the South over extending slavery without an equivalent concession to the North. It also shattered the fragile sectional accommodation of 1850 and made future compromises less likely. From then on, northern sectionalists would be fighting to regain what they had lost, while southerners would battle to maintain rights already conceded.

The act also destroyed what was left of the second-party system. The weakened and tottering Whig party disintegrated when its congressional representation split along sectional lines on the Kansas-Nebraska issue. The Democratic party survived, but its ability to act as a unifying national force was impaired. Northern desertions and southern gains (resulting from the recruitment of proslavery Whigs) destroyed the sectional balance within the party, placing it under southern control.

The Kansas-Nebraska furor also doomed the Pierce administration's efforts to revive an expansionist foreign policy. Pierce and Secretary of State William Marcy wanted to acquire Cuba from Spain. But northerners interpreted the administration's plan, made public in a memorandum known as the Ostend Manifesto, as an attempt to create a "Caribbean slave empire." The resulting storm of protest forced Pierce and his cohorts to abandon their scheme.

Quick Check

✓ Why did the Kansas-Nebraska Act divide the Democratic party along sectional lines and lead to the demise of the Whig party?

Kansas and the Rise of the Republicans

The new Republican party was an outgrowth of the anti-Nebraska coalition of 1854. A new political label was required because Free-Soil Democrats—who were important in the Midwest—refused to march under the Whig banner or support any candidate for high office who called himself a Whig.

In 1854–1855, some ex-Whigs had joined the short-lived nativist party known as the "Know-Nothings." The Know-Nothing party was founded in 1849 as an anti-immigrant vehicle. Massive immigration of Irish and Germans, most of whom were Catholic, led to increasing tension among ethnic groups during the 1840s and early 1850s. Native-born and even immigrant Protestants viewed the newcomers as bearers of alien cultures. Political nativism first emerged in the form of local "American" parties protesting immigrant influence in cities such as New York and Philadelphia. The Know-Nothings sought to extend the period of naturalization to undercut immigrant voting strength and keep aliens in their place.

When the Know-Nothing party split over the Kansas-Nebraska issue in 1856, most northern nativists became Republicans. The Republican argument that the "slave-power conspiracy" was a greater threat to American liberty and equality than an alleged "popish plot" proved persuasive. But Republican nativists did not have to abandon their ethnic and religious prejudices; the party showed a clear commitment to the values of native-born evangelical Protestants. On the local level, Republicans generally supported causes that reflected an anti-immigrant or anti-Catholic bias—such as banning the sale of alcoholic beverages, observance of the Sabbath, defense of Protestant Bible-reading in schools, and opposition to state aid for parochial education.

The Republican leaders were seasoned professional politicians, men who had earlier been prominent Whigs or Democrats. Adept at organizing the grass roots, building coalitions, and employing the techniques of popular campaigning, they built up an effective party apparatus in an amazingly short time. By 1856, the new party was well established throughout the North and was preparing to make a serious bid for the presidency.

The Republicans' position on slavery in the territories explains their rapid and growing appeal. Republicans viewed the unsettled West as a land of opportunities, a place to which the ambitious and hardworking could migrate to improve their social and economic position. But if slavery was permitted to expand, it would deny the rights of "free labor." Slaveholders would monopolize the best land, use their slaves to compete unfairly with free white workers, and block commercial and industrial development. They could also use their control of new western states to dominate the federal government in the interest of the "slave power." Republicans also pandered to racial prejudice: They presented their policy as a way to keep African Americans out of the territories, thus preserving the new lands for whites.

Although the Kansas-Nebraska Act raised the territorial issue and gave birth to the Republican party, the turmoil associated with attempts to implement popular sovereignty in Kansas enabled the Republicans to increase their following

View the **Closer Look**
The Compromise of 1850 on
myhistorylab.com

throughout the North. When Kansas was organized in 1854, a bitter contest began to control the territorial government between militant Free-Soilers from New England and the Midwest and slaveholding settlers from Missouri. In the first territorial elections, thousands of Missouri residents crossed the border to vote illegally. The result was a decisive victory for the slave-state forces. The legislature not only legalized slavery but made it a crime to speak or act against it.

Free-Soilers were already a majority of the actual residents of the territory when this legislature denied them the right to agitate against slavery. To defend themselves and their convictions, they took up arms and established a rival territorial government under a constitution that outlawed slavery.

A small-scale civil war then broke out between the rival regimes, culminating in May 1856 when proslavery adherents raided the free-state capital at Lawrence. Portrayed in Republican propaganda as "the sack of Lawrence," this incursion resulted in substantial property damage but no loss of life. More bloody was the reprisal by the antislavery zealot John Brown. After the attack on Lawrence, Brown and a few followers murdered five proslavery settlers in cold blood, in what became known as the Pottawatomie Massacre. During the next few months—until an effective territorial governor arranged a truce in 1856—a hit-and-run guerrilla war raged between free-state and slave-state factions.

The Republican press had a field day with the events in Kansas, exaggerating the violence but correctly pointing out that the federal government was favoring a proslavery minority over a Free-Soil majority. Since the "sack of Lawrence" occurred about the same time that Preston Brooks assaulted Charles Sumner on the Senate floor, the Republicans launched their 1856 campaign under twin slogans: "Bleeding Kansas" and "Bleeding Sumner." The image of an evil and aggressive "slave power," using violence to deny constitutional rights to its opponents, aroused northern sympathies and won votes.

Read the **Document**
John Gihon, Kansas Begins to Bleed on **myhistorylab.com**

Quick Check

✓ What positions did the new Republican party take regarding immigration, western expansion, and slavery?

Sectional Division in the Election of 1856

The Republican nominating convention revealed the strictly sectional nature of the new party. Only a handful of delegates from the slave states attended, all from the upper South. The platform called for liberating Kansas from the slave power and congressional prohibition of slavery in all territories. The nominee was John C. Frémont, explorer of the West and one of the conquerors of California during the Mexican-American War.

The Democratic convention dumped Pierce, passed over Stephen A. Douglas, and nominated James Buchanan of Pennsylvania, who had a long career in public service. The platform endorsed popular sovereignty in the territories. The American party, a Know-Nothing remnant that survived mainly as the rallying point for anti-Democratic conservatives in the border states and the South, chose ex-President Millard Fillmore as its standard-bearer and received the backing of those northern Whigs who refused to become Republicans and hoped to revive the tradition of sectional compromise.

TABLE 14.3 The Election of 1856

Candidate	Party	Popular Vote	Electoral Vote
Buchanan	Democratic	1,832,955	174
Frémont	Republican	1,339,932	114
Fillmore	American (Know-Nothing)	871,731	8

The election was really two separate races—one in the North, where the main contest was between Frémont and Buchanan; the other in the South, between Fillmore and Buchanan. Buchanan won, outpolling Fillmore in every slave state except Maryland and edging out Frémont in five northern states—Pennsylvania, New Jersey, Indiana, Illinois, and California. But Frémont won 11 of the 16 free states, sweeping the upper North with substantial majorities and winning more northern popular votes than either of his opponents. (See Table 14.3) Since the free states had a majority in the electoral college, a future Republican candidate could win the presidency by overcoming a slim Democratic edge in the lower North.

In the South, where the possibility of a Frémont victory had revived talk of secession, the results of the election brought relief tinged with anxiety. The very existence of a sectional party committed to restricting the expansion of slavery constituted an insult to the southerners' way of life. That such a party was popular in the North raised doubts about the security of slavery within the Union. The continued success of a unified Democratic party under southern control was widely viewed as the last hope for maintaining sectional balance and "southern rights."

Quick Check

✓ How was the election of 1860 really "two separate races"?

THE HOUSE DIVIDED, 1857–1860

The sectional quarrel became virtually irreconcilable between Buchanan's election in 1856 and Lincoln's victory in 1860. A series of incidents provoked one side or the other, heightened the tension, and ultimately brought the crisis to a head. Behind the panicky reaction to public events lay a growing sense that North and South were so different in culture and so opposed in basic interests that they could no longer coexist in the same nation.

How did the institution of slavery go beyond political and economic debates?

Cultural Sectionalism

Signs of cultural and intellectual cleavage had appeared well before the triumph of sectional politics. In the mid-1840s, the Methodist and Baptist churches split into northern and southern denominations because of differing attitudes toward slaveholding. Presbyterians and Episcopalians remained formally united but had informal northern and southern factions that went their separate ways on the slavery issue. Instead of unifying Americans around a common Protestant faith, the churches became nurseries of sectional discord. Northern preachers and congregations denounced slaveholding as a sin, while most southern churchmen rallied to a biblical defense of the peculiar institution and became apologists for the southern way of life. Prominent religious leaders—such as Henry Ward Beecher, George B. Cheever, and Theodore Parker in the North, and James H. Thornwell and Bishops Leonidas Polk and Stephen Elliott in the South—were in the forefront of sectional mobilization. As men of God, they helped to turn political questions into moral issues and reduced the prospects for a compromise.

American literature also became sectionalized during the 1840s and 1850s. Southern men of letters, including such notable figures as novelist William Gilmore Simms and Edgar Allan Poe, wrote proslavery polemics. Popular novelists produced a flood of "plantation romances" that glorified southern civilization and sneered at that of the North. The notion that planter "cavaliers" were superior to money-grubbing Yankees was the message that most southerners derived from the homegrown literature they read. In the North, prominent men of letters—Emerson, Thoreau, James Russell Lowell, and Herman Melville—expressed antislavery sentiments in prose and poetry, particularly after the outbreak of the Mexican-American War.

Literary abolitionism climaxed in 1852 when Harriet Beecher Stowe published *Uncle Tom's Cabin*, an enormously successful novel (it sold more than 300,000 copies in one year) that fixed in the northern mind the image of the slaveholder as a brutal Simon Legree. Much of its emotional impact came from its portrayal of slavery as a threat to the family and the Cult of Domesticity. When the saintly Uncle Tom was sold away from his adoring wife and children, northerners shuddered with horror, and some southerners felt a twinge of conscience.

Southern defensiveness gradually hardened into cultural and economic nationalism. Southern schools banished northern textbooks in favor of those with a prosouthern slant; young men of the planter class were induced to stay in the South for higher education rather than go North to universities (as had been the custom); and a movement developed to encourage southern industry and commerce to reduce dependence on the North. Almost without exception, prominent southern educators and intellectuals of the late 1850s rallied behind southern sectionalism, and many even endorsed the idea of an independent southern nation.

Watch the **Video**
Harriet Beecher Stowe and the Making Of Uncle Tom's Cabin on **myhistorylab.com**

Quick Check

✓ What aspects of American culture became sectionalized in the 1850s?

The Dred Scott Case

When James Buchanan was inaugurated on March 4, 1857, the dispute over the legal status of slavery in the territories was an open door through which sectional fears and hatreds could enter the political arena. Buchanan hoped to close that door by encouraging the Supreme Court to resolve the constitutional issue once and for all.

The Court was about to render its decision in the case of *Dred Scott v. Sandford*. Dred Scott was a Missouri slave who sued for his freedom on the grounds that he had lived for years in an area where the Missouri Compromise had outlawed slavery. The Court could have decided the issue on the narrow ground that a slave was not a citizen and therefore had no right to sue in federal courts. But President-elect Buchanan encouraged the Court to render a broader decision.

On March 6, Chief Justice Roger B. Taney announced that the majority had ruled against Scott. Taney argued that no African American—slave or free—could be a citizen of the United States. But the real bombshell was the ruling that Dred Scott would not have won his case even if he had been a legal plaintiff. His residence in the Wisconsin Territory established no right to freedom because Congress had no power to prohibit slavery there. The Missouri Compromise was thus unconstitutional and so, implicitly, was the plank in the Republican platform that called for excluding slavery from all federal territories.

In the North, and especially among Republicans, the Court's verdict was viewed as the latest diabolical act of the "slave-power conspiracy." Circumstantial evidence supported the charge that the decision was a political maneuver. Five of the six judges who voted in the majority were proslavery southerners. Their resolution of the territorial issue was close to the extreme southern-rights position John C. Calhoun had advocated in 1850.

Republicans denounced the decision as "a wicked and false judgment," "the greatest crime in the annals of the republic." But they stopped short of openly defying the Court's authority. Instead, they argued on narrow technical grounds that the decision as written was not binding on Congress, which could still enact a ban on slavery in the territories. The decision actually helped the Republicans build support; it lent credence to their claim that an aggressive slave power was dominating all branches of the federal government and attempting to use the Constitution to achieve its own ends.

Watch the **Video**
Dred Scott and the Crises that Led to the Civil War on
myhistorylab.com

Quick Check

✓ What did chief justice Taney argue in his opinion, and what impact did this have on American sectionalism?

Debating the Morality of Slavery

In the aftermath of the Dred Scott decision, Stephen Douglas faced a tough reelection campaign to the Senate from Illinois in 1858. His opponent was the former Whig Congressman Abraham Lincoln. Their battle became a forum for the debate over slavery in the territories.

In the famous speech that opened his campaign, Lincoln tried to distance himself from his opponent by taking a more radical position: "A house divided against itself cannot stand. I believe this government cannot endure, permanently half *slave* and half *free*." Lincoln then described the chain of events between the Kansas-Nebraska Act and the Dred Scott decision as evidence of a plot to extend and nationalize slavery and tried to link Douglas to this proslavery conspiracy by pointing

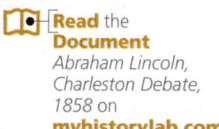

Read the **Document**
Abraham Lincoln, Charleston Debate, 1858 on
myhistorylab.com

Little Giant Stephen Douglas, the "Little Giant" from Illinois, won election to Congress when he was just 30 „years old. Four years later, he was elected to the Senate.

to his rival's unwillingness to take a stand on the morality of slavery, to his professed indifference about whether slavery was voted up or down in the territories. For Lincoln, the only security against the triumph of slavery and the slave power was moral opposition to human bondage.

In the series of debates that focused national attention on the Illinois contest, Lincoln hammered away at the theme that Douglas was a covert defender of slavery because he was not a principled opponent of it. Douglas accused Lincoln of endangering the Union by his talk of putting slavery on the path to extinction. Denying that he was an abolitionist, Lincoln distinguished between tolerating slavery in the South, where the Constitution protected it, and allowing it to expand to places where it could legally be prohibited. The Founders had restricted slavery, he argued. Douglas and the Democrats had departed from the great tradition of containing an evil that could not be immediately eliminated.

In the debate at Freeport, Illinois, Lincoln questioned Douglas on how he could reconcile popular sovereignty with the Dred Scott decision. The Little Giant responded that slavery could not exist without supportive legislation to sustain it and that territorial legislatures could simply not pass a slave code if they wanted to keep it out. Historians formerly believed that Douglas's "Freeport doctrine" alienated his southern supporters. In truth, Douglas had already undermined his popularity in the slave states. But the Freeport speech hardened southern opposition to his presidential ambitions.

Douglas's most effective debating point was to charge that Lincoln's moral opposition to slavery implied a belief in racial equality. Lincoln, facing a racist electorate, affirmed his commitment to white supremacy. He would grant blacks the right to the fruits of their own labor while denying them the "privileges" of full citizenship. Douglas made the most of this inherently contradictory position.

Although Republican candidates for the state legislature won a majority of the popular vote, the Democrats carried more counties and thus were able to reelect Douglas. Lincoln lost an office, but he won respect in Republican circles throughout the country. By stressing the moral dimension of the slavery question and under-cutting any possibility of fusion between Republicans and Douglas Democrats, he had sharpened his party's ideological focus and stiffened its resolve not to compromise its Free-Soil position.

Slavery remained an emotional and symbolic issue. Events in late 1859 and early 1860 turned southern anxiety about northern attitudes and policies into a "crisis of fear." The most significant event was John Brown's raid on Harpers Ferry, Virginia, in October 1859. Brown led 18 men, including five free blacks, in seizing the federal arsenal and armory in Harpers Ferry, hoping to start an uprising against slavery. While he failed at that, and was hanged for treason, the sympathy and admiration he aroused in the North stunned southerners. Within the South, the raid and its aftermath touched off a frenzy of fear, repression, and mobilization.

Read the **Document**
Garrison on John Brown's Raid on **myhistorylab.com**

Quick Check

✓ What was the basis of Lincoln's opposition to slavery?

The Election of 1860

The Republicans, sniffing victory and insensitive to the depth of southern feeling against them, met in Chicago on May 16 to nominate a presidential candidate. The initial front-runner, Senator William H. Seward of New York, had two strikes against him: He had a reputation for radicalism and a record of opposition to nativism. Most of the delegates wanted a less controversial nominee who could win two or three of the northern states that the Democratic had carried in 1856. Lincoln met their specifications: He was from Illinois, a state the Republicans needed to win; he seemed more moderate than Seward; and he had kept his distaste for Know-Nothingism to himself. He was also a self-made man, whose rise from frontier poverty to legal and political prominence embodied the Republican ideal of equal opportunity for all.

The Republican platform, like the nominee, was meant to broaden the party's appeal in the North. Although the platform retained a commitment to halt the expansion of slavery, it gave economic matters more attention than in 1856. It called for a high protective tariff, endorsed free homesteads, and supported federal aid for internal improvements, especially a transcontinental railroad. The platform was designed to attract enough ex-Whigs and renegade Democrats to give the Republicans a solid majority in the North.

The Democrats failed to present a united front against this formidable challenge. When the party first met in the sweltering heat of Charleston in late April, Douglas commanded a majority of the delegates but not the two-thirds required for nomination because of southern opposition. The convention did endorse popular sovereignty, but the price was a walkout by Deep South delegates who favored a federal slave code for the territories.

Unable to agree on a nominee, the convention reconvened in Baltimore in June. There, the pro-Douglas forces won a fight over whether to seat newly selected pro-Douglas delegations from some Deep South states in place of the

A Rising Star Abraham Lincoln, shown here in his first full-length portrait. Although Lincoln lost the contest for the Senate seat in 1858, the Lincoln–Douglas debates established his reputation as a rising star of the Republican party.

bolters from the first convention. But that led to another and more massive southern walkout. The Democratic party fractured. The delegates who remained nominated Douglas and reaffirmed the party's commitment to popular sovereignty. The bolters nominated John Breckinridge of Kentucky on a platform of federal protection for slavery in the territories.

By the time the campaign was under way, four parties were running presidential candidates. In addition to the Republicans, the Douglas Democrats, and the "Southern Rights" Democrats, John Bell of Tennessee ran under the banner of the Constitutional Union party, a remnant of conservative Whigs and Know-Nothings. Taking no explicit stand on slavery in the territories, the Constitutional Unionists tried to represent the spirit of sectional accommodation that had led to compromise in 1820 and 1850. In effect, the race became two separate two-party contests: In the North, the real choice was between Lincoln and Douglas; in the South, it was between Breckinridge and Bell.

The result was a stunning Republicans victory. By gaining the electoral votes of all the free states, except those from three districts of New Jersey that voted for Douglas, Lincoln won a decisive majority over his combined opponents. In the North, his 54 percent of the popular vote annihilated Douglas. In the South, where Lincoln was not even on the ballot, Breckinridge triumphed everywhere except in Virginia, Kentucky, and Tennessee, which went for Bell. (See Map 14.3) The Republican strategy of seeking power by winning decisively in the majority section had succeeded. Although less than 40 percent of those who went to the polls throughout the nation voted for Lincoln, his support in the North was so solid that he would have won in the electoral college even if he had faced a single opponent.

Most southerners saw the election as a catastrophe. A candidate and a party with no support in their own section had won the presidency on a platform viewed as insulting to southern honor and hostile to southern interests. Since the birth of the republic, southerners had either sat in the White House or influenced those who did. Those days might now be gone forever. Rather than accept permanent minority status in American politics and face the resulting dangers to black slavery and white "liberty," the political leaders of the lower South launched a movement for immediate secession from the Union.

CONCLUSION: EXPLAINING THE CRISIS

Generations of historians have searched for the underlying causes of the crisis leading to disruption of the Union but have failed to agree on what these causes were. Some have stressed the clash of economic interests between agrarian and industrializing regions. But this interpretation does not reflect the way people at the time expressed their concerns. The main issues in the sectional debates of the 1850s were whether slavery was right or wrong and whether it should be extended or contained. Disagreements over protective tariffs and other economic measures benefiting one section or the other were secondary.

Another group of historians blame the crisis on "irresponsible" politicians and agitators on both sides of the Mason–Dixon Line. Public opinion was whipped into a frenzy over issues that competent statesmen could have resolved. But this viewpoint fails to acknowledge the depths of feeling that the slavery question aroused and underestimates the obstacles to a peaceful solution.

The dominant modern view is that the crisis was rooted in profound ideological differences over the morality and utility of slavery as an institution. Most interpreters agree that the roots of the conflict lay in the fact that the South was a slave society and determined to stay one, while the North was equally committed to a free-labor system. No other differences divided the regions in this decisive way. It is hard to imagine that secessionism would have developed if the South like the North had abolished slavery after the Revolution.

Nevertheless, the existence or nonexistence of slavery will not explain why the crisis came when and how it did. Why did the conflict become irreconcilable in

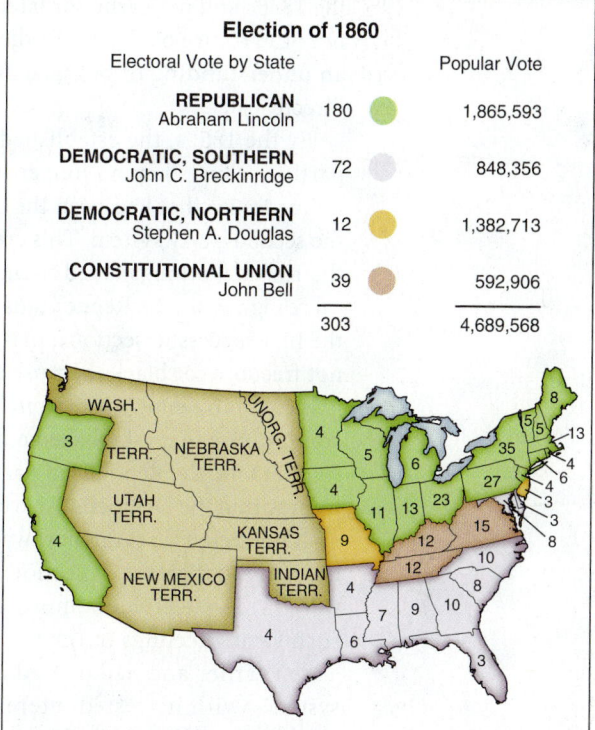

Map 14.3 *The Election of 1860* Many observers have said that the election of 1860 was really two elections: one in the North and one in the South. From this map, can you see why the candidate who won the northern election became president?

the 1850s and not earlier or later? Why did it take the form of a political struggle over the future of slavery in the territories? Answers to both questions require an understanding of political developments that tensions over slavery did not directly cause.

By the 1850s, the established Whig and Democratic parties were in trouble, partly because they no longer offered the voters clear-cut alternatives on economic issues that had been the bread and butter of politics during the heyday of the second-party system. This created an opening for new parties and issues. After the Know-Nothings failed to make hostility to immigrants the basis for a political realignment, the Republicans used the issue of slavery in the territories to build the first successful sectional party in American history. They called for "free soil," not freedom for blacks because abolitionism conflicted with the northern majority's commitment to white supremacy and its respect for the original constitutional compromise that established a hands-off policy toward slavery in the South. For southerners, the Republican party now became the main issue, and they fought it from within the Democratic party.

If politicians seeking new ways to mobilize an apathetic electorate are seen as the main instigators of sectional crisis, we still have to ask why certain appeals were more effective than others. Why did the slavery extension issue arouse such strong feelings in the two sections during the 1850s? The same issue had arisen earlier and had proved adjustable, even in 1820 when the second-party system—with its vested interest in compromise—had not yet emerged. If the expansion of slavery had been as vital and emotional a question in 1820 as it was in the 1850s, the moribund Federalist party presumably would have revived in the form of a northern sectional party adamantly opposed to admitting slave states to the Union.

Ultimately, therefore, we must recognize that the crisis of the 1850s had both a deep social and cultural dimension and a purely political one. Beliefs and values had diverged significantly in the North and the South between the 1820s and the 1850s. Both sections continued to profess allegiance to the traditional "republican" ideals of individual liberty and independence, and both were influenced by evangelical religion. But differences in the economic and social development of each region transformed a common culture into two conflicting cultures. In the North, a rising middle class adapted to the new market economy with the help of an evangelical Christianity that sanctioned self-discipline and social reform (see Chapter 12). The South, on the other hand, embraced slavery as a foundation for white liberty and independence. Its evangelicalism encouraged personal piety but not social reform and gave only limited attention to building the kind of personal character that made for commercial success. The notion that white liberty and equality depended on resisting social and economic change and—to get to the heart of the matter—continuing to have enslaved blacks to do menial labor became more entrenched.

When politicians appealed to sectionalism during the 1850s, therefore, they could evoke conflicting views of what constituted the good society. The South—with its allegedly idle masters, degraded unfree workers, and shiftless poor whites—seemed to most northerners to be in flagrant violation of the Protestant work ethic and the ideal of open competition in "the race of life." From the dominant southern point of view, the North was a land of hypocritical money-grubbers who denied the obvious fact that the virtue, independence, and liberty of free citizens was possible only when dependent laboring classes—especially racially inferior ones—were kept under the kind of rigid control that only slavery could provide. Once these contrary views of the world had become the main themes of political discourse, sectional compromise was no longer possible.

14 STUDY RESOURCES

((•—Listen to the **Chapter Audio** for Chapter 14 on **myhistorylab.com**

TIMELINE

CHAPTER REVIEW

THE COMPROMISE OF 1850

How did territorial expansion intensify the conflict over slave ownership?

Manifest Destiny raised questions about states' rights. The Constitution did not permit the federal government to override state slavery laws, but the Wilmot Proviso attempted and failed to ban slavery in the Mexican cession. Despite that defeat, California was admitted as a free state under the Compromise of 1850, while the Fugitive Slave Law appeased the South. *(p. 336)*

POLITICAL UPHEAVAL, 1852–1856

How did the two-party system change during this period?

The Whig candidate lost in 1852 for supporting the antislavery cause, while the Kansas-Nebraska Act sought to repeal the Missouri Compromise—a move most northerners and some southerners considered abominable. This gave rise to Republicanism, which adhered to native Protestant values while supporting development in the West and opposing slavery. The 1856 election was largely a choice between rivals, one northern and one southern. *(p. 341)*

THE HOUSE DIVIDED, 1857–1860

How did the institution of slavery go beyond political and economic debates?

Slavery divided American society culturally, legally, and morally. Religious congregations broke up, while literature expressed increasingly the sentiments surrounding slaveholding. The Dred Scott decision stripped American blacks—free and slave alike—of most legal rights. Finally, Lincoln chose to oppose slavery on moral grounds, making freedom a human (and not simply legal) right. *(p. 347)*

KEY TERM QUESTIONS

1. How did the Wilmot Proviso blur party lines in Congress? (p. 337)

2. How did popular sovereignty try to resolve the slavery question? (p. 338)

3. What did the South and the North each gain from the Compromise of 1850? (p. 339)

4. Why were northerners so angry about the Fugitive Slave Law? (p. 340)

5. Why did the Kansas-Nebraska Act divide the Democratic Party along sectional lines and lead to the demise of the Whig Party? (p. 343)

6. Why was the Ostend Manifesto so controversial? (p. 344)

MyHistoryLab CONNECTIONS

Visit **www.myhistorylab.com** for a customized Study Plan to build your knowledge of *The Sectional Crisis*

Question for Analysis

1. Why is the Fugitive Slave Act significant?

    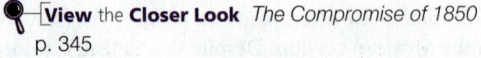 **Read** the **Document** *The Fugitive Slave Act* p. 339

2. Was the Compromise of 1850 truly a compromise?

    View the **Closer Look** *The Compromise of 1850* p. 345

Other Resources from this Chapter

Read the **Document** *John C. Calhoun's Proposal to Preserve the Union*

View the **Image** *Stephen Douglas*

3. Why did *Uncle Tom's Cabin* become a bestseller?

   👁—Watch the Video *Harriet Beecher Stowe and the Making of Uncle Tom's Cabin* p. 348

4. What was decided in the Dred Scott Supreme Court case?

   👁—Watch the Video *Dred Scott and the Crises that Led to the Civil War* p. 349

5. How do you think the audience reacted to Lincoln's introductory speech in Charleston?

   📖—Read the Document *Abraham Lincoln, Charleston Debate in 1858* p. 349

📖—Read the Document *John Gihon, Kansas Begins to Bleed*

📖—Read the Document *Garrison on John Brown's Raid*

15

Secession and the Civil War

1860–1865

Contents and Spotlight Questions

((•—[Listen to the **Chapter Audio** for Chapter 15 on **myhistorylab.com**

THE EMERGENCE OF LINCOLN

The man elected to the White House in 1860 was 6 feet, 4 inches tall and seemed even taller because of his disproportionately long legs and his habit of wearing a high silk "stovepipe" hat. But Abraham Lincoln's previous career provided no guarantee he would tower over most of the other presidents in more than height. When Lincoln sketched the events of his life for a campaign biographer in June 1860, he was modest almost to the point of self-deprecation. Regretting his "want of education," he assured the biographer that "he does what he can to supply the want."

Born to poor and illiterate parents on the Kentucky frontier in 1809, Lincoln received only two years of formal schooling in Indiana after the family moved there in 1816. But mostly he educated himself, reading and rereading treasured books by firelight. In 1831, when the

Matthew Brady's Lincoln On February 27, 1860, Abraham Lincoln gave a campaign speech at Cooper Union in front of 1500 people that helped him win the Presidency. In this forceful, hour-long speech, he proved that the Founders intended to regulate slavery. On his way there, he stopped at photographer Matthew Brady's studio. Brady's "Cooper Union Portrait" became the iconic image of President Lincoln. (Portrait of Abraham Lincoln, Matthew Brady, Library of Congress) family migrated to Illinois, he left home to make a living in the struggling settlement of New Salem, where he worked as a surveyor, shopkeeper, and postmaster. His brief career as a merchant was disastrous: He went bankrupt and was saddled with debt for years. But he found success in law and politics. While studying law on his own in New Salem, he was elected to the state legislature. In 1837, he moved to Springfield, a growing town that offered bright prospects for a young lawyer-politician. Lincoln combined exceptional political and legal skills with a down-to-earth, humorous way of addressing jurors and voters. He became a leader of the Whig party in Illinois and one of the most sought after lawyers in the central Illinois judicial circuit.

The high point of his political career as a Whig was one term in Congress (1847–1849). Lincoln did not seek reelection, but he would have faced certain defeat if he had. His opposition to the Mexican-American War alienated his constituency, and the voters elected a Democrat to succeed him in 1848. In 1849, President Zachary Taylor, for whom Lincoln had campaigned vigorously, did not give him a patronage job he coveted. Having been repudiated by the electorate and ignored by the national leadership of a party he had served loyally and well, Lincoln built his law practice.

The Kansas-Nebraska Act of 1854, with its advocacy of popular sovereignty, provided Lincoln with a heaven-sent opportunity to return to politics with a stronger base of support. For the first time, his ambition for political success and convictions about what was best for the country were easy to reconcile. Lincoln had long believed slavery was unjust and should be tolerated only to the extent the Constitution and the tradition of sectional compromise required. He attacked Douglas's plan of popular sovereignty because it broke with precedents for federal containment or control of the growth of slavery. After trying to rally Free-Soilers around the Whig standard, Lincoln threw in his lot with the Republicans, became leader of the new party in Illinois, attracted national attention in his bid for Douglas's Senate seat in 1858, and had the right qualifications when the Republicans chose a presidential nominee in 1860. That he had split rails with an axe as a young man was used in the campaign to show that he was a man of the people.

After Lincoln's election provoked southern secession and plunged the nation into the greatest crisis in its history, many people were skeptical of his abilities: Was he up to the responsibilities he faced? Lincoln had less experience relevant to a wartime presidency than any previous or future chief executive; he had never been a governor, senator, cabinet officer, vice president, or high-ranking military officer. But his training as a prairie politician would prove useful in the years ahead.

Lincoln was also an effective war leader because he identified wholeheartedly with the northern cause and could inspire others to make sacrifices for it. In his view, the issue in the conflict was nothing less than the survival of the kind of political system that gave men like himself a chance for high office.

The Civil War put on trial the very principle of democracy at a time when most European nations had rejected political liberalism and accepted the conservative view that popular government would inevitably collapse into anarchy. It also showed the shortcomings of a purely white man's democracy and brought the first hesitant steps toward black citizenship. As Lincoln put it in the Gettysburg Address in 1863, the only cause great enough to justify the enormous sacrifice of life on the battlefields was the struggle to preserve and extend the democratic ideal, to ensure that "government of the people, by the people, for the people, shall not perish from the earth."

THE STORM GATHERS

Lincoln's election provoked the secession of seven states of the Deep South but did not lead immediately to armed conflict. Before the sectional quarrel would turn from a cold war into a hot one, two things had to happen: A final effort to defuse the conflict by compromise and conciliation had to fail, and the North needed to develop a firm resolve to maintain the Union by military action.

The Deep South Secedes

South Carolina, which had long been in the forefront of southern rights and proslavery agitation, was the first state to secede. On December 20, 1860, a convention in Charleston declared unanimously that "the union now subsisting between South Carolina and other states, under the name of the 'United States of America,' is hereby dissolved." The constitutional theory behind secession was that the Union was a "compact" among sovereign states, each of which could withdraw from it by the vote of a convention similar to the one that had ratified the Constitution in the first place. The South Carolinians justified secession by charging that "a sectional party" had elected a president "whose opinions and purposes are hostile to slavery."

Other states of the Cotton Kingdom felt similar outrage at Lincoln's election but less certainty about how to respond to it. Cooperationists, who believed the slave states should act as a unit, opposed those who advocated immediate secession by each state individually. If the cooperationists had triumphed, secession would have been delayed until a southern convention had agreed on it. Some of these moderates hoped to extort major concessions from the North and thus remove the need for dissolving the Union. But South Carolina's unilateral action weakened their cause.

Elections for delegates to secession conventions in six other Deep South states were hotly contested. Cooperationists did well in Georgia, Louisiana, and Texas. But secessionists won a majority in every state. By February 1, six other states had left the Union—Alabama, Mississippi, Florida, Georgia, Louisiana, and Texas. In the upper South, however, calls for immediate secession failed; majority opinion in Virginia, North Carolina, Tennessee, and Arkansas did not think that Lincoln's election was a sufficient reason for breaking up the Union. These states had stronger ties to the northern economy, and moderate leaders were more willing to seek a sectional compromise.

Delegates from the Deep South met in Montgomery, Alabama, on February 4 to establish the Confederate States of America. The convention acted as a provisional government while drafting a constitution. Relatively moderate leaders, most of whom had not supported secession until *after* Lincoln's election, dominated the proceedings and defeated or modified the pet schemes of extreme southern nationalists. Voted down were proposals to reopen the Atlantic slave trade, abolish the three-fifths clause (in favor of counting all slaves in determining congressional representation), and prohibit admitting free states to the new Confederacy.

What developments and events drew the Union toward Civil War?

Watch the **Video**
What caused the Civil War? on
myhistorylab.com

Read the
Document
South Carolina Declaration of the Causes of Secession on
myhistorylab.com

📖 **Read** the
Document
Confederate Constitution, 1861 on
myhistorylab.com

The resulting constitution was surprisingly similar to that of the United States. Most of the differences merely spelled out traditional southern interpretations of the federal charter: The central government was denied the authority to impose protective tariffs, subsidize internal improvements, or interfere with slavery in the states and was required to protect slavery in the territories. As president and vice president, the convention chose Jefferson Davis of Mississippi and Alexander Stephens of Georgia, men who had resisted secessionist agitation.

The moderation shown in Montgomery resulted in part from a desire to win support in the upper South. But it also revealed that proslavery reactionaries had never won a majority. Most southerners had opposed dissolving the Union so long as slavery seemed safe from northern interference.

Lincoln's election destroyed that sense of security. But the Montgomery convention made it clear that the new converts to secessionism did not want to establish a slaveholder's reactionary utopia. They wanted to re-create the Union as it had been before the rise of the Republican party. They opted for secession only when it seemed the only way to achieve their aim. The decision to allow free states to join the Confederacy reflected a hope that the old Union could be reconstituted under southern direction. Some optimists even predicted that all of the North except New England would transfer its loyalty to the new government.

Men of Moderation Jefferson Davis, inaugurated as president of the Confederacy on February 18, 1861, was a West Point graduate and had served as secretary of war under President Franklin Pierce and as a U.S. senator.

Secession and the formation of the Confederacy thus amounted to a conservative and defensive kind of "revolution." The only justification for southern independence on which a majority could agree was the need for greater security for the "peculiar institution." Vice President Stephens spoke for all the founders of the Confederacy when he described the cornerstone of the new government as "the great truth that the negro is not equal to the white man—that slavery—subordination to the superior race—is his natural condition."

✓ **Quick Check**

How did secessionists conceive of the U.S. constitution, and how did their new constitution differ?

The Failure of Compromise

While the Deep South was opting for independence, moderates in the North and border slave states were trying to devise a compromise that would stem the secessionist tide. In December 1860, Senator John Crittenden of Kentucky presented the Crittenden compromise, which advocated extending the Missouri Compromise line to the Pacific to protect slavery in the southwestern territories. The federal government would compensate the owners of escaped slaves, and a constitutional amendment would forever prohibit the federal government from abolishing or regulating slavery in the states.

Congressional Republicans seemed willing take the proposals seriously. However, their support evaporated when President-elect Lincoln adamantly opposed extending the compromise line. In the words of a fellow Republican, he stood "firm as an oak."

Lincoln's resounding "no" to the central provision of the Crittenden plan and similar proposals stiffened the backbone of congressional Republicans, and they voted against compromise as members of the committees both houses set up to avert war. Also voting against the Crittenden plan, and thereby ensuring its defeat, were the remaining senators and congressmen of the seceding states, who had vowed to support no compromise unless the majority of Republicans also endorsed it. Their purpose in taking this stand was to obtain guarantees that the northern sectional party would end its attacks on "southern rights." The Republicans did agree to support Crittenden's "un-amendable" amendment guaranteeing that slavery would be immune from federal interference. But this was not really a concession to the South, because Republicans had always acknowledged that the federal government had no constitutional authority to meddle with slavery in the states.

Lincoln and those who took his advice had what they considered good reasons for not making territorial concessions. They mistakenly believed that the secession movement was a conspiracy that reflected only a minority opinion in the South and that a strong stand would rally southern Unionists and moderates. However, Lincoln and the dedicated Free-Soilers for whom he spoke would probably not have given ground even if they had realized the secession movement was genuinely popular in the Deep South. In their view, extending the Missouri Compromise line of 36°30′ to the Pacific would not halt agitation for extending slavery. South of the line were Cuba and Central America, where southern expansionists dreamed of a Caribbean slave empire. The only way to resolve the crisis over the future of slavery and reunite the "house divided" was to remove any chance that slaveholders could enlarge their domain.

Lincoln was also convinced that backing down in the face of secessionist threats would undermine the democratic principle of majority rule. In his inaugural address of March 4, 1861, he recalled that during the winter, "patriotic men" had urged him to accept a compromise that would "shift the ground" on which he had been elected. But that would have signified that a victorious presidential candidate "cannot be inaugurated till he betrays those who elected him by breaking his pledges, and surrendering to those who tried and failed to defeat him at the polls." Such a concession would mean that "this government and all popular government is already at an end."

Quick Check

✓ What was the Crittenden compromise, and why was it rejected?

And the War Came

By the time of Lincoln's inauguration, the Confederacy had seized most federal installations in the Deep South without firing a shot. President James Buchanan had denied the right of secession but had also refused to use "coercion" to maintain federal authority. Many in the North shared his doubts about whether a Union held together by force was worth preserving. The business community feared breaking commercial links with the cotton-producing South, and some antislavery Republicans and abolitionists thought the nation might be better off if "the erring sisters" were allowed "to depart in peace."

The collapse of compromise efforts eliminated the option of maintaining the Union peacefully and narrowed the choices to separation between the sections with or without war. By early March, public opinion was beginning to shift in favor of action to preserve the Union. Once the business community realized conciliation would not keep the cotton states in the Union, it put its weight behind coercion, reasoning that a temporary disruption of commerce was better than the permanent loss of the South as a market and source of raw materials.

In his inaugural address, Lincoln called for a cautious use of force. He would defend federal forts not yet in Confederate hands but would not attempt to recapture the ones already taken. He thus tried to shift the burden for beginning hostilities to the Confederacy, which would have to attack before it would be attacked.

As Lincoln spoke, U.S. forces held only four military installations within the seceded states. Two in the remote Florida Keys attracted little attention. The others were Fort Pickens on an island outside Pensacola in northwest Florida and Fort Sumter inside Charleston Harbor. Attention focused on Sumter because the Confederacy, egged on by South Carolina, was demanding the surrender of a garrison that was within easy reach of shore batteries and running low on supplies. Shortly after taking office, Lincoln was informed that Sumter could not hold out much longer and that he would have to decide whether to reinforce it or let it fall.

Initially, Lincoln's cabinet opposed reinforcing or provisioning Sumter, on the grounds that it was indefensible. Secretary of State Seward was so certain this would be the decision that he so advised Confederate representatives. But on April 4, Lincoln ordered that the beleaguered troops in Charleston Harbor be resupplied. Two days later, he notified the governor of South Carolina that a relief expedition was being sent.

The expedition sailed on April 8 and 9, but before it arrived, Confederate authorities decided that sending supplies was a hostile act and attacked the fort. On the morning of April 12, shore batteries opened fire; the bombardment continued for 40 hours without loss of life but with heavy damage to the fort. Finally, on April 13, the Union forces under Major Robert Anderson surrendered, and the Confederate flag was raised over Fort Sumter. The South had won a victory but had also assumed responsibility for firing the first shot.

On April 15, Lincoln proclaimed that an insurrection against federal authority existed in the Deep South and called on the militia of the loyal states to provide 75,000 troops for short-term service to put it down. Two days later, a Virginia

View the **Image**
Fort Sumter on
myhistorylab.com

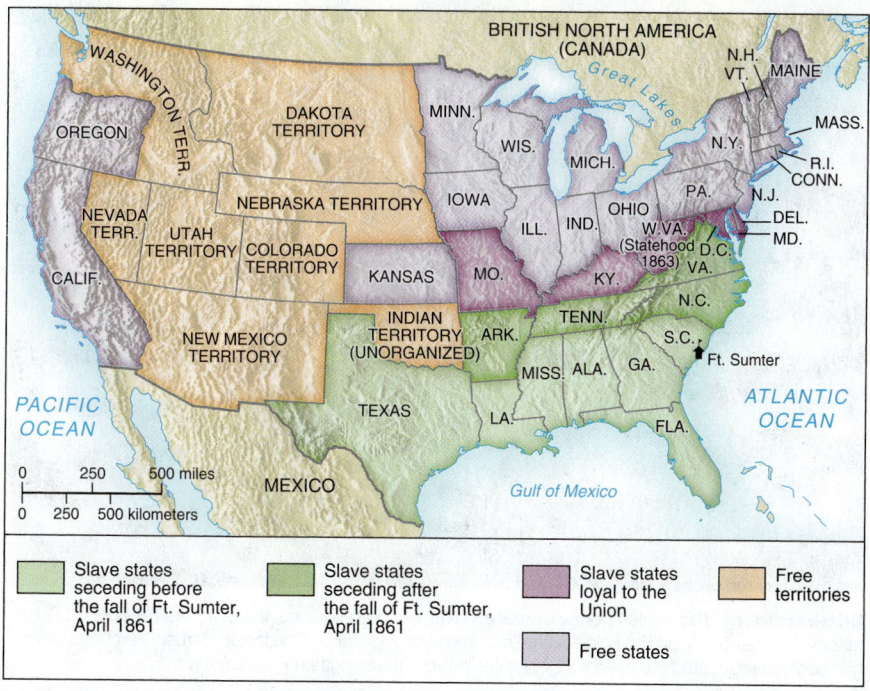

Map 15.1 *Secession* The fall of Fort Sumter was a watershed for the secessionist movement.

convention that had rejected secession in February voted to join the Confederacy. Within five weeks, Arkansas, Tennessee, and North Carolina followed suit. These slave states of the upper South had been unwilling to secede just because Lincoln was elected, but when he called on them to provide troops to "coerce" other southern states, they had to choose sides. Believing that secession was a constitutional right, they cut their ties with a government that opted to use force to maintain the Union and asked them to join the effort. (See Map 15.1)

In the North, the firing on Sumter evoked an outpouring of patriotism and dedication to the Union. "It seems as if we were never alive till now; never had a country till now," wrote a New Yorker; and a Bostonian noted, "I never before knew what a popular excitement can be." Stephen A. Douglas, Lincoln's former political rival, pledged his full support for the crusade against secession and literally worked himself to death rallying midwestern Democrats behind the government. By firing on the flag, the Confederacy united the North. Everyone assumed the war would be short and not very bloody. Whether Unionist fervor could be sustained through a long and costly struggle remained to be seen.

The Confederacy, which now moved its capital to Richmond, Virginia, contained only 11 of the 15 states in which slavery was lawful. In the border slave states of Maryland, Delaware, Kentucky, and Missouri, local Unionism and federal intervention thwarted secession. Kentucky, the most crucial of these states, proclaimed

Bombardment This contemporary Currier and Ives lithograph depicts the bombardment of Fort Sumter on April 12–13, 1861. The soldiers are firing from Fort Moultrie in Charleston Harbor, which the Union garrison had evacuated the previous December in order to strengthen Fort Sumter.

its neutrality. It eventually sided with the Union, mainly because Lincoln, who was careful to respect this tenuous neutrality, provoked the South into violating it first by invading the state. Maryland surrounded the nation's capital and provided it with access to the free states. More ruthless methods, which included martial law to suppress Confederate sympathizers, kept it in the Union. In Missouri, regular troops, aided by a staunchly pro-Union German immigrant population, stymied the secession movement. But pro-Union forces failed to establish order in this deeply divided frontier state. Guerrilla fighting made wartime Missouri an unsafe and bloody place.

Hence the Civil War was not, strictly speaking, a struggle between slave and free states. Nor did it simply pit states that could not tolerate Lincoln's election against those that could. More than anything else, conflicting views on secession determined the division of states and the choices individuals made in areas where sentiment was divided. General Robert E. Lee, for example, was neither a defender of slavery nor a southern nationalist. But he followed Virginia out of the Union because he was the loyal son of a "sovereign state." General George Thomas, another Virginian, chose the Union because he believed it was indissoluble. Although concern about the future of slavery had driven the Deep South to secede in the first place, the actual lineup of states and supporters meant the two sides would initially define the war less as a struggle over slavery than as a contest to determine whether the Union was indivisible.

Quick Check

✓ What was Lincoln's attitude toward the use of force, and why did he want the south to initiate any hostilities that might occur?

ADJUSTING TO TOTAL WAR

The Civil War was a "total war" involving every aspect of society because the North could restore the Union only by defeating the South so thoroughly that its separatist government would collapse. It was a long war because the Confederacy put up "a hell of a fight" before it would agree to be put to death. Total war is a test of societies, economies, and political systems, as well as a battle of wits between generals and military strategists—and the Civil War was no exception.

What challenges did "total war" bring for each side?

Mobilizing the Home Fronts

North and South faced similar problems in trying to create the vast support systems armies in the field needed. (See Figure 15.1) At the beginning of the conflict, both sides had more volunteers than they could arm and outfit. But as hopes for a short and easy war faded, the pool of volunteers began to dry up. Many of the early recruits, who had been enrolled for short terms, were reluctant to reenlist. To resolve this problem, the Confederacy passed a conscription law in April 1862, and in July, Congress gave Lincoln the power to assign manpower quotas to each state and resort to conscription if they were not met.

To produce the materials of war, both governments relied mainly on private industry. In the North, especially, the system of contracting with private firms and individuals to supply the army resulted in corruption and inefficiency. The government bought shoddy uniforms that disintegrated in heavy rain, defective rifles, and

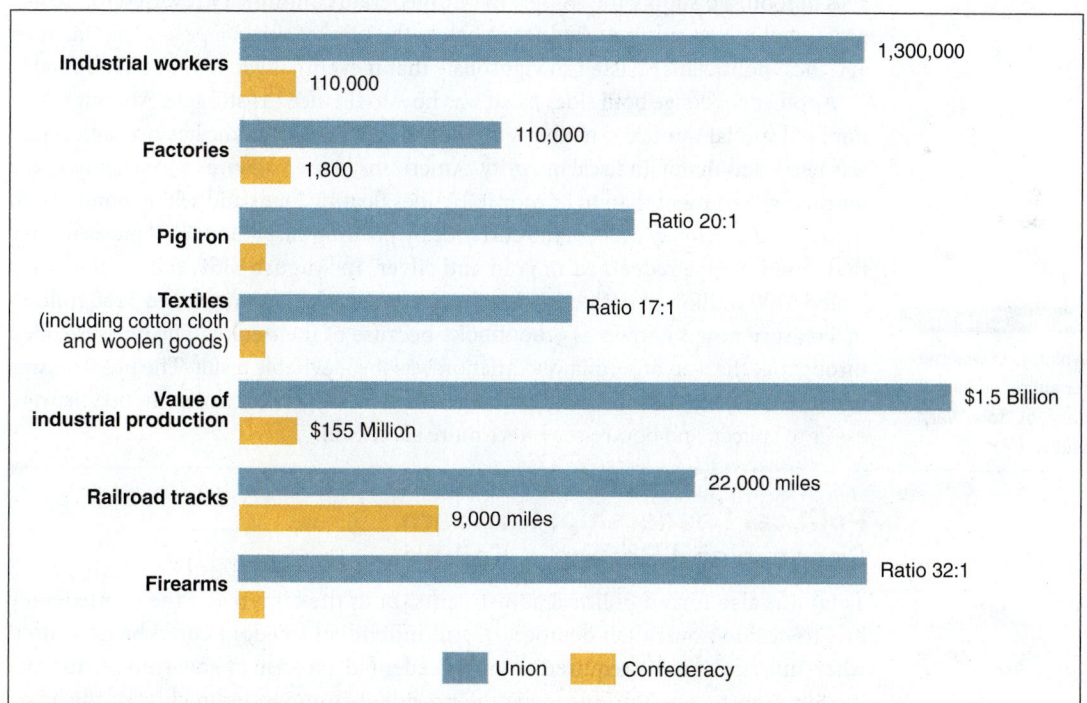

Figure 15.1 Resources of the Union and the Confederacy, 1861

horses unfit for service. But the North's economy was strong at the core. By 1863, its factories and farms were producing more than enough to provision the troops without lowering the living standards of the civilian population.

The southern economy was less adaptable to the needs of a total war. The South of 1861 imported most of its manufactured goods. As the Union blockade became more effective, the Confederacy had to rely on a government-sponsored crash program to produce war materials. The government encouraged and promoted private initiatives and built its own munitions plants. Astonishingly, the Confederate Ordnance Bureau, under the able direction of General Josiah Gorgas, produced or procured sufficient armaments to keep southern armies well supplied throughout the conflict.

Southern agriculture, however, failed to meet the challenge. Planters were reluctant to shift from staples that could no longer be readily exported to urgently needed foodstuffs. But more significant was the South's inadequate internal transportation system. Its limited rail network was designed to link plantation regions to port cities rather than to connect food-producing areas with centers of population, the way the North's was. Railroad construction during the war did not resolve the problem; most of the new lines facilitated the movement of troops, not the distribution of food.

Read the **Document**
Diary Of Joseph Addison Waddell on **myhistorylab.com**

When northern forces penetrated the South, they created new gaps in the system. As a result, much of the corn or livestock that was raised could not reach the people who needed it. Although well armed, Confederate soldiers were increasingly undernourished, and by 1863, civilians in urban areas were rioting to protest shortages of food. To supply the troops, the Confederate commissary resorted to the impressment of agricultural produce at below the market price, a policy that farmers and local politicians resisted so vigorously that it eventually had to be abandoned.

Another challenge both sides faced was how to finance the struggle. Although they imposed special war taxes, neither side was willing to resort to the heavy taxation that was needed to maintain fiscal integrity. Americans, it seems, were more willing to die for their government than to pay for it. Besides floating loans and selling bonds, both treasuries deliberately inflated the currency by printing vast amounts of paper money that could not be redeemed in gold and silver. In August 1861, the Confederacy issued $100 million of such currency. In early 1862, the Union printed $150 million in Treasury notes, known as **greenbacks** because of their color. The presses rolled throughout the war, and runaway inflation was the inevitable result. The problem was less severe in the North because its economy was stronger, war taxes on income were easier to collect, and bond issues were more successful.

Quick Check

✔ Which side was better suited economically for "total war," and why?

Political Leadership: Northern Success and Southern Failure

Total war also forced political adjustments. Both the Union and the Confederacy had to decide how much democracy and individual freedom could be permitted when military success required an unprecedented exercise of government authority. Since both constitutions made the president commander in chief of the army and navy, Lincoln and Jefferson Davis took actions that would have been regarded as arbitrary or even tyrannical in peacetime.

Lincoln was especially bold in assuming new executive powers. After the fighting started at Fort Sumter, he expanded the regular army and advanced public money to private individuals without congressional authorization. On April 27, 1861, he declared martial law, which enabled the military to arrest civilians suspected of aiding the enemy, and suspended the writ of habeas corpus in the area between Philadelphia and Washington, because of mob attacks on Union troops in Baltimore. Suspending the writ enabled the government to arrest Confederate sympathizers and hold them without trial. In September 1862, Lincoln extended this authority to all parts of the United States where "disloyal" elements were active. Such willingness to interfere with civil liberties was unprecedented and possibly unconstitutional, but Lincoln argued that "necessity" justified a flexible interpretation of his war powers. For critics of suspension, he had a question: "Are all the laws, *but one*, to go unexecuted, and the government itself to go to pieces, lest that one be violated?" In fact, however, most of the thousands of civilians military authorities arrested were not exercising their right to criticize the government but were suspected deserters and draft dodgers, refugees, smugglers, or people simply found wandering in areas under military control.

For the most part, the Lincoln administration tolerated a broad spectrum of political dissent. Although the government briefly closed down a few newspapers when they allegedly published false information or military secrets, anti-administration journals were allowed to criticize the president and his party at will. A few politicians were arrested for pro-Confederate activity, but many "Peace Democrats"—who called for restoring the Union by negotiation rather than force—ran for office and sat in Congress and state legislatures. They had ample opportunity to present their views to the public. In fact, vigorous two-party competition in the North during the Civil War strengthened Lincoln's hand. Since his war policies were also the platform of his party, he could usually rely on unified partisan backing for his most controversial decisions.

Lincoln was singularly adept at the art of party leadership; he accommodated factions and defined party issues and principles in a way that would encourage unity and dedication to the cause. Since the Republican party was the main vehicle for mobilizing and maintaining devotion to the Union effort, these political skills were crucial. When a majority of the party came around to the view that freeing the slaves was necessary to the war effort, Lincoln complied with their wishes while minimizing the disenchantment of the conservative minority. Lincoln held the party together by persuasion, patronage, and flexible policymaking; this cohesiveness was essential to Lincoln's success in unifying the nation by force.

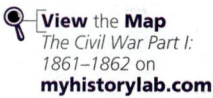

View the **Map**
The Civil War Part I: 1861–1862 on
myhistorylab.com

Jefferson Davis, most historians agree, was a less effective war leader. He defined his powers as commander in chief narrowly and literally, which meant he personally directed the armed forces but left policymaking for mobilizing and controlling the civilian population primarily to the Confederate Congress. Unfortunately, he overestimated his capacities as a strategist and lacked the tact to handle field commanders who were as proud and testy as he was.

Davis's greatest failing, however, was his lack of initiative and leadership in dealing with the home front. He devoted little attention to a deteriorating economic situation that caused great hardship and sapped Confederate morale. Although division and disloyalty were more serious in the South than in the North, he was extremely cautious in his use of martial law.

Quick Check

✓ In what ways did Lincoln assume stronger executive powers than a peacetime president, and was he justified in doing so?

As the war dragged on, Davis's support eroded. State governors who resisted conscription and other policies that violated the tradition of states' rights opposed and obstructed him. Southern newspapers and the Confederate Congress attacked Davis's conduct of the war. His authority was further undermined because he did not have an organized party behind him, for the Confederacy never developed a two-party system. As a result, it was difficult to mobilize the support hard decisions and controversial policies required.

Early Campaigns and Battles

The war's first major battle was a disaster for northern arms. Against his better judgment, General Winfield Scott, the aged army commander, responded to the "On to Richmond" clamor and ordered poorly trained Union troops under General Irvin McDowell to advance against the Confederate forces gathered at Manassas Junction, Virginia. They attacked the enemy position near Bull Run Creek on July 21, 1861. Confederate General Thomas J. Jackson earned the nickname "Stonewall" for holding the line against the northern assault until reinforcements routed the invading force. The raw Union troops stampeded back to safety in Washington.

This humiliating defeat led to a shake-up of the northern high command. George McClellan replaced McDowell as commander of troops in the Washington area and then became general in chief when Scott was eased into retirement. In the West, however, Union forces won important victories. In February 1862, a joint military–naval operation, under General Ulysses S. Grant, captured Fort Henry on the Tennessee River and Fort Donelson on the Cumberland along with 14,000 prisoners. The Confederate army withdrew from Kentucky and middle Tennessee. Southern forces in the West then massed at Corinth, Mississippi, just across the border from Tennessee. When a slow-moving Union army arrived just north of the Mississippi state line, the South attacked on April 6. In the battle of Shiloh, one of the bloodiest of the war, only the arrival of reinforcements prevented the annihilation of Union troops backed up against the Tennessee River. After a second day of fierce fighting, the Confederates retreated to Corinth, leaving the enemy battered and exhausted.

Although Shiloh halted the Union's effort to seize the Mississippi Valley, on April 26, a Union fleet from the Gulf captured New Orleans. The occupation of New Orleans, besides securing the mouth of the Mississippi and the largest city in the South, climaxed a series of naval and amphibious operations around the edges of the Confederacy. Bases were now available to enforce a blockade of the southern coast.

But Union forces made little headway on the eastern front. In May, Robert E. Lee took command of the Confederate Army of Northern Virginia, and in June

Casualties of War Alexander Gardner took this photograph of dead Confederate soldiers lined up for burial at Antietam, in Maryland, after the deadliest one-day battle of the war. Photographers working with Mathew Brady accompanied Union troops in battle. Their visual records of the campaigns and casualties stand as a testament to the hardships and horrors of war.

he began an all-out effort to expel Union forces from the outskirts of Richmond. All summer, Lee's forces battled McClellan's up and down the peninsula southeast of the city until McClellan withdrew. In September, Lee invaded Maryland, hoping to isolate Washington from the rest of the North. The bloodiest one-day battle of the war ensued. When the smoke cleared at Antietam on September 17, almost 5,000 men had been killed on the two sides and more than 18,000 wounded. The result was a draw, but Lee was forced to fall back south of the Potomac to protect his supply lines. McClellan was slow in pursuit, and Lincoln blamed him for letting the enemy escape. He replaced McClellan with General Ambrose E. Burnside, who was responsible for a disastrous assault on Confederate forces at the Battle of Fredericksburg, Virginia in December 1862. This Union defeat ended a year of bitter failure for the North in the East.

Quick Check

✓ What strategic choices did Union generals make in the early fighting that led to severe losses and heavy casualties?

FIGHT TO THE FINISH

The last two and a half years of the struggle saw the implementation of more radical war measures. The most dramatic and important of these was Lincoln's decision to free the slaves and bring the black population into the war on the Union side. The tide of battle turned decisively in the summer of 1863, but the South resisted valiantly for two more years until the sheer weight of the North's advantages in manpower and resources finally overcame it.

How did the Union finally attain victory, and what role did emancipation play in it?

The Road to Liberty In this allegorical painting, President Lincoln extends a copy of his proclamation to the goddess of liberty, who is driving her chariot, Emancipation.

The Coming of Emancipation

At the beginning of the war, when the North still hoped for a quick and easy victory, only dedicated abolitionists favored turning the struggle for the Union into a crusade against slavery. In summer 1861, Congress almost unanimously affirmed that the war was being fought only to preserve the Union, not to change the domestic institutions of any state. But as it became clear how hard subduing the "rebels" was going to be, sentiment developed for striking at the South's economic and social system by freeing its slaves. In July 1862, Congress authorized the confiscation of slaves whose masters supported the Confederacy. By this time, the slaves themselves were voting for freedom with their feet by deserting plantations in areas where the Union forces were close enough to offer a haven. They thus put pressure on the government to determine their status and, in effect, offered themselves as a source of manpower to the Union on the condition that they be made free.

Although Lincoln favored freedom for blacks as an ultimate goal, he was reluctant to commit his administration to immediate emancipation. In the fall of 1861 and spring of 1862, he had reversed the orders of field commanders who sought to free slaves in areas their forces occupied, thus angering abolitionists and the strongly antislavery Republicans known as Radicals. Lincoln's caution stemmed from fear of alienating Unionists in the border slave states and from his own preference for a gradual, compensated form of emancipation.

Lincoln was also aware that the racial prejudice of most whites in the North and the South was an obstacle to any program leading to emancipation. Although personally more tolerant than most white Americans, Lincoln was pessimistic about equality for blacks in the United States. He therefore coupled a proposal for gradual emancipation with a plea for government subsidies to support the voluntary "colonization" of freed blacks outside of the United States, and he sought places that would accept them.

But the slaveholding states that remained loyal to the Union refused to endorse Lincoln's gradual plan, and the failure of Union arms in the 1862 increased the clamor for striking directly at the South's peculiar institution. The Lincoln administration also realized that emancipation would win sympathy for the Union cause in Britain and France and might counter the threat that they would come to the aid of the Confederacy. In July, Lincoln read an emancipation proclamation to his cabinet, but Secretary of State Seward persuaded him not to issue it until the North had won a victory and could not be accused of acting out of desperation.

Finally, on September 22, 1862, Lincoln issued his preliminary **Emancipation Proclamation.** McClellan's success at Antietam provided the occasion, but the president was also responding to political pressures. Most Republican politicians were now committed to emancipation, and many were on the verge of repudiating the administration for its inaction. Had Lincoln failed to act, his party would have split, and he would have been in the minority faction. The proclamation gave the Confederate states 100 days to give up the struggle without losing their slaves. In December, Lincoln proposed that Congress approve constitutional amendments providing for gradual, compensated emancipation and subsidized colonization.

Since there was no response from the South and little enthusiasm in Congress for Lincoln's gradual plan, the president went ahead on January 1, 1863, and declared that all slaves in those areas under Confederate control "shall be … thenceforward, and forever free." He justified the final proclamation as an act of "military necessity" sanctioned by the war powers of the president, and he authorized the enlistment of freed slaves in the Union army. The language and tone of the document—one historian has described it as having "all the moral grandeur of a bill of lading"—made it clear that blacks were being freed for reasons of state and not out of humanitarian conviction.

Despite its uninspiring origin and limited application—it did not extend to slave states loyal to the Union or to occupied areas and thus did not immediately free a single slave—the proclamation did commit the Union to abolishing slavery as a war aim. It also accelerated the breakdown of slavery as a labor system, a process that was already under way by early 1863. The blacks who had remained in captured areas or deserted their masters to cross Union lines before 1863 had been kept in a kind of way station between slavery and freedom, in accordance with the theory that they were "contraband of war." As word spread among the slaves that emancipation was now official policy, more of them were inspired to run off and seek the protection of northern armies. One slave who crossed the Union lines summed up their motives: "I wants to

Read the **Document**
The Emancipation Proclamation (1863) on
myhistorylab.com

Quick Check

✓ Why was Lincoln skeptical of immediate emancipation, and what changed his mind?

be free. I came in from the plantation and don't want to go back; ... I don't want to be a slave again." Approximately one-quarter of the slave population gained freedom during the war under the terms of the Emancipation Proclamation and thus deprived the South of an important part of its agricultural workforce.

African Americans and the War

Almost 200,000 African Americans, most of them newly freed slaves, eventually served in the Union forces and made a vital contribution to the North's victory. Without them it is doubtful that the Union could have been preserved. Although enrolled in segregated units under white officers, initially paid less than their white counterparts, and used disproportionately for garrison duty or heavy labor behind the lines, "blacks in blue" fought heroically in major battles during the last two years of the war.

Read the **Document** H. Ford Douglas to Frederick Douglass's Monthly (1863) on **myhistorylab.com**

Those freed during the war who did not serve in the military were often conscripted as contract wage laborers on cotton plantations that "loyal" white planters owned or leased within occupied areas of the Deep South. Abolitionists protested that the coercion military authorities used to get blacks back into the cotton fields amounted to slavery in a new form, but those in power argued that the necessities of war and the northern economy required such "temporary" arrangements. Regimentation of the freedmen within the South also assured racist northerners, especially in the Midwest, that emancipation would not result in a massive migration of black refugees to their region of the country.

The heroic performance of African American troops and the easing of northern fears of being swamped by black migrants deepened the commitment to permanent and comprehensive emancipation. Realizing that his proclamation had a shaky constitutional foundation and might apply only to slaves actually freed while the war was going on, Lincoln sought to organize and recognize loyal state governments in southern areas under Union control on condition that their constitutions abolished slavery.

Black Soldiers This 1890 lithograph by Kurz and Allison commemorates the 54th Massachusetts Colored Regiment charging Fort Wagner, South Carolina, in July 1863. The 54th was the first African-American unit recruited during the war. Charles and Lewis Douglass, sons of Frederick Douglass, served with this regiment.

Finally, Lincoln pressed for an amendment to the Constitution outlawing involuntary servitude. After supporting its inclusion as a central plank in the Republican platform of 1864, Lincoln won congressional approval for the Thirteenth Amendment, which was passed by Congress in January 1865 and ratified in December. The cause of freedom for blacks and the cause of the Union had at last become one and the same. Lincoln, despite his earlier hesitations and misgivings, had earned the right to be called the Great Emancipator.

Quick Check

✓ What effect did African American troops have on the war in battle and on the homefront?

The Tide Turns

By 1863, the Confederate economy was in shambles. The social order of the South was also buckling. Masters were losing control of their slaves, and non-slaveholding whites were becoming disillusioned with the hardships of what some described as "a rich man's war and a poor man's fight." Yet the North had its own morale problems. The long series of eastern defeats had engendered war weariness, and the new policies that "military necessity" forced the government to adopt encountered fierce opposition.

The Enrollment Act of March 1863, which provided for outright conscription of white males but permitted men to hire substitutes or pay a fee to avoid military service, provoked a violent response from those unable to buy their way out of

Read the Document
If it were Not For My Trust In Christ, I do Not on
myhistorylab.com

THE RIOTS IN NEW YORK : THE MOB LYNCHING A NEGRO IN CLARKSON-STREET.—SEE PAGE 142.

An 1863 draft call in New York provoked violence against African Americans, viewed by the rioters as the cause of an unnecessary war, and rage against the rich men who had been able to buy exemptions from the draft. This 1863 illustration from *Harper's Weekly* depicts a mob lynching a black man on Clarkson Street in New York City.

service and unwilling to fight for blacks. Antidraft riots broke out, culminating in one of the bloodiest domestic disorders in American history—the New York Riot of July 1863. The New York mob, composed mainly of Irish-American laborers, burned the draft offices, the homes of Republicans, and a black orphanage. They also lynched more than a dozen defenseless blacks. At least 120 people died before federal troops restored order. Besides racial prejudice, the draft riots also reflected working-class anger at the wartime privileges and prosperity of the middle and upper classes; they exposed deep divisions on the administration's conduct of the war.

To fight dissension and "disloyalty," the government used martial law to arrest a few alleged ringleaders, including Democratic Congressman Clement Vallandigham of Ohio. Private organizations also issued propaganda attacking what they believed was a vast secret conspiracy to undermine the northern war effort. Historians disagree about the extent of covert and illegal antiwar activity. No vast conspiracy existed, but militant advocates of "peace at any price"— popularly known as Copperheads—were active in some areas, especially among the immigrant working classes of large cities and in southern Ohio, Indiana, and Illinois.

The only effective way to overcome the disillusionment that fed the peace movement was to win battles and convince the northern public that victory was assured. Before this could happen, the North suffered another humiliating defeat in the East. In May 1863, a Confederate army less than half their size routed Union forces under General Joseph Hooker at Chancellorsville, Virginia. Again, Lee demonstrated his superior generalship, this time by dividing his forces and sending Stonewall Jackson to make a surprise attack on the Union right. The Confederacy prevailed, but Jackson himself died from wounds received in the battle.

In the West, however, a major Union triumph was taking shape. For more than a year, General Ulysses S. Grant had been trying to capture Vicksburg, Mississippi, the almost inaccessible Confederate bastion that stood between the North and control of the Mississippi River. Finally, in late March 1863, he crossed to the west bank north of the city and moved his forces to south of it, where he joined up with naval forces that had run the Confederate batteries mounted on Vicksburg's high bluffs. In one of the boldest campaigns of the war, Grant crossed the river, deliberately cutting himself off from his sources of supply, and marched into the interior of Mississippi. Living off the land and out of communication with an anxious and perplexed Lincoln, his troops defeated two Confederate armies and advanced on Vicksburg from the east. After unsuccessfully assaulting the city, Grant settled down for a siege on May 22.

Meanwhile, President Davis approved Lee's plan to invade the Northeast. Although this would not relieve Vicksburg, it might win a victory that would more than compensate for the probable loss of the Mississippi stronghold. Lee's army crossed the Potomac in June and kept going until it reached Gettysburg, Pennsylvania. There Lee confronted a Union army that had taken up defensive positions on Cemetery Ridge and Culp's Hill.

On July 2, Confederate attacks failed to dislodge Union troops from the high ground they occupied. The following day, Lee decided to attack the strongest part of the Union line. The resulting charge on Cemetery Ridge was disastrous; Confederate soldiers dropped like flies under Union fire. The few who made it to the Union lines were killed or captured. Lee withdrew his battered troops, but because the Union army did not pursue him vigorously, he escaped again. Vicksburg fell to Grant on July 4, the same day Lee began his retreat. Northerners rejoiced that on Independence Day, the Union had secured control of the Mississippi and had finally won a major battle in the East. But Lincoln's joy turned to frustration when he learned his generals had missed the chance to end to the war.

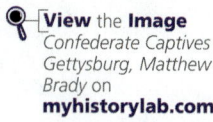

View the **Image**
Confederate Captives Gettysburg, Matthew Brady on **myhistorylab.com**

Quick Check

✓ How did the tide turn against the Confederate army in the middle of 1863?

Last Stages of the Conflict

In 1863, the North also finally gained control of the middle South, where indecisive fighting had been going on since the conflict began. The main Union target was Chattanooga, "the gateway to the Southeast." In September, Union troops managed to maneuver the Confederates out of the city but were in turn surrounded and besieged there by southern forces. Grant arrived from Vicksburg to break the encirclement with assaults on the Confederate positions on Lookout Mountain and Missionary Ridge. The North was now poised to invade Georgia.

Grant's victories in the West earned him promotion to general in chief of the Union armies. In March 1864, he ordered a multipronged offensive to finish off the Confederacy. Its main movements were a thrust on Richmond under Grant's personal command and another by the western armies, under General William Tecumseh Sherman, toward Atlanta and the heart of Georgia.

View the **Map**
The Civil War Part II: 1863–1865 on **myhistorylab.com**

In May and June, Grant and Lee fought a series of bloody battles in northern Virginia that tended to follow a set pattern. Lee would take up an entrenched position in the path of the invading force, and Grant would attack it, sustaining heavy losses but also inflicting casualties the Confederate army could ill afford. When his direct assault had failed, Grant would move to his left, hoping in vain to maneuver Lee into a less defensible position. In the battles of the Wilderness, Spotsylvania, and Cold Harbor, the Union lost about 60,000 men—more than twice the number of Confederate casualties—without opening the road to Richmond. After losing thousands of soldiers in three days at Cold Harbor, Grant moved his army south of Richmond. There he drew up before Petersburg, a rail center that linked Richmond to the rest of the Confederacy; after failing to take it by assault, he settled down for another siege.

The siege of Petersburg was a drawn-out affair, and northern morale plummeted during the summer of 1864. Lincoln was facing reelection, and his failure to end the war dimmed his prospects. Although nominated with ease in June—with Andrew Johnson, a pro-administration Democrat from Tennessee, as his running mate—Lincoln confronted growing opposition within his own party, especially from Radicals who disagreed with his lenient approach to restoring seceded states to the Union (see Chapter 16).

TABLE 15.1 The Election of 1864

Candidate	Party	Popular Vote	Electoral Vote*
Lincoln	Republican	2,213,655	212
McClellan	Democratic	1,805,237	21

*Out of a total of 233 electoral votes. The 11 secessionist states—Alabama, Arkansas, Florida, Georgia, Louisiana, Mississippi, North Carolina, South Carolina, Tennessee, Texas, and Virginia—did not vote.

The Democrats made a strong bid for the White House. Their platform appealed to war weariness by calling for a cease-fire followed by negotiations to reestablish the Union. The party's nominee, General George McClellan, announced he would not be bound by the peace plank and would pursue the war. But he promised to end the conflict sooner than Lincoln could because he would not insist on emancipation as a condition for reunion. By late summer, Lincoln thought that he would lose.

But northern victories changed the political outlook. Sherman's invasion of Georgia went well. On September 2, Atlanta fell, and northern forces occupied the hub of the Deep South. The news unified the Republican party behind Lincoln. The election itself was almost an anticlimax: Lincoln won 212 of a possible 233 electoral votes and 55 percent of the popular vote. The Republican cause of "liberty and Union" was secure. (See Table 15.1)

The concluding military operations revealed the futility of further southern resistance. Sherman marched unopposed through Georgia to the sea, destroying almost everything of military or economic value in a corridor 300 miles long and 60 miles wide. The Confederate army that had opposed him at Atlanta moved into Tennessee, where Union forces almost destroyed it at Nashville in mid-December. Sherman captured Savannah on December 25. He then carried his scorched-earth policy into South Carolina with the aim of continuing through North Carolina and joining up with Grant at Petersburg.

While Sherman was invading the Carolinas, Grant finally forced the starving and exhausted Confederates to abandon Petersburg and Richmond on April 2, 1865. Grant then pursued them west for 100 miles, and cut off their line of retreat to the south. Recognizing the hopelessness of further resistance, Lee surrendered his army at Appomattox Courthouse on April 9. (See Map 15.2)

But the joy of the victorious North turned to sorrow and anger when John Wilkes Booth, a pro-Confederate actor, assassinated Abraham Lincoln as the president watched a play at Ford's Theater in Washington on April 14. Although Booth had a few accomplices, popular theories that the assassination was the result of a vast conspiracy involving Confederate leaders or Radical Republicans have never been substantiated.

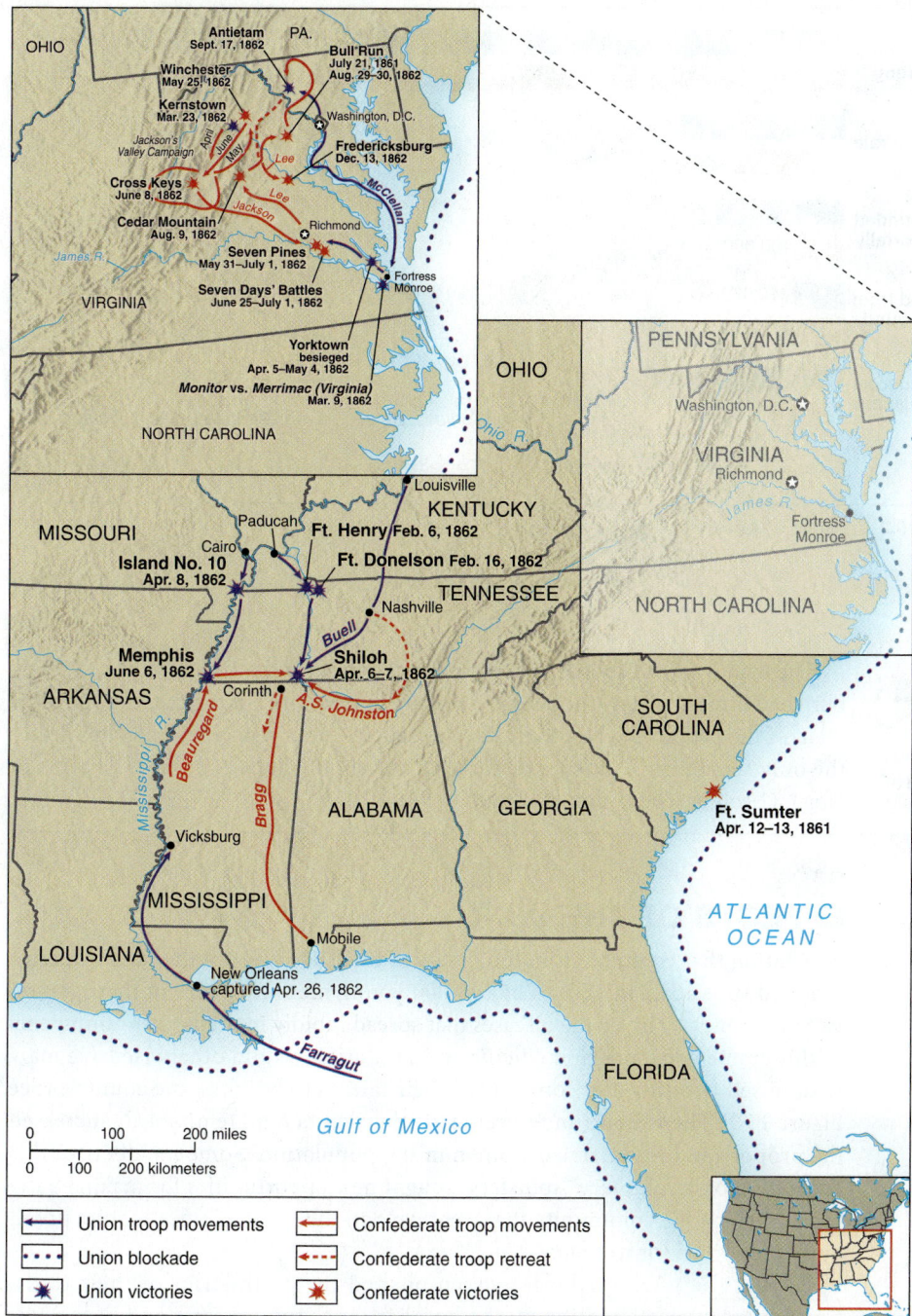

Map 15.2 Civil War, 1861–1865 In the western theater of war, Grant's victories at Port Gibson, Jackson, and Champion's Hill cleared the way for his siege of Vicksburg. In the east, after the hard-won Union victory at Gettysburg, the South never again invaded the North. In 1864 and 1865, Union armies gradually closed in on Lee's Confederate forces in Virginia. Leaving Atlanta in flames, Sherman marched to the Georgia coast, took Savannah, then moved his troops north through the Carolinas. Grant's army, though suffering enormous losses, moved on toward Richmond, marching into the Confederate capital on April 3, 1865, and forcing surrender.

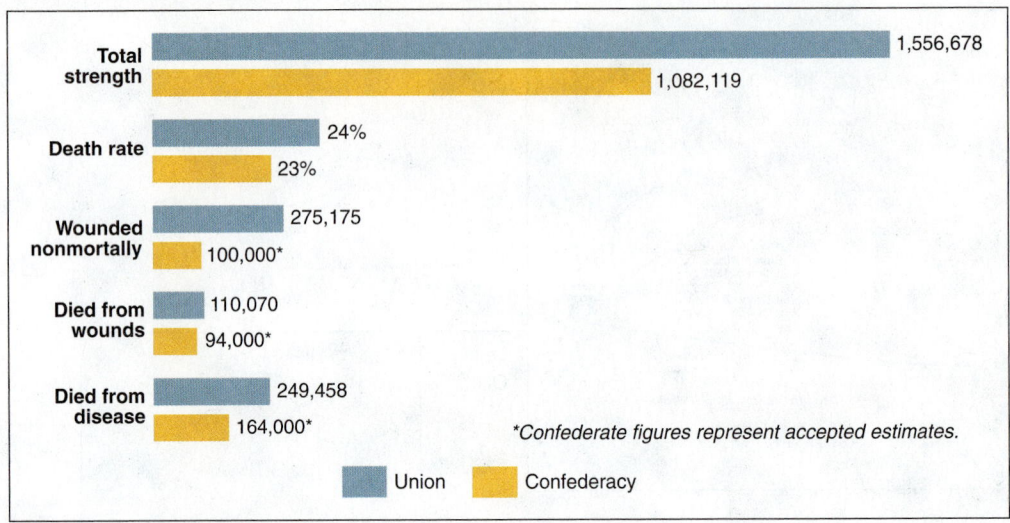

Figure 15.2 Casualties of war

Quick Check

✓ How did Generals Grant and Sherman affect the election of 1864?

The man who had spoken of the need to sacrifice for the Union cause at Gettysburg had himself given "the last full measure of devotion" to the cause of "government of the people, by the people, for the people." Four days after Lincoln's death, the only remaining Confederate force of any significance laid down its arms in North Carolina. The Union was saved.

EFFECTS OF THE WAR

How did the outcome of the war affect America socially and politically?

The nation that emerged from four years of total war was not the same America that had split apart in 1861. The 618,000 young men who were in their graves, victims of enemy fire or the diseases that spread rapidly in military encampments in this era before modern medicine and sanitation, would otherwise have married, raised families, and contributed their talents to building the country. (See Figure 15.2) The widows and sweethearts they left behind temporarily increased the proportion of unmarried women in the population. Some members of this generation of involuntary "spinsters" sought new opportunities for making a living or serving the community that went beyond the purely domestic roles previously prescribed for women.

During the war, northern women pushed the boundaries of their traditional roles by participating on the home front as fund-raisers and in the rear lines as army nurses and members of the Sanitary Commission. The Sanitary Commission promoted health in the northern army's camps through attention to cleanliness, nutrition, and medical care. Northern women simultaneously utilized their traditional position as nurturers to participate in the war effort while they advanced new ideas about their role in society. The many who had served as nurses or volunteer workers during the war were especially responsive to calls for broadening "the woman's sphere." Some northern women who were prominent in wartime service organizations led postwar philanthropic and reform movements. The war did not destroy the traditional barriers to sexual equality in American society, but women's efforts during the Civil War broadened beliefs about what women could accomplish outside of the home.

The war had a different effect on white women in the Confederacy. Southern women had always been involved in administering farms and plantations, but the war forced them to shoulder even greater burdens. Wealthy plantation mistresses had to run huge plantations without the benefit of extensive training or the assistance of male relatives. Farmers' wives found it hard to survive at all, especially at harvest time when they often had to do all the work themselves. The loss of fathers and brothers, the advance of Union troops, and the difficulty of controlling a slave labor force destroyed many southern women's allegiance to the Confederate cause. As in the North, the Civil War changed the situation of women in society. The devastation of the southern economy forced many women to play a more conspicuous public and economic role. They formed associations to assist returning soldiers, became teachers, and established benevolent and reform societies or temperance organizations. Although these changes created a more visible presence for southern women in public, the South remained more conservative in its views about women's "proper place" than did the North.

At enormous human and economic cost, the nation had emancipated four million African Americans from slavery, but it had not yet resolved that they would be equal citizens. At the time of Lincoln's assassination, most northern states still denied blacks equality under the law and the right to vote. Whether the North would extend more rights to southern freedmen than it had granted to "free Negroes" was an open question.

The impact of the war on white working people was also unclear. Those in the industrializing parts of the North had suffered and lost ground economically because prices had risen faster than wages during the conflict. But Republican rhetoric stressing "equal opportunity" and the "dignity of labor" raised hopes that the crusade against slavery could be broadened into a movement to improve the lot of working people in general. Foreign-born workers had additional reason to be optimistic; that so many immigrants had fought and died for the Union cause had—for the moment—weakened nativist sentiment and encouraged tolerance.

What the war definitely decided was that the federal government was supreme over the states and had broad constitutional authority to act for "the general welfare." The southern principle of state sovereignty and strict construction died at Appomattox. The United States was becoming a true nation-state with an effective central government. States still had primary responsibility for most government functions, and the Constitution limited what the national government could do; questions would continue to arise about where federal authority ended and states' rights began. Still, the war had determined where ultimate authority rested.

👁 Watch the **Video**
The Lives Of Southern Women on
myhistorylab.com

A broadened definition of federal powers had its greatest impact in economic policy. During the war, the Republican-dominated Congresses passed legislation to stimulate and direct the nation's economic development. Taking advantage of the absence of southern opposition, Republicans rejected the pre–Civil War tradition of virtual laissez-faire and enacted a Whiggish program of active support for business and agriculture. In 1862, Congress passed a high protective tariff, approved a homestead act to encourage settlement of the West by providing free land to settlers, granted huge tracts of public land to railroads to support building a transcontinental railroad, and gave the states land for agricultural colleges. In 1863, Congress set up a national banking system that required member banks to keep adequate reserves and invest one-third of their capital in government securities. The notes the national banks issued became the country's first standardized and reliable circulating paper currency.

These wartime achievements decisively shifted the relationship between the federal government and private enterprise. The Republicans changed a limited government that sought to do little more than protect the marketplace from the threat of monopoly into an activist state that promoted and subsidized the ambitious and industrious.

CONCLUSION: AN ORGANIZATIONAL REVOLUTION

The most pervasive effect of the war on northern society was to encourage an "organizational revolution." Aided by government policies, venturesome businessmen took advantage of the new national market military procurement created to build larger firms that could operate across state lines; some of the huge corporate enterprises of the postwar era began to take shape. Philanthropists also developed more effective national associations; the most notable of these were the Sanitary and Christian Commissions that ministered to the physical and spiritual needs of the troops. Efforts to care for the wounded influenced the development of the modern hospital and the rise of nursing as a female profession. Both the men who served in the army and those men and women who supported them behind the lines became accustomed to working in large, bureaucratic organizations that had scarcely existed before the war.

The North won the war mainly because it had shown a greater capacity than the South to organize, innovate, and "modernize." Its victory meant the nation as a whole would now embrace the concept of progress that the North had affirmed in its war effort—its advances in science and technology and its success in bringing together and managing large numbers of men and women for economic and social goals. The Civil War was thus a catalyst for the transformation of American society from an individualistic society of small producers into the more highly organized and "incorporated" America of the late nineteenth century.

15 STUDY RESOURCES

((•—Listen to the **Chapter Audio** for Chapter 15 on **myhistorylab.com**

TIMELINE

1860 South Carolina secedes from the Union (December), p. 361

1861 Rest of Deep South secedes, p. 361
- Confederacy founded (January–February), p. 361
- Confederate forces fire on Fort Sumter (April), p. 364
- Upper South secedes (April–May), p. 365
- South wins first Battle of Bull Run (July), p. 370

1862 Grant captures forts Henry and Donelson (February), p. 370
- Union navy captures New Orleans (April), p. 370
- McClellan leads unsuccessful campaign on the peninsula (March–July), p. 371
- McClellan stops Lee at Battle of Antietam (September), p. 371
- Lee defeats Union army at Fredericksburg (December), p. 371

1863 Lincoln issues Emancipation Proclamation (January), p. 373
- North gains major victories at Gettysburg and Vicksburg (July), p. 377
- Grant defeats Confederate forces at Chattanooga (November), p. 377

1864 Grant and Lee battle in northern Virginia (May–June), p. 377
- Atlanta falls to Sherman (September), p. 378
- Lincoln reelected president (November), p. 378
- Sherman marches through Georgia (November–December), p. 378

1865 Grant captures Petersburg and Richmond; Lee surrenders at Appomattox (April), p. 378

- Lincoln assassinated by John Wilkes Booth (April), p. 378

CHAPTER REVIEW

THE STORM GATHERS

What developments and events drew the Union toward Civil War?

Lincoln's election prompted the secession of seven states. In South Carolina, "cooperationism" was defeated, sparking other states to follow. Republicans rejected compromise on the question of slavery in new states, and Lincoln resolved to use force should the South strike first. At Fort Sumter in 1861 it did. (p. 361)

ADJUSTING TO TOTAL WAR

What challenges did "total war" bring for each side?

Total war meant no cease-fire until the southern separatists were defeated. The North, with its large population, heavy industry, and agriculture, was better suited for the long conflict. The South struggled to feed itself and lacked wealth, yet put up a strong fight. Meanwhile, Lincoln maintained northern unity. (p. 367)

FIGHT TO THE FINISH

How did the Union finally attain victory, and what role did emancipation play in it?

Lincoln was skeptical of emancipation, although he favored it morally. Later he saw the strategic benefit of opposing slavery, so he declared the freedom of slaves in unoccupied areas in the January 1863 Emancipation Proclamation. Many African Americans escaped slavery and joined the Union Army, helping to turn the tide of the war. Union victories helped reelect Lincoln in 1864. *(p. 371)*

EFFECTS OF THE WAR

How did the outcome of the war affect America socially and politically?

The Civil War changed the status of many social groups, including women, who took on new social roles after the death of male family members, and blacks, who were adjusting to free status in a white society. New national institutions, including benevolent organizations and banks, contributed to an "organizational revolution." The federal government grew stronger than ever. *(p. 380)*

KEY TERM QUESTIONS

1. Why did the cooperationists lose out to those who advocated immediate secession? (p. 361)

2. Why was the Crittenden compromise rejected? (p. 363)

3. Why did the Union issue greenbacks beginning in 1862? (p. 368)

4. Why did Lincoln issue the Emancipation Proclamation? (p. 373)

5. How did the government deal with Copperheads and others indifferent or hostile to the Union in the Civil War? (p. 376)

6. What was the Sanitary Commission during the Civil War? (p. 380)

MYHISTORYLAB CONNECTIONS

Visit **www.myhistorylab.com** for a customized Study Plan to build your knowledge of *Secession and the Civil War*

Question for Analysis

1. Did the South's idea of what caused the Civil War change after the war?

   Watch the **Video** *What Caused the Civil War?* p. 361

2. How did the Emancipation Proclamation alter the wartime objectives of the Union?

   Read the **Document** *Emancipation Proclamation* p. 373

3. What were the key battles of the Civil War from 1863 to 1865?

   View the **Map** *The Civil War Part II, 1863-1865* p. 377

Other Resources from this Chapter

Read the **Document** *South Carolina Declaration of the Causes*

Read the **Document** *Confederate Constitution, 1861*

View the **Image** *Ft. Sumter*

Read the **Document** *Diary of Joseph Addison Waddell*

View the **Map** *The Civil War, 1861-1862*

Read the **Document** *H. Ford Douglas to Fredrick Douglass*

4. What factors impacted the lives of southern women in the period leading up to the Civil War?

Watch the **Video** *The Lives of Southern Women* p. 382

Read the **Document** *"If It Were Not For My Trust in Christ I Do Not Know How I Could Have Endured It"*

View the **Image** *Confederate Captives, Gettysburg, Matthew Brady*

Contents and Spotlight Questions

((•—[**Listen** to the **Chapter Audio** for Chapter 16 on **myhistorylab.com**

ROBERT SMALLS AND BLACK POLITICIANS DURING RECONSTRUCTION

During the Reconstruction period immediately following the Civil War, African Americans struggled to become equal citizens of a democratic republic. Remarkable black leaders won public office. Robert Smalls of South Carolina was perhaps the most famous and widely respected southern black leader of the era.

Born a slave in 1839, Smalls was allowed as a young man to live and work independently, hiring his own time from a master who may have been his half brother. Smalls worked as a sailor and trained

Robert Smalls With the help of several black crewmen, Robert Smalls—then twenty-three years old—commandeered the Planter, a Confederate steamship used to transport guns and ammunition, and surrendered it to the Union vessel, USS Onward. Smalls provided distinguished service to the Union during the Civil War and after the war went on to become a successful politician and businessman.

himself to be a pilot in Charleston Harbor. When the Union navy blockaded Charleston in 1862, Smalls, who was working on a Confederate steamship called the *Planter*, saw a chance to win his freedom. At three o'clock in the morning on May 13, 1862, when the white officers were ashore, he took command of the vessel and its slave crew, sailed it out of the fortified harbor, and surrendered it to the Union navy. Smalls immediately became a hero to antislavery northerners who were seeking evidence that the slaves were willing and able to serve the Union. The *Planter* became a Union army transport, and Smalls was made its captain after being commissioned as an officer. During the remainder of the war, he rendered conspicuous and gallant service as captain and pilot of Union vessels off the coast of South Carolina.

Like other African Americans who fought for the Union, Smalls had a distinguished political career during Reconstruction, serving in the South Carolina constitutional convention, the state legislature, and the U.S. Congress. He was also a shrewd businessman and owned extensive properties in Beaufort, South Carolina, and its vicinity. The electoral organization Smalls established was so effective that he controlled local government and was elected to Congress even after the election of 1876 had placed the state under the control of white conservatives bent on depriving blacks of political power. Organized mob violence defeated him in 1878, but he bounced back to win a contested congressional election in 1880. He did not leave the House of Representatives for good until 1886, when he lost another contested election.

To defeat him, Smalls's white opponents charged that he had a hand in the corruption that was allegedly rampant in South Carolina during Reconstruction. But careful historical investigation shows that he was, by the standards of the time, an honest and responsible public servant. In the South Carolina convention of 1868 and in the state legislature, he championed free and compulsory public education. In Congress, he fought for federal civil rights laws. Not especially radical on social questions, he sometimes bent over backward to accommodate what he regarded as the legitimate interests and sensibilities of South Carolina whites. Like other middle-class black political leaders in Reconstruction-era South Carolina, he can perhaps be faulted for not doing more to help poor blacks gain access to land of their own. But in 1875, he sponsored congressional legislation that opened for purchase at low prices the land in his own district that the federal government had confiscated during the war. As a result, blacks soon owned three-fourths of the land in the Beaufort area.

Robert Smalls spent the later years of his life as U.S. collector of customs for the port of Beaufort, a beneficiary of the patronage that the Republican party continued to provide for a few loyal southern blacks. But the loss of real political clout for Smalls and men like him was a tragic consequence of the fall of Reconstruction.

For a few years, black politicians such as Robert Smalls exercised more power in the South than they would for another century. But political developments on the national and regional stage made Reconstruction "an unfinished revolution," promising but not delivering true equality for newly freed African Americans. National party politics; shifting priorities among northern Republicans; white southerners' commitment to white supremacy, which was backed by legal restrictions and massive extralegal violence against blacks, all combined to stifle the promise of Reconstruction.

Yet during the Reconstruction era, American society was transformed—new ways of organizing labor and family life, new institutions within and outside the government, and new ideologies about the role of institutions and government in social and economic life. Many of the changes begun during Reconstruction would revolutionize American life.

THE PRESIDENT VERSUS CONGRESS

Reconstructing the Union after the South's defeat was one of the most difficult challenges American policymakers ever faced. The Constitution provided no firm guidelines, for the Framers had not anticipated that the country would divide into warring sections. After emancipation became a northern war aim, a new issue compounded the problem: How far should the federal government go to secure freedom and civil rights for 4 million former slaves?

What conflicts arose among Lincoln, Johnson, and Congress during Reconstruction?

The debate led to a major political crisis. Advocates of a minimal Reconstruction policy favored quickly restoring the Union with no protection for the freed slaves except prohibiting slavery. Proponents of a more radical policy demanded guarantees that "loyal" men would displace the Confederate elite in power and that blacks would acquire basic rights of American citizenship as preconditions for readmitting the southern states. The White House favored the minimal approach. Congress came to endorse the more radical and thoroughgoing form of Reconstruction. The resulting struggle between Congress and the chief executive was the most serious clash between two branches of government in the nation's history.

Wartime Reconstruction

Tension between the president and Congress over how to reconstruct the Union began during the war. Preoccupied with achieving victory, Lincoln never set forth a final and comprehensive plan to bring rebellious states back into the fold. But he favored a lenient and conciliatory policy toward southerners who would give up the struggle and repudiate slavery. In December 1863, he issued a Proclamation of Amnesty and Reconstruction, which offered a full pardon to all southerners (except certain Confederate leaders) who would take an oath of allegiance to the Union and accept emancipation. This Ten Percent Plan provided that once ten percent or more of the voting population of any occupied state had taken the oath, they could set up a loyal government. By 1864, Louisiana and Arkansas, states that Union troops occupied, had established Unionist governments. Lincoln's policy was meant to shorten the war. He hoped to weaken the southern cause by making it easy for disillusioned or lukewarm

Confederates to switch sides and support emancipation by insisting that the new governments abolish slavery.

Congress was unhappy with Lincoln's Reconstruction experiments and in 1864 refused to seat the Unionists that Louisiana and Arkansas elected to the House and Senate. A minority of congressional Republicans—the strongly antislavery **Radical Republicans**—favored protection for black rights (especially black male suffrage) as a precondition for readmitting southern states. But a larger group of congressional moderates opposed Lincoln's plan because they did not trust the repentant Confederates who would play a major role in the new governments. Congress also believed the president was exceeding his authority by using executive powers to restore the Union. Lincoln operated on the theory that secession, being illegal, did not place the Confederate states outside the Union in a constitutional sense. Since individuals and not states had defied federal authority, the president could use his pardoning power to certify a loyal electorate, which could then function as the legitimate state government.

After refusing to recognize Lincoln's ten percent governments, Congress passed a Reconstruction bill of its own in July 1864. Known as the **Wade–Davis Bill**, it required that 50 percent of the voters take a loyalty oath before the restoration process could begin. Once this had occurred, those who could swear they had never willingly supported the Confederacy could vote in an election for delegates to a constitutional convention. The bill did not require black suffrage, but it gave federal courts the power to enforce emancipation. Faced with this attempt to nullify his own program, Lincoln exercised a pocket veto by refusing to sign the bill before Congress adjourned. He said that he did not want to be committed to any single Reconstruction plan. The bill's sponsors responded angrily, and Lincoln's relations with Congress reached their low point.

Congress and the president remained stalemated on the Reconstruction issue for the rest of the war. During his last months in office, however, Lincoln showed a willingness to compromise. He tried to obtain recognition for the governments he had nurtured in Louisiana and Arkansas but seemed receptive to setting other conditions—perhaps including black suffrage—for readmitting those states in which wartime conditions had prevented execution of his plan. However, he was assassinated before he made his intentions clear, leaving historians to speculate whether his quarrel with Congress would have been resolved. Given Lincoln's record of flexibility, the best bet is that he would have come to terms with the majority of his party.

Quick Check

✓ On what matters did Lincoln and Congress disagree?

Andrew Johnson at the Helm

Andrew Johnson, the man an assassin's bullet suddenly made president, attempted to put the Union back together on his own authority in 1865. But his policies set him at odds with Congress and the Republican party and provoked the most serious crisis in the history of relations between the executive and legislative branches of the federal government.

Johnson's background shaped his approach to Reconstruction. Born in poverty in North Carolina, he migrated to eastern Tennessee, where he worked as a tailor. Lacking formal schooling, he was illiterate until adult life. Entering politics as a Jacksonian Democrat, his railing against the planter aristocracy made him the spokesman for Tennessee's non-slaveholding whites and the most successful politician in the state. He advanced from state legislator to congressman to governor and then the U.S. Senate in 1857.

In 1861, Johnson was the only senator from a Confederate state who remained loyal to the Union and continued to serve in Washington. But his Unionism and defense of the common people did not include antislavery sentiments. Nor was he friendly to blacks. In Tennessee, he had objected only to the fact that slaveholding was the privilege of a wealthy minority. He wished that "every head of family in the United States had one slave to take the drudgery and menial service off his family."

During the war, while acting as military governor of Tennessee, Johnson endorsed Lincoln's emancipation policy to destroy the power of the hated planter class rather than as a recognition of black humanity. He was chosen as Lincoln's running mate in 1864 because a pro-administration Democrat, who was a southern Unionist in the bargain, would strengthen the ticket. No one expected this fervent white supremacist to become president. Radical Republicans initially welcomed Johnson's ascent to the nation's highest office. Their hopes made sense given Johnson's fierce loyalty to the Union and his apparent agreement with the Radicals that ex-Confederates should be severely treated. Unlike Lincoln, who had spoken of "malice toward none and charity for all," Johnson seemed likely to punish southern "traitors" and prevent them from regaining political influence. Only gradually did the deep disagreement between the president and the Republican congressional majority become evident.

View the Image
Andrew Johnson Brady on **myhistorylab.com**

The Reconstruction policy that Johnson initiated on May 29, 1865, created uneasiness among the Radicals, but most Republicans were willing to give it a chance. Johnson placed North Carolina, and eventually other states, under appointed provisional governors chosen mostly from among prominent southern politicians who had opposed the secession movement and had rendered no conspicuous service to the Confederacy. The governors were responsible for calling constitutional conventions and ensuring that only "loyal" whites could vote for delegates. Participation required taking the oath of allegiance that Lincoln had prescribed earlier. Confederate leaders and officeholders had to apply for individual presidential pardons to regain their political and property rights. Johnson made one significant addition to the list of the excluded: all those possessing taxable property exceeding $20,000 in value. He thus sought to prevent his longtime adversaries—the wealthy planters—from participating in the Reconstruction of southern state governments.

Johnson urged the convention delegates to declare the ordinances of secession illegal, repudiate the Confederate debt, and ratify the Thirteenth Amendment abolishing slavery. After governments had been reestablished under constitutions meeting these conditions, the president assumed that the Reconstruction process would be complete and that the ex-Confederate states could regain their full rights under the Constitution.

📖 **Read** the
Document
The Mississippi Black Code (1865) on
myhistorylab.com

The results of the conventions, which prewar Unionists and backcountry yeoman farmers dominated, were satisfactory to the president but troubling to many congressional Republicans. Delegates in several states approved Johnson's recommendations only grudgingly or with qualifications. Furthermore, all the constitutions limited suffrage to whites, disappointing the many northerners who hoped, as Lincoln had, that at least some African Americans—perhaps those who were educated or had served in the Union army—would be given the vote. Republican uneasiness turned to anger when the new state legislatures passed Black Codes restricting the freedom of former slaves. Especially troubling were vagrancy and apprenticeship laws that forced African Americans to work and denied them a free choice of employers. Blacks in some states could not testify in court on the same basis as whites and were subject to a separate penal code. The Black Codes looked like slavery under a new guise. More upsetting to northern public opinion in general was the election of prominent ex-Confederates to Congress in 1865.

Johnson himself was partly responsible for these events. Despite his lifelong feud with the planter class, he was generous in granting pardons to members of the old elite who came to him, hat in hand, and asked for them. When former Confederate Vice President Alexander Stephens and other proscribed ex-rebels were elected to Congress even though they had not been pardoned, Johnson granted them special amnesty so they could serve.

Quick Check

✓ Why did Northerners and Republicans grow uneasy and disillusioned with Johnson's approach to reconstruction?

The growing rift between the president and Congress came into the open in December, when the House and Senate refused to seat the recently elected southern delegations. Instead of recognizing the state governments Johnson had called into being, Congress established a joint committee to review Reconstruction policy and set further conditions for readmitting the seceded states.

Congress Takes the Initiative

The struggle over how to reconstruct the Union ended with Congress setting policy all over again. The clash between Johnson and Congress was a matter of principle and could not be reconciled. Johnson, an heir of the Democratic states' rights tradition, wanted to restore the prewar federal system as quickly as possible and without change except that states would not have the right to legalize slavery or to secede.

Most Republicans wanted guarantees that the old southern ruling class would not regain regional power and national influence by devising new ways to subjugate blacks. They favored a Reconstruction policy that would give the federal government authority to limit the political role of ex-Confederates and protect black citizenship.

Republican leaders—except for a few extreme Radicals such as Charles Sumner—lacked any firm conviction that blacks were inherently equal to whites. They did believe, however, that in a modern democratic state, all citizens must have the same basic rights and opportunities, regardless of natural abilities. Principle coincided with political expediency; southern blacks, whatever their alleged shortcomings, were likely to be loyal to the Republican party that had emancipated them and thus increase that party's power in the South.

The disagreement between the president and Congress became irreconcilable in early 1866, when Johnson vetoed two bills that had passed with overwhelming Republican support. The first extended the life of the Freedmen's Bureau—a temporary agency set up to provide relief, education, legal help, and assistance in obtaining land or work to former slaves. The second was a civil rights bill to nullify the Black Codes and guarantee to freedmen "full and equal benefit of all laws and proceedings for the security of person and property as is enjoyed by white citizens."

Johnson's vetoes shocked moderate Republicans. He succeeded in blocking the Freedmen's Bureau bill, although a modified version later passed. But his veto of the Civil Rights Act was overridden, signifying that the president was now hopelessly at odds with most of the legislators from what was supposed to be his own party. Congress had not overridden a presidential veto since Franklin Pierce was president in the early 1850s.

Johnson soon revealed that he intended to place himself at the head of a new conservative party uniting the few Republicans who supported him with a reviving Democratic party that was rallying behind his Reconstruction policy. In preparation for the elections of 1866, Johnson helped found the National Union movement to promote his plan to readmit the southern states to the Union without further qualifications. A National Union convention in Philadelphia called for electing men to Congress who endorsed the presidential plan for Reconstruction.

Meanwhile, the Republican majority on Capitol Hill, fearing that Johnson would not enforce civil rights legislation or that the courts would declare such laws unconstitutional, passed the Fourteenth Amendment. This, perhaps the most important of all the constitutional amendments, gave the federal government responsibility for guaranteeing equal rights under the law to all Americans. Section 1 defined national citizenship for the first time as extending to "all persons born or naturalized in the United States." The states were prohibited from abridging the rights of American citizens and could not "deprive any person of life, liberty, or property, without due process of law; nor deny to any person … equal protection of the laws." The amendment was sent to the states with the understanding that southerners would have no chance of being readmitted to Congress unless their states ratified it. (See Table 16.1)

Read the **Document** *Thirteenth, Fourteenth, and Fifteenth Amendments* on **myhistorylab.com**

The congressional elections of 1866 served as a referendum on the Fourteenth Amendment. Johnson opposed the amendment on the grounds that it created a "centralized" government and denied states the right to manage their own affairs; he also counseled southern state legislatures to reject it, and all except Tennessee followed his advice. But bloody race riots in New Orleans and Memphis weakened the president's case for state autonomy. These and other atrocities against blacks made it clear that the southern state governments were failing abysmally to protect the "life, liberty, or property" of the ex-slaves.

TABLE 16.1   Reconstruction Amendments, 1865–1870

Amendment	Main Provisions	Congressional Passage (2/3 majority in each house required)	Ratification Process (3/4 of all states required, including ex-Confederate states)
13	Slavery prohibited in United States	January 1865	December1865 (27 states, including 8 southern states)
14	National citizenship; state representation in Congress reduced proportionally to number of voters disfranchised; former Confederates denied right to hold office; Confederate debt repudiated	June 1866	Rejected by 12 southern and border states, February 1867; Radicals make readmission of southern states hinge on ratification; ratified July 1868
15	Denial of franchise because of race, color, or past servitude explicitly prohibited	February 1869	Ratification required for readmission of Virginia, Texas, Mississippi, Georgia; ratified March 1870

Johnson further hurt his cause by taking the stump on behalf of candidates who supported his policies. In his notorious "swing around the circle," he toured the nation, slandering his opponents in crude language and engaging in undignified exchanges with hecklers. Enraged by southern inflexibility and the antics of a president who acted as if he were still campaigning in the backwoods of Tennessee, northern voters repudiated the administration. The Republican majority in Congress increased to a solid two-thirds in both houses, and the Radical wing of the party gained strength at the expense of moderates and conservatives.

Quick Check

✓ What events caused Congress to take the initiative in passing the Fourteenth Amendment?

Congressional Reconstruction Plan Enacted

Congress now implemented its own plan of Reconstruction. In 1867 and 1868, it nullified the president's initiatives and reorganized the South. Generally referred to as Radical Reconstruction, the measures actually represented a compromise between genuine Radicals and more moderate Republicans.

Radicals such as Senator Charles Sumner of Massachusetts and Congressmen Thaddeus Stevens of Pennsylvania and George Julian of Indiana wanted to reshape southern society before readmitting ex-Confederates to the Union. Their program of "regeneration before Reconstruction" required an extended period of military rule, confiscation and redistribution of large landholdings among the freedmen, and federal aid for schools to educate blacks and whites for citizenship. But most Republican congressmen found such a program unacceptable because it broke too sharply with American traditions of federalism and regard for property rights, and might take decades.

The First Reconstruction Act, passed over Johnson's veto on March 2, 1867, reorganized the South into five military districts. (See Map 16.1.) But military rule would last for only a short time. Subsequent acts allowed for quickly readmitting any state that framed and ratified a new constitution providing for black suffrage. Ex-Confederates disqualified from holding federal office under the Fourteenth Amendment were prohibited from voting for delegates to the constitutional conventions or in the elections to ratify the conventions' work. Since blacks could participate in this process, Republicans thought they had ensured that "loyal" men would dominate the new governments. Radical Reconstruction was based on the dubious assumption that once blacks had the vote, they would be able to protect themselves against white supremacists' efforts to deny them their rights. The Reconstruction Acts thus signaled a retreat from the true Radical position that sustained federal authority was needed to complete the transition from slavery to freedom and prevent the resurgence of the South's old ruling class Most Republicans were unwilling to embrace centralized government and an extended period of military rule over civilians. Yet a genuine spirit of democratic idealism did give legitimacy and

View the **Map**
Reconstruction on
myhistorylab.com

Map 16.1 *Reconstruction*   During the Reconstruction era, the southern state governments passed through three phases: control by white ex-Confederates; domination by Republican legislators, both white and black; and, finally, the regaining of control by conservative white Democrats.

Quick Check

✓ What was "Radical Reconstruction", and how did it differ from previous plans?

fervor to the cause of black male suffrage. Enabling people who were so poor and downtrodden to have access to the ballot box was a bold and innovative application of the principle of government by the consent of the governed. The problem was enforcing equal suffrage under conditions then existing in the postwar South.

The Impeachment Crisis

The first obstacle to enforcing Congressional Reconstruction was resistance from the White House. Johnson sought to thwart the will of Congress by obstructing the plan. He dismissed officeholders who sympathized with Radical Reconstruction and countermanded the orders of generals in charge of southern military districts who zealously enforced the new legislation. Conservative

THE PAROQUET OF THE WH—E HO—E.

Impeached Andrew Johnson's successful defense against conviction in his impeachment case centered on his invocation of the Constitution to defend his presidential rights and powers. Impeached in 1868, Johnson escaped conviction by a single vote.

Democrats replaced Radical generals. Congress then passed laws to limit presidential authority over Reconstruction. The Tenure of Office Act required Senate approval for the removal of officials whose appointment had needed the consent of the Senate. Another measure limited Johnson's authority to issue orders to military commanders.

Johnson objected that the restrictions violated the constitutional doctrine of the separation of powers. When it became clear that the president was resolute in fighting for his powers and using them to resist establishing Radical regimes in the southern states, congressmen began to call for his impeachment. A preliminary effort foundered in 1867, but when Johnson tried to discharge Secretary of War Edwin Stanton—the only Radical in the cabinet—and persisted in his efforts despite the disapproval of the Senate, the pro-impeachment forces gained in strength.

In January 1868, Johnson ordered General Grant, who already commanded the army, to replace Stanton as head of the War Department. But Grant had his eye on the Republican presidential nomination and refused to defy Congress. General Lorenzo Thomas then agreed to serve. Faced with this violation of the Tenure of Office Act, the House impeached the president on February 24, and he went on trial before the Senate.

Because seven Republican senators broke with the party leadership and voted for acquittal, the effort to convict Johnson and remove him from office fell one vote short of the necessary two-thirds. This outcome resulted in part from a skillful defense. Attorneys for the president argued that the constitutional provision that a president could be impeached only for "high crimes and misdemeanors" referred only to indictable offenses and that the Tenure of Office Act did not apply to Stanton because Lincoln, not Johnson, had appointed him.

The core of the prosecution case was that Johnson had abused the powers of his office to sabotage congressional Reconstruction. Obstructing the will of the legislative branch, they claimed, was grounds for conviction even if no crime had been committed. The Republicans voting for acquittal could not endorse such a broad view of the impeachment power. They feared that removing a president for essentially political reasons would threaten the constitutional balance of powers and allow legislative supremacy over the executive.

Failure to remove Johnson from office embarrassed Republicans, but the episode did ensure that Reconstruction in the South would proceed as the majority in Congress intended. Johnson influenced the verdict by pledging to enforce the Reconstruction Acts, and he held to this promise during his remaining months in office. Unable to depose the president, the Radicals had at least neutralized his opposition to their program.

Quick Check

✓ What Prompted Congress to initiate impeachment against Johnson, and what was the outcome of that action?

RECONSTRUCTING SOUTHERN SOCIETY

The Civil War left the South devastated, demoralized, and destitute. Slavery was dead, but what this meant for future relationships between whites and blacks was unclear. Most southern whites wanted to keep blacks adrift between slavery and freedom—without rights, like the "free Negroes" of the Old South. Blacks

What problems did southern society face during Reconstruction?

sought to be independent of their former masters and viewed acquiring land, education, and the vote as the best means of achieving this goal. The thousands of northerners who went south after the war for materialistic or humanitarian reasons hoped to extend Yankee "civilization" to what they considered an unenlightened and barbarous region. For most of them, this meant aiding the freed slaves.

The struggle between these groups bred chaos, violence, and instability. This was scarcely an ideal setting for an experiment in interracial democracy, but one was attempted nonetheless. Its success depended on massive and sustained federal support. To the extent that this was forthcoming, progressive reform could be achieved. When it faltered, the forces of reaction and white supremacy were unleashed.

Read the **Document**
Carl Schurz, Report on the Condition of the South (1865) on **myhistorylab.com**

Reorganizing Land and Labor

The Civil War scarred the southern landscape and wrecked its economy. One devastated area—central South Carolina—looked to an 1865 observer "like a broad black streak of ruin and desolation." Atlanta, Columbia, and Richmond were gutted by fire. Factories were dismantled or destroyed. Railroads were torn up.

Investment capital for rebuilding was inadequate. The wealth represented by Confederate currency and bonds had melted away, and emancipation had divested the propertied classes of their most valuable and productive assets—the slaves. According to some estimates, the South's per capita wealth in 1865 was only about half what it had been in 1860.

Watch the **Video**
The Schools the Civil War and Reconstruction Created on **myhistorylab.com**

Recovery could not begin until a new labor system replaced slavery. Most northerners and southerners assumed that southern prosperity still depended on cotton and that the plantation was the most efficient unit for producing the crop. Hindering efforts to rebuild the plantation economy were lack of capital, the conviction of southern whites that blacks would work only under compulsion, and the freedmen's resistance to labor conditions that recalled slavery.

Blacks preferred to determine their own economic relationships, and for a time they had reason to hope the federal government would support their ambitions. The freed slaves were, in effect, fighting a two-front war. Although they were grateful for federal aid in ending slavery, freed slaves' ideas about freedom often contradicted the plans of their northern allies. Many ex-slaves wanted to hold on to the family-based communal work methods that they used during slavery. Freed slaves in South Carolina, for example, attempted to maintain the family task system rather than adopt the individual piecework system northern capitalists pushed. Many ex-slaves opposed plans to turn them into wage laborers who produced exclusively for a market. Finally, freed slaves often wanted to stay on the land their families had spent generations farming rather than move elsewhere to occupy land as individual farmers.

While not guaranteeing all of the freed slaves' hopes for economic self-determination, the northern military attempted to establish a new economic base for them. General Sherman, hampered by the many black fugitives that followed his army on its famous march, issued an order in January 1865 that set aside the islands and coastal areas of Georgia and South Carolina for exclusive black occupancy on 40-acre plots. Furthermore, the Freedmen's Bureau was given control of hundreds of thousands of acres of abandoned or confiscated land and was authorized to make 40-acre grants to black settlers for three-year periods, after which they could buy at low prices. By June 1865, 40,000 black farmers were working on 300,000 acres of what they thought would be their own land.

But for most of them, the dream of "40 acres and a mule," or some other arrangement that would give them control of their land and labor, was not to be realized. President Johnson pardoned the owners of most of the land Sherman and the Freedmen's Bureau consigned to the ex-slaves, and Congress rejected proposals for an effective program of land confiscation and redistribution. Among the considerations prompting congressional opposition to land reform were a

Sharecropping The Civil War brought emancipation to slaves, but the sharecropping system kept many of them economically bound to their employers. At the end of a year the sharecropper tenants might owe most—or all—of what they had made to their landlord. Here, a sharecropping family poses in front of their cabin. Ex-slaves often built their living quarters near woods in order to have a ready supply of fuel for heating and cooking. The cabin's chimney lists away from the house so that it can be easily pushed away from the living quarters should it catch fire.

tenderness for property rights, fear of sapping the freedmen's initiative by giving them something they allegedly had not earned, and the desire to restore cotton production as quickly as possible to increase agricultural exports and stabilize the economy. Consequently, most blacks in physical possession of small farms failed to acquire title, and the mass of freedmen did not become landowners. As an ex-slave later wrote, "they were set free without a dollar, without a foot of land, and without the wherewithal to get the next meal even."

Despite their poverty and landlessness, ex-slaves were reluctant to settle down and commit themselves to wage labor for their former masters. Many took to the road, hoping to find something better. Some were still expecting land, but others were simply trying to increase their bargaining power. One freedman recalled that an important part of being free was that "we could move around [and] change bosses." By the end of 1865, many freedmen had still not signed up for the coming season; anxious planters feared that blacks were plotting to seize land by force. Within weeks, however, most holdouts signed for the best terms they could get.

One common form of agricultural employment in 1866 was a contract labor system. Under this system, workers committed themselves for a year in return for fixed wages, much of which was withheld until after the harvest. Since many planters drove hard bargains, abused their workers, or cheated them at the end of the year, the Freedmen's Bureau reviewed and enforced the contracts. But bureau officials had differing notions of what it meant to protect African Americans from exploitation. Some stood up for the rights of the freedmen; others served as allies of the planters.

An alternative capital–labor relationship—sharecropping—eventually replaced the contract system. First in small groups known as "squads" and later as individual families, black sharecroppers worked a piece of land for a fixed share of the crop, usually one-half. Credit-starved landlords liked this arrangement because it did not require much expenditure before the harvest, and the tenant shared the risks of crop failure or a fall in cotton prices.

African Americans initially viewed sharecropping as a step toward landownership. But during the 1870s, it evolved into a new kind of servitude. Croppers had to live on credit until their cotton was sold, and planters or merchants "provisioned" them at high prices and exorbitant interest. Creditors deducted what was owed to them out of the tenant's share of the crop. This left most sharecroppers with no net profit at the end of the year—and often with a debt they had to work off in subsequent years.

Black Codes: A New Name for Slavery?

While landless rural blacks were being reduced to economic dependence, those in towns and cities were living in an increasingly segregated society. The Black Codes of 1865 attempted to require separation of the races in public places and facilities; when federal authorities overturned most of the codes as violations of the Civil Rights Act of 1866, private initiative and community pressure often achieved the

Read the
Document
*A Sharecrop Contract
(1882)* on
myhistorylab.com

Quick Check

✔ What were the conflicting visions of the planters, the Freedmen's Bureau agents, and the freed slaves with regard to what a new labor system should look like?

same end. In some cities, blacks resisted being consigned to separate streetcars by appealing to the military when it still exercised authority or by organizing boycotts. But they found it almost impossible to gain admittance to most hotels, restaurants, and other private establishments catering to whites. Although separate black, or "Jim Crow," cars were not yet the rule on railroads, African Americans were often denied first-class accommodations. After 1868, black-supported Republican governments required equal access to public facilities, but made little effort to enforce the legislation.

The Black Codes had other onerous provisions to control African Americans and return them to quasi-slavery. Most codes made black unemployment a crime, which meant blacks had to make long-term contracts with white employers or be arrested for vagrancy. Others limited the rights of African Americans to own property or engage in occupations other than those of servant or laborer. Congress, the military, and the Freedmen's Bureau set the codes aside, but vagrancy laws remained in force across the South.

Furthermore, private violence and discrimination against blacks continued on a massive scale, unchecked by state authorities. Whites murdered hundreds, perhaps thousands, of blacks in 1865–1866, and few perpetrators were brought to justice. Military rule was designed to protect former slaves from such violence and intimidation, but the task was beyond the capacity of the few thousand troops stationed in the South. When new constitutions were approved and states readmitted to the Union under the congressional plan in 1868, the problem became more severe. White opponents of Radical Reconstruction adopted systematic terrorism and mob violence to keep blacks from the polls.

The freed slaves, in the face of opposition from both their Democratic enemies and some Republican allies, tried to defend themselves by organizing their own militia groups and to assert their political rights. However, the militias were too weak to overcome the anti-Republican forces. And as the military presence was reduced, the new Republican regimes fought a losing battle against armed white supremacists.

Quick Check

✓ What were the Black Codes, and how did they compare to the conditions of slavery?

Republican Rule in the South

Hastily organized in 1867, the southern Republican party dominated the constitution-making of 1868 and the regimes it produced. The party was an attempted coalition of three social groups (which varied in their relative strength from state to state). One was the same class that was becoming the backbone of the Republican party in the North—businessmen who wanted government aid for private enterprise. Many Republicans of this stripe were recent arrivals from the North—the so-called carpetbaggers—but some were scalawags, former Whig planters or merchants who were born in the South or had immigrated there before the war and now saw a chance to realize their dreams for commercial and industrial development.

Poor white farmers, especially those from upland areas where Unionist sentiment had been strong during the Civil War, were a second element in the original coalition. These owners of small farms expected the party to favor their interests at the expense of the wealthy landowners and pass special legislation when—as often happened in this period of economic upheaval—creditors attempted to seize their homesteads. Newly enfranchised blacks were the third group to which the Republicans appealed. Blacks formed most of the Republican rank and file in most states and were concerned mainly with education, civil rights, and landownership.

Under the best conditions, these coalitions would have been fragile. Each group had its own goals and did not fully support those of the others. White yeomen, for example, had a deep resistance to black equality. And for how long would essentially conservative businessmen support costly measures to elevate or relieve the lower classes of either race? In some states, astute Democrats exploited these divisions by appealing to disaffected white Republicans.

But during the relatively brief period when they were in power in the South—from one to nine years depending on the state—the Republicans chalked up notable achievements. They established (on paper at least) the South's first adequate systems of public education, democratized state and local government, and expanded public services and responsibilities.

As important as these social and political reforms were, they took second place to the Republicans' major effort—fostering economic development and restoring prosperity by subsidizing the construction of railroads and other internal improvements. But the policy of aiding railroads turned out to be disastrous, even though it addressed the region's real economic needs and was initially popular. Extravagance, corruption, and routes laid out in response to political pressure rather than on sound economic grounds increased public debt and taxation.

The policy did not produce the promised payoff of efficient, cheap transportation. Subsidized railroads went bankrupt, leaving the taxpayers holding the bag. When the Panic of 1873 brought many southern state governments to the verge of bankruptcy, and railroad building ended, it was clear the Republicans' "gospel of prosperity" through state aid to private enterprise had failed. Their political opponents, many of whom had favored such policies, now took advantage of the situation, charging that Republicans had ruined the southern economy.

In general, the Radical regimes failed to conduct public business honestly and efficiently. Embezzlement of public funds and bribery of state lawmakers or officials were common. State debts and tax burdens rose enormously, mainly because governments had undertaken heavy new responsibilities, but also because of waste and graft. The situation varied from state to state: Ruling cliques in Louisiana and South Carolina were guilty of much wrongdoing; Mississippi had a relatively honest and frugal regime.

Furthermore, southern corruption was not exceptional, nor was it a result of extending suffrage to uneducated African Americans, as critics of Radical

Reconstruction have claimed. It was part of a national pattern during an era when private interests considered buying government favors as part of the cost of doing business, and politicians expected to profit by obliging them.

Many Reconstruction-era scandals started at the top. President Grant's first-term vice president, Schuyler Colfax of Indiana, was directly involved in the notorious Credit Mobilier scandal. Credit Mobilier was a construction company that actually served as a fraudulent device for siphoning off profits that should have gone to the stockholders of the Union Pacific Railroad, which had received massive federal land grants. Credit Mobilier distributed stock to influential congressmen, including Colfax before he became vice president, in order to keep Congress from inquiring into this shady arrangement. In 1875, during President Grant's second administration, his private secretary was indicted in a conspiracy to defraud the government of millions of dollars in liquor taxes, and his secretary of war was impeached for taking bribes. While there is no evidence that Grant profited personally from these misdeeds, he failed to take firm action against the wrongdoers and participated in covering up their crimes.

The new African American public officials were only minor participants in this rampant corruption. Although 16 blacks served in Congress—two in the Senate—between 1869 and 1880, only in South Carolina were blacks a majority of even one house of the legislature. Furthermore, no black governors were elected during Reconstruction (although Pinckney B. S. Pinchback was acting governor of Louisiana in 1872–1873). The biggest grafters were opportunistic whites. Businessmen offering bribes included members of the prewar gentry who were staunch opponents of Radical programs. Some black legislators went with the tide and accepted "loans" from railroad lobbyists who would pay most for their votes, but the same men would usually vote the will of their constituents on civil rights or education.

Blacks served or supported corrupt and wasteful regimes because the alternative was dire. Although the Democrats, or Conservatives as they called themselves in some states, made sporadic efforts to attract African American voters, it was clear that if they won control, they would strip blacks of their civil and political rights. But opponents of Radical Reconstruction capitalized on racial prejudice and persuaded many Americans that "good government" was synonymous with white supremacy.

Contrary to myth, the few African Americans elected to state or national office during Reconstruction demonstrated on the average more integrity and competence than their white counterparts. Most were fairly well educated, having been free or unusually privileged slaves before the war. Among the most capable were Robert Smalls (whose career was described earlier); Blanche K. Bruce of Mississippi, elected to the U.S. Senate in 1874 after rising to prominence in the Republican party of his home state; Congressman Robert Brown Elliott of South Carolina, an adroit politician who was also a consistent champion of civil rights; and Congressman James T. Rapier of Alabama, who stirred the nation in 1873 with his appeals for federal aid to southern education and new laws to enforce equal rights for African Americans.

Quick Check

✓ What were the three social groups that made up the southern Republican party?

Claiming Public and Private Rights

The ways that freed slaves claimed rights for themselves were as important as party politics to the changing political culture of the Reconstruction South. Ex-slaves fought for their rights not only in negotiations with employers and in public meetings and convention halls, but also through the institutions they created and, perhaps most important, the households they formed.

Read the **Document** *Slave Narrative, "The Story of Mattie J. Jackson"* on **myhistorylab.com**

Some ex-slaves used institutions formerly closed to them like the courts to assert rights they considered part of citizenship. Many ex-slaves rushed to formalize their marriages before the law, and they used their new status to fight for custody of children who had been taken from them under the apprenticeship provisions of the Black Clodes. Ex-slaves sued white people and other blacks over domestic violence, child support, assault, and debt. Freed women sued their husbands for desertion and alimony and enlisted the Freedmen's Bureau to help them claim property from men. Immediately after the war, freed people created institutions that had been denied to them under slavery: churches, fraternal and benevolent associations, political organizations, and schools. Many joined all-black denominations such as the African Methodist Episcopal (AME) church, which provided freedom from white dominance and more congenial worship. Black women formed all-black chapters

Freedmen's Schools A Freedmen's school, one of the more successful endeavors the Freedmen's Bureau supported. The bureau, working with teachers from northern abolitionist and missionary societies, founded thousands of schools for freed slaves and poor whites.

of organizations such as the Women's Christian Temperance Union and created their own women's clubs to oppose lynching and promote "uplift" in the black community.

A top priority for most ex-slaves was education for their children; the first schools for freed people were all-black institutions the Freedmen's Bureau and northern missionary societies established. Having been denied education during the antebellum period, most blacks viewed separate schooling as an opportunity rather than as a form of discrimination. However, these schools were precursors to the segregated public school systems first instituted by Republican governments. Only at city schools in New Orleans and the University of South Carolina were serious attempts made during Reconstruction to bring white and black students together in the same classrooms.

In many ways, African American men and women during Reconstruction asserted freedom in the "private" realm and the public sphere by claiming rights to their own families and building their own institutions. They did so despite the efforts of their former masters and the new government agencies to control their private lives and shape their new identities as husbands, wives, and citizens.

Quick Check

✓ What new rights and institutions did free blacks create and use following emancipation?

RETREAT FROM RECONSTRUCTION

The era of Reconstruction began to end almost before it got started. Although it was only three years after the end of the Civil War, the impeachment crisis of 1868 was the high point of popular interest in Reconstruction. That year, Ulysses S. Grant, a popular general, was elected president. Many historians blame Grant for the corruption of his administration and for the inconsistency and failure of his southern policy. He had neither the vision nor the sense of duty to tackle the difficult challenges the nation faced. From 1868 on, political issues other than southern Reconstruction moved to the forefront of national politics, and the plight of African Americans in the South receded in white consciousness.

Why did Reconstruction end?

Final Efforts of Reconstruction

The Republican effort to make equal rights for blacks the law of the land culminated in the Fifteenth Amendment. Passed by Congress in 1869 and ratified by the states in 1870, it prohibited any state from denying a male citizen the right to vote because of race, color, or previous condition of servitude. A more radical version, requiring universal manhood suffrage, was rejected partly because it departed too sharply from traditional federal–state relations. States therefore could still limit the suffrage by imposing literacy tests, property qualifications, or poll taxes allegedly applying to all racial groups; such devices would eventually be used to strip southern blacks of the right to vote. But the authors of the amendment did not foresee this. They believed it would prevent future

View the **Closer Look**
The First Vote on
myhistorylab.com

Black Voting *The First Vote*, drawn by A. H. Ward for *Harper's Weekly*, November 16, 1867.

Congresses or southern constitutional conventions from repealing or nullifying the provisions for black male suffrage included in the Reconstruction Acts. A secondary aim was to enfranchise African Americans in northern states that still denied them the vote.

Many feminists were bitter that the amendment did not extend the vote to women. A militant wing of the women's rights movement, led by Elizabeth Cady Stanton and Susan B. Anthony, was so angered that the Constitution was being amended to, in effect, make gender a qualification for voting that they campaigned against ratification of the amendment. Other feminists led by Lucy Stone supported the amendment, saying this was "the Negro's hour" and that women could afford to wait a few years for the vote. This disagreement divided the woman suffrage movement for a generation.

The Grant administration was charged with enforcing the amendment and protecting black men's voting rights in the reconstructed states. Since survival of the Republican regimes depended on African American support, political partisanship dictated federal action, even though the North's emotional and ideological commitment to black citizenship was waning.

Read the
Document
*The State of the
South (1872)* on
myhistorylab.com

Quick Check

✓ What did the Fifteenth
Amendment stipulate,
and whom did it
benefit?

A Reign of Terror Against Blacks

Between 1868 and 1872, the Ku Klux Klan and other secret societies bent on restoring white supremacy by intimidating blacks who sought to exercise their political rights were the main threat to Republican regimes. Founded in Tennessee in 1866, the Klan spread rapidly, adopting lawless and brutal tactics. A grassroots vigilante movement, not a centralized conspiracy, the Klan thrived on local initiative and support from whites of all social classes. Its secrecy, decentralization, popular support, and ruthlessness made it difficult to suppress. As soon as blacks had been granted the right to vote, hooded "night riders" began to visit the cabins of active Republicans. Some victims were only threatened. Others were whipped or murdered.

Such methods were first used effectively in the presidential election of 1868. Grant lost in Louisiana and Georgia mainly because the Klan—or the Knights of the White Camellia, as the Louisiana variant was called—launched a reign of terror to prevent blacks from voting. In Louisiana, political violence claimed more than 1,000 lives. In Arkansas, which Grant did carry, more than 200 Republicans, including a congressman, were killed.

Thereafter, Klan terrorism was directed mainly at Republican state governments. Virtual insurrections broke out in Arkansas, Tennessee, North Carolina, and parts of South Carolina. Republican governors called out the state militia to fight the Klan, but only the Arkansas militia brought it to heel. In Tennessee, North Carolina, and Georgia, Klan activities enabled Democrats to come to power by 1870.

In 1870–1871, Congress provided federal protection for black suffrage and authorized using the army against the Klan. The Force Acts, also known as the Ku Klux Klan acts, made interference with voting rights a federal crime and provided for federal supervision of elections. The legislation also empowered the president to call out troops and suspend the writ of habeas corpus to quell insurrection. In 1871–1872, the military or U.S. marshals arrested thousands of suspected Klansmen, and the writ was suspended in nine counties of South Carolina that the Klan had virtually taken over. Although most of the accused Klansmen were never tried, were acquitted, or received suspended sentences, the enforcement effort did put a damper on hooded terrorism and ensure relatively fair and peaceful elections in 1872.

A heavy black turnout in these elections enabled the Republicans to hold on to power in most of the Deep South, despite Democratic-Conservative efforts to cut into the Republican vote by taking moderate positions on racial and economic issues. This setback prompted the Democratic-Conservatives to change their strategy and ideology. They stopped trying to take votes away from the Republicans by proclaiming support for black suffrage and government aid to business. Instead they began to appeal openly to white supremacy and the traditional Democratic and agrarian hostility to government promotion of economic development. They were thus able to attract part of the white Republican electorate, mostly small farmers.

Read the **Document**
Hannah Irwin Describes Ku Klux Klan Ride on **myhistorylab.com**

Ku Klux Klan This 1868 photograph shows typical regalia of members of the Ku Klux Klan, a secret white supremacist organization. Before elections, hooded Klansmen terrorized African Americans to discourage them from voting.

This new strategy dovetailed with a resurgence of violence to reduce Republican, especially black Republican, voting. Its agents no longer wore masks but acted openly. They were effective because the northern public was increasingly disenchanted with federal intervention to prop up what were widely viewed as corrupt and tottering Republican regimes. Grant used force in the South for the last time in 1874 when an overt paramilitary organization in Louisiana, known as the White League, tried to overthrow a Republican government accused of stealing an election. When another unofficial militia in Mississippi instigated bloody race riots before the state elections of 1875, Grant refused the governor's request for federal troops. As a result, black voters were intimidated—one county registered only seven Republican votes where there had been a black majority of 2,000—and Mississippi fell to the Democratic-Conservatives.

By 1876, partly because of Grant's hesitant and inconsistent use of presidential power, but mainly because the northern electorate would no longer tolerate military action to sustain Republican governments and black voting rights, Radical Reconstruction was collapsing.

Quick Check

✓ How important was the Ku Klux Klan in influencing elections and policies in the South?

REUNION AND THE NEW SOUTH

The end of Radical Reconstruction in 1877 opened the way to a reconciliation of North and South. But the costs of reunion were high for less privileged groups in the South. The civil and political rights of African Americans, left unprotected, were relentlessly stripped away by white supremacist regimes. Lower-class whites saw their interests sacrificed to those of capitalists and landlords. Despite the rhetoric hailing a prosperous "New South," the region remained poor and open to exploitation by northern business interests.

Who benefited and who suffered from the reconciliation of the North and South?

The Compromise of 1877

The election of 1876 pitted Rutherford B. Hayes of Ohio, a Republican governor untainted by the scandals of the Grant era, against Governor Samuel J. Tilden of New York, a Democratic reformer who had fought corruption in New York City. Honest government was apparently the electorate's highest priority. When the returns came in, Tilden had won the popular vote and seemed likely to win a narrow victory in the electoral college. But the returns from the three southern states the Republicans still controlled—South Carolina, Florida, and Louisiana—were contested. If Hayes were awarded these three states, plus one contested electoral vote in Oregon, Republican strategists realized, he would triumph in the electoral college by a single vote. (See Map 16.2)

The election remained undecided for months, plunging the nation into a political crisis. To resolve the impasse, Congress appointed a 15-member commission to determine who

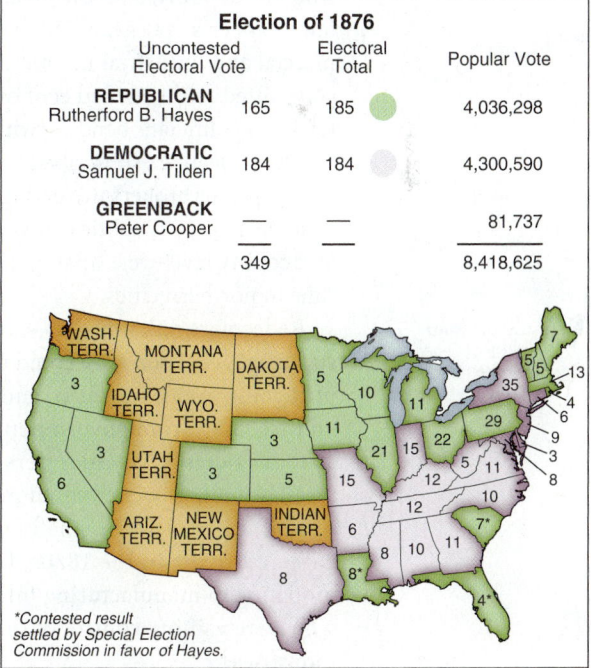

Election of 1876

	Uncontested Electoral Vote	Electoral Total	Popular Vote
REPUBLICAN Rutherford B. Hayes	165	185	4,036,298
DEMOCRATIC Samuel J. Tilden	184	184	4,300,590
GREENBACK Peter Cooper	—	—	81,737
		349	8,418,625

*Contested result settled by Special Election Commission in favor of Hayes.

Map 16.2

would receive the votes of the disputed states. Originally composed of seven Democrats, seven Republicans, and an independent, the commission fell under Republican control when the independent member resigned to run for the Senate and a Republican replaced him. The commission split along party lines and voted eight to seven to award Hayes all the disputed votes. But both houses of Congress still had to ratify the decision, and in the House, there was strong Democratic opposition. To ensure Hayes's election, Republican leaders struck an informal bargain with conservative southern Democrats that historians have dubbed the Compromise of 1877. What precisely was agreed to and by whom remains in dispute, but both sides understood that Hayes would be president and that southern blacks would be abandoned to their fate. President Hayes immediately ordered the army not to resist a Democratic takeover of state governments in South Carolina and Louisiana. Thus fell the last of the Radical governments. White Democrats firmly controlled the entire South. The trauma of the war and Reconstruction had destroyed the chances for renewing two-party competition among white southerners.

Quick Check

✔ Who agreed upon the Compromise of 1877, and why?

"Redeeming" a New South

The men who took power after Radical Reconstruction fell in one southern state after another are usually referred to as the Redeemers. Their backgrounds and previous loyalties differed. Some were members of the Old South's ruling planter class who had supported secession and now sought to reestablish the old order with as few changes as possible. Others, of middle-class origin or outlook, favored commercial and industrial interests over agrarian groups and called for a New South committed to diversified economic development. A third group consisted of professional politicians bending with the prevailing winds.

The Redeemers subscribed to no single coherent ideology but are best characterized as power brokers mediating among the dominant interest groups of the South to serve their own political advantage. The "rings" that they established on the state and county level were analogous to the political machines developing at the same time in northern cities.

View the **Map**
The Rise of Tenancy in the South, 1880 on **myhistorylab.com**

Redeemers did, however, endorse two basic principles: laissez-faire and white supremacy. Laissez-faire could unite planters, frustrated at seeing direct state support going to businessmen, and capitalist promoters, who realized that low taxes and freedom from government regulation were even more advantageous than state subsidies. The Redeemers responded only to privileged and entrenched interest groups, especially landlords, merchants, and industrialists, and offered little or nothing to tenants, small farmers, and working people. As industrialization gathered steam in the 1880s, Democratic regimes became increasingly accommodating to manufacturing interests and hospitable to agents of northern capital who were gaining control of the South's transportation system and its extractive industries.

White supremacy was the rallying cry that brought the Redeemers to power. Once in office, they stayed there by charging that opponents of ruling Democratic cliques were trying to divide "the white man's party" and open the way for a return to "black domination." Appeals to racism also deflected attention from the economic grievances of groups without political clout.

The new governments were more economical than those of Reconstruction, mainly because they drastically cut appropriations for schools and other public services. But they were scarcely more honest—embezzlement and bribery remained rife. The Redeemer regimes of the late 1870s and 1880s neglected small white farmers. Whites, as well as blacks, were suffering from the notorious crop lien system, which gave local merchants who advanced credit at high interest during the growing season the right to take possession of the harvested crop on terms that buried farmers deeper and deeper in debt. As a result, many whites lost title to their homesteads and were reduced to tenancy. When a depression of world cotton prices added to the burden of a ruinous credit system, agrarian protesters began to challenge the ruling elite, first through the Southern Farmers' Alliance of the late 1880s and then by supporting its political descendant—the Populist party of the 1890s (see Chapter 20).

Quick Check

✓ Which principles divided, and which united, the new "Redeemer" governments?

The Rise of Jim Crow

The new order imposed the greatest hardships on African Americans. The dark night of racism fell on the South. From 1876 to 1910, southern states imposed restrictions on black civil rights known as Jim Crow laws. The term "Jim Crow" came from an antebellum minstrel show figure first popularized by Thomas "Daddy" Rice, who blackened his face and sang a song called "Jump Jim Crow." By the 1850s, Jim Crow was a familiar figure in minstrel shows, and had become a synonym for a black person in popular white speech. It was a short step to referring to segregated railroad cars for black people as Jim Crow cars. While segregation and disfranchisement began as informal arrangements in the immediate aftermath of the Civil War, they culminated in a legal regime of separation and exclusion that took firm hold in the 1890s. (See Chapter 19.)

The rise of Jim Crow in the political arena was especially bitter for southern blacks who realized that only political power could ensure other rights. The Redeemers promised, as part of the understanding that led to the end of federal intervention in 1877, that they would respect the rights of blacks as set forth in the Fourteenth and Fifteenth Amendments. Governor Wade Hampton of South Carolina pledged that the new regimes would not reduce African Americans to second-class citizenship. But when blacks tried to vote Republican in the "redeemed" states, they encountered violence and intimidation. "Bulldozing" African American voters remained common in state elections during the late 1870s and early 1880s; those blacks who withstood the threat of losing their jobs or being evicted from tenant farms if they voted for the party of Lincoln were

Watch the **Video**
The Promise and Failure of Reconstruction on **myhistorylab.com**

visited at night and literally whipped into line. The message was clear: Vote Democratic, or vote not at all.

Furthermore, white Democrats now controlled the electoral machinery and manipulated the black vote by stuffing ballot boxes, discarding unwanted votes, or reporting fraudulent totals. Some states imposed complicated voting requirements to discourage black participation. Full-scale disfranchisement did not occur until literacy tests and other legalized obstacles to voting were imposed from 1890 to 1910, but by then, less formal and comprehensive methods had already made a mockery of the Fifteenth Amendment.

Nevertheless, blacks continued to vote freely in some localities until the 1890s; a few districts, like the one Robert Smalls represented, even elected black Republicans to Congress during the immediate post-Reconstruction period. The last of these, Representative George H. White of North Carolina, served until 1901. His farewell address eloquently conveyed the agony of southern blacks in the era of Jim Crow (strict segregation):

> These parting words are in behalf of an outraged, heart-broken, bruised, and bleeding but God-fearing people, faithful, industrious, loyal people—rising people, full of potential force.... The only apology that I have to make for the earnestness with which I have spoken is that I am pleading for the life, the liberty, the future happiness, and manhood suffrage of one-eighth of the entire population of the United States.

Quick Check

✓ What aspects of southern society did the Jim Crow Laws regulate?

CONCLUSION: HENRY MCNEAL TURNER AND THE "UNFINISHED REVOLUTION"

The career of Henry McNeal Turner sums up the bitter side of the black experience in the South during and after Reconstruction. Born free in South Carolina in 1834, Turner became a minister of the AME Church just before the Civil War. During the war, he recruited African Americans for the Union army and served as chaplain for black troops. After the war, he went to Georgia to work for the Freedmen's Bureau but encountered racial discrimination from white officers and left government service for church work and Reconstruction politics. Elected to the 1867 Georgia constitutional convention and to the state legislature in 1868, he was one of many black clergymen who became leaders among the freedmen. But whites won control of the Georgia legislature and expelled all the black members. As the inhabitant of a state in which blacks never gained the power that they achieved in other parts of the South, Turner was one of the first black leaders to see the failure of Reconstruction as the betrayal of African American hopes for citizenship.

Becoming a bishop of the AME Church in 1880, Turner emerged as the era's leading proponent of black emigration to Africa. Because he believed that white Americans would never grant blacks equal rights, Turner became

Henry McNeal Turner, who was born in freedom, became a bishop of the African Methodist Episcopal Church and was elected to the Georgia legislature.

an early advocate of black nationalism and a total separation of the races. Emigration became popular among southern blacks, who were especially hard hit by terror and oppression just after the end of Reconstruction. Still, most blacks in the nation as a whole and even in Turner's own church refused to give up the hope of eventual equality on American soil. But Bishop Turner's anger and despair were the understandable responses of a proud man to how he and his fellow African Americans had been treated in the post–Civil War period.

By the late 1880s, the wounds of the Civil War were healing, and white Americans were seized by the spirit of sectional reconciliation and their common Americanism. But whites could reunite only because northerners had tacitly agreed to give southerners a free hand to reduce blacks to servitude. The "outraged, heartbroken, bruised, and bleeding" African Americans of the South paid the heaviest price for sectional reunion.

16 Study Resources

((•─ **Listen** to the **Chapter Audio** for Chapter 16 on **myhistorylab.com**

Timeline

1863 Lincoln sets forth 10 percent Reconstruction plan, p. 389

1864 Lincoln pocket vetoes Wade–Davis Bill, p. 390

1865 President Andrew Johnson moves to reconstruct the South on his own initiative, p. 391
- Congress refuses to seat representatives and senators from states reestablished under presidential plan (December), p. 392
- **1866** Johnson vetoes Freedmen's Bureau Bill (February), p. 392
- Civil Rights Act passed over Johnson's veto (April), p. 393
- Congress passes Fourteenth Amendment (June), p. 393
- Republicans increase their congressional majority, p. 393

1867 First Reconstruction Act passed over Johnson's veto (March), p. 395

1868 Johnson is impeached but avoids conviction by one vote (February–May), p. 396
- Southern blacks vote and serve in constitutional conventions, p. 405
- Ulysses S. Grant elected president, p. 405

1869 Congress passes Fifteenth Amendment, p. 405

1870–1871 Force Acts protect black voting rights in the South, p. 407

1872 Grant reelected president, p. 407

1876–1877 Disputed presidential election resolved in favor of Republican Rutherfrod B. Hayes, p. 409

1877 Compromise of 1877 ends Reconstruction, p. 409

Chapter Review

THE PRESIDENT VERSUS CONGRESS

What conflicts arose between Lincoln and Johnson and Congress during Reconstruction?

Both Lincoln and Johnson had their own notions of how Reconstruction should be governed. Radical Republicans who sought more protection for black rights challenged Lincoln's Ten Percent Plan. Later, when Johnson hesitated to renew the Freedmen's Bureau and fight the Black Codes, Congress passed the Fourteenth Amendment to ensure equal rights to all Americans. *(p. 389)*

RECONSTRUCTING SOUTHERN SOCIETY

What problems did southern society face during Reconstruction?

The immediate problems facing the South were economic and physical devastation, and providing for the mass of freed slaves. While former slaveholders hoped to reduce ex-slaves to conditions not unlike slavery, northern Republicans wanted to reorganize southern land and labor on a northern free-labor model. Freedmen's Bureau agents emphasized that ex-slaves had to sign contracts and work for wages. The freed slaves hoped instead to own land. Sharecropping was a compromise. *(p. 397)*

RETREAT FROM RECONSTRUCTION

Why did Reconstruction end?

Although intended to protect civil rights, the Fifteenth Amendment allowed states to limit local suffrage through difficult voting prerequisites. Further, the

Ku Klux Klan intimidated black voters and representation. By 1876, these tactics had defeated the Republicans in most southern states and Reconstruction was nearly dead. *(p. 405)*

REUNION AND THE NEW SOUTH

Who benefited and who suffered from the reconciliation of North and South?

Reunion came at the expense of African Americans. The Compromise of 1877 restored autonomous government in the South to resolve the 1876 election. The North would no longer enforce unpopular civil rights, allowing the Redeemers to bring back laissez-faire economics and restore white supremacy through the Jim Crow laws. *(p. 408)*

KEY TERM QUESTIONS

1. Why was Congress unhappy with the Ten Percent Plan proposed by Lincoln? (p. 389)

2. What were the core beliefs of the Radical Republicans? (p. 390)

3. How did the Wade–Davis Bill passed by Congress in 1864 differ from the Ten Percent Plan? (p. 390)

4. Why did President Johnson assume that the Thirteenth Amendment would, almost on its own, be enough to end the Reconstruction process? (p. 391)

5. Why were the southern states able to pass Black Code laws so easily? (p. 392)

6. What were the successes and failures of the Freedmen's Bureau? (p. 393)

7. Why is the Fourteenth Amendment regarded as perhaps the most important of all the constitutional amendments? (p. 393)

8. How did Radical Reconstruction differ from previous plans? (p. 394)

9. How did sharecropping work in practice to keep many blacks from ever owning land? (p. 400)

10. Why were many feminists disappointed with the passage of the Fifteenth Amendment? (p. 405)

11. Why did Ku Klux Klan members disguise themselves in hoods and robes? (p. 406)

12. How did the Force Acts attack the Ku Klux Klan? (p. 407)

13. What was the most significant result of the Compromise of 1877? (p. 409)

14. Which principles divided, and which united, the new Redeemer governments? (p. 409)

15. How did the Jim Crow laws come to serve as a second racial caste system? (p. 410)

MYHISTORYLAB CONNECTIONS

Visit **www.myhistorylab.com** for a customized Study Plan to build your knowledge of *The Agony of Reconstruction*

Question for Analysis

1. What was the significance of The Mississippi Black Code?

   Read the **Document** *Mississippi Black Code, 1865* p. 392

Other Resources from this Chapter

View the **Image** *Andrew Johnson, Brady Photo*

Read the **Document** *Thirteenth, Fourteenth, and Fifteenth Amendments*

2. How were the Southern states readmitted to the Union during Reconstruction?

   View the **Map** *Reconstruction* p. 395

3. How did the nature of education change in America during Reconstruction?

   Watch the **Video** *The Schools that the Civil War and Reconstruction Created* p. 398

4. Why was the federal government unable to protect African American civil rights despite the passage of the Civil Rights Act of 1875?

   View the **Closer Look** *The First Vote* p. 405

5. Why did Reconstruction ultimately fail?

   Watch the **Video** *The Promise and Failure of Reconstruction* p. 410

Read the **Document** *Carl Schurz, Report on the Condition of the South*

Read the **Document** *Sharecrop Contract, 1882*

Read the **Document** *Slave Narrative, The Story of Mattie Jackson*

Read the **Document** *State of the South, 1872*

Read the **Document** *Hannah Irwin Describes KKK Ride*

View the **Map** *The Rise of Tenancy in the South, 1880*

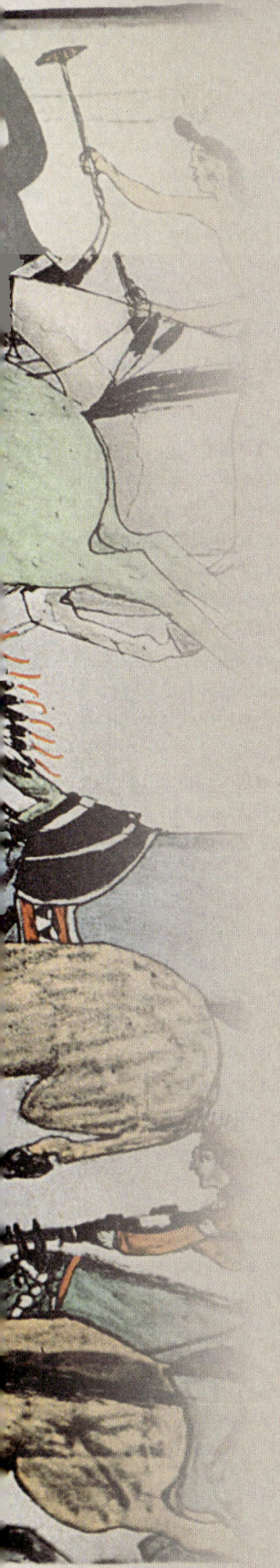

Content and Spotlight Questions

BEYOND THE FRONTIER PG. 420

What were the challenges of settling the country west of the Mississippi?

CRUSHING THE NATIVE AMERICANS PG. 421

How did white Americans crush the culture of the Native Americans as they moved west?

SETTLEMENT OF THE WEST PG. 428

Why did Americans and others move to the West?

THE BONANZA WEST PG. 433

Why was the West a bonanza of dreams and get-rich-quick schemes?

((•—Listen to the **Chapter Audio** for Chapter 17 on **myhistorylab.com**

LEAN BEAR'S CHANGING WEST

In 1863, federal Indian agents took a delegation of Cheyenne, Arapaho, Comanche, Kiowa, and Plains Apache to visit the eastern United States, hoping to impress them with the power of the white man. The visitors were, in fact, impressed. In New York City, they stared at the tall buildings and crowded streets, so different from the wide-open plains to which they were accustomed. They visited the museum of the great showman Phineas T. Barnum, who in turn put them on display; they even saw a hippopotamus.

In Washington, they met President Abraham Lincoln. Lean Bear, a Cheyenne chief, assured Lincoln that Indians wanted peace but were worried about the numbers of white people who were pouring into their country. Lincoln swore friendship, said the Indians would be better off if they began to farm, and promised to do his best to keep the peace. But, he said, smiling at Lean Bear, "You know it is not always possible for any father to have his children do precisely as he wishes them to do."

This Pictogram by Oglala Sioux Amos Bad Heart Bull is a Native American version of the Battle of the Little Bighorn, also known as Custer's Last Stand.

Lean Bear, who had children of his own, understood what Lincoln said, at least in a way. A year later, back on his own lands, he watched federal troops, Lincoln's "children," approach his camp. Wearing a peace medal that Lincoln had given him, Lean Bear rode slowly toward the troops to again offer his friendship. When he was 20 yards away, they opened fire, then rode closer and fired again and again into his fallen body.

As Lean Bear had feared, in the last three decades of the nineteenth century, a flood of settlers ventured into the vast lands across the Mississippi River. Prospectors searched for "pay dirt," railroads crisscrossed the continent, eastern and foreign capitalists invested in cattle and land bonanzas, and farmers took up the promise of free western lands. In 1867, Horace Greeley, editor of the New York *Tribune,* told New York City's unemployed: "If you strike off into the broad, free West, and make yourself a farm from Uncle Sam's generous domain, you will crowd nobody, starve nobody, and neither you nor your children need evermore beg for something to do."

With the end of the Civil War in 1865, white Americans again claimed a destiny to expand across the continent. In the process, they crushed the culture of the Native Americans and ignored the contributions of people of other races, such as Chinese miners and laborers and Mexican herdsmen. As millions moved west, the states of Colorado, Washington, Montana, North and South Dakota, Idaho, Wyoming, and Utah were carved out of the lands across the Mississippi. By 1900, only Arizona, New Mexico, and Oklahoma remained as territories.

The West became a great colonial empire, harnessed to eastern capital and tied increasingly to national and international markets. Its raw materials, sent east by wagon, train, and ship, helped fuel eastern factories. Westerners' economies relied heavily on the federal government, which subsidized their railroads, distributed their land, and spent millions of dollars for the upkeep of soldiers and Indians.

By the 1890s, the lands west of the Mississippi had changed substantially. In place of buffalo and unfenced vistas, there were cities and towns, health resorts, homesteads, sheep ranches, and, in the arid regions, the beginnings of the irrigated agriculture that would reshape the West in the twentieth century. Ghost towns, abandoned farms, and the scars in the earth left by miners and farmers spoke to the less favorable side of settlement. As the new century dawned, the West had become a place of conquest and exploitation, as well as a mythic land of cowboys and quick fortunes.

BEYOND THE FRONTIER

What were the challenges of settling the country west of the Mississippi?

The line of white settlement had reached the edge of the Missouri timber country by 1840. Beyond lay an enormous land of rolling prairies, parched deserts, and rugged, majestic mountains. Emerging from the timber country, travelers first encountered the Great Plains—treeless, nearly flat, an endless "sea of grassy hillocks" extending from the Mississippi River to the Rocky Mountains.

Running from Alaska to central New Mexico, the Rockies presented a formidable barrier, and most travelers crossed the northern passes, emerging in the desolate basin of present-day southern Idaho and Utah. On the west, the lofty Cascades and Sierra Nevada held back rainfall; beyond was the temperate Pacific coast.

Map 17.1 *Physiographic Map of the United States*   In the Great Plains and Rocky Mountains, the topography, altitudes, crops, and climate—especially the lack of rain west of the rainfall line shown here—led to changes in mode of settlement, which had been essentially uniform from the Atlantic coast through Kentucky, Ohio, and Missouri. The traditional rectangular land surveys and quarter-section lots could not accommodate Great Plains conditions.

Few rivers cut through the Plains; those that did raged in the winter and trickled in the summer. Rainfall usually did not reach 15 inches a year, not enough to support extensive agriculture. There was little lumber for homes and fences, and the tools of eastern settlement—the cast-iron plow, the boat, and the ax—were virtually useless on the tough and treeless Plains soil. "East of the Mississippi," historian Walter Prescott Webb noted, "civilization stood on three legs—land, water, and timber; west of the Mississippi not one but two of these legs were withdrawn—water and timber—and civilization was left on one leg—land." (See Map 17.1.)

CRUSHING THE NATIVE AMERICANS

When Greeley urged New Yorkers to move west and "crowd nobody," he—like almost all white Americans—ignored the fact that many people already lived there. At the close of the Civil War, Native Americans inhabited nearly half the United States. By 1880, they had been driven onto smaller and smaller reservations and were no longer an independent people. A decade later, even their culture had crumbled under white domination.

In 1865, nearly 250,000 Native Americans lived in the western half of the country. Tribes such as the Winnebago, Menominee, Cherokee, and Chippewa were resettled there, forced out of their eastern lands by advancing white settlement. Other tribes were native to the region. In the Southwest were the Pueblo groups, including

How did white Americans crush the culture of the Native Americans as they moved west?

the Hopi, Zuni, and Rio Grande Pueblos. Peaceful farmers and herders, they had built up complex traditions around a settled way of life.

More nomadic were the Camp Dwellers, the Jicarilla Apache and Navajo, who roamed Arizona, New Mexico, and western Texas. The Navajo herded sheep and produced beautiful ornamental silver, baskets, and blankets. Fierce fighters, Apache horsemen were feared by whites and fellow Indians across the southwestern Plains.

Farther west were the tribes that inhabited present-day California. Divided into many small bands, they eked out a difficult existence living on roots, grubs, berries, acorns, and small game. In the Pacific Northwest, where fish and forest animals made life easier, the Klamath, Chinook, Yurok, and Shasta tribes developed a rich civilization. They built plank houses and canoes, worked extensively in wood, and evolved a complex social and political organization.

By the 1870s, most of these tribes had been destroyed or beaten into submission. The powerful Ute, crushed in 1855, ceded most of their Utah lands to the United States and settled on a small reservation near the Great Salt Lake. The Navajo and Apache fought back fiercely, but between 1865 and 1873, they too were confined to reservations. The Native Americans of California succumbed to the contagious diseases whites carried during the Gold Rush of 1849. Miners burned their villages, and by 1880, fewer than 20,000 Indians lived in California.

Life of the Plains Indians

In the mid-nineteenth century, nearly two-thirds of the Native Americans lived on the Great Plains. The Plains tribes included the Sioux of present-day Minnesota and the Dakotas; the Blackfoot of Idaho and Montana; the Cheyenne, Crow, and Arapaho of the central Plains; the Pawnee of western Nebraska; and the Kiowa, Apache, and Comanche of present-day Texas and New Mexico.

Nomadic and warlike, the Plains Indians depended on the buffalo and horse. The modern horse, first brought by Spanish explorers in the 1500s, spread north from Mexico onto the Plains, and by the 1700s, horses had changed the Plains Indians' way of life. The Plains tribes gave up farming almost entirely and hunted the buffalo on horseback, ranging widely over the rolling plains. The men became superb warriors and horsemen, among the best light cavalry in the world.

Migratory in culture, the Plains Indians formed tribes of several thousand people but lived in smaller bands of 300–500. The bands followed and lived off the buffalo. Buffalo provided food, clothing, and shelter; the Indians, unlike later white hunters, used every part of the animal. The meat was dried or "jerked" in the hot Plains air. The skins made tepees, blankets, and robes. Buffalo bones became knives; tendons were made into bowstrings; horns and hooves were boiled into glue. Buffalo "chips"—dried manure—were burned as fuel.

The Plains tribes divided labor tasks according to gender. Men hunted, traded, supervised ceremonial activities, and cleared ground for planting. They usually held the positions of authority, such as chief or medicine man. Women were responsible for child rearing and artistic activity. They also did the camp work, grew vegetables,

View the **Map**
Native Americans, 1850–1896 on
myhistorylab.com

Listen to the
Audio File
Rituals of the Maize on
myhistorylab.com

After the buffalo was killed, women skinned the hide, cut up the meat, and then cured the hide, as shown in the painting *Halcyon Days* by George Catlin. Women also decorated the tepees and preserved the meat by drying it in the sun.

prepared buffalo meat and hides, and gathered berries and roots. In most tribes, women played an important role in political, economic, and religious activities. Among the Navajo and Zuni, kinship descended from the mother's side, and Navajo women were in charge of most of the family's property. In tribes such as the Sioux, there was little difference in status. Men were respected for hunting and war, women for their artistic skills with quill and paint.

Quick Check

✓ What characterized the life of the Plains Indians?

Searching for an Indian Policy

Before the Civil War, Americans used the land west of the Mississippi as "one big reservation." The government named the area "Indian Country," moved eastern tribes there with firm treaty guarantees, and in 1834 prohibited any white person from entering Indian country without a license.

This changed in the 1850s. Wagon trains wound their way to California and Oregon, miners pushed into western goldfields, and there was talk of a transcontinental railroad. To clear the way for settlement, the federal government in 1851 abandoned the "one big reservation" in favor of a new policy of concentration. For the first time, it assigned definite boundaries to each tribe. The Sioux, for example, were given the

Dakota country north of the Platte River, the Crow a large area near the Powder River, and the Cheyenne and Arapaho the Colorado foothills between the North Platte and Arkansas Rivers for "as long as waters run and the grass shall grow."

The concentration policy lasted only a few years. Accustomed to hunting widely for buffalo, many Native Americans refused to stay within their assigned areas. White settlers poured into Indian lands, then called on the government to protect them. Indians were pushed out of Kansas and Nebraska in the 1850s, even as white reformers fought to hold those territories open for free blacks. In 1859, gold miners moved into the Pikes Peak country, touching off warfare with the Cheyenne and Arapaho.

In 1864, tired of the fighting, the two tribes asked for peace. Certain that the war was over, Chief Black Kettle led his 700 followers to camp on Sand Creek in southeastern Colorado. Early on the morning of November 29, 1864, Colorado militia led by Colonel John M. Chivington attacked the sleeping group. "Kill and scalp all, big and little," Chivington told his men. "Nits make lice." Black Kettle tried to stop the ambush, raising first an American flag and then a white flag. Neither worked. Men, women, and children were clubbed, stabbed, and scalped.

The Chivington massacre set off angry protests in Colorado and the East. Congress appointed an investigating committee, and the government concluded a treaty with the Cheyenne and Arapaho, condemning "the gross and wanton outrages." Still, the two tribes had to surrender their Sand Creek reservation in exchange for lands elsewhere. The Kiowa and Comanche were also ousted from areas they had been granted "forever" only a few years before. As the Sioux chief Spotted Tail said, "Why does not the Great Father put his red children on wheels so that he can move them as he will?"

Before long, the powerful Sioux were on the warpath in the great Sioux War of 1865–1867. Again, an invasion of gold miners touched off the war, which flared even more intensely when the federal government announced plans to connect the various mining towns by building the Bozeman Trail through the heart of the Sioux hunting grounds in Montana. Red Cloud, the Sioux chief, determined to stop the trail. In December 1866, he lured an army column under Captain William J. Fetterman deep into the wilderness, ambushed it, and wiped out all 82 soldiers in Fetterman's command.

The Fetterman massacre, coming so soon after the Chivington massacre, sparked a debate over Indian policy. Like the policy itself, the debate reflected differing white views of the Native Americans. In the East, some reform, humanitarian, and church groups wanted a humane peace policy, directed toward educating and "civilizing" the tribes. Many white people, in the East and West, questioned this approach, convinced that Native Americans were savages unfit for civilization. Westerners, of course, had reason to fear Indian attacks, and the fears often fed on wild rumors of scalped settlers and besieged forts. As a result, Westerners in general favored firm control over the Native Americans, including swift punishment of any who rebelled.

In 1867, the peace advocates won the debate. Halting construction on the Bozeman Trail, Congress created a Peace Commission of four civilians and three generals to end the Sioux War and eliminate the causes of Indian wars. The Peace Commissioners agreed that only one policy offered a permanent solution: "small

Read the
Document
Chief Red Cloud's Speech on
myhistorylab.com

Read the
Document
Congressional Report on the Sand Creek Massacre (1867) on
myhistorylab.com

Map 17.2 *Native Americans in the West* Major Battles and Reservations "They made us many promises, more than I remember, but they never kept but one; they promised to take our land, and they took it." So said Red Cloud of the Oglala Sioux, summarizing Native American–white relations in the 1870s.

reservations" to isolate the Native Americans on distant lands, teach them to farm, and "civilize" them.

The Kiowa, Comanche, Cheyenne, and Arapaho agreed to the plan in 1867, the Sioux in 1868. The policy was extended beyond the Plains, and the Ute, Shoshone, Bannock, Navajo, and Apache also accepted small reservations. (See Map 17.2.)

Quick Check

✓ How did American policy toward the Indians evolve in these years?

Final Battles on the Plains

Few Native Americans settled peacefully into life on the new reservations. The reservation system not only changed their age-old customs; it impoverished and isolated them. Young warriors and minor chiefs denounced the treaties and drifted back to the open countryside. In late 1868, warfare broke out again, and it took more than a decade of violence to beat the Indians into submission.

On the northern Plains, fighting resulted from the Black Hills Gold Rush of 1875. As prospectors tramped across Native American hunting grounds, the Sioux gathered to stop them. They were led by Rain-in-the-Face, the great war chief Crazy Horse, and the famous medicine man Sitting Bull. The army sent troops after the

 **View** the **Map**
*Resources and Conflict
in the West* on
myhistorylab.com

**Watch** the **Video**
Sioux Ghost Dance on
myhistorylab.com

Indians, but one column, under flamboyant Lieutenant Colonel George Armstrong Custer, pushed recklessly ahead, eager to claim the victory. On the morning of June 25, 1876, thinking he had a small band of Native Americans surrounded in their village on the banks of the Little Bighorn River in Montana, Custer divided his column and took 265 men toward it. Instead of a small band, he had stumbled on the main Sioux camp, with 2,500 warriors. It was the largest Native American army ever assembled in the United States.

By mid-afternoon Custer and his men were dead. Custer was largely responsible for the loss, but "Custer's Last Stand" set off a nationwide demand for revenge. Within months, the Sioux were surrounded and beaten, 3,000 of them surrendering in October 1876. Sitting Bull and a few followers who had fled to Canada gave up in 1881.

The Sioux War ended major Indian warfare in the West, but occasional outbreaks still recurred. In 1890, many of the Teton Sioux of South Dakota, bitter and starving, turned to the Ghost Dances, rites that grew from a vision of a Paiute messiah named Wovoka. The dances, Wovoka said, would bring back Native American lands and make the whites disappear. All Native Americans would unite, the earth would be covered with dust, and a new earth would come upon the old. The buffalo would return in great herds.

Read the
Document
*Benjamin Harrison,
Report on Wounded
Knee and Decrease
in Indian Land
Acreage* on
myhistorylab.com

The army intervened to stop the dancing, touching off violence that killed Sitting Bull and other warriors. Frightened Native Americans fled southwest to join other Ghost Dancers under the aging chief Big Foot. The Seventh Cavalry, Custer's old regiment, caught up with Big Foot's band and took them to the army camp on Wounded Knee Creek in South Dakota. A Native American, it is thought, fired the first shot, but the army's new machine guns, firing a shell a second, shredded tepees and people. In the infamous Wounded Knee Massacre, about 200 men, women, and children were killed in the snow.

Quick Check

✓ What were the final battles on the Plains?

The End of Tribal Life

The final step in Indian policy came in the 1870s and 1880s. Reformers had long argued against segregating the Native Americans on reservations, urging instead that the nation assimilate them individually into white culture. "Assimilationists" wanted to use education, land policy, and federal law to eradicate tribal society.

Congress began to adopt the policy in 1871 when it stopped making treaties with Native American tribes. Since tribes were no longer separate nations, they lost many of their political and judicial functions, and the power of the chiefs was weakened.

Read the
Document
*Autobiographical
Narrative of Zitakala
School in Indiana* on
myhistorylab.com

While Congress worked to break down the tribes, educators trained young Native Americans to adjust to white culture. In 1879, 50 Pawnee, Kiowa, and Cheyenne youths were brought to the new Carlisle Indian School in Carlisle, Pennsylvania. Other Native American schools soon opened, including the Haskell Institute in Kansas and numerous day schools on the western reservations. The schools taught students to fix machines and farm; they forced young Indians to trim their long hair and made them speak English, banned wearing tribal paint or clothes, and forbade tribal ceremonies and dances. "Kill the Indian and save the man," said Richard H. Pratt, the army officer who founded the Carlisle School.

Tom Torlino A Navajo Indian, photographed before and after his "assimilation." Torlino attended the Carlisle Indian School in Pennsylvania.

Land ownership was the final and most important link in the new policy. Native Americans who owned land, it was thought, would become responsible, self-reliant citizens. Deciding to give each Native American a farm, Congress in 1887 passed the Dawes Severalty Act, the most important legal development in Indian–white relations in more than three centuries.

To end tribal life, the Dawes Act divided tribal lands into small plots for distribution among members of the tribe. Each family head received 160 acres, single adults 80 acres, and children 40 acres. Once the land was distributed, any surplus was sold to white settlers, with the profits going to Native American schools.

Through the Dawes Act, 47 million acres of land were distributed to Native Americans and their families, but many Native Americans knew little about farming. Their tools were rudimentary, and in Plains Indians' culture, men had not ordinarily participated in farming. In 1934, the government returned to the idea of tribal land ownership, but by then 138 million acres of Indian land had shrunk to 48 million acres, half of which was barren.

The final blow to tribal life was the virtual extermination of the buffalo, the

Huge buffalo herds grazing along railroads in the West frequently blocked passing trains. Passengers often killed for sport, shooting at the beasts with "no intention of using or removing the animal carcasses."

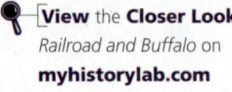

View the **Closer Look**
Railroad and Buffalo on
myhistorylab.com

Plains Indians' chief resource and the basis for their unique way of life. The killing began in the 1860s as the transcontinental railroads pushed west, and it stepped up as settlers found they could harm the Indians by wiping out the buffalo. "Kill every buffalo you can," an army officer said. "Every buffalo dead is an Indian gone." Then, in 1871, a Pennsylvania tannery discovered that buffalo hides made valuable leather. Professional hunters such as William F. "Buffalo Bill" Cody swarmed across the Plains, killing millions of the beasts.

Between 1872 and 1874, professional hunters slaughtered 3 million buffalo a year. By 1883, the buffalo were almost gone. When the government set out to produce the famous "buffalo nickel," the designer had to go to the Bronx Zoo in New York City to find a buffalo.

By 1900, only 250,000 Native Americans lived in the U.S. (There had been 600,000 within the limits of the present-day United States in 1800, and more than 5 million in 1492, when Columbus first set foot in the New World.) Most of the Indians lived on reservations. Many lived in poverty. Alcoholism and unemployment were growing problems, and Native Americans, no longer able to live off the buffalo, became wards of the state. They lost their cultural distinctiveness. Once possessors of the entire continent, they had been crowded into smaller and smaller areas, overwhelmed by the demand to become settled, literate, and English-speaking. "Except for the internment of the West Coast Japanese during World War II," said historian Roger L. Nichols, "Indian removal is the only example of large-scale government-enforced migration in American history. For the Japanese, the move was temporary; for the Indians it was not."

Even as the Native Americans lost their identity, they entered the romantic folklore of the West. Dime novels, snapped up by readers young and old, told tales of Indian fighting on the Plains. "Buffalo Bill" Cody turned it all into a profitable business. Beginning in 1883, his Wild West Show played to millions of viewers in the United States, Canada, and Europe for more than three decades. It featured Plains Indians chasing buffalo, performing a war dance, and attacking a settler's cabin. In 1885, Sitting Bull himself, victor over Custer at the Battle of the Little Bighorn, performed in the show.

Quick Check

✓ What events and measures ended tribal life?

SETTLEMENT OF THE WEST

Why did Americans and others move to the West?

Between 1870 and 1900, white—and some African, Hispanic, and Asian—Americans settled the 430 million acres west of the Mississippi; they took over more land than Americans had occupied in all the years before 1870.

People moved west for many reasons. Some sought adventure; others wanted to escape the drab routine of factory or city life. Many moved to California for their health. The Mormons settled Utah to escape religious persecution. Others followed the mining camps, the advancing railroads, and the farming and cattle frontier.

Whatever the specific reason, most people moved west to better their lot. On the whole, their timing was good, for as the nation's population grew, so did demand for the livestock and the agricultural, mineral, and lumber products of the expanding West. Contrary to older historical views, the West did not act as a major "safety valve," an outlet for social and economic tensions. The poor and unemployed could not afford to move there and establish farms.

Men and Women on the Overland Trail

The first movement west aimed not for the nearby Plains but for California and Oregon on the continent's far shore. It started in the Gold Rush of 1849, and in the next three decades, perhaps 500,000 people made the long journey over the Overland Trail, a network of trails leading west. Some walked; others rode horses alone or in small groups. About half joined great caravans, numbering 150 wagons or more, that inched across the 2,000 miles between the Missouri River and the Pacific coast.

More often than not, men made the decision to make the crossing, but, except for the stampedes to the mines, migration was usually a family affair. Wives were consulted, though in some cases they had little choice. They could either go along or live alone at home. While many women regretted leaving family and friends, they agreed to the trip, sometimes as eagerly as the men. Most people traveled in family groups, including in-laws, grandchildren, aunts, and uncles. As one historian had said, "The quest for something new would take place in the context of the very familiar."

Individuals and wagon trains set out from points along the Missouri River. During April, travelers assembled in camp just across the Missouri River, waiting for the new grass to ripen into forage. They packed and repacked the wagons and elected the trains' leaders, who would set the line of march, look for water and campsites, and impose discipline. Some trains adopted detailed rules, fearing a lapse into savagery in the wild lands across the Missouri. "Every man to carry with him a Bible and other religious books, as we hope not to degenerate into a state of barbarism," one agreement said.

Setting out in early May, travelers divided the route into manageable portions. The first leg of the journey followed the Platte River west to Fort Kearney in central Nebraska Territory, a distance of about 300 miles. From a distance, the white-topped wagons seemed driven by a common force, but, in fact, internal discipline broke down almost immediately. Arguments erupted over the pace of the march, the choice of campsites, the number of guards to post, whether to rest or push on. Elected leaders quit; new ones were chosen. Every train was filled with individualists, and as the son of one train captain said, "If you think it's any snap to run a wagon train of 66 wagons with every man in the train having a different idea of what is the best thing to do, all I can say is that some day you ought to try it."

Men, women, and children had different tasks on the trail. Men concerned themselves almost entirely with hunting, guard duty, and transportation. They rose at 4 A.M. to hitch the wagons, and after breakfast began the day's march. At noon, they stopped and set the teams to graze. After the midday meal, the march continued until sunset. Then, while the men relaxed, the women fixed dinner and the next day's lunch, and the children kindled the fires, fetched water, and searched for wood or other fuel. Walking 15 miles a day, in searing heat and mountain cold, travelers were exhausted by late afternoon.

For women, the trail was lonely, and they worked to exhaustion. Some adjusted their clothing to the harsh conditions, adopting the new bloomer pants, shortening their skirts, or wearing "wash dresses"—so called because they had shorter hemlines that did not drag on the wet ground on washday. Other women continued to wear their long dresses, thinking bloomers "indecent." Both men and women carried firearms in case of Indian attacks, but most emigrants saw few Indians en route.

What they often did see was trash, miles of it, for the wagon trains were an early example of the impact of migration and settlement on the western environment. On the Oregon and other trails, travelers sidestepped mounds of garbage, tin cans, furniture, cooking stoves, kegs, tools, and clothing discarded by people who had passed through before.

The first stage of the journey was deceptively easy, and travelers usually reached Fort Kearney by late May. The second leg led another 300 miles up the Platte River to Fort Laramie on the eastern edge of Wyoming Territory. The heat of June had dried the grass, and there was no wood. Anxious to beat the early snowfalls, travelers rested a day or two at the fort, then hurried on to South Pass, 280 miles to the west, the best route through the forbidding Rockies. It was now mid-July, but the mountain nights were so cold that ice formed in the water buckets.

Beyond South Pass, some emigrants turned south to the Mormon settlements on the Great Salt Lake, but most headed 340 miles north to Fort Hall on the Snake River in Idaho. It took another three months to cover the remaining 800 miles. California-bound travelers followed the Humboldt River through the summer heat of Nevada. Well into September, they began the final arduous push: first, a 55-mile stretch of desert; then 70 difficult miles up the eastern slopes of the Sierra Nevada, laboriously hoisting wagons over massive outcrops of rock; and finally the last 100 miles down the western slopes to the welcome sight of California's Central Valley in October.

Under the best conditions the trip took six months, 16 hours a day, dawn to dusk, of grueling labor. Walking halfway across the continent was no easy task, a never-to-be-forgotten experience for those who did it. The wagon trains, carrying the dreams of thousands of individuals, reproduced society in small focus: individualistic, hopeful, mobile, divided by age and gender roles, apprehensive, yet willing to strike out for the distant and new.

View the **Image**
Great Western Migration on
myhistorylab.com

Quick Check

✔ What was life like on the Overland Trail?

Land for the Taking

As railroads pushed west in the 1870s and 1880s, locomotive trains replaced wagon trains, but the shift was gradual, and until the end of the century, emigrants often combined both modes of travel. Early railroad transportation was expensive, and the average farm family could not afford to buy tickets and ship supplies. Many Europeans traveled by rail to designated outfitting places and then proceeded west with wagons and oxen.

Traffic flowed in all directions, belying the image of a simple "westward" movement. Many people did go west, of course, but others, such as migrants from Mexico, became westerners by moving north, and Asian Americans moved eastward from the Pacific coast. Whatever their route, they all ended up in the meeting ground of cultures that formed the modern West.

Why did they come? "The motive that induced us to part with the pleasant associations and the dear friends of our childhood days," explained Phoebe Judson, an early emigrant, "was to obtain from the government of the United States a grant of land that 'Uncle Sam' had promised to give to the head of each family who settled in this new country." A popular camp song reflected the same motive:

> Come along, come along—don't be alarmed,
> Uncle Sam is rich enough to give us all a farm.

Uncle Sam owned about one billion acres of land in the 1860s, much of it mountain and desert unsuited for agriculture. By 1900, land laws had distributed half of it. Between 1862 and 1890, the government gave away 48 million acres to western farmers, sold about 100 million acres to private citizens and corporations, granted 128 million acres to railroad companies to tempt them to build across the unsettled West, and sold huge tracts to the states.

The Homestead Act of 1862 gave 160 acres of land to anyone who would pay a $10 registration fee and pledge to live on the land and cultivate it for five years. The offer set off a mass migration of land-hungry Europeans, dazzled by a country that gave its land away. Americans also seized on the act's provisions, and between 1862 and 1900, nearly 600,000 families claimed free homesteads under it.

Yet the Homestead Act did not work as Congress had hoped. Few farmers and laborers had the cash to move to the frontier, buy farm equipment, and wait out the year or two before the farm became self-supporting. Tailored to the timber and water conditions of the East, the act worked less well in the semiarid West. In the fertile valleys of the Mississippi, 160 acres provided a generous farm. A farmer on the Great Plains needed either a larger farm for dry farming or a smaller one for irrigation.

Speculators made ingenious use of the land laws. Sending agents in advance of settlement, they moved along choice river bottoms or irrigable areas, accumulating large holdings to be held for high prices. In the arid West, where control of water meant control of the surrounding land, shrewd ranchers plotted their holdings accordingly. In Colorado, one cattleman, John F. Iliff, owned only 105 small parcels of land, but by placing them around the few water holes, he effectively dominated a 6,000-square-mile empire.

Water, in fact, became a dominant issue, since much of the trans-Mississippi West received less than 20 inches of rainfall annually. People speculated in water as if it were gold and planned great irrigation systems in Utah, eastern Colorado, and California's Central Valley to "make the desert bloom."

Irrigators received a major boost in 1902 when the National Reclamation Act (Newlands Act) set aside most of the proceeds from the sale of public lands in 16 western states to finance irrigation projects in the arid states. Dams, canals, and irrigation systems channeled water into dry areas, creating a "hydraulic" society that was rich in crops and cities (such as Los Angeles and Phoenix), but ever thirstier and in danger of outrunning the precious water on which it all depended.

As beneficiaries of government land grants for railway construction, the railroad companies were the West's largest landowners. Eager to have immigrants settle on the land they owned near the railroad right-of-way, and eager to boost their freight and passenger business, the companies sent agents to the East and Europe.

Quick Check

✓ By what measures did the government distribute land in the West?

In all, half a billion acres of western land were given or sold to speculators and corporations. Only 600,000 homestead patents were issued, covering 80 million acres. Thus, only one acre in every nine grants initially went to individual pioneers, the intended beneficiaries of the nation's largesse. Two-thirds of all homestead claimants before 1890 failed to farm their new land.

The Spanish-Speaking Southwest

In the nineteenth century, almost all Spanish-speaking people in the United States lived in California, Arizona, New Mexico, Texas, and Colorado. Their numbers were small—California had only 8,086 Mexican residents in 1900—but the influence of their culture and institutions was large. In some respects, the southwestern frontier was more Spanish American than Anglo American.

Pushing north from Mexico, the Spanish gradually established the present-day economic structure of the Southwest. They brought with them techniques of mining, stock raising, and irrigated farming. After winning independence in the 1820s, the Mexicans brought new laws and ranching methods as well as chaps and the burro. Both Spanish and Mexicans created the legal framework for distributing land and water. They gave large grants of land to communities for grazing, to individuals as rewards for service, and to the Native American pueblos.

In southern California, the Californios, descendants of the original colonizers, began after the 1860s to lose their vast landholdings to drought and mortgages. As they died out, Mexican Americans continued the Spanish–Mexican influence. In 1880, one-fourth of the residents of Los Angeles County were Spanish speaking.

Throughout the Southwest, the Spanish–Mexican heritage shaped society. Men headed the families and dominated economic life. Women had substantial economic rights (though few political ones) and enjoyed a status their English American counterparts lacked. Wives kept full control of property acquired before their marriage and held half title to all property in a marriage, which later caused many southwestern states to pass community property laws.

The Spanish–Mexican heritage also fostered a modified economic caste system, a strong Roman Catholic influence, and the Spanish language. Continuous immigration from Mexico kept

Invitation to the Dance In this painting by Theodore Gentilz, a young woman stands in the doorway of her San Antonio, Texas, home to greet the caballeros riding up on their horses and making music on the violin and guitar. The caballeros' flared trousers, known as *calzoneras*, were well suited for riding and dancing. Note the distinctive architectural style of the white building at the left, where a couple is dancing.

language and cultural ties strong. Spanish names and customs spread, even among Anglos. David Starr Jordan, arriving from Indiana in 1891 to become the first president of Stanford University in California, bestowed Spanish names on streets, houses, and a dormitory. Spanish was the region's first or second language. Confronted by Sheriff Pat Garrett in 1881 in a darkened room, New Mexico's famous outlaw Billy the Kid died asking, "Quién es? Quién es?" ("Who is it? Who is it?").

Quick Check

✓ In what ways did the Spanish–Mexican heritage of the Southwest shape its development?

THE BONANZA WEST

Between 1850 and 1900, waves of newcomers swept across the trans-Mississippi West. There were riches for the taking, hidden in gold-washed streams, spread lushly over grass-covered prairies, or in the gullible minds of greedy newcomers. The nineteenth-century West took shape in the search for mining, cattle, and land bonanzas that drew eager settlers from around the world.

Why was the West a bonanza of dreams and get-rich-quick schemes?

As with all bonanzas, the consequences in the West were uneven growth, boom-and-bust economic cycles, and wasted resources. Society seemed constantly in the making. People moved here and there, following river bottoms, gold strikes, railroad tracks, and other opportunities. "Instant cities" arose. San Francisco, Salt Lake City, and Denver were the most spectacular examples, but every cow town and mining camp witnessed similar spurts of growth. Boston needed more than two centuries to attract 300,000 people; San Francisco did the same in a little more than 20 years.

Many Westerners had left home to get rich quickly, and they adopted institutions that reflected that goal. The West was an idea as well as a region, and the idea molded westerners as much as they molded it.

The Mining Bonanza

Mining was the first important magnet to attract people to the West. Many hoped to "strike it rich" in gold and silver, but at least half the newcomers had no intention of working in the mines. Instead, they provided food, clothing, and services to the thousands of miners.

The California Gold Rush of 1849 set the pattern for subsequent mining booms. Individual prospectors made the first strikes, discovering gold along streams flowing westward from the Sierra Nevada. To get the gold, they used placer mining, which required little skill, technology, or capital. A placer miner needed only a shovel, a washing pan, and a good claim. As the placers gave out, much gold remained, but it was locked in quartz or buried deep in the earth. Mining became an expensive business, far beyond the reach of the average miner.

Large corporations moved in to dig the deep shafts and finance costly equipment. Quartz mining required heavy rock crushers, mercury vats to dissolve the gold, and large retorts to recapture it. Eastern and European financiers took control, labor became unionized, and mining towns took on some of the characteristics of the industrial city. Individual prospectors meanwhile dashed on to the next find. Unlike other frontiers, the mining frontier moved from west to east, as the original California miners—the "yonder-siders"—hurried eastward in search of the big strike.

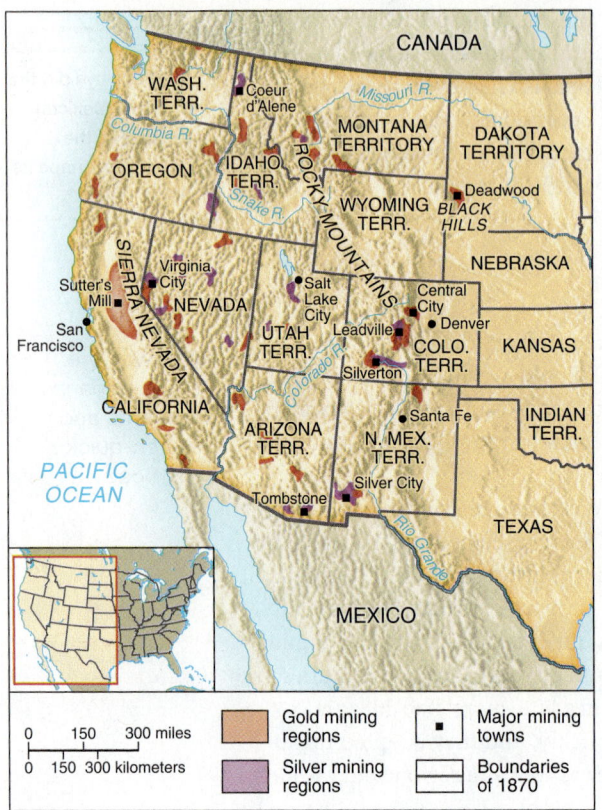

Map 17.3 Mining Regions of the West Gold and silver mines dotted the West, drawing settlers and encouraging political organization.

In 1859, fresh strikes near Pikes Peak in Colorado and in the Carson River Valley of Nevada set off wild migrations—100,000 miners were in Pikes Peak country by June 1859. The gold there quickly played out, but the Nevada find uncovered a thick bluish black ore that was almost pure silver and gold. A quick-witted drifter named Henry T. P. Comstock talked his way into partnership in the claim, and word of the **Comstock Lode**—a fabulous mine with ore worth $3,876 a ton—flashed over the mountains.

Thousands of miners climbed the Sierra Nevada that summer; but the biggest strike was yet to come. In 1873, John W. Mackay and three partners formed a company to dig deep into the mountain, and at 1,167 feet they hit the Big Bonanza, a seam of gold and silver more than 54 feet wide. It was the richest discovery in the history of mining. Between 1859 and 1879, the Comstock Lode produced gold and silver worth $306 million. Most of it went to financiers and corporations. Mackay became the richest person in the world.

In the 1860s and 1870s, important strikes were made in Washington, Idaho, Nevada, Colorado, Montana, Arizona, and Dakota. Miners flocked from strike to strike, and new camps and mining towns sprang up overnight. (See Map 17.3.)

The final fling came in the Black Hills rush of 1874 to 1876. The army had tried to keep miners out of the area, the heart of the Sioux hunting grounds, and even sent a scientific party under Colonel George Armstrong Custer to disprove the rumors of gold and stop the miners' invasion. Instead, Custer found gold all over the hills, and the rush was on. Miners, gamblers, desperadoes, and prostitutes flocked to Deadwood, the most lawless of all the mining camps. There, Martha Jane Canary—a crack shot who, as Calamity Jane, won fame as a scout and teamster—fell in love with "Wild Bill" Hickok. Hickok himself—a western legend who had tamed Kansas cow towns, killed an unknown number of men, and toured in Buffalo Bill's Wild West Show—died in Deadwood, shot in the back of the head. He was 39 years old.

Towns such as Deadwood, in the Dakota Territory; Virginia City, Nevada; Leadville, Colorado; and Tombstone, Arizona, demonstrated a new development process in the frontier experience. The farming frontier had developed naturally in a rural setting. On the mining frontier, the germ of a city—the camp—appeared almost simultaneously with the first "strike." Periodicals, the latest fashions, theaters, schools, literary clubs, and lending libraries came quickly to the camps, providing civilized refinements not available on other frontiers. Urbanization also created the need for municipal government, sanitation, and law enforcement.

Read the **Document**
John Lester, "Hydraulic Mining" on
myhistorylab.com

A simple democracy governed mining camps. Soon after a strike, the miners organized a mining "district" and adopted rules governing behavior in it. Rules regulated the size and boundaries of claims, established procedures for settling disputes, and set penalties for crimes. Petty criminals were banished; serious offenders were hanged. For a major dispute, the whole camp gathered, chose legal counsel for both sides, and heard the evidence. If all else failed, miners formed secret vigilance committees to hang a few offenders as a lesson to the rest. Early visitors to the mining country were struck by how miners, solitary and competitive, joined together, founded a camp, and created a society.

The camps were mostly male, made up of "men who can rough it" and a few "ladies of spirit and energy." In 1870, men outnumbered women in the mining districts by more than two to one; there were few children. Prostitutes followed the camps around the West, and a "respectable" woman was a curiosity. Some women worked claims, but more often they took jobs as cooks, housekeepers, and seamstresses—for wages considerably higher than in the East.

In most camps, between one-quarter and one-half of the population was foreign born. The lure of gold drew many Chinese, Chileans, Peruvians, Mexicans, French, Germans, and English. Experienced miners, the Latin Americans brought valuable mining techniques. At least 6,000 Mexicans joined the California rush of 1849, and by 1852, there were 25,000 Chinese in California. Painstaking, the Chinese profitably worked claims others had abandoned. In the 1860s, almost one-third of the miners in the West were Chinese.

Hostility often surfaced against foreign miners, particularly the French, Latin Americans, and Chinese. Riots against Chinese laborers occurred in the 1870s and 1880s in Los Angeles, San Francisco, Seattle, Reno, and Denver. Responding to pressure, Congress passed the Chinese Exclusion Act of 1882, which suspended immigration of Chinese laborers for ten years. The number of Chinese in the United States fell drastically.

By the 1890s, the early mining bonanza was over. All told, the western mines contributed billions of dollars to the economy. They had helped finance the Civil War and industrialization. The vast boost in silver production from the Comstock Lode changed the relative value of gold and silver, the base of American currency. Disputes over the currency affected politics and led to the famous "battle of the standards" in the presidential election of 1896 (see Chapter 20).

The mining frontier populated portions of the West and sped up its political organization. Nevada, Idaho, and Montana were granted early statehood because of mining. Merchants, editors, lawyers, and ministers moved with the advancing frontier, establishing permanent settlements. Women in the mining camps helped foster family life and raised the moral tone by campaigning against drinking, gambling, and prostitution. But the industry also left painful scars in the form of invaded Indian reservations, pitted hills, and ghost towns.

Quick Check

✓ What were the characteristics of the mining industry?

The Cattle Bonanza

"There's gold from the grass roots down," said California Joe, a guide in the gold districts of Dakota in the 1870s, "but there's more gold from the grass roots up." Ranchers

Charles M. Russell *Cowboy Camp During Roundup*, ca. 1885–1887. Artist Charles Russell here documents the cowboys' activities during the annual spring roundup. Before setting off on the long trek to drive cattle to market, the cowboys had to rope and break in horses that might have gone wild over the winter.

began to recognize the potential of the vast western grasslands. The Plains were covered with buffalo or grama grass, a wiry variety with short, hard stems. Cattle thrived on it.

For 20 years after 1865, cattle ranching dominated the "open range," a vast fenceless area from the Texas Panhandle north into Canada. The techniques of the business came from Mexico. Long before American cowboys moved herds north, their Mexican counterparts, the vaqueros, developed the essential techniques of branding, roundups, and roping. The cattle themselves, the famous Texas longhorns, also came from Mexico. Spreading over the grasslands of southern Texas, the longhorns multiplied rapidly. Although their meat was coarse and stringy, they fed a nation hungry for beef at the end of the Civil War.

The problem was getting the beef to eastern markets, and Joseph G. McCoy, a livestock shipper from Illinois, solved it. To market Texas beef, McCoy conceived the idea of taking the cattle to railheads in Kansas. He talked first with the president of the Missouri Pacific, who ordered him out of his office, and then with the head of the Kansas Pacific, who laughed at the idea. McCoy finally signed a contract in 1867 with the Hannibal and St. Joseph Railroad. Searching for an appropriate rail junction, he settled on the sleepy Kansas town of Abilene, "a very small, dead place," he remembered, with about a dozen log huts and one nearly bankrupt saloon.

In September 1867, McCoy shipped the first 20 cars of longhorn cattle. By the end of the year, 1,000 carloads had followed, all headed for Chicago markets. In 1870, 300,000 head of Texas cattle reached Abilene, followed the next year—the peak year—by 700,000 head. The Alamo Saloon, crowded with tired cowboys at the end of the drive, employed 75 bartenders, working three eight-hour shifts.

The profits were enormous. Drivers bought cheap Texas steers for $4 a head and sold them for $30 or $40 a head at the northern railhead. The most famous trail, the

Chisholm, ran from southern Texas through Oklahoma Territory to Ellsworth and Abilene, Kansas, on the Kansas Pacific Railroad. Dodge City, Kansas, became the prime shipping center between 1875 and 1879. (See Map 17.4)

Cowboys pushed steers northward in herds of 2,000–3,000. Novels and films have portrayed the cowboys as white, but at least a quarter of them were black, and possibly another quarter were Mexicans. A typical crew on the trail north might have eight men, half of them black or Mexican. Most of the trail bosses were white; they earned about $125 a month.

Like miners, cattlemen lived beyond the formal reach of the law. So they established their own. Before each drive, Charles Goodnight drew up rules governing behavior on the trail. A cowboy who shot another was hanged on the spot. Ranchers adopted rules for cattle ownership, branding, roundups, and drives, and they formed associations to enforce them. The Wyoming Stock Growers' Association,

👁 **Watch** the **Video**
Cowboys and Cattle on **myhistorylab.com**

Map 17.4 Cattle Trails Cattle raised in Texas were driven along the cattle trails to the northern railheads where trains carried them to market.

the largest and most formidable, had 400 members owning 2 million cattle; its reach extended into Colorado, Nebraska, Montana, and the Dakotas. Throughout this vast territory, the "laws" of the association were often the law of the land.

By 1880, more than 6 million cattle had been driven to northern markets. But the era of the great cattle drive was ending. Farmers were planting wheat on the old buffalo ranges; barbed wire, a recent invention, cut across the trails and divided up the big ranches. Mechanical improvements in slaughtering, refrigerated transportation, and cold storage modernized the industry. Ranchers bred the Texas longhorns with heavier Hereford and Angus bulls, and as the new breeds proved profitable, more and more ranches opened on the northern ranges. Stories of vast profits attracted outside capital. Large investments transformed ranching into big business, often controlled by absentee owners and subject to new problems.

By 1885, however, experienced cattle ranchers were growing alarmed. The winter of 1885–1886 was cold, and the following summer was one of the hottest on record. Water holes dried up; the grass turned brown. Beef prices fell.

The winter of 1886–1887 was one of the worst in western history. Temperatures dropped to 45 degrees below zero, and cattle that once would have saved themselves by drifting ahead of the storms came up against the new barbed wire fences. Herds jammed together, pawing the frozen ground or stripping bark from trees in search of food. Tens of thousands of cattle died. In the spring of 1887, when the snows thawed, ranchers found carcasses piled up against the fences.

The melting snows did, however, produce lush grass for the survivors. The cattle business recovered, but it took different directions. Outside capital, so plentiful in the boom years, dried up. Ranchers began fencing their lands, reducing their herds, and growing hay for winter food.

The last roundup on the northern ranges took place in 1905. Ranches grew smaller, and some ranchers, at first in the scrub country of the Southwest, then on the Plains themselves, switched to raising sheep. By 1900, there were nearly 38 million sheep west of the Missouri River, far more than there were cattle.

Ranchers and sheepherders fought to control the grazing lands, but they had one problem in common: The day of the open range was over. Homesteaders, armed with barbed wire and new strains of wheat, were pushing onto the Plains.

Quick Check

✓ What characterized the growth of the cattle business in these years?

The Farming Bonanza

Like miners and cattle ranchers, millions of farmers moved into the West after 1870 to seek crop bonanzas and new ways of life. Some realized their dreams; many fought just to survive.

Between 1870 and 1900, farmers cultivated more land than ever before in American history. They peopled the Plains from the Dakotas to Texas, pushed the Indians out of their last sanctuary in Oklahoma, and poured into the basins and foothills of the Rockies. By 1900, the western half of the nation contained almost 30 percent of the population, compared to less than 1 percent in 1850.

Unlike mining, farm settlement often followed predictable patterns, taking population from states east of the settlement line and moving westward. Crossing the Mississippi, farmers settled first in western Iowa, Minnesota, Nebraska, Kansas, Texas, and South Dakota. The movement slumped during the depression of the 1870s, but then a new wave of optimism carried thousands more west. Years of above-average rainfall convinced farmers that the Dakotas, western Nebraska and Kansas, and eastern Colorado were the "rain belt of the Plains." Between 1870 and 1900, the population on the Plains tripled.

Some newcomers were blacks who had fled the South, fed up with beatings and murders, crop liens, and the Black Codes that institutionalized their subordination. In 1879, about 6,000 African Americans known as the Exodusters left Louisiana, Mississippi, and Texas to establish new and freer lives in Kansas, the home of John Brown and the Free-Soil campaigns of the 1850s. Once there, they farmed or worked as laborers; women worked in the fields alongside the men or cleaned houses and took in washing to make ends meet. All told, the Exodusters homesteaded 20,000 acres of land, and though they met prejudice, it was less extreme than they had known in the South.

Other African Americans moved to Oklahoma, thinking they might establish the first African American state. Whether headed for Oklahoma or Kansas, they picked up and moved in sizable groups based on family units; they took with them the customs they had known, and in their new homes, they were able, for the first time, to enjoy some measure of self-government.

For blacks and whites alike, farming on the Plains presented new problems. There was little surface water, and wells ranged between 50 and 500 feet deep. Well drillers charged up to $2 a foot. Taking advantage of the steady Plains winds, windmills brought the water to the surface, but they too were expensive, and until 1900, many farmers could not afford them. Lumber for homes and fences was also scarce.

Unable to afford wood, farmers often started out in dreary sod houses. Cut into 3-foot sections, the thick prairie sod was laid like brick, with space for two windows and a door. Since glass was scarce, cloth covered the windows; a blanket was hung from the ceiling to make two rooms. Sod houses were small, provided little light and air, and were impossible to keep clean. Rain water seeped through the roof. But a sod house cost only $2.78 to build.

Outside, the Plains environment tested the men and women who moved there. In the winters, savage storms swept the open grasslands. Ice caked on the cattle until their heads were too heavy to hold up. Summer temperatures stayed near 110 degrees for weeks. Fearsome rainstorms, building in the heat, beat down the young corn and wheat. Summers also brought grasshoppers in clouds so huge they shut out the sun. The grasshoppers ate everything in sight: crops, clothing, mosquito netting, tree bark, even plow handles. In 1874, they ate everything on the Plains "but the mortgage," as one farmer said, from Texas to the Dakotas.

Farmers adopted new techniques to meet these conditions. Most importantly, they needed cheap and effective fencing material, and in 1874, Joseph F. Glidden, a farmer from De Kalb, Illinois, provided it with the invention of barbed wire. By 1883, his factory was turning out 600 miles of barbed wire every day, and farmers were buying it faster than it could be produced. Barbed wire fences helped them pen their own stock in and keep other animals out.

View the Image
Exodusters on
myhistorylab.com

Quick Check
✓ What was farming like on the Plains?

Discontent on the Farm

Touring the farming areas in the 1860s, Oliver H. Kelley, a clerk in the U.S. Department of Agriculture, was struck by the drabness of rural life. In 1867, he founded the National Grange of the Patrons of Husbandry, known simply as the Grange. The Grange provided social, cultural, and educational activities for its members. Its constitution banned involvement in politics, but Grangers often ignored the rules and supported railroad regulation and other measures.

The Grange grew rapidly during the depression of the 1870s, and by 1875, it had more than 800,000 members in 20,000 local Granges. Most were in the Midwest and South. The Granges set up cooperative stores, grain elevators, warehouses, insurance companies, and farm machinery factories. Many of these failed, but the organization made its mark. Picking up where the Grange left off, groups such as the Farmers' Alliance, with branches in both the South and West, attracted followers.

Like the cattle boom, the farming boom ended abruptly after 1887. A severe drought that year cut harvests, and more droughts in 1889 and 1894 wiped out thousands of new farmers on the western Plains. Between 1888 and 1892, more than half the population of western Kansas left. Angry and restless farmers complained about declining crop prices, rising railroad rates, and heavy mortgages.

Although many farmers were unhappy, the peopling of the West in those years transformed American agriculture. The states beyond the Mississippi became the nation's garden. California sent fruit, wine, and wheat to eastern markets. Under the Mormons, Utah flourished with irrigation. Texas beef stocked the country's tables, and vast wheat fields, stretching to the horizon, covered Minnesota, the Dakotas, Montana, and eastern Colorado. All produced more than Americans could consume. By 1890, American farmers were exporting large amounts of wheat and other crops.

Farmers became more commercial and scientific. They needed to know more and work harder. Mail-order houses and rural free delivery diminished their isolation and tied them ever closer to the national future. "This is a new age to the farmer," said a statistician in the Department of Agriculture in 1889. "He is now, more than ever before, a citizen of the world."

Quick Check

✓ Why were so many farmers unhappy in the last decades of the nineteenth century, and what did they try to do about it?

The Final Fling

As the West filled in with people, pressure mounted to open the last Indian territory, Oklahoma, to settlers. In March 1889, Congress forced the Creek and Seminole tribes, which had been moved into Oklahoma in the 1820s, to surrender their rights to the land. President Benjamin Harrison announced the opening of the Oklahoma District as of noon, April 22, 1889.

On the morning of April 22, nearly 100,000 people lined the Oklahoma borders. At noon, the starting flag dropped. Bugles and cannon signaled the opening of the "last" territory. Horsemen lunged forward; overloaded wagons collided and overturned. By sunset, settlers claimed 12,000 homesteads, and the 1.92 million acres of the Oklahoma District were officially settled. The "Boomers" (those who waited for the signal) and "Sooners" (those who had jumped the gun) reflected the speed of western settlement. "Creation!" a character in Edna Ferber's novel *Cimarron* declared. "Hell! That took six days. This was done in one. It was History made in an hour—and I helped make it."

Quick Check

✓ Who were the "Boomers," and Who were the "Sooners"?

CONCLUSION: THE MEANING OF THE WEST

Between the Civil War and 1900, the West witnessed one of the greatest migrations in history. With the Native Americans driven into smaller and smaller areas, farms, ranches, mines, and cities took over the vast lands from the Mississippi to the Pacific. The 1890 census noted that for the first time in American history, "there can hardly be said to be a frontier line." Picking up the theme, Frederick Jackson Turner, a young historian at the University of Wisconsin, examined its importance in an influential 1893 paper, "The Significance of the Frontier in American History."

Read the **Document**
Frederick Jackson Turner, "The Significance of the Frontier in American History" on **myhistorylab.com**

"The existence of an area of free land," Turner wrote, "its continuous recession, and the advance of American settlement westward, explain American development." It shaped customs and character; gave rise to independence, self-confidence, and individualism; and fostered invention and adaptation. Historians have modified Turner's thesis by pointing to frontier conservatism and imitativeness, the influence of racial groups, and the persistence of European ideas and institutions. Most recently, they have shown that family and community loomed as large as individualism on the frontier; men, women, and children played much the same roles as they had back home.

Rejecting Turner almost completely, a group of "new Western historians" has advanced a different and complex view of the West, and one with few heroes and heroines. Emphasizing the region's racial and ethnic diversity, these historians stress the role of women as well as men, trace struggles between economic interests instead of fights between gunslingers, and question the impact of development on the environment. White English-speaking Americans, they suggest, could be said to have conquered the West rather than settled it.

The West, in this view, was not settled by a wave of white migrants moving west across the continent (Turner's "frontier") but by a set of waves—Anglo, Mexican American, African American, Asian American, and others—moving in many directions and interacting with each other and with Native American cultures to produce the modern West. Nor did western history end in 1890 as Turner would have it. Instead, migration, development, and economic exploitation continued into the twentieth and twenty-first centuries, illustrated by the fact that many more people moved to the West after 1900 than before.

In the nineteenth, twentieth, and twenty-first centuries, there can be no doubt that the image of the frontier and the West influenced American development. Western lands attracted European, Latin American, and Asian immigrants, adding to the society's talent and diversity. The mines, forests, and farms of the West fueled the economy, sent raw materials to eastern factories, and fed the growing cities. Though defeated in warfare, the Native Americans and Mexicans influenced art, architecture, law, and western folklore. The West was the first American empire, and it profoundly affected the American mind and imagination.

17 STUDY RESOURCES

((•—Listen to the **Chapter Audio** for
Chapter 17 on **myhistorylab.com**

TIMELINE

1849 Gold Rush to California, p. 528

1862 Homestead Act encourages western settlement, p. 431

1864 Colonel John Chivington massacres Indians at Sand Creek, Colorado, p. 424

1865–1867 Sioux War against white miners and U.S. Army, p. 424

1866 "Long drive" touches off cattle bonanzas, p. 424

1867 Horace Greeley urges easterners to "Go West, young man," p. 424
  • National Grange of the Patrons of Husbandry (the Grange) founded to enrich farmers' lives, p. 440

1867–1868 Policy of "small reservations" for Indians adopted, p. 425

1873 Comstock Lode discovered in Nevada, p. 434

1874 Joseph F. Glidden invents barbed wire, p. 431
  • Discovery of gold in Dakota Territory sets off Black Hills Gold Rush, p. 425

1876 Sioux defeat and kill Custer at Battle of the Little Bighorn (June), p. 426

1883 Museum expedition discovers fewer than 200 buffalo in the West, p. 428

1886–1887 Severe weather damages cattle and farming bonanzas, p. 440

1887 Dawes Severalty Act makes Indians individual landowners, p. 427

1889 Oklahoma Territory opened to settlement, p. 437

1890 Teton Sioux massacred at Battle of Wounded Knee, South Dakota (December), p. 426

1893 Historian Frederick Jackson Turner analyzes closing of the frontier, p. 441

1902 National Reclamation Act (the Newlands Act), p. 431

CHAPTER REVIEW

BEYOND THE FRONTIER

What were the challenges of settling the country west of the Mississippi?

West of the Mississippi River, settlers encountered new conditions, including vast treeless plains and towering mountain ranges. Above all, they left behind the water and timber on which they had depended in the East, forcing them to devise new ways to deal with the different challenges. *(p. 420)*

CRUSHING THE NATIVE AMERICANS

How did white Americans crush the culture of the Native Americans as they moved west?

Native Americans had a complex culture suited to the various environments in which they lived. The United States government and white settlers employed various methods—political, military, legal, and cultural—to oust the Indians from their lands, "civilize" them, and contain and control them. *(p. 421)*

SETTLEMENT OF THE WEST

Why did Americans and others move to the West?

Americans moved west for many reasons, including a desire to get rich, seek religious freedom, and improve health. The federal government helped out with generous land laws and laws favoring irrigation in the arid West. In the Southwest a proud culture took shape around Spanish laws and customs, involving water, the rights of women, and the sale, ownership, and use of land. *(p. 428)*

THE BONANZA WEST

Why was the West a bonanza of dreams and get-rich-quick schemes?

The West attracted many people seeking a better economic life. Many failed, but others found bonanzas in mining, cattle ranching, and farming. In many of these areas, western development paralleled trends in the rest of the nation: larger and larger businesses, new uses for technology, and the employment of outside capital. *(p. 433)*

KEY TERM QUESTIONS

1. What were the Ghost Dances supposed to achieve? (p. 426)

2. What was the root cause of the Wounded Knee Massacre? (p. 426)

3. How did the Dawes Severalty Act affect Indian life? (p. 427)

4. How did the Gold Rush of 1849 affect the development of the West? (p. 429)

5. What was life like on the Overland Trail? (p. 429)

6. How did the Homestead Act of 1862 contribute to the development of the West? (p. 431)

7. How did the National Reclamation Act (Newlands Act) help create a "hydraulic society" in the West? (p. 431)

8. What was placer mining? (p. 433)

9. What was the Comstock Lode? (p. 434)

10. Why did Congress pass the Chinese Exclusion Act of 1882? (p. 435)

11. Why did the Exodusters migrate to Kansas? (p. 439)

12. What did the National Grange of the Patrons of Husbandry provide for its members? (p. 440)

13. What role did the existence of the frontier play in Turner's thesis? (p. 441)

MyHistoryLab CONNECTIONS

Visit **www.myhistorylab.com** for a customized Study Plan to build your knowledge of *The West: Exploiting an Empire*

Questions for Analysis

1. How did Native Americans respond to increasing white settlement in the West?

   View the **Map** *Native Americans, 1850-1896* p. 422

2. What was the reason for performing the Sioux Ghost Dance?

   Watch the **Video** *Sioux Ghost Dance* p. 426

3. How does Benjamin Harrison describe Native Americans in his report?

   Read the **Document** *Benjamin Harrison, Report on Wounded Knee and Decrease in Indian Land Acreage (1891)* p. 426

4. Why was the railroad critical to rapid westward expansion?

   View the **Closer Look** *Railroad and Buffalo* p. 428

5. What support does Frederick Jackson Turner provide for his argument that the settlement of the frontier made the American nation unique?

   Read the **Document** *Frederick Jackson Turner, "The Significance of the Frontier in American History" (1893)* p. 441

Other Resources from this Chapter

Listen to the **Audio File** *Ritual of the Maize*

Read the **Document** *Congressional Report on the Sand Creek Massacre, 1867*

Read the **Document** *Chief Red Cloud's Speech*

View the **Map** *Resources and Conflict in the West*

Read the **Document** *Autobiographical Narrative of Zitakala School in Indiana*

View the **Image** *Great Western Migration*

Read the **Document** *John Lester, Hydraulic Mining*

Watch the **Video** *Cowboys and Cattle*

View the **Image** *Exodusters*

18

THE INDUSTRIAL SOCIETY

1850–1901

GEO. H. CORLISS   PROVIDENCE, R.

Contents and Spotlight Questions

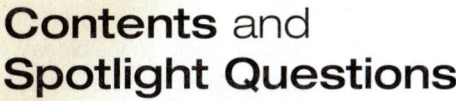 **Listen** to the **Chapter Audio** for Chapter 18 on **myhistorylab.com**

A MACHINE CULTURE

In 1876, Americans celebrated their first century of independence. Survivors of a recent civil war, they observed the centenary proudly and self-consciously, in song and speech, and above all in a grand Centennial Exposition held in Philadelphia, Pennsylvania.

Spread over hundreds of acres, the exposition occupied 180 buildings and attracted 9 million visitors, about one-fifth of the country's population.

The Corliss Engine A "mechanical marvel" at the Centennial Exposition of 1876, the Corliss engine was a prime example of the giantism the public admired. (*Source: "The Corliss Engine," The Metropolitan Museum of Art, New York, NY, U.S.A. Image copyright © The Metropolitan Museum of Art/Art Resource, NY.*)

Significantly, it focused more on the present than the past. Fairgoers strolled through exhibits of life in colonial times, then hurried off to the main attractions: machines, inventions, and products of the new industrial era. They saw linoleum, a new, easy-to-clean floor covering made of linseed oil and canvas. For the first time, they tasted root beer, supplied by a young druggist named Charles Hires, and the exotic banana, wrapped in foil and selling for a dime. They saw their first bicycle, an awkward high-wheeled contraption with solid tires.

A Japanese pavilion generated widespread interest in that country's culture. A women's building, the first one ever in a major exposition, displayed paintings and sculpture by women artists, and textile machinery staffed by female operators.

Machinery was the focus of the entire exposition, and Machinery Hall was the most popular building. Here were the products of an ever-improving civilization. Long lines waited to see the telephone, Alexander Graham Bell's new device. ("My God, it talks!" the emperor of Brazil exclaimed.) Thomas A. Edison displayed recent inventions, while nearby, machines turned out bricks, chewing tobacco, and other products. Fairgoers saw the first public display of the typewriter, Elisha Otis's new elevator, and the Westinghouse railroad air brake.

But above all, they crowded around the mighty Corliss engine, the exposition's focal point. A giant steam engine, its twin vertical cylinders towered almost four stories high, dwarfing everything else in Machinery Hall. Alone, it supplied power for the 8,000 other machines, large and small, on the exposition grounds. Poorly designed, the Corliss was soon obsolete, but it captured the nation's imagination. It symbolized swift movement toward an industrial and urban society. John Greenleaf Whittier, the aging poet from rural New England, likened it to the snake in the biblical Garden of Eden and refused to see it.

As Whittier feared, the United States was fast becoming an industrial society. Developments earlier in the century laid the basis, but the most spectacular advances in industrialization came during the three decades after the Civil War. At the start of the war in 1861, the country lagged behind industrializing nations such as Britain, France, and Germany. By 1900, its manufacturing output exceeded that of its three European rivals combined. Over the same years, cities grew, technology advanced, and farm production rose. Developments in manufacturing, mining, agriculture, transportation, and communications changed society.

In this change, railroads, steel, oil, and other industries, all shaped by the hands of labor, played a leading role. Many Americans welcomed the new directions. The Corliss awed the novelist William Dean Howells when he visited the Exposition. Howells preferred the machine to the artworks on display: "It is in these things of iron and steel that the national genius most freely speaks."

INDUSTRIAL DEVELOPMENT

What enabled the United States to build an industrial economy?

American industry owed its remarkable growth to several considerations. It fed on an abundance of natural resources: coal, iron, timber, petroleum, waterpower. An iron manufacturer likened the nation to "a gigantic bowl filled with treasure." Labor was also abundant, drawn from American farm families and the European immigrants who flocked to American mines, cities, and factories. Nearly 8 million immigrants arrived in the 1870s and 1880s; another 15 million came between 1890 and 1914—large figures for a nation whose population in 1900 was about 76 million.

The burgeoning population led to expanded markets, which new devices such as the telegraph and telephone helped to exploit. The growing cities devoured goods, and the railroads linked the cities together and opened a national market. Within its boundaries, the United States had the largest free trade market in the world, while tariff barriers protected its producers from outside competition.

Expansive market and labor conditions buoyed the confidence of European and American investors, who provided large amounts of capital. Technological progress doomed some older industries (tallow, for example) but increased productivity in others (like kerosene), and created entirely new ones like electric lights. Inventions such as the harvester and the combine strengthened the agricultural base, on which industrialization depended.

Eager to promote economic growth, government at all levels—federal, state, and local—gave manufacturers money, land, and other resources. The American system of government also provided stability, commitment to private property, and, initially at least, a reluctance to regulate industry. Unlike their European counterparts, American manufacturers faced few legal or social barriers. Their main domestic rivals, the southern planters, had lost power in the Civil War.

In this atmosphere, entrepreneurs flourished. Taking steps crucial for industrialization, they organized, managed, and assumed the financial risks of the new enterprises. Admirers called them captains of industry; foes labeled them robber barons. To some degree, they were both—creative *and* acquisitive. If sometimes they seemed larger than life, it was because they dealt in concepts, distances, and quantities often unknown to earlier generations.

Industrial growth was not simple, steady, or inevitable. It involved human decisions and entailed social benefits and costs. Growth varied from industry to industry and from year to year. It was concentrated in the Northeast, where in 1890 more than 85 percent of America's manufactured goods originated. The more sparsely settled West provided raw materials. The South, although making gains in the manufacture of iron, textiles, and tobacco, had to rebuild after wartime devastation.

Still, industry developed quickly. Between 1865 and 1914, the real gross national product—the total monetary value of all goods and services produced in a year, with prices held stable—grew at more than 4 percent a year, increasing about eightfold overall. As Robert Higgs, an economic historian, noted, "Never before had such rapid growth continued for so long."

AN EMPIRE ON RAILS

Genuine revolutions are rare, but a major one occurred in the nineteenth century: a revolution in transportation and communications. When the century began, people traveled and communicated much as they had for centuries before; when it ended, the railroad, the telegraph, the telephone, and the steamship had wrought enormous changes.

How and why did the railroad system grow?

The steamship sliced in half the time it took to cross the Atlantic and introduced new regularity in moving goods and passengers. The telegraph, flashing messages almost instantaneously along miles of wire (400,000 miles of it in the early 1880s), transformed communications, as did the telephone a little later. But the railroad worked the largest changes of all. Along with Bessemer steel, it was the century's most significant technical innovation.

Advantages of the Railroad

The railroad dramatically affected economic and social life. Economic growth would have occurred without it, of course; canals, inland steamboats, and the country's superb system of interior waterways already provided the outlines of an effective transportation network. But the railroad contributed advantages all its own.

Those advantages included more direct routes, greater speed, safety, and comfort than other modes of land travel, more dependable schedules, a larger volume of traffic, and year-round service. A day's travel on stagecoach or horseback might cover 50 miles. The railroad covered 50 miles in about an hour, 700 miles in a day. It went where canals and rivers did not go—directly to the loading platforms of factories or across the arid West. As construction crews pushed tracks onward, vast areas opened for settlement.

Consequently, American railroads differed from European ones. In Europe, railroads were usually built between cities and towns that already existed; they carried mostly the same goods that earlier forms of transportation had. American railroads did that and more: They often created the towns they then served. They carried cattle from Texas, fruit from Florida, and goods that had never been carried before.

Linking widely separated cities and villages, the railroad ended the relative isolation and self-sufficiency of the country's "island communities." It tied people together, brought in outside products, fostered interdependence, and encouraged economic specialization. The railroad made possible a national market and thus pointed the way toward mass production and mass consumption, two hallmarks of twentieth-century society. It also pointed the way toward business development.

A railroad corporation, far-flung and complex, was a new kind of business. It stretched over thousands of miles, employed thousands of people, dealt with countless customers, and required an unprecedented scale of organization and decision making. Railroad managers never met most of their customers or even many of their employees. This created new problems in marketing and labor relations. Year by year, railroad companies consumed large quantities of iron, steel, coal, lumber, and glass, stimulating growth and employment in numerous industries.

No wonder the railroad captured so completely the country's imagination. For nearly a hundred years—the railroad era lasted through the 1940s—children gathered at depots, paused in the fields to wave as the fast express flashed by, listened at night to far-off whistles, and wondered what lay down the tracks. They lived in a world grown smaller.

Quick Check

✓ What advantages did the railroad have over earlier forms of transportation?

Building the Empire

When Robert E. Lee surrendered at Appomattox in 1865, the country already had 35,000 miles of track, and much of the railroad system east of the Mississippi was in place. Farther west, the rail network stood poised on the edge of settlement. Although the Civil War had reduced southern railroads to shambles, the United States had nearly as much railroad track as the rest of the world combined.

After the Civil War, rail construction boomed. From 35,000 miles in 1865, the network expanded to 193,000 miles in 1900—more than in all Europe, including Russia. Mileage peaked at 254,037 miles in 1916, just before the industry began its long decline into the mid-twentieth century. (See Figure 18.1)

Building such an empire took vast amounts of capital. American and European investors provided some of the money; government supplied the rest. The federal government loaned nearly $65 million to a half dozen western railroads and donated millions of acres of the public domain.

Almost 90 percent of the federal land grants lay in 20 states west of the Mississippi. Federal land grants helped build 18,738 miles of track, less than 8 percent of the system. The land was frequently distant and difficult to market. Railroad companies sold it to raise cash, but more often they used it as security for bonds or loans.

Beyond doubt, the grants of cash and land promoted waste and corruption. The companies built fast and wastefully, eager to collect government subsidies for each mile of track they laid. The grants also enabled railroads to build into territories that the government had pledged to the Indians, thus helping to destroy Indian life.

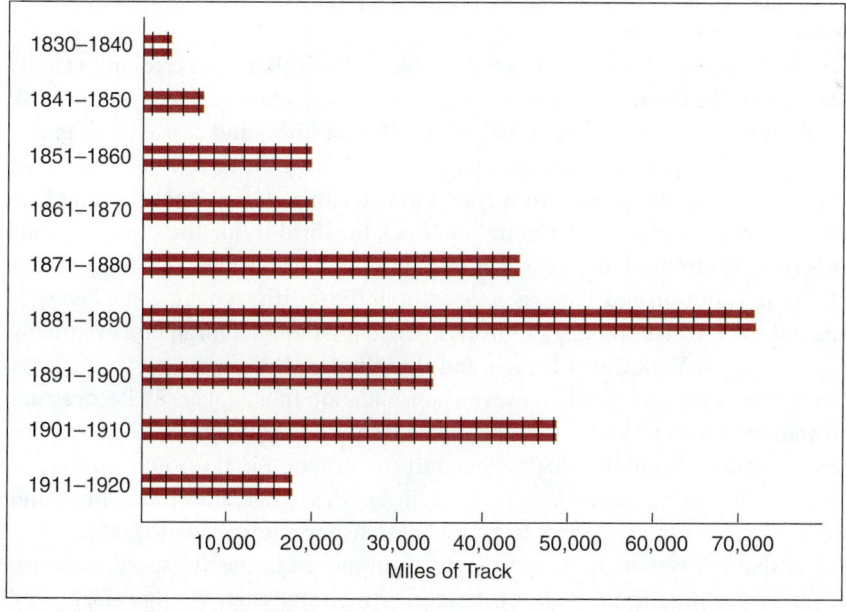

Figure 18.1 Railroad Construction, 1830–1920
Source: U.S. Bureau of the Census, *Historical Statistics of the United States, Colonial Times to 1970*, Bicentennial Edition, Washington, DC, 1975.

Yet the grants probably worked more benefits than evils. As Congress had hoped, the grants stimulated railroad building across the rugged, unsettled West, where the railroads' revenues would not repay their construction for years. Farmers, ranchers, and merchants poured into the newly opened areas, boosting the value of government and private land. The grants seemed necessary in a nation that, unlike most of Europe, expected private enterprise to build the railroads. In return for government aid, Congress required the railroads to carry government freight, troops, and mail at reduced rates—saving the government almost $1 billion between 1850 and 1945. In no other cases of federal subsidies to carriers—canals, highways, and airlines—did Congress exact specific benefits in return.

Quick Check

✓ How did the railroad empire grow?

Linking the Nation via Trunk Lines

The early railroads may seem to have linked different regions, but in fact they did not. Built with little regard for through traffic, they were designed more to protect local interests than to tap outside markets. Many extended less than 50 miles. To avoid cooperating with other lines, they adopted conflicting schedules, built separate depots, and above all, used different gauges. Gauges, the distance between the rails, ranged from 4 feet 8.5 inches, which became the standard, to 6 feet. Without special equipment, trains of one gauge could not run on tracks of another.

The Civil War showed the value of fast long-distance transportation, and after 1865, railroad managers worked to provide it. In a burst of consolidation, the large companies swallowed the small; integrated rail networks became a reality. Railroads also adopted standard schedules, signals, and equipment and finally, in 1886, the standard gauge.

In the Northeast, four great trunk lines took shape, all intended to link eastern seaports with the Great Lakes and western rivers. Like a massive river system, trunk lines drew traffic from dozens of tributaries (feeder lines) and carried it to major markets. The Baltimore and Ohio (B&O), which reached Chicago in 1874, was one; the Erie Railroad, which ran from New York to Chicago, was another. The Erie competed with the New York Central Railroad, the third trunk line, and Cornelius Vanderbilt, its multimillionaire owner from the shipping business.

J. Edgar Thomson and Thomas A. Scott built the fourth trunk line, the Pennsylvania Railroad, which initially ran from Philadelphia to Pittsburgh and eventually extended to New York City, Chicago, and Washington, D.C.

In the war-damaged South, however, consolidation took longer. As Reconstruction waned, northern and European capital rebuilt and integrated the southern lines, especially during the 1880s, when rail construction in the South led the nation. By 1900, five large systems connected the South's major cities and farming and industrial regions and tied them to a national transportation network.

Over that rail system, passengers and freight moved in relative speed, comfort, and safety. Automatic couplers, air brakes, refrigerator cars, dining cars, heated cars, electric switches, and stronger locomotives transformed railroad service. George Pullman's lavish sleeping cars became popular on overnight routes.

View the **Image**
Pullman Car Works on
myhistorylab.com

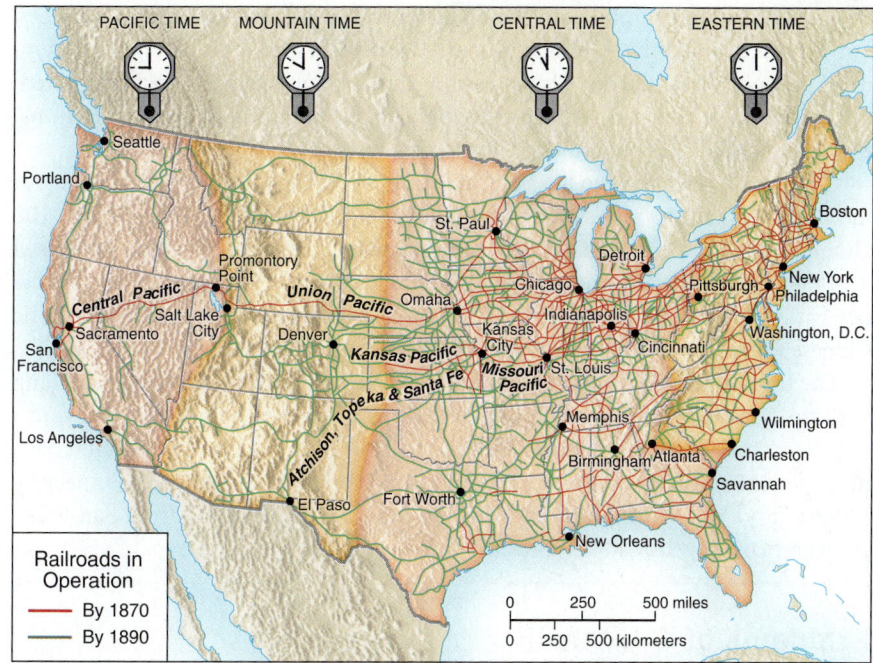

Map 18.1 Railroads, 1870 and 1890 In the last quarter of the nineteenth century, railroads expanded into Texas, the far Southwest, and the Northwest, carrying settlers, businesses, and government to the far-flung areas.

In November 1883, the railroads even changed time. Ending the country's crazy quilt jumble of local times that caused scheduling nightmares, the American Railway Association divided the country into four time zones and adopted the modern system of standard time. Congress took 35 years longer; it finally adopted standard time in 1918, during World War I. (See Map 18.1)

Quick Check
✓ How did the railroad tie the nation together?

Rails Across the Continent

The dream of a transcontinental railroad, linking the Atlantic and Pacific Oceans, had always been lost to sectional quarrels over the route. In 1862 and 1864, with the South out of the picture, Congress moved to build the first transcontinental railroad. It chartered the Union Pacific Railroad Company to build westward from Nebraska and the Central Pacific Railroad Company to build eastward from California.

Construction began simultaneously at Omaha and Sacramento in 1863, lagged during the war, and became a race after 1865, each company vying for land, loans, and markets. General Grenville M. Dodge, a tough Union army veteran, was construction chief for the Union Pacific. Charles Crocker, a former Sacramento dry goods merchant, led the Central Pacific crews. Dodge organized 10,000 workers, many of them ex-soldiers and Irish immigrants. Pushing rapidly westward, his crews were attacked by Native Americans defending their lands, but he had the advantage of building over flat prairie.

Crocker had to contend with the high Sierra Nevada along California's eastern border. He decided that Chinese laborers worked best and hired 6,000 of them, most brought directly from China. "I built the Central Pacific," Crocker boasted, but the Chinese crews in fact did the work. Under the most difficult conditions, they dug, blasted, and pushed their way slowly east.

On May 10, 1869, the two lines met at Promontory, Utah, near the northern tip of the Great Salt Lake. Dodge's crews had built 1,086 miles of track, Crocker's 689. The Union Pacific and Central Pacific presidents hammered in a golden spike (both missed it on the first try), and the dreamed-of connection was made. The telegraph flashed the news east and west, setting off celebrations. A photograph was taken, but it left out the Chinese who had worked so hard to build the road; they were asked to step aside.

The transcontinental railroad symbolized American unity and progress. Along with the Suez Canal in Egypt, completed the same year, it helped knit the world together. Three more railroads reached the coast in 1883: the Northern Pacific, running from Minnesota to Oregon; the Atchison, Topeka, and Santa Fe, connecting Kansas City and Los Angeles; and the Southern Pacific, running from San Francisco and Los Angeles to New Orleans.

Quick Check

✓ What characterized the building and completion of the transcontinental railroads?

Problems of Growth

Overbuilding during the 1870s and 1880s caused problems for the railroads. Competition was severe, and managers fought desperately for traffic. They offered special rates and favors: free passes for large shippers; low rates on bulk freight, carload lots, and long hauls; and, above all, rebates—secret discounts below published rates. Rate wars convinced managers that ruthless competition helped no one. They tried to arrange pooling agreements, sharing traffic to control competition, but none of these agreements survived the pressures of competition.

Railroad owners next tried to consolidate. Through purchase, lease, and merger, they gobbled up competitors and built "self-sustaining systems" that dominated entire regions. But many of the systems, expensive and unwieldy, collapsed in the economic Panic of 1893, which led to a depression that paralyzed the country (see Chapter 20). By mid-1894, a quarter of the railroads were bankrupt, including such legendary names as the Erie, B&O, Santa Fe, Northern Pacific, and Union Pacific.

View the **Image**
J. P. Morgan on
myhistorylab.com

Needing money, the railroads turned to bankers, who finally imposed order. J. Pierpont Morgan, head of the New York investment house of J. P. Morgan and Company, took the lead. Massively built, with eyes so piercing they seemed like the headlights of an onrushing train, Morgan was the most powerful figure in American finance. He liked efficiency, combination, and order. He disliked "wasteful" competition.

After 1893, Morgan and other bankers refinanced ailing railroads and took control of the industry. Fixed costs and debt were cut, new stock was issued to provide capital, rates were stabilized, rebates and competition were eliminated; and control was vested in a "voting trust" of handpicked trustees. Between 1894 and 1898, Morgan reorganized—critics said "Morganized"—the Southern Railway, the Erie, the Northern Pacific, and the B&O. By 1900, he was a dominant figure in American railroading.

The Meeting of the Central Pacific and Union Pacific Railroads After the last spike was hammered in at Promontory, Utah, the pilots of the two locomotives exchanged champagne toasts. The chief engineers of the two lines are shaking hands. Absent from the photograph are the Chinese laborers who helped build the railroad.

As the new century began, the railroads had pioneered the patterns most other industries followed. Seven giant systems controlled nearly two-thirds of the mileage. They in turn answered to a few investment banks such as the house of Morgan. For good and ill, a national transportation network, centralized and relatively efficient, was now in place.

Quick Check

✓ What problems did railroads face as they grew?

AN INDUSTRIAL EMPIRE

The new industrial empire was based on a number of dramatic innovations, including steel, oil, and inventions of all kinds that transformed ordinary life. Steel was as important as the railroads. Harder and more durable than other kinds of iron, steel changed manufacturing, agriculture, transportation, and architecture. It permitted construction of longer bridges, taller buildings, stronger railroad track, deadlier weapons, better plows, heavier machinery, and faster ships. Made in great furnaces by strong men, it symbolized the tough, often brutal nature of industrial society. From the 1870s onward, steel output became the worldwide measure of industrial progress, and nations vied for leadership in steel production. (See Figure 18.2)

The Bessemer process, developed in the late 1850s by Henry Bessemer in England and independently by William Kelly in the United States, increased steel production. Bessemer and Kelly discovered that a blast of air forced through molten

What were the main characteristics of the new steel and oil industries?

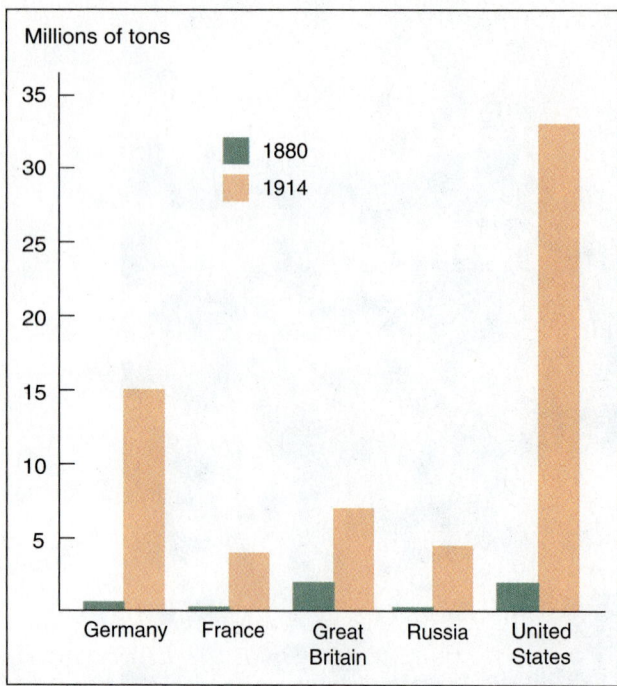

Figure 18.2 International Steel Production, 1880–1914

iron burned off carbon and other impurities, resulting in more uniform and durable steel. The discovery transformed the industry. Earlier methods produced amounts a person could lift. A Bessemer converter handled 5 tons of molten metal at a time. The mass production of steel was now possible.

Carnegie and Steel

Bessemer plants demanded extensive capital investment, abundant raw materials, and sophisticated techniques. Using chemical and other processes, the plants also required research departments, which became critical components of American industries. Costly to build, Bessemer plants limited entry into the industry to the few who could afford them.

Great steel districts arose in Pennsylvania, Ohio, and Alabama—in each case around large coal deposits that fueled the huge furnaces. Pittsburgh became the center of the industry. Its giant mills employed thousands of workers. Output soared. In 1874, the United States produced less than half the amount of pig iron, which was used to make steel, that Britain produced. By 1900, it produced four times as much as Britain.

Like the railroads, steel companies grew larger and larger. In 1880, only nine companies could produce more than 100,000 tons a year. By the early 1890s, several companies exceeded 250,000 tons, and two—including the great Carnegie Steel Company—produced more than 1 million tons a year. As operations expanded, managers needed more complex skills. Product development, marketing, and consumer preferences became important.

Andrew Carnegie became the master of the industry. Born in Scotland, he came to the United States in 1848 at age 12. Settling near Pittsburgh, he worked as a bobbin boy in a cotton mill, earning $1.20 a week. He soon took a job in a telegraph office, where in 1852 his hard work and skill caught the eye of Thomas A. Scott of the Pennsylvania Railroad. Starting as Scott's personal telegrapher, Carnegie spent 12 years with the Pennsylvania, a training ground for managers. By 1859, he had become a divisional superintendent. He was 24 years old.

Rich from shrewd investments, Carnegie plunged into the steel industry in 1872. He attracted able partners and subordinates such as Henry Clay Frick and Charles M. Schwab, whom he drove hard and paid well. Although he had written articles defending the rights of workers, Carnegie kept the wages of the laborers in his mills low and disliked unions. With the help of Frick, he crushed a violent strike at his Homestead works near Pittsburgh in 1892 (see p. 466).

In 1878, he won the steel contract for the Brooklyn Bridge. During the next decade, as city building boomed, he converted the huge Homestead works to making structural beams and angles, which went into the New York City elevated railway, the first skyscrapers, and the Washington Monument. In 1900, Carnegie Steel alone produced more steel than Britain. Employing 20,000 people, it was the largest industrial company in the world.

In 1901, Carnegie sold it. Believing that wealth brought social obligations, he wanted to devote his time to philanthropy. He found a buyer in J. Pierpont Morgan, who had put together several steel companies, including Federal Steel, Carnegie's chief rival. In mid-1900, when a price war loomed between the two interests, Morgan decided to buy Carnegie out. In January 1901, Morgan told Charles M. Schwab: "Go and find his price." Schwab cornered Carnegie on the golf course; Carnegie listened. The next day he handed Schwab a note, asking for almost a half billion dollars. Morgan glanced at it and said, "I accept this price."

Drawing other companies into the combination, Morgan on March 3, 1901, created the United States Steel Corporation. The new firm was capitalized at $1.4 billion, the first billion-dollar company. It absorbed more than 200 other companies, employed 168,000 people, produced 9 million tons of iron and steel a year, and controlled three-fifths of the country's steel business. Soon other giants also appeared, including Bethlehem Steel, Republic Steel, and National Steel. By 1900, steel products—rare just 30 years before—had altered the landscape. Huge firms, investment bankers, and professional managers dominated the industry.

Read the **Document**
Andrew Carnegie, "Wealth" (1889) on **myhistorylab.com**

Quick Check
✓ What were the main characteristics of the growth of the steel industry?

Rockefeller and Oil

Petroleum also changed the economic and social landscape, although mostly after 1900. Distilled into oil, it lubricated the machinery of the industrial age. There seemed little use for gasoline (the internal combustion engine had only just been developed). But kerosene, another major distillate of petroleum, brought inexpensive illumination into almost every home. Whale oil, cottonseed oil, and even tallow candles were so expensive to burn that many people went to bed at nightfall. Kerosene lamps opened the evenings to activity, altering the patterns of life.

Like other changes in these years, the oil boom happened quickly. In 1859, Edwin L. Drake drilled the first oil well near Titusville in northwest Pennsylvania, and "black gold" fever struck. Chemists soon discovered ways to transform petroleum into lubricating oil, grease, paint, wax, varnish, naphtha, and paraffin. A world market in oil arose.

At first, the industry was chaotic. Early drillers and refiners produced for local markets. Since drilling wells and even erecting refineries cost little, competition flourished. Output and prices fluctuated, with devastating effect.

A young merchant from Cleveland named John D. Rockefeller imposed order on the industry. "I had an ambition to build," he recalled. Beginning in 1863 at age 24, he built the Standard Oil Company, a corporate titan. Like Morgan, Rockefeller considered competition wasteful, small-scale enterprise inefficient, and consolidation vital. Methodically, he absorbed or destroyed competitors. As ruthless as Carnegie, he lacked the steel master's charm.

King of a New Industry John D. Rockefeller, satirized in a 1901 *Puck* cartoon, is enthroned on oil, the base of his empire; other holdings gird his crown.

Rockefeller triumphed over his competitors by marketing high-quality products at the lowest unit cost. But he also employed other, less savory methods. He threatened rivals and bribed politicians. He used spies to harass competitors' customers. Above all, he extorted railroad rebates that lowered his transportation costs and undercut competitors. By 1879, he controlled 90 percent of the country's oil-refining capacity.

Vertically integrated, Standard Oil owned wells, timberlands, barrel and chemical plants, refineries, warehouses, pipelines, and fleets of tankers and oil cars. Its marketing organization was the model for the industry. Standard exported oil to Asia, Africa, and South America; its 5-gallon kerosene tin, like Coca-Cola bottles and cans of a later era, was familiar in the most distant parts of the world.

To manage it all, the company developed a new business organization, the trust, which had profound significance for American business. In 1881, Samuel C. T. Dodd, Standard's attorney, set up the Standard Oil Trust. Its nine trustees were empowered "to hold, control, and manage" all Standard's properties. Stockholders exchanged their stock for trust certificates, on which dividends were paid. On January 2, 1882, the first modern trust was born. As Dodd intended, it immediately centralized control of Standard's far-flung empire.

Competition almost disappeared; profits soared. A trust movement swept the country. Industries with similar problems—whiskey, lead, and sugar, among others—followed Standard's example. The word *trust* became synonymous with monopoly, amid vehement protests from the public. *Antitrust* became a watchword for a generation of reformers, from the 1880s through the era of Woodrow Wilson. But Rockefeller's purpose had been *management* of a monopoly, not monopoly itself, which he had already achieved.

Other companies organized their own trusts, including American Sugar Refining, the Northern Securities Company, and the National Biscuit Company. Merger followed merger. By 1900, 1 percent of the nation's companies controlled more than one-third of its industrial production.

In 1897, Rockefeller retired with nearly $900 million, but for Standard Oil and petroleum in general, the most expansive period was yet to come. The great oil pools of Texas and Oklahoma had not yet been discovered. Plastics and other oil-based synthetics were in the future. The country had only four usable automobiles. The day of the gasoline engine, automobile, and airplane lay just ahead.

Quick Check

✓ How did John D. Rockefeller transform the oil industry?

The Business of Invention

"America has become known the world around as the home of invention," boasted the commissioner of patents in 1892. It had not always been so; until the late nineteenth century, the country had imported most of its technology. Then an extraordinary group of inventors and tinkerers—"specialists in invention," as Thomas A. Edison, the most famous of them all, called them—began to study the world around them. Some of their inventions gave rise to new industries; a few changed the quality of life.

In the very act of inventing, Edison and others drew on a deeper "invention," a realization that people could mold nature to their own ends. As a result, the number of patents issued to inventors soared. During the 1850s, fewer than 2,000 patents were issued each year. By the 1880s and 1890s, the figure reached more than 20,000 a year. Between 1790 and 1860, the U.S. Patent Office issued just 36,000 patents; in the 1890s alone, it issued more than 200,000.

Some of the inventions transformed communications. In 1866, Cyrus W. Field improved the transatlantic cable linking the telegraph networks of Europe and the United States. By the early 1870s, land and submarine cables ran to Brazil, Japan, and the China coast; by the 1890s, they reached Africa and spread across South America. Diplomats and business leaders in Washington and New York could now "talk" to their counterparts in Berlin or Hong Kong. Even before the telephone, the cables quickened the pace of foreign affairs, revolutionized journalism, and allowed businesses to expand and centralize.

The typewriter (1867), stock ticker (1867), cash register (1879), calculating machine (1887), and adding machine (1888) facilitated business transactions. High-speed spindles, automatic looms, and electric sewing machines transformed the clothing industry, which for the first time in history turned out ready-made clothes for the masses. In 1890, the Census Bureau first used machines to sort and tabulate data on punched cards, a portent of a new era of information storage and processing.

In 1879, George Eastman patented a process for coating gelatin on photographic dry plates, which led to celluloid film and motion pictures. By 1888, he was marketing the Kodak camera, which weighed 35 ounces, took 100 exposures, and cost $25. Even though early Kodaks had to be returned to the factory, camera and all, for film developing, they revolutionized photography. Now almost anyone could snap a picture.

Other innovations changed the diet. There were new processes for flour, canned meat and vegetables, condensed milk, and even beer (from an offshoot of Louis Pasteur's discoveries about bacteria). Packaged cereals appeared on breakfast tables. Refrigerated railroad cars, ice-cooled, brought fresh fruit from Florida and California to all parts of the country. In the 1870s, Gustavus F. Swift, a Chicago meat packer, hit on the idea of using the cars to distribute meat nationwide. Setting up "disassembly" factories to butcher meat (Henry Ford later copied them for his famous automobile "assembly" lines (see Chapter 25), Swift started an "era of cheap beef."

No innovation, however, rivaled the importance of the telephone and the use of electricity for light and power. The telephone was the work of Alexander Graham Bell, a shrewd and genial Scot who settled in Boston in 1871. Interested in the problems of the deaf, Bell experimented with ways to transmit speech electrically. He eventually developed electrified metal disks that, like the human

View the **Image**
Model of Bell's Telephone on
myhistorylab.com

ear, converted sound waves to electrical impulses and back again. On March 10, 1876, he transmitted the first sentence over a telephone: "Mr. Watson, come here; I want you." Later that year, he exhibited the new device to excited crowds at the Centennial Exposition.

In 1878—when a telephone was installed in the White House—the first telephone exchange opened in New Haven, Connecticut. Fighting off competitors who challenged the patent, the young Bell Telephone Company dominated the growing industry. By 1895, there were about 310,000 phones; a decade later, there were 10 million—about one for every ten people. American Telephone and Telegraph Company, formed by the Bell interests in 1885, became another vast holding company, consolidating more than 100 local systems.

If the telephone dissolved communication barriers as old as the human race, Thomas Alva Edison, the "Wizard of Menlo Park," invented processes and products of comparable significance. Born in 1847, Edison had little formal education, although he was an avid reader. Like Carnegie, he went into the new field of telegraphy. Tinkering in his spare time, he made improvements, including a telegraph capable of sending four messages over a single wire. Gathering specialists to work on specific problems, Edison built the first modern research laboratory at Menlo Park, New Jersey. It may have been his most important invention.

The laboratory, Edison promised, would turn out "a minor invention every ten days and a big thing every six months or so." In 1877, it turned out a big thing, the phonograph. Those unable to afford a phone, Edison thought, could record their voices for replay from a central telephone station. Using tin foil wrapped around a grooved, rotating cylinder, he shouted the verses of "Mary Had a Little Lamb" and then listened in awe as the machine played them back. "I was never so taken aback in all my life," he said. "Everybody was astonished. I was always afraid of things that worked the first time." For the first time in history, people could listen again and again to a favorite symphony or a song. The phonograph made human experience repeatable in a way never before possible.

In 1879 came an even larger triumph, the incandescent lamp. Sir Joseph William Swan, an English inventor, had already experimented with the carbon filament, but Edison set out to do nothing less than change light. A trial-and-error inventor, he tested 1,600 materials before producing the carbon filament he wanted. Then he devised a complex system of conductors, meters, and generators to distribute electricity to homes and businesses.

With the backing of J. P. Morgan, he organized the Edison Illuminating Company and built the Pearl Street power station in New York City, the testing ground of the new apparatus. On September 4, 1882, as Morgan and others watched, Edison threw a switch and lit the house of Morgan, the stock exchange, the *New York Times*, and other buildings. A *Times* reporter marveled that writing stories in the office at night "seemed almost like writing in daylight." By 1900, 2,774 power stations were lighting 2 million electric lights around the country. In a nation alive with light, the habits of centuries changed. A flick of the switch lit homes and factories at any hour of the day or night.

Electricity could light a lamp or illuminate a skyscraper, pull a streetcar or drive a railroad, run a sewing machine or power an assembly line. Transmitted easily over long distances, it freed factories and cities from dependence on water power or coal. Electricity, in short, brought a revolution.

Frank J. Sprague, a young engineer, electrified the Richmond, Virginia, streetcar system in 1887. Other cities followed. Electric-powered subway systems opened in Boston in 1897 and New York City in 1904. Overhead wires and third rails made urban transportation quieter, faster, and cleaner. Buried under pavement or strung from pole to pole, wires of every description—trolley, telephone, and power—marked the birth of the modern city.

Read the **Document**
Thomas Edison, The Success of the Electric Light on **myhistorylab.com**

Quick Check

✓ What were the most important inventions of the years between 1870 and 1900?

THE SELLERS

The increased output of the industrial age alone was not enough to ensure huge profits. The products still had to be sold, and that gave rise to a new "science" of marketing. Some business leaders—such as Swift in meatpacking, James B. Duke in tobacco, and Rockefeller in oil—built their own marketing organizations. Others relied on retailers, merchandising techniques, and advertising to convince consumers to buy.

In 1867, businesses spent about $50 million on advertising. In 1900, they spent more than $500 million, and the figure was increasing rapidly. The rotary press (1875) churned out newspapers and introduced a new era in newspaper advertising. Bringing producer and consumer together, nationwide advertising was the final link in the national market. From roadside signs to newspaper ads, it pervaded American life.

The idea of consumption became prominent. R. H. Macy in New York, John Wanamaker in Philadelphia, and Marshall Field in Chicago turned the department store into a national institution. There people could browse (a new concept) and buy. Innovations in pricing, display, and advertising helped customers develop wants they did not know they had. In 1870, Wanamaker took out the first full-page newspaper ad, and Macy, an aggressive advertiser, touted "goods suitable for the millionaire at prices in reach of the millions."

In similar fashion, Sears, Roebuck and Montgomery Ward sold to rural customers through mail-order catalogs—a means of selling that depended on effective transportation and a high level of customer literacy. As a traveler for a dry goods firm, Aaron Montgomery Ward had seen an unfulfilled need among rural westerners. He started the mail-order trend in 1872 with a one-sheet price list offered from a Chicago loft. By 1884, he offered almost 10,000 items in a 240-page catalogue.

Richard W. Sears also entered the mail-order business, starting with watches and jewelry. In the 1880s, he moved to Chicago and with Alvah C. Roebuck founded Sears, Roebuck and Company. Sears sold anything and everything, prospering in a business that relied on mutual trust between unseen customers and distant distributors. Sears catalogs, soon more than 500 pages long, exploited four-color illustration and other new techniques. By the early 1900s, Sears distributed 6 million catalogs annually.

Why were the new methods of advertising so important?

View the **Image**
The Department Store: Another View on **myhistorylab.com**

Advertising, brand names, chain stores, and mail-order houses brought Americans into a national market. Even as the country grew, a homogeneity of goods bound it together, touching cities and farms, East and West, rich and poor. There was a common language of consumption. Americans had become a community of consumers, surrounded by goods unavailable a few decades before, and able to purchase them. They had learned to make, want, and buy. "Because you see the main thing today is—shopping," Arthur Miller, a twentieth-century playwright, said in *The Price*:

> Years ago a person, he was unhappy, didn't know what to do with himself— he'd go to church, start a revolution—something. Today you're unhappy? Can't figure it out? What is the salvation? Go shopping.

THE WAGE EARNERS

Who were the wage earners in the new economy?

Although entrepreneurs were important, the labor of millions of men and women built the new industrial society. In their individual stories, nearly all unrecorded, lay much of the achievement, drama, and pain of these years.

In some respects, their lot improved during the last quarter of the nineteenth century. Real wages rose, working conditions got better, and the workers' influence in national affairs increased. Workers also benefited from expanding health and educational services.

Working Men, Working Women, Working Children

Still, life was hard. Before 1900, most wage earners worked at least ten hours a day, six days a week. If skilled, they earned about 20 cents an hour; if unskilled, half that. On average, workers earned between $400 and $500 a year. To live decently, a family of four needed about $600. Construction workers, machinists, government employees, printers, clerical workers, and western miners made more than the average. Eastern coal miners, agricultural workers, garment workers, and unskilled factory hands made less.

There were few holidays or vacations and little respite from the grueling routine. Safety standards were low, and accidents were common—more common, in fact, than in any other industrial nation in the world. On the railroads, one in every 26 workers was injured and one in every 399 was killed each year. Thousands suffered without knowing why from chronic illness, victims of dust, chemicals, and other pollutants at their jobs. In the early 1900s, Dr. Alice Hamilton established a link between jobs and disease, but meanwhile, illness weakened or struck down many a breadwinner.

The breadwinner might be a woman or a child; both worked in increasing numbers. In 1870, about 15 percent of women over the age of 16 were employed for wages; in 1900, 20 percent were. Of 303 occupations in the 1900 census, women were represented in 296. The textile industry was their largest employer. Between 1870 and 1900, the number of working children more than doubled. In 1900, one out of every ten girls and one out of every five boys between the ages of 10 and 15 held jobs.

So many children were in the labor force that when people spoke of child labor, they often meant boys and girls under the age of 14. Boys were paid little enough, but girls made even less. Girls, it was argued, were headed for marriage; those who worked were just doing so to help out their families. "We try to employ girls who are members of families," a box manufacturer said, "for we don't pay the girls a living wage in this trade."

Most working women were young and single. Many began working at 16 or 17, worked a half dozen years or so, married, and quit. In 1900, only 5 percent of all married women were employed outside the home, although 25 percent of married African American women worked, usually on southern farms or as low-paid laundresses or servants. As clerical work expanded, women learned new skills such as typing and stenography. Moving into formerly male occupations, they became secretaries, bookkeepers, typists, telephone operators, and clerks in the new department stores.

A few women—very few—became ministers, lawyers, and doctors. Arabella Mansfield, admitted to the Iowa bar in 1869, was the country's first woman lawyer. But change was slow. In the 1880s, law schools still were refusing to admit women because they "had not the mentality to study law." Most women in the professions became nurses, schoolteachers, and librarians. These fields became "feminized": most workers were women, a few men took the management roles, and most men left for other jobs, lowering the profession's status.

New Jobs for Women As demand for workers grew, women took over many of the duties formerly performed by men. Despite their performance in the workplace, however, the women were usually overseen by male supervisors.

In most jobs, status and pay were divided unequally between men and women. Many of both sexes thought a woman's place was in the home. When employed in factories, women tended to occupy jobs that were viewed as natural extensions of household activity. They made clothes and textiles, food products, cigars, tobacco, and shoes. In the garment industry, which employed many women, they were the sewers and finishers, doing jobs that paid less; men were the higher-paid cutters and pressers.

In general, adults earned more than children, the skilled more than the unskilled, native born more than foreign born, Protestants more than Catholics or Jews, and whites more than blacks or Asians. On average, women made a little more than half as much as men, according to contemporary estimates. Some employers defended

📖 **Read** the
Document
*Chinese Exclusion
Act (1882)* on
myhistorylab.com

Quick Check

✔ What were condi-
tions like for working
men, women, and
children?

the differences—the foreign born, for example, might not speak English—but most simply reflected biases against race, creed, or gender. In the industrial society, white, native-born Protestant men—the bulk of the male population—reaped the greatest rewards.

Blacks labored on the fringes, usually in menial jobs. The last hired and first fired, they earned less than other workers at almost every level of skill. On the Pacific coast, the Chinese—and later the Japanese—lived in enclaves and suffered from discrimination. In 1882, the **Chinese Exclusion Act** prohibited the immigration of Chinese workers for ten years.

CULTURE OF WORK

How did wage
earners organize
in this period, and
what demands did
they make?

Among almost all groups, industrialization shattered age-old patterns, including work habits and the culture of work. As Herbert G. Gutman, a social historian, noted, it made people adapt "older work routines to new necessities and strained those wedded to premodern patterns of labor." Adaptation was difficult and often demeaning. Virtually everyone endured it, and newcomers repeated the experiences of those who came before.

Men and women fresh from farms were not accustomed to the factory's disciplines. Now they worked indoors rather than out, paced themselves to the clock rather than the sun, and followed the needs of the market rather than the natural rhythms of the seasons. They had supervisors, hierarchies, and strict rules.

As industries grew larger, work became more impersonal. Machines displaced skilled artisans, and the unskilled tended the machines for employers they never saw. Workers picked up and left their jobs with startling frequency. Factories drew on a churning, mobile labor supply. Historian Stephan Thernstrom, who studied the census records, found that only about half the people recorded in any census still lived in the same community ten years later: "The country had an enormous reservoir of restless and footloose men, who could be lured to new destinations when opportunity beckoned."

There was also economic and social mobility. The rags-to-riches stories of Horatio Alger had always celebrated it. Careers of men such as Andrew Carnegie—the impoverished immigrant boy who made good—seemed to confirm it. The actual record was more limited. Most business leaders came from well-to-do or middle-class families of old American stock. Of 360 iron and steel barons in Pittsburgh, Carnegie's own city, only five fit the Carnegie characteristics, and one of those was Carnegie himself. Still, if few workers became steel magnates, many workers made progress during their lifetimes. Thernstrom discovered that a quarter of the manual laborers rose to middle-class positions. Working-class children were even more likely to move up the ladder.

The chance for advancement played a vital role in American industrial development. It gave workers hope, wedded them to the system, and tempered their response to the appeal of labor unions and working-class agitation. Few workers rose from rags to riches, but many rose to better jobs and higher status.

Labor Unions

Weak throughout the nineteenth century, labor unions never included more than 2 percent of the total labor force or more than 10 percent of industrial workers. To many workers, unions seemed "foreign," radical, and out of step with the American tradition of individual advancement. Craft, ethnic, and other differences fragmented the labor force, and its extraordinary mobility made organization difficult. Employers opposed unions. "I have always had one rule," said an executive of U.S. Steel. "If a worker sticks up his head, hit it."

As the national economy emerged, however, so did national labor unions. In 1869, Uriah S. Stephens and Philadelphia garment workers founded the Noble and Holy Order of the **Knights of Labor**, known simply as the **Knights of Labor**. A secret fraternal order, it grew slowly, until Terence V. Powderly, the new Grand Master Workman elected in 1879, ended the secrecy and began to recruit aggressively. The Knights welcomed everyone who "toiled," regardless of skill, creed, sex, or color. Unlike most unions, it organized women workers, and at its peak, it had 60,000 black members.

Harking back to the Jacksonians (see Chapter 10), the Knights set the "producers" against monopoly and special privilege. As members they excluded only "nonproducers"—bankers, lawyers, liquor dealers, and gamblers. Since employers were "producers," they could join; and since workers and employers had common interests, the Knights maintained that workers should not strike. The order's platform included the eight-hour day and the abolition of child labor, but more often it focused on uplifting, utopian reform. Powderly, the eloquent and idealistic leader, spun dreams of a new era of harmony and cooperation.

In March 1885, ignoring Powderly's dislike of strikes, Knights in St. Louis, Kansas City, and other cities won a victory against Jay Gould's Missouri Pacific Railroad, and membership increased. But in 1886, the wily Gould crushed the Knights on the Texas and Pacific Railroad. This defeat punctured the union's growth and revealed the ineffectiveness of its national leaders. Tens of thousands of unskilled laborers deserted the ranks. The Haymarket Riot turned public sympathy against unions like the Knights. By 1890, the order had shrunk to 100,000 members. A few years later, it was virtually defunct.

Even as the Knights waxed and waned, a more enduring organization emerged. Founded in 1886, the **American Federation of Labor (AFL)** was a loose alliance of national craft unions. It organized only skilled workers along craft lines, avoided politics, and worked for specific practical objectives. "I have my own philosophy and my own dreams," said Samuel Gompers, its founder and longtime president, "but first and foremost I want to increase the workingman's welfare year by year."

View the Image
American Federation of Labor on
myhistorylab.com

Born in a London tenement in 1850, Gompers was a child of the union movement. Settling in New York, he worked as a cigar maker, participated in union activities, and experimented with socialism and working-class politics. As leader of the AFL, he adopted a pragmatic approach to labor's needs. Gompers accepted capitalism and did not argue for fundamental changes in it. For labor he wanted simply a recognized place within the system and more of the rewards.

Unlike Powderly, Gompers and the AFL assumed that most workers would re-main workers throughout their lives. The goal was to improve lives in "practical" ways: higher wages, shorter hours, and better working conditions. The AFL reas-sured employers. As a trade union, it would use the strike and boycott, but only for limited gains. If treated fairly, the AFL would provide a stable labor force. It would not oppose monopolies and trusts, as Gompers said, "so long as we obtain fair wages."

By the 1890s, the AFL was the most important labor group in the country. Gompers remained its president, except for one year, until his death in 1924. By then, the AFL included almost one-third of the country's skilled workers. Most workers—skilled and unskilled—remained unorganized, but Gompers and the AFL had become a significant force.

The AFL either ignored or opposed women workers. Only two of its national affiliates—the Cigar Makers' Union and the Typographical Union—accepted women members; others prohibited them outright. Gompers himself complained that women workers undercut the pay scales for men.

The AFL did not forbid blacks from joining, but member unions used high ini-tiation fees, technical examinations, and other means to discourage black mem-bership. The AFL's informal exclusion practices were a sorry record, but Gompers defended his policy toward blacks, women, and the unskilled by pointing to the dangers unions faced. Only by restricting membership, he argued, could the union succeed.

Quick Check

✓ What was the history of the Knights of Labor and the Ameri-can Federation of Labor during the late nineteenth century?

Labor Unrest

Workers adjusted to the factory age in various ways. To the dismay of managers and "efficiency" experts, employees often dictated the pace and quality of their work and set the tone of the workplace. Friends and relatives of newly arrived im-migrants found jobs for them, taught them how to deal with factory conditions, and humanized the workplace.

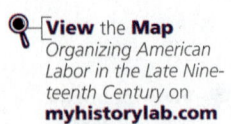

View the **Map**
Organizing American Labor in the Late Nine-teenth Century on
myhistorylab.com

Workers also formed their own institutions to deal with their jobs. Over-coming differences of race or ethnic origin, they often helped each other. They joined social or fraternal organizations. Their unions offered companionship, news of job openings, and insurance plans for sickness, accident, or death. Workers went to the union hall to play cards or pool, sing union songs, and hear older workers tell of past labor struggles. Unions provided food for sick members. There were dances, picnics, and parades. Unions also argued for higher wages.

Many employers, however, believed in an "iron law of wages" in which supply and demand, not their workers' welfare, dictated wages. Employers wanted a docile labor force and would often fire union members, hire scabs to replace strikers, and obtain court injunctions to quell strikes.

The injunction, which forbade workers to interfere with their employers' busi-ness, was used to break the great Pullman Strike of 1894, and the Supreme Court upheld use of the injunction in 1895.

As employers' attitudes hardened, strikes and violence broke out. The United States had the greatest number of violent confrontations between capital and labor in the industrial world. Between 1880 and 1900, more than 23,000 strikes involved 6.6 million workers. (See Map 18.2) The great railroad strike of 1877 paralyzed railroads from West Virginia to California, resulted in the deaths of more than 100 workers, and required federal troops to suppress it.

The worst incident took place at Haymarket Square in Chicago, where workers had been campaigning for an eight-hour workday. In May 1886, police shot and killed two workers in a strike at the McCormick Harvester works. The next evening, May 4, labor leaders called a protest meeting at Haymarket Square near downtown Chicago. The meeting was peaceful, even dull. About 3,000 people attended. Police ordered them to disperse, but someone threw a bomb that killed one policeman and fatally wounded six others. Police fired into the crowd and killed four people.

The authorities never discovered who threw the bomb, but many Americans—not just business leaders—demanded action against labor "radicalism." Cities strengthened their police forces and armories. Eight Chicago anarchists were convicted of murder. Although there was no evidence of their guilt, four were hanged, one committed suicide, and three remained in jail until the governor pardoned them in 1893. Linking labor and anarchism in the public mind, the Haymarket Riot weakened the labor movement because the public associated labor with anarchism.

Violence again broke out in the unsettled conditions of the 1890s. In 1892, Carnegie and Henry Clay Frick, Carnegie's partner and manager, cut wages nearly 20 percent at the Homestead steel plant. The Amalgamated Iron and Steel Workers, an AFL affiliate, struck. Frick locked the workers out of the plant. The workers

View the **Image**
Handbill Haymarket Square Bombing on **myhistorylab.com**

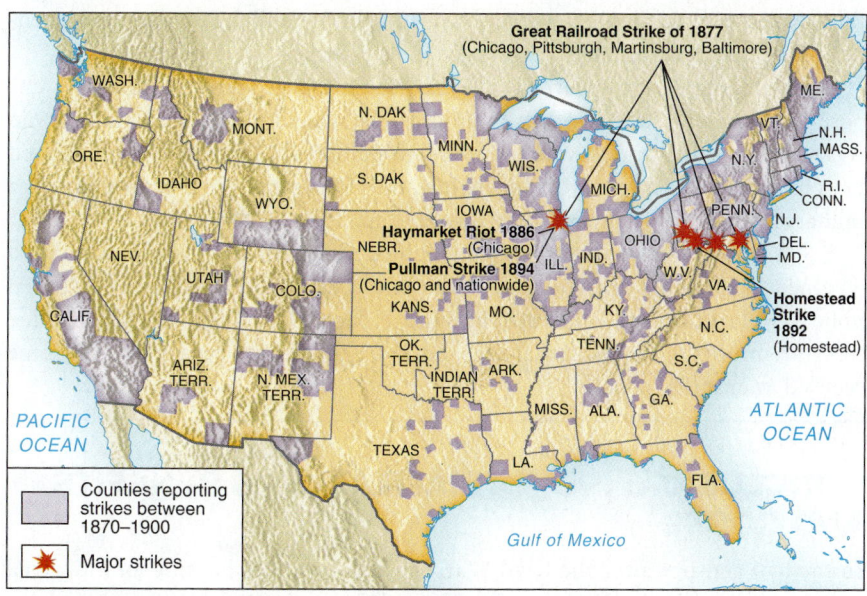

Map 18.2 Labor Strikes, 1870–1900 More than 14,000 strikes occurred in the 1880s and early 1890s, involving millions of workers.

The Riot in Hay Market Square In the rioting that followed the bomb explosion in Haymarket Square in Chicago, seven police officers and five workers died and more than 60 officers were wounded, many of them by fellow police.

surrounded it, and Frick hired an army of Pinkerton detectives to drive them off. But workers pinned the Pinkertons down with gunfire and forced them to surrender. Three detectives and ten workers died in the battle.

A few days later, the governor of Pennsylvania ordered the state militia to impose peace at Homestead. On July 23, an anarchist named Alexander Berkman, who was not one of the strikers, walked into Frick's office, shot him twice, and stabbed him. Incredibly, Frick survived. In late July, the Homestead works reopened under military guard. In November the strikers gave up.

Events like the Homestead Strike troubled many Americans who wondered whether the benefits of industrialization might carry too heavy price in social upheaval, class tensions, and outright warfare. Most workers did not share in the immense profits of the industrial age, and as the nineteenth century ended, some rebelled against the inequity.

Quick Check

✓ What major strikes occurred between the 1870s and the 1890s?

CONCLUSION: INDUSTRIALIZATION'S BENEFITS AND COSTS

In the half century after the Civil War, the United States became an industrial nation—the leading one in the world. On one hand, industrialization meant "progress," growth, world power, and in some sense, fulfillment of the American promise of abundance. National wealth grew from $16 billion in 1860 to $88 billion in 1900; wealth per capita more than doubled. For the bulk of the population, the standard of living—a particularly American concept—rose.

But industrialization also meant rapid change, social instability, exploitation of labor, and growing disparity in income between rich and poor. Industry flourished, but control rested in fewer and fewer hands. Maturing quickly, the young system became a new corporate capitalism: giant businesses, interlocking in ownership, managed by a new professional class, and selling an expanding variety of goods in an increasingly controlled market. As goods spread through society, so did a sharpened, aggressive materialism. Workers felt the strains of the shift to a new social order.

In 1902, a well-to-do New Yorker named Bessie Van Vorst decided to see what it was like to work for a living in a factory. Disguising herself in coarse woolen clothes, a shabby felt hat, a cheap piece of fur, and an old shawl and gloves, she got a job in a Pittsburgh canning factory. She worked ten hours a day, six days a week, including four hours on Saturday afternoons when she and the other women, on their hands and knees, scrubbed the tables, stands, and factory floor. For that she earned $4.20 a week, $3 of which went for food.

Van Vorst was lucky—when she tired of the life, she went back to her home in New York. The working men and women around her were less fortunate. They stayed on the factory floor, and, by dint of their labor, created the new industrial society.

18 STUDY RESOURCES

((•–Listen to the **Chapter Audio** for Chapter 18 on **myhistorylab.com**

TIMELINE

1859 First oil well drilled near Titusville, Pennsylvania, p. 454

1869 Transcontinental railroad completed at Promontory, Utah, p. 452
- Knights of Labor organize, p. 463

1876 Alexander Graham Bell invents the telephone, p. 457
- Centennial Exposition held in Philadelphia, p. 458

1877 Railroads cut workers' wages, leading to bloody and violent strikes, p. 465

1879 Thomas A. Edison invents the incandescent lamp, p. 458

1882 Rockefeller's Standard Oil Company becomes nation's first trust, p. 456

1883 Railroads introduce standard time zones, p. 451

1886 Samuel Gompers founds American Federation of Labor (AFL), p. 463
- Violent labor protest erupts in Haymarket Riot in Chicago, p. 465
- Railroads adopt standard gauge, p. 450

1892 Workers strike at Homestead steel plant in Pennsylvania, p. 466

CHAPTER REVIEW

INDUSTRIAL DEVELOPMENT

What enabled the United States to build an industrial economy?

The United States had an abundance of natural resources, plentiful labor from Europe and American farms, numerous inventions, a national market, plentiful capital, favorable government policies, and entrepreneurs who saw the possibilities in developing a national economy. *(p. 446)*

AN EMPIRE ON RAILS

How and why did the railroad system grow?

Through the infusion of foreign and domestic capital, and the help of local, state, and federal government, a railroad system grew that dwarfed those in other countries. It changed the economic, political, and social landscape, creating a different nation from the country that had come before. *(p. 447)*

AN INDUSTRIAL EMPIRE

What were the main characteristics of the new steel and oil industries?

In the late nineteenth century, an industrial empire took shape, centered around steel and oil, leading to the importance of the automobile in the twentieth century. The result was larger and more complex business organizations and greater concentrations of wealth, capital, and control by a relatively few individuals and companies. *(p. 453)*

THE SELLERS

Why were the new methods of advertising so important?

Advertising, a relatively new industry, helped to sell the goods of the new industrial economy. Americans learned to buy goods they did not even know they wanted. When bored or troubled, they went to a store—today's mall—to shop. *(p. 459)*

THE WAGE EARNERS

Who were the wage earners in the new economy?

The hard work of millions of men and women built the new factory society. Their work was grueling and often dangerous. Men, women, and children often worked for low wages in unsafe conditions. *(p. 460)*

CULTURE OF WORK

How did wage earners organize in this period, and what demands did they make?

Laborers faced many challenges in the new economy, including work that followed the clock, bigger industries, machines, and wages. Unions formed, including the American Federation of Labor (AFL), which still exists. Labor unrest for better wages and safer working conditions took peaceful forms, but also resulted in violence that disturbed other Americans. *(p. 462)*

KEY TERM QUESTIONS

1. How did the trunk lines help spur large-scale industrialization across the United States? (p. 450)

2. How did the trust affect American business? (p. 456)

3. What were the successes and failures of the Knights of Labor? (p. 463)

4. Why was the American Federation of Labor (AFL) more successful than the Knights of Labor? (p. 463)

5. Why was the Homestead Strike so violent? (p. 466)

MYHISTORYLAB CONNECTIONS

Visit **www.myhistorylab.com** for a customized Study Plan to build your knowledge of *The Industrial Society*.

Questions for Analysis

1. According to Andrew Carnegie, what is the duty of wealthy individuals?

   Read the **Document** *Andrew Carnegie, Wealth* p. 455

2. Why was Thomas Edison's invention of the light bulb so significant?

   Read the **Document** *Thomas Edison, The Success of the Electric Light* p. 459

3. Why did the federal government aim to restrict Chinese immigration more so than European immigration?

   Read the **Document** *Chinese Exclusion Act, 1882* p. 462

4. In what states did labor strikes occur most frequently?

   View the **Map** *Organizing American Labor in the Late Nineteenth Century* p. 464

Other Resources from this Chapter

View the **Image** *Pullman Car Works*

View the **Image** *J.P Morgan*

View the **Image** *Model of Bell's Telephone*

View the **Image** *The Department Store, Another View*

View the **Image** *American Federation of Labor*

View the **Image** *Handbill Haymarket Square Bombing*

19
TOWARD AN URBAN SOCIETY
1877–1900

Contents and Spotlight Questions

((•—Listen to the **Chapter Audio** for Chapter 19 on **myhistorylab.com**

THE OVERCROWDED CITY

One day around 1900, Harriet Vittum, a settlement house worker in Chicago, went to help a young Polish girl who lived in a nearby slum. The girl, aged 15, had discovered she was pregnant and had taken poison. An ambulance was on the way, and Vittum rushed over to do what she could.

She raced up three flights of stairs to the floor where the girl and her family lived. Pushing open the door, she found the father, male boarders, and small boys asleep on the kitchen floor. In the next room, the mother was also on the floor among women boarders and small children. Another building was so close Vittum could reach out the window and touch it.

The girl lay in a third room, along with two more children who were asleep. Vittum thought about the girl's life in the crowded tenement. Should she even try to save her and bring her back "to the misery and hopelessness of the life she was living in that awful place"?

Life in the Slums The kitchen of a tenement apartment was often a multipurpose room. Here the tenement dwellers prepared and ate their meals; the room might also serve as a workroom, and sleeping quarters for one or more members of the family. (Source: © The Museum of the City of New York, The Byron Collection).

The young girl died, and Vittum often retold her story. It was easy to see why. The girl's life in the slum, the children on the floor, the need for boarders to make ends meet, the way the mother and father collapsed at the end of a workday that began before sunup—all reflected the lives of millions in America's cities.

Vittum and people like her were responding to the challenges of the nation's burgeoning cities. People poured into cities in the late nineteenth century, lured by glitter and excitement, by friends and relatives who were already there, and, above all, by the opportunities for jobs and higher wages. Between 1860 and 1910, the rural population of the United States almost doubled, but the number of people living in cities increased sevenfold. Little of the increase came from natural growth, since urban families had high rates of infant mortality, a declining fertility rate, and a high death rate from injury and disease. Many of the newcomers came from rural America, many more from Europe, Latin America, and Asia. In the 1880s, in one of the most significant migrations in American history, thousands of African Americans began to move from the rural South to northern cities. By 1900, New York, Baltimore, Philadelphia, Chicago, Washington, D.C., and other cities had large black communities. Yet to come was the even greater black migration during World War I.

Two major forces reshaped American society between 1870 and 1920: industrialization and urbanization, the headlong rush of people from their rural roots into the modern urban environment. In these years, cities grew upward and outward, attracting millions of newcomers and influencing politics, education, entertainment, and family life. By 1920, they had become the center of American economic, social, and cultural life.

THE LURE OF THE CITY

Why did cities in the United States grow between 1880 and 1900?

Between 1870 and 1900, the city—like the factory—became a symbol of a new America. Drawn from farms, small towns, and foreign lands, newcomers swelled the population of older cities and created new ones almost overnight. At the beginning of the Civil War in 1861, only one-sixth of the American people lived in cities of 8,000 people or more. By 1900, one-third did; by 1920, one-half.

Growth was explosive. Thousands of years of history had produced only a handful of cities with more than 500,000 in population. In 1900, the United States had six such cities, including three—New York, Chicago, and Philadelphia—with populations greater than 1 million.

Skyscrapers and Suburbs

As it did so many things in these years, a revolution in technology transformed the city. Beginning in the 1880s, the age of steel and glass produced the skyscraper, and the streetcar produced the suburbs and new residential patterns.

On the eve of the change, American cities were a crowded jumble of small buildings. Church steeples soared above the roofs of factories and office buildings.

Buildings were usually made of masonry, and since the massive walls had to support their own weight, they could only be a dozen or so stories tall. But steel frames and girders allowed buildings to go higher and higher. "Curtain walls," which concealed the steel framework, were no longer load bearing; they were pierced by many windows that let in fresh air and light.

To a group of talented Chicago architects, the new trends were a springboard for innovative forms. The leaders of the movement were John Root and Louis H. Sullivan, both of whom were attracted by the chance to rebuild Chicago after a great fire destroyed much of the city in 1871. Noting that the fire had fed on fancy exterior ornamentation in buildings, Root developed a plain, stripped-down style, bold in mass and form—the keynotes of modern architecture. He had another important insight: In an age of business, the office tower, more than a church or government building, symbolized the society, and he designed office buildings that embodied, as he said, "the ideas of modern business life: simplicity, stability, breadth, dignity."

Sullivan had studied at the Massachusetts Institute of Technology (MIT) and in Paris before settling in Chicago. In 1886, at age 30, he began work on the Chicago Auditorium, one of the last great masonry buildings. "Then came the flash of imagination which saw the single thing," he later said. "The trick was turned; and there swiftly came into being something new under the sun." Sullivan's "flash of imagination"—skyscrapers—changed the urban skyline.

Electric elevators, first used in 1871, carried passengers upward in the new skyscrapers. During the same years, streetcars, another innovation, transformed urban life by carrying people outward.

Cities were no longer largely "walking cities," confined to a radius of two or three miles, the distance a person might walk. Streetcar systems extended the city's radius and changed the urban habitat. Cable lines, electric surface lines, and elevated rapid transit brought shoppers and workers into central business districts and sped them home. For a modest five-cent fare with a free transfer, the mass transit systems fostered commuting, and widely separated business and residential districts sprang up. The middle class moved farther and farther out to the leafy greenness of the suburbs.

As the middle class left the cities, the immigrants and working class poured in. They turned the older brownstones, row houses, and workers' cottages into the slums of the central city. In the cities of the past, classes and occupations had been thrown together; without streetcars and subways, they had no other choice. The streetcar city, sprawling and specialized, became a more fragmented and stratified society with middle-class residential rings surrounding a business and working-class core.

Quick Check

✓ How did cities change between the 1870s and 1900?

Tenements and the Problems of Overcrowding

In the shadow of the skyscrapers, grimy rows of tenements crowded people into cramped apartments in the central city. In the late 1870s, architect James E. Ware won a competition for tenement design with the "dumbbell tenement." Seven or eight stories high, the dumbbell tenement packed about 30 four-room apartments on a 25-by-100-foot lot. Between four and 16 families lived on a floor with two toilets in the hall of each floor. Narrowed at the middle, the tenement was shaped like a giant dumbbell.

View the **Image**
Slum Children on
myhistorylab.com

In 1890, nearly half the dwellings in New York City were tenements. That year, more than 1.4 million people lived on Manhattan Island, one of whose wards had a population density of 334,000 people per square mile. Many people lived in alleys and basements so dark they could not be photographed until flashlight photography was invented in 1887. Exploring the city, the novelist William Dean Howells inhaled "the stenches of the neglected street … [and] the yet fouler and dreadfuller poverty smell which breathes from the open doorways."

Howells smelled more than poverty. In the 1870s and 1880s, cities stank. One problem was horse manure, hundreds of tons of it a day in every city. Another was the outdoor toilet or privy, "a single one of which," said a leading authority on public health, "may render life in a whole neighborhood almost unendurable in the summer."

Baltimore smelled "like a billion polecats," recalled H. L. Mencken, who grew up there. Said one New York City resident, "The stench is something terrible." Another wrote that "the stink is enough to knock you down." In 1880, the Chicago *Times* said that a "solid stink" pervaded the city. "No other word expresses it so well as stink. A stench means something finite. Stink reaches the infinite and becomes sublime in the magnitude of odiousness."

Cities dumped their wastes into the nearest body of water, then drew drinking water from the same site. Many built purified waterworks but could not keep pace with spiraling growth. In 1900, fewer than one in ten city dwellers drank filtered water. Factories, the pride of the era, polluted the urban air.

Crime was another problem. The nation's homicide rate nearly tripled in the 1880s, much of the increase coming in the cities. Slum youths formed street gangs with names such as the Hayes Valley Gang in San Francisco and the Baxter Street Dudes, the Daybreak Boys, and the Alley Gang in New York. After remaining constant for decades, the suicide rate rose steadily between 1870 and 1900, according to a study of Philadelphia. Alcoholism also rose, especially among men, though studies have shown that for working-class men, the urban saloon was as much a gathering spot as a place to drink. Nonetheless, in 1905, Chicago had as many saloons as grocery stores, meat markets, and dry goods stores combined.

Quick Check

✔ What were the main challenges of life in the overcroweded city?

Strangers in a New Land

While some of the new city dwellers came from farms and small towns, many more came from abroad. Most came from Europe, where unemployment, food shortages, and threats of war sent millions fleeing across the Atlantic to make a fresh start. Often they knew someone already in the United States, a friend or relative who had written them about jobs and freer lives in a new land.

View the **Map**
*Immigration,
1880–1920* on
myhistorylab.com

The immigration figures were staggering. Between 1877 and 1890, more than 6.3 million people entered the United States. In 1882 alone, almost 789,000 people came. By 1890, about 15 percent of the population, 9 million people, were foreign born.

Most newcomers were job seekers. Nearly two-thirds were males, most between the ages of 15 and 40. Most were unskilled laborers who settled on the east coast. In 1901, the Industrial Relocation Office was established to relieve overcrowding in eastern cities; opening Galveston, Texas, as a port of entry, it attracted Russian Jews to Texas and the Southwest. But most immigrants preferred the shorter, more familiar journey to New York. Entering through Ellis Island in New York harbor, as four in every ten immigrants did, most of them crowded into northern and eastern cities, settling among others of their nationality or religion.

Watch the Video
Ellis Island Immigrants on
myhistorylab.com

Cities had increasingly large foreign-born populations. In 1900, four-fifths of Chicago's population was foreign born or of foreign-born parentage, two-thirds of Boston's, and one-half of Philadelphia's. New York City, where most immigrants arrived and many stayed, had more Italians than Naples, more Germans than Hamburg, and twice as many Irish as Dublin. Four out of five New York City residents in 1890 were of foreign birth or foreign parentage. (See Map 19.1)

Beginning in the 1880s, immigration shifted away from northern and western Europe, the chief source of immigration for more than two centuries. More and more immigrants now came from southern and eastern Europe: Italy, Greece, Austria-Hungary, Poland, and Russia. Between 1880 and 1910, approximately 8.4 million people came from these lands. (See Figure 19.1.) The new immigrants tended to be Catholics or Jews rather than Protestants. Like their predecessors, most were unskilled rather than skilled, and they often spoke "strange" languages. Most were poor and uneducated; they clung to their native customs, languages, and religions in close-knit communities.

More than any previous group, the so-called new immigrants troubled mainstream society. Could they be assimilated? Did they share "American" values? Such questions preoccupied groups like the American Protective Association, a

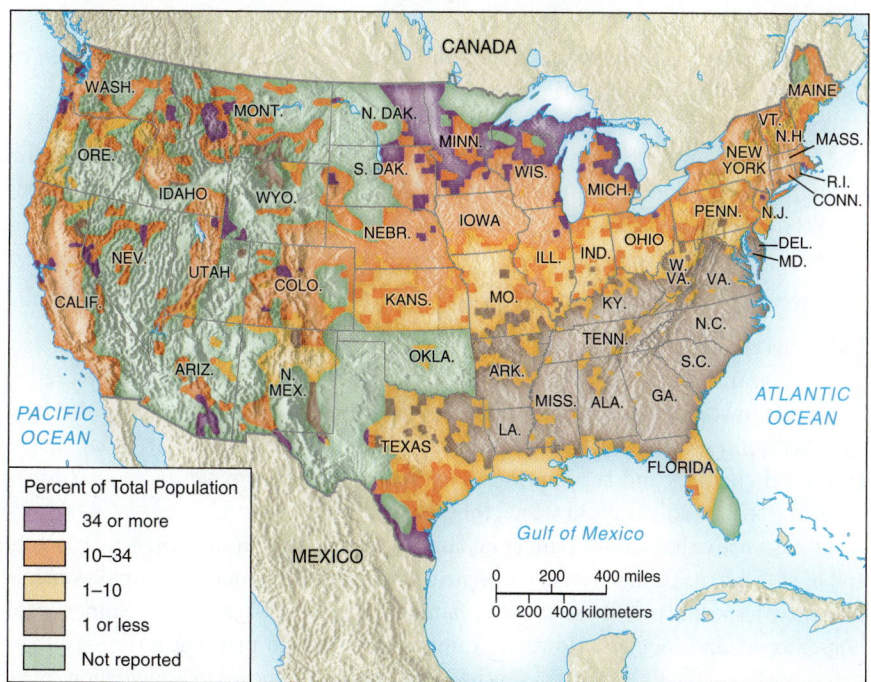

Map 19.1 Foreign-Born Population, 1890 Immigrants tended to settle in regions where jobs were relatively plentiful or conditions were similar to those in their homelands. Cities of the Northeast, Midwest, and West offered job opportunities, while land available for cultivation drew immigrant farmers to the plains and prairies of the nation's midsection.

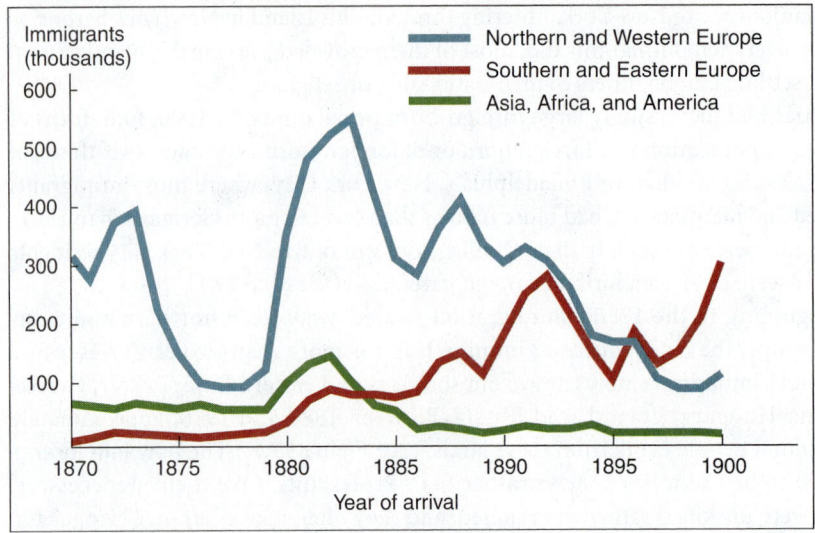

Figure 19.1 Immigration to the United States, 1870–1900
Note: For purposes of classification, "Northern and Western Europe" includes Great Britain, Ireland, Scandinavia, the Netherlands, Belgium, Luxembourg, Switzerland, France, and Germany. "Southern and Eastern Europe" includes Poland, Austria-Hungary, Russia and the Baltic States, Romania, Bulgaria, European Turkey, Italy, Spain, Portugal, and Greece. "Asia, Africa, and America" includes Asian Turkey, China, Japan, India, Canada, the Caribbean, Latin America, and all of Africa.
Source: U.S. Bureau of the Census, *Historical Statistics of the United States, Colonial Times to 1970,* Bicentennial Edition, Washington, DC, 1975.

midwestern anti-Catholic organization that expanded in the 1890s and worked to limit or end immigration.

Anti-Catholicism and anti-Semitism flared up again, as they had in the 1850s. The Immigration Restriction League, founded in 1894, demanded a literacy test for immigrants from southern and eastern Europe. Congress passed such a law in 1896, but President Grover Cleveland vetoed it as violating the country's traditions.

Quick Check

✓ What drew the river of immigrants to the United States?

Immigrants and the City

Industrial capitalism—the world of factories, foremen, and grimy machines—tested the immigrants and their families. Many immigrants came from peasant societies where life proceeded according to outdoor routine and age-old tradition. In their new city homes, they found new freedoms and confinements, a different language, and novel customs and expectations. Historians have only recently begun to discover the remarkable ways in which they learned to adjust.

Like the native born, most immigrant families were nuclear in structure—two parents and their children. Though variations occurred from group to group, men's and women's roles were also similar to those in native families: Men were wage earners; women were housekeepers and mothers. However, immigrants tended to marry at a later age than natives and to have more children, which worried nativists opposed to immigration.

Immigrants shaped the city as much as it shaped them. Most of them tried to retain their traditional culture for themselves and their children while adapting to life in their new country. To do this, they spoke their native language, practiced their religion, read their own newspapers, and established parochial or other schools. They observed traditional holidays and formed myriad social organizations to maintain ties within the group.

Immigrant associations—every city had many of them—offered fellowship in a strange land. They helped newcomers find jobs and homes; they provided services such as unemployment insurance and health insurance. In a Massachusetts textile town, the Irish Benevolent Society said, "We visit our sick, and bury our dead." Some groups were no larger than a neighborhood; others spread nationwide. In 1914, the Deutsch-Amerikanischer Nationalbund (German-American National Association), the largest of the associations, had more than 2 million members in dozens of cities and towns. Many women belonged to and participated in the immigrant associations' work. There were also groups exclusively for women, such as the Polish Women's Alliance, the Society of Czech Women, and the National Council of Jewish Women.

Every major city had dozens of foreign-language newspapers. The first newspaper in the Lithuanian language appeared in the United States, not in Lithuania. Eagerly read, the papers not only carried news of the homeland but also reported on local ethnic leaders, told readers how to vote and become citizens, and gave practical tips on adjusting to life in the United States.

Read the **Document** *Letter to the* Jewish Daily Forward on **myhistorylab.com**

The church and the school were the most important institutions in every immigrant community. Eastern European Jews established synagogues and religious schools wherever they settled; they taught Hebrew and raised their children in a heritage they did not want to leave behind. Among such groups as the Irish and the Poles, the Roman Catholic Church provided spiritual and educational guidance. In parish schools, Polish priests and nuns taught Polish American children about Polish as well as American culture in the Polish language.

Church, school, and fraternal societies shaped how immigrants adjusted to life in America. By preserving language, religion, and heritage, they also shaped the country itself.

Quick Check

✓ In what specific ways did immigrants respond to the American city?

Urban Political Machines

Closely connected with urban growth was the emergence of the powerful city political machine. As cities grew, lines of responsibility in city governments became hopelessly confused, increasing the opportunity for corruption and greed. Burgeoning populations required streets, buildings, and public services; immigrants needed even more services. In this situation, political party machines flourished.

The machines traded services for votes. A strong leader—the "boss"—tied together a loose network of ward and precinct captains, each of whom looked after his local constituents. In New York, "Honest" John Kelly, Richard Croker, and Charles F. Murphy led Tammany Hall, the famous Democratic party organization that dominated city politics from the 1850s to the 1930s. Other bosses included "Hinky Dink" Kenna and "Bathhouse John" Coughlin in Chicago, James McManes in Philadelphia, and Christopher A. Buckley—the notorious "Blind Boss," who used an exceptional memory for voices to make up for his failing eyesight—in San Francisco.

Read the **Document** *George Washington Plunkitt of Tammany Hall* on **myhistorylab.com**

William M. Tweed, head of the famed Tweed Ring in New York, provided the model for them all. Nearly six feet tall, weighing almost 300 pounds, Tweed rose through the ranks of Tammany Hall. He served in turn as city alderman, member of Congress, and New York State assemblyman. A warm, cultured man, he moved easily between the rough back alleys of New York and the parlors and clubs of the city's elite. Behind the scenes, he headed a ring that plundered New York for tens of millions of dollars.

The role of the political bosses can be overemphasized. Power structures in the turn-of-the-century city involved many people and institutions. Banks, real estate investors, insurance companies, architects, and engineers, among others, played roles in governing the city. Many city governments were remarkably successful. With populations that in some cases doubled every decade, city governments provided water and sewer lines, built parks and playgrounds, and paved streets. They gave Boston the world's largest public library and New York City the Brooklyn Bridge and Central Park, two of the finest achievements in city planning and architecture of any era. By the 1890s, New York also had 660 miles of water lines, 464 miles of sewers, and 1,800 miles of paved streets, far more than comparable cities in Europe.

Why did voters keep the bosses in power? The answers are complex, but two reasons were skillful political organization and the fact that immigrants and others made up the bosses' constituency. Most immigrants had little experience with democratic government and proved easy prey for well-oiled machines. However, the bosses stayed in power mostly because they paid attention to the needs of the least privileged city voters. They offered valued services in an era when neither government nor business lent a hand.

If an immigrant, tired and bewildered after crossing the ocean, came looking for a job, bosses like Tweed or Buckley found him one in city offices or local businesses. If a family's breadwinner died or was injured, the bosses donated food and clothing and saw the family through the crisis.

Most bosses became wealthy; they were not Robin Hoods who took from the rich to give to the poor. They also took for themselves. Reformers occasionally ousted them. Tweed fell from power in 1872, "Blind Boss" Buckley in 1891, Croker in 1894. But the reformers rarely stayed in power. Drawn mainly from the middle and upper classes, they did not understand the needs of the poor.

Quick Check

✓ What role did politicians play in American cities?

"What tells in holdin' your grip on your district," Tammany's George Washington Plunkitt once said, "is to go right down among the poor families and help them in the different ways they need help.... It's philanthropy, but it's politics, too—mighty good politics.... The poor are the most grateful people in the world."

SOCIAL AND CULTURAL CHANGE, 1877–1900

How did the growth of American cities affect social, cultural, and political life?

The rise of cities and industry between 1877 and the 1890s affected all aspects of American life. Customs changed; family ties loosened. Factories turned out consumer goods, and the newly invented cash register rang up record sales. Public and private educational systems burgeoned, illiteracy declined, life expectancy increased. While many people worked harder just to survive, others had more leisure time. The roles of women and children changed, and the family took on functions it had not had before. Thanks to technological advances, news flashed across the oceans, and for the first time in history, people read of the day's events in distant lands in their daily newspapers.

The population continued to grow. In 1877, the country had 47 million people. In 1900, it had nearly 76 million. Nine-tenths of the population was white; just under one-tenth was black. There were 66,000 American Indians, 108,000 Chinese, and 148 Japanese. The bulk of the white population, most of whom were Protestant, came from the so-called Anglo-Saxon countries of northern Europe: Britain, Germany, and Scandinavia. WASPs—white Anglo-Saxon Protestants—dominated American society.

Though the rush to the cities was about to begin, most people in 1877 still lived on farms or in small towns. Their lives revolved around the farm, the church, and the general store. In 1880, nearly 75 percent of the population lived in communities of fewer than 2,500 people. In 1900, despite city growth, 60 percent still did. The average family in 1880 had three children, dramatically fewer than in 1800. Life expectancy was about 43 years. By 1900, improved health care and sanitation had raised it to 47 years. For blacks and other minorities, who often lived in unsanitary rural areas, life expectancy was only 33 years.

Meals tended to be heavy, and so did people. Even breakfast had several courses and could include steak, eggs, fish, potatoes, toast, and coffee. Food was cheap. Families ate fresh homegrown produce in the summer and "put up" their fruits and vegetables for the long winters. Toward the end of the century, eating habits changed. Packaged breakfast cereals became popular; fresh fruit and vegetables came in on fast trains from Florida and California; and commercially canned food became safer and cheaper. The newfangled icebox, cooled by blocks of ice, kept food fresher and added new treats such as ice cream.

Medical science was undergoing a revolution. Louis Pasteur's discovery that germs cause infection and disease created the new science of microbiology and led the way to new vaccines and other preventive measures. But tuberculosis, typhoid, diphtheria, and pneumonia—all now curable—were still the leading causes of death. Infant mortality gradually declined between 1877 and 1900, but a great drop did not come until after 1920.

There were few hospitals and no hospital insurance. Most patients stayed at home, although medical practice, especially surgery, expanded rapidly. Once brutal and dangerous, surgery became relatively safe and painless. Anesthetics—ether and chloroform— eliminated pain, and antiseptics helped prevent postoperative infections. Antiseptic practices at childbirth

Changing Styles for Women Victorian fashion ideals for women emphasized elaborate, confining dress styles with a tiny waistline and full skirts that reached to the floor. Throughout the 1890s, as women began to participate in sports or work in factories, stores, or business offices, styles gradually became less restrictive. This 1900 cover of *Ladies' Home Journal* shows women wearing tailored jackets and simple pleated skirts hemmed above the ankle, playing golf with men.

reduced puerperal fever, an infection that for centuries had killed women and newborns. The new science of psychology began to explore the mind, hitherto uncharted. William James, a leading American psychologist and philosopher, laid the foundations of modern behavioral psychology, which stressed the importance of the environment on human development.

Manners and Mores

Victorian morality, its name derived from the British queen who reigned from 1837 to 1901, set the tone for the era. The code prescribed strict standards of dress, manners, and sexual behavior. It was both obeyed and disobeyed and reflected the tensions of a generation whose moral standards were changing.

In 1877, children were to be seen and not heard. They spoke only when spoken to, listened rather than chattered—or at least that was the rule. Older boys and girls were often chaperoned, although they could always find moments alone. They played post office and spin the bottle; they puffed cigarettes behind the barn. Journalist William Allen White recalled his boyhood high jinks. He and his friends smeared their naked bodies with mud and leaped out in full view of passing trains. Counterbalancing such youthful exuberance was pride in virtue and self-control. "Thank heaven I am absolutely pure," Theodore Roosevelt, the future president, wrote in 1880 after proposing to Alice Lee. "I can tell Alice everything I have ever done."

Middle-class gentlemen dressed in heavy black suits, derby hats, and white shirts with paper collars. Women wore tight corsets, long dark dresses, and black shoes reaching well above the ankles. As with so many things, styles changed dramatically toward 1900, spurred in part by new sporting fads such as golf, tennis, and bicycling, which required looser clothing. By the 1890s, a middle-class woman wore a tailored suit or a dark skirt and a blouse, called a shirtwaist, modeled after men's shirts. Her skirts still draped about the ankles, but she increasingly removed or loosened the corset, the dread device that squeezed internal organs into fashionable 18-inch waistlines.

Religious and patriotic values were strong. A center of community life, the church often set the tenor for family and social relationships. In the 1880s, eight out of ten church members were Protestants; most of the rest were Roman Catholics.

With slavery abolished, reformers turned their attention to new moral and political issues. One group, known as the Mugwumps, worked to end corruption in politics. Other zealous reformers campaigned for prohibiting the sale of intoxicating liquors, hoping to end the social evils that stemmed from drunkenness. In 1874, women who advocated total abstinence from alcoholic beverages formed the Women's Christian Temperance Union (WCTU). Frances E. Willard was president of the group from 1879 until her death in 1898. By then, the WCTU had 500,000 members.

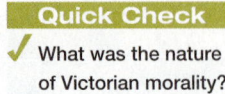

Quick Check

✓ What was the nature of Victorian morality?

Leisure and Entertainment

In the 1870s, people rose early. They washed from a pitcher and bowl in the bedroom. After dressing and eating, they went to work and school. Without refrigerators, housewives marketed almost daily. In the evening, families gathered in the "second parlor" or living room, where the children did their lessons, played games, sang around the piano, and listened to that day's verse from the Bible.

Cards, dominoes, backgammon, chess, and checkers were popular. Many homes had a packet of "author cards" that required knowledge of books, authors, and quotations. The latest fad was the stereopticon or "magic lantern," which brought three-dimensional life to art, history, and nature. Like author cards and other games, it was both instructional and entertaining.

Sentimental ballads such as "Silver Threads Among the Gold" (1873) remained the most popular musical form, but the insistent syncopated rhythms of ragtime reflected the influence of the new urban culture. By the time Scott Joplin's "Maple Leaf Rag" (1899) popularized ragtime, critics complained that "a wave of vulgar, filthy and suggestive music has inundated the land." Classical music flourished. The New England Conservatory (1867), the Cincinnati College of Music (1878), and the Metropolitan Opera (1883) were new sources of civic pride; New York, Boston, and Chicago launched first-rate symphony orchestras between 1878 and 1891.

Fairs, horse races, balloon ascensions, bicycle tournaments, and football and baseball contests attracted avid fans. The popularity of organized spectator sports between 1870 and 1900 reflected both the rise of the city and new uses of leisure. Baseball's first professional team, the Cincinnati Red Stockings, appeared in 1869, and baseball soon became the preeminent national sport. Fans sang songs about it ("Take Me Out to the Ballgame"), wrote poems about it ("Casey at the Bat"), and made up riddles about it ("What has 18 feet and catches flies?"). Modern rules were adopted. Umpires were designated to call balls and strikes; catchers wore masks and chest protectors and moved closer to the plate instead of staying back to catch the ball on the bounce. Fielders had to catch the ball on the fly rather than on one bounce in their caps. By 1890, professional baseball games were drawing crowds of 60,000. In 1901, the American League was organized. Two years later the Boston Red Sox beat the Pittsburgh Pirates in the first modern World Series.

In 1869, Princeton and Rutgers played the first intercollegiate football game. Soon, other schools picked up the sport. By the 1890s, crowds of 50,000 or more attended the most popular contests. Basketball, invented in 1891, gained a large following.

As gas and electric lights brightened the night, and streetcars crisscrossed city streets, leisure habits changed. Delighted with the new technology, people took advantage of an increasing variety of things to do. They stayed home less often. New York City's first electric sign—"Manhattan Beach Swept by Ocean Breezes"—appeared in 1881. At night people filled the streets on their way to the theater, vaudeville shows, and dance halls or just out for a stroll.

Watch the **Video**
College Football, 1903 on
myhistorylab.com

Quick Check
✓ In a period of increasing leisure, what did people do in their free time?

Changes in Family Life

Industrialization and urbanization were changing family relationships. On the farm, parents and children worked more or less together, and the family was a producing unit. In factories and offices, family members rarely worked together. In working-class families, mothers, fathers, and children separated at dawn and returned, exhausted, at dark.

Late-nineteenth-century working-class families, like that of the young Polish girl that Harriet Vittum saw, often lived in complex household units—taking in relatives and boarders to pay the rent. As many as one-third of all households contained people who were not members of the immediate family. Although the daily routine separated its members, working-class families tended to retain strong family ties, cemented by the need to survive in the industrial economy.

Middle-class wives and children, however, became increasingly isolated from the world of work, and the middle-class family became more self-contained. Older children spent more time in adolescence, and formal schooling lengthened. Families took in fewer apprentices and boarders. By 1900, more middle-class offspring lived with their parents into their late teens and twenties than do today.

Fewer middle-class wives participated directly in their husbands' work. As a result, they and their children occupied what contemporaries called a "separate sphere of domesticity," set apart from the masculine sphere of income-producing work. The family home became a "walled garden," a retreat from the crass materialism of the outside world. Middle-class fathers began to move their families out of the city to the suburbs, commuting to work on the new streetcars, leaving wives and children at home and school.

The middle-class family had once functioned in part to transmit a craft or skill, arrange marriages, and care for dependent kin. As these functions declined, the family took on new emotional and ideological responsibilities. In a society that worried about the weakening hold of other institutions, the family became an important means of social control.

Magazines such as the *Ladies' Home Journal*, which started in 1889, glorified motherhood and the home, and its articles and ads featured women as homebound, child-oriented consumers. While society's leaders praised the value of homemaking, housewives' status declined under the factory system, which emphasized money rewards and devalued household labor.

Underlying these changes was one of the modern world's most important trends, a decline in fertility rates that lasted from 1800 to 1939. Though blacks, immigrants, and rural dwellers had more children than white native-born city dwellers, the trend affected all classes and races; among white women, the birthrate fell from seven in 1800 to just over four in 1880 to about three in 1900. People everywhere tended to marry later and to have fewer children.

Since contraceptives were not yet widely used, the decline reflected abstinence and a conscious decision to postpone or limit families. Some women decided to devote greater attention to fewer children, others to pursue careers. The number of young unmarried women working for wages, attending school, delaying marriage, or not marrying at all increased, while rates of illegitimacy and premarital pregnancy declined.

The decline in fertility largely stemmed from people's responses to social and economic forces, the rise of cities and industry. Couples decided to have fewer children, and the result reshaped American society.

Quick Check

✓ How did the process of urbanization affect the family?

Changing Views: A Growing Assertiveness Among Women

In and out of the family, self-sufficient women, employed in factories, telephone exchanges, or offices, were increasingly entering the workforce. Most were single and worked because they had to rather than chose to.

Many regarded this "new woman" as a corruption of the ideal vision of the American woman, in which man worshiped "a diviner self than his own," innocent, helpless, and good. Women were to be better than the world around them. They were brought up, said Ida Tarbell, a leading political reformer, "as if wrongdoing were impossible to them."

Views changed, albeit slowly. One important change occurred in the legal codes, particularly in the common law doctrine of *femme couverte.* Under that doctrine, wives were their husbands' chattel; they could not legally control their own earnings, property, or children unless they had a specific contract before marriage. By 1890, many states had revised the doctrine to allow wives control of their earnings and inherited property. The new laws also recognized divorced women's rights to custody or joint custody of their children. Although divorce was still not socially acceptable, divorce rates more than doubled during the last third of the century. By 1905, one in 12 marriages ended in divorce.

In the 1870s and 1880s, more women were asserting their own humanness. They fought for the vote, lobbied for equal pay, and sought self-fulfillment. The new interest in psychology and medicine strengthened their causes. Charlotte Perkins Gilman, author of *Women and Economics* (1898), argued that the ideal of womanly "innocence" actually meant ignorance. In medical and popular literature, menstruation, sexual intercourse, and childbirth were becoming discussed as natural functions instead of taboo topics. For example, Edward Bliss Foote's *Plain Home Talk of Love, Marriage, and Parentage*, a best-seller between the 1880s and 1900, challenged Victorian notions that sexual intercourse was unhealthy and intended solely to produce children.

Women espoused causes with new fervor. Susan B. Anthony, a veteran of many reform campaigns, tried to vote in the 1872 presidential election and was fined $100, which she refused to pay. In 1890, she helped form the National American Woman Suffrage Association to work for the enfranchisement of women.

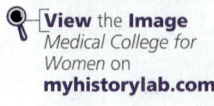

View the Image
Medical College for Women on
myhistorylab.com

Quick Check

✓ In what ways did women respond to life in the urban-industrial society?

Educating the Masses

Continuing a trend that stretched back a century, childhood was becoming a more distinct time of life. Adolescence—the special nature of the teenage years— was still only a vague concept, but the role of children was changing. Less and less were children perceived as "little adults," valued for the financial gain they might bring the family. Now children were to grow, learn, and be nurtured rather than rushed into adulthood.

As a result, schooling became more important, and universal education for American children came closer than ever before. By 1900, 31 states and territories (out of 51) had made school compulsory, though most required attendance only until age 14. In 1870, there were only 160 public high schools; in 1900, there were 6,000. Illiteracy declined from 20 percent to just over 10 percent of the population. Still, even in 1900, the average adult had only five years of schooling.

A Regimented Education Schools, regarded primarily as training grounds for a life of work, stressed conformity and deportment—feet on the floor, hands folded and resting atop the desk. The teacher was drillmaster and disciplinarian as well as instructor.

Educators saw the school as the primary means to train people for life and work in an industrializing society. Hence teachers focused on basic skills—reading and mathematics—and on values—obedience and attentiveness to the clock. Most schools had a highly structured curriculum, built around discipline and routine. In 1892, Joseph Rice, a pediatrician, toured 1,200 classrooms in 36 cities. In a typical classroom, he reported, the atmosphere was "damp and chilly," the teacher strict. "The unkindly spirit of the teacher is strikingly apparent; the pupils being completely subjugated to her will, are silent and motionless." One teacher asked her pupils, "How can you learn anything with your knees and toes out of order?"

School began early; boys attended all day, but girls often stayed home after lunch, since they were thought to need less learning. Many children dropped out of school, and not just to earn money. Helen Todd, a factory inspector in Chicago, found young girls working in a hot, stuffy attic. When she asked why they were not in school, Tillie Isakowsky, who was 14, said, "School! School is de fiercest t'ing youse kin come up against. Factories ain't no cinch, but schools is worst." Todd asked 500 children whether they would go to school or work in a factory if their families did not need the money—412 preferred the factory.

The South lagged far behind in education. The average family size was about twice as large as in the North, and a greater proportion of the population lived in isolated rural areas. State and local authorities mandated fewer weeks in the average school year, and many southern states refused to adopt compulsory education laws. Most important, southerners insisted on maintaining segregated school systems—North Carolina and Alabama in 1876, South Carolina and Louisiana in 1877, Mississippi in 1878, and Virginia in 1882. Supreme Court decisions in the 1880s and 1890s upheld the legality of segregation. In the Civil Rights Cases (1883), the Court ruled that the Fourteenth Amendment barred state governments from discriminating on account of race but did not prevent private individuals or organizations from doing so. In *Plessy v. Ferguson* (1896), the Court established the "separate but equal" doctrine and upheld a Louisiana law requiring different seating in railroad cars for whites and blacks. In *Cumming v. County Board of Education* (1899), the Court approved the creation of separate schools for whites, even if there were no comparable schools for blacks. Segregated schooling added a devastating financial burden to education in the South.

Southern school laws often implied that the schools would be "separate but equal," and they were often separate but rarely equal. Black schools were usually dilapidated, and black teachers were paid considerably less than white teachers. In 1890, only 35 percent of black children attended school in the South; 55 percent of white children did. That year nearly two-thirds of the country's black population was illiterate.

Educational techniques changed after the 1870s. Educators paid more attention to early elementary education, a trend that placed young children in school and helped the growing number of mothers who worked outside the home. The kindergarten movement, started in St. Louis in 1873, spread across the country. In kindergartens, 4- to 6-year-olds learned by playing, not by keeping their knees and toes in order. For older children, social reformers advocated "practical" courses in manual training and homemaking.

Read the **Document**
Opinion of the Supreme Court for Plessy v. Ferguson (1896) on **myhistorylab.com**

Quick Check
✓ In what ways did ideas about education change during these years?

Higher Education

Nearly 150 new colleges and universities opened between 1880 and 1900. The Morrill Land Grant Act of 1862 gave the states land to establish colleges to teach "agriculture and the mechanic arts." The act fostered 69 "land-grant" institutions, including the great state universities of Wisconsin, California, Minnesota, and Illinois.

Private philanthropy, born of the large fortunes of the industrial age, also spurred growth in higher education. Leland Stanford gave $24 million to endow Stanford University on his California ranch, and John D. Rockefeller, founder of the Standard Oil Company, gave $34 million to found the University of Chicago. Other industrialists established Cornell (1865), Vanderbilt (1873), and Tulane (1884).

As colleges expanded, their function changed, and their curriculum broadened. No longer did they exist primarily to train young men for the ministry. They moved away from the classical curriculum of rhetoric, mathematics, Latin, and Greek toward "reality and practicality," as President David Starr Jordan of Stanford University said. MIT, founded in 1861, focused on science and engineering.

Women still had to fight for educational opportunities. Some formed study clubs, an important movement that spread rapidly between 1870 and 1900. Club members read Virgil and Chaucer, studied history and architecture, and discussed women's rights.

Read the **Document**
M. Carey Thomas, higher education for women" on **myhistorylab.com**

Clubs sprang up almost everywhere there were women: in Caribou, Maine; Tyler, Texas; and Leadville, Colorado—as well as San Francisco, New York, and Boston. Although they were usually small, study clubs sparked interest in education among women and their daughters and contributed to a rapid rise in the number of women entering college in the early 1900s.

Before the Civil War, only three private colleges admitted women to study with men. After the war, educational opportunities increased for women. Women's colleges opened, including Vassar (1865), Wellesley (1875), Smith (1875), Bryn Mawr (1885), Barnard (1889), and Radcliffe (1893). The land-grant colleges of the Midwest, open to women from the outset, spurred a nationwide trend toward coeducation, although some physicians, such as Harvard Medical School's Dr. Edward H. Clarke in his popular *Sex in Education* (1873), argued that the strain of learning

Growth in Higher Education A physics lecture at the University of Michigan in the late 1880s or early 1890s. The land-grant university admitted women, but seating in the lecture hall was segregated by gender—although not by race. Note that both whites and African Americans are seated in the back rows of the men's section.

made women sterile. By 1900, women made up about 40 percent of college students, and four out of five colleges admitted them.

Fewer opportunities existed for African Americans and other minorities. Jane Stanford encouraged the Chinese who had worked on her husband's Central Pacific Railroad to apply to Stanford University, but that was unusual. Most colleges did not accept minority students, and only a few applied. W. E. B. Du Bois, the brilliant African American sociologist and civil rights leader, attended Harvard in the late 1880s but found the social life of Harvard Yard closed to him. Disdained and disdainful, he "asked no fellowship of my fellow students." Chosen as one of the commencement speakers, Du Bois picked as his topic "Jefferson Davis," the president of the Confederacy, treating it, said an onlooker, with "an almost contemptuous fairness."

Most black students turned to black colleges such as the Hampton Normal and Industrial Institute in Virginia and the Tuskegee Institute in Alabama. Whites who favored manual training for blacks often supported these colleges. Booker T. Washington, an ex-slave, put his educational ideas into practice at Tuskegee, which opened in 1881. Washington began Tuskegee with limited funds, four run-down buildings, and only 30 students; by 1900, it was a model industrial and agricultural school. Spread over 46 buildings, it offered instruction in 30 trades to 1,400 students.

Washington stressed patience, manual training, and hard work. "The wisest among my race understand," he said in an acclaimed speech to a white audience at the Atlanta Cotton States Exposition in 1895, "that the agitation of questions of social equality is the extremest folly." Blacks should focus on economic gains; they should go to school, learn skills, and work their way up the ladder: "No race can prosper till it learns that there is as much dignity in tilling a field as in writing a poem. It is at the bottom of life we must begin, and not at the top." Southern whites should help out because they would then have "the most patient, faithful, law-abiding, and unresentful people that the world has seen."

Washington's philosophy became known as the Atlanta Compromise, and many whites and some blacks welcomed it. Acknowledging white domination, it called for slow progress through self-improvement, not through lawsuits or agitation. Rather than fighting for equal rights, blacks should acquire property and show they were worthy of their rights. But Washington did believe in black equality. He worked behind the scenes to organize black voters and lobby against harmful laws. In his own way, he bespoke a racial pride that contributed to the rise of black nationalism in the twentieth century.

Watch the **Video**
Conflict between Booker T. Washington and W. E. B. Du Bois on **myhistorylab.com**

Du Bois wanted a more aggressive strategy. Born in Massachusetts in 1868, the son of poor parents, he studied at Fisk University in Tennessee and the University of Berlin in Germany before attending Harvard. Unable to find a teaching job in a white college, he took a low-paying research position at the University of Pennsylvania. He had no office but did not need one. Du Bois used the new discipline of sociology, which emphasized factual observation in the field, to study the condition of blacks.

Notebook in hand, he examined crime in Philadelphia's black seventh ward. He interviewed 5,000 people, mapped and classified neighborhoods, and produced *The Philadelphia Negro* (1898). The first study of the effect of urban life on blacks, it cited a wealth of statistics, all suggesting that crime in the ward stemmed not from inborn degeneracy but from the environment in which blacks lived. Change the environment, and people would change, too; education was a good way to go about it.

Educational Opportunities for African Americans Booker T. Washington, who served as the first president of Tuskegee Institute, advocated work efficiency and practical skills as keys to advancement for African Americans. Students like these at Tuskegee studied academic subjects and received training in trades and professions.

In The *Souls of Black Folk* (1903), Du Bois openly attacked Booker T. Washington and the philosophy of the Atlanta Compromise. He urged African Americans to aspire to professional careers, fight for their civil rights, and get a college education. Calling for integrated schools with equal opportunity for all, Du Bois urged blacks to educate their "talented tenth," a highly trained intellectual elite, to lead them.

Du Bois was not alone in promoting careers in the professions. Throughout higher education there was increased emphasis on professional training, particularly in medicine, dentistry, and law. Enrollments swelled, even as standards of admission tightened. The number of medical schools in the country rose from 75 in 1870 to 160 in 1900, and the number of medical students—including more women—almost tripled. Nursing schools grew from only 15 in 1880 to 432 in 1900. Doctors, lawyers, and others became part of a growing middle class that shaped the concerns of the Progressive Era of the early twentieth century.

Although less than 5 percent of the college-age population attended college in 1877–1890, the new trends had great impact. A generation of men and women encountered new ideas that changed their views of themselves and society. Courses never before offered, such as Philosophy II at Harvard, "The Ethics of Social Reform," which students called "drainage, drunkenness, and divorce," heightened interest in social problems and the need for reform. Some students burned with a desire to cure society's ills. "My life began … at Johns Hopkins University," Frederic C. Howe, an influential reformer, recalled. "I came alive, I felt a sense of responsibility to the world, I wanted to change things."

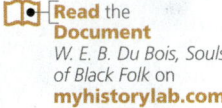

Read the
Document
W. E. B. Du Bois, Souls of Black Folk on
myhistorylab.com

Quick Check
✓ What were the trends in higher education between the 1870s and 1900?

Why did Jim Crow laws spread across the South after the end of Reconstruction?

THE SPREAD OF JIM CROW

Though Washington and Du Bois differed widely in their views, both of them fought the growing restrictions on black civil rights known as Jim Crow laws (see Chapter 16). While segregation and disfranchisement began as informal arrangements in the immediate aftermath of the Civil War, they soon culminated in a legal regime of separation and exclusion that took firm hold in the 1890s.

Throughout the South, the new measures lent the sanction of law to a racial ostracism that included voting booths, churches, schools, housing, and jobs. Touching virtually all parts of life, they affected public transportation, hospitals, prisons, and asylums—even funeral homes and cemeteries.

A number of influences lay behind their rapid growth. By the 1870s, many northerners had lost interest in guarding the rights of blacks. Weariness with Civil War issues played a role in this trend, as did beliefs in Anglo-Saxon superiority and, after the Spanish-American War of 1898, the acquisition of colonial subjects—called, revealingly, "the white man's burden"—in Hawaii, Guam, Puerto Rico, and the Philippines.

As a result, the North and the federal government did little to stem the tide. Supreme Court decisions between 1878 and 1898 gutted the Reconstruction amendments and the legislation passed to enforce them, leaving blacks virtually defenseless against political and social discrimination. (See Table 19.1.)

Most visible in areas like voting, Jim Crow laws soon penetrated nearly every aspect of Southern life. In 1915 a South Carolina code banned textile factories from allowing laborers of different races to work together in the same room or to use the same entrances, exits,

Lynching Perhaps no event better expresses the cruel and barbaric nature of the racism and white supremacy that swept the South after Reconstruction than lynching. Although lynchings were not confined to the South, most occurred there, and African American men were the most frequent victims. Here two men lean out of a barn window above a black man who is about to be hanged. Others below prepare to set on fire the pile of hay at the victim's feet. Lynchings were often public events, drawing huge crowds to watch the victim's agonizing death.

toilets, and drinking water. That year, Oklahoma required telephone companies to maintain separate phone booths for whites and blacks. North Carolina and Florida ordered separate textbooks for black and white children. Florida even required that the books be segregated while they were in storage. A New Orleans ordinance placed black and white prostitutes in separate districts of the city. There were Jim Crow Bibles for African American witnesses in Atlanta courts and Jim Crow elevators in Atlanta buildings.

Jim Crow laws expanded during the 1920s and 1930s. Mississippi segregated white and black patients in hospitals and mandated that nurses could tend only the sick of their own race. City ordinances required Jim Crow taxis in Jacksonville, Florida, in 1929; Birmingham, Alabama, in 1930; and Atlanta, Georgia, in 1940. In 1930, a Birmingham ordinance forbade blacks and whites from playing each other at dominoes or checkers.

Lynchings also spread. Between 1889 and 1899, an average of 187 blacks were lynched every year for alleged offenses against white supremacy. Many blacks (and whites) convicted of petty crimes were leased out to private contractors whose brutality rivaled that of the most sadistic slaveholders. The convict-lease system enabled entrepreneurs, such as mine owners and lumber companies, to rent prisoners from the state and treat them as they saw fit. Unlike slaveowners, they suffered no loss when a forced laborer died from overwork.

TABLE 19.1 Supreme Court Decisions Affecting Black Civil Rights, 1875–1900

Case	Effects of Court's Decisions
Hall v. DeCuir (1878)	Struck down Louisiana law prohibiting racial discrimination by "common carriers" (railroads, steamboats, buses). Declared the law a "burden" on interstate commerce, over which states had no authority.
United States v. Harris (1882)	Declared federal laws to punish crimes such as murder and assault unconstitutional. Declared such crimes to be the sole concern of local government. Ignored the frequent racial motivation behind such crimes in the South.
Civil Rights Cases (1883)	Struck down Civil Rights Act of 1875. Declared that Congress may not legislate on civil rights unless a state passes a discriminatory law. Declared the Fourteenth Amendment silent on racial discrimination by private citizens.
Plessy v. Ferguson (1896)	Upheld Louisiana statute requiring "separate but equal" accommodations on railroads. Declared that segregation is *not* necessarily discrimination.
Williams v. Mississippi (1898)	Upheld state law requiring a literacy test to qualify for voting. Refused to find any implication of racial discrimination in the law, although it permitted illiterate whites to vote if they "understood" the Constitution. Using such laws, southern states rapidly disfranchised blacks.

Racism, of course, was not limited to the South, as race riots in East St. Louis, Illinois, (1917) and Chicago (1919), among other events, attested. In 1903, the New York public school system banned *Uncle Tom's Cabin* from its reading lists, saying that Harriet Beecher Stowe's depiction of antebellum slavery "does not belong to today but to an unhappy period of our country's history, the memory of which it is not well to revive in our children." Encountering the racism of the North—far less brutal but racism nonetheless—blacks who had migrated there called it James Crow.

THE STIRRINGS OF REFORM

How did life in the growing cities lead to ideas of reform?

When Henry George, a leading reformer, asked a friend what could be done about political corruption in American cities, his friend replied: "Nothing! You and I can do nothing at all…. We can only wait for evolution. Perhaps in four or five thousand years evolution may have carried men beyond this state of things."

This stress on the slow pace of change reflected the doctrine of social Darwinism, which argued against the usefulness of reform, and was based on the writings of the English philosopher Herbert Spencer. In influential books, Spencer applied Charles Darwin's principles of natural selection to society. He combined biological evolution and sociology to develop a theory of "social selection" that tried to explain human progress. Like animals, society evolved, slowly, by adapting to the environment. The "survival of the fittest"—Spencer's term, not Darwin's—preserved the strong and weeded out the weak.

Social Darwinism had a number of influential followers in the United States, including William Graham Sumner, a professor of political and social science at Yale University. One of the country's best known academics, Sumner was forceful and eloquent. In writings such as *What Social Classes Owe to Each Other* (1883) and "The Absurd Effort to Make the World Over" (1894), he argued that government action to help the poor or weak interfered with evolution and sapped the species. Reform tampered with the laws of nature.

Social Darwinism's impact on American thinking has been exaggerated, but in the powerful hands of Sumner and others it did influence some journalists, ministers, and policymakers. Between 1877 and the 1890s, however, social Darwinism came under increasing attack. In religion, economics, politics, literature, and law, thoughtful people questioned established conditions and advocated reform.

Progress and Poverty

Read and reread, passed from hand to hand, Henry George's best-seller *Progress and Poverty* (1879) led to a more critical appraisal of American society in the 1880s and beyond. The book jolted traditional thought.

Disturbed by an economic depression in the 1870s and by labor upheavals such as the great railroad strikes of 1877 (see Chapter 18), George saw modern society—rich, complex, with material goods hitherto unknown—as sadly flawed: "The wealthy class is becoming more wealthy; but the poorer class is becoming more dependent. The gulf between the employed and the employer is growing wider; social contrasts are becoming sharper… ."

George proposed a simple solution. Land, he thought, formed the basis of wealth, and a few people could grow wealthy just because the price of their land rose. Since the rise in price did not result from any effort on their part, it represented an "unearned increment" that should be taxed for the good of society. A "single tax" on the increment, replacing all other taxes, would help equalize wealth and raise revenue to aid the poor. "Single-tax" clubs sprang up around the country, but George's solution, simplistic and unappealing, had much less impact than his analysis of the problem itself. He raised questions a generation of readers set out to answer.

Quick Check

✓ What was Henry George's solution to economic inequity in the late nineteenth century?

New Currents in Social Thought

George's emphasis on the effects of deprivation in the social environment excited a young country lawyer in Ohio—Clarence Darrow. Unlike the social Darwinists, Darrow was sure that criminals were made and not born. They grew out of "the unjust condition of human life." In the mid-1880s, he left for Chicago and a 40-year career working to convince people that poverty lay at the root of crime. "There is no such thing as crime as the word is generally understood," he told startled prisoners in the Cook County jail. "If every man, woman and child in the world had a chance to make a decent, fair, honest living there would be no jails and no lawyers and no courts."

Edward Bellamy also dreamed of a cooperative society that eradicated poverty, greed, and crime. A lawyer from western Massachusetts, in 1887, Bellamy published *Looking Backward, 2000–1887* and became a national reform figure overnight. The novel's protagonist, Julian West, falls asleep in 1887 and awakes in 2000 to find himself in a socialist utopia: The government owns the means of production, and citizens share the material rewards. Cooperation, not competition, is the watchword.

Read the **Document**
Edward Bellamy, from Looking Backward on **myhistorylab.com**

The world of *Looking Backward* had limits; it was regimented, paternalistic, and filled with the gadgets and material concerns of Bellamy's own day. But it enthralled readers. The book sold 10,000 copies a week, and its followers formed Nationalist Clubs to work for its objectives. By 1890, there were such clubs in 27 states, calling for the nationalization of public utilities and a wider distribution of wealth.

Despite these ideas, some Protestant sects stressed individual salvation and a better life in the next world, not in this one. Poverty was evidence of sinfulness; the poor had only themselves to blame. "God has intended the great to be great and the little to be little," said Henry Ward Beecher, the country's best known pastor. Wealth and destitution, suburbs and slums—all formed part of God's plan.

Challenging those traditional doctrines, churches in the 1880s began establishing missions in city slums. Living among the poor and homeless, urban missionaries grew impatient with religious doctrines that endorsed the status quo.

A religious philosophy known as the Social Gospel reflected many of the new trends. As the name suggests, the Social Gospel focused on society as well as individuals, on improving living conditions as well as saving souls. Sermons in Social Gospel churches called on church members to fulfill their social obligations, and adults met before and after the regular service to discuss social and economic problems. Children were excused from sermons, organized into age groups, and encouraged to make the church a center for social and religious activity. Soon churches included dining halls, gymnasiums, and even theaters.

Quick Check

✓ What new ideas did Henry George and others offer, and what effect did those ideas have?

The Settlement Houses

Like Tweed and other bosses, social reformers living in the urban slums appreciated the dependency of the poor; unlike them, they wanted to eradicate the conditions that underlay it. To do so, they formed settlement houses in the slums and lived in them to experience the problems they were trying to solve.

Youthful, idealistic, and mostly middle class, these social workers took as their model Toynbee Hall, founded in 1884 in the slums of east London to provide community services to the British poor. Stanton Coit, a moody and poetic graduate of Amherst College, was the first American to borrow the settlement house idea; in 1886, he opened the Neighborhood Guild on New York's Lower East Side. The idea spread. By 1900, there were more than 100 settlements in the country; five years later, more than 200, and by 1910, more than 400.

The settlements included Jane Addams's famous Hull House in Chicago (1889), Robert A. Woods's South End House in Boston (1892), and Lillian Wald's Henry Street Settlement in New York (1893). The reformers wanted to bridge the socioeconomic gap between rich and poor and bring education, culture, and hope to the slums. They sought to create in the heart of the city the values and sense of community of small-town America.

Many of the settlement workers were women, some of them college graduates, who found that society had little use for their talents and energy. Jane Addams, a graduate of Rockford College in Illinois, opened Hull House on South Halsted Street in the heart of the Chicago slums. Twenty-nine years old, forceful and winning, she intended "to share the lives of the poor" and humanize the industrial city. "American ideals," she said, "crumbled under the overpowering poverty of the overcrowded city."

Occupying an old, rundown house, Hull House stressed education, offering classes in elementary English and Shakespeare, lectures on ethics and the history of art, and courses in cooking, sewing, and manual skills. A pragmatist, Addams believed in investigating a problem and then doing something to solve it. Noting the lack of medical care in the area, she established an infant welfare clinic and free medical dispensary. Because the tenements lacked bathtubs, she installed showers in the basement of Hull House and built a bathhouse. Because there was no local library, she opened a reading room. Hull House eventually occupied a dozen buildings, sprawling over more than a city block.

OPENING OF

HULL=HOUSE
PLAY GROUND

Polk Street, Near Halsted

Saturday, May 1st, 1897,

AT 3 O'CLOCK, P. M.

" The air is warm, the skies are clear,
Birds and blossoms all are here,
Come old and young with spirits gay,
To welcome back the charming May."

MUSIC BY THE BRASS BAND

...Kindergarten Games---May Pole Dance...

ALL KINDS OF RACES

The Settlement House, a Revolution and Social Reform Jane Addams founded Chicago's Hull House in 1889. The settlement house provided recreational and day-care facilities; offered extension classes in academic, vocational, and artistic subjects; and, above all, sought to bring hope to poverty-stricken slum dwellers.

Like settlement workers in other cities, Addams and her colleagues studied the immigrants in nearby tenements. Laboriously, they identified the background of every family in a one-third-square-mile area around Hull House. Finding people of 18 different nationalities, they taught them American history and the English language, yet Addams also encouraged them—through folk festivals and art—to preserve their own heritage.

But the settlement house movement had its limits. Although Hull House, one of the best, attracted 2,000 visitors a week, this was still just a fraction of the 70,000 people who lived within six blocks of it. Immigrants sometimes resented the middle-class "strangers" who told them how to live. Dressed always in a brown suit and dark stockings, Harriet Vittum, the head resident of Chicago's Northwestern University Settlement (who told the story of the suicide victim at the beginning of this chapter), was known as "the police lady in brown." She once stopped a dance because it was too wild, and then was disgusted when the boys made "vulgar sounds with their lips." Though her attempts to help were sincere, in private Vittum called the people she was trying to help "ignorant foreigners, who live in an atmosphere of low morals ... surrounded by anarchy and crime."

Quick Check

✓ What were the causes and characteristics of the numerous settlement houses formed in these years?

Although Addams tried to offer programs for blacks, most white reformers did not, and after 1900, a number of black reformers opened their own settlements. Like the whites, they offered employment information, medical care, and recreational facilities, along with concerts, lectures, and other educational events. White and black, the settlement workers made important contributions to urban life.

A Crisis in Social Welfare

The depression of 1893 jarred the young settlement workers, many of whom had just begun their work. In cities and towns across the country, traditional methods of helping the needy foundered in the crisis. Churches, charity organization societies, and Community Chests did what they could, but their resources were limited, and they functioned on traditional lines. Many of them still tried to change rather than aid individual families, and people were often reluctant to call on them for help.

Gradually, a new class of professional social workers filled the need. Unlike the church and charity volunteers, these social workers wanted not only to feed the poor but to study their condition and alleviate it. Revealingly, they called themselves "case workers" and collected data on the income, housing, jobs, health, and habits of the poor. Prowling tenement districts, they gathered information about the number of rooms and occupants, ventilation, and sanitation of the buildings in tenement districts, putting together a fund of useful data.

Studies of the poor popped up everywhere. Du Bois did his pioneering study of urban blacks; Lillian Pettengill worked as a servant to see "the ups and downs of this particular dog-life from the dog's end of the chain." Others became beggars, miners, lumberjacks, and factory laborers.

William T. Stead, a prominent British editor, visited the Chicago World's Fair in 1893 and stayed to examine the city. He roamed the flophouses and tenements and dropped in at Hull House to drink hot chocolate and talk over conditions with Jane Addams at Hull House. Later he wrote an influential book, *If Christ Came to Chicago* (1894), and in a series of mass meetings during 1893, he called for a civic revival. In response, Chicagoans formed the Civic Federation, a group of 40 leaders who aimed to make Chicago "the best governed, the healthiest city in this country." Setting up task forces for philanthropy, moral improvement, and legislation, they helped spawn the National Civic Federation (1900), a nationwide organization devoted to reforming urban life.

Quick Check

✓ What effect did the panic and depression of the 1890s have on social thought?

CONCLUSION: THE PLURALISTIC SOCIETY

"The United States was born in the country and moved to the city," historian Richard Hofstadter said. Much of that move occurred during the nineteenth century when the United States was the most rapidly urbanizing nation in the Western world. American cities bustled with energy; they absorbed millions of migrants from Europe and other parts of the world. That migration, and the urban growth that accompanied it, reshaped American politics and culture.

The 1920 census showed that, for the first time, most Americans lived in cities. By then, too, almost half the population was descended from people who had arrived after the American Revolution. As European, African, and Asian cultures met in the American city, a culturally pluralistic society emerged. Dozens of nationalities produced a culture whose members considered themselves Polish Americans, African Americans, and Irish Americans. The melting pot sometimes softened distinctions among the groups, but it only partially blended them into a unified society.

"Ah, Vera," said a character in Israel Zangwill's popular play *The Melting Pot* (1908), "what is the glory of Rome and Jerusalem where all nations and races come to worship and look back, compared with the glory of America, where all races and nations come to labour and look forward!" Critics scorned the play as "romantic claptrap," and indeed it was. But the metaphor of the melting pot depicted a new national image. In the decades after the 1870s a jumble of ethnic and racial groups struggled for a place in society.

That society, it is clear, experienced a crisis between 1870 and 1900. Together, the growth of cities and the rise of industrial capitalism brought jarring change, the exploitation of labor, ethnic and racial tensions, poverty—and, for a few, wealth beyond imagination. There was often open warfare between capital and labor. As reformers struggled to mediate the situation, they turned to state and federal government to look after human welfare, a tendency the Supreme Court resisted. In the midst of the crisis, the depression of the 1890s added to the turmoil, straining American institutions. Tracing the changes waves of urbanization and industrialization wrought, Henry George described the country as "the House of Have and the House of Want," almost a paraphrase of Abraham Lincoln's earlier metaphor of the "house divided" over slavery. The question was, could this house, unlike that one, stand?

19 STUDY RESOURCES

((•—Listen to the **Chapter Audio** for Chapter 19 on **myhistorylab.com**

TIMELINE

1881 Booker T. Washington opens Tuskegee Institute in Alabama, p. 486

1883 Metropolitan Opera opens in New York, p. 481

1887 Edward Bellamy promotes socialist utopia in *Looking Backward, 2000–1887*, p. 491

1889 Jane Addams opens Hull House in Chicago, p. 492

1890 National American Woman Suffrage Association formed, p. 483

1894 Immigration Restriction League formed to limit immigration from southern and eastern Europe, p. 476

1896 Supreme Court in *Plessy v. Ferguson* establishes constitutionality of "separate but equal" facilities, p. 484

Chapter Review

THE LURE OF THE CITY

Why did cities expand in the United States between 1880 and 1900?

American cities grew by leaps and bounds between 1880 and 1900. Among the reasons for the growth were the needs of an industrializing society; technological change in the form of electricity, elevators, steel beams, and other advances; and the arrival of millions of immigrants. Politically, city bosses retained power by responding to the needs of immigrants and other urban voters. *(p. 472)*

SOCIAL AND CULTURAL CHANGE, 1877–1900

How did the growth of American cities affect social, cultural, and political life?

The rapid growth of cities changed how Americans thought and acted. Cities opened up new areas of entertainment, employment, and behavior. They reshaped the family, brought more women into the workforce, and emphasized education. *(p. 478)*

THE SPREAD OF JIM CROW

Why did Jim Crow laws spread across the South after Reconstruction?

After Reconstruction ended in 1877, northern weariness with Civil War issues, a series of Supreme Court decisions, and growing racism led the federal government to stop trying to uphold civil rights legislation in the South. This enabled Southern states and cities to pass and enforce Jim Crow laws that mandated rigid separation between blacks and whites. *(p. 488)*

THE STIRRINGS OF REFORM

How did life in the growing city lead to reform?

Urban life, which forced many people close together, made social problems unprecedentedly visible. The city could not hide the contrasts between rich and poor, the dirtiness and dangers of factory life, and the woeful lot of millions of immigrants. Reformers argued for change. Some of them, like Jane Addams, opened urban settlement houses where they lived among the poor. *(p. 490)*

Key Term Questions

1. What drew the flow of new immigrants to the United States? (p. 475)

2. What were the Mugwumps trying to change in American society? (p. 480)

3. What was the Women's Christian Temperance Union (WCTU) trying to change in American society? (p. 480)

4. What was the main goal of the American Woman Suffrage Association? (p. 483)

5. What was the most significant outcome of the Civil Rights Cases? (p. 484)

6. What is the principle reaffirmed in Plessy v. Ferguson? (p. 484)

7. How did Herbert Spencer's social Darwinism help stir the cause for reform in America? (p. 490)

8. What were the goals of those who believed in the philosophy known as the Social Gospel? (p. 492)

9. What were the characteristics of the numerous settlement houses formed in the late 1800s? (p. 492)

MyHistoryLab Connections

Visit **www.myhistorylab.com** for a customized Study Plan to build your knowledge of *Toward an Urban Society*

Questions for Analysis

1. What was the experience of arriving at Ellis Island like for immigrants in the early Twentieth Century?

   Watch the **Video** *Ellis Island Immigrants, 1903* p. 475

2. According to George Washington Plunkitt, how does one become a successful big city politician?

   Read the **Document** *George Washington Plunkitt of Tammany Hall, (1905)* p. 477

3. How did the ideologies of Booker T. Washington and W.E.B. Du Bois differ?

   Watch the **Video** *The Conflict between Booker T. Washington and W.E.B. Du Bois* p. 486

4. To what extent does Edward Bellamy's fictional society in *Looking Backward* mirror modern American society?

   Read the **Document** *Edward Bellamy, from Looking Backward (1888)* p. 491

Other Resources from this Chapter

Read the **Document** *Letters to the Jewish Daily Forward*

View the **Image** *Medical College for Women*

Watch the **Video** *College Football, 1903*

View the **Image** *Plessy v. Ferguson*

Read the **Document** *M. Carey Thomas, Higher Education for Women*

Read the **Document** *W.E.B. Du Bois, Souls of Black Folk*

Contents and Spotlight Questions

((•━ **Listen** to the **Chapter Audio** for Chapter 20 on **myhistorylab.com**

Wealth and Poverty Tiny children peddling newspapers and women domestics serving the rich—their meager earnings were desperately needed.

HARDSHIP AND HEARTACHE

In June 1894, Susan Orcutt, a young farm woman from western Kansas, wrote the governor of her state a letter. She was desperate. The nation was in the midst of a devastating economic depression, and, like thousands of others, she had no money and nothing to eat. "I take my Pen In hand to let you know that we are Starving to death," she wrote. Hail had ruined the Orcutts' crops, and none of the household could find work. "My Husband went away to find work and came home last night and told me that we would have to Starve. [H]e has bin in ten countys and did not Get no work . . . . I havent had nothing to Eat today and It is three oclock[.]"

We do not know what happened to the Orcutts, but conditions were no better in the cities. "There are thousands of homeless and starving men in the streets," reported a Chicago journalist in the winter of 1893. "I have seen more misery in this last week than I ever saw in my life before." Charity societies and churches could not handle the huge numbers who were in need. The records of the Massachusetts state medical examiner told a grim story:

K.R., 29   Suicide by drowning
Boston   October 2, 1896

Out of work and despondent for a long while. Body found floating in the Charles [River].

F.S., 29   Suicide by arsenic
Boston   January 1, 1896

Much depressed for several weeks. Loss of employment. At 7:50 A.M. Jan. 1, she called her father and told him she had taken poison and wished to die.

L.M., 38   Hanging suicide
E. Boston   October 15, 1895

Had been out of work for several weeks and was very despondent. Wife went to market at about 11 A.M. and upon returning at about 12 P.M. found him hanging from bedroom door. . . . Slipped noose about his neck and [fell] forward upon it.

R.N., 23   Suicide by bullet wound of brain
Boston   June 22, 1896

Out of work. Mentally depressed. About 3 P.M. June 21 shot himself in right temple. . . . Left a letter explaining that he killed himself to save others the trouble of caring for him.

Lasting until 1897, the depression was the decisive event of the decade. At its height, 3 million people were unemployed—20 percent of the workforce. The human costs were enormous, even among the well-to-do. "They were for me years of simple Hell," shattering "my whole scheme of life," said Charles Francis Adams, Jr., the descendant of two American presidents. "I was sixty-three years old and a tired man when at last the effects of the 1893 convulsion wore themselves out."

Like the Great Depression of the 1930s that gave rise to the New Deal, the depression of the 1890s had profound and lasting effects. Bringing to a head many of the tensions that had been building in the society, it increased rural hostility toward the cities, provoked a bitter fight over the currency, and changed attitudes to government, unemployment, and reform. There were outbreaks of warfare between capital and labor; farmers demanded a fairer share of economic and social benefits; the new immigrants came under fresh attack. The depression of the 1890s changed the course of American history, as did another event of that decade: the war with Spain in 1898.

The impact of the depression changed American history. It led to a stronger impulse toward reform, a larger role for the presidency, help for farmers and laborers. The depression brought to fruition a realignment of the American political system that had been developing since the end of Reconstruction in 1877, establishing new patterns that gave rise to the Progressive Era and have endured into the twenty-first century.

POLITICS OF STALEMATE

Politics fascinated late-nineteenth-century Americans. Political campaigns involved the whole community, even though in most states only men could vote. During the weeks before an election, there were rallies, parades, picnics, and torchlight processions. In the six presidential elections from 1876 to 1896, an average of almost 79 percent of the electorate voted, a higher percentage than before or after.

White males made up the bulk of the electorate; until after 1900, women could vote in national elections only in Wyoming, Utah, Idaho, and Colorado. The National Woman Suffrage Association sued for the vote, but in 1875, the Supreme Court (*Minor v. Happersett*) upheld the power of the states to deny them this right. Congress refused to pass a constitutional amendment for woman suffrage, and between 1870 and 1910, nearly a dozen states defeated referenda to grant women the vote.

Black men were also kept from the polls. In 1877, Georgia adopted the poll tax to make voters pay an annual tax for the right to vote. The technique, aimed at disenfranchising impoverished blacks, quickly spread across the South.

In 1890, Mississippi required voters to be able to read and interpret the Constitution to the satisfaction of registration officials, all of them white. Such literacy tests, which the Supreme Court upheld in *Williams v. Mississippi* (1898), excluded poor white voters as well as blacks. To get around this, in 1898, Louisiana adopted the infamous "grandfather clause," which used a literacy test to disqualify black voters but permitted men who had failed the test to vote anyway if their fathers and grandfathers had voted before 1867—a time, of course, when no blacks could vote. The tactics worked. Black voters almost disappeared in the South. In 1896, there were 130,334 registered black voters in Louisiana; in 1904, there were 1,342.

The Party Deadlock

The Civil War generation, the unusual group of men who rose to power in the turbulent 1850s, still dominated politics in the 1870s and 1880s. In both North and South, they had ruled longer than most generations, aware that the war had set them apart. Five of the six presidents elected between 1865 and 1900 had served in the

Why was there a stalemate between Republicans and Democrats until the mid-1890s?

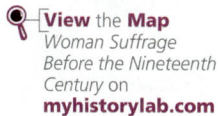

View the **Map**
Woman Suffrage Before the Nineteenth Century on
myhistorylab.com

Political Toys A toy scale pitting the presidential candidates of 1888 (Harrison and Cleveland) against each other. More than a plaything, this scale symbolizes the high level of voter participation during the late nineteenth century when elections hung in balance until the last vote was counted.

Quick Check

✓ What were the characteristics of politics in the 1870s, 1880s, and 1890s?

Civil War, as had many civic, business, and religious leaders. In 1890, over 1 million veterans of the Union army and hundreds of thousands of Confederates were still alive.

Party loyalties—rooted in Civil War traditions, ethnic and religious differences, and perhaps class distinctions—were strong. Voters clung to their old parties, shifts were infrequent, and there were relatively few "independent" voters. Although linked to the defeated Confederacy, the Democrats revived quickly after the war. They rested on a less sectional base than the Republicans. Identification with civil rights and military rule cut Republican strength in the South, but the Democratic party's principles of states' rights, decentralization, and limited government won supporters everywhere.

While Democrats wanted to keep government local and small, the Republicans pursued policies for the nation as a whole, in which government was an instrument to promote moral progress and material wealth. The Republicans passed the Homestead Act (1862), granted subsidies to the transcontinental railroads, and pushed other measures to encourage economic growth. They enacted legislation and constitutional amendments to protect civil rights. They advocated a high protective tariff as a tool of economic policy, to keep out foreign products while "infant industries" grew.

In national elections, 16 states, mostly in New England and the North, consistently voted Republican; 14 states, mostly in the South, consistently voted Democratic. A handful of "doubtful" states therefore could swing elections. These states—New York, New Jersey, Connecticut, Ohio, Indiana, and Illinois—received special attention during elections. Politicians lavished money and time on them; presidential candidates usually came from them. From 1868 to 1912, eight of the nine Republican presidential candidates and six of the seven Democratic candidates came from the "doubtful" states, especially New York and Ohio.

The two parties were evenly matched, and elections were closely fought. In three of the five presidential elections from 1876 to 1892, the victor won by less than 1 percent of the vote; in 1876 and 1888, the losing candidates actually had more popular votes than the winners but lost in the electoral college. Only twice during these years did one party control both the presidency and both houses of Congress—the Republicans in 1888 and the Democrats in 1892.

Reestablishing Presidential Power

Andrew Johnson's impeachment in 1868, the scandals of the Grant administrations in the 1870s, and the controversy over the 1876 election weakened the presidency. In the 1880s and 1890s, presidents fought to reassert their authority. By 1900, under William McKinley, they had largely succeeded. The late 1890s, in fact, marked the birth of the modern powerful presidency.

TABLE 20.1 The Election of 1880

Candidate	Party	Popular Vote	Electoral Vote
Garfield	Republican	4,454,416	214
Hancock	Democrat	4,444,952	155
Weaver	Greenback	308,578	0

The disputed election of 1876 clouded Rutherford B. Hayes' title to the presidency, but he soon began to reassert his authority (see Chapter 16). Hayes worked to reform the civil service, appointed reformers to high office, and ended military Reconstruction. Committed to the gold standard, a monetary system based on gold—the only basis, Hayes thought, of a sound currency—in 1878 he vetoed a bill calling for the partial coinage of silver. Congress passed this Bland-Allison Silver Purchase Act, requiring coinage of silver, over his veto.

James A. Garfield, a Union army hero and long-time member of Congress from Ohio, succeeded Hayes in 1881. (See Table 20.1.) Winning by a handful of votes, he took office determined to unite the Republican party (which was split by personality differences and disagreements over the tariff and the South), lower the tariff to cut taxes, and assert American interests in Latin America. Garfield had looked forward to the presidency, yet within weeks he told friends, "My God! What is there in this place that a man should ever want to get into it?"

Office seekers, hordes of them, caused Garfield's anguish. Each wanted a government job and thought nothing of cornering the president on every occasion. Garfield planned to leave Washington on July 2, 1881, for a New England vacation. Walking toward his train, he was shot in the back by Charles J. Guiteau, a deranged lawyer and disappointed office seeker. Suffering through the summer, Garfield died on September 19, 1881, and Vice President Chester A. Arthur—an ally of Senator Roscoe Conkling from New York—became president.

Arthur was a better president than many had expected. In 1883, with his backing, Congress passed the Pendleton Act to reform the civil service. In part a reaction to Garfield's assassination, the act created a bipartisan Civil Service Commission to administer competitive examinations and appoint officeholders on the basis of merit. It laid the basis for the expansion of the civil service.

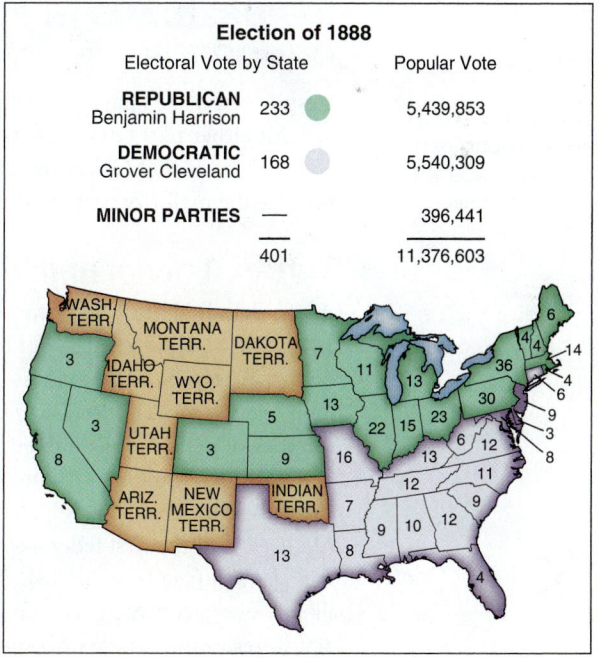

Election of 1888

	Electoral Vote by State	Popular Vote
REPUBLICAN Benjamin Harrison	233	5,439,853
DEMOCRATIC Grover Cleveland	168	5,540,309
MINOR PARTIES	—	396,441
	401	11,376,603

Map 20.1

TABLE 20.2 The Election of 1884

Candidate	Party	Popular Vote	Electoral Vote
Cleveland	Democrat	4,874,986	219
Blaine	Republican	4,851,981	182
Butler	Greenback	175,370	0
St. John	Prohibition	150,369	0

Quick Check

✓ How did each of the presidents from Rutherford B. Hayes to Benjamin Harrison work to regain the powers of his office, diminished during the impeachment of president Andrew Johnson?

In the election of 1884, Grover Cleveland, the Democratic governor of New York, won a narrow victory. (See Table 20.2.) The first Democratic president since 1861, Cleveland reflected his party's desire to curtail federal activities. He vetoed more than two-thirds of the bills presented to him, more than all his predecessors combined.

In 1887, he committed himself and the Democratic party to lowering the tariff, "the vicious, inequitable, and illogical source of unnecessary taxation." The Republicans accused him of undermining American industries. In 1888, they nominated for the presidency Benjamin Harrison of Indiana, a defender of the tariff. Cleveland garnered 90,000 more popular votes than Harrison but carried only two northern states, Connecticut and New Jersey, and the South. Harrison won the electoral vote 233 to 168. (See Map 20.1)

REPUBLICANS IN POWER: THE BILLION-DOLLAR CONGRESS

How did the Republican party's vision shape the "Billion-Dollar Congress"?

Despite Harrison's narrow margin, the election of 1888 was the most sweeping victory for either party in almost twenty years; it gave the Republicans the presidency and both houses of Congress. They had broken, it seemed, the party stalemate and become the majority party in the country.

Tariffs, Trusts, and Silver

As if a dam had burst, law after law poured out of the Republican Congress during 1890. The McKinley Tariff Act raised tariff duties about 4 percent, higher than ever before. A Dependent Pensions Act granted pensions to Union army veterans and their widows and children. The pensions were modest—$6 to $12 a month—but the number of pensioners doubled by 1893, when nearly one million people received about $160 million in pensions.

With little debate, the Republicans and Democrats joined in passing the Sherman Antitrust Act, the first federal attempt to deal with the problem of trusts and industrial growth (see Chapter 18). The act shaped all later antitrust policy. It declared illegal "every contract, combination in the form of trust or otherwise, or conspiracy, in restraint of trade or commerce." Experimental in nature, the act's terms were often vague, leaving precise interpretation to later experience and the courts.

The Sherman Antitrust Act made the United States virtually the only industrial nation to regulate business combinations. It tried to harness big business without harming it. Many members of Congress did not expect the new law to have much effect, and for a decade it did not. The Justice Department rarely filed suit under it, and in the first judicial interpretation of the law in 1895, the Supreme Court crippled it. Though the E. C. Knight Co. controlled 98 percent of sugar refining in the country, the Court sharply distinguished commerce from manufacturing, holding that the company, as a manufacturer, was not subject to the law. But judicial interpretations changed after 1900, and the Sherman Antitrust Act gained fresh power.

Another measure, the Sherman Silver Purchase Act, tried to solve the problem silver presented. Together with gold, silver had played a large role in currencies around the world. But by the mid-1800s, silver coinage had slipped into disuse. With the discovery of the great bonanza mines in Nevada (see Chapter 18), American silver production quadrupled between 1870 and 1890, glutting the world market, lowering the price of silver, and persuading many European nations to abandon

The Battle of the Standards In this 1886, cartoon illustrating the silver standard versus gold standard controversy, Uncle Sam bicycles to national bankruptcy on an enormous silverite dollar.

silver coinage in favor of the scarcer metal, gold, and thus restrict the amount of money in circulation.

Support for silver coinage was especially strong in the South and West, where people thought it might inflate the currency, raise wages and crop prices, make it cheaper to repay debts, and challenge the power of the gold-oriented Northeast, which favored high prices for its manufactured goods. Eager to avert the so-called free coinage of silver, which would require the U.S. mints to buy all the silver available for coinage, President Harrison and other Republicans pressed for a compromise that took shape in the Sherman Silver Purchase Act of 1890.

The act directed the Treasury to purchase 4.5 million ounces of silver a month and issue legal tender in the form of Treasury notes in payment for it. This satisfied both sides. Opponents of silver were pleased that it did not include free coinage. Silverites were delighted that the monthly purchases would buy up most of the country's silver production. The Treasury notes, moreover, could be cashed for either gold or silver at a bank, a gesture toward a bimetallic coinage system based on silver and gold.

Quick Check

✓ What were the three most important measures of the "Billion-Dollar Congress"?

The 1890 Elections

The Republican Congress of 1890 was one of the most important Congresses in American history. It passed a record number of laws that helped shape later policy and asserted the authority of the federal government to a degree the country would not then accept. Sensing the public unease, the Democrats labeled it the "Billion-Dollar Congress" for spending that much in appropriations and grants.

Quick Check

✓ Why were the 1890 elections among the most important midterm elections in American history?

"This is a billion-dollar country," Speaker of the House Thomas B. Reed of Maine replied, but the voters disagreed. The 1890 elections crushed the Republicans, who lost 78 seats in the House. Political veterans went down to defeat, and new leaders vaulted into prominence. Nebraska elected a Democratic governor for the first time in its history. Iowa, once so staunchly Republican that an Iowa Republican had predicted that "Iowa will go Democratic when Hell goes Methodist," went Democratic in 1890.

THE RISE OF THE POPULIST MOVEMENT

What factors led to the formation and growth of the Farmers' Alliance and People's party?

The elections of 1890 drew attention to a fast-growing movement among farmers that came to be known as populism. That summer, thousands of farm families in the South and West met on campgrounds and picnic areas to socialize and discuss problems. They were weary of drought, mortgages, and low crop prices, and they listened to recruiters from the National Farmers' Alliance and Industrial Union, which promised united action to solve agricultural problems.

One thousand farmers a week were joining the Alliance; the Kansas Alliance alone claimed 130,000 members in 1890. The summer of 1890 became "that wonderful picnicking, speech-making Alliance summer," a time of fellowship and spirit farmers long remembered.

The Farm Problem

Farm discontent was a worldwide phenomenon between 1870 and 1900. The new means of transportation and communication enmeshed farmers everywhere in a complex international market they neither controlled nor entirely understood.

American farmers complained bitterly about declining prices for their products, rising railroad rates to ship them, and burdensome mortgages. Some of their grievances were valid. Farm profits were low; agriculture in general tends to produce low profits because the ease of entry into the industry fosters competition. But even though farmers received less for their crops, their purchasing power actually increased in these years.

The farmers' second grievance—rising railroad rates—was not entirely justified. Railroad rates actually fell during these years, benefiting shippers of all products. Farm mortgages, the farmers' third grievance, were common because many farmers mortgaged their property to expand their holdings or buy new machinery. While certainly burdensome, most mortgages were short, with a term of four years or less, after which farmers could renegotiate at new rates. The new machinery farmers bought enabled them to triple their output and increase their income.

Some farmers did have valid grievances, though many understandably exaggerated them. More important, many farmers felt their condition had declined, and this perception—as bitterly real as any actual fact—sparked a growing anger. Equally upsetting, everyone in the 1870s and 1880s seemed excited about factories, not farms. A literature of disillusionment described the drabness of farm life.

Quick Check

✓ What was the situation of farmers between 1870 and 1900?

The Fast-Growing Farmers' Alliance

By the late 1880s, different farm societies had formed into two major organizations: the National Farmers' Alliance, located on the Plains west of the Mississippi and known as the Northwestern Alliance, and the Farmers' Alliance and Industrial Union, based in the South and known as the Southern Alliance.

The Southern Alliance spread rapidly across the South, where farmers were fed up with crop liens, depleted lands, and sharecropping. In 1890, the Southern Alliance claimed more than a million members. It welcomed the farmers' "natural friends"—country doctors, teachers, preachers, and mechanics. It excluded lawyers, bankers, cotton merchants, and warehouse operators.

Read the **Document** *Proceedings of Grange Session (1879)* on **myhistorylab.com**

The Southern Alliance published its own newspaper and distributed material to hundreds of local newspapers. In five years its lecturers spoke to 2 million farm families in 43 states and territories. It was "the most massive organizing drive by any citizen institution of nineteenth-century America."

Loosely affiliated with the Southern Alliance, a separate Colored Farmers' National Alliance and Cooperative Union enlisted black farmers in the South. Claiming more than 1 million members, it probably had about 250,000, but even that was sizable in an era when "uppity" blacks faced not merely hostility, but death. In 1891, black cotton pickers struck for higher wages in Tennessee. Led by Ben Patterson, a 30-year-old picker, they walked off several plantations. A posse hunted them down and, following violence on both sides, lynched 15 strikers, including Patterson. The abortive strike ended the Colored Farmers' Alliance.

On the Plains, the Northwestern Alliance, a smaller organization, was formed in 1880. Its objectives were similar to those of the Southern Alliance, but it disagreed with the southerners' emphasis on secrecy, centralized control, and separate organizations for blacks. In 1889, the Southern Alliance changed its name to the National Farmers' Alliance and Industrial Union and persuaded the three strongest state alliances on the Plains—those in the Dakotas and Kansas—to join. Thereafter, it dominated the Alliance movement.

The Alliance mainly sponsored social and economic programs, but it turned early

The Farmers' Alliance The Alliance movement grew quickly in the late 1800s among discontented farmers. This photograph shows Southern Alliance members meeting at the site of their first formal meeting in 1877 in Lampasas County, Texas. The cabin was later uprooted and exhibited at the World's Columbian Exposition in Chicago in 1893.

to politics. In the West, its leaders rejected both the Republicans and Democrats and organized their own party; in June 1890, Kansas Alliance members formed the first major People's party. The Southern Alliance resisted forming a new party lest it divide the white vote and undercut white supremacy. Instead, the southerners followed leaders such as Benjamin F. "Pitchfork" Tillman of South Carolina, who wanted to capture control of the dominant Democratic party.

The Alliance leadership was highly qualified. Thomas E. Watson, a talented orator and organizer, urged Georgia farmers, black and white, to unite against their oppressors. The president of the National Farmers' Alliance, Leonidas L. Polk, a former Confederate officer from North Carolina, believed in scientific farming and cooperative action. In Kansas, Mary E. Lease helped head a movement remarkably open to female leadership. A captivating speaker, she made 160 speeches during the summer of 1890, calling on farmers to resist Wall Street and the industrial East.

Read the **Document**
Ocala Platform 1890 on **myhistorylab.com**

Meeting in Ocala, Florida, in 1890, the Alliance adopted the Ocala Demands, a platform the organization pushed as long as it existed. First and foremost, it demanded the creation of a "sub-treasury system," to allow farmers to store their crops in government warehouses. In return, they could claim Treasury notes for up to 80 percent of the local market value of the crop. They would repay this loan when the crops were sold. Farmers could thus hold their crops until they could get the best price. The Ocala Demands also urged the free coinage of silver, an end to protective tariffs and national banks, a federal income tax, the direct election of senators by voters instead of state legislatures, and tighter regulation of railroads.

The Alliance strategy worked well in the elections of 1890. In Kansas, the Alliance-related People's party elected four congressmen (out of eight) and a U.S. senator. Across the South, the Alliance won victories based on the "Alliance yardstick," a demand that Democratic candidates support Alliance measures. Alliance leaders claimed 38 Alliance supporters elected to Congress, with at least a dozen more pledged to Alliance principles.

Quick Check

✔ What brought farmers to join the Farmers' Alliance?

The People's Party

After the 1890 elections, Northern Alliance leaders wanted to form a national third party to promote reform. In July 1892, a convention in Omaha, Nebraska, formed the new People's (or Populist) party. Southern Alliance leaders finally joined, convinced that the Democrats exploited Alliance popularity but failed to adopt its reforms.

In the South, some Populists worked for a time to unite black and white farmers. "They are in the ditch just like we are," a white Texas Populist said. Blacks and whites served on Populist election committees, spoke from the same platforms, and ran on the same tickets. Populist sheriffs called blacks for jury duty, an unheard-of practice in the South.

For president, the Omaha convention nominated James B. Weaver of Iowa, a former congressman, Union army general, and third-party candidate for president in 1880. Weaver won 1,027,329 votes, the first third-party presidential candidate ever to attract more than a million, and 22 electoral votes, a measure of agrarian unrest. The Populists elected governors in Kansas and North Dakota, ten congressmen, five senators, and about 1,500 state legislators.

Despite the Populists' victories, the election brought disappointment. Southern Democrats used intimidation, fraud, and manipulation to hold Weaver to less than a quarter of the vote in every southern state except Alabama. In most of the country, he lost heavily in urban areas except for mining towns in the Far West. He even failed to win over most farmers.

In 1892, many voters did switch parties, but they tended to realign with the Democrats rather than the Populists, whose platform on silver and other issues had little appeal among city dwellers or factory workers. Although the Populists ran candidates in the next three presidential elections, 1892 was their peak. Farmers' Alliance membership dropped. The organization, which was once the breeding ground of the People's party, was broken.

But while it lived, the Alliance was one of the most powerful protest movements in American history. Catalyzing the feelings of hundreds of thousands of farmers, it attempted to solve specific economic problems while advancing a larger vision of harmony and community, in which people who cared about each other were rewarded for what they produced.

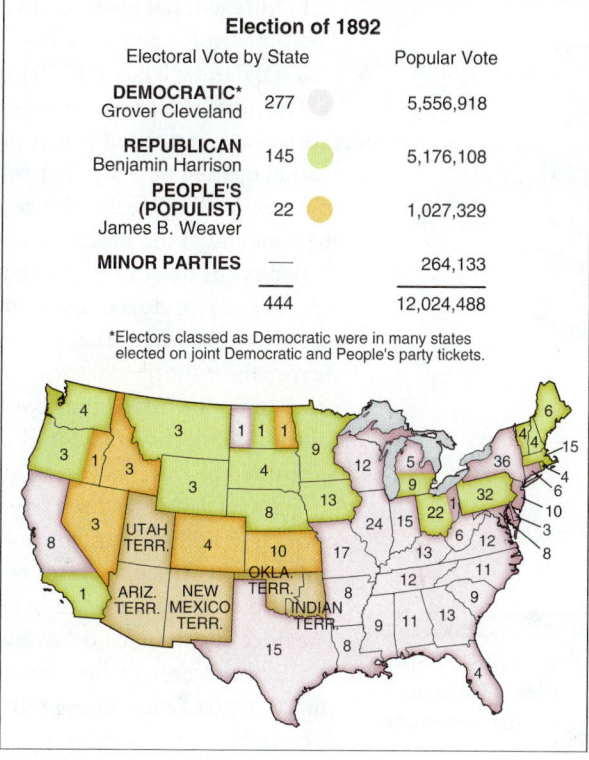

Map 20.2

Quick Check

✓ What happened to the People's party?

THE CRISIS OF THE DEPRESSION

Economic crisis, however, not harmony and community, dominated the 1890s. Responding to the heady forces of industrialization, the American economy had expanded too rapidly in the 1870s and 1880s. Railroads had overbuilt, gambling on future growth. Companies had outgrown their markets; farms and businesses had borrowed heavily for expansion.

What were the main political and labor effects of the panic and depression of the 1890s?

The Panic of 1893

The mood changed in mid-February 1893, when panic suddenly hit the New York stock market. In one day, investors dumped one million shares of the Philadelphia and Reading Railroad, and it went bankrupt. Investment dropped sharply in the railroad and construction industries, touching off the worst economic downturn to that point in the country's history.

Frightened, people sold stocks and other assets to buy gold. On April 22, the Treasury's gold reserve, which represented the government's commitment to the gold standard, fell below $100 million for the first time since the 1870s.

The news shattered business confidence—the stock market broke. On May 3, railroad and industrial stocks plummeted. Major firms went bankrupt. When the market opened on May 5, crowds filled its galleries, anticipating a panic. Within minutes, leading stocks plunged to record lows, and there was pandemonium on the floor and in the streets outside.

Banks cut back on loans. Unable to get capital, businesses failed at an average rate of two dozen a day in May. On July 26, the Erie Railroad, one of the leading names in railroading history, failed. August 1893 was the worst month. Across the country, factories and mines shut down. On August 15, the Northern Pacific Railroad went bankrupt; the Union Pacific and the Santa Fe soon followed. An estimated 2 million people, or nearly 15 percent of the labor force, were unemployed.

The year 1894 was even worse. The gross national product dropped again. By midyear, 3 million workers, one out of every five, were unemployed. A heat wave and drought struck the farm belt west of the Mississippi, creating conditions unmatched until the devastating Dust Bowl of the 1930s. Corn withered in the fields. The price of cotton fell below five cents a pound, far below the break-even point.

People became restless and angry. As one newspaper said in 1896: "On every corner stands a man whose fortune in these dull times has made him an ugly critic of everything and everybody." There was talk of revolution and bloodshed.

Quick Check

✓ What were the effects of the panic and depression after 1893?

The Pullman Strike

The great **Pullman strike**—one of the largest strikes in the country's history—began in May 1894 when the employees of the Pullman Palace Car Company struck to protest wage cuts and layoffs. On June 26, the American Railway Union (ARU) under Eugene V. Debs joined the strike by refusing to handle trains that carried Pullman sleeping cars.

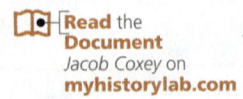

Read the
Document
Jacob Coxey on
myhistorylab.com

Within hours, the strike paralyzed the western half of the nation. Grain and livestock could not reach markets. Factories shut down for lack of coal. The strike extended into 27 states and territories, tying up the economy and renewing talk of class warfare. In Washington, President Grover Cleveland, who had been reelected in 1892, decided to break the strike on the grounds that it obstructed delivery of the mail.

On July 2, he secured a court injunction against the ARU and ordered troops to Chicago, the center of the strike. When they arrived on the morning of Independence Day, the city was peaceful. Before long, however, violence broke out. Mobs, composed mostly of nonstrikers, overturned freight cars, looted, and burned. Restoring order, the army occupied railroad yards in Illinois, California, and other places. By late July, the strike was over; Debs was jailed for violating the injunction.

The Pullman strike had far-reaching consequences for the labor movement. Workers resented Cleveland's actions in the strike, particularly as it became apparent that he sided with the railroads. Upholding Debs's sentence in *In re Debs* (1895), the Supreme Court endorsed the use of the injunction in labor disputes, thus giving business and government an effective antilabor weapon that hindered union growth.

Quick Check

✓ What were the three most important causes and events of the Pullman Strike?

A Beleaguered President

Building on the Democratic party's triumph in the midterm elections of 1890, Grover Cleveland decisively defeated James B. Weaver, and the incumbent president, Benjamin Harrison, in 1892. He won by nearly 400,000 votes, a large margin for the era. The Democrats increased their strength in the cities and among working-class voters. For the first time since the 1850s, they controlled the White House and both branches of Congress.

The Democrats, it now seemed, had broken the party stalemate, but unfortunately for Cleveland, the Panic of 1893 struck almost as he took office. He blamed the Sherman Silver Purchase Act of 1890 for damaging business confidence, draining the Treasury's gold reserve, and causing the panic. The solution to the depression was simple: Repeal the act.

View the **Image**
Grover Cleveland on **myhistorylab.com**

In June 1893, Cleveland summoned Congress into special session. British-ruled India had just closed its mints to silver. Mexico was now the only country with free silver coinage. The silverites pleaded for a compromise. But Cleveland pushed the repeal bill through Congress, and on November 1, 1893, he signed it into law. Always sure of himself, he had staked everything on a single measure—a winning strategy if he succeeded, a devastating one if he did not.

Repeal of the Sherman Silver Purchase Act was probably necessary. It responded to the realities of international finance, reduced the flight of gold out of the country, and, over the long run, boosted business confidence. But in the short term, it contracted the currency and led to deflation at a time when inflation might have helped. The stock market remained listless, businesses continued to close, unemployment spread, and farm prices dropped. "We are hourly expecting the arrival of the benevolent man who is to pay ten cents a pound for cotton," a Virginia newspaper said.

By discrediting the conservative Democrats who had dominated the party since the 1860s, the repeal battle of 1893 reshaped politics. It confined the Democratic party largely to the South, helped the Republicans become the majority party in 1894, and strengthened the silver Democrats in their bid for the presidency in 1896. It also focused national attention on the silver issue and thus intensified the sentiment for silver that Cleveland had intended to dampen. Repeal did not even solve the Treasury's gold problem. By January 1894, the reserve had fallen to $65 million. A year later, it was $44.5 million.

The Democrats' morale fell further when they failed to reduce the tariff. Despite their efforts, the Wilson-Gorman Tariff Act in August 1894 reduced duties only modestly. It also imposed a small income tax, a provision the Supreme Court overturned in 1895 (*Pollock v. Farmer's Loan and Trust Co.*). Few Democrats, including Cleveland, were pleased with the measure. The president let it become law without his signature.

Quick Check

✓ How did President Grover Cleveland respond to the difficult events of the 1890s?

Breaking the Party Deadlock

The elections of 1894 crushed the Democrats. In the greatest defeat in congressional history, they lost 113 House seats, while the Republicans gained 117. In 24 states, not one Democrat was elected to Congress. Only one Democrat (Boston's John F. Fitzgerald, the grandfather of President John F. Kennedy) came from all of New England. The Democrats even lost some of the "solid South." In the Midwest, a crucial battleground, the party was virtually destroyed.

Wooing labor and the unemployed, the Populists gained in the South and West. Yet in a year in which thousands of voters switched parties, the People's party elected only four senators and four congressmen. Southern Democrats again used fraud and violence to keep the Populists' totals down. In the Midwest, the Populists won double the number of votes they had received in 1892, yet still attracted less than 7 percent of the vote. Across the country, the discontented tended to vote for the Republicans, not the Populists, a discouraging sign for the Populist party.

For millions of people, Grover Cleveland became a scapegoat for the country's economic ills. Fearing attack, he placed police barracks on the White House grounds. The Democratic party split. Southern and western Democrats deserted him.

The elections of 1894 broke the party deadlock that had existed since the 1870s. The Democrats lost, the Populists gained somewhat, and the Republicans became the majority party in the country. In the midst of the depression, the Republican doctrines of activism and national authority, which voters had repudiated in 1890, became more attractive. As Americans became more accepting of the use of government power to regulate the economy and safeguard individual welfare, the way lay open to the reforms of the Progressive Era, the New Deal, and beyond.

Quick Check

✓ What was the outcome and significance of the midterm elections of 1894?

CHANGING ATTITUDES

What changes in outlook did the panic and depression of the 1890s bring about?

The depression, brutal and far-reaching, did more than shift political alignments. Across the country, it undermined traditional views about government, the economy, and society. As men and women concluded that established ideas had failed to deal with the depression, they looked for new ones.

In prosperous times, Americans had thought of unemployment as a personal failure, affecting primarily the lazy and immoral. In the depression, such views were harder to hold. Everyone knew people who were both worthy and unemployed.

People debated issues they had long taken for granted. New and reinvigorated local institutions—discussion clubs, women's clubs, reform societies, university extension centers, church groups, farmers' societies—gave people a place to discuss alternatives to the existing order. Pressures for reform increased, and demand grew for government intervention to help the poor and unemployed.

Women and Children in the Labor Force

Women and children had been entering the labor force for years, and the depression accelerated the trend. As husbands and fathers lost their jobs, more women and children went to work. Even as late as 1901, well after the depression had ended, a study of working-class families showed that more than half the principal breadwinners were out of work. So many women and children worked that "Everybody Works But Father" was a popular song in 1905.

During the 1890s, the number of working women rose from 4 million to 5.3 million. To make ends meet, they took in boarders and worked as laundresses, cleaners, and domestics or in offices and factories. More black urban women than white worked to supplement their husbands' meager earnings. Men still dominated business offices, but during the 1890s, more employers noted that female labor was cheaper. The number of women telegraph and telephone operators nearly tripled during the decade. Women worked as clerks in the new five-and-tens and department stores, and as nurses; in 1900, 500,000 were teachers. They became stenographers and typists in offices.

The depression also caused more children to work. During the 1890s, the number of children in southern textile mills jumped more than 160 percent. Boys and girls under 16 years old were nearly one-third of the mills' labor force. Youngsters of 8 and 9 years worked 12 hours a day for pitiful wages. However, most children worked in farming and on city streets as peddlers and shoe shiners.

Concerned about child labor, middle-class women in 1896 formed the League for the Protection of the Family, which called for compulsory education to get children out of factories and into classrooms. The Mothers Congress of 1896 gave rise to the National Congress of Parents and Teachers, the spawning ground of thousands of local Parent–Teacher Associations. The National Council of Women and the General Federation of Women's Clubs took up similar issues. By the late 1890s, the Federation had 150,000 members who worked for reforms in child welfare, education, and sanitation.

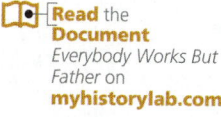

Read the
Document
Everybody Works But Father on
myhistorylab.com

Quick Check

✓ In what ways did the depression of the 1890s affect women and children?

Changing Themes in Literature

The depression also gave point to a growing movement in literature toward realism and naturalism. In the years after the Civil War, literature was often sentimental and unrealistic. Horatio Alger's novels about poor boys who succeeded through hard work, thrift, honesty, and luck attracted many readers. Louisa May Alcott's *Little Women* (1868–1869) related the daily lives of four girls in a New England family, and Anna Sewell's *Black Beauty* (1877) charmed readers with the story of an abused horse that found a happy home.

After the 1870s, however, talented authors began to reject romanticism and escapism, turning instead to realism. Determined to portray life as it was, they studied local dialects, wrote regional stories, and emphasized "true" relationships between people. This reflected broader social trends, such as industrialism; evolutionary theory, which emphasized the effect of the environment on humans; and pragmatism, which stressed the relativity of values.

Regionalist authors such as Joel Chandler Harris and George Washington Cable depicted life in the South. Hamlin Garland described the grimness of life on the Great Plains. Sarah Orne Jewett wrote about everyday life in rural New England. Another regionalist, Bret Harte, achieved fame with stories about the California mining camps, particularly in his popular tale "The Outcasts of Poker Flat."

Mark Twain became the country's most outstanding realist author. Growing up along the Mississippi River in Missouri, the young Samuel Langhorne Clemens observed life with a humorous and skeptical eye. Adopting a pen name from the river term "mark twain" (two fathoms), his works drew on his own experiences. In *The Adventures of Tom Sawyer* (1876) and *The Adventures of Huckleberry Finn* (1884), Twain used dialect and common speech instead of literary language, a technique that changed American prose style.

Other writers, the naturalists, became impatient even with realism. Pushing Darwinian theory to its limits, they wrote of a world in which a merciless environment determined human fate. Often focusing on economic hardship, naturalist writers studied the poor, the lower classes, and the criminal mind; they brought to their writing the social worker's passion for direct and honest experience.

Stephen Crane spent a night in a seven-cent lodging house on the Bowery in New York City and in "An Experiment in Misery" captured the smells and sounds of the poor. Crane depicted the carnage of war in *The Red Badge of Courage* (1895) and the impact of poverty in *Maggie: A Girl of the Streets* (1893). Jack London, another naturalist author, traced the power of nature over civilized society in *The Sea Wolf* (1904) and *The Call of the Wild* (1903), his classic tale of a sled dog that preferred the harsh wilderness to the world of human beings.

Theodore Dreiser, the foremost naturalist writer, portrayed human beings tossed about by forces beyond their understanding or control. In *Sister Carrie* (1901), he followed the moral decline of a young farm girl who takes an exhausting job in a Chicago shoe factory, is seduced by men, and embarks on a successful but morally bankrupt career.

Like other naturalists, Dreiser focused on environment and character. He thought writers should tell the truth about human affairs, not fabricate romance. *Sister Carrie*, he said, was "not intended as a piece of literary craftsmanship, but was a picture of conditions."

Quick Check

✓ What were some of the major changes in literature during these years?

THE PRESIDENTIAL ELECTION OF 1896

The election of 1896 was known as the "battle of the standards" because it focused primarily on the gold versus silver standards of money. It was exciting and decisive. New voting patterns replaced old, a new majority party confirmed its dominance, and national policy shifted to suit new realities.

Why was the presidential election of 1896 so important?

The Mystique of Silver

Support for free silver coinage grew swiftly after 1894, dominating the South and West, appearing even in the farming regions of New York and New England. Pro-silver literature flooded the country. Pamphlets issued by the millions argued silver's virtues.

People wanted quick solutions to the economic crisis. During 1896, unemployment shot up, and farm income and prices fell to the lowest point in the decade. "I can remember back as far as 1858," an Iowa hardware dealer said in February

1896, "and I have never seen such hard times as these are." Prosilver people offered a solution, simple but compelling: the free and independent coinage of silver at the ratio of 16 ounces of silver to every ounce of gold. Free coinage meant that the U.S. mints would coin all the silver offered for sale to them. Independent coinage meant that the country would coin silver regardless of the policies of other nations, nearly all of which were on the gold standard.

It is difficult now to understand the faith the silverites placed in silver as a cure for the depression. But faith it was, and observers compared it to religious fervor. Underlying it all was a belief in a quantity theory of money: The silverites believed the amount of money in circulation determined the level of activity in the economy. If money was short, that meant there was a limit on economic activity and ultimately a depression. Coining silver and gold meant more money in circulation, more business for everyone, and thus prosperity. Farm prices would rise; laborers would find work.

By 1896, silver was also a symbol. It had moral and patriotic dimensions—by going to a silver standard, the United States could assert its independence in the world—and it stood for a wide range of popular grievances. For many, it reflected rural values rather than urban ones, would shift power away from the Northeast, and favored the downtrodden instead of the well-to-do.

Silver was more than just a political or economic issue. It was a social movement, one of the largest in American history, but its life span turned out to be brief. As a mass phenomenon, it flourished between 1894 and 1896, then succumbed to electoral defeat, the return of prosperity, and the onset of fresh concerns. But in its time, the silver movement bespoke a national mood and won millions of followers.

> **Quick Check**
> ✓ Why did so many people believe in silver?

The Republicans and Gold

Scenting victory over the discredited Democrats, numerous Republicans fought for the party's presidential nomination, including a Republican favorite, William McKinley of Ohio.

Able, calm, and affable, McKinley had served in the Union army during the Civil War. In 1876, he won a seat in Congress, where he became the chief sponsor of the tariff act named for him. Marcus A. Hanna, his campaign manager and friend, built a powerful national organization that featured McKinley as "the advance agent of prosperity," an alluring slogan during a depression. When the Republican convention met in June, McKinley had the nomination in hand. He backed a platform that favored the gold standard against the free coinage of silver.

Republicans favoring silver proposed a prosilver platform, but the convention overwhelmingly defeated it. Twenty-three silverite Republicans, far fewer than prosilver forces had hoped, marched out of the convention hall. The remaining delegates waved handkerchiefs and flags and shouted "Good-bye" and "Put them out." Hanna stood on a chair screaming "Go! Go! Go!" William Jennings Bryan, who was there as a special correspondent for a Nebraska newspaper, climbed on a desk to get a better view.

> **Quick Check**
> ✓ How did McKinley gain the presidential nomination?

A Crucial Election This cartoon satirizes the religious symbolism in Bryan's "Cross of Gold" speech, but his stirring rhetoric captivated his audience and won him the Democratic presidential nomination in 1896.

The Democrats and Silver

Silver, meanwhile, had captured large segments of the Democratic party in the South and West. Despite President Cleveland's opposition, more than 20 Democratic state platforms called for free silver in 1894. Power in the party shifted to the South, where it remained for decades. The party's base narrowed; its outlook increasingly reflected southern views on silver, race, and other issues. In effect, the Democrats became a sectional—no longer a national—party.

The anti-Cleveland Democrats had their issue, but they lacked a leader. Out in Nebraska, William Jennings Bryan, a young former congressman, saw the opportunity to take on that role. He was barely 36 years old and had relatively little political experience. But he had spent months wooing support, and he was a captivating public speaker—tall, slender, and handsome, with a resounding voice that, in an era without microphones, projected easily into every corner of an auditorium.

The silver Democrats were in charge of the 1896 Democratic convention. Their platform stunned the party's Cleveland wing. It demanded the free coinage of silver, attacked Cleveland's actions in the Pullman strike, and censured his sales of gold bonds. On July 9, as delegates debated the platform, Bryan's moment came. Striding to the stage, he raised a hand for silence, waiting for the applause to die down. He would not contend with the previous speakers, he began, for "this is not a contest between persons. The humblest citizen in all the land, when clad in the armor of a righteous cause, is stronger than all the hosts of error. I come to speak to you in defense of a cause as holy as the cause of liberty—the cause of humanity."

The delegates were captivated. Like a trained choir, they rose, cheered each point, and sat back to listen for more. Easterners, Bryan said, liked to praise businessmen but forgot that plain people—laborers, miners, and farmers—were businessmen, too. Shouts rang through the hall, and delegates pounded on chairs. Savoring each cheer, Bryan defended silver. Then came the famous closing: "Having behind us the producing masses of this nation and the world . . . we will answer their demand for a gold standard by saying to them: 'You shall not press down upon the brow of labor this crown of thorns, you shall not crucify mankind upon a cross of gold.'"

Read the **Document**
William Jennings Bryan, "Cross of Gold" Speech (1896) on **myhistorylab.com**

Bryan moved his fingers down his temples, suggesting blood trickling from his wounds. He ended with his arms outstretched as on a cross. Letting the silence hang, he dropped his arms, stepped back, then started to his seat. Suddenly, there was pandemonium. Delegates shouted and cheered. When the tumult subsided, they adopted the anti-Cleveland platform, and the next day, Bryan won the presidential nomination.

Quick Check

✓ What won William Jennings Bryan the Democratic nomination in 1896?

Campaign and Election

The Democratic convention presented the Populists with a dilemma. The People's party had assumed that neither major party would endorse silver. Now it faced a painful choice: Nominate an independent ticket and split the silverite forces, or nominate Bryan and give up its separate identity as a party.

View the **Closer Look**
Republican Campaign Poster of 1896, William McKinley on
myhistorylab.com

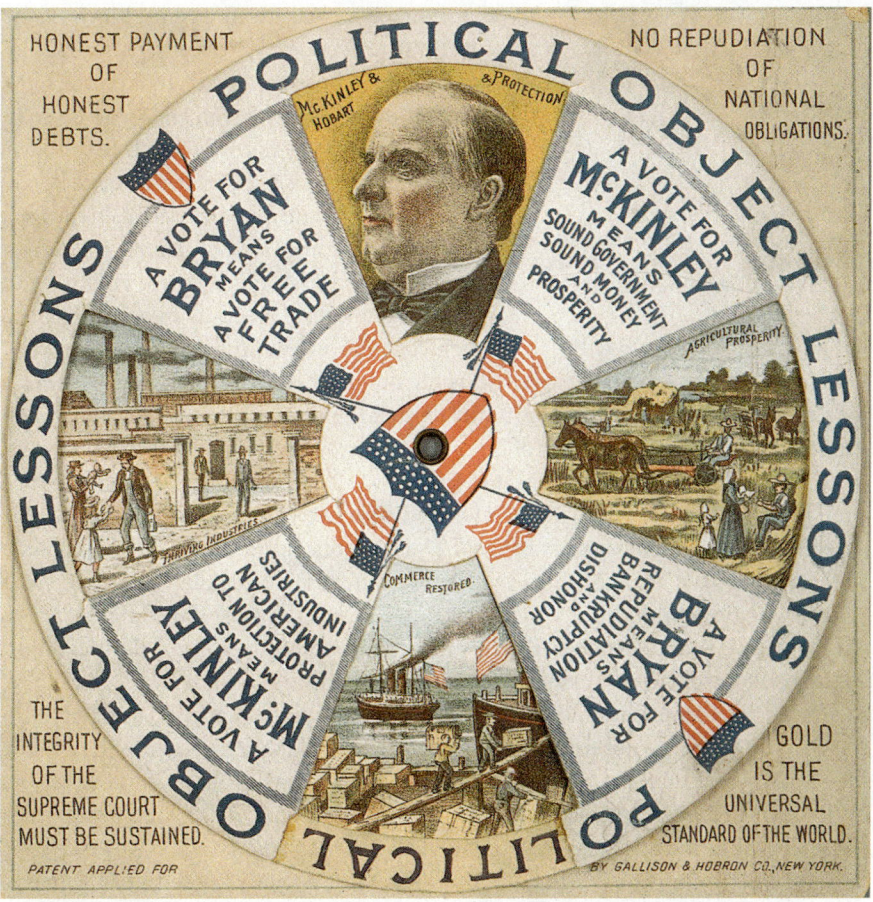

Political Conflict in 1896 This campaign card from the 1896 presidential election predicts that Republican candidate William McKinley's protariff, protectionist policy will lead to prosperity and thriving industrialism while Democratic candidate William Jennings Bryan's free trade and free silver policies will lead to economic ruin.

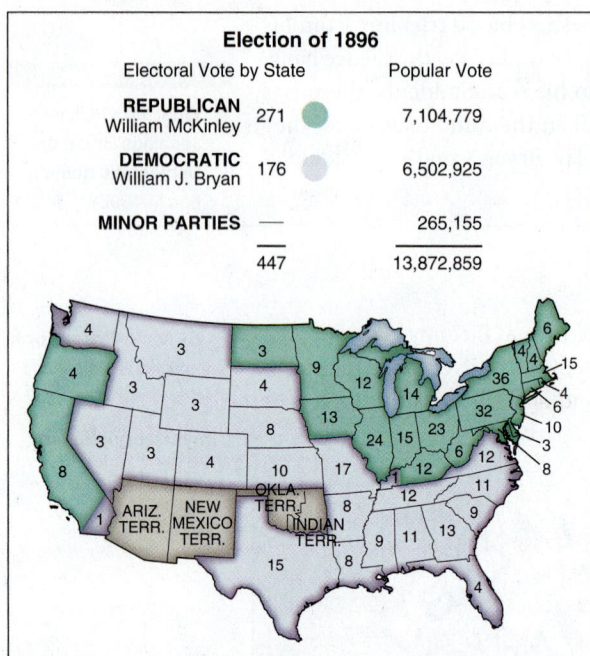

Election of 1896

	Electoral Vote by State		Popular Vote
REPUBLICAN William McKinley	271		7,104,779
DEMOCRATIC William J. Bryan	176		6,502,925
MINOR PARTIES	—		265,155
	447		13,872,859

Map 20.3 This map illustrates McKinley's victories over a large swatch of states in the North, Midwest and Pacific Coast. It also shows the greater reach of the Democratic party under William Jennings Bryan, though the states he carried in the West tended to have few electoral votes.

The choice shattered the People's party. Its convention nominated Bryan, but rather than accept the Democratic candidate for vice president, it named Tom Watson instead. The Populists' endorsement probably hurt Bryan as much as it helped. It won him relatively few votes, since many Populists would have voted for him anyway. It also identified him as a Populist, which he was not, allowing the Republicans to accuse him of heading a ragtag army of malcontents. The squabble over Watson seemed to prove that the Democratic–Populist alliance could never stay together long enough to govern.

In August 1896, Bryan's set off on a campaign that became an American legend. Much of the conservative Democratic eastern press had deserted him. So he went directly to the voters, the first presidential candidate in history to do so in a systematic way. By his own count, Bryan traveled 18,009 miles, visited 27 states, and spoke 600 times to 3 million people. He built skillfully on a new "merchandising" style of campaign in which he worked to educate and persuade voters.

Bryan summoned voters to an older America, where farms were as important as factories, where the virtues of rural and religious life outweighed the lure of the city, where common people ruled, and opportunity existed for all. He drew on the Jeffersonian tradition of rural virtue, distrust of central authority, and faith in human reason.

Urged to take the stump against Bryan, McKinley replied, "I might just as well put up a trapeze on my front lawn and compete with some professional athlete as go out speaking against Bryan." The Republican candidate let voters come to him. Railroads brought them by the thousands into McKinley's hometown of Canton, Ohio, and he spoke to them from his front porch. Through the press, he reached as many people as Bryan's more strenuous effort. Appealing to labor, immigrants, well-to-do farmers, businessmen, and the middle class, McKinley defended economic nationalism and the advancing urban-industrial society.

On election day, voter turnout was extraordinarily high, a measure of the intense interest. By nightfall, the outcome was clear: McKinley won 50 percent of the vote to Bryan's 46 percent. He won the Northeast and Midwest and carried four border states. In the cities, McKinley crushed Bryan. (See Map 20.3.)

The election struck down the Populists, whose totals sagged nearly everywhere. Many Populist proposals were later adopted under different leadership. The graduated income tax, crop loans to farmers, the secret ballot, and direct election of U.S. senators all were early Populist ideas. But the People's party never could win a majority of the voters, and failing that, it vanished after 1896.

Quick Check

✓ What were the most important results of the 1896 election?

THE MCKINLEY ADMINISTRATION

The election of 1896 cemented the voter realignment of 1894 and initiated a generation of Republican rule. For more than three decades after 1896, with only a brief Democratic resurgence under Woodrow Wilson, the Republicans remained the country's majority party.

McKinley took office in 1897 under favorable circumstances. To everyone's relief, the economy had begun to revive. The stock market rose, factories again churned out goods, and farmers prospered. Farm prices climbed sharply during 1897 on bumper crops of wheat, cotton, and corn. Gold discoveries in Australia and Alaska—together with a new cyanide process for extracting gold from ore—enlarged the world's gold supply, decreased its price, and inflated the currency as the silverites had hoped. For the first time since 1890, the 1897 Treasury statements showed a comfortable gold reserve.

McKinley and the Republicans basked in the glow. They became the party of progress and prosperity, an image that helped them win victories until another depression hit in the 1930s. McKinley's popularity soared. An activist president, he set the policies of the administration. Conscious of the limits of power, he maintained close ties with Congress and worked to educate the public on national choices and priorities. McKinley established new relations with the press and traveled far more than previous presidents. In some ways, he began the modern presidency.

Shortly after taking office, he summoned Congress into special session to revise the tariff. In July 1897, the Dingley Tariff raised average tariff duties to a record level. As the final burst of nineteenth-century protectionism, it caused trouble for the Republican party. By the end of the 1890s, consumers, critics, and the Republicans themselves were questioning the tariff's usefulness in the maturing American economy.

From the 1860s to the 1890s, the Republicans had built their party on a pledge to *promote* economic growth through the use of state and national power. By 1900, with the industrial system firmly in place, the focus had shifted. The need to *regulate*, to control the effects of industrialism, became a central public concern. McKinley prodded the Republicans to meet that shift, but he died before his plans matured.

McKinley toyed with lowering the tariff, but one obstacle stood in the way: The government needed revenue, and tariff duties were one of the few taxes the public would support. The Spanish–American War of 1898 persuaded people to accept greater federal power and, with it, new forms of taxation. In 1899, McKinley spoke of lowering tariff barriers in a world that technology had made smaller. "God and man have linked the nations together," he said in his last speech at Buffalo, New York, in 1901. "Isolation is no longer possible or desirable."

In 1898 and 1899, the McKinley administration focused on the war with Spain, the peace treaty that followed, and the dawning realization that the war had made the United States a world power. In March 1900, Congress passed the Gold Standard Act, which declared gold the standard of currency and ended the silver controversy that had dominated the 1890s.

The presidential campaign of 1900 replayed the McKinley–Bryan fight of 1896. McKinley's running mate was Theodore Roosevelt, hero of the Spanish–American

What did McKinley accomplish that placed the results of the 1896 election on a solid basis?

TABLE 20.3	The Election of 1900		
Candidate	**Party**	**Popular Vote**	**Electoral Vote**
McKinley	Republican	7,207,923	292
Bryan	Democrat	6,358,133	155
Woolley	Prohibition	209,004	0
Debs	Socialist	94,768	0

War and governor of New York, who was nominated for vice president to capitalize on his popularity and, his enemies hoped, to sidetrack his political career into oblivion. Bryan stressed imperialism and the trusts; McKinley stressed his record at home and abroad. The result in 1900 was a landslide. (See Table 20.3.)

On September 6, 1901, six months after his second inauguration, McKinley stood in a receiving line at the Pan-American Exposition in Buffalo, New York. Leon Czolgosz, a 28-year-old unemployed laborer and anarchist, moved through the line and, reaching the president, shot him. Surgeons probed the wound but could find nothing. A recent discovery called the X ray was on display at the exposition, but it was not used. On September 14, McKinley died, and Vice President Theodore Roosevelt became president. A new century had begun.

CONCLUSION: A DECADE'S DRAMATIC CHANGES

As the funeral train carried McKinley's body back to Ohio, Mark Hanna, McKinley's old friend and ally, sat slumped in his parlor car. "I told William McKinley it was a mistake to nominate that wild man at Philadelphia," he mourned. "I asked him if he realized what would happen if he should die. Now look, that damned cowboy is president of the United States!"

Hanna's world had changed, and so had the nation's—not so much because "that damned cowboy" was suddenly president, but because events in the 1890s had powerful effects. In the course of that decade, political patterns shifted, the presidency acquired fresh power, and massive unrest prompted social change. The war with Spain brought a new empire and worldwide responsibilities. Economic hardship posed difficult questions about industrialization, urbanization, and the quality of American life. Worried, people embraced new ideas and causes. Reform movements begun in the 1890s flowered in the Progressive Era after 1900.

Technology continued to alter how Americans lived. In 1896, Henry Ford produced a two-cylinder, four-horsepower car, the first of the famous line that bore his name. In 1899, the first automobile salesroom opened in New York, and some innovative thinkers were already imagining a network of service stations to keep the new cars running. At Kitty Hawk, North Carolina, Wilbur and Orville Wright, two bicycle manufacturers, neared the birth of powered flight.

The realignments that peaked in the 1890s seem distant, yet decisions in those years shaped nearly everything that followed them. In character and influence, the 1890s still have repercussions in the twenty-first century.

20 STUDY RESOURCES

((•—Listen to the **Chapter Audio** for Chapter 20 on **myhistorylab.com**

TIMELINE

1876 Mark Twain publishes *The Adventures of Tom Sawyer*, p. 514

1877 Disputed election of 1876 awards presidency to Republican Rutherford B. Hayes, p. 503

1880 Republican James A. Garfield elected president, p. 503

1881 Garfield assassinated; Vice President Chester A. Arthur becomes president, p. 503

1884 Democrat Grover Cleveland elected president, p. 504

1888 Republican Benjamin Harrison elected president, p. 504

1889 National Farmers' Alliance and Industrial Union formed, p. 506

1890 Republican "Billion-Dollar" Congress enacts McKinley Tariff Act, Sherman Antitrust Act, and Sherman Silver Purchase Act, p. 504
  • Farmers' Alliance adopts the Ocala Demands, p. 508

1892 Grover Cleveland regains presidency, p. 509
  • People's party formed, p. 508

1893 Financial panic touches off depression lasting until 1897, p. 501
  • Sherman Silver Purchase Act repealed, p. 505

1894 Pullman strike, p. 510

1896 Republican William McKinley defeats William Jennings Bryan, Democratic and Populist candidate, in "battle of the standards," p. 514

1897 Gold discovered in Alaska, p. 519
  • Dingley Tariff Act raises duties, p. 519

1900 McKinley reelected, p. 519
  • Gold Standard Act establishes gold as standard of currency, p. 519

1901 McKinley assassinated; Theodore Roosevelt becomes president, p. 520
  • Theodore Dreiser publishes *Sister Carrie*, p. 514

CHAPTER REVIEW

POLITICS OF STALEMATE

Why was there a stalemate between Republicans and Democrats until the mid-1890s?

For more than two decades after Reconstruction, there was a stalemate, in which the Democrats and Republicans fought for votes and focused on a handful of "doubtful" states. In general, Democrats dominated the South, and Republicans controlled crucial sections of the North. Presidents reestablished the authority of their office. *(p. 501)*

REPUBLICANS IN POWER: THE BILLION-DOLLAR CONGRESS

How did the Republican party's vision shape the "Billion-Dollar Congress"?

In control of both the presidency and Congress after 1888, Republicans enacted their activist policies, only to discover that voters were not ready for them. The congressional elections of 1890 restored the Democrats to power. *(p. 504)*

THE RISE OF THE POPULIST MOVEMENT

What factors led to the formation and growth of the Farmers' Alliance and People's party?

In the late 1880s and early 1890s, farmers in the South and West joined the Farmers' Alliance, and later the People's party. The People's party failed, as voters turned to the Democrats in the presidential election of 1892. *(p. 506)*

THE CRISIS OF THE DEPRESSION

What were the main political and labor effects of the panic and depression of the 1890s?

The depression encouraged people to rethink their views on the causes of poverty and unemployment. It discredited President Cleveland and crushed the Democrats in the midterm elections of 1894, giving the Republican party a long-term lease on power. *(p. 509)*

CHANGING ATTITUDES

What changes in outlook did the panic and depression of the 1890s bring about?

The depression led people to reconsider the roles of the government, the economy, and society. They had once thought that people lost their jobs because of their own failings; now they knew that economic forces were at fault. People joined organizations like women's clubs, church groups, and farm societies to discuss cures for the situation. More women and children worked. Realism and naturalism dominated American literature. *(p. 512)*

THE PRESIDENTIAL ELECTION OF 1896

Why was the presidential election of 1896 so important?

The election of 1896 brought to a head the fight between supporters of silver and gold, established the Republicans as the majority party, and shaped the nation's politics until 1932. *(p. 514)*

THE MCKINLEY ADMINISTRATION

What did McKinley accomplish that placed the results of the 1896 election on a solid basis?

The McKinley administration profited from economic recovery. It enacted the gold standard, passed a new tariff, and defeated Spain. How to *regulate* big business instead of simply promoting it became a new challenge. *(p. 519)*

KEY TERM QUESTIONS

1. How did the Bland–Allison Silver Purchase Act try to satisfy supporters of both gold and silver coinage? (p. 503)

2. How did the Pendleton Act begin to reform the Civil Service (p. 503)

3. Why is the Sherman Antitrust Act so important? (p. 504)

4. How did the Sherman Silver Purchase Act attempt to resolve the argument over gold versus silver coinage? (p. 505)

5. Why did farmers join the National Farmers' Alliance and Industrial Union? (p. 506)

6. Which of the Ocala Demands were enacted? (p. 508)

7. Why did the People's (or Populist) party disintegrate by 1892? (p. 508)

8. What were the most important causes of the Pullman strike? (p. 510)

9. How did the Gold Standard Act affect U.S. monetary policy? (p. 519)

MyHistoryLab Connections

Visit **www.myhistorylab.com** for a customized Study Plan to build your knowledge of *Political Realignments*

Questions for Analysis

1. In what states were women not voting at all prior to the Nineteenth Amendment?

   View the **Map** *Woman Suffrage Before the Nineteenth Amendment?* p. 501

2. What were some of the injustices experienced by farmers in the late Nineteenth Century?

   Read the **Document** *Proceedings of the Thirteenth Session of the National Grange of the Patrons of Husbandry (1879)* p. 507

3. What were some of the demands of the Ocala Platform?

   Read the **Document** *Ocala Platform, 1890* p. 508

4. Why did William Jennings Bryan's "Cross of Gold" speech captivate the audience?

   Read the **Document** *William Jennings Bryan, "Cross of Gold" Speech (1896)* p. 516

5. How did the expansion of the railroads and rapid growth of industry excite national politics in the late Nineteenth Century?

   View the **Closer Look** *Republican Campaign Poster of 1896, William McKinley* p. 517

Other Resources from this Chapter

Read the **Document** *Jacob Coxey*

View the **Image** *Grover Cleveland*

Read the **Document** *Everybody Works But Father*

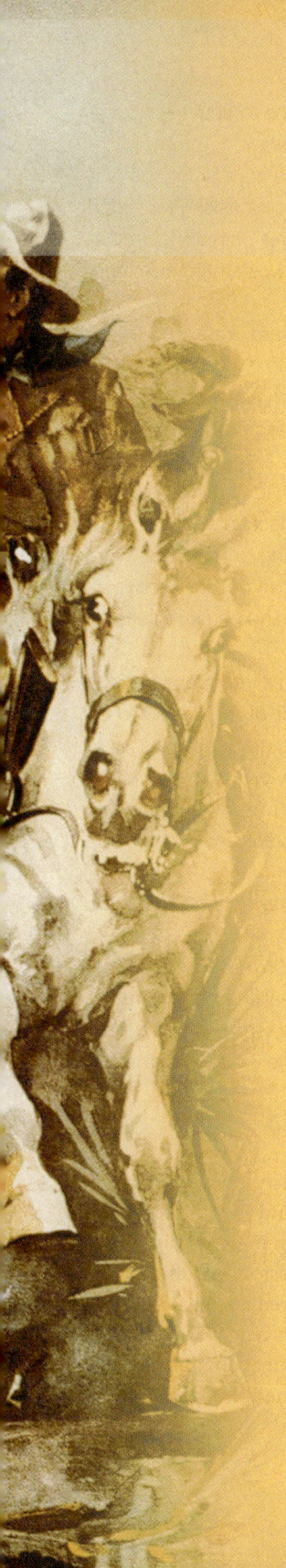

Contents and Spotlight Questions

((•—[**Listen** to the **Chapter Audio** for Chapter 21 on **myhistorylab.com**

ROOSEVELT AND THE ROUGH RIDERS

Many Americans regretted the start of the war with Spain that began in April 1898, but many others welcomed it. Many highly respected people believed that nations must fight every now and then to prove their power and test their spirit.

Theodore Roosevelt, 39 years old in 1898, was one of them. Nations needed to fight in order to survive, he thought. Roosevelt argued strenuously for war with Spain for three reasons: first, to free Cuba and expel Spain from the hemisphere; second, because of "the benefit done to our people by giving them something to think of which isn't material gain"; and third, because the army and navy needed the practice.

In 1898, Roosevelt was serving in the important post of assistant secretary of the navy. When war broke out, he resigned to join the army, rejecting the advice of Secretary of the Navy John Long, who warned he would only "ride a horse and brush mosquitoes from his neck in the Florida

TR and the Rough Riders in Action A blend of Ivy League athletes and Western frontiersmen, the Rough Riders, became the most famous military unit in the war.

sands." Long was wrong—dead wrong—and later had the grace to admit it: "Roosevelt was right. His going into the Army led straight to the Presidency."

Roosevelt chose to enlist his own regiment. After telephone calls to friends and telegrams to the governors of Arizona, New Mexico, and Oklahoma asking for "good shots and good riders," he had more than enough men. The First United States Volunteer Cavalry, an intriguing mixture of Ivy League athletes and western frontiersmen, was born.

Known as the Rough Riders, it included men from the Harvard, Yale, and Princeton clubs of New York City, the Somerset Club of Boston, and New York's exclusive Knickerbocker Club. Former college athletes—football players, tennis players, and track stars—enlisted. Woodbury Kane, a wealthy yachtsman, signed up and volunteered for kitchen duty.

Other volunteers came from the West—natural soldiers, Roosevelt called them, "tall and sinewy, with resolute, weather-beaten faces, and eyes that looked a man straight in the face without flinching." Among the cowboys, hunters, and prospectors were Bucky O'Neill, a legendary Arizona sheriff and Indian fighter; a half dozen other sheriffs and Texas Rangers; many Indians; a famous broncobuster; and an ex-marshal of Dodge City, Kansas.

Eager for war, the men trained hard, played harder, and rarely passed up a chance for an intellectual discussion—if Roosevelt's memoir of the war is to be believed. Once, he overhead Bucky O'Neill and a Princeton graduate "discussing Aryan word roots together, and then sliding off into a review of the novels of Balzac, and a discussion as to how far Balzac could be said to be the founder of the modern realistic school of fiction." Discipline was lax, and enlisted men got on easily with the officers.

The troops howled with joy when orders came to join the invasion army for Cuba. They set sail on June 14, 1898, and Lieutenant Colonel Roosevelt, who had performed a war dance for the troops the night before, caught their mood: "We knew not whither we were bound, nor what we were to do; but we believed that the nearing future held for us many chances of death and hardship, of honor and renown. If we failed, we would share the fate of all who fail; but we were sure that we would win, that we should score the first great triumph in a mighty world-movement."

That "world-movement," Roosevelt was sure, would establish the United States as a world power, whose commerce and influence would extend around the globe, particularly in Latin America and Asia. As he hoped, the nation in the 1890s underwent dramatic expansion, building on the foreign policy decisions of administrations from Lincoln to William McKinley. Policymakers fostered business interests abroad, strengthened the navy, and extended American influence into Latin America and the Pacific. Differences over Cuba resulted in a war with Spain that brought new colonies and colonial subjects, establishing for the first time an American overseas empire.

AMERICA LOOKS OUTWARD

The overseas expansion of the 1890s differed in several important respects from earlier expansion. From its beginning, the American republic had been expanding. After the first landings in Jamestown and Plymouth, settlers pushed westward: into the trans-Appalachian region, the Louisiana Territory, Florida, Texas, California, Arizona, and New Mexico. Most of these lands were contiguous with United States territory, and most were intended for settlement, usually agricultural.

The expansion of the 1890s was different. It involved island possessions, most of them already thickly populated. The new territories were intended less for settlement than for use as naval bases, trading outposts, or commercial centers on major trade routes. Most were viewed as colonies, not as states-in-the-making.

Historian Samuel F. Bemis described the overseas expansion of the 1890s as "the great aberration," a time when the country adopted expansionist policies that did not fit with its history. Other historians, pointing to expansionist tendencies in thought and foreign policy that surfaced during the last half of the nineteenth century, have found a developing pattern that led naturally to the overseas adventures of the 1890s. In the view of Walter LaFeber, "the United States did not set out on an expansionist path in the late 1890s in a sudden, spur-of-the-moment fashion. The overseas empire that Americans controlled in 1900 was not a break in their history, but a natural culmination."

Catching the Spirit of Empire

Throughout history, most people have tended to focus on domestic concerns, and after the Civil War, Americans were no exception. Among other things, they focused on Reconstruction, the movement westward, and simply making a living. Throughout the nineteenth century, Americans enjoyed "free security" without fully appreciating it. Sheltered by two oceans and the British navy, they could enunciate bold policies such as the Monroe Doctrine, which instructed European nations to stay out of the affairs of the Western Hemisphere, while remaining virtually impregnable to foreign attack.

In those circumstances a sense of isolationism spread, fostering a desire to avoid foreign entanglements. Some people even wanted to abolish the foreign service, considering it an unnecessary expenditure, a dangerous profession that might lead to involvement in the struggles of the world's great powers.

In the 1870s and after, however, Americans' interest in events abroad increased. There was a growing sense of internationalism, which stemmed in part from the telegraphs, telephones, and undersea cables that kept people better informed about political and economic developments in distant lands. Many Americans wanted to expand the country's borders, but relatively few were interested in imperialism. Expansion meant the kind of growth that had brought California and Oregon into the American system. Imperialism meant imposing control over other peoples through annexation, military conquest, or economic domination.

Why did Americans look outward in the last half of the nineteenth century?

Watch the **Video**
Roosevelt's Rough Riders on **myhistorylab.com**

Quick Check
✓ Why did Americans resist for a long time involvement in events abroad?

Reasons for Expansion

Several developments in these years shifted attention outward across the seas. The end of the frontier, announced officially in the census report of 1890, sparked fears about diminishing opportunities at home. Further growth, it seemed to some, must take place abroad. Factories and farms multiplied, producing more goods than the domestic market could consume. Both farmers and industrialists looked for new overseas markets, and the growing volume of exports—including more manufactured goods—changed American trade relations with the world. In 1898, the United States exported more than it imported, beginning a trend that lasted through the 1960s.

To some extent, Americans were also caught up in a worldwide scramble for empire. In the last third of the century, Britain, France, and Germany divided up Africa and looked covetously at Asia. The idea of imperialistic expansion was in the air, and the great powers measured their greatness by the colonies they acquired.

Adherents of expansion drew on Charles Darwin's theories of evolution. They pointed, for example, to *The Origin of Species*, whose subtitle was *The Preservation of Favoured Races in the Struggle for Life*. Applied to human and social development, biological concepts seemed to call for the triumph of the fit and the elimination of the unfit. "In this world," said Theodore Roosevelt, who considered himself one of the fit, "the nation that has trained itself to a career of unwarlike and isolated ease is bound, in the end, to go down before other nations which have not lost the manly and adventurous qualities."

John Fiske, a popular writer and lecturer, argued for Anglo-Saxon racial superiority, a result of the process of natural selection. The English and Americans, Fiske said, would occupy every land on the globe that was not already "civilized," bringing the advances of commerce and democratic institutions.

Read the **Document**
Josiah Strong from "Our Country" on **myhistorylab.com**

The career of Josiah Strong, a Congregational minister and fervent expansionist, suggested the strength of these developing ideas. A champion of overseas missionary work, Strong traveled through the West for the Home Missionary Society, and in 1885, drawing on his experiences, he published *Our Country: Its Possible Future and Its Present Crisis* and became a national celebrity. An immediate bestseller, *Our Country* argued for expanding American trade and dominion. Trade was important, Strong said, because the desire for material things was a hallmark of civilized people. So was the Christian religion. By exporting both trade and religion, Americans could civilize and Christianize "inferior" races around the world. As Anglo-Saxons, they were members of a God-favored race destined to lead the world.

Taken together, these currents in social, political, and economic thought prepared Americans for a larger role in the world. The change was gradual, and there was never a day when people woke up with a sudden interest in overseas expansion. But change there was, and by the 1890s, Americans were ready to reach out into the world in a more determined and deliberate fashion than ever before. For almost the first time, they felt the need for a foreign "policy."

Quick Check

✓ What were some of the factors that led Americans in the late nineteenth century to become more willing to get involved in events abroad?

Foreign Policy Approaches, 1867–1900

Rarely consistent, American foreign policy in the last half of the nineteenth century took different approaches to different areas of the world. In relation to Europe, seat of the dominant world powers, policymakers promoted trade and tried to avoid diplomatic entanglements. In North and South America, they based policy on the Monroe Doctrine, a recurrent dream of annexing Canada or Mexico, a hope for trade, and Pan-American unity against the nations of the Old World. In the Pacific, they coveted Hawaii and other outposts on the sea-lanes to China.

Secretary of State William Henry Seward, who served from 1861 to 1869, pushed an expansive foreign policy. "Give me . . . fifty, forty, thirty more years of life," he told a Boston audience in 1867, "and I will give you possession of the American continent and control of the world." Seward, it turned out, had only five more years of life, but he developed a vision of an American empire stretching south into Latin America and west to the shores of Asia. His vision included Canada and Mexico; Caribbean islands as bases to protect a canal across Central America; and Hawaii and other islands as stepping-stones to Asia, which Seward and others considered a bottomless market for farm and manufactured goods.

In 1867, he concluded a treaty with Russia to purchase Alaska (which was promptly labeled "Seward's Folly"), partly to sandwich western Canada between American territory and lead to its annexation. As the American empire spread, Seward thought, Mexico City would become its capital.

James G. Blaine served briefly as secretary of state under Presidents James Garfield and Chester Arthur in 1881 and laid plans to establish closer commercial relations with Latin America. His successor, Frederick T. Frelinghuysen, changed Blaine's approach but not his strategy. Like Blaine, Frelinghuysen wanted to find Caribbean markets for American goods; he negotiated separate reciprocity treaties with Mexico, Spanish-ruled Cuba and Puerto Rico, the British West Indies, Santo Domingo, and Colombia. Using these treaties, Frelinghuysen hoped not only to obtain markets for American goods but to bind these countries to American interests.

When Blaine returned to the State Department in 1889 under President Benjamin Harrison, he moved again to expand markets in Latin America. Drawing on earlier ideas, he envisaged a hemispheric system of peaceful intercourse, arbitration of disputes, and expanded trade. He also wanted to annex Hawaii.

Harrison and Blaine toyed with acquiring naval bases in the Caribbean and elsewhere, but in general they focused on Pan-Americanism and tariff reciprocity. Blaine presided over the first Inter-American Conference in Washington on October 2, 1889, where delegates from 19 American nations negotiated agreements to promote trade and created the International Bureau of the American Republics, later renamed the Pan-American Union, to exchange political, scientific, and cultural knowledge. The conference, a major step in hemispheric relations, led to later meetings promoting trade and other agreements.

Grover Cleveland, Harrison's successor, also pursued an aggressive policy toward Latin America. In 1895, he brought the United States precariously close to war with Britain over a boundary dispute between Venezuela and British Guiana. Cleveland sympathized with Venezuela, and he and Secretary of State Richard Olney urged Britain to arbitrate the dispute. When Britain failed to act, Olney drafted a stiff diplomatic note affirming the Monroe Doctrine, asserting United States' predominance in the Western Hemisphere, and denying European nations the right to meddle in its affairs.

Four months passed before Lord Salisbury, the British prime minister and foreign secretary, replied. Rejecting Olney's arguments, he sent two letters. The first bluntly repudiated the Monroe Doctrine as international law. The second, carefully reasoned and sometimes sarcastic, rejected Olney's arguments for the Venezuelan boundary. Enraged, Cleveland defended the Monroe Doctrine and asked Congress for authority to appoint a commission to decide the boundary and enforce its decision.

Preoccupied with larger diplomatic problems in Africa and Europe, Britain changed its position. In November 1896, the two countries signed a treaty of arbitration, under which Britain and Venezuela divided the disputed territory. Though Cleveland's approach was clumsy—throughout the crisis, for example, he rarely consulted Venezuela—the incident demonstrated a growing determination to exert American power in the Western Hemisphere. Cleveland and Olney had persuaded Britain to recognize the United States' dominance, and they had increased American influence in Latin America. The Monroe Doctrine assumed new importance. In averting war, an era of Anglo-American friendship was also begun.

> **Quick Check**
>
> ✓ What were the main characteristics of American foreign policy between 1867 and 1900?

The Lure of Hawaii

The Hawaiian Islands offered a tempting way station to Asian markets. (See Map 21.1.) In the early 1800s, they were already called the "Crossroads of the Pacific," and ships of many nations stopped there. In 1820, the first American missionaries arrived to convert the islanders to Christianity. Like missionaries elsewhere, they advertised Hawaii's economic and other benefits and attracted new settlers. Their children later dominated Hawaiian political and economic life and played an important role in annexation.

After the Civil War, the United States tightened its connections with the islands. The reciprocity treaty of 1875 allowed Hawaiian sugar to enter the United States free of duty and bound the Hawaiian monarchy to make no territorial or economic concessions to other powers. The treaty made Hawaii economically dependent on the United States; its political clauses effectively made Hawaii an American protectorate. In 1887, a new treaty reaffirmed these arrangements and granted the United States exclusive use of Pearl Harbor, a magnificent harbor that had early caught the eye of naval strategists.

Following the 1875 treaty, white Americans in Hawaii became more and more influential in the islands' political life. The McKinley Tariff Act of 1890 ended the special status given Hawaiian

Map 21.1 *Hawaiian Islands* The Hawaiian Islands provided the United States with both a convenient stopping point on the way to Asian markets and a strategic naval station in the Pacific.

sugar and awarded American producers a bounty of two cents a pound. Hawaiian sugar production dropped dramatically, unemployment rose, and property values fell. The following year, the weak King Kalakaua died. His successor Queen Liliuo-kalani was a strong-willed nationalist. Resentful of white minority rule, she decreed a new constitution that gave greater power to native Hawaiians.

View the **Image**
Queen Liliuokalani on **myhistorylab.com**

In response, the American residents revolted in January 1893 and called on the United States for help. John L. Stevens, the American minister in Honolulu, sent 150 marines ashore from the cruiser *Boston* to help the rebels, and within three days, the bloodless revolution was over. Queen Liliuokalani surrendered "to the superior force of the United States," and the victorious rebels set up a provisional government. On February 14, 1893, President Harrison's secretary of state, John W. Foster, and delegates of the new government signed a treaty annexing Hawaii to the United States.

View the **Image**
Iolani Palace, Hawaii on **myhistorylab.com**

But only two weeks remained in Harrison's term, and the Senate refused to ratify the agreement. President Cleveland promptly withdrew the treaty; he then sent a representative to investigate the rebellion. The investigation revealed that the Americans' role in it had been improper, and Cleveland decided to restore the queen to her throne. He made the demand, but the provisional government in Hawaii refused and instead established the Republic of Hawaii, which the embarrassed Cleveland had to recognize.

The debate over Hawaiian annexation, continuing through the 1890s, foreshadowed the later debate over the treaty to end the Spanish-American War. People in favor of annexation pointed to Hawaii's strategic location, argued that Japan, Germany, or Britain might seize the islands if the United States did not, and suggested that Americans had a responsibility to civilize and Christianize the native Hawaiians. Opponents warned that annexation might lead to a colonial army and colonial problems, the inclusion of a "mongrel" population in the United States, and rule over an area not destined for statehood.

Annexation finally came in 1898 in the midst of excitement over victories in the Spanish-American War. The year before, President William McKinley had sent a treaty of annexation to the Senate, but opponents stalled it.

The Last Hawaiian Queen The first step toward American annexation of Hawaii came in 1893 when Queen Liliuokalani was overthrown. Hawaii was annexed to the United States as a possession in 1898 and became a U.S. territory in 1900. This photograph from c. 1898 shows the former queen with guests and members of her household at Washington Place, her residence from 1896 until her death in 1917.

Quick Check

✓ For what three reasons were the Hawaiian Islands important to American policymakers?

In 1898, annexationists redoubled arguments about Hawaii's commercial and military importance. McKinley and congressional leaders switched strategies to seek a joint resolution, rather than a treaty, for annexation. A joint resolution required only a majority of both houses, while a treaty needed a two-thirds vote in the Senate. The annexation measure then moved quickly through Congress, and McKinley signed it on July 7, 1898. His signature, giving the United States a naval and commercial base in the mid-Pacific, achieved a goal policymakers had sought since the 1860s.

The New Navy

Navies were vital in the scramble for colonies, and in the 1870s, the United States had almost no naval power. One of the world's most powerful fleets during the Civil War, the American navy had fallen into rapid decline. By 1880, there were fewer than 2,000 vessels, only 48 of which could fire a gun. Ships rotted, and many officers left the service.

Conditions changed during the 1880s. A group of rising young officers, steeped in a new naval philosophy, argued for an expanded, fast, aggressive fleet capable of fighting battles across the seas. Big-navy proponents pointed to the growing fleets of Britain, France, and Germany, arguing that the United States needed to protect its economic and other interests in the Caribbean and Pacific.

In 1883, Congress authorized construction of four steel ships, marking the beginning of the new navy. Between 1885 and 1889, Congress budgeted funds for 30 more ships. The initial building program focused on lightly armored fast cruisers for raiding enemy merchant ships and protecting American shores, but after 1890, it shifted to constructing a seagoing offensive battleship navy capable of challenging the strongest fleets of Europe.

Alfred Thayer Mahan and Benjamin F. Tracy were two of the main advocates for the new navy. Austere and scholarly, Mahan was the era's most influential naval strategist. After graduating from the Naval Academy in 1859, he devoted a lifetime to studying the influence of sea power in history; for more than two decades, he headed the Newport Naval War College, where officers imbibed the latest strategic thinking. A clear, logical writer, Mahan summarized his beliefs in major books, including *The Influence of Sea Power upon History, 1660–1783* (1890) and *The Interest of America in Sea Power* (1897).

Read the **Document**
Alfred Thayer Mahan, The Interest of America in Sea Power on **myhistorylab.com**

Mahan's reasoning was simple and, to that generation, persuasive. Industrialism, he argued, produced vast surpluses of agricultural and manufactured goods, for which markets must be found. Markets involved distant ports; reaching them required a large merchant marine and a powerful navy to protect it. Navies, in turn, needed coaling stations and repair yards. Coaling stations meant colonies, and colonies became strategic bases, the foundation of a nation's wealth and power. The bases might serve as markets themselves, but they were more important as stepping-stones to other objectives, such as the markets of Latin America and Asia.

Mahan called attention to the worldwide race for power, a race, he warned, the United States could not afford to lose. To compete in the struggle, Mahan argued, the United States must expand. It needed strategic bases, a powerful oceangoing

New Steel Navy *Return of the Conquerors* by Edward Moran celebrates the triumphant return of America's Great White Fleet. The fleet of 16 white-hulled battleships and supporting craft set off in December 1907 on a 14-month, round-the-world cruise as a dramatic show of America's naval strength.

navy, a canal across Central America to link the East Coast with the Pacific, and Hawaii as a way station on the route to Asia.

Mahan influenced a generation of policymakers in the United States and Europe; one of them, Benjamin F. Tracy, became Harrison's secretary of the navy in 1889. Tracy organized the Bureau of Construction and Repair to design and build new ships, established the Naval Reserve in 1891, and built the first American submarine in 1893. He also adopted the first heavy rapid-fire guns, smokeless powder, torpedoes, and heavy armor. Above all, Tracy joined with big-navy advocates in Congress to push for a far-ranging battleship fleet capable of attacking distant enemies. He wanted two fleets of battleships, eight ships in the Pacific and 12 in the Atlantic. He got four first-class battleships.

In 1889, when Tracy entered office, the United States ranked twelfth among world navies; in 1893, when he left, it ranked seventh and was climbing rapidly. "The sea," he predicted in 1891, "will be the future seat of empires. And we shall rule it as certainly as the sun doth rise." By the end of the 1890s, the navy had 17 steel battleships, six armored cruisers, and many smaller craft. It ranked third in the world.

Quick Check

✓ What led the United States to build a new steel navy?

WAR WITH SPAIN

What were the causes and results of the war with Spain?

The war with Spain in 1898 bolstered national confidence, altered older, more insular patterns of thought, and reshaped how Americans saw themselves and the world. Its outcome pleased some people but troubled others, who raised questions about war itself, colonies, and subject peoples. The war left a lingering strain of isolationism and antiwar feeling that affected later policy. It also left an American empire, small by European standards, but new to the American experience because it was overseas. When the war ended, American possessions stretched into the Caribbean and deep into the Pacific. American influence went further still, and the United States was recognized as a "world power."

The Spanish-American War established the United States as a dominant force for the twentieth century. It brought America colonies, millions of colonial subjects, and the responsibilities of governing an empire and protecting it. For better or worse, it involved the country in other nations' arguments and affairs. The war strengthened the office of the presidency, swept up the nation in a tide of emotion, and confirmed Americans' long-standing belief in the superiority of the New World over the Old. When it was over, Americans looked outward as never before, touched, they were sure, with a special destiny.

A War for Principle

By the 1890s, Cuba and the nearby island of Puerto Rico comprised nearly all that remained of Spain's once vast empire in the New World. Cuban insurgents had repeatedly rebelled against Spanish rule, including a decade-long rebellion from 1868 to 1878 (the Ten Years' War) that failed to achieve independence. The depression of 1893 damaged the Cuban economy, and the Wilson-Gorman Tariff of 1894 prostrated it. The tariff raised duties on sugar, Cuba's lifeblood, 40 percent. With the island's sugar market in ruins, discontent with Spanish rule heightened. In February 1895, revolt again broke out.

Recognizing the importance of the nearby United States, Cuban insurgents established a junta in New York City to raise money, buy weapons, and wage a propaganda war to sway American opinion. Conditions in Cuba were grim.

In January 1896, Spain sent a new commander to Cuba, General Valeriano Weyler y Nicolau. Relentless and brutal, Weyler gave the rebels ten days to lay down their arms. He then put into effect a "reconcentration" policy designed to move the native population into camps and destroy the rebellion's popular base. Herded into fortified areas, Cubans died by the thousands, victims of unsanitary conditions, overcrowding, and disease.

There was a wave of sympathy for the insurgents, stimulated by the newspapers; but so-called yellow journalism, sensationalist reporting practiced mainly by a handful of newspapers in New York City that were eager to increase sales, did not cause the war. The conflict stemmed from larger disputes in policies and perceptions between Spain and the United States. Grover Cleveland, under whose administration the rebellion began, preferred Spanish rule to the kind of turmoil that might invite foreign intervention. Opposed to the annexation of Cuba, he issued a proclamation of neutrality and tried to restrain public opinion.

Taking office in March 1897, President McKinley also urged neutrality but leaned slightly toward the insurgents. He sent an aide on a fact-finding mission to Cuba; the aide reported in mid-1897 that Weyler's policy had wrapped Cuba "in the stillness of death and the silence of desolation." McKinley then offered to mediate between Spain and the rebels, but, concerned over the suffering, he criticized Spain's "uncivilized and inhuman" conduct. The United States, he made clear, did not contest Spain's right to fight the rebellion but insisted it be done within humane limits.

Late in 1897, a new government in Madrid recalled Weyler and agreed to offer the Cubans autonomy. It also declared an amnesty for political prisoners and released Americans from Cuban jails. The new initiatives pleased McKinley, though he again warned Spain that it must find a humane end to the rebellion. In January 1898, however, Spanish army officers led riots in Havana against the new autonomy policy, shaking the president's confidence in Madrid's control over conditions in Cuba.

McKinley ordered the battleship *Maine* to Havana to demonstrate strength and protect American citizens if necessary. On February 9, 1898, the *New York Journal*, a leader of the yellow press, published a letter stolen from Enrique Dupuy de Lôme, the Spanish minister in Washington. In the letter, which was private correspondence to a friend, de Lôme called McKinley "weak," "a would-be politician," and "a bidder for the admiration of the crowd." The insult angered Americans; McKinley himself was more worried about sections of the letter that revealed Spanish insincerity in the negotiations. De Lôme immediately resigned and went home, but the damage was done.

A few days later, at 9:40 in the evening of February 15, an explosion tore through the hull of the *Maine*, riding at anchor in Havana harbor. The ship, a trim symbol of the new steel navy, sank quickly; 266 lives were lost. McKinley cautioned patience and promised an immediate investigation. Crowds gathered on Capitol Hill and outside the White House, mourning the lost men. Soon there was a new slogan: "Remember the *Maine* and to Hell with Spain!"

The most recent study of the *Maine* incident blames the sinking on an accidental internal explosion, caused perhaps by spontaneous combustion in poorly ventilated coal bunkers. In 1898, Americans blamed it on Spain. Spaniards were hanged in effigy in many communities. Roosevelt, William Jennings Bryan, and others urged war, but McKinley hoped that Spain might yet agree to an armistice and perhaps Cuban independence.

In early March 1898, to be ready for war if it came, McKinley asked for $50 million in emergency defense appropriations, a request Congress promptly approved. The unanimous vote stunned Spain; allowing the president a latitude that was highly unusual for the era, Congress appropriated the money "for the National defense and for each and every purpose connected therewith to be expended at the discretion of the President." In late March, the report of the investigating board blamed the sinking of the *Maine* on an external (and thus presumably Spanish) explosion. Pressure for war increased.

Watch the Video
Burial of the Maine Victims on
myhistorylab.com

On March 27, McKinley cabled Spain his final terms. He asked Spain to declare an armistice, end the reconcentration policy, and—implicitly—move toward Cuban independence. When the Spanish answer came, it conceded some things, but not, in McKinley's judgment, the important ones. Spain offered to suspend hostilities but left its commander in Cuba to set the length and terms of the suspension. It also revoked the reconcentration policy. But Spain made no mention of a true armistice, McKinley's offer to mediate, or Cuba's independence.

Reluctantly McKinley asked Congress on April 11, 1898, for authority to send American troops to Cuba. On April 19, Congress passed a joint resolution declaring Cuba independent and authorizing the president to use the army and navy to expel the Spanish from it. The Teller Amendment, offered by Colorado Senator Henry M. Teller, pledged that the United States had no intention of annexing Cuba.

On April 21, in response to an American ultimatum to grant Cuba independence, Spain severed diplomatic relations. The following day, McKinley proclaimed a blockade of Cuba and called for 125,000 volunteers. On Monday, April 25, Congress passed a declaration of war, and McKinley signed it.

Some historians have suggested that in leading the country toward war, McKinley was weak and indecisive, a victim of war hysteria in Congress and the country; others have called him a wily manipulator for war and imperial gains. In truth, he was neither. Throughout the crisis, McKinley pursued a moderate course that sought to end the suffering in Cuba, promote Cuba's independence, and allow Spain time to adjust to the loss of the remnant of its American empire. He wanted peace, as did Spain, but in the end, the conflicting national interests of the two countries brought them to war.

Quick Check

✓ What were the three main causes of the war with Spain in 1898?

The Spanish-American War

📖● **Read** the **Document**
Spanish-American War on **myhistorylab.com**

Ten weeks after the declaration of war, the fighting was over. For Americans, they were ten glorious, dizzying weeks, with victories to fill every headline and slogans to suit every taste. No war can be a happy occasion for those who fight it, but the Spanish-American War came closer than most. Declared in April, it ended in August. Relatively few Americans died in the fighting, and the quick victory seemed to verify burgeoning American power, though the author Sherwood Anderson suggested that fighting a weakened Spain was "like robbing an old gypsy woman in a vacant lot at night after a fair." John Hay, soon to be McKinley's secretary of state, called it "a splendid little war."

At the outset, the United States was militarily unprepared. The regular army consisted of only 28,000 officers and men, most of them more experienced in quelling Indian uprisings than fighting large-scale battles.

When McKinley called for 125,000 volunteers, as many as 1 million young Americans responded. Ohio alone had 100,000 volunteers. Keeping the regular army units intact, War Department officials enlisted the volunteers in National

Guard units that were then integrated into the national army. Men clamored to join. William Jennings Bryan, a pacifist by temperament, took command of a regiment of Nebraska volunteers; Roosevelt chafed to get to the front. The secretary of war feared "there is going to be more trouble to satisfy those who are not going than to find those who are willing to go."

In an army inundated with men, problems of equipment and supply quickly appeared. The regulars had the new .30-caliber Krag-Jorgensen rifles, but National Guard units carried Civil War Springfield rifles that used old black-powder cartridges. The cartridges gave off a puff of smoke when fired, neatly marking the troops' position. Spanish troops had modern Mausers with smokeless powder, which they used to devastating effect. Food and sickness were also problems. Tropical disease felled many soldiers. Scores took ill after landing in Cuba and the Philippines, and half a regiment was sometimes unable to answer the bugle call.

Americans then believed that "a foreign war should be fought by the hometown military unit acting as an extension of their community." Soldiers identified with their hometowns, dressed in the local fashion, and thought of themselves as members of a town unit in a national army. The poet Carl Sandburg, 20 years old in 1898, rushed to join the army and called his unit a "living part" of his hometown of Galesburg, Illinois. And the citizens of Galesburg, for their part, took a special interest in Sandburg's unit, in a fashion repeated in countless towns across the country.

Not surprisingly, then, National Guard units mirrored the social patterns of their communities. Since everyone knew each other, there was an easygoing familiarity, tempered by the deference that went with hometown wealth, occupation, education, and length of residence. Enlisted men resented officers who grabbed too much authority, and they expected officers and men to call each other by their first names. Sandburg knew most of the privates in his unit, had worked for his corporal, and had gone to school with the first lieutenant.

Each community thought of the hometown unit as its own unit, an extension of itself. In later wars, the government censored news and dominated press relations. There was little censorship in the war with Spain, and the freshest news arrived in the latest letter home. Small-town newspapers printed news of the men, and townswomen knit special red or white bellybands of stitched flannel, thought to ward off tropical fevers. Towns sent food, clothing, and occasionally even local doctors to the front.

Quick Check

✓ What was the nature of this "Splendid Little War," as Mckinley's secretary of state described it?

African American Soldiers in the War

View the **Image**
African American Troops in Spanish-American War on
myhistorylab.com

When the invasion force sailed for Cuba, nearly one-fourth of it was African American. In 1898, the regular army included four African American regiments: the Twenty-fourth and Twenty-fifth Infantry and the Ninth and Tenth Cavalry. Black regiments had served with distinction against the Indians in the West, where most African American troops were posted. No eastern community would accept them. A troop of the Ninth Cavalry was stationed in Virginia in 1891, but it was ordered back to the West after whites complained.

When the war broke out, the War Department called for five black volunteer regiments. Military authorities were sure that blacks had a natural immunity to the

The Battle of San Juan Hill *Charge of the 24th and 25th Colored Infantry and Rescue of the Rough Riders at San Juan Hill, July 2, 1898,* colored lithograph by Kurz and Allison, 1899 (above). The Twenty-fourth and Twenty-fifth Colored Infantry regiments served with exceptional gallantry in the Spanish-American War. Charles Young (left), an 1889 graduate of West Point, was the only African American officer in the army during the war except for a few chaplains.

climate and diseases of the tropics. But most state governors refused to accept black volunteers. African American leaders protested the discrimination. The McKinley administration intervened, and in the end, the volunteer army included more than 10,000 black troops.

The four black regiments in the West were ordered to camps in the South to prepare for the invasion of Cuba. Crowds and cheers followed the troop trains across the Plains, but as they crossed into Kentucky and Tennessee, the cheering stopped, and the troops were hustled onward. Station restaurants refused to serve them; waiting rooms were segregated.

Many black soldiers were not prepared to put up with this treatment. Those stationed near Chickamauga Park, Tennessee, shot "at some whites who insulted them" and forcibly desegregated the railroad cars on the line into Chattanooga. Troops training near Macon, Georgia, refused to ride in the segregated "trailers" attached to the trolleys, and fights broke out.

More than 4,000 black troops training near Tampa and Lakeland, Florida, found segregated saloons, cafés, and drugstores. "Here the Negro is not allowed to purchase over the same counter in some stores as the white man purchases over," Chaplain George W. Prioleau charged. "Why sir, the Negro of this country is a freeman and yet a slave. Talk about fighting and freeing poor Cuba and of Spain's brutality; of Cuba's murdered thousands, and starving reconcentradoes. Is America any better than Spain?"

When the invasion force sailed, segregation continued on some of the troopships. Blacks were assigned to the lowest decks, or whites and blacks were placed on different sides of the ship. But the confusion of war often ended the problem, if only temporarily. Blacks took command as white officers died, and Spanish troops soon came to fear the "smoked Yankees," as they called them. Black soldiers played a major role in the Cuban campaign and probably staved off defeat for the Rough Riders at San Juan Hill. In Cuba, they won 26 Certificates of Merit and five Congressional Medals of Honor.

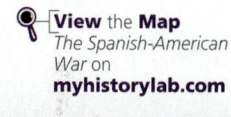

Quick Check

✓ What role did African American troops play in the Spanish-American war?

The Course of the War

🔍 **View** the **Map**
The Spanish-American War on
myhistorylab.com

Mahan's Naval War College had begun studying strategy for a war with Spain in 1895. By 1898, it had a detailed plan for operations in the Caribbean and Pacific. Naval strategy was simple: Destroy the Spanish fleet, damage Spain's merchant marine, and harry the colonies or the coast of Spain. Planners were excited; two steam-powered armored fleets had yet to meet in battle anywhere in the world. The army's task was more difficult. It had to defend the United States, invade Cuba and probably Puerto Rico, and undertake possible action in far-flung places such as the Philippines or Spain itself.

Even before war was declared, the secretary of war arranged joint planning between the army and navy. Military intelligence was accurate, and planners knew the numbers and locations of the Spanish troops. Earlier they had rejected a proposal to send an officer in disguise to map Cuban harbors; such things, they said, were simply not done in peacetime. Still, the War Department's new Military Information Division, a sign of the increasing professionalization of the army, had detailed diagrams of Spanish fortifications in Havana and other points. On April 20, 1898, McKinley summoned the strategists to the White House. To the dismay of those who wanted a more aggressive policy, they decided on the limited strategy of blockading Cuba, arming the insurgents, and annoying the Spanish with small thrusts by the army.

African Americans in the War with Spain Charles Young an 1889 graduate of West Point, was the only African American officer in the army during the Spanish-American War except for a few chaplains.

Victories soon changed the strategy. In case of war, long-standing naval plans had called for a holding action against the Spanish base in the Philippines. On May 1, 1898, with the war barely a week old, Commodore George Dewey, commander of the Asiatic Squadron based at Hong Kong, destroyed the Spanish fleet in Manila Bay. Suddenly, Manila and the Philippines lay within American grasp. At home, Dewey portraits, songs, and poems blossomed everywhere, and his calm order to the flagship's captain—"You may fire when ready, Gridley"—hung on every tongue. Dewey had four modern cruisers, two gunboats, and a Civil War paddle steamer. He sank eight obsolete Spanish warships. Dewey had no troops to attack the Spanish army in Manila, but the War Department, stunned by the speed and size of the victory, quickly raised an expeditionary force. On August 13, 1898, the troops accepted the surrender of Manila, and with it, the Philippines. (See Map 21.2.)

McKinley and his aides were worried about Admiral Pascual Cervera's main Spanish fleet, thought to be headed across the Atlantic for an attack on Florida. On May 13, the navy found Cervera's ships near Martinique in the Caribbean but then lost them again. A few days later, Cervera slipped secretly into the harbor of Santiago de Cuba, a city on the island's southern coast. A spy in the Havana telegraph office alerted the Americans, and on May 28, a superior American force under Admiral William T. Sampson bottled Cervera up.

In early June, Marines seized Guantánamo Bay, the great harbor on the south of the island. They established depots for the navy to refuel and pinned down Spanish troops in the area. On June 21, an invasion force of about 17,000 landed at Daiquiri on Cuba's southeastern coast. All was confusion, but the Spanish offered no resistance. Helped by Cuban insurgents, the Americans pushed west toward Santiago, which they hoped to surround and capture.

The first battle broke out at Las Guasimas, a crossroads on the Santiago road. After a sharp fight, the Spanish fell back. On July 1, the Rough Riders, troops from the four black regiments, and the other regulars reached the fortifications at El Caney and San Juan Hill. Black soldiers of the Twenty-fifth Infantry charged the El Caney blockhouses, surprising the Spanish defenders with Comanche yells. For the better part of a day, the defenders held back the army's elite corps. In the confusion of battle, Roosevelt rallied an assortment of infantry and cavalry to take Kettle Hill, adjacent to San Juan Hill.

They charged directly into the Spanish guns, Roosevelt at their head, mounted on a

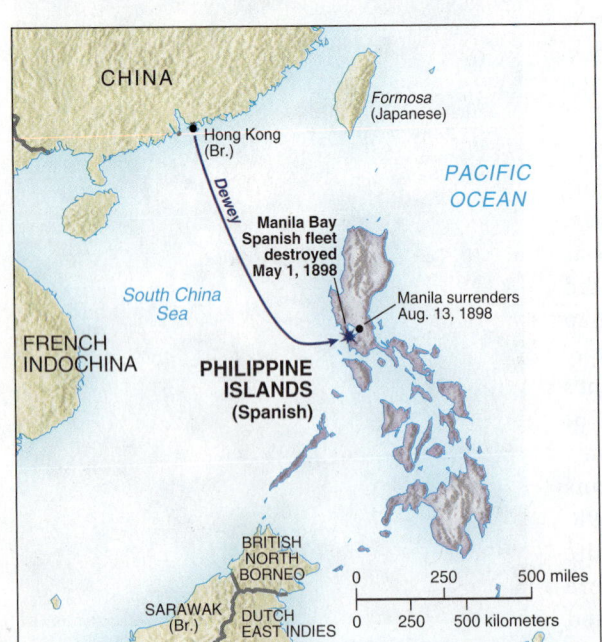

Map 21.2 Spanish-American War: Pacific Theater Commodore Dewey, promoted to admiral immediately after the naval victory at Manila Bay, was the first hero of the war.

horse, a blue polka-dot handkerchief floating from the brim of his sombrero. "I waved my hat and we went up the hill with a rush," he recalled in his autobiography. Actually, it was less easy. Losses were heavy: 89 Rough Riders were killed or wounded in the attack. Dense foliage concealed the enemy and smokeless powder gave no clue to their position. At nightfall, the surviving Spanish defenders withdrew, and the Americans prepared for the counterattack.

American troops now occupied the ridges overlooking Santiago. They were weakened by sickness, a fact unknown to the Spanish, who decided the city was lost. The Spanish command in Havana ordered Cervera to run for the open sea, although he knew the attempt was hopeless. On the morning of July 3, Cervera's squadron steamed down the bay and out through the harbor's narrow channel, but the waiting American fleet closed in, and in a few hours every Spanish vessel was destroyed. Two weeks later, Santiago surrendered. (See Map 21.3.)

Soon thereafter, troops, meeting little resistance, occupied Puerto Rico. Cervera had commanded Spain's only battle fleet, and when it sank, Spain was helpless against attacks on the colonies or even its own shores. The war was over. Lasting 113 days, it took relatively few lives, most of them the result of accident, yellow fever, malaria, and typhoid in Cuba. Of the 5,500 Americans who died in the war, only 379 were killed in battle. The navy lost one man in the battle at Santiago Bay and only one to heatstroke in the stunning victory in Manila Bay.

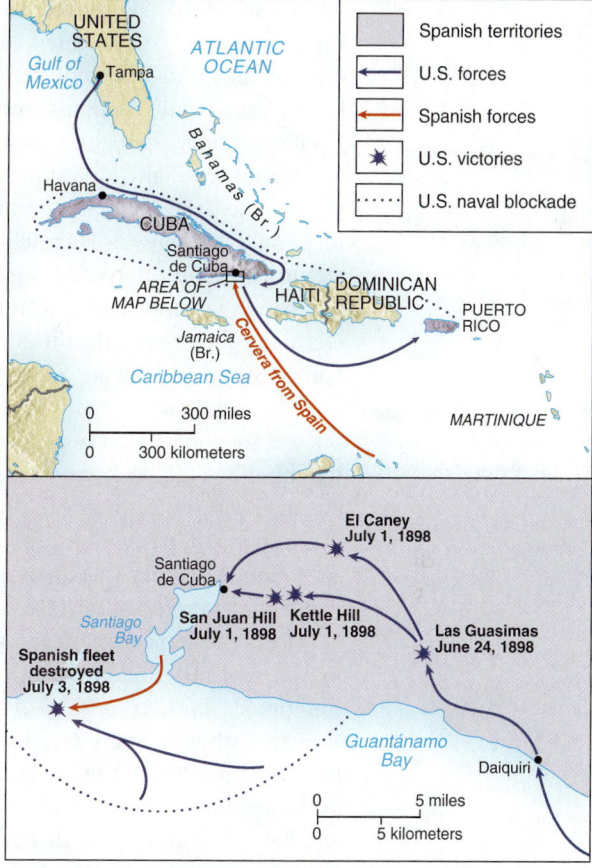

Map 21.3 *Spanish-American War:* Caribbean Theater President McKinley set up a "war room" in the White House, following the action on giant maps with red and white marking pins.

Quick Check

✓ What were the main events of the war itself?

ACQUISITION OF EMPIRE

Late in the afternoon of August 12, 1898, representatives of Spain and the United States met in McKinley's White House office to sign the preliminary instrument of peace. Secretary of State William R. Day beckoned a presidential aide over to a large globe, remarking, "Let's see what we get by this."

What the United States got was more territory and even more responsibilities. According to the preliminary agreement, Spain granted independence to Cuba, ceded Puerto Rico and the Pacific island of Guam to the United States, and allowed

What were the various viewpoints about the acquisition of empire after the war with Spain?

Americans to occupy Manila until the two countries reached final agreement on the Philippines. To McKinley, the Philippines were the problem. Puerto Rico was close to the mainland, and even many opponents of expansion wanted to take it. Guam was too small and unknown to merit attention. The Philippines, on the other hand, were huge, sprawling, populous, and thousands of miles from America.

McKinley weighed a number of alternatives for the Philippines, but he liked none of them. He believed he could not give the islands back to Spain; public opinion would not allow it. He might turn them over to another nation, but then they would fall, as he later said, "a golden apple of discord, among the rival powers." Germany, Japan, Britain, and Russia had all expressed interest in acquiring them. Germany even sent a fleet to Manila and laid plans to take the Philippines if the United States let them go.

View the **Closer Look**
American Empire on
myhistorylab.com

Rejecting those alternatives, McKinley considered independence for the islands but was soon talked out of it. People who had been there, reflecting the era's racism, told him the Filipinos were not ready for independence. He thought of establishing an American protectorate but discarded the idea, convinced it would bring American responsibilities without full American control. Finally, McKinley decided the only practical policy was to annex the Philippines, with an eye to future independence after a period of tutelage.

At first hesitant, American opinion was swinging to the same conclusion. Religious and missionary organizations appealed to McKinley to hold on to the Philippines in order to "Christianize" them, although most Filipinos were already Roman Catholics. Some merchants and industrialists saw the islands as the key to the China market and the wealth of Asia. Many Americans simply regarded them as the legitimate fruits of war. In October 1898, representatives of the United States and Spain met in Paris to discuss a peace treaty. Spain agreed to recognize Cuba's independence, assume the Cuban debt, and cede Puerto Rico and Guam to the United States.

On instructions from McKinley, the American representatives also demanded the cession of the Philippines: "Grave as are the responsibilities and unforeseen as are the difficulties which are before us, the President can see but one plain path of duty—the acceptance of the archipelago," the instructions said. In return, the United States offered to pay $20 million. Spain resisted but had little choice. On December 10, 1898, American and Spanish representatives signed the Treaty of Paris.

The Treaty of Paris Debate

Submitted to the Senate for ratification, the treaty set off a storm of debate. Industrialist Andrew Carnegie, reformer Jane Addams, labor leader Samuel Gompers, Mark Twain, and many others argued forcefully against annexing the Philippines. Annexation, the anti-imperialists protested, violated the very principles of independence and self-determination on which the United States was founded.

Some labor leaders feared cheap labor from new Pacific colonies. Gompers warned about the "half-breeds and semi-barbaric people" who might undercut wages and the union movement. Other anti-imperialists argued against assimilation of different races: "Spanish-Americans," as one said, "with all the mixture of Indian and negro blood, and Malays and other unspeakable Asiatics, by the tens of millions!" Such racist views were also common among those favoring expansion, and the anti-imperialists usually focused on different arguments. If the United States established a tyranny abroad, they were sure, there would soon be tyranny at home.

William Jennings Bryan scoffed at the argument that colonies were good for trade: "It is not necessary to own people to trade with them." Many thought the country's republican ideals could not be reconciled with subjugating people abroad. To Booker T. Washington, the country had more important things to think about at home, including its treatment of Indians and blacks. Carnegie was so upset that he offered to buy Filipino independence with a personal check for $20 million.

In November 1898, opponents of expansion formed the Anti-Imperialist League to fight the treaty. Membership centered in New England; the cause was less popular in the West and South. It enlisted more Democrats than Republicans, though never a majority of either. Their lack of a coherent program weakened the anti-imperialists. Some favored keeping naval bases in the conquered areas. Some wanted Hawaii and Puerto Rico but not the Philippines. Others wanted nothing at all to do with any colonies. Most simply wished that Dewey had sailed away after beating the Spanish at Manila Bay.

The debate in the Senate lasted a month. Pressing for ratification, McKinley toured the South to rally support and consulted closely with senators. Though opposed to taking the Philippines, Bryan supported ratification in order to end the war; his support influenced some Democratic votes. Still, on the final weekend before the vote, the treaty was two votes short. That Saturday night, news reached Washington that fighting had broken out between American troops and Filipino insurgents who demanded immediate independence. The news increased pressure to ratify the treaty, which the Senate did on February 6, 1899, with two votes to spare. An amendment promising independence as soon as the Filipinos established a stable government lost by one vote. The United States had a colonial empire. (See Map 21.4.)

> **Quick Check**
> ✓ What were the main arguments on each side in the debate over the treaty that ended the war?

Guerrilla Warfare in the Philippines

Historians rarely write of the Philippine-American War, a guerrilla war between American troops and the newly freed Filipinos, but it was an important event in American history. The war with Spain was over three months after it began, but war with the Filipinos lasted more than three years. Four times as many American soldiers fought in the Philippines as in Cuba. For the first time, Americans fought men of a different color in an Asian guerrilla war. The Philippine-American War of 1898–1902 took a heavy toll: 4,300 American lives and thousands of Filipino lives (estimates range from 50,000 to 200,000).

Emilio Aguinaldo, the Filipino leader, was 29 years old in 1898. An early organizer of resistance to Spain, he had gone into exile in Hong Kong, from where he welcomed the outbreak of the Spanish-American War. Certain the United States would grant independence, he worked for an American victory. Filipino insurgents helped guide Dewey into Manila Bay, and Dewey sent a ship to Hong Kong to bring back Aguinaldo to lead an uprising against the Spanish. On June 12, 1898, the insurgents proclaimed their independence.

Cooperating with the Americans, they drove the Spanish out of many areas. In the liberated regions, Aguinaldo established local governments and appointed

Map 21.4 *American Empire, 1900* With the Treaty of Paris, the United States gained an expanded colonial empire stretching from the Caribbean to the far Pacific. It embraced Puerto Rico, Alaska, Hawaii, part of Samoa, Guam, the Philippines, and a chain of Pacific islands. The dates on the map refer to the date of U.S. acquisition.

provincial governors. He waited for American recognition, but McKinley and others had concluded that the Filipinos were not ready. Soon, warfare broke out between the Filipinos and Americans over Filipino independence.

By late 1899, the American army had dispersed the organized Filipino army, but claims of victory proved premature. Aguinaldo shifted to guerrilla tactics, striking suddenly and then melting into the jungle or friendly native villages. In many areas, the Americans ruled the day, the guerrillas the night. Both sides committed atrocities. The Americans used brutal, Weyler-like tactics. After any attack on an American patrol, the Americans burned all the houses in the district. They tortured people and executed prisoners. They herded people into protected "zones." Seizing or destroying food outside the zones, they starved guerrillas into submission.

Bryan tried to turn the election of 1900 into a debate over imperialism, but the attempt failed. For one thing, he himself refused to give up the silver issue, which cost him support among anti-imperialists in the Northeast who were for gold (see Chapter 20). McKinley, moreover, took advantage of the surging economy and defended expansion as an accomplished fact. Riding a wave of patriotism and prosperity, McKinley won the election handily—by an even larger margin than he had in 1896.

In 1900, McKinley sent a special commission to the islands under William Howard Taft, a prominent Ohio judge. Directed to establish a civil government, the commission organized municipal administrations and, in stages, created a government for the Philippines. In March 1901, five American soldiers tricked their way into Aguinaldo's camp deep in the mountains and took him prisoner. Back in Manila, he urged his

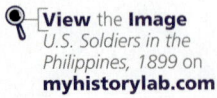

View the **Image**
U.S. Soldiers in the Philippines, 1899 on **myhistorylab.com**

View the **Image**
Emilio Aguinaldo on **myhistorylab.com**

people to end the fighting. Some guerrillas held out for another year, but to no avail. On July 4, 1901, authority was transferred from the army to Taft, who was named civilian governor of the islands, and his civilian commission. McKinley reaffirmed his purpose to grant the Filipinos self-government as soon as they were deemed ready for it.

Given broad powers, the Taft Commission introduced many changes. New schools provided education and vocational training for Filipinos of all social classes. The Americans built roads and bridges, reformed the judiciary, restructured the tax system, and introduced sanitation and vaccination programs. They established local governments built on Filipino traditions and hierarchies. Taft encouraged Filipino participation in government. Over the next 40 years, other measures broadened Filipino rights. Independence finally came on July 4, 1946, nearly 50 years after Aguinaldo proclaimed it.

Quick Check

✓ What were the causes and consequences of the Philippine-American War?

The Open Door

Poised in the Philippines, the United States had become an Asian power on the doorstep of China. Weakened by years of warfare and rebellion, China in 1898 and 1899 was unable to resist foreign influence. Japan, Britain, France, Germany, and Russia eyed it covetously, dividing parts of the country into "spheres of influence." They forced China to grant "concessions" that allowed them exclusive rights to develop particular areas and threatened American hopes for trade.

McKinley first outlined a new China policy in 1898 when he said that Americans sought trade, "but we seek no advantages in the Orient which are not common to all. Asking only the open door for ourselves, we are ready to accord the open door to others." In September 1899, Secretary of State John Hay addressed identical diplomatic notes to Britain, Germany, and Russia, and later to France, Japan, and Italy, asking them to join the United States in establishing the Open Door policy. This policy urged three agreements: Nations possessing a sphere of influence would respect the rights and privileges of other nations in that sphere; the Chinese government would continue to collect tariff duties in all spheres; and nations would not discriminate against other nations in levying port dues and railroad rates within their respective spheres of influence.

Under the Open Door policy, the United States would retain many commercial advantages it might lose if China were partitioned into spheres of influence. McKinley and Hay also attempted to preserve for the Chinese some semblance of national authority. Britain most nearly accepted the principle of the Open Door. Russia declined to approve it. The other powers, sending evasive replies, stated they would agree only if all the other nations did. Hay tried to turn the situation to American advantage by boldly announcing in March 1900 that all the powers had accepted the Open Door policy.

U.S. Policy in Asia In this 1899 cartoon, "Putting His Foot Down" from *Puck*, the nations of Europe are getting ready to cut up China to expand their spheres of influence, but Uncle Sam stands firm on American commitments to preserve China's sovereignty.

The policy's first test came three months later with the outbreak of the Boxer Rebellion in Peking (now Beijing). In June 1900, a secret, intensely nationalistic Chinese society called the Boxers tried to oust all foreigners from their country. Overrunning Peking, they drove foreigners into their legations and penned them up for nearly two months. In the end, the United States, Britain, Germany, Japan, and other powers sent troops to lift the siege.

Fearing that the rebellion gave some nations, especially Germany and Russia, an excuse to expand their spheres of influence, Hay sent off another round of Open Door notes affirming U.S. commitment to equal commercial opportunity and respect for China's independence. While the first Open Door notes had implied recognition of China's continued independence, the second notes explicitly stated the need to preserve it. Together, the two notes comprised the Open Door policy, which became a central element in American diplomacy in the Far East.

The policy tried to help China, but it also led to further American meddling in Chinese affairs. Moreover, by committing itself to a policy that Americans were not prepared to defend militarily, the McKinley administration laid the basis for later controversy with Japan and other expansion-minded powers in the Pacific.

Quick Check

✓ What was the "Open Door" policy toward China?

CONCLUSION: OUTCOME OF THE WAR WITH SPAIN

The war with Spain over, Roosevelt and the Rough Riders sailed for home in mid-August 1898. They sauntered through the streets of New York, the heroes of the city. A few weeks later, Roosevelt bade them farewell. They presented him with a reproduction of Frederick Remington's famed bronze *The Bronco-Buster*, and, close to tears, he told them, "I am proud of this regiment beyond measure." Roosevelt was soon governor of New York and on his way to the White House.

Other soldiers were also glad to be home, although they sometimes resented the reception they found. "The war is over now," said Winslow Hobson, a black trooper from the Ninth Ohio, "and Roosevelt . . . and others (white of course) have all there is to be gotten out of it." Bravery in Cuba and the Philippines won some recognition for black soldiers, but the war itself set back the cause of civil rights. It spurred talk about "inferior" races, at home and abroad, and united whites in the North and South. "The Negro might as well know it now as later," a black editor said, "the closer the North and South get together by this war, the harder he will have to fight to maintain a footing." A fresh outburst of segregation laws and lynching occurred during the decade after the war.

McKinley and the Republican party soared to new heights of popularity. Firmly established, the Republican majority dominated politics until 1932. Scandals arose about the food provided for the troops and the conduct of the War Department, but there was none of the sharp sense of deception and betrayal that was to mark the years after World War I. In a little more than a century, the United States had grown from 13 states stretched along a thin Atlantic coastline into a world power that reached from the Caribbean to the Pacific. As Seward and others had hoped, the nation now dominated its own hemisphere, dealt with European powers on more equal terms, and was a major power in Asia. (See Map 21.5.)

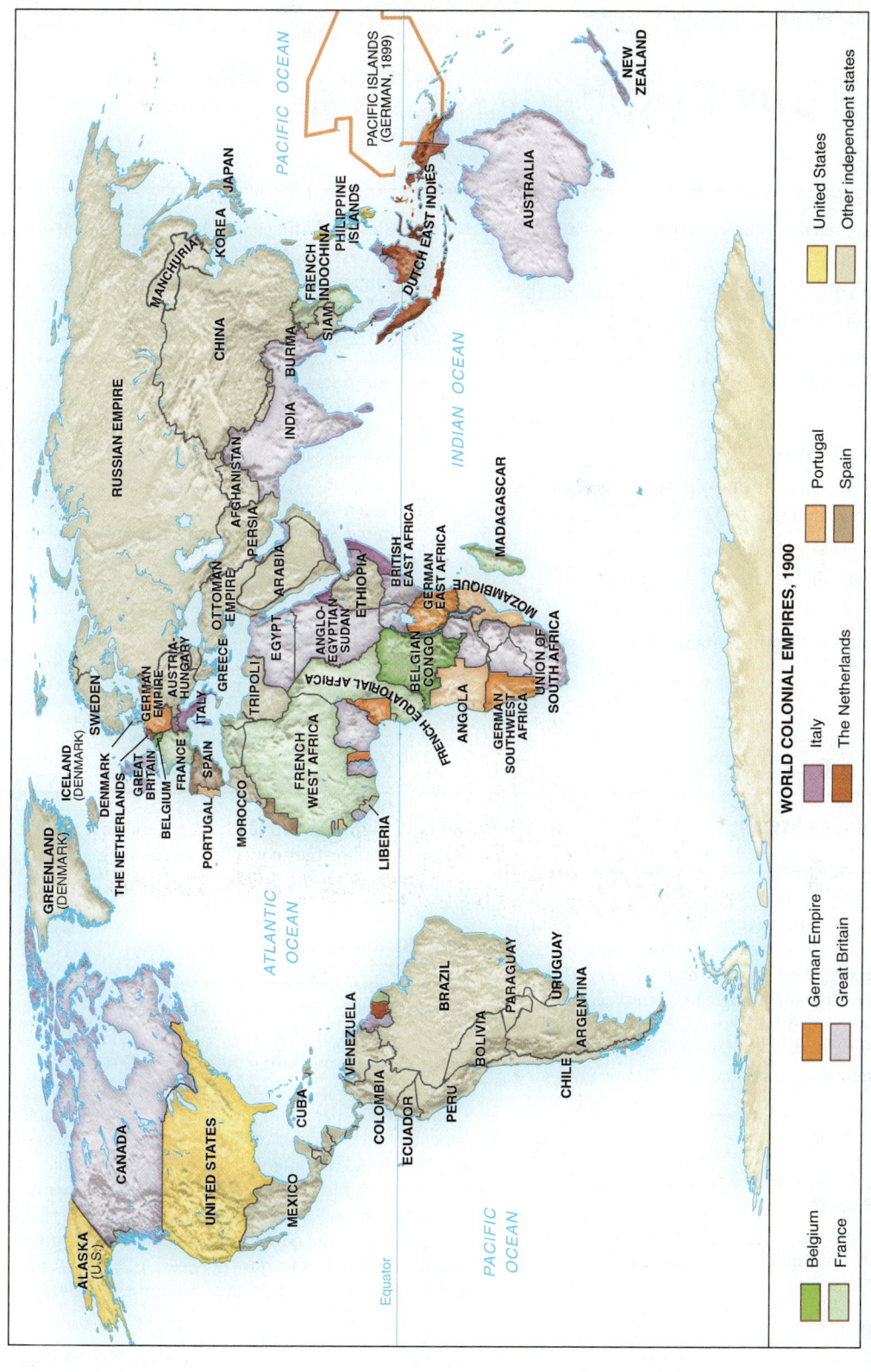

Map 21.5 World Colonial Empires, 1900 Events of the nineteenth century increased European hegemony over the world. By 1900, most independent African nations had disappeared and the major European nations had divided the continent among themselves. In the East, the European powers and Japan took advantage of China's internal weakness to gain both trading ports and economic concessions.

WORLD COLONIAL EMPIRES, 1900

- Belgium
- France
- German Empire
- Great Britain
- Italy
- The Netherlands
- Portugal
- Spain
- United States
- Other independent states

Map labels

PACIFIC OCEAN

PACIFIC ISLANDS (GERMAN, 1899)

NEW ZEALAND

AUSTRALIA

MANCHURIA

KOREA

JAPAN

CHINA

RUSSIAN EMPIRE

BURMA

FRENCH INDOCHINA

SIAM

PHILIPPINE ISLANDS

DUTCH EAST INDIES

INDIAN OCEAN

INDIA

AFGHANISTAN

PERSIA

ARABIA

OTTOMAN EMPIRE

GREECE

MADAGASCAR

MOZAMBIQUE

BRITISH EAST AFRICA

GERMAN EAST AFRICA

ETHIOPIA

ANGLO-EGYPTIAN SUDAN

EGYPT

TRIPOLI

ITALY

AUSTRIA-HUNGARY

GERMAN EMPIRE

SWEDEN

DENMARK

ICELAND (DENMARK)

GREAT BRITAIN

THE NETHERLANDS

BELGIUM

FRANCE

SPAIN

PORTUGAL

MOROCCO

FRENCH WEST AFRICA

FRENCH EQUATORIAL AFRICA

BELGIAN CONGO

ANGOLA

GERMAN SOUTHWEST AFRICA

UNION OF SOUTH AFRICA

LIBERIA

GREENLAND (DENMARK)

ATLANTIC OCEAN

ALASKA (U.S.)

CANADA

UNITED STATES

MEXICO

CUBA

VENEZUELA

COLOMBIA

ECUADOR

PERU

BOLIVIA

BRAZIL

PARAGUAY

URUGUAY

ARGENTINA

CHILE

PACIFIC OCEAN

Equator

Map 21.5 World Colonial Empires, 1900 Events of the nineteenth century increased European hegemony over the world. By 1900, most independent African nations had disappeared and the major European nations had divided the continent among themselves. In the East, the European powers and Japan took advantage of China's internal weakness to gain both trading ports and economic concessions.

547

21 STUDY RESOURCES

((•—Listen to the **Chapter Audio** for Chapter 21 on **myhistorylab.com**

TIMELINE

CHAPTER REVIEW

AMERICA LOOKS OUTWARD

Why did Americans look outward in the last half of the nineteenth century?

In the late nineteenth century, Americans increasingly looked overseas, influenced by the example of other nations and confidence in what their country could offer other peoples, including Christianity, commerce, and American values. Policymakers were sure that the nation needed a navy, colonial outposts, foreign markets, and a new foreign policy. *(p. 527)*

WAR WITH SPAIN

What were the causes and results of the war with Spain?

In 1898, the United States fought a war with Spain, which resulted in a quick victory and enormous changes for American society, including a larger military, an increased role for the federal government in American life, the acquisition of colonies, and increased power for the presidency. *(p. 534)*

ACQUISITION OF EMPIRE

What were the various viewpoints about the acquisition of empire after the war with Spain?

In the peace treaty ending the war with Spain, the United States acquired a new empire, including Puerto Rico, Guam, and the Philippines. For the first time, the United States owned territories overseas, to which it did not intend to grant statehood. That, together with historical, racial, and other arguments, caused an angry debate between those in favor and those opposing the new colonies. Adding to the furor was the outbreak of warfare between American troops and Filipino insurgents in the Philippines. *(p. 541)*

KEY TERM QUESTIONS

1. Why did Americans prefer isolationism for such a long time? (p. 527)

2. Why did Americans become interested in imperialism in the late nineteenth century? (p. 527)

3. How did yellow journalism influence the outbreak of the Spanish-American War? (p. 534)

4. What was the Teller Amendment? (p. 536)

5. What did the U.S. gain from the Treaty of Paris? (p. 542)

6. Why did the Anti-Imperialist League oppose the Treaty of Paris? (p. 543)

7. What was the Philippine-American War? (p. 543)

8. Why did the U.S. propose the Open Door policy? (p. 545)

MYHISTORYLAB CONNECTIONS

Visit **www.myhistorylab.com** for a customized Study Plan to build your *knowledge of Toward Empire*

Questions for Analysis

1. Who were the members of the "Rough Riders"?

   Watch the **Video** *Roosevelt's Rough Riders* p. 527

2. How does Josiah Strong support his argument that white Anglo-Saxons are superior to all others?

   Read the **Document** *Josiah Strong, from Our Country* p. 528

3. What was Alfred Thayer Mahan's reasoning behind his belief in the importance of sea power?

   Read the **Document** *Alfred Thayer Mahan, The Interest of America in Sea Power* p. 532

4. What was the significance of the sinking of the *Maine*?

   Watch the **Video** *Burial of the Maine Victims* p. 535

5. What were the primary motives behind the American Empire?

   View the **Closer Look** *American Empire* p. 542

Other Resources from this Chapter

Read the **Document** *Theodore Roosevelt, "The Strenuous Life" (1900)*

View the **Image** *Queen Liliuokalani*

View the **Image** *Iolani Palace, Hawaii*

Read the **Document** *Spanish American War*

View the **Image** *African American Troops in the Spanish-American War*

View the **Map** *The Spanish-American War, 1898-1899*

View the **Image** *U.S. Soldiers in the Philippines, 1899*

View the **Image** *Emilio Aguinaldo*

Contents and Spotlight Questions

((•⁻ **Listen** to the **Chapter Audio** for Chapter 22 on **myhistorylab.com**

MUCKRAKERS CALL FOR REFORM

In 1902, Samuel S. McClure, the shrewd owner of *McClure's Magazine*, sensed something astir in the country that his reporters were not covering. Like *Life*, *Munsey's*, the *Ladies' Home Journal*, and *Cosmopolitan*, *McClure's* was reaching more and more people—more than 250,000 readers a month. Americans were snapping up the new popular magazines filled with eye-catching illustrations and up-to-date fiction. Advances in photoengraving during the 1890s reduced the cost of illustrations; income from advertisements also rose sharply. By 1900, some magazines earned $60,000 an issue from advertising alone, and publishers could price them as low as 10 cents a copy.

McClure was always chasing new ideas and readers, and in 1902, certain that something was happening in the public mood, he told one of his editors, 36-year-old Lincoln Steffens, a former Wall Street reporter,

The Muckrakers At the beginning of the twentieth century magazines enjoyed increasing popularity. *McClure's Magazine* pioneered investigative journalism. The November 1902 edition featured the first installment of Ida Tarbell's two-year series on Standard Oil that exposed the corrupt practices and deals that had helped create the company.

to find out what it was: "Get out of here, travel, go—somewhere. Buy a railroad ticket, get on a train, and there, where it lands you, there you will learn to edit a magazine."

Steffens went west. In St. Louis, he came across a young district attorney, Joseph W. Folk, who had found a trail of corruption linking politics and some of the city's respected business leaders. Eager for help, Folk named names to the editor from New York. "It is good business men that are corrupting our bad politicians," he stressed. "It is the leading citizens that are battening on our city." Steffens's story, "Tweed Days in St. Louis," appeared in the October 1902 issue of *McClure's*.

The November *McClure's* carried the first installment of Ida Tarbell's scathing "History of the Standard Oil Company." In January 1903, Steffens was back with "The Shame of Minneapolis," another tale of corrupt partnership between business and politics. McClure had what he wanted, and in the January issue he printed an editorial, "Concerning Three Articles in This Number of *McClure's*, and a Coincidence That May Set Us Thinking." Steffens on Minneapolis, Tarbell on Standard Oil, and an article on abuses in labor unions—all, McClure said, on different topics but actually on the same theme: corruption in American life: "Capitalists, workingmen, politicians, citizens—all breaking the law, or letting it be broken."

▶ **Read** the
Document
*Upton Sinclair from
The Jungle* on
myhistorylab.com

Readers were enthralled, and articles and books by other **muckrakers**—Theodore Roosevelt coined the term in 1906 to describe the writers who made a practice of exposing the corruption of public and prominent figures—spread swiftly. *Collier's* had articles on questionable stock market practices, patent medicines, and the beef trust. Novelist Upton Sinclair tackled the meatpackers in *The Jungle* (1906). In 1904, Steffens collected his *McClure's* articles in *The Shame of the Cities*, with an introduction expressing confidence that reform was possible, "that our shamelessness is superficial, that beneath it lies a pride which, being real, may save us yet."

Muckraking flourished from 1903 to 1909, and while it did, good writers and bad investigated almost every corner of American life: government, labor unions, big business, Wall Street, health care, the food industry, child labor, women's rights, prostitution, ghetto life, and life insurance.

The muckrakers were a journalistic voice of a larger movement in American society. Called **progressivism**, it lasted from the mid-1890s through World War I. Like muckraking itself, progressivism reflected worry about society, the effects of industrialization and urbanization, social disorder, political corruption, and many other issues. With concerns so large, progressivism often had a sense of crisis and urgency, although it was rooted in a spirit of hopefulness and confidence in human progress. For varying reasons, thousands of people became concerned about their society. Separately and together, they set out to cure the ills they saw around them. The efforts of the so-called progressives changed the nation and gave the era its name.

THE CHANGING FACE OF INDUSTRIALISM

As the new century turned, conditions in America were better than just a few years before. Farms and factories were prosperous again; in 1901, for the first time in years, the economy reached full capacity. Farm prices rose almost 50 percent-between 1900 and 1910. Unemployment dropped. "In the United States of today," a Boston newspaper said in 1904, "everyone is middle class. The resort to force, the wild talk of the nineties are over. Everyone is busily, happily getting ahead."

Everyone, of course, was not middle class, nor was everyone getting ahead. "Wild talk" persisted. Many of the problems that had angered people in the 1890s continued into the new century, and millions of Americans still suffered from poverty and disease. Racism sat even more heavily on African Americans in both South and North, and hostility to immigrants from southern and eastern Europe, Mexico, and Asia was increasing. Yet economic conditions were better for many people, and as a result, prosperity became one of the keys to understanding the era and the nature of progressive reform.

The start of the new century was another key, for it influenced people to take a fresh look at themselves and their times. Excited about beginning the twentieth century, people believed technology and enterprise would shape a better life. Savoring the word *new*, they talked of the new poetry, new cinema, new history, new democracy, new woman, new art, new immigration, new morality, and new city. Presidents Theodore Roosevelt and Woodrow Wilson called their political programs the New Nationalism and the New Freedom, respectively.

The word *mass* also cropped up frequently. Victors in the recent war with Spain, Americans took pride in teeming cities, burgeoning corporations, and other marks of the mass society. They enjoyed the fruits of mass production, read mass circulation newspapers and magazines, and took mass transit from the growing spiral of suburbs into the central cities.

Behind mass production lay significant changes in the nation's industrial system. Businesses grew at a rapid rate. They were large in the three decades after the Civil War, but between 1895 and 1915, industries became mammoth, employing thousands of workers and equipped with assembly lines to turn out huge quantities of the company's product. Inevitably, changes in management attitudes, business organization, and worker roles influenced the entire society. Inevitably, too, the growth of giant businesses gave rise to a widespread fear of "trusts" and a desire among many progressive reformers to break them up or regulate them.

How did industrialism change after 1900?

The Innovative Model T

In the movement toward large-scale business and mass production, the automobile industry was one of those that led the way. In 1895, there were only four cars on the nation's roads; in 1917, there were nearly 5 million, and the automobile had already helped work a small revolution in industrial methods and social mores.

In 1903, Henry Ford and a few associates formed the Ford Motor Company, the firm that transformed the business. That year, Ford sold the first Ford car.

Rise of Mass Production Henry Ford built his first car in 1896, then produced improved models, each designated by a letter of the alphabet. Shown here are Henry Ford and a friend in a 1905 Model N, Ford's best-selling model before the Model T debuted in 1908. The "Tin Lizzie" was Ford's "motorcar for the multitudes," affordably priced so that every family could own one. The automobile changed American life and the American landscape as it spawned the development of paved roads, traffic lights, and numerous auto-related businesses.

The price was high, and in 1905, Ford raised prices still higher. Sales plummeted. In 1907, he lowered the price; sales and revenues rose. Ford learned an important lesson of the modern economy: A smaller unit profit on a large number of sales meant enormous revenues. In 1908, he introduced the Model T, a four-cylinder, 20-horsepower "Tin Lizzie," costing $850, and available only in black. The first year 11,000 were sold.

"I am going to democratize the automobile," Ford proclaimed. "When I'm through everybody will be able to afford one, and about everyone will have one." The key was mass production, and after many experiments, Ford copied the techniques of meatpackers who moved carcasses along overhead trolleys from station to station. Adapting the process to automobile assembly, Ford in 1913 set up moving assembly lines in his plant in Highland Park, Michigan, that dramatically reduced the time and cost of producing cars. Emphasizing continuous movement, he strove for a nonstop flow from raw material to finished product. In 1914, he sold 248,000 Model Ts.

That year, Ford workers assembled a car in 93 minutes, one-tenth the time it had taken just eight months before. On a single day in 1925, Ford set a record by turning out 9,109 Model Ts, a new car every 10 seconds of the workday.

Quick Check

✓ How did Henry Ford revolutionize the automobile industry?

The Burgeoning Trusts

As businesses like Ford's grew, capital and organization became increasingly important, and the result was the formation of a growing number of trusts. Standard Oil started the trend in 1882, but the greatest momentum came two decades later. Between 1898 and 1903, a series of mergers and consolidations swept the economy. Many smaller firms disappeared, swallowed up in giant corporations. By 1904, large-scale combinations of one form or another controlled nearly two-fifths of the capital in manufacturing in the country. (See Figure 22.1.)

The result was not monopoly but oligopoly—control of a commodity or service by a small number of large, powerful companies. Six great financial groups dominated the railroad industry; a handful of holding companies controlled utilities and steel. Rockefeller's Standard Oil owned about 85 percent of the oil business. After 1898, financiers and industrialists formed the Amalgamated Copper Company, Consolidated Tobacco, U.S. Rubber, and many others. By 1909, just 1 percent of the industrial firms were producing nearly half of all manufactured goods.

Though the trend has been overstated, finance capitalists such as J. P. Morgan tended to replace the industrial capitalists of an earlier era. Able to finance the mergers and reorganizations, investment bankers played a greater and greater role in the economy. A multibillion-dollar financial house, J. P. Morgan and Company operated a network of control that ran from New York City to every industrial and financial center in the nation. Like other investment firms, it held directorships in many corporations, creating "interlocking directorates" that allowed it to control many businesses.

Massive business growth set off a decade-long debate over what government should do about the trusts. Some critics who believed that the giant companies were responsible for stifling individual opportunity and raising prices wanted to break them up into small competitive units. Others argued that large-scale business was a mark of the times, and that it produced more goods and better lives.

The debate over the trusts was one of the issues that shaped the Progressive Era, but it was never a simple contest between high-minded reformers and greedy business titans. Some progressives favored big business; others wanted it broken up. Business leaders themselves were divided. Some welcomed reformers' assaults on giant competitors. As a rule, both progressives and business leaders drew on similar visions of the country: complex, expansive, hopeful, managerially minded, and oriented toward results and efficiency. They both believed in private property and the importance of economic progress. In fact, in working for reform, the progressives often drew on the managerial methods of a business world they sought to regulate.

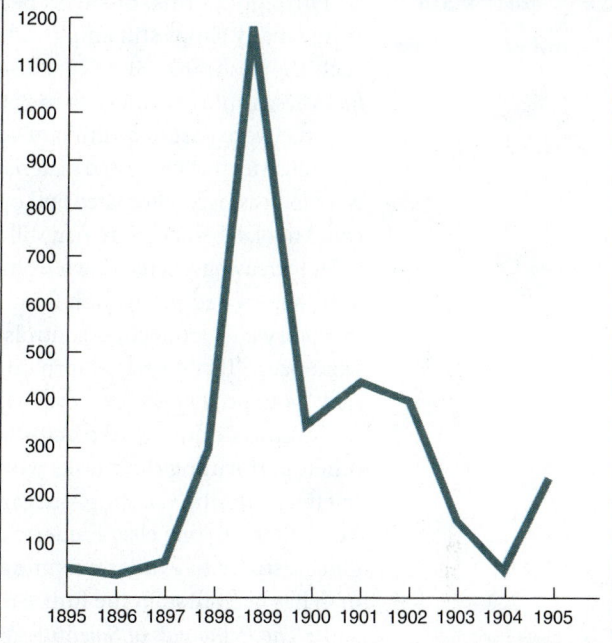

Figure 22.1 Business Consolidations (Mergers), 1895–1905

Quick Check

✓ What factors led to the rapid growth of trusts?

Managing the Machines

Mass production changed the direction of American industry. Size, system, organization, and marketing became increasingly important. Management focused on speed and product, not on workers. Assembly-line technology changed tasks and, to some extent, values. The goal was no longer to make a unique product that would be better than the one before. "The way to make automobiles," Ford said as early as 1903, "is to make one automobile like another automobile, to make them all alike, to make them come through the factory just alike."

In a development that rivaled assembly lines in importance, businesses established industrial research laboratories where scientists and engineers developed new products. General Electric founded the first one in 1900, housed in a barn. It soon attracted experts who improved light bulbs, invented the cathode-ray tube, worked on early radio, and even tinkered with atomic theory. Du Pont opened its labs in 1911, Eastman Kodak in 1912, and Standard Oil in 1919. As the source of new ideas and technology, the labs altered life in the twentieth and twenty-first centuries.

👁 **Watch** the **Video**
Punching the Clock on
myhistorylab.com

Through all this, business became large-scale, mechanized, and managed. While many shops still employed fewer than a dozen workers, the proportion of such shops shrank. By 1920, close to one-half of all industrial workers toiled in factories employing more than 250 people. More than one-third worked in factories that were part of multiplant companies.

Industries that processed materials—iron and steel, paper, cement, and chemicals—were increasingly automated and operated continuously. Workers in those industries could not fall behind. Foremen still managed the laborers on the factory floor, but the rules increasingly came down from a central office where trained professional managers supervised production flow. Systematic record keeping, cost accounting, and inventory and production controls became widespread. Workers lost control of the work pace. "If you need to turn out a little more," a manager at Swift and Company said, "you speed up the conveyor a little and the men speed up to keep pace."

Folkways of the workplace—workers passing job-related knowledge to each other, performing their tasks with little supervision, setting their own pace, and in effect running the shop—began to give way to "scientific" labor management. More than anyone else, Frederick Winslow Taylor, an inventive mechanical engineer, strove to extract maximum efficiency from each worker: "In the past the man has been first; in the future the system must be first."

📖 **Read** the
Document
*Frederick Winslow
Taylor, Scientific
Management
(1911)* on
myhistorylab.com

In *The Principles of Scientific Management* (1911), Taylor proposed two major reforms. First, management must take responsibility for job-related knowledge and classify it into "rules, laws, and formulae." Second, management should control the workplace "through *enforced* standardization of methods, *enforced* adoption of the best implements and working conditions, and *enforced* cooperation." Although few factories wholly adopted Taylor's principles, the doctrines of scientific management spread through American industry.

Tragedy at the Triangle Company Fire nets were of no avail to the workers at the Triangle Shirtwaist Company who jumped from the upper stories to escape the flames. Speaking to a mass meeting after the fire, labor organizer Rose Schneiderman inveighed against a system that treated human beings as expendable commodities.

Workers caught up in the changing industrial system experienced the benefits of efficiency and productivity; in some industries, they earned more. But they also suffered important losses. Performing repetitive tasks, they seemed part of the machinery, moving to the pace and needs of their mechanical pacesetters. Bored, they might easily lose pride of workmanship, though many workers, it is clear, did not. Efficiency engineers experimented with tools and methods, a process many workers found unsettling.

Jobs became not only monotonous but dangerous. As machines and assembly lines sped up, boredom or miscalculation could bring disaster. In March 1911, a fire at the Triangle Shirtwaist Company in New York focused nationwide attention on unsafe working conditions. When the fire started, 500 men and women, mostly Italians and eastern European Jews, were just finishing their workday. Firefighters arrived within minutes, but they were already too late. Terrified seamstresses raced to the exits to escape the flames, but the company had locked most exit doors to prevent theft and to shut out union organizers. Many died in the stampede down the narrow stairways or the single fire escape. Others, trapped on the top stories far above the reach of the fire department's ladders, jumped to their deaths on the street below: 146 people died.

A few days later, 80,000 people marched silently in the rain in a funeral procession up Fifth Avenue. A quarter million people watched. At a mass meeting to protest factory working conditions, Rose Schneiderman, a 29-year-old organizer for the Women's Trade Union League, told New York City's civic and religious leaders that they had not done enough, they had not cared: "We have tried you good people of the public and we have found you wanting. . . . Every week I must learn of the untimely death of one of my sister workers. Every year thousands of us are maimed. The life of men and women is so cheap and property is so sacred."

The outcry impelled New York's governor to appoint a State Factory Investigating Commission that recommended laws to shorten the workweek and improve safety in factories and stores.

Quick Check
✓ What methods emerged to help manage the workers and machinery on the factory floor?

SOCIETY'S MASSES

Spreading consumer goods through society, mass production not only improved people's lives but sometimes cost lives, too. Tending the machines, as Rose Schneiderman pointed out, took hard, painful labor, often under dangerous conditions. As businesses expanded, the labor force increased tremendously to keep up with the demand for workers in the factories, mines, and forests. Women, African Americans, Asian Americans, and Mexican Americans played larger and larger roles. Immigration soared. Between 1901 and 1910, nearly 8.8 million immigrants entered the United States; between 1911 and 1920, another 5.7 million came.

For many of these people, life was harsh, spent in crowded slums and long hours on the job. Fortunately, the massive unemployment of the 1890s was over, and in many skilled trades, such as cigar making, there was plenty of work to go around. Though the economic recovery helped nearly everyone, the less skilled continued to be the less fortunate. Migrant workers, lumberjacks, ore shovelers, and others struggled to find decent-paying jobs.

How did mass production affect women, children, immigrants, and African Americans?

Under such circumstances, many people fought to make a living, and many, too, fought to improve their lot. Their efforts, along with those of the reform-minded people who came to their aid, became another important hallmark of the Progressive Era.

Better Times on the Farm

While people continued to flee the farms—by 1920, fewer than one-third of all Americans lived on farms, and fewer than one-half lived in rural areas—farmers themselves prospered, the beneficiaries of greater production and expanding urban markets. Rural free delivery (RFD), begun in 1896, helped diminish the farmers' sense of isolation and changed farm life. The delivery of mail to the farm door opened that door to a wider world; it exposed farmers to urban thinking, national advertising, and political events. In 1911, more than one billion newspapers and magazines were delivered over RFD routes.

Watch the **Video**
Rural Free Delivery Mail on
myhistorylab.com

Parcel post (1913) permitted the sending of packages through the U.S. mail. Mail-order houses flourished; rural merchants suffered. Within a year, 300 million packages were being mailed annually. While telephones and electricity did not reach most rural areas for decades, better roads, mail-order catalogs, and other innovations knit farmers into the larger society. Early in the new century, Mary E. Lease—who in her Populist days had urged Kansas farmers to raise less corn and more hell—moved to Brooklyn.

Farmers still had problems. Land prices rose with crop prices, and farm tenancy increased, especially in the South. Tenancy grew from one-quarter of all farms in 1880 to more than one-third in 1910. Many southern tenant farmers were African Americans, and they suffered from farm-bred diseases. In one of the reforms of the Progressive Era, in 1909, the Rockefeller Sanitary Commission, acting on recent scientific discoveries, began a sanitation campaign that eventually wiped out the hookworm disease.

In the arid West, irrigation transformed the land as the federal government and private landholders joined to import water from mountain watersheds. The dry lands bloomed, and so did a rural class structure that sharply separated owners from workers. Under the Newlands Act of 1902, the secretary of the interior formed the U.S. Reclamation Service, which gathered a staff of thousands of engineers and technicians, "the largest bureaucracy ever assembled in irrigation history."

Quick Check

✓ Why did conditions on the farm improve after 1900?

Dams and canals channeled water into places such as California's Imperial Valley. As the water streamed in, cotton, cantaloupes, oranges, tomatoes, lettuce, and other crops streamed out to national markets. By 1920, Idaho, Montana, Utah, Wyoming, Colorado, and Oregon had extensive irrigation systems, all drawing on scarce water supplies; California, the foremost importer of water, had 4.2 million acres under irrigation, many of them picked by migrant workers from Mexico, China, and Japan.

Women and Children at Work

Watch the **Video**
Women in the Workplace, 1904 on
myhistorylab.com

More women worked. In 1900, more than 5 million worked—one-fifth of all adult women—and among those aged 14 to 24, the employment rate was almost one-third. Of those employed, single women outnumbered married women by seven to one, yet more than one-third of married women worked. Most women held service jobs. Only a few held higher-paying jobs as professionals or managers.

In the 1890s, women made up more than one-quarter of medical school graduates. Using a variety of techniques, men gradually squeezed them out, and by the 1920s, only about 5 percent of the graduates were women. Few women taught in colleges and universities, and those who did were expected to resign if they married.

More women than men graduated from high school. With professions like medicine and science largely closed to them, they often turned to the new "business schools" that offered training in stenography, typing, and bookkeeping. In 1920, more than one-quarter of all employed women held clerical jobs. Many others taught school.

Far more black women than white women had always worked. The reason was usually economic; an African American man or woman alone could rarely support a family. Unlike many white women, black women tended to remain in the labor force after marriage or the start of a family. They also had less opportunity for job advancement. In 1920, between one-third and one-half of all African American women who were working were restricted to personal and domestic service jobs.

Critics charged that women's employment endangered the home, threatened their reproductive functions, and even, as one man said, stripped them of "that modest demeanor that lends a charm to their kind." Adding to these fears, the birthrate continued to drop between 1900 and 1920, and the divorce rate soared, in part because more working-class men took advantage of the newer moral freedom and deserted their families. By 1916, there was one divorce for every nine marriages as compared to one for 21 in 1880.

Many children also worked. In 1900, about 3 million children—nearly 20 percent of those between ages 5 and 15—held full-time or almost full-time jobs. Twenty-five thousand boys under 16 worked in mining; 20,000 children under 12, mainly girls, worked in southern cotton mills. But as public indignation grew, the use of child labor shrank.

Determined to do something about the situation, the Women's Trade Union League lobbied the federal Bureau of Labor to investigate the conditions under which women and children worked. Begun in 1907, the investigation took four years and produced 19 volumes of data, some of it shocking, all of it factual. In 1911, spurred by the data, the Children's Bureau was formed within the U.S. Bureau of Labor, with Grace Abbott, a social worker, at its head.

Numerous middle-class women became involved in the fight for reform. Many others, reflecting the ongoing changes in the family, took

> **Read** the **Document**
> *John Spargo, "The Bitter Cries of the Children" on* **myhistorylab.com**

Child Labor Breaker boys, who picked out pieces of slate from the coal as it rushed past, often became bent-backed and suffered respiratory diseases such as bronchitis and tuberculosis after years of working 14 hours a day in the coal mines. Accidents—and deaths—were common in the mines.

Quick Check

✓ In what conditions
did women and chil-
dren work in the early
twentieth century?

increasing pride in homemaking and motherhood. Mother's Day, the national holi-
day, was formally established in 1913. Women who preferred fewer children turned
increasingly to birth control, which became more acceptable. Margaret Sanger,
a nurse and outspoken social reformer, led a campaign to give physicians broad
discretion in prescribing contraceptives.

The Niagara Movement and the NAACP

Read the
Document
*The Niagara Move-
ment Declaration
of Principles* on
myhistorylab.com

In 1900, eight of every ten African Americans still lived in rural areas, mainly in
the South. Most were poor sharecroppers. Jim Crow laws segregated many schools,
railroad cars, hotels, and hospitals. Poll taxes and other devices disfranchised blacks
and many poor whites. Violence was common; from 1900 to 1914, white mobs
murdered more than 1,000 black people.

Many African Americans labored on the cotton farms and in the railroad
camps, sawmills, and mines of the South under conditions of peonage. Peons
traded their lives and labor for food and shelter. Often illiterate, they were forced
to sign contracts allowing the planter "to use such force as he or his agents may
deem necessary to require me to remain on his farm and perform good and satisfactory services." Armed guards patrolled the camps and whipped those trying
to escape.

Few blacks belonged to labor unions, and blacks almost always earned less
than whites in the same job. In Atlanta, white electricians earned $5.00 a day,
blacks $3.50. Black songs such as "I've Got a White Man Workin' for Me" (1901)
voiced more hope than reality. Illiteracy among African Americans dropped
from 45 percent in 1900 to 30 percent in 1910, but nowhere were they given
equal school facilities, teachers' salaries, or educational materials. In 1910,
scarcely 8,000 African American youths attended high schools in all the states
of the Southeast.

African American leaders grew increasingly impatient with this kind of treatment, and in 1905 a group of them, led by sociologist W. E. B. Du Bois, met near
Niagara Falls, New York (they met on the Canadian side of the Falls, since no hotel
on the American side would take them). There they pledged action on equal access
to voting, economic opportunity, integration, and equality before the law. Rejecting Booker T. Washington's gradualist approach, the Niagara Movement claimed
"every single right that belongs to a freeborn American, political, civil and social;
and until we get these rights we will never cease to protest."

The Niagara Movement focused on equal rights and the education of African
American youth: "They have a right to know, to think, to aspire." Keeping alive a
program of militant action, it spawned later civil rights movements. Du Bois was its
inspiration. In *The Souls of Black Folk* (1903) and other works, he called eloquently
for justice and equality.

Still, race riots broke out in Atlanta, Georgia, in 1906 and Springfield, Illinois, in
1908, the latter the home of Abraham Lincoln. Unlike the riots of the 1960s, white
mobs invaded black neighborhoods, burning, looting, and killing. They lynched
two blacks—one 84 years old—in Springfield.

William E. Walling, a wealthy southerner and settlement house worker; Mary Ovington, a white anthropology student; and Oswald Garrison Villard, grandson of the famous abolitionist William Lloyd Garrison, were outraged. With other reformers, white and black (among them Jane Addams and John Dewey), they called for the conference that organized the National Association for the Advancement of Colored People (NAACP), which swiftly became the most important civil rights organization in the country. Created in 1909, within five years the NAACP had 50 branches and more than 6,000 members. Walling headed it, and Du Bois, the only African American among the top officers, directed publicity and edited its magazine, *The Crisis*.

Joined by the National Urban League, which was created in 1911, the NAACP pressured employers, labor unions, and the government on behalf of African Americans. It had some victories. In 1918, during World War I, the NAACP and the National Urban League persuaded the federal government to form a special Bureau of Negro Economics within the Labor Department to look after the interests of African American workers.

Despite these gains, African Americans continued to experience disfranchisement, poor job opportunities, and segregation. As Booker T. Washington said in 1913, "I have never seen the colored people so discouraged and so bitter as they are at the present time."

> **Quick Check**
> ✓ What were the main causes for the formation of the Niagara Movement and the NAACP in the early twentieth century?

Immigrants in the Labor Force

While more women and African Americans were working, much of the huge increase in the labor force in these years came from outside the country, particularly from Europe and Mexico. Between 1901 and 1920, 14.5 million immigrants entered the country, more than in any previous 20-year period. Continuing the trend begun in the 1880s, many came from southern and eastern Europe. Still called the "new" immigrants, they met hostility from "older" immigrants of northern European stock who questioned their values, religion (often Catholic or Jewish), traditions, and appearance. (See Figure 22.2.)

Immigrant patterns often departed from traditional stereotypes. Immigrants, for example, moved both to and from their homelands. Fifty percent or more of the members of some groups returned home, although the proportion varied. Jews and Czechs often brought their families to resettle in America; Serbs and Poles tended to come singly, intent on earning enough money to make a fresh start at home. Some migrants—Italian men, in particular—virtually commuted, returning home every slack season. These temporary migrants became known as birds of passage. The outbreak of World War I trapped thousands who had planned to return to Europe.

Older residents lumped the newcomers together, ignoring geographic, religious, and other differences. Preserving important regional distinctions, Italians, for example, tended to settle as Calabreses, Venetians, Abruzzis, and Sicilians. Yet to old-stock Americans, they were all simply Italians. Henry Ford and other employers tried to erase the differences through English classes and "Americanization" programs. The Ford Motor Company ran a school where immigrant employees were

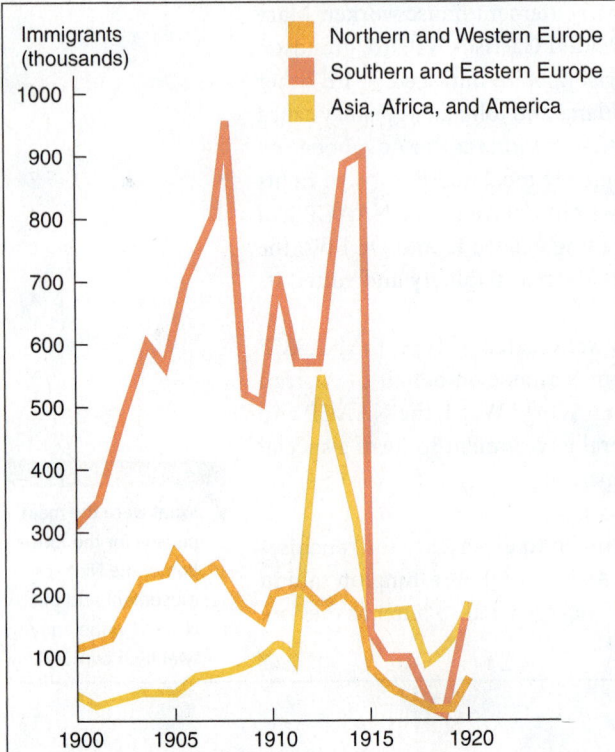

Figure 22.2   Immigration to the United States, 1900–1920 (by area of origin)

Note: For purposes of classification, "Northern and Western Europe" includes Great Britain, Ireland, Scandinavia, the Netherlands, Belgium, Luxembourg, Switzerland, France, and Germany. "Southern and Eastern Europe" includes Poland, Austria-Hungary, Russia and the Baltic States, Romania, Bulgaria, European Turkey, Italy, Spain, Portugal, and Greece. "Asia, Africa, and America" includes Asian Turkey, China, Japan, India, Canada, the Caribbean, Latin America, and all of Africa.
Source: U.S. Bureau of the Census, *Historical Statistics of the United States, Colonial Times to 1970*, Bicentennial Edition, Washington, DC, 1975.

first taught to say, "I am a good American." At the graduation ceremony, the pupils acted out a gigantic pantomime in which, clad in their old-country dress, they filed into a large "melting pot." When they emerged, they were wearing identical American-made clothes, and each was waving an American flag.

Labor groups soon learned to counter these techniques. The Women's Trade Union League (WTUL) urged workers to ignore business-sponsored English lessons because they did not "tell the girl worker the things she really wants to know. They do not suggest that $5 a week is not a living wage. They tell her to be respectful to her employer."

In another significant development at the beginning of the twentieth century, for the first time, many Mexicans immigrated, especially after a revolution in Mexico in 1910 forced them to flee across the border into Texas, New Mexico, Arizona, and California. Their exact numbers were unknown. American officials did not count border crossings until 1907, and even then, many migrants avoided the official immigration stations. Almost all came from the Mexican lower class, eager to escape peonage and violence in their native land. Labor agents called *coyotes*—usually in the employ of large corporations or ranchers—recruited Mexican workers.

Between 1900 and 1910, the Mexican population of Texas and New Mexico nearly doubled; in Arizona, it more than doubled; in California, it quadrupled. In all four states, it doubled again between 1910 and 1920. After 1900, almost 10 percent of the population of Mexico moved to the American Southwest. (See Figure 22.3.)

In time, these Mexican Americans and their children transformed the Southwest. They built most of the early highways in Texas, New Mexico, and Arizona; dug the irrigation ditches that watered crops; laid railroad track; and picked the cotton and vegetables that clothed and fed millions of Americans. Many lived in shacks and shanties along the railroad tracks, isolated in a separate Spanish-speaking world. Like other immigrant groups, they also formed enclaves in the cities; these *barrios* became cultural islands of family life, foods, church, and festivals.

Fewer people emigrated from China in these years, deterred in part by anti-Chinese laws and hostility. Like many other immigrants, most Chinese who came wanted to make money and return home. They mined, farmed, and worked as common

View the **Image**
Chinese Americans in California on
myhistorylab.com

laborers. In their willingness to work hard for low wages, their desire to preserve clan and family associations from China, and their strong ties to their home villages, Chinese Americans resembled other immigrant groups, but they differed in two important respects. As late as 1920, men outnumbered women by ten to one in the Chinese American population, and with a male median age of 42, the elderly dominated their communities.

The Chinese-American population differed in another respect as well. Unlike other immigrant groups, whose numbers tended to grow, the number of Chinese Americans shrank in these years—from about 125,000 in the early 1880s to just over 60,000 in 1920. After 1910, the U.S. government set up a special immigration facility at Angel Island in San Francisco Bay, but unlike European immigrants who landed at Ellis Island in New York and were quickly sent on, Chinese immigrants were kept for weeks and months, examined and reexamined, before being allowed to cross the narrow band of water to San Francisco.

Many Japanese also arrived at Angel Island, and though at first fewer in numbers than the Chinese, they developed communities along the Pacific coast, where they settled mainly on farms. The number of Japanese Americans grew. In 1907, the heaviest year of immigration from Japan, nearly 31,000 Japanese entered the United States; by 1920, there were 111,000 Japanese in the country, nearly three-quarters of them in California.

As the newcomers arrived from Asia, Europe, and Mexico, nativist sentiment, which had criticized earlier waves of immigrants, intensified. Old-stock Americans sneered at their dress and language. Racial theories emphasized the superiority of northern Europeans, and the new "science" of eugenics suggested the need to control the population growth of "inferior" peoples. Hostility to Catholics and Jews was common but also touched other groups.

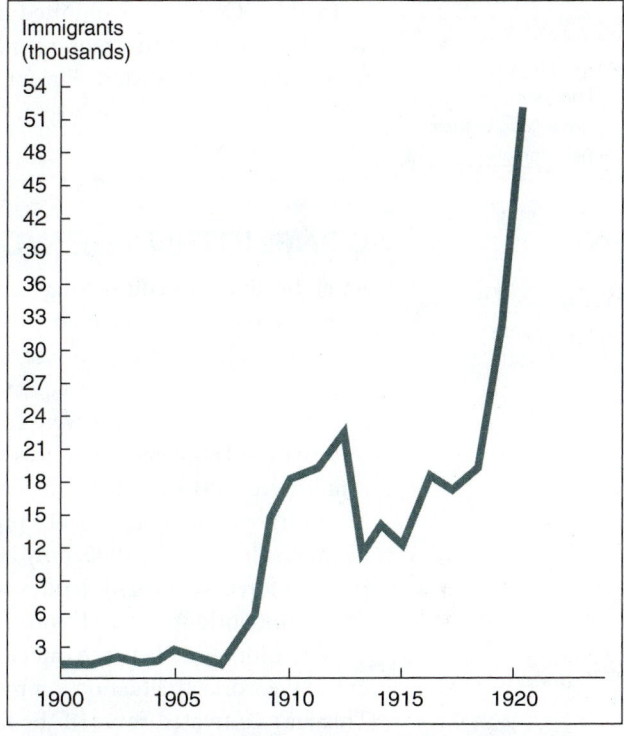

Figure 22.3   Mexican Immigration to the United States, 1900–1920

Immigrants from Asia Japanese immigrants wait with a Methodist deaconess in the administration building of the immigration station at Angel Island, near San Francisco. Quota systems and exclusionary laws limited Asian immigration, while other laws placed restrictions on the immigrants, curtailing their right to own or even rent agricultural land. Some Asian immigrants, after months of detention at Angel Island, were refused permission to enter the United States and were forced to return to their homelands. (*Source: Courtesy of the California Historical Society, FN-18240.*)

In 1902, Congress prohibited immigration from China. Presidents Taft and Wilson vetoed statutes requiring literacy tests designed to curtail immigration from southern and eastern Europe in 1913 and 1915. In 1917, another such measure passed despite Wilson's veto. Other measures tried to limit immigration from Mexico and Japan.

CONFLICT IN THE WORKPLACE

Why were there so many strikes in this period?

Assembly lines, speedups, long hours, and low pay increased American industrial output (and profits) after 1900; they also gave rise to strikes and other labor unrest. Sometimes unions led strikes; sometimes workers just walked off the job. Whatever the cause, strikes were frequent. In one industry, in one city—the meatpacking industry in Chicago—there were 251 strikes in 1903 alone.

Strikes and absenteeism increased after 1910; labor productivity dropped 10 percent between 1915 and 1918, the first such decline in memory. In many industries, labor turnover became a serious problem; workers changed jobs in droves. Union membership grew. In 1900, only about a million workers—less than 4 percent of the workforce—belonged to unions. By 1920, 5 million workers belonged, 13 percent of the workforce. (See Figure 22.4.)

Read the **Document**
Samuel Gompers, The American Labor Movement (1914) on **myhistorylab.com**

As tensions grew between capital and labor, some middle-class people feared that, unless the workers' situation improved, there might be violence or even revolution. This fear motivated some of the labor-oriented reforms of the Progressive Era. While some reform supporters genuinely wanted to improve labor's lot, others embraced reform because they were afraid of violent upheaval.

Organizing Labor

Samuel Gompers's American Federation of Labor (AFL), by far the largest union organization, remained devoted to the interests of skilled craftspeople. While it sought better wages and working conditions, it also sought to limit entry into the crafts and protect worker prerogatives. Within limits, the AFL found acceptance among giant business corporations eager for conservative policies and labor stability.

Of the 8 million female workers in 1910, only 125,000 belonged to unions. Gompers continued to resist organizing them, saying they were too emotional and, as union organizers, "had a way of making serious mistakes." Margaret Dreier Robins, an organizer of proven skill, scoffed at that: "These men died twenty years ago and are just walking around dead!"

Robins helped found the Women's Trade Union League in 1903. The WTUL led the effort to organize women into trade unions, lobby for legislation

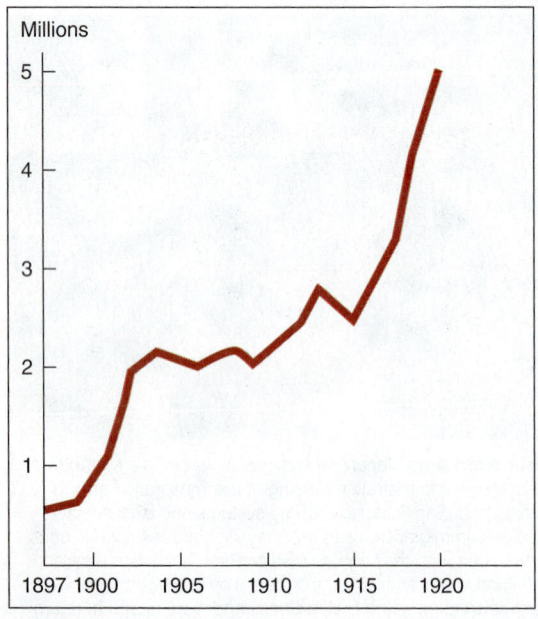

Figure 22.4 Labor Union Membership, 1897–1920
Source: U.S. Bureau of the Census, *Statistical Abstract of the United States: 1982–1983,* 103rd ed., Washington, DC, 1982.

protecting female workers, and educate the public on the problems and needs of working women. It accepted all working women who would join, regardless of skill (although not, at first, African American women), and it won crucial financial support from well-to-do women such as Anne Morgan, daughter of the feared financier J. P. Morgan. Robins's close friend Jane Addams belonged, as did Mary McDowell, the "Angel of the Stockyards," who worked with slaughterhouse workers in Chicago; Julia Lathrop, who tried to improve the lot of wage-earning children; and Dr. Alice Hamilton, a pioneer in American research on the causes of industrial disease.

The WTUL never had more than a few thousand members, but its influence extended far beyond its membership. In 1909, it supported the "Uprising of the 20,000," a strike of shirtwaist workers in New York City. When female employees of the Triangle Shirtwaist Company tried to form a union, the company fired them, and they walked out; 20,000 men and women in 500 other shops followed. Strike meetings were conducted in three languages—English, Yiddish, and Italian—and before being forced to go back to work, the strikers won a shorter workweek and a few other gains. Sadly, the Triangle women lost out on another important demand—for unlocked shop doors and safe fire escapes. Their loss proved lethal in the famous Triangle Shirtwaist Company fire of 1911.

The WTUL also backed a strike in 1910 against Hart, Schaffner and Marx, Chicago's largest manufacturer of men's clothing. One day, Annie Shapiro, the 18-year-old daughter of Russian immigrants, was told her wages were being cut from $7 a week to $6.20. That was a large cut, and along with 16 other young women, Shapiro refused to accept it and walked out. "We had to be recognized as people," she said later. Other women joined them, and the revolt spread.

Within days, 40,000 garment workers were on strike, about half of them women. Manufacturers hurried to negotiate, and the result was the important Hart, Schaffner agreement, which created an arbitration committee composed of management and labor to handle grievances and settle disputes. The first successful experiment in collective bargaining, it became the model for agreements that govern industrial relations today.

Another union, the Industrial Workers of the World (IWW), attracted the most attention (and fears) in these years. Unlike the WTUL, it welcomed everyone regardless of gender or race. Unlike the AFL, it tried to organize the unskilled and foreign-born who worked in the mass production industries. Founded in Chicago in 1905, it aimed to unite the American working class into a mammoth union to promote labor's interests. Its motto—"An injury to one is an injury to all"—stressed labor solidarity, as had

A Radical Union Holding signs and banners that proudly display their union allegiance, including a sign with the slogan, "An injury to one is an injury to all," women of the IWW participate in a strike at the Oliver Iron and Steel Company in Pittsburgh, Pennsylvania, in 1913. The Clayton Act in 1914 legalized picketing and other union activity.

the earlier Knights of Labor. But unlike the Knights, the IWW, or Wobblies as they were known, urged social revolution.

"It is our purpose to overthrow the capitalist system by forcible means if necessary," William D. "Big Bill" Haywood, one of its founders, said; and he went on in his speeches to say he knew of nothing a worker could do that "will bring as much anguish to the boss as a little sabotage in the right place." IWW leaders included Mary Harris ("Mother") Jones, a famous veteran of battles in the Illinois coalfields; Elizabeth Gurley Flynn, a fiery young radical who joined as a teenager; and Haywood himself, the strapping one-eyed founder of the Western Federation of Miners.

The IWW led a number of major strikes. Strikes in Lawrence, Massachusetts (1912), and Paterson, New Jersey (1912), attracted national attention: in Lawrence, when the strikers sent their children, ill-clad and hungry, out of the city to stay with sympathetic families; in Paterson, when they rented New York's Madison Square Garden for a massive labor pageant. IWW leaders welcomed the revolutionary tumult sweeping Russia and other countries. In the United States, they thought, a series of local strikes would provoke capitalist repression, then a general strike, and eventually a workers' commonwealth.

The IWW fell short of these objectives, but during its lifetime—from 1905 to the mid-1920s—it made major gains among immigrant workers in the Northeast, migrant farm laborers on the Plains, and loggers and miners in the South and Far West. In factories like Ford's, it recruited workers resentful of the speedups on the assembly lines. Although IWW membership probably amounted to no more than 100,000 at any one time, workers came and left so often that its total membership may have reached 1 million.

Concerned about labor unrest, some business leaders used violence and police action to keep workers in line, but others turned to the new fields of applied psychology and personnel management. A school of industrial psychology emerged. As had Taylor, industrial psychologists studied workers' routines and showed that job satisfaction also affected output. As a result, some businesses established industrial relations departments, hired public relations firms to improve their corporate image, and linked productivity to job safety and worker happiness.

To please employees, companies printed newsletters and organized softball teams; they awarded prizes and celebrated retirements. Ford created a "sociology department" staffed by 150 experts who showed workers how to budget their incomes and care for their health. They even taught them how to shop for meat.

On January 5, 1914, Ford took another significant step. He announced the $5 day, "the greatest revolution," he said, "in the matter of rewards for workers ever known to the industrial world." With a stroke, he doubled the wage rate for common labor, reduced the work day from nine hours to eight, and established a personnel department to place workers in appropriate jobs. The next day, 10,000 applicants stood outside the gates.

As a result, Ford had the pick of the labor force. Turnover declined; absenteeism, previously as much as one-tenth of all Ford workers every day, fell to 0.3 percent. Output increased; the IWW at Ford collapsed. The plan increased wages, but it also gave the company greater control over a more stable labor force. Workers had to meet a behavior code to qualify for the $5 day. At first scornful of the "utopian" plan, business leaders across the country soon copied it, and on January 2, 1919, Ford announced the $6 day.

Quick Check

✓ How did labor organize to protect its interests, and how did some businesses, like Ford, respond?

A NEW URBAN CULTURE

For many Americans, the quality of life improved significantly between 1900 and 1920. Jobs were relatively plentiful, and, in a development of great importance, more and more people were entering the professions as doctors, lawyers, teachers, and engineers. With comfortable incomes, a growing middle class could take advantage of new lifestyles, inventions, and forms of entertainment. Mass production could not have worked without mass consumption, and Americans in these years increasingly became a nation of consumers.

What happened to art and culture in these years so filled with change?

Production and Consumption

In 1900, business firms spent about $95 million on advertising; 20 years later, they spent more than $500 million. Ads and billboards touted cigarettes, cars, perfumes, and cosmetics. Advertising agencies boomed. Using new sampling techniques, they developed modern concepts of market testing and research. Sampling customer preferences also made businesses more responsive to public opinion on social and political issues.

Mass production swept the clothing industry and dressed more Americans better than any people ever had been before. Using lessons learned in making uniforms during the Civil War, manufacturers for the first time developed standard clothing and shoe sizes that fit most bodies. Clothing prices dropped; the availability of inexpensive "off-the-rack" clothes lessened distinctions between rich and poor. By 1900, nine of every ten men and boys wore the new "ready-to-wear" clothes.

In 1900, manufacturing workers earned on average $418 a year. In 1920, they earned $1,342 a year, though inflation took much of the increase. While the middle class expanded, the rich also grew richer. In 1920, the new income tax showed the first accurate tabulation of income, and it confirmed what many had suspected all along. Five percent of the population received almost one-fourth of all income.

Quick Check

✓ What were some of the characteristics of mass production?

Living and Dying in an Urban Nation

In 1920, the median age of the population was only 25. (It is now 35.) Immigration accounted for part of the population's youthfulness, since most immigrants were young. Thanks to medical advances and better living conditions, the death rate dropped, and the average life span increased. Between 1900 and

1920, life expectancy rose from 49 to 56 years for white women and from 47 to 54 years for white men. It rose from 33 to 45 years for blacks and other racial minorities.

Despite the increase in life expectancy, infant mortality remained high; nearly 10 percent of white babies and 20 percent of minority babies died in the first year of life. In comparison to today, fewer babies on average survived to adolescence, and fewer people survived beyond middle age. In 1900, the death rate among people between 45 and 65 was more than twice the modern rate. As a result, there were relatively fewer older people—in 1900, only 4 percent of the population was older than 65, compared to nearly 13 percent today. Fewer children than today knew their grandparents. Still, improvements in health care helped people live longer, and as a result, the incidence of cancer and heart disease increased.

Cities grew, and by any earlier standards, they grew on a colossal scale. Downtowns became a central hive of skyscrapers, department stores, warehouses, and hotels. Strips of factories radiated from the center. As street railways spread, cities took on a systematic pattern of socioeconomic segregation, usually in rings. The innermost ring filled with immigrants, circled by a belt of working-class housing. The remaining rings marked areas of rising affluence outward toward wealthy suburbs, which themselves formed around shopping strips and grid patterns of streets that restricted social interaction.

The giants were New York, Chicago, and Philadelphia, industrial cities that turned out every kind of product from textiles to structural steel. Smaller cities such as Rochester, New York, or Cleveland, Ohio, specialized in manufacturing a specific line of goods or processing regional products for the national market. Railroads instead of highways tied things together; in 1916, the rail network, the largest in the world, reached its peak—254,000 miles of track that carried more than three-fourths of all intercity freight tonnage.

Step by step, cities adopted their twentieth-century forms. Between 1909 and 1915, Los Angeles, a city of 300,000 people, passed ordinances that gave rise to modern urban zoning. For the first time, the ordinances divided a city into three districts of specified use: a residential area, an industrial area, and an area open to residence and a limited list of industries. Other cities followed. Combining several features, the New York zoning law of 1916 became the model for the nation; within a decade, 591 cities copied it.

Zoning ordered city development, keeping skyscrapers out of factory districts, factories out of the suburbs. It also had social repercussions. In the South, zoning became a tool to extend racial segregation; in northern cities, it acted against ethnic minorities. Jews in New York, Italians in Boston, Poles in Detroit and African Americans in Chicago—zoning laws held them all at arm's length. Like other migrants, African Americans often preferred to settle together, but zoning also helped put them there. By 1920, ten districts in Chicago were more than three-quarters black. In Los Angeles, Cleveland, Detroit, and Washington, D.C., most blacks lived in only two or three wards.

Quick Check

✓ What were some of the characteristics of the new urban culture?

Popular Pastimes

Thanks to changing work rules and mechanization, many Americans enjoyed more leisure time. The average workweek for manufacturing laborers fell from 60 hours in 1890 to 51 in 1920. By the early 1900s, white-collar workers might spend only 8 to 10 hours a day at work and a half day on Saturday. Greater leisure time gave more people more opportunity for play, and people flocked to places of entertainment. Baseball entrenched itself as the national pastime. Automobiles and streetcars carried fans to ballparks; attendance at major league games doubled between 1903 and 1920. Football also drew fans, although critics attacked its violence and the use of "tramp athletes," nonstudents whom colleges paid to play. In 1905, the worst year, 18 players were killed and 150 seriously injured.

Alarmed, President Theodore Roosevelt—who had once said, "I am the father of three boys [and] if I thought any one of them would weigh a possible broken bone against the glory of being chosen to play on Harvard's football team I would disinherit him"—called a White House conference to clean up college sports. The conference founded the Intercollegiate Athletic Association, which in 1910 became the National Collegiate Athletic Association (NCAA).

Movie theaters opened everywhere. By 1910, there were 10,000 of them, drawing a weekly audience of 10 million people. Admission was usually 5 cents, and movies stressing laughter and pathos appealed to a mass market. In 1915, D. W. Griffith, a talented and creative director—as well as a racist—produced the first movie spectacular: *Birth of a Nation*. Griffith adopted new film techniques, including close-ups, fade-outs, and artistic camera angles.

Phonographs brought ready-made entertainment into the home. By 1901, phonograph and record companies included the Victor Talking Machine Company, the Edison Speaking Machine Company, and Columbia Records. Ornate mahogany Victrolas became standard fixtures in middle-class parlors. Early records were usually of vaudeville skits; orchestral recordings began in 1906. In 1919, 2.25 million phonographs were produced; two years later, more than 100 million records were sold.

As record sales grew, families sang less and listened more. Music became a business. In 1909, a copyright law provided a 2-cent royalty on each piece of music on phonograph records or piano rolls. The royalty, small as it was, offered welcome income to composers and publishers, and in 1914, composer Victor Herbert and others formed the American Society of Composers, Authors, and Publishers (ASCAP) to protect musical rights and royalties.

Vaudeville, increasingly popular after 1900, matured around 1915. Drawing on the immigrant experience, it voiced the variety of city life and included skits, songs, comics, acrobats, and magicians. Dances and jokes showed an earthiness new to mass audiences. By 1914, stage runways extended into the crowd; women performers had bared their legs and were beginning to show glimpses of the midriff.

In songs like "St. Louis Blues" (1914), W. C. Handy took the black southern folk music of the blues to northern cities. Gertrude "Ma" Rainey, the daughter of

Watch the **Video**
A Vaudeville Act on
myhistorylab.com

minstrels, sang in black vaudeville for nearly 35 years. Performing in Chattanooga, Tennessee, about 1910, she came across a 12-year-old orphan, Bessie Smith, who became the "Empress of the Blues." Smith's voice was huge and sweeping. She made more than 80 records for the Race division of Columbia Records that together sold nearly ten million copies.

Another musical innovation came north from New Orleans. Charles (Buddy) Bolden, a cornetist; Ferdinand "Jelly Roll" Morton, a pianist; and a youngster named Louis Armstrong played an improvisational music that had no formal name. Reaching Chicago, it became "jas," then "jass," and finally "jazz." Jazz jumped, and jazz musicians relied on feeling and mood.

Quick Check

✓ How did people use their new leisure time?

Experimentation in the Arts

"There is a state of unrest all over the world in art as in all other things," the director of New York's Metropolitan Museum said in 1908. "It is the same in literature, as in music, in painting, and in sculpture."

Isadora Duncan and Ruth St. Denis transformed dance. Departing from traditional ballet steps, both women stressed improvisation, emotion, and the human form. The lofts and apartments of New York's Greenwich Village attracted artists, writers, and poets interested in experimentation and change. To these artists, the city was the focus of national life and the sign of a new culture. Robert Henri and the realist painters known to their critics as the Ashcan School—relished the city's excitement. They wanted, a friend said, "to paint truth and to paint it with strength and fearlessness and individuality."

To the realists, a painting carried into the future the look of life as it happened. Their paintings depicted street scenes, colorful crowds, and slum children swimming in the river. In paintings such as the *Cliff Dwellers*, George W. Bellows captured the color and excitement of the tenements; John Sloan, one of Henri's most talented students, painted the vitality of ordinary people and familiar scenes.

In 1913, a show at the New York Armory presented 1,600 modernist paintings, prints, and sculptures. The work of Picasso, Cézanne, Matisse, Brancusi, Van Gogh, and Gauguin dazed and dazzled American observers. Critics attacked the show as worthless and depraved; a Chicago official wanted it banned because the "idea that people can gaze at this sort of thing without [it] hurting them is all bosh."

The postimpressionists changed the direction of twentieth-century art and influenced adventuresome American painters. John Marin, Max Weber, Georgia O'Keeffe, Arthur Dove, and other modernists experimented in ways foreign to Henri's realists. Defiantly avant-garde, they shook off convention and experimented with new forms. Using bold colors and abstract patterns, they worked to capture the energy of urban life.

There was also an extraordinary outburst of poetry. In 1912, Harriet Monroe started the magazine *Poetry* in Chicago, the hotbed of the new poetry; Ezra Pound and Vachel Lindsay, both daring experimenters with ideas and verse, published in the first issue. T. S. Eliot published the classic "Love Song of J. Alfred Prufrock" in *Poetry* in 1915. Others experimenting with new techniques in poetry included Robert Frost (*North of Boston*, 1914), Edgar Lee Masters (*Spoon River Anthology*, 1915), and Carl Sandburg (*Chicago Poems*, 1916). Sandburg's poem "Chicago" celebrated the vitality of the city.

Quick Check

✓ What were some of the important changes in the arts in the period?

CONCLUSION: A FERMENT OF DISCOVERY AND REFORM

Manners and morals change slowly, and many Americans overlooked the importance of the first two decades of the twentieth century. Yet sweeping change was under way; anyone who doubted it could visit a gallery, see a film, listen to music, or read one of the new literary magazines. Garrets and galleries were filled with a breathtaking sense of change. "There was life in all these new things," Marsden Hartley, a modernist painter, recalled. "There was excitement, there was healthy revolt, investigation, discovery, and an utterly new world out of it all."

The ferment of progressivism in city, state, and nation reshaped the country. In a burst of reform, people built playgrounds, restructured taxes, regulated business, won the vote for women, shortened working hours, altered political systems, opened kindergartens, and improved factory safety. They tried to fulfill the national promise of dignity and liberty.

Marsden Hartley, it turned out, had voiced a mood that went well beyond painters and poets. Across society, people in many walks of life were experiencing a similar sense of excitement and discovery. Racism, repression, and labor conflict were present, to be sure, but there was also talk of hope, progress, and change. In politics, science, journalism, education, and a host of other fields, people believed for a time that they could make a difference, and in trying to do so, they became part of the progressive generation.

22 STUDY RESOURCES

((•—**Listen** to the **Chapter Audio** for Chapter 22 on **myhistorylab.com**

TIMELINE

1898 Mergers and consolidations begin to sweep the business world, leading to fear of trusts, p. 554

1903 Ford Motor Company formed, p. 553
- W. E. B. Du Bois's *The Souls of Black Folk*, p. 560
- Women's Trade Union League (WTUL) formed, p. 562

1905 Industrial Workers of the World (IWW) established, p. 565
- African American leaders inaugurate the Niagara Movement, p. 560

1909 Shirtwaist workers in New York City strike in the Uprising of the 20,000, p. 557

CHAPTER REVIEW

THE CHANGING FACE OF INDUSTRIALISM

How did industrialism change after 1900?

As prosperity returned after the late 1890s, the American industrial system underwent important changes. Mass production, spurred by the spread of the moving assembly line, turned out more and more products for American and foreign consumers. New management methods organized workers on the factory floor. Jobs became both routine and more dangerous. Trusts grew. *(p. 553)*

SOCIETY'S MASSES

How did mass production affect women, children, immigrants, and African Americans?

While life improved for many people in the post-1900 industrial society, many others faced challenges: women and children in the workforce, and laborers in their efforts to organize. Between 1901 and 1920, some 14.8 million immigrants entered the country and began the difficult process of adjusting to life in their new home. All of these people faced difficult challenges due to low wages, dangerous working conditions, and the steady demands of the factory system. *(p. 557)*

CONFLICT IN THE WORKPLACE

Why were there so many strikes in the period?

Low wages, speeded-up assembly lines, and dangerous conditions in the workplace brought about numerous attempts to organize workers for their own defense. The Women's Trade Union League had many successes. The International Workers of the World, a radical union, wanted to place workers in control. In the end, Samuel Gompers and the American Federation of Labor won the allegiance of most workers. *(p. 564)*

A NEW URBAN CULTURE

What happened to art and culture in these years so filled with change?

In the dozen years after 1900, American culture changed in important ways. Cities took on their modern form. Suburbs flourished. Sports became increasingly popular, reflecting people's increased leisure time. Experimentation occurred in literature, poetry, painting, and the arts. *(p. 567)*

KEY TERM QUESTIONS

1. Why did magazines feature articles by muckrakers in the early twentieth century? (p. 552)

2. What social and political problems did progressivism seek to remedy? (p. 552)

3. What was the Niagara Movement? (p. 560)

4. How did the NAACP try to combat discrimination against African Americans? (p. 561)

5. Who were the birds of passage? (p. 561)

6. Why was the Women's Trade Union League (WTUL) so influential? (p. 565)

7. What were the goals of the Industrial Workers of the World (IWW)? (p. 565)

8. Why was the Ashcan School so interested in depicting urban life? (p. 570)

MyHistoryLab Connections

Visit **www.myhistorylab.com** for a customized Study Plan to build your knowledge of *The Progressive Era*

Questions for Analysis

1. How does Upton Sinclair describe the conditions of the meatpacking plant?

   Read the **Document** *Upton Sinclair, from The Jungle (1905)* p. 552

2. What was a typical work day like for women in the early Twentieth Century?

   Watch the **Video** *Women in the Workplace, 1904* p. 558

3. What were some of the achievements of the American Labor Movement by 1914?

   Read the **Document** *Samuel Gompers, American Labor Movement: Its Makeup, Achievements, and Aspirations (1914)* p. 564

4. Why was Vaudeville such a popular form of entertainment in America?

   Watch the **Video** *A Vaudeville Act* p. 569

Other Resources from this Chapter

Watch the **Video** *Punching the Clock*

Read the **Document** *Frederick Taylor, Scientific Management*

Watch the **Video** *Rural Free Delivery Mail*

Read the **Document** *John Spargo, "The Bitter Cries of the Children"*

Read the **Document** *The Niagara Movement, Declaration of Principals*

View the **Image** *Chinese Americans in California*

Contents and Spotlight Questions

((•─ Listen to the **Chapter Audio** for Chapter 23 on **myhistorylab.com**

THE REPUBLICANS SPLIT

On a sunny spring morning in 1909, Theodore Roosevelt, wearing the greatcoat of a colonel of the Rough Riders, left New York for a safari in Africa. An ex-president at age 50, he had turned over the White House to his chosen successor, William Howard Taft, and was now off for "the joy of wandering through lonely lands, the joy of hunting

The Troubles of William Howard Taft A 1910 Puck cartoon shows Taft snarled in the intricacies of office as his disappointed mentor looks on.

Conservationist as Hunter Teddy Roosevelt, with his hunting party in Africa, poses with one of the nearly three hundred animals he and his group took down. As president, Roosevelt had supported measures protecting wildlife in the United States, including designating Pelican Island, Florida, as the nation's first wildlife refuge.

the mighty and terrible lords" of Africa, "where death broods in the dark and silent depths."

Some of Roosevelt's enemies hoped he would not return. "I trust some lion will do its duty," Wall Street magnate J. P. Morgan said. Always prepared, Roosevelt took nine extra pairs of eyeglasses, and, just in case, brought expert hunters along with him. When the nearsighted Roosevelt took aim, three others aimed at the same animal. "Mr. Roosevelt had a fairly good idea of the general direction," the safari leader said, "but we couldn't take chances with the life of a former president."

It was all good fun, and afterward Roosevelt set off on a tour of Europe. He attended the funeral in London of King Edward VII of Britain with the crowned heads of Europe, dined with the king and queen of Italy in Rome—an experience he likened to "a Jewish wedding on the East Side of New York"—and happily spent five hours reviewing troops of the German Empire in Berlin. Less happily, he followed events back home, where, many friends told him, Taft was not working out as president. Gifford Pinchot, Roosevelt's close companion in the conservation movement, came to Italy to complain personally about Taft, and at almost every stop, letters awaited him from other disappointed Republicans.

Taft was puzzled by it all. Honest and warmhearted, he had intended to continue Roosevelt's policies, even writing Roosevelt that he would "see to it that your judgment in selecting me as your successor and bringing about that succession shall be vindicated." But the conservative and progressive wings of the Republican party split, and Taft often sided with the conservatives. Among progressive Republicans, Taft's troubles stirred talk of a Roosevelt "back from Elba" movement, akin to Napoleon's return from exile in 1815.

Thousands gathered to greet Roosevelt on his return from Europe. He sailed into New York harbor on June 18, 1910, to the sound of naval guns and cheers. Characteristically, he had helped make the arrangements: "If there is to be a great crowd, do arrange it so that the whole crowd has a chance to see me and that there is as little disappointment as possible." Greeting Pinchot, one of Taft's leading opponents, with a hearty "Hello, Gifford," Roosevelt slipped away to his home in Oyster Bay, New York, where other friends awaited him.

He carried with him a touching letter from Taft, received just before he left Europe: "I have had a hard time—I do not know that I have had harder luck than other Presidents, but I do know that thus far I have succeeded far less than have others. I have been conscientiously trying to carry out your policies but my method of doing so has not worked smoothly." Taft invited Teddy to spend a night or two at the White House, but Roosevelt declined, saying that ex-presidents should not visit Washington. Relations between the two friends cooled.

A year later, there was no thought of friendship, only a desperate fight between Taft and Roosevelt for the Republican presidential nomination. Taft won, but, angry and ambitious, Roosevelt bolted and helped form the Progressive (or "Bull Moose") party, to unseat Taft and recapture the White House. With Taft, Roosevelt, Woodrow Wilson (the Democratic party's candidate), and Socialist party candidate Eugene V. Debs all in the race, the election of 1912 became one of the most exciting in American history.

It was also one of the most important. People were worried about the social and economic effects of urban-industrial growth. The election of 1912 provided a forum for those worries, and, to a degree unusual in American politics, it pitted deeply opposed candidates against one another and outlined differing views of the nation's future. In the battle between Roosevelt and Wilson, it also brought to the forefront some of the currents of progressive reform.

Those currents built on a number of important developments, including the rise of a new professional class, reform movements designed to cure problems in the cities and states, and the activist, achievement-oriented administrations of Roosevelt and Wilson. Together they produced the age of progressivism.

THE SPIRIT OF PROGRESSIVISM

One way or another, progressivism touched all aspects of society. Politically, it fostered a reform movement that sought cures for the problems of city, state, and nation. Intellectually, it drew on the expertise of the new social sciences and reflected a shift from older absolutes such as religion to newer schools of thought that emphasized relativism and the role of the environment in human development. Culturally, it inspired fresh modes of expression in dance, film, painting, literature, and architecture. Touching individuals in different ways, progressivism became a set of attitudes as well as a definable movement.

What were the six major characteristics of progressivism?

Though it was broad and diverse, six characteristics defined progressivism as a whole. First, the progressives acted out of concern about the effects of industrialization and the conditions of industrial life. While their viewpoints varied, their goals were to humanize and regulate big business, not harm it.

In pursuing these objectives, the progressives displayed a second characteristic: a fundamental optimism about human nature, the possibilities of progress, and people's capacity to recognize problems and take action to solve them. Progressives believed they could "investigate, educate, and legislate"—learn about a problem, inform people about it, and, with the help of an informed public, find and enforce a solution.

Third, more than many earlier reformers, the progressives were confident that they had the right to intervene in people's lives. They knew best, some of them thought, and as a result, their ideas had an element of coercion. Fourth, while progressives preferred if possible to achieve reform through voluntary means, they tended to turn to the authority of the state and government at all levels to effect the reforms they wanted.

Fifth, many progressives drew on a combination of evangelical Protestantism (which gave them the desire—and, they thought, the duty—to purge the world of sins like prostitution and drunkenness) and the natural and social sciences (whose theories made them confident that they could understand and control the environment in which people lived). Progressives tended to view the environment as a key to reform, thinking—as some economists, sociologists, and other social scientists were suggesting—that if they could change the environment, they could change the individual.

Finally, progressivism was distinctive because it touched virtually the whole nation. Not everyone, of course, was a progressive, and there were many who opposed or ignored progressives' ideas. There were also those who were untouched by progressive reforms and those whom the movement overlooked. But in one way or another, a remarkable number of people were caught up in it, giving progressivism a national reach and a mass base.

That was one of the features, in fact, that set it off from populism, which had appealed mostly to the rural South and West. Progressivism drew support from across society. "The thing that constantly amazed me," said William Allen White, a leading progressive journalist, "was how many people were with us." Progressivism appealed to the expanding middle class, prosperous farmers, and skilled laborers; it also attracted significant support in the business community.

The progressives believed in progress and disliked waste. No single issue or concern united them all. Some wanted to clean up city governments, others to clean up city streets. Some wanted to purify politics or control corporate abuses, others to eradicate poverty or prostitution. Some demanded social justice in the form of women's rights, child labor laws, temperance, and factory safety. They were Democrats, Republicans, Socialists, and independents.

Progressives believed in a better world and in people's ability to achieve it. They paid people, as a friend said of social reformer Florence Kelley, "the high compliment of believing that, once they knew the truth, they would act upon it." Progress depended on knowledge. The progressives stressed individual morality and collective action, the scientific method, and the value of expert opinion. Like contemporary business leaders, they valued system, planning, management, and predictability. They wanted not only reform but efficiency.

The Rise of the Professions

Progressivism fed on an organizational impulse that encouraged people to join forces, share information, and solve problems. Between 1890 and 1920, a host of national societies and associations took shape—nearly four hundred of them in just three decades. Groups such as the National Child Labor Committee, which lobbied for legislation to regulate the employment and working conditions of children, were formed to attack specific issues. Other groups reflected one of the most significant developments in American society at the turn of the century—the rise of the professions.

Growing rapidly in these years, the professions—law, medicine, religion, business, teaching, and social work—provided the leadership of much of the progressive movement. The professions attracted young, educated men and women, who in turn were part of a larger trend: a dramatic increase in the number of people working in administrative and professional jobs. In businesses, these people were managers, architects, technicians, and accountants. In city governments, they were experts in everything from education to sanitation. They organized and ran the urban-industrial society.

These professionals formed part of a new middle class whose members did not derive their status from birth or inherited wealth, as had many members of the older middle class. Instead, they moved ahead through education and personal accomplishment and worked to become doctors, lawyers, ministers, and teachers. Proud of their skills, they were ambitious and self-confident, and they thought of themselves as experts who could use their knowledge to benefit society.

To assert their status, they formed professional societies to look after their interests and govern entry into their professions. Just a few years before, for example, a doctor had become a doctor simply by stocking up on patent medicines and hanging out a sign. Now doctors began to insist they were part of a medical profession, and they wanted to set educational requirements and minimum standards for practice. In 1901, they reorganized the American Medical Association (AMA) and made it into a modern national professional society.

Other groups and professions showed the same pattern. Lawyers formed bar associations, created examining boards, and lobbied for regulations restricting entry into the profession. Teachers organized the National Education Association (1905) and pressed for teacher certification and compulsory education laws. Social workers formed the National Federation of Settlements (1911); business leaders created the National Association of Manufacturers (1895) and the U.S. Chamber of Commerce (1912); and farmers joined the National Farm Bureau Federation to spread information about farming and improve their lot.

Quick Check

✓ What were the causes and results of the rise of the professions?

The Social-Justice Movement

Progressivism began in the cities during the 1890s. It first took form around settlement workers and others interested in freeing individuals from the crushing impact of cities and factories.

Ministers, intellectuals, social workers, and lawyers joined in a social-justice movement that focused national attention on the need for tenement house laws, more stringent child labor legislation, and better working conditions for women. They pressured municipal agencies for more and better parks, playgrounds, day nurseries, schools, and community services. Blending private and public action, settlement leaders turned increasingly to government aid.

Social-justice reformers were more interested in social cures than individual charity. Unlike earlier reformers, they saw problems as endless and interrelated; individuals became part of a city's larger patterns. With that insight, social-service casework shifted from a focus on an individual's well-being to a scientific analysis of neighborhoods, occupations, and classes.

Social-justice reformers, banding together to work for change, formed the National Conference of Charities and Corrections, which in 1915 became the National Conference of Social Work. Controlled by social workers, the conference reflected the growing professionalization of reform. Through it, social workers shared experiences and methodology and tried to establish themselves as a separate field within the social sciences. Once content with informal training sessions in a settlement house living room, they now founded professional schools at Chicago, Harvard, and other universities. After 1909, they had their own professional magazine, the *Survey*, and instead of piecemeal reforms, they aimed at a comprehensive program of minimum wages, maximum hours, workers' compensation, and widows' pensions.

Quick Check

✓ What were the aims of the social-justice movement?

The Purity Crusade

Working in city neighborhoods, social-justice reformers were often struck by the degree to which alcohol affected those they were trying to help. Workers drank away their wages; some men spent more time in saloons than at home. Drunkenness caused violence and angered employers who did not want intoxicated workers on the job. In countless ways, alcohol wasted human resources, the reformers believed, and with business leaders, ministers, and others, they crusaded to remove the evils of drink from American life.

At the head of the crusade was the Women's Christian Temperance Union (WCTU). Founded in the 1870s, by 1911 the WCTU had nearly 250,000 members and was the largest organization of women in American history to that time. In 1893, it was joined by the Anti-Saloon League, and together the groups pressed to abolish alcohol and the places where it was consumed. By 1916, they had succeeded in 19 states, but as drinking continued elsewhere, they pushed for a nationwide law. In the moral fervor of World War I, they succeeded, and the Eighteenth Amendment, prohibiting the manufacture, sale, and transportation of intoxicating liquors, took effect in January 1920.

📖 **Read** the **Document**
Report of the Vice Commission (1915) on **myhistorylab.com**

The amendment encountered troubles in the 1920s as the social atmosphere changed, but when it passed, progressives thought Prohibition was a major step toward eliminating social instability and moral wrong. In a similar fashion, some progressive reformers also worked to eliminate prostitution, convinced that poverty and ignorance drove women to the trade. By 1915, nearly every state had banned brothels, and in 1910, Congress passed the Mann Act, which prohibited the interstate transportation of women for immoral purposes. Like that against liquor, the campaign against prostitution reflected the era's desire to purify and elevate, often through the instrument of government action.

Quick Check

✓ What motivated people who opposed alcohol, and what measures did they achieve?

Woman Suffrage, Women's Rights

Women played a large role in the social-justice movement. Feminists were particularly active, especially in the political sphere, between 1890 and 1914—more active then, in fact, than at any other time until the 1960s. Some working-class women pushed for higher wages and better working conditions. College-educated women—5,000 a year graduated after 1900—took up careers in the professions, from which some of them supported reform. From 1890 to 1910, the work of a

number of national women's organiza-
tions, including the National Council of
Jewish Women, the National Congress of
Mothers, and the Women's Trade Union
League, furthered the aims of the progressive
movement.

Excluded from most of these organizations, African American women formed
their own groups. The National Association
of Colored Women was founded in 1895, 14
years before the better-known, male-oriented
NAACP. The women's organization was the
first African American social-service agency
in the country.

From 200,000 members in 1900, the General Federation of Women's Clubs grew to
more than 1 million by 1912. The clubs met,
as they had before, for coffee and literary
conversation, but they also began to look closely at conditions around them.

Progressivism in Action An Infant Welfare Society nurse treats
the baby of an immigrant family in Chicago. Medical discoveries and
improvements in the quality of medical education fostered an interest in
public health work among the social-justice reformers.

Forming an Industrial Section and a Committee on Legislation for Women and
Children, the federation supported reforms to safeguard child and women workers, improve schools, ensure pure food, and beautify the community. Reluctantly
at first, in 1914, the federation finally supported woman suffrage, a cause that dated
back to the first women's rights convention in Seneca Falls, New York, in 1848.
Divided over tactics since the Civil War, the suffrage movement suffered from disunity, male opposition, indecision over whether to act at the state or national level,
resistance from the Catholic Church, and opposition from liquor interests, who
linked the cause to Prohibition.

Because politics was an avenue for reform, growing numbers of women activists became involved in the suffrage movement. After years of disagreement, the
two major suffrage organizations, the National Woman Suffrage Association and
the American Woman Suffrage Association, merged in 1890 to form the **National
American Woman Suffrage Association** under Susan B. Anthony. The merger
opened a new phase of the suffrage movement, characterized by unity and a tightly
controlled national organization.

In 1900, Carrie Chapman Catt, a superb organizer, became president of the
National American Woman Suffrage Association. By 1920 it had nearly 2 million members. Catt and Anna Howard Shaw, who became the association's head in
1904, believed in organization and peaceful lobbying to win the vote. Alice Paul and
Lucy Burns, founders of the Congressional Union, were more militant; they inter-
rupted public meetings, focused on Congress rather than the states, and in 1917
picketed the White House.

Significantly, Catt, Paul, and others changed the argument for woman suffrage.
Nineteenth-century suffragists had claimed the vote as a natural right, owed to
women as much as men. Now, they stressed a pragmatic argument: Since women

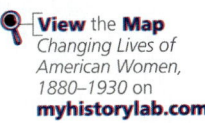

View the **Map**
*Changing Lives of
American Women,
1880–1930* on
myhistorylab.com

were more sensitive to moral issues than men, they would use their votes to help create a better society. They would support temperance, clean government, laws to protect workers, and other reforms. This argument attracted progressives who believed the women's vote would purify politics. In 1918, Congress passed a constitutional amendment stating simply that the right to vote shall not be denied "on account of sex." Enough states followed, and, after three generations of suffragist efforts, the Nineteenth Amendment took effect in 1920. (See Map 23.1.)

A Ferment of Ideas: Challenging the Status Quo

A dramatic shift in ideas became one of the most important forces behind progressive reform. Most of the ideas focused on the role of the environment in shaping human behavior. Progressive reformers accepted society's growing complexity, called for factual treatment of piecemeal problems, allowed room for new theories, and, above all, rejected age-encrusted divine or natural "laws" in favor of thoughts and actions that worked.

A new doctrine called pragmatism, based on dealing with things practically to see if they worked, emerged in this ferment of ideas. It came from William James, a brilliant Harvard psychologist who became the key figure in American thought from the 1890s to World War I. Warm and tolerant, James was impatient with theories that regarded truth as abstract. Truth, he believed, should work for the individual, and it worked best not in abstraction, but in action.

The environment, James thought, not only shaped people; they shaped it. In *Pragmatism* (1907), he praised "tough-minded" individuals who could live in a world with no easy answers. The tough-minded accepted change; they knew how to pick manageable problems, gather facts, discard ideas that did not work, and act on those that did. Ideas that worked became truth.

The most influential educator of the Progressive Era, John Dewey, applied pragmatism to educational reform. A friend and disciple of William James, he argued that thought evolves in relation to the environment and that education is directly related to experience. In 1896, Dewey founded a separate School of Pedagogy at the University of Chicago, with a laboratory in which educational theory based on the newer philosophical and psychological studies could be tested and practiced.

Dewey introduced an educational revolution that stressed children's needs and capabilities. He opposed memorization, rote learning, and dogmatic, authoritarian teaching methods; he

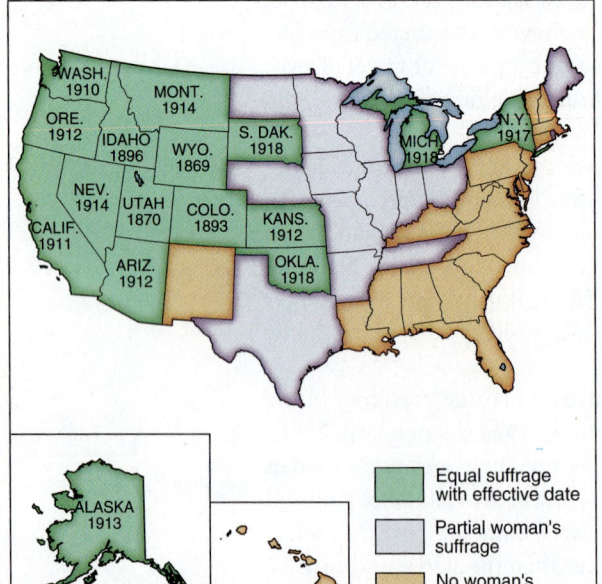

Map 23.1 *Woman Suffrage Before 1920* State-by-state gains in woman suffrage were mainly limited to the Far West and were agonizingly slow in the early twentieth century.

Equal suffrage with effective date

Partial woman's suffrage

No woman's suffrage

emphasized personal growth, free inquiry, and creativity.

Rejecting the older view of the law as universal and unchanging, lawyers and legal theorists instead viewed it as a reflection of the environment—an instrument for social change. Law reflected the environment that shaped it. Judges began to favor "sociological jurisprudence" that related the law to social reform.

In Denver, Colorado, after Judge Ben Lindsey sentenced a boy to reform school for stealing coal, the boy's mother, grief-stricken, beat her head against the wall. Lindsey investigated the case and found that the father was a smelting worker dying of lead poisoning; the family needed coal for heat. From such experiences, Lindsey concluded that children were not born with a genetic tendency to crime; the environment in which they grew made them good or bad. Lindsey "sentenced" youthful offenders to education and good care. He worked for playgrounds, slum clearance, public baths, and technical schools. Known as the "Kids' Judge," he attracted visitors from as far away as Japan, who wanted to study and copy his methods.

Votes for Women Woman suffrage was a key element in the social-justice movement. Without the right to vote, women working for reform had little power to influence elected officials to support their endeavors.

Socialism, a reformist political philosophy, grew dramatically before World War I. Eugene V. Debs, president of the American Railway Union, in 1896 formed the Social Democratic party. Gentle and reflective, not at all the popular image of the wild-eyed radical, Debs was thrust into prominence by the Pullman strike (see Chapter 20). In 1901, he organized the Socialist Party of America. Neither Debs nor the party ever developed a cohesive platform, nor was Debs an effective organizer. But he was eloquent, passionate, and visionary.

Although torn by factions, the Socialist party doubled in membership between 1904 and 1908, then tripled by 1912. Running for president, Debs garnered 100,000 votes in 1900; 400,000 in 1904; and 900,000 in 1912, the party's peak year.

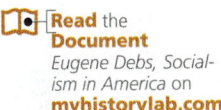 **Read** the **Document**
Eugene Debs, Socialism in America on **myhistorylab.com**

Quick Check

✓ In what ways did ideas change in the years after 1900 and open up new avenues to reform?

REFORM IN THE CITIES AND STATES

Progressive reformers realized government could be a crucial agent in accomplishing their goals. They wanted to curb the influence of "special interests" and, through political reforms such as the direct primary and the direct election of senators, make government follow the public will. Once it did, they welcomed government action at whatever level was appropriate.

What methods did progressive reformers use to attack problems in the cities and states?

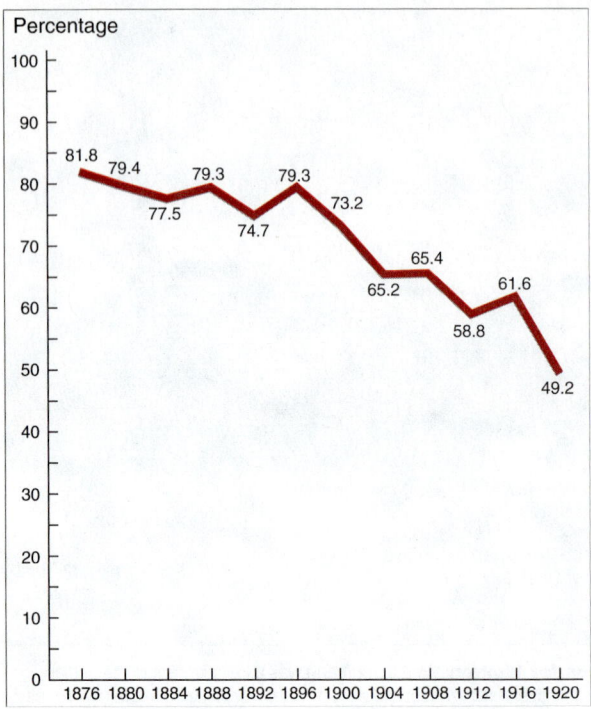

Figure 23.1 Voter Participation in Presidential Elections, 1876–1920

As a result of this thinking, the use of federal power increased, as did the power and prestige of the presidency. Progressives not only lobbied for government-sponsored reform but also worked in their home neighborhoods, cities, and states; much of the significant change occurred in local settings, outside the national limelight. Most important, the progressives believed in experts' ability to solve problems. At every level—local, state, and federal—thousands of commissions and agencies took form. Staffed by trained experts, they oversaw a multitude of matters from railroad rates to public health.

Interest Groups and the Decline of Popular Politics

Placing government in the hands of experts was one way to get it out of the hands of politicians and political parties. The direct primary, which allowed voters rather than parties to choose candidates, was another way. These initiatives and others like them were part of a fundamental change in how Americans viewed their political system.

As one sign of the change, fewer and fewer people were going to the polls. Voter turnout dropped dramatically after 1900, when the intense partisanship of the decades after the Civil War gave way to media-oriented political campaigns based largely on the candidates' personalities. From 1876 to 1900, the average turnout in presidential elections was 77 percent. From 1900 to 1916, it was 65 percent. In the 1920s, it dropped to 52 percent, close to the average today. (See Figure 23.1.) Turnout was lowest among young people, immigrants, the poor, and, ironically, newly enfranchised women.

The falloff had many causes, but among the most important was that people had found another way to achieve some of the objectives they had once assigned to political parties. The "interest group" became important in this era and a major feature of politics ever after. Professional societies, trade associations, labor organizations, farm lobbies, and other interest groups worked outside the party system to pressure government for things their members wanted. Social workers, women's clubs, reform groups, and others learned to apply similar pressure, and the result was much significant legislation of the Progressive Era.

Quick Check

✓ What brought about the dramatic drop in voter turnout in these years?

Reform in the Cities

During the early twentieth century, urban reform movements, many of them born in the depression of the 1890s, spread across the nation. In 1894, the National Municipal League was organized. It became the forum for debate over civic reform, changes in the tax laws, and municipal ownership of public utilities. Within a few years, nearly every city had a variety of clubs and organizations directed at improving the quality of city life.

In the 1880s, reformers would call a conference, pass resolutions, and go home; after 1900, they formed associations, adopted long-range policies, and hired a staff to achieve them. In the mid-1890s, only Chicago had an urban reform league with a full-time paid executive; within a decade, every major city had such leagues.

In city after city, reformers reordered municipal government. Tightening controls on corporate activities, they broadened the scope of utility regulation and restricted city franchises. They updated tax assessments, often skewed in favor of corporations, and tried to clean up the electoral machinery. Devoted to efficiency, they developed a trained civil service to oversee planning and operations. The generation of the 1880s also had believed in civil service, but the goal then was mostly negative: to get spoilsmen out and "good" people in. Now the goal was efficiency and, above all, results.

In constructing their model governments, urban reformers often turned to recent advances in business management and organization. They stressed continuity and expertise, a system in which professional experts staffed a government overseen by elected officials. At the top, the elected leader surveyed the breadth of city, state, or national affairs and defined directions. Below, a corps of experts—trained in the various disciplines of the new society—funneled those directions into specific scientifically based policies.

Reformers created a growing number of regulatory commissions and municipal departments. They hired engineers to oversee utility and water systems, physicians and nurses to improve health, and city planners to develop parks and highways.

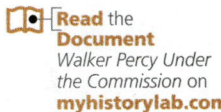
Read the **Document**
Walker Percy Under the Commission on **myhistorylab.com**

Quick Check

✓ What methods did reformers use to improve life in their cities?

Action in the States

Reformers soon discovered, however, that many problems lay beyond a city's boundaries, and they turned to the state governments. From the 1890s to 1920, reformers worked to stiffen state laws regulating the labor of women and children, create and strengthen commissions to regulate railroads and utilities, impose corporate and inheritance taxes, improve mental and penal institutions, and allocate more funds for state universities, which were viewed as the training ground for the experts and educated citizenry the new society needed.

To regulate business, virtually every state created regulatory commissions to examine corporate books and hold public hearings. Building on earlier experience, state commissions after 1900 were given new power to initiate actions, rather than await complaints, and in some cases to set maximum prices and rates. Dictating company practices, they pioneered regulatory methods later adopted in federal legislation of 1906 and 1910.

Historians have long praised the regulation movement, but the commissions did not always act wisely or even in the public interest. Elected commissioners often knew little about corporate affairs. To win election, some promised specific rates or reforms, obligations that might bias the commission's investigative functions.

Appointive commissions sometimes fared better, but they too had to oversee extraordinarily complex businesses such as the railroads.

To the progressives, commissions offered a way to end the corrupt alliance between business and politics. Another way to do that was to "democratize" government by reducing the power of politicians and increasing the influence of the electorate. To achieve that, progressives backed three measures: the initiative, which allowed voters to propose new laws; the referendum, which allowed them to accept or reject a law at the ballot box; and the recall, which enabled them to remove an elected official.

Oregon adopted the initiative and referendum in 1902; by 1912, 12 states had them. 1n 1913 the Seventeenth Amendment provided for the direct election of U.S. senators. By 1916, all but three states had direct primaries, which allowed the people, rather than nominating conventions, to choose candidates for office.

As governor of Wisconsin between 1901 and 1906, Robert M. La Follette developed the "Wisconsin Idea," one of the most important reform programs in the history of state government. He established an industrial commission, the first in the country, to regulate factory safety and sanitation. He improved education, workers' compensation, public utility controls, and resource conservation. He lowered railroad rates and raised railroad taxes. Under his prodding, Wisconsin became the first state to adopt a direct primary for all political nominations and a state income tax. Theodore Roosevelt called La Follette's Wisconsin "the laboratory of democracy," and the Wisconsin Idea soon spread to many other states.

After 1905, the progressives looked more and more to Washington. For one thing, Teddy Roosevelt was there, with his zest for publicity and his alluring grin. But progressives also sensed that many concerns—corporations and conservation, factory safety and child labor—crossed state lines. Federal action seemed desirable; specific reforms fit into a larger plan perhaps best seen from the nation's center. In 1906, La Follette became a U.S. senator, and the focus of progressivism shifted to Washington.

Quick Check

✓ How did the states respond to the new industrial society?

THE REPUBLICAN ROOSEVELT

How would you describe the personality and programs of Theodore Roosevelt?

When President William McKinley died of gunshot wounds in September 1901, Vice President Theodore Roosevelt succeeded him in the White House. The new president initially vowed to carry on McKinley's policies. He continued some, developed others of his own, and brought to them all the exuberance of his own personality.

At age 42, Roosevelt was then the youngest president in American history. In contrast to the dignified McKinley, he was open, aggressive, and high-spirited. At his desk by 8:30 every morning, he worked through the day, usually with visitors for breakfast, lunch, and dinner. Politicians, labor leaders, industrialists, poets, artists, and writers paraded through the White House.

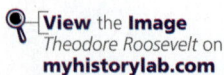

View the **Image**
Theodore Roosevelt on
myhistorylab.com

If McKinley reduced presidential isolation, Roosevelt virtually ended it. The presidency, he thought, was the "bully pulpit," a forum of ideas and leadership for the nation. The president was "a steward of the people bound actively and affirmatively to do all he could for the people." Self-confident, Roosevelt enlisted talented associates, including Elihu Root, secretary of war and later secretary of state; William Howard Taft, secretary of war; Gifford Pinchot, the nation's chief forester and leading conservationist; and Oliver Wendell Holmes, Jr., whom he named to the Supreme Court.

In 1901, Roosevelt invited Booker T. Washington to dinner at the White House. Many southerners protested—"a crime equal to treason," a newspaper said—and they protested again when Roosevelt appointed several African Americans to important federal offices in South Carolina and Mississippi. At first, Roosevelt considered building a biracial "black-and-tan" southern Republican party, thinking it would foster racial progress and his own renomination in 1904.

But Roosevelt soon retreated. In parts of the South, he supported "lily-white" Republican organizations, and his policies often reflected his own belief in African American inferiority. He said nothing when 12 people died in a race riot in Atlanta in 1906. He blamed African American soldiers stationed near Brownsville, Texas, after a night of violence there in August 1906. Acting on little evidence, he discharged "without honor" three companies of African American troops, six of whom held the Congressional Medal of Honor.

Busting the Trusts

"There is a widespread conviction in the minds of the American people that the great corporations known as trusts are in certain of their features and tendencies hurtful to the general welfare," Roosevelt reported to Congress in 1901. Like most people, however, the president wavered on the trusts. Large-scale production and industrial growth, he believed, were natural and beneficial; they needed only to be controlled. Still, he distrusted the trusts' impact on local enterprise and individual opportunity. Distinguishing between "good" and "bad" trusts, he pledged to protect the former while controlling the latter.

In 1903, Roosevelt asked Congress to create a Department of Commerce and Labor, with a Bureau of Corporations to investigate interstate commerce. Congress balked; Roosevelt called in reporters and, in an off-the-record interview, charged that John D. Rockefeller had organized the opposition to the measure. The press spread the word, and in the outcry that followed, the proposal passed easily. Roosevelt was delighted. With the new Bureau of Corporations publicizing its findings, he thought, the glare of publicity would eliminate most corporate abuses.

Roosevelt also undertook direct legal action. In 1902, he instructed the Justice Department to sue the Northern Securities Company for violating the Sherman Antitrust Act. It was a shrewd move. A mammoth holding company, Northern Securities

Trust-Buster A cartoon illustrating Theodore Roosevelt's promise to break up only those "bad trusts" that were hurtful to the general welfare. Despite his reputation as a "trustbuster," Roosevelt dissolved relatively few trusts.

Quick Check

✓ What were Theodore Roosevelt's views on the trusts?

controlled the massive rail networks of the Northern Pacific, Great Northern, and Chicago, Burlington & Quincy railroads.

In 1904, the Supreme Court ordered the company dissolved. Roosevelt was jubilant and he initiated several other antitrust suits. In 1902, he had also moved against the beef trust, an action western farmers and urban consumers both applauded. After a lull, he initiated suits in 1906 and 1907 against the American Tobacco Company, the Du Pont Corporation, the New Haven Railroad, and Standard Oil.

But Roosevelt's policies were not always clear, nor his actions consistent. He asked for (and received) business support in his bid for reelection in 1904. Industrial leaders gave large donations. J. P. Morgan himself later testified that he gave $150,000 to Roosevelt's campaign. In 1907, acting in part to avert a threatened financial panic, the president permitted Morgan's U.S. Steel to absorb the Tennessee Coal and Iron Company, an important competitor.

Roosevelt, in truth, was not a trustbuster, although he was frequently called that. William Howard Taft, his successor in the White House, initiated 43 antitrust indictments in four years—nearly twice the 25 Roosevelt did in the seven years of his presidency. Instead, Roosevelt used antitrust threats to keep businesses within bounds. Regulation, he believed, was a better way to control large-scale enterprise.

"Square Deal" in the Coalfields

A few months after announcing the Northern Securities suit, Roosevelt intervened in a major labor dispute involving the anthracite coal miners of northeastern Pennsylvania. Led by John Mitchell, a moderate, the United Mine Workers demanded wage increases, an eight-hour workday, and company recognition of the union. The coal companies refused, and in May 1902, 140,000 miners walked off the job. The mines closed.

As the months passed and the strike continued, coal prices rose. With winter coming on, schools, hospitals, and factories ran short of coal. Public opinion turned against the companies. Morgan and other industrial leaders privately urged them to settle, but the companies refused.

Roosevelt was furious. Complaining of the companies' arrogance, he invited both sides in the dispute to an October 1902 conference at the White House. There,

View the **Image**
TR as "Jack the Giant Killer"—Puck Cartoon on **myhistorylab.com**

Mitchell took a moderate tone and offered to submit the issues to arbitration, but the companies would not budge. Roosevelt ordered the army to prepare to seize the mines and then leaked word of his intent to Wall Street leaders.

Alarmed, Morgan and others again urged a settlement, and the companies finally agreed to accept the recommendations of an independent commission the president would appoint. In late October, the strikers returned to work. In March 1903, the commission awarded them a 10 percent wage increase and a cut in working hours. It recommended, however, against union recognition. The coal companies, in turn, were encouraged to raise prices to offset the wage increase.

More and more, Roosevelt saw the federal government as an honest and impartial "broker" between powerful elements in society. Rather than leaning toward labor, he pursued a middle way to curb corporate and labor abuses, abolish privilege, and enlarge individual opportunity. Conservative by temperament, he sometimes backed reforms in part to head off more radical measures.

During the 1904 campaign, Roosevelt called his actions in the coal miners' strike a "square deal" for both labor and capital, a term that stuck to his administration. Roosevelt was not the first president to take a stand for labor, but he was the first to bring opposing sides in a labor dispute to the White House to settle it. He was also the first to threaten to seize a major industry and to appoint an arbitration commission whose decision both sides agreed to accept.

Quick Check

✓ In what ways did Theodore Roosevelt enlarge presidential power by intervening in the 1902 coal strike?

ROOSEVELT PROGRESSIVISM AT ITS HEIGHT

In the election of 1904, the popular Roosevelt crushed his Democratic opponent, Alton B. Parker of New York, and the Socialist Eugene V. Debs of Indiana. (See Table 23.1.) On election night, overjoyed, he pledged that "under no circumstances will I be a candidate for or accept another nomination," a statement he later regretted.

What were the major measures of Theodore Roosevelt's term from 1905 to 1909?

Regulating the Railroads

After his election, Roosevelt laid out a reform program that included railroad regulation, employers' liability for federal employees, greater federal control over corporations, and laws regulating child labor, factory inspection, and slum

TABLE 23.1 The Election of 1904

Candidate	Party	Popular Vote	Electoral Vote
T. Roosevelt	Republican	7,623,486	336
Parker	Democrat	5,077,911	140
Debs	Socialist	402,400	0
Swallow	Prohibition	258,596	0

clearance in the District of Columbia. He turned first to railroad regulation. In the Midwest and Far West, the issue was popular, and reform governors like La Follette urged federal action. Roosevelt maneuvered cannily. As the legislative battle opened, he revealed that Standard Oil had reaped $750,000 a year from railroad rebates. He also skillfully traded congressional support for a strong railroad measure in return for his promise to postpone reducing the tariff, a stratagem that came back to plague Taft.

Triumph came with passage of the **Hepburn Act** of 1906. A significant achievement, the act strengthened the rate-making power of the Interstate Commerce Commission (ICC), increased the number of commissioners from five to seven, empowered it to fix reasonable maximum railroad rates, and broadened its jurisdiction to include oil pipeline, express, and sleeping car companies. ICC orders were binding, pending court appeals, thus placing the burden of proof of injustice on the companies. Delighted, Roosevelt viewed the Hepburn Act as a major step in his plan for expert federal control over industry.

Quick Check

✓ Why and how did Theodore Roosevelt want to regulate the railroads?

Cleaning Up Food and Drugs

📖 **Read** the **Document**
Upton Sinclair from The Jungle on **myhistorylab.com**

Soon Roosevelt was dealing with two other important bills aimed at regulating the food and drug industries. Muckraking articles had cited filthy conditions in meatpacking houses, but Upton Sinclair's *The Jungle* (1906) set off a storm of indignation. Ironically, Sinclair had set out to write a novel about the packinghouse workers, the "wage slaves of the Beef Trust," hoping to do for wage slavery what Harriet Beecher Stowe had done for chattel slavery. But readers largely ignored his story of the workers and seized instead on his graphic descriptions of what went into their meat.

Sinclair was disappointed: "I aimed at the public's heart, and by accident I hit it in the stomach." He had, indeed. After reading *The Jungle*, Roosevelt ordered an investigation. The result, he said, was "hideous," and he threatened to publish the entire "sickening report" if Congress did not act. Meat sales plummeted in the United States and Europe. Demand for reform grew. Alarmed, the meat packers themselves supported a reform law, which they hoped would be just strong enough to still the clamor. The Meat Inspection Act of 1906, stronger than the packers wanted, set rules for sanitary meatpacking and government inspection of meat products.

A second measure, the Pure Food and Drug Act, passed more easily. Samuel Hopkins Adams, a muckraker, exposed the dangers of patent medicines in several sensational articles in Collier's. Patent medicines, Adams pointed out, contained mostly alcohol, drugs, and "undiluted fraud." Dr. Harvey W. Wiley, the chief chemist in the Department of Agriculture, led a "poison squad" of young assistants who experimented with the medicines. With evidence in hand, Wiley pushed for regulation; Roosevelt and the recently reorganized AMA joined the fight, and the act passed in 1906. Requiring manufacturers to list certain ingredients on labels, it was a pioneering effort to ban the manufacture and sale of adulterated, misbranded, or unsanitary food or drugs.

Quick Check

✓ What laws regulated the food and drug industries?

Conserving the Land

An expert on birds, Roosevelt loved nature and the wilderness, and some of his most enduring accomplishments came in the field of conservation, an effort to preserve nature. Working closely with Gifford Pinchot, chief of the Forest Service, he established the first comprehensive national conservation policy. To Roosevelt, conservation meant the wise use of natural resources, not locking them away, so those who thought that wilderness should be preserved rather than developed generally opposed his policies. But when Roosevelt took office in 1901, there were 45 million acres in government preserves. By 1908, there were almost 195 million. (See Map 23.2.)

As 1908 approached, Roosevelt became increasingly strident in his demand for reforms. He attacked "malefactors of great wealth," urged greater federal regulatory powers, criticized the federal courts' conservatism, and called for laws protecting factory workers. Many business leaders blamed him for a severe financial panic in 1907, and conservatives in Congress stiffened their opposition. Divisions between Republican conservatives and progressives grew.

Immensely popular, Roosevelt prepared in 1908 to turn over the White House to William Howard Taft, his close friend and colleague. As expected, Taft soundly defeated William Jennings Bryan, who was making his third try for the presidency. (See Table 23.2.) The Republicans retained control of Congress. Taft seemed ready and willing to carry on the Roosevelt legacy.

Quick Check

✓ What did Theodore Roosevelt accomplish with regard to the environment?

Map 23.2 National Parks and Forests During the presidency of Theodore Roosevelt, who considered conservation his most important domestic achievement, millions of acres of land were set aside for national parks and forests.

TABLE 23.2 The Election of 1908

Candidate	Party	Popular Vote	Electoral Vote
Taft	Republican	7,678,908	321
Bryan	Democrat	6,409,104	162
Debs	Socialist	402,820	0
Chafin	Prohibition	252,821	0

THE ORDEAL OF WILLIAM HOWARD TAFT

Why was the presidency of William Howard Taft so difficult for him?

Taking office in 1909, Taft felt "just a bit like a fish out of water." The son of a distinguished Ohio family and a graduate of Yale Law School, he became an Ohio judge, solicitor general of the United States, and a judge of the federal circuit court. In 1900, McKinley asked him to head the Philippine Commission (see Chapter 21), charged with the difficult and challenging task of forming a civil government in the Philippines. Later, Taft was named the first governor general of the Philippines. In 1904, Roosevelt appointed him secretary of war. In all these positions, Taft was a skillful administrator. He worked quietly behind the scenes, avoided controversy, and shared none of Roosevelt's zest for politics. A good-natured man, Taft had personal charm and infectious humor. He fled from fights rather than seeking them out, and he preferred quiet solitude to political maneuvering: "I don't like politics," he said. "I don't like the limelight."

Weighing close to 300 pounds, Taft enjoyed conversation, golf and bridge, good food, and plenty of rest. Compared to the hardworking Roosevelt and Woodrow Wilson, he was lazy. He was also honest, kindly, and amiable, and in his own way, he knew how to get things done.

Taft's years as president were not happy. As it turned out, he presided over a Republican party torn with tensions that Roosevelt had either brushed aside or concealed. The tariff, business regulation, and other issues split conservatives and progressives, and Taft often wavered or sided with the conservatives. Taft revered the past and distrusted change; although an ardent supporter of Roosevelt, he never had Roosevelt's faith in government's ability to impose reform and alter individual behavior. He named five corporation attorneys to his cabinet, leaned toward business over labor, and spoke of a desire to "clean out the unions."

Taft's reputation has suffered by comparison to the flair of Roosevelt and the moral majesty of Wilson. Taft was an honest and sincere president who—sometimes firm, sometimes befuddled—faced a series of important and troublesome problems.

Party Insurgency

Taft started his term with an attempt to curb the powerful Republican speaker of the House, Joseph "Uncle Joe" Cannon of Illinois. Using the powers of his position, Cannon had been setting House procedures, appointing committees, and virtually dictating legislation. Straightforward and crusty, he often opposed reform. In March 1909, 30 Republican congressmen joined Taft's effort to curb Cannon's power, and the president sensed success. But Cannon retaliated and, threatening to block all tariff bills, forced a compromise. Taft stopped the anti-Cannon campaign in return for Cannon's pledge to help with tariff cuts.

Opposition to high rates was growing among Republicans. The House passed a bill lowering rates, but in the Senate, Nelson W. Aldrich of Rhode Island added more than 800 amendments raising the rates the House had approved.

La Follette and other Republicans attacked the bill as the child of special interests. In speeches on the Senate floor they called themselves "progressives," invoked Roosevelt's name, and urged Taft to defeat the high-tariff proposal. Taft tried to compromise, but in the end, he backed Aldrich. The Payne–Aldrich Act, passed in November 1909, called for higher rates than the original House bill, though it lowered them from the Dingley Tariff of 1897. An unpopular law, Payne–Aldrich helped discredit Taft and revealed the tensions in the Republican party.

Republican progressives and conservatives drifted apart. Taft resented the persistent pinpricks of the progressives, who criticized virtually everything he did. He tried to find middle ground but leaned more and more toward the conservatives. During a nationwide speaking tour in 1909, he praised Aldrich, scolded the low-tariff insurgents, and called the Payne–Aldrich Act "the best bill that the Republican party ever passed."

By early 1910, progressive Republicans in Congress no longer looked to Taft for leadership. They again challenged Cannon, and again Taft wavered. In an outcome embarrassing to the president, the progressives managed to curtail Cannon's authority to dictate committee assignments and schedule debate. In progressive circles, talk grew of a Roosevelt return to the White House.

Quick Check

✓ What were the motives of the Republicans in Congress who opposed William Howard Taft?

The Ballinger–Pinchot Affair

The conservation issue further damaged relations between Roosevelt and Taft. In 1909, Richard A. Ballinger, Taft's secretary of the interior, put up for sale a million acres of public land that Pinchot, who had stayed on as Taft's chief forester, had withdrawn from sale. Pinchot, fearing that Ballinger would hurt conservation programs, protested. Seizing on a report that Ballinger had helped sell Alaskan coal lands to a syndicate that included J. P. Morgan, he asked Taft to intervene. After investigating, Taft supported Ballinger, although he asked Pinchot to remain in office.

Pinchot refused to drop the matter. He provided material for two anti-Ballinger magazine articles and wrote a critical public letter that Senator Dolliver of Iowa read to the Senate. Taft then fired the insubordinate Pinchot, which, though appropriate, lost the president more support. Newspapers followed the controversy for months, and muckrakers assailed the administration's "surrender" to Morgan and other "despoilers of the national heritage."

The controversy obscured Taft's contributions to conservation. He won from Congress the power to remove lands from sale and conserved more land than Roosevelt did. Still, the controversy tarred Taft and upset Roosevelt.

Quick Check

✓ What was the Ballinger–Pinchot Controversy?

Taft Alienates the Progressives

In 1910, Taft backed a bill to empower the ICC to fix maximum railroad rates. Progressive Republicans favored that plan but attacked Taft's proposal for a special Commerce Court to hear appeals from ICC decisions because most judges were conservative and rejected attempts to regulate railroad rates. Progressives also thought the railroads had been consulted too closely in drawing up the bill. Democratic and Republican progressives tried to strengthen the bill; Taft made support of it a test of party loyalty.

The Mann–Elkins Act of 1910 gave something to everyone. It gave the ICC power to set rates, stiffened long- and short-haul regulations, and placed telephone and telegraph companies under ICC jurisdiction. These provisions delighted progressives. In a trade-off, conservative Republican senators pledged to support statehood for Arizona and New Mexico, which were both predicted to be Democratic. In return, enough Democratic senators voted for the Commerce Court provision to pass the bill. While pleased with the act, Taft and the Republican party lost further ground. In key votes, progressive Republicans defied Taft.

Taft attempted to defeat the progressive Republicans in the 1910 elections. He helped form anti-progressive organizations and campaigned against progressive Republican candidates for the Senate. Progressive Republicans organized a nationwide network of anti-Taft Progressive Republican Clubs.

The 1910 election results were a major setback for Taft and conservative Republicans. The high cost of living gave an edge to the progressive wings in both major parties, lending support to their attack on the tariff and the trusts. In party primaries, progressive Republicans overwhelmed most Taft candidates. In the general election, they fared better than the conservatives, which increased progressive influence in the Republican party.

For Republicans of all persuasions, however, it was a difficult election. The Democrats swept the urban-industrial states. New York, New Jersey, Indiana, and even Taft's Ohio elected Democratic governors. For the first time since 1894, Republicans lost control of both the House and the Senate. Taft called it "not only a landslide, but a tidal wave and holocaust all rolled into one general cataclysm."

Despite the defeat, Taft pushed through important measures before his term ended. With Democratic help, he backed laws to regulate safety in mines and on railroads, create a Children's Bureau in the federal government, establish employers' liability for all work done on government contracts, and mandate an eight-hour day for government workers.

In 1909, Congress initiated the Sixteenth Amendment authorizing an income tax, which, along with woman suffrage, was one of the most significant legislative measures of the twentieth century. The amendment took effect in 1913.

An ardent supporter of competition, Taft relentlessly campaigned against trusts. The Sherman Antitrust Act, he said in 1911, "is a good law that ought to be enforced, and I propose to enforce it." That year, the Supreme Court in cases against Standard Oil and American Tobacco established the "rule of reason," which allowed the Court to determine whether a business presented "reasonable" restraint on trade. Taft thought the decisions gave the Court too much discretion and pushed ahead with the antitrust effort.

In October 1911, he sued U.S. Steel for acquiring the Tennessee Coal and Iron Company in 1907. Roosevelt had approved the acquisition, and the suit seemed designed to impugn his action. Enraged, he attacked Taft, who, for once, fought back. He accused Roosevelt of undermining the conservative tradition in the country and began to undercut progressive Republicans. Anti-Taft Republicans increasingly urged Roosevelt to run for president. In February 1912, he announced, "My hat is in the ring."

> **Quick Check**
> ✓ How did Taft lose the support of Republican progressives?

Differing Philosophies in the Election of 1912

Delighted Democrats looked on as Taft and Roosevelt fought for the Republican nomination. As the incumbent, Taft controlled the party machinery, and when the Republican convention met in June 1912, he took the nomination. In July, the Democrats met in Baltimore and, confident of victory, struggled through 46 ballots before finally nominating Woodrow Wilson, the reform-minded governor of New Jersey.

A month later, anti-Taft and progressive Republicans—now calling themselves the Progressive party—whooped it up in Chicago. Naming Roosevelt for president at its convention, the Progressive party—soon known as the Bull Moose party—set the stage for the first important multi-party presidential contest since 1860.

Taft was out of the running before the campaign even began: "I think I might as well give up so far as being a candidate is concerned," he said in July. "There are so many people in the country who don't like me." He stayed home and made no speeches before the election. Roosevelt campaigned strenuously, even completing one speech after being shot in the chest by an anti–third-term fanatic. "I have a message to deliver," he said, "and will deliver it as long as there is life in my body."

Roosevelt called his program the New Nationalism. An important phase in the shaping of twentieth-century American political thought, it demanded a national approach to the country's affairs and a strong president to deal with them. The New Nationalism called for efficiency in government and society. It exalted the executive and the expert; urged social-justice reforms to protect workers, women, and children; and accepted "good" trusts. The New Nationalism encouraged large concentrations of labor and capital, serving the nation's interests under a forceful federal executive.

The Bull Moose Campaign "I'm feeling like a bull moose!" declared Teddy Roosevelt while campaigning in 1912 as a Progressive, inadvertently renaming the new political party. The patch depicts a strong, independent animal, much like Roosevelt himself. In 1904, Roosevelt had won re-election by promising to give Americans a "square deal."

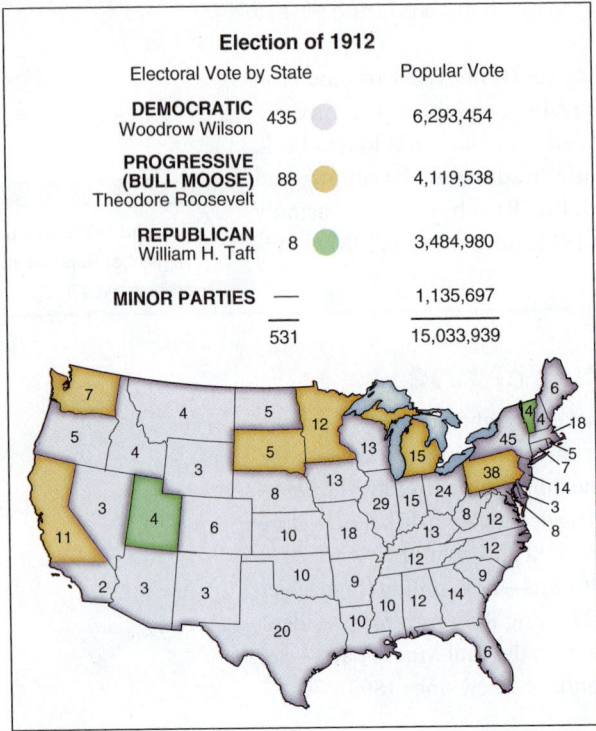

Election of 1912

	Electoral Vote by State	Popular Vote
DEMOCRATIC Woodrow Wilson	435	6,293,454
PROGRESSIVE (BULL MOOSE) Theodore Roosevelt	88	4,119,538
REPUBLICAN William H. Taft	8	3,484,980
MINOR PARTIES	—	1,135,697
	531	15,033,939

Map 23.3

👁 **Watch** the **Video**
Bull Moose Campaign Speech on
myhistorylab.com

Quick Check

✓ What were the two opposing philosophies in the presidential election of 1912?

For the first time in history, a major political party enlisted women in its organization. Jane Addams, the well-known settlement worker (see Chapter 22), seconded Roosevelt's nomination at Chicago, and she and other women played a leading role in the Progressive campaign. Some labor leaders who saw potential for union growth and some business leaders who saw relief from destructive competition and labor strife supported the new party.

Wilson called his program the New Freedom. It emphasized business competition and small government. A states' rights Democrat, he wanted to rein in federal authority, using it only to sweep away special privilege, release individual energies, and restore competition. Drawing on the thinking of Louis D. Brandeis, the brilliant legal reformer, he echoed the Progressive party's social-justice objectives, while attacking Roosevelt's planned state. For Wilson, the vital issue was not a planned economy but a free one: "The history of liberty is the history of the limitation of governmental power. If America is not to have free enterprise, then she can have freedom of no sort whatever."

In the New Nationalism and New Freedom, the election of 1912 offered competing philosophies of government. Both Roosevelt and Wilson saw the central problem of the American nation as economic growth and its effect on individuals and society. Both focused on the government's relation to business, both believed in bureaucratic reform, and both wanted to use government to protect the ordinary citizen. But Roosevelt welcomed federal power, national planning, and business growth; Wilson distrusted them all.

On election day, Wilson won 6.3 million votes to 4.1 million for Roosevelt, and 900,000 for Eugene V. Debs, the Socialist party candidate. Taft finished third with 3.5 million votes. The Democrats also won control of both houses of Congress. (See Map 23.3.)

WOODROW WILSON'S NEW FREEDOM

What were the central principles of Woodrow Wilson's New Freedom?

If under Roosevelt social reform took on the excitement of a circus, "under Wilson it acquired the dedication of a sunrise service." Born in Virginia in 1856 and raised in the South, Wilson was the son of a Presbyterian minister. As a young man, he wanted a career in public service, and he trained himself carefully in history and oratory. A moralist, he reached judgments easily. Once reached, almost nothing shook them. Opponents called him stubborn and smug.

From 1890 to 1902 he served as professor of jurisprudence and political economy at Princeton. In 1902, he became president of the university. Eight years later, he was governor of New Jersey, where he campaigned to reform election procedures, abolish corrupt practices, and strengthen railroad regulation.

Wilson's rise was rapid, though he knew relatively little about national issues and personalities. But he learned fast, and in some ways, the lack of experience served him well. He had few political debts to repay and brought fresh perspectives to older issues. Ideas intrigued Wilson; details bored him. Although outgoing at times, he could also be cold and aloof, and aides soon learned that he preferred loyalty and flattery to candid criticism.

Prone to self-righteousness, Wilson often turned differences of opinion into bitter personal quarrels. Like Roosevelt, he believed in strong presidential leadership. A scholar of the party system, he cooperated closely with Democrats in Congress, and he was among the most effective presidents in terms of passing bills that he supported. Forbidding in individual conversation, Wilson could move crowds with graceful oratory. Unlike Taft, and to a greater degree than Roosevelt, he could inspire.

The New Freedom in Action

On the day of his inauguration, Wilson called Congress into special session to lower the tariff. When the session opened on April 8, 1913, Wilson himself was there, the first president since John Adams in 1801 to appear personally before Congress. In forceful language, he urged Congress to reduce tariff rates.

As the bill moved through Congress, Wilson showed exceptional skill. He worked closely with congressional leaders, and when lobbyists threatened the bill in the Senate, he appealed for popular support. The result was a triumph for Wilson and the Democratic party. The Underwood Tariff Act lowered tariff rates about 15 percent and removed duties from sugar, wool, and other consumer goods.

To make up for lost revenue, the act also levied a modest graduated income tax, authorized under the new Sixteenth Amendment. Marking a significant shift in the American tax structure, it imposed a 1 percent tax on individuals and corporations earning more than $4,000 annually and an additional 1 percent tax on incomes of more than $20,000. Above all, the act reflected a new unity within the Democratic party, which had worked together to pass a difficult tariff law.

Encouraged by his success, Wilson decided to keep Congress in session through the hot Washington summer. Now he focused on banking reform, and the result in December 1913 was the Federal Reserve Act, the most important domestic law of his administration.

To provide the United States with a sound yet flexible currency, the act established the country's first efficient banking system since Andrew Jackson killed the second Bank of the United States in 1832. It created 12 regional banks, each to serve the banks of its district. A Federal Reserve Board, appointed by the president, governed the nationwide system.

Read the **Document**
Woodrow Wilson, from The New Freedom (1913) on **myhistorylab.com**

A compromise law, the act blended public and private control of the banking system. Private bankers owned the federal reserve banks but answered to the presidentially appointed Federal Reserve Board. The reserve banks were authorized to issue currency, and through the discount rate—the interest rate at which they loaned money to member banks—they could raise or lower the amount of money in circulation. Monetary affairs no longer depended solely on the price of gold. Within a year, nearly half the nation's banking resources were in the Federal Reserve System.

The Clayton Antitrust Act (1914) completed Wilson's initial legislative program. It prohibited unfair trade practices, forbade pricing policies that created monopoly, and made corporate officers personally responsible for antitrust violations. Delighting Samuel Gompers and the labor movement, the act declared that unions were not conspiracies in restraint of trade, outlawed the use of injunctions in labor disputes except to protect property, and approved lawful strikes and picketing.

In November 1914, Wilson proudly announced the completion of his New Freedom program. Tariff, banking, and antitrust laws promised a brighter future, he said, and it was now "a time of healing because a time of just dealing." Many progressives were aghast. That Wilson could think society's ills were so easily cured, the *New Republic* said, "casts suspicion either upon his own sincerity or upon his grasp of the realities of modern social and industrial life."

Quick Check

✓ What characterized Woodrow Wilson's New Freedom program?

Wilson Moves Toward the New Nationalism

Distracted by the start of war in Europe, Wilson gave less attention to domestic issues for more than a year. When he took up reform again, he increasingly adopted Roosevelt's New Nationalism and blended it with the New Freedom to set it off from his earlier policies.

One of Wilson's problems was Congress. To his dismay, the Republicans gained substantially in the 1914 elections. Reducing the Democratic majority in the House, they swept key industrial and farm states. A recession also struck the economy, which had been hurt by the outbreak of the European war in August 1914. Some business leaders blamed the tariff and other New Freedom laws.

Preoccupied with such problems, Wilson blocked significant action in Congress through most of 1915. He refused to support minimum wages for women workers, sidetracked a child labor bill as unconstitutional, and opposed a bill to establish long-term credits for farmers. He also refused to endorse woman suffrage, arguing that it was a state matter, not a federal one.

Wilson's record on race disappointed African Americans and many progressives. He had appealed to African American voters in 1912, and a number of African American leaders campaigned for him. Soon after the inauguration, Oswald Garrison Villard, a leader of the NAACP, proposed a National Race Commission to study race relations. Initially sympathetic, Wilson rejected the idea because he feared losing southern Democratic votes in Congress. He appointed many southerners to high office, and for the first time since the Civil War, southern views on race dominated Washington.

At one of Wilson's first cabinet meetings, the postmaster general proposed segregating African American federal workers. No one dissented, including Wilson. Government bureaus began to segregate offices, shops, rest rooms, and restaurants. Employees who objected were fired. African American leaders, progressives, and clergymen protested. Wilson backed away from the policy, although he insisted that segregation benefited African Americans.

As 1916 began, Wilson again pushed for reforms. The result was a river of reform laws, which began the second, more national-minded phase of the New Freedom. With scarcely a backward glance, Wilson embraced parts of Roosevelt's New Nationalism campaign.

In part, he was motivated by the approaching presidential election. Wilson owed his victory in 1912 to the Republican split, but Roosevelt was moving back into Republican ranks, and he might use issues connected with the war in Europe against Wilson. Moreover, many progressives were disappointed with Wilson's failure to support reform legislation on farm credits, child labor, and woman suffrage.

But Wilson was popular within the labor movement. Where Roosevelt had sought a balance between business and labor, Wilson defended union recognition and collective bargaining. In 1913, he appointed William B. Wilson, a respected leader of the United Mine Workers, as the first head of the Labor Department and strengthened its Division of Conciliation.

In August 1916, a threatened railroad strike revealed Wilson's sympathies with labor. Like Roosevelt, he invited the two sides to the White House, where he urged the railroad companies to grant an eight-hour day and labor leaders to abandon the demand for overtime pay. Labor leaders accepted the proposal; railroad leaders did not. "I pray God to forgive you, I never can," Wilson said as he left the room. Ending the threat of a strike, the Adamson Act imposed the eight-hour day on interstate railways and established a federal commission to study the railroad problem. The act was a milestone in the expansion of the federal government's authority to regulate industry.

In September, Wilson signed the Tariff Commission Act creating an expert commission to recommend tariff rates. The same month, the Revenue Act of 1916 boosted income taxes and furthered tax reform. Four thousand members of the National American Woman Suffrage Association cheered when Wilson finally supported woman suffrage. Two weeks later he endorsed the eight-hour day for all workers.

The 1916 presidential election was close, but Wilson won it on the issues of peace and progressivism. By the end of 1916, he and the Democratic party had enacted most of the important parts of Roosevelt's Progressive party platform of 1912. To do it, Wilson accepted much of the activism of the New Nationalism, including greater federal power and commissions governing trade and tariffs, in place of much of the restraint of the New Freedom. In mixing the two programs, he blended some of the competing doctrines of the Progressive Era, established the primacy of the federal government, and foreshadowed Franklin D. Roosevelt's pragmatic New Deal of the 1930s.

Watch the **Video**
Charles E. Hughes,
1916 Presidential
Campaign Speech on
myhistorylab.com

Quick Check
✓ In what five ways did Wilson move more closely to Theodore Roosevelt's ideas of New Nationalism?

CONCLUSION: THE FRUITS OF PROGRESSIVISM

The election of 1916 showed how deeply progressivism had reached into American society. "We have in four years," Wilson said that fall, "come very near to carrying out the platform of the Progressive party as well as our own; for we are also progressives."

In retrospect, however, 1916 also marked the beginning of progressivism's decline. At most, the years of progressive reform lasted from the 1890s to 1921, and they were largely compressed into a single decade between 1906 and American entry into World War I in 1917. Many problems the progressives addressed but did not solve; and some important ones, such as race, they did not even tackle. Yet their regulatory commissions, direct primaries, city improvements, and child labor laws marked an era of important and measured reform.

The institution of the presidency expanded. From the White House radiated executive departments that guided many activities. Independent commissions, operating within flexible laws, supplemented executive authority.

These developments owed much to both Roosevelt and Wilson. To manage a complex society, Roosevelt developed a simple formula: expert advice; growth-minded policies; a balancing of business, labor, and other interests; the use of publicity to gather support; and stern but often permissive oversight of the economy. Roosevelt strengthened the executive office, and he called on the newer group of professional, educated, public-minded citizens to help him: "I believe in a strong executive," he said; "I believe in power."

At first, Wilson had different ideas, wanting to dismantle much of Roosevelt's governing apparatus. But, driven by outside forces and changes in his own thinking, he soon moved in directions similar to those Roosevelt had championed. Starting out to disperse power, he eventually consolidated it.

Through such movements, government at all levels accepted responsibility for the welfare of various elements in the social order. A reform-minded and bureaucratic society took shape, in which men and women, labor and capital, political parties and social classes competed for shares in the expansive framework of twentieth-century life. But reform had limits. As both Roosevelt and Wilson found, the new government agencies, understaffed and underfinanced, depended on the responsiveness of those they sought to regulate.

Soon a far darker cloud appeared on the horizon. The spirit of progressivism rested on a belief in human potential, peace, and progress. After Napoleon's defeat in 1815, a century of peace began in western Europe. War seemed a dying phenomenon. "It looks as though this were going to be the age of treaties rather than the age of wars," an American said in 1912, "the century of reason rather than the century of force." It was not to be. Two years later, the most devastating of wars broke out in Europe, and in 1917, Americans were fighting on the battlefields of France.

23 STUDY RESOURCES

((•—Listen to the **Chapter Audio** for Chapter 23 on **myhistorylab.com**

TIMELINE

1894 National Municipal League formed to work for reform in cities, p. 584

1901 Theodore Roosevelt becomes president, p. 586
- Robert M. La Follette elected governor of Wisconsin, p. 586
- Doctors reorganize the American Medical Association, p. 579
- Socialist Party of America organized, p. 583

1902 Roosevelt sues Northern Securities Company, p. 587
- Coal miners in Pennsylvania strike, p. 588

1904 Roosevelt elected president, p. 589

1906 Hepburn Act strengthens Interstate Commerce Commission (ICC), p. 590
- Upton Sinclair attacks meatpacking industry in *The Jungle*, p. 590
- Congress passes Meat Inspection and Pure Food and Drug Acts, p. 590

1908 Taft elected president, p. 591

1909 Payne–Aldrich Tariff Act divides Republican party, p. 593

1910 Mann–Elkins Act regulates railroads, p. 594
- Taft fires Gifford Pinchot, head of U.S. Forest Service, p. 593
- Democrats sweep midterm elections, p. 594

1912 Progressive party nominates Roosevelt for president, p. 595
- Woodrow Wilson elected president, p. 596

1913 Underwood Tariff Act lowers rates, p. 597
- Federal Reserve Act reforms U.S. banking system, p. 597
- Sixteenth Amendment authorizes income tax, p. 594
- Seventeenth Amendment provides for direct election of U.S. senators, p. 586

1914 Clayton Act strengthens antitrust legislation, p. 598

1916 Wilson reelected president, p. 596

1920 Nineteenth Amendment gives women the right to vote, p. 582

CHAPTER REVIEW

THE SPIRIT OF PROGRESSIVISM

What were the six major characteristics of progressivism?

Progressivism sought cures for social and economic problems and was defined by six major characteristics: (1) a desire not to harm big business but to humanize and regulate it; (2) optimism about human nature; (3) a willingness to intervene in people's lives; (4) a tendency to stress the authority of the state and the government; (5) belief in the environment as a key to reform; and (6) a nationwide base. *(p. 577)*

REFORM IN THE CITIES AND STATES

What methods did progressive reformers use to attack problems in the cities and states?

Progressive reformers turned increasingly to the government to carry out their measures. At the same time, ironically, fewer people tended to vote. Reformers focused on life in the growing cities. Robert M. La Follette of Wisconsin personified the movement. His focus was on improving factory safety, regulating the railroads, and adopting political reforms. *(p. 583)*

THE REPUBLICAN ROOSEVELT

How would you describe the personality and programs of Theodore Roosevelt?

Roosevelt attacked some trusts and, through the courts, broke up a railroad holding company. His intervention in the coal strike of 1902 reflected his active, energetic personality and represented an advance in presidential power. *(p. 586)*

ROOSEVELT PROGRESSIVISM AT ITS HEIGHT

What were the major measures of Theodore Roosevelt's term from 1905 to 1909?

Winning easy election in 1904, Roosevelt persuaded Congress to improve railroad regulation, backed pure food and drug laws, and enlarged national parks. In all these actions, he reflected the values of the progressive generation: a reliance on experts, a faith in government power to initiate reform, and a desire to tame big business. *(p. 589)*

THE ORDEAL OF WILLIAM HOWARD TAFT

Why was the presidency of William Howard Taft so difficult for him?

Roosevelt had left Taft a variety of difficult problems, including the tariff and a widening split between progressive and conservative Republicans. Taft increasingly alienated the progressives and Roosevelt. In the election of 1912, Taft finished third behind Woodrow Wilson and Roosevelt. *(p. 592)*

WOODROW WILSON'S NEW FREEDOM

What were the central principles of Woodrow Wilson's New Freedom?

Victorious in 1912, Wilson set out to put into effect the central principles of his New Freedom program, including tariff reform, an antitrust law, and the Federal Reserve Act, a measure that still guides our economy today. By 1916, however, Wilson found greater value in Roosevelt's New Nationalism, which had emphasized government intervention and measures to protect women, labor, and other groups. *(p. 596)*

Key Term Questions

1. Why did Roosevelt and his supporters form the Progressive (or "Bull Moose") party? (p. 577)

2. What did the social-justice movement aim to achieve? (p. 579)

3. Why did the National American Woman Suffrage Association argue that women deserved the right to vote? (p. 581)

4. What was pragmatism? (p. 582)

5. Why was the Hepburn Act of 1906 a significant achievement for Roosevelt? (p. 590)

6. Why did Roosevelt support conservation? (p. 591)

7. How did the New Nationalism aim to achieve society and government? (p. 595)

8. How did Wilson's New Freedom program differ from Roosevelt's New Nationalism? (p. 596)

9. What did the Underwood Tariff Act accomplish? (p. 597)

10. Why was the establishment of the Federal Reserve Act so important? (p. 597)

11. What did the Clayton Antitrust Act of 1914 accomplish? (p. 598)

MyHistoryLab Connections

Visit **www.myhistorylab.com** for a customized Study Plan to build your knowledge of *From Roosevelt to Wilson in the Age of Progressivism.*

Questions for Analysis

1. What was the ideology behind the anti-vice crusades?

   Read the **Document** *Report of the Vice Commission, 1915* p. 580

2. How did life change for American women between 1880 and 1930?

   View the **Map** *Changing Lives of American Women, 1880–1930* p. 581

3. Why did Eugene Debs believe America was ripe for Socialism in 1900?

   Read the **Document** *Eugene V. Debs, from "The Outlook for Socialism in America" (1900)* p. 583

4. What was Woodrow Wilson's "New Freedom" ideology?

   Read the **Document** *Woodrow Wilson, from The New Freedom (1913)* p. 597

5. What were Charles E. Hughes political viewpoints in 1916?

   Watch the **Video** *Charles E. Hughes 1916 Presidential Campaign Speech* p. 599

Other Resources from this Chapter

Read the **Document** *Walker Percy, "Birmingham Under the Commission Plan" (1911)*

View the **Image** *Theodore Roosevelt*

View the **Image** *TR as Jack the Giant Killer*

Read the **Document** *Upton Sinclair, from The Jungle (1905)*

Watch the **Video** *Bull Moose Campaign Speech*

New York Tribune

GUARANTEE

Vol. LXXV ... No. 25,010. [Copyright, 1915, By The Tribune Association.] SATURDAY, MAY 8, 1915. PRICE

First to Last—the Truth: News · Editorials · Advertisements

900 Die as Lusitania Goes to Bott
400 Americans on Board Torpedo
Washington Stirred as When M

CAPITAL AROUSED, SITUATION GRAVEST YET FACED IN WAR

Washington Determined That Germany Shall Not Be Allowed to Shirk Responsibility for Deaths.

GREATLY FEARS LOSS OF AMERICANS

President Shows Nervousness as Bulletins of Disaster Come In—Strongest Protest Yet Made Planned Even if No U.S. Citizens Were Lost

From The Tribune Bureau!

Washington, May 7.—The news of the heavy loss of life on the Lusitania stirred Washington as it has not been stirred since the sinking of the Maine. The earlier reports that both passengers and crew had been landed safely had quieted apprehensions of an immediate crisis in the relations of the United States and Germany. But when it became clear that Americans—undoubtedly a considerable number of them—were to be counted among the victims of German savagery at sea the full significance of the tragedy off Queenstown struck home.

President Wilson made little effort to conceal his feelings. At 8 o'clock to-night the President received the following dispatch from the United States Consul at Cork:

"Lusitania sank at 2:30 o'clock. Probably many survivors. Rescue work proceeding favorably. Shall I send you list of survivors?"

As soon as he read it he put on his hat and walked out of the White House without the knowledge of the Secret Service men who are guarding him. The President walked up Sixteenth Street to Corcoran Street, crossed over to Fifteenth Street and back to the White House, where he went into his study to await further information and to turn over in his mind the message that it is expected he will send to the German Foreign Office as soon as all the details of the

THE LUSITANIA, SUNK BY GERMAN TORPEDO, WITH HEAVY LOSS OF LIFE.

GERMANS TOAST 'VICTORY' AMID 'HOCHS' IN CAFES

U. S. OWES IT TO SELF-RESPECT TO ACT, SAYS ROOSEVELT; 'PIRACY ON VAST SCALE'

[From a Staff Correspondent of The Tribune]

Syracuse, May 7.—After the appalling details of the Lusitania disaster had been told to Colonel Roosevelt late to-night he said: "It seems inconceivable that we should refrain from

MANY NOTED NEW YORKERS ON LUSITANIA

WEATHER

FAIR TO-DAY AND TO-MORROW;
SOUTHWEST TO WEST WINDS.
Yesterday's Temperature:
High, 64, Low, 55.
Full report on Page 15.

In City of New York, Newark, Jersey City and Hoboken,
ELSEWHERE TWO CENTS

;

Ship;

e Sank

ed Brought in with Other
eenstown—Some Landed
le and Clonakilty.

S FIRED, SAYS STEWARD

Eight Miles from Irish Coast In
and in Fine Weather—Sur-
Bravery of Cunard Officers.

able to The Tribune.]
. m.—At least 900 lives were lost when
oed without warning in broad dayligh
German submarine, according to esti
estimate of First Officer Jones puts the

than two hundred are supposed to be
d there were about 400 on board.
eenstown sent out at midnight says:
620 passengers from the Lusitania ha
boats. Ten or eleven boatloads came
ected."

abeth has arrived at Kinsale and reports
ked up two lifeboats containing 63 and
nia, respectively. A Cork tug took the
They were mostly women and childre
ot launch many of her lifeboats.
Kinsale and Clonakilty, and the instit
own are jammed with survivors from th
ctually wounded suffering terribly from
r now rests on the bottom of the ocean,
le Head and twenty miles from the en
bor.

Y GIVES OUT NEWS.

filtering into London last night an
that the rescued are being brought t
ers. The Admiralty says between fr
dy been landed at Clonakilty and Kin

Contents and Spotlight Questions

((•— **Listen** to the **Chapter Audio** for Chapter 24 on **myhistorylab.com**

THE SINKING OF THE *LUSITANIA*

On May 1, 1915, the German embassy took out the following advertisement in the *New York World* as a warning to Americans and other voyagers setting sail for England:

A Fateful Torpedo With the sinking of the *Lusitania,* the American people learned firsthand of the horrors of total war. President Wilson's decision to protest the incident through diplomacy kept the United States out of the war—but only temporarily.

605

NOTICE—

Travellers intending to embark on the Atlantic voyage are reminded that a state of war exists between Germany and her allies and Great Britain and her allies; that the zone of war includes the waters adjacent to the British Isles; that, in accordance with formal notice given by the Imperial German Government, vessels flying the flag of Great Britain, or of any of her allies, are liable to destruction in those waters and that travelers sailing in the war zone on ships of Great Britain or her allies do so at their own risk.

At 12:30 that afternoon, the British luxury steamship *Lusitania* set sail from New York to Liverpool. Secretly, it carried a load of ammunition as well as passengers.

The steamer left two hours late, but it held several speed records and could easily make up the time. The passenger list of 1,257 was the largest since the outbreak of war in Europe in August 1914. It took six days for it to reach the coast of Ireland. German U-boats (submarines) were known to patrol the dangerous waters there. When the war began, Britain imposed a naval blockade of Germany. In return, Germany in February 1915 declared the area around the British Isles a war zone; all enemy vessels, armed or unarmed, were at risk. Germany had only a handful of U-boats, but they were a new and frightening weapon. On February 10, President Woodrow Wilson warned Germany of its "strict accountability" for American losses from U-boat attacks.

Off Ireland, the passengers lounged on the deck of the *Lusitania*. As if it were peacetime, the ship sailed straight ahead, with no zigzag maneuvers to throw off pursuit. But the U-20 was there, and its commander, seeing a large ship, fired a single torpedo. Seconds after it hit, a boiler exploded and blew a hole in the *Lusitania*'s side. The ship listed immediately, hindering the launching of lifeboats, and in 18 minutes it sank. Nearly 1,200 people died, including 128 Americans. As the ship's bow lifted and went under, the U-20 commander for the first time read the name: *Lusitania*.

The sinking, the worst marine disaster since the *Titanic* went down with 1,500 people in 1912, horrified Americans. Theodore Roosevelt called it "an act of piracy" and demanded war. Most Americans, however, wanted to stay out of war; like Wilson, they hoped negotiations could solve the problem. "There is such a thing," Wilson said a few days after the sinking, "as a man being too proud to fight. There is such a thing as a nation being so right that it does not need to convince others by force."

In a series of diplomatic notes, Wilson demanded a change in German policy. The first *Lusitania* note (May 13, 1915) called on Germany to abandon unrestricted submarine warfare, disavow the sinking, and compensate for lost American lives. Germany sent an evasive reply, and Wilson drafted a second note (June 9) insisting on specific pledges. Fearful the demand would lead to war, Secretary of State William Jennings Bryan resigned. Wilson sent it anyway and followed with a third note (July 21)—almost an ultimatum—warning Germany that the United States would view similar sinkings as "deliberately unfriendly."

Unbeknownst to Wilson, Germany had already ordered U-boat commanders not to sink passenger liners without warning. In August 1915, a U-boat mistakenly torpedoed the British liner *Arabic*, killing two Americans. Wilson protested, and Germany, eager to keep the United States out of the war, backed down. The *Arabic* pledge (September 1) promised that U-boats would stop and warn liners, unless they tried to resist or escape. Germany also apologized for American deaths on the *Arabic*, and for the rest of 1915, U-boats hunted freighters, not passenger liners.

Although Wilson had achieved his immediate goal, the *Lusitania* and *Arabic* crises contained the elements that led to war. Trade and travel tied the world together, and Americans no longer hid behind safe ocean barriers. New weapons, such as the submarine, strained old rules of international law. But while Americans sifted the conflicting claims of Britain and Germany, they hoped for peace. A generation of progressives, confident of human progress, did not easily accept war.

Wilson also hated war, but he found himself caught up in a worldwide crisis that demanded the best in American will and diplomacy. In the end, diplomacy failed, and in April 1917, the United States entered a war that changed the nation's history. Building on several major trends in American foreign policy since the 1890s, the years around World War I established the United States as a world power, confirmed its dominance in Latin America, and ended with a war with Germany and its allies that had far-reaching results.

A NEW WORLD POWER

As they had in the late nineteenth century, Americans after 1900 paid relatively little attention to foreign affairs. Newspapers and magazines ran stories every day about events abroad, but people were more concerned with what was going on at home.

For Americans at the time, foreign policy was something to be left to the president, an attitude the presidents themselves favored. Foreign affairs became an arena in which they could exert a free hand, largely unchallenged by Congress or the courts, and Roosevelt, Taft, and Wilson all did so.

The foreign policy they pursued from 1901 to 1920 was aggressive and nationalistic. During these years, the United States intervened in Europe, the Far East, and Latin America. It dominated the Caribbean.

In 1898, the United States left the peace table after the war with Spain possessing the Philippines, Puerto Rico, and Guam. Holding distant possessions required a colonial policy; it also required a change in foreign policy, reflecting an outward approach. From the Caribbean to the Pacific, policymakers paid attention to issues and countries they had earlier ignored. Like other nations in these years, the United States built a large navy, protected its colonial empire, and became increasingly involved in economic ventures abroad.

What were the main events that showed the United States was becoming a world power?

Building the Panama Canal

Convinced the United States should take a more active international role, Theodore Roosevelt spent his presidency preparing the nation for world power. Working with Secretary of War Elihu Root, he modernized the army, using lessons learned from the war with Spain. Roosevelt and Root established the Army War College, imposed stiff tests for promotion, and in 1903 created a general staff to oversee military

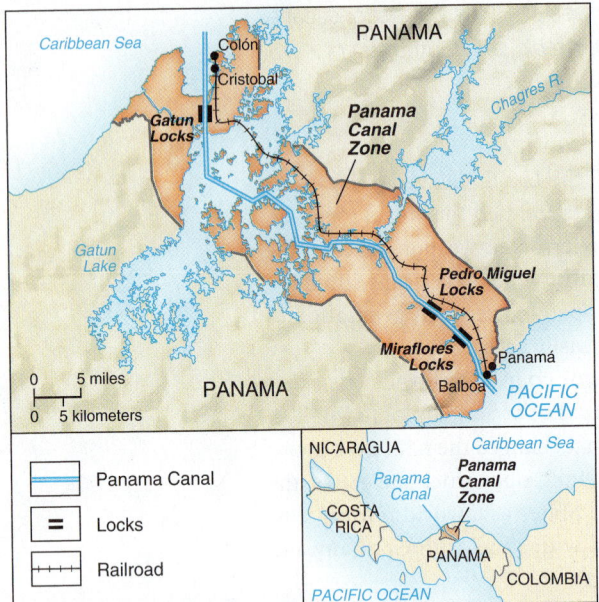

PANAMA

Caribbean Sea

Colón
Cristobal
Gatun Locks
Panama Canal Zone
Chagres R.
Gatun Lake
Pedro Miguel Locks
Miraflores Locks
Panamá
Balboa
PACIFIC OCEAN
PANAMA

0   5 miles
0   5 kilometers

— Panama Canal
= Locks
+++ Railroad

NICARAGUA
Caribbean Sea
Panama Canal
Panama Canal Zone
COSTA RICA
PANAMA
COLOMBIA
PACIFIC OCEAN

Map 24.1   The Panama Canal Zone Construction of the canal began in 1904, and despite landslides, steamy weather, and yellow fever, work was completed in 1914.

planning and mobilization. Determined to end dependence on the British fleet, Roosevelt doubled the strength of the navy during his term in office.

Stretching his authority to the limits, Roosevelt took steps to consolidate the country's new position in the Caribbean and Central America. European powers, which had long resisted American initiatives there, now accepted American supremacy. Preoccupied with problems in Europe, Asia, and Africa, Britain agreed to U.S. plans for an isthmian canal in Central America and withdrew much of its forces from the area.

Roosevelt wanted a canal to link the Atlantic and Pacific oceans across the isthmus connecting North and South America. Secretary of State John Hay negotiated with Britain the Hay–Pauncefote Treaty of 1901, which permitted the United States to construct and control an isthmian canal, provided it would be open to ships of all nations.

Delighted, Roosevelt began selecting the route. One route, 50 miles long, traversed the rough, swampy Panama region of Colombia. A French company had tried and failed to dig a canal there. To the northwest, another route ran through mountainous Nicaragua. Although 200 miles long, it followed natural waterways, which would make construction easier.

In 1899, an Isthmian Canal Commission recommended the shorter route through Panama. Roosevelt agreed and authorized Hay to negotiate an agreement with the Colombian representative in Washington, Thomas Herrán. The Hay–Herrán Convention (1903) gave the United States a 99-year lease, with option for renewal, on a canal zone 6 miles wide. In exchange, the United States would pay Colombia a one-time fee of $10 million and an annual rental of $250,000.

To Roosevelt's dismay, the Colombian Senate rejected the treaty because it infringed on Colombian sovereignty and because the Colombians wanted more money. Calling them "jack rabbits" and "contemptible little creatures," Roosevelt considered seizing Panama, then hinted he would welcome a Panamanian revolt. In November 1903, the Panamanians took the hint, and Roosevelt quickly supported them. Sending the cruiser *Nashville* to prevent Colombian troops from putting down the revolt, he recognized the new Republic of Panama.

Two weeks later, the Hay–Bunau–Varilla Treaty with Panama granted the United States control of a canal zone 10 miles wide across the Isthmus of Panama. In return, the United States guaranteed the independence of Panama and agreed to pay the same fees offered Colombia. On August 15, 1914, the first ocean steamer sailed through the canal, which had cost $375 million to build. (See Map 24.1.)

Roosevelt took great pride in the canal, calling it "by far the most important action in foreign affairs." Defending his methods, he said in 1911, "If I had followed traditional conservative methods, I would have submitted a dignified state paper of 200 pages to Congress and the debate on it would have been going on yet; but I took the Canal Zone and let Congress debate; and while the debate goes on the Canal does also."

From 1903 to 1920, the United States intervened often in Latin America to protect the canal, promote regional stability, and exclude foreign influence. One problem was Latin American debts to European powers. Many countries in the Western Hemisphere owed money to European governments and banks, and often these nations were poor, unstable, and unable to pay. The situation invited European intervention. In 1902, Venezuela defaulted on debts; Britain, Germany, and Italy sent Venezuela an ultimatum and blockaded its ports. American pressure forced a settlement, but foreign debts remained a problem.

In 1904, when the Dominican Republic defaulted on its debts, Roosevelt made a major announcement. Known as the **Roosevelt Corollary** to the Monroe Doctrine, the new policy warned Latin American nations to keep their affairs in order or face American intervention.

Applying his corollary immediately, Roosevelt in 1905 took charge of the Dominican Republic's revenue system. American officials collected customs and used them to pay the country's debts. Within two years, Roosevelt also established protectorates in Cuba and Panama. In 1912, the Senate added the Lodge Corollary, which warned foreign corporations not to purchase harbors and other sites of military significance in Latin America. The Roosevelt Corollary guided American policy in Latin America until the 1930s, when Franklin D. Roosevelt's Good Neighbor policy replaced it.

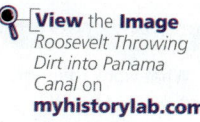

View the **Image**
Roosevelt Throwing Dirt into Panama Canal on
myhistorylab.com

Quick Check

✓ What did Theodore Roosevelt do to build the Panama Canal?

Ventures in the Far East

The Open Door policy toward China and possession of the Philippines shaped American actions in the Far East. Congress refused to fortify the Philippines, and the islands were vulnerable to Japanese attack. Roosevelt wanted to balance Russian and Japanese power, and he was not unhappy when war broke out between them in 1904. As Japan won victory after victory, however, Roosevelt grew worried. Acting on a request from Japan, he offered to mediate the conflict. Both Russia and Japan accepted: Russia because it was losing, Japan because it was financially drained.

In August 1905, Roosevelt convened a peace conference at Portsmouth, New Hampshire.

TR's Big Stick A cartoon from *Judge* titled "The World's Constable." The Roosevelt Corollary claimed the right of the United States to exercise "an international police power," enforced by what many referred to as a "big stick" diplomacy.

The conference ended the war, but Japan emerged as the dominant force in the Far East. Roosevelt then sent Secretary of War Taft to Tokyo to negotiate the Taft–Katsura Agreement (1905), which recognized Japan's dominance over Korea in return for its promise not to invade the Philippines. Giving Japan a free hand in Korea violated the Open Door policy, but Roosevelt argued that he had little choice.

To show Japan his determination, Roosevelt sent 16 battleships of the new American fleet around the world, including a stop in Tokyo in October 1908. European naval experts felt certain Japan would attack the fleet, but the Japanese welcomed it. In 1908, the two nations reached the Root–Takahira Agreement, in which they promised to maintain the status quo in the Pacific, uphold the Open Door, and support Chinese independence.

Quick Check

✓ What were Theodore Roosevelt's policies toward China and Japan?

Taft and Dollar Diplomacy

📖 **Read** the **Document**
Dollar Diplomacy on **myhistorylab.com**

In foreign as well as domestic affairs, President Taft tried to continue Roosevelt's policies. For secretary of state he chose Philander C. Knox, Roosevelt's attorney general, and together they pursued a policy of "dollar diplomacy" to promote American financial and business interests abroad. The policy had profit-seeking motives, but it also aimed to substitute economic ties for military alliances.

Intent, like Roosevelt, on supremacy in the Caribbean, Taft worked to replace European loans with American ones, thereby reducing the danger of outside meddling. In the Far East, Knox worked closely with Willard Straight, an agent of American bankers, who argued that dollar diplomacy was the financial arm of the Open Door. Straight had close ties to Edward H. Harriman, the railroad magnate, who wanted to build railroads in Manchuria in northern China. Knox approached Britain, Japan, and Russia to organize an international syndicate to loan China money to purchase the Manchurian railroads, but in January 1910, all three turned him down.

This was a blow to American policy and prestige in Asia. Russia and Japan cooperated with each other and staked out spheres of influence in violation of the Open Door. Japan resented Taft's initiatives in Manchuria, and China's distrust of the United States deepened. Instead of cultivating friendship, as Roosevelt had envisioned, Taft had started an intense rivalry with Japan for commercial advantage in China.

Quick Check

✓ What was the essential idea behind Taft's "dollar diplomacy"?

FOREIGN POLICY UNDER WILSON

What did Woodrow Wilson mean by "moral diplomacy"?

When he took office in 1913, Woodrow Wilson knew little about foreign policy. During the 1912 campaign he mentioned foreign policy only when it affected domestic concerns. "It would be the irony of fate if my administration had to deal chiefly with foreign affairs," he said to a friend before becoming president. And so it was. During his two terms, Wilson faced crisis after crisis in foreign affairs, including the outbreak of World War I.

The idealistic Wilson believed in an ethical world in which militarism, colonialism, and war were brought under control. He stressed morality over material interests and said during one crisis, "The force of America is the force of moral principle." Rejecting dollar diplomacy, Wilson initially chose moral diplomacy to bring right to the world, preserve peace, and extend the blessings of democracy.

Troubles Across the Border

William Jennings Bryan, whom Wilson appointed secretary of state, was also an amateur in foreign relations and a fervent pacifist. Like Wilson, he believed in the American duty to "help" less favored nations.

Wilson and Bryan promised a dramatic new approach in Latin America, concerned not with the "pursuit of material interest" but with "human rights" and "national integrity." Yet in the end, Wilson, distracted by other problems and impatient with the results of his idealistic approach, continued the Roosevelt–Taft policies. He defended the Monroe Doctrine, gave unspoken support to the Roosevelt Corollary, and intervened in Latin America more than had either Roosevelt or Taft. (See Map 24.2.)

Wilson's moral diplomacy encountered one of its greatest challenges across the border in Mexico. Porfirio Díaz, president of Mexico for 37 years, was overthrown in 1911, and a liberal reformer, Francisco I. Madero, became president. But Madero

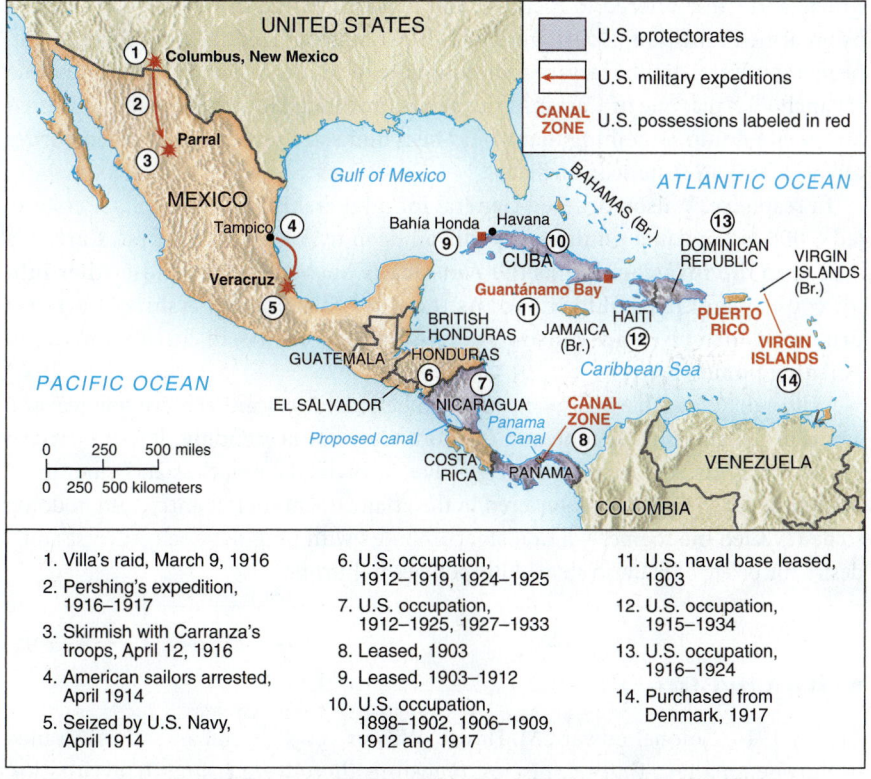

Map 24.2 *Activities of the United States in the Caribbean, 1898–1930*   During the first three decades of the twentieth century, the United States policed the Caribbean, claiming the right to take action when it judged Latin American countries were doing a bad job of running their affairs.

could not keep order. With support from wealthy landowners, the army, and the Catholic Church, General Victoriano Huerta ousted Madero in 1913 and arranged his murder. Most European nations recognized Huerta, but Wilson, calling him a "butcher," refused. Instead, he announced a new policy: To win American recognition, revolutionary regimes in Latin America must not only exercise power but be "a just government based upon law, not upon arbitrary or irregular force."

On that basis, Wilson maneuvered to oust Huerta. In 1914, he stationed warships off Mexico's ports to cut off arms shipments to the Huerta regime. Trouble followed. On April 9, 1914, several American sailors, who had gone ashore in Tampico to purchase supplies, were arrested. They were promptly released, but the American admiral demanded an apology and a 21-gun salute to the American flag. Huerta agreed—if the Americans also saluted the Mexican flag.

Wilson asked Congress for authority to use military force if needed; then, just as Congress acted, he learned that a German ship was landing arms at Veracruz on Mexico's eastern coast. With Wilson's approval, American warships shelled the harbor, and marines took the city against heavy resistance. Outraged, Mexicans of all factions denounced the invasion, and the two countries hovered on the edge of war.

Retreating, Wilson explained that he desired only to help Mexico. Argentina, Brazil, and Chile offered to mediate, and tensions eased. In July 1914, weakened by an armed rebellion, Huerta resigned. Wilson recognized the new government, headed by Venustiano Carranza, an associate of Madero. But in 1916, Francisco ("Pancho") Villa, one of Carranza's generals, revolted. Hoping to goad the United States into doing something that would help him seize power, Villa raided border towns, killing 18 American civilians.

In response, Wilson ordered General John J. Pershing to seize Villa. Pershing led 6,000 troops on a punitive expedition deep into Mexico. At first, Carranza agreed to the invasion, but as the Americans pushed farther and farther into his country, he changed his mind. As the wily Villa eluded Pershing, Carranza protested bitterly, and Wilson, worried about events in Europe, ordered Pershing home.

Wilson had laudable goals; he wanted to help the Mexicans achieve political and agrarian reform. But his tone and methods were condescending. Wilson tried to impose progressive reform on a society sharply divided along class and other lines. With little forethought, he interfered in the affairs of another country, and in doing so he revealed the themes—moralism, combined with pragmatic self-interest and a desire for peace—that also shaped his policies in Europe.

Quick Check

✓ How and why did Wilson get Involved in Mexico, and how did his involvement reflect his "moral diplomacy"?

What were the reasons behind and dangers of Wilson's neutrality policy?

TOWARD WAR

In May 1914, Colonel Edward M. House, Wilson's close friend and adviser, sailed to Europe on a fact-finding mission. Tensions there were rising. "The situation is extraordinary," he reported to Wilson. "There is too much hatred, too many jealousies."

In Germany, the ambitious Kaiser Wilhelm II coveted a world empire to match those of Britain and France. Germany had military treaties with Turkey and Austria-Hungary, a sprawling, multinational central European empire. In another alliance, Britain, France, and Russia agreed to aid each other in case of attack.

On June 28, 1914, an assassin linked to Serbia murdered Archduke Franz Ferdinand, heir to the Austro-Hungarian throne. Within weeks, Germany, Turkey, and Austria-Hungary (the Central Powers) were at war with Britain, France, and Russia (the Allied Powers). Americans were shocked at the events. Wilson immediately proclaimed neutrality and asked Americans to remain "impartial in thought as well as in action." The war, he said, was one "with which we have nothing to do, whose causes cannot touch us."

In private, Wilson was stunned. A man who loved peace, he had long admired the British parliamentary system, and he respected the leaders of the British Liberal party, who supported social programs akin to his own. "Everything I love most in the world," he said, "is at stake."

Watch the **Video**
The Outbreak of World War I on
myhistorylab.com

The Neutrality Policy

In general, Americans accepted neutrality. They saw no need to enter the conflict, especially after the Allies in September 1914 halted the first German drive toward Paris. America resisted involvement in other countries' problems, except for Latin America, and had a tradition of avoiding foreign entanglements.

Many of the nation's large number of progressives saw additional reasons to resist. They thought war violated the very spirit of progressive reform. Why demand safer factories in which people could work and then kill them by the millions in war? To many progressives, moreover, Britain represented international finance, which they detested. Germany, on the other hand, had pioneered some of their favorite social reforms, including health insurance, universal education, and old age pensions. Above all, progressives were sure that war would end reform. It consumed money and attention; it inflamed emotions.

As a result, Jane Addams, Florence Kelley, and other progressives fought to keep the United States out of war. In late 1915, they formed the American Union Against Militarism, to throw, they said, "a monkey wrench into the machinery" of war. In 1915, Addams helped organize the League to Limit Armament, and she and Carrie Chapman Catt formed the Woman's Peace Party to organize women against the war.

The war's outbreak also tugged at the emotions of millions of Americans. At the deepest level, most, bound by common language and institutions, sympathized with the Allies and blamed Germany for the war. Like Wilson, many Americans admired English literature, customs, and law; they remembered Lafayette and France's help during the American Revolution. Germany seemed arrogant and militaristic. When the war began, it invaded Belgium to strike at France and violated a treaty that the German chancellor called "just a scrap of paper."

Quick Check

✓ What were the factors behind Wilson's neutrality policy?

Both sides tried to sway American opinion. German propaganda tended to stress strength and will; Allied propaganda called on historical ties and publicized German atrocities, real and alleged. In the end, the propaganda probably made little difference. Ties of heritage and the course of the war, not propaganda, decided the American position. At the outset, no matter which side they cheered for, Americans preferred simply to remain at peace.

Freedom of the Seas

The demands of trade tested American neutrality and confronted Wilson with difficult choices. Under international law, neutral countries could trade in nonmilitary goods with all belligerent countries. But Britain controlled the seas, and it intended to cut off shipments of war materials to the Central Powers.

As soon as war broke out, Britain blockaded German ports and limited what Americans could sell to Germany. American ships had to carry cargoes to neutral ports from which, after examination, they could be carried to Germany. As time passed, Britain forbade the shipment to Germany of all foodstuffs and most raw materials, seized and censored mail, and "blacklisted" American firms that dealt directly with the Central Powers.

Again and again, Wilson protested against such infringements on neutral rights. Sometimes Britain complied, sometimes not, and Wilson often grew angry. But, needing American support and supplies, Britain was careful to disrupt German-American trade without disrupting Anglo-American relations. When necessary, it also promised to reimburse American businesses after the war.

Other than the German U-boats, there were no constraints on trade with the Allies, and a flood of Allied war orders fueled the American economy. To finance the purchases, the Allies borrowed from American bankers. By 1917, loans to Allied governments exceeded $2 billion; loans to Germany came to only $27 million.

Quick Check

✓ In what ways did the demands of trade test American neutrality?

In a development that influenced Wilson's policy, the war produced the greatest economic boom in the nation's history. Loans and trade drew the United States ever closer to the Allied cause. And although Wilson often protested British maritime policy, the protests involved American goods and money; U-boats threatened American lives.

The U-Boat Threat

A relatively new weapon, the *Unterseeboot*, or submarine, strained international law. Legally, a submarine had to surface, warn a ship to stop, send a boarding party to check papers and cargo, then allow passengers and crew to board lifeboats before sinking the vessel. Flimsy and slow, however, submarines could ill afford to surface while the prey radioed for help.

When Germany announced its submarine campaign in February 1915, Wilson protested sharply, calling the sinking of merchant ships without checking cargo "a wanton act." The Germans promised not to sink American ships—an agreement that lasted until 1917—and thereafter the issue became Americans' right to sail on the ships of belligerent nations. In March 1915, an American citizen aboard the

British liner *Falaba* perished when the ship was torpedoed off the Irish coast. Bryan urged Wilson to forbid Americans to travel in the war zones, but the president, determined to stand by the principles of international law, refused.

Wilson reacted more harshly in May and August of 1915 when U-boats sank the *Lusitania* and the *Arabic*. He demanded that the Germans protect passenger vessels and pay for American losses. At odds with Wilson's understanding of neutrality, Bryan resigned as secretary of state in June 1915. Robert Lansing, a lawyer and counselor in the State Department, replaced him. Lansing brought a very different spirit to the job. He favored the Allies and believed that a German-dominated world would threaten democracy. He urged strong stands against German violations of American neutrality.

The U-Boat A new and terrifying weapon of the war was the German U-boat, which attacked silently and without warning.

In February 1916, Germany declared unrestricted submarine warfare against all armed ships. Lansing told Germany it would be held strictly accountable for American losses. A month later, a U-boat torpedoed the unarmed French steamer *Sussex* without warning, drowning several Americans. Arguing that the sinking violated the *Arabic* pledge, Lansing urged Wilson to break relations with Germany. Wilson refused, but on April 18, he sent an ultimatum to Germany, stating that unless the Germans immediately ceased attacking cargo and passenger ships, the United States would sever relations.

The German government yielded. In the *Sussex* pledge of May 4, 1916, it promised to shoot on sight only enemy warships.

A short period of friendly relations between Germany and the United States ensued. The pledge applied not only to passenger liners but to all merchant ships, belligerent or not. There was one problem: Wilson had taken such a strong position that if Germany renewed submarine warfare on merchant shipping, war was likely. Most Americans, however, viewed the agreement as a diplomatic stroke for peace by Wilson, and the issues of peace and preparedness dominated the presidential election of 1916.

Read the **Document** *Adolf K. G. E. von Spiegel, U-boat 202 (1919)* on **myhistorylab.com**

Quick Check

✓ How did German submarines threaten to involve the United States in the war?

The Election of 1916

The "preparedness" issue pitted antiwar groups against those who wanted to prepare for war. Bellicose as always, Teddy Roosevelt led the preparedness campaign. He called Wilson "yellow" for not pressing Germany harder after the *Lusitania* sinking, but Wilson refused to be stampeded.

Both sides attacked his position. Preparedness advocates charged cowardice; pacifists denounced any attempt at military readiness. The difficulty of his situation, plus the growing U-boat crisis, soon changed Wilson's mind. In mid-1915, he

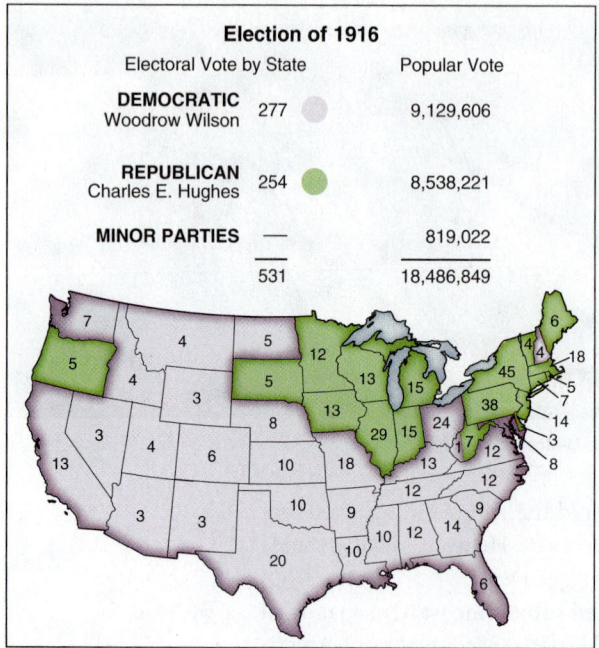

Election of 1916

	Electoral Vote by State		Popular Vote
DEMOCRATIC Woodrow Wilson	277		9,129,606
REPUBLICAN Charles E. Hughes	254		8,538,221
MINOR PARTIES	—		819,022
	531		18,486,849

Map 24.3

asked the War Department to increase military planning, and later that year, approved large increases in the army and navy, which upset peace-minded progressives.

For their standard-bearer in 1916, the Republicans nominated Charles Evans Hughes, a moderate justice of the Supreme Court. Hughes seemed to have all the qualifications for victory. A former reform governor of New York, he could lure back the Roosevelt progressives and appeal to Republican conservatives. To woo the Roosevelt wing, Hughes called for a tougher line against Germany, thus allowing the Democrats to label him the "war" candidate. Even so, Roosevelt and others considered Hughes a "bearded iceberg," a dull campaigner who wavered on important issues.

The Democrats renominated Wilson in a convention marked by spontaneous demonstrations for peace. Picking up the theme, Wilson said in October, "I am not expecting this country to get into war." The campaign slogan "He kept us out of war" was repeated endlessly, and just before the election, the Democrats took full-page ads in leading newspapers:

> You Are Working—Not Fighting!
> Alive and Happy—Not Cannon Fodder!
> Wilson and Peace with Honor?
> or
> Hughes with Roosevelt and War?

On election night, Hughes swept most of the East, and Wilson retired at 10 P.M. thinking he had lost. During the night, the results came in from California, New Mexico, and North Dakota; all supported Wilson—California by just 3,773 votes. Holding the Democratic South, he carried key states in the Midwest and West and took much of the labor and progressive vote. Women—who were then allowed to vote in presidential elections in 12 states—also voted heavily for Wilson. (See Map 24.3.)

Quick Check

✓ What were the two key issues and the main results of the 1916 presidential election?

The Final Months of Peace

Just before election day, Britain further limited neutral trade, and there were reports Germany was going to renew unrestricted submarine warfare. Fresh from his victory, Wilson redoubled his efforts for peace. Aware that time was running out, he hoped to start negotiations to end the bloodshed and create a peaceful postwar world.

In December 1916, he asked both sides to state their war aims. Should they do so, he pledged the "whole force" of the United States to end the war. The Allies refused, although they promised privately to negotiate if the German terms were reasonable. The Germans replied evasively and in January 1917 revealed their real objectives. Close to forcing Russia out of the war, Germany sensed victory and wanted territory in eastern Europe and Africa.

On January 22, in an eloquent speech before the Senate, Wilson called for a "peace without victory." Outlining his own ambitious aims, he urged respect for all nations, freedom of the seas, arms limitations, and a League of Nations to keep the peace: "Only a peace between equals can last, only a peace the very principle of which is equality and a common participation in a common benefit." Many Europeans were impressed, but it was too late. The Germans had already decided to unleash the submarines and gamble on a quick end to the war. Even as Wilson spoke, U-boats were in the Atlantic west of Ireland, preparing to attack.

On January 31, the German ambassador in Washington informed Lansing that beginning February 1, U-boats would sink on sight all ships—passenger or merchant, neutral or belligerent, armed or unarmed—in the waters around Britain and France. Staking everything on a last effort, the Germans calculated that if they could sink 600,000 tons of shipping a month, they could defeat Britain in six months. As he had pledged in 1916, Wilson severed relations with Germany, although he still hoped for peace.

On February 25, the British government privately gave Wilson a telegram intercepted from Arthur Zimmermann, the German foreign minister, to the German ambassador in Mexico. A day later, Wilson asked Congress for authority to arm merchant ships to deter U-boat attacks. When La Follette and a handful of others threatened to filibuster, Wilson published the Zimmermann telegram. It proposed an alliance with Mexico in case of war with the United States, offering financial support and recovery of Mexico's "lost territory" in New Mexico, Texas, and Arizona.

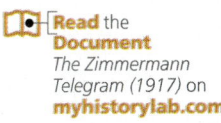

Read the **Document**
The Zimmermann Telegram (1917) on **myhistorylab.com**

Spurred by a wave of public indignation toward the Germans, the House passed Wilson's measure, but La Follette and others still blocked action in the Senate. On March 9, 1917, Wilson ordered merchant ships armed on his own authority. On March 13, the navy instructed all vessels to fire on submarines. Between March 12 and March 21, U-boats sank five American ships, and Wilson decided on war.

He called Congress into special session and on April 2, 1917, asked for a declaration of war. Pacifists in Congress managed to postpone a vote for four days. Finally, on April 6, the declaration of war passed, with 50 members of the House and six senators voting against it. Even then, the country was divided over entry into the war.

Quick Check

✓ How did the United States finally get involved in the war?

OVER THERE

With a burst of patriotism, the United States entered a war its new allies were in danger of losing. In April, the Germans sank 881,000 tons of Allied shipping, the greatest amount for any one month during the war. There were mutinies in the

How did the United States' entry affect the course of World War I?

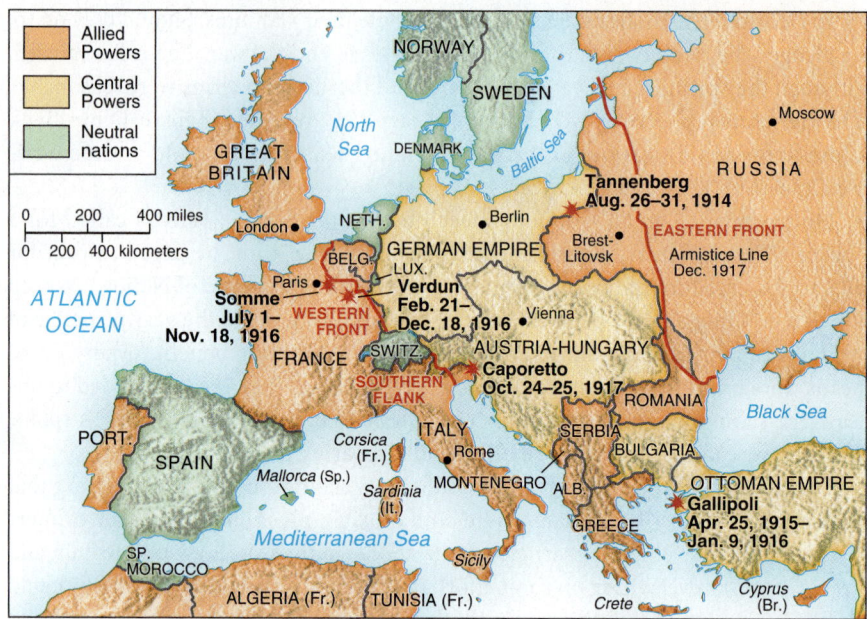

Map 24.4 *European Alliances and Battlefronts, 1914–1917* Allied forces suffered early defeats on the eastern front (Tannenberg) and in the Dardanelles (Gallipoli). In 1917, the Allies were routed in the Alps (Caporetto); the western front then became the critical theater of the war.

Watch the **Video**
American Entry into WWI on
myhistorylab.com

French army and a costly British failure in Flanders. In November, the Bolsheviks seized power in Russia, and, led by V. I. Lenin, they signed a separate peace treaty with Germany in March 1918, freeing German troops to fight in the West. German and Austrian forces routed the Italian army in the Alps, and the Allies braced for a spring 1918 offensive. (See Map 24.4.)

Mobilization

The United States was not prepared for war. Some Americans hoped the declaration of war itself might daunt the Germans; others thought that naval escorts of Allied shipping or supplying money and arms to the Allies would produce victory without sending troops.

Listen to the
Audio File
"Over There" on
myhistorylab.com

Bypassing older generals, Wilson named John J. ("Black Jack") Pershing, leader of the Mexican campaign, to head the American Expeditionary Force (AEF). Pershing inherited an army unready for war. In April 1917, it had 200,000 officers and men, equipped with 300,000 old rifles, 1,500 machine guns, 55 obsolete airplanes, and two field radio sets. Its most recent battle experience had been chasing Pancho Villa around northern Mexico. It had not caught him.

Although some in Congress preferred a voluntary army of the kind that had fought in the Spanish-American War, Wilson turned to conscription, which he considered both efficient and democratic. In May 1917, the **Selective Service Act** required all men between the ages of 21 and 30 (later changed to 18 and 45) to register. In June, 9.5 million men registered for the draft. By the end of the war, 24.2 million men had registered, and about 2.8 million were inducted into the army.

The draft included black men as well as white, and four African American regiments were among the first sent into action in France. Despite their contributions, however, American commanders allowed no black soldiers to march in the victory celebrations that eventually took place in Paris.

View the **Closer Look**
Mobilizing the Home Front on
myhistorylab.com

Quick Check

✓ How did the United States mobilize for war?

War in the Trenches

World War I may have been the most terrible war of all time, more terrible even than World War II and its vast devastation. After the early offensives, the European armies dug themselves into trenches only hundreds of yards apart in places. Artillery, poison gas, hand grenades, flame throwers, and a new weapon—rapid-fire machine guns—kept them pinned down.

Even in moments of respite, the mud, rats, cold, fear, and disease took a heavy toll. Deafening bombardments shook the earth, and shell shock was common. From time to time, troops went "over the top" of the trenches to attack the enemy's lines, but the costs were enormous. The German offensive at Verdun in 1916 killed 600,000 men; the British lost 20,000 on the first day of an offensive on the Somme.

The first American soldiers reached France in June 1917. By March 1918, 300,000 Americans were there. By war's end, 2 million men had crossed the Atlantic.

As expected, on March 21, 1918, the Germans launched a massive assault in western Europe. With help from troops from the Russian front, by May the Germans were just 50 miles from Paris. In their first action, the Americans blocked the Germans at Château-Thierry and four weeks later forced them out of Belleau Wood, a crucial stronghold. On July 15, the Germans threw everything into a last drive for Paris, but they were halted at the Marne River, and in three days of battle they were finished. "On the 18th," the German chancellor said, "even the most optimistic among us knew that all was lost. The history of the world was played out in three days."

With the German drive stalled, the Allies counterattacked along the entire front. On September 12, 500,000 Americans and a smaller contingent of French drove the Germans from the St. Mihiel salient. Two weeks later, 896,000 Americans attacked between the Meuse River and the Argonne Forest. Focusing on a main railroad supply line for the German army, American troops broke through in early November, cut the line, and drove the Germans back along the whole front. (See Map 24.5.)

The German high command knew that the war was lost. On October 6, 1918, Germany appealed to Wilson for an armistice. By the end of the month, Turkey, Bulgaria, and Austria-Hungary were out of the war. At 4 A.M. on November 11,

View the **Image**
Trench Warfare on
myhistorylab.com

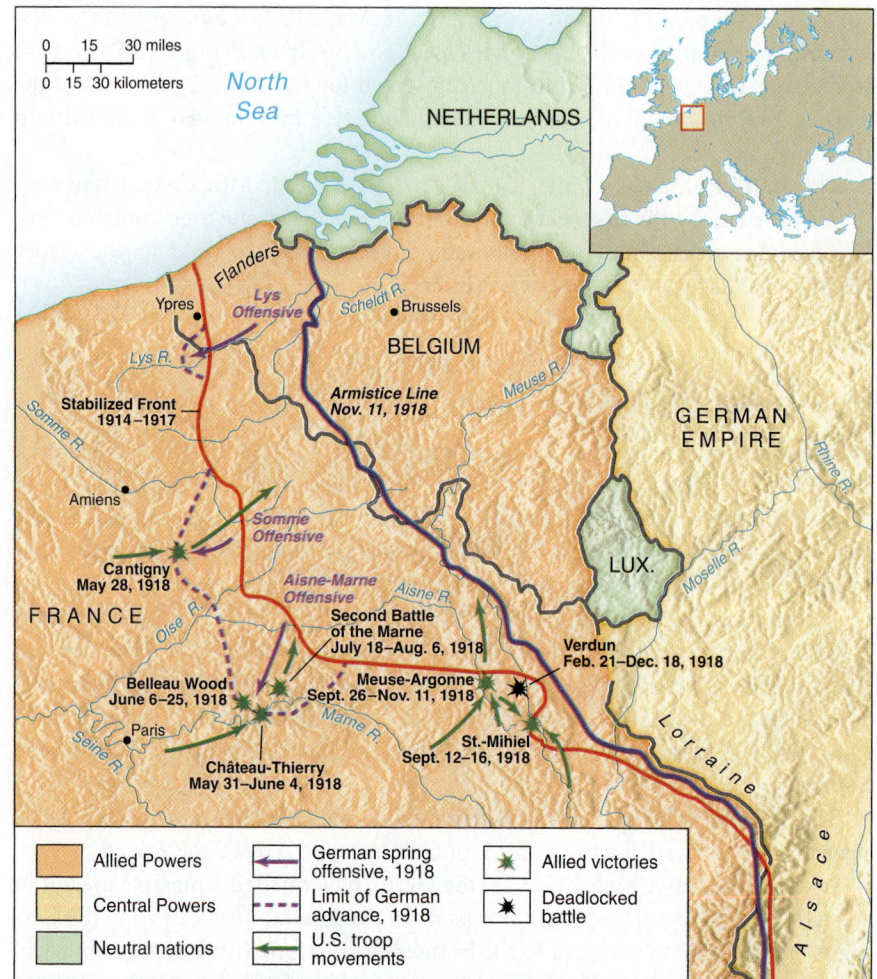

Map 24.5 *The Western Front: U.S. Participation, 1918* The turning point of the war came in July, when the German advance was halted at the Marne. The "Yanks," now a fighting force, were thrown into the breach. They helped stem the tide and mount the counteroffensives that ended the war.

Quick Check

✓ Why might World War I have been the most terrible war of all time?

Germany signed the armistice. The Americans had lost 48,909 dead and 230,000 wounded; losses to disease brought the total of dead to more than 112,000.

The American contribution, although small compared to the enormous costs to European nations, was vital. Fresh, enthusiastic American troops raised Allied morale; they helped turn the tide at a crucial point in the war.

OVER HERE

What programs and changes did World War I bring at home?

Victory at the front depended on economic and emotional mobilization at home. Consolidating federal authority, Wilson moved quickly in 1917 and 1918 to organize war production and distribution. An idealist who knew how to sway public opinion, he also recognized the need to enlist American emotions. To him, the war for people's minds, the "conquest of their convictions," was as vital as the battlefield.

The Conquest of Convictions

A week after war was declared, Wilson formed the Committee on Public Information (CPI) to mobilize support for the war, and asked George Creel, an outspoken progressive journalist, to head it. Creel hired progressives such as Ida Tarbell and Ray Stannard Baker and recruited thousands of people in the arts, advertising, and film industries to publicize the war. He worked out a system of voluntary censorship with the press, plastered walls with colorful posters, and issued more than 75 million pamphlets.

Wartime Hatred Anti-German sentiment escalated dramatically after the United States entered the war in April 1917. A wave of verbal and physical attacks on German Americans was accompanied by a campaign to repress German culture. In this photograph from 1917, children stand in front of an anti-German sign posted in the Edison Park community of Chicago, Illinois. As the sign suggests, some Americans questioned the loyalty of their German American neighbors.

Stoked by the propaganda campaign, anti-German sentiment spread. Many schools stopped teaching the German language—California's state education board called it a language "of autocracy, brutality, and hatred." Sauerkraut became "liberty cabbage"; saloonkeepers removed pretzels from the bar. Orchestral works by Bach, Beethoven, and Brahms vanished from concert halls.

Wilson encouraged anti-German sentiment. "Woe be to the man or group of men that seeks to stand in our way," he told peace advocates soon after the war began. The Espionage Act of 1917 imposed sentences of up to 20 years for persons found guilty of aiding the enemy, obstructing military recruitment, or encouraging disloyalty. It allowed the postmaster general to remove from the mails materials that incited treason or insurrection. The Trading-with-the-Enemy Act of 1917 authorized the government to censor the foreign language press.

In 1918, the Sedition Act imposed harsh penalties on anyone using "disloyal, profane, scurrilous, or abusive language" about the government, flag, or armed forces uniforms. In all, more than 1,500 persons were arrested under the new laws.

The sedition laws clearly went beyond any clear or present danger. There were, to be sure, German spies in the country, and Germans who wanted to encourage strikes in American arms factories. Moreover, the government and national leaders were painfully aware of how divided Americans had been about entering the war. They set out to promote unity—by force, if necessary—to convince Germany that the nation was united.

But none of this warranted a nationwide program of repression. Conservatives took advantage of wartime feelings to try to stamp out American socialists, who were vulnerable because, unlike European socialists, they continued to oppose the war even after their country had entered it. Using the sedition laws, conservatives harried the Socialist party and the Industrial Workers of the World.

((•── **Listen** to the
Audio File
*The Speech that
Sent Debs to Jail* on
myhistorylab.com

Quick Check

✓ What measures did
Wilson pass to sway
American opinions?

Wilson's postmaster general banned from the mails more than a dozen socialist publications, including the *Appeal to Reason*, which went to more than 500,000 people weekly. In 1918, Eugene V. Debs, the Socialist party leader, delivered a speech denouncing capitalism and the war. He was convicted of violating the Espionage Act and spent the war in a penitentiary. Nominated as the Socialist party candidate for president in 1920, Debs—prisoner 9653—won nearly a million votes, but the Socialist movement never fully recovered from the repression of the war.

Opposition to the War Eugene V. Debs, serving time in an Atlanta penitentiary for speaking against the war, is shown here after receiving word of his nomination for the presidency. Debs campaigned in 1920 from behind bars.

▢│▢─ **Read** the
Document
*Newton D. Baker,
Treatment of German
Americans (1918)* on
myhistorylab.com

A Bureaucratic War

Quick, effective action was needed to win the war. To meet the need, Wilson and Congress set up nearly 5,000 new federal agencies. Staffed largely by businessmen, the agencies had unprecedented funds and powers.

By the time the war ended, it had cost $32 billion in direct war expenses—in an era when the entire federal budget rarely exceeded $1 billion. To raise the money, the administration sold about $23 billion in "Liberty Bonds" and, using the new Sixteenth Amendment, boosted taxes on corporations and personal incomes.

At first, Wilson tried to organize the wartime economy along decentralized lines like his early New Freedom thinking. But that proved unworkable, and he moved instead to a series of highly centralized planning boards, each with broad authority over a specific area of the economy. Boards controlled virtually every aspect of transportation, agriculture, and manufacturing. Though only a few of them were as effective as Wilson had hoped, they did coordinate the war effort to some degree.

The War Industries Board (WIB), one of the most powerful of the new agencies, oversaw the production of all American factories. Headed by millionaire Bernard M. Baruch, a Wall Street broker and speculator, it determined priorities, allocated raw materials, and fixed prices. It told manufacturers what they could and could not make. The WIB set the output of steel and regulated the number of stops on elevators. Working closely with business, Baruch for a time acted as the dictator of the American economy.

Herbert Hoover, the hero of a campaign to feed starving Belgians after Germany invaded Belgium in 1914 and cut it off from most of its supplies of imported food, headed a new Food Administration. He set out with customary energy to supply food to the armies overseas. Appealing to the "spirit of self-sacrifice," Hoover convinced people to observe "meatless" and "wheatless" days. He fixed prices to boost production, bought and distributed wheat, and encouraged people to plant "victory gardens" behind homes, churches, and schools.

At another new agency, the Fuel Administration, Harry A. Garfield, the president of Williams College, introduced daylight saving time, rationed coal and oil, and imposed gasless days when motorists could not drive. The Railroad Administration dictated traffic over nearly 400,000 miles of track—standardizing rates, limiting passenger travel, and speeding arms shipments. The War Shipping Board coordinated shipping, the Emergency Fleet Corporation supervised shipbuilding, and the War Trade Board oversaw foreign trade.

As never before, the government intervened in American life. Businessmen flocked to Washington to run the new agencies, and the partnership between government and business \grew closer. As government expanded, so did business. Industries such as steel, aluminum, and cigarettes boomed, and wartime contracts increased corporate profits threefold between 1914 and 1919.

Quick Check

✓ What were the main bureaucratic measures that shaped American war policy in World War I?

Labor in the War

Labor also entered into a partnership with government, although the results were more limited than in the business–government alliance. Samuel Gompers, president of the AFL, served on Wilson's Council of National Defense, an advisory group formed to unify business, labor, and government. Gompers hoped to trade labor peace for labor advances, and he formed a War Committee on Labor to enlist workers' support for the war. With the blessing of the Wilson administration, membership in the AFL and other unions grew from about 2.7 million in 1916 to more than 4 million in 1919.

Hoping to encourage production and avoid strikes, Wilson adopted many of the objectives of the social-justice reformers. He supported an eight-hour day in war-related industries and improved wages and working conditions. In May 1918, he named Felix Frankfurter, a brilliant young law professor, to head a new War Labor Board (WLB). The agency standardized wages and hours, and it protected the right of labor to organize and bargain collectively.

The WLB also ordered equal pay for equal work for women in war industries. In 1914, the war stopped the flow of European immigrants, and in 1917, the draft began to

Read the **Document**
Abrams v. United States on
myhistorylab.com

Women at Work Housewives did not leave home for the factory en masse in 1917 as they did during World War II, but many women already employed outside the home found new, well-paying opportunities in jobs previously held by men.

Watch the Video
*The Great
Migration* on
myhistorylab.com

take many American men. Women, African Americans, and Mexican Americans filled the resulting labor shortage. One million women worked in war industries. Some took jobs men had held, but most moved from one set of "women's jobs" into another.

Still, there were new opportunities and in some cases higher pay. In food, airplane, and electrical plants, women made up one-fifth or more of the workforce. As their wages increased, so did their expectations; some became more militant and clashed with male co-workers.

Looking for more people to fill wartime jobs, corporations recruited southern blacks. Beginning in 1916, northern labor agents traveled across the South, promising jobs, high wages, and free transportation. Soon the movement northward became a flood. Between 1916 and 1918, more than 450,000 African Americans left the Old South for the booming industrial cities of St. Louis, Chicago, Detroit, and Cleveland. In the decade before 1920, Detroit's black population grew by more than 600 percent, Cleveland's by more than 300 percent, and Chicago's by 150 percent. (See Map 24.6.)

Most of the newcomers were young, unmarried, and skilled or semiskilled. The men found jobs in factories, railroad yards, steel mills, packinghouses, and coal mines; black women worked in textile factories, department stores, and restaurants. In their new homes, African Americans found greater racial freedom but also different living conditions. If the South was often hostile, the North could be impersonal and lonely. Accustomed to the pace of the farm—ruled by the seasons and the sun—blacks who entered the industrial sector now worked for hourly

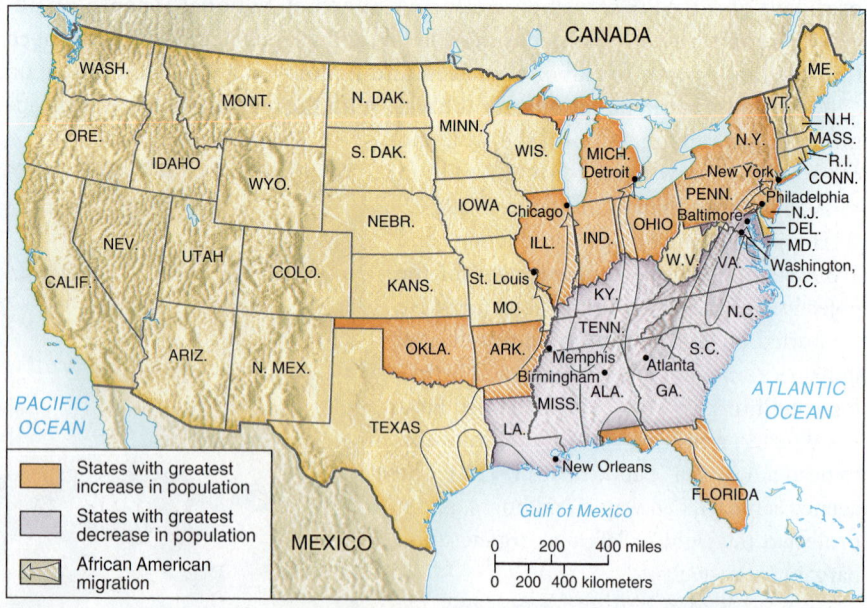

Map 24.6 *African American Migration Northward, 1910–1920* The massive migration of African Americans from the South to the North during World War I changed the dynamics of race relations in the United States.

wages in mass production industries, where time clocks and line supervisors dictated the daily routine.

Growing competition for housing and jobs increased racial tensions. In mid-1917, a race war in East St. Louis, Illinois, killed nine whites and about 40 blacks. Chicago, New York City, Omaha, and other cities had race riots. Lynch mobs killed 48 blacks in 1917, 63 in 1918, and 78 in 1919. Ten of the victims in 1919 were war veterans, several still in uniform.

Blacks were increasingly inclined to fight back. Two hundred thousand blacks served in France—42,000 as combat troops. Returning home, they expected better treatment. "I'm glad I went," a black veteran said. "I done my part and I'm going to fight right here till Uncle Sam does his."

Heroes of the War The 369th infantry regiment returning from the war on the *Stockholm* in February 1919. France awarded them its highest medal for valor, the Croix de Guerre, for bravery in the Meuse-Argonne.

"Lift Ev'ry Voice and Sing," composed in 1900, became known as the "Negro National Anthem." Parents bought black dolls for their children, and W. E. B. Du Bois spoke of a "New Negro," proud and more militant: "We return. We return from fighting. We return fighting."

Eager for cheap labor, farmers and ranchers in the Southwest persuaded the federal government to relax immigration restrictions. Between 1917 and 1920, more than 100,000 Mexicans migrated into Texas, Arizona, New Mexico, and California. The Mexican American population grew from 385,000 in 1910 to 740,000 in 1920. Tens of thousands of Mexican Americans moved to Chicago, St. Louis, Omaha, and other northern cities to take wartime jobs. Often scorned and insecure, they created urban barrios similar to the Chinatowns and Little Italys around them.

Like most wars, World War I affected patterns at home as much as abroad. Business profits grew, factories expanded, and industries turned out huge amounts of war goods. Government authority swelled, and people came to expect different things of their government. Labor, women, and blacks made gains. Society assimilated some of the shifts, but social and economic tensions grew, and when the war ended, they spilled over in the strikes and violence of the Red Scare (see Chapter 25).

The United States emerged from the war the strongest economic power in the world. In 1914, it was a debtor nation. Americans owed foreign investors about $3 billion. Five years later, the United States had become a creditor nation. Foreign governments owed more than $10 billion, and foreign citizens owed American investors nearly $3 billion. The war marked a shift in economic power rarely equaled in history.

Quick Check

✓ What were four effects the war had on labor?

THE TREATY OF VERSAILLES

What mistakes did Wilson make in negotiating the Treaty of Versailles?

Long before the fighting ended, Wilson began to plan for the peace. Like many others, he was disconcerted when the Bolsheviks in Russia began revealing the secret agreements among Britain, France, Italy, and czarist Russia to divide up Turkey and Germany's colonies. To place the war on a higher plane, he outlined a far-reaching, nonpunitive settlement before Congress on January 8, 1918. Wilson's Fourteen Points were generous and far-sighted, but they failed to satisfy wartime emotions for vindication. (See Table 14.1.)

Britain and France distrusted Wilsonian idealism as a basis for peace. They had lost huge amounts of blood and treasure during the war. They wanted Germany disarmed and crippled; they wanted its colonies; and they were skeptical of the principle of self-determination. As the war ended, the Allies, who had in fact made secret commitments with one another, balked at making the Fourteen Points the basis of peace. When Wilson threatened to negotiate a separate treaty with Germany, however, they appeared to give in.

TABLE 24.1   Woodrow Wilson's Fourteen Points, 1918: Success and Failure in Implementation

1. Open covenants of peace openly arrived at	Not fulfilled
2. Absolute freedom of navigation on the seas in peace and war	Not fulfilled
3. Removal of all economic barriers to the equality of trade among nations	Not fulfilled
4. Reduction of armaments to the level needed only for domestic safety	Not fulfilled
5. Impartial adjustments of colonial claims	Not fulfilled
6. Evacuation of all Russian territory; Russia to be welcomed into the society of free nations	Not fulfilled
7. Evacuation and restoration of Belgium	Fulfilled
8. Evacuation and restoration of all French lands; return of Alsace-Lorraine to France	Fulfilled
9. Readjustment of Italy's frontiers along lines of Italian nationality	Compromised
10. Self-determination for the former subjects of the Austro-Hungarian Empire	Compromised
11. Evacuation of Rumania, Serbia, and Montenegro; free access to the sea for Serbia	Compromised
12. Self-determination for the former subjects of the Ottoman Empire; secure sovereignty for Turkish portion	Compromised
13. Establishment of an independent Poland, with free and secure access to the sea	Fulfilled
14. Establishment of a League of Nations affording mutual guarantees of independence and territorial integrity	Not fulfilled

Sources: Data from G. M. Gathorne-Hardy, *The Fourteen Points and the Treaty of Versailles* (Oxford Pamphlets on World Affairs, no. 6, 1939), pp. 8–34; Thomas G. Paterson et al., *American Foreign Policy: A History Since 1900,* 2nd ed., vol. 2, pp. 282–293.

Wilson had won an important victory, but difficulties lay ahead. As Georges Clemenceau, the 78-year-old French premier, said, "God gave us the Ten Commandments, and we broke them. Wilson gives us the Fourteen Points. We shall see."

A Peace at Paris

Unfortunately, Wilson made a grave error just before the peace conference began. He appealed to voters to elect a Democratic Congress in November 1918, saying that any other result would be "interpreted on the other side of the water as a repudiation of my leadership." Republicans were furious, especially those who had supported the Fourteen Points; Wilson's problems deepened when the Democrats lost both the House and Senate.

Two weeks after the elections, Wilson announced he would attend the peace conference. This was a dramatic break from tradition, and Republicans attacked his personal involvement.

They renewed criticism when he named the rest of the delegation: Secretary of State Lansing; Colonel House; General Tasker H. Bliss, a military expert; and Henry White, a career diplomat. Wilson named no senator; the only Republican was White.

In selecting the delegation, Wilson passed over Henry Cabot Lodge, the powerful Republican senator from Massachusetts who opposed the Fourteen Points and would soon head the Senate Foreign Relations Committee. He also decided not to appoint Elihu Root or ex-President Taft, both of them enthusiastic internationalists. Never good at accepting criticism or delegating authority, Wilson wanted a delegation he could control—an advantage at the peace table but not in a battle over the treaty at home.

Wilson received a tumultuous welcome in London, Paris, and Rome. Never before had such crowds acclaimed a democratic political figure. In Paris, two million people lined the Champs-Elysees, threw flowers, and shouted, "Wilson le Juste [the just]" as his carriage drove by. Overwhelmed, Wilson was sure that Europeans shared his goals and would force their leaders to accept his peace. He was wrong. Like their leaders, many people on the Allied side hated Germany and wanted revenge and a peace that reflected victory.

Opening in January 1919, the Peace Conference at Paris continued until May. Although 27 nations were represented, the "Big Four" dominated it: Wilson; Clemenceau of France, tired and stubborn, determined to end the German threat forever; David Lloyd George, the crafty British prime minister who had pledged to squeeze Germany "until the pips squeak"; and the Italian prime minister, Vittorio Orlando. A clever negotiator, Wilson traded various "small" concessions for his major goals—national self-determination, a reduction in tensions, and a League of Nations to enforce the peace.

Wilson still had to surrender some important principles. Violating the principle of self-determination, the treaty created two new nations—Poland and Czechoslovakia—with large German-speaking populations. It divided up the German colonies in Asia and Africa. Instead of a peace without victory, it made Germany accept responsibility for the war and demanded enormous reparations—which eventually totaled $33 billion. It made no mention of disarmament, free trade, or freedom of the seas. Instead of an open covenant openly arrived at, the treaty was drafted behind closed doors. (See Map 24.7.)

Read the
Document
President Wilson's Fourteen Points on
myhistorylab.com

Map 24.7 *Europe after the Treaty of Versailles, 1919* The treaty changed the map of Europe, creating new and reconstituted nations. (Note the boundary changes from the map on p. 618.)

(Note the boundary changes from the map on p. 618.)

Quick Check

✓ What were the main considerations in the negotiatons over the peace treaty to end the war?

But Wilson deflected some of the most extreme Allied demands, and he won his coveted League of Nations, "to achieve international peace and security." The League included a general assembly; a nine-member council composed of the United States, Britain, France, Italy, Japan, and four nations elected by the assembly; and a court of international justice. League members pledged to submit to arbitration every dispute threatening peace and to impose military and economic sanctions against nations resorting to war. Article X, for Wilson the heart of the League, obliged members to protect one another's independence and territorial integrity.

Wilson returned home in February 1919 to discuss the draft treaty with Congress and the people. Most Americans, the polls showed, favored the League; 33 governors endorsed it. But over dinner with the Senate and House Foreign Relations Committees, Wilson learned of the strength of congressional opposition. On March 3, Senator Lodge produced a "round robin" signed by 37 senators declaring they would not vote for the treaty without amendment. Should the numbers hold, Lodge had enough votes to defeat it.

Returning to Paris, Wilson attacked his critics, while he worked for changes to improve the chances of Senate approval. In return for major concessions, the Allies agreed that domestic affairs remained outside League jurisdiction (exempting the Monroe Doctrine) and allowed nations to withdraw after two years' notice. On June 28, 1919, they signed the treaty in the Hall of Mirrors at Versailles, and Wilson went home for his most difficult fight.

Rejection in the Senate

There were 96 senators in 1919, 49 of them Republicans. William E. Borah of Idaho led 14 Republican "irreconcilables" who opposed the League on any grounds. Twelve "mild reservationists" led by Frank B. Kellogg of Minnesota accepted the treaty but wanted amendments that would not greatly weaken the treaty. Finally, 23 Lodge-led "strong reservationists" wanted major changes that the Allies would have to approve.

Only four Democratic senators opposed the treaty. Democrats and Republicans willing to compromise had enough votes to ratify it, once a few reservations were inserted. Bidding for time to allow public opposition to grow, Lodge scheduled lengthy hearings and spent two weeks reading the 268-page treaty aloud.

Democrats urged Wilson to appeal to the Republican "mild reservationists," but he refused: "Anyone who opposes me in that I'll crush!"

In September, Wilson took his case directly to the people. In the Midwest, his speeches aroused little emotion, but on the Pacific Coast he won ovations, which heartened him. In Pueblo, Colorado, he delivered one of the most eloquent speeches of his career. People wept as he talked of Americans who had died in battle and the hope that they would never fight again in foreign lands. But that night Wilson felt ill. On October 2, Mrs. Wilson found him unconscious on the White House floor. A stroke had paralyzed his left side.

The Treaty of Versailles Sir William Orpen, The Signing of Peace in the Hall of Mirrors, Versailles, 28th of May 1919. Although the United States played a major role in drafting the treaty, the Senate never ratified the document. Instead, the United States made a separate peace with Germany in 1921.

After the stroke, Wilson could not work more than an hour or two at a time. Only family members, his secretary, and his physician could see him. For more than seven months, he did not meet with the cabinet. Focusing his remaining energy on the fight over the treaty, Wilson lost touch with other issues, and critics charged that his wife, Edith Bolling Wilson, ran the government.

On November 6, 1919, while Wilson convalesced, Lodge finally reported the treaty out of committee, along with "Fourteen Reservations," one for each of Wilson's points. The most important reservation stipulated that implementation of Article X, Wilson's key article, required congressional approval before any American intervention abroad.

On November 19, the treaty—with the Lodge reservations—failed, 39 to 55. Following Wilson's instructions, the Democrats voted against it. A motion to approve without the reservations lost 38 to 53, with only one Republican voting in favor. The defeat brought pleas for compromise, but neither Wilson nor Lodge would back down. When the treaty with reservations again came up for a vote on March 19, 1920, Wilson ordered the Democrats to oppose it. Although 21 of them defied him, enough obeyed his orders to defeat it, 49 to 35, seven votes short of the necessary two-thirds majority.

To Wilson, walking now with a cane, one chance remained: the presidential election of 1920. He thought of running for a third term, but his party shunted him aside. The Democrats nominated Governor James M. Cox of Ohio, with the young and popular Franklin D. Roosevelt, assistant secretary of the navy, for vice president. Wilson called for "a great and solemn referendum" on the treaty. The Democratic platform endorsed the treaty but agreed to accept reservations that clarified the American role in the League.

Senator Warren G. Harding of Ohio, who had nominated Taft in 1912, won the Republican nomination. Harding waffled on the treaty, but that made little

TABLE 24.2   The Election of 1920

Candidate	Party	Popular Vote	Electoral Vote
Harding	Republican	16,152,200	404
Cox	Democrat	9,147,353	127
Debs	Socialist	917,799	0

Quick Check

✓ Why was the treaty defeated in the Senate?

difference. Voters wanted a change. Harding took 61 percent of the vote and beat Cox by seven million votes. (See Table 24.2.) Without a peace treaty, the United States remained technically at war. In July 1921, almost three years after the last shot was fired, Congress finally passed a joint resolution ending the war.

CONCLUSION: POSTWAR DISILLUSIONMENT

After 1919, disillusionment set in. World War I was feared before it started, popular while it lasted, and hated when it ended. To a whole generation that followed, it appeared futile, killing without cause, sacrificing without benefit. Books, plays, and movies depicted it as waste, horror, and death.

The war and its aftermath damaged the humanitarian, progressive spirit of the early years of the century. It killed "something precious and perhaps irretrievable in the hearts of thinking men and women." Progressivism survived into the 1920s and the New Deal, but the old conviction and popular support were gone. Fights over the war and the League drained people's energy and enthusiasm.

Confined to bed, Woodrow Wilson died in Washington in 1924, three years after Harding, the new president, promised "not heroics but healing; not nostrums but normalcy; not revolution but restoration." Nonetheless, the "war to end all wars" and the spirit of Woodrow Wilson left an indelible imprint on the country.

24 STUDY RESOURCES

((•—Listen to the **Chapter Audio** for Chapter 24 on **myhistorylab.com**

TIMELINE

1901 Hay–Pauncefote Treaty with Britain empowers United States to build isthmian canal, p. 608

1904 Theodore Roosevelt's corollary to Monroe Doctrine, p. 609

1904–1905 Russo-Japanese War, p. 609

1905 Taft–Katsura Agreement recognizes Japanese power in Korea, p. 610

1908 Root–Takahira Agreement to maintain status quo in the Pacific, p. 610
• Roosevelt sends the fleet around the world, p. 610

CHAPTER REVIEW

A NEW WORLD POWER

What were the main events that showed the United States was becoming a world power?

After winning the Spanish-American War, American presidents began to exert more influence in the world. Roosevelt took extraordinary steps to build the Panama Canal. He enlarged the country's role in the Western Hemisphere and tried to deal with the growing power of Japan. Taft focused on protecting American economic interests abroad. *(p. 607)*

FOREIGN POLICY UNDER WILSON

What did Woodrow Wilson mean by "moral diplomacy"?

Wilson hoped to focus on domestic affairs but was soon involved in crises abroad. He first tried what he called "moral diplomacy," asking the United States and other countries to treat each other in a moral manner, especially in Europe and Mexico. In Mexico, he had praiseworthy aims but misjudged the country. *(p. 610)*

TOWARD WAR

What were the reasons behind and dangers of Wilson's neutrality policy?

With the outbreak of war in Europe in 1914, Wilson proclaimed neutrality, which was difficult to maintain. Neutrality, he hoped, would favor neither side and keep the United States out of war. Progressives knew that war would distract attention from reform. Submarine warfare offered new threats, which Wilson tried to control but could not. On April 6, 1917, the United States joined the war. *(p. 612)*

OVER THERE

How did the United States' entry affect World War I?

The United States entered the war at a crucial time for the Allies. American troops helped stop the last German offensive in 1918. Entry into the war gave the United States a stake in the peace treaty. *(p. 617)*

OVER HERE

What programs and changes did World War I bring at home?

American participation in World War I drew on many of the techniques of progressive reformers, including using people with expertise and exploiting bureaucracy. The War Industries Board oversaw the production of all American factories; the Food Administration Board looked after food for the armies overseas. The government played a larger role in American life than ever before. *(p. 620)*

THE TREATY OF VERSAILLES

What mistakes did Wilson make in negotiating the Treaty of Versailles?

Wilson's Fourteen Points sought to reduce armaments, lower trade barriers, provide for self-determination, and establish a League of Nations to prevent further wars. He was forced to compromise at Versailles, but the Senate refused to ratify the peace treaty when he would not compromise on issues such as the League of Nations. *(p. 626)*

KEY TERM QUESTIONS

1. How did the Hay–Bunau–Varilla Treaty lead to the building of the Panama Canal? (p. 608)

2. What was the Roosevelt Corollary? (p. 609)

3. What did Taft's "dollar diplomacy" attempt to achieve? (p. 610)

4. How did Wilson's involvement in Mexico reflect his "moral diplomacy"? (p. 611)

5. Why did Congress pass the Selective Service Act? (p. 619)

6. How did the Committee on Public Information (CPI) work to ensure public support for the war effort? (p. 621)

7. How did the Espionage Act of 1917 seek to repress opposition to the war? (p. 621)

8. Was the Sedition Act necessary? (p. 621)

9. What was the purpose of the War Industries Board (WIB)? (p. 622)

10. While heading the Food Administration, how did Herbert Hoover convince people to save food? (p. 623)

11. What did Wilson's Fourteen Points call for and why did they fail? (p. 626)

MYHISTORYLAB CONNECTIONS

Visit **www.myhistorylab.com** for a customized Study Plan to build your knowledge of *The Nation at War*

Questions for Analysis

1. How did World War I start?

   ◉ **Watch** the **Video** *The Outbreak of World War I* p. 613

2. How did the United States become involved in World War I?

   ◉ **Watch** the **Video** *American Entry into World War I* p. 618

3. In what way was World War I a "total" war?

   View the **Closer Look** *Mobilizing the Home Front* p. 619

Other Resources from this Chapter

View the **Image** *Roosevelt Throwing Dirt into the Panama Canal*

Read the **Document** *Dollar Diplomacy*

Read the **Document** *Adolf KGE von Spiegel, U-boat 202*

Read the **Document** *Zimmerman Telegram*

Listen to the **Audio File** *Over There*

View the **Image** *Trench Warfare*

4. How were German Americans treated during World War I?

📖● Read the Document *Newton D. Baker, Treatment of German Americans (1918)* p. 622

5. What did Woodrow Wilson's Fourteen Points aim to accomplish?

📖● Read the Document *Woodrow Wilson, The Fourteen Points (1918)* p. 627

((•● Listen to the Audio File *"The Speech that Sent Debs to Jail"*

📖● Read the Document *Abrams vs. U.S.*

👁 Watch the Video *The Great Migration*

Contents and Spotlight Questions

((•—Listen to the **Chapter Audio** for Chapter 25 on **myhistorylab.com**

WHEELS FOR THE MILLIONS

The moving assembly line that Henry Ford opened at Highland Park, Michigan, in 1913 to manufacture the Model T cars marked only the first step toward full mass production and the beginning of America's worldwide industrial supremacy. A year later, Ford began buying large plots of land along the Rouge River southeast of Detroit. He envisioned a vast industrial tract where machines, moving through a sequence of carefully arranged operations, would transform raw materials into finished cars, trucks, and tractors. The key would be control over the flow of goods at each step along the way—from lake steamers and railroad cars bringing in the coal and iron ore, to overhead conveyor belts and huge turning tables carrying the moving parts past the stationary workers on the assembly line. "Everything must move," Ford commanded, and by the mid-1920s at River Rouge, as the plant became known, it did.

On the assembly line at Ford's River Rouge plant, workers performed repetitive tasks on the car chassis that moved by at a rate of 6 feet per minute. (*Source: From the Collections of Henry Ford Museum and Greenfield Village, Neg. # P.833.51079.*)

Ford began fulfilling his industrial dream in 1919 when he built a blast furnace and foundry to make engine blocks for both the Model T and his tractors. By 1924, more than 40,000 workers were turning out nearly all the metal parts used to make Ford vehicles. One tractor factory took just over 28 hours to convert raw ore into a new farm implement.

Visitors from all over the world marveled at River Rouge. Some were disturbed by the jumble of machines (by 1926, there were 43,000 in operation) and the apparent congestion on the plant floor, but industrial experts recognized that the arrangement led to incredible productivity because "the work moves and the men stand still." A trained engineer summed it up best when he wrote that a visitor to the plant "sees each unit as a carefully designed gear which meshes with other gears and operates in synchronism with them, the whole forming one huge, perfectly-timed, smoothly-operating industrial machine of almost unbelievable efficiency."

In May 1927, after producing more than 15 million Model Ts, Ford closed the assembly line at Highland Park. For the next six months, his engineers worked on a more compact and efficient assembly line at River Rouge for the Model A, which went into production in November. By then, River Rouge had more than justified Ford's vision. "Ford had brought together everything at a single site and on a scale no one else had ever attempted," concluded historian Geoffrey Perrett. "The Rouge plant became to a generation of engineers far more than a factory. It was a monument."

Mass production, born in Highland Park in 1913 and perfected at River Rouge in the 1920s, became the hallmark of American industry. Other carmakers copied Ford's methods, and soon his emphasis on the flow of parts moving past stationary workers became the standard in nearly every American factory. The moving assembly line—with its emphasis on uniformity, speed, precision, and coordination—took away the last vestiges of craftsmanship and turned workers into near robots. It led to amazing efficiency that produced both high profits for manufacturers and low prices for buyers. By the mid-1920s, the price of the Model T had dropped from $950 to $290.

Most important, mass production contributed to a consumer goods revolution. American factories turned out a flood of automobiles, electrical appliances, and other items that made life easier and more pleasant for most Americans. The result was the creation of a distinctively modern America, one marked by the material abundance that has characterized American society ever since.

But the abundance came at a price. The 1920s have been portrayed as a decade of escape and frivolity, and for many Americans they were just that. But those years also were an era of transition: a time when the old America of traditional rural values gave way to a new America of sometimes unsettling urban values. The transition was often wrenching, and many Americans clung desperately to the old ways. Modernity won, but not without a struggle.

THE SECOND INDUSTRIAL REVOLUTION

The first Industrial Revolution in the late nineteenth century had catapulted the United States to the forefront among the world's richest and most developed nations. With the advent of the new consumer goods industries, the American people by the 1920s enjoyed the highest standard of living on earth. After a brief postwar depression, a great boom began in 1922, peaked in 1927, and lasted until 1929. In this brief period, American industrial output nearly doubled, and the gross national product rose by 40 percent. Most of this explosive growth took place in industries producing consumer goods—automobiles, appliances, furniture, and clothing. Equally important, the national per capita income increased by 30 percent to $681 in 1929. American workers became the highest paid in history. Combined with the expansion of installment credit that allowed customers to buy now and pay later, this income growth sparked a purchasing spree like nothing the nation had ever experienced.

The key to the new affluence lay in technology. The moving assembly line Ford pioneered became a standard feature in American plants. Electric motors replaced steam engines as the basic source of energy in factories; by 1929, electricity supplied 70 percent of industrial power. Efficiency experts used time and motion studies to break down the industrial process into minute parts, and then showed managers and workers how to maximize the output of their labor. Production per worker-hour increased an amazing 75 percent: In 1929, a workforce no larger than that of 1919 was producing almost twice as many goods.

What was new about the American economy in the 1920s?

The Automobile Industry

The automobile industry, which became the nation's largest in the 1920s, exemplifies the nature of the consumer goods revolution. Rapid growth was its hallmark. In 1920, the nation had 10 million cars; by 1929, 26 million were on the road. Production jumped from fewer than 2 million units a year to more than 5 million.

The automobile boom, at its peak from 1922 to 1927, depended on Americans' apparently insatiable appetite for cars. But the market became saturated as more and more of those who could afford the new luxury became car owners. Marketing became as crucial as production. Automobile makers began to rely heavily on advertising and annual model changes, seeking to make customers dissatisfied with their old vehicles and eager to order new ones. Despite these efforts, sales slumped in 1927 when Ford stopped making the Model T, picked up the next year with the new Model A, but began to slide again in 1929. The new industry revealed a basic weakness in the consumer goods economy; once people had bought an item with a long life—what economists call a durable good—they would not buy another one for a few years. The consumer revolution also bypassed much of rural America, where farmers struggled against falling prices.

Amid the urban affluence, few noticed the underlying problems. Instead, contemporary observers focused on how the automobile stimulated the rest of the economy. The mass production of cars required huge quantities of steel; new rolling mills had to be built to supply sheet steel for car bodies. Rubber factories boomed with the demand for tires, and paint and glass suppliers had more business than ever before. The auto changed the pattern of city life, leading to a suburban explosion. Real estate developers, no longer dependent on streetcars and railway lines, could now build houses in ever wider concentric circles around the central cities.

The automobile affected all aspects of American life in the 1920s. Filling stations replaced smithies and stables on the main streets. In Kansas City, Missouri, Jess D. Nichols built the first shopping center, Country Club Plaza, and set an example other suburban developers quickly followed.

Even in smaller communities, the car ruled. In Muncie, Indiana, site of a famous sociological survey in the 1920s, one elder replied when asked what was taking place, "I can tell you what's happening in just four letters: A-U-T-O!" A nation that had always revered symbols of movement, from the *Mayflower* to the covered wagon, now had a new icon to worship.

Read the **Document** *The Automobile Comes to Middletown* on **myhistorylab.com**

Quick Check
✓ How did the auto industry drive the rest of the economy?

Patterns of Economic Growth

Automobiles were the most conspicuous of the consumer products that flourished in the 1920s, but certainly not the only ones. The electrical industry grew almost as quickly. Central power stations, where massive steam generators converted coal into electricity, brought current into the homes of city and town dwellers. Two-thirds of all American families enjoyed electricity by 1929, and they spent vast sums on washing machines, vacuum cleaners, refrigerators, and ranges. The new appliances made housework easier and ushered in an age of leisure.

Radio broadcasting and motion picture production also boomed. The early success of KDKA in Pittsburgh stimulated the growth of more than 800 independent radio stations, and by 1929, NBC had formed the first successful radio network. Five nights a week, *Amos 'n' Andy*, a comic serial featuring two "blackface" white vaudevillians, held the attention of millions of Americans. The film industry thrived in Hollywood, reaching its maturity in the mid-1920s when every large city had huge theaters seating as many as 4,000 people. With the advent of the "talkies" by 1929, average weekly movie attendance climbed to nearly 100 million.

Other industries also prospered. Production of light metals such as aluminum and magnesium became a major business. Chemical engineering came of age with the invention of synthetics, ranging from rayon for clothing to cellophane for packaging. Americans found a new spectrum of products to buy—cigarette lighters, wristwatches, heat-resistant glass cooking dishes, and rayon stockings, to name a few.

The most distinctive feature of the new consumer-oriented economy was the emphasis on marketing. Advertising earnings rose from $1.3 billion in 1915 to $3.4 billion in 1926. Skillful practitioners such as Edward Bernays and Bruce Barton sought to control public taste and consumer spending by identifying the good life with the possession of the latest product of American industry, whether it was a car, a refrigerator, or a brand of cigarettes. Chain stores advanced rapidly at the expense of small retail shops. A&P dominated the retail food industry, growing from 400 stores in 1912 to 15,500 by 1932. Woolworth's "five-and-tens" spread almost as rapidly, while such drugstore chains as Rexall and Liggetts—both owned by one huge holding company—opened outlets in nearly every town and city.

Uniformity and standardization, the characteristics of mass production, now prevailed. The farmer in Kansas bought the same kind of car, the same groceries, and the same pills as the factory worker in Pennsylvania. Sectional differences in dress, food, and furniture began to disappear. Even regional accents were threatened with extinction by the advent of radio and films, which promoted a standard national dialect devoid of local flavor.

Despite all these changes, the New Era, as business leaders labeled the decade, was less prosperous than it appeared. The revolution in consumer goods disguised the decline of many traditional industries in the 1920s. Hardest hit of all was agriculture. By 1921, farm exports had fallen by more than $2 billion. In addition, during the decade, factory wages rose only a modest 11 percent; in 1929, nearly half of American families earned less than $1,500 a year. Organized labor proved unable to advance the interests of workers, and union membership fell. In fact, middle- and upper-class Americans were the only groups who thrived in the 1920s. The rewards of this second Industrial Revolution went to the managers—the engineers, bankers, and executives—who directed it. All these factors contributed to economic instability. The boom of the 1920s would end in a great crash.

View the **Closer Look**
The Great White Way—
Times Square on
myhistorylab.com

Quick Check
✓ What other industries contributed to the boom of the 1920s?

CITY LIFE IN THE ROARING TWENTIES

The city replaced the countryside as the focal point of American life in the 1920s. The 1920 census revealed that for the first time, slightly more than half of the population lived in cities (defined broadly to include all places of more than 2,500 people). During the decade, the metropolitan areas grew rapidly as both rural whites and blacks migrated to find jobs in the new consumer industries. Between 1920 and 1930, cities with populations of 250,000 or more added some 8 million people to their ranks. New York City grew by nearly 25 percent, while Detroit's population more than doubled.

How did life in the cities change after World War I?

In the cities, life was different. The old community ties of home, church, and school were absent, but important gains replaced them—new ideas, new creativity, new perspectives. Some city dwellers became lost and lonely without the old institutions; others thrived.

Women and the Family

The urban culture of the 1920s witnessed important changes in the American family. This vital institution began to break down under the impact of economic and social change. A new freedom for women and children seemed to be emerging in its wake.

Although World War I accelerated the process by which women left the home for work, the postwar decade witnessed a return to the slower pace of the prewar years. During the 1920s the percentage of working women barely changed. Two million more women were employed in 1930 than in 1920, but this represented an increase of only 1 percent. Most women workers, moreover, had low-paying jobs, ranging from stenographers to maids. The number of women doctors actually decreased, and even though women earned nearly one-third of all graduate degrees, only 4 percent of full professors were female. For the most part, men monopolized the professions, with women relegated to such fields as teaching and nursing.

Women had won the right to vote in 1920, but the Nineteenth Amendment had less impact than its proponents had hoped. Adoption of the amendment robbed women of a unifying cause, and the exercise of the franchise itself did little to change sex roles. Men remained the principal breadwinners in the family; women cooked, cleaned, and reared the children. "The creation and fulfillment of a successful home," a *Ladies Home Journal* writer advised women, "is a bit of craftsmanship that compares favorably with building a beautiful cathedral."

The feminist movement, however, still showed signs of vitality. Social feminists pushing for humanitarian reform won enactment of the Sheppard–Towner Act of 1921, which provided for federal aid to establish state programs for maternal and infant health care. Although the failure to enact the child labor amendment in 1925 marked the beginning of a decline in humanitarian reform, for the rest of the decade, women's groups worked for good-government measures, the inclusion of women on juries, and consumer legislation.

Other women looked beyond politics to express themselves. In the larger cities, some quickly adopted what critic H. L. Mencken called the flapper image, portrayed most strikingly by artist John Held, Jr. Cutting their hair short, raising their skirts above the knee, and binding their breasts, "flappers" set out to compete on equal terms with men on the golf course and in the speakeasy. Young women delighted in shocking their elders—they rouged their cheeks and danced the Charleston. Women smoked cigarettes and drank alcohol in public more freely than before. The flappers assaulted the traditional double standard, demanding that equality with men should include sexual fulfillment before and during marriage. New and more liberal laws doubled the divorce rate; by 1928, there were 166 divorces for every 1,000 marriages, compared to only 81 in 1900.

The family also changed in other ways. The average family became smaller as easier access to effective birth control methods enabled couples to limit the number of their offspring. More married women took jobs outside the home, bringing in income and gaining a measure of independence (although their pay was always lower than men's). Young people, who had once joined the labor force in their teens, now discovered adolescence as a stage of life. A high school education was no longer uncommon, and college attendance increased.

Prolonged adolescence led to new strains on the family in the form of youthful revolt. Freed of the burden of earning a living at an early age, youths went on a spree. Heavy drinking, casual sex, and a constant search

View the **Image**
McClure's Magazine Featuring a Flapper on **myhistorylab.com**

Read the **Document**
Wembridge Petting and the Campus on **myhistorylab.com**

After passage of the Nineteenth Amendment, activist Alice Paul and the National Woman's Party continued to fight for women's equality. Here, 50 NWP members visit the White House to request President Harding's support for equal rights legislation.

for excitement became the hallmarks of the upper-class youth F. Scott Fitzgerald immortalized. "I have been kissed by dozens of men," one of his characters commented. "I suppose I'll kiss dozens more." The theme of rebellion against parental authority, which ran through all aspects of the 1920s, was at the heart of the youth movement.

Quick Check

✓ How did women's lives change during the 1920s?

Popular Culture in the Jazz Age

Excitement ran high in the cities as both crime waves and highly publicized sports events flourished. Prohibition ushered in such distinctive features of the decade as speakeasies, bootleggers, and bathtub gin. Crime rose sharply as middle- and upper-class Americans broke the law to gain access to alcoholic beverages. City streets became the scene of violent shootouts between rival bootleggers; by 1929, Chicago had witnessed more than 500 gangland murders. Underworld czars controlled illicit empires; Al Capone's empire produced revenue of $60 million a year.

Sports became a national mania as people found more leisure time. Golf boomed, with some 2 million men and women playing on nearly 5,000 courses. Spectator sports attracted even more attention. Boxing drew huge crowds to see fighters such as Jack Dempsey and Gene Tunney. Baseball attendance soared. More than 20 million fans attended games in 1927, the year Babe Ruth became a national idol by hitting 60 home runs. On college campuses, football became more popular than ever. Universities vied to build massive stadiums, seating upward of 70,000 people.

New dances were introduced on the dance floors of ballrooms and clubs in the 1920s jazz era. One of the most popular new dances was the Charleston—a dance associated with the rebellious image of the "flapper." Here, two daring flappers dance the Charleston on the roof of Chicago's Hotel Sherman in 1926.

The arts also flourished. Authors Ernest Hemingway, F. Scott Fitzgerald, John Dos Passos, and Sinclair Lewis chronicled the experience of the post–World War I generation. In New York City, the Harlem Renaissance—an outpouring of African American literature, theater, visual arts, and music, especially jazz—made Manhattan seem the most exciting place on earth.

👁 **Watch** the **Video**
The Harlem Renaissance on **myhistorylab.com**

In what Frederick Lewis Allen called "the ballyhoo years," the popular yearning for release led people to seek vicarious thrills in all kinds of ways—applauding Charles Lindbergh's solo flight across the Atlantic, cheering Gertrude Ederle's swim across the English Channel, and flocking to such bizarre events as six-day bicycle races, dance marathons, and flagpole sittings. It was a time of pure pleasure-seeking, when people sought to escape from the increasingly drab world of the assembly line by worshiping heroes.

Sex became a popular topic as Victorian standards crumbled. Sophisticated city dwellers seemed to be intent on exploring a new freedom in sexual expression. Plays and novels focused on adultery, and the new urban tabloids—led by the *New York Daily News*—delighted in telling their readers about love nests and kept women. The popular songs of the decade, such as "Hot Lips" and "Burning Kisses," were less romantic and more explicit than those of years before. Hollywood exploited the obsession with sex by producing movies with such provocative titles as *Up in Mabel's Room*, *A Shocking Night*, and *Women and Lovers*. Theda Bara and Clara Bow, the "vamp" and the "It" girl, set the model for feminine seductiveness, while the actor Rudolph Valentino became the heartthrob of millions of American women. Young people embraced the new permissiveness, with the automobile giving couples an easy way to escape parental supervision.

Quick Check

✓ What did people do with their spare time during the decade?

THE CONSERVATIVE COUNTERATTACK

How did conservatives resist the changes of the decade?

The shift of population from the countryside to the city heightened social tensions. Intent on preserving traditional values, rural Americans saw in the city all that was evil in contemporary life. Saloons, whorehouses, little Italys and little Polands, communist cells, free love, and atheism—all were identified with the city. Accordingly, the countryside struck back, aiming to restore the primacy of the Anglo-Saxon and predominantly Protestant culture it revered. This counterattack won considerable support in the cities from those who were recently uprooted from their rural backgrounds.

Other factors intensified the counterattack. The war had unleashed a nationalistic spirit that craved unity and conformity. In a nation where one-third of the people were foreign born, the attack on immigrants and the call for 100 percent Americanism took on a frightening zeal. When the war was over, groups such as the American Legion tried to root out "un-American" behavior and insisted on cultural and political conformity. The prewar progressive reform spirit added to the social tension. Stripped of much of its idealism, progressivism focused on such social problems as drinking and illiteracy to justify repressive measures such as prohibition and immigration restriction. The result was tragic. Amid the emergence of a new urban culture, the movements that aimed to preserve the values of an earlier America only complicated an already difficult period of cultural transition.

The Fear of Radicalism

The first and most intense outbreak of national alarm, an anti-radical hysteria known as the Red Scare, came in 1919. The heightened nationalism of World War I, which aimed to achieve unity at the expense of ethnic diversity, found a new target in communism. The Russian Revolution of 1917 and the triumph of Marxism frightened many Americans. A growing turn to communism among American radicals (especially the foreign born) heightened these fears. Although their numbers were tiny—at most there were 60,000 communists in the United States in 1919—some communists were highly visible in the cities. Labor unrest seemed to magnify their influence.

A general strike in Seattle, a police strike in Boston, and a violent strike in the iron and steel industry alarmed Americans in the spring and summer of 1919. A series of bombings led to panic. First the mayor of strikebound Seattle received a small brown package containing a homemade bomb; then an alert New York postal employee detected 16 bombs addressed to famous citizens (including John D. Rockefeller); and finally, on June 2, a bomb shattered the front of Attorney General A. Mitchell Palmer's home. Although the man who delivered it was blown to pieces, authorities quickly identified him as an Italian anarchist from Philadelphia.

The explosion in Wall Street on September 16, 1920, left 33 dead and nearly 200 wounded. Attorney General Palmer saw the blast as the work of a communist conspiracy, but relatively few Americans subscribed to his view.

In the ensuing outcry, Palmer led the attack on the alien threat. A Quaker and a progressive, Palmer abandoned his earlier liberalism to launch a massive roundup of foreign-born radicals. In raids that began on November 7, federal agents seized suspected anarchists and communists and held them for deportation with no regard for due process of law. In December, 249 aliens—including such well-known radical leaders as Emma Goldman and Alexander Berkman—were sent to Russia aboard the *Buford*, dubbed the "Soviet Ark" by the press. Nearly all were innocent of the charges against them. A month later, Palmer rounded up nearly 4,000 suspected communists in one evening. Federal agents broke into homes, meeting halls, and union offices without search warrants. Many native-born Americans were caught in the dragnet and spent days in jail before being released; aliens were deported without hearings or trials.

For a time, the Red Scare seemed to reflect the views of the American people. Instead of condemning their government's action, citizens voiced their approval and urged more drastic steps. One patriot said his solution to the alien problem was simple: "S.O.S.—ship or shoot." General Leonard Wood, the former army chief of staff, favored placing Bolsheviks on "ships of stone with sails of lead," while evangelist Billy Sunday preferred to take "these ornery, wild-eyed Socialists" and "stand them up before a firing squad and save space on our ships." Inflamed by such public statements, legionnaires in Centralia, Washington, dragged a radical from the town jail, castrated him, and hanged him from a railway bridge. The coroner's report blandly stated that the victim "jumped off with a rope around his neck and then shot himself full of holes."

The very extremism of the Red Scare led to its rapid demise. In early 1920, courageous officials from the Department of Labor insisted on due process and full hearings before anyone else was deported. Prominent leaders spoke out against the

Read the **Document**
A. Mitchell Palmer on the Menace of Communism (1920) on **myhistorylab.com**

acts of terror. Charles Evans Hughes, the defeated GOP candidate for president in 1916, offered to defend six socialists expelled from the New York legislature; Ohio Senator Warren G. Harding, the embodiment of middle-class values, declared that "too much has been said about bolshevism in America." Finally, Palmer himself, with evident presidential ambition, went too far. In April 1920, he warned of a revolution to occur on May 1; the entire New York City police force, 11,000 strong, was placed on duty to prepare for imminent disaster. When no bombings or violence took place on May Day, the public began to react against Palmer's hysteria. Despite an explosion on Wall Street in September that killed 33 people, the Red Scare died out by the end of 1920. Palmer passed into obscurity, factionalism splintered the tiny Communist party, and the American people tried to forget their loss of balance.

Yet the Red Scare exerted a continuing influence on American society in the 1920s. The foreign born knew that they were viewed with hostility and suspicion. Two Italian aliens in Massachusetts, Nicola Sacco and Bartolomeo Vanzetti, were arrested in May 1920 for a payroll robbery and murder. The prosecutor and jury condemned them more for their radical ideas than for any evidence of criminal conduct, and the judge referred to them as "those anarchist bastards." Despite a worldwide effort that became the chief liberal cause of the 1920s, the courts rejected all appeals. Sacco, a shoemaker, and Vanzetti, a fish peddler, were electrocuted on August 23, 1927. Their fate symbolized the bigotry and intolerance that made the 1920s one of the least attractive decades in American history.

Quick Check

✓ What was the "Red Scare"?

Prohibition

In December 1917, Congress passed the Eighteenth Amendment, prohibiting the manufacture and sale of alcoholic beverages, and then sent the amendment to the states for ratification. In January 1919, Nebraska became the necessary thirty-sixth state to ratify it, and prohibition became the law of the land.

Effective January 16, 1920, the Volstead Act, which implemented prohibition, banned most commercial production and distribution of beverages containing more than one-half of 1 percent of alcohol by volume. (Exceptions were made for medicinal and religious uses of wine and spirits. Production for one's private use was also allowed.) Prohibition was the result of both a rural effort of the Anti-Saloon League, backed by Methodist and Baptist clergymen, and the urban progressive concern over the social disease of drunkenness, especially among industrial workers. The moral issue had already led to the enactment of prohibition laws in 26 states by 1920; the effort to extend this "noble experiment" to the cities, where ethnic groups such as the Germans and Irish resented it and the well-to-do and sophisticated almost totally ignored it, was a tragedy.

((•─ **Listen** to the
Audio File
*Prohibition Is a
Failure* on
myhistorylab.com

Drinking did decline under prohibition. Americans consumed much less alcohol in the 1920s than in the prewar years. Rural areas became almost totally dry, and in the cities, the consumption of alcoholic beverages dropped sharply among the lower classes, who could not afford the high prices for bootleg liquor. Among the middle class and the wealthy, however, drinking became fashionable. Bootleggers supplied whiskey, which quickly replaced lighter drinks such as wine and beer. The alcohol was either smuggled from abroad (a $40 million a year business by 1924) or illicitly manufactured in America. Exotic products such as Jackass Brandy, Soda Pop Moon, and Yack Yack Bourbon were common—and could be fatal. Despite the risk of illness or death from extraordinarily high alcohol content or poor distillation, Americans consumed some 150 million quarts of liquor a year in the 1920s. Bootleggers took in nearly $2 billion annually, about 2 percent of the gross national product.

Urban resistance to prohibition finally led to its repeal in 1933. But in the intervening years, it bred a profound disrespect for the law. The flamboyant excesses of bootleggers were only the more obvious evils prohibition spawned. In city after city, police openly tolerated the traffic in liquor, and judges and prosecutors let bootleggers pay merely token fines, creating almost a system of licenses. Prohibition satisfied the countryside's desire for vindication, yet rural and urban America alike suffered from this overzealous attempt to legislate morals.

Quick Check

✓ How effective was prohibition?

The Ku Klux Klan

The most ominous expression of protest against the new urban culture was the rebirth of the Ku Klux Klan. On Thanksgiving night in 1915, on Stone Mountain in Georgia, Colonel William J. Simmons and 34 followers founded the modern Klan. Only "native born, white, gentile Americans" could join "the Invisible Empire, Knights of the Ku Klux Klan." Membership grew slowly during World War I, but after 1920, fueled by postwar fears and shrewd promotional techniques, the Klan mushroomed. In villages, towns, and small cities across the nation, Anglo-Saxon Protestant men flocked into the Klan's new chapters, seeking to relieve their anxiety over a changing society by embracing the Klan's

A 1925 Ku Klux Klan demonstration in Cincinnati, Ohio, attended by nearly 30,000 robed members and marked by the induction of 8,000 young boys in the Junior Order. The original Klan, formed during the Reconstruction era to terrorize former slaves, disbanded in 1869. The Klan that formed in 1915 declined after the mid-1920s but did not officially disband until 1944.

rituals and demonstrating their hatred of blacks, aliens, Jews, and Catholics.

The Klan of the 1920s, unlike the night riders of the post–Civil War era, was not just anti-black; the threat to American culture, as Klansmen perceived it, also came from aliens—Italians and Russians, Jews and Catholics. They attributed much of the tension and conflict in society to the prewar flood of immigrants, foreigners who spoke different languages, worshiped in strange churches, and lived in distant, threatening cities. The Klansmen struck back by coming together and enforcing their own values. They punished blacks who did not know their place, women who practiced the new morality, and aliens who refused to conform. Beating, flogging, burning with acid—even murder—were condoned. They also tried more peaceful coercion, formulating codes of behavior and seeking communitywide support.

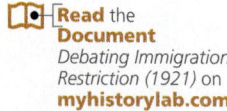View the Image
KKK March on Washington on
myhistorylab.com

The Klan entered politics, at first hesitantly, then with growing confidence. The KKK gained control of the legislatures in Texas, Oklahoma, Oregon, and Indiana; in 1924, it blocked a resolution of censure at the Democratic national convention. With an estimated 5 million members by the mid-1920s, the Klan seemed to be fully established.

Its appeal lay in the sanctuary it offered to insecure and anxious people. Protestant to the core, the members found in the local Klavern a reassurance missing in their churches. The poor and ignorant became enchanted with the titles, ranging from Imperial Wizard to Grand Dragon, and gloried in the ritual that centered around the letter K: Each Klan had its own "Klalendar," held its weekly "Klonklave" in the local "Klavern," and followed the rules set forth in the Kloran. Members found a sense of identity in the group activities, whether they were peaceful picnics, ominous parades in white robes, or fiery cross burnings at night.

Read the
Document
"Creed of Klans-women" (1924) on
myhistorylab.com

Although it was a men's organization, the Klan did not neglect the family. There was a Women's Order, a Junior Order for boys, and a Tri-K Klub for girls. Members had to be born in America, but foreign-born Protestants could join a special Krusaders affiliate. Only blacks, Catholics, Jews, and prostitutes were beyond redemption to these lonely and anxious men who chanted:

United we stick

Divided we're stuck.

The better we stick

The better we Klux!

The Klan fell even more quickly than it rose. Its more violent activities—which included kidnapping, lynching, burning synagogues and Catholic churches, and murdering a priest—began to offend the nation's conscience. Misuse of funds and sexual scandals among Klan leaders, notably in Indiana, repelled many of the rank and file; counterattacks by traditional politicians ousted the KKK from control in Texas and Oklahoma. Membership declined sharply after 1925; by 1929, the Klan had virtually disappeared. But its spirit lived on, testimony to the recurring demons of nativism and hatred that have surfaced periodically throughout the American experience.

Quick Check

✓ What groups did the Ku Klux Klan persecute during the 1920s?

Immigration Restriction

The nativism, or hostility to things foreign, that permeated the Klan found its most successful outlet in the immigration legislation of the 1920s. The sharp increase in immigration in the late nineteenth century had led to a broad-based movement, spearheaded by organized labor and New England aristocrats such as Henry Cabot Lodge, to restrict the flow of people from Europe. In 1917, over President Wilson's veto, Congress enacted a literacy test that reduced the number of immigrants allowed into the country. The war caused a much more drastic decline—from an average of 1 million a year between 1900 and 1914 to only 110,000 in 1918.

Read the
Document
Debating Immigration Restriction (1921) on
myhistorylab.com

After the armistice, however, rumors spread of a flood of people seeking to escape war-ravaged Europe. Kenneth Roberts, a popular historical novelist, warned that all Europe was on the move, with only the limits of steamship space likely to stem the flow. Worried congressmen spoke of a "barbarian horde" and a "foreign tide" that would inundate the United States with "dangerous and deadly enemies of the country." Even though the actual number of immigrants, 810,000 in 1920 (fewer than the prewar yearly average), did not match these projections, Congress in 1921 passed an emergency immigration act, which restricted immigration from Europe to 3 percent of the number of nationals from each country living in the United States in 1910.

The nativists were not satisfied. The quotas still permitted more than 500,000 Europeans to come to the United States in 1923, nearly half of them from southern and eastern Europe. The declining percentage of Nordic immigrants alarmed writers such as Madison Grant, who warned the American people that lesser breeds with inferior genes were about to overwhelm the Anglo-Saxon stock that had founded the nation: "These immigrants adopt the language of the native American, they wear his clothes and are beginning to take his women, but they seldom adopt his religion or understand his ideals."

Psychologists, relying on primitive IQ tests the army had used in World War I, confirmed this judgment. One senator claimed that all the nation's ills were due to an "intermingled and mongrelized people" as he demanded that racial purity replace the older reliance on the melting pot. In 1924, the National Origins Quota Act limited immigration from Europe to 150,000 a year; allocated most of the available slots to Great Britain, Ireland, Germany, and Scandinavia; and banned Asian immigrants. The measure passed Congress with overwhelming rural support.

The new restrictive legislation marked the most enduring achievement of the rural counterattack. Unlike the Red Scare, prohibition, and the Klan, the quota system would survive until the 1960s, enforcing a racist bias that excluded Asians and limited the immigration of Italians, Greeks, and Poles to a few thousand a year while permitting a steady stream of Irish, English, and Scandinavian immigrants. Large corporations, no longer dependent on armies of unskilled immigrant workers, did not object to the 1924 law; the machine had replaced the immigrant on the assembly line. Yet the victory was incomplete. A growing tide of Mexican laborers, exempt from the quota act, flowed across the Rio Grande to fill the continuing need for unskilled workers on farms and in the service trades. Mexican immigrants, as many as 100,000 a year, strengthened an element in the national ethnic mosaic that would grow until it became a major force in American society.

Quick Check

✓ What was the National Origins Quota Act?

The Fundamentalist Challenge

Another significant—and the longest-lasting—challenge to the new urban culture was rooted in the traditional religious beliefs of millions of Americans who felt alienated from city life, science, and much of what modernization entailed. Sometimes this challenge was direct, as when Christian fundamentalists campaigned against teaching evolution in the public schools. Their success in Tennessee touched off a court battle, the Scopes trial, that drew the attention of the entire country to the small town of Dayton in the summer of 1925, when a high school biology teacher was prosecuted for teaching evolution. The trial court convicted John Scopes, affirming the fundamentalist view, but the spectacle drew the derision of many Americans who saw nothing threatening about Darwin's theory.

Other aspects of the fundamentalist challenge were more subtle but no less important in countering the modernizing trend. As middle- and upper-class Americans

View the Image
Clarence Darrow at Scopes Trial on **myhistorylab.com**

drifted into a genteel Christianity that stressed good works and respectability, the Baptist and Methodist churches clung to the old faith. Aggressive fundamentalist sects such as the Churches of Christ, the Pentecostals, and Jehovah's Witnesses grew rapidly. While church membership increased from 41.9 million in 1916 to 54.5 million in 1926, the number of churches actually declined during the decade. More and more rural dwellers drove their cars into town on Sundays instead of attending the local crossroads chapel.

Many of those who came to the city in the 1920s brought their religious beliefs with them and found new outlets for them. Thus, evangelist Aimee Semple McPherson enjoyed amazing success in Los Angeles with her Church of the Four-Square Gospel, building the Angelus Temple to seat more than 5,000 worshipers. And in Fort Worth, the Reverend J. Frank Norris erected a 6,000-seat sanctuary for the First Baptist Church, bathing it in spotlights so it could be seen for 39 miles across the North Texas prairie.

Far from dying out, as divinity professor Thomas G. Oden noted, biblical fundamentalism retained "remarkable grassroots strength among the organization men and the industrialized mass society of the 20th century." The rural counterattack, while challenged by the city, enabled older American values to survive amidst the new mass production culture.

Quick Check

✓ How did the Scopes trial reflect the strength of conservative religious thought?

REPUBLICAN POLITICS

The tensions between city and countryside also shaped politics in the 1920s. On the whole, it was a Republican decade. The GOP ("Grand Old Party") controlled the White House from 1921 to 1933 and had majorities in both houses of Congress from 1919 to 1931. The Republicans used their return to power after World War I to halt further reform legislation and establish a friendly relationship between government and business.

How did the politics of the 1920s reflect changes in the economy and in American society?

Harding, Coolidge, and Hoover

Watch the **Video** *Warren G. Harding* on **myhistorylab.com**

The Republicans regained the White House in 1920 with the election of Warren G. Harding of Ohio. Harding won the nomination when he became the compromise choice after the convention deadlocked. Handsome and dignified, Harding reflected both the virtues and the blemishes of small-town America. Originally a newspaper publisher in Marion, he had made many friends and few enemies throughout his career as a legislator, lieutenant governor, and finally, after 1914, U.S. senator. Conventional in outlook, Harding was a genial man who lacked the capacity to govern and who, as president, broadly delegated power.

He made some good cabinet choices, notably Charles Evans Hughes as secretary of state and Herbert C. Hoover as secretary of commerce, but two corrupt officials—Attorney General Harry Daugherty and Secretary of the Interior Albert Fall—sabotaged his administration. Daugherty became involved in questionable deals that led to his forced resignation; Fall was the chief figure in the Teapot Dome scandal. In return for nearly $400,000 in loans and bribes, he helped two oil promoters secure leases on naval oil reserves in Elk Hills, California, and Teapot Dome, Wyoming. The scandal came to light after Harding's death from a heart attack in 1923. Fall served a year in jail, and the reputation of the Harding administration never recovered.

Vice President Calvin Coolidge assumed the presidency upon Harding's death, and his honesty and integrity reassured the nation. Coolidge, born in Vermont of old Yankee stock, had gained national attention in 1919 as governor of Massachusetts when he had dealt firmly with a Boston police strike by declaring, "There is no right to strike against the public safety by anybody, anywhere, any time." A reserved, reticent man, Coolidge became famous for his epigrams, which contemporaries mistook for wisdom. "The business of America is business," he proclaimed. "The man who builds a factory builds a temple; the man who works there worships there." He believed his duty was to preside benignly over, not govern, the nation. "Four-fifths of all our troubles in this life would disappear," he said, "if we would just sit down and be still." Calvin Coolidge, one observer noted, "aspired to become the least President the country ever had; he attained his desire." Satisfied with the prosperity of the mid-1920s, the people reelected Coolidge to a full term by a wide margin in 1924.

When Coolidge announced in 1927 that he did not "choose to run" again, Herbert Hoover became the Republican choice to succeed him. The ablest GOP leader of the decade, Hoover epitomized the American myth of the self-made man. Orphaned as a boy, he had worked his way through Stanford University and had gained wealth and fame as a mining engineer. During World War I, he had displayed administrative skills in directing Wilson's food program at home and relief activities abroad. Sober, intelligent, and hardworking, Hoover embodied the nation's faith in individualism and free enterprise.

As secretary of commerce under Harding and Coolidge, he had sought cooperation between government and business. He helped American manufacturers and exporters expand their overseas trade and supported a trade association movement to encourage cooperation rather than cutthroat competition among smaller American companies. He saw business and government not as antagonists, but as partners, working together to achieve efficiency and affluence for all Americans. His optimistic view of the future led him to declare in his speech accepting the Republican presidential nomination in 1928 that "we in America today are nearer to the final triumph over poverty than ever before in the history of any land."

> **Quick Check**
> ✓ Who were the Republican presidents of the 1920s?

A New Kind of Conservatism

During the 1920 campaign, Harding urged a return to "not heroism, but healing, not nostrums, but normalcy." Misreading his speechwriter's "normality," he coined a new word that became the theme for the Republican administrations of the 1920s. Aware that the public was tired of zealous, reform-minded presidents such as Teddy Roosevelt and Woodrow Wilson, Harding and his successors sought a return to traditional Republican policies. In some areas they were successful, but in others the Republican leaders had to adjust to the new realities of a mass production society. The result was a mixture of traditional and innovative measures that was neither wholly reactionary nor entirely progressive.

The most obvious attempt to go back to the Republicanism of William McKinley came in tariff and tax policy. Fearful of a flood of postwar European imports, Congress passed an emergency tariff act in 1921 and followed it a year later with the protectionist

Fordney–McCumber Tariff Act. The net effect was to raise the basic rates substantially over the moderate Underwood Tariff schedules of the Wilson period.

Secretary of the Treasury Andrew Mellon, a wealthy Pittsburgh banker and industrialist, worked hard to achieve a similar return to normalcy in taxation. Condemning the high wartime tax rates on businesses and wealthy individuals, Mellon pressed for repealing an excess profits tax on corporations and slashing personal rates on the rich. Using the new budget system Congress adopted in 1921, he reduced government spending from its World War I peak of $18 billion to just over $3 billion by 1925, creating a slight surplus. Congress responded in 1926 by cutting the highest income tax bracket to a modest 20 percent.

The revenue acts of the 1920s greatly reduced the burden of taxation; by 1929, the government was collecting one-third less than it had in 1921, and the number of people paying income taxes dropped from more than 6.5 million to 4 million. Yet the greatest relief went to the wealthy. The public was shocked to learn in the 1930s that J. P. Morgan, Jr., and his 19 partners had paid no income tax at all during the depths of the Great Depression.

The growing crisis in American farming during the decade forced the Republican administrations to seek new solutions. The end of the European war led to a sharp decline in farm prices and a return to overproduction. Southern and western lawmakers formed a farm bloc in Congress to press for special legislation for American agriculture. The farm bloc supported the higher tariffs, which included protection for constituents' crops, and helped pass legislation to create federal supervision over stockyards, packinghouses, and grain trading.

This special-interest legislation failed to get at the root of overproduction, however. Farmers then supported more controversial measures to raise domestic crop prices by having the government sell the surplus overseas at low world prices. Coolidge vetoed the legislation on grounds that it involved unwarranted government interference in the economy.

Yet the government's role in the economy increased in the 1920s. Republicans widened the scope of federal activity and nearly doubled the ranks of government employees. Hoover led the way in the Commerce Department, establishing new bureaus to help make American industry more efficient in housing, transportation, and mining. Under his leadership, the government encouraged corporations to develop welfare programs that undercut trade unions, and he tried to minimize labor disturbances by devising new federal machinery to mediate disputes. Instead of going back to the laissez-faire tradition of the nineteenth century, the Republican administrations of the 1920s were pioneering a close relationship between government and private business.

Quick Check

✓ What was new about the Republican approach to government?

The Election of 1928

To challenge Hoover in 1928, the Democrats selected Al Smith of New York. Born on the Lower East Side of Manhattan of mixed Irish-German ancestry, Smith was the prototype of the urban Democrat. He was Catholic; he was associated with a big-city machine; he was a "wet" who wanted to end prohibition. Starting out working in the Fulton Fish Market as a boy, he had joined Tammany Hall (the Democratic party in New York City) and climbed the political ladder, rising from subpoena server to state legislator to governor, a post he held with distinction for nearly a decade. But as the embodiment of the big-city East, Smith had to struggle to gain the support of the West and South. His lack of education, poor grammar, and distinctive New York accent all hurt him, as did his eastern provincialism. When reporters asked him about his appeal in the states west of the Mississippi, he replied, "What states are west of the Mississippi?"

The choice facing the American voter in 1928 seemed unusually clear-cut. Hoover was a Protestant, a dry, and an old-stock American, who stood for efficiency and individualism; Smith was a Catholic, a wet, a descendant of immigrants, and was associated with big-city politics. Just as Smith appealed to new voters in the cities, so Hoover won the support of many old-line Democrats who feared the city, Tammany Hall, and the pope.

Yet beneath the surface, as Allan J. Lichtman points out, there were "striking similarities between Smith and Hoover." Both were self-made

Election of 1928

	Electoral Vote by State		Popular Vote
REPUBLICAN Herbert C. Hoover	444	🟠	21,391,381
DEMOCRATIC Alfred E. Smith	87	🟣	15,016,443
MINOR PARTIES	—		330,725
	531		36,738,549

Map 25.1

men who embodied the American belief in freedom of opportunity and upward mobility. Neither advocated significant economic change or redistribution of national wealth or power. Though religion proved to be the most important issue for the voters, hurting Smith far more than prohibition or his identification with the city, the Democratic candidate's failure to spotlight the growing cracks in prosperity or offer alternative economic policies ensured his defeat.

The 1928 election was a dubious victory for the Republicans. Hoover won easily, defeating Smith by more than 6 million votes and carrying such Democratic states as Oklahoma, Texas, and Florida. (See Map 25.1.) But Smith for the first time won a majority for the Democrats in the nation's 12 largest cities. A new Democratic electorate was emerging, consisting of Catholics and Jews, Irish and Italians, Poles and Greeks. The task was to unite the traditional Democrats of the South and West with the urban voters of the Northeast and Midwest.

Quick Check

✓ How did the election of 1928 summarize the divisions of the period?

CONCLUSION: THE OLD AND THE NEW

Prohibition and the president-elect's natural reserve muted election night celebrations at Hoover's campaign headquarters. Had Hoover known what lay ahead for the country and his presidency, no doubt the party would have been even more somber.

During the 1920s, America struggled to enter the modern era. The economics of mass production and the politics of urbanization drove the country forward, but the persistent appeal of individualism and rural-based values held it back.

Watch the **Video** *Prosperity of the 1920s and the Great Depression* on **myhistorylab.com**

Americans achieved greater prosperity than ever before, but it was unevenly distributed. Further, as the outbursts of nativism, bigotry, and intolerance revealed, prosperity hardly guaranteed generosity or unity. Nor did it guarantee continued prosperity, even for those who benefited initially. As much as America changed during the 1920s, in one crucial respect the country remained as before. The American economy, for all its remarkable productive capacity, was astonishingly fragile. This was the lesson Hoover was soon to learn.

25 Study Resources

(((•— Listen to the **Chapter Audio** for Chapter 25 on **myhistorylab.com**

Timeline

1919 U.S. agents arrest 1,700 in Red Scare raids, p. 642
- Eighteenth Amendment (prohibition) ratified, p. 644

1920 Nineteenth Amendment grants women the right to vote, p. 640
- WWJ-Detroit broadcasts first commercial radio program (November), p. 638

1923 Newspapers expose Ku Klux Klan graft, torture, and murder, p. 646

1924 Senate probes Teapot Dome scandal, p. 648
- National Origins Quota Act restricts immigration from Europe and bans immigration from Asia, p. 647

1925 John Scopes convicted of teaching theory of evolution in violation of Tennessee law (July), p. 647

1927 Charles Lindbergh completes first nonstop transatlantic flight from New York to Paris (May), p. 641
- Sacco and Vanzetti executed (August), p. 644

Chapter Review

THE SECOND INDUSTRIAL REVOLUTION

What was new about the American economy in the 1920s?

The American economy in the 1920s underwent a second industrial revolution. Powered by electricity and featuring the mass production of automobiles and other consumer goods, the second industrial revolution lifted the American standard of living to new heights. (p. 637)

CITY LIFE IN THE ROARING TWENTIES

How did life in the cities change after World War I?

During the 1920s, the focus of American life shifted to the cities, which for the first time contained most of the American population. Women found new opportunities to express themselves, and sports, music, literature, and the arts flourished as never before. (p. 639)

THE CONSERVATIVE COUNTERATTACK

How did conservatives resist the changes of the decade?

The changes of the 1920s alarmed many conservatives, who tried to resist them. The police and courts cracked down on radicals; prohibition outlawed liquor; the Ku Klux Klan attacked immigrants and minorities; Congress restricted immigration; and fundamentalist Christians decried the changing code of morality and the teaching of evolution in the schools. (p. 642)

REPUBLICAN POLITICS

How did the politics of the 1920s reflect changes in the economy and in American society?

The 1920s were a decade of Republican politics. Presidents Harding, Coolidge, and Hoover favored business and the wealthy. In the election of 1928, voters had a clear choice between Hoover, the candidate of the countryside and conservatism, and Al Smith, the candidate of the cities and change, Hoover won in a landslide. *(p. 648)*

KEY TERM QUESTIONS

1. How did the Harlem Renaissance reflect the Jazz Age? (p. 641)

2. Why did the Red Scare follow World War I? (p. 642)

3. Why was prohibition repealed? (p. 644)

4. Why did nativism become more prevalent in the early decades of the twentieth century? (p. 646)

5. How did the National Origins Quota Act affect immigration? (p. 647)

6. Why did the Scopes Trial occur? (p. 647)

7. What was the Teapot Dome scandal? (p. 648)

MyHistoryLab Connections

Visit **www.myhistorylab.com** for a customized Study Plan to build your knowledge of *Transition to Modern America*

Questions for Analysis

1. On what basis could artists of the 1920s condemn American society for being overly materialistic?

   View the **Closer Look** *The Great White Way— Times Square* p. 639

2. What was the Harlem Renaissance?

   Watch the **Video** *The Harlem Renaissance* p. 641

3. What were A. Mitchell Palmer's views on communism?

   Read the **Document** *A. Mitchell Palmer on the Menace of Communism (1920)* p. 643

4. What reasons did congressman provide for supporting immigration restriction in 1921?

   Read the **Document** *Debating Immigration Restriction (1921)* p. 646

5. How did the onset of the Great Depression change the life style that most Americans were accustomed to during the 1920s?

   Watch the **Video** *Prosperity of the 1920s and the Great Depression* p. 651

Other Resources from this Chapter

Read the **Document** *The Automobile Comes to Middletown*

View the **Image** *McClure's Magazine featuring a Flapper*

Read the **Document** *Wembridge, Petting and the Campus*

Listen to the **Audio File** *Prohibition is a Failure*

View the **Image** *KKK March on Washington*

Read the **Document** *Creed of Klanswomen, 1924*

View the **Image** *Clarence Darrow at the Scopes Trial*

Watch the **Video** *Warren G. Harding*

Contents and Spotlight Questions

((•—| **Listen** to the **Chapter Audio** for Chapter 26 on **myhistorylab.com**

THE STRUGGLE AGAINST DESPAIR

Oscar Heline never forgot the terrible waste of the Great Depression. "Grain was being burned," he told interviewer Studs Terkel. "It was cheaper than coal." Heline lived in Iowa, in the heart of the farm belt. "A county just east of here, they burned corn in their courthouse all winter. . . . You couldn't hardly buy groceries for corn." Farmers, desperate for higher prices, resorted to destruction. "People were determined to withhold produce from the market—livestock, cream, butter, eggs, what not. If they would dump the produce, they would force the market to a higher level. The farmers would man the highways, and cream cans were emptied in ditches and eggs dumped out. They burned the trestle bridge, so the trains wouldn't be able to haul grain."

During the Great Depression, market prices for produce were so low that farmers could scarcely afford to harvest their crops. Many resorted to destroying produce in an attempt to limit supplies and force prices higher, among them were these striking dairy farmers in Illinois dumping cans of milk into the street.

Film critic Pauline Kael recounted a different memory of the 1930s. Kael, a college student in California during the Great Depression, was struck by how many students were missing fathers: "They had wandered off in disgrace because they couldn't support their families. Other fathers had killed themselves, so the family could have the insurance. Families had totally broken down." Kael and many of her classmates struggled to stay in school: "There were kids who didn't have a place to sleep, huddling under bridges on the campus. I had a scholarship, but there were times when I didn't have any food. The meals were often three candy bars."

Howard Worthington resorted to trickery after losing his job in Chicago. One Easter Sunday during the Depression, when his son was four years old, Worthington couldn't afford enough eggs for a proper egg hunt. So he devised a plan: "I hid a couple in the piano and all around. Tommy got his little Easter basket, and as he would find the eggs, I'd steal 'em out of the basket and re-hide them. . . . He hunted Easter eggs for three hours and he never knew the difference."

No American who lived through the Great Depression ever forgot it. As the stories of Heline, Kael, and Worthington show, the memories were of hard times, but also of determination, adaptation, and survival.

The depression decade had an equally profound effect on American institutions. To cope with poverty and dislocation, Americans looked to government as never before, and in doing so transformed American politics and public life. The agent of the transformation—the man America turned to in its moment of trial—was Franklin D. Roosevelt (FDR). His answer to the country's demands for action was an ambitious program called the New Deal.

THE GREAT DEPRESSION

What were the causes and effects of the Great Depression?

The depression of the 1930s shocked Americans who had grown used to prosperity. The consumer revolution of the 1920s had fostered confidence that the American way of life would continue to improve. But following the collapse of the stock market in late 1929, factories closed, machines fell silent, and millions of Americans looked for jobs that didn't exist.

The Great Crash

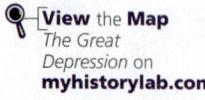

View the **Map**
The Great Depression on
myhistorylab.com

The consumer goods revolution contained the seeds of its own demise. The productive capacity of the automobile and appliance industries grew faster than the effective demand for the products they produced. Each year after 1924, fewer cars, refrigerators, and ranges were sold, a natural consequence as more and more people already owned these durable goods. Production faltered, and in 1927, a mild recession occurred. The sale of durable goods declined, and construction of houses and buildings fell slightly.

Even so, individuals with ready cash invested heavily in the stock market. The market had advanced in spurts during the 1920s; the value of all stocks listed on the New York Stock Exchange rose from $27 billion in 1925 to $67 billion in early

1929. The strongest surge began in the spring of 1928, when investors believed they could make a killing in the market despite the declining production figures. People bet their savings on speculative stocks. Corporations used their cash reserves to lend money to brokers who in turn lent it to investors on margin; in 1929, for example, the Standard Oil Company of New Jersey loaned out $69 million a day in this fashion.

Investors could now play the market on credit, buying stock listed at $100 a share with $10 down and $90 on margin, using the broker's loan for the balance. If the stock advanced to $150, the investor could sell and reap a 500-percent gain on the $10 investment. And in the bull market climate of the 1920s, everyone was sure the market would go up.

By 1929, it seemed the whole nation was engaged in speculation. In city after city, brokers opened branches, each complete with a stock ticker and a huge board showing the latest Wall Street quotations. People filled the seats in the customers' rooms in these offices, cheering the advances of their favorite stocks. Newspapers printed the stock averages on their front pages.

In reality, though, more people were spectators than speculators; fewer than three million Americans owned stocks in 1929, and only about 500,000 were active buyers and sellers. But the bull market became a national obsession, assuring everyone that the economy was healthy and preventing serious analysis of its flaws. When the market soared to more than $80 billion in total value by mid-summer, the *Wall Street Journal* proclaimed: "The outlook for the fall months seems brighter than at any time."

And then things changed, almost overnight. On October 24—later known as Black Thursday—the rise in stock prices faltered, and investors nervously began to sell. Such leading stocks as RCA and Westinghouse lost nearly half their value in a single day. Speculators panicked as their creditors demanded new collateral, and the panic caused prices to plummet still further. Within weeks the gains of the previous two years had vanished.

The great stock market crash soon spilled over into the larger economy. Banks and other financial institutions suffered heavy losses in the market and curtailed lending for consumer purchases. As consumers stopped buying, factories cut back production, laying off workers and reducing hours. The layoffs and cutbacks lowered purchasing power even further, so fewer people bought cars and appliances. More factory layoffs resulted, and some plants closed entirely, making even less money available to purchase consumer goods.

This downward economic spiral continued for four years. By 1932, 25 percent of the workforce was unemployed. (See Figure 26.1.) Steel production was down to 12 percent of capacity. The vast assembly lines in Detroit produced only a trickle of cars each day. The gross national product fell to 67 percent of the 1929 level. The bright dream of mass production had become a nightmare.

The basic explanation for the Great Depression is overproduction: U.S. factories produced more goods than the American people could consume. The problem was not that the market for such products was fully saturated. In 1929, millions of Americans still did not own cars, radios, or refrigerators. But many of them could not afford the new products. There were other contributing causes—unstable

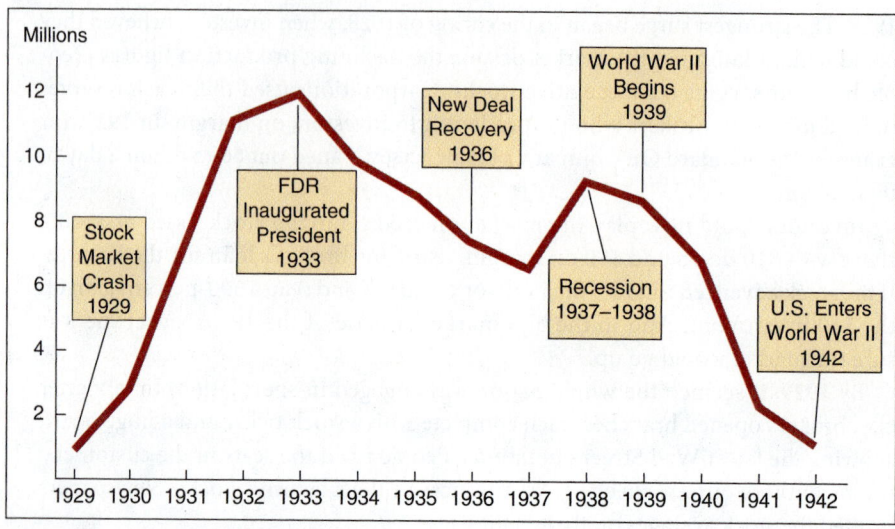

Millions

Stock Market Crash 1929

FDR Inaugurated President 1933

New Deal Recovery 1936

World War II Begins 1939

Recession 1937–1938

U.S. Enters World War II 1942

1929 1930 1931 1932 1933 1934 1935 1936 1937 1938 1939 1940 1941 1942

Figure 26.1 U.S. Unemployment, 1929–1942

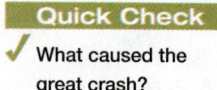

Quick Check
✓ What caused the great crash?

economic conditions in Europe, the agricultural decline since 1919, corporate misman-agement, and excessive speculation—but it all came down to the fact that people did not have enough money to buy the consumer products coming off the assembly lines.

The Effect of the Depression

Read the Document
Women on the Breadlines on **myhistorylab.com**

It is difficult to measure the human cost of the Great Depression. The material hardships were bad enough. Men and women lived in lean-tos made of scrap wood and metal. Families went without meat and fresh vegetables for months, existing on soup and beans. The psychological burden was even greater: Americans suffered through year after year of grinding poverty with no letup. The unemployed stood in line for hours waiting for relief checks; veter-ans sold apples or pencils on street corners, their manhood—once prized so highly by the nation—in question. People left the city for the countryside but found no refuge on the farm. Crops rotted in the fields because prices were too low to make harvesting worthwhile; sheriffs fended off angry crowds as banks foreclosed long-overdue mortgages on once prosperous farms.

Few escaped the suffering. African Ameri-cans who had left the poverty of the rural South for factory jobs in the North were among the first to be laid off. Mexican im-migrants, who had replaced European

The Great Depression devastated millions who lost their jobs and often the means to provide food and shelter for themselves and their families. Local and private charities could not keep up with the demands for assistance, and many looked to the federal government. Breadlines stretched as far as the eye could see.

immigrants, competed with angry citizens now willing to do stoop labor in the fields and lay tracks on the railroads. Immigration officials used technicalities to halt and even reverse the flow across the Rio Grande; nearly 500,000 Mexicans were deported in the 1930s, including families with children born in the United States.

The poor—black, brown, and white—survived because they knew better than most Americans how to exist in poverty. They stayed in bed in cold weather to keep warm and avoid burning calories; they patched their shoes with rubber from discarded tires, heated only the kitchens of their homes, and ate scraps that others would reject.

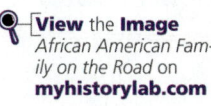
View the **Image**
African American Family on the Road on
myhistorylab.com

The middle class, which had always lived with high expectations, was hit hard. Professionals and white-collar workers refused to ask for charity even while their families went hungry. One New York dentist and his wife committed suicide and left a note saying, "We want to get out of the way before we are forced to accept relief money." People who fell behind in their mortgage payments lost their homes and faced eviction when they could not pay the rent. Health care declined. Middle-class people stopped going to doctors and dentists regularly, unable to pay in advance for services rendered.

Even the well-to-do were affected, giving up many of their former luxuries and weighed down with guilt as they watched former friends and business associates become impoverished. "My father lost everything in the depression" became an all-too-familiar refrain among young people who dropped out of college.

Many Americans sought escape in movement. Men, boys, and women rode the rails in search of jobs, hopping freights to move south in the winter or west in the summer. On the Missouri Pacific alone, vagrants increased from just over 13,000 in 1929 to nearly 200,000 in 1931. One town in the Southwest hired special police to keep vagrants from leaving the boxcars. Tramps had to keep on the move, but they did find a sense of community in the hobo jungles that sprang up along the major railroad routes. Here they could find a place to eat and sleep and people with whom to share their misery. Louis Banks, a black veteran, told interviewer Studs Terkel what these informal camps were like:

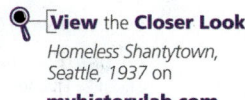
View the **Closer Look**
Homeless Shantytown, Seattle, 1937 on
myhistorylab.com

> Black and white, it didn't make any difference who you were, 'cause everybody was poor. All friendly, sleep in a jungle. We used to take a big pot and cook food, cabbage, meat and beans all together. We all set together, we made a tent. Twenty-five or thirty would be out on the side of the rail, white and colored: They didn't have no mothers or sisters, they didn't have no home, they were dirty, they had overalls on, they didn't have no food, they didn't have anything.

Quick Check
✓ How did the Great Depression affect individual lives?

FIGHTING THE DEPRESSION

The Great Depression presented an enormous challenge for American political leadership. The Republicans' inability to overcome the economic catastrophe enabled the Democrats to regain power. Although they failed to achieve full recovery before the outbreak of World War II, the Democrats did alleviate some of the suffering and establish political dominance.

How did Franklin Roosevelt fight the Depression?

The Emergence of Roosevelt

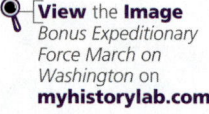

Watch the **Video**
Responding to the Great Depression: Whose New Deal? on **myhistorylab.com**

View the **Image**
Bonus Expeditionary Force March on Washington on **myhistorylab.com**

The Great Depression took Herbert Hoover by surprise. At first the Republican president relied on the natural working of the economy to restore prosperity. When this failed, he called for voluntary cooperation among businesses to maintain wages and employment. To relieve the suffering of the unemployed, he looked to local governments and private charities. Eventually, and reluctantly, Hoover agreed to federal assistance to business, but by then the depression had become overwhelming. His mishandling of the Bonus Army—jobless World War I veterans who traveled to Washington seeking federal help and were forcibly dispersed by General Douglas MacArthur and the regular army—made Hoover the most unpopular man in America by 1932.

His successor as president was Franklin D. Roosevelt. Born into the old Dutch aristocracy of New York, FDR was a distant cousin of the Republican Teddy Roosevelt. He grew up with all the advantages of wealth: private tutors, his own sailboat and pony, trips to Europe, and education at elite private schools. His strong-willed mother gave him a priceless sense of self-confidence. After graduation from Harvard, he attended law school but left to plunge into politics. He served in the New York legislature and then went to Washington as assistant secretary of the navy under Wilson, a post he filled capably during World War I. Defeated as the Democratic vice presidential candidate in 1920, Roosevelt had just begun a banking career when polio struck in 1921. He fought back bravely, and though he never again walked unaided, he reentered politics and was elected governor of New York in 1928.

Roosevelt's dominant trait was his ability to persuade and motivate other people. He possessed a deep, rich voice; a winning smile; and a buoyant confidence he transmitted to others. Some believed he was too vain and superficial as a young man, but his bout with polio gave him both an understanding of human suffering and a broad political appeal as a man who had overcome heavy odds. He understood the give-and-take of politics, knew how to use flattery to win over doubters, and was especially effective in exploiting the media, whether bantering with reporters or reaching out to the American people on the radio. Although his mind was quick and agile, he had little patience with philosophical nuances; he dealt with perceptions of issues, not their deeper substance, and displayed a flexibility toward political principles that often dismayed even his warmest admirers.

Roosevelt took advantage of the opportunity the Great Depression offered. With the Republicans discredited, he cultivated the two wings of the divided Democrats, appealing to both the traditionalists from the South and West and the new urban elements in the North. After winning the party's nomination in 1932, he broke

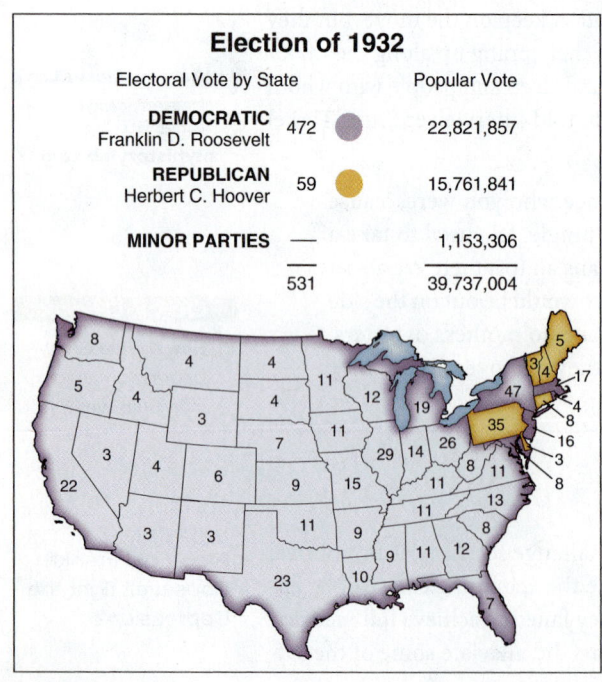

Election of 1932

	Electoral Vote by State		Popular Vote
DEMOCRATIC Franklin D. Roosevelt	472		22,821,857
REPUBLICAN Herbert C. Hoover	59		15,761,841
MINOR PARTIES	—		1,153,306
	531		39,737,004

Map 26.1

with tradition by flying to Chicago and accepting in person, telling the cheering delegates, "I pledge you—I pledge myself to a new deal for the American people."

In the fall, he defeated Herbert Hoover in a landslide. (See Map 26.1.) Farmers and workers, Protestants and Catholics, immigrants and native born rallied behind the new leader who promised to restore prosperity.

Quick Check

✓ How did Franklin Roosevelt's background prepare him to deal with the Great Depression?

The Hundred Days

When Franklin Roosevelt took office on March 4, 1933, the nation's economy was on the brink of collapse. Unemployment stood at nearly 13 million, one-fourth of the labor force; banks were closed in 38 states. On inauguration morning, the governors of New York and Illinois closed the banks in the nation's two largest cities, thus bringing the country's financial transactions to a halt. Speaking from the steps of the Capitol, FDR declared boldly, "First of all, let me assert my firm belief that the only thing we have to fear is fear itself—nameless, unreasoning, unjustified terror." Then he announced he would call Congress into special session and request "broad executive power to wage a war against the emergency, as great as the power that would be given to me if we were in fact invaded by a foreign foe."

Within the next ten days, Roosevelt won his first great New Deal victory by saving the nation's banks. On March 5, he issued a decree closing the banks and called Congress back into session. His aides presented new banking legislation to Congress on March 9; both houses passed it within hours, and FDR signed it that evening. The measure provided for government supervision and aid to the banks. Strong ones would be reopened with federal support, weak ones closed. Government loans would bolster those in difficulty.

On March 12, FDR addressed the nation by radio in the first of his fireside chats. In conversational tones, he told the public what he had done. Some banks would reopen the next day, with the government standing behind them. Other banks, once they became solvent, would open later, and the American people could safely put their money back into these institutions. The next day, March 13, the nation's largest and strongest banks reopened their doors; at the end of the day, customers had deposited more cash than they withdrew. The crisis was over; gradually, other banks opened, and the bank runs and failures ceased.

"Capitalism was saved in eight days," boasted one of Roosevelt's advisers. Most surprising was the conservative nature of FDR's action. Instead of nationalizing the banks, he had simply thrown the government's resources behind them and preserved private ownership. Though other New Deal measures would be more radical, Roosevelt set a tone in the banking crisis. He was out to reform and restore the American economic system, not change it drastically. He drew on the progressive tradition and his experience with World War I mobilization to fashion a moderate program of government action.

For the next three months, until it adjourned in June, Congress responded to presidential initiatives. During these "Hundred Days," Roosevelt sent 15 major requests to Congress and received back 15 pieces of legislation. A few created agencies that have become part of American life. The Tennessee Valley Authority (TVA) was

◉—Watch the **Video**
FDR's First Inaugural Address on
myhistorylab.com

one of the most ambitious of Roosevelt's New Deal measures. This innovative effort at regional planning built dams in seven states to control floods, ease navigation, and produce electricity. (See Map 26.2.) The Civilian Conservation Corps (CCC) put jobless young men from cities to work in the forests planting trees, fighting fires, and building roads and trails. Though not part of the Hundred Days, the final commitment to the idea of work relief came in 1935 when Roosevelt established the Works Progress Administration (WPA) to spend nearly $5 billion authorized by Congress for emergency relief. The WPA put the unemployed on the federal payroll, so they could earn enough to meet their basic needs and stimulate the stagnant economy.

Other New Deal agencies were temporary measures to meet specific economic problems of the depression. None were completely successful; the depression would continue for another six years, immune even to Roosevelt's magic. But psychologically, the nation turned the corner in the spring of 1933. Under FDR, the government seemed to be responding to the economic crisis, enabling people for the first time since 1929 to look to the future with hope.

Quick Check

✔ What were the principal accomplishments of the hundred days?

Steps Toward Recovery

View the **Map**
The Tennessee Valley Authority on
myhistorylab.com

Two major New Deal programs launched during the Hundred Days were aimed at industrial and agricultural recovery. The first was the National Recovery Administration (NRA), FDR's attempt to achieve economic advance through planning and cooperation among government, business, and labor. In the midst of the depression, business owners were intent on stabilizing production and raising prices. Labor leaders were equally determined to spread work through maximum hours and to put a floor under workers' income with minimum wages.

The NRA hoped to achieve both goals by permitting companies in each major industry to cooperate in writing codes of fair competition that would set realistic limits on production, allocate percentages to individual producers, and set firm guidelines for prices. Section 7a of the enabling act mandated protection for labor in all the codes by establishing maximum hours, minimum wages, and the guarantee of collective bargaining by unions. No company could be compelled to join, but the New Deal sought complete participation by appealing to patriotism. Each firm that took part could display a blue eagle and stamp the symbol on its products. Under Hugh Johnson, the NRA quickly enrolled the nation's leading companies and unions. By the summer of 1933, more than 500 industries had adopted codes that covered 2.5 million workers.

Map 26.2 *The Tennessee Valley Authority* The Tennessee Valley Authority (TVA) served a seven-state region in the Southeast.

But the NRA bogged down in a huge bureaucratic morass. The codes were too detailed to enforce easily. Written by the largest companies, the rules favored big business over smaller competitors. Labor became disenchanted with Section 7a. The minimum wages were often near starvation level, while business avoided collective bargaining by creating company unions that did not represent workers' real needs. After a brief upsurge in early 1933, industrial production began to sag as disillusionment with the NRA grew. By 1934, more and more business owners were complaining, calling the agency the "National Run Around." Few mourned when the Supreme Court invalidated the NRA in 1935 on constitutional grounds. Self-interest and greed had defeated the idea of trying to overcome the depression by relying on voluntary cooperation between competing businesses and labor leaders.

Farm recovery fared better. Henry A. Wallace, FDR's secretary of agriculture, came up with an answer to the farmers' old dilemma of overproduction. The government would set production limits for wheat, cotton, corn, and other leading crops. The Agricultural Adjustment Administration (AAA), created by Congress in

The National Recovery Administration blue eagle signaled a firm's participation in the National Recovery Act. Roosevelt's innovative program met resistance, and signs modeled on this original example attempted to make participation patriotic and respectable.

May 1933, allocated acreage among individual farmers, paying them subsidies (raised by a tax on food production) to take land out of production. Unfortunately, Wallace preferred not to wait until the 1934 planting season to implement this program. So farmers were paid in 1933 to plow under crops they had already planted and kill livestock they were raising. Faced with the problem of hunger in the midst of plenty, the New Deal seemed to respond by destroying the plenty.

The AAA program worked better in 1934 and 1935 as land removed from production led to smaller harvests and rising prices for crops. Farm income rose for the first time since World War I, increasing from $2 billion in 1933 to $5 billion by 1935. Severe weather, especially Dust Bowl conditions on the Great Plains, contributed to the crop-limitation program, but most of the gain in farm income came from the subsidy payments themselves rather than from higher market prices. Though the Supreme Court in 1936 ruled the AAA unconstitutional, Congress reenacted its essential features in acceptable form.

Read the
Document
*An Attack on New
Deal Farm Policies* on
myhistorylab.com

Quick Check

✓ How did the new
deal try to promote
recovery of industry
and agriculture?

On the whole, large farmers benefited most from the New Deal's agricultural program. Possessing the capital to buy machinery and fertilizer, they could farm more efficiently than before on fewer acres of land. Small farmers, tenants, and sharecroppers fared less well, receiving little of the government payments and often being driven off the land as owners took the acreage previously cultivated by tenants and sharecroppers out of production. Some 3 million people left the land in the 1930s, crowding into the cities where they swelled the relief rolls. In the long run, the New Deal reforms improved the efficiency of American agriculture, but at a human cost.

REFORMING AMERICAN LIFE

How did the
New Deal reform
American life?

During his first two years in office, FDR had concentrated on fighting the Great Depression by shoring up the sagging American economy. Only a few new agencies, notably TVA, sought to make permanent changes in national life. Roosevelt was developing a "broker-state" concept of government, responding to pressures from organized elements such as corporations, labor unions, and farm groups while ignoring the needs and wants of the dispossessed, who had no clear political voice. The early New Deal tried to assist bankers and industrialists, large farmers, and union members, but it did little to help the elderly and the poor.

The continuing depression and high unemployment began to create pressure for more sweeping changes. Roosevelt either had to provide more radical programs to end historical inequities in American life, or defer to others' solutions to the nation's ills.

Federal work relief programs helped millions maintain their self-respect. Workers in the CCC received $30 a month for planting trees and building parks and trails.

Challenges to FDR

Discontent was widespread by 1935. In the upper Midwest, progressives and agrarian radicals, led by Minnesota governor Floyd Olson, were calling for government action to raise farm and labor income. "I am a radical in the sense that I want a definite change in the system," Olson declared. "I am not satisfied with patching." Upton Sinclair, the muckraking novelist, was nearly elected governor of California in 1934 on the slogan "End poverty in California." A violent strike shut down textile plants in 20 states. The most serious challenge to Roosevelt's leadership, however, came from three demagogues who captured national attention in the mid-1930s.

The first was Father Charles Coughlin, a Roman Catholic priest from Detroit, who had originally supported FDR. In his rich, melodious voice, Coughlin appealed to the discontented with a mixture of crank monetary schemes and anti-Semitism. He denounced the New Deal in late 1934 as the "Pagan Deal" and founded his own National Union for Social Justice. Increasingly vitriolic, he called for monetary inflation and nationalizing the banking system in his weekly radio sermons to a rapt audience of more than 30 million.

A more benign but equally influential figure appeared in California. Francis Townsend, a 67-year-old physician, developed a scheme in 1934 to assist the elderly, who were suffering greatly during the depression. The Townsend Plan proposed giving everyone over age 60 a monthly pension of $200 with the proviso that it must be spent within 30 days. Although the plan was designed less as an old-age pension than as a way to stimulate the economy, the elderly embraced the proposal as a holy cause, joining Townsend Clubs across the country. Despite the criticism from economists that the plan would transfer more than half the national income to less than 10 percent of the population, more than 10 million people signed petitions endorsing the Townsend Plan. Few politicians dared oppose it.

Huey Long, the flamboyant senator from Louisiana, was the third new voice of protest. Like Coughlin, an original supporter of the New Deal, Long had become a major political threat to the president by 1935. A shrewd, ruthless, yet witty man, Long mocked those in power. The Kingfish (a nickname he borrowed from a character on the *Amos 'n' Andy* radio show) announced a nationwide "Share the Wealth" movement in 1934. He spoke grandly of taking from the rich to make "every man a king," guaranteeing each American a home worth $5,000 and an annual income of $2,500. To finance the plan, Long advocated seizing all fortunes of more than $5 million and taxing incomes greater than $1 million at 100 percent. By 1935, Long claimed to have 27,000 Share the Wealth clubs and a mailing list of more than 7 million people, including workers, farmers, college professors, and even bank presidents. Democratic leaders feared that if Long ran as a third-party candidate in 1936 he might attract 3 to 4 million votes, possibly enough to swing the election to the Republicans. Although an assassin killed Huey Long in Louisiana in September 1935, his popularity showed that the New Deal needed to do more to help those in distress.

> **Watch** the **Video**
> *President Roosevelt Focuses on America's Youth* on **myhistorylab.com**

> **Quick Check**
> ✓ Who were Charles Coughlin, Francis Townsend, and Huey Long, and what did they want?

Social Security

When the new Congress met in January 1935, Roosevelt was ready to support reform measures to take the edge off national dissent. In the midterm elections, the Republicans had lost 13 seats in the House and retained less than one-third of the Senate. Many of the Democrats were to the left of Roosevelt, favoring increased spending and more sweeping federal programs. "Boys—this is our hour," exulted FDR's assistant Harry Hopkins. "We've got to get everything we want . . . now or never." Congress quickly appropriated $4.8 billion for the WPA and was prepared to enact virtually any proposal that Roosevelt offered.

The most significant reform enacted in 1935, and the most important reform of the entire New Deal, was the Social Security Act. The Townsend movement had reminded Americans that the United States, alone among modern industrial nations,

Despite the administration's boosterism, many believed that Social Security could not fulfill its promises.

Read the **Document**
Frances Perkins and the Social Security Act (1935, 1960) on **myhistorylab.com**

had never developed a welfare system to aid the aged, disabled, and unemployed. A cabinet committee began studying the problem in 1934. Roosevelt sent its recommendations to Congress the following January.

The proposed legislation had three major parts. First, it provided for old-age pensions financed equally by a tax on employers and workers. It also gave states federal matching funds to provide modest pensions for the destitute elderly. Second, it set up a system of unemployment compensation on a federal–state basis, with employers paying a payroll tax and each state setting benefit levels and administering the program locally. Finally, it provided for direct federal grants to the states, on a matching basis, for welfare payments to the blind, handicapped, needy elderly, and dependent children.

Although conservatives mourned the passing of traditional American reliance on self-help and individualism, others argued that the measure did not go far enough. Democratic leaders, however, defeated efforts to incorporate Townsend's proposal for $200 monthly pensions and increases in unemployment benefits. Congress then passed the Social Security Act by overwhelming margins.

Critics pointed out its shortcomings. The old-age pensions were paltry. Designed to begin in 1942, they ranged from $10 to $85 a month. Many of those who most needed protection in their old age, such as farmers and domestic servants, were excluded. And all participants, regardless of income or economic status, paid in at the same rate, with no supplement from the general revenue. The trust fund also took out of circulation money that was desperately needed to stimulate the economy in the 1930s.

Other portions of the act were equally questionable. The cumbersome unemployment system offered no aid to those currently out of work, only to people who would lose their jobs in the future, and the benefits (depending on the state) ranged from barely adequate to substandard. The outright grants to the handicapped and dependent children were minute; in New York City, for example, a blind person received only $5 a week in 1937.

The conservative nature of the legislation reflected not only Roosevelt's fiscal orthodoxy, but his political realism. Despite the severity of the depression, he realized that establishing a system of federal welfare went against deep American convictions. A tax on participants gave those involved in the pension plan a vested interest in Social Security. He wanted them to feel they had earned their pensions and that no one would dare take them away. "With those taxes in there," he explained privately, "no damned politician can ever scrap my social security program." Above all, FDR had established the principle of government responsibility for the aged, the handicapped, and the unemployed. Whatever its defects, Social Security was a landmark of the New Deal, creating a system to provide for the welfare of individuals in a complex industrial society.

Quick Check

✓ What motivated the Social Security Act, and what did it accomplish?

THE IMPACT OF THE NEW DEAL

The New Deal influenced the quality of life in the United States in the 1930s. Government programs reached into areas hitherto untouched. Many of them brought about long-overdue improvements, but others failed to reduce historic inequities. The most important advances came with the growth of labor unions; conditions for working women and minorities in non-unionized industries showed no comparable advance.

What was the lasting impact of the New Deal?

The Rise of Organized Labor

At the onset of the Great Depression, trade unions had fewer than 3 million workers. Most were in the American Federation of Labor (AFL), composed of craft unions for skilled workers. Basic industries, such as steel and automobiles, were unorganized; wages and working conditions for the great mass of unskilled workers were poor. Section 7a of the NRA had increased the AFL's ranks, but the union's conservative leaders, eager to cooperate with business, failed to organize the mass-production industries.

John L. Lewis took the lead in forming mass unions. The son of a Welsh coal miner, Lewis was dynamic and ruthless. He had led the United Mine Workers since 1919 and was determined to spread the benefits of unions throughout industry. Lewis first battled with the leadership of the AFL. After being expelled, he renamed his group the Congress of Industrial Organizations (CIO) and announced that he would use the Wagner Act, which provided federal support for efforts to unionize workers, to extend collective bargaining to the auto and steel industries.

Within five years, Lewis had scored remarkable victories. Some came easily. The big steel companies, led by U.S. Steel, surrendered without a fight in 1937; management realized that federal support put the unions in a strong position. The automobile industry was less obliging. When General Motors, the first target, resisted, the new United Automobile Workers (UAW) developed an effective strike technique. In December 1936, GM workers in Flint, Michigan, simply sat down in the factory, refusing to leave until the company recognized their union, and threatening to destroy the tools and machines if they were removed forcibly. When the governor refused to call out the National Guard to break the strike, GM conceded and signed a contract with the UAW. So did Chrysler. But Henry Ford chose to fight, hiring

▶ **Read** the **Document**
Bob Stinson, Flint Sit Down Strike, 1936 on **myhistorylab.com**

strikebreakers and beating up organizers. Ford did not recognize the UAW until 1941. Smaller steel companies, led by Republic Steel, also resisted even more violently; in 1937, police shot ten strikers. The companies eventually reached a settlement with the steelworkers' union in 1941.

By the end of the 1930s, the CIO had some five million members, slightly more than the AFL. In addition to the automaking and steel unions, the CIO and the AFL had organized the textile, rubber, electrical, and metal industries. For the first time, unskilled as well as skilled workers were unionized. Women and African Americans benefited from the creation of the CIO, not because the union followed enlightened policies, but because they were a large part of the unskilled workforce that the CIO organized.

Yet despite these impressive gains, only 28 percent of all Americans (excluding farmworkers) belonged to unions by 1940. Millions in the restaurant, retail, and service trades remained unorganized, working long hours for low wages. Employer resistance and traditional hostility to unions blocked progress, as did the aloof attitude of FDR, who pronounced, "A plague on both your houses," for labor and management, during the steel strike. The Wagner Act in 1935 had helped open the way, but labor leaders such as Lewis, Philip Murray of the Steel Workers Organizing Committee, and Walter Reuther of the UAW deserved most of the credit for union achievements.

Quick Check

✓ How did the New Deal benefit organized labor?

The New Deal Record on Help to Minorities

The Roosevelt administration's attempts to aid the downtrodden were least effective with racial minorities. The Great Depression had hit blacks hard. Sharecroppers and tenant farmers had seen the price of cotton drop from 18 to 6 cents a pound, far below the level needed to sustain a family on the land. In the cities, the saying "Last hired, first fired" proved all too true; by 1933, more than 50 percent of urban blacks were unemployed. Hard times sharpened racial prejudice. "No jobs for niggers until every white man has a job" became a rallying cry for whites in Atlanta.

The New Deal helped African Americans survive the depression, but it never tried to confront racial injustice in the federal relief programs. Although New Deal programs served blacks and whites, southern blacks received much smaller weekly payments. In the early days, NRA codes permitted lower wage scales for blacks, while the AAA led to the eviction of thousands of black tenants and sharecroppers. African American leaders referred to the NRA as standing for "Negro Robbed Again" and dismissed the AAA as "a continuation of the same old raw deal." Nor did later reform measures help much. Neither the minimum wage nor Social Security covered farmers or domestic servants, who comprised 65 percent of all African American workers. An NAACP official said that Social Security "looks like a sieve with the holes just large enough for the majority of Negroes to fall through."

Yet African Americans still rallied behind Roosevelt's leadership, abandoning their historic ties to the Republican party. In 1936, more than 75 percent of those African Americans who voted supported FDR. In part, this switch came in response to Roosevelt's appointment of prominent African Americans to high-ranking positions, such as William H. Hastie in the Interior Department and Mary McLeod Bethune (founder and president of Bethune-Cookman College) in the National Youth Administration. Eleanor Roosevelt denounced racial discrimination throughout the decade, most notably in 1939 when the Daughters of the American Revolution refused to let African American contralto Marian Anderson sing in Constitution Hall. The first lady and Interior Secretary Harold Ickes arranged for Anderson to perform at the Lincoln Memorial, where 75,000 people heard her on Easter Sunday.

Perhaps the most influential factor in African Americans' political switch was the color-blind policy of Harry Hopkins. He had more than one million blacks working for the WPA by 1939, many of them as teachers and artists. The New Deal provided assistance to 40 percent of the nation's blacks during the depression. Uneven as his record was, Roosevelt had still done more to aid this oppressed minority than any president since Lincoln. One African American newspaper commented that while "relief and WPA are not ideal, they are better than the Hoover bread lines and they'll have to do until the real thing comes along."

With the statue of Abraham Lincoln as a backdrop, African-American contralto Marian Anderson sang on the steps of the Lincoln Memorial in a concert given April 9, 1939.

The New Deal did far less for Mexican Americans. Most of them were agricultural laborers, and their wages in California fields dropped from 35 to 14 cents an hour by 1933. The pool of unemployed migrant labor expanded rapidly with Dust Bowl conditions in the Great Plains and the flight of "Okies" and "Arkies" to the cotton fields of Arizona and the truck farms of California. The Roosevelt administration cut off any further influx from Mexico by barring any immigrant "likely to become a public charge"; local authorities shipped migrants back to Mexico to reduce the welfare rolls.

The New Deal relief program did aid thousands of Mexican Americans in the Southwest in the 1930s, although migrant workers had difficulty meeting state requirements. The WPA hired Mexican Americans for construction and cultural programs, but after 1937, such employment was denied to aliens. Overall, Mexican Americans suffered economic hardship and got little federal assistance.

Native Americans, after decades of neglect, fared slightly better under the New Deal. Roosevelt appointed John Collier, a social worker who championed Indian rights, as commissioner of Indian affairs. In 1934, the Indian Reorganization Act

Quick Check

✓ What did the New
Deal accomplish, and
not accomplish, for
minorities?

stressed tribal unity and autonomy instead of attempting (as previous policy had) to transform Indians into self-sufficient farmers by granting them small plots of land. Collier employed more Native Americans in the Indian Bureau, supported education on the reservations, and encouraged tribes to produce native handiwork such as blankets and jewelry. Despite modest gains, however, Indians—who numbered about a third of a million—remained the most impoverished citizens in America.

THE NEW DEAL'S END

How and why did
the New Deal end?

The New Deal reached its high point in 1936, when Roosevelt was overwhelmingly reelected and the Democrats strengthened their hold on Congress. This triumph was deceptive. In the next two years, Roosevelt met with defeats in Congress. Yet he remained a popular political leader who had restored American self-confidence as he strove to meet the challenges of the Great Depression.

The Supreme Court Fight

Roosevelt's resounding reelection went to his head. In 1937, he attempted to remove the one obstacle remaining in his path—the Supreme Court. During his first term, the Court had ruled several New Deal programs unconstitutional, most notably the NRA and

Courtesy, D. R. Fitzpatrick. *St. Louis Post-Dispatch*, June 28, 1935

FDR's battle with the Supreme Court provoked both sympathy and contempt among political cartoonists of the day. In the cartoon on the right, the NRA blue eagle lies dead, nailed to the wall by the Supreme Court. The cartoon on the left, titled "Do We Want a Ventriloquist Act in the Supreme Court?" satirizes FDR's "court-packing" scheme.

the AAA. Only three of the nine justices were sympathetic to the need for emergency measures in the midst of the depression. Two others were unpredictable. Four justices were bent on using the Constitution to block Roosevelt's proposals. All were elderly men. Justice Willis Van Devanter had planned to retire in 1932 but remained on the Court because he believed Roosevelt to be "unfitted and unsafe for the Presidency."

When Congress convened in 1937, the president offered a startling proposal to overcome the Court's threat to the New Deal. Instead of seeking a constitutional amendment either to limit the Court's power or to clarify the constitutional issues, FDR chose an oblique attack. Declaring the Court was falling behind schedule because of the age of its members, he asked Congress to appoint a new justice for each member of the Court over the age of 70, up to a maximum of six.

Although this "court-packing" scheme, as critics dubbed it, was perfectly legal, it outraged conservatives and liberals, who realized it could set a dangerous precedent. Republicans let prominent Democrats such as Senator Burton Wheeler of Montana lead the fight against Roosevelt's plan. Despite pressure from the White House, the Senate blocked early action on the proposal.

The Court defended itself well. Chief Justice Charles Evans Hughes pointed out to the Senate Judiciary Committee that in fact the Court was not behind schedule as Roosevelt charged. The Court then surprised observers by approving such controversial measures as the Wagner Act and Social Security. In the midst of the struggle, Justice Van Devanter resigned, enabling FDR to make his first appointment to the Court since taking office in 1933. Believing he had proved his point, the president allowed his court-packing plan to die in the Senate.

By 1939, four more vacancies occurred, and Roosevelt was able to appoint such distinguished jurists as Hugo Black, William O. Douglas, and Felix Frankfurter to the Supreme Court. Yet the price was high. The Court fight had weakened the president's relations with Congress, opening deep rifts among Democrats. Senators and representatives who had voted reluctantly for Roosevelt's measures during the depths of the Great Depression now felt free to oppose further New Deal reforms.

Quick Check

✓ What prompted Roosevelt to try to "Pack" the Supreme Court, and how did the effort turn out?

The New Deal in Decline

The legislative record during Roosevelt's second term was meager. Aside from laws on minimum wages and maximum hours, Congress did not extend the New Deal into any new areas. Attempts to institute national health insurance and pass anti-lynching legislation failed. Disturbed by the congressional resistance, Roosevelt set out in 1938 to defeat conservative Democratic congressmen and senators, primarily in the South. His targets gleefully charged the president with interference in local politics; only one of them lost in the primaries. The failure of this attempted purge further strained Roosevelt's relations with Congress.

The worst blow came in the economic sector. The slow but steady improvement in the economy suddenly gave way to a sharp recession in late summer 1937. In the following ten months, industrial production fell by one-third, and nearly 4 million workers lost their jobs. Critics of the New Deal labeled the downturn "the Roosevelt recession," and business executives claimed that it reflected a lack of confidence in FDR's leadership.

The criticism was overblown but not without basis. To reduce budget deficits, Roosevelt had cut back on WPA and other government programs after the election. Federal contributions to consumer purchasing power fell from $4.1 billion in 1936 to less than $1 billion in 1937. For months, Roosevelt refused to restore government spending. Finally, in April 1938, he asked Congress for a $3.75 billion relief appropriation, and the economy began to revive. But FDR's premature attempt to balance the budget had meant two more years of hard times and had marred his reputation as the energetic foe of the depression.

The political result of the attempted purge and the recession was a Republican upsurge. In 1938, the GOP gained 81 seats in the House, eight in the Senate, and 13 governorships. The party many thought dead suddenly had new life. The Democrats still held a sizable majority in Congress, but their margin in the House was deceptive. There were 262 Democratic representatives to 169 Republicans, but 93 southern Democrats held the balance of power. Increasingly after 1938, anti–New Deal southerners voted with Republican conservatives to block social and economic reforms. Thus, not only was the New Deal over by the end of 1938, but a new bipartisan conservative coalition that would prevail for a quarter century had formed in Congress.

Quick Check

✓ How did the New Deal end?

CONCLUSION: THE NEW DEAL AND AMERICAN LIFE

The New Deal lasted just five years, and most of its measures came in two legislative bursts in the spring of 1933 and summer of 1935. Yet nearly every aspect of economic, social, and political development in the decades that followed bore the imprint of Roosevelt's leadership.

The least impressive achievement of the New Deal came in the economic realm. Whatever credit Roosevelt is given for relieving human suffering during the Great Depression must be balanced against his failure to restore prosperity in the 1930s. The moderate nature of his programs, especially the unwieldy NRA, led to slow and halting industrial recovery. Although government spending was responsible for much of the improvement that was made, FDR never embraced the concept of planned deficits, striving instead for a balanced budget. As a result, by 1939, the nation had barely reached the 1929 level of production, and nearly ten million men and women were still unemployed.

Roosevelt also refused to make sweeping changes in the American economic system. Aside from the TVA, there were no broad experiments in regional planning and no attempts to alter free enterprise beyond imposing limited forms of government regulation. The New Deal did nothing to alter the basic distribution of wealth and power in the nation. The outcome preserved the traditional capitalist system under a thin overlay of federal control.

More significant change occurred in American society. With Social Security, the government acknowledged its responsibility to provide for those unable to care for themselves in an industrial society. The Wagner Act stimulated the growth of labor unions to balance corporate power, and the minimum wage law provided a needed floor for many workers.

◉ **Watch** the **Video**
Dorothea Lange and Migrant Mother on **myhistorylab.com**

Yet the New Deal tended to help only more vocal and organized groups, such as union members and commercial farmers. Those without effective voices or political clout—African Americans, Mexican Americans, women, sharecroppers, restaurant and laundry workers—received little help. For all the appealing rhetoric about the "forgotten man," Roosevelt did little more than Hoover for the long-term needs of the dispossessed.

The most lasting impact of the Roosevelt leadership came in politics. Taking advantage of the emerging power of ethnic voters and capitalizing on the frustration growing out of the depression, FDR was a genius at forging a new coalition. Overcoming the friction between rural and urban Democrats that had prolonged Republican supremacy in the 1920s, he attracted new groups to the Democratic party, principally African Americans and organized labor. His political success led to a major realignment that lasted long after he left the scene.

His political achievement also revealed the true nature of Roosevelt's success. He was a brilliant politician who recognized the essence of leadership in a democracy—appealing directly to the people and giving them a sense of purpose. He infused them with the same indomitable courage and jaunty optimism that had marked his own battle with polio. Thus, despite his limitations as a reformer, Roosevelt was the leader the American people needed in the 1930s—a president who provided the psychological lift that helped them endure and survive the Great Depression.

26 STUDY RESOURCES

((•—[Listen to the **Chapter Audio** for Chapter 26 on **myhistorylab.com**

TIMELINE

1932 Franklin D. Roosevelt (FDR) elected president, p. 660

1933 Emergency Banking Relief Act passed in one day (March), p. 661

1935 Wagner Act grants workers collective bargaining rights (July), p. 667
• Social Security Act passed (August), p. 665

1936 FDR reelected president, p. 670

1937 United Automobile Workers sit-down strike forces General Motors contract (February), p. 667
• FDR loses court-packing battle (July), p. 671
• "Roosevelt recession" begins (August), p. 671

CHAPTER REVIEW

THE GREAT DEPRESSION

What were the causes and effects of the Great Depression?

The Great Depression resulted from imbalances in the American economy that developed during the 1920s.

Wealth was unequally distributed, depriving millions of the purchasing power necessary to keep America's factories and farms operating at full capacity. The depression threw millions out of work, out of their homes, and into despair. *(p. 656)*

FIGHTING THE DEPRESSION

How did Franklin Roosevelt fight the Depression?

Roosevelt persuaded Congress to pass relief, recovery, and reform measures known collectively as the New Deal. Begun during the Hundred Days, the New Deal stabilized the banks, reorganized American industry, assisted American agriculture, and put Americans to work conserving and restoring the nation's resources. *(p. 659)*

REFORMING AMERICAN LIFE

How did the New Deal reform American life?

In responses to the challenges of Charles Coughlin, Francis Townsend, and Huey Long, Roosevelt persuaded Congress to approve sweeping measures to reform American life. The Social Security Act established old-age and disability pensions to alleviate poverty among the elderly and those unable to work. *(p. 664)*

THE IMPACT OF THE NEW DEAL

What was the lasting impact of the New Deal?

The New Deal encouraged the emergence of organized labor as a major force in American economic life. It modestly improved the lot of African Americans, although it failed to tackle the racial prejudice that was at the heart of much black poverty. It did little for Mexican Americans, and only a bit more for Native Americans. *(p. 667)*

THE NEW DEAL'S END

How and why did the New Deal end?

After a high point in 1936, the New Deal declined as a result of Roosevelt's overreaching in the court-packing effort, growing resistance from conservatives, and a recession in 1937 that reminded the country that the New Deal had not ended the Great Depression. *(p. 670)*

KEY TERM QUESTIONS

1. What was the New Deal? (p. 656)

2. Why did the Bonus Army march on Washington in 1932? (p. 660)

3. What was the purpose of Roosevelt's fireside chats? (p. 661)

4. Why was the Tennessee Valley Authority created? (p. 661)

5. What was the Civilian Conservation Corps (CCC)? (p. 662)

6. What was the main objective of the Works Progress Administration (WPA)? (p. 662)

7. How did the National Recovery Administration (NRA) try to regulate businesses and labor? (p. 662)

8. How did the Agricultural Adjustment Administration (AAA) affect American farmers? (p. 663)

9. Why was the Social Security Act so important? (p. 665)

10. How did the Wagner Act benefit organized labor? (p. 667)

11. What was FDR's "court-packing" scheme and why did it fail? (p. 671)

MyHistoryLab Connections

Visit **www.myhistorylab.com** for a customized Study Plan to build your knowledge of *Franklin D. Roosevelt and the New Deal, 1929–1939*

Questions for Analysis

1. How does Le Sueur describe the despair she found among unemployed women in Minneapolis?

   📖 **Read** the **Document** *Women on the Breadlines* p. 658

2. What were the strengths and limitations of Roosevelt's New Deal policies?

   🔍 **View** the **Closer Look** *Homeless Shantytown, Seattle, 1937* p. 659

3. How did ordinary Americans bring about change during the 1930s?

   👁 **Watch** the **Video** *Responding to the Great Depression: Whose New Deal?* p. 660

4. What was the significance of the passage of the Social Security Act in 1935?

   📖 **Read** the **Document** *Francis Perkins and the Social Security Act (1935, 1960)* p. 666

5. Why is Dorothea Lange's "Migrant Mother" such an iconic photograph in American history?

   🔍 **View** the **Map** *Dorothea Lange and Migrant Mother* p. 672

Other Resources from this Chapter

🔍 **View** the **Map** *The Great Depression*

🔍 **View** the **Image** *African American Family on the Road*

🔍 **View** the **Image** *Bonus Expeditionary Force, March on Washington*

👁 **Watch** the **Video** *FDR's First Inaugural Address*

🔍 **View** the **Map** *The Tennessee Valley Authority*

📖 **Read** the **Document** *An Attack on New Deal Farm Policies*

👁 **Watch** the **Video** *President Roosevelt Focuses on America's Youth*

📖 **Read** the **Document** *Bob Stinson, Flint Sit-Down Strike, 1936*

Contents and Spotlight Questions

((•—|**Listen** to the **Chapter Audio** for Chapter 27 on **myhistorylab.com**

A PACT WITHOUT POWER

On August 27, 1928, U.S. Secretary of State Frank B. Kellogg, French Premier Aristide Briand, and representatives of 12 other nations met in Paris to sign a treaty outlawing war. Hundreds of spectators crowded into the ornate clock room of the French Foreign Ministry to watch the ceremony. Six huge klieg lights enabled photographers to record the moment for a world eager for peace. Briand declared, "Peace is proclaimed." Then Kellogg signed the document with a foot-long gold pen given to him by French citizens as a token of Franco-American friendship. In the United States, a senator called the **Kellogg–Briand Pact** "the most telling action ever taken in human history to abolish war."

In reality, the pact was the result of American determination to avoid involvement in the European alliance system. In June 1927, Briand had invited the United States to sign a treaty outlawing war between the two nations. The invitation struck a sympathetic response, especially among pacifists who had advocated outlawing war throughout the 1920s, but the State Department feared correctly that Briand's true intention was to strengthen ties between France and the United States. The French had already created a network of alliances with the smaller countries of eastern Europe; an antiwar treaty with the United States would at least ensure American sympathy, if not involvement, in case another war broke out in Europe. Kellogg outmaneuvered Briand by proposing to extend the pledge against war to all nations. Briand, who had wanted a bilateral treaty with the United States, had to agree, and the diplomatic charade culminated in the elaborate signing ceremony in Paris.

Eventually nearly every nation in the world signed the Kellogg–Briand Pact, but the effect was negligible. All promised to renounce war as an instrument of national policy, except of course, as the British made clear, in self-defense. Enforcement of the treaty relied solely on the moral force of world opinion. The pact was, as one senator shrewdly commented, only "an international kiss."

Unfortunately, the pact was also symbolic of American foreign policy immediately following World War I. Instead of asserting the role of world leadership its resources and power commanded, the United States went its own way, extending its trade and economic dominance but refusing to take the lead in maintaining world order. This retreat from responsibility seemed unimportant in the 1920s, when exhaustion from World War I ensured relative peace and tranquility. But in the 1930s, when aggressive powers threatened world order in Europe and Asia, the American people retreated even deeper, searching for an isolationist policy that would spare them the agony of another great war.

There was no place to hide in the modern world, however. The Nazi onslaught in Europe and Japanese expansion in Asia finally convinced America to reverse its isolationism and enter World War II in December 1941, when the chances for an Allied victory seemed most remote. With incredible swiftness, the nation mobilized its military and industrial strength. American armies were soon fighting on three continents, the U.S. Navy controlled the world's oceans, and American factories were sending war supplies to more than 20 Allied countries.

When victory came in 1945, the United States was the most powerful nation in the world. But the end of the war brought a new era of tension and rivalry. This time the United States could not retreat from responsibility. World War II was a coming of age for American foreign policy.

ISOLATIONISM

What was isolationism, and why was it so appealing to Americans in the 1920s and 1930s?

American disillusionment with international affairs became evident soon after World War I. The Senate's rejection of the Treaty of Versailles left the United States outside the League of Nations, where it remained for the life of that ill-fated organization. American financial connections to Europe grew during the 1920s, but the United States kept its distance politically. The retreat from an active world policy in the 1920s turned into a headlong flight back to isolationism in the 1930s. Two factors were responsible. First, the depression made foreign policy seem remote and unimportant. As unemployment increased and the economic crisis intensified after 1929, many people grew apathetic about events abroad. Second, when the danger of war abroad did finally penetrate the American consciousness, it only strengthened the desire to stay out of it.

Three powerful and discontented nations were on the march in the 1930s—Germany, Italy, and Japan. In Germany, Adolf Hitler came to power in 1933 as the head of the National Socialist, or Nazi, movement. A shrewd and charismatic leader, Hitler capitalized on both domestic discontent and bitterness over World War I. Blaming the Jews for Germany's ills and asserting the supremacy of the "Aryan" race of blond, blue-eyed Germans, he quickly imposed a totalitarian dictatorship in which the Nazi party ruled, and he, the Leader or *Führer*, was supreme. At first, his foreign policy seemed harmless, but as he consolidated his power, the threat he represented to world peace became clear. Hitler took Germany out of the League of Nations, reoccupied the Rhineland, and formally denounced the Treaty of Versailles. His massive rearmament and boasts of uniting all Germans into a Greater Third Reich that would last 1,000 years terrified his European opponents, blocking any effective challenge to his regime.

Watch the Video
Hitler and Roosevelt on
myhistorylab.com

In Italy, another dictator, Benito Mussolini, had come to power in 1922. Emboldened by Hitler's success, he embarked on an aggressive foreign policy in 1935. His invasion of the independent African nation of Ethiopia led its emperor, Haile Selassie, to call on the League of Nations for support. With Britain and France far more concerned about Hitler than events in East Africa, the League's halfhearted measures failed to halt Mussolini's conquest of all of Ethiopia. "Fifty-two nations had combined to resist aggression," commented historian A. J. P. Taylor; "all they accomplished was that Haile Selassie lost all his country instead of only half." Collective security had failed its most important test.

Japan was the third threat to world peace. Militarists began to dominate the government in Tokyo by the mid-1930s, intimidating and even assassinating their liberal opponents. By 1936, Japan had also left the League of Nations. A year later, its armies invaded China, marking the beginning of the Pacific phase of World War II.

The resurgence of militarism in Germany, Italy, and Japan undermined the Versailles settlement and destroyed the balance of power. Britain and France in Europe proved as powerless as China in Asia to stop the tide of aggression. In 1937, the three totalitarian nations signed a pact forming a Berlin–Rome–Tokyo axis. This alliance of the **Axis Powers** ostensibly was aimed at communism and the Soviet Union, but it threatened the entire world. Only a determined American response could unite the other nations against the Axis threat. Unfortunately, the United States deliberately avoided this leadership until it was nearly too late.

The Lure of Pacifism and Neutrality

The danger of war abroad increased American desire for peace and noninvolvement. Memories of World War I were vivid. Erich Maria Remarque's novel *All Quiet on the Western Front*, and the movie based on it, reminded people of the brutality of war.

The pacifism that swept college campuses in the 1930s touched students at the University of Chicago. These undergraduates hold placards bearing antiwar slogans as they wait to join a parade as part of a nationwide demonstration against war.

Historians began to treat the Great War as a mistake, criticizing Wilson for not preserving American neutrality and claiming the British had duped the United States into entering the war. Walter Millis's *America's Road to War, 1914–1917*, published in 1935, was hailed for exposing how "a peace-loving democracy, muddled but excited, misinformed and whipped to a frenzy, embarked upon its greatest foreign war."

American youth were determined not to repeat their elders' mistakes. Pacifism swept college campuses. At Brown University, 72 percent of the students opposed military service in wartime. At Princeton, undergraduates formed the Veterans of Future Wars, a parody on veterans' groups, to demand a bonus of $1,000 apiece before they marched off to a foreign war. In April 1934, students and professors walked out of class to attend massive antiwar rallies, which became an annual rite of spring in the 1930s. Demonstrators carried signs reading "Abolish the R.O.T.C." and "Build Schools—Not Battleships." Pacifist orators urged students to pledge not to support their country "in any war it might conduct."

The pacifist movement found a scapegoat in the munitions industry. Books exposing the unsavory tactics of large arms dealers such as Krupp in Germany and Vickers in Britain led to a demand to curb these "merchants of death." Senator Gerald Nye of North Dakota headed a Senate committee that spent two years investigating American munitions dealers. The committee revealed the enormous profits firms such as Du Pont reaped from World War I, but Nye also charged that bankers and munitions makers were responsible for American intervention in 1917. No proof was forthcoming, but the public—prepared to believe the worst of businessmen during the Great Depression—accepted the "merchants of death" thesis.

The Nye Committee's revelations culminated in legislation. Congress passed three neutrality acts to keep the United States out of war. A 1935 law banned the sale of arms to nations at war and warned Americans not to sail on belligerent ships. In 1936, a second act banned loans to countries at war. A third neutrality act in 1937 made these prohibitions permanent and required, on a two-year trial basis, that all trade, other than in munitions, between the U.S. and belligerent powers be conducted on a cash-and-carry basis. American ships were forbidden to carry any goods or passengers to the ports of any nation at war or fighting a civil war.

Quick Check

✓ What was the purpose of the neutrality acts?

War in Europe

The neutrality legislation played directly into Hitler's hands. Bent on conquering Europe, he could now proceed without worrying about American interference. In

March 1938, he seized Austria in a bloodless coup. Six months later, he demanded the Sudetenland, a province of Czechoslovakia with a largely German population. When the British and French leaders agreed to meet with Hitler at Munich to resolve the crisis, FDR approved. Roosevelt kept the United States aloof from the decision to appease Hitler by surrendering the Sudetenland. But he gave his tacit approval of appeasement by telling the British prime minister that he shared his "hope and belief that there exists today the greatest opportunity in years for the establishment of a new order based on justice and on law."

Six months after the meeting at Munich, Hitler violated his promises by seizing nearly all of what remained of Czechoslovakia. In the United States, Roosevelt permitted the State Department to press for revising the neutrality acts. The administration's proposal to repeal the arms embargo and place all trade with belligerents, including munitions, on a cash-and-carry basis met stubborn resistance from isolationists. They argued that cash-and-carry would favor Britain and France, who controlled the sea. The House rejected the measure by a narrow margin, and the Senate's Foreign Relations Committee voted 12 to 11 to postpone neutrality revision.

In July 1939, Roosevelt finally abandoned his aloof position and pleaded with Senate leaders to reconsider. The president's and secretary of state's warnings that war in Europe was imminent failed to impress the isolationists. Senator William Borah, who had led the fight against the League of Nations in 1919, responded that he believed the chances for war in Europe were remote. Vice President John Nance Garner told FDR that neutrality revision was dead: "You haven't got the votes, and that's all there is to it."

On September 1, 1939, Hitler began World War II by invading Poland. Two days later, Britain and France declared war, although they could not prevent the German conquest of Poland. Russia had refused Western overtures for a common front against Germany and signed a nonaggression treaty with Hitler in late August. This Nazi–Soviet Pact enabled Germany to avoid a two-front war; the Russians' reward was half of Poland.

Roosevelt proclaimed American neutrality, but the successful aggression by Nazi Germany brought into question the isolationist assumption that American well-being did not depend on the European balance of power. Strategic and ideological considerations undermined the belief that the United States could safely pursue a policy of neutrality and noninvolvement. The long retreat from responsibility was about to end as Americans came to realize that their own democracy and security were at stake in the European war.

View the **Map**
World War II in Europe on
myhistorylab.com

Quick Check

✓ What was the American response to the outbreak of war in Europe?

THE ROAD TO WAR

For two years, the United States tried to remain at peace while war raged in Europe and Asia. In contrast to the mood in 1914–1917, when Wilson attempted to be impartial during World War I, the American people this time displayed overwhelming sympathy for the Allies and distaste for Germany and Japan. Roosevelt openly favored an Allied victory, but fear of isolationist criticism compelled him to move slowly, and often deviously, in helping Britain and France.

How did the United States go from neutrality in the 1930s to war in 1941?

Kneeling at the Capitol Plaza in Washington, members of the "Mothers' Crusade" conduct a pray-in to protest the passage of the Lend-Lease Act.

From Neutrality to Undeclared War

Two weeks after the outbreak of war in Europe, Roosevelt called Congress into special session to revise the neutrality legislation. He wanted to supply weapons to Britain and France, but he refused to state this openly. Instead, he again asked Congress to replace the arms embargo with cash-and-carry regulations. Belligerents could purchase war supplies in the United States, but they would have to pay cash and transport the goods in their own ships. Public opinion supported the president, and Congress passed the legislation in November 1939.

Dramatic German victories profoundly affected American opinion. Quiet during the winter of 1939–1940, the Germans struck in the spring. In April, they seized Denmark and Norway. On May 10, they unleashed the *blitzkrieg* (lightning war) on the western front. Using tanks, infantry, and dive-bombers in close coordination, the German army overran the Netherlands, Belgium, and Luxembourg en route to France. It split the British and French forces, driving the British off the continent at Dunkirk. In June, France fell to Hitler's war machine.

Americans were stunned. Hitler had taken only six weeks to achieve what Germany had failed to do in four years in World War I. Suddenly they realized they had a stake in the outcome; if Britain fell, Hitler might gain control of the British navy. Instead of a barrier, the Atlantic would be a highway for German penetration of the New World.

Roosevelt responded with a policy of all-out aid to the Allies, short of war. In a speech at Charlottesville, Virginia, in June (just after Italy invaded France), he denounced Germany and Italy as representing "the gods of force and hate. . . . The whole of our sympathies lies with those nations that are giving their life blood in combat against these forces." It was too late to help France, but in September, FDR transferred 50 old destroyers to Britain in exchange for rights to build air and naval bases in the British West Indies. Giving warships to a belligerent nation was a breach of neutrality, but Roosevelt stressed the importance of guarding the Atlantic approaches, calling the destroyers-for-bases deal "the most important action in the reinforcement of our national defense that has been taken since the Louisiana Purchase."

Isolationists attacked this departure from neutrality. The *St. Louis Post-Dispatch* proclaimed, "Dictator Roosevelt Commits Act of War." The America First Committee protested the drift toward war. Such diverse individuals as aviator-hero Charles Lindbergh, conservative Senator Robert A. Taft of Ohio, socialist leader Norman Thomas, and liberal educator Robert M. Hutchins condemned FDR for involving the United States in a foreign conflict. Voicing belief in a "Fortress America," they denied that Hitler threatened American security and claimed that the nation could defend itself regardless of what happened in Europe.

Opponents of the isolationists organized the Committee to Defend America by Aiding the Allies. Eastern Anglophiles, moderate New Dealers, and liberal Republicans made up the bulk of the membership. Kansas newspaper editor William Allen White was chairman. The White Committee, as it became known, advocated unlimited assistance to Britain short of war, although some of its members favored entering the conflict. Above all, the interventionists challenged the isolationist premise that events in Europe did not affect American security. "The future of western civilization is being decided upon the battlefield of Europe," White declared.

In the ensuing debate, the American people gradually sided with the interventionists. The Battle of Britain—Germany's air assault on Britain—helped. "Every time Hitler bombed London, we got a couple of votes," noted one interventionist. In 1940, Congress increased the defense budget from $2 billion to $10 billion and approved the first peacetime draft in American history.

The sense of crisis affected domestic politics. Roosevelt ran for an unprecedented third term in 1940 because of the European war; the Republicans nominated Wendell Willkie, a former Democratic businessman who shared FDR's commitment to aid Britain. Both candidates appealed to peace sentiment during the campaign, but Roosevelt's decisive victory made it clear that the nation supported his departure from neutrality. (See Table 27.1.)

After the election, FDR took his boldest step. Responding to Prime Minister Winston Churchill's warning that Britain was running out of money, the president asked Congress to approve a new program to provide goods and weapons to countries fighting aggressors. Roosevelt's call for America to become "the great arsenal of democracy" seemed straightforward enough, but he acted deviously by calling it Lend-Lease and comparing it to loaning a neighbor a garden hose to put out a fire.

Isolationists denounced Lend-Lease as unnecessary and untruthful. "Lending war equipment is a good deal like lending chewing gum," commented Senator Taft. "You don't want it back." In March 1941, however, Congress authorized the president to "sell, transfer title to, exchange, lease, lend, or otherwise dispose of" war supplies to "any country the President deems vital to the defense of the United States." A $7 billion appropriation ended the "cash" part of cash-and-carry and assured Britain full access to American war supplies.

The "carry" problem remained. German submarines were sinking more than 500,000 tons of shipping a month. Britain desperately needed the help of the American navy in escorting convoys across the U-boat–infested North Atlantic. Roosevelt, fearful of isolationist reaction, responded with naval patrols in the western half of the ocean. Hitler placed his submarine commanders under strict restraints to

Read the **Document**
Charles Lindbergh, Radio Address (1941) on **myhistorylab.com**

Read the **Document**
Franklin D. Roosevelt, "The Four Freedoms" (1941) on **myhistorylab.com**

TABLE 27.1   The Election of 1940

Candidate	Party	Popular Vote	Electoral Vote
Roosevelt	Democratic	27,244,160	449
Willkie	Republican	22,305,198	82

avoid drawing America into the European war. Nevertheless, incidents occurred. In September 1941, after a U-boat narrowly missed torpedoing an American destroyer tracking it, Roosevelt denounced the German submarines as the "rattlesnakes of the Atlantic" and ordered the navy to convey British ships halfway across the ocean.

Undeclared naval war followed. On October 17, 1941, a German submarine damaged the U.S. destroyer *Kearney*; ten days later, another U-boat sank the *Reuben James*, killing more than 100 American sailors. FDR ordered the destroyers to shoot U-boats on sight. He also asked Congress to repeal the "carry" section of the neutrality laws and permit American ships to deliver supplies to Britain. In mid-November, Congress approved these moves by slim margins. Now American merchant ships would also become targets. By December, it seemed that repeated sinkings would soon lead to a formal declaration of war against Germany.

In leading the nation to the brink of war in Europe, Roosevelt opened himself to criticism from both sides in the domestic debate. Interventionists believed he had been too cautious in dealing with the danger Nazi Germany posed. Isolationists claimed he had misled the American people by professing peace while plotting war. Roosevelt was certainly less than candid, relying on executive discretion to engage in provocative acts in the North Atlantic. He agreed with the interventionists that a German victory would threaten American security. But he also was aware that a poll in September 1941 showed nearly 80 percent of the American people wanted to stay out of World War II. Realizing that leading a divided nation into war would be disastrous, FDR played for time, inching the country toward war while waiting for the Axis nations to make the ultimate move. Japan finally obliged at Pearl Harbor.

Quick Check

✓ How did FDR overcome the opposition to war?

Showdown in the Pacific

Japan had taken advantage of the war in Europe to expand in Asia. Although they had conquered the populous coastal areas of China, the Japanese had been unable to overcome Chiang Kai-shek, whose Nationalist forces retreated into the vast interior of the country. The German defeat of France and the Netherlands in 1940, however, left their colonies in the East Indies and Indochina defenseless. Japan now set out to incorporate these territories—rich in oil, tin, and rubber—into what it called a Greater East Asia Co-Prosperity Sphere.

The Roosevelt administration countered with economic pressure. Japan depended heavily on the United States for petroleum and scrap metal. In July 1940, Roosevelt set up a licensing and quota system for exporting these crucial materials to Japan and banned the sale of aviation gasoline altogether. With Britain fighting for survival and France and the Netherlands occupied by Germany, the United States was now employing economic sanctions to defend Southeast Asia against Japanese expansion.

Tokyo appeared unimpressed. In September, Japanese troops occupied bases in northern French Indochina, and Japan signed the Tripartite Pact with Germany and Italy, a defensive treaty that confronted the United States with a possible two-ocean war. The new Axis pact confirmed American suspicions that Japan was part of a worldwide totalitarian threat. Roosevelt and his advisers, however, saw Germany as the primary danger; thus they pursued a policy of all-out aid to Britain while hoping that economic measures alone would deter Japan.

The embargo on aviation gasoline, extended to include scrap iron and steel in late September 1940, was a burden Japan could bear, but banning all oil shipments was different. Japan was entirely dependent on petroleum imports from the United States and the Dutch East Indies. To ease the economic pressure through negotiation, Japan sent a new envoy to Washington in spring 1941. But the talks broke down. Tokyo wanted a free hand in China and an end to American sanctions; the United States insisted that Japan evacuate all of China.

In July 1941, Japan occupied all of Indochina, beginning the chain of events that led to war. Washington knew of this aggression before it occurred. Naval intelligence had broken the Japanese diplomatic code and was reading all messages between Tokyo and its embassy in Washington. On July 25, 1941, Roosevelt froze all Japanese assets in the United States. This step, intended only as a temporary warning, became a permanent embargo due to positive public reaction and State Department zeal. Trade with Japan, including the vital oil shipments, stopped. When the Dutch government-in-exile took similar action, Japan faced a dilemma: To get oil shipments resumed, Tokyo would have to end its aggression; the alternative would be to seize the needed petroleum supplies in the Dutch East Indies, which would mean war.

After a final diplomatic effort failed, General Hideki Tojo, an army militant, became the new premier of Japan. To mask its war preparations, Tokyo sent yet another envoy to Washington with new proposals. Code breaking enabled American diplomats to learn that the Japanese terms were unacceptable even before they were presented. Military leaders urged President Roosevelt to reach at least a temporary settlement with Japan to give them time to prepare American defenses in the Pacific. Secretary of State Cordell Hull, however, refused any concession; on November 26, he again demanded Japan withdraw from China.

The Japanese response came two weeks later. On the evening of December 6, 1941, the first 13 parts of the reply to Hull's note arrived at the Japanese embassy in Washington, with the fourteenth part to follow the next morning. Naval intelligence decoded the message faster than the embassy clerks. Roosevelt read it that night and commented, "This means war." The next day, December 7, the fourteenth part revealed that Japan rejected the American position.

Officials in Washington immediately sent warnings to American bases in the Pacific, but they arrived too late. At 7:55 in the morning, just before 1 P.M. in Washington, Japanese

Four American battleships were destroyed in the surprise attack on Pearl Harbor, December 7, 1941. Caught completely off guard, U.S. forces still managed to shoot down 29 enemy planes.

carrier-based planes caught the American fleet at Pearl Harbor by surprise. In little more than an hour, they crippled the Pacific fleet and its major base, sinking four battleships, damaging four more, and killing more than 2,400 American sailors.

In Washington, the Japanese envoys had requested a meeting with Secretary Hull at 1 P.M. Just before the meeting, news arrived of the attack on Pearl Harbor. Hull read the note the Japanese handed him and then, unable to restrain himself any longer, burst out, "In all my fifty years of public service, I have never seen a document that was more crowded with infamous falsehoods and distortions—on a scale so huge that I never imagined until today that any government was capable of uttering them."

Speaking before Congress the next day, President Roosevelt termed December 7 "a date which will live in infamy" and asked for a declaration of war on Japan. With only one dissenting vote, both branches passed the measure. On December 11, Germany and Italy declared war against the United States; the nation was now fully involved in World War II.

Quick Check

✓ What led Japan to attack Pearl Harbor?

TURNING THE TIDE AGAINST THE AXIS

How did America and its allies halt the advances of Germany and Japan?

The outlook for victory was bleak. Hitler's armies controlled Europe, from Norway in the north to Greece in the south. Despite their nonaggression pact, Germany had invaded Russia in June 1941. Although they had failed to capture either Moscow or Leningrad, the Nazi forces had conquered Ukraine and by 1942 were threatening to cross the Volga River and seize vital oil fields in the Caucasus. In North Africa, General Erwin Rommel's Afrika Korps had pushed the British back into Egypt and threatened the Suez Canal (see Map 27.1).

The situation was no better in Asia. Within three months after Pearl Harbor, the Japanese had conquered British Malaya and Burma and the Dutch East Indies, with its valuable oil fields, and were pressing the British back in New Guinea. American forces under General Douglas MacArthur had been overwhelmed in the Philippines. With the American navy still recovering from Pearl Harbor, Japan controlled the Pacific as far as Hawaii (see Map 27.2).

Over the next two years, the United States and its allies would halt the German and Japanese offensives in Europe and Asia. But then they faced the challenge of driving back the enemy, freeing the conquered areas, and defeating the Axis powers on their home territory. The struggle would require sacrifice and heavy losses; World War II would test American will and resourcefulness to the utmost.

Wartime Partnerships

The greatest single advantage that the United States and its partners possessed was their willingness to form a genuine coalition to defeat the Axis powers. Although the wartime alliance was often strained, it still permitted considerable coordination. In contrast, Germany and Japan each fought a separate war without any attempt at cooperation.

The United States and Britain achieved a complete partnership. A Combined Chiefs of Staff, headquartered in Washington, directed Anglo-American military

Map 27.1 *World War II in the Pacific*   The tide of battle turned in the Pacific the same year as in Europe. The balance of sea power shifted back to the United States from Japan after the naval victories of 1942.

operations. The close cooperation between Roosevelt and Churchill ensured a common strategy. The leaders decided that a German victory was the greater danger and thus gave priority to the war in Europe. In December 1941, Roosevelt and Churchill signed a Declaration of the United Nations, to which 26 countries eventually subscribed, that pledged them to defeat the Axis powers.

Relations with the other members of the United Nations coalition in World War II were less harmonious. The decision to defeat Germany first displeased the Chinese, who had been fighting Japan since 1937. Roosevelt tried to appease Chiang Kai-shek with a trickle of supplies, flown in at great risk by Americans over the Himalayas from India. France posed a more delicate problem. FDR virtually ignored the Free French government-in-exile under General Charles de Gaulle. Roosevelt preferred to deal with the pro-German regime at Vichy in France, because it controlled the French fleet and most of France's overseas territories.

The greatest strain within the wartime coalition was with the Soviet Union. Although Roosevelt had recognized the Soviet regime in 1933, ties were not close.

Map 27.2 *World War II in Europe and North Africa*   The tide of battle shifted in this theater during the winter of 1942–1943. At Stalingrad the Russians turned back massive German assault on the eastern front, and the Allied forces recaptured North Africa.

The Russian refusal to pay prerevolutionary debts and Soviet support of communists in the United States in the 1930s intensified American distaste for Stalin's regime. The great Russian purge trials and the Nazi–Soviet alliance from 1939 to 1941, along with deep-seated cultural and ideological differences, made wartime cooperation difficult.

Ever the pragmatist, Roosevelt tried to establish a more cordial relationship with Russia during the war. Even before Pearl Harbor, he extended Lend-Lease aid to Russia, and after American entry into the war, only the difficulty of delivering the supplies limited this economic assistance. Eager to keep Russia in the war, the president promised in May 1942 that the United States would create a second front in Europe by the end of that year—a pledge he could not fulfill. But in January 1943, Roosevelt and Churchill met in Casablanca, Morocco, where they demanded

At their meeting at Casablanca, Morocco, in January 1943, President Roosevelt and British Prime Minister Winston Churchill announced that the unconditional surrender of the Axis powers would be the only acceptable basis for ending the war.

unconditional surrender, vowing that the Allies would fight until the Axis nations were completely defeated.

Despite these promises, the Soviet Union bore the brunt of battle against Hitler, fighting alone against two-thirds of the German army. The United States and Britain, grateful for the respite to build up their forces, could only promise future help and send supplies. The result was a rift that never healed—one that did not prevent the defeat of Germany but did ensure future tensions between the Soviet Union and the West.

Quick Check

✓ What countries were America's principal allies during the war?

Halting the German Blitz

From the outset, the United States favored an invasion across the English Channel. Army planners, led by Chief of Staff George C. Marshall and his protégé, Dwight D. Eisenhower, were convinced such a frontal assault would be the quickest way to win the war. Roosevelt concurred, in part because it fulfilled his second-front commitment to the Soviets.

Eisenhower's initial plan called for a full-scale invasion of Europe in the spring of 1943 and a temporary beachhead in France in the fall of 1942 if necessary to keep Russia in the war. But the British, remembering the heavy casualties of trench warfare in World War I, and hoping to protect the route to India, their most important colony, preferred a perimeter approach. Air and naval attacks around the edge of the continent, especially in the Mediterranean, would be a prelude to an invasion of Germany. British strategists wanted to invade North Africa first. Roosevelt also wanted American troops fighting Germans before the end of 1942 to offset pressure at home to concentrate on the Pacific; hence, he overruled objections from his military advisers, and American and British troops landed in Morocco and Algeria in November 1942.

The British also attacked Rommel at El Alamein in Egypt and soon forced the Afrika Korps to retreat to Tunisia. Eisenhower, delayed by poor roads and bad weather, was slow in bringing up his forces from the west, and in their first encounter with Rommel at the Kasserine Pass south of Tunis, inexperienced American troops suffered a humiliating defeat. General George Patton rallied the demoralized soldiers, and by May 1943, Germany had been driven from Africa, leaving behind nearly 300,000 prisoners.

During these same months, the Soviets had broken the back of German military power in the Battle of Stalingrad. Turned back at the critical bend in the Volga, Hitler had poured in division after division in what was ultimately a lost cause.

At Churchill's insistence, FDR agreed to follow up the North African campaign by invading Sicily and then Italy in the summer of 1943. Italy dropped out of the war when Mussolini fled to Germany, but the Italian campaign was a strategic dead end. Germany sent in enough divisions to establish a strong defense, and Allied troops had to fight their way slowly up the peninsula, suffering heavy casualties.

Moreover, these Mediterranean operations delayed the second front until June 1944. Meanwhile, the Soviets began to push the Germans out of Russia and looked forward to the conquest of eastern Europe, where they could establish "friendly" communist regimes. Having borne the brunt of the fighting against Nazi Germany, Russia was ready to claim its reward—the postwar domination of eastern Europe.

Quick Check

✓ Where did the Allies achieve early victories over Germany?

Checking Japan in the Pacific

Both the decision to defeat Germany first and the vast expanses of the Pacific dictated the nature of the war against Japan. The United States conducted amphibious island-hopping campaigns rather than attempt to reconquer Southeast Asia and China. There would be two separate American offensives. One, led by Douglas MacArthur, would move from New Guinea back to the Philippines, while the other, commanded by Admiral Chester Nimitz, was directed at key Japanese islands in the Central Pacific. The original plan called for the two offensives to come together for the final invasion of the Japanese home islands.

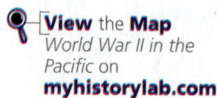

View the **Map**
*World War II in the
Pacific* on
myhistorylab.com

Success in the Pacific depended on control of the sea. The devastation at Pearl Harbor gave Japan the edge, but fortunately, the United States had not lost any of its four aircraft carriers. In the Battle of the Coral Sea in May 1942, American naval forces blocked a Japanese thrust to outflank Australia. The turning point came one month later at Midway. A Japanese task force threatened this remote American outpost more than 1,000 miles west of Pearl Harbor; Japan's real objective was to destroy what remained of the American Pacific fleet. Superior air power enabled

Nimitz's forces to engage the enemy at long range. Japanese fighters shot down 35 of 41 attacking torpedo bombers, but a second wave of dive-bombers sank three Japanese carriers. In all, Japan lost four carriers at Midway compared to the loss of just one American carrier. It was the first defeat the modern Japanese navy had ever suffered, and it left the United States in control of the Central Pacific.

American forces then launched their first Pacific offensive in the Solomon Islands, east of New Guinea, in August 1942. Both sides suffered heavy losses, but six months later, the Japanese were driven from the key island of Guadalcanal. MacArthur also began the long, slow, bloody job of driving the Japanese back along the north coast of New Guinea.

By early 1943, Japan was on the defensive, and the United States was preparing to penetrate the Gilbert, Marshall, and Caroline Islands and recapture the Philippines. Just as Russia had broken German power in Europe, so the United States, fighting alone except for Australia and New Zealand, had halted the Japanese. And, like the USSR in eastern Europe, America expected to reap the rewards of victory by dominating the Pacific in the future.

> **Quick Check**
> ✓ How did the United States break Japan's momentum in the Pacific?

THE HOME FRONT

World War II affected American life more than the Great Depression had. While American soldiers and sailors fought overseas, the nation underwent sweeping social and economic changes. American industry worked to capacity to meet the need for war materials. Increased production in industry and agriculture benefited workers and farmers. The expansion of war-related industries encouraged people to move to where new jobs had sprung up. Women entered the paid workforce; rural dwellers relocated to urban areas; and northerners and easterners sought new opportunities and homes in the South and West. FDR also benefited from the return to prosperity the war brought on. The economic recovery helped him win a fourth term in 1944.

How did American domestic life change during World War II?

The Arsenal of Democracy

American industry made the nation's most important contribution to victory. Although more than 15 million Americans served in the armed forces, it was the nearly 60 million who worked on farms and factories who achieved the miracle of production that ensured the defeat of Germany and Japan. Manufacturing plants that had run at half capacity through the 1930s now hummed with activity. In Detroit, automobile assembly lines were converted to produce tanks and airplanes. At Henry Ford's giant Willow Run factory, covering 67 acres, 42,000 workers turned out a B-24 bomber every hour. Henry J. Kaiser, a California industrialist who constructed huge West Coast shipyards to meet the demand for cargo vessels and landing craft, operated on an equally large scale. His plant in Richmond, California, reduced the time to build a merchant ship from 105 to 14 days. In part, America won the battle of the Atlantic by building ships faster than German U-boats could sink them.

View the **Image**
Heel Hitler Poster on
myhistorylab.com

This vast industrial expansion, however, created problems. In 1942, President Roosevelt appointed Donald Nelson, a Sears, Roebuck executive, to head a War Production Board (WPB). A jovial, easygoing man, Nelson soon was outmaneuvered by the army and navy, which preferred to negotiate directly with large corporations. The WPB allowed business to claim rapid depreciation, and thus huge tax credits, for new plants and awarded lucrative cost-plus contracts for urgently needed goods. Shortages of critical materials such as steel, aluminum, and copper led to an allocation system based on military priorities. Rubber, cut off by the Japanese conquest of Southeast Asia, was particularly scarce; the administration finally began gasoline rationing in 1943 to curb pleasure driving and prolong tire life. The government built 51 synthetic-rubber plants, which by 1944 were producing nearly a million tons a year for the tires of American airplanes and military vehicles. All in all, the nation's factories turned out twice as many goods as did German and Japanese industry combined.

Roosevelt revealed the same tendency toward compromise in directing the economic mobilization as he did in shaping the New Deal. When the Office of Price Administration—which tried to curb inflation by controlling prices and rationing scarce goods such as sugar, canned food, and shoes—clashed with the WPB, FDR appointed James Byrnes to head an Office of Economic Stabilization. Byrnes, a former South Carolina senator and Supreme Court justice, used political judgment to settle disputes between agencies and keep all groups happy. The president also compromised with Congress, which pared down the administration's requests for large tax increases. Borrowing financed half the cost of the war, although taxes did rise. A $7 billion tax increase in 1942 included so many new taxpayers that in 1943 the Treasury Department instituted a new practice—withholding income taxes from workers' wages.

Quick Check

✓ How was industry reorganized during the war?

A Nation on the Move

The war led to a vast migration of the American population. Young men left home for training camps and service overseas. Defense workers and their families, 9 million people in all, moved to work in the booming war industries. Norfolk, Virginia; San Diego, California; Mobile, Alabama; and other centers of defense production grew by more than 50 percent in just a year or two. Rural areas lost population while coastal regions, especially along the Pacific and the Gulf of Mexico, drew millions of people. Putting army camps, aircraft factories, and shipyards in the South and West created boom conditions in the future Sunbelt. California's population increased by nearly 2 million in less than five years.

This massive relocation caused severe social problems. Housing was in short supply. Migrating workers crowded into house trailers and boardinghouses, bringing unexpected windfalls to landlords. In one boomtown, a reporter described an old Victorian house that had five bedrooms on the second floor: "Three of them held two cots apiece, the two others held three cots." But the owner revealed that "the third floor is where we pick up the velvet. . . . We rent to workers in different shifts . . . three shifts a day . . . seven bucks a week apiece."

Family life suffered under these conditions. The number of marriages increased, as young people searched for something to hang on to amidst wartime turmoil, but so did the divorce rate. The baby boom that would peak in the 1950s began during the war and brought its own problems. Few publicly funded day-care centers were available, and working mothers worried about their "latchkey children." Schools in boom areas could not cope with the influx of new students; a teacher shortage, intensified by the lure of higher wages in war industries, compounded the education crisis.

Despite these problems, women found the war a time of economic opportunity. Women's employment outside the home rose from 14 million in 1940 to 19 million by 1945. Most of the new women workers were married, and many were middle-aged, thus broadening the composition of the female workforce, which in the past had been composed primarily of young single women. Women entered industries once viewed as exclusively male; by the end of the war, they tended blast furnaces in steel mills and welded hulls in shipyards alongside men. Few challenged the traditional view of gender roles, yet the wartime experience temporarily undermined the concept that woman's proper place was in the home. Women enjoyed the hefty weekly paychecks, which rose by 50 percent from 1941 to 1943, and they took pride in their contributions to the war effort. "To hell with the life I have had," commented a former fashion designer. "This war is too damn serious, and it is too damn important to win it."

African Americans shared in the wartime migration, but racial prejudice limited their social and economic gains. Nearly one million served in the armed forces, but relatively few saw combat. The army placed black soldiers in segregated units, usually led by white officers, and used them for service and construction tasks. The navy relegated them to menial jobs until late in the war. African Americans were denied the chance to become petty officers, Secretary of the Navy Frank Knox explained, because "men of the colored race . . . cannot maintain discipline among men of the white race."

Watch the **Video**
Rosie the Riveter on
myhistorylab.com

African American civilians fared better. In 1941, black labor leader A. Philip Randolph threatened a massive march on Washington to force President Roosevelt to end racial discrimination in defense industries and government employment and to integrate the armed forces. FDR persuaded Randolph to call off the march and drop his integration demand in return for an executive order creating a Fair Employment Practices Committee (FEPC) to ban racial discrimination in war industries. As a result, African American employment by the federal government rose from 60,000 in 1941 to 200,000 by 1945. The FEPC was less successful in the private

As men left for military service in World War II and U.S. industry expanded to keep up with the defense needs, millions of women joined the paid labor force. The women shown here are operating a bolt-cutting machine at a factory in Erie, Pennsylvania.

sector. Underfunded and understaffed, it could act on only one-third of the 8,000 complaints it received. The nationwide shortage of labor did more than the FEPC to raise black employment during wartime. African Americans moved from the rural South to northern and western cities, finding jobs in the automobile, aircraft, and shipbuilding industries.

The movement of an estimated 700,000 people helped transform black–white relations from a regional issue into a national concern that could no longer be ignored. The limited housing and recreational facilities for both black and white war workers created tensions that led to urban race riots. On a hot Sunday evening in June 1943, blacks and whites began exchanging insults and then blows near Belle Isle recreation park in Detroit. The next day, a full-scale riot broke out in which 23 blacks and nine whites died. The fighting raged for 24 hours until national guard troops restored order. Later that summer, only personal intervention by New York Mayor Fiorello LaGuardia quelled a Harlem riot in which six blacks died.

Read the
Document
Jim Crow in the Army Camps on
myhistorylab.com

These outbursts of racial violence fueled the resentments that would grow into the postwar civil rights movement. For most African Americans, despite economic gains, World War II was a reminder of the inequality of American life. "Just carve on my tombstone," remarked one black soldier in the Pacific, "'Here lies a black man killed fighting a yellow man for the protection of a white man.'"

More than 300,000 Mexican Americans served in the armed forces and shared some of the same experiences as African Americans. Although they were not as segregated, many served in the 88th Division, made up largely of Mexican American officers and troops, which earned the nickname "Blue Devils" in the Italian campaign. At home, Spanish-speaking people left rural Texas, New Mexico, and California for jobs in the cities, especially in aircraft plants and petroleum refineries. Despite low wages and union resistance, they improved their economic position substantially. But they still faced discrimination based on skin color and language, most notably in the Los Angeles "zoot suit" riots in 1943 when white sailors attacked Mexican American youths dressed in their distinctive outfits—long jackets worn with pants tightly pegged at the ankles. The racial prejudice heightened feelings of ethnic identity and led returning Mexican American veterans to form organizations such as the American G.I. Forum to press for equal rights.

Native Americans joined the military in large numbers relative to their share of the population. Citing their warrior heritage, many enlisted without waiting for the draft to select them. "Since when has it been necessary for Blackfeet to draw lots to fight?" one member of that tribe asked scornfully. Native Americans fought in various theaters; among the most celebrated were the Navajo "code talkers," radiomen of the U.S. Marine Corps who employed their tribal language to frustrate Japanese eavesdropping.

Read the
Document
Japanese relocation order on
myhistorylab.com

A tragic counterpoint to the voluntary movement of American workers in search of jobs was the forced relocation of 120,000 Japanese Americans from the West Coast. Responding to racial fears in California after Pearl Harbor, President Roosevelt approved an army order in February 1942 to move all Japanese Americans on the West Coast to concentration camps in the interior. More than two-thirds of those detained were Nisei, native-born Americans whose only "crime" was their Japanese ancestry. Forced to sell their farms and businesses at distress prices, the Japanese Americans lost their worldly goods and their liberty. Herded into ten hastily built detention centers in seven western and southern states, they became prisoners in flimsy barracks behind barbed wire, guarded by armed troops.

Appeals to the Supreme Court proved fruitless; in 1944, six justices upheld relocation on grounds of national security in wartime. Beginning in 1943, individual Nisei could win release by pledging their loyalty and finding a job away from the West Coast. Some 35,000 left the camps during the next two years, including more than 13,000 who joined the armed forces. The all-Nisei 442nd Combat Team served gallantly in Europe, losing more than 500 men in battle and winning more than 1,000 citations for bravery. One World War II veteran remembers that when his unit was in trouble, the commander would issue a familiar appeal: "Call in the Japs."

For other Nisei, the experience was bitter. More than 5,000 renounced their American citizenship and chose to live in Japan after the war. The government did not close down the last detention center until March 1946. Japanese Americans never experienced the torture and mass death of the German concentration camps, but their treatment was a disgrace to a nation fighting for freedom and democracy. Finally, in 1988, Congress voted an indemnity of $1.2 billion for the estimated 60,000 surviving Japanese Americans detained during World War II. Susumi Emori, who had been moved with his wife and four children from his farm in Stockton, California, to a camp in Arkansas, felt vindicated. "It was terrible," he said, with tears in his eyes, "but it was a time of war. Anything can happen. I didn't blame the United States for that."

> **Quick Check**
> ✓ How did the war affect women and minorities?

VICTORY

World War II ended with surprising swiftness. By 1943, the Axis tide had been turned in Europe and Asia, and Russia, the United States, and Britain mounted the offensives that began to drive Germany and Japan back across the vast areas they had conquered to their final defeat.

> **How** did the war end, and what were its consequences?

The long-awaited second front finally came in June 1944. For two years, the United States and Britain built up a force of nearly three million troops and an armada of ships and landing craft to carry them across the English Channel. Hoping to catch Hitler by surprise, Eisenhower chose the Normandy peninsula, where the lack of good harbors had led to lighter German fortifications. Allied aircraft bombed northern France for six weeks preceding the assault to block German reinforcements once the invasion began.

D-Day, when the invasion would begin, was set for June 5, but bad weather forced a delay. Relying on a forecasted break in the storm, Eisenhower gambled on going ahead on June 6. During the night, three divisions parachuted behind the German defenses; at dawn, American, British, and Canadian troops fought their way ashore at five points along a 60-mile stretch of beach, encountering stiff resistance. By the end of the day, however, Eisenhower had won his beachhead; a week later, more than 300,000 men were pushing back the Germans through the hedgerows of Normandy. The breakthrough came on July 25 when General Omar Bradley decimated the

View the **Closer Look**
D-Day Landing, June 6, 1944 on
myhistorylab.com

enemy with a massive artillery and aerial bombardment at Saint-Lô, opening a gap for George Patton's Third Army. American tanks raced across the French country-side, trapping thousands of Germans and liberating Paris by August 25. Allied troops reached the Rhine River by September, but a shortage of supplies, especially gasoline, forced a three-month halt.

Hitler took advantage of this breathing spell to counterattack in what became known as the Battle of the Bulge. In mid-December, the remaining German ar-mored divisions burst through a weak point in the Allied lines in the Ardennes For-est, hoping to reach the coast and cut off nearly one-third of Eisenhower's forces. Tactical surprise and bad weather, which prevented Allied air support, led to a huge bulge in the American lines. But an airborne division at the key crossroads of Bas-togne, in Belgium, held off a much larger German force. Allied reinforcements and air power then broke the attack. By committing nearly all his reserves to this offen-sive, Hitler had delayed Eisenhower's advance into Germany by a few months, but he also had fatally weakened German resistance.

The end came quickly. American and British bombers had been pounding Ger-man cities for many months. Hamburg had been leveled in 1943; Dresden joined the list in early 1945. The destruction included tens of thousands of civilian lives and provoked controversy then and later, but it also hindered the German war ef-fort during the critical final phase. A massive Russian offensive in mid-January swept toward Berlin. Bradley's troops, finding a bridge the Germans had left intact, crossed the Rhine on March 7. Although the British favored a concentrated drive on Berlin, the Allied forces advanced on a broad front, capturing the industrial Ruhr basin and breaking the Nazi death grip on prisoner populations, including the tragic remnant of the Nazi Holocaust, the slaughter of 6 million Jews and other per-sons whom Hitler's regime despised. The Americans and British met the Russians at the Elbe River in late April. With the Red Army already in the streets of Berlin, Hitler committed suicide on April 30. A week later, on May 7, 1945, Eisenhower accepted the unconditional surrender of all German forces. Just 11 months and a day after the landings in Normandy, the Allies had brought the war in Europe to a successful conclusion.

War Aims and Wartime Diplomacy

The American contribution to Hitler's defeat was relatively minor compared to the damage the Soviet Union inflicted. At the height of the German invasion of Russia, more than 300 Soviet divisions had battled 250 German ones. The United States and Britain used only 58 divisions in the Normandy invasion. As his armies over-ran Poland and the Balkans, Stalin was determined to control this region, which had been the historic pathway for Western invasions of Russia. Delay in opening the second front and an innate distrust of the West convinced the Soviets that they should maximize their gains by imposing communist regimes on eastern Europe.

American postwar goals were different. Now believing the failure to join the League of Nations in 1919 had led to the coming of World War II, the American people and their leaders vowed to put their faith in a new attempt at collective security. At Moscow in 1943, Secretary of State Cordell Hull had won Russian agreement to participate in a world organization at the war's end. The first wartime Big Three conference brought together Roosevelt, Churchill, and Stalin at Tehran, Iran, in late 1943. Stalin reaffirmed this commitment and promised to enter the war against Japan once Germany was defeated.

By the time the Big Three met again in February 1945 at the Yalta Conference, the military situation favored the Russians. While British and American forces were still recovering from the Battle of the Bulge, the Red Army was within 50 miles of Berlin. Stalin drove hard bargains. He refused to give up communist domination of Poland and the Balkans, although he did agree to Roosevelt's request for a Declaration of Liberated Europe, which called for free elections without providing for enforcement or supervision. Stalin also promised to enter the Pacific war three months after Germany surrendered. In return, Roosevelt offered concessions in Asia, including Russian control over Manchuria. While neither a sellout nor a betrayal, as some critics have charged, Yalta was a diplomatic triumph for the Soviets—one that reflected Russia's major contribution to victory in Europe.

For the president, the long journey to Yalta proved too much. His health continued to fail after his return to Washington. In April, FDR left for Warm Springs, Georgia, where he had always been able to relax. He was sitting for his portrait at midday on April 12, 1945, when he complained of a "terrific headache," slumped forward, and died.

The nation mourned a man who had gallantly met the challenges of the Depression and global war. Unfortunately, FDR had not prepared his successor for the problems that lay ahead. The defeat of Nazi Germany dissolved the strongest bond between the United States and the Soviet Union. With different histories, cultures, and ideologies, the two nations were bound to drift apart. The inexperienced Harry Truman had to manage the rivalry that was destined to develop into the future Cold War.

Watch the **Video**
The Big Three, Yalta Conference on
myhistorylab.com

Quick Check

✓ How did the objectives of the United States and the Soviet Union conflict?

Triumph and Destruction in the Pacific

The total defeat of Germany in May 1945 turned eyes toward Japan. Although the combined chiefs of staff had estimated it would take 18 months after Germany's surrender to conquer Japan, American forces moved faster. Admiral Nimitz swept through the Gilbert, Marshall, and Caroline Islands in 1944, securing bases and building airfields for American B-29s to bombard the Japanese home islands. MacArthur cleared New Guinea of the last Japanese defender in early 1944, and American troops landed in the Philippines on October 20. Manila fell in early February 1945. The Japanese navy, in a Pacific version of the Battle of the Bulge, launched a daring three-pronged attack on the American invasion fleet in Leyte Gulf. The U.S. Navy blunted all three thrusts, sinking four carriers and ending any further Japanese naval threat.

Japan's defeat was now inevitable. The United States had three possible ways to proceed. The military favored a full-scale invasion, beginning on the southernmost island of Kyushu in November 1945 and culminating with a climactic battle for Tokyo in 1946; hundreds of thousands of casualties were expected. Diplomats, in

The atomic bomb dropped on Nagasaki, a provincial capital and naval base in southern Japan, on August 9, 1945, virtually obliterated the city and killed more than 60,000 people. Only buildings made with reinforced concrete remained standing after the blast.

Read the **Document**
Albert Einstein, Letter to President Roosevelt (1939) on **myhistorylab.com**

Watch the **Video**
Truman on the End of World War II on **myhistorylab.com**

Quick Check

✔ What was the role of the atomic bomb in ending the war against Japan?

contrast, urged the United States to modify the unconditional surrender formula to permit Japan to retain its emperor.

The third option involved the **Manhattan Project**, the top-secret program that developed the atom bomb. Scientists, many of them refugees from Europe, had worked since 1939 to perfect this deadly new weapon. In the New Mexico desert on July 16, 1945, they successfully tested the first atomic bomb, creating a fireball brighter than several suns and a telltale mushroom cloud that rose some 40,000 feet above an enormous crater in the desert floor.

Truman had been unaware of the Manhattan Project before he became president. Now he simply followed the recommendation of a committee headed by Secretary of War Henry L. Stimson to drop the bomb on a Japanese city. The committee rejected inviting the Japanese to observe a demonstration shot at a remote Pacific site or giving advance notice of the bomb's destructive power. Neither Truman nor Stimson had qualms about dropping the bomb without warning. They viewed it as a legitimate wartime measure to save the lives of hundreds of thousands of Americans—and Japanese—that would be lost in a full-scale invasion.

Weather conditions on August 6 dictated the choice of Hiroshima as the bomb's target. The explosion incinerated four square miles of the city, killing more than 60,000. Two days later, Russia entered the war against Japan. On August 9, the United States dropped a second bomb on Nagasaki. No more atomic bombs were available, but no more were needed. The emperor personally commanded his ministers to surrender unconditionally on August 14, 1945. Three weeks later, Japan signed a formal capitulation on the decks of the battleship *Missouri* in Tokyo Bay. World War II was over.

Years later, scholars charged that Truman had more in mind than defeating Japan when he decided to use the atomic bomb. Citing air force and naval officers who claimed a blockade or conventional air attacks could defeat Japan, these revisionists suggested the bomb was really dropped to impress the Soviet Union with the United States' exclusive possession of the ultimate weapon. The evidence indicates that while Truman and his associates were aware of the possible effect on the Soviet Union, their primary motive was to end World War II as quickly and effortlessly as possible. Saving American lives, along with a desire for revenge for Pearl Harbor, were uppermost in the decision to bomb Hiroshima and Nagasaki. Yet in using the atomic bomb to defeat Japan, the United States virtually guaranteed a postwar arms race with the Soviet Union.

CONCLUSION: THE TRANSFORMING POWER OF WAR

The second great war of the twentieth century changed American life. For the first time, the nation had achieved its military potential. In 1945, the United States was unquestionably the strongest country on earth, with 12 million men and women in uniform; a vast array of shipyards, aircraft plants, and munitions factories in full production; and a monopoly over the atomic bomb. For better or worse, it was now launched on a global career. In the future, the United States would be involved in all parts of the world, from Western Europe to remote jungles in Asia, from the nearby Caribbean to the distant Persian Gulf. And despite its enormous strength in 1945, the nation's new world role would encompass failure and frustration as well as power and dominion.

The war's legacy was equally strong at home. Four years of fighting brought about industrial recovery and unparalleled prosperity. The old pattern of unregulated free enterprise was as much a victim of the war as of the New Deal; big government and huge deficits had now become the norm. Economic control passed from New York and Wall Street to Washington and Pennsylvania Avenue. Far-reaching changes in American society would become apparent only decades later. Such distinctive patterns of recent American life as the baby boom and the growth of the Sunbelt began during wartime. World War II was a watershed in twentieth-century America, ushering in a new age of global concerns and domestic upheaval.

27 STUDY RESOURCES

((•—[Listen to the **Chapter Audio** for Chapter 27 on **myhistorylab.com**

TIMELINE

1928 Kellogg–Briand Pact outlaws war (August), p. 677

1936 Hitler's troops reoccupy Rhineland, p. 679

1937 FDR signs permanent Neutrality Act (May), p. 680

1938 Munich Conference appeases Hitler (September), p. 681

1939 Germany invades Poland; World War II begins, p. 681

1941 Japan attacks Pearl Harbor; United States enters World War II, p. 686

1942 U.S. defeats Japanese at Battle of Midway (June), p. 691
- Allies land in North Africa (November), p. 690

1943 Soviets smash Nazis at Stalingrad, p. 690

1944 Allies land on Normandy beachheads, p. 695

1945 Big Three meet at Yalta (February), p. 697
- FDR dies; Harry Truman becomes president (April), p. 692
- Germany surrenders unconditionally (May), p. 696
- United States drops atomic bombs on Hiroshima and Nagasaki; Japan surrenders (August), p. 698

CHAPTER REVIEW

ISOLATIONISM

What was isolationism, and why was it so appealing to Americans in the 1920s and 1930s?

Disillusionment with the outcome of World War I led to a policy of isolationism, by which Americans hoped to avoid responsibility for the peace of Europe and Asia, and to spare themselves the agony of war if peace failed. Isolationism had traditionally served Americans well, and many Americans expected that it would continue to do so. *(p. 678)*

THE ROAD TO WAR

How did the United States go from neutrality in the 1930s to war in 1941?

FDR gradually led the United States from neutrality in the 1930s to war in 1941, responding to German and Japanese aggression with careful political and diplomatic steps, including aid to Britain, an undeclared naval war against Germany, and economic pressure on Japan, which lashed out by attacking Pearl Harbor. *(p. 681)*

TURNING THE TIDE AGAINST THE AXIS

How did America and its allies halt the advances of Germany and Japan?

The United States formed an alliance with Britain and the Soviet Union against Germany and Japan. American and British forces fought the Germans in North Africa and Italy, while Soviet forces beat back the Germans in Russia. American ships and planes defeated Japanese forces at the Coral Sea and Midway. *(p. 686)*

THE HOME FRONT

How did American domestic life change during World War II?

During the war American industry churned out equipment at a rate unimagined before 1941. Record numbers of women and minorities entered the workforce. But 120,000 Japanese Americans were forced into concentration camps. *(p. 691)*

VICTORY

How did the war end, and what were its consequences?

The war in Europe ended in May 1945 after Allied and Soviet forces overran Germany. The war in the Pacific ended after the atomic bombing of Hiroshima and Nagasaki, and left the United States in undisputed control of Japan. *(p. 695)*

KEY TERM QUESTIONS

1. Why did the Kellogg–Briand Pact include no method to enforce its provisions? (p. 677)

2. What did the Axis Powers represent? (p. 679)

3. What did the neutrality acts aim to achieve? (p. 680)

4. Why did Roosevelt enact the Lend-Lease plan and what were the criticisms leveled against it? (p. 683)

5. What effect did the attack on Pearl Harbor have on American attitudes? (p. 686)

6. How successful was the D-Day invasion? (p. 695)

7. How did Allied forces discover the Nazi Holocaust toward the end of the war? (p. 696)

8. What decisions were made at the Yalta Conference? (p. 697)

9. Who comprised the Manhattan Project and what were they aiming to accomplish? (p. 698)

MyHistoryLab Connections

Visit **www.myhistorylab.com** for a customized Study Plan to build your knowledge of *America and the World*

Questions for Analysis

1. Were there any similarities between Adolf Hitler and Franklin D. Roosevelt?

   👁 **Watch** the **Video** *Hitler and Roosevelt* p. 679

2. What were Franklin D. Roosevelt's "Four Freedoms"?

   📖 **Read** the **Document** *Franklin D. Roosevelt, "The Four Freedoms" (1941)* p. 683

3. In what parts of Europe did the most intense fighting of the war occur?

   🔍 **View** the **Map** *World War II in Europe* p. 681

4. What was military life like for African Americans?

   📖 **Read** the **Document** *Jim Crow in the Army Camps (1940) and Jim Crow Army (1941)* p. 694

5. What is the significance of the United States' superior development of landing craft and amphibious vessels to the outcome of World War II?

   🔍 **View** the **Closer Look** *D-Day Landing, June 6, 1944* p. 695

Other Resources from this Chapter

📖 **Read** the **Document** *Charles Lindbergh, Radio Address*

🔍 **View** the **Map** *World War II in the Pacific*

🔍 **View** the **Image** *Heel Hitler Poster*

👁 **Watch** the **Video** *Rosie the Riveter*

📖 **Read** the **Document** *Japanese Relocation Order*

👁 **Watch** the **Video** *The Big Three, Yalta Conference*

📖 **Read** the **Document** *Albert Einstein, Letter to the President*

👁 **Watch** the **Video** *Truman on the End of World War II*

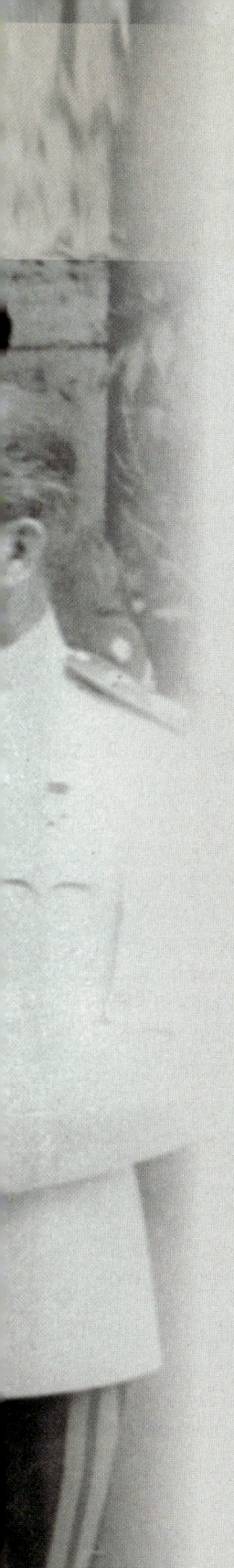

Contents and Spotlight Questions

((•— **Listen** to the **Chapter Audio** for Chapter 28 on **myhistorylab.com**

THE POTSDAM SUMMIT

"I am getting ready to go see Stalin and Churchill," President Truman wrote to his mother in July 1945, "and it is a chore." On board the cruiser *Augusta*, the new president complained in his diary about the upcoming Potsdam Conference: "How I hate this trip! But I have to make it win, lose, or draw and we must win. I am giving nothing away except to save starving people and even then I hope we can only help them to help themselves."

Halfway around the world, Joseph Stalin left Moscow a day late because of a slight heart attack. The Soviet leader hated to fly, so he traveled by rail. Moreover, he ordered the heavily guarded train to detour around Poland for fear of an ambush, further delaying his arrival. When he arrived in Potsdam, a suburb of Berlin miraculously spared the total destruction that the Allies had wrought in the German capital, he was ready to claim the spoils of war.

These two men, one the veteran revolutionary who had been in power for two decades, the other an untested leader in office for barely three months, symbolized the enormous differences that now separated the wartime allies. Stalin was above all a realist. Brutal in securing total control at home, he was more flexible in his foreign policy, bent on exploiting Russia's victory in World War II rather than aiming at world domination. Cunning and caution were

Churchill, Truman, and Stalin during the Potsdam Conference in July 1945.

the hallmarks of his diplomatic style. Short and ungainly, he waited, catlike, behind his unassuming facade, ready to pounce on an opponent with his "brilliant, terrifying tactical mastery." Truman, in contrast, personified traditional Wilsonian idealism. Lacking Roosevelt's guile, the new president placed his faith in international cooperation. Like many Americans, he took his country's innate goodness for granted. Self-assured to the point of cockiness, he came to Potsdam clothed in the armor of self-righteousness.

Truman and Stalin met for the first time on July 17, 1945. "I told Stalin that I am no diplomat," the president recorded in his diary, "but usually said yes and no to questions after hearing all the argument." The Russian dictator's reaction to Truman remains a mystery, but Truman believed the first encounter went well: "I can deal with Stalin. He is honest—but smart as hell."

Together with Winston Churchill and his replacement as prime minister, Clement Attlee, whose Labour party had just triumphed in British elections, Truman and Stalin clashed for the next ten days over such difficult issues as reparations, the Polish borders, and Eastern Europe. Truman presented the ideas and proposals formulated by his advisers; he saw his task as essentially procedural, and when he presided, he moved the agenda along briskly. After he had "banged through" three items one day, he commented, "I am not going to stay around this terrible place all summer, just to listen to speeches. I'll go home to the Senate for that." In an indirect, roundabout way, he informed Stalin of the existence of the atomic bomb, tested successfully in the New Mexico desert just before the conference began. Truman offered no details, and the impassive Stalin asked for none, commenting only that he hoped the United States would make "good use of it against the Japanese."

Reparations were the crucial issue at Potsdam. The Russians wanted to rebuild their war-ravaged economy with German industry; the United States feared it would be saddled with the entire cost of caring for the defeated Germans. A compromise was finally reached. Each side would take reparations primarily from its own occupation zone, a solution that foreshadowed the division of Germany. "Because they could not agree on how to govern Europe," wrote historian Daniel Yergin, "Truman and Stalin began to divide it." The other issues were referred to a Council of Foreign Ministers, which would meet in the fall in London.

The Potsdam Conference thus ended on a note of harmony; beneath the surface, however, the bitter antagonism of the Cold War was festering. A dozen years later, Truman described himself as "an innocent idealist" surrounded by wolves. He claimed that all the agreements reached at Potsdam were "broken as soon as the unconscionable Russian Dictator returned to Moscow!" He added ruefully, "And I liked the little son of a bitch."

Potsdam marked the end of the wartime alliance. America and Russia, each distrusting the other, began a long, bitter confrontation. For the next decade, the two superpowers would vie to control postwar Europe, and later clash over the spread of communism to Asia. When Truman's and Stalin's successors met for the next summit conference, at Geneva in 1955, the Cold War was at its height.

THE COLD WAR BEGINS

The conflict between the United States and the Soviet Union began gradually. For two years, the nations tried to negotiate their differences over the division of Europe and the atomic bomb. The Council of Foreign Ministers provided the forum. Beginning in London in 1945 and meeting with their Russian counterparts in Paris, New York, and Moscow, American diplomats searched for a way to live in peace with a suspicious Soviet Union.

How did the Cold War begin?

The Division of Europe

The fundamental disagreement was over control of postwar Europe. In the east, the Red Army had swept over Poland and most of the Balkans, laying the basis for Soviet domination there. American and British forces had liberated Western Europe from Scandinavia to Italy. The Russians, mindful of past invasions from the west across the plains of Poland, were intent on imposing communist governments loyal to Moscow in the Soviet sphere. The United States, on the other hand, upheld the principle of national self-determination, insisting the people in each country should freely elect their postwar rulers. The Soviets saw this demand as subversive, since they knew that popularly chosen regimes would be unfriendly to Russia. Suspecting American duplicity, Stalin brought down an Iron Curtain (Churchill's phrase for the suppression of individual rights in Eastern Europe) and created satellite governments. (See Map 28.1.)

Germany was the key. The temporary zones of occupation hardened into permanent divisions. Ignoring the Potsdam agreement that the country be treated as an economic unit, the United States, Britain, and France were by 1946 refusing to permit the Russians to take reparations from the industrial western zones. The initial harsh occupation policy gave way to more humane treatment of the German people and a slow but steady economic recovery. The United States, Britain, and France merged their zones and championed the unification of all Germany. Russia, fearing a resurgence of German military power, responded by intensifying the communization of its zone, which included the jointly occupied city of Berlin. By 1947, Britain, France, and the United States were planning to transfer their authority to an independent West Germany.

The Soviet Union also consolidated its grip on Eastern Europe in 1946 and 1947. One by one, communist regimes replaced coalition governments in Poland, Hungary, Romania, and Bulgaria. Moving cautiously to avoid provoking the West, Stalin used communism to dominate half of Europe, both to protect the Soviet state and to advance its power. The climax came in March 1948 when a communist coup in Czechoslovakia overthrew a democratic government and gave the Soviets a strategic foothold in central Europe.

The division of Europe was an inevitable aftereffect of World War II. Both sides were intent on imposing their values in the areas their troops liberated. The Russians were no more likely to withdraw from Eastern Europe than the United States and Britain were from Germany, France, and Italy. A frank recognition of competing spheres of influence might have avoided escalating tension. But the Western

Read the **Document**
Churchill's "Iron Curtain" Speech (March 5, 1946) on **myhistorylab.com**

Map 28.1 *Europe after World War II*   The heavy red line splitting Germany shows in graphic form the division of Europe between the Western and Soviet spheres of influence. "From Stettin in the Baltic to Trieste in the Adriatic," said Winston Churchill in a speech at Fulton, Missouri, in 1946, "an iron curtain has descended across the Continent."

nations, remembering Hitler's aggression in the 1930s, began to see Stalin as an equally dangerous threat to their well-being. Instead of accepting him as a cautious leader bent on protecting Russian security, they perceived him as an aggressive dictator leading a communist drive for world domination.

Quick Check
✓ What caused the division of Europe after World War II?

The Atomic Dilemma

Overshadowing all else was the atomic bomb. Used by the United States with deadly success at Hiroshima and Nagasaki, the new weapon raised problems that would have been difficult for even friendly nations to resolve. Given Soviet-American tensions, the effect was disastrous.

The wartime policy followed by Roosevelt and Churchill ensured a postwar nuclear arms race. Instead of informing their major ally of the developing atomic bomb, they kept it secret. Stalin learned of the Manhattan Project through espionage and started a Soviet atomic program in 1943. By the time Truman informed Stalin of the weapon's existence at Potsdam, the Russians, aided by information from spies in the United States, were on the way to making their own bomb.

After the war, the United States developed a disarmament plan that would turn control of fissionable material, then the processing plants, and ultimately the American stockpile of bombs over to an international agency. When President Truman appointed financier Bernard Baruch to present this proposal to the United Nations, Baruch added sanctions against violators and exempted the international agency from the UN veto. Ignoring scientists who pleaded for a more cooperative position, Baruch followed instead the advice of Army Chief of Staff Dwight D. Eisenhower, who cited the rapid demobilization of the American armed forces (from nearly 12 million personnel in 1945 to fewer than 2 million in 1947) to argue that "we cannot at this time limit our capability to produce or use this weapon." In effect, the Baruch Plan, with its multiple stages and emphasis on inspection, would preserve the American atomic monopoly indefinitely.

The Soviets responded predictably. Ambassador Andrei Gromyko presented a simple plan calling for a total ban on producing and using the new weapon and destroying all existing bombs. The Russian proposal reflected the same perception of national self-interest as the Baruch Plan. Russia still had nearly 3 million men under arms in 1947 and wanted to maximize its conventional strength by outlawing the atomic bomb.

No agreement was possible. Neither the United States nor the Soviet Union could abandon its position without surrendering a vital interest. To preserve its monopoly, America stressed inspection and control; to neutralize the U.S. advantage, Russia advocated immediate disarmament. The nuclear dilemma, inherent in the Soviet-American rivalry, blocked any negotiated settlement. Instead, the two superpowers agreed to disagree, and each concentrated on taking maximum advantage of its wartime gains. Thus the Russians exploited the territory they had conquered in Europe while the United States retained its economic and strategic advantages over the Soviet Union. The result was the Cold War.

Quick Check
✓ How did the atomic bomb influence international relations?

CONTAINMENT

What was
containment,
and why was it
adopted?

A major departure in American foreign policy occurred in January 1947, when General George C. Marshall, the wartime army chief of staff, became secretary of state. Calm, mature, and orderly, Marshall had the capability—honed in World War II—to think in broad strategic terms. An extraordinarily good judge of ability, he relied on gifted subordinates to implement his policies, and on two men in particular: Dean Acheson and George Kennan.

Acheson, an experienced Washington lawyer and bureaucrat, was appointed undersecretary of state and given free rein by Marshall to conduct American diplomacy. Acheson seemed more British than American, with his patrician manners, impeccable Ivy League clothes, and bushy mustache. Keenly intelligent, he had a carefully cultivated reputation for arrogance and a low tolerance for mediocrity. An ardent Anglophile, he wanted the United States to take over a faltering Britain's role as the arbiter of world affairs. Recalling the lessons of Munich, he opposed appeasement and advocated negotiating only from strength.

George Kennan, Marshall's other mainstay, headed the new Policy Planning Staff. A career diplomat, Kennan had become a Soviet expert, mastering Russian language, history, and culture. He had served in Moscow in the 1930s and during World War II and distrusted the Soviet regime. In a crucial telegram in 1946, he warned that the Kremlin believed "that there can be no compromise with rival power," arguing that only sustained resistance could halt the expansion of Russian power. As self-assured as Acheson, Kennan believed that neither Congress nor public opinion should interfere with the experts' conduct of foreign policy.

In the spring of 1947, a sense of crisis impelled Marshall, Acheson, and Kennan to set a new course in American diplomacy. Dubbed containment, after an article by Kennan in *Foreign Affairs*, the new policy both consolidated the evolving postwar anticommunism and established guidelines that would shape America's role in the world for more than two decades. Kennan proposed "a long-term, patient but firm, and vigilant containment of Russian expansive tendencies." Such a policy would not lead to immediate victory, Kennan warned. In the long run, however, he believed that the United States could force the Soviet Union to adopt more reasonable policies and live in peace with the West.

The Truman Doctrine

The initial step toward containment came in response to an urgent appeal. Since March 1946, Britain had been supporting the Greek government in a bitter civil war against communist guerrillas. On February 21, 1947, the British informed the United States that they could no longer afford to aid Greece or Turkey, the latter under Soviet pressure for access to the Mediterranean. Believing the Russians responsible for the strife in Greece (in fact, they were not), Marshall, Acheson, and Kennan decided the United States would have to assume Britain's traditional role as the dominant power in the eastern Mediterranean.

Worried about congressional support, especially since the Republicans had gained control of Congress in 1946, Marshall met with the legislative leadership in February.

👁 **Watch** the **Video**
*President Truman and
the Threat of Commu-
nism* on
myhistorylab.com

He outlined the problem; then Acheson warned that "a highly possible Soviet break-through might open three continents to Soviet penetration." Comparing the situation in Greece to one rotten apple spoiling an entire barrel, Acheson warned that "the corruption of Greece would infect Iran and all to the east. It would also carry infection to Africa through Asia Minor and Egypt, and to Europe through Italy and France." Claiming that the Soviets were "playing one of the greatest gambles in history," Acheson concluded that "we and we alone were in a position to break up the play."

The bipartisan group of congressional leaders was impressed. Finally, Republican Senator Arthur M. Vandenberg said he would support the president, but added that to ensure public backing, Truman would have to "scare hell" out of the American people.

The president followed that advice. On March 12, 1947, he asked Congress for $400 million for military and economic assistance to Greece and Turkey. In what became known as the Truman Doctrine, he made clear that the stakes were far higher than just these two countries: "It must be the policy of the United States to support free peoples who are resisting attempted subjugation by armed minorities or by outside pressure." Both the House and the Senate approved the program by margins of better than three to one.

The Truman Doctrine was an informal declaration of cold war against the Soviet Union. Truman used the crisis to secure congressional approval and build a national consensus for the policy of containment. The Greek civil war ended in 1949, but the American commitment to oppose communist expansion, whether by internal subversion or external aggression, placed the United States on a collision course with the Soviet Union around the globe.

Read the **Document** *Truman Doctrine* on **myhistorylab.com**

Quick Check
✓ What was the significance of the Truman Doctrine?

The Marshall Plan

Western Europe, however, was far more vital to U.S. interests than was the eastern Mediterranean. Yet by 1947, many Americans believed that Western Europe was open to Soviet penetration. The problem was economic. Despite $9 billion in piecemeal American loans, the European countries had difficulty recovering from World War II. Food was scarce, with millions existing on less than 1,500 calories a day; industrial machinery was broken down and obsolete; years of depression and war had demoralized workers. The cruel winter of 1947, the worst in 50 years, compounded the problem. Resentment and discontent led to votes for communist parties, especially in Italy and France. It seemed as though all Europe might drift into the communist orbit.

In the weeks following the proclamation of the Truman Doctrine, American officials dealt with this problem. Secretary of State Marshall, returning from a frustrating meeting in Moscow, warned that "the patient is sinking while the doctors deliberate." Acheson believed that it was time to extend American "economic power" in Europe, "to call an effective halt to the Soviet Union's expansionism" and "to create a basis for political stability and economic well-being." The experts drew up a plan for the massive infusion of American capital to finance the recovery of Europe. Speaking at Harvard on June 5, 1947, Marshall offered economic aid to all the nations of Europe if they could agree on ways to achieve "the revival of a working economy in the world so as to permit the emergence of political and social conditions in which free institutions can exist."

Read the **Document** *George Marshall, The Marshall Plan (1947)* on **myhistorylab.com**

The fate of the Marshall Plan, as the aid program was called, depended on the reaction of the Soviet Union and Congress. Marshall had taken, as one American diplomat said, "a hell of a gamble" by including Russia in his offer of aid. At a meeting in Paris in July 1947, the Soviet foreign minister ended the suspense. Neither the Soviet Union nor its satellites would take part, apparently because Moscow saw the Marshall Plan as an American attempt to weaken its control over Eastern Europe. The other European countries then formally requested $17 billion in assistance over the next four years.

Congress appointed a special joint committee to investigate the proposal. The administration pointed out that the Marshall Plan would help the United States by stimulating trade with Europe and check Soviet expansion. The latter argument proved decisive. When the Czech coup touched off a war scare in March 1948, Congress approved the Marshall Plan by heavy majorities. Over the next four years, the huge American investment generated an industrial revival in Western Europe that became self-sustaining by the 1950s. The communist threat faded, and a prosperous Europe became a bonanza for American farmers, miners, and manufacturers.

Quick Check

✓ What was the purpose of the Marshall Plan?

The Western Military Alliance

The third and final phase of containment came in 1949 with the North Atlantic Treaty Organization (NATO). NATO grew out of European fears of Russian military aggression.

Recalling Hitler's tactics in the 1930s, Western Europeans wanted assurance that the United States would protect them from attack as they began to achieve economic recovery. American diplomats were sympathetic. "People could not go ahead and make investments for the future," commented Averell Harriman, the American ambassador in Moscow, "without some sense of security."

Britain, France, Belgium, the Netherlands, and Luxembourg began the process in March 1948 with the Brussels Treaty, providing for collective self-defense. In January 1949, President Truman called for a broader defense pact; ten European nations, from Norway to Italy, joined the United States and Canada in signing the North Atlantic Treaty in Washington on April 4, 1949. This departure from the traditional policy of isolation—the United States had not signed such a treaty since the French alliance in the eighteenth century—caused debate, but the Senate ratified it in July by a vote of 82 to 13.

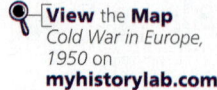

View the **Map**
Cold War in Europe, 1950 on
myhistorylab.com

NATO had two main features. First, the United States committed itself to defend Europe, The key clause stated: "an armed attack against one or more shall be considered an attack against them all." In effect, the United States was extending its atomic shield over Europe. The second feature was designed to reassure Europeans that the United States would honor this commitment. In late 1950, Truman appointed Dwight D. Eisenhower NATO supreme commander and stationed four American divisions in Europe as the nucleus of the NATO army. It was believed the threat of American troop involvement in any Russian assault would deter the Soviet Union from attacking.

The NATO alliance escalated the Cold War. Whatever its advantage in building a sense of security among Europeans, it represented an overreaction to the Soviet danger. Americans and Europeans alike were attempting to apply the lessons of Munich—that appeasement of aggressors led to more aggression—to the Cold War. But Stalin was not Hitler, and the Soviets were not the Nazis. There was no evidence of any Russian plan to invade Western Europe, and given the American atomic bomb, none was likely. NATO intensified Russian fears of the West and thus increased international tension.

Quick Check

✓ What were the important features of NATO?

The Berlin Blockade

The main Russian response to containment came in 1948 at the West's most vulnerable point. American, British, French, and Soviet troops each occupied a sector of Berlin, but the city was more than 100 miles within the Russian zone of Germany (see Map 28.1). Stalin decided to test his opponents' resolve by cutting off rail and road traffic to Berlin on June 20, 1948.

The Berlin blockade caught Truman unprepared. He had his hands full resisting efforts to force him off the Democratic ticket and faced a difficult reelection against Republican Governor Thomas E. Dewey of New York. The alternatives were unappealing. The United States could withdraw its forces and lose not just a city but the confidence of all Europe; it could try to send in reinforcements and fight for Berlin; or it could attempt to find a diplomatic solution. Characteristically, Truman told the military that there would be no pulling out. "We were going to stay, period," an aide reported him saying.

The president and his advisers then implemented the decision. Rejecting proposals to send an armored column down the main highway, the administration adopted a two-phase policy. The first part was a massive airlift of food, fuel, and supplies for the 10,000 troops and the 2 million civilians in Berlin. Fifty-two C-54s and 80 C-47s carried 2,500 tons to Berlin every 24 hours. To guard against Soviet interruption of the Berlin airlift, Truman transferred 60 American B-29s, capable of delivering atomic bombs, to bases in Britain. The president was bluffing; the B-29s were not equipped with atomic bombs, but the threat was effective.

The world teetered on the edge of war. Stalin did not disrupt the flights to Berlin, but he rejected American diplomatic initiatives. Although the Russians could have halted it by jamming radar or shooting down the defenseless cargo planes, the airlift increased to more than 7,000 tons a day. Dewey supported the president, thus removing foreign policy from the campaign. Yet the tension was fierce. In September, Truman asked his advisers to brief him "on bases, bombs, Moscow, Leningrad, etc." "I have a terrible feeling afterward that we are very close to war," he confided in his diary. "I hope not."

The Berlin airlift of 1948–1949 broke the Soviet blockade. Called Operation Vittles, it provided food and fuel for West Berliners. Here, children atop a pile of rubble wave to an American cargo plane flying overhead.

Slowly, the tension eased. The Russians did not shoot down any planes, and the daily airlift climbed to nearly 7,000 tons. Truman, a decided underdog, won a surprising second term in November over a complacent Dewey, in part because the Berlin crisis had rallied the nation behind his leadership. In early 1949, the Soviets ended the blockade in return for another meeting of the Council of Foreign Ministers on Germany—a conclave that was as unproductive as all the earlier ones.

The Berlin crisis marked the end of the initial phase of the Cold War. The airlift had shown the world the triumph of American ingenuity over Russian stubbornness. Yet the Cold War had still cut Europe in two. Behind the Iron Curtain, the Russians had consolidated control over the areas their troops won in the war, while the United States had used the Marshall Plan to revitalize Western Europe. But a divided continent was a far cry from the wartime hopes for a peaceful world. And the rivalry that began in Europe would spread into a worldwide contest between the superpowers.

> **Quick Check**
> ✓ How did the United States respond to the Berlin blockade?

THE COLD WAR EXPANDS

How did the Cold War expand from Europe to Asia?

The rivalry between the United States and the Soviet Union grew in the late 1940s and early 1950s. Both sides rebuilt their military forces with new methods and weapons. The diplomatic competition spread as each of the superpowers sought to enhance its influence in East Asia. By the time Truman left office in 1953, the Cold War had become global.

The Military Dimension

After World War II, American leaders were intent on reforming the nation's military system. Two goals were uppermost. First, nearly everyone agreed in the aftermath of Pearl Harbor that the U.S. armed services should be unified into an integrated system. The Cold War reinforced this decision. Without unification, declared George Marshall in 1945, "there can be little hope that we will be able to maintain through the years a military posture that will secure for us a lasting peace." Planners also realized the need for new institutions to coordinate military and diplomatic strategy, so the nation could counter threats to its security.

In 1947, the National Security Act established a Department of Defense, headed by a civilian secretary of cabinet rank presiding over three separate services—the army, the navy, and the new air force. The act also created the Central Intelligence Agency (CIA) to coordinate the intelligence-gathering activities of government agencies and a National Security Council (NSC)—composed of the service secretaries, the secretary of defense, and the secretary of state—to advise the president regarding the nation's security.

Despite the appearance of equality among the services, the air force became the dominant power in the atomic age, based on its capability both to deter an enemy from attacking and to wage war if deterrence failed. President Truman, intent on reducing defense expenditures, allotted the air force more than one-half the total of his 1949 military budget. After the Czech coup and the resulting war scare, Congress granted an additional $3 billion to the military. The appropriation included funds for a new B-36 to replace the B-29 as the nation's primary strategic bomber.

> 📖 **Read** the **Document**
> *National Security Council Memorandum Number 68 (1950)* on **myhistorylab.com**

American military planners received even greater support in 1949 after the Soviet Union exploded its first atomic bomb. Truman appointed a committee to explore an all-out effort to build a hydrogen bomb to maintain American nuclear supremacy.

Some scientists had technical objections to the H-bomb. Others opposed it on moral grounds, claiming that its enormous destructive power (intended to be 1,000 times greater than the atomic bomb) made it unthinkable. George Kennan suggested a new effort at international arms control with the Soviets, but Dean Acheson—who succeeded Marshall as secretary of state in 1949—believed the United States had to develop the hydrogen bomb before the Soviet Union. When Acheson presented the committee's favorable report to the president in January 1950, Truman took only seven minutes to decide to go ahead.

Acheson also ordered the Policy Planning Staff (headed by Paul Nitze after Kennan resigned in protest) to draw up a new national defense policy. **NSC-68**, as the document became known, was based on the premise that the Soviet Union sought "to impose its absolute authority over the rest of the world" and thus "mortally challenged" the United States. Rejecting appeasement or a return to isolation, Nitze advocated massive expansion of American military power to overcome the Soviet

The explosion of a U.S. test bomb over an uninhabited island in the Pacific on November 1, 1952, demonstrated to the world the fearsome power of the hydrogen bomb. This early H-bomb could destroy a city the size of Washington, D.C.

Quick Check

✓ What changes did the Cold War prompt in American military institutions and policies?

threat. Contending the nation could afford to spend "upward of 50 percent of its gross national product" for security, NSC-68 proposed increasing defense spending from $13 to $45 billion annually. Approved in principle by the National Security Council in April 1950, NSC-68 symbolized the Truman administration's determination to win the Cold War regardless of cost.

The Cold War in Asia

The Soviet-American conflict developed more slowly in Asia. At Yalta, the two superpowers had agreed to a Far Eastern balance of power, with the Russians dominating northeast Asia and the Americans controlling the Pacific, including Japan and its former island empire.

The United States quickly consolidated its sphere of influence. General Douglas MacArthur denied the Soviet Union any role in reconstructing Japan. Instead, he supervised the transition of the Japanese government into a constitutional democracy along Western lines, in which communists were barred from government. The Japanese renounced war in their new constitution, relying on American forces to protect their security. American policy was equally nationalistic in the Pacific. A trusteeship arrangement with the United Nations disguised the United States' control over the Marshall, Mariana, and Caroline Islands. American scientists conducted atomic bomb tests at Bikini atoll in 1946, and by 1949, MacArthur declared that the Pacific "had become an Anglo-Saxon lake and our line of defense runs through the chain of islands fringing the coast of Asia."

China lay between the Soviet and American spheres. When World War II ended, the country was torn between Chiang Kai-shek's Nationalists in the south and Mao Zedong's communists in the north. Chiang had American political and economic backing and official Soviet recognition. But corruption was widespread among the Nationalist leaders, and inflation that soon reached 100 percent a year devastated the Chinese middle classes and eroded Chiang's support. Mao used discipline and patriotic appeals to strengthen his hold on the peasantry and extend his influence. When the Soviets vacated Manchuria in 1946, after stripping it of the industrial machinery Japan had installed there, Mao got control of this rich northern province. Ignoring American advice, Chiang occupied Manchurian cities, overextending his supply lines and exposing his forces to communist counterattack.

American policy sought to prevent a Chinese civil war. Before he became secretary of state, George Marshall tried to form a coalition government between Chiang and Mao. For a few months in 1946, Marshall appeared to have succeeded, but in reality, compromise was impossible. Chiang insisted he "was going to liquidate communists," while Mao tried to play the United States against Russia. By 1947, as China plunged into full-scale civil war, the Truman administration had given up trying to influence the outcome. Political mediation had failed, military intervention was out of the question so soon after World War II, and continued American economic aid served only to appease domestic supporters of Chiang; 80 percent of the military supplies ended up in communist hands.

In late 1948, Mao drove the Nationalists out of Manchuria. By mid-1949, the communists had crossed the Yangtze River. Acheson reported that the civil war "was beyond the control of the government of the United States." An American military adviser told Congress that the Nationalist defeat was due to "the world's worst leadership" and "a complete loss of will to fight." Republican senators, however, blamed American diplomats for sabotaging the Nationalists and termed Acheson's report "a 1054-page white-wash of a wishful, do-nothing policy." While the debate raged over responsibility for the "loss" of China, Chiang's forces fled the mainland for sanctuary on Formosa (Taiwan) in December 1949. Two months later, Mao and Stalin signed a treaty that seemed to place China in the Russian orbit.

The American response was twofold. First, the State Department refused to recognize the new regime in Beijing, maintaining instead formal diplomatic relations with the Nationalists on Formosa. Citing the Sino-Soviet alliance, Assistant Secretary of State Dean Rusk called the Beijing regime "a colonial Russian government" and declared, "It is not the Government of China. It does not pass the first test. It is not Chinese." Second, to compensate for the loss of China, the United States focused on Japan as its main ally in Asia. The State Department encouraged the buildup of Japanese industry. The Pentagon expanded bases on the Japanese home islands and Okinawa. A Japanese-American security pact led to the end of American occupation by 1952. The Cold War had now split East Asia in two.

Quick Check

✓ What was the role of the United States in China's civil war?

The Korean War

The showdown between the United States and the Soviet Union in Asia came in Korea. Traditionally the cockpit of international rivalry in northeast Asia, Korea had been divided at the 38th parallel in 1945. The Russians installed a communist government under Kim Il-Sung in the industrial north. In the agrarian south, Syngman Rhee, a conservative nationalist, became the American-sponsored ruler. Neither regime heeded a UN call for elections to unify the country. The two superpowers pulled out most of their forces by 1949. The Russians, however, helped train a well-equipped army in the north, while the United States—fearful Rhee would seek unification through war—gave only limited military assistance to South Korea.

On June 25, 1950, the North Korean army suddenly crossed the 38th parallel in strength. Stalin had approved this aggression. In January 1950, he had told Mao Zedong that he was ready to overthrow the Yalta settlement in the Far East ("and to hell with it," he exclaimed to Mao). In April, when Kim Il-Sung came to Moscow, Stalin backed the assault, apparently thinking that the United States would abandon Syngman Rhee. But Stalin warned Kim not to count on Soviet assistance: "If you should get kicked in the teeth, I shall not lift a finger. You have to ask Mao for all the help." In May, despite reservations, Mao also approved the North Korean aggression.

Both Stalin and Mao had miscalculated the American response. Truman saw the invasion as a clear-cut case of Soviet aggression reminiscent of the 1930s: "Communism was acting in Korea just as Hitler, Mussolini, and the Japanese had acted ten, fifteen, and twenty years earlier." Following Acheson's advice, the president convened the UN Security Council and, taking advantage of a Soviet boycott, secured a resolution condemning North Korea as an aggressor and calling on the member nations to engage in a collective security action. Within days, American troops from

View the **Map**
The Korean War, 1950–1953 on
myhistorylab.com

Japan were in combat in South Korea. The conflict, which would last for more than three years, was technically a police action fought under UN auspices; in reality, the United States was at war with a Soviet satellite in Asia. (See Map 28.2.)

At first the North Koreans drove down the peninsula. But by August, American forces had halted them near Pusan. In September, General MacArthur launched an amphibious assault at Inchon, on the waist of Korea, cutting off and destroying most of the North Korean army in the south. Truman then began to shift from his original goal of restoring the 38th parallel to unifying Korea by military force.

The administration ignored Beijing's repeated warnings not to invade North Korea. "I should think it would be sheer madness for the Chinese to intervene," commented Acheson. Despite CIA reports of a massive Chinese force assembling in Manchuria, Truman and his advisers believed that the Soviet Union, not ready for all-out war, would restrain China. MacArthur was equally certain that China would not attack his troops in Korea. "We are no longer fearful of their intervention," he told Truman in October, adding that if they crossed the Yalu River into Korea, "there would be the greatest slaughter."

Rarely has an American president received worse advice. China was not a Soviet puppet. When UN forces crossed the 38th parallel and moved toward the Yalu, a Chinese counterattack in late November caught MacArthur by surprise and drove his armies out of North Korea by the end of the year. MacArthur finally stabilized the fighting near the 38th parallel, but when Truman decided to give up his attempt to unify Korea, the general protested to Congress, calling for a renewed offensive and proclaiming, "There is no substitute for victory."

Truman then relieved the popular hero of the Pacific of his command on April 11, 1951. At first, MacArthur seemed likely to force the president to back down. Huge crowds welcomed him home and heard him call for victory over the communists in Asia. At a congressional hearing, the administration warned that MacArthur's strategy would expose all Europe to Soviet attack. General Omar Bradley, Truman's chief military adviser, pointed out that a "showdown" with communism in Asia would be "the wrong war, at the wrong place, at the wrong time, and with the wrong enemy."

Congress and the American people accepted MacArthur's recall. The Korean War became

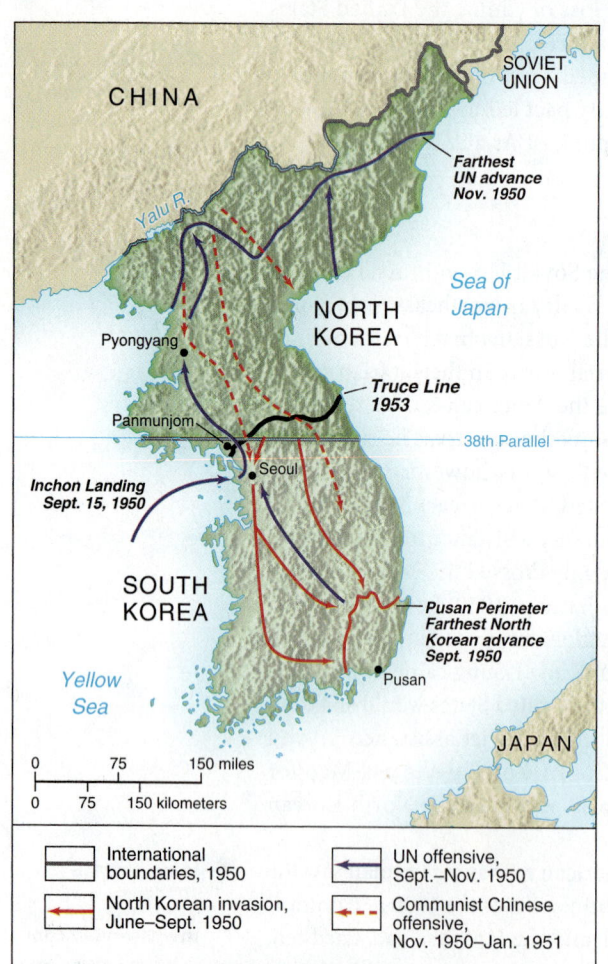

Map 28.2 The Korean War, 1950–1953 After a year of rapid movement up and down the Korean peninsula, the fighting stalled just north of the 38th parallel.

a stalemate near the 38th parallel as truce talks bogged down. The president had achieved his primary goal, defense of South Korea and the principle of collective security. Yet by taking the gamble to unify Korea by force, he had confused the American people and humiliated the United States in the eyes of the world.

The most significant result of the Korean conflict was massive American rearmament. The war led to the implementation of NSC-68—the army expanded to 3.5 million troops, the defense budget increased to $50 billion a year by 1952, and the United States acquired military bases from Saudi Arabia to Morocco. America was now committed to waging a global contest against the Soviet Union with arms as well as words.

Watch the **Video**
The Korean War Armistice on
myhistorylab.com

Quick Check

✓ How did the Korean war begin? How did it end?

THE COLD WAR AT HOME

The Cold War cast a long shadow over American life in the late 1940s and early 1950s. Truman tried to carry on the New Deal reform tradition he had inherited from FDR, but the American people were more concerned about events abroad. The Republicans used dissatisfaction with postwar economic adjustment and fears of communist penetration of the United States to regain control of the White House in 1952 for the first time in 20 years.

How did the Cold War affect life in America?

Truman's Troubles

Matching his foreign policy successes with equal achievements at home was not easy for Harry S. Truman. As a loyal supporter of Franklin D. Roosevelt's New Deal during his Senate career, Truman had a reputation for being hardworking, reliable, and intensely partisan. But he was relatively unknown to the general public, and his background as a Missouri county official associated with Kansas City machine politics did not inspire confidence in his ability to lead the nation. Surprisingly well-read—especially in history and biography—Truman possessed sound judgment, the ability to reach decisions quickly, and a fierce and uncompromising sense of right and wrong.

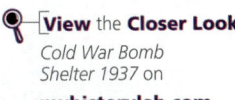

View the **Closer Look**
Cold War Bomb Shelter 1937 on
myhistorylab.com

Two weaknesses marred his performance in the White House. One was a fondness for old friends, which resulted in the appointment of Missouri and Senate cronies to high office. Attorney General Tom Clark, Secretary of the Treasury Charles Snyder, and White House military aide Harry Vaughn brought little credit to the administration, while the loss of such effective public servants as Secretary of the Interior Harold Ickes and Labor Secretary Frances Perkins hurt it. The president also lacked political vision. Failing to pursue a coherent legislative program of his own, he tried to perpetuate FDR's New Deal and fought a running battle with Congress.

The postwar mood was not conducive to extending New Deal reforms. Americans were weary of shortages and sacrifices; they wanted the consumer goods denied them under wartime conditions. But in the rush to convert industry from producing planes and tanks to cars and appliances, problems emerged. Prices and wages rose quickly as Congress ended wartime controls. With prices going up 25 percent in two years, workers demanded higher wages to offset the loss of overtime pay. Labor unrest swept the country in the spring of 1946, culminating in a walkout by coal miners that threatened to close down much of American industry and a paralyzing strike by railroad workers.

Truman was caught in the middle. Sensitive to union demands, he let businesses negotiate large pay increases for their workers and then pass on the cost to consumers as higher prices. He criticized Congress for weakening wartime price controls, but failed to offer anything else to curb inflation. Homemakers blamed him for the rising price of food. Organized labor called him as the country's "No. 1 Strikebreaker" when he asked Congress for power to draft striking railway workers into the army.

Given this discontent, Truman's efforts to extend the New Deal met with little success. Congress ignored his September 1945 call for measures to ensure economic security and enacted only the Employment Act of 1946. This legislation created the Council of Economic Advisers to assist the president and asserted government responsibility for the state of the economy, but it failed to address Truman's original goal of mandatory federal planning to achieve full employment.

The Republicans took advantage of postwar economic woes to attack the Democrats. "To err is Truman," the GOP proclaimed and then adopted a two-word slogan for the 1946 congressional elections: "Had enough?" The American people, weary of inflation and labor unrest, elected Republican majorities in both the House and Senate for the first time since 1930.

Quick Check

✓ What troubles did the country encounter on converting from war to peace?

Truman Vindicated

The president's relations with Congress became even stormier after the 1946 elections. Truman vetoed two GOP measures to give large tax cuts to the wealthy, but Congress overrode his veto of the Taft–Hartley Act in 1947, which outlawed specific union activities—including the closed shop and secondary boycotts. It also permitted the president to invoke an 80-day cooling-off period to delay strikes that might endanger national health or safety. Despite Truman's claim that it was a "slave-labor" bill, unions survived.

Truman's political fortunes reached their nadir in early 1948. Former vice president Henry A. Wallace, claiming to represent the New Deal, announced his third-party (Progressive) candidacy in the coming presidential contest. Worried Democrats sought to persuade Truman to step aside and allow General Dwight D. Eisenhower to become the Democratic candidate. When Eisenhower turned down bids from both parties, the Democrats reluctantly nominated Truman. His prospects for victory in the fall, however, looked dim—especially after disgruntled southerners bolted the Democratic party to protest a progressive civil rights platform. The Dixiecrats, as they became known, nominated Governor Strom Thurmond of South Carolina on a states' rights party ticket.

Election of 1948

Electoral Vote by State		Popular Vote
DEMOCRATIC Harry S. Truman	303	24,105,695
REPUBLICAN Thomas E. Dewey	189	21,969,170
STATES' RIGHTS Strom Thurmond	39	1,169,021
MINOR PARTIES	—	1,296,898
	531	48,537,784

Map 28.3

The defection of the Dixiecrats in the South and of Wallace's liberal followers in the North led experts to predict a Republican victory. Governor Thomas E. Dewey of New York, the GOP candidate, was so sure of winning that he waged a cautious and bland campaign designed to give him a free hand once he was in the White House. With nothing to lose, Truman barnstormed around the country denouncing the "do-nothing" Republican Eightieth Congress. The president's "give 'em hell" tactics reminded voters of how much they owed the Democrats for helping them survive the Great Depression. To the amazement of the pollsters, Truman won in November. The old Roosevelt coalition—farmers, organized labor, urban ethnic groups, and blacks—had held together, enabling Truman to remain in the White House and the Democrats to regain control of Congress. (See Map 28.3.)

There was one more reason for Truman's victory. During this election, held at the height of the Berlin crisis, the GOP failed to challenge Truman's conduct of the Cold War. Locked in a tense rivalry with the Soviet Union, the American people saw no reason to reject a president who had countered aggression overseas with the Truman Doctrine and the Marshall Plan. The Republicans, committed to support the bipartisan policy of containment, had allowed the Democrats to preempt the foreign policy issue. Until they found a way to challenge Truman's Cold War policies, GOP leaders had little chance to regain the White House.

Quick Check

✓ What were the key issues in the 1948 presidential election?

The Loyalty Issue

Despite Truman's surprising victory, the Democrats were vulnerable in one area. Fear of communism abroad that had led to the bipartisan containment policy could be used against them at home by politicians who were more willing to exploit the public's anxiety.

Fear of radicalism had been a recurrent feature of American life since the early republic. Federalists had tried to suppress dissent with the Alien and Sedition Acts in the 1790s; the Know-Nothings had campaigned against foreigners and Catholics in the 1850s; and the Red Scare after World War I had targeted both aliens and radicals. The Cold War heightened traditional fears that subversion from abroad endangered the republic. The Truman administration's portrayal of the men in the Kremlin as revolutionaries bent on world conquest frightened Americans. They viewed the Soviet Union as a successor to Nazi Germany—a totalitarian police state that threatened the liberties of a free people.

Revelations of communist espionage stoked these fears, sparking a second Red Scare. Canadian officials uncovered a Soviet spy ring in 1946, and the House Un-American Activities Committee (HUAC) held hearings indicating that communist agents had flourished in the Agriculture and Treasury Departments in the 1930s.

Truman tried to dismiss the loyalty issue as a "red herring," but felt compelled to take protective measures, thus lending substance to the charges of subversion. In March 1947, he had initiated a loyalty program, ordering security checks of government employees to root out communists. Intended to remove subversives for whom "reasonable grounds exist for belief that the person involved is disloyal," within four years the Loyalty Review Board was dismissing workers as security risks if there was "reasonable doubt" of their loyalty. Thousands of government workers lost their jobs, charged with guilt by association with radicals or with membership in left-wing organizations. Often they had no opportunity to face their accusers.

Read the
Document
Truman Loyalty Order on
myhistorylab.com

The most famous disclosure came in August 1948, when Whittaker Chambers, a repentant communist, accused Alger Hiss of having been a Soviet spy in the 1930s. When Hiss, who had been a prominent diplomat, denied the charges, Chambers led investigators to a hollowed-out pumpkin on his Maryland farm. Inside were microfilms of confidential government documents. Chambers claimed that Hiss had passed these materials to him in the late 1930s. Although the statute of limitations prevented a charge of treason against Hiss, he was convicted of perjury in January 1950 and sentenced to a five-year prison term.

In 1948, the Justice Department charged 11 officials of the Communist party with advocating the violent overthrow of the government. After a long trial, the jury found them guilty, and they received prison sentences and heavy fines; in 1951, the Supreme Court upheld the convictions as constitutional.

Such repression failed, however, to reassure the nation. Events abroad intensified the sense of danger. The communist triumph in China in 1949 came as a shock; there were charges that "fellow travelers" in the State Department were responsible for "the loss of China." In September 1949, after the Russians had detonated their first atomic bomb, the end of America's nuclear monopoly was blamed on Soviet espionage. In early 1950, Klaus Fuchs—a British scientist who had worked on the Manhattan Project—admitted giving the Russians vital information about the A-bomb.

A few months later, the government charged American communists Ethel and Julius Rosenberg with conspiracy to transmit atomic secrets to the Soviet Union. In 1951, a jury found the Rosenbergs guilty of espionage, and Judge Irving Kaufman sentenced them to die for their "loathsome offense." Despite their claims of innocence and worldwide appeals on their behalf, the Rosenbergs were electrocuted on June 19, 1953. Thus by the early 1950s, nearly all the ingredients were at hand for a new outburst of hysteria—fear of Russia, evidence of espionage, and a belief in a vast conspiracy. Only a leader to release the intolerance was missing.

McCarthyism in Action

On February 12, 1950, Senator Joseph R. McCarthy of Wisconsin delivered a routine Lincoln's Birthday speech in Wheeling, West Virginia. This little-known Republican attracted national attention when he declared, "I have here in my hand a list of 205—a list of names that were made known to the secretary of state as being members of the Communist party and who nevertheless are still working and shaping policy in the State Department." The charge of communists in the State Department—repeated on different occasions with the number changed to 57, then 81—was never substantiated. But McCarthy's speech triggered a four-and-a-half-year crusade to hunt down alleged communists in government. The stridency and sensationalism of the senator's accusations soon won the name McCarthyism.

McCarthy's basic technique was the multiple untruth. He made charges of treasonable activities in government. While officials were refuting his initial accusations, he made new ones, so the corrections never caught up with the latest blast. He failed to unearth a single confirmed communist in government, but he kept the Truman administration in turmoil. Drawing on an army of informers, primarily disgruntled federal workers with grievances against their colleagues and superiors, McCarthy charged government agencies with harboring and protecting communist agents and accused the State Department of deliberately losing the Cold War. His briefcase bulged with documents, but he did little actual research, relying instead on reports (often outdated) from earlier congressional investigations. He exploited the press, combining current accusations with promises of future disclosures to guarantee headlines.

The secret of McCarthy's power was the fear he engendered in his Senate colleagues. In 1950, Maryland Senator Millard Tydings, who headed a committee critical of McCarthy's activities, lost reelection when McCarthy opposed him; other senators then ran scared. McCarthy delighted in making sweeping, startling charges of communist sympathies against prominent figures. A favorite target was patrician Secretary of State Dean Acheson, whom McCarthy ridiculed as the "Red Dean," with his "cane, spats and tea-sipping little finger"; he even claimed that General George Marshall was an agent of the communist conspiracy. Nor were fellow Republicans immune. He called one GOP senator "a living miracle in that he is without question the only man who has lived so long with neither brains nor guts."

The attacks on the wealthy, famous, and privileged won McCarthy a devoted following, though at the height of his influence in early 1954, only 50 percent of the respondents in a Gallup poll approved of him. McCarthy drew

Senator Joseph McCarthy maintained a stream of unsubstantiated charges, always ready to make new accusations of communist infiltration before the preceding ones could be proven untrue.

disproportionate backing from working-class Catholics and ethnic groups, especially the Irish, Poles, and Italians, who normally voted Democratic. He offered a simple solution to the complicated Cold War: Defeat the enemy at home rather than continue to engage in costly foreign aid programs and entangling alliances abroad. Above all, McCarthy appealed to conservative Republicans in the Midwest who shared his right-wing views and felt cheated by Truman's upset victory in 1948. Even GOP leaders who viewed McCarthy with distaste, such as Robert A. Taft of Ohio, encouraged him to attack the vulnerable Democrats.

Quick Check

✓ How did Joseph McCarthy use the power of fear to win a devoted following?

The Republicans in Power

In 1952, the GOP capitalized on national frustration to capture the presidency. The stalemate in Korea and the second Red Scare created a desire for political change;

Eisenhower's landslide victories in 1952 and 1956 seemed to prove his slogan that Americans did, indeed, "like Ike," as expressed on this campaign pennant.

revelations of scandals involving individuals close to Truman intensified the feeling that someone needed to clean up "the mess in Washington." In Dwight D. Eisenhower, the Republican party found the perfect candidate to explore what one senator called K1C2—Korea, communism, and corruption.

Popular because of his amiable manner, winning smile, and heroic stature, Eisenhower alone appeared to have the ability to unite a divided nation. In the 1952 campaign, Ike displayed hidden gifts as a politician in running against Adlai Stevenson, the eloquent Illinois governor, whose appeal was limited to diehard Democrats and liberal intellectuals. Eisenhower allowed his young running mate, Senator Richard M. Nixon of California, to hammer away at the Democrats on the communist and corruption issues, but he himself delivered the most telling blow of all on the Korean War. Speaking in Detroit in late October, just after the fighting had intensified again in Korea, Ike promised to go personally to the battlefield "to bring the Korean War to an early and honorable end."

"That does it—Ike is in," reporters exclaimed after they heard this pledge. The hero of World War II had clinched his election by committing himself to end an unpopular war. Ten days later, he won the presidency handily, carrying 39 states, including four in the formerly solid Democratic South. (See Table 28.1.) The Republicans, however, fared less well in Congress; they gained just a slight edge in the House and controlled the Senate by only one seat.

Watch the **Video**
Ike for President: Campaign Ad, 1952 on
myhistorylab.com

TABLE 28.1 The Election of 1952

Candidate	Party	Popular Vote	Electoral Vote
Eisenhower	Republican	33,778,963	442
Stevenson	Democratic	27,314,992	89

Eisenhower fulfilled his campaign pledge. He spent three days in early December touring the battlefront in Korea, ruling out the new offensive the military favored: "Small attacks on small hills would not end the war." Instead he turned to diplomacy, relying on hints to China on the use of nuclear weapons to break the stalemated peace talks. These tactics, together with Stalin's death in March, finally led to an armistice on July 27, 1953, which ended the fighting but left Korea divided—as it had been before the war—near the 38th parallel.

The new president was less effective in dealing with McCarthy's continuing witch-hunt. Instead of toning down his anticommunist crusade after the Republican victory in 1952, McCarthy used his new position as chairman of the Senate Committee on Government Operations to ferret out communists on the federal payroll. He made charges against the foreign affairs agencies and demanded that books be purged from American information libraries overseas. Eisenhower's advisers urged the president to use his prestige to stop McCarthy. But Ike refused: "I will not get into a pissing contest with a skunk." Instead he played for time, hoping the American people would come to their senses.

The Wisconsin senator finally overreached himself. In early 1954, he uncovered an army dentist suspected of disloyalty and attacked the upper echelons of the army, telling one much-decorated general that he was "not fit to wear the uniform." The controversy culminated in the televised Army–McCarthy hearings. For six weeks, the senator exhibited his crude bullying to the American people. Viewers were repelled by his frequent outbursts that began with the insistent cry, "Point of order, Mr. Chairman, point of order," and by his attempt to smear the reputation of a young lawyer associated with army counsel Joseph Welch. Welch condemned McCarthy for his "reckless cruelty" and asked rhetorically, as millions watched, "Have you no sense of decency, sir?"

Courageous Republicans, led by Senators Ralph Flanders of Vermont and Margaret Chase Smith of Maine, joined Democrats to censure McCarthy in December 1954, by a vote of 67 to 22. McCarthy fell quickly from prominence. He died three years later virtually unnoticed and unmourned.

Yet his influence was profound. He paralyzed national life with what a Senate subcommittee described as "the most nefarious campaign of half-truth and untruth in the history of the Republic." He also helped impose a political and cultural conformity that froze dissent for the rest of the 1950s. Long after his passing, the nation tolerated loyalty oaths for teachers, banning left-wing books from public libraries, and blacklisting entertainers in radio, television, and films. Freedom of expression was inhibited, and new ideas and approaches stifled. The United States settled into a sterile Cold War consensus.

While Eisenhower could claim that his policy of giving McCarthy enough rope to hang himself had worked, a bolder and more forthright presidential attack on the senator might have spared the nation some of the excesses of the second Red Scare.

Quick Check

✔ What foreign and domestic issues influenced the election of Eisenhower in 1952?

CONCLUSION: THE CONTINUING COLD WAR

Eisenhower's election calmed things at home but did not end the Cold War abroad. During Ike's presidency the United States extended its policy of containment and expanded its nuclear arsenal. Eisenhower himself wondered where it all would lead. In his second term, he tried to defuse tensions with the Soviet Union, and he warned about the danger of massive military spending in his farewell address to the American people: "In the councils of government, we must guard against the acquisition of unwarranted influence, whether sought or unsought, by the military-industrial complex. The potential for the disastrous rise of misplaced power exists and will persist."

Rarely has an American president been more prophetic. Defense spending would skyrocket as the Cold War escalated. Eisenhower had kept the peace, but he had failed to halt the momentum of the Cold War he had inherited from Truman.

28 STUDY RESOURCES

((•—[**Listen** to the **Chapter Audio** for
Chapter 28 on **myhistorylab.com**

TIMELINE

1945 Truman meets Stalin at Potsdam Conference (July), p. 703

1947 Truman Doctrine announced (March), p. 708
- Truman orders loyalty program for government employees (March), p. 719
- George Marshall outlines Marshall Plan (June), p. 709

1948 Soviets begin blockade of Berlin (June), p. 711
- Truman elected president, p. 720

1949 NATO treaty signed in Washington (April), p. 708
- Soviet Union tests its first atomic bomb (August), p. 713

1950 Truman authorizes developing hydrogen bomb (January), p. 713
- Senator Joseph McCarthy claims communists in government (February), p. 720
- North Korea invades South Korea (June), p. 715

1951 Truman recalls MacArthur from Korea, p. 716

1952 Dwight D. Eisenhower elected president, p. 724

CHAPTER REVIEW

THE COLD WAR BEGINS

How did the Cold War begin?

The Cold War began as the United States and the Soviet Union discovered that their interests in Europe conflicted. Each feared the other and, acting on its fears, took steps that heightened the other's fears. Atomic weapons made the mistakes of miscalculation far greater than in the past and everyone more fearful. (p. 705)

CONTAINMENT

What was containment, and why was it adopted?

Containment was the American policy of preventing Soviet power and influence from expanding. It was

adopted to preserve American interests without excessively risking war. (p. 708)

THE COLD WAR EXPANDS

How did the Cold War expand from Europe to Asia?

The United States and the Soviet Union took opposite sides in the Chinese civil war. Shortly after the communist victory in China, communist North Korea battled anticommunist South Korea. The United States sided with South Korea. The Soviet Union and Communist China backed North Korea. (p. 712)

THE COLD WAR AT HOME

How did the Cold War affect life in America?

The Cold War spawned fears of communist subversion. It led to a campaign to ensure loyalty, and fostered McCarthyism, an exaggerated effort to find communists in every corner of American life. Although McCarthyism eventually burned itself out, it contributed to Eisenhower's election in 1952, which ended 20 years of Democratic control of the White House. *(p. 717)*

KEY TERM QUESTIONS

1. How did the Potsdam Conference reveal the tensions that would produce the Cold War? (p. 703)

2. What was the Iron Curtain? (p. 705)

3. Why did the Soviets reject the Baruch Plan? (p. 707)

4. Why was containment adopted and how successful was it? (p. 708)

5. What was the Truman Doctrine? (p. 708)

6. What was the Marshall Plan and how well did it work? (p. 710)

7. Why did the U.S. sponsor the North Atlantic Treaty Organization (NATO)? (p. 710)

8. Why was the Berlin airlift carried out and how successful was it? (p. 711)

9. Why was the National Security Act passed and what were its key provisions? (p. 712)

10. What was the purpose of NSC-68 and why is it significant? (p. 713)

11. Why did organized labor oppose the Taft–Hartley Act? (p. 718)

12. What was McCarthyism? (p. 720)

MyHistoryLab CONNECTIONS

Visit **www.myhistorylab.com** for a customized Study Plan to build your knowledge of *The Onset of the Cold War*

Questions for Analysis

1. Why did Winston Churchill deliver the Iron Curtain Speech?

    Read the **Document** *Winston Churchill, from Iron Curtain Speech, 1946* p. 705

2. What do AA batteries, Campbell's soup, and Legos have to do with the House Committee on Un-American Activities?

    View the **Closer Look** *Cold War Bomb Shelter* p. 717

3. How did Truman believe the United States should confront the threat of communism?

    Watch the **Video** *President Truman and the Threat of Communism* p. 708

4. Why and how did the Korean War end in 1953?

    View the **Map** *The Korean War, 1950–1953* p. 715

5. What did Ronald Reagan tell the House Committee on Un-American Activities?

    Read the **Document** *Ronald Reagan, Testimony before HUAC (1947)* p. 720

Other Resources from this Chapter

Watch the **Video** *Atomic Age Begins*

Read the **Document** *Truman Doctrine*

Read the **Document** *George Marshall, The Marshall Plan*

View the **Map** *Cold War in Europe, 1950*

Read the **Document** *National Security Council Memorandum Number 68*

Watch the **Video** *The Korean War Armistice*

Read the **Document** *Truman Loyalty Order*

Listen to the **Audio File** *Joseph P. McCarthy Speech*

Watch the **Video** *Ike for President: Eisenhower Campaign Ad, 1952*

Contents and Spotlight Questions

((•— Listen to the **Chapter Audio** for Chapter 29 on **myhistorylab.com**

LEVITTOWN: THE FLIGHT TO THE SUBURBS

On May 7, 1947, William Levitt announced plans to build thousands of rental houses in a former potato field on Long Island, 30 miles from Midtown Manhattan. Using mass production techniques he had learned while erecting navy housing during the war, Levitt quickly built 4,000 homes and rented them to young veterans and their wives eager to leave crowded city apartments or their parents' homes to begin raising families. A change in government financing regulations led him to offer his houses for sale in 1948 for a small amount down and a low monthly payment. Young couples, many of them the original renters, quickly bought the first 4,000. By the time Levittown—as he called the new community—was completed in 1951, it contained more than 17,000 houses. So many babies were born there that it was called "Fertility Valley" and "the Rabbit Hutch."

Levitt built two more Levittowns, in Pennsylvania and New Jersey; each contained the same curving streets, neighborhood parks and playgrounds, and community swimming pools characteristic of his first development. The secret of Levittown's appeal was the basic house, a 720-square-foot Cape Cod design built on a concrete slab. It had a kitchen, two bedrooms, a bath, a living room with a fireplace and 16-foot picture window, and an expansion

The houses of Levittown spread over 1,200 acres of former potato fields on Long Island, New York.

attic with room for two more bedrooms. Each house had the same interior, but four different exterior facades broke the monotony. The original house sold for $6,990 in 1948; even the improved ranch-style model sold for less than $10,000 in 1951.

Levitt's houses were ideal for young people starting out in life. They were cheap, comfortable, and efficient, and each house came with a refrigerator, stove, and washing machine. Despite the houses' conformity, the three Levittowns became surprisingly diverse communities; residents had a wide variety of religious, ethnic, and occupational backgrounds. African Americans, however, were rigidly excluded. In time, as the more successful families moved on to larger homes in more expensive neighborhoods, the Levittowns became enclaves for lower-middle-class families.

Levittown symbolized the most significant social trend of the postwar era in the United States—the flight to the suburbs. The residential areas surrounding cities such as New York and Chicago nearly doubled in the 1950s. While the population of central cities remained relatively stagnant, suburbs grew by 46 percent; by 1960, 60 million people, one-third of the nation, lived in suburban rings around the cities. A baby boom that started during World War II accompanied the massive shift in population from the central cities. Young married couples began to have three, four, or even five children (compared with only one or two children in American families during the 1930s). As a result, the nation's population grew by 19 percent between 1950 and 1960, the highest growth rate since 1910. (See Figure 29.1.)

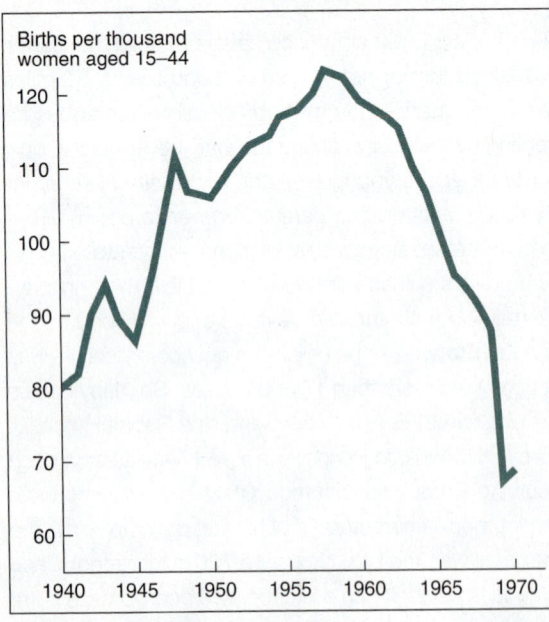

Figure 29.1 Birthrate, 1940–1970

Source: Compiled from U.S. Bureau of the Census, *Historical Statistics of the United States, Colonial Times to 1970*, Bicentennial Edition, Washington, DC, 1975.

The economy also boomed as residential construction soared. By 1960, one-fourth of all existing houses were less than ten years old, and factories were turning out large quantities of appliances and television sets for the new households. New consumer products—ranging from frozen foods to filter cigarettes, from high-fidelity phonographs to cars with automatic transmissions and tubeless tires—appeared. In the suburbs, the corner grocery gave way to the supermarket carrying a vast array of items that provided families with a more varied diet.

Affluence replaced the poverty and hunger of the Great Depression for most Americans, but memories of the 1930s still haunted many. The obsession with material goods became almost desperate, as if houses, cars, and appliances could guarantee that the nightmare of depression would never return. Critics condemned the conformity of suburban life, charging the newly affluent with forsaking traditional American individualism to live in identical houses, drive look-alike cars, and accumulate the same material possessions.

Events abroad added to postwar anxiety. Nuclear war became a frightening possibility. The rivalry with the Soviet Union had led to the second Red Scare and charges of treason and disloyalty being leveled at loyal Americans. Many Americans joined Senator Joseph McCarthy in searching for the communist enemy at home rather than abroad. Loyalty oaths and book burnings revealed how insecure Americans had become in the Cold War. The 1950s also witnessed a growing demand by African Americans for equal opportunity in an age of abundance. The civil rights movement, and strident criticism of the consumer culture, revealed that forces for change were at work beneath the bland surface of suburban affluence.

THE POSTWAR BOOM

For 15 years following World War II, the nation experienced unparalleled economic growth. Pent-up demand for consumer goods fueled industrial expansion. Government spending during the Cold War also stimulated the economy, offsetting brief recessions in 1949 and 1953 and moderating a steeper one in 1957–1958. By 1960, the American people had achieved an affluence that finally erased the lingering fears of the Great Depression.

How did the American economy evolve after World War II?

Postwar Prosperity

Two long-term factors accounted for the economy's upward surge. First, American consumers—after being held in check by depression and wartime scarcities—finally were able to indulge their appetites for material goods. At the war's end, personal savings in the United States stood at more than $37 billion, providing a powerful stimulus to consumption. American factories could not turn out enough automobiles and appliances to satisfy the horde of buyers until 1950. In that year, the gross national product (GNP) reached $318 billion (50 percent higher than in 1940).

The Cold War provided the additional stimulus the economy needed when postwar expansion slowed. The Marshall Plan and other foreign aid programs financed a heavy export trade. The Korean War helped reverse a brief recession and ensured continued prosperity as the government spent massively on weapons and munitions. In 1952, the nation spent $44 billion, two-thirds of the federal budget, on national defense. Although Eisenhower managed to effect modest reductions, defense spending continued at a level of $40 billion throughout the decade.

The affluence of the 1950s made the fear of another Great Depression seem irrational. The baby boom and the spectacular growth of suburbia were great stimulants to the consumer goods industries. Manufacturers turned out an ever-increasing number of refrigerators, washing machines, and dishwashers to equip the kitchens of Levittown and its many imitators. The automobile industry thrived as two-car suburban families became common. In 1955, when oil was abundant and gasoline sold for less than 30 cents a gallon, Detroit sold a record eight million cars. The electronics industry also boomed. Consumers were eager to acquire the latest marvel of home entertainment—the television set.

Businesses snapped up office machines and the first generation of computers; industry installed electronic sensors and processors as automation grew, and the military appetite for electronic devices for its planes and ships was insatiable. As a result, American industry averaged more than $10 billion a year in capital investment, and the number of persons employed rose above the long-sought goal of 60 million nationwide.

Yet the economic abundance of the 1950s was not without its problems. While some sections of the nation (notably the Pacific Northwest and the emerging Sunbelt areas of the South and West) benefited enormously from the growth of the aircraft and electronics industries, older manufacturing regions, such as New England, fared less well. The steel industry increased its capacity during the decade, but fell behind the rate of national growth. Agriculture experienced bumper crops and low prices, so rural regions, like the vast Plains states, failed to share in the general affluence. Despite the boom, unemployment rose to more than 7 percent in a sharp recession that began in late 1957 and lasted through the summer of 1958. Economic growth slowed after 1955, causing concern about the continuing vitality of the economy.

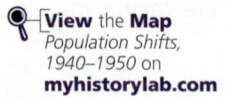

View the **Map**
*Population Shifts,
1940–1950* on
myhistorylab.com

None of these flaws, however, could disguise a prosperity that no one had dreamed possible in the 1930s. The GNP grew to $440 billion by 1960, more than double the 1940 level. More important, workers now labored fewer than 40 hours a week; they rarely worked on Saturdays, and nearly all enjoyed an annual two-week paid vacation. By the mid-1950s, the average American family had twice as much real income to spend as its counterpart had possessed in the boom years of the 1920s. From 1945 to 1960, per capita disposable income rose by $500—to $1,845—for every man, woman, and child in the country. The American people, in one generation, had moved from poverty and depression to the highest standard of living the world had ever known.

Quick Check

✓ What drove the prosperity of the postwar decades?

Life in the Suburbs

Sociologists had difficulty describing the nature of suburban society in the 1950s. Some saw it as classless, while others noted the absence of both the very rich and the very poor and labeled it "middle class." Rather than forming a homogeneous social group, though, the suburbs contained a surprising variety of people, whether classified as "upper lower," "lower middle," and "upper middle," or simply as blue collar, white collar, and professional. Doctors and lawyers often lived in the same developments as salesclerks and master plumbers. The traditional distinctions of ancestry, education, and size of residence no longer differentiated people as easily as they once had.

Yet suburbs could vary widely, from working-class communities clustered near factories built in the countryside to old, elitist areas such as Scarsdale, New York, and Shaker Heights, Ohio. Most were almost exclusively white and Christian, but suburbs such as Great Neck on Long Island and Richmond Heights outside Miami enabled Jews and blacks to take part in the flight from the inner city.

Suburban life depended on the automobile. Highways and expressways allowed fathers to commute to jobs in the cities, often an hour or more away. Children might ride buses to and from school, but mothers had to drive them to piano lessons and

Little League games. Two cars became a necessity for almost every suburban family, spurring the boom in automobile production. In 1948, only 59 percent of American families owned a car; a few years later, nearly every suburban family had at least one vehicle, and many had several.

In the new drive-in culture, people shopped at the stores that grew up first in "miracle miles" along the highways and later at the shopping centers that spread across the countryside in the 1950s. In 1946, the entire country had only eight shopping centers; hundreds appeared over the next 15 years, including Poplar Plaza in Memphis, with one large department store, 30 retail shops, and parking for more than 500 cars. In 1956, the first enclosed air-conditioned mall, the Southdale Shopping Center, opened outside Minneapolis.

Despite the increased mobility the car provided, the home became the focus for activities and aspirations. The postwar housing shortage that often forced young couples to live with their parents created an intense demand for new houses in the suburbs. Prospective buyers expressed a desire for "more space," "comfort and roominess," and "privacy and freedom of action" in their new residences. Men and women who moved to the suburbs prized the new kitchens with their built-in dishwashers, electric ovens, and gleaming counters; the extra bedrooms that ensured privacy from and for the children; the large garages that could be converted into recreation rooms; and the small, neat lawns that gave them an area for outdoor activities and a new way to compete with their neighbors. "Togetherness" became the code word of the 1950s. Families did things together, whether gathering around the TV sets that dominated living rooms, attending community activities, or taking vacations in huge station wagons.

But the new suburban lifestyle also had less attractive consequences. The extended family, in which several generations had lived in close proximity, was a casualty of the boom in small detached homes. As historian Kenneth Jackson noted, suburban life "ordained that most children would grow up in intimate contact only with their parents and siblings." For many families, grandparents, aunts and uncles, cousins, and more distant relatives would become remote figures, seen only on special occasions.

The nuclear family, typical of the suburb, did little to encourage feminism. After the war, many women who had entered the workforce returned to the home, where the role of wife and mother remained the ideal for women in the 1950s. Trends toward getting married earlier and having larger families reinforced the pattern of women devoting their efforts to housework and child raising rather than acquiring professional skills and pursuing careers outside the home. Adlai Stevenson, the Democratic presidential candidate in 1952 and 1956, extolling "the humble role of housewife," told Smith College graduates that there was much they could do "in the living room with a baby in your lap or in the kitchen with a can opener in your hand." Dr. Benjamin Spock's 1946 bestseller, *Baby and Child Care*, became a fixture in millions of homes, while the traditional women's magazines such as *McCall's* and *Good Housekeeping* thrived with articles on natural childbirth and inspirational pieces such as "Homemaking Is My Vocation."

Read the **Document**
Ladies Home Journal, "Young Mother" (1956) on **myhistorylab.com**

Quick Check

✓ How did the growth
of suburbs change
the way Americans
lived?

Nonetheless, the number of working wives doubled between 1940 and 1960. By 1960, 40 percent of American women, and nearly one-third of married women, had jobs outside the home. The expense of rearing and educating children led wives and mothers to seek to augment the family income, inadvertently preparing the way for a new demand for equality in the 1960s.

THE GOOD LIFE?

How did
American culture
change after the
war?

Consumerism became the dominant social theme of the 1950s. Yet even with an abundance of creature comforts and more leisure time, many Americans remained anxious and dissatisfied.

Areas of Greatest Growth

Organized religion flourished in the 1950s. Ministers, priests, and rabbis noted the rise in church and synagogue attendance in the new communities. Sociologist Will Herberg claimed that religious affiliation had become the primary identifying feature of modern American life, dividing the nation into three segments—Protestant, Catholic, and Jewish.

Observers condemned the bland, secular nature of suburban churches, which seemed to be part of the consumer society. "On weekdays one shops for food," wrote one critic, "on Saturdays one shops for recreation, and on Sundays one shops for the Holy Ghost." But the popularity of the Rev. Norman Vincent Peale, who urged people to "start thinking faith, enthusiasm and joy," suggested that the new churches filled a genuine if shallow human need. But the emergence of neo-orthodoxy in Protestant seminaries, notably through the ideas of Reinhold Niebuhr, who sought to accommodate Christian teaching to the atomic age, and the spread of radical fundamentalism such as the Assemblies of God, indicated that millions of Americans still were searching for a more personal religious faith.

One of the most popular television programs of the 1950s was *I Love Lucy*, a situation comedy featuring the real-life husband-and-wife team of Lucille Ball and Desi Arnaz portraying the fictional couple Lucy and Ricky Ricardo.

Schools were a problem for the growing new suburban communities. The increase in the number of school-age children, from 20 to 30 million in the first eight grades, overwhelmed many local districts, leading to demands for federal aid. Congress granted limited help for areas affected by defense plants and military bases, but Eisenhower's reluctance to unbalance the budget—along with traditional adherence to state control over public education—blocked further federal assistance before 1957, when the government reacted to *Sputnik*, the Soviet satellite that ushered in the space age, by sharply increasing federal support for science education.

A controversy also arose over education in the 1950s. Critics of "progressive" education called for sweeping educational reforms and a new stress on traditional academic subjects. Suburban communities had bitter fights; affluent parents demanded kindergarten enrichment programs and grade school foreign language instruction, while working-class people resisted such costly innovations. The one thing all seemed to agree on was the desirability of a college education. College enrollment increased from 1.5 million in 1940 to 3.6 million in 1960.

The largest advances were made in the exciting new medium of television. From a shaky start just after the war, TV boomed in the 1950s, pushing radio aside and undermining magazines. By 1957, three networks controlled the airwaves, reaching 40 million sets over nearly 500 stations. Advertisers soon took charge of the new medium, using techniques first pioneered in radio—including taped commercials, quiz shows, and soap operas.

At first, the insatiable demand for programs encouraged creativity. Playwrights such as Reginald Rose, Rod Serling, and Paddy Chayefsky wrote notable dramas for *Playhouse 90*, *Studio One*, and the *Goodyear Television Playhouse*. Broadcast live from cramped studios, these productions thrived on tight dramatic structures, movable scenery, and frequent close-ups of the actors.

Advertisers, however, quickly became disillusioned with the live dramatic programs, which usually dealt with controversial subjects or focused on ordinary people and events. Sponsors wanted shows that featured excitement, glamour, and instant success. Aware that contestants with unusual expertise (a shoemaker answering tough questions on operas, a grandmother stumping experts on baseball) fascinated audiences, producers began giving away huge cash prizes on *The $64,000 Question* and *Twenty-One*. In 1959, Charles Van Doren, a Columbia University professor, confessed he had been given the answers in advance to win $129,000 on *Twenty-One*. The three networks quickly replaced the big-prize quiz programs with comedy, action, and adventure shows such as *The Untouchables* and *Bonanza*. Despite its early artistic promise, television became a technologically sophisticated but safe conveyor of the consumer culture.

View the **Closer Look**
A 1950s Family Watching I love Lucy on
myhistorylab.com

Read the **Document**
The Teenage Consumer on
myhistorylab.com

Quick Check
✓ What was the effect of television on American life?

Critics of the Consumer Society

One striking feature of the 1950s was the disenchantment many authors and artists expressed. This disenchantment reached its most eloquent expression with the beats, literary groups that rebelled against the era's materialism. Jack Kerouac's novel *On the Road*, published in 1957, and Allen Ginsburg's poem *Howl* set the tone for the new movement. The name "beats" came from the quest for beatitude, a state of inner grace sought in Zen Buddhism. Flouting the respectability of suburbia, the "beatniks"—as middle America termed them—were easily identified by their long hair and bizarre clothing; they also had a penchant for sexual promiscuity and drugs. They were conspicuous dropouts from a society they found senseless. Poet Lawrence Ferlinghetti, who held forth in the City Lights Bookshop in San

Francisco (a favorite beats' resort), summed it up: "I was a wind-up toy someone had dropped wound up into a world already running down."

The social protest inherent in the books and poems of the beats found its counterpart in the rise of abstract expressionism. Abstract expressionists emphasized individuality and freedom from the constraints of representational, realistic art. Painters Jackson Pollock and Mark Rothko, among others, challenged mainstream America's notions about the form and function of art. For Pollock, the act of creating a painting was as important as the painting itself. Rothko pioneered a style known as color field painting; his works in this style are monumental pieces in which enormous areas of color lacking any distinct structure or central focus create a mood.

Despite the disapproval of mainstream Americans, the beat generation had compassion for their detractors. "We love everything," Kerouac proclaimed, "Billy Graham, the Big Ten, Rock and Roll, Zen, apple pie, Eisenhower—we dig it all." Yet, as highly visible nonconformists in an era of stifling conformity, the beats demonstrated a style of social protest that would flower into the counterculture of the 1960s.

> **Quick Check**
>
> ✓ What did critics find lacking in American postwar culture?

THE STRUGGLE OVER CIVIL RIGHTS

How did the civil rights movement develop in the 1940s and 1950s?

The questioning of American life was most evident in race relations, where the white majority continued to deny basic rights to the black minority. The contradiction between denouncing the Soviet Union for its human rights violations and the second-class status of African Americans began to arouse the national conscience. Fighting for freedom against communist tyranny abroad, Americans had to acknowledge the denial of freedom to a submerged minority at home.

African Americans had benefited economically from World War II, but they were still seriously disadvantaged. Those who had left the South for northern and western cities were concentrated in blighted and segregated neighborhoods, working at low-paying jobs, suffering discrimination, and not sharing fully in the postwar prosperity. African Americans' rising expectations in the postwar years led them to challenge racial segregation and inequality.

In the South, conditions were worse. State laws forced blacks to live almost totally segregated from white society. Not only did African Americans attend separate (and inferior) schools, but they also were rigidly segregated in all public facilities. They were forced to use separate waiting rooms in train stations, separate seats on all forms of transportation, separate drinking fountains, and even separate telephone booths and cemeteries. "Segregation was enforced at all places of public entertainment, including libraries, auditoriums, and circuses," Chief Justice Earl Warren noted. "There was segregation in the hospitals, prisons, mental institutions, and nursing homes. Even ambulance service was segregated."

Civil Rights as a Political Issue

Truman was the first president to attempt to alter the pattern of racial discrimination in the United States. In 1946, he appointed a presidential commission on civil rights. In 1947, in a report titled "To Secure These Rights," the commission recommended reinstating the wartime Fair Employment Practices Committee (FEPC), establishing a permanent civil rights commission, and denying federal aid to any state that segregated schools and public facilities. The president's ten-point legislative program proposed in 1948 included some of these measures, notably the establishment of a permanent FEPC and a civil rights commission. But southern resistance blocked action by Congress, and the inclusion of a strong civil rights plank in the 1948 Democratic platform led to the walkout of southern delegations and a separate States' Rights (Dixiecrat) ticket that fall.

African American voters in the North overwhelmingly backed Truman over Dewey in 1948. The African American vote in Los Angeles, Cleveland, and Chicago ensured the Democratic victory in California, Ohio, and Illinois. Truman responded by including civil rights legislation in his Fair Deal program in 1949. Again, however, southerners blocked congressional action on both a permanent FEPC and an anti-lynching measure.

Even though Truman was unable to secure significant legislation, he made civil rights an integral part of the Democratic reform program. Truman also used his executive power to assist African Americans. He strengthened the civil rights division of the Justice Department, which helped black groups challenge school segregation and restrictive housing covenants in the courts. Most important, in 1948 Truman ordered the desegregation of the armed forces. The navy and the air force quickly complied, but the army resisted until the personnel needs of the Korean War finally overcame its objections. By 1960, the armed forces were far more integrated than American society at large.

Watch the **Video**
The Desegregation of the Military and Blacks in Combat on **myhistorylab.com**

Quick Check
✓ How did civil rights shape the politics of the postwar years?

Desegregating the Schools

Schools soon became the primary target of civil rights advocates. The NAACP concentrated first on universities, winning admission for qualified African Americans to state graduate and professional schools. Led by Thurgood Marshall, NAACP lawyers then attacked segregation in the public schools. Challenging *Plessy v. Ferguson*, the 1896 Supreme Court decision that upheld the constitutionality of separate but equal public facilities (see Chapter 19), Marshall argued that even substantially equal but separate schools did profound psychological damage to African American children and thus violated the Fourteenth Amendment.

In 1954, in the case of ***Brown v. Board of Education of Topeka,*** the Supreme Court unanimously agreed. Chief Justice Earl Warren, recently appointed by President Eisenhower, flatly declared that "separate educational facilities are inherently unequal." To divide grade school children "solely because of their race," he argued, "generates a feeling of inferiority as to their status in the community that may affect their hearts and minds in a way unlikely ever to be undone." Despite this sweeping language, Warren realized that changing historic patterns of segregation would be difficult. Accordingly, in 1955 the Court ruled that school desegregation should proceed "with all deliberate speed" and left the details to the lower federal courts.

"All deliberate speed" proved to be agonizingly slow. The border states quickly complied with the Court's ruling, but the Deep South responded with massive resistance. White citizens' councils organized to retain racial separation; 101

Read the **Document**
Brown v. Board of Education of Topeka, Kansas (1954) on **myhistorylab.com**

Demonstrators supporting the Supreme Court's 1954 *Brown v. Board of Education* ruling to desegregate the nation's schools. The ruling also sparked protests, many of them violent and destructive, by opponents of integration.

representatives and senators signed a Southern Manifesto in 1956 denouncing the *Brown* decision as "a clear abuse of judicial power." School boards found ways to evade the Court's ruling. Pupil placement laws enabled officials to assign individual students to schools on the basis of scholastic aptitude, ability to adjust, and "morals, conduct, health and personal standards." These tactics led to long disputes in the federal courts; by 1960, less than 1 percent of the black children in the Deep South attended school with whites.

A conspicuous lack of presidential support further weakened the desegregation effort. Eisenhower believed that "cold law making" could not alter people's attitudes. Change could only come "by appealing to reason, by prayer, and by constantly working at it through our own efforts." Quietly, he worked to desegregate federal facilities, particularly in veterans' hospitals, navy yards, and the District of Columbia school system. Yet he refrained from endorsing *Brown*, which he believed had "set back progress in the South at least fifteen years."

Southern leaders mistook Ike's silence for support of segregation. In 1957, Governor Orval Faubus of Arkansas called out the National Guard to prevent the integration of Little Rock's Central High School on grounds of a threat to public order. After 270 troops turned back nine African American students, a federal judge ordered the guardsmen removed; but when the black students entered the school, a mob of 500 jeering whites surrounded the building. Eisenhower, who had told Faubus that "the Federal Constitution will be upheld by me by every legal means at my command," sent in 1,000 paratroopers to ensure the rights of the Little Rock Nine to attend Central High. The students finished the school year under armed guard. Then Little Rock authorities closed the school for two years; when it reopened, only three African Americans were in attendance.

Despite the snail's pace of school desegregation, the *Brown* decision led to other advances. In 1957, the Eisenhower administration proposed the first general civil rights legislation since Reconstruction. Senate Majority Leader Lyndon B. Johnson overcame strong southern resistance to avoid a filibuster, but at the expense of weakening the measure. The act, however, did create a permanent Commission for Civil Rights, one of Truman's original goals. It also provided for federal efforts aimed at "securing and protecting the right to vote." A second civil rights act in 1960 slightly strengthened the voting rights section.

Like the desegregation effort, the attempt to ensure African American voting rights in the South was still largely symbolic. Southern registrars used devices, ranging from intimidation to unfair tests, to deny African Americans suffrage. Yet the actions of Congress and the Supreme Court marked a turning point in national policy toward racial justice.

Quick Check

✓ What was the importance of the case of *Brown v. Board of Education of Topeka*?

The Beginnings of Black Activism

African Americans themselves were the most dynamic force for change. The shift from legal struggles in the courts to protest in the streets began in Montgomery, Alabama. On December 1, 1955, Rosa Parks—a black seamstress who had been active in the local NAACP—violated a city ordinance by refusing to give up her seat to a white man on a city bus. Her action, often viewed as spontaneous, grew out of a long tradition of black protest against rigid segregation in the South. Rosa Parks herself had been ejected from a bus a decade earlier for refusing to obey the driver's command, "Niggers move back." In 1953, black ministers in Baton Rouge, Louisiana, had mounted a weeklong boycott of that city's bus system and succeeded in modifying the segregated seating rules.

In Montgomery, Parks's arrest sparked a massive protest. Black women were particularly important in the movement, printing and handing out 50,000 leaflets to rally the African American community behind Parks. The protest also led to Martin Luther King, Jr.'s emergemce as an eloquent spokesman for African Americans.

King agreed to lead a bus boycott. The son of a famous Atlanta preacher, he had recently taken his first church in Montgomery after earning a Ph.D. in theology at Boston University. Now he combined his wide learning with charismatic appeal to achieve a practical goal—fair treatment for the African Americans who made up the bulk of the riders on the city's buses.

The Montgomery bus boycott began with a modest goal. Instead of challenging the legality of segregated seating, King simply asked that seats be taken on a first-come, first-served basis, with African Americans being seated from the back and whites from the front of each bus. As the protest continued, however, and as protesters endured harassment and violence, the protesters became more assertive. Car pools enabled them to avoid using the buses. Soon protesters were insisting on an end to segregated seating as they sang their new song of protest:

Ain't gonna ride them buses no more
Ain't gonna ride no more
Why in the hell don't the white folk know
That I ain't gonna ride no more.

View the **Map**
Civil Rights Movement on **myhistorylab.com**

Watch the **Video**
African American Women and The Struggle For Civil Rights on **myhistorylab.com**

Rosa Parks's refusal to surrender her seat to a white man on a Montgomery, Alabama, bus led to a citywide bus boycott that brought Rev. Martin Luther King, Jr., to prominence as a leader of the civil rights movement. Parks is shown here being fingerprinted in February 1956 after her arrest for violating an anti-boycott law.

Read the
Document
Jo Ann Gibson,
Bus Boycott on
myhistorylab.com

The boycott ended in victory when the Supreme Court ruled in November 1956 that the Alabama segregated seating law was unconstitutional. The protest movement had dented the wall of southern segregation, and Martin Luther King, Jr., had emerged as the leader of a new civil rights movement—to worldwide acclaim. In 1957, King founded the Southern Christian Leadership Conference (SCLC) to direct the crusade against segregation. He visited Third World leaders in Africa and Asia and paid homage to India's Mahatma Gandhi, who had influenced his reliance on nonviolent civil disobedience. He led a triumphant Prayer Pilgrimage to Washington on the third anniversary of the *Brown* decision, stirring the crowd of 30,000 with his demand for the right to vote. His cry "Give us the ballot" boomed in salvos that historian Taylor Branch likened to "cannon bursts in a diplomatic salute." King's remarkable voice became familiar to the entire nation. Unlike many African American preachers, King never shouted, yet his passion and a compelling cadence captured his audiences. "Though still a boy to many of his older listeners," Branch noted, "he had the commanding air of a burning sage."

Even more important, King's strategy and message fitted perfectly with the plight of his followers. Drawing on sources as diverse as Gandhi and Henry David Thoreau, King came out of the bus boycott with the concept of passive resistance. "If cursed," he had told protesters in Montgomery, "do not curse back. If struck, do not strike back, but evidence love and goodwill at all times." The essence of his strategy was to turn the apparent weakness of southern blacks—their lack of power—into a conquering weapon. His message to southern whites was unmistakable: "We will match your capacity to inflict suffering with our capacity to endure suffering. We will meet your physical force with soul force. We will not hate you, but we will not obey your evil laws. We will soon wear you down by pure capacity to suffer."

King's goal was to unite the broken community through bonds of Christian love. He hoped to use nonviolence to appeal to middle-class white America, "to the conscience of the great decent majority who through blindness, fear, pride or irrationality have allowed their consciences to sleep." The result, King prophesied, would enable future historians to say of the effort, "There lived a great people—a black people—who injected new meaning and dignity into the veins of civilization."

Read the
Document
Student Nonviolent
Coordinating Com-
mittee, Statement on
myhistorylab.com

King was not alone in championing civil rights. Jo Ann Robinson helped pave the way in Montgomery with the Women's Political Caucus, and leaders as diverse as Bayard Rustin and Ella Baker advanced the cause at the grassroots level.

In February 1960, another spontaneous event sparked a further advance for passive resistance. Four African American students from North Carolina Agricultural and Technical College sat down at a lunch counter in Greensboro, North Carolina, and refused to move after being denied service. Other students, whites and blacks, joined in similar "sit-ins" across the South, as well as "kneel-ins" at churches and "wade-ins" at swimming pools. By 1961, 50,000 young people had desegregated public facilities in more than 100 southern cities. Thousands of the demonstrators were arrested and jailed, but the movement led to the formation of the **Student Nonviolent Coordinating Committee (SNCC)** in April 1960. The SCLC and SNCC, with their tactic of direct, though peaceful, confrontation, replaced the NAACP and its reliance on court action in the forefront of the civil rights movement. The change would eventually lead to success for the movement, but it also heightened social turmoil in the 1960s.

In February 1960, black students from North Carolina A&T College staged a sit-in at a "whites only" lunch counter in Greensboro, North Carolina. Their nonviolent protest spurred similar demonstrations in public spaces across the South.

Quick Check

✓ By what means did African American individuals and groups challenge segregation?

CONCLUSION: RESTORING NATIONAL CONFIDENCE

In 1959, President Eisenhower appointed a Commission on National Goals "to develop a broad outline of national objectives for the next decade and longer." Ten prominent citizens, led by Henry W. Wriston of Brown University, issued a report that called for increased military spending abroad, greater economic growth at home, broader educational opportunities, and more government support for scientific research and the arts. The consensus seemed to be that rather than a change of direction, all the United States needed was a renewed commitment to the pursuit of excellence.

The 1950s ended with the national mood less troubled than when the decade began amid the turmoil of the second Red Scare and the Korean War, yet less tranquil or confident than Eisenhower had hoped it would be. The American people felt reassured about the economy, no longer fearing a return of the Great Depression. However, they were also aware that abundance did not guarantee the quality of everyday life and realized that there was still a huge gap between American ideals and the reality of race relations, in the North and the South.

29 STUDY RESOURCES

((•─Listen to the **Chapter Audio** for Chapter 29 on **myhistorylab.com**

TIMELINE

1947 William Levitt announces first Levittown, p. 727

1948 Truman desegregates the armed forces, p. 735

1954 Supreme Court orders schools desegregated in *Brown v. Board of Education of Topeka*, p. 735

1955 African Americans begin boycott of Montgomery, Alabama, buses (December), p. 737

1957 Congress passes first Civil Rights Act since Reconstruction, p. 737

CHAPTER REVIEW

THE POSTWAR BOOM

How did the American economy evolve after World War II?

The American economy boomed after World War II, as the nation recovered from the Great Depression and the war. The GNP doubled between 1940 and 1960. Individuals spent heavily on housing, automobiles, and consumer goods, and the government on defense. New communities emerged in the suburbs and the Sunbelt states of the West and South. (*p. 729*)

THE GOOD LIFE?

How did American culture change after the war?

American culture reflected both the promise of material prosperity and the failure of material goods to yield true happiness. More people went to church than ever; more young people went to college. Television provided endless information and entertainment. But suburban life exhibited a shallow sameness that prompted critics to question if it was worthwhile. (*p. 732*)

THE STRUGGLE OVER CIVIL RIGHTS

How did the civil rights movement develop in the 1940s and 1950s?

Civil rights became a major issue after World War II. Truman desegregated the military, and federal courts ordered the desegregation of schools. Black activists such as Rosa Parks and Martin Luther King, Jr., led protests against segregation on buses and other public facilities. Students organized sit-ins. (*p. 734*)

KEY TERM QUESTIONS

1. How did Levittown symbolize the postwar era? (p. 727)

2. How did the baby boom affect postwar America? (p. 728)

3. Why was the decision in *Brown v. Board of Education of Topeka* so important? (p. 735)

4. What was the significance of the Montgomery bus boycott? (p. 737)

5. What was the Southern Christian Leadership Conference (SCLC)? (p. 738)

6. How did passive resistance to segregation give rise to the Student Nonviolent Coordinating Committee (SNCC)? (p. 739)

MyHistoryLab Connections

Visit **www.myhistorylab.com** for a customized Study Plan to build your knowledge of *Affluence and Anxiety*

Questions for Analysis

1. Why did certain shows like *I love Lucy* grab the attention of American families?

🔍 **View** the **Closer Look** *A 1950s Family Watching I Love Lucy* p. 733

2. What factors contributed to the development and growth of teenage consumer culture?

📖 **Read** the **Document** *The Teenage Consumer*

3. What was the short and long term significance of the *Brown v. Board of Education* Supreme Court decision?

📖 **Read** the **Document** *Brown v. Board of Education of Topeka, Kansas (1954)* p. 735

4. How did African American women contribute to the efforts of the Civil Rights Movement?

👁 **Watch** the **Video** *African American Women and the Struggle for Civil Rights* p. 737

5. In which states did the number of African American voters increase the most from 1960 to 1971?

🔍 **View** the **Map** *Civil Rights Movement* p. 737

Other Resources from this Chapter

🔍 **View** the **Map** *Population Shifts, 1940–1950*

📖 **Read** the **Document** *Ladies Home Journal, Young Mother*

👁 **Watch** the **Video** *The Desegregation of the Military and Blacks in Combat*

📖 **Read** the **Document** *Jo Ann Gibson, Bus Boycott*

📖 **Read** the **Document** *Student Nonviolent Coordinating Committee Statement*

Contents and Spotlight Questions

((•⎯ **Listen** to the **Chapter Audio** for Chapter 30 on **myhistorylab.com**

KENNEDY VERSUS NIXON: THE FIRST TELEVISED PRESIDENTIAL CANDIDATE DEBATE

On Monday evening, September 26, 1960, John F. Kennedy and Richard M. Nixon faced each other in the nation's first televised debate between two presidential candidates. Kennedy, the relatively unknown Democratic challenger, had proposed the debates; Nixon, confident of his mastery of television, had accepted even though, as

Eisenhower's vice president and the front-runner in the election, he had more to lose and less to gain.

Nixon arrived an hour early at the CBS studio in Chicago, looking tired and ill at ease. He was still recovering from a knee injury that had slowed his campaign and left him pale and weak. Makeup experts offered to hide Nixon's heavy beard and soften his prominent jowls, but instead he let an aide apply a light coat of "Lazy Shave," a pancake cosmetic. Kennedy, tanned from campaigning in California and well rested, wore light makeup. He also wore a dark blue suit better adapted to the intense television lighting.

At 8:30 P.M. central time, moderator Howard K. Smith welcomed an estimated 77 million viewers. Kennedy, echoing Abraham Lincoln, said that the nation faced the question of "whether the world will exist half-slave and half-free." Although the rules limited the first debate to domestic issues, Kennedy argued that foreign and domestic policy were inseparable. He accused the Republicans of letting the country drift at home and abroad: "I think it's time America started moving again." Nixon, caught off guard, seemed to agree with Kennedy's assessment of the nation's problems, but he contended that he had better solutions: "Our disagreement is not about the goals for America but only about the means to reach those goals."

For the rest of the hour, the two candidates answered questions from journalists. Radiating self-assurance, Kennedy used statistics and details to create the image of a man deeply knowledgeable about government. Nixon defended the Eisenhower record but seemed unsure of himself. The reaction shots of each candidate listening to the other's remarks showed Kennedy calm and serene, Nixon tense and uncomfortable.

Polls revealed a sharp swing to Kennedy. His performance impressed Democrats and independents who had thought him too young or inexperienced. Nixon suffered more from his unattractive image than from what he said; radio listeners thought the Republican candidate more than held his own. In three additional debates, Nixon improved his performance, wearing makeup to soften his appearance and taking the offensive. But the damage had been done. A postelection poll revealed that of 4 million voters whom the debates influenced, 3 million voted for Kennedy.

The televised debates were only one of many factors influencing the 1960 election. In essence, Kennedy won because he took advantage of all his opportunities. Lightly regarded by Democratic leaders, he won the nomination by appealing to the rank and file in the primaries. Then he astutely chose Lyndon Johnson of Texas as his running mate to blunt Nixon's southern strategy.

During the fall campaign, Kennedy promised to stimulate the economy and reform education, health care, and civil rights under the banner of the New Frontier. Abroad, he vowed he would lead the nation to victory over the Soviet Union in the Cold War. He met the issue of his Catholicism head on, telling Protestant ministers in Houston that as president he would always place country above religion. In his

◉ **Watch** the **Video**
Kennedy–Nixon Debate on
myhistorylab.com

shrewdest move, he won over African American voters by helping to secure the release of Martin Luther King, Jr., from a Georgia jail where the civil rights leader was being held on a trumped-up charge.

The Democratic victory in 1960 was paper-thin. Kennedy's edge in the popular vote was only .02 percent, and voting irregularities in several states—notably Illinois and Texas—which went Democratic by slender majorities, tainted his wide margin in the electoral college (303 to 219). (See Map 30.1.) Yet Kennedy's triumph marked a sharp political shift. In contrast to the aging Eisenhower, Kennedy symbolized youth, energy, and ambition. His mastery of the new medium of television reflected his sensitivity to the changes taking place in American life in the 1960s. He promised reform at home and advances abroad. Over the next eight years, he and Lyndon Johnson achieved many of their goals. Yet angry protests, violent demonstrations, and sweeping social change made the 1960s one of the stormiest decades in American history.

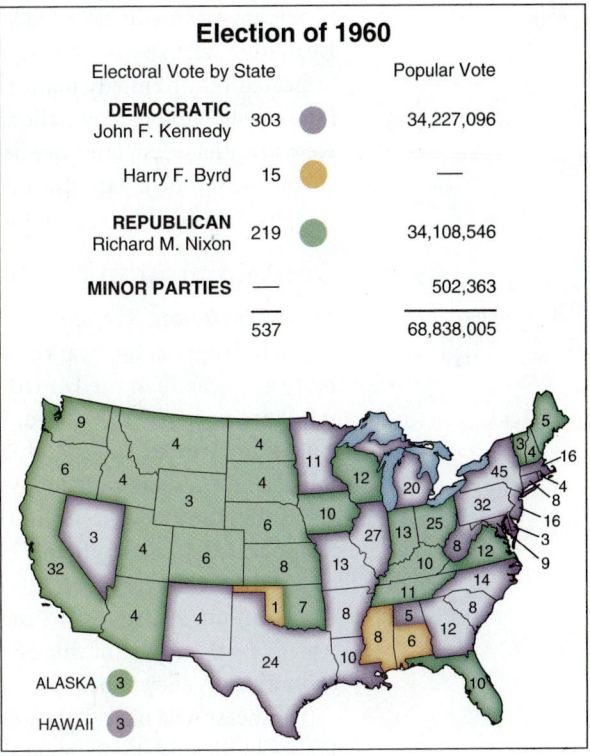

Election of 1960

	Electoral Vote by State		Popular Vote
DEMOCRATIC John F. Kennedy	303	●	34,227,096
Harry F. Byrd	15	●	—
REPUBLICAN Richard M. Nixon	219	●	34,108,546
MINOR PARTIES	—		502,363
	537		68,838,005

Map 30.1

KENNEDY INTENSIFIES THE COLD WAR

John F. Kennedy was determined to succeed where he believed Eisenhower had failed. Critical of his predecessor for holding down defense spending and apparently allowing the Soviet Union to open up a dangerous lead in nuclear missiles (in fact, it had not), Kennedy sought to warn the nation of its peril and lead it to victory in the Cold War.

How did the Cold War intensify under Kennedy?

In his inaugural address, the young president sounded the alarm. Ignoring the domestic issues aired during the campaign, he dealt primarily with the world: "Let every nation know, whether it wishes us well or ill, that we shall pay any price, bear any burden, meet any hardship, support any friend, oppose any foe to assure the survival and success of liberty. We will do all this and more."

From the start, Kennedy gave foreign policy top priority. In part, the decision reflected the perilous world situation, the immediate dangers ranging from troubles over Berlin to the emergence of Fidel Castro as a Soviet ally in Cuba. But it also corresponded to Kennedy's personal priorities. As a congressman and senator, he had been an intense cold warrior. Bored by committee work and legislative details, he had focused on foreign policy, gaining a seat on the Senate Foreign Relations Committee and publishing a book of speeches, *The Strategy of Peace*, in 1960.

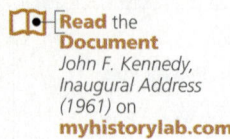

His appointments reflected his determination to win the Cold War. His choice of
Dean Rusk, an experienced but unassertive diplomat, to head the State Department
indicated that Kennedy planned to be his own secretary of state. He surrounded
himself with young, pragmatic advisers who prided themselves on toughness. These
New Frontiersmen, later dubbed "the best and the brightest" by journalist David
Halberstam, took a hard line on the Soviet Union and they believed that American
security depended on superior force and the willingness to use it.

Containment in Southeast Asia

Two weeks before Kennedy's inauguration, Soviet Premier Nikita Khrushchev declared his support for "wars of national liberation." His words were actually aimed
more at China than the United States; the two communist nations were rivals for
influence in the Third World. But Kennedy, ignoring the Sino-Soviet split, concluded the United States and Russia were locked in a struggle for the hearts and
minds of the uncommitted in Asia, Africa, and Latin America.

Calling for a new policy of nation building, Kennedy advocated financial and
technical assistance to help Third World nations modernize and achieve stable
pro-Western governments. Measures ranging from the idealistic Peace Corps to
the ambitious Alliance for Progress—a massive economic aid program for Latin
America—were part of this effort. Unfortunately, Kennedy relied even more on
counterinsurgency to beat back the communist challenge in the Third World.

Southeast Asia offered the gravest test. After Vietnam gained independence from
France in the mid-1950s, an anticommunist government emerged in the south, under Ngo Dinh Diem. A communist regime, headed by Ho Chi Minh, controlled the
north. The United States supported Diem and South Vietnam and opposed Ho and
North Vietnam.

When Kennedy entered the White House, North Vietnam was directing the insurgency of Vietcong rebels in the south. As the guerrilla war intensified in 1961,
the president sent two trusted advisers, Walt Rostow and General Maxwell Taylor,
to South Vietnam. They favored dispatching 8,000 American combat troops. "As an
area for the operation of U.S. troops," Taylor reported, "SVN [South Vietnam] is
not an excessively difficult or unpleasant place to operate. . . . The risks of backing
into a major Asian war by way of SVN are present but are not impressive."

The president decided against sending in combat troops, but he increased economic aid to Diem and the size of the U.S. military mission in Saigon. American
advisers in Vietnam grew from fewer than 1,000 in 1961 to more than 16,000 by late
1963. The flow of supplies and the creation of "strategic hamlets," fortified villages
to protect the peasantry from the Vietcong, slowed the communist momentum. But
by 1963, the situation had again become critical. Diem, a Christian aristocrat, had
lost the support of his own people; Buddhist monks set themselves aflame in protests against him, and his own generals plotted his overthrow.

Kennedy was in a quandary. He realized that only the Vietnamese could
determine the fate of South Vietnam: "In the final analysis, it is their war. They are
the ones who have to win it or lose it." But Kennedy was not prepared to accept the
possible loss of all Southeast Asia. It would be "a great mistake" to withdraw from

South Vietnam, he told reporters: "Strongly on our mind is what happened in the case of China at the end of World War II, where China was lost. We don't want that." Although aides later claimed he planned to pull out after the 1964 election, Kennedy tacitly approved a coup that led to Diem's overthrow and murder on November 1, 1963. The resulting power vacuum in Saigon made further American involvement in Vietnam almost certain.

Quick Check

✓ What was Kennedy's dilemma in vietnam?

Containing Castro: The Bay of Pigs Fiasco

Kennedy's determination to check global communist expansion peaked in Cuba. In the 1960 campaign, pointing to the ties between the Soviet Union and Fidel Castro's regime, he had accused the Republicans of permitting a "communist satellite" on "our very doorstep." Kennedy had even backed "anti-Castro exile forces," calling them "fighters for freedom" who could overthrow Castro.

In fact, the Eisenhower administration had been training Cuban exiles in Guatemala since March 1960 as part of a CIA plan to topple Castro. Eisenhower had employed the CIA to oust unfriendly regimes in Iran in 1953 and Guatemala in 1954. Those successes caused Eisenhower and then Kennedy to dismiss skeptics who thought Castro would be harder to overthrow, and who contended that, in any case, covert operations damaged America's reputation. Senator J. William Fulbright of Arkansas, chairman of the Foreign Relations Committee, was especially critical, saying, "The Castro regime is a thorn in the flesh, but it is not a dagger in the heart." Kennedy, however, decided to proceed.

On April 17, 1961, 1,400 Cuban exiles landed at the Bay of Pigs in southern Cuba. Even though the United States had masterminded the operation, Kennedy insisted on covert action, even canceling an American air strike on the beachhead. Castro's forces easily quashed the invasion. They killed nearly 500 exiles and captured the rest, in what became known as the Bay of Pigs.

Kennedy took personal responsibility for the defeat. In his address to the American people, however, he showed no remorse for violating a neighboring country's sovereignty, only regret at the outcome, and he warned the Soviets that "our restraint is not inexhaustible." He asserted that the United States would resist "communist penetration" in the Western Hemisphere, terming it part of the "primary obligations . . . to the security of our nation." For the remainder of his presidency, Kennedy harassed the Castro regime, imposing an economic blockade on Cuba, supporting raids by exiles from Florida, and failing to stop the CIA from launching bizarre plots to assassinate Castro.

Quick Check

✓ What was the Bay of Pigs affair?

Containing Castro: The Cuban Missile Crisis

The climax of Kennedy's crusade came in October 1962 with the Cuban missile crisis. The Soviets had engaged in a massive arms buildup in Cuba, ostensibly to protect Castro from an American invasion. Republican candidates in the 1962 congressional elections called for a firm response; Kennedy contented himself with warning against introducing offensive weapons, believing their presence would threaten American security. Khrushchev denied any such intent, but secretly built sites for 24 medium-range (1,000-mile) and 18 intermediate-range (2,000-mile) missiles in Cuba. Later he claimed his purpose was purely defensive, but he was probably responding to pressures from his own military to close the enormous strategic gap in nuclear striking power that Kennedy's arms buildup had opened up.

Unfortunately, the Kennedy administration had stopped overflights of Cuba by U-2 spy planes in August. Fearful that Soviet surface-to-air missiles could bring down the American spy plane and create an international incident, the White House, over the objections of the CIA, limited U-2 flights to the air space bordering the island. When direct overflights resumed on October 14, they showed indisputable photographic evidence of the missile sites, which were nearing completion.

Kennedy decided to keep this development secret while he consulted with close advisers about how to respond. Their initial preference for an immediate air strike gave way to discussion of either a full-scale invasion or naval blockade of Cuba. The president and his advisers rejected a proposal to withdraw obsolete American Jupiter missiles from Turkey in return for a similar Russian pullout in Cuba. Kennedy finally agreed to a two-step procedure. He would proclaim a quarantine of Cuba to prevent new missiles from arriving and threaten a nuclear confrontation to force the removal of those already there. If the Russians did not cooperate, the United States would invade Cuba and dismantle the missiles.

On October 22, the president told the nation about the Soviet missiles and his plans to remove them. He blamed Khrushchev for "this clandestine, reckless, and provocative threat to world peace" and made it clear that a missile attack from Cuba would lead to "a full retaliatory response upon the Soviet Union."

Read the **Document**
John F. Kennedy, Cuban Missile Crisis Address on **myhistorylab.com**

For the next six days, the world hovered on the brink of nuclear catastrophe. Khrushchev replied defiantly, accusing Kennedy of pushing mankind "to the abyss of a world nuclear-missile war." Sixteen Soviet ships continued toward Cuba, while the American navy deployed to intercept them 500 miles from the island. In Florida, nearly 250,000 men were being concentrated in the largest invasion force ever assembled in the continental United States.

The first break came at midweek when the Soviet ships halted to avert a confrontation at sea. "We're eyeball to eyeball," commented Secretary of State Dean Rusk, "and I think the other fellow just blinked." On Friday, Khrushchev sent Kennedy a long, rambling letter offering a face-saving way out: Russia would remove the missiles in return for an American promise never to invade Cuba.

Aerial photographs taken by a U-2 reconnaissance plane flying over Cuba revealed the presence of Russian missile sites under construction on the island. Recently released information about the type and number of Soviet nuclear warheads in Cuba reveals just how imminent was the threat of nuclear war had the Soviets not capitulated to U.S. demands for removal of the missiles.

The president was ready to accept when a second Russian message insisted that the Jupiter missiles be withdrawn from Turkey. Heeding the advice of his brother, Attorney General Robert Kennedy, the president refused to bargain; Khrushchev had endangered world peace by putting the missiles in Cuba secretly, and he must take them out immediately. Nevertheless, while the military went ahead with plans to invade Cuba, the president, again heeding his brother's advice, made one last appeal for peace. Ignoring the second Russian message, he cabled Khrushchev accepting his original offer.

On Saturday, October 27, Robert Kennedy told Soviet Ambassador Anatoly Dobrynin it was the last chance to avert nuclear confrontation: "We had to have a commitment by tomorrow that those bases would be removed. He should understand that if they did not remove those bases, we would remove them." If Khrushchev did not back down, "there would be not only dead Americans but dead Russians as well."

In reality, Kennedy was not ready to risk nuclear war. His brother assured Dobrynin that the Jupiter missiles would soon be removed from Turkey. The president preferred that the missile swap be done privately, but 25 years later, Dean Rusk revealed that JFK had instructed him to arrange a deal through the United Nations involving "the removal of both the Jupiters and the missiles in Cuba." In recently released transcripts of his meetings with his advisers, the president reaffirmed his intention to make a missile trade with Khrushchev publicly as a last resort to avoid nuclear war: "We can't very well invade Cuba with all its toil when we could have gotten them out by making a deal on the same missiles in Turkey."

Kennedy never had to make this concession. At nine the next morning, Khrushchev agreed to remove the missiles in return only for Kennedy's promise not to invade Cuba. The crisis was over.

The world, however, had come close to a nuclear conflict. We now know the Soviets had nuclear warheads in Cuba, not only for 20 of the medium-range missiles, but also for short-range tactical launchers for use against an American invasion. If Kennedy had approved the military's recommendations to invade Cuba, the consequences might have been disastrous.

The peaceful resolution of the crisis became a triumph for Kennedy. His party overcame the Republican challenge in the November elections, and his popularity soared. The American people, on the defensive since *Sputnik*, felt that they had proved their superiority over the Russians. Arthur Schlesinger, Jr., Kennedy's confidant and biographer, claimed that the Cuban crisis showed the "the ripening of an American leadership unsurpassed in the responsible management of power. . . . It was this combination of toughness and restraint, of will, nerve and wisdom, so brilliantly controlled, so matchlessly calibrated, that dazzled the world."

The Cuban missile crisis also had more substantial results. Shaken by their close call, Kennedy and Khrushchev installed a "hot line" for direct communication between Washington and Moscow in an emergency. Stalled negotiations over reducing nuclear testing resumed, leading to the limited test ban treaty of 1963, which outlawed tests in the atmosphere while still permitting them underground. Above all, Kennedy displayed a new maturity. In a speech in June 1963,

Watch the **Video**
President John F. Kennedy and the Cuban Missile Crisis on **myhistorylab.com**

Read the **Document**
John F. Kennedy Space Program Speech on **myhistorylab.com**

he shifted from the rhetoric of confrontation to that of conciliation. Speaking of the Russians, he said, "Our most basic common link is the fact that we all inhabit this planet. We all breathe the same air. We all cherish our children's future. And we are all mortal."

But the missile crisis also had an unfortunate consequence. Those who believed that the Russians understood only the language of force were confirmed in their penchant for a hard line. Hawks who had backed Kennedy's military buildup believed events had justified a policy of nuclear superiority. The Russians drew similar conclusions. Aware the United States had a four-to-one advantage in nuclear striking power during the Cuban crisis, one Soviet official told his American counterpart, "Never will we be caught like this again." The Soviets embarked on a crash program to build up their navy and overtake the American lead in nuclear missiles. Within five years, they had the nucleus of a modern navy and more ICBMs than the United States. Kennedy's fleeting triumph thus escalated the arms race. His legacy was bittersweet: short-term success and long-term anxiety.

Quick Check

✓ What were the causes and consequences of the Cuban missile crisis?

THE NEW FRONTIER AT HOME

What was the "New Frontier," and what did it accomplish?

Kennedy hoped to change history at home and abroad. His election marked the arrival of a new generation of leaders. For the first time, people born in the twentieth century and had entered political life after World War II were in charge of national affairs. Kennedy's inaugural call to get the nation moving again was particularly attractive to young people, who had shunned political involvement under Eisenhower.

The new administration reflected Kennedy's aura of youth and energy. Major cabinet appointments went to activists—notably Connecticut governor Abraham Ribicoff as secretary of health, education, and welfare; labor lawyer Arthur J. Goldberg as secretary of labor; Arizona congressman Stuart Udall as secretary of the interior; and Robert McNamara as secretary of defense. The most controversial choice was Robert Kennedy for attorney general. Critics scoffed at his lack of legal experience, leading JFK to joke that he wanted to give Bobby "a little experience before he goes out to practice law." In fact, the president prized his brother's loyalty and advice.

Equally important were the members of the White House staff who handled domestic affairs. Like their counterparts in foreign policy, these New Frontiersmen—Kenneth O'Donnell, Theodore Sorensen, Richard Goodwin, and Walter Heller—prided themselves on being tough and pragmatic. In contrast to Eisenhower, Kennedy relied heavily on academics and intellectuals to help him infuse the nation with energy and direction.

Kennedy's greatest asset was his own personality. A cool, attractive, and intelligent man, his sense of style endeared him to the American public. Encouraged by his wife, Jacqueline, the president invited artists and musicians to White House functions and sprinkled his speeches with references to Emerson and Shakespeare.

He seemed to be a new Lancelot, bent on calling forth the best in national life; admirers likened his inner circle to King Arthur's Camelot. Reporters loved him, both for his fact-filled and candid press conferences and for his wit. After an embarrassing foreign policy failure, when his standing in the polls actually went up, he remarked, "It's just like Eisenhower. The worse I do, the more popular I get."

Moving Slowly on Civil Rights

Kennedy faced a dilemma over civil rights. Despite his lack of a strong record in the Senate, he had portrayed himself during the 1960 campaign as a crusader for African American rights. He promised to attack segregation in the Deep South, but his fear of alienating southern Democrats forced him to downplay civil rights legislation.

The attempts of African Americans to end discrimination and secure their civil rights met with violent resistance in Birmingham, Alabama, where police used snarling dogs, fire hoses, clubs, and electric cattle prods to turn back the unarmed demonstrators.

The president's solution was to defer congressional action in favor of executive leadership. Robert Kennedy expanded the Eisenhower administration's efforts to achieve voting rights for southern blacks. To register disfranchised citizens, the Justice Department worked with the civil rights movement—notably the Student Nonviolent Coordinating Committee (SNCC)—in the Deep South. In two years, the Kennedy administration increased the number of voting rights suits fivefold. Yet the attorney general could not force the FBI to protect the civil rights volunteers who risked their lives by encouraging African Americans to register. "SNCC's only contact with federal authority," noted one observer, "consisted of the FBI agents who stood by taking notes while local policemen beat up SNCC members."

Watch the Video
Photographing the Civil Rights Movement on **myhistorylab.com**

Other efforts had equally mixed results. Vice President Lyndon Johnson headed a presidential Commission on Equal Employment Opportunities that worked with defense industries and other government contractors to increase jobs for African Americans. But a limited budget and a reliance on voluntary cooperation prevented dramatic gains; African American employment improved only in direct proportion to economic growth in the early 1960s.

Kennedy did appoint African Americans to high positions: Robert Weaver became chief of the federal housing agency. Thurgood Marshall, who pleaded the *Brown* school desegregation case before the Supreme Court, was named to the U.S. Court of Appeals. On the other hand, Kennedy also appointed as federal judge a Mississippi jurist who referred to African Americans in court as "niggers" and once compared them to "a bunch of chimpanzees."

The civil rights movement rejected Kennedy's indirect approach. In May 1961, the Congress of Racial Equality (CORE) sponsored a freedom ride in which a

Rev. Martin Luther King, Jr., addresses the crowd at the March on Washington in August 1963. In his speech, King recounted the difficulties of blacks' struggle for freedom, then stirred the crowd with the description of his dream for America: "I have a dream that one day this nation will rise up and live out the true meaning of its creed—we hold these truths to be self-evident, that all men are created equal."

Quick Check

✓ What was Kennedy's response to the civil rights movement?

biracial group tested a Supreme Court decision outlawing segregation in all bus and train stations used in interstate commerce. In Birmingham, Alabama, a mob of angry whites attacked the freedom riders. The attorney general dispatched hundreds of federal marshals to protect them, but the president was more upset at the distraction the protesters created. Kennedy directed one of his aides to call the leaders of CORE: "Tell them to call it off. Stop them."

In September, after the attorney general convinced the Interstate Commerce Commission to ban segregation in interstate terminals and buses, the **freedom rides** ended. The Kennedy administration then sought to prevent further confrontations by involving civil rights activists in its voting drive.

A pattern of belated reaction to southern racism marked the Kennedys' basic approach. When James Meredith sought admission to the all-white University of Mississippi in 1962, the president and the attorney general worked with Mississippi Governor Ross Barnett to avoid violence. However, the night before Meredith enrolled at the university, a mob attacked the federal marshals and National Guard troops sent to protect him. The violence left two dead and 375 injured, including 166 marshals and 12 guardsmen, but Meredith attended the university and graduated.

In 1963, Kennedy sent the deputy attorney general to face down Governor George C. Wallace, a segregationist who had promised "to stand in the schoolhouse door" to prevent the integration of the University of Alabama. After a brief confrontation, Wallace yielded, and two African American students desegregated the university.

"I Have a Dream"

Martin Luther King, Jr., finally forced Kennedy to openly support racial justice. In the spring of 1963, King began a massive protest in Birmingham, one of the South's most segregated cities. Marches and demonstrations aimed at integrating public facilities and opening up jobs for African Americans led to police harassment and arrests, including that of King himself. Police Commissioner Eugene "Bull" Connor was determined to crush the civil rights movement; King was equally determined to prevail. Writing from his cell in Birmingham, he vowed to bring the issue of racial injustice to national attention.

Connor played directly into King's hands. On May 3, as 6,000 children marched in place of the jailed protesters, authorities responded with clubs, police dogs, and high-pressure water hoses strong enough to take the bark off a tree. With a horrified nation watching this brutality on television, the Kennedy administration arranged a settlement that ended the violence and granted most of the protesters' demands.

More important, Kennedy finally called for action. "We are confronted primarily with a moral issue," he told the nation on June 11. "It is as old as the Scriptures and is as clear as the American Constitution." Eight days later, the administration sponsored civil rights legislation providing equal access to all public accommodations and an extension of voting rights for African Americans.

Despite pleas from the government to stop demonstrations and protests, civil rights leaders kept pressure on the administration. On August 28, more than 200,000 marchers gathered in a March on Washington for a daylong rally in front of the Lincoln Memorial. The climax was Martin Luther King, Jr.'s eloquent description of his dream for America:

> When we let freedom ring, when we let it ring from every village and every hamlet, from every state and every city, we will be able to speed up that day when all God's children, black men and white men, Jews and Gentiles, Protestants and Catholics, will be able to join hands and sing, in the words of that old Negro spiritual, "Free at last! Free at last! Thank God almighty, we are free at last!"

Watch the Video
Civil Rights March on Washington on
myhistorylab.com

Watch the Video
Rev. Dr. Martin Luther King, Jr.'s Speech at the March on Washington, August, 1963 on
myhistorylab.com

Quick Check
✓ How did King's role evolve during the Kennedy years?

LBJ'S GREAT SOCIETY

The New Frontier came to a violent end on November 22, 1963, when Lee Harvey Oswald assassinated Kennedy as the president rode in a motorcade in Dallas. The shock stunned the world. The American people were bewildered by the rapid sequence of events: the brutal killing of their young president; the televised slaying of Oswald by Jack Ruby in the basement of the Dallas police headquarters; Jacqueline Kennedy's composure and dignity at the state funeral; and the hurried Warren Commission report, which identified Oswald as the lone assassin. Critics would later charge that Oswald had been part of a vast conspiracy, but at the time, the prevailing national reaction was a numbing sense of loss.

Lyndon B. Johnson quickly filled the vacuum left by Kennedy's death. Sworn in aboard Air Force One as he returned to Washington, Johnson reassured world leaders of American political stability. Five days after the tragedy in Dallas, Johnson spoke eloquently to a joint session of Congress: "Today in the moment of new resolve, I would say to all my fellow Americans, 'Let us continue.'" Asking Congress to enact Kennedy's tax and civil rights bills as a tribute to the fallen leader, LBJ concluded, "Let us here highly resolve that John Fitzgerald Kennedy did not live or die in vain."

What were Johnson's domestic priorities, and what were his achievements?

JOHNSON IN ACTION

Johnson suffered from the inevitable comparison with his young and stylish predecessor. LBJ was aware of his own lack of polish; he surrounded himself with Kennedy advisers and insiders, hoping their air of sophistication would rub off on him. Johnson's assets were real—he possessed an intimate knowledge of Congress, incredible energy and determination to succeed, and a fierce ego. When a young marine officer tried to direct him to the proper helicopter, saying, "This one is yours," Johnson replied, "Son, they are all my helicopters."

LBJ's height and intensity gave him a powerful presence; he dominated any room he entered and delighted in using his physical power of persuasion. One Texas politician explained why he had given in to Johnson: "Lyndon got me by the lapels and put his face on top of mine and he talked and talked and talked. I figured it was either getting drowned or joining."

Yet LBJ could not project his intelligence and vitality to large audiences. Unlike Kennedy, his televised speeches were stilted and awkward. Trying to belie his reputation as a riverboat gambler, he came across like a foxy grandpa, clever, calculating, and not to be trusted. He lacked Kennedy's wit and charm. Reporters delighted in describing how he berated his aides or shocked the nation by showing the scar from an operation.

 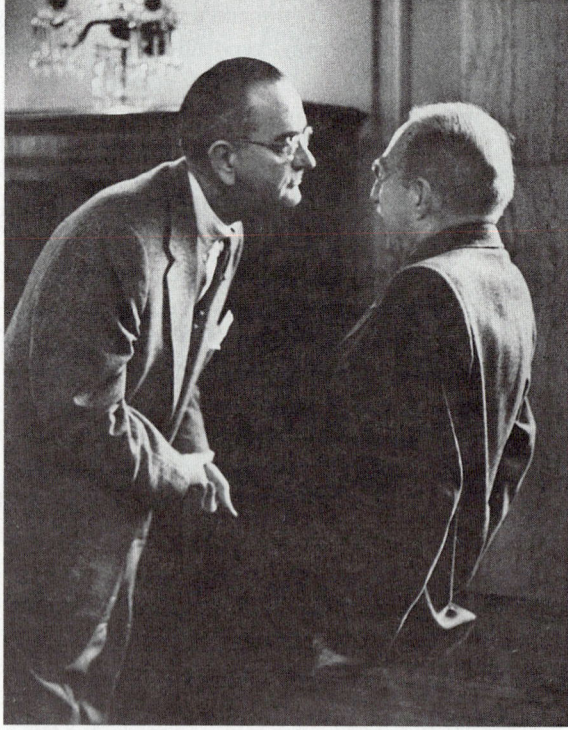

President Johnson applies the "Johnson treatment" to Senator Theodore Francis Green of Rhode Island. A shrewd politician and master of the legislative process, Johnson always knew which votes he could count on, those he couldn't, and where and how to apply pressure to swing votes his way.

Whatever his shortcomings in style, however, Johnson's ability to deal with Congress was far greater than Kennedy's. He had more than 30 years of experience in Washington as a legislative aide, congressman, and senator. His encyclopedic knowledge of the legislative process and his shrewd manipulation of senators had made him the most influential Senate leader in history. Famed for "the Johnson treatment," a legendary ability to use personal persuasion to reach his goals, Johnson in fact relied more on his ties with the Senate's power brokers—or "whales," as he called them—than on his exploitation of the "minnows."

Above all, Johnson sought consensus. Indifferent to ideology, he had moved easily from New Deal liberalism to oil-and-gas conservatism as his career advanced. He had cultivated Richard Russell of Georgia, leader of the Dixie bloc, but he also had taken Hubert Humphrey, a Minnesota liberal, under his wing. He had performed a balancing act on civil rights, working with the Eisenhower administration to pass the 1957 Voting Rights Act, yet weakening it to avoid alienating southern Democrats. When Kennedy dashed Johnson's own presidential ambitions in 1960, LBJ had gracefully agreed to be his running mate and had endured the disappointment of the vice presidency loyally and silently. Thrust into power, Johnson used his gifts wisely. Citing his favorite scriptural passage from Isaiah, "Come now, and let us reason together, saith the Lord," he concentrated on passing Kennedy's tax and civil rights bills in 1964.

The tax cut came first. Aware of the power Senate Finance Committee Chairman Harry Byrd, a Virginia conservative, wielded, Johnson astutely lowered Kennedy's projected $101.5 billion budget for 1965 to $97.9 billion. Although Byrd voted against the tax cut, he let the measure out of his committee, telling Johnson, "I'll be working for you behind the scenes." In February, Congress reduced personal income taxes by more than $10 billion, touching off an economic boom. Consumer spending increased by $43 billion during the next 18 months, and new jobs opened up at the rate of one million a year.

Johnson was even more influential in passing the Kennedy civil rights measure. Staying in the background, he encouraged liberal amendments that strengthened the bill in the House. With Hubert Humphrey leading the floor fight in the Senate, Johnson refused all efforts at compromise, counting on public pressure to force northern Republicans to abandon their traditional alliance with southern Democrats. Everett M. Dirksen of Illinois, the GOP leader in the Senate, finally led a Republican vote to end a 57-day filibuster.

The 1964 Civil Rights Act, signed on July 2, outlawed segregation in public facilities, established an Equal Employment Opportunity Commission to lessen racial discrimination in employment, and protected African American voting rights. An amendment sponsored by segregationists to obstruct the bill added gender to the prohibition of discrimination in Title VII of the act; women's groups would use the clause to secure government support for greater equality in employment and education

Quick Check

✓ How did Johnson's personality influence his politics?

The Election of 1964

Johnson now wanted to win the presidency in his own right—and to win by a landslide.

Watch the **Video**
Lyndon Johnson Presidential Campaign Ad: Little Girl vs. Mushroom Cloud on
myhistorylab.com

Searching for a cause of his own, LBJ found one in poverty. Economists had been warning since the late 1950s that the prevailing affluence disguised persistent and deep-seated poverty. Johnson made proposals that Kennedy had been developing his own. In his January 1964 State of the Union address, LBJ announced, "This administration, today, here and now, declares unconditional war on poverty in America." During the next eight months, Johnson fashioned a comprehensive poverty program under the direction of R. Sargent Shriver, Kennedy's brother-in-law. The president added $500 million to existing programs to come up with a $1 billion effort that Congress passed in August 1964.

The new Office of Economic Opportunity (OEO) set up programs ranging from Head Start for preschoolers to the Job Corps to give high school dropouts vocational training. The emphasis was on self-help, with the government providing money and know-how so the poor could benefit from day care centers, consumer education classes, legal aid services, and adult remedial reading programs. The level of funding was never high enough to meet the OEO's ambitious goals, and an attempt to include representatives of the poor in the Community Action Program led to bitter feuding with city and state officials. Nonetheless, the **war on poverty**, along with the economic growth the tax cut provided, helped reduce the ranks of the poor by nearly 10 million between 1964 and 1967.

Read the
Document
Lyndon Johnson "War On Poverty" on
myhistorylab.com

The new programs established Johnson's reputation as a reformer in an election year, but he still faced two challenges. The first came from Robert Kennedy, who remained attorney general but who wanted to become vice president and Johnson's successor in the White House. Desperate to succeed without Kennedy help, LBJ commented, "I don't need that little runt to win" and chose Hubert Humphrey as his running mate. Kennedy then left the cabinet and was elected U.S. senator from New York.

The second challenge was posed by the Republican candidate, Senator Barry Goldwater, an outspoken conservative from Arizona. An attractive and articulate man, Goldwater advocated a rejection of the welfare state and a return to unregulated free enterprise. To Johnson's delight, Goldwater placed ideology ahead of political expediency. The senator attacked the Tennessee Valley Authority, denounced Social Security, and favored a hawkish foreign policy. "In Your Heart, You Know He's Right," read the Republican slogan, to which Democrats replied, "Yes, Far Right." In reference to a careless Goldwater comment about using nuclear weapons, Johnson backers also punned, "In Your Heart, You Know He Might."

Johnson stuck to the middle of the road, embracing the liberal reform program—which he now called the **Great Society**—while stressing balanced budgets and fiscal orthodoxy. The more Goldwater sagged in the polls, the harder Johnson campaigned, determined to achieve his landslide. On election day, LBJ received 61.1 percent of the popular vote and an overwhelming majority in the electoral college; Goldwater carried only Arizona and five Deep South states (see Table 30.1).

TABLE 30.1	The Election of 1964		
Candidate	**Party**	**Popular Vote**	**Electoral Vote**
Johnson	Democratic	43,126,506	486
Goldwater	Republican	27,176,799	52

The Democrats also won huge gains in Congress, controlling the House by 295 to 140 and the Senate by 68 to 32. Kennedy's legacy and Goldwater's candor had enabled Johnson to break the conservative grip on Congress for the first time in a quarter century.

Quick Check

✓ What were the key issues in the election of 1964?

The Triumph of Reform

LBJ moved quickly to secure his legislative goals. Despite solid majorities in both houses, including 70 first-term Democrats who had ridden into office on his coattails, Johnson knew he would have to enact the Great Society as swiftly as possible: "Doesn't matter what kind of majority you come in with. You've got just one year when they treat you right, and before they start worrying about themselves."

Johnson gave two traditional Democratic reforms—health care and education—top priority. Aware of strong opposition to a comprehensive medical program, LBJ settled for Medicare, which mandated health insurance under the Social Security program for Americans over age 65 and for the disabled, and a supplementary Medicaid program for the poor. To symbolize the end of a long struggle, Johnson flew to Independence, Missouri, so Harry Truman could witness the ceremonial signing of the Medicare law, which had its origins in Truman's 1949 health insurance proposal.

LBJ overcame the religious hurdle on education by supporting a child-benefit approach, allocating federal money for the education of students in parochial and public schools. The Elementary and Secondary Education Act of 1965 provided more than $1 billion in federal aid, the largest share going to school districts with the most impoverished pupils.

Civil rights was the most difficult test of Johnson's leadership. Martin Luther King, Jr., concerned that 3 million southern blacks were still denied the right to vote, in early 1965 chose Selma, Alabama, as a test case. The white authorities in Selma, led by Sheriff James Clark, broke up the demonstrations with cattle prods and bullwhips. More than 2,000 African Americans were jailed. In March, after TV cameras showed deputies brutally halting a march from Selma to Montgomery, the president ordered the Alabama National Guard to federal duty to protect the demonstrators, had the Justice Department draw up a new voting rights bill, and addressed Congress on civil rights: "I speak tonight for the dignity of man and the destiny of democracy." Calling the denial of the right to vote "deadly wrong," LBJ vowed, "Their cause must be our cause, too. Because it is not just Negroes, but really it is all of us who must overcome the crippling legacy of bigotry and injustice."

Five months later, Congress passed the Voting Rights Act of 1965. Again Johnson had worked with Senate Republicans to break a southern filibuster and assure its passage. The act banned literacy tests in states and counties in which less than half the population had voted in 1964 and provided for federal registrars in these areas to assure African Americans the franchise.

The results were dramatic. In less than a year, 166,000 African Americans were added to the voting rolls in Alabama; African American registration went up 400 percent in Mississippi. By 1970, the percentage of eligible African American voters who had registered had risen from 40 to 65 percent. For the first time since Reconstruction, African Americans had become active participants in southern politics.

Before the 89th Congress ended its first session in 1965, it had passed 89 bills. These included measures to create two new cabinet departments (Transportation and Housing and Urban Development); acts to provide for highway safety and clean air and water; large appropriations for higher education, public housing, and the war on poverty; and sweeping immigration reform. In nine months, Johnson had enacted the entire Democratic reform agenda.

The man responsible for this great leap forward, however, had not won the public adulation he craved. His legislative skills had made the most of the 1964 Democratic landslide, but the people denied Johnson the warmth and praise they had showered on Kennedy. Reporters continued to portray him as a crude wheeler-dealer; as a maniac who drove around Texas back roads at 90 miles an hour, one hand on the wheel and the other holding a beer; or as a bully who picked up his dog by the ears. No one was more aware of this lack of affection than LBJ himself. His public support, he told an aide, is "like a Western river, broad but not deep."

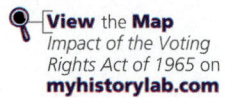

View the **Map**
Impact of the Voting Rights Act of 1965 on
myhistorylab.com

Johnson's realization of the fragility of his popularity was accurate. The Cold War began to divert his attention from domestic concerns and eventually, in the case of Vietnam, would overwhelm him. Yet his legislative achievements were remarkable. In one brief outburst of reform, he had accomplished more than any president since FDR.

Difficulties abroad would dim the luster of the Johnson presidency, but they could not diminish the impact of the Great Society on American life. Federal aid to education, Medicare and Medicaid, and the civil rights acts of 1964 and 1965 changed the nation irrevocably. The aged and the poor were guaranteed medical care; federal funds improved education; and African Americans could attend integrated schools, enjoy public facilities, and gain political power by exercising the right to vote. But even at this moment of triumph for liberal reform, dissent and rebellion were brewing.

Quick Check

✓ What were the major reforms of Johnson's great society?

JOHNSON ESCALATES THE VIETNAM WAR

How did Johnson's Vietnam policy evolve?

Johnson stressed continuity in foreign policy just as he had in enacting Kennedy's domestic reforms. He shared his fallen predecessor's Cold War convictions. And, feeling less confident about dealing with international issues, he relied heavily on Kennedy's advisers—notably Secretary of State Rusk, Secretary of Defense McNamara, and McGeorge Bundy (the national security adviser until the even more hawkish Walt Rostow replaced him in 1966).

Johnson had broad exposure to national security affairs. He had served on the Naval Affairs Committee in the House before and during World War II, and as Senate majority leader he had been consulted on the crises of the 1950s. A confirmed cold warrior, he had seen in the 1940s how the communist triumph in China had damaged the Democratic party. "I am not going to lose Vietnam," he told the American ambassador to Saigon in 1963. "I am not going to be the president who saw Southeast Asia go the way China went."

Aware of the problems Castro had caused Kennedy, LBJ moved to contain communism in the Western Hemisphere. When a military junta overthrew a leftist regime in Brazil, Johnson offered covert aid and open encouragement. He also forced Panama to restrain rioting aimed at the American presence in the Canal Zone.

In 1965, to block the possible emergence of a Castro-type government, LBJ sent 20,000 troops to the Dominican Republic. Johnson's flimsy justifications—ranging from the need to protect American tourists to a dubious list of suspected communists among the rebel leaders—alienated liberal critics in the United States, particularly Senator Fulbright, a former Johnson favorite. The intervention ended in 1966 with the election of a conservative government. Fulbright, however, attacked Johnson's foreign policy in *The Arrogance of Power*, a biting analysis of the fallacies of containment. Fulbright's defection symbolized a growing gap between the president and liberal intellectuals; the more LBJ struggled to uphold Kennedy's Cold War policies, the more Congress, the media, and the universities attacked him.

The Vietnam Dilemma

But Vietnam, not Latin America, became Johnson's obsession and led ultimately to his downfall. Inheriting a commitment that dated back to Eisenhower to support South Vietnam, the new president believed he had to continue Kennedy's policy there. Diem's overthrow only three weeks before Kennedy's assassination led to a power struggle in Saigon that prevented Johnson from thoroughly reassessing the strategic alternatives in Southeast Asia. In 1964, seven different governments ruled South Vietnam; power changed hands three times within one month. According to an American officer, Saigon "fairly smelled of discontent," with "workers on strike, students demonstrating, [and] the local press pursuing a persistent campaign of criticism of the new government."

View the **Map**
Vietnam War on
myhistorylab.com

Resisting pressure for direct military involvement, LBJ continued Kennedy's policy of economic and technical assistance. He sent 7,000 more military advisers and an additional $50 million in aid. While he insisted the Vietnamese themselves had to win the war, he expanded American support for covert operations, including amphibious raids on the North.

These undercover activities led to the Gulf of Tonkin affair. On August 2, 1964, North Vietnamese torpedo boats attacked the *Maddox*, an American destroyer engaged in intelligence gathering in the Gulf of Tonkin. The North Vietnamese believed the American ship had been involved in a South Vietnamese raid nearby. The *Maddox* escaped unscathed, but the navy sent in another destroyer, the *C. Turner Joy*. On August 4, the two destroyers, responding to sonar and radar contacts, opened fire on North Vietnamese gunboats. Johnson ordered retaliatory air strikes on North Vietnamese naval bases. Later investigation indicated that the North Vietnamese gunboats had not launched a second attack on the American ships.

The next day, the president asked Congress to authorize "all necessary measures to repel any armed attack against the forces of the United States and to prevent further aggression." He did not need this authority; he had already ordered the retaliatory air strike. Later, critics charged that LBJ wanted a blank check from Congress to escalate the Vietnam War, but such a motive is unlikely. He had already rejected immediate intervention. In part, he wanted the Gulf of Tonkin Resolution to demonstrate to North Vietnam the American determination to defend South Vietnam. "The challenge we face in Southeast Asia today," he told Congress, "is the same challenge that we have faced with courage and that we have met with strength in Greece and Turkey, in Berlin and Korea." He also wanted to preempt the issue from Barry Goldwater, who had been advocating a tougher policy. By taking a firm stand on the Gulf of Tonkin incident, Johnson could both impress the North Vietnamese and outmaneuver a rival at home.

Congress responded with alacrity. The House acted unanimously, while only two senators voted against the resolution. Johnson's standing in the Gallup poll shot up from 42 to 72 percent, and he had blocked Goldwater from exploiting Vietnam as a campaign issue.

In the long run, however, this easy victory proved costly. Having used force once against North Vietnam, LBJ was more likely to do so in the future. And although he apparently had no intention of widening the conflict in August 1964, the congressional resolution was broad enough to enable him to use whatever level of force he wanted—including unlimited military intervention. Above all, when he did wage war in Vietnam, he left himself open to the charge of deliberately misleading Congress. Presidential credibility became Johnson's Achilles' heel; his downfall began with the Gulf of Tonkin Resolution.

Quick Check

✓ What happened in the gulf of tonkin, and how did it reflect Johnson's vietnam problem?

Escalation

Full-scale American involvement in Vietnam began in 1965 in a series of steps designed primarily to prevent a North Vietnamese victory. (See Map 30.2.) With the political situation in Saigon growing more hopeless every day, the president's advisers urged the bombing of the north. American air attacks would block North Vietnamese infiltration routes, make Hanoi pay a heavy price, and encourage the South Vietnamese. But most important, as McGeorge Bundy reported after a visit to Pleiku (site of a Vietcong attack on an American base), "Without new U.S. action defeat appears inevitable—probably not in a matter of weeks or perhaps even months, but within the next year or so." In February 1965, Johnson cited the Pleiku attack in ordering a long-planned aerial bombardment of North Vietnamese targets.

The air strikes proved ineffective. In April, Johnson authorized using American combat troops in South Vietnam to protect American air bases. The Joint Chiefs then pressed the president for both unlimited bombing of the north and the aggressive use of American ground forces in the south. In mid-July, Secretary of Defense McNamara recommended sending 100,000 combat troops to Vietnam. He believed this escalation would lead to a "favorable outcome," but he also warned that an additional 100,000 soldiers might be needed in 1966 and that American battle deaths could be 500 a month (by 1968, they were 500 a week).

Other advisers, most notably Undersecretary of State George Ball, advocated a political settlement. Warning that the United States was likely to suffer "national humiliation," Ball told the president that he had "serious doubt that an army of westerners can successfully fight Orientals in an Asian jungle."

Johnson was torn: "Are we starting something that in two to three years we simply can't finish?" But he decided he had to persevere in Vietnam. Although he pared down McNamara's troop request, LBJ settled on a steady military escalation to compel Hanoi to accept a diplomatic solution. In July, the president increased the bombing of North Vietnam and allowed American commanders to conduct offensive operations in the south. He also approved the dispatch of 50,000 troops and the future commitment of 50,000 more.

These decisions formed "an open-ended commitment to employ American military forces as the situation demanded," wrote historian George Herring. They were "the closest thing to a formal decision for war in Vietnam." Convinced that withdrawal would destroy American credibility and that an invasion of the north would lead

Map 30.2 Southeast Asia and the Vietnam War   American combat forces in South Vietnam rose from 16,000 in 1963 to 500,000 in 1968, but a successful conclusion to the conflict was no closer.

to World War III, Johnson opted for large-scale but limited military intervention. He also feared the domestic consequences of either extreme. A pullout could cause a political backlash at home, as conservatives condemned him for betraying South

Vietnam to communism. All-out war, however, would mean the end of his social programs. Once Congress focused on the conflict, he explained to biographer Doris Kearns Goodwin, "that bitch of a war" destroyed "the woman I really loved—the Great Society." So he settled for a limited war, committing 500,000 American troops to battle in Southeast Asia, while pretending it was a minor engagement and refusing to ask the American people for the support and sacrifice victory required.

Johnson was not solely responsible for the Vietnam War. He inherited both a policy that assumed Vietnam was a vital national interest and a deteriorating situation in Saigon that demanded a more active American role. Truman, Eisenhower, and Kennedy had taken the United States deep into the Vietnam maze; Johnson's fate was to have to find a way out. But LBJ bears full responsibility for how he tried to resolve his dilemma. The failure to confront the people with the stark choices the nation faced in Vietnam, the insistence on secrecy and deceit, the refusal to acknowledge that he had committed the United States to a dangerous military involvement—these were Johnson's sins in Vietnam. His lack of self-confidence in foreign policy and fear of domestic reaction led to his undoing.

Quick Check

✓ How and why did Johnson escalate American involvement in Vietnam?

Stalemate

For the next three years, Americans waged an intensive war in Vietnam and succeeded only in preventing a communist victory. Bombing proved ineffective. The rural, undeveloped nature of the North Vietnamese economy meant there were few industrial targets; a refusal to bomb the main port of Haiphong allowed Soviet and

U.S. troops wade through marshland during an operation on South Vietnam's Mekong Delta. Although the United States conducted thousands of air strikes over North Vietnam and committed a half million troops to the South, it failed to win the advantage.

Chinese arms to flow freely into the country. The efforts to destroy supply lines were equally unsuccessful. American planes pounded the Ho Chi Minh Trail that ran down through Laos and Cambodia, but the jungle canopy hid North Vietnamese shipments and their massive efforts to repair roads and bridges. In fact, the American air attacks, with their inadvertent civilian casualties, gave North Vietnam a propaganda weapon to rouse world opinion against the United States.

The war in the south went no better. American ground forces increased from 184,000 in late 1965 to more than 500,000 by early 1968, but the Vietcong still controlled much of the countryside. The search-and-destroy tactics the American commander, General William Westmoreland, employed proved ineffective. The Vietcong, aided by North Vietnamese regulars, were waging an insurgent war, ambushing and avoiding fixed positions. Westmoreland used superior American firepower wantonly, devastating the countryside and driving the peasantry into the arms of the guerrillas. Inevitably, these tactics led to the slaughter of innocent civilians, most notably at the hamlet of My Lai. In March 1968, an American company led by Lieutenant William Calley, Jr., massacred more than 200 unarmed villagers.

Westmoreland tried to wage a war of attrition that would finally reach a "crossover point" when communist losses each month would be greater than the number of new troops they could recruit. He hoped to lure the enemy into pitched battles in which American firepower would inflict heavy casualties. But the communists decided where and when the fighting would take place, provoking American attacks in remote areas of South Vietnam that favored the defenders and made Westmoreland pay heavily in American lives. By the end of 1967, the nearly 500,000 troops Johnson had sent to Vietnam had only achieved a bloody stalemate that was gradually turning the American people against a war they had once eagerly embraced.

View the Image
Johnson in Vietnam on
myhistorylab.com

Quick Check
✓ What was the result of the escalation?

YEARS OF TURMOIL

The Vietnam War became the focal point for youthful protests that made the 1960s the most turbulent decade of the twentieth century. Disenchantment with middle-class values, an increase in college enrollments as a result of the baby boom, a reaction against the crass materialism of the affluent society—with its endless suburbs and shopping malls—led American youth to embrace an alternative lifestyle based on the belief that people are "sensitive, searching, poetic, and capable of love." They were ready to create a counterculture.

The agitation of the 1960s was at its height between 1965 and 1968, during the escalation of the Vietnam War. Disturbances on college campuses reflected discontent in other parts of society, from the urban ghettos to the lettuce fields of the Southwest. All who felt disadvantaged and dissatisfied—students, African Americans, Hispanics, Native Americans, women, hippies—took to the streets.

Why were there protests in the 1960s?

Protesting the Vietnam War

The most dramatic aspect of the youthful rebellion came in opposing the Vietnam War. The first student "teach-ins"—organized but informal discussions and debates—began at the University of Michigan in March 1965 and spread across the nation. More than 20,000 protesters, under the auspices of the Students for a Democratic Society (SDS), a radical student organization, gathered in Washington in April to hear Joan Baez and Judy Collins sing antiwar songs. "End the War in Vietnam Now, Stop the Killing" read the signs.

One of the ironies of the Vietnam War was the system of draft deferments, which enabled most college students to avoid military service. As a result, the children of the well-to-do, who were more likely to attend college, were able to escape the draft. One survey revealed that men from disadvantaged families, including a disproportionately large number of black and Hispanic Americans, were twice as likely to be drafted and fight in Vietnam as those from more privileged backgrounds. Consequently, a sense of guilt led many college activists whose student status saved them from Vietnam to take the lead in denouncing an unjust war.

Watch the **Video**
Protests Against the Vietnam War on
myhistorylab.com

As the fighting in Southeast Asia intensified in 1966 and 1967, the protests grew larger and the slogans more extreme. "Hey, hey, LBJ, how many kids did you kill today?" chanted students as they proclaimed, "Hell, no, we won't go!" At the Pentagon in October 1967, more than 100,000 demonstrators—mainly male students but also housewives, teachers, and young professionals—confronted military policemen guarding the heart of the nation's war machine.

The climax came in the spring of 1968. Driven by opposition to the war and concern for social justice, the SDS and African American radicals at Columbia University joined forces in April. They seized five buildings, paralyzing one of the country's leading colleges. After eight tense days, the New York City police regained control. The brutal repression inflamed protest elsewhere. Students held sit-ins and marches at more than 100 colleges.

The students failed to stop the war, but they did gain a voice in their education. Administrations allowed undergraduates to sit on faculty curriculum-planning committees and gave up their rigid control of dormitory and social life. But the students' greatest impact lay outside politics and the campus. They spawned a cultural uprising that transformed the manners and morals of America.

Quick Check

✓ What forms did opposition to the war in vietnam take?

The Cultural Revolution

In contrast to the elitist political revolt of the SDS, the cultural rebellion by youth in the 1960s was pervasive. Led by college students, young people challenged the prevailing adult values in clothing, hairstyles, sexual conduct, work, and music. Blue jeans and love beads replaced business suits and wristwatches; long hair and unkempt beards for men, bare feet and bralessness for women became a uniform of protest. "Flower children" communes emerged.

Listen to the
Audio File
Timothy Leary, "Going Out" (1966) on
myhistorylab.com

Music became the touchstone of the new departure. Folksingers such as Joan Baez and Bob Dylan, popular for their social protest songs in the mid-1960s, gave way first to rock groups such as the Beatles, whose lyrics were often suggestive of drug use, and then to "acid rock" as symbolized by the Grateful Dead. The climactic event of the decade was the Woodstock concert in upstate New York, when 400,000 young people indulged in a three-day festival of rock music, drugs, and public sex.

Former Harvard psychology professor Timothy Leary encouraged youth to join him in trying out the drug scene. Millions accepted his invitation to "tune in, turn on, drop out" literally, as they experimented with marijuana and LSD, a chemical hallucinogen. The ultimate expression of insurgency was the Yippie movement, led by Jerry Rubin and Abbie Hoffman. Shrewd buffoons who mocked the consumer culture, they capitalized on the mood of social protest to win attention. When testifying before a congressional committee investigating internal subversion, Rubin dressed as a Revolutionary War soldier; Hoffman appeared in the gallery of the New York Stock Exchange in 1967, raining money down on the cheering brokers.

Quick Check

✓ How did young people challenge adult culture during the 1960s?

"Black Power"

The civil rights movement, which had spawned the mood of protest in the 1960s, fell on hard times later in the decade. The legislative triumphs of 1964 and 1965 were relatively easy victories over southern bigotry; now the movement faced the more complex problem of achieving economic equality in the cities of the North, where more than half of the nation's African Americans lived in poverty. The civil rights movement had raised the expectations of urban African Americans; frustration mounted as they failed to experience significant economic gain.

The first sign of trouble came in the summer of 1964, when African American teenagers in Harlem and Rochester, New York, rioted. The next summer, an outburst of rage and destruction swept over the Watts area of Los Angeles as the inhabitants burned buildings and looted stores. Riots in the summer of 1966 were less destructive, but in 1967, the worst ones yet took place in Newark and Detroit, where 43 were killed and thousands injured. The mobs attacked shops and stores, expressing a burning grievance against a consumer society from which their poverty excluded them.

The civil rights coalition fell apart, a victim of both its legislative success and economic failure. Black militants took over SNCC; they disdained white help and even reversed Martin Luther King's insistence on nonviolence. Their new leader, Stokely Carmichael, told blacks they should seize power in those parts of the South where they outnumbered whites: "I am not going to beg the white man for anything I deserve. I'm going to take it." His calls for "black power" became a rallying cry for more militant blacks who advocated the need for African Americans to form "our own institutions, credit unions, co-ops, political parties" and even write "our own history."

Others went further. H. Rap Brown, who replaced Carmichael as the leader of SNCC in 1967, told African Americans in Cambridge, Maryland, to "get your guns" and "burn this town down"; Huey Newton, a founder of the militant Black Panther party, proclaimed, "We make the statement, quoting from Chairman Mao, that Political Power comes through the Barrel of a Gun."

Read the **Document**
Stokely Carmichael and Charles V. Hamilton, from Black Power on **myhistorylab.com**

King suffered the most from this extremism. His denunciation of the Vietnam War cost him the support of the Johnson administration and alienated him from the more conservative civil rights groups such as the NAACP and the Urban League. He finally seized on poverty as the enemy to attack, but before he could lead his Poor People's March on Washington in 1968, he was assassinated in Memphis in April.

Blacks and whites realized the nation had lost its most eloquent voice for racial harmony. His tragic death made King a martyr, but it also led to one last outbreak of urban violence. African Americans exploded in riots in 125 cities; in Washington, D.C., buildings were set on fire within a few blocks of the White House. "It was as if the city were being abandoned to an invading army," wrote a British journalist. "Clouds of smoke hung over the Potomac, evoking memories of the London blitz."

Yet the emotions black nationalism engendered had a positive side. Leaders urged African Americans to take pride in their ethnic heritage, to embrace their blackness. African Americans began to wear Afros and dress in dashikis, stressing their African roots. Students demanded black studies programs in colleges; the word *Negro*—identified with white supremacy—disappeared from usage overnight, replaced by *Afro-American* or *black*. Singer James Brown expressed the sense of racial identity: "Say It Loud—I'm Black and I'm Proud."

Quick Check

✓ What was "Black Power," and what did it represent?

Ethnic Nationalism

Other groups emulated the African American phenomenon. Native Americans decried the callous use of their identity as football mascots; in response, universities such as Stanford changed their symbols. Puerto Ricans demanded their history be included in textbooks. Polish, Italian, and Czech groups insisted on respect for their nationalities. Congress acknowledged these demands with the Ethnic Heritage Studies Act of 1972. Instead of trying to melt all groups down into a standard American type, Congress now gave what one sponsor of the measure called "official recognition to ethnicity as a positive constructive force in our society today."

Mexican Americans were in the forefront of the ethnic groups that became active in the 1960s. The primary impulse came from the efforts of César Chávez to organize the poorly paid grape and lettuce pickers in California into the National Farm Workers Association (NFWA). Chávez appealed to ethnic nationalism in mobilizing Mexican American field hands to strike against grape growers in the San Joaquin Valley in 1965. A national boycott of grapes by Mexican Americans and their sympathizers led to hard-fought victories over the growers. The five-year struggle resulted in a union victory in 1970, but at an enormous cost—95 percent of the farmworkers involved had lost

In March 1966, César Chávez, shown here talking with workers, led striking grape pickers on a 250-mile march from Delano, California, to the state capital at Sacramento to dramatize the plight of the migrant farmworkers.

their homes and cars. Nevertheless, the hourly wage of farmworkers in California rose from $1.20 in 1965 to $3.53 by 1977.

Chávez's efforts helped spark an ethnic consciousness among Mexican Americans that swept through the urban barrios of the Southwest. Mexican American leaders campaigned for bilingual programs and improved educational opportunities. Young activists began to call themselves Chicanos, which had previously been a derogatory term, and take pride in their heritage; in 1968, they established the first Mexican American studies program at California State College at Los Angeles. Campus leaders called for reform, urging high school students to insist on improvements. Heeding such appeals, nearly 10,000 students at East Los Angeles high schools walked out of class in March 1968. Similar movements in San Antonio and Phoenix led to bilingual programs in grade schools and the hiring of more Chicano teachers.

Quick Check

✓ What did Cesar Chavez want, and what did he get?

Women's Liberation

Active as they were in the civil rights and antiwar movements, women soon learned that the male leaders of these causes were like corporate executives—they expected women to cook and type the communiqués while the men made the decisions. Women realized that they could only achieve respect and equality by mounting their own protest.

In some ways, the position of women in American society was worse in the 1960s than it had been in the 1920s. After 40 years, a lower percentage of women were enrolled in the nation's colleges and professional schools. Women were still relegated to stereotyped occupations such as nursing and teaching; there were few female lawyers and even fewer doctors. And gender roles, as portrayed in television commercials, assumed the husband was the breadwinner and the wife the homemaker.

Betty Friedan was one of the first to seize on the sense of grievance and discrimination that white middle-class women felt in the 1960s. In her 1963 book *The Feminine Mystique*, she called the American home "a comfortable concentration camp" and attacked the prevailing view that women were completely contented with housekeeping and child-rearing, claiming that housewives had no self-esteem or sense of identity. "I'm a server of food and putter on of pants and a bedmaker," a mother of four told Friedan, "somebody who can be called on when you want something. But who am I?"

The 1964 Civil Rights Act made it illegal to discriminate in employment on the basis of gender. Women filed suit for equal wages, demanded that companies provide day care for their infants and preschool children, and entered politics to lobby against laws that—in the guise of protecting a weaker gender—were unfair to women. As the women's liberation movement grew, its advocates began to attack laws banning abortion and fought to toughen the enforcement of rape laws.

The women's movement met many of the same obstacles as other protest groups in the 1960s. Women with more extreme views soon challenged the moderate

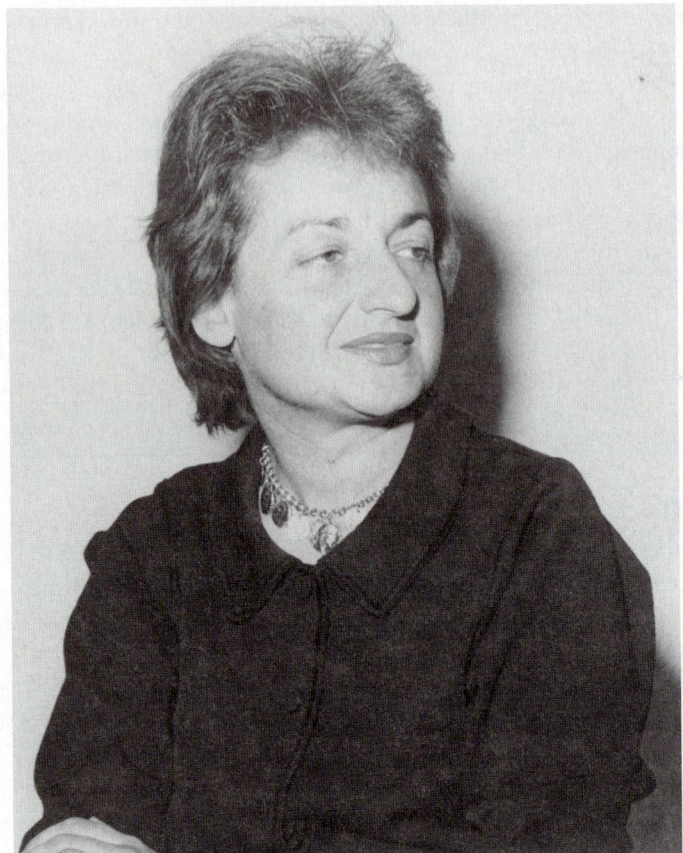

Betty Friedan authored the groundbreaking book, *The Feminine Mystique*. In the work, Friedan castigated advertisers, educators, and others for promoting what she labeled the feminine mystique—the idea that women could find fulfillment only in their roles as wives and mothers.

Quick Check

✓ What were the aims of the women's rights movement?

leadership of the National Organization for Women (NOW), founded by Friedan in 1966. Ti-Grace Atkinson and Susan Brownmiller attacked revered institutions—the family and the home—and called sexual intercourse with men a method of male domination. Many women were repelled by the harsh rhetoric of the extremists and expressed satisfaction with their lives. But despite these disagreements, most women supported the effort to achieve equal status with men.

THE RETURN OF RICHARD NIXON

How did the Vietnam War influence American politics?

The turmoil of the 1960s reached a crescendo in 1968 as the American people responded to the two dominant events of the decade—the war in Vietnam and the cultural insurgency at home. In an election marked by riots and the assassination of Robert Kennedy, Richard Nixon won the post denied him in 1960.

Vietnam Undermines Lyndon Johnson

A Vietcong offensive in 1968 broke the stalemate in Vietnam and drove Lyndon Johnson from office. The North Vietnamese began a prolonged siege of an American marine base at Khe Sanh, deep in the northern interior. Fearing a decisive defeat, Westmoreland sent more than 40 percent of all American infantry and armored battalions into the two northernmost provinces of South Vietnam.

The Vietcong then used the traditional lull in the fighting at Tet, the Buddhist lunar New Year, to attack the cities. Beginning on January 30, 1968, the Vietcong struck at 36 of the 44 provincial capitals. The most daring raid came at the American embassy in Saigon. Although the guerrillas were unable to penetrate the embassy proper, for six hours television cameras caught the fighting in the courtyard before troops finally overcame the attackers.

Although caught off guard, American and South Vietnamese forces repulsed the Tet offensive everywhere except in Hue, the old capital, which was retaken only after three weeks of heavy fighting that left this beautiful city, in the words of one observer, "a shattered, stinking hulk, its streets choked with rubble and rotting bodies."

Tet was the turning point of the Vietnam War. Although the communists suffered heavy losses, they had scored a political victory. For months, Johnson had been telling the American people victory was in sight; suddenly the war appeared to be nearly lost. CBS-TV newscaster Walter Cronkite went to Saigon to find out what had happened. Horrified at what he saw, he exclaimed to his guides, "What the hell is going on? I thought we were winning the war." He returned to tell the American people, "It seems now more certain than ever that the bloody experience of Vietnam is to end in a stalemate."

Johnson reluctantly came to the same conclusion after the Joint Chiefs of Staff requested an additional 205,000 troops after the Tet offensive. He began to listen to his new secretary of defense, Clark Clifford, who had replaced McNamara in January 1968. In mid-March, after receiving advice from the "wise men," experienced cold warriors who included such illustrious figures as Dean Acheson and Omar Bradley, the president decided to limit the bombing of North Vietnam and negotiate with Hanoi. In a speech on March 31, 1968, Johnson outlined his plans for a new effort to end the war peacefully and then said, as proof of his sincerity, "I shall not seek, and I will not accept, the nomination of my party for another term as your president."

Three years of inconclusive fighting and mounting losses had disillusioned the American people and cost Lyndon Johnson the presidency. And the full price the nation would have to pay for its folly in Southeast Asia was still unknown—the Vietnam experience would cast a shadow over American life for years to come.

Quick Check

✓ How did vietnam bring Johnson down?

The Republican Resurgence

The primary beneficiary of Johnson's Vietnam troubles was Richard Nixon. Written off as politically dead after his defeat for governor of California in 1962, Nixon had rebuilt his place within the party by working for Barry Goldwater in 1964 and for GOP congressional candidates two years later. Positioning himself squarely in the middle, he became the front-runner for the Republican nomination. At the GOP convention in Miami Beach, Nixon won an easy first-ballot nomination and chose Maryland governor Spiro Agnew as his running mate. Agnew, little known on the national scene, had won conservative support by taking a strong stand against African American rioters.

In the campaign, Nixon opened up a wide lead by avoiding controversy and capitalizing on discontent with the Vietnam War. He appeared to advocate an end to the conflict without taking a definite stand, hinting he had a secret formula for peace but never revealing what it was. Above all, he chose the role of reconciler for a nation torn by emotion, a leader who promised to reunite a divided country.

Vice President Hubert Humphrey, in contrast, seemed the symbol of division. Humphrey won the Democratic nomination after a bruising primary season that turned tragic when a deranged gunman assassinated Robert Kennedy in Los Angeles, and a bitter party convention that convulsed Chicago in antiwar protests and riots. Humphrey had Johnson's lukewarm support but was handicapped by LBJ's refusal to halt the bombing of North Vietnam. Only when Humphrey broke with Johnson in September by announcing that if elected he would "stop the bombing of North Vietnam as an acceptable risk for peace" did his campaign gain momentum.

Unfortunately for Humphrey, a third-party candidate cut deeply into the normal Democratic majority. George C. Wallace had gained national attention as the racist governor of Alabama whose motto was "Segregation now . . . segregation tomorrow . . . segregation forever." In 1964, he had shown surprising strength in northern Democratic primaries. By attacking black leaders and their liberal white allies, Wallace appealed to the sense of powerlessness among the urban working classes: "Liberals, intellectuals, and longhairs have run the country for too long. When I get to Washington, I'll throw all these phonies and their briefcases into the Potomac."

Running on the ticket of the American Independent Party, Wallace had support from more than 20 percent of the electorate in the September polls. But as the election neared, his following declined. Humphrey continued to gain, especially after Johnson agreed in late October to stop bombing North Vietnam. By November, the outcome was too close to call.

Nixon won with the smallest share of the popular vote of any winning candidate since 1916. But he swept a broad band of states from Virginia and the Carolinas to the Pacific for a clear-cut victory in the electoral college. Humphrey held on to the urban Northeast; Wallace took just five states in the Deep South, but his inroads into blue-collar districts in the North shattered the New Deal coalition. (See Map 30.3.)

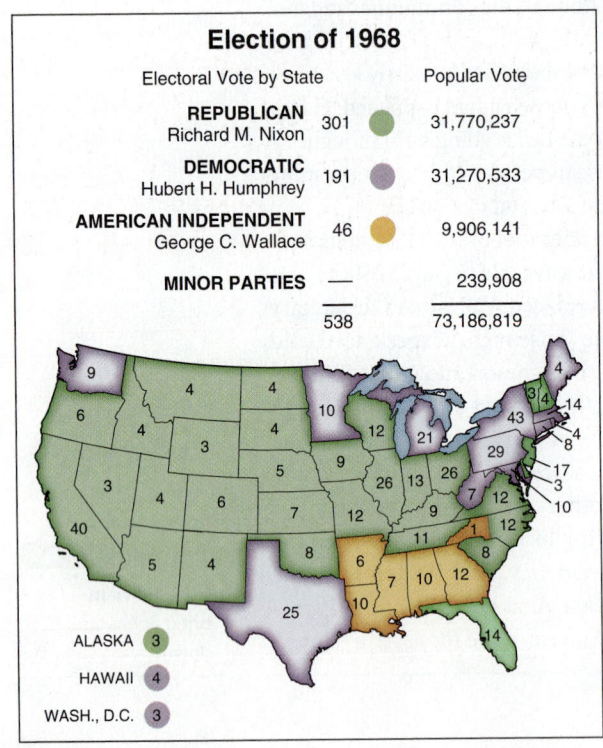

Map 30.3

Read the Document
Richard Nixon, Vietnamization on **myhistorylab.com**

Election of 1968

	Electoral Vote by State		Popular Vote
REPUBLICAN Richard M. Nixon	301	🟢	31,770,237
DEMOCRATIC Hubert H. Humphrey	191	🟣	31,270,533
AMERICAN INDEPENDENT George C. Wallace	46	🟠	9,906,141
MINOR PARTIES	—		239,908
	538		73,186,819

ALASKA 3
HAWAII 4
WASH., D.C. 3

Quick Check

✔ How did Nixon capitalize on Johnson's troubles?

CONCLUSION: THE END OF AN ERA

The election of 1968 repudiated the politics of protest and the cultural insurgency of the mid-1960s. The combined popular vote for Nixon and Wallace, 56.5 percent of the electorate, signified that a silent majority was fed up with violence and confrontation. Concern over psychedelic drugs, rock music, long hair, and sexual permissiveness had offset the usual Democratic advantage on economic issues and led to the election of a Republican president.

Nixon's victory marked the passing of two concepts that had guided American life since the 1930s. First, the liberal reform impulse, which reached its zenith with the Great Society legislation in 1965, had run its course. Civil rights, Medicare, and federal aid to education would remain, but Nixon's election signaled a reaction against the growth of federal power. The Vietnam debacle also spelled the end of an activist foreign policy that had begun with American entry into World War II. Containment, so successful in protecting Western Europe against the Soviet threat, had proved a disastrous failure when applied on a global scale. The last three decades of the twentieth century would witness a struggle to replace outmoded liberal internationalism with new policies at home and abroad.

30 STUDY RESOURCES

((•—[Listen to the **Chapter Audio** for Chapter 30 on **myhistorylab.com**

TIMELINE

1961 Cubans crush U.S.-backed Bay of Pigs invasion (April), p. 747

1962 Cuban missile crisis takes world to brink of nuclear war (October), p. 747

1963 JFK assassinated; Lyndon B. Johnson sworn in as president (November), p. 753

1964 Johnson declares war on poverty (January), p. 756
- Civil Rights Act (July), p. 755
- Congress passes Gulf of Tonkin Resolution (August), p. 760
- Johnson wins presidency in landslide (November), p. 756

1965 LBJ commits 50,000 American troops to combat in Vietnam (July), p. 763
- Congress enacts Medicare and Medicaid (July), p. 758
- Voting Rights Act (August), p. 758

1966 National Organization for Women (NOW) formed, p. 768

1967 Riots in Detroit kill 43, injure 2,000, leave 5,000 homeless (July), p. 765

1968 Vietcong launch Tet offensive (January), p. 769
- Johnson announces he will not seek reelection (March), p. 768
- Martin Luther King, Jr., assassinated (April), p. 765

CHAPTER REVIEW

KENNEDY INTENSIFIES THE COLD WAR

How did the Cold War intensify under Kennedy?

Kennedy increased American support to South Vietnam and pressured the Cuban government of Fidel Castro.

Kennedy raised troop levels in Vietnam and authorized the overthrow of Diem. He ordered a covert operation against Castro at the Bay of Pigs (which failed) and delivered an ultimatum to the Soviets to pull their missiles out of Cuba (which succeeded). *(p. 745)*

THE NEW FRONTIER AT HOME

What was the "New Frontier," and what did it accomplish?

The "New Frontier" was Kennedy's domestic program, and on its most important issue, civil rights, it achieved mixed results. Kennedy supported civil rights, but hesitantly. Black activists, especially Martin Luther King, Jr., pushed the cause of racial equality farther than Kennedy was prepared to take it. *(p. 750)*

LBJ'S GREAT SOCIETY

What were Johnson's domestic priorities, and what were his achievements?

Johnson's "Great Society" included the 1964 Civil Rights Act and the 1965 Voting Rights Act; Medicare, which provided health insurance for the elderly; and federal aid to education. *(p. 753)*

JOHNSON ESCALATES THE VIETNAM WAR

How did Johnson's Vietnam policy evolve?

Johnson seized upon an ambiguous incident in the Gulf of Tonkin to persuade Congress to grant him authority to escalate American involvement in Vietnam. He initiated a major troop buildup and air attacks against North Vietnam. The escalation produced only a bloody stalemate. *(p. 758)*

YEARS OF TURMOIL

Why were there protests in the 1960s?

During the 1960s, students protested the war in Vietnam. Many young people also rebelled against the values of their parents, experimenting with new kinds of music, clothing styles, and drugs. Black militants demanded faster progress toward racial equality, and sometimes employed violence to achieve it. César Chávez improved the lot of Mexican American farmworkers. Feminists sought greater equality for women. *(p. 763)*

THE RETURN OF RICHARD NIXON

How did the Vietnam War influence American politics?

Johnson's failure in Vietnam discredited his administration and produced desire for change. He abandoned plans to run for reelection in 1968, opening the door to Richard Nixon. *(p. 768)*

KEY TERM QUESTIONS

1. What was Kennedy's New Frontier? (p. 744)

2. Why was the Bay of Pigs a failure? (p. 747)

3. What were the causes and consequences of the Cuban missile crisis? (p. 747)

4. What were the freedom rides and how successful were they? (p. 752)

5. Why did Martin Luther King, Jr., sponsor the March on Washington? (p. 753)

6. What was Lyndon Johnson's war on poverty? (p. 756)

7. What were the main achievements of Lyndon Johnson's Great Society? (p. 756)

8. What benefits does Medicare provide? (p. 757)

9. Why was the Voting Rights Act of 1965 so significant? (p. 758)

10. Why was the Gulf of Tonkin Resolution a key turning point in the escalation of the Vietnam War? (p. 760)

11. What did Students for a Democratic Society (SDS) stand for and how successful were they? (p. 764)

12. What were the aims of the National Organization for Women (NOW) and how successful was it? (p. 768)

13. Why was the Tet offensive a decisive turning point in the Vietnam War? (p. 769)

MyHistoryLab Connections

Visit **www.myhistorylab.com** for a customized Study Plan to build your knowledge of *The Turbulent Sixties*

Questions for Analysis

1. Why is the Kennedy-Nixon television debate so significant?

   👁—**Watch** the **Video** *Kennedy-Nixon Debate* p. 744

2. How do you think the American people reacted to John F. Kennedy's Cuban Missile Crisis address?

   📖—**Read** the **Document** *John F. Kennedy, Cuban Missile Crisis Address (1962)* p. 748

3. How did the photographs from Birmingham in 1963 affect American public opinion about the Civil Rights Movement?

   👁—**Watch** the **Video** *Photographing the Civil Rights Movement* p. 751

4. Where were the major battles of the Vietnam War fought?

   🔍—**View** the **Map** *The Vietnam War* p. 759

5. What was a typical Vietnam War protest like?

   👁—**Watch** the **Video** *Protests Against the Vietnam War* p. 764

Other Resources from this Chapter

📖—**Read** the **Document** *John F. Kennedy Inaugural Address*

📖—**Read** the **Document** *Policy Statement about U.S. Objectives in Southeast Asia*

📖—**Read** the **Document** *John F. Kennedy, Space Program Speech*

👁—**Watch** the **Video** *Civil Rights March on Washington*

👁—**Watch** the **Video** *President John F. Kennedy and the Cuban Missile Crisis*

👁—**Watch** the **Video** *Reverend Dr. Martin Luther King, Jr.'s Speech at the March on Washington*

👁—**Watch** the **Video** *Lyndon Johnson Presidential Campaign Ad: Little Girl vs. Mushroom Cloud*

📖—**Read** the **Document** *Lyndon Johnson, War on Poverty*

🔍—**View** the **Map** *Impact of the Voting Rights Act of 1965*

🔍—**View** the **Image** *Johnson in Vietnam*

((•—**Listen** to the **Audio File** *"Going Out"*

📖—**Read** the **Document** *Stokely Carmichael*

📖—**Read** the **Document** *Richard Nixon, Vietnamization*

Contents and Spotlight Questions

((•— **Listen** to the **Chapter Audio** for Chapter 31 on **myhistorylab.com**

REAGAN AND AMERICA'S SHIFT TO THE RIGHT

I n October 1964, the Republican National Committee sponsored a televised address by Ronald Reagan on behalf of Barry Goldwater's presidential candidacy. Reagan's speech had originally been aired on a Los Angeles station; the resulting outpouring of praise and campaign contributions led to its national rebroadcast.

In contrast to Goldwater's strident rhetoric, Reagan put the case for a return to individual freedom in relaxed, confident, and persuasive terms.

Ronald Reagan and his wife Nancy wave to the crowd during the 1980 Republican convention in Detroit.

Instead of the usual choice between increased government activity and less government involvement, often couched in terms of the left and the right, Reagan presented the options of either going up or down—"up to the maximum of human freedom consistent with law and order, or down to the ant heap of totalitarianism." Then, borrowing a phrase from FDR, he told his audience: "You and I have a rendezvous with destiny. We can preserve for our children this the last best hope of man on earth, or we can sentence them to take the first step into a thousand years of darkness."

Although the speech did not rescue Goldwater's candidacy, it marked the beginning of Ronald Reagan's political career. A popular actor whose movie career had begun to fade in the 1950s, Reagan had become a television performer as host of *The General Electric Theater.* His political views, once liberal, moved steadily to the right as he became a spokesperson for a major American corporation. In 1965, wealthy friends persuaded him to run for the California governorship.

Reagan was an attractive candidate. His approachable manner and mastery of television enabled him to present his strongly conservative message without appearing to be a rigid right-wing ideologue. He won handily by appealing to middle-class suburban resentment over taxes, welfare programs, and bureaucratic regulation.

In two terms as governor, Reagan displayed natural ability as a political leader. Instead of trying to implement all of his conservative beliefs, he proved flexible. Faced with a Democratic legislature, he yielded on raising taxes and increasing state spending while trimming the welfare rolls. Symbolic victories were his specialty, For example, he confronted campus radicals and fired Clark Kerr, chancellor of the University of California, while generously funding higher education.

When Reagan left the governor's office in 1974, signs pointed to a growing conservative mood across the nation. In a popular rebellion in 1978, California's voters passed Proposition 13, which slashed property taxes in half and resulted in a reduction in social services. The 1962 Supreme Court ruling in *Engel v. Vitale* outlawing school prayer on the grounds that it was "no part of the business of government to compose official prayers" outraged religious leaders. In the South, where prayers were the customary way to begin the school day, the reaction was intense. One Alabama congressman denounced the Supreme Court justices: "They put the Negroes in the schools and now they're driving God out."

Concern over school prayer, along with rising abortion and divorce rates, impelled religious groups to engage in political activity to defend what they viewed as traditional family values. Jerry Falwell, a Virginia radio and television evangelist, founded the **Moral Majority,** a fundamentalist group dedicated to preserving the "American way of life."

View the **Map**
Postwar Migration to the Sunbelt on
myhistorylab.com

The population shift of the 1970s, especially the rapid growth of the Sunbelt region in the South and West, added momentum to the conservative upsurge. Those moving to the Sunbelt tended to be white, middle- and upper-class suburbanites—skilled workers, young professionals, and business executives attracted by both economic opportunity and a political climate stressing low taxes, less government regulation, and more reliance on the marketplace. The political impact of population shifts from East to West and North to South during the 1970s was reflected in the congressional gains (17 seats) by Sunbelt and Far West states after the 1980 census.

Conservatives also, for the first time since World War II, made their cause intellectually respectable. Scholars and academics on the right flourished in new "think tanks"; William Buckley and economist Milton Friedman became effective advocates of conservative causes in print and on television. **Neoconservatism,** led by Norman Podhoretz's magazine *Commentary*, became fashionable among intellectuals who were former liberal stalwarts. They denounced liberals for being too soft on the communist threat abroad and too willing to compromise high standards at home in the face of demands for equality from African Americans, women, and the disadvantaged. Neoconservatives called for reaffirming capitalism and emphasizing what was right about America rather than an obsessive concern with social ills.

By the end of the 1970s, a decade marked by military defeat in Vietnam, political scandal that destroyed the administration of Richard Nixon, economic ills that vexed the country under Gerald Ford and Jimmy Carter, and unprecedented strains on families and traditional institutions, millions of Americans had come to believe that Cold War liberalism had run its course. Ronald Reagan, as the acknowledged leader of the conservative resurgence, was ideally placed to capitalize on this discontent. His charm softened the hard edges of his right-wing call to arms, and his conviction that America could regain its self-confidence by reaffirming basic ideals had a broad appeal to a nation facing new challenges at home and abroad. In 1976, Reagan had barely lost to President Ford at the Republican convention; four years later, he won the GOP nomination handily.

In his acceptance speech at the Republican convention in Detroit, Reagan set forth the themes that endeared him to conservatives: less government, a balanced budget, family values, and peace through greater military spending. Unlike Barry Goldwater, whose rigid ideology frightened people, Reagan offered reassurance and hope for the future. He spoke of restoring to the federal government "the capacity to do the people's work without dominating their lives." As historian Robert Dallek pointed out, Reagan "assured his listeners that he was no radical idealist courting defeat, but a sensible, thoroughly likable American with a surefire formula for success that would please everyone." In Ronald Reagan, the Republicans had found the perfect figure to lead Americans into a new conservative era.

THE TEMPTING OF RICHARD NIXON

Following the divisive campaign of 1968, Nixon's presidency proved to be one of the most controversial in American history. Though he broke new ground in relations with China and the Soviet Union and ended American fighting in Vietnam, the Watergate scandal forced him to resign the presidency.

What were the major accomplishments and failures of the Nixon presidency?

Détente

Foreign policy was Nixon's pride and joy. He had thought long about the state of the world and was determined to improve it. To assist him, he appointed Henry Kissinger to be national security adviser. A refugee from Nazi Germany, Kissinger had become a professor of government at Harvard, the author of influential books, and an authority on international affairs. Nixon and Kissinger approached foreign policy from a practical, realistic perspective. They saw the Cold War not as an ideological struggle for survival with communism but as a traditional great-power rivalry, to be managed rather than won.

Nixon and Kissinger had a grand design. Realizing that recent events, especially the Vietnam War and the rapid Soviet arms buildup of the 1960s, had eroded America's primacy in the world, they planned a strategic retreat. Russia had military strength, but its economy was weak and it had a rival in China. Nixon planned to use American trade—notably grain and technology—to induce Soviet cooperation, while improving U.S. relations with China.

Nixon and Kissinger shrewdly played the China card as their first step toward achieving **détente**—a relaxation of tension—with the Soviets. In February 1972, accompanied by a planeload of reporters and camera crews, Nixon visited China, meeting with the communist leaders and ending more than two decades of Sino-American hostility. He established an American liaison mission in Beijing as a step toward diplomatic recognition.

The Soviets, who viewed China as a dangerous adversary, responded by agreeing to an arms control pact with the United States. The **Strategic Arms Limitation Talks (SALT)** had been under way since 1969. During a visit to Moscow in May 1972, Nixon signed two vital documents with Soviet leader Leonid Brezhnev. The first limited the two superpowers to 200 antiballistic missiles (ABMs) apiece; the second froze the number of offensive ballistic missiles for five years. These SALT I agreements recognized the existing Soviet lead in missiles, but the American deployment of multiple independently targeted reentry vehicles (MIRVs) ensured a strategic advantage for the United States.

The SALT I agreements were most important as a symbolic first step toward control of the nuclear arms race. They signified that the United States and the Soviet Union were trying to settle their differences peacefully.

Quick Check

✓ What was Détente and why did it appeal to Nixon?

Ending the Vietnam War

Vietnam remained the one foreign policy challenge that Nixon could not overcome. He had a three-part plan to end the conflict—gradual withdrawal of American troops, accompanied by training South Vietnamese forces to take over the combat role; renewed bombing; and a hard line in negotiations with Hanoi. The number of American soldiers in Vietnam fell from 540,000 in early 1969 to fewer than 30,000 by 1972; domestic opposition to the war declined sharply with the accompanying drop in casualties and reductions in the draft call.

Renewed bombing was the most controversial part of the plan. As early as the spring of 1969, Nixon secretly ordered raids on communist supply lines in neutral Cambodia. Then in April 1970, he launched both air and ground strikes into Cambodia, causing an outburst of antiwar protests at home. Students demonstrated on campuses across the nation. Tragedy struck at Kent State University in Ohio in May. After rioters had firebombed an ROTC building, the governor sent in National Guard troops, who were taunted and harassed. The guardsmen then opened fire,

The renewed bombing of North Vietnam and the invasion of Cambodia ordered by Nixon precipitated student protests at many campuses. At Kent State University in Ohio, national guardsmen killed four students.

killing four students and wounding 11 more. The victims were innocent bystanders; two were young women caught in the fusillade between classes. A week later, two African American student demonstrators were killed at Jackson State College in Mississippi; soon riots and protests raged on more than 400 campuses.

Nixon had no sympathy for the demonstrators, calling the students "bums" intent on "blowing up the campuses." The "silent majority" to whom he appealed seemed to agree; one poll showed that most Americans blamed the students, not the National Guard, for the deaths at Kent State. An "Honor America Day" program in Washington, D.C., on July 4, attracted 250,000 people, who heard Billy Graham and Bob Hope endorse the president's policies. Nixon's Cambodian invasion did little to shorten the Vietnam War, but the public reaction reinforced his resolve not to surrender.

The third tactic, negotiation with Hanoi, finally proved successful. Beginning in the summer of 1969, Kissinger held secret meetings with North Vietnam's foreign minister. In 1972, the two sides neared agreement, but South Vietnam blocked a settlement before the 1972 election. When the North Vietnamese tried to make last-minute changes, Nixon ordered heavy B-52 raids on Hanoi that finally led to the signing of a truce on January 27, 1973. In return for the release of all American prisoners of war, the United States agreed to remove its troops from South Vietnam within 60 days. The North Vietnamese, however, could keep their troops in the South, thus virtually guaranteeing future communist control of all Vietnam.

For two years after the accords, the communists waited. The Watergate scandal (see below) weakened Nixon's grip on foreign policy. By the time he was forced from office in August 1974, most Americans wanted to forget Vietnam. The following spring the communists mounted a major offensive and in just weeks took over all of Vietnam. Ten years after the American escalation of the war, and after the loss of 60,000 American lives, the effort to preserve South Vietnam from communism had proved a tragic failure.

Quick Check

✓ How did the Vietnam war end?

The Watergate Scandal

Nixon's Vietnam problems and especially his formulation of détente made him sensitive to the unauthorized release of information about American foreign policy. Leaks might tip the administration's hand in sensitive negotiations with the communists. When leaks did occur, Nixon demanded that they be stopped. The White House established an informal office of covert surveillance—the so-called "plumbers"—which began by investigating national security breaches but, during the presidential campaign of 1972, branched out into spying on Nixon's Democratic opponents and engaging in political dirty tricks.

Five of the "plumbers" were arrested in June 1972 during a break-in at the headquarters of the Democratic National Committee at the Watergate office complex in Washington. The White House took pains to conceal its connection to what its spokesman dismissed as a "third-rate burglary attempt." Nixon personally ordered the cover-up. "I want you to stonewall it, let them plead the Fifth Amendment, cover-up, or anything else," Nixon told John Mitchell, his campaign director and former attorney general.

The cover-up succeeded long enough to ensure Nixon's landslide reelection victory over Democrat George S. McGovern of South Dakota (see Map 31.1), but then began to unravel. James McCord, one of the Watergate burglars, broke the silence. Sentenced to a long jail term by Judge John Sirica, McCord asked for leniency, informing Sirica that he had received money from the White House and had been promised a presidential pardon in return for his silence. By April 1973, Nixon was compelled to fire aide John Dean, who had directed the cover-up but refused to become a scapegoat. Two other aides, H. R. Haldeman and John Ehrlichman, resigned.

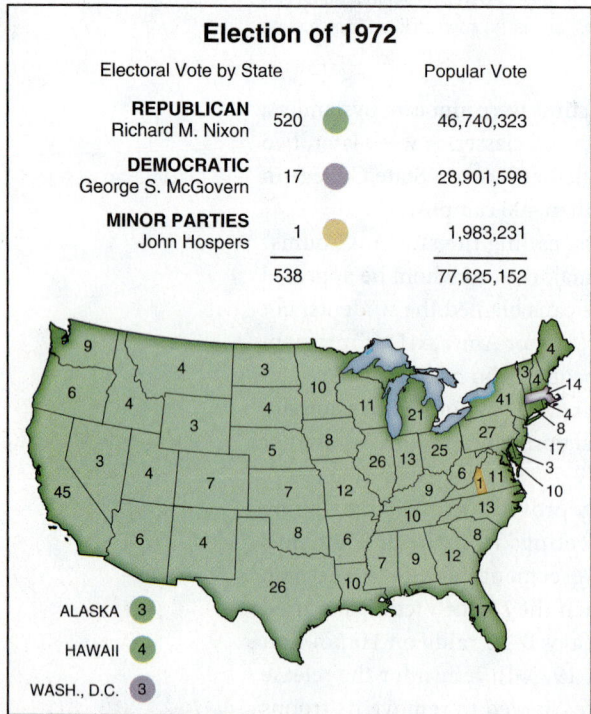

Election of 1972

Electoral Vote by State		Popular Vote
REPUBLICAN Richard M. Nixon	520	46,740,323
DEMOCRATIC George S. McGovern	17	28,901,598
MINOR PARTIES John Hospers	1	1,983,231
	538	77,625,152

ALASKA 3
HAWAII 4
WASH., D.C. 3

Map 31.1

The Senate then appointed a special committee to investigate the Watergate scandal. In dramatic testimony, Dean revealed the president's personal involvement in the cover-up. Still, it was basically a matter of whose word to believe—the president's or a discredited aide's—and Nixon hoped to weather the storm.

The committee's discovery of tape recordings of conversations in the Oval Office, made regularly since 1970, doomed Nixon. At first, the president invoked executive privilege to withhold the tapes. When Archibald Cox, the Watergate special prosecutor, demanded their release, Nixon fired him. Yet the new prosecutor, Leon Jaworski, continued to press for the tapes.

In an April 29, 1974, television address, Nixon announced that he would release Watergate tape transcripts, shown stacked in the background, to the House Judiciary Committee's impeachment probe. The transcripts were edited versions of taped conversations in the Oval Office.

Nixon tried to release only a few of the less damaging ones, but the Supreme Court ruled unanimously in July 1974 that the tapes had to be turned over to Jaworski.

By this time, the House Judiciary Committee had voted three articles of impeachment, charging Nixon with obstruction of justice, abuse of power, and contempt of Congress. Faced with the release of tapes that directly implicated him in the cover-up, the president resigned on August 9, 1974.

Nixon's resignation proved to be the culmination of the Watergate scandal. The episode revealed the weaknesses and strengths of the American political system. Most regrettable was the abuse of presidential authority—a reflection both of the power of the modern presidency and of fatal flaws in Nixon's character. Unlike previous executive branch scandals, Watergate involved a lust for power rather than money. Having become president, Nixon did everything possible to retain his hold on the office. He used the plumbers to maintain executive secrecy and directed the Internal Revenue Service and the Justice Department to punish his enemies and reward his friends.

But Watergate also demonstrated the vitality of a democratic society. The press showed how investigative reporting could unlock even the most closely guarded executive secrets. Judge Sirica proved that an independent judiciary was still the best bulwark for individual freedom. And Congress rose to the occasion, both by investigating executive misconduct and by following a scrupulous and nonpartisan impeachment process that left Nixon with no chance to escape his fate.

The nation survived Watergate with its institutions intact. John Mitchell and 25 presidential aides went to jail. Congress, in decline since Lyndon Johnson's exercise of executive dominance, was rejuvenated, with its members now intent on extending congressional authority into other areas of American life.

Read the **Document**
Watergate Special Prosecution Force Memo (August 9, 1974) on **myhistorylab.com**

Watch the **Video**
Richard Nixon, "I am not a crook" on **myhistorylab.com**

Quick Check
✓ Why was Nixon forced to resign?

OIL AND INFLATION

How were oil and inflation linked during the 1970s?

In the midst of Watergate, war in the Middle East threatened a vital national interest: the unimpeded and inexpensive flow of oil to the United States. The resulting energy crisis helped spark raging inflation that profoundly affected the economy and American society.

War and Oil

On October 6, 1973, Egypt and Syria attacked Israel. The fighting followed decades of conflict between Israel and its Arab neighbors, which had only grown worse after the Israeli victory in the Six Day War of 1967. In that conflict, the Israelis seized the Golan Heights from Syria, the Sinai Peninsula from Egypt, and Jerusalem and the West Bank from Jordan. The Arabs ached for revenge, and in 1973, the Egyptians and Syrians caught Israel off guard. They won early battles but lost the initiative and were forced to give up the ground they had recovered. The Israelis would have won another victory if not for the diplomatic intervention of Nixon and Kissinger, who, despite America's support for Israel, believed a decisive Israeli victory would further destabilize the Middle East.

An unforeseen consequence of the October War (also called the Yom Kippur War because it started on that Jewish holy day) offset the American diplomatic triumph, however. On October 17, the Arab members of the Organization of the Petroleum Exporting Countries (OPEC) announced a 5 percent cut in oil production, and vowed additional cuts of 5 percent each month until Israel surrendered the lands it had taken in 1967. Three days later, following Nixon's announcement of an emergency aid package for Israel, Saudi Arabia cut off oil shipments to the United States.

The Arab oil embargo had a disastrous impact on the American economy. With Arab producers cutting oil production by 25 percent from the September 1973 level, world supplies fell by 10 percent. For the United States, which imported one-third of its daily consumption, this meant a loss of nearly 2 million barrels a day. Long lines formed at gas stations as motorists who feared running out of fuel kept filling their tanks.

Oil prices also rose dramatically. After the Arab embargo began, OPEC, led by the shah of Iran, raised crude oil prices fourfold. In the United States, gasoline prices at the pumps nearly doubled, while home heating fuel rose even more.

Nixon responded with temporary measures, including pleas to Americans to turn down their thermostats and avoid driving for pleasure. When the Arab oil embargo ended in March, after Kissinger negotiated an Israeli pullback in the Sinai, the American public relaxed. Gasoline became plentiful, thermostats were raised, and people resumed their love affair with the automobile.

The energy crisis, however, did not end with the lifting of the embargo. The Arab action marked the beginning of a new era in American history. The United States, with only 6 percent of the world's population, had been responsible for nearly 40 percent of the world's energy consumption. In 1970, domestic oil production began to decline; the embargo only highlighted the nation's dependence on other countries, notably those in the Persian Gulf, for its economic well-being. A nation that based its way of life on abundance and expansion suddenly was faced with the reality of limited resources and economic stagnation.

Quick Check
✓ Why did oil prices quadruple in the 1970s?

The Great Inflation

The price spike from the October War was merely the first of the "oil shocks" of the 1970s. Cheap energy had been a primary contributor to the relentless growth of the American economy after World War II. The GNP had more than doubled between 1950 and 1973; the American people had come to base their standard of living on oil prices that yielded gas at about 35 cents a gallon. Large cars, sprawling suburbs, detached houses heated by fuel oil and natural gas and cooled by central air-conditioning produced a dependence on inexpensive energy that Americans took for granted.

The quadrupling of oil prices in 1973–1974 suddenly put all this at risk. Because oil or its equivalent in energy is required to produce and transport manufactured goods, the rising oil prices increased the prices of nearly everything else, including most services. (See Figure 31.1.)

Other factors added to the trend of rising prices. The Vietnam War and the Great Society produced federal budget deficits that grew from $63 billion for the entire decade of the 1960s to $420 billion for the 1970s. Rapid population increases and poor harvests around the globe in the mid-1970s triggered a 20 percent rise in American food prices in 1973 alone. But the primary source of the great inflation of the 1970s was the increase in petroleum prices.

The impact on consumers was staggering. The price of an automobile jumped 72 percent between 1973 and 1978. During the 1970s, the price of a hamburger doubled, milk went from 28 to 59 cents a quart, and a loaf of bread—the proverbial staff of life—rose from 24 to 89 cents. Wage increases failed to keep pace with inflation; in 1980, the real income of the average American family fell by 5.5 percent.

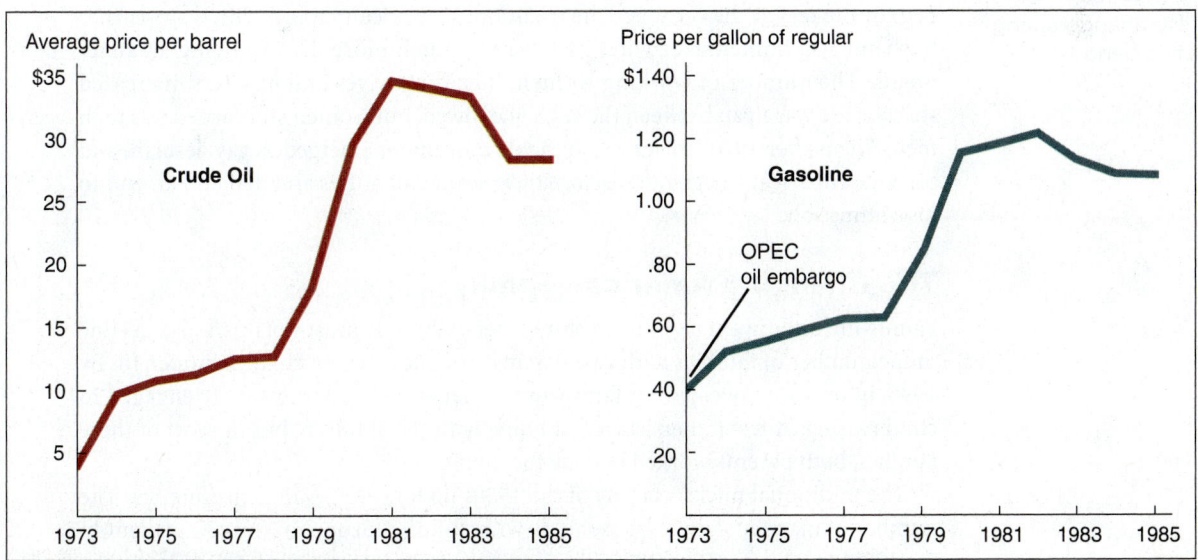

Figure 31.1 The Oil Shocks: Price Increases for Crude Oil and Gasoline, 1973–1985

Often inflation signals economic exuberance, and rising prices indicate rapid growth. But the inflation of the 1970s reflected economic weakness. The great inflation contributed to a severe recession. American GNP dropped by 6 percent in 1974, and unemployment rose to more than 9 percent, the highest level since the Great Depression of the 1930s.

President Gerald R. Ford, who followed Richard Nixon into the White House (see below), responded belatedly to the economic crisis by proposing a tax cut to stimulate consumer spending. Congress passed a $23 billion reduction in taxes in early 1975, which led to a gradual recovery by 1976. The resulting budget deficits, however, helped keep inflation above 5 percent and prevented a return to full economic health.

Jimmy Carter of Georgia, who succeeded Ford, had little more success in reviving the economy. Federal deficits and relatively high interest rates kept the economy sluggish throughout 1977 and 1978. Then in 1979, the Iranian Revolution and the overthrow of the shah touched off another oil shock. OPEC took advantage of the situation to double prices over the next 18 months. A barrel of crude oil now cost more than $30. Gasoline prices climbed to more than $1 a gallon at American service stations, leading to greater inflation than in 1973.

Finally, in late 1979, the Federal Reserve Board, led by Carter appointee Paul Volcker, began an effort to halt inflation by mandating increased bank reserves to curtail the supply of money in circulation. The new tight-money policy only heightened inflation in the short run by driving interest rates up to record levels. By the spring of 1980, the prime interest rate reached 20 percent.

Quick Check

✓ How did rising oil prices help trigger the inflation of the 1970s?

PRIVATE LIVES, PUBLIC ISSUES

How did private life change during this period?

Sweeping changes in the private lives of Americans began in the 1970s and continued for the rest of the century. The traditional American family, with wage-earner husband and homemaker wife, gave way to much more diverse living arrangements. The number of working women, including wives and mothers, increased sharply; the wage gap between the sexes narrowed, but women still earned less than men. Then, after 1970, an active gay rights movement emerged as gay, lesbian, and bisexual Americans began to disclose their sexual identities and demand an end to discrimination.

The Changing American Family

Family life underwent significant shifts after 1970. The most notable was a decline in the number of families with two parents and one or more children under 18. By 1990, in only one two-parent family out of five was the mother solely engaged in child rearing. A few fathers stayed at home with the children, but in most of these families, both parents worked outside the home.

The traditional nuclear family of the 1950s no longer prevailed in America. The number of married couple households with children dropped from 30 percent in the 1970s to 23 percent by 2000. The number of unmarried couples doubled in the

1990s, while adults living alone surpassed the number of married couples with children for the first time in American history. "Being married is great," commented demographer William H. Frey, "but being married with kids is tougher in today's society with spouses in different jobs and expensive day care and schools."

The divorce rate, which doubled between the mid-1960s and the late 1970s, leveled off for the rest of the century. Nevertheless, half of all first marriages still ended in divorce. After a sharp fall in the 1970s, the birthrate climbed again as the baby boom generation matured. The number of births to women over age 30 increased, and single mothers comprised 7 percent of all households by 2000, a 25 percent increase since 1990. Conservatives, alarmed by the decline of the nuclear family, called for change. "We need to discourage people from living together outside of marriage," observed Bridget Maher of the Family Research Council, "and encourage them to have children within marriage."

For better or worse, the American family structure changed significantly in the last three decades of the twentieth century, with many people either never marrying or postponing marriage until late in the childbearing period. The traditional family unit, with the working father and the mother rearing the children at home, declined. Most mothers worked outside the home, and many were the sole support for their children. The proportion of children living with only one parent doubled in 20 years. Women without partners headed more than one-third of all impoverished families, and children made up 40 percent of the nation's poor. Although politicians, especially Republicans, would hail family values during campaigns, those values underwent great stress due to social changes in the last third of the twentieth century, and children suffered disproportionately.

Quick Check

✓ How did American family life change during the 1970s?

Gains and Setbacks for Women

American women experienced significant changes in their way of life and their place in society in the last quarter of the twentieth century. There was a rapid movement of women into the labor force in the 1970s; six million more married women held jobs by 1980 as two incomes became increasingly necessary to keep up with inflation. The trend continued through the 1980s. Women filled 61 percent of the nearly 19 million new jobs created during that decade; many of these new jobs, however, were entry-level or low-paying service positions.

Women scored some impressive breakthroughs. They began to enter corporate boardrooms, became presidents of major universities, and were admitted to the nation's military academies. Women entered blue-collar, professional, and small-business fields traditionally dominated by men. Ronald Reagan's appointment of Sandra Day O'Connor to the Supreme Court in 1981 marked a historic first.

Yet women also encountered resistance. Most women continued to work in female-dominated fields—as nurses, secretaries, teachers, and waitresses. Those who entered such "male" areas as management and administration soon hit the so-called glass ceiling, which kept them from advancing beyond mid-level executive status. In 1990, only 4.3 percent of corporate officers were women. Most women in business worked at the middle and lower rungs of management in personnel and

During the 1970s and 1980s employment opportunities expanded for women, including jobs in fields traditionally dominated by men. This photograph from 1980 shows a woman working as a union electrician in Harlem.

public relations, not key operational positions in sales and marketing that would lead to the boardroom; women held fewer than 3 percent of the top jobs in *Fortune* 500 companies. The economic boom of the 1990s, however, increased the number of women executives by 514,000 in 1998.

Even with these gains, however, by 2009 women's wages still averaged only 80 percent of men's earnings. Younger women did best; those between 16 and 24 earned 92 cents for every dollar paid to a male in the same age group, and in certain large cities young women earned more than young men. But the overall gap remained, and experts predicted that it would take years to close.

The most encouraging development for women came in business ownership, as more women went into business for themselves. The number of female business owners increased 40 percent between 1987 and 1992, twice the national rate of business growth. A women's trade group estimated that in 1996 women owned almost eight million businesses, employing more than 18 million workers—one out of four American workers. A speaker at the first National Women's Economic Summit in 1996 exaggerated only slightly in crediting her group with restoring prosperity, claiming that "the American economy has been revitalized in good measure because of the participation of and contributions of women business owners."

Beyond economic opportunity, the women's movement had two goals. The first was ratification of the **Equal Rights Amendment (ERA)**. Approved by Congress in 1972, the ERA stated simply, "Equality of rights under the law shall not be denied or abridged by the United States or any state on account of sex." Within a year, 22 states had approved the amendment, but the effort gradually stalled. Opposition came in part from working-class women who feared, as one union leader explained, that "maids, laundry workers, hospital cleaners, or dishwashers" would lose the protection of state laws that regulated wages and hours of work for women. Right-wing activist Phyllis Schlafly led an effort to defeat the ERA, claiming the amendment would lead to unisex toilets, homosexual marriages, and the drafting of women. The National Organization for Women (NOW) persuaded Congress to extend the time for ratification by three years, but the deadline for ratification passed on June 30, 1982, with the ERA forces still three states short (see Map 31.2.). NOW leader Eleanor Smeal vowed to fight on: "The crusade is not over. We know that we are the wave of the future."

The women's movement devoted even more of its energies to protecting *Roe v. Wade,* the 1973 Supreme Court decision that guaranteed women's right to abortion. Right-to-life groups, consisting mainly of orthodox Catholics, fundamentalist Protestants, and conservatives, fought back. In 1978, with support from President Carter, Congress passed the Hyde amendment, which denied the use of federal funds to pay for abortions for poor women. Nevertheless, pro-choice groups organized privately funded family planning agencies and abortion clinics to give more women a chance to exercise their constitutional right to abortion.

As Presidents Reagan and Bush appointed more conservative judges to the Court, however, pro-choice groups began to fear the overturn of *Roe v. Wade.* The Court avoided a direct challenge, contenting itself with upholding the rights of states to regulate abortion clinics, imposing a 24-hour waiting period, and requiring the approval of a parent or judge before a minor could have an abortion. Abortion became an issue in presidential contests, with the Republicans upholding a pro-life position and the Democrats taking a pro-choice stand. Bill Clinton's election and appointment of Ruth Bader Ginsburg to the Court appeared to end the challenge to *Roe v. Wade,* but in 2000, the Court margin in rejecting a Nebraska law forbidding certain late-term abortions fell to a bare majority, 5–4. And the often violent protests of pro-life groups outside abortion clinics made getting an abortion difficult and dangerous. For many women, abortion was a hard-won right they had to struggle to protect.

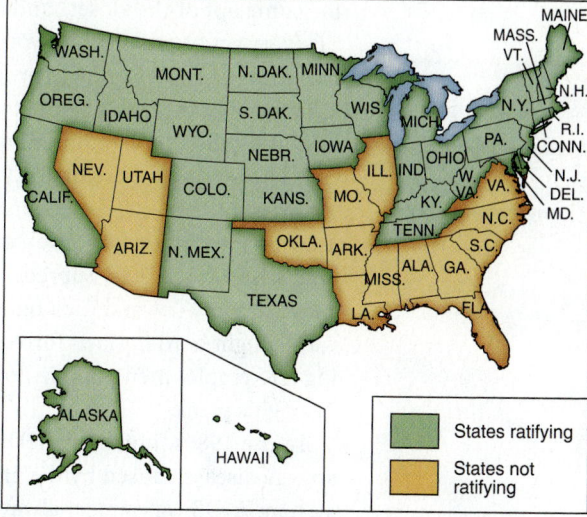

Map 31.2   *Voting on the Equal Rights* Amendment By the end of 1974, 34 states had ratified the ERA; Indiana finally approved the amendment in 1977, but the remaining 15 states held out, leaving ratification three states short of the required three-fourths majority.

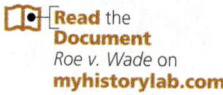

Read the **Document**
Roe v. Wade on **myhistorylab.com**

Quick Check
✓ What new challenges and opportunites faced women during the decade?

The Gay Liberation Movement

On the night of June 27, 1969, New York police raided the Stonewall Inn, a Greenwich Village bar frequented by "drag queens" and lesbians. As the patrons were being herded into vans, gay onlookers began to jeer and taunt the police. A riot broke out. "Beer cans and bottles were heaved at the windows and a rain of coins descended on the cops," reported the *Village Voice.* "Almost by signal the crowd erupted into cobblestone and bottle heaving." The next night, more than 400 police officers battled 2,000 gay demonstrators in Greenwich Village. The two-day Stonewall Riots marked the beginning of the modern gay liberation movement. Refusing to be victims any longer, gays and lesbians affirmed their sexual orientation and demanded an end to discrimination against homosexuals.

Within days, two new organizations were formed in New York, the Gay Liberation Front and the Gay Activist Alliance, with branches and offshoots in cities across the country. The basic theme of gay liberation was to urge all homosexuals to "come out of the closet" and affirm their sexual identity with pride not shame. The very act of coming out would bring freedom and self-respect. "Come out for freedom! Come out now!" proclaimed the Gay Liberation Front's newspaper. "Come out of the closet before the door is nailed shut!"

View the **Image**
*Sign at a Gay Pride
March on*
myhistorylab.com

During the 1970s, hundreds of thousands of gays and lesbians responded to this call. They formed more than 1,000 local clubs and organizations and won notable victories. In 1974, the American Psychiatric Association stopped classifying homosexuality as a mental disorder, and by 1980, half the states had repealed their sodomy statutes. The 2003 Supreme Court decision in *Lawrence v. Texas* struck down a Texas sodomy law and declared private consensual sex a matter of personal liberty. Gays fought hard for laws forbidding discrimination against homosexuals in housing and employment, and in 1980, the Democratic National Platform included a gay rights plank.

In the 1980s, however, AIDS put the gay liberation movement on the defensive. A disease caused by the HIV retrovirus that destroyed the human immune system, AIDS was almost always fatal until the introduction of new drugs in the mid-1990s. And because it was first diagnosed among male homosexuals, the gay community faced new condemnation at a time when its members were trying desperately to care for the many victims of the disease within their ranks. The gay organizations formed in the 1970s to win new rights now channeled their energies into caring for the ill, promoting safer sex practices, and fighting for more public funding to help conquer AIDS. In 1986, ACT UP (AIDS Coalition to Unleash Power) began violent demonstrations to shock the nation into doing more about AIDS. Its members disrupted public meetings, chained themselves to a New York Stock Exchange balcony, and spray-painted outlines of corpses on the streets of San Francisco to call attention to those who had died of AIDS.

The movement also continued to stimulate gay consciousness in the 1980s. In 1987, an estimated 600,000 gays and lesbians took part in a march on Washington on behalf of gay rights. Every year afterward, gay groups held a National Coming Out Day in October to encourage homosexuals to proclaim proudly their sexual identity. In a more controversial move, some gay leaders encouraged "outing"—releasing the names of prominent homosexuals, primarily politicians and movie stars—to make the nation aware of how many Americans were gay or lesbian. Gay leaders claimed there were more than 20 million gays and lesbians in the nation, basing this estimate on a Kinsey report that had stated in the late 1940s that one in ten American males had engaged in homosexual behavior. On the other hand, a sociological survey released in 1993 contradicted those numbers, finding only 1.1 percent of American males exclusively homosexual. Whatever the actual number, it was clear by the 1990s that gays and lesbians formed a significant minority that had forced the nation, however grudgingly, to respect its rights.

However, one victory eluded the gay liberation movement. In the 1992 election, gays and lesbians strongly backed Democratic candidate Bill Clinton, who promised, if elected, to end the ban on homosexuals in the military. In his first days in office, however, President Clinton stirred up resistance in the Pentagon and Congress when he tried to issue an executive order forbidding such discrimination. The Joint

Chiefs of Staff and many Democrats, led by Georgia Senator Sam Nunn, claimed accepting gays and lesbians would destroy morale and weaken the armed forces. Clinton finally settled for the Pentagon's compromise "Don't ask, don't tell" policy that would permit homosexuals to serve in the military as they had in the past as long as they did not reveal their sexual preference and refrained from homosexual conduct. However disappointed gays and lesbians were in Clinton's retreat, their leaders understood that the real problem was the resistance of mainstream America to full acceptance of homosexuality.

Public attitudes toward gays and lesbians changed in the 1990s, but the growing tolerance had limits. In a 1996 poll, 85 percent of those questioned believed that gays should be treated equally in the workplace, up from 76 percent in 1992. Violence against gays, however, continued, most notably in the 1998 fatal beating of Matthew Shepard, a 21-year-old gay college student, in Wyoming. That attack spurred calls for hate-crime legislation, and the judge in the case, banning a so-called gay-panic defense, sentenced Shepard's assailants to two consecutive terms of life imprisonment.

The issue of same-sex marriage came to a head at the end of the century. In 1996, President Clinton signed the Defense of Marriage Act, which decreed that states did not have to recognize same-sex marriages performed elsewhere. But in 2000, following a state supreme court ruling, the Vermont legislature legalized civil unions between individuals of the same sex, enabling gays and lesbians to receive all the legal benefits available to married couples. Whether sanctioned by law or not, the number of gay and lesbian households steadily increased; the 2000 census revealed that there were nearly 600,000 homes in America headed by same-sex couples. While nearly one-quarter were in California and New York, there was at least one gay or lesbian couple living in 99 percent of the nation's counties.

> **Quick Check**
> ✓ What was "Gay Liberation," and how did the movement develop?

POLITICS AND DIPLOMACY AFTER WATERGATE

The era's economic and social disruptions contributed to problems of governance left over from Watergate. Even as many Americans worried about shrinking paychecks and disintegrating families, Congress challenged the prerogatives of the presidency. This made life in the White House difficult for Richard Nixon's immediate successors—and it made solving America's problems nearly impossible.

> **Why** did the presidencies of Ford and Carter largely fail?

The Ford Administration

Gerald R. Ford was the first president who had never been elected to national office. Nixon had appointed him to the vice presidency to succeed Spiro Agnew, who had been forced to resign to avoid prosecution for accepting bribes while he was governor of Maryland. Ford, an amiable and unpretentious Michigan congressman who was House minority leader, seemed ready to restore confidence in the presidency when he replaced Nixon in August 1974.

But his honeymoon lasted only a month. On September 8, 1974, he shocked the nation by granting Richard Nixon a full and unconditional pardon for all federal crimes he may have committed. Some critics charged that Nixon and Ford had made a secret bargain; others pointed out how unfair it was for Nixon's aides to go to prison while the chief criminal went free. Ford apparently wanted to end the bitterness over Watergate, but his attempt backfired, eroding confidence in his leadership and linking him indelibly with the scandal.

Ford soon found himself fighting an equally difficult battle on behalf of the CIA. The Watergate scandal and the Vietnam fiasco had eroded confidence in the government and lent credibility to startling disclosures about covert actions. The president allowed the CIA to confirm some of the charges but then made things worse by blurting out to the press the juiciest item of all: The CIA had been involved in plots to assassinate foreign leaders.

Senate and House committees investigating the CIA now focused on the assassination issue, eventually charging that the agency had been involved in no fewer than eight separate attempts to kill Fidel Castro. The chairman of the Senate committee, Frank Church of Idaho, worried that the revelations would damage the reputations of Presidents Kennedy and Johnson; he likened the CIA to "a rogue elephant on the rampage."

In late 1975, Ford appointed George H. W. Bush, then a respected former Republican congressman, as the CIA's new director and gave him the authority to reform the agency and strengthen its role in shaping national security policy. Ford also issued an executive order outlawing assassination as an instrument of American foreign policy. To prevent future abuses, Congress created permanent House and Senate intelligence committees to exercise general oversight for covert CIA operations.

Ford proved less successful in his dealings with Congress on other issues. Although he prided himself on his good relations with members of both houses, he opposed Democratic measures such as federal aid to education and control over strip mining, and vetoed 39 separate bills. In fact, Ford, who as a congressman had opposed virtually every Great Society measure, proved far more conservative than Nixon in the White House.

○● Watch the **Video**
Gerald Ford Presidential Campaign Ad: Feeling Good About America on
myhistorylab.com

Quick Check
✓ What ended Ford's honeymoon with the American people?

Carter and American Malaise

Ford's lackluster record and the legacy of Watergate made the Democratic nomination a prize in 1976. Many candidates entered the contest, but a virtual unknown, former Georgia Governor James Earl Carter, became the front-runner. Aware of the voters' disgust with politicians of both parties, Carter ran as an outsider who could give the nation fresh and untainted leadership. On television, the basic Carter commercial showed him at his Georgia peanut farm, dressed in blue jeans, looking directly into the camera and saying, "I'll never tell a lie."

○● Watch the **Video**
Jimmy Carter and the Crisis of Confidence on
myhistorylab.com

Voters took Carter at his word and elected him over Ford in a close contest (see Table 31.1). Unfortunately, Carter's outsider status, while attractive in a campaign, made governing as president difficult. He had no discernible political philosophy, no clear sense of direction. He called himself a populist, but that label meant little more than an appeal to the common man, an ironic appeal, given Carter's wealth. "The idea of a millionaire populist has always amused me," commented his attorney general, fellow Georgian Griffin Bell.

TABLE 31.1 The Election of 1976			
Candidate	Party	Popular Vote	Electoral Vote
Jimmy Carter	Democratic	40,828,587	297
Gerald Ford	Republican	39,147,613	241

The Carter administration had little chance to succeed. The president strove for a balanced budget but had to accept mounting deficits. Federal agencies fought to save the environment and help consumers but only angered industry.

Joseph Califano, secretary of health, education, and welfare (HEW), failed repeatedly to effect long-overdue reforms. His attempts to overhaul the nation's welfare program, which had become a $30 billion annual operation serving 30 million Americans, won little support from the White House. Carter's unwillingness to take the risks involved in revamping the overburdened Social Security system by reducing benefits and raising the retirement age blocked Califano's efforts. And the HEW secretary finally gave up his attempt to draw up a national health insurance plan.

Informed by his pollsters in 1979 that he was losing the nation's confidence, Carter sought to redeem himself. After consulting advisers, he gave a speech in which he seemed to accuse the American people of creating "a crisis of confidence . . . that strikes at the very heart and soul and spirit of our national will." Then, a week after what his critics termed the "national malaise" speech, he requested the resignation of Califano and the secretary of the treasury. But neither the attempt to pin responsibility on the American people nor firing cabinet members could hide Carter's failure, despite good intentions and hard work, to provide the leadership the nation needed.

Quick Check

✓ What mood did Carter detect in American society?

Troubles Abroad

After the Vietnam War, most Americans wanted to have little to do with the world. Military intervention had failed in Southeast Asia, and with the economy in trouble, the country's economic leverage appeared minimal. Moreover, the point of détente was to diminish the need for American intervention abroad by directing the superpower contest with the Soviet Union into political channels.

Yet groups in the Third World didn't get the message of détente. In Central America, for example, there were uprisings against entrenched authoritarian regimes. In mid-1979, the Sandinistas in Nicaragua overthrew dictator Antonio Somoza. Despite American attempts to moderate the Sandinista revolution, the new regime moved steadily to the left, developing close ties with Cuba. In El Salvador, a leftist insurgency against a repressive regime put the United States in an awkward position. Unable to find an alternative between the extremes of reactionary dictatorship and radical revolution in Central America, Carter tried to encourage the military junta in El Salvador to carry out democratic reforms. But after the guerrillas launched a major offensive in January 1981, he authorized large-scale military assistance to the government, setting a precedent for the future.

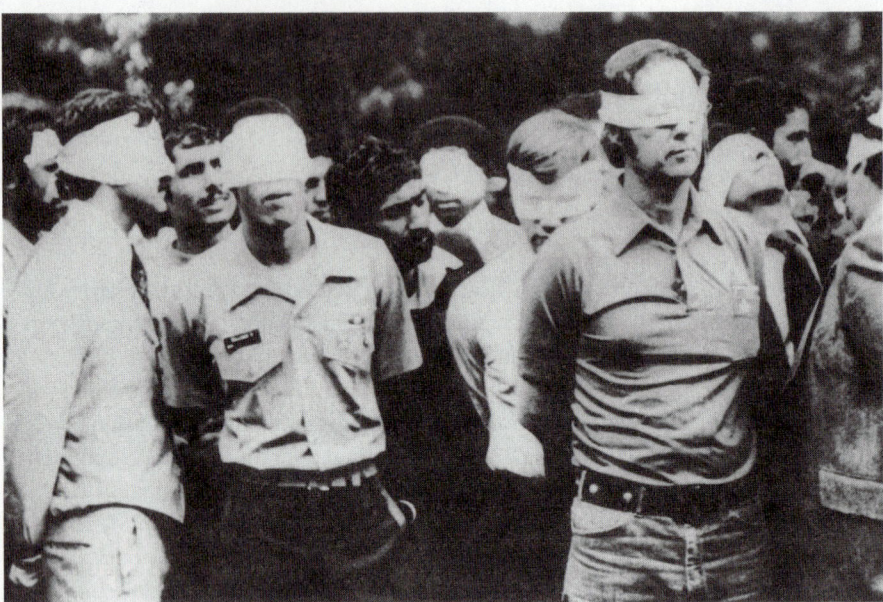

Blindfolded American hostages stand among their Iranian captors after militants captured the American embassy in Tehran on November 4, 1979. The Iranians' capture of 53 American hostages and their violent attacks on the embassy shocked U.S. citizens.

View the **Image**
The Signing of the Camp David Accords on **myhistorylab.com**

Carter initially had better luck in the Middle East. In 1978, he invited Egyptian President Anwar Sadat and Israeli Prime Minister Menachem Begin to negotiate a peace treaty under his guidance at Camp David. For 13 days, Carter met with them, finally emerging with the Camp David accords. A framework for negotiations rather than an actual peace settlement, the accords nonetheless paved the way for a 1979 treaty between these antagonists. The treaty provided for the return of the Sinai to Egypt but left the fate of the Palestinians, the Arab inhabitants of the West Bank and the Gaza Strip, unsettled.

The Iranian Revolution in 1979 offset any sense of progress in the Middle East. Under Nixon and Kissinger, the United States had depended heavily on the shah for defense of the Persian Gulf. Carter continued this close relationship, despite growing domestic discontent with the shah's leadership. By 1978, Iran was in chaos as the exiled Ayatollah Ruholla Khomeini led a fundamentalist Muslim revolt that forced the shah to flee the country in January 1979.

In October 1979, Carter let the shah enter the United States for medical treatment. Mobs in Iran denounced the United States, and on November 4, militants seized the U.S. embassy in Tehran and took 53 Americans prisoner. The ensuing Iranian hostage crisis revealed the decline of American power in the 1970s. Carter relied first on diplomacy and economic reprisals in a vain attempt to free the hostages. In April 1980, he authorized a desperate rescue mission that failed when helicopters broke down in the Iranian desert and an accident killed eight crewmen. The hostage crisis dragged on through 1980, a symbol of American weakness and a handicap to Carter in the presidential election.

Quick Check

✓ What happened at Camp David, and why were Americans taken hostage in Iran?

THE REAGAN REVOLUTION

After the turmoil of the 1960s, the economic and political troubles of the 1970s made Americans' turn to conservatism almost inevitable. The Watergate scandal won the Democrats a reprieve, but with Ronald Reagan, a decisive Republican victory was essentially assured.

What was the "Reagan revolution"?

The Election of 1980

In 1980, Jimmy Carter, who had used the Watergate trauma to win the presidency, found himself in trouble. Inflation, touched off by the second oil shock of the 1970s, reached double-digit figures. The Federal Reserve Board's tighter money supply had led to a recession, with unemployment climbing to nearly 8 percent by July 1980. What Ronald Reagan dubbed the "misery index," the combined rate of inflation and unemployment, hit 28 percent early in 1980 and stayed above 20 percent throughout the year.

Watch the **Video** *Jimmy Carter Presidential Campaign Ad: Burning the Midnight Oil* on **myhistorylab.com**

Foreign policy proved almost as damaging to Carter. The Soviet invasion of Afghanistan in 1979 had exploded hopes for continued détente and made Carter appear naive. The hostage crisis in Iran underlined the administration's helplessness.

Reagan and his running mate, George H. W. Bush, hammered away at the state of the economy and the world. Reagan scored heavily among traditionally Democratic blue-collar groups by blaming Carter for inflation, which robbed workers of any gain in real wages. Reagan also accused Carter of allowing the Soviets to outstrip the United States militarily and promised a massive buildup of American forces if he was elected. The independent candidacy of liberal Republican John Anderson, who appealed to voters disenchanted with Carter but not yet ready to embrace Reagan, further hurt Carter.

The president claimed that Reagan was too reckless to conduct American foreign policy in the nuclear age. Charging that the election would decide "whether we have peace or war," Carter tried to portray his Republican challenger as a warmonger. Reagan summarized the case against the administration by asking voters a simple question: "Are you better off now than you were four years ago?"

The answer was "no." Reagan carried 44 states and gained 51 percent of the popular vote. Carter won only six states and 41 percent of the popular vote. Anderson received the remaining 8 percent but failed to carry a single state. (See Map 31.3.) The growing political power of the Sunbelt helped Reagan; he carried every state west of the Mississippi except Minnesota, the

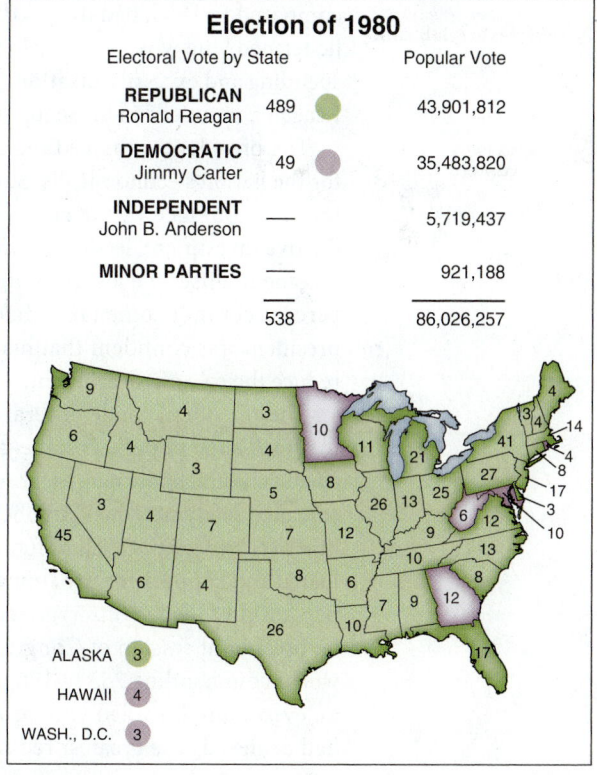

Election of 1980

	Electoral Vote by State	Popular Vote
REPUBLICAN Ronald Reagan	489	43,901,812
DEMOCRATIC Jimmy Carter	49	35,483,820
INDEPENDENT John B. Anderson	—	5,719,437
MINOR PARTIES	—	921,188
	538	86,026,257

ALASKA 3
HAWAII 4
WASH., D.C. 3

Map 31.3

home state of Carter's running mate, Walter Mondale. In the South, Reagan lost only Georgia, Carter's home state. Even more impressive were Reagan's inroads into the old New Deal coalition. He received 50.5 percent of the blue-collar vote and 46 percent of the Jewish vote, the best showing by a Republican since 1928. Only one group remained loyal to Carter: African American voters gave him 85 percent of their ballots.

Republican gains in Congress were even more surprising. For the first time since 1954, the GOP gained control of the Senate, 53 to 46, and the party picked up 33 seats in the House.

Though the full implications of the 1980 election remained to be seen, the outcome suggested that the Democratic coalition that had dominated American politics since FDR was falling apart. In the eight presidential elections from 1952 to 1980, Republican candidates received 52.3 percent of the popular vote, compared with 47.7 percent for the Democrats. Reagan's victory thus marked the culmination of a Republican presidential realignment that ended a half-century of Democratic dominance.

Quick Check

✓ Why did Americans find Reagan so attractive?

Cutting Taxes and Spending

Read the **Document**
Ronald Reagan, First Inaugural Address on **myhistorylab.com**

When Ronald Reagan took office in January 1981, inflation had devastated the economy. Interest rates hovered near 20 percent, while the value of the dollar, compared to 1960, had dropped to just 36 cents. The new president blamed what he termed "the worst economic mess since the Great Depression" on high federal spending and excessive taxation. "Government is not the solution to our problems," Reagan announced in his inaugural address. "Government is the problem."

Read the **Document**
Paul Craig Roberts, The Supply-Side Revolution (1984) on **myhistorylab.com**

The president embraced the concept of supply-side economics as the remedy for the nation's economic ills. Supply-side economists believed that the private sector, if encouraged by tax cuts, would shift its resources from tax shelters to productive investment, leading to an economic boom that would provide enough new income to offset the lost revenue. Although many economists worried that the 30 percent cut in income taxes that Reagan favored would lead to large deficits, the president was confident that his program would both stimulate the economy and reduce the role of government.

The president made federal spending his first target. Quickly deciding not to attack such popular middle-class entitlement programs as Social Security and Medicare, and sparing critical social services for the "truly deserving needy," the so-called safety net, the Republicans slashed $41 billion from the budget by cutting other social services such as food stamps and reducing public service jobs, student loans, and support for urban mass transit. Reagan used his charm and powers of persuasion to woo conservative Democrats from the West and South. Appearing before a joint session of Congress only weeks after an attempt on his life, Reagan won a commanding 253 to 176 margin of victory for his budget in the House, and an even more lopsided vote of 78 to 20 in the Senate. A jubilant Reagan said he had achieved "the greatest reduction in government spending that has ever been attempted."

The president proved equally successful in trimming taxes. He initially advocated annual cuts of 10 percent in personal income taxes for three consecutive years. When the Democrats countered with a two-year plan that would reduce taxes by only 15 percent, Reagan compromised with a proposal to cut taxes by 5 percent the first year but insisted on the full 10 percent reduction for the second and third years. In July, both houses passed the tax cut.

The president's economic program yielded mixed results. A sharp recession in 1981–1982 (engineered partly by the Federal Reserve to reduce inflation) drove unemployment to its highest level since World War II, and the tax cuts contributed to record federal budget deficits. But the overall performance of the economy in the 1980s was decidedly better than in the 1970s, with inflation down and jobs up. And in getting the policies he wanted, Reagan demonstrated his ability to wield presidential power. As *Time* magazine commented, no president since FDR had "done so much of such magnitude so quickly to change the economic direction of the country."

Quick Check

✓ What was Reagan's philosophy on taxes?

REAGAN AND THE WORLD

Reagan was determined to reverse American policy abroad no less than at home. He believed that under Carter, American prestige and standing in the world had dropped to an all-time low. Intent on restoring American pride and influence, Reagan devoted himself to strengthening America's defenses and recapturing world supremacy from the Soviet Union.

How did Reagan reshape American foreign relations?

Challenging the "Evil Empire"

The president scored his first foreign policy victory on the day he took office, thanks to diplomatic efforts begun under Carter. On January 20, 1981, Iran released the American hostages and enabled Reagan to begin his presidency on a positive note.

He built upon this accomplishment by embarking on a major military expansion. Here again he continued efforts begun by Carter, who after the Soviet invasion of Afghanistan had persuaded Congress to fund a 5 percent increase in defense spending. But the Reagan expansion went beyond Carter's. Secretary of Defense Caspar Weinberger proposed more than doubling defense spending. The emphasis was on new weapons, ranging from the B-1 bomber and the controversial MX nuclear missile to the expansion of the navy from 456 to 600 ships. Despite opposition in Congress, Reagan and Weinberger got most of what they wanted, and by 1985 the defense budget exceeded $300 billion.

The justification for this spending was Reagan's belief that the Soviet Union threatened the well-being and security of the United States. Reagan saw the Russians as bent on world revolution, ready "to commit any crime, to lie, to cheat" to advance their cause. Citing what he called a "record of tyranny," Reagan denounced the Russians before the UN in 1982, claiming that "Soviet-sponsored guerrillas and terrorists are at work in Central and South America, in Africa, the Middle East, in the Caribbean and in Europe, violating human rights and unnerving the world with violence."

Read the
Document
*Ronald Reagan,
Speech to the
House of Commons
(1982)* on
myhistorylab.com

Given his view of Russia as "the evil empire," it is not surprising that Reagan continued the hard line that Carter had adopted after the invasion of Afghanistan. Abandoning détente, Reagan implemented a 1979 decision to place 572 Pershing II and cruise missiles in Western Europe within range of Moscow and other Russian cities to match Soviet deployment of medium-range missiles aimed at NATO countries. Despite Soviet protests, uneasiness in Europe, and a vocal opposition at home, the United States began putting the weapons in Britain and Germany in 1983. The Soviets, claiming the move gave them only ten minutes of warning time if America attacked, broke off disarmament negotiations in Geneva.

The nuclear arms race was now more dangerous than ever. The United States stepped up research and development of the Strategic Defense Initiative (SDI), an antimissile system based on the use of lasers and particle beams to destroy incoming missiles in outer space. The media dubbed it "star wars." Critics doubted that SDI could be perfected, but they warned that even if it were, it would escalate the arms race by forcing the Russians to build more offensive missiles to overcome the American defense system. The Reagan administration, however, defended SDI as a legitimate attempt to free the United States from the deadly trap of deterrence, with its reliance on the threat of nuclear retaliation to keep the peace. Meanwhile, the Soviet Union kept deploying larger and more accurate land-based ICBMs. Although both sides observed the unratified SALT II agreements, the two superpowers had nearly 50,000 nuclear warheads between them.

Quick Check
✓ Why did Reagan think
the Soviet Union was
evil, and what did he
intend to do about it?

Confrontation in Central America

Reagan saw the Soviet challenge as global. In Central America, an area of extremes of wealth, with a small landowning elite and masses of poor peasants, the United States had traditionally looked for moderate, middle-class regimes to support. But these were hard to find, and Washington often ended up backing right-wing dictatorships rather than the leftist groups that advocated land reform and redistribution of wealth. Yet oppression by U.S.-supported regimes often drove reformers to embrace revolution. (See Map 31.4.)

View the **Map**
*Conflict in Central
America, 1970–1998* on
myhistorylab.com

This was what happened in Nicaragua. To strengthen the middle-class elements in the Sandinista government and avoid forcing Nicaragua into the Cuban and Soviet orbit, Carter had extended American economic aid.

The Reagan administration reversed this policy. Secretary of State Alexander Haig cut off aid to Nicaragua in 1981, accusing the Sandinistas of driving out the moderates, welcoming Cuban advisers and Soviet military assistance, and supporting leftist guerrillas in El Salvador. The criticism became a self-fulfilling prophecy as Nicaragua grew even more dependent on Cuba and the Soviet Union.

The United States and Nicaragua were soon on a collision course. In April 1983, declaring that "the national security of all the Americas is at stake in Central America," Reagan asked Congress for the money and authority to oust the Sandinistas. When Congress, fearful of repeating the Vietnam fiasco, refused, Reagan opted for covert action. The CIA began supplying the Contras, exiles fighting the Sandinistas from bases in Honduras and Costa Rica. The U.S.-backed rebels tried to disrupt the Nicaraguan economy, raiding villages, blowing up oil

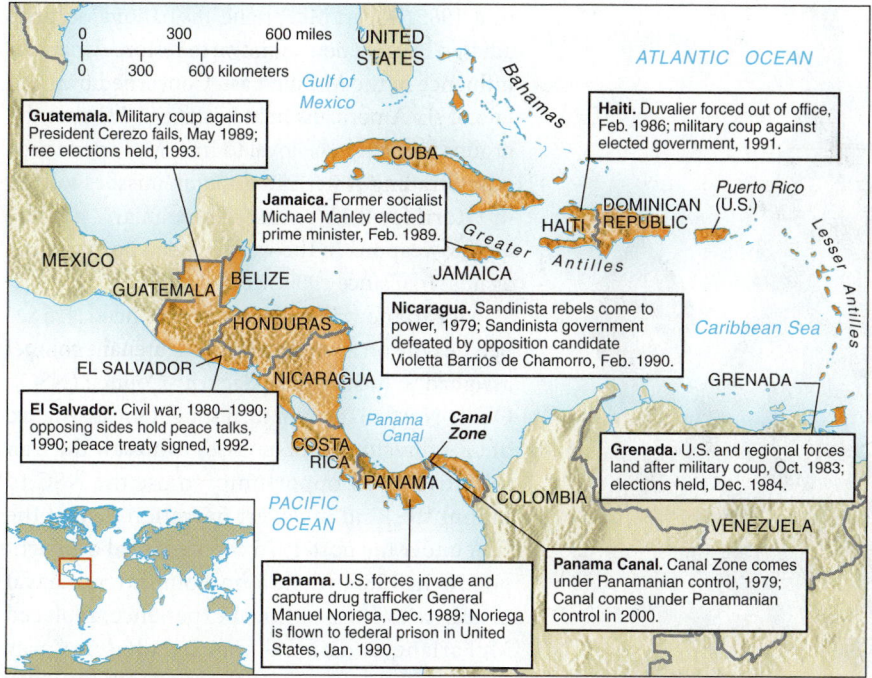

Map 31.4 Trouble Spots in Central America and the Caribbean U.S. involvement in Central American trouble spots intensified in the 1980s and early 1990s.

tanks, and mining harbors. Then, in 1984, Congress passed the Boland Amendment, prohibiting any U.S. agency from spending money in Central America. The withdrawal of U.S. financial backing left the Contras in a precarious position.

Quick Check

✓ How did Reagan deal with leftists in Central America?

Trading Arms for Hostages

Reagan was reelected easily in 1984. Voters gave him credit for reviving the economy and challenging communism. Democratic candidate Walter Mondale provided a jolt to the campaign by choosing Representative Geraldine Ferraro of New York as his running mate. But even the presence of the first woman on the national ticket of a major American party couldn't dent Reagan's popularity. He won 59 percent of the popular vote and every state but Mondale's home, Minnesota (see Table 31.2).

Yet the troubles abroad persisted. Not long after Reagan's second inauguration, his policies in the Middle East and Central America converged in the Iran-Contra affair. In

View the **Map**
The Middle East in the 1980s and 1990s on
myhistorylab.com

TABLE 31.2	The Election of 1984		
Candidate	**Party**	**Popular Vote**	**Electoral Vote**
Reagan	Republican	54,455,075	525
Mondale	Democratic	37,577,185	13

Reagan and Gorbachev in Red Square. During the summits between the two leaders, the American public grew to admire the Soviet premier for his policies of *perestroika* (restructuring) and *glasnost* (openness).

👁 **Watch** the **Video** *Oliver North Hearing* on **myhistorylab.com**

Quick Check

✓ What was the Iran-Contra affair?

mid-1985, Robert McFarlane, the national security adviser, began a new initiative to restore American influence in the Middle East. Concerned over the fate of six Americans held hostage in Lebanon by groups thought to be loyal to Iran, McFarlane proposed trading American antitank missiles to Iran in return for their release. The Iranians, desperate for weapons in the war they had been waging against Iraq since 1980, seemed willing to comply.

McFarlane was soon in over his head. He relied heavily on a young marine lieutenant colonel assigned to the National Security Council (NSC), Oliver North. North in turn sought the assistance of CIA director William Casey, who saw the Iran initiative as an opportunity to use the NSC to mount the kind of covert operation denied the CIA under the post-1975 congressional oversight policy. In 1986, when John Poindexter, a naval officer with little political experience, replaced McFarlane as national security adviser, Casey persuaded the president to ship TOW antitank missiles and HAWK anti-aircraft missiles to Iran.

The arms deal with Iran was bad policy, but what came next was criminal. Ever since the Boland Amendment had cut off congressional funding, the Reagan administration had been searching for ways to supply the Contras in Nicaragua. North was put in charge of soliciting donations from wealthy right-wing Americans. In early 1986, North had what he later described as a "neat idea" (apparently shared by Casey)—he could use profits from selling weapons to Iran (charging as much as $10,000 for a TOW that cost the United States only $3,500) to finance the Contras. North's ploy was both illegal and unconstitutional, since it meant usurping the congressional power of the purse.

Ultimately the secret got out. Officials tried to shield Reagan, and it was unclear whether the president had approved the Contra diversion. Reagan's reputation was tarnished. Subordinates, including North and Poindexter, were prosecuted. Casey died of a brain tumor.

Reagan the Peacemaker

Americans' tolerance of Reagan's mistakes in the Iran-Contra affair resulted in part from the progress he was making in U.S.-Soviet relations. Elected as an anticommunist hardliner, Reagan advocated cooperation with Moscow during his second term.

A change in leadership in the Soviet Union had much to do with the change in Reagan's approach. The death of Leonid Brezhnev in 1982, followed in rapid succession by the deaths of his aged successors, Yuri Andropov and Konstantin Chernenko, led to the selection of Mikhail Gorbachev, a younger and more dynamic Soviet leader, in 1985. Gorbachev was intent on improving relations with the United States as part of his policy of *perestroika* (restructuring the Soviet economy) and *glasnost* (political openness). Soviet economic performance was deteriorating, and the war in Afghanistan had become a running sore. Gorbachev needed a breathing spell in the arms race and a reduction in Cold War tensions to carry out his domestic reforms.

Summit meetings between Reagan and Gorbachev broke the chill in superpower relations and led in December 1987 to an **Intermediate Nuclear Forces Treaty (INF)**, by which the two sides agreed to remove and destroy all intermediate-range missiles in Europe. The most important arms-control agreement since SALT I in 1972, the INF treaty raised hopes that an end to the Cold War was in sight.

During the president's last year in office, the Soviets cooperated with the United States in pressuring Iran and Iraq to end their long war. Gorbachev also pulled the last Soviet troops out of Afghanistan in 1989. By the time Reagan left office, his foreign policy triumphs had offset the Iran-Contra fiasco and helped redeem his presidency.

Quick Check

✓ What did the INF Treaty do?

CONCLUSION: CHALLENGING THE NEW DEAL

Though trouble dogged the final years of his presidency, Reagan's two terms reshaped American politics. The Democratic coalition forged by FDR during the New Deal finally broke down as the Republicans captured the South and made inroads into organized labor.

More significantly, Reagan challenged the liberal premises of the New Deal by asserting that the private sector, rather than the federal government, ought to be the source of remedies to most of America's ills. Reagan left intact the centerpieces of the welfare state—Social Security and Medicare—but trimmed other programs and made any comparable expansion of federal authority nearly impossible for 20 years. By the time he left office, small-government conservatism seemed the undeniable wave of the American future.

31 STUDY RESOURCES

((•—[Listen to the **Chapter Audio** for Chapter 31 on **myhistorylab.com**

TIMELINE

1969 Stonewall Riots in New York City's Greenwich Village spark gay rights movement (June), p. 787

1970 U.S. invades Cambodia (April), p. 778
 • Ohio National Guardsmen kill four students at Kent State University (May), p. 778

1972 President Nixon visits China (February), p. 778
 • U.S. and USSR sign SALT I accords in Moscow (May), p. 778

• White House "plumbers" break into Democratic headquarters in Watergate complex (June), p. 780

• Nixon wins landslide reelection (November), p. 780

1973 U.S. and North Vietnam sign truce (January), p. 779
 • Arab oil embargo creates energy crisis in the U.S. (October), p. 782

CHAPTER REVIEW

THE TEMPTING OF RICHARD NIXON

What were the major accomplishments and failures of the Nixon presidency?

Nixon opened diplomatic relations with China and initiated détente with the Soviet Union. He withdrew American troops from Vietnam, terminating a quarter-century of American involvement. But his role in the Watergate scandal led to a constitutional crisis that forced him from office in disgrace. *(p. 777)*

OIL AND INFLATION

How were oil and inflation linked during the 1970s?

Oil prices jumped dramatically in the 1970s, as a result of growing demand for oil and turmoil in the Middle East. Rising oil prices contributed to the worst inflation in modern American history. *(p. 782)*

PRIVATE LIVES, PUBLIC ISSUES

How did private life change during this period?

The divorce rate rose significantly, and the number of married couples with children declined. More women entered the professions, and *Roe v. Wade* guaranteed their right to an abortion. Gay men and lesbians achieved greater freedom than before, though they still lacked rights accorded to heterosexuals. *(p. 784)*

POLITICS AND DIPLOMACY AFTER WATERGATE

Why did the presidencies of Ford and Carter largely fail?

Ford and Carter had to deal with the aftermath of Vietnam and Watergate and the economic disruptions that followed the oil price rises of the 1970s. Ford alienated many Americans by pardoning Nixon, and Carter fumbled the hostage crisis in Iran. *(p. 789)*

THE REAGAN REVOLUTION

What was the "Reagan revolution"?

The Reagan revolution was the return to conservatism in American politics and diplomacy upon Reagan's 1980 election as president. Reagan pledged to reduce the role of government in American life, and restore American honor and confidence abroad. *(p. 793)*

REAGAN AND THE WORLD

How did Reagan reshape American foreign relations?

Reagan rejected détente and challenged the Soviet Union more directly than any American president in decades. He called for the creation of the SDI missile system, and he waged covert war against leftists in Central America. The Iran-Contra affair, in which Reagan traded arms for hostages, tarnished his reputation, but he also negotiated the INF treaty with the Soviet Union. *(p. 795)*

KEY TERM QUESTIONS

1. Why did Jerry Falwell form the Moral Majority? (p. 776)

2. How does neoconservatism differ from other political ideologies? (p. 777)

3. Was détente successful and why did it appeal to Nixon? (p. 777)

4. Were the Strategic Arms Limitation Talks (SALT) successful? (p. 778)

5. How did the Watergate scandal come about and how was it unfolded by investigators? (p. 781)

6. Why is the Organization of Petroleum Exporting Countries (OPEC) significant? (p. 782)

7. Why did the Equal Rights Amendment (ERA) ultimately fail? (p. 786)

8. What was the ruling in *Roe v. Wade* and why was it significant? (p. 787)

9. Why were the Camp David accords a breakthrough in the relationship between Israel and Egypt? (p. 792)

10. Why were Americans seized in the Iranian hostage crisis and how did Carter respond to the crisis? (p. 792)

11. Why did Reagan advocate supply-side economics and how successful was it? (p. 794)

12. What prompted Reagan's Strategic Defense Initiative (SDI)? (p. 796)

13. What caused the Iran-Contra affair? (p. 797)

14. What did the Intermediate Nuclear Forces Treaty (INF) aim to do? (p. 799)

MyHISTORYLAB CONNECTIONS

Visit **www.myhistorylab.com** for a customized Study Plan to build your knowledge of *To a New Conservatism*

Questions for Analysis

1. Which states saw their population increase the most during the postwar migration to the Sunbelt?

   View the **Map** *Postwar Migration to the Sunbelt and the West Coast* p. 776

2. What was the significance of the Roe v. Wade Supreme Court decision?

   Read the **Document** *Roe v. Wade* p. 787

3. Why did Jimmy Carter feel that America was suffering from a "Crisis of Confidence"?

   Watch the **Video** *Jimmy Carter and the "Crisis of Confidence"* p. 790

4. What was the "Supply-Side" Revolution?

   Read the **Document** *Paul Craig Roberts on the Supply-Side Revolution* p. 794

5. Why did U.S. relations with the Middle East become more complex in the 1980s and 1990s?

   View the **Map** *The Middle East in the 1980s and 1990s* p. 797

Other Resources from this Chapter

Read the **Document** *Watergate Special Prosecution Force Memo*

Watch the **Video** *Richard Nixon, "I am not a Crook"*

View the **Image** *Sign at a Gay Pride March*

Watch the **Video** *Gerald Ford Presidential Campaign Ad: Feeling Good About America*

View the **Image** *The Signing of the Camp David Accords*

Watch the **Video** *Jimmy Carter Presidential Campaign Ad*

Read the **Document** *Ronald Reagan, First Inaugural Address*

Read the **Document** *Ronald Reagan, Speech to the House of Commons*

View the **Map** *Conflict in Central America, 1970–1998*

Watch the **Video** *Oliver North Hearing*

Contents and Spotlight Questions

((•─ **Listen** to the **Chapter Audio** for Chapter 32 on **myhistorylab.com**

"THIS WILL NOT STAND": FOREIGN POLICY IN THE POST–COLD WAR ERA

On the evening of August 1, 1990, George H. W. Bush sat in a T-shirt in the medical office in the basement of the White House. Bush was an avid golfer, but his duties as president kept him from playing as much as he would have liked, and when he did find time to squeeze in a round or some practice, he tended to overdo things. This summer day he had strained a shoulder muscle hitting practice balls, and now he rested

President George Bush confers with National Security Advisor Brent Scowcroft (left), White House Chief of Staff John Sununu (center), and Vice President Dan Quayle (right) at the Oval Office on August 1, 1990, following the Iraqi invasion of Kuwait.

on the exam table while a therapist applied deep heat. He planned a quiet evening and hoped the soreness would be gone by morning.

Two unexpected visitors altered his plans. Brent Scowcroft, Bush's national security adviser, and Richard Haass, the Middle East expert of the National Security Council, appeared at the door of the exam room. Bush had known Scowcroft for years, and the look on his face told him something was amiss. Scowcroft's words confirmed the impression: "Mr. President, it looks very bad. Iraq may be about to invade Kuwait."

For months the Bush administration had been monitoring a territorial and financial dispute between Iraq and Kuwait. Iraqi dictator Saddam Hussein was rattling the saber against much smaller Kuwait, but he had rattled sabers before without actually using them. The previous week Saddam had met with the American ambassador in Iraq, April Glaspie, who came away with the belief that his bellicose talk was chiefly for political effect. The United States had indicated its displeasure with Saddam's threats, and Glaspie judged that he had gotten the message. "He does not want to further antagonize us," she wrote to Washington.

Saddam's decision to invade Kuwait at the beginning of August therefore caught the Bush administration by surprise. American intelligence agencies detected Iraq's mobilization; this was what brought Scowcroft and Haass to the White House on August 1. Haass suggested that the president call Saddam and warn him not to attack. But even as Bush considered this suggestion, Scowcroft received a message that the American embassy in Kuwait had reported shooting in Kuwait City. "So much for calling Saddam," Bush said. Within hours the Iraqi forces crushed Kuwaiti resistance.

Bush, Scowcroft, and other American officials recognized that the Iraqi takeover of Kuwait constituted the first crisis of the post–Cold War era. As Lawrence Eagleburger, the deputy secretary of state, asserted in an emergency meeting of the National Security Council, "This is the first test of the postwar system. As the bipolar world is relaxed, it permits this, giving people more flexibility because they are not worried about the involvement of the superpowers." During the Cold War, a de facto division of labor had developed, with the United States and the Soviet Union each generally keeping its clients and allies in line, typically by threatening to withhold weapons or other assistance. Had the Soviet Union still been a superpower, Saddam, a longtime recipient of Soviet aid, likely would have heeded Moscow's warnings to settle his dispute with Kuwait peacefully. But in 1990, the Soviet system was disintegrating, and the Kremlin's clients were on their own. "Saddam Hussein now has greater flexibility because the Soviets are tangled up in domestic issues," Eagleburger explained. The world was watching. "If he succeeds, others may try the same thing."

This belief shaped the Bush administration's response to the crisis. The president and his advisers understood that they were entering uncharted territory after the Cold War. As the sole remaining superpower, the United States could employ its military and economic resources more freely than at any time in history. But with that freedom came unprecedented responsibility. During the Cold War the United States could cite the threat of Soviet retaliation as reason to avoid intervening in the affairs of other countries; with that threat gone, American leaders would have to weigh each prospective intervention on its own merits. If one country attacked another, should the United States defend the victim? If the government of a country oppressed its own people, should the United States move to stop the oppression? These questions—and the answers American presidents gave to them—would define American foreign policy in the era after the Cold War.

Bush sensed the importance of the United States' responses, and he responded accordingly. He convened his principal deputies for a series of White House meetings. The particular stakes with Iraq and in the surrounding Persian Gulf were discussed at length. "The rest of the world badly needs oil," Defense Secretary Dick Cheney observed, stating the obvious. Saddam's seizure of Kuwait gave him control of much of the world's oil supply, but the real prize was Saudi Arabia. "Saudi Arabia and others will cut and run if we are weak," Cheney predicted.

Bush consulted America's oldest allies. Britain's Margaret Thatcher urged the president to oppose Saddam most vigorously: "If Iraq wins, no small state is safe. We must win this. . . . We cannot give in to dictators."

Bush asked his generals what his military options were. "Iraq is not ten feet tall, but it is formidable," Norman Schwarzkopf, the U.S. commander for the Middle East, replied. American air power could punish Saddam and perhaps soften him up, but ground forces—in large numbers—would be required to guarantee victory.

By August 5, Bush had made up his mind. As he exited the helicopter that brought him back to the White House from another high-level meeting, reporters crowded the South Lawn. They asked what he was planning to do.

"I'm not going to discuss what we're doing in terms of moving forces, anything of that nature," Bush answered. "But I view it very seriously, not just that but any threat to any other countries." Bush was no orator, and these remarks were unscripted. But one sentence summarized the policy that soon began to unfold: "This will not stand, this aggression against Kuwait."

THE FIRST PRESIDENT BUSH

Elected on the strength of his association with Ronald Reagan, George H. W. Bush appeared poised to confirm the ascendancy of the conservative values Reagan forced to the center stage of American life. But events, especially abroad, distracted Bush, whose principal contribution proved to be in foreign affairs. Bush brought the Cold War to a peaceful and triumphant conclusion, and he launched America toward the twenty-first century, an era when the United States faced new opportunities and new challenges.

What were the important issues in George H. W. Bush's presidency, and how were they handled?

Republicans at Home

Democrats approached the 1988 presidential election with high hopes, having regained control of the Senate in 1986 and not having to face the popular Reagan. But Vice President George H. W. Bush proved a stronger candidate than almost anyone had expected, and in a contest that confirmed the Republicans' hold on the Sunbelt, he defeated Massachusetts Governor Michael Dukakis. (See Table 32.1.)

Many people expected the policies of the Bush administration to reflect the reputation of the new president—bland and cautious, lacking in vision but safely predictable. At home, he lived up (or down) to his reputation, sponsoring few initiatives in education, health care, or environmental protection, while continuing the Reagan theme of limiting federal interference in the everyday lives of Americans. He vetoed family leave legislation, declined to endorse meaningful health care reform, and watered down civil rights proposals in Congress. The one exception was the Americans with Disabilities Act (ADA), passed in 1990, which prohibited discrimination against the disabled in hiring, transportation, and public accommodations. Beginning in July 1992, ADA called for all public buildings, restaurants, and stores to be made accessible to those with physical handicaps and required that businesses with 25 or more workers hire new employees without regard to disability.

The soaring federal budget deficit took up much of Bush's time on domestic affairs. The deficits Bush inherited from Reagan topped $150 billion per year, and conventional financial wisdom dictated that something be done to bring them down. In campaigning for president, Bush had promised "no new taxes," but in 1990, he broke the pledge. In a deal negotiated with the Congress, he agreed to a budget that included new taxes and substantial spending cuts, especially on the military. The resulting agreement projected a savings of $500 billion over five years, half from reduced spending and half from new revenue generated mainly by increasing the top tax rate from 28 percent to 31 percent and raising the gasoline tax by 5.1 cents a gallon.

Unfortunately for the president, the budget deal coincided with the beginning of a slow but painful recession that ended the Republican prosperity of the 1980s. Not only did Bush face recriminations from voters for breaking a campaign pledge not to raise taxes, but the economic decline led to greatly reduced government revenues. As a result, the deficit continued to soar, rising from $150 billion in fiscal year 1989 to just under $300 billion in 1992. Despite the 1990 budget agreement, the national debt increased by more than $1 trillion during Bush's presidency.

Quick Check

✓ How did Bush help end the Cold War?

Ending the Cold War

Bush might have accomplished more in domestic affairs had not the international developments begun during the Reagan years accelerated dramatically. Bush had been in office only months when the communist system of the Cold War began

TABLE 32.1   The Election of 1988

Candidate	Party	Popular Vote	Electoral Vote
Bush	Republican	48,886,097	426
Dukakis	Democratic	41,809,074	111

falling apart. In country after country in eastern Europe, communism gave way to democracy as the old order collapsed more quickly than anyone had expected.

An early attempt at anticommunist liberation failed. In May 1989, Chinese students began a month-long demonstration for democracy in Beijing's Tiananmen Square that attracted worldwide attention. Watching American television coverage of Gorbachev's visit to China in mid-May, Americans were fascinated to see the Chinese students call for democracy with a hunger strike and a replica of the Statue of Liberty. But on June 4, the Chinese leaders sent tanks and troops to Tiananmen Square to crush the demonstration. By the next day, full-scale repression swept over China; hundreds of protesters were killed, and thousands injured. Martial law quelled the dissent and shattered hopes for a democratic China.

Bush responded cautiously. He wanted to preserve American influence with the Chinese government. Hence, despite denouncing the crackdown, Bush sent National Security Adviser Brent Scowcroft to Beijing to maintain a working relationship with the Chinese leaders.

A far more promising trend toward freedom began in Europe in mid-1989. In June, Lech Walesa and his Solidarity movement won free elections in Poland. Soon the winds of change were sweeping over the former Iron Curtain countries. Hungary opened its borders to the West in September, allowing thousands of East Germans to flee to freedom. One by one, the repressive governments of East Germany, Czechoslovakia, Bulgaria, and Romania fell. The most heartening scene took place in East Germany in early November when new communist leaders suddenly announced the opening of the Berlin Wall. Workers quickly demolished a 12-foot-high section of this despised symbol of the Cold War, joyously singing a German version of "For He's a Jolly Good Fellow."

Most people realized that Mikhail Gorbachev was responsible for the liberation of eastern Europe. In late 1988, the Soviet leader signaled the spread of his reforms to the Soviet satellites by announcing that the Brezhnev doctrine, which called for Soviet control of eastern Europe, was now replaced with "the Sinatra doctrine," which meant that the people of this region could do things "their way." Gorbachev's refusal to use armed force to keep repressive regimes in power permitted the long-delayed liberation of the captive peoples of eastern Europe.

View the **Closer Look**
Opening the Wall, Berlin on
myhistorylab.com

Yet by the end of 1991, both Gorbachev and the Soviet Union had become victims of the demise of communism. On August 19, 1991, hardline communists placed Gorbachev under arrest. Boris Yeltsin, the newly elected president of the Russian Republic, broke up the coup by mounting a tank in Moscow and demanding Gorbachev's release. The Red Army rallied to Yeltsin's side. The coup failed, and Gorbachev was released, only to resign in December 1991 after the 15 republics in the old USSR dissolved the Soviet Union. Russia, by far the largest and most powerful of these republics, joined with ten others to form a loose alignment called the Commonwealth of Independent States (CIS). Yeltsin then disbanded the Communist party and continued Gorbachev's reforms to establish democracy and a free market system in Russia.

The Bush administration, although criticized for its caution, welcomed the demise of communism. Bush facilitated the reunification of Germany and offered economic assistance to Russia and the other members of the CIS. On the critical issue of nuclear weapons, Bush and Gorbachev in 1991 signed START I, agreeing to reduce nuclear warheads to fewer than 10,000 apiece. In 1992, Bush and Yeltsin agreed on the terms of START II, which would eliminate land missiles with multiple warheads and reduce the number of nuclear weapons on each side to just over 3,000, a level not seen since the mid-1960s.

The Gulf War

Amid the disintegration of the Soviet system, Iraq in August 1990 invaded Kuwait. Although Bush quickly concluded that Saddam Hussein's aggression must be reversed, removing Iraq from Kuwait took time and effort. The president started by persuading Saudi Arabia to accept a huge American troop buildup, dubbed Desert Shield. This would prevent Saddam from advancing into Saudi Arabia and allow the United States to launch a ground attack against Iraqi forces.

While the American buildup mounted, Bush arranged an international coalition to condemn the Iraqi invasion and endorse economic sanctions against Iraq. Not every member of the coalition subscribed to the "new world order" that Bush said the liberation of Kuwait would help establish, but all concurred in the general principle of deterring international aggression. Essential to the success of Bush's diplomatic offensive was the support of the Soviet Union, which during the Cold War had regularly blocked American initiatives in the United Nations. Soviet leaders may have wished to see Saddam punished, but they also hoped to receive American aid in restructuring their economy.

Read the **Document**
George Bush, Address to the Nation on Persian Gulf (1991) on
myhistorylab.com

Congress required more convincing. Many Democrats supported economic sanctions against Iraq but opposed using force. Yet as the troop buildup in the Persian Gulf proceeded—as Operation Desert Shield evolved into Operation Desert Storm—and as the sanctions failed to dislodge Iraq from Kuwait, some skeptics came around. After securing UN support for military action, Bush persuaded Congress (with just five votes to spare in the Senate) to approve using force to liberate Kuwait.

On January 17, 1991, the president unleashed a devastating aerial assault on Iraq. After knocking out the Iraqi air defense network in a few hours, F-117A stealth fighters and Tomahawk cruise missiles hit key targets in Baghdad. The air attack wiped out command and control centers and enabled the bombers of the United States and its coalition partners (chiefly Britain) to demoralize the enemy troops.

After five weeks of this, Bush gave the order for the ground assault. Led by General Schwarzkopf, American and allied armored units swept across the desert in a great

Anti-aircraft fire lights up the sky over Baghdad, Iraq, during the Persian Gulf War. A month of strikes on Iraqi targets was followed by a ground offensive that lasted only 100 hours before Iraqi troops began to surrender and President Bush ordered a ceasefire.

flanking operation while U.S. marines and Saudi troops drove directly into Kuwait City. In just 100 hours, the American-led offensive liberated Kuwait and sent Saddam Hussein's vaunted Republican Guard fleeing back into Iraq.

President Bush, acting on the advice of General Colin Powell, chairman of the Joint Chiefs of Staff, then halted the advance and agreed to an armistice with Iraq. Critics claimed that with just a few more days of fighting, perhaps even just a few more hours, American forces could have ended Saddam's cruel regime. But the president, fearful of disrupting the allied coalition and of becoming mired down in a guerrilla war, stopped when he had achieved his announced goal of liberating Kuwait. Moreover, he hoped that a chastened Saddam would help balance the threat of Iran in the volatile Persian Gulf region.

Quick Check

✓ What provoked the Gulf War of 1991, and how did it turn out?

THE CHANGING FACES OF AMERICA

From the *Mayflower* to the covered wagon and beyond, movement has always characterized the American people. The late twentieth and early twenty-first centuries witnessed two significant shifts in the American population: continued movement internally to the Sunbelt region of the South and West, and an influx of immigrants from developing nations. These changes led to increased urbanization, greater ethnic diversity, and growing social unrest.

How did the American population shift and grow between 1990 and 2010?

A People on the Move

By the 1990s, a majority of Americans lived in the Sunbelt of the South and West. Best defined as a broad band running across the country below the 37th parallel from the Carolinas to Southern California, the Sunbelt had begun to flourish with the buildup of military bases and defense plants during World War II. Rapid population growth continued with the stimulus of heavy Cold War defense spending and accelerated in the 1970s when lower labor costs and the favorable climate of the Sunbelt states attracted both high-technology firms and more established industries. Florida, Texas, and California led the way, each gaining more than 2 million new residents in the 1970s.

◉ View the **Map**
Americans Move to the Sunbelt on
myhistorylab.com

The flow continued over the next two decades. The Northeast and the Middle West continued losing people to the South and West, and in 1994, Texas surpassed New York as the nation's second most populous state. The 2000 census revealed that while all regions had gained population in the 1990s, the South and West had expanded by nearly 20 percent, compared to around 6 percent for the Northeast and Middle West. Phoenix, Arizona, was typical of the phenomenal growth of Sunbelt cities, adding a million residents in the 1990s to grow at a 45 percent rate. "Phoenix is flat and it's easy," explained a geographer who saw no end in sight. "You stick a shovel in the ground and pour a slab and you have a house."

The increasing urbanization of America had positive and negative aspects. People living in the large metropolitan areas were both more affluent and better educated than their rural counterparts. Family income among people living in the bigger cities and their suburbs was $9,000 a year higher, and three-fourths of the urban population had graduated from high school, compared to two-thirds of other

Americans. A metropolitan American was twice as likely to be a college graduate as a rural resident. Yet higher urban crime rates, longer commutes in heavy traffic, and higher living costs offset these advantages. Nevertheless, the big cities and their suburbs continued to thrive, accounting for 80 percent of all Americans by 2000.

Another striking population trend was the rise in the number of the elderly. In 1900, only 4.1 percent of the population was aged 65 or older; by 2010, those over 65 made up more than 13 percent of the population. Census Bureau projections suggest that by 2030, one out of every five Americans will be over age 65.

Quick Check

✓ Why did Americans migrate to the Sunbelt?

The Revival of Immigration

The flow of immigrants into the United States grew dramatically between 1990 and 2010. By 2010, a record high of 38 million foreign-born persons lived in the United States, constituting 12 percent of the population.

Read the **Document** *Illegal Immigration Reform and Immigrant Responsibility Act of 1996 on* **myhistorylab.com**

The new immigrants came mainly from Latin America and Asia. By 2010, over half the foreign-born population of the United States came from Latin America, about one-quarter from Asia, and about one out of seven from Europe. The new immigrants tended to settle in urban areas in six states—California, Texas, New York, Florida, Illinois, and New Jersey. In California especially, the influx of immigrants from Asia and Mexico created growing pressure on public services.

The arrival of so many immigrants was bound to lead to controversy over whether immigrants were a benefit or a liability to American society. A study by the National Academy of Sciences in 1997 reported that while government services

Newly sworn-in citizens of the United States wave U.S. flags during a naturalization ceremony in Miami on April 28, 2006. Days later, more than a million immigrants participated in a nationwide boycott called "A Day Without Immigrants" to protest the proposed tightening of U.S. immigration laws.

used by immigrants—schools, welfare, health clinics—cost more initially than was collected from them in taxes, in the long run, immigrants and their families more than paid their way. Immigrants tended to help consumers and employers by working for relatively low wages in restaurants, the textile industry, and farming, but they hurt low-skilled U.S. workers, notably high school dropouts and many African Americans, by keeping wages low. Economist George J. Borjas, a refugee from Cuba, claimed that immigrants from developing countries lacked the education and skills to achieve the prosperity previous newcomers attained; instead of entering mainstream American life, they were likely to remain a permanent underclass.

Quick Check
✓ What prompted the renewed growth in immigration?

Emerging Hispanics

Hispanics became the nation's largest ethnic group in 2002, surpassing African Americans for the first time. The Hispanic population climbed to over 49 million by 2010, accounting for 16 percent of the nation's population. "It doesn't surprise me," commented the leader of the League of Latin American Citizens. "Anybody that travels around . . . can see Latinos everywhere, working everywhere, trying to reach the American dream."

The Census Bureau identified four major Hispanic groups: Mexican Americans, Puerto Ricans, Cuban Americans, and other Hispanics, including many from Central America. Even though most of the Hispanic population was concentrated in cities such as New York, Los Angeles, San Antonio, and Miami, recent data showed a surprising geographical spread. Hispanics made up 20 percent of the population in individual counties in states such as Georgia, Iowa, and Minnesota. "The Latinization of the country is not just happening in New York, Miami, or L.A.," observed a Puerto Rican leader. "Its greatest impact is in the heartland in places like Reading, Pennsylvania; Lorain, Ohio; and Lowell, Massachusetts."

The Hispanic groups had several features in common. All were relatively youthful, with a median age of 27 (compared to 37 for the nation as a whole) and a high fertility rate. They tended to be relatively poor, with one-fourth falling below the poverty line, and to be employed in low-paying positions as manual laborers, domestic servants, and migrant workers. Although their position had improved considerably in the boom years of the 1980s and 1990s, Hispanics still lagged behind mainstream America. The poverty rate among Hispanics was twice the national average, and family median income in 2009 was $38,000 (against $50,000 for the country as a whole).

Lack of education was a key factor in preventing economic progress. Fewer Hispanics graduated from high school than other minorities, and their school dropout rate was the nation's highest at more than 50 percent. Hispanic leaders warned that these figures boded ill not just for their own group, but for society as a whole. "You either educate us," claimed a San Antonio activist, "or you pay for building more jails or for more welfare."

The entry of millions of illegal immigrants from Mexico, once derisively called "wetbacks" and now known as undocumented aliens, created a social problem for the nation and especially for the Southwest. Critics charged that the flagrant violation of the nation's border with Mexico had led to a subculture beyond the boundaries of law and ordinary custom. They argued that the aliens took jobs from U.S. citizens, kept wages artificially low, and received welfare and medical benefits that strained budgets in states such as Texas and California.

Defenders of the undocumented aliens contended that the nation gained from the abundant supply of workers who were willing to work in fields and factories at backbreaking jobs most Americans shunned. Moreover, defenders stated, illegal entrants usually paid sales and withholding taxes but rarely used government services for fear of being deported. Whichever view was correct, an exploited class of illegal aliens was living on the edge of poverty. As the *Wall Street Journal* observed, "The people who benefit the most from this situation are certainly the employers, who have access to an underground market of cheap, productive labor, unencumbered by minimum wage laws, union restrictions, or pension requirements."

Concern over economic competition from Mexican "illegals" had led Congress in 1986 to penalize employers who hired undocumented workers. Congress permitted those aliens who could show that they were living in the United States before 1982 to become legal residents; nearly 3 million accepted this offer of amnesty to become legal residents. Nevertheless, undocumented workers continued to flow north from Mexico in the 1990s and early 2000s—more than 500,000 in some years. The most widely accepted estimates indicated that about 11 million foreigners, mainly from Mexico and Central America, were living illegally in the United States in 2010.

Despite stepped-up border enforcement after the September 11, 2001, terrorist attacks, illegal immigrants continued to move north from Mexico and Central America. The trip could be dangerous, even lethal. Border Patrol agents counted as many as 500 deaths per year among migrants attempting to enter the United States illegally during the first decade of the twenty-first century. In Pima County, Arizona, alone, authorities discovered 40 bodies during two weeks in the summer of 2010. Yet the movement continued. As one Mexican official said, "There are great problems in the countryside. And that famous American dream keeps calling."

Quick Check

✓ Why was immigration from Mexico so controversial?

Advance and Retreat for African Americans

African Americans formed the second largest ethnic minority. In 2010, the United States had 39 million blacks, 12.5 percent of the population. Although the heaviest concentration of African Americans was in northern cities, notably New York and Chicago, there was a significant movement back to the South. This shift, which began in the 1970s and accelerated during the 1990s, meant that by 2010 more than half of those identifying themselves as black for the census lived in the 16 states of the Sunbelt. Family ties and ancestral roots explained much of this movement, but it also reflected the same economic incentives that drew so many other Americans to the Sunbelt.

African Americans made gains in certain areas of life. In 2010, more than 80 percent of blacks aged 25 and older had earned a high school diploma, a substantial increase during the previous generation. Nearly one in five African Americans possessed a college degree. The number of black-owned businesses grew significantly.

Yet in other respects African Americans did less well. The black poverty rate was nearly 25 percent, and the median income for black families was less than two-thirds of that for whites. Blacks remained clustered in entry-level jobs, where they faced competition from immigrants. The African American incarceration rate was much higher than the national average; in 2010, more than 10 percent of black males aged 25 to 29 were in prison, and, at current rates, one out of three black men could expect to spend time in a state or federal prison during his life. Blacks were also more likely to be victims of crime, especially violent crime. Homicide was the leading cause of death among black males between the ages of 15 and 34.

Two events, one from 1991 and the other from 2005, summarized the frustration African Americans felt. In March 1991, a bystander videotaped four Los Angeles policemen beating Rodney King, an African American who had been stopped for a traffic violation. The pictures of the rain of blows on King shocked the nation. Nearly a year later, when an all-white jury acquitted the four officers of charges of police brutality, rioting erupted in South Central Los Angeles that threatened the entire city when the police failed to respond promptly. In the aftermath of the riot, which took 53 lives (compared to 34 deaths in the 1965 riot in nearby Watts) and did more than $1 billion in damage, government and state agencies promised new help for inner-city dwellers. But the efforts produced little, and life for many urban blacks remained difficult and dangerous.

A tragedy of a different sort occurred 14 years later. In August 2005, Hurricane Katrina ravaged the Gulf Coast and broke levees in New Orleans. The high winds

In August 2005, the catastrophic Hurricane Katrina devastated much of the Louisiana and Mississippi Gulf Coast. In the wake of the storm, the levee system of New Orleans failed and flooded nearly 80 percent of the city. Particularly hard hit were low-lying areas such as the Lower Ninth Ward, where police rescue boats are shown here rescuing residents.

and water killed more than 1,000 persons, destroyed hundreds of thousands of homes, and forced millions of men, women, and children to evacuate. Television cameras captured the plight of the thousands who took refuge in the New Orleans Superdome, only to be stranded when state and federal relief efforts failed. Most of those suffering the worst in New Orleans were black. Their neighborhoods were the lowest-lying in the city, and hence the worst flooded. Many lacked the cars to flee the city in advance of the hurricane; others lacked the means to pay for hotels or apartments had they been able to get out. Though the relief efforts were largely color-blind (despite allegations to the contrary), the experience demonstrated that poverty in America was not.

Quick Check

✓ How did Hurricane Katrina reveal problems of African American life?

Americans from Asia and the Middle East

Asian Americans were the fastest-growing minority in 2000. As of 2010, there were more than 15 million Americans of Asian or Pacific Island descent. Although only 5 percent of the total population, they were increasing at seven times the national rate, and projections indicated that by 2050 one in ten Americans would be of Asian ancestry.

The Chinese formed the largest single group of Asian Americans, followed by Filipinos, Japanese, Indians, Koreans, and Vietnamese. Immigration was the primary reason for the rapid growth of all these groups except the Japanese; during the 1980s, Asia had provided nearly half of all immigrants to the United States. Though the influx slowed, the immigrants' children added to the Asian numbers.

Compared to other minorities, Asian Americans were well educated and affluent. Three out of four Asian youths graduated from high school, compared to fewer than one out of two blacks and Hispanics. Asian Americans also had the highest percentage of college graduates and doctoral degrees of any minority group; in fact, they were better represented in colleges and universities than the white majority. Many Asians entered professions, and the median income for Asian American families in 2010 was nearly 30 percent higher than the national average.

Not all fared so well, however. Refugees from Southeast Asia experienced hardship and persecution. The median family income for Vietnamese Americans was below the national average. Nearly half the Laotian refugees in Minnesota were unemployed because of difficulty learning to read and write English. Vietnamese fishermen on the Gulf Coast of Texas and Louisiana experienced repeated attacks on their livelihood and their homes. In the Los Angeles riots in 1992, Korean stores and shops were looted and firebombed.

But the overall experience of Asian Americans was positive. They came to America seeking economic opportunity, "to climb the mountain of gold." "People are looking for a better life," a Chinese spokeswoman explained. "It's as simple as that, and we will continue to come here, especially if the situations over there [in Asia] stay tight, or get worse."

The number of Americans from the Middle East grew almost as fast as those from Asia. By 2010, some 2 million Americans claimed Middle Eastern ancestry, 200,000 more than a generation earlier. Most came from Arab countries, Israel,

View the **Map**
Immigration to the United States on
myhistorylab.com

and Iran. Concentrated in California, New York, and Michigan, Middle Eastern Americans were well educated; nearly half had college degrees. Many Arab Americans felt nervous after the terrorist attacks of September 11, 2001, committed by Arab extremists; some were assaulted by persons who blamed anyone of Arab descent for the mass murders. Yet most Arab Americans carried on as before, pursuing their interpretation of the American dream.

Quick Check

✓ How did the new immigration from Asia and the Middle East differ from earlier phases of immigration?

THE NEW DEMOCRATS

The Democrats, political victims of the runaway inflation of the 1970s, became the beneficiaries of the lingering recession of the early 1990s. Moving away from its traditional liberal reliance on big government, the party regained strength by choosing moderate candidates and tailoring its programs to appeal to the hard-pressed middle class. These tactics enabled the Democrats to regain the White House in 1992 and retain it in 1996, despite a Republican sweep of Congress in 1994. The key figure in this political shift was Bill Clinton, who overcame early setbacks to reap the rewards of a sustained economic boom.

What were the accomplishments and failures of the Clinton administration?

Clinton and Congress

A recession that began in 1990 soured voters on George H. W. Bush, allowing Clinton to defeat him in a three-way race that included eccentric Texas billionaire H. Ross Perot. Clinton proved to be the most adept politician since Franklin Roosevelt. Born in Hope, Arkansas, in 1946, Clinton weathered a difficult childhood with an alcoholic stepfather by developing skills at dealing with people and using personal charm to achieve his goals. Intelligent and ambitious, he completed his undergraduate work at Georgetown University, studied law at Yale, and spent two years as a Rhodes scholar at Oxford University in England. Entering politics, he was elected Arkansas attorney general and then governor. Defeated after his first term in 1980, Clinton won the nickname "Comeback Kid" by regaining the governor's office in 1982. He was elected three more times, earning a reputation as one of the nation's most successful young political leaders.

Watch the **Video**
Bill Clinton's First Inauguration on
myhistorylab.com

In keeping with the theme of his 1992 campaign, Clinton concentrated at first on the economy. In February 1993, he called for tax increases and spending cuts to achieve a balanced budget. Congress was skeptical of such unpopular measures, but Clinton cajoled, shamed, and threatened sufficient members to win approval of $241 billion in new taxes and $255 billion in spending cuts, for a total deficit reduction of $496 billion over four years. This earned Clinton the confidence of financial markets and helped fuel the economic boom of the 1990s.

Clinton scored another victory when Congress approved the North American Free Trade Agreement (NAFTA) in 1993. NAFTA, initiated and nearly completed by Bush, was a free trade plan that united the United States, Mexico, and Canada into a common market without tariff barriers. Clinton endorsed the treaty to secure American prosperity and spread American values. Critics complained that free trade would cost American workers their jobs as American companies moved production overseas; Ross Perot, the defeated 1992 third-party candidate, predicted a "giant sucking sound" as American jobs went south to Mexico. But Clinton won a bruising fight in the House and an easier contest in the Senate.

Although Clinton's NAFTA coalition included many congressional Republicans, on other issues the GOP opposed the president. Republicans said his budget entailed "the biggest tax increase in the history of the world," and they scuttled an ambitious attempt to revamp the nation's health care system. Leading the opposition was a young congressman from Georgia, Newton Leroy "Newt" Gingrich, who asked all GOP candidates in the 1994 congressional races to sign a ten-point Contract with America. The contract consisted of familiar conservative goals, including a balanced budget amendment to the Constitution, term limits for members of Congress, a line-item veto for the president, and a middle-class tax cut. For the first time in recent political history, a party sought to win Congress on ideological issues rather than relying on individual personalities.

Embarrassing disclosures involving Clinton's character made this tactic particularly effective. During the 1992 campaign, the *New York Times* had raised questions about a bankrupt Arkansas land development called Whitewater in which the Clintons had lost a modest investment. Other alleged scandals cropped up over activities that had taken place after Clinton was elected president. Travelgate was the name given to the firing, apparently at the urging of First Lady Hillary Clinton, of White House employees who arranged travel for the press covering the president. Then in early 1994, Paula Jones, a former Arkansas state employee, filed a sexual harassment suit, charging that in 1991 then-Governor Clinton had made sexual advances to her.

The outcome of the November 1994 vote stunned political observers. The Republicans gained nine seats in the Senate and 53 in the House to take control of both houses. Newt Gingrich became speaker of the House. The GOP also captured 32 governorships, including those of New York, California, and Texas, where George W. Bush, the son of the man Clinton beat in 1992, won handily.

The Republicans claimed a mandate to resume the Reagan revolution: to cut taxes, diminish the scope of government, and empower the private sector. Clinton and the Democrats managed to check the Republicans on matters of substance, but the Republicans in turn contrived to hobble Clinton. The administration and the Republicans collaborated on welfare reform and a modest increase in the minimum wage, but otherwise deadlock descended on Washington.

Clinton turned the deadlock to his benefit in 1996 after the Republicans, having failed to force him to accept cuts in Medicare, college loans, and other social services, refused to pass a budget bill, and thereby shut down the federal government. Clinton persuaded voters that the Republicans were to blame and carried this theme into his 1996 reelection campaign. The Republican nominee, Robert Dole of Kansas, lacked Clinton's charisma and failed to shake the impression that the Republicans were flint-hearts who wanted to cut the pet programs of the American

Quick Check

✓ What victories did Clinton score in domestic affairs?

people. Clinton won decisively, even while the Republicans continued to control Congress. (See Map 32.1.)

Scandal in the White House

Despite Clinton's reelection, rumors of wrong-doing clung to his presidency. The special prosecutor appointed to probe the Whitewater transactions, Kenneth Starr, turned over stone after stone in search of malfeasance, until he came across rumors that Clinton had had an affair with a White House intern, Monica Lewinsky.

Clinton initially denied the affair. "I did not have sexual relations with that woman, Miss Lewinsky," he said in January 1998. But Starr subpoenaed Lewinsky, who eventually gave a detailed account of her sexual encounters with the president and provided crucial physical evidence implicating Clinton.

Realizing that he could no longer deny the affair, the president sought to limit the damage.

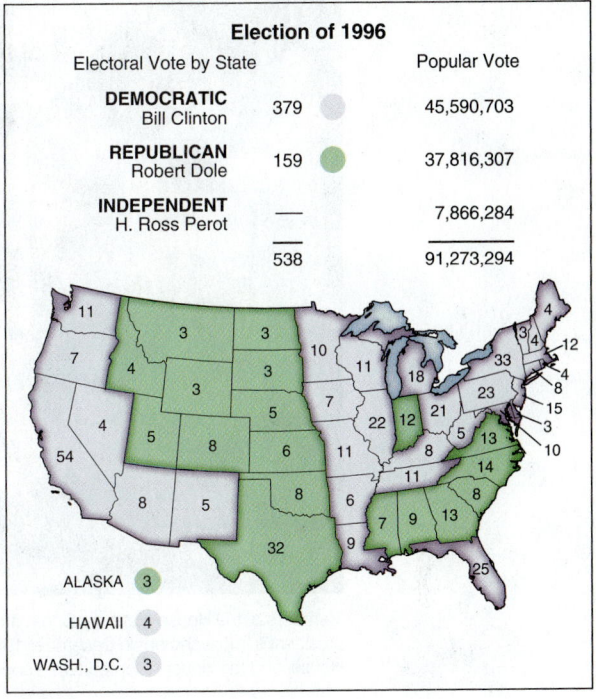

Map 32.1

On August 17, 1998, he appeared before Starr's grand jury and admitted to having "inappropriate intimate contact" with Lewinsky. That evening Clinton spoke briefly to the nation. Claiming that he had given the grand jury "legally accurate" answers, the president admitted to a relationship with Lewinsky that was "not appropriate" and "wrong." He said he regretted misleading the people and especially his wife, but he refused to apologize for his behavior or his false denials.

But just when Clinton seemed most vulnerable, the special prosecutor inadvertently rescued him. In September, Starr sent a 452-page report to Congress outlining 11 possible impeachment charges against Clinton. The key one was perjury, and Starr provided painstakingly graphic detail on the sexual encounters between Clinton and Lewinsky to prove that the president had lied when he denied engaging in sexual relations with the intern.

Many Americans condemned Starr rather than the president. Shocked by the sordid details, they blamed the prosecutor for exposing families to distasteful sexual practices on the evening news. When Hillary Clinton stood staunchly by her husband, a majority of the public seemed to conclude that president's conduct was a private matter to be settled between a husband and a wife, not in the public arena.

Republican leaders ignored this sentiment and pressed ahead with impeachment proceedings. In December, the House (where the 1998 midterm elections had

Read the **Document**
Exhibition of Articles of Impeachment (1999) on **myhistorylab.com**

Read the **Document**
Bill Clinton, Answers to the Articles of Impeachment on **myhistorylab.com**

Members of the House Judiciary Committee listen to Clinton's testimony during the hearings on the president's impeachment in December 1998. The committee sent four articles of impeachment to the full House, and the House adopted two—one count of perjury and one of obstruction of justice.

narrowed the GOP advantage to six) approved two articles of impeachment—perjury and obstruction of justice—by nearly straight party-line votes.

The showdown in the Senate was anticlimactic. With a two-thirds vote required to find the president guilty and remove him from office, there was no chance of conviction in the highly charged partisan mood. On February 12, 1999, the GOP was unable to muster even a majority on the perjury charge, with 45 in favor and 55 opposed. After a second, closer vote, 50 to 50, on obstruction of justice, the presiding officer, Chief Justice William Rehnquist, declared, "Acquitted of the charges."

Clinton had survived the Lewinsky affair, but his presidency was damaged. His final two years in office would be devoted to a concerted effort to restore his reputation. Desperate for a legacy to mark his White House years, Clinton failed to realize that he had already created an enduring one—he would be remembered as the president who dishonored his office by his affair with a young intern.

Quick Check

✓ Why was Clinton impeached?

REPUBLICANS RESURGENT

How did George W. Bush become president, and what did he do in the White House?

Clinton's eight years in the White House gave Democrats hope that the conservative gains of the 1980s had been temporary. They pointed to the booming economy and the absence of a serious threat to American security as reasons for voters to leave the presidency in Democratic hands. The election of 2000 proved a bitter disappointment—all the more bitter because of how it made Republican George W. Bush president.

The Disputed Election of 2000

If history had been the guide, the prosperity of the 1990s should have guaranteed victory to Clinton's protégé, Vice President Al Gore. The state of the economy generally determines the outcome of presidential elections, and entering 2000 the American economy had never appeared stronger. The stock market soared, spreading wealth among tens of millions of Americans; the federal deficit of the Reagan years had given way to large and growing surpluses.

But Clinton's personal problems muddled the issue. Clinton had survived his impeachment trial, yet the experience tainted his record and left many voters unwilling to reward the Democrats by promoting his vice president.

Other domestic problems also unnerved voters. The 1995 bombing of a federal building in Oklahoma City by two domestic terrorists killed 168 people and suggested that irrational violence threatened ordinary Americans. This feeling was reinforced by a 1999 shooting rampage at Columbine High School near Denver, which left 12 students and a teacher dead, besides the two shooters, who killed themselves. The apparent conflict between material abundance and eroding personal values resulted in the closest election in more than a century.

The two candidates, Vice President Gore of Tennessee and Governor Bush of Texas, had little in common beyond being the sons of successful politicians. Gore had spent 18 years in Washington as a congressman, senator, and vice president. Somewhat stiff and aloof, he had mastered the intricacies of all the major policy issues and had the experience and knowledge to lead the nation. Bush, by contrast, had pursued a business career before winning the governorship of Texas in 1994. Personable and outgoing, Bush had the temperament for leadership but lacked not only experience but a full grasp of national issues. Journalists were quick to seize on the weaknesses of both men, accusing Gore of frequent and misleading exaggeration and Bush of mangling words and speaking only in generalities.

The candidacy of consumer advocate Ralph Nader, who ran on the Green party ticket, complicated the political reckoning. Nader never seemed likely to win more than a small percentage of the votes, but in a close election, a few points could make the difference. Nader's mere presence pushed Gore to the left, leaving room for Bush among independent-minded swing voters.

On election night, Gore seemed the winner when the major television networks predicted a Democratic victory in Florida. They reconsidered as Bush swept the South, including the Clinton–Gore home states of Arkansas and Tennessee. After midnight, the networks again called Florida, but this time for Bush, and the vice president telephoned the governor to concede, only to recant an hour later when it became clear that the Bush margin in Florida was paper thin.

There things stuck, and for the next month all eyes were on Florida. Gore had 500,000 more popular votes nationwide than Bush, and 267 electoral votes to Bush's 246. Yet with Florida's 25 electoral votes, Bush could win the presidency. (See Map 32.2.) Both sides sent lawyers to Florida. Bush's team, working with Florida's Republican secretary of state, sought to certify the results that showed the GOP candidate with a lead of 930 votes out of nearly six million cast. Citing voting problems disclosed by the media, Gore asked for a recount in three heavily Democratic

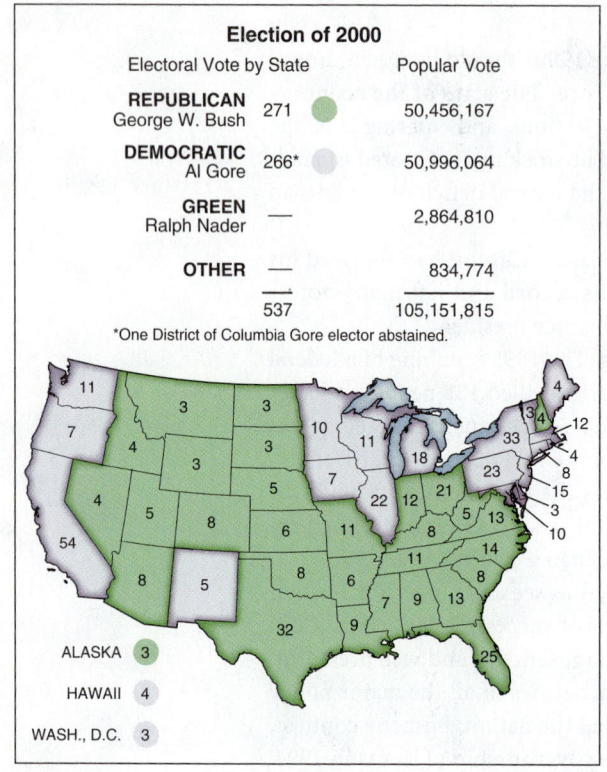

Election of 2000

	Electoral Vote by State	Popular Vote
REPUBLICAN George W. Bush	271	50,456,167
DEMOCRATIC Al Gore	266*	50,996,064
GREEN Ralph Nader	—	2,864,810
OTHER	—	834,774
	537	105,151,815

*One District of Columbia Gore elector abstained.

ALASKA 3
HAWAII 4
WASH., D.C. 3

Map 32.2

counties in south Florida. All three used antiquated punch card machines that resulted in some ballots not being clearly marked for any presidential candidate when the chads, the bits of paper removed when a card is punched, were not completely detached from the cards. For weeks the results in Florida, and hence of the entire election, appeared to depend on how one divined the intent of a voter based on hanging, dimpled, or bulging chads.

The decision finally came in the courts. Democrats appealed the initial attempt to certify Bush as the victor to the Florida Supreme Court. The Florida court twice ordered recounts, the second time for all counties in the state, but Bush's lawyers appealed to the United States Supreme Court. On December 12, five weeks after the election, the Court overruled the state court's call for a recount, in a 5 to 4 decision that reflected a long-standing ideological divide among the nine justices. The next day, Gore gracefully conceded, and Bush finally became president-elect.

Bush's narrow victory revealed deep divisions in American life. The rural West and South went for Bush, along with a few key Midwest and border states, while Gore won the urban states along both coasts. There was an equally strong divide along economic lines, with the poor voting for Gore, the rich for Bush, and the middle class dividing evenly between the two candidates. Gore benefited from the gender gap, winning 54 percent of the women's vote, and he won an even larger share of the black vote, 90 percent, than Clinton in 1996. Bush managed to narrow the Democratic margin among Hispanic voters, taking 35 percent, compared to only 28 percent for Dole four years earlier. The two candidates split the suburban vote evenly, while Bush reclaimed the Catholic vote for Republicans.

Quick Check

✓ What was controversial about the 2000 election?

George W. Bush at Home

Bush's first order of business was a large tax cut, which required intense lobbying from the White House. The president had to win over enough conservative southern Democrats to compensate for losing Republican moderates who insisted on reducing the federal debt before cutting taxes. Bush managed the feat, and in June 2001, Congress slashed taxes by a staggering $1.35 trillion over a ten-year period. Many of the cuts would take effect only in future years, but Congress offered an immediate stimulus to the economy by authorizing rebates to taxpayers: $600 for couples and $300 for individuals earning more than $6,000 a year. While critics saw this measure as a betrayal of the long effort to balance the budget, Bush contended that future surpluses would more than offset the loss of tax revenue.

A slowdown in the American economy, triggered by the bursting of the 1990s high-tech bubble, soon turned the projected budget surplus into annual deficits. But it failed to halt the Bush administration's tax cut momentum. In 2003, arguing that a further reduction in taxes would stimulate the stalled economy, Bush prevailed upon Congress to adopt another $350 billion in cuts. Like the 2001 cuts, the new reductions were temporary to preserve the possibility of a balanced budget by 2010. Opponents charged that if a future Congress made these tax cuts permanent, as seemed likely, the total cost would rise to nearly $1 trillion. While Clinton had favored eliminating the deficit, Bush made tax reduction the centerpiece of his economic policy.

The president also succeeded in persuading Congress to enact education reform. Borrowing the label "No Child Left Behind" from liberal Democrats, the administration pushed hard for a new policy requiring states to give annual performance tests to all elementary school students. Democrats countered with demands for increased federal funding of public education to assist states and local school boards in raising their standards. Bush shrewdly cultivated the support of Senator Edward Kennedy, a leading liberal Democrat, to forge a bipartisan consensus. The final measure increased federal aid to education by $4 billion, to a total of $22 billion annually, and mandated state tests in reading and math for all students in grades three through eight, and at least once during grades ten to twelve.

By this time the economic slowdown had become a full-blown recession, the first in ten years. A glut of unsold goods forced manufacturers to curtail production and lay off workers. Unemployment rose to six percent, despite the Federal Reserve's efforts to stem the decline by cutting interest rates. The tax rebates had boosted the economy slightly during the summer of 2001, but then the September 11 terrorist attacks led to a further decline. In 2002, the economy began to recover, only to relapse amid concern over the threat of war with Iraq.

One of the most troubling aspects of the economic downturn was the implosion of major corporations and the revelation of shocking financial practices. WorldCom, Inc., a telecommunications company, became the largest corporation in American history to declare bankruptcy, while a New York grand jury charged executives of Tyco International, an electronics company, with stealing more than $600 million from shareholders.

These scandals, however, paled before the misdeeds of Enron, a Houston energy company that failed in late 2001 as the result of astonishingly corrupt practices, including fraudulent accounting and private partnerships designed to inflate profits and hide losses. When investors began to sell their overvalued Enron stock, shares that were once worth nearly $100 fell to less than $1. Enron declared bankruptcy. The remaining shareholders lost over $50 billion, while rank-and-file employees lost not only their jobs but much of their retirement savings, invested largely in now worthless Enron stock.

Quick Check

✓ What was George W. Bush's tax policy?

The War on Terrorism

View the **Closer Look**
World Trade Center,
Sept. 11, 2001 on
myhistorylab.com

On the morning of September 11, 2001, 19 Islamic terrorists hijacked four U.S. air-liners and turned them to attack targets in New York City and Washington, D.C. The hijackers took over two planes flying out of Boston's Logan Airport en route to California, and flew them into the World Trade Center (WTC) in New York. One plane slammed into the north tower just before 9:00 A.M., and the second hit the south tower only 20 minutes later. Within two hours, both towers had collapsed, killing nearly 3,000 victims trapped in the buildings or crushed by the debris and more than 300 rescue workers who had attempted to save them.

In Washington, an American Airlines flight that left Dulles Airport for Los Angeles met a similar fate. Taken over by five terrorists, it plowed into the Pentagon, destroying one wing of the building and killing 189 workers. The terrorists had seized a fourth plane, United Airlines flight 93, scheduled to fly from Newark, New Jersey, to San Francisco. Over Pennsylvania, as the hijackers attempted to turn the plane toward the nation's capital, the passengers fought to regain control of it. They failed to do so, but prevented the plane from hitting another target in Washington—perhaps the White House or the Capitol. Flight 93 crashed in southern Pennsylvania, killing all 44 passengers and crew as well as the hijackers.

"None of us will forget this day," President Bush told the American people in a televised speech that evening. Bush vowed to find and punish those responsible for the attacks and any who assisted them: "We will make no distinction between those who planned these acts and those who harbor them."

 Read the
Document
George Bush Address
to the Nation on
myhistorylab.com

Bush didn't have to look long to discover the mastermind behind the September 11 attacks. Osama bin Laden, a wealthy Saudi, released videotapes claiming responsibility on behalf of his terrorist organization, al Qaeda ("the Base" in Arabic). Bin Laden had been part of the international Muslim resistance to the Soviet invasion of Afghanistan, which had received support from the CIA in the 1980s. He turned against the United States during the Persian Gulf War, outraged by the presence of American troops in his native Saudi Arabia. Evidence linked bin Laden and al Qaeda to the bombing of two American embassies in East Africa in 1998 and to an attack on the American destroyer USS *Cole* in Yemen in 2000.

The United States had been trying to neutralize al Qaeda for a decade without success. Ordered out of Saudi Arabia in 1991, bin Laden had sought refuge in Sudan and in Afghanistan after the Taliban, another extremist Muslim group, took over that country. In Afghanistan, bin Laden set up camps to train hundreds of would-be terrorists, mainly from Arab countries but including recruits from the Philippines, Indonesia, and Central Asia. After the 1998 embassy bombings, President Clinton ordered cruise missile attacks on these camps. The al Qaeda leader survived, though, leaving one of the targets only hours before the strike.

Bush's determination to go after those harboring terrorists made Afghanistan the prime target. The president ordered the Pentagon and the CIA, which already had agents on the scene, to destroy the Taliban, wipe out al Qaeda, and capture or kill Osama bin Laden.

In October 2001, the CIA and Army Special Forces began the operation, rely-ing on the Northern Alliance, an Afghan political coalition resisting the Taliban.

Using methods ranging from bribes of local warlords to air strikes, American forces routed the Taliban and by December had installed a friendly regime in Kabul. Most of Afghanistan, however, remained in chaos, and despite near misses, bin Laden avoided capture.

While waging the **war on terror** abroad, the Bush administration also focused on securing the United States from further terrorist assaults. At the president's urging, Congress approved a new Department of Homeland Security, combining the Customs Bureau, the Coast Guard, the Immigration and Naturalization Service (INS), and other government bureaus.

A primary focus of homeland security was ensuring the safety of airline travel. In November 2001, Bush signed legislation replacing private companies with government employees at all airport screening stations. The airlines were required to replace cockpit doors with secure barriers and permit armed air marshals to ride among the passengers. The public fear of flying after September 11 nevertheless devastated the airline industry. Despite a $15 billion government bailout, the airlines experienced heavy losses. Several, including United Airlines, filed for bankruptcy. Although air travel began to revive in 2002, the industry, along with other forms of tourism, continued to be a drag on an already sluggish economy.

The war on terror raised an even more fundamental question than economic stagnation. Attorney General John Ashcroft, using new powers granted by Congress under the Patriot Act, conducted a broad crackdown on possible terrorists, detaining many Muslim Americans on flimsy evidence and insisting that concern for national security outweighed traditional civil liberties. Opponents argued that the terrorists would win their greatest victory if the United States violated its own historic principles of individual freedom in the name of fighting terrorism. The debate troubled many Americans who had difficulty reconciling the need for security with respect for civil liberties.

> **Quick Check**
> ✓ What prompted America's war on terrorism?

Widening the Battlefield

The terrorist attacks on the United States were the catalyst for a major change in foreign policy. The Bush administration initiated a new global policy of American preeminence. For the first time since the end of the Cold War, the United States had a clear, if controversial, blueprint for international affairs.

The new administration rejected traditional forms of international cooperation. President Bush ended U.S. participation in the Kyoto Protocol to control global warming and announced plans to terminate the 1972 Antiballistic Missile (ABM) treaty with Russia. And he was outspoken in refusing to expose American military personnel to the jurisdiction of the International Criminal Court for possible crimes committed in worldwide peacekeeping efforts.

The new direction of American foreign policy became clear on January 29, 2002, when Bush delivered his second State of the Union address. He repeated his vow to punish all nations sponsoring terrorism and denounced Iraq, Iran, and North Korea as constituting an "axis of evil." Nine months later, in September 2002, the Bush administration released a statement of its new world policy, "National Security Strategy (NSS) of the United States." The goal it declared was to "extend the peace by encouraging free and open societies on every continent."

There were two main components of the new strategy, which critics quickly called unilateralism. The first was to accept the role the nation had been playing since the end of the Cold War: global policeman. The United States would defend freedom anywhere in the world—with allies if possible, by itself if necessary. To implement this policy, the NSS asserted that the Bush administration would maintain "military strength beyond challenge. . . . Our forces will be strong enough to dissuade potential adversaries from pursuing a military buildup in hopes of surpassing, or equaling, the power of the United States."

As world cop, Bush and his advisers asserted the right to use preventive force. Reacting to September 11, the NSS continued, "We cannot let our enemies strike first." Although promising to seek the support of the international community before using force, "we will not hesitate to act alone, if necessary, to exercise our right of self-defense." In other words, the Bush administration, aware that the United States was far stronger militarily and economically than any other nation, asserted America's role as final arbiter of all international disputes.

Iraq quickly became the test case for this shift in American foreign policy. After his "axis of evil" speech, Bush focused on what he and his Pentagon advisers called weapons of mass destruction (WMD) that they claimed Saddam Hussein had been secretly amassing. The United States demanded that Iraq permit UN inspectors (forced out of the country in 1998) to search for such weapons. Meanwhile, the Bush administration perfected plans for a unilateral American military solution to the Iraq question.

Slowly, but inexorably, the United States moved toward war with Iraq. Congress approved a resolution in October 2002 authorizing the president to use force against Saddam Hussein's regime. A month later, the UN Security Council voted unanimously to send its team of inspectors back into Iraq, warning Saddam of "severe consequences" if he failed to comply. Despite the failure of the international inspectors to find evidence of chemical, biological, or nuclear weapons in Iraq, the Bush administration kept pressing for a Security Council resolution authorizing the use of force to compel Saddam to disarm. When France and Russia vowed to veto any such measure, Bush and his advisers decided to proceed on their own. Preventive war would have its first real test.

The ensuing conflict with Iraq surprised both the backers and the critics of unilateralism. In March 2003, 65,000 American troops began to invade Iraq from Kuwait. Britain, the only major power to join the United States in the fighting, helped by besieging the city of Basra and taking control of southern Iraq. By April 8, just three weeks after the fighting had begun, marines marched virtually unopposed into the heart of Baghdad. Americans watched joyous Iraqis toppling a statue of Saddam. An Iraqi major summed up the magnitude of his country's defeat: "Losing a war is one thing, but losing Baghdad is another. It was like losing the dearest thing in life."

In a memorable image from the war in Iraq, Iraqi civilians and U.S. soldiers pull down a statue of Saddam Hussein in Baghdad on April 9, 2003.

The rapid success seemed to confirm the wisdom of Bush's decision for war. But the subsequent failure to find weapons of mass destruction led critics to question the validity of the war. In response, the president's defenders stressed the importance of deposing Saddam by pointing to his brutal prisons and to the killing fields south of Baghdad where thousands of Shi'ite rebels had been slaughtered in 1991.

The problems of restoring order and rebuilding the shattered Iraqi economy quickly overshadowed the debate over the war's legitimacy. Daily attacks on American troops in the Sunni triangle north of Baghdad began in the summer of 2003 and increased during the fall, killing an average of three American soldiers each week. By October, more troops had died from these attacks than had been killed during combat in March and April. Looting, sabotage of oil pipelines, and difficulties in repairing and operating outdated power plants and oil facilities made economic recovery slow and halting. Efforts to involve occupation forces from other UN members yielded few troops.

The December 2003 arrest of Saddam, who had eluded capture, revived American optimism. Yet the overall situation remained troubling. Despite slow but steady progress in restoring public services such as electric power and the gradual recovery of the Iraqi oil industry, the armed insurrection continued. Mortar attacks on Baghdad hotels, roadside bombs aimed at American armored convoys, and handheld missile attacks on American helicopters made Iraq a dangerous place. Conflicts between Shi'ite and Sunni Muslims, and the

Quick Check

✓ Why did Bush order the invasion of Iraq?

Kurdish demand for autonomy, threatened the American goal of creating a stable Iraqi government.

Bush Reelected

Not surprisingly, the war in Iraq became the central issue in the 2004 presidential race. Bush cast himself as the resolute commander in the war on terror; he and his supporters contended that it would be reckless to change commanders in mid-conflict. Democrats initially favored former Vermont governor Howard Dean, who had opposed the invasion of Iraq and strongly criticized Bush's conduct of the war. But the nomination ultimately went to Senator John Kerry of Massachusetts, a decorated Vietnam War veteran who had voted for the war but later criticized Bush for misleading the country regarding the causes of the conflict, and who contended that the war in Iraq, rather than contributing to the war on terror, actually distracted from it.

The campaign was the most vitriolic in years. Democrats accused Bush of having stolen the election of 2000 (with the help of the Supreme Court) and of lying about Saddam's weapons. Republicans called Kerry's belated opposition to the war in Vietnam an insult to those Americans who had died there, and they cited his votes in the Senate as evidence of a fatal inconsistency. Both sides (following the example of Howard Dean in the primaries) employed the Internet to rally the faithful, raise money, and spread rumors.

The strong emotions produced a record turnout: 12 million more than in 2000. Bush won the popular vote by 2.5 percent, becoming the first victor since his father in 1988 to gain an absolute popular majority. The electoral race was comparably close, with 286 for Bush and 252 for Kerry. Together with the congressional elections, which increased the Republican majorities in both houses, the 2004 race confirmed a "red state/blue state" split in America, with the Republicans dominating the South, the Plains, and the Rockies, while the Democrats carried the Northeast, the Great Lakes, and the West Coast. (See Map 32.3.)

Despite his modest margin of victory, Bush claimed a mandate. He proposed to privatize part of the Social Security system and promised to stay the course in Iraq. His Social Security plan went nowhere, but the situation in Iraq eventually improved. Following a new round of insurgent attacks, Bush in 2007 ordered an increase in American troop strength; this "surge," combined with a divide-and-conquer policy toward the insurgents, diminished the violence and made credible Bush's claim that Iraq had turned a corner toward democratic self-government.

Quick Check

✓ How did Bush win re-election?

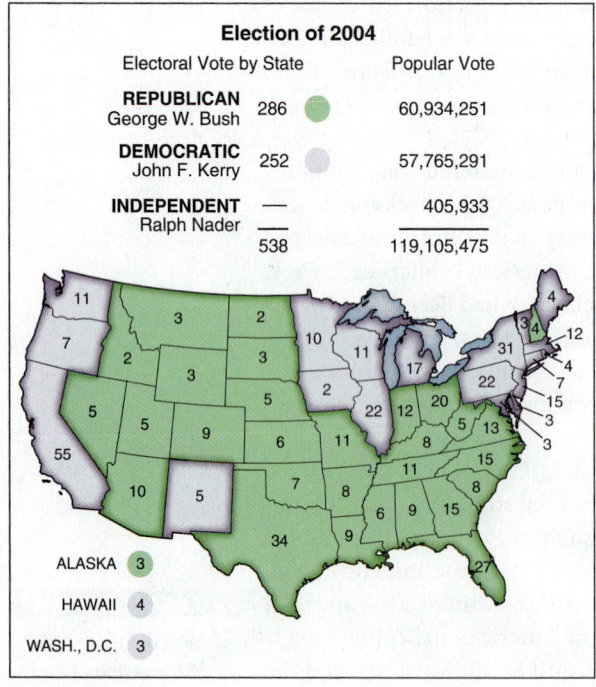

Election of 2004

Electoral Vote by State		Popular Vote
REPUBLICAN George W. Bush	286	60,934,251
DEMOCRATIC John F. Kerry	252	57,765,291
INDEPENDENT Ralph Nader	—	405,933
	538	119,105,475

ALASKA 3
HAWAII 4
WASH., D.C. 3

Map 32.3

BARACK OBAMA'S TRIUMPH AND TRIALS

By then, however, Americans faced a new problem—one that looked much like an old problem. A booming real estate market in the early 2000s tempted banks and other investors to borrow and lend more than was prudent; when the real estate bubble burst in 2007, the financial markets reeled. Wall Street's panic evoked grim memories of the Great Depression of the 1930s and produced a comparable result at the ballot box: the replacement of a Republican president by a Democratic one. That this new president was the first African American to occupy the White House made his accession even more historic. But it didn't make the problems he inherited less daunting.

> **What** challenges faced Barack Obama the American people during the first decade of the twenty-first century?

The Great Recession

Wall Street's troubles reached the crisis stage in the summer and autumn of 2008. Major lenders, including the government-backed twins the Federal National Mortgage Association and the Federal Home Mortgage Corporation (nicknamed Fannie Mae and Freddie Mac), teetered on the brink of bankruptcy. The Bush administration, fearful of the consequences that might follow their collapse, threw the two a life-preserver of federal loans. The panic nonetheless spread, bringing down Wall Street giants Bear Stearns and Lehman Brothers and frightening the administration and Congress into crafting a broader rescue package for the financial sector, totaling hundreds of billions of dollars.

Watch the **Video**
*The Historical Sig-
nificance of the 2008
Election* on
myhistorylab.com

The bailout package averted chaos but left voters shaken. Until this point the Republican nominee for president, Senator John McCain of Arizona, appeared the favorite in the 2008 contest. His war-hero background from the Vietnam era reassured Americans worried about the ongoing wars in Afghanistan and Iraq. But the floundering economy neutralized McCain's advantage and made voters take a second look at the Democratic candidate, Senator Barack Obama of Illinois. Obama ran a brilliant campaign, summarized in the catchword "Hope" and the promise "Yes, We Can." More important was the fact that he was from the opposite party to that which had held the White House during the boom and bust. Obama garnered 53 percent of the popular vote and defeated McCain handily. (See Map 32.4.)

Obama's supporters hoped for great things from the new president. And indeed his inauguration was historic and moving. "God calls on us to shape an uncertain destiny," Obama said. "This is the meaning of our liberty and our creed; why men and women and children of every race and every faith can join in celebration across this magnificent Mall, and why a man whose father less than 60 years ago might not have been served at a local restaurant can now stand before you to take a most sacred oath."

But the warm feeling soon wore off in the cold wind of the bleak economy. The rescue package helped stabilize the financial sector, but unemployment rose inexorably, peaking at 10 percent in 2009 and sticking near there for the next year. Obama and the Democratic majority in Congress pushed through an economic stimulus package, which may have kept unemployment from going even higher but did little to bring it down.

Obama and the Democrats also achieved something Democratic presidents since Harry Truman had been attempting: passage of a comprehensive program of medical insurance for nearly all Americans. But the measure, passed in the face of bitter resistance from Republicans in Congress, prompted a backlash among voters. Together with the lengthening recession, it contributed to the rebuke the Democrats received in the 2010 midterm elections, in which the Republicans reclaimed control of the House of Representatives, gained six seats in the Senate, and carried most of the governor's races.

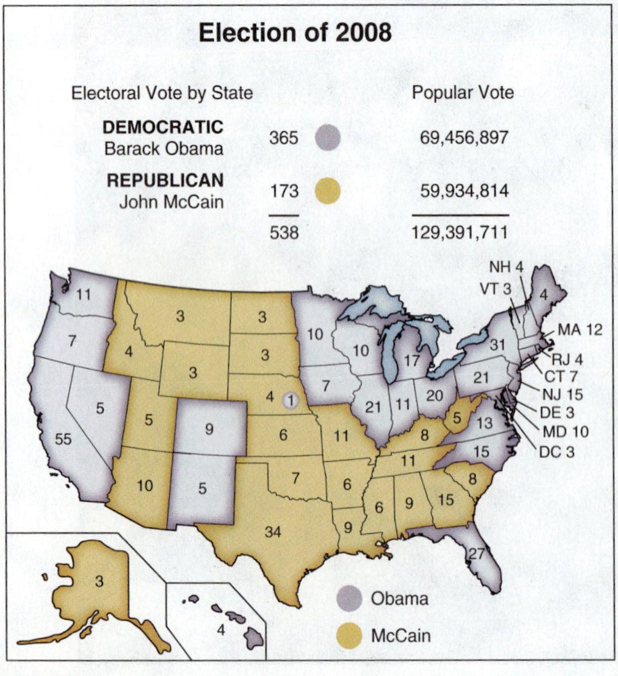

New Challenges and Old

Meanwhile, the Great Recession knocked the federal budget wildly out of balance. Government revenues fell as unemployed workers no longer paid income taxes; government spending rose to cover unemployment compensation and other recession-related expenses. By 2010, the annual deficit topped $1 trillion. Reducing the deficit seemed the first priority to many voters and elected officials, but if reducing the deficit required

Election of 2008

Electoral Vote by State

DEMOCRATIC
Barack Obama   365

REPUBLICAN
John McCain   173

Popular Vote

69,456,897

59,934,814

538   129,391,711

Obama
McCain

Map 32.4

laying off government workers, as it seemed certain to do, it might aggravate the recession. The problem, for the moment, defied solution.

Other problems had deeper roots but no easier solutions. The race question remained alive and contentious, despite the presence of an African American in the White House. Affirmative action policies—policies designed to ensure greater participation by minorities—had been under scrutiny for years. The *Bakke v. Regents of the University of California* decision of 1978 had allowed the use of race as one factor in determining admission to colleges and universities, so long as rigid racial quotas weren't employed. This dissatisfied many conservatives, who during the 1980s and 1990s attacked affirmative action politically and in the courts. In 1992, Cheryl Hopwood, an unsuccessful white applicant to the University of Texas Law School, challenged her rejection, contending that the school had admitted less-qualified African Americans. In 1996, the Fifth Circuit Court of Appeals decided in her favor, and the *Hopwood* decision raised the hopes of anti–affirmative action groups that the Supreme Court would overturn *Bakke*. But in a 2003 case involving the University of Michigan, the Supreme Court ruled that "student body diversity is a compelling state interest that can justify the use of race in university admissions." In other words, affirmative action in higher education could continue. But the narrowness of the 5–4 vote suggested that affirmative action would continue to spark controversy, as indeed it did.

Even more controversial was abortion. The issue had roiled American politics for decades, but it did so particularly after the 2005 death of Chief Justice William Rehnquist and the nearly concurrent retirement of Associate Justice Sandra Day O'Connor. The two vacancies on the Supreme Court allowed George W. Bush to nominate their replacements. Rehnquist had been a reliable conservative, but O'Connor was a swing vote, and liberals feared that a more conservative successor would tip the balance against abortion rights, among other contentious issues. Yet John Roberts, Bush's nominee for chief justice, and Samuel Alito, the nominee for associate justice, dodged Democrats' questions in hearings, and both nominations succeeded. Almost immediately, the South Dakota legislature essentially banned abortion, hoping to persuade the newly reconfigured court to revisit the 1973 *Roe* decision, which guaranteed abortion rights. South Dakota voters subsequently overturned the state law, but the issue remained highly charged.

Gay rights provoked fresh controversy as gay advocates pushed for equal marital rights. After the Massachusetts Supreme Court in 2004 struck down a state law barring same-sex marriages, gay advocates celebrated, but conservatives in dozens of states pressed for laws and constitutional amendments reaffirming traditional views on the subject and defining marriage as the union of one man and one woman. Nearly all these efforts were successful, suggesting that, on this front at least, the advances gay men and women had achieved since the 1960s had hit a wall. The issue of military service proved similarly controversial. Bill Clinton had achieved a minor breakthrough with the "don't ask, don't tell" policy, which allowed gay service as long as the men and women in question kept their sexual orientation to themselves. Barack Obama campaigned to let gays come out of the military closet, but the Republican party resisted. Finally, however, in the lame duck session of Congress in December 2010, the legislature approved and Obama signed a measure repealing the "don't ask, don't tell" policy and permitting gays to serve openly in the armed forces.

Read the
Document
Dissent Within the World Episcopal Church Over Gay Rights on
myhistorylab.com

Science and religion continued to battle in America's classrooms. Opponents of evolution revised their challenge to Darwin, replacing creationism with "intelligent design" and demanding that biology classes air this version of their beliefs. School board elections hinged on the issue; Ohio embraced intelligent design only to reject it following an adverse 2005 court decision in a case from the Dover school district. For the moment the evolutionists held their own, but given that public-opinion polls consistently showed most Americans rejecting evolution in favor of divine creation, the fight was sure to continue.

Quick Check

✓ What were the principal issues in the culture wars of the early twenty-first century?

Doubting the Future

During most of American history, every generation had been better off materially than the generation before. Events of the early twenty-first century called this implicit guarantee into question. The stubbornness of the Great Recession made Americans wonder whether the economy would ever recover its resiliency. The towering federal deficit imperiled such cherished programs as Social Security and Medicare and put the myriad other contributions the federal government had long made to American life even more at risk.

Demographics didn't help. As the baby boom generation neared retirement, the load on the Social Security system increased. Everyone realized that something would have to be done to keep the pension program afloat, but no one could figure out how to make the necessary changes politically palatable. Middle-aged Americans faced the prospect of delayed retirement, smaller pensions, or both. Not surprisingly, they objected. Younger Americans resisted the tax increases that could have spared their elders such sacrifice.

The trend in health care costs was even more alarming. For years, medical costs had grown rapidly, and as the population aged, the costs appeared certain to claim an ever-larger share of the nation's income. The health care law enacted by Congress at Obama's behest promised to rein in medical costs, but many observers doubted the promises, and the Republicans vowed to repeal it.

Immigration remained controversial. Efforts to reduce the number of illegal entries—by tighter enforcement at the border, by sanctions on employers hiring undocumented aliens, by temporary visas for guest workers—stalled on the opposition of immigrant advocates, businesses, and other groups. The cloud of the Great Recession had at least one silver lining: As jobs grew scarce in America, the flow of illegal immigrants diminished. But no one doubted that the immigration issue would resurface or that it would provoke heated debate.

Environmental problems demanded attention, which they got, and solutions, which they didn't. A broad consensus emerged among the scientific community that global warming had to be addressed, but the proposed solutions—higher mileage standards for automobiles, a "carbon tax" on emissions of greenhouse gases, greater reliance on nuclear energy, among others—were costly, intrusive, unproven, or environmentally problematic in their own ways. And though the scientists mostly agreed that humans were causing global warning, the politicians did not. As on other problems facing the country, the consequence was deadlock.

Quick Check

✓ What questions clouded America's future?

CONCLUSION: THE END OF THE AMERICAN FUTURE—OR NOT?

From before its eighteenth-century birth as an independent nation, America had been the land of the future. Immigrants to America left their pasts behind as they traveled to the new country; native-born Americans treated the future as though they owned it. And to nearly everyone in the country, the future almost invariably looked bright.

By 2010, however, the American future didn't look bright at all. The terrorist attacks of 2001 had made Americans feel vulnerable; nine years later they had suffered no comparable assaults, but they still felt vulnerable. They waited in long lines at airport security checkpoints, and they paid hundreds of billions of dollars to support the armies their leaders had sent to Afghanistan and Iraq to combat terrorism. The recession darkened America's economic horizons like nothing since the Great Depression, and American officials could not agree how to restore prosperity. A poll released in November 2010 revealed that 47 percent of Americans believed that their country's best days were in the past, up from 12 percent more than two years earlier.

Not everyone despaired, though. Immigrants still came to America, seeking its promise of a better life for themselves and their children. Young people went to college in search of fulfilling jobs. Young men and women got married and had children, hoping the little ones would fare well in the decades ahead.

Those who knew history tended to be the most optimistic. The country had been through difficult times in the past. The American Revolution, the Civil War, the Great Depression, and two world wars had tested Americans' mettle and faith in the future. Each time the country had survived, typically stronger for the trial. No one could guarantee that America would emerge from its twenty-first-century trial stronger than before, but Americans had never required guarantees.

32 STUDY RESOURCES

((•—[Listen to the **Chapter Audio** for Chapter 32 on **myhistorylab.com**

TIMELINE

1989 Berlin Wall crumbles (November), p. 807

1990 Americans with Disabilities Act (July), p. 806
- Saddam Hussein invades Kuwait (August), p. 805
- Bush breaks "no new taxes" campaign pledge, supports $500 billion budget deal (November), p. 806

1991 Operation Desert Storm frees Kuwait and crushes Iraq (January–February), p. 808
- Soviet Union replaced by Commonwealth of Independent States (December), p. 807

1992 Riots devastate South Central Los Angeles after verdict in Rodney King case (May), p. 813
- Bill Clinton elected president (November), p. 815

1994 Republicans gain control of both houses of Congress (November), p. 815

1996 Clinton signs major welfare reform measure (August), p. 816

1999 Senate acquits Clinton of impeachment charges (February), p. 818

2000 George W. Bush wins contested presidential election, p. 818

2001 American economy goes into recession, ending the longest period of expansion in U.S. history (March), p. 815
- Terrorist attacks on World Trade Center and the Pentagon (September 11), p. 822
- U. S. military action against the Taliban regime in Afghanistan (October–December), p. 822

2002 Department of Homeland Security created (November), p. 825

2003 U.S. troops invade Iraq and overthrow Saddam Hussein (March–April), p. 824
- Saddam Hussein captured (December), p. 825

2004 Insurgency in Iraq escalates, p. 826
- Global warming gains international attention, p. 823
- George W. Bush reelected (November), p. 826

2005 Bush's plan for Social Security reform fails, p. 826
- Hurricane Katrina (August) devastates Gulf Coast and forces evacuation of New Orleans, p. 813

2006 Proposed constitutional amendment to ban same-sex marriage fails to achieve two-thirds majority in the Senate, p. 829

2007 U.S. troop "surge" in Iraq reduces violence in that country, p. 826.

2008 Financial crisis shakes economy (October), p. 827.
- Barack Obama elected president (November), p. 828.

2009 Recession drives unemployment rate to 10 percent (October), p. 828

2010 Republicans regain control of House (November), p. 828

Chapter Review

THE FIRST PRESIDENT BUSH

What were the important issues in George H. W. Bush's presidency, and how were they handled?

In domestic affairs, the first President Bush focused on fixing the savings and loan industry and balancing the budget. In foreign affairs, he managed the end the Cold War peacefully and successfully. The Gulf War of 1991 liberated Kuwait and weakened the Iraqi regime of Saddam Hussein, but didn't remove Saddam from power in Baghdad. *(p. 805)*

THE CHANGING FACES OF AMERICA

How did the American population shift and grow between 1990 and 2010?

Americans continued to migrate to the Sunbelt in the 1990s and early 2000s, and immigration continued to grow. Hispanics formed the largest segment of the immigrant population and included millions of illegal immigrants. African Americans gained ground economically but still suffered from poverty, as Hurricane Katrina demonstrated. *(p. 809)*

THE NEW DEMOCRATS

What were the accomplishments and failures of the Clinton administration?

Clinton balanced the federal budget and helped revive the economy, which boomed during the 1990s. The North American Free Trade Agreement eliminated tariff barriers among the United States, Canada, and Mexico. But personal scandals led to Clinton's impeachment, which he survived, although not without damage to his own reputation and that of the Democrats. *(p. 815)*

REPUBLICANS RESURGENT

How did George W. Bush become president, and what did he do in the White House?

George W. Bush became president in an election that turned on a ballot dispute in Florida, which was resolved only by the Supreme Court. As president, Bush persuaded Congress to cut taxes and, after the terrorist attacks of September 11, 2001, to authorize invasions of Afghanistan and Iraq. The war in Iraq bogged down amid an insurgency against the American-supported government in Baghdad. *(p. 818)*

BARACK OBAMA'S TRIUMPH AND TRIALS

What challenges faced Barack Obama the American people during the first decade of the twenty-first century?

The culture wars between conservatives and liberals continued into the twenty-first century, with abortion, affirmative action, gay rights, and evolution provoking controversy. The Great Recession shook the economy, and Americans wondered how to deal with problems of health care, retirement, illegal immigration, and the environment. *(p. 827)*

KEY TERM QUESTIONS

1. How did disabled Americans benefit from the Americans with Disabilities Act (ADA)? (p. 806)

2. Why did the U.S. and its allies launch Operation Desert Storm? (p. 808)

3. What is the Sunbelt and why did its population grow so dramatically after World War II? (p. 809)

4. Why have many Americans become concerned about the mass influx of undocumented aliens into the U.S.? (p. 811)

5. What was the Contract with America? (p. 816)

6. Why did President George W. Bush institute the war on terror? (p. 823)

7. Why did the Bush administration base its foreign policy on unilateralism after the terrorist attacks of September 11, 2001? (p. 824)

8. Why is affirmative action so controversial? (p. 829)

MYHISTORYLAB CONNECTIONS

Visit **www.myhistorylab.com** for a customized Study Plan to build your knowledge of *Into the Twenty-first Century*

Questions for Analysis

1. How was President Reagan able to garner so much popular support at home and abroad?

   View the **Closer Look** *Opening the Wall, Berlin* p. 807

2. What was the primary objective of the Illegal Immigration Reform and Immigrant Responsibility Act of 1996?

   Read the **Document** *Illegal Immigration and Immigrant Responsibility Act of 1996* p. 810

3. What have been the promises and pitfalls of globalization in the twenty-first century?

   View the **Closer Look** *World Trade Center, September 11, 2001* p. 822

4. What was George W. Bush's response to the terrorist attacks of September 11, 2001?

   Read the **Document** *George Bush, Address to the Nation (2001)* p. 822

5. Why was the presidential election of 2008 so significant?

   Watch the **Video** *The Historical Significance of the 2008 Presidential Election* p. 828

Other Resources from this Chapter

Watch the **Video** *George Bush Presidential Campaign Ad*

Read the **Document** *George H.W. Bush, Allied Military Action in the Persian Gulf (1991)*

View the **Map** *Immigration to the United States*

Watch the **Video** *Bill Clinton's First Inauguration*

Read the **Document** *Articles of Impeachment against William Jefferson Clinton*

Read the **Document** *Bill Clinton Answers to the Articles of Impeachment*

Read the **Document** *Dissent within the World Episcopal Church Over Gay Rights*

Appendix

For additional reference material, go to
www.pearsonamericanhistory.com
The on-line appendix includes the following:

~~~

THE DECLARATION OF INDEPENDENCE
In Congress, July 4, 1776

The Unanimous Declaration of the Thirteen United States of America,
When, in the course of human events, it becomes necessary for one people to dissolve the political bonds which have connected them with another, and to assume, among the powers of the earth, the separate and equal station to which the laws of nature and of nature's God entitle them, a decent respect to the opinions of mankind requires that they should declare the causes which impel them to the separation.

We hold these truths to be self-evident: That all men are created equal; that they are endowed by their Creator with certain unalienable rights; that among these are life, liberty, and the pursuit of happiness; that, to secure these rights, governments are instituted among men, deriving their just powers from the consent of the governed; that whenever any form of government becomes destructive of these ends, it is the right of the people to alter or to abolish it, and to institute new government, laying its foundation on such principles, and organizing its powers in such form, as to them shall seem most likely to effect their safety and happiness. Prudence, indeed, will dictate that governments long established should not be changed for light and transient causes; and accordingly all experience hath shown that mankind are more disposed to suffer, while evils are sufferable, than to right themselves by abolishing the forms to which they are accustomed. But when a long train of abuses and usurpations, pursuing invariably the same object, evinces a design to reduce them under absolute despotism, it is their right, it is their duty, to throw off such government, and to provide new guards for their future security. Such has been the patient sufferance of these colonies; and such is now the necessity which constrains them to alter their former systems of government. The history of the present King of Great Britain is a history of repeated injuries and usurpations, all having in direct object the establishment of an absolute tyranny over these states. To prove this, let facts be submitted to a candid world.

He has refused his assent to laws, the most wholesome and necessary for the public good.

He has forbidden his governors to pass laws of immediate and pressing importance, unless suspended in their operation till his assent should be obtained; and, when so suspended, he has utterly neglected to attend to them.

He has refused to pass other laws for the accommodation of large districts of people, unless those people would relinquish the right of representation in the legislature, a right inestimable to them, and formidable to tyrants only.

He has called together legislative bodies at places unusual, uncomfortable, and distant from the depository of their public records, for the sole purpose of fatiguing them into compliance with his measures.

He has dissolved representative houses repeatedly, for opposing, with manly firmness, his invasions on the rights of the people.

He has refused for a long time, after such dissolutions, to cause others to be elected; whereby the legislative powers, incapable of annihilation, have returned to the people at large for their exercise; the state remaining, in the mean time, exposed to all the dangers of invasions from without and convulsions within.

He has endeavored to prevent the population of these states; for that purpose obstructing the laws for naturalization of foreigners; refusing to pass others to encourage their migration hither, and raising the conditions of new appropriations of lands.

He has obstructed the administration of justice, by refusing his assent to laws for establishing judiciary powers.

He has made judges dependent on his will alone, for the tenure of their offices, and the amount and payment of their salaries.

He has erected a multitude of new offices, and sent hither swarms of officers to harass our people and eat out their substance.

He has kept among us, in times of peace, standing armies, without the consent of our legislatures.

He has affected to render the military independent of, and superior to, the civil power.

He has combined with others to subject us to a jurisdiction foreign to our constitution, and unacknowledged by our laws, giving his assent to their acts of pretended legislation:

For quartering large bodies of armed troops among us;

For protecting them, by a mock trial, from punishment for any murder which they should commit on the inhabitants of these states;

For cutting off our trade with all parts of the world;

For imposing taxes on us without our consent;

For depriving us, in many cases, of the benefits of trial by jury;

For transporting us beyond seas, to be tried for pretended offenses;

For abolishing the free system of English laws in a neighboring province, establishing therein an arbitrary government, and enlarging its boundaries, so as to render it at once an example and fit instrument for introducing the same absolute rule into these colonies;

For taking away our charters, abolishing our most valuable laws, and altering fundamentally the forms of our governments;

For suspending our own legislatures, and declaring themselves invested with power to legislate for us in all cases whatsoever.

He has abdicated government here, by declaring us out of his protection and waging war against us.

He has plundered our seas, ravaged our coasts, burned our towns, and destroyed the lives of our people.

He is at this time transporting large armies of foreign mercenaries to complete the works of death, desolation, and tyranny already begun with circumstances of cruelty and perfidy scarcely paralleled in the most barbarous ages, and totally unworthy the head of a civilized nation.

He has constrained our fellow-citizens, taken captive on the high seas, to bear arms against their country, to become the executioners of their friends and brethren, or to fall themselves by their hands.

He has excited domestic insurrection among us, and has endeavored to bring on the inhabitants of our frontiers the merciless Indian savages, whose known rule of warfare is an undistinguished destruction of all ages, sexes, and conditions.

In every stage of these oppressions we have petitioned for redress in the most humble terms; our repeated petitions have been answered only by repeated injury. A prince, whose character is thus marked by every act which may define a tyrant, is unfit to be the ruler of a free people.

Nor have we been wanting in our attentions to our British brethren. We have warned them, from time to time, of attempts by their legislature to extend an unwarrantable jurisdiction over us. We have reminded them of the circumstances of our emigration and settlement here. We have appealed to their native justice and magnanimity; and we have conjured them, by the ties of our common kindred, to disavow these usurpations, which would inevitably interrupt our connections and correspondence. They, too, have been deaf to the voice of justice and of consanguinity. We must, therefore, acquiesce in the necessity which denounces our separation, and hold them, as we hold the rest of mankind, enemies in war, in peace friends.

We, therefore, the representatives of the United States of America, in General Congress assembled, appealing to the Supreme Judge of the world for the rectitude of our intentions, do, in the name and by the authority of the good people of these colonies, solemnly publish and declare, that these United Colonies are, and of right ought to be, FREE AND INDEPENDENT STATES; that

John Hancock

Button Gwinnett	George Wythe	Geo. Ross	Saml. Adams
Lyman Hall	Richard Henry Lee	Caesar Rodney	John Adams
Geo. Walton	Th. Jefferson	Geo. Read	Robt. Treat Paine
Wm. Hooper	Benj. Harrison	Tho. M'kean	Elbridge Gerry
Joseph Hewes	Thos. Nelson, Jr.	Wm. Floyd	Step. Hopkins
John Penn	Francis Lightfoot Lee	Phil. Livingston	William Ellery
Edward Rutledge	Carter Braxton	Frans. Lewis	Roger Sherman
Thos. Heyward, Junr.	Robt. Morris	Lewis Morris	Sam'el Huntington
Thomas Lynch, Junr.	Benjamin Rush	Richd. Stockton	Wm. Williams
Arthur Middleton	Benja. Franklin	Jno. Witherspoon	Oliver Wolcott
Samuel Chase	John Morton	Fras. Hopkinson	Matthew Thornton
Wm. Paca	Geo. Clymer	John Hart	
Thos. Stone	Jas. Smith	Abra. Clark	
Charles Carroll of	Geo. Taylor	Josiah Bartlett	
Carrollton	James Wilson	Wm. Whipple	

they are absolved from all allegiance to the British crown, and that all political connection between them and the state of Great Britain is, and ought to be, totally dissolved; and that, as free and independent states, they have full power to levy war, conclude peace, contract alliances, establish commerce, and do all other acts and things which independent states may of right do. And for the support of this declaration, with a firm reliance on the protection of Divine Providence, we mutually pledge to each other our lives, our fortunes, and our sacred honor.

THE ARTICLES OF CONFEDERATION

Between the States of New Hampshire, Massachusetts Bay, Rhode Island and Providence Plantations, Connecticut, New York, New Jersey, Pennsylvania, Delaware, Maryland, Virginia, North Carolina, South Carolina, Georgia

ARTICLE 1

The stile of this confederacy shall be "The United States of America."

ARTICLE 2

Each State retains its sovereignty, freedom and independence, and every power, jurisdiction, and right, which is not by this confederation expressly delegated to the United States, in Congress assembled.

ARTICLE 3

The said states hereby severally enter into a firm league of friendship with each other for their common defence, the security of their liberties and their mutual and general welfare; binding themselves to assist each other against all force offered to, or attacks made upon them, or any of them, on account of religion, sovereignty, trade, or any other pretence whatever.

ARTICLE 4

The better to secure and perpetuate mutual friendship and intercourse among the people of the different states in this union, the free inhabitants of each of these states, paupers, vagabonds, and fugitives from justice excepted, shall be entitled to all privileges and immunities of free citizens in the several states; and the people of each State shall have free ingress and regress to and from any other State, and shall enjoy therein all the privileges of trade and commerce, subject to the same duties, impositions, and restrictions, as the inhabitants thereof respectively; provided, that such restrictions shall not extend so far as to prevent the removal of property, imported into any State, to any other State of which the owner is an inhabitant; provided also, that no imposition, duties, or restriction, shall be laid by any State on the property of the United States, or either of them.

If any person guilty of, or charged with treason, felony, or other high misdemeanor in any State, shall flee from justice and be found in any of the United States, he shall, upon demand of the governor or executive power of the State from which he fled, be delivered up and removed to the State having jurisdiction of his offence.

Full faith and credit shall be given in each of these states to the records, acts, and judicial proceedings of the courts and magistrates of every other State.

ARTICLE 5

For the more convenient management of the general interests of the United States, delegates shall be annually appointed, in such manner as the legislature of each State shall direct, to meet in Congress, on the 1st Monday in November in every year, with a power reserved to each State to recall its delegates, or any of them, at any time within the year, and to send others in their stead for the remainder of the year.

No State shall be represented in Congress by less than two, nor by more than seven members; and no person shall be capable of being a delegate for more than three years in any term of six years; nor shall any person, being a delegate, be capable of holding any office under the United States, for which he, or any other for his benefit, receives any salary, fees, or emolument of any kind.

Each State shall maintain its own delegates in a meeting of the states, and while they act as members of the committee of the states.

In determining questions in the United States, in Congress assembled, each State shall have one vote.

Freedom of speech and debate in Congress shall not be impeached or questioned in any court or place out of Congress: and the members of Congress shall be protected in their persons from arrests and imprisonments, during the time of their going to and from, and attendance on Congress, except for treason, felony, or breach of the peace.

ARTICLE 6

No State, without the consent of the United States, in Congress assembled, shall send any embassy to, or receive any embassy from, or enter into any conference, agreement, alliance, or treaty with any king, prince, or state; nor shall any person, holding any office of profit or trust under the United States, or any of them, accept of any present, emolument, office or title, of any kind whatever, from any king, prince, or foreign state; nor shall the United States, in Congress assembled, or any of them, grant any title of nobility.

No two or more states shall enter into any treaty, confederation, or alliance, whatever, between them, without the consent of the United States, in Congress assembled, specifying accurately the purposes for which the same is to be entered into, and how long it shall continue.

No State shall lay any imposts or duties which may interfere with any stipulations in treaties entered into by the United States, in Congress assembled, with any king, prince, or state, in pursuance of any treaties already proposed by Congress to the courts of France and Spain.

No vessels of war shall be kept up in time of peace by any State, except such number only as shall be deemed necessary by the United States, in Congress assembled, for the defence of such State or its trade; nor shall any body of forces be kept up by any State, in time of peace, except such number only as, in the judgment of the United States, in Congress assembled, shall be deemed requisite to garrison the forts necessary for the defence of such State; but every State shall always keep up a well regulated and disciplined militia, sufficiently armed and accoutred, and shall provide, and constantly have ready for use, in public stores, a due number, of field pieces and tents, and a proper quantity of arms, ammunition and camp equipage.

No State shall engage in any war without the consent of the United States, in Congress assembled, unless such State be actually invaded by enemies, or shall have received certain advice of a resolution being formed by some nation of Indians to invade such State, and the danger is so imminent as not to admit of a delay till the United States, in Congress assembled, can be consulted; nor shall any State grant commissions to any ships or vessels of war, nor letters of marque or reprisal, except it be after a declaration of war by the United States, in Congress assembled, and then only against the kingdom or state, and the subjects thereof, against which war has been so declared, and under such regulations as shall be established by the United States, in Congress assembled, unless such States be infested by pirates, in which case vessels of war may be fitted out for that occasion, and kept so long as the danger shall continue, or until the United States, in Congress assembled, shall determine otherwise.

ARTICLE 7

When land forces are raised by any State for the common defence, all officers of or under the rank of colonel, shall be appointed by the legislature of each State respectively, by whom such forces shall be raised, or in such manner as such State shall direct; and all vacancies shall be filled up by the State which first made the appointment.

ARTICLE 8

All charges of war and all other expences, that shall be incurred for the common defence or general welfare, and allowed by the United States, in Congress assembled, shall be defrayed out of a common treasury, which shall be supplied by the several states, in proportion to the value of all land within each State, granted to or surveyed for any person, as such land and the buildings and improvements thereon shall be estimated according to such mode as the United States, in Congress assembled, shall, from time to time, direct and appoint.

The taxes for paying that proportion shall be laid and levied by the authority and direction of the legislatures of the several states, within the time agreed upon by the United States, in Congress assembled.

ARTICLE 9

The United States, in Congress assembled, shall have the sole and exclusive right and power of determining on peace and war, except in the cases mentioned in the 6th article; of sending and receiving ambassadors; entering into treaties and alliances, provided that no treaty of commerce shall be made, whereby the legislative power of the respective states shall be restrained from imposing such imposts and duties on foreigners as their own people are subjected to, or from prohibiting the exportation or importation of any species of goods or commodities whatsoever; of establishing rules for deciding, in all cases, what captures on land or water shall be legal, and in what manner prizes, taken by land or naval forces in the service of the United States, shall be divided or appropriated; of granting letters of marque and reprisal in times of peace; appointing courts for the trial of piracies and felonies committed on the high seas, and establishing courts for receiving and determining, finally, appeals in all cases of captures; provided, that no member of Congress shall be appointed a judge of any of the said courts.

The United States, in Congress assembled, shall also be the last resort on appeal in all disputes and differences now subsisting, or that hereafter may arise between two or more states concerning boundary, jurisdiction or any other cause whatever; which authority shall always be exercised in the manner following: whenever the legislative or executive authority, or lawful agent of any State, in controversy with another, shall present a petition to Congress, stating the matter in question, and praying for a hearing, notice thereof shall be given, by order of Congress, to the legislative or executive authority of the other State in controversy, and a day assigned for the appearance of the parties by their lawful agents, who shall then be directed to appoint, by joint consent, commissioners or judges to constitute a court for hearing and determining the matter in question; but, if they cannot agree, Congress shall name three persons out of each of the United States, and from the list of such persons each party shall alternately strike out one, in the petitioners beginning, until the number shall be reduced to thirteen; and from that number not less than seven, nor more than nine names, as Congress shall direct, shall, in the presence of Congress, be drawn out by lot; and the persons whose names shall be drawn, or any five of them, shall be commissioners or judges to hear and finally determine the controversy, so always as a major part of the judges who shall hear the cause shall agree in the determination; and if either party shall neglect to attend at the day appointed, without shewing reasons which Congress shall judge sufficient, or, being present, shall refuse to strike, the Congress shall proceed to nominate three persons out of each State, and the secretary of Congress shall strike in behalf of such party absent or refusing; and the judgment and sentence of the court to be appointed, in the manner before prescribed, shall be final and conclusive; and if any of the parties shall refuse to submit to the authority of such court, or to appear or defend their claim or cause, the court shall nevertheless proceed to pronounce sentence or judgment, which shall, in like manner, be final and decisive, the judgment or sentence and other proceedings being, in either case, transmitted to Congress, and lodged among the acts of Congress for the security of the parties concerned: provided, that every commissioner, before he sits in judgment, shall take an oath, to be administered by one of the judges of the supreme or superior court of the State where the cause shall be tried, "well and truly to hear and determine the matter in question, according to the best of his judgment, without favor, affection, or hope of reward": provided, also, that no State shall be deprived of territory for the benefit of the United States.

All controversies concerning the private right of soil, claimed under different grants of two or more states, whose jurisdictions, as they may respect such lands and the states which passed such grants, are adjusted, the said grants, or either of them, being at the same time claimed to have originated antecedent to such settlement of jurisdiction, shall, on the petition of either party to the Congress of the United States, be finally determined, as near as may be, in the same manner as is before prescribed for deciding disputes respecting territorial jurisdiction between different states.

The United States, in Congress assembled, shall also have the sole and exclusive right and power of regulating the alloy and value of coin struck by their own authority, or by that of the respective states; fixing the standard of weights and measures throughout the United States; regulating the trade and managing all affairs with the Indians not members of any of the states; provided that the legislative right of any State within its own limits be not infringed or violated; establishing and regulating post offices from one State to another throughout all the United States, and exacting such postage on the papers passing through the same as may be requisite to defray the expences of the said office; appointing all officers of the land forces in the service of the United States, excepting regimental officers; appointing all the officers of the naval forces, and commissioning all officers whatever in the service of the United States; making rules for the government and regulation of the said land and naval forces, and directing their operations.

The United States, in Congress assembled, shall have authority to appoint a committee to sit in the recess of Congress, to be denominated "a Committee of the States," and to consist of one delegate from each State, and to appoint such other committees and civil officers as may be necessary for managing the general affairs of the United States, under their direction; to appoint one of their number to preside; provided that no person be allowed to serve in the office of president more than one year in any term of three years; to ascertain the necessary sums of money to be raised for the service of the United States, and to appropriate and apply the same for defraying the public expences; to borrow money or emit bills on the credit of the United States, transmitting, every half year, to the respective states, an account of the sums of money so borrowed or emitted; to build and equip a navy; to agree upon the number of land forces, and to make requisitions from each State for its quota, in proportion to the number of white inhabitants in such State; which requisitions shall be binding; and, thereupon, the legislature of each State shall appoint the regimental officers, raise the men, and cloathe, arm, and equip them in a soldier-like manner, at the expence of the United States; and the officers and men so cloathed, armed, and equipped, shall march to the place appointed and within the time agreed on by the United States, in Congress assembled; but if the United States, in Congress assembled, shall, on consideration of circumstances, judge proper that any State should not raise men, or should raise a smaller number than its quota, and that any other State should raise a greater number of men than the quota thereof, such extra number shall be raised, officered, cloathed, armed, and equipped in the same manner as the quota of such State, unless the legislature of such State shall judge that such extra number cannot be safely spared out of the same, in which case they shall raise, officer, cloathe, arm, and equip as many of such extra number as they judge can be safely spared. And the officers and men so cloathed, armed, and equipped, shall march to the place appointed and within the time agreed on by the United States, in Congress assembled.

The United States, in Congress assembled, shall never engage in a war, nor grant letters of marque and reprisal in time of peace, nor enter into any treaties or alliances, nor coin money, nor regulate the value thereof, nor ascertain the sums and expences necessary for the defence and welfare of the United States, or any of them: nor emit bills, nor borrow money on the credit of the United States, nor appropriate money, nor agree upon the number of vessels of war to be built or purchased, or the number of land or sea forces to be raised, nor appoint a commander in chief of the army or navy, unless nine states assent to the same; nor shall a question on any other point, except for adjourning from day to day, be determined, unless by the votes of a majority of the United States, in Congress assembled.

The Congress of the United States shall have power to adjourn to any time within the year, and to any place within the United States, so that no period of adjournment be for a longer duration than the space of six months, and shall publish the journal of their proceedings monthly, except such parts thereof, relating to treaties, alliances or military operations, as, in their judgment, require secrecy; and the yeas and nays of the delegates of each State on any question shall be entered on the journal, when it is desired by any delegate; and the delegates of a State, or any of them, at his, or their request, shall be furnished with a transcript of the said journal, except such parts as are above excepted, to lay before the legislatures of the several states.

ARTICLE 10

The committee of the states, or any nine of them, shall be authorized to execute, in the recess of Congress, such of the powers of Congress as the United States, in Congress assembled, by the consent of nine states, shall, from time to time, think expedient to vest them with; provided, that no power be delegated to the said committee for the exercise of which by the articles of confederation, the voice of nine states, in the Congress of the United States assembled, is requisite.

ARTICLE 11

Canada acceding to this confederation, and joining in the measures of the United States, shall be admitted into and entitled to all the advantages of this union; but no other colony shall be admitted into the same, unless such admission be agreed to by nine states.

ARTICLE 12

All bills of credit emitted, monies borrowed and debts contracted by, or under the authority of Congress before the assembling of the United States, in pursuance of the present confederation, shall be deemed and considered as a charge against the United States, for payment and satisfaction whereof the said United States and the public faith are hereby solemnly pledged.

ARTICLE 13

Every State shall abide by the determinations of the United States, in Congress assembled, on all questions which, by this confederation, are submitted to them. And the articles of this confederation shall be inviolably observed by every State, and the union shall be perpetual; nor shall any alteration at any time hereafter be made in any of them, unless such alteration be agreed to in a Congress of the United States, and be afterwards confirmed by the legislatures of every State.

These articles shall be proposed to the legislatures of all the United States, to be considered, and if approved of by them, they are advised to authorize their delegates to ratify the same in the Congress of the United States; which being done, the same shall become conclusive.

THE CONSTITUTION OF THE UNITED STATES OF AMERICA

PREAMBLE

We the People of the United States, in Order to form a more perfect Union, establish Justice, insure domestic Tranquility, provide for the common defence, promote the general Welfare, and secure the Blessings of Liberty to ourselves and our Posterity, do ordain and establish this Constitution for the United States of America.

ARTICLE 1

Section 1

All legislative Powers herein granted shall be vested in a Congress of the United States, which shall consist of a Senate and House of Representatives.

Section 2

The House of Representatives shall be composed of Members chosen every second Year by the People of the several States, and the Electors in each State shall have the Qualifications requisite for Electors of the most numerous Branch of the State Legislature.

No Person shall be a Representative who shall not have attained to the Age of twenty five Years, and been seven Years a Citizen of the United States, and who shall not, when elected, be an inhabitant of that State in which he shall be chosen.

Representatives and direct Taxes shall be apportioned among the several States which may be included within this Union, according to their respective Numbers, *which shall be determined by adding to the whole Number of free Persons, including those bound to Service for a Term of Years, and excluding Indians not taxed, three fifths of all other Persons.** The actual Enumeration shall be made within three Years after the first Meeting of the Congress of the United States, and within every subsequent Term of ten Years, in such Manner as they shall by Law direct. The Number of Representatives shall not exceed one for every thirty Thousand, but each State shall have at Least one Representative; *and until such enumeration shall be made, the State of New Hampshire shall be entitled to chuse three, Massachusetts eight, Rhode-Island and Providence Plantations one, Connecticut five, New York six, New Jersey four, Pennsylvania eight, Delaware one, Maryland six, Virginia ten, North Carolina five, South Carolina five, and Georgia three.*

When vacancies happen in the Representation from any State, the Executive Authority thereof shall issue Writs of Election to fill such Vacancies.

The House of Representatives shall chuse their Speaker and other Officers; and shall have the sole Power of Impeachment.

Section 3

The Senate of the United States shall be composed of two Senators from each State, *chosen by the Legislature thereof,* for six Years; and each Senator shall have one Vote.

*Passages no longer in effect are printed in italic type.

Immediately after they shall be assembled in Consequence of the first Election, they shall be divided as equally as may be into three Classes. The Seats of the Senators of the first Class shall be vacated at the Expiration of the second Year, of the second Class at the Expiration of the fourth Year, and of the third Class at the Expiration of the sixth Year so that one third may be chosen every second Year; and if Vacancies happen by Resignation, or otherwise, during the Recess of the Legislature of any state, the Executive thereof may make temporary Appointments until the next Meeting of the Legislature, which shall then fill such Vacancies.

No Person shall be a Senator who shall not have attained to the Age of thirty Years, and been nine Years a Citizen of the United States, and who shall not, when elected, be an Inhabitant of that State for which he shall be chosen.

The Vice President of the United States shall be President of the Senate, but shall have no Vote, unless they be equally divided.

The Senate shall chuse their other Officers, and also a President *pro tempore,* in the Absence of the Vice President, or when he shall exercise the Office of President of the United States.

The Senate shall have the sole Power to try all Impeachments. When sitting for that Purpose, they shall be on Oath or Affirmation. When the President of the United States is tried the Chief Justice shall preside: And no Person shall be convicted without the Concurrence of two thirds of the Members present.

Judgment in Cases of Impeachment shall not extend further than to removal from Office, and disqualification to hold and enjoy any Office of honor, Trust or Profit under the United States: but the Party convicted shall nevertheless be liable and subject to Indictment, Trial, Judgment and Punishment, according to Law.

Section 4

The Times, Places and Manner of holding Elections for Senators and Representatives, shall be prescribed in each State by the Legislature thereof; but the Congress may at any time by Law make or alter such Regulations, except as to the Places of chusing Senators.

The Congress shall assemble at least once in every Year, *and such Meeting shall be on the first Monday in December, unless they shall by Law appoint a different Day.*

Section 5

Each House shall be the Judge of the Elections, Returns and Qualifications of its own Members, and a Majority of each shall constitute a Quorum to do Business; but a smaller Number may adjourn from day to day, and may be authorized to compel the Attendance of absent Members, in such Manner, and under such Penalties as each House may provide.

Each House may determine the Rules of its Proceedings, punish its Members for disorderly Behaviour, and, with the Concurrence of two thirds, expel a Member.

Each House shall keep a Journal of its Proceedings, and from time to time publish the same, excepting such Parts as may in their Judgment require Secrecy; and the Yeas and Nays of the Members of either House on any question shall, at the Desire of one fifth of those Present, be entered on the Journal.

Neither House, during the Session of Congress, shall, without the Consent of the other, adjourn for more than three days, nor to any other Place than that in which the two Houses shall be sitting.

Section 6

The Senators and Representatives shall receive a Compensation for their Services, to be ascertained by Law, and paid out of the Treasury of the United States. They shall in all Cases, except Treason, Felony and Breach of the Peace, be privileged from Arrest during their Attendance at the Session of their respective Houses, and in going to and returning from the same; and for any Speech or Debate in either House, they shall not be questioned in any other Place.

No Senator or Representative shall, during the Time for which he was elected, be appointed to any civil Office under the Authority of the United States, which shall have been created, or the Emoluments whereof shall have been encreased during such time, and no Person holding any Office under the United States, shall be a Member of either House during his Continuance in Office.

Section 7

All Bills for raising Revenue shall orginate in the House of Representatives; but the Senate may propose or concur with Amendments as on other Bills.

Every Bill which shall have passed the House of Representatives and the Senate, shall, before it become a Law, be presented to the President of the United States; If he approve he shall sign it, but if not he shall return it, with his Objections to the House in which it shall have originated, who shall enter the Objections at large on their Journal, and proceed to reconsider it. If after such Reconsideration two thirds of that House shall agree to pass the Bill, it shall be sent, together with the Objections, to the other House, by which it shall likewise be reconsidered, and if approved by two thirds of that House, it shall become a Law. But in all such Cases the Votes of both Houses shall be determined by yeas and Nays, and the Names of the Persons voting for and against the Bill shall be entered on the Journal of each House respectively. If any Bill shall not be returned by the President within ten Days (Sundays excepted) after it shall have been presented to him, the Same shall be a Law, in like Manner as if he had signed it, unless the Congress by their Adjournment prevent its Return, in which Case it shall not be a Law.

Every Order, Resolution, or Vote to which the Concurrence of the Senate and House of Representatives may be necessary (except on a question of Adjournment) shall be presented to the President of the United States; and before the Same shall take Effect, shall be approved by him, or being disapproved by him, shall be repassed by two thirds of the Senate and House of Representatives, according to the Rules and Limitations prescribed in the Case of a Bill.

Section 8

The Congress shall have Power To lay and collect Taxes, Duties, Imposts and Excises, to pay the Debts and provide for the common Defence and general Welfare of the United States; but all Duties, Imposts and Excises shall be uniform throughout the United States;

To borrow Money on the credit of the United States;

To regulate Commerce with foreign Nations, and among the several States, and with the Indian Tribes;

To establish an uniform Rule of Naturalization, and uniform Laws on the subject of Bankruptcies throughout the United States;

To coin Money, regulate the Value thereof, and of foreign Coin, and fix the Standard of Weights and Measures;

To provide for the Punishment of counterfeiting the Securities and current Coin of the United States;

To establish Post Offices and post Roads;

To promote the Progress of Science and useful Arts, by securing for limited Times to Authors and Inventors the exclusive Right to their respective Writings and Discoveries;

To constitute Tribunals inferior to the supreme Court;

To define and punish Piracies and Felonies committed on the high Seas, and Offences against the Law of Nations;

To declare War, grant Letters of Marque and Reprisal, and make Rules concerning Captures on Land and Water;

To raise and support Armies, but no Appropriation of Money to that Use shall be for a longer Term than two Years;

To provide and maintain a Navy;

To make Rules for the Government and Regulation of the land and naval Forces;

To provide for calling forth the Militia to execute the Laws of the Union, suppress Insurrections and repel Invasions;

To provide for organizing, arming, and disciplining, the Militia, and for governing such Part of them as may be employed in the Service of the United States, reserving to the States respectively, the Appointment of the Officers, and the Authority of training the Militia according to the discipline prescribed by Congress;

To exercise exclusive Legislation in all Cases whatsoever, over such District (not exceeding ten Miles square) as may, by Cession of particular States, and the Acceptance of Congress, become the Seat of the Government of the United States, and to exercise like Authority over all Places purchased by the Consent of the Legislature of the State in which the Same shall be, for the Erection of Forts, Magazines, Arsenals, dock-Yards, and other needful Buildings;—And

To make all Laws which shall be necessary and proper for carrying into Execution the foregoing Powers, and all other Powers vested by this Constitution in the Government of the United States, or in any Department of Officer thereof.

Section 9

The Migration or Importation of such Persons as any of the States now existing shall think proper to admit, shall not be prohibited by the Congress prior to the Year one thousand eight hundred and eight, but a Tax or duty may be imposed on such Importation, not exceeding ten dollars for each Person.

The Privilege of the Writ of Habeas Corpus shall not be suspended, unless when in Cases of Rebellion or Invasion the public Safety may require it.

No Bill of Attainder or ex post facto Law shall be passed.

No Capitation, or other direct, Tax shall be laid, unless in Proportion to the Census or Enumeration herein before directed to be taken.

No Tax or Duty shall be laid on Articles exported from any State.

No Preference shall be given by any Regulation of Commerce or Revenue to the Ports of one State over those of another: nor shall Vessels bound to, or from, one State, be obliged to enter, clear, or pay Duties in another.

No Money shall be drawn from the Treasury, but in Consequence of Appropriations made by Law; and a regular Statement and Account of the Receipts and Expenditures of all public Money shall be published from time to time.

No Title of Nobility shall be granted by the United States: And no Person holding any Office of Profit or Trust under them, shall, without the Consent of the Congress, accept of any present, Emolument, Office, or Title, of any kind whatever, from any King, Prince, or foreign State.

Section 10

No State shall enter into any Treaty, Alliance, or Confederation; grant Letters of Marque and Reprisal;

coin Money; emit Bills of Credit; make any Thing but gold and silver Coin a Tender in Payment of Debts; pass any Bill of Attainder, ex post facto Law, or Law impairing the obligation of Contracts, or grant any Title of Nobility.

No State shall, without the Consent of the Congress, lay any Imposts or Duties on Imports or Exports, except what may be absolutely necessary for executing its inspection Laws: and the net Produce of all Duties and Imposts, laid by any State on Imports or Exports, shall be for the Use of the Treasury of the United States; and all such Laws shall be subject to the Revision and Controul of the Congress.

No State shall, without the Consent of Congress, lay any Duty of Tonnage, keep Troops, or Ships of War in time of Peace, enter into any Agreement or Compact with another State, or with a foreign Power, or engage in War, unless actually invaded, or in such imminent Danger as will not admit of delay.

ARTICLE 2

Section 1

The executive Power shall be vested in a President of the United States of America. He shall hold his Office during the Term of four Years, and, together with the Vice President, chosen for the same Term, be elected, as follows:

Each State shall appoint, in such Manner as the Legislature thereof may direct, a Number of Electors, equal to the whole Number of Senators and Representatives to which the State may be entitled in the Congress: but no Senator or Representative, or Person holding an Office of Trust or Profit under the United States, shall be appointed an Elector.

The Electors shall meet in their respective States, and vote by Ballot for two Persons, of whom one at least shall not be an Inhabitant of the same State with themselves. And they shall make a List of all the Persons voted for, and of the Number of Votes for each; which List they shall sign and certify, and transmit sealed to the Seat of the Government of the United States, directed to the President of the Senate. The President of the Senate shall, in the Presence of the Senate and House of Representatives, open all the

Certificates, and the Votes shall then be counted. The Person having the greatest Number of Votes shall be the President, if such Number be a Majority of the whole number of Electors appointed; and if there be more than one who have such Majority, and have an equal Number of Votes, then the House of Representatives shall immediately chuse by Ballot one of them for President; and if no Person have a Majority, then from the five highest on the List the said House shall in like Manner chuse the President. But in chusing the President, the Votes shall be taken by States, the Representation from each State having one Vote; A quorum for this Purpose shall consist of a Member or Members from two thirds of the States, and a Majority of all the States shall be necessary to a Choice. In every Case, after the Choice of the President, the Person having the greatest Number of Votes of the Electors shall be the Vice President. But if there should remain two or more who have equal Votes, the Senate shall chuse from them by Ballot the Vice President.

The Congress may determine the time of chusing the Electors, and the Day on which they shall give their Votes; which Day shall be the same throughout the United States.

No person except a natural born Citizen, *or a Citizen of the United States, at the time of the Adoption of this Constitution,* shall be eligible to the Office of President; neither shall any Person be eligible to that Office who shall not have attained to the Age of thirty five Years, and been fourteen Years a Resident within the United States.

In Case of the Removal of the President from Office, or of his Death, Resignation, or Inability to discharge the Powers and Duties of the said Office, the Same shall devolve on the Vice President, and the Congress may by Law provide for the Case of Removal, Death, Resignation or Inability, both of the President and Vice President, declaring what Officer shall then act as President, and such Officer shall act accordingly, until the Disability be removed, or a President shall be elected.

The President shall, at stated Times, receive for his Services, a Compensation, which shall neither be encreased nor diminished during the Period for which he shall have been elected, and he shall not receive within that period any other Emolument from the United States, or any of them.

Before he enter on the Execution of his Office, he shall take the following Oath or Affirmation:—"I do solemnly swear (or affirm) that I will faithfully execute the Office of President of the United States, and will to the best of my Ability, preserve, protect and defend the Constitution of the United States."

Section 2

The President shall be Commander in Chief of the Army and Navy of the United States, and of the Militia of the several States, when called into the actual Service of the United States; he may require the Opinion, in writing, of the principal Officer in each of the executive Departments, upon any Subject relating to the Duties of their respective Offices, and he shall have Power to grant Reprieves and Pardons for Offences against the United States, except in Cases of Impeachment.

He shall have Power, by and with the Advice and Consent of the Senate, to make Treaties, provided two thirds of the Senators present concur; and he shall nominate, and by and with the Advice and Consent of the Senate, shall appoint Ambassadors, other public Ministers and Consuls, Judges of the supreme Court, and all other Officers of the United States, whose Appointments are not herein otherwise provided for, and which shall be established by Law: but the Congress may by Law vest the Appointment of such inferior Officers, as they think proper in the President alone, in the Courts of Law, or in the Heads of Departments.

The President shall have Power to fill up all Vacancies that may happen during the Recess of the Senate, by granting Commissions which shall expire at the End of their next Session.

Section 3

He shall from time to time give to the Congress Information of the State of the Union, and recommend to their Consideration such Measures as he shall judge necessary and expedient; he may, on extraordinary Occasions, convene both Houses, or either of them, and in Case of disagreement between them, with Respect to the Time of Adjournment, he may adjourn them to such Time as he shall think proper; he shall receive Ambassadors and other public Ministers; he shall take Care that the Laws be faithfully executed, and shall Commission all the officers of the United States.

Section 4

The President, Vice President and all civil Officers of the United States, shall be removed from Office on Impeachment for, and Conviction of, Treason, Bribery or other high Crimes and Misdemeanors.

ARTICLE 3

Section 1

The judicial Power of the United States, shall be vested in one supreme Court, and in such inferior Courts as the Congress may from time to time ordain and establish. The Judges, both of the supreme and inferior Courts, shall hold their offices during good Behaviour, and shall, at stated Times, receive for their Services, a Compensation, which shall not be diminished during their Continuance in Office.

Section 2

The judicial Power shall extend to all Cases, in Law and Equity, arising under this Constitution, the Laws of the United States, and Treaties made, or which shall be made, under their Authority;—to all Cases affecting Ambassadors, other public Ministers and Consuls;—to all Cases of admiralty and maritime Jurisdiction;—to Controversies to which the United States shall be a Party;—to Controversies between two or more States;—*between a State and Citizens of another State;*—between Citizens of different States;—between Citizens of the same State claiming Lands under Grants of different States, and between a State, or the Citizens thereof, and foreign States, Citizens or Subjects.

In all Cases affecting Ambassadors, other public Ministers and Consuls, and those in which a State shall be Party, the supreme Court shall have original Jurisdiction. In all the other Cases before mentioned, the supreme Court shall have appellate Jurisdiction, both as to Law and Fact, with such Exceptions, and under such Regulations as the Congress shall make.

The Trial of all Crimes, except in Cases of Impeachment, shall be by Jury; and such Trial shall be held in the State where the said Crimes shall have been committed, but when not committed within any State, the Trial shall be at such Place or Places as the Congress may by Law have directed.

Section 3

Treason against the United States, shall consist only in levying War against them, or in adhering to their Enemies, giving them Aid and Comfort. No person shall be convicted of Treason unless on the Testimony of two Witnesses to the same overt Act, or on Confession in open Court.

The Congress shall have Power to declare the Punishment of Treason, but no Attainder of Treason shall work Corruption of Blood, or Forfeiture except during the Life of the Person attainted.

ARTICLE 4

Section 1

Full Faith and Credit shall be given in each State to the public Acts, Records, and judicial Proceedings of every other State. And the Congress may by general Laws prescribe the Manner in which such Acts, Records and Proceedings shall be proved, and the Effect thereof.

Section 2

The Citizens of each State shall be entitled to all Privileges and Immunities of Citizens in the several States.

A Person charged in any State with Treason, Felony, or other Crime, who shall flee from Justice, and be found in another State, shall on Demand of the executive Authority of the State from which he fled, be delivered up, to be removed to the State having Jurisdiction of the Crime.

No Person held to Service or Labour in one State, under the Laws thereof, escaping into another, shall, in Consequence of any Law or Regulation therein, be discharged from such Service or Labour, but shall be delivered up on Claim of the Party to whom such Service or Labour may be due.

Section 3

New States may be admitted by the Congress into this Union; but no new State shall be formed or erected within the Jurisdiction of any other State; nor any State be formed by the Junction of two or more States, or Parts of States, without the Consent of the Legislatures of the States concerned as well as of the Congress.

The Congress shall have Power to dispose of and make all needful Rules and Regulations respecting the Territory or other Property belonging to the United States; and nothing in this Constitution shall be so construed as to Prejudice any Claims of the United States, or of any particular States.*

Section 4

The United States shall guarantee to every State in this Union a Republican Form of Government, and shall protect each of them against Invasion; and on Application of the Legislature, or of the Executive (when the Legislature cannot be convened) against domestic violence.

ARTICLE 5

The Congress, whenever two thirds of both Houses shall deem it necessary, shall propose Amendments to this Constitution, or, on the Application of the Legislatures of two thirds of the several States, shall call a Convention for proposing Amendments, which, in either Case, shall be valid to all Intents and Purposes, as Part of this Constitution, when ratified by the Legislatures of three fourths of the several States, or by Conventions in three fourths thereof, as the one or the other Mode of Ratification may be proposed by the Congress; Provided *that no Amendment which may be made prior to the Year One thousand eight hundred and eight shall in any Manner affect the first and fourth Clauses in the Ninth Section of the first Article;* and that no State, without its Consent, shall be deprived of its equal Suffrage in the Senate.

---

*The Constitution was submitted on September 17, 1787, by the Constitutional Convention, was ratified by the Convention of several states at various dates up to May 29, 1790, and became effective on March 4, 1789.

ARTICLE 6

All Debts contracted and Engagements entered into, before the Adoption of this Constitution, shall be as valid against the United States under this Constitution, as under the Confederation.

This Constitution, and Laws of the United States which shall be made in Pursuance thereof; and all Treaties made, or which shall be made, under the Authority of the United States, shall be the supreme Law of the Land; and the Judges in every State shall be bound thereby, any Thing in the Constitution or Laws of any State to the Contrary notwithstanding.

The Senators and Representatives before mentioned, and the Members of the several State Legislatures, and all executive and Judicial Officers, both of the United States and of the several States, shall be bound by Oath or Affirmation, to support this Constitution; but no religious Test shall ever be required as a Qualification to any Office of public Trust under the United States.

ARTICLE 7

The Ratification of the Conventions of nine States, shall be sufficient for the Establishment of this Constitution between the States so ratifying the Same.

Done in Convention by the Unanimous Consent of the States present the Seventeenth Day of September in the Year of our Lord one thousand seven hundred and Eighty seven and of the Independence of the United States of America the Twelfth* IN WITNESS whereof We have hereunto subscribed our Names,

George Washington President and Deputy from Virginia

Delaware
George Read
Gunning Bedford, Jr.
John Dickinson
Richard Bassett
Jacob Broom

Maryland
James McHenry
Daniel of St. Thomas Jenifer
Daniel Carroll

Virginia
John Blair
James Madison, Jr

North Carolina
William Blount
Richard Dobbs Spraight
Hugh Williamson

South Carolina
John Rutledge
Charles Cotesworth Pinckney
Charles Pinckney
Pierce Butler

Georgia
William Few
Abraham Baldwin

New Hampshire
John Langdon
Nicholas Gilman

Massachusetts
Nathaniel Gorham
Rufus King

Connecticut
William Samuel Johnson
Roger Sherman

New York
Alexander Hamilton

New Jersey
William Livingston
David Brearley
William Paterson
Jonathan Dayton
Pennsylvania
Benjamin Franklin
Thomas Mifflin
Robert Morris
George Clymer
Thomas FitzSimons
Jared Ingersoll
James Wilson
Gouverneur Morris

*The Constitution was submitted on September 17, 1787, by the Constitutional Convention, was ratified by the Convention of several states at various dates up to May 29, 1790, and became effective on March 4, 1789.

AMENDMENTS TO THE CONSTITUTION

AMENDMENT I

Congress shall make no law respecting an establishment of religion, or prohibiting the free exercise thereof; or abridging the freedom of speech, or of the press; or the right of the people peaceably to assemble, and to petition the Government for a redress of grievances.

AMENDMENT II

A well regulated Militia being necessary to the security of a free State, the right of the people to keep and bear Arms, shall not be infringed.

AMENDMENT III

No Soldier shall, in time of peace be quartered in any house, without the consent of the Owner, nor in time of war, but in a manner to be prescribed by law.

AMENDMENT IV

The right of the people to be secure in their persons, houses, papers, and effects, against unreasonable searches and seizures, shall not be violated, and no Warrants shall issue, but upon probable cause, supported by Oath or affirmation, and particularly describing the place to be searched, and the persons or things to be seized.

AMENDMENT V

No person shall be held to answer for a capital, or otherwise infamous crime, unless on a presentment or indictment of a Grand Jury, except in cases arising in the land or naval forces, or in the Militia, when in actual service in time of War or public danger; nor shall any person be subject for the same offense to be twice put in jeopardy of life or limb; nor shall be compelled in any criminal case to be a witness against himself, nor be deprived of life, liberty, or property, without due process of law; nor shall private property be taken for public use, without just compensation.

AMENDMENT VI

In all criminal prosecutions, the accused shall enjoy the right to a speedy and public trial, by an impartial jury of the State and district wherein the crime shall have been committed, which district shall have been previously ascertained by law, and to be informed of the nature and cause of the accusation; to be confronted with the witnesses against him; to have compulsory process for obtaining witnesses in his favor, and to have the Assistance of Counsel for his defence.

AMENDMENT VII

In Suits at common law, where the value in controversy shall exceed twenty dollars, the right of trial by jury shall be preserved, and no fact tried by a jury, shall be otherwise reexamined in any Court of the United States, than according to the rules of the common law.

AMENDMENT VIII

Excessive bail shall not be required, nor excessive fines imposed, nor cruel and unusual punishments inflicted.

AMENDMENT IX

The enumeration in the Constitution, of certain rights, shall not be construed to deny or disparage others retained by the people.

AMENDMENT X*

The powers not delegated to the United States by the Constitution, nor prohibited by it to the States, are reserved to the States respectively, or to the people.

AMENDMENT XI [ADOPTED 1798]

The Judicial power of the United States shall not be construed to extend to any suit in law or equity, commenced or prosecuted against one of the United States by Citizens of another State, or by Citizens or Subjects of any Foreign State.

*The first ten amendments (the Bill of Rights) were ratified and their adoption was certified on December 15, 1791.

AMENDMENT XII [ADOPTED 1804]

The Electors shall meet in their respective states, and vote by ballot for President and Vice President, one of whom, at least, shall not be an inhabitant of the same state with themselves; they shall name in their ballots the person voted for as President, and in distinct ballots the person voted for as Vice President, and they shall make distinct lists of all persons voted for as President, and of all persons voted for as Vice President, and of the number of votes for each, which lists they shall sign and certify, and transmit sealed to the seat of the government of the United States, directed to the President of the Senate;—The President of the Senate shall, in the presence of the Senate and House of Representatives, open all the certificates and the votes shall then be counted;—The person having the greatest number of votes for President, shall be the President, if such number be a majority of the whole number of Electors appointed; and if no person have such majority, then from the persons having the highest numbers not exceeding three on the list of those voted for as President, the House of Representatives shall choose immediately, by ballot, the President. But in choosing the President, the votes shall be taken by states, the representation from each state having one vote; a quorum for this purpose shall consist of a member or members from two-thirds of the states, and a majority of all the states shall be necessary to a choice. And if the House of Representatives shall not choose a President whenever the right of choice shall devolve upon them, before *the fourth day of March* next following, then the Vice President shall act as President, as in the case of the death or other constitutional disability of the President.—The person having the greatest number of votes as Vice President, shall be the Vice President, if such number be a majority of the whole number of Electors appointed, and if no person have a majority, then from the two highest numbers on the list, the Senate shall choose the Vice President; a quorum for the purpose shall consist of two-thirds of the whole number of Senators, and a majority of the whole number shall be necessary to a choice. But no person constitutionally ineligible to the office of President shall be eligible to that of Vice President of the United States.

AMENDMENT XIII [ADOPTED 1865]

Section 1

Neither slavery nor involuntary servitude, except as a punishment for crime whereof the party shall have been duly convicted, shall exist within the United States, or any place subject to their jurisdiction.

Section 2

Congress shall have power to enforce this article by appropriate legislation.

AMENDMENT XIV [ADOPTED 1868]

Section 1

All persons born or naturalized in the United States, and subject to the jurisdiction thereof, are citizens of the United States and of the State wherein they reside. No State shall make or enforce any law which shall abridge the privileges or immunities of citizens of the United States; nor shall any State deprive any person of life, liberty, or property, without due process of law; nor deny to any person within its jurisdiction the equal protection of the laws.

Section 2

Representatives shall be apportioned among the several States according to their respective numbers, counting the whole number of persons in each State, excluding Indians not taxed. But when the right to vote at any election for the choice of electors for President and Vice President of the United States, Representatives in Congress, the Executive and Judicial officers of a State, or the members of the Legislature thereof, is denied to any of the male inhabitants of such State, being twenty-one years of age, and citizens of the United States, or in any way abridged, except for participation in rebellion, or other crime, the basis of representation therein shall be reduced in the proportion which the number of such male citizens shall bear to the whole number of male citizens twenty-one years of age in such State.

Section 3

No person shall be a Senator or Representative in Congress, or elector of President and Vice President, or hold any office, civil or military, under the United States, or under any State, who, having previously taken an oath, as a member of Congress, or as an officer of the United States, or as a member of any State legislature, or as an executive or judicial officer of any State, to support the Constitution of the United States, shall have engaged in insurrection or rebellion against the same, or given aid or comfort to the enemies thereof. But Congress may by a vote of two-thirds of each House, remove such disability.

Section 4

The validity of the public debt of the United States, authorized by law, including debts incurred for payment of pensions and bounties for services in suppressing insurrection or rebellion, shall not be questioned. But neither the United States nor any State shall assume or pay any debt or obligation incurred in aid of insurrection or rebellion against the United States, or any claim for the loss or emancipation of any slave; but all such debts, obligations and claims shall be held illegal and void.

Section 5

The Congress shall have power to enforce, by appropriate legislation, the provisions of this article.

AMENDMENT XV [ADOPTED 1870]

Section 1

The right of citizens of the United States to vote shall not be denied or abridged by the United States or by any State on account of race, color, or previous condition of servitude.

Section 2

The Congress shall have power to enforce this article by appropriate legislation.

AMENDMENT XVI [ADOPTED 1913]

The Congress shall have power to lay and collect taxes on incomes, from whatever source derived, without apportionment among the several States, and without regard to any census or enumeration.

AMENDMENT XVII [ADOPTED 1913]

The Senate of the United States shall be composed of two Senators from each State, elected by the people thereof, for six years; and each Senator shall have one vote. The electors in each State shall have the qualifications requisite for electors of the most numerous branch of the State legislatures.

When vacancies happen in the representation of any State in the Senate, the executive authority of such State shall issue writs of election to fill such vacancies: *Provided*, That the legislature of any State may empower the executive thereof to make temporary appointments until the people fill the vacancies by election as the legislature may direct.

This amendment shall not be so construed as to affect the election or term of any Senator chosen before it becomes valid as part of the Constitution.

AMENDMENT XVIII [ADOPTED 1919, REPEALED 1933]

Section 1

After one year from the ratification of this article the manufacture, sale, or transportation of intoxicating liquors within, the importation thereof into, or the exportation thereof from the United States and all territory subject to the jurisdiction thereof for beverage purposes is hereby prohibited.

Section 2

The Congress and the several States shall have concurrent power to enforce this article by appropriate legislation.

Section 3

This article shall be inoperative unless it shall have been ratified as an amendment to the Constitution by the legislatures of the several States, as provided in the Constitution, within seven years from the date of the submission hereof to the States by the Congress.

AMENDMENT XIX [ADOPTED 1920]

The right of citizens of the United States to vote shall not be denied or abridged by the United States or by any State on account of sex.

Congress shall have power to enforce this article by appropriate legislation.

AMENDMENT XX [ADOPTED 1933]

Section 1

The terms of the President and Vice President shall end at noon on the 20th day of January, and the terms of Senators and Representatives at noon on the 3d day of January, of the years in which such terms would have ended if this article had not been ratified and the terms of their successors shall then begin.

Section 2

The Congress shall assemble at least once in every year, and such meeting shall begin at noon on the 3d day of January, unless they shall by law appoint a different day.

Section 3

If, at the time fixed for the beginning of the term of the President, the President elect shall have died, the Vice President elect shall become President. If a President shall not have been chosen before the time fixed for the beginning of his term, or if the President elect shall have failed to qualify, then the Vice President elect shall act as President until a President shall have qualified; and the Congress may by law provide for the case wherein neither a President elect nor a Vice President elect shall have qualified, declaring who shall then act as President, or the manner in which one who is to act shall be selected, and such person shall act accordingly until a President or Vice President shall have qualified.

Section 4

The Congress may by law provide for the case of the death of any of the persons from whom the House of Representatives may choose a President whenever the right of choice shall have devolved upon them, and for the case of the death of any of the persons from whom the Senate may choose a Vice President whenever the right of choice shall have devolved upon them.

Section 5

Sections 1 and 2 shall take effect on the 15th day of October following the ratification of this article.

Section 6

This article shall be inoperative unless it shall have been ratified as an amendment to the Constitution by the legislatures of three fourths of the several States within seven years from the date of its submission.

AMENDMENT XXI [ADOPTED 1933]

Section 1

The eighteenth article of amendment to the Constitution of the United States is hereby repealed.

Section 2

The transportation or importation into any State, Territory, or possession of the United States for delivery or use therein of intoxicating liquors in violation of the laws thereof, is hereby prohibited.

Section 3

This article shall be inoperative unless it shall have been ratified as an amendment to the Constitution by conventions in the several States, as provided in the Constitution, within seven years from the date of the submission hereof to the States by the Congress.

AMENDMENT XXII [ADOPTED 1951]

Section 1

No person shall be elected to the office of the President more than twice, and no person who has held the office of President, or acted as President, for more than two years of a term to which some other person was elected President shall be elected to the office of the President more than once. But this Article shall not apply to any person holding the office of President when this Article was proposed by the Congress, and shall not prevent any person who may be holding the office of President, or acting as President, during the term within which this Article becomes operative from holding the office of President or acting as President during the remainder of such term.

Section 2

This article shall be inoperative unless it shall have been ratified as an amendment to the Constitution by the legislatures of three-fourths of the several States within seven years from the date of its submission to the States by the Congress.

AMENDMENT XXIII [ADOPTED 1961]

Section 1

The District constituting the seat of Government of the United States shall appoint in such manner as the Congress shall direct:

A number of electors of President and Vice President equal to the whole number of Senators and Representatives in Congress to which the District would be entitled if it were a State, but in no event more than the least populous State; they shall be in addition to those appointed by the States, but they shall be considered, for the purposes of the election of President and Vice President, to be electors appointed by a State; and they shall meet in the District and perform such duties as provided by the twelfth article of amendment.

Section 2

The Congress shall have power to enforce this article by appropriate legislation.

AMENDMENT XXIV [ADOPTED 1964]

Section 1

The right of citizens of the United States to vote in any primary or other election for President or Vice President, for electors for President or Vice President, or for Senator or Representative in Congress, shall not be denied or abridged by the United States or any state by reason of failure to pay any poll tax or other tax.

Section 2

The Congress shall have the power to enforce this article by appropriate legislation.

AMENDMENT XXV [ADOPTED 1967]

Section 1

In case of the removal of the President from office or his death or resignation, the Vice President shall become President.

Section 2

Whenever there is a vacancy in the office of the Vice President, the President shall nominate a Vice President who shall take the office upon confirmation by a majority vote of both houses of Congress.

Section 3

Whenever the President transmits to the President pro tempore of the Senate and the Speaker of the House of Representatives his written declaration that he is unable to discharge the powers and duties of his office, and until he transmits to them a written declaration to the contrary, such powers and duties shall be discharged by the Vice President as Acting President.

Section 4

Whenever the Vice President and a majority of either the principal officers of the executive departments or of such other body as Congress may by law provide, transmit to the President pro tempore of the Senate and the Speaker of the House of Representatives their written declaration that the President is unable to discharge the powers and duties of his office, the Vice President shall immediately assume the powers and duties of the office as Acting President.

Thereafter, when the President transmits to the President pro tempore of the Senate and the Speaker of the House of Representatives his written declaration that no inability exists, he shall resume the powers and duties of his office unless the Vice President and a majority of either the principal officers of the executive department or of such other body as Congress may by law provide, transmit within four days to the President pro tempore of the Senate and the Speaker of the House of Representatives their written declaration that the President is unable to discharge the powers and duties of his office. Thereupon Congress shall decide the issue, assembling within 48 hours for that purpose if not in session. If the Congress, within 21 days after receipt of the latter written declaration, or, if Congress is not in session, within 21 days after Congress is required to assemble, determines by two-thirds vote of both houses that the President is unable to discharge the powers and duties of his office, the Vice President shall continue to discharge the same as Acting President; otherwise, the President shall resume the powers and duties of his office.

AMENDMENT XXVI [ADOPTED 1971]

Section 1

The right of citizens of the United States, who are 18 years of age or older, to vote shall not be denied or abridged by the United States or any state on account of age.

Section 2

The Congress shall have the power to enforce this article by appropriate legislation.

AMENDMENT XXVII [ADOPTED 1992]

No law, varying the compensation for the services of the Senators and Representatives shall take effect, until an election of Representatives shall have intervened.

Presidential Elections

Year	Candidates	Parties	Popular Vote	Electoral Vote	Voter Participation
1789	George Washington		*	69	
	John Adams			34	
	Others			35	
1792	George Washington		*	132	
	John Adams			77	
	George Clinton			50	
	Others			5	
1796	John Adams	Federalist	*	71	
	Thomas Jefferson	Democratic-Republican		68	
	Thomas Pinckney	Federalist		59	
	Aaron Burr	Dem.-Rep.		30	
	Others			48	
1800	Thomas Jefferson	Dem.-Rep.	*	73	
	Aaron Burr	Dem.-Rep.		73	
	John Adams	Federalist		65	
	C. C. Pinckney	Federalist		64	
	John Jay	Federalist		1	
1804	Thomas Jefferson	Dem.-Rep.	*	162	
	C. C. Pinckney	Federalist		14	
1808	James Madison	Dem.-Rep.	*	122	
	C. C. Pinckney	Federalist		47	
	George Clinton	Dem.-Rep.		6	
1812	James Madison	Dem.-Rep.	*	128	
	De Witt Clinton	Federalist		89	
1816	James Monroe	Dem.-Rep.	*	183	
	Rufus King	Federalist		34	
1820	James Monroe	Dem.-Rep.	*	231	
	John Quincy Adams	Dem.-Rep.		1	
1824	John Quincy Adams	Dem.-Rep.	108,740 (30.5%)	84	26.9%
	Andrew Jackson	Dem.-Rep.	153,544 (43.1%)	99	
	William H. Crawford	Dem.-Rep.	46,618 (13.1%)	41	
	Henry Clay	Dem.-Rep.	47,136 (13.2%)	37	

(continued)

Presidential Elections *(continued)*

Year	Candidates	Parties	Popular Vote	Electoral Vote	Voter Participation
1828	Andrew Jackson	Democratic	647,286 (56.0%)	178	57.6%
	John Quincy Adams	National Republican	508,064 (44.0%)	83	
1832	Andrew Jackson	Democratic	688,242 (54.2%)	219	55.4%
	Henry Clay	National Republican	473,462 (37.4%)	49	
	John Floyd	Independent		11	
	William Wirt	Anti-Mason	101,051 (7.8%)	7	
1836	Martin Van Buren	Democratic	762,198 (50.8%)	170	57.8%
	William Henry Harrison	Whig	549,508 (36.6%)	73	
	Hugh L. White	Whig	145,342 (9.7%)	26	
	Daniel Webster	Whig	41,287 (2.7%)	14	
	W. P. Magnum	Independent		11	
1840	William Henry Harrison	Whig	1,274,624 (53.1%)	234	80.2%
	Martin Van Buren	Democratic	1,127,781 (46.9%)	60	
	J. G. Birney	Liberty	7069	—	
1844	James K. Polk	Democratic	1,338,464 (49.6%)	170	78.9%
	Henry Clay	Whig	1,300,097 (48.1%)	105	
	J. G. Birney	Liberty	62,300 (2.3%)	—	
1848	Zachary Taylor	Whig	1,360,967 (47.4%)	163	72.7%
	Lewis Cass	Democratic	1,222,342 (42.5%)	127	
	Martin Van Buren	Free-Soil	291,263 (10.1%)	—	
1852	Franklin Pierce	Democratic	1,601,117 (50.9%)	254	69.6%
	Winfield Scott	Whig	1,385,453 (44.1%)	42	
	John P. Hale	Free-Soil	155,825 (5.0%)	—	
1856	James Buchanan	Democratic	1,832,955 (45.3%)	174	78.9%
	John C. Frémont	Republican	1,339,932 (33.1%)	114	
	Millard Fillmore	American	871,731 (21.6%)	8	
1860	Abraham Lincoln	Republican	1,865,593 (39.8%)	180	81.2%
	Stephen A. Douglas	Democratic	1,382,713 (29.5%)	12	
	John C. Breckinridge	Democratic	848,356 (18.1%)	72	
	John Bell	Union	592,906 (12.6%)	39	
1864	Abraham Lincoln	Republican	2,213,655 (55.0%)	212†	73.8%
	George B. McClellan	Democratic	1,805,237 (45.0%)	21	
1868	Ulysses S. Grant	Republican	3,012,833 (52.7%)	214	78.1%
	Horatio Seymour	Democratic	2,703,249 (47.3%)	80	

Presidential Elections *(continued)*

Year	Candidates	Parties	Popular Vote	Electoral Vote	Voter Participation
1872	Ulysses S. Grant	Republican	3,597,132 (55.6%)	286	71.3%
	Horace Greeley	Dem.; Liberal Republican	2,834,125 (43.9%)	66‡	
1876	Rutherford B. Hayes§	Republican	4,036,298 (48.0%)	185	81.8%
	Samuel J. Tilden	Democratic	4,300,590 (51.0%)	184	
1880	James A. Garfield	Republican	4,454,416 (48.5%)	214	79.4%
	Winfield S. Hancock	Democratic	4,444,952 (48.1%)	155	
1884	Grover Cleveland	Democratic	4,874,986 (48.5%)	219	77.5%
	James G. Blaine	Republican	4,851,981 (48.2%)	182	
1888	Benjamin Harrison	Republican	5,439,853 (47.9%)	233	79.3%
	Grover Cleveland	Democratic	5,540,309 (48.6%)	168	
1892	Grover Cleveland	Democratic	5,556,918 (46.1%)	277	74.7%
	Benjamin Harrison	Republican	5,176,108 (43.0%)	145	
	James B. Weaver	People's	1,029,329 (8.5%)	22	
1896	William McKinley	Republican	7,104,779 (51.1%)	271	79.3%
	William Jennings Bryan	Democratic People's	6,502,925 (47.7%)	176	
1900	William McKinley	Republican	7,207,923 (51.7%)	292	73.2%
	William Jennings Bryan	Dem.-Populist	6,358,133 (45.5%)	155	
1904	Theodore Roosevelt	Republican	7,623,486 (57.9%)	336	65.2%
	Alton B. Parker	Democratic	5,077,911 (37.6%)	140	
	Eugene V. Debs	Socialist	402,400 (3.0%)	—	
1908	William H. Taft	Republican	7,678,908 (51.6%)	321	65.4%
	William Jennings Bryan	Democratic	6,409,104 (43.1%)	162	
	Eugene V. Debs	Socialist	402,820 (2.8%)	—	
1912	Woodrow Wilson	Democratic	6,293,454 (41.9%)	435	58.8%
	Theodore Roosevelt	Progressive	4,119,538 (27.4%)	88	
	William H. Taft	Republican	3,484,980 (23.2%)	8	
	Eugene V. Debs	Socialist	900,672 (6.0%)	—	
1916	Woodrow Wilson	Democratic	9,129,606 (49.4%)	277	61.6%
	Charles E. Hughes	Republican	8,538,221 (46.2%)	254	
	A. L. Benson	Socialist	585,113 (3.2%)	—	
1920	Warren G. Harding	Republican	16,152,200 (60.4%)	404	49.2%
	James M. Cox	Democratic	9,147,353 (34.2%)	127	
	Eugene V. Debs	Socialist	917,799 (3.4%)	—	
1924	Calvin Coolidge	Republican	15,725,016 (54.0%)	382	48.9%
	John W. Davis	Democratic	8,386,503 (28.8%)	136	
	Robert M. La Follette	Progressive	4,822,856 (16.6%)	13	

(continued)

Presidential Elections *(continued)*

Year	Candidates	Parties	Popular Vote	Electoral Vote	Voter Participation
1928	Herbert Hoover	Republican	21,391,381 (58.2%)	444	56.9%
	Alfred E. Smith	Democratic	15,016,443 (40.9%)	87	
	Norman Thomas	Socialist	267,835 (0.7%)	—	
1932	Franklin D. Roosevelt	Democratic	22,821,857 (57.4%)	472	56.9%
	Herbert Hoover	Republican	15,761,841 (39.7%)	59	
	Norman Thomas	Socialist	884,781 (2.2%)	—	
1936	Franklin D. Roosevelt	Democratic	27,751,597 (60.8%)	523	61.0%
	Alfred M. Landon	Republican	16,679,583 (36.5%)	8	
	William Lemke	Union	882,479 (1.9%)	—	
1940	Franklin D. Roosevelt	Democratic	27,244,160 (54.8%)	449	62.5%
	Wendell L. Willkie	Republican	22,305,198 (44.8%)	82	
1944	Franklin D. Roosevelt	Democratic	25,602,504 (53.5%)	432	55.9%
	Thomas E. Dewey	Republican	22,006,285 (46.0%)	99	
1948	Harry S Truman	Democratic	24,105,695 (49.5%)	304	53.0%
	Thomas E. Dewey	Republican	21,969,170 (45.1%)	189	
	J. Strom Thurmond	State-Rights Democratic	1,169,021 (2.4%)	38	
	Henry A. Wallace	Progressive	1,157,326 (2.4%)	—	
1952	Dwight D. Eisenhower	Republican	33,778,963 (55.1%)	442	63.3%
	Adlai E. Stevenson	Democratic	27,314,992 (44.4%)	89	
1956	Dwight D. Eisenhower	Republican	35,575,420 (57.6%)	457	60.6%
	Adlai E. Stevenson	Democratic	26,033,066 (42.1%)	73	
	Other	—	—	1	
1960	John F. Kennedy	Democratic	34,227,096 (49.9%)	303	62.8%
	Richard M. Nixon	Republican	34,108,546 (49.6%)	219	
	Other	—	—	15	
1964	Lyndon B. Johnson	Democratic	43,126,506 (61.1%)	486	61.7%
	Barry M. Goldwater	Republican	27,176,799 (38.5%)	52	
1968	Richard M. Nixon	Republican	31,770,237 (43.4%)	301	60.6%
	Hubert H. Humphrey	Democratic	31,270,533 (42.7%)	191	
	George Wallace	American Indep.	9,906,141 (13.5%)	46	

Presidential Elections

Year	Candidates	Parties	Popular Vote	Electoral Vote	Voter Participation
1972	Richard M. Nixon	Republican	46,740,323 (60.7%)	520	55.2%
	George S. McGovern	Democratic	28,901,598 (37.5%)	17	
	Other	—	—	1	
1976	Jimmy Carter	Democratic	40,828,587 (50.0%)	297	53.5%
	Gerald R. Ford	Republican	39,147,613 (47.9%)	241	
	Other	—	1,575,459 (2.1%)	—	
1980	Ronald Reagan	Republican	43,901,812 (50.7%)	489	52.6%
	Jimmy Carter	Democratic	35,483,820 (41.0%)	49	
	John B. Anderson	Independent	5,719,437 (6.6%)	—	
	Ed Clark	Libertarian	921,188 (1.1%)	—	
1984	Ronald Reagan	Republican	54,455,075 (59.0%)	525	53.3%
	Walter Mondale	Democratic	37,577,185 (41.0%)	13	
1988	George H. W. Bush	Republican	48,886,097 (53.4%)	426	57.4%
	Michael S. Dukakis	Democratic	41,809,074 (45.6%)	111	
1992	William J. Clinton	Democratic	44,908,254 (43%)	370	55.0%
	George H. W. Bush	Republican	39,102,343 (37.5%)	168	
	H. Ross Perot	Independent	19,741,065 (18.9%)	—	
1996	William J. Clinton	Democratic	45,590,703 (50%)	379	48.8%
	Robert Dole	Republican	37,816,307 (41%)	159	
	Ross Perot	Reform	7,866,284	—	
2000	George W. Bush	Republican	50,456,167 (47.88%)	271	51.2%
	Al Gore	Democratic	50,996,064 (48.39%)	266"	
	Ralph Nader	Green	2,864,810 (2.72%)	—	
	Other	834,774 (less than 1%)	—		
2004	George W. Bush	Republican	60,934,251 (51.0%)	286	50.0%
	John F. Kerry	Democratic	57,765,291 (48.0%)	252	
	Ralph Nader	Independent	405,933 (less than 1%)	—	
2008	Barack Obama	Democractic	69,456,897 (52.9%)	365	62%
	John McCain	Republican	59,934,814 (45.7%)	173	

*Electors selected by state legislatures.

†Eleven secessionist states did not participate.

‡Greeley died before the electoral college met. His electoral votes were divided among the four minor candidates.

§Contested result settled by special election.

"One District of Columbia Gore elector abstained. Popular Vote

Presidents and Vice Presidents

	President	Vice President	Term
1.	George Washington	John Adams	1789–1793
	George Washington	John Adams	1793–1797
2.	John Adams	Thomas Jefferson	1797–1801
3.	Thomas Jefferson	Aaron Burr	1801–1805
	Thomas Jefferson	George Clinton	1805–1809
4.	James Madison	George Clinton (d. 1812)	1809–1813
	James Madison	Elbridge Gerry (d. 1814)	1813–1817
5.	James Monroe	Daniel Tompkins	1817–1821
	James Monroe	Daniel Tompkins	1821–1825
6.	John Quincy Adams	John C. Calhoun	1825–1829
7.	Andrew Jackson	John C. Calhoun	1829–1833
	Andrew Jackson	Martin Van Buren	1833–1837
8.	Martin Van Buren	Richard M. Johnson	1837–1841
9.	William H. Harrison (d. 1841)	John Tyler	1841
10.	John Tyler	—	1841–1845
11.	James K. Polk	George M. Dallas	1845–1849
12.	Zachary Taylor (d. 1850)	Millard Fillmore	1849–1850
13.	Millard Fillmore	—	1850–1853
14.	Franklin Pierce	William R. King (d. 1853)	1853–1857
15.	James Buchanan	John C. Breckinridge	1857–1861
16.	Abraham Lincoln	Hannibal Hamlin	1861–1865
	Abraham Lincoln (d. 1865)	Andrew Johnson	1865
17.	Andrew Johnson	—	1865–1869
18.	Ulysses S. Grant	Schuyler Colfax	1869–1873
	Ulysses S. Grant	Henry Wilson (d. 1875)	1873–1877
19.	Rutherford B. Hayes	William A. Wheeler	1877–1881
20.	James A. Garfield (d. 1881)	Chester A. Arthur	1881
21.	Chester A. Arthur	—	1881–1885
22.	Grover Cleveland	Thomas A. Hendricks (d. 1885)	1885–1889
23.	Benjamin Harrison	Levi P. Morton	1889–1893
24.	Grover Cleveland	Adlai E. Stevenson	1893–1897
25.	William McKinley	Garret A. Hobart (d. 1899)	1897–1901
	William McKinley (d. 1901)	Theodore Roosevelt	1901
26.	Theodore Roosevelt	—	1901–1905
	Theodore Roosevelt	Charles Fairbanks	1905–1909
27.	William H. Taft	James S. Sherman (d. 1912)	1909–1913
28.	Woodrow Wilson	Thomas R. Marshall	1913–1917
	Woodrow Wilson	Thomas R. Marshall	1917–1921

Presidents and Vice Presidents

	President	Vice President	Term
29.	Warren G. Harding (d. 1923)	Calvin Coolidge	1921–1923
30.	Calvin Coolidge	—	1923–1925
	Calvin Coolidge	Charles G. Dawes	1925–1929
31.	Herbert Hoover	Charles Curtis	1929–1933
32.	Franklin D. Roosevelt	John N. Garner	1933–1937
	Franklin D. Roosevelt	John N. Garner	1937–1941
	Franklin D. Roosevelt	Henry A. Wallace	1941–1945
	Franklin D. Roosevelt (d. 1945)	Harry S Truman	1945
33.	Harry S Truman	—	1945–1949
	Harry S Truman	Alben W. Barkley	1949–1953
34.	Dwight D. Eisenhower	Richard M. Nixon	1953–1957
	Dwight D. Eisenhower	Richard M. Nixon	1957–1961
35.	John F. Kennedy (d. 1963)	Lyndon B. Johnson	1961–1963
36.	Lyndon B. Johnson	—	1963–1965
	Lyndon B. Johnson	Hubert H. Humphrey	1965–1969
37.	Richard M. Nixon	Spiro T. Agnew	1969–1973
	Richard M. Nixon (resigned 1974)	Gerald R. Ford	1973–1974
38.	Gerald R. Ford	Nelson A. Rockefeller	1974–1977
39.	Jimmy Carter	Walter F. Mondale	1977–1981
40.	Ronald Reagan	George H. W. Bush	1981–1985
	Ronald Reagan	George H. W. Bush	1985–1989
41.	George H. W. Bush	J. Danforth Quayle	1989–1993
42.	William J. Clinton	Albert Gore, Jr.	1993–1997
	William J. Clinton	Albert Gore, Jr.	1997–2001
43.	George W. Bush	Richard Cheney	2001–2005
	George W. Bush	Richard Cheney	2005–2009
44.	Barack Obama	Joe Biden	2009-

Glossary

Abolitionist movement (p. 303) Reform movement dedicated to the immediate and unconditional end of slavery in the United States.

Adams–Onís Treaty (p. 223) Signed by Secretary of State John Quincy Adams and Spanish minister Luis de Onís in 1819, this treaty allowed for U.S. annexation of Florida.

Affirmative action (p. 829) The use of laws or regulations to achieve racial, ethnic, gender, or other diversity, as in hiring or school admissions. Such efforts are often aimed at improving employment or educational opportunities for women and minorities.

African Methodist Episcopal (AME) Church (p. 148) Richard Allen founded the African Methodist Episcopal Church in 1816 as the first independent black-run Protestant church in the United States. The AME Church was active in the abolition movement and founded educational institutions for free blacks.

Agricultural Adjustment Administration (AAA) (p. 663) Created by Congress in 1933 as part of the New Deal, this agency attempted to restrict agricultural production by paying farmers subsidies to take land out of production. The object was to raise farm prices, and it did, but the act did nothing for tenant farmers and sharecroppers. The Supreme Court declared it unconstitutional in 1936.

Agricultural Revolution (p. 7) The gradual shift from hunting and gathering to cultivating basic food crops that occurred worldwide from 7,000 to 9,000 years ago.

Alamo (p. 317) In 1835, Americans living in Mexican-ruled Texas fomented a revolution. Mexico lost the resulting conflict, but not before its troops defeated and killed a group of American rebels at the Alamo, a fortified mission in San Antonio.

Albany Plan (p. 106) Plan of intercolonial cooperation proposed by prominent colonists including Benjamin Franklin at a conference in Albany, New York, in 1754. The plan called for a Grand Council of elected delegates from the colonies that would have powers to tax and provide for the common defense. Although rejected by the colonial and British governments, it was a prototype for colonial union.

Alien and Sedition Acts (p. 191) Collective name given to four laws Congress passed in 1798 to suppress criticism of the federal government and curb liberties of foreigners living in the United States.

American Colonization Society (p. 282) Founded in 1817, the society advocated the relocation of free blacks and freed slaves to the African colony of Monrovia, present-day Liberia.

American Federation of Labor (AFL) (p. 463) Founded by Samuel Gompers in 1886, the AFL organized skilled workers by craft and worked for specific practical objectives, such as higher wages, shorter hours, and better working conditions. The AFL avoided politics, and while it did not expressly forbid blacks and women from joining, it used exclusionary practices to keep them out.

Americans with Disabilities Act (ADA) (p. 806) Passed by Congress in 1991, this act banned discrimination against the disabled in employment and mandated easy access to all public and commercial buildings.

Antifederalists (p. 163) Critics of the Constitution who were concerned that it included no specific provisions to protect natural and civil rights.

Anti-Imperialist League (p. 543) An organization formed in 1898 to fight the **Treaty of Paris** ending the Spanish-American War. Members opposed acquiring overseas colonies, believing it would subvert American ideals and institutions. Membership centered in New England; the cause was less popular in the South and West.

Antinomianism (p. 46) Religious belief rejecting traditional moral law as unnecessary for Christians who possess saving grace and affirming that a person could experience divine revelation and salvation without the assistance of formally trained clergy.

Articles of Confederation (p. 153) Ratified in 1781, this document was the United States' first constitution, providing a framework for national government. The articles limited central authority by denying the national government any taxation or coercive power.

Ashcan School (p. 570) Early twentieth-century realist painters who portrayed the slums and streets of the nation's cities and the lives of ordinary urban dwellers. They often advocated political and social reform.

Axis Powers (p. 679) During World War II, the alliance between Italy, Germany, and Japan was known as the "Rome–Berlin–Tokyo axis," and the three members were called the Axis Powers. They fought against the Allied Powers, led by the United States, Britain, and the Soviet Union.

Baby boom (p. 728) The rise in births following World War II. Children born to this generation are referred to as "baby boomers."

Backcountry (p. 87) In the eighteenth century, the edge of settlement extending from western Pennsylvania to Georgia. This region formed the second frontier as settlers moved west from the Atlantic coast into the interior.

Bacon's Rebellion (p. 77) An armed rebellion in Virginia (1675–1676) led by Nathaniel Bacon against the colony's royal governor, Sir William Berkeley. Although some of his followers called for an end to special privilege in government, Bacon was chiefly interested in gaining a larger share of the lucrative Indian trade.

Bank of the United States (p. 179) National bank proposed by Secretary of the Treasury Alexander Hamilton and established in 1791. It served as a central depository for the U.S. government and had the authority to issue currency.

Bank War (p. 259) Between 1832–1836, Andrew Jackson used his presidential power to fight and ultimately destroy the second Bank of the United States.

Baruch Plan (p. 707) In 1946, Bernard Baruch presented an American plan to control and eventually outlaw nuclear weapons. The plan called for UN control of nuclear weapons in three stages before the United States gave up its stockpile. Soviet insistence on immediate nuclear disarmament without inspection doomed the Baruch Plan and led to a nuclear arms race between the United States and the Soviet Union.

Battle of New Orleans (p. 218) Battle that occurred in 1815 at the end of the War of 1812 when U.S. forces defeated a British attempt to seize New Orleans.

Bay of Pigs (p. 747) In April 1961, a group of Cuban exiles organized and supported by the CIA landed on the southern coast of Cuba in an effort to overthrow Fidel Castro. When the invasion ended in disaster, President Kennedy took full responsibility for it.

Benevolent empire (p. 296) Collection of missionary and reform societies that sought to stamp out social evils in American society in the 1820s and 1830s.

Beringia (p. 5) Land bridge formerly connecting Asia and North America that is now submerged beneath the Bering Sea.

Berlin airlift (p. 711) In 1948, in response to a Soviet land blockade of Berlin, the United States carried out a massive effort to supply the 2 million Berlin citizens by air. The airlift forced the Soviets to end the blockade in 1949.

Bill of Rights (p. 167) The first ten amendments to the Constitution, adopted in 1791 to preserve the rights and liberties of individuals.

Birds of passage (p. 561) Immigrants who came to the United States to work and save money and then returned to their native countries during the slack season.

Black Codes (p. 392) Laws passed by southern states immediately after the Civil War to maintain white supremacy by restricting the rights of the newly freed slaves.

Bland–Allison Silver Purchase Act (p. 503) This 1878 act called for the partial coinage of silver. Those favoring silver coinage argued that it would increase the money supply and help farmers and workers repay their debts. Opponents advocated a restricted money supply based solely on gold and pointed out that few other major countries accepted silver coinage. Congress passed the bill over President Rutherford B. Hayes's veto.

Bonus Army (p. 660) In June 1932, a group of 20,000 World War I veterans marched on Washington, D.C., to demand immediate payment of their "adjusted compensation" bonuses voted by Congress in 1924. Congress rejected their demands, and President Herbert Hoover had the Bonus Army forcibly dispersed.

Boston Massacre (p. 124) A violent clash between British troops and a Boston mob on March 5, 1770. Five citizens were killed when the troops fired into the crowd. The incident inflamed anti-British sentiment in Massachusetts.

Boston Tea Party (p. 126) Raid on British ships in which Patriots disguised as Mohawks threw hundreds of chests of tea owned by the East India Company into Boston Harbor to protest British taxes.

Brown v. Board of Education of Topeka (p. 735) In 1954, the Supreme Court reversed the *Plessy v. Ferguson* decision (1896), which established the "separate but equal" doctrine. The *Brown* decision found segregation in schools inherently unequal and initiated a long and difficult effort to integrate the nation's public schools.

Camp David Accords (p. 792) In 1978, President Jimmy Carter mediated a peace agreement between the leaders of Egypt and Israel at Camp David. In 1979, Israel and Egypt signed a peace treaty based on the accords.

Chinese Exclusion Act of 1882 (p. 435) Legislation passed in 1882 that excluded Chinese immigrants for ten years and denied U.S. citizenship to Chinese nationals. It was the first U.S. exclusionary law aimed at a specific racial group.

Civilian Conservation Corps (CCC) (p. 662) One of the most popular **New Deal** programs, the CCC provided 300,000 young men between the ages of 18 and 25 with government jobs in reforestation and other conservation projects..

Civil Rights Cases (p. 484) A group of cases in 1883 in which the Supreme Court ruled that the Fourteenth Amendment barred state governments from discriminating on the basis of race but did not prevent private individuals or organizations from doing so. The ruling dealt a major blow to efforts to protect African Americans.

Clayton Antitrust Act (p. 598) This law outlawed interlocking directorates (in which the same people served as directors for several competing companies), forbade policies that created monopolies, and made corporate officers responsible for antitrust violations. It also declared that unions were not conspiracies in restraint of trade and outlawed the use of injunctions in labor disputes unless they were necessary to protect property.

Coercive Acts (p. 126) Also known as the Intolerable Acts, the four pieces of legislation passed by Parliament in response to the Boston Tea Party to punish Massachusetts.

Columbian Exchange (p. 12) The exchange of plants, animals, and diseases between Europe and the Americas from first contact throughout the era of exploration.

Committee of correspondence (p. 125) Communication network formed in Massachusetts and other colonies to communicate grievances and provide colonists with evidence of British oppression.

Committee on Public Information (CPI) (p. 621) Created in 1917 by President Wilson and headed by progressive journalist George Creel, this organization rallied support for American involvement in World War I through art, advertising, and film. Creel worked out a system of voluntary censorship with the press and distributed posters and pamphlets.

Common Sense **(p. 129)** Revolutionary tract written by Thomas Paine in 1776. It called for independence and a republican government in America.

Compromise of 1850 (p. 339) Five federal laws that temporarily calmed the sectional crisis. The compromise made California a free state, ended the slave trade in the District of Columbia, and strengthened the Fugitive Slave Law.

Compromise of 1877 (p. 410) Compromise struck during the contested presidential election of 1876, in which Democrats accepted the election of Rutherford B. Hayes (Republican) in exchange for the withdrawal of federal troops from the South and the end of Reconstruction.

Comstock Lode (p. 434) Discovered in 1859 near Virginia City, Nevada, this ore deposit was the richest discovery in the history of mining. Named after T. P. Comstock, the deposit produced silver and gold worth more than $306 million.

Conquistadores (p. 16) Sixteenth-century Spanish adventurers, often of noble birth, who subdued the Native Americans and created the Spanish empire in the New World.

Conservation (p. 591) President Theodore Roosevelt made this principle one of his administration's top goals. Conservation in his view aimed at protecting the nation's natural resources, but called for the wise use of them rather than locking them away.

Consumer revolution (p. 96) Period between 1740 and 1770 when English exports to the American colonies increased by 360 percent to satisfy Americans' demand for consumer goods.

Containment (p. 708) First proposed by George Kennan in 1947, containment became the basic strategy of the United States throughout the Cold War. Kennan argued that firm American resistance would eventually compel Moscow to adopt more peaceful policies.

Contract with America (p. 816) In the 1994 congressional elections, Congressman Newt Gingrich had Republican candidates sign a document in which they pledged support for such things as a balanced budget amendment, term limits for members of Congress, and a middle-class tax cut.

Cooperationists (p. 361) Southerners in 1860 who advocated secession by the South as a whole rather than unilateral secession by each state.

Copperheads (p. 376) Northern Democrats suspected of being indifferent or hostile to the Union cause in the Civil War.

Cotton gin (p. 285) Invented by Eli Whitney in 1793, this device for separating the seeds from the fibers of short-staple cotton enabled a slave to clean fifty times more cotton as by hand, which reduced production costs and gave new life to slavery in the South.

Coureurs de bois **(p. 21)** Fur trappers in French Canada who lived among the Native Americans.

"Court-packing" scheme (p. 671) Concerned that the conservative Supreme Court might declare all his New Deal programs unconstitutional, President Franklin D. Roosevelt asked Congress to allow him to appoint additional justices to the Court. Both Congress and the public rejected this "court-packing" scheme.

Crittenden compromise (p. 363) Introduced by Kentucky Senator John Crittenden in 1861 in an attempt to prevent secession and civil war, it would have extended the Missouri Compromise line west to the Pacific.

Cuban missile crisis (p. 747) In October 1962, the United States and the Soviet Union came close to nuclear war when President John F. Kennedy insisted that Nikita Khrushchev remove the 42 missiles he had secretly deployed in Cuba. The Soviets eventually did so, and the crisis ended.

Cult of Domesticity (p. 297) Term used to characterize the dominant gender role for white women in the antebellum period. It stressed the virtue of women as guardians of the home, which was considered their proper sphere.

Dartmouth College v. Woodward **(p. 237)** In this 1819 case, the Supreme Court ruled that the Constitution protected charters given to corporations by states.

Dawes Severalty Act (p. 427) Legislation passed by Congress in 1887 that aimed to break up traditional Indian life by promoting individual land ownership. It divided tribal lands into small plots that were distributed among members of each tribe. Provisions were made for education and eventual citizenship. The law led to corruption and exploitation and weakened tribal culture.

D-Day (p. 695) June 6, 1944, the day Allied troops crossed the English Channel and opened a second front in western Europe during World War II. The "D" stands for "disembarkation": to leave a ship and go ashore.

Desert Storm (p. 808) Desert Storm was the code name used the United States and its coalition partners used in the war against Iraq in 1991 to liberate Kuwait.

Détente (p. 778) President Richard Nixon and Henry Kissinger pursued a policy of détente, a French word meaning a relaxation of tension, with the Soviet Union to lessen the possibility of nuclear war in the 1970s.

"Dollar diplomacy" (p. 610) The Taft administration's policy in the early 1900s to promote U.S. financial and business interests abroad, especially in Latin America.

Dominion of New England (p. 78) Incorporation of the New England colonies under a single appointed royal governor that lasted from 1686–1689.

Eastern Woodland Cultures (p. 9) Term given to Indians from the Northeast region who lived on the Atlantic coast and supplemented farming with seasonal hunting and gathering.

Emancipation Proclamation (p. 373) On January 1, 1863, President Abraham Lincoln proclaimed that the slaves of the Confederacy were free. Since the South had not yet been defeated, the proclamation did not immediately free anyone, but it made emancipation an explicit war aim of the North.

Embargo Act (p. 213) In response to a British attack on an American warship off the coast of Virginia, this 1807 law prohibited foreign commerce.

***Encomienda* system (p. 19)** An exploitative system by Spanish rulers that granted conquistadors control of Native American villages and their inhabitants' labor.

Enlightenment (p. 93) Philosophical and intellectual movement that began in Europe during the eighteenth century. It stressed the use of reason to solve social and scientific problems.

Enumerated goods (p. 74) Raw materials, such as tobacco, sugar, and rice, that were produced in the British colonies and under the Navigation Acts had to be shipped only to England or its colonies.

Equal Rights Amendment (ERA) (p. 786) A proposed constitutional amendment passed by Congress in 1972 to guarantee women equal treatment under the law. The amendment failed to be ratified in 1982.

Era of Good Feeling (p. 234) A description of the two terms of President James Monroe (1817–1823) during which partisan conflict abated and federal initiatives suggested increased nationalism.

Espionage Act (p. 621) This law, passed after the United States entered World War I, imposed sentences of up to 20 years on anyone found guilty of aiding the enemy, obstructing recruitment of soldiers, or encouraging disloyalty. It allowed the postmaster general to remove from the mail any materials that incited treason or insurrection.

Exodusters (p. 439) A group of about 6,000 African Americans who left Louisiana, Mississippi, and Texas in 1879, for freer lives as farmers or laborers in Kansas.

Farewell Address (p. 186) In this 1796 document, President George Washington announced his intention not to seek a third term. He also stressed federalist interests and warned Americans against political factions and foreign entanglements.

Federal Reserve Act (p. 597) This 1913 act created a central banking system, consisting of 12 regional banks governed by the Federal Reserve Board. It was an attempt to provide the United States with a sound yet flexible currency.

Federalist (p. 163) Supporter of the Constitution who advocated its ratification.

Fifteenth Amendment (p. 393) Ratified in 1870, it prohibits the denial or abridgment of the right to vote by the federal or state governments on the basis of race, color, or prior condition as a slave. It was intended to guarantee African Americans the right to vote in the South.

Fireside chats (p. 661) Radio addresses by President Franklin D. Roosevelt from 1933 to 1944, in which he spoke to the American people about such issues as the banking crisis, Social Security, and World War II. The chats enhanced Roosevelt's popularity among ordinary Americans.

First Continental Congress (p. 127) A meeting of delegates from 12 colonies in Philadelphia in 1774, the Congress denied

Parliament's authority to legislate for the colonies, condemned British actions toward the colonies, created the Continental Association, and endorsed a call to take up arms.

Food Administration (p. 623) A government agency that encouraged Americans to save food during World War II.

Force Acts (p. 407) Designed to protect black voters in the South from the Ku Klux Klan in 1870–1871, these laws placed state elections under federal jurisdiction and imposed fines and punished those guilty of interfering with any citizen exercising his right to vote.

Fourteen Points (p. 626) In January 1918, President Woodrow Wilson presented these terms for a far-reaching, nonpunitive settlement of World War I and the establishment of a League of Nations. While generous and optimistic, the Points did not satisfy wartime hunger for revenge and were largely rejected by European nations.

Fourteenth Amendment (p. 393) Ratified in 1868, it provided citizenship to ex-slaves after the Civil War and constitutionally protected equal rights under the law for all citizens. Radical Republicans used it to enact a congressional Reconstruction policy in the former Confederate states.

Freedmen's Bureau (p. 393) Agency established by Congress in March 1865 to provide freedmen with shelter, food, and medical aid and to help them establish schools and find employment. The Bureau was dissolved in 1872.

Freedom ride (p. 751) Sponsored by the Congress of Racial Equality (CORE), freedom rides on buses by civil rights advocates in 1961 in the South were designed to test the enforcement of federal regulations that prohibited segregation in interstate public transportation.

French Revolution (p. 182) A social and political revolution in France (1789–1799).

Fugitive Slave Law (p. 340) Passed in 1850, this federal law made it easier for slaveowners to recapture runaway slaves; it also made it easier for kidnappers to take free blacks. The law became an object of hatred in the North.

Ghost Dances (p. 426) A religious movement that arose in the late nineteenth century under the prophet Wavoka, a Paiute Indian. Its followers believed that dances and rites would cause white men to disappear and restore lands to the Native Americans. The U.S. government outlawed the Ghost Dances, and army intervention to stop them led to the **Wounded Knee Massacre**.

***Gibbons v. Ogden* (p. 238)** In this 1824 case, the Supreme Court expanded the power of the federal government to regulate interstate commerce.

Glorious Revolution (p. 78) Replacement of James II by William III and Mary II as English monarchs in 1688, marking the beginning of constitutional monarchy in Britain.

Gold Rush of 1849 (p. 429) Prospectors made the first gold strikes along the Sierra Nevada Mountains in California in 1849, touching off a mining boom that set the pattern for subsequent strikes in other regions.

Gold Standard Act (p. 519) Passed by Congress in 1900, this law made all currency redeemable in gold. The United States remained on the gold standard until 1933.

Great Awakening (p. 98) Widespread evangelical religious revival movement of the mid-1700s. It divided congregations and weakened the authority of established churches in the colonies.

Great Migration (p. 44) Migration of 16,000 Puritans from England to the Massachusetts Bay Colony during the 1630s.

Great Society (p. 756) President Lyndon Johnson's name for his version of the Democratic reform program. In 1965, Congress passed many Great Society measures, including **Medicare**, civil rights legislation, and federal aid to education.

Greenbacks (p. 368) Paper currency issued by the Union during the Civil War.

Gulf of Tonkin Resolution (p. 760) After a North Vietnamese attack on an American destroyer in the Gulf of Tonkin in 1964, Congress gave President Lyndon authority in this resolution to use force in Vietnam.

Harlem Renaissance (p. 641) An African American cultural, literary, and artistic movement centered in Harlem, in New York City, in the 1920s. Harlem, the largest black community in the world outside of Africa, was considered the cultural capital of African Americans.

Hartford Convention (p. 218) An assembly of New England Federalists who met in Hartford, Connecticut, in December 1814 to protest President James Madison's foreign policy in the War of 1812, which had undermined commercial interests in the North. They proposed amending the Constitution to prevent future presidents from declaring war without a two-thirds majority in Congress.

Hay–Bunau–Varilla Treaty (p. 608) This 1903 treaty with Colombia granted the United States control over a canal zone ten miles wide across the Isthmus of Panama.

Headright (p. 37) System of land distribution in which settlers were granted a 50-acre plot of land from the colonial government for each servant or dependent they transported to the New World. It encouraged the recruitment of a large servile labor force.

Hepburn Act (p. 590) A 1906 law that strengthened the power of the **Interstate Commerce Commission (ICC)** to regulate the railroads.

Homestead Act of 1862 (p. 431) Legislation granting 160 acres to anyone who paid a $10 fee and pledged to live on and cultivate the land for five years. Between 1862 and 1900, nearly 600,000 families claimed homesteads under its provisions.

Homestead Strike (p. 466) In July 1892, wage-cutting at Andrew Carnegie's Homestead Steel Plant in Pittsburgh provoked a violent strike in which three company-hired detectives and ten workers died. Using ruthless force and strikebreakers, company officials broke the strike and destroyed the union.

House of Burgesses (p. 37) The elective representative assembly in colonial Virginia.

Imperialism (p. 527) The policy of extending a nation's power over other areas through military conquest, economic domination, or annexation.

Implied powers (p. 179) Powers the Constitution did not explicitly grant the federal government, but that it could be interpreted to grant.

Indentured servants (pp. 37) Persons who agreed to serve a master for a set number of years in exchange for the cost of transport to America. Indentured servitude was the dominant form of labor in the Chesapeake colonies before slavery.

Industrial Workers of the World (IWW) (p. 565) Founded in 1905, this radical union, also known as the Wobblies, aimed to unite the American working class into one union. It organized unskilled and foreign-born laborers, advocated social revolution, and led strikes.

Intermediate Nuclear Forces Treaty (p. 799) Signed by President Ronald Reagan and Soviet President Mikhail Gorbachev in late 1987, this agreement provided for the destruction of all intermediate-range nuclear missiles and permitted on-site inspection for the first time during the Cold War.

Iran-Contra affair (p. 797) The Iran-Contra affair involved officials in the Reagan administration secretly and illegally selling arms to Iran and using the proceeds to finance the Contra rebels in Nicaragua.

Iranian hostage crisis (p. 792) In 1979, Iranian fundamentalists seized the American embassy in Tehran and held 53 Americans hostage for over a year. The hostages were released on January 20, 1981, the day Ronald Reagan became president.

Iron Curtain (p. 705) Winston Churchill coined the phrase "Iron Curtain" to refer to the boundary in Europe that divided Soviet-dominated Eastern and Central Europe from Western Europe.

Isolationism (p. 527) A belief that the United States should avoid entanglements with other nations.

Itinerant preachers (p. 99) These charismatic preachers spread revivalism throughout America during the Great Awakening.

Jay's Treaty (p. 183) Treaty with Britain negotiated by Chief Justice John Jay in 1794. Though the British agreed to surrender forts on U.S. territory, the treaty provoked a storm of protest in America.

Jim Crow laws (p. 411) Segregation laws enacted by southern states after Reconstruction.

Joint-stock company (p. 33) Business enterprise that enabled investors to pool money for commerce and funding for colonies.

Judicial review (p. 206) The authority of the Supreme Court to determine the constitutionality of statutes.

Kansas-Nebraska Act (p. 343) This 1854 act repealed the Missouri Compromise, split the Louisiana Purchase into two territories, and allowed its settlers to accept or reject slavery by popular sovereignty.

Kellogg–Briand Pact (p. 677) Also called the Pact of Paris, this 1928 agreement was the brainchild of U.S. Secretary of State

Frank B. Kellogg and French premier Aristide Briand. Its signatories, eventually including nearly all nations, pledged to shun war as an instrument of policy. It had little effect on the conduct of world affairs.

Kentucky and Virginia Resolutions (p. 192) Statements penned by Thomas Jefferson and James Madison to mobilize opposition to the Alien and Sedition Acts, which they argued were unconstitutional. Jefferson's statement (the Kentucky Resolution) suggested that states could declare null and void congressional acts they deemed unconstitutional. (See **Nullification**.)

Knights of Labor (p. 463) Founded in 1869, this labor organization pursued broad-gauged reform and practical issues such as improved wages and hours. The Knights welcomed all laborers regardless of race, gender, or skill.

Ku Klux Klan (p. 407) A secret terrorist society first organized in Tennessee in 1866. The original Klan's goals were to disfranchise African Americans, stop Reconstruction, and restore the prewar social order of the South. The Ku Klux Klan re-formed in the twentieth century to promote white supremacy and combat aliens, Catholics, and Jews.

Lend-Lease (p. 683) In 1941, Congress gave President Franklin D. Roosevelt the authority to sell, lend, lease, or transfer war materials to any country whose defense he declared vital to that of the United States.

Levittown (p. 727) In 1947, William Levitt used mass production techniques to build inexpensive houses in suburban New York to help relieve the postwar housing shortage. Levittown became a symbol of the postwar move to the suburbs.

Lewis and Clark Expedition (p. 207) Overland expedition to the Pacific coast (1804–1806) led by Meriwether Lewis and William Clark. Commissioned by President Thomas Jefferson, it collected scientific data about the country and its resources.

Louisiana Purchase (p. 207) U.S. acquisition of the Louisiana Territory from France in 1803 for $15 million. The purchase secured American control of the Mississippi River and doubled the size of the nation.

Loyalists (p. 117) Colonists sided with Britain during the American Revolution.

Manhattan Project (p. 698) The top-secret World War II program that produced the first atomic weapons.

Manifest Destiny (p. 315) Coined in 1845, this term referred to a doctrine in support of territorial expansion based on the belief that the United States should expand to encompass all of North America.

Marbury v. Madison **(p. 209)** In this 1803 landmark decision, the Supreme Court first asserted the power of judicial review by declaring an act of Congress unconstitutional.

March on Washington (p. 753) In August 1963, civil rights leaders organized a massive rally in Washington to urge passage of President John F. Kennedy's civil rights bill. The high point was Martin Luther King, Jr.'s "I Have a Dream" speech.

Marshall Plan (p. 710) In 1947, A massive aid program to rebuild the war-torn economies of Western Europe. The plan was motivated by both humanitarian concerns and fear of communism.

Mayflower Compact (p. 41) Agreement among the Pilgrims aboard the Mayflower in 1620 to create a civil government at Plymouth Colony.

McCarthyism (p. 720) A sensationalist campaign by Senator Joseph McCarthy against supposed communists in government that began in 1950 and ended when the Senate censured him in 1954.

McCulloch v. Maryland **(p. 238)** This 1819 ruling asserted the supremacy of federal power over state power and the legal doctrine that the Constitution could be broadly interpreted. (See **Implied powers**.)

Medicare (p. 757) The 1965 Medicare Act provided Social Security funding for hospitalization insurance for people over age 65 and the disabled and a voluntary plan to cover doctor bills paid in part by the federal government.

Mercantilism (p. 73) An economic theory that shaped imperial policy throughout the colonial period, mercantilism assumed that the supply of wealth was fixed. To increase its wealth, a nation needed to export more goods than it imported. Favorable trade and protective economic policies and colonial possessions rich in raw materials were important in achieving this balance.

Mexican-American War (p. 321) Conflict (1846–1848) between the United States and Mexico after the U.S. annexation of Texas. As victor, the United States acquired vast new territories from Mexico.

Middle ground (p. 90) A geographical area where two distinct cultures meet and merge with neither bolding a clear upper hand.

Missouri Compromise (p. 235) A sectional compromise in 1820 that admitted Missouri to the Union as a slave state and Maine as a free state. It also banned slavery in the remainder of the Louisiana Purchase territory above the latitude of 36°30'.

Monroe Doctrine (p. 240) A key foreign policy declaration made by President James Monroe in 1823, it declared the Western Hemisphere off limits to new European colonization; in return, the United States promised not to meddle in European affairs.

Montgomery bus boycott (p. 737) In late 1955, African Americans led by Martin Luther King, Jr., boycotted the buses in Montgomery, Alabama, after seamstress Rosa Parks was arrested for refusing to move to the back of a bus. The boycott, which ended when the Supreme Court ruled in favor of the protesters, marked the beginning of a new, activist phase of the civil rights movement.

Moral diplomacy (p. 611) Policy of President Woodrow Wilson that rejected "**dollar diplomacy**." Rather than focusing mainly on economic ties with other nations, Wilson sought to practice morality in international relations, preserve peace, and extend to other peoples the blessings of democracy.

Moral Majority (p. 776) In 1979, the Reverend Jerry Falwell founded the Moral Majority to combat "amoral liberals," drug abuse, "coddling" of criminals, homosexuality, communism, and abortion. The Moral Majority represented the rise of political activism among organized religion's radical right wing.

Muckrakers (p. 552) Writers who made a practice between 1903 and 1909 of exposing the wrongdoings of public figures and corporations and highlighting social and political problems.

Mugwumps (p. 480) Educated and upper-class reformers who crusaded for lower tariffs, limited federal government, and civil service reform. They were best known for helping elect Grover Cleveland president in 1884.

National American Woman Suffrage Association (pp. 483) Founded by Susan B. Anthony in 1890, this organization worked to secure women the right to vote. It stressed careful organization and peaceful lobbying.

National Association for the Advancement of Colored People (NAACP) (p. 561) Created in 1909, this organization became the most important civil rights organization in the country.

National Farmers' Alliance and Industrial Union (p. 506) The Alliance sought to organize farmers in the South and West to fight for reforms that would improve their lot, including measures to overcome low crop prices, burdensome mortgages, and high railroad rates. The Alliance ultimately organized the People's (Populist) party.

National Grange of the Patrons of Husbandry (p. 440) Founded by Oliver H. Kelly in 1867, the Grange sought to relieve the drabness of farm life by providing a social, educational, and cultural outlet for its members. It also set up grain elevators, cooperative stores, warehouses, insurance companies, and farm machinery factories.

National Organization for Women (NOW) (p. 768) Founded in 1966, NOW called for equal employment opportunity and equal pay for women. It also championed the legalization of abortion and an equal rights amendment to the Constitution.

National Origins Quota Act (p. 647) This 1924 law established a quota system that restricted immigration from Asia and southern and Eastern Europe and reduced the annual total of immigrants.

National Reclamation Act (Newlands Act) (p. 431) Passed in 1902, this legislation set aside most of the proceeds from the sale of public land in 16 Western states to fund irrigation projects.

National Recovery Administration (NRA) (p. 662) This New Deal agency was created in 1933 to promote economic recovery and revive industry during the Great Depression. It permitted manufacturers to establish industrywide codes of "fair business practices" setting prices and production levels. It also provided for minimum wages and maximum working hours for labor and guaranteed labor the right to organize and bargain collectively (Section 7a). The Supreme Court declared it unconstitutional in 1935.

National Security Act (p. 712) Congress passed the National Security Act in 1947 in response to perceived threats from the Soviet Union after World War II. It established the Department of Defense and created the Central Intelligence Agency (CIA) and National Security Council.

Nativism (p. 646) Hostility to things foreign.

Natural rights (p. 151) Fundamental rights over which the government should exercise no control.

Navigation Acts (p. 74) Commercial restrictions that regulated colonial commerce to favor England's accumulation of wealth. (See **Mercantilism**.)

Nazi Holocaust (p. 696) The slaughter of six million Jews and other persons by Hitler's regime.

Neoconservatism (p. 777) Former liberals who advocated a strong stand against communism abroad and free market capitalism at home. These intellectuals stressed the positive values of American society in contrast to those liberals who emphasized social problems.

Neutrality Acts (p. 680) Laws in the 1930s that forbade selling munitions or lending money to belligerents. The 1937 act required that all other trade with countries at war be conducted on a cash-and-carry basis.

New Deal (p. 656) President Franklin Delano Roosevelt's program to combat the Great Depression.

New Freedom (p. 596) President Woodrow Wilson's program, which emphasized business competition and small government. It sought to rein in federal authority, release individual energy, and restore competition. It achieved many of the progressive social-justice objectives while pushing for a free economy rather than a planned one.

New Frontier (p. 744) President John F. Kennedy's program to revitalize the stagnant economy and enact reform legislation in education, health care, and civil rights.

New immigrants (p. 475) Starting in the 1880s, immigration into the United States began to shift from northern and Western Europe to southern and eastern Europe. These new immigrants were mostly poor, non-Protestant, and unskilled; they tended to stay in close-knit communities and retain their language, customs, and religions. Between 1880 and 1910, approximately 8.4 million of these so-called new immigrants came to the United States.

New Nationalism (p. 595) President Theodore Roosevelt's program calling for a national approach to the country's affairs and a strong president to deal with them; efficiency in government and society; and protection of children, women, and workers. It accepted "good" trusts; and exalted the expert and the executive. It also encouraged large concentrations of capital and labor.

Niagara Movement (p. 560) A movement, led by W. E. B. Du Bois, that focused on equal rights for and the education of African American youth. Rejecting the gradualist approach of Booker T. Washington, it favored militant action and claimed for African Americans all the rights afforded to other Americans.

North American Free Trade Agreement (NAFTA) (p. 815) A free trade plan among the United States, Canada, and Mexico enacted by Congress in 1993.

North Atlantic Treaty Organization (NATO) (p. 710) In 1949, the United States, Canada, and ten European nations formed this military mutual-defense pact.

Northwest Ordinance (p. 155) Legislation in 1787 that established governments in America's northwest territories, defined a procedure for their admission to the Union as states, and prohibited slavery north of the Ohio River.

NSC-68 (p. 713) National Security Council planning paper No. 68 redefined America's national defense policy. Adopted in 1950, it committed the United States to a massive military buildup to meet the challenge posed by the Soviet Union.

Nullification (p. 258) The supposed right of any state to declare a federal law inoperative within its boundaries. In 1832, South Carolina nullified the federal tariff.

Ocala Demands (p. 508) Adopted by the Farmers' Alliance in 1890 in Ocala, Florida, these demands became the organization's main platform. They called for a sub-treasury system to allow farmers to store their crops until they could get the best price, the free coinage of silver, an end to protective tariffs and national banks, a federal income tax, the direct election of senators by voters, and tighter regulation of railroads. (See **People's party**.)

Open Door Policy (p. 545) This policy established free trade between the United States and China in 1900 and attempted to induce European nations and Japan to recognize the territorial integrity of China. It marked a departure from the American tradition of **isolationism** and signaled the country's growing involvement in the world.

Organization of the Petroleum Exporting Countries (OPEC) (p. 782) A cartel of oil-exporting nations.

Ostend Manifesto (p. 344) Written by American diplomats in 1854, this secret memorandum urged acquiring Cuba by any means necessary. When it became public, northerners claimed it was a plot to extend slavery, and the manifesto was disavowed.

Overland Trail (p. 429) The route from the Mississippi Valley to the Pacific Coast in the last half of the nineteenth century.

Panic of 1837 (p. 262) A financial depression that lasted until the 1840s.

Parliamentary sovereignty (p. 116) Principle that emphasized Parliament's power to govern colonial affairs.

Peace of Paris of 1763 (p. 108) Treaty ending the French and Indian War by which France ceded Canada to Britain.

Pearl Harbor (p. 686) On December 7, 1941, Japanese warplanes attacked the U.S. fleet at Pearl Harbor, Hawaii. The attack marked America's entrance into World War II.

Pendleton Act (p. 503) This 1883 law created a bipartisan Civil Service Commission to administer competitive exams for civil service jobs and appoint officeholders based on merit. It also outlawed compulsory political contributions from appointed officials.

People's (or Populist) party (p. 508) This political party was organized in 1892 by farm, labor, and reform leaders, mainly from the Farmers' Alliance. It offered a broad-based reform platform reflecting the **Ocala Demands**. After 1896, it became identified as a one-issue party focused on free silver and gradually died away.

Perfectionism (p. 294) The doctrine that a state of freedom from sin is attainable on earth.

Philippine-American War (p. 543) A war fought from 1899 to 1903 to quell Filipino resistance to U.S. control of the Philippine Islands.

Placer mining (p. 433) Mining that included using a shovel and washing pan to separate gold from the ore in streams and riverbeds. Placer miners worked as individuals or in small groups.

Plessy v. Ferguson **(p. 484)** A Supreme Court case in 1896 that established the doctrine of "separate but equal." The Court applied it to schools in *Cumming v. County Board of Education* (1899) . The doctrine was finally overturned in 1954, in *Brown v. Board of Education of Topeka*.

Popular sovereignty (p. 338) The concept that the settlers of a newly organized territory had the right to decide (through voting) whether to accept slavery.

Potsdam Conference (p. 703) The final wartime meeting of the leaders of the United States, Britain, and the Soviet Union was held at Potsdam, outside Berlin, in July, 1945. Their failure to agree about the future of Europe led to the Cold War.

Pragmatism (p. 582) An early twentieth-century doctrine, based on the ideas of William James. Pragmatists were impatient with the concept of truth as an abstract reality. They believed that truth should work for the individual and that people were not only shaped by their environment but also helped to shape it. If an idea worked, it became truth.

Preemption (p. 225) The right of first purchase of public land. Settlers enjoyed this right even if they squatted on the land in advance of government surveyors.

Progressive (or "Bull Moose") party (p. 577) This political party was formed by Theodore Roosevelt to advance progressive ideas and unseat President William Howard Taft in 1912.

Progressivism (p. 552) Movement for social change between the late 1890s and World War I. Its orgins lay in a fear of big business and corrupt government and a desire to improve living conditions. Progressives set out to cure the social ills brought about by industrialization and urbanization, social disorder, and corruption.

Prohibition (p. 644) The ban on the manufacture, sale, and transportation of alcoholic beverages in the United States. The Eighteenth Amendment, adopted in 1919, established prohibition. It was repealed by the Twenty-First Amendment in 1933.

Protestant Reformation (p. 21) Sixteenth-century religious movement to reform and challenge the spiritual authority of the Roman Catholic Church.

Pullman strike (p. 510) Beginning in May 1894, this strike at the Pullman Palace Car Company near Chicago was one of the largest strikes in American history. Workers struck to protest wage cuts, high rents for company housing, and layoffs. The American Railway Union, led by Eugene V. Debs, joined the strike in June. Extending into 27 states and territories, it paralyzed the western half of the nation. President Grover Cleveland secured an injunction to break the strike on the grounds that it obstructed the mail, and sent federal troops to enforce it.

Puritans (p. 42) Members of a reformed Protestant sect in Europe and America that insisted on removing all vestiges of Catholicism from religious practice.

Quakers (p. 51) Members of a radical religious group, formally known as the Society of Friends, that rejects formal theology and stress each person's "inner light," a spiritual guide to righteousness.

Quasi-war (p. 188) Undeclared war between the United States and France in the late 1790s.

Radical Reconstruction (p. 394) The Reconstruction Acts of 1867 divided the South into five military districts. They required the states to guarantee black male suffrage and to ratify the **Fourteenth Amendment** as a condition of their readmission to the Union.

Radical Republicans (p. 390) Congressional Republicans who insisted on black suffrage and federal protection of civil rights of African Americans.

Red Scare (p. 642) A wave of anticommunist, antiforeign, and antilabor hysteria that swept over America in 1919. It resulted in the deportation of many alien residents and violated the civil liberties of many of its victims.

Redeemers (p. 410) A loose coalition of prewar Democrats, Confederate veterans, and Whigs who took over southern state governments in the 1870s, supposedly "redeeming" them from the corruption of Reconstruction. They shared a commitment to white supremacy and laissez-faire economics.

Republicanism (p. 144) Concept that ultimate political authority is vested in the citizens of the nation.

Roe v. Wade **(p. 787)** The 1973 Supreme Court decision that women have a constitutional right to abortion during the early stages of pregnancy.

Roosevelt Corollary (p. 609) A corollary to the Monroe Doctrine, which asserted that the United States would intervene in Latin American affairs if those countries could not keep their affairs in order.

Royal African Company (p. 70) Slaving company created to meet colonial planters' demands for black laborers.

Sanitary Commission (p. 380) An association chartered by the government during the Civil War to promote health in the northern army's camps though cleanliness, nutrition, and medical care.

Scopes trial (p. 647) Also called the "monkey trial," the 1924 Scopes trial was a contest between modern liberalism and religious fundamentalism. John T. Scopes was prosecuted for teaching Darwinian evolution in defiance of Tennessee state law. He was found guilty and fined $100. Scopes's conviction was later set aside on a technicality.

Second Continental Congress (p. 128) A gathering of colonial representatives in Philadelphia in 1775 that organized the Continental Army and began requisitioning men and supplies for the war effort.

Second Great Awakening (p. 292) Evangelical Protestant revivals that swept over America in the early nineteenth century.

Second-party system (p. 263) Historians' term for the national two-party rivalry between Democrats and **Whigs**. The second-party system began in the 1830s and ended in the 1850s with the demise of the Whigs and the rise of the Republican party.

Sedition Act (p. 621) A World War I law that imposed harsh penalties on anyone using "disloyal, profane, scurrilous, or abusive language about the U.S. government, flag, or armed forces.

Selective Service Act (p. 619) This 1917 law required all American men between the ages of 21 and 30 to register for a military draft. The age limits were later changed to 18 and 45.

Seneca Falls Convention (p. 308) An 1848 gathering of women's rights advocates that culminated in the adoption of a Declaration of Sentiments demanding voting and property rights for women.

Settlement houses (p. 492) Located in poor districts, these community centers tried to soften the impact of urban life for immigrant and other families. Often run by young, educated women, they provided social services and a political voice for their neighborhoods. Chicago's Hull House, founded by Jane Addams in 1889, was the most famous of them.

Seven Years' War (p. 106) Worldwide conflict (1756–1763) that pitted Britain against France. With help from the American colonists, the British won the war and eliminated France as a power on the North American continent. Also known as the French and Indian War. (See **Peace of Paris of 1763**.)

Sharecropping (p. 400) After the Civil War, the southern states adopted a sharecropping system as a compromise between former slaves who wanted land of their own and former slave owners who needed labor. The landowners provided land, tools, and seed to a farming family, who in turn provided labor. The resulting crop was divided between them, with the farmers receiving a "share" of one-third to one-half of the crop.

Shays's Rebellion (p. 158) Armed insurrection of farmers in western Massachusetts led by Daniel Shays. Intended to prevent state courts from foreclosing on debtors unable to pay their taxes, the rebellion was put down by the state militia. Nationalists used the event to call a constitutional convention to strengthen the national government.

Sherman Antitrust Act (p. 504) This 1890 act was the first major U.S. attempt to deal with the problem of the increasing size of business. It declared illegal "every contract, combination in the form of trust or otherwise, or conspiracy, in restraint of trade or commerce."

Sherman Silver Purchase Act (p. 505) An 1890 act that attempted to resolve the controversy over silver coinage by requiring the Treasury to purchase 4.5 million ounces of silver each month and issue legal tender (in the form of Treasury notes) for it. The act pleased opponents of silver because it did not call for free coinage; it pleased proponents of silver because it bought up most of the nation's silver production.

Social Darwinism (p. 490) Adapted by English social philosopher Herbert Spencer from Charles Darwin's theory of evolution, this theory held that the "laws" of evolution applied to human life, that change or reform therefore took centuries, and that the "fittest" would succeed in business and social relationships. It promoted competition and individualism, saw government intervention into human affair as futile, and was used by the economic and social elite to oppose reform.

Social Gospel (p. 492) Preached by urban Protestant ministers, the Social Gospel focused as much on improving the conditions of life on earth as on saving souls for the hereafter. Its adherents worked for child-labor laws and measures to alleviate poverty.

Social Security Act (p. 665) The 1935 Social Security Act established a system of old age, unemployment, and survivors' insurance funded by wage and payroll taxes.

Social-justice movement (p. 579) During the 1890s and after, this movement attracted followers who sought to free people from the often devastating impact of urban life. It focused on the need for housing reform, more stringent child labor regulations, and better working conditions for women.

Southern Christian Leadership Conference (SCLC) (p. 738) An organization founded by Martin Luther King, Jr., to fight segregation through passive resistance, nonviolence, and peaceful confrontation.

Spectral evidence (p. 79) In the Salem witch trials, the court allowed reports of dreams and visions in which the accused appeared as the devil's agent to be introduced as testimony. The accused had no defense against this kind of "evidence." When the judges later disallowed this testimony, the executions for witchcraft ended.

Stamp Act Congress (p. 121) Meeting of colonial delegates in New York City in October 1765 to protest the Stamp Act, a law passed by Parliament to raise revenue in America.

Stamp Act of 1765 (p. 120) Placed a tax on newspapers and printed matter produced in the colonies, causing mass opposition by colonists.

Strategic Arms Limitations Talks (SALT) (p. 836) In 1972, the United States and the Soviet Union culminated four years of SALT by signing a treaty limiting the deployment of antiballistic missiles (ABM) and an agreement to freeze the number of offensive missiles for five years.

Strategic Defense Initiative (SDI) (p. 796) Popularly known as "Star Wars," President Ronald Reagan's SDI proposed to construct an elaborate computer-controlled antimissile defense system capable of destroying enemy missiles in outer space.

Student Nonviolent Coordinating Committee (SNCC) (p. 739) A group organized by students to work for equal rights for African Americans. It spearheaded peaceful sit-ins and marches in the early 1960s, but later grew more radical and changed its name to the Student National Coordinating Committee.

Students for a Democratic Society (SDS) (p. 764) Founded in 1962, the SDS was a popular college student organization that protested shortcomings in American life, notably racial injustice and the Vietnam War. It led thousands of protests before it split apart in the late 1960s.

Sunbelt (p. 809) A broad band of states running across the South from Florida to Texas, extending west and north to include California and the Pacific Northwest. Beginning in the 1970s, it experienced rapid economic and population growth.

Supply-side economics (p. 794) The theory that tax cuts would stimulate the economy by giving individuals more incentive to earn more money, which would lead to greater investment and eventually larger tax revenues at a lower rate.

Taft–Hartley Act (p. 718) This 1947 anti-union legislation outlawed the closed shop and secondary boycotts. It also authorized the president to seek injunctions to prevent strikes that threatened national security.

Tariff of abominations (p. 252) An 1828 protective tariff, or tax on imports, that angered southern free traders.

Teapot Dome scandal (p. 648) A 1924 scandal in which Secretary of the Interior Albert Fall was convicted of accepting bribes in exchange for leasing government-owned oil lands in Wyoming (Teapot Dome) and California (Elks Hill) to private businessmen.

Teller Amendment (p. 536) In this amendment to the declaration of war on Spain in 1898, the United States pledged that it did not intend to annex Cuba and that it would recognize Cuban independence after the Spanish-American War.

Temperance movement (p. 480) Temperance—moderation or abstention in the consumption of alcoholic beverages—attracted many advocates in the early nineteenth century. (See **Second Great Awakening**.)

Ten Percent Plan (p. 389) Reconstruction plan proposed by President Abraham Lincoln as a quick way to readmit the former Confederate States. It called for pardon of all southerners except Confederate leaders, and readmission to the Union for any state after 10 percent of its voters signed a loyalty oath and the state abolished slavery.

Tennessee Valley Authority (TVA) (p. 661) A **New Deal** effort created in 1933 to build dams and power plants on the Tennessee River. Its programs helped raise the standard of living for millions in the Tennessee River valley.

Tet offensive (p. 769) In February 1968, the Viet Cong launched a major offensive in the cities of South Vietnam. Although caught by surprise, American and South Vietnam forces quashed this attack. But the Tet offensive was a blow to American public opinion and led President lyndon Johnson to seek a negotiated peace.

The Spanish Armada (p. 25) Spanish fleet sent to invade England in 1588.

Thirteenth Amendment (p. 391) Ratified in 1865, it prohibits slavery and involuntary servitude.

Three-fifths rule (p. 160) Constitutional provision that for every five slaves a state would receive credit for three free voters in determining seats for the House of Representatives.

Trail of Tears (p. 256) In the winter of 1838–1839, the Cherokee were forced to evacuate their lands in Georgia and travel under military guard to present-day Oklahoma. Exposure and disease killed roughly one-quarter of the 16,000 forced migrants en route.

Treaty of Guadalupe Hidalgo (p. 322) Signed in 1848, this treaty ended the Mexican-American War. Mexico relinquished its claims to Texas and ceded an additional 500,000 square miles to the United States for $15 million.

Treaty of Paris (p. 542) Treaty in December 1898 ending the Spanish-American War. Under its terms, Spain recognized Cuba's independence, assumed the Cuban debt, and ceded Puerto Rico, Guam, and the Philippines to the United States.

Treaty of Paris of 1783 (p. 138) Agreement establishing American independence after the Revolutionary War. It also transferred territory east of the Mississippi River, except for Spanish Florida, to the new republic.

Treaty of Tordesillas (p. 17) Treaty negotiated by the pope in 1494 that divided the world along a north–south line in the middle of the Atlantic Ocean, granting Spain all lands west of the line and Portugal lands east of the line.

Truman Doctrine (p. 709) In 1947, President Truman asked Congress for money to aid the Greek and Turkish governments that were then threatened by communist rebels. Truman asserted that the United States was committed to support free people everywhere against communist attack or rebellion.

Trunk lines (p. 450) Four major railroad networks that emerged after the Civil War to connect the eastern seaports to the Great Lakes and western rivers. They reflected the growing integration of transportation across the country that helped spur large-scale industrialization.

Trust (p. 456) A device to centralize and make more efficient the management of diverse and far-flung business operations. It allowed stockholders to exchange their stock certificates for trust certificates, on which dividends were paid. John D. Rockefeller organized the first major trust, the Standard Oil Trust, in 1882.

Turner's thesis (p. 441) Put forth by historian Frederick Jackson Turner in 1893, this thesis asserted that the existence of a frontier and its settlement had shaped American character; given rise to individualism, independence, and self-confidence; and fostered the American spirit of invention and adaptation. Later historians modified the thesis by pointing out the environmental and other consequences of frontier settlement, the federal government's role in peopling the West, and the clash of races and cultures that took place on the frontier.

Underground Railroad (p. 274) A network of safe houses organized by abolitionists (usually free blacks) to help slaves escape to the North or Canada.

Underwood Tariff Act (p. 597) This 1913 law reduced tariff rates and levied a graduated income tax to make up for the lost revenue.

Undocumented aliens (p. 811) Illegal immigrants, mainly from Mexico and Central America.

Unilateralism (p. 824) A national policy of acting alone without consulting others.

Vesey conspiracy (p. 274) An unsuccessful 1822 plot to burn Charleston, South Carolina, and initiate a general slave revolt, led by a free African American, Denmark Vesey.

Virgin of Guadalupe (p. 20) Apparition of the Virgin Mary that has become a symbol of Mexican nationalism.

Virginia Plan (p. 159) Offered by James Madison and the Virginia delegation at the Constitutional Convention, this proposal called for a strong executive office and two houses of Congress, each with representation proportional to a state's population.

Voting Rights Act of 1965 (p. 758) The 1965 Voting Rights Act banned literacy tests for voting rights and provided for federal registrars to assure the franchise to minority voters.

Wade–Davis Bill (p. 390) In 1864, Congress passed the Wade-Davis bill to counter Lincoln's **Ten Percent Plan** for Reconstruction. The bill required that a majority of a former Confederate state's white male population take a loyalty oath and guarantee equality for African Americans. President Lincoln pocket-vetoed the bill.

Wagner Act (p. 667) The 1935 Wagner Act, formally known as the National Labor Relations Act, created the National Labor Relations Board to supervise union elections and designate winning unions as official bargaining agents. The board could also issue cease-and-desist orders to employers who dealt unfairly with their workers.

War Hawks (p. 216) Congressional leaders who, in 1811 and 1812, called for war against Britain.

War Industries Board (WIB) (p. 622) This government agency oversaw the production of American factories during World War I.

War of 1812 (p. 217) War between Britain and the United States. U.S. justifications for war included British violations of American maritime rights, impressment of seamen, provocation of the Indians, and defense of national honor.

War on poverty (p. 756) President Lyndon Johnson declared war on poverty in his 1964 State of the Union address. A new Office of Economic Opportunity (OEO) oversaw programs to help the poor.

War on terror (p. 823) Initiated by President George W. Bush after the attacks of September 11, 2001, the broadly defined war on terror aimed to weed out terrorist operatives and their supporters throughout the world.

Watergate scandal (p. 781) A break-in at the Democratic National Committee offices in the Watergate complex in Washington was carried out under the direction of White House employees. Disclosure of the White House involvement in the break-in and subsequent cover-up forced President Richard Nixon to resign in 1974.

Weapons of mass destruction (WMD) (p. 824) Biological, chemical, and nuclear weapons capable of widespread destruction.

Whigs (p. 115) In mid-eighteenth century Britain, the Whigs were a political faction that dominated Parliament. Generally, they opposed royal influence in government and wanted to increase the power of Parliament. In America, a Whig party coalesced in the 1830s in opposition to President Andrew

Jackson. The American Whigs supported federal power and internal improvements but not territorial expansion. The Whig party collapsed in the 1850s.

Whiskey Rebellion (p. 185) Protests in 1794 by western Pennsylvania farmers against a federal tax on whiskey. The uprising was suppressed when President George Washington called an army of 15,000 troops to the area.

Wilmot Proviso (p. 337) In 1846, shortly after outbreak of the **Mexican-American War**, Congressman David Wilmot of Pennsylvania introduced this amendment banning slavery in any lands won from Mexico.

Women's Christian Temperance Union (WCTU) (p. 480) This organization campaigned to end drunkenness and the social ills that accompanied it. By 1898, it had 10,000 branches and 500,000 members. The WCTU illustrated the role women played in politics and reform long before they won the right to vote.

Women's Trade Union League (WTUL) (p. 564) Founded in 1903, this group worked to organize women into trade unions. It also lobbied for laws to safeguard female workers and backed strikes, especially in the garment industry. While it never attracted many members, its leaders were influential enough to give the union considerable power.

Works Progress Administration (WPA) (p. 662) New Deal agency to provide work relief for the unemployed.

Wounded Knee Massacre (p. 426) In December 1890, troopers of the Seventh Cavalry, under orders to stop the **Ghost Dance** religion among the Sioux, took Chief Big Foot and his followers to a camp on Wounded Knee Creek in South Dakota. It is uncertain who fired the first shot, but 200 Native Americans were killed.

XYZ Affair (p. 189) A diplomatic incident in which American peace commissioners sent to France by President John Adams in 1797 were insulted with bribe demands from their French counterparts, dubbed X, Y, and Z in American newspapers. The incident heightened war fever against France.

Yalta Conference (p. 697) A wartime conference in February 1945 in which the Allies agreed to final plans for the defeat of Germany and the terms of its occupation. The Soviets agreed to allow free elections in Poland, but they were never held.

Yellow journalism (p. 534) To sell newspapers before and during the Spanish-American War, publishers William Randolph Hearst and Joseph Pulitzer engaged in blatant sensationalization of the news, which became known as "yellow journalism." Although it did not cause the war, it helped turn U.S. public opinion against Spain.

Yeomen (p. 65) Southern small landholders who owned no slaves, and who lived primarily in the foothills of the Appalachian and Ozark mountains. They were self-reliant and grew mixed crops, although they usually did not produce a substantial amount to be sold on the market.

Yorktown (p. 137) Virginia market town on a peninsula bounded by the York and James rivers, where Lord Cornwallis's army was trapped by the Americans and French in 1781.

Young America (p. 313) In the 1840s and early 1850s, many public figures—especially younger members of the Democratic party—used this term to describe their program of territorial expansion and industrial growth.

Credits

Chapter 1

2 North Wind Picture Archives/Alamy **7** Scala/Art Resource, NY **14** AP Photo/Clement N'Taye **21** From Theodor d Bry, "America" New York Public Library, Astor, Lenox, and Tilden Foundations **22** The Granger Collection, NYC. All rights reserved. **27** The Trustees of the British Museum

Chapter 2

30 MPI/Archive Photos/Getty Image **35** Ashmolean Museum, University of Oxford **38** Historic St. Mary's City **44** Eliot Elisofon/Time Life Pictures/Getty Images **50** Lebrecht Music and Arts Photo Library/Alamy **53** Mary Evans Picture Library / The Image Works

Chapter 3

60 © Fine Arts Museums of San Francisco **70** Colonial Williamsburg Foundation **72T** © National Maritime Museum Greenwich, UK **72B** © National Maritime Museum Greenwich, UK **73** Abby Aldrich Rockefeller Folk Art Museum, The Colonial Williamsburg Foundation, Williamsburg, Va. **79** Art Resource, NY

Chapter 4

82 William Byrd II (oil on canvas), Hysing, Hans (1678-1753)/Virginia Historical Society, Richmond, Virginia, USA/The Brid-geman Art Library **90** Richard Cummins/CORBIS **92** Oil on canvas, 36 × 27", Charles Willson Peale, 1789, Gift of James J. Barclay, 1852, Historical Society of Pennsylvania Collection, Portrait/Science, The Philidelphia History Museum at the Atwater Kent. **93** New York Public Library/Art Resource, **96** © National Portrait Gallery, London **102** The British Library **104** Library of Congress

Chapter 5

110 New Hampshire Historical Society **114** Courtesy of the John Carter Brown Library at Brown University **121** Library of Congress **122** Library of Congress **128** Atwater Kent Museum of Philadelphia **135** Anne S. K. Brown Military Collection, Brown University Library

Chapter 6

140 The Granger Collection, NYC. All rights reserved. **143** Library of Congress Rare Books and Special Collections **146** Art Resource, NY/The New York Public Library, Rare Book Division **148** Abigail Smith Adams, c.1766 (pastel on paper), Blyth, Benjamin (fl.1740-87)/© Massachusetts Historical Society, Boston, MA, USA/The Bridgeman Art Library **156** National Portrait Gallery, Smithsonian Institution/Art Resource, NY

Chapter 7

168 MPI/Getty Images **177** Art Resource, NY **183** North Wind/North Wind Picture Archives **185** U.S. Department of the Interior **187** Library of Congress

Chapter 8

194 National Museum of American History/Smithsonian Institution **197** Senator John Heinz Pittsburgh Regional History Center **198** Library of Congress **199** Library of Congress **207** Colonial Williamsburg Foundation **215** MPI/Getty Images

Chapter 9

220 Courtesy, Winterthur Museum, Funds provided by H.F. DuPont **226** Library of Congress **227** Library of Congress **229** The New York Public Library/Art Resource, NY **230** The Granger Collection, NYC. All rights reserved. **233T** Colonial Williamsburg Foundation **233B** American Textile History Museum, Lowell, MA

Chapter 10

244 Courtesy, Winterthur Museum, Funds provided by H.F. DuPont **250** Stump Speaking (oil on canvas), Bingham, George Caleb (1811–79)/Private Collection/The Bridgeman Art Library **255** Library of Congress **256** Woolaroc Museum **261** The New-York Historical Society

Chapter 11

268 Library of Congress **271** The New-York Historical Society **273** Library of Congress **277** The Collection of the Shadows-On-The-Teche, New Iberia, Louisiana. A National Trust Historic Site **282** Daughters of the Republic of Texas Library **284** Colonial Williamsburg Foundation **288** Library of Congress

Chapter 12

290 The Granger Collection, NYC. All rights reserved **296** Published courtesy of Fruitlands Museum, Harvard, MA **306** National Portrait Gallery, Smithsonian Institution/Art Resource, NY **307** Sophia Smith Collection, Smith College **308** Bettmann/CORBIS

Chapter 13

312 Harvard University, Houghton Library **314** The New York Public Library/Art Resource, NY **318** World History Archive/Newscom **326** Neg.# ICHi-00013/Chicago History Museum **330** Bettmann/CORBIS

Chapter 14

334 Art Resource, NY/The New York Public Library **339** The Granger Collection, NYC. All rights reserved. **341** Library of Congress **350** Library of Congress **352** Library of Congress

Chapter 15

358 Library of Congress **362** Library of Congress **366** Library of Congress **371** Library of Congress **372** Francis G. Mayer/Corbis Art/CORBIS **374** Library of Congress **375** The New-York Historical Society

Chapter 16

386 Library of Congress **396** Stock Montage, Inc./Historical Pictures Collection **399** Collection of The New-York Historical Society, negative number 50475 **404** Valentine Richmond History Center **406** The Granger Collection, NYC. All rights reserved. **408** Rutherford B. Hayes Presidential Center **413** Time & Life Pictures/Getty Images

Index

PRESENT DAY UNITED STATES

WASHINGTON
Olympia • Seattle • Tacoma
Spokane •
Portland • Salem
OREGON

IDAHO
Boise

MONTANA
Helena
• Billings

NORTH DAKOTA
Bismark

SOUTH DAKOTA
Pierre

NEBRASKA

WYOMING
Cheyenne

COASTAL RANGES
SIERRA NEVADA

NEVADA
Sacramento
Carson City
San Francisco
Stockton
Fresno •
CALIFORNIA
Bakersfield •
Las Vegas •
Los Angeles •
San Diego

Great Salt Lake
Salt Lake City

UTAH

ROCKY MOUNTAINS
COLORADO
Denver
Colorado Springs
Pueblo

KANSAS

ARIZONA
Phoenix • Mesa
Tucson •

NEW MEXICO
Santa Fe
Albuquerque •

OKLA
Oki
City

Amarillo •

Lubbock •

El Paso •

TEXAS

San An

PACIFIC OCEAN

MEXICO

Columbia R.
Missouri R.
Snake R.
Colorado R.
Arkansas R.
Brazos R.
Rio Grande

Alaska inset

ARCTIC OCEAN
RUSSIA
ALASKA
CANADA
Yukon R.
Anchorage
Juneau
Bering Strait
Bering Sea
Gulf of Alaska
Kodiak Island
Aleutian Islands

0   200   400 mi
0   200   400 km

Hawaii inset

Kauai
Oahu
Honolulu
Molokai
Lanai
Maui
PACIFIC OCEAN
HAWAII
Hawaii

0   50   100 mi
0   50   100 km

CANADA

NESOTA

Lake Superior

St. Paul
neapolis

WISCONSIN
Madison
Milwaukee

MICHIGAN
Grand Rapids
Lansing
Detroit

Lake Michigan

Lake Huron

VERMONT

MAINE
Augusta
Montpelier
Portland

NEW
HAMPSHIRE
Concord

NEW YORK
Albany
Syracuse
Buffalo

Lake Ontario

Boston
MASSACHUSETTS
Providence
Hartford
RHODE ISLAND
CONNECTICUT

IOWA
Des Moines
Davenport

ILLINOIS
Peoria
Springfield
Chicago
Gary

Indianapolis
INDIANA
Louisville

Lake Erie
Cleveland
Toledo

OHIO
Columbus
Cincinnati

PENNSYLVANIA
Harrisburg
Pittsburgh

Newark
New York City
Trenton
Philadelphia
Baltimore
Dover
Annapolis
Washington D.C.
Richmond
Newport News

NEW JERSEY
DELAWARE
MARYLAND

WEST VIRGINIA
Charleston

Frankfort
Lexington
KENTUCKY

Kansas City
Jefferson City
St. Louis

MISSOURI

Ohio R.

Tennessee R.

VIRGINIA
Norfolk

Raleigh

NORTH CAROLINA
Charlotte

Nashville
Knoxville
TENNESSEE
Chattanooga
Memphis
Huntsville

ARKANSAS
Little Rock

A P P A L A C H I A N   M T S.

Columbia
SOUTH CAROLINA
Charleston

Atlanta

GEORGIA
Columbus

Birmingham

Savannah

ATLANTIC OCEAN

MISSISSIPPI
Jackson
Shreveport

ALABAMA
Montgomery

LOUISIANA
Mobile
Baton Rouge
New Orleans
Houston

Tallahassee
FLORIDA
Jacksonville

Gulf of Mexico

Orlando
St. Petersburg
Tampa

BAHAMAS

Lake Okeechobee
Fort Lauderdale
Miami

Key West

Straits of Florida

CUBA

Mississippi R.

INSET:

ATLANTIC OCEAN

San Juan
Bayamon
Carolina
Isla de Culebra

PUERTO RICO

Ponce

Isla de Vieques

Caribbean Sea

0   20   40 mi
0 20 40 km

Legend	
—	National boundary
—	State boundary
⊛	National capital
★	State capital
●	Other city

Scale: 0 — 200 — 400 mi / 0 — 200 — 400 km

St. Lawrence R.

PRESENT DAY WORLD

ARCTIC
OCEAN

GREENLAND

Beaufort
Sea

Baffin
Bay

ALASKA
(U.S.)

ICELAND

Bering
Sea

Gulf of
Alaska

Hudson
Bay

Labrador
Sea

CANADA

Great
Lakes

UNITED STATES

ATLANTIC
OCEAN

MOROC

WESTERN
SAHARA

MEXICO

Gulf
of
Mexico

MAURITANIA

PACIFIC
OCEAN

CAPE
VERDE

SENEGAL
THE GAMBIA

Hawaiian Is. (U.S.)

BELIZE

SURINAME

GUINEA
BISSAU

GUINE

SIERRA
LEONE

GUATEMALA

FRENCH
GUIANA
(FR.)

LIBERIA

EL SALVADOR

CÔTE
D'IVOIRE

Kiribati

Galapagos Is. (EQ.)

GHANA

Tokelau

French
Polynesia

ECUADOR

SÃO TO
PRÍNC

Samoa

Cook
Is.

PERU

BRAZIL

Am.
Samoa

Tonga

BOLIVIA

PARAGUAY

CHILE

URUGUAY

ARGENTINA

Falkland Is. (U.K.)

South Georgia (U.K.)

UNITED
STATES

0   200   400   600 mi
0 200 400 600 km

BAHAMAS

ATLANTIC
OCEAN

Turks and
Caicos Is. (U.K.)

CUBA

DOMINICAN
REPUBLIC

Cayman Is. (U.K.)

U.S. Virgin Is.

Antigua and
Barbuda

JAMAICA

HAITI

PUERTO
RICO

Guadaloupe

Dominica

HONDURAS

Martinique

St. Lucia

Caribbean
Sea

St. Vincent and
the Grenadines

Barbados

NICARAGUA

Curaco

Grenada

COSTA
RICA

Trinidad
and Tobago

Weddell
Sea

VENEZUELA

GUYANA

ANTARCTICA

PANAMA   COLOMBIA

SVALBARD IS. (NOR.)

Novaya
Zemlya

*Barents
Sea*

*Kara
Sea*

*Laptev
Sea*

New Siberian Is.

*ARCTIC
OCEAN*

*East
Siberian
Sea*

0   1000   2000   3000 mi
0   1000   2000 3000 km

RUSSIA

*Lake
Baikal*

*Sea
of
Okhotsk*

KAZAKHSTAN

*Aral
Sea*   *Lake
Balkhash*

MONGOLIA

Sakhalin

N. KOREA

PEOPLE'S
REPUBLIC
OF CHINA

S. KOREA

JAPAN

AFGHAN

PAKISTAN

NEPAL

BHUTAN

*East
China
Sea*

TAIWAN

*PACIFIC
OCEAN*

NISIA
LIBYA

ISRAEL
JORDAN
EGYPT   IRAQ
BAHRAIN
QATAR
SAUDI
ARABIA

IRAN

U.A.E.
OMAN

INDIA

BANG.

BURMA
(MYANMAR)

MACAO
LAOS
VIETNAM

*Philippine
Sea*

PHILIPPINES

Northern
Mariana
Is.

CHAD

SUDAN

ERITREA YEMEN

DJIBOUTI
SOMALIA

*Arabian
Sea*

*Bay of
Bengal*

THAILAND

*South
China
Sea*

Marshall
Is.

CENT.
AFRICAN REP.
MEROON

ETHIOPIA

SRI
LANKA

CAMBODIA

MALAYSIA

BRUNEI

EQUA.
GUINEA   UGANDA
KENYA

SINGAPORE

PAPUA
NEW GUINEA

Nauru

DEM. REP.
OF
CONGO   RWANDA
BURUNDI
TANZANIA

INDONESIA

ANGOLA
ZAMBIA   MALAWI

*INDIAN
OCEAN*

Solomon Is.

Tuvalu

AMBIA
BOTSWANA   ZIMB.

MADAGASCAR

MAURITIUS

*Coral
Sea*

Vanuatu

Fiji

SOUTH
AFRICA   MOZAMBIQUE

SWAZILAND

LESOTHO

AUSTRALIA

New Caledonia (FR.)

*Tasman
Sea*

NEW
ZEALAND

N

NORWAY   FINLAND

SWEDEN

ESTONIA

0   200   400   600   800 mi
0 200 400 600 800 km

IRELAND

*North
Sea*

DENMARK

LATVIA

*Baltic
Sea*   LITHUANIA
RUSSIA

RUSSIA

*ATLANTIC
OCEAN*

UNITED
KINGDOM

NETHERLANDS
BELGIUM   GERMANY

POLAND

BELARUS

LUX.
FRANCE

CZECH
REPUBLIC
LIECHT.
SWITZ. AUSTRIA
SLOVENIA   SLOVAKIA
HUNGARY

UKRAINE

MOLDOVA

PORTUGAL

SPAIN

CROATIA
BOSNIA
HERZ.   SERBIA

ROMANIA

Black Sea

GEORGIA

ARMENIA

Caspian Sea

ITALY

MACEDONIA
ALBANIA

BULGARIA

TURKEY

AZERBAIJAN

GREECE

MONTENEGRO

*Mediterranean
Sea*

CYPRUS

SYRIA

IRAQ

LEBANON